LOUISE BROOKS

BARRY PARIS

ALFRED A. KNOPF   NEW YORK

1989

THIS IS A BORZOI BOOK
PUBLISHED BY ALFRED A. KNOPF, INC.

Copyright © 1989 by Barry Paris
All rights reserved under International and Pan-American Copyright Conventions. Published
in the United States by Alfred A. Knopf, Inc., New York, and simultaneously in Canada by
Random House of Canada Limited, Toronto. Distributed by Random House, Inc., New York.

The author gratefully acknowledges the assistance of the Louise Brooks estate, Daniel Brooks
and Benjamin Phelosof, co-executors, and the Theodore R. Brooks family of Wichita, Kansas, for
access to the Louise Brooks letters, logs, and photographs, and thanks them for their invaluable
cooperation throughout the research and writing of this book. All rights, including copyright,
to these books, articles, letters, logs, and photographs by Louise Brooks are owned by
the Estate of Louise Brooks. All rights reserved.

Library of Congress Cataloging-in-Publication Data
Paris, Barry.
Louise Brooks/Barry Paris.—1st ed.
p.   cm.
"Louise Brooks filmography": p.
Includes bibliographical references.
ISBN: 0-394-55923-1: $24.95
1. Brooks, Louise, 1906–1985. 2. Motion picture actors and actresses—United States—
Biography. I. Title.
PN2287.B694P37   1989
791.43'028'092—dc20   89-45540
[B]   CIP

Owing to limitations of space, all acknowledgments for permission to reprint
previously published material may be found on pages 607-8.

Manufactured in the United States of America
Published October 31, 1989
Reprinted Once
Third Printing, November 1989

54 4 5 5

"In writing the history of a life, I believe absolutely that the reader cannot understand the character and deeds of the subject unless he is given a basic understanding of that person's sexual loves and hates and conflicts. It is the only way the reader can make sense out of innumerable apparently senseless actions. To paraphrase Proust: how often do we change the whole course of our lives in pursuit of a love that we will have forgotten within a few months. We flatter ourselves when we assume that we have restored the sexual integrity which was expurgated by the Victorians . . . .

"I too am unwilling to write the sexual truth that would make my life worth reading. I cannot unbuckle the Bible Belt. That is why I will never write my memoirs."

— LOUISE BROOKS

LOUISE BROOKS

CONTENTS

Contents

PREFACE

I should speak in somber tones of the great burden of assembling the
Louise Brooks papers from far and wide, on two continents—but it would
be a sham. Hundreds of individuals and institutions made the task easier
at every step. Their names are to be found in the full Acknowledgments
section and my gratitude to all of them is enormous.

But certain key people provided encouragement and assistance far beyond the call, and without them, there would be no book.

Foremost among them are James Card and Kevin Brownlow, who
shared not only their vast knowledge of silent films but their relationships and correspondence with Louise Brooks. Their generosity with time
and research materials was as invaluable as their close reading of the
manuscript.

John Kobal, William K. Everson, and Ricky Leacock—three other
major names in film chronicling—likewise shared their knowledge and
their stormy friendships with Louise. It was fortunate, indeed, that she
numbered the best of film historians among her friends, including the late
George C. Pratt, a tireless and brilliant researcher who lives on as an
inspiration to all writers interested in separating fact from myth.

Jane Sherman Lehac, dancer and dance historian, made certain that
the Denishawn period of Brooksie's life was accurate, and was both delightful and indefatigable in her critiques.

Jan-Christopher Horak, film curator at Eastman House, never failed to
make that facility's treasures available. Also indispensable were the ongo-
ing counsel of Lawrence J. Quirk, Lothar Wolff, Jan Wahl, David Stenn,
and Tom Graves and the very kind cooperation of Roddy McDowall,
William S. Paley, John Minary, Francis Lederer, and Joan Rivers. Among
my "support systems," the most vital were the research, photographic, and
technical service of Maria Ciaccia and the consultation of Dr. Rose
Hayden.

For the creation and shaping of the book itself, I am forever indebted
to Robert Gottlieb, Martha Kaplan, and Daniel Strone, and to my patient
editor, Susan Ralston, who pulled it all together.

Finally, two families were required to bring this book into existence. Of the Brooks clan in Kansas, the joyful ghost of Louise's brother Theodore sustained me throughout. His wife Margaret, son Daniel, and daughter Roseanna extended every courtesy throughout, as did Louise's sister, June Brooks Lashley, and the Louise Brooks Estate, Benjamin Phelosof and Daniel Brooks, co-executors.

The second crucial family was my own, of whom John Barba and Lina Basquette were an integral part. From day one, Claire and Wyoming B. Paris inspired me to pursue this shooting star, while I was repeatedly rescued along the way by my daughter, Merica, my son, Ben, and my beloved wife and critic, Myrna.

Act One

___

E VERY
L ITTLE
B REEZE

Louise at twelve in her original Bubble Dance at the Wheat Show, Wichita, 1919

1 · Flashbacks

I have a gift for enraging people.
— LOUISE BROOKS

NOBODY burned more bridges than Louise Brooks, or left prettier blazes on two continents. People around her scrambled for cover, but she watched the flames with a child's pyromaniacal glee—the star of a flicker gone wild. With the advent of talkies, her name would largely disappear, but her face would not: a girl in a Prince Valiant bob, with electrifying eyes that drilled straight to the heart from the silent screen and left you weak when you met their gaze. Eyes that beckoned not so much "come hither" as "I'll come to you."

They danced in the face of a perfect little dancer who shared the stage at sixteen with Ted Shawn and Martha Graham. The eyes snared Florenz Ziegfeld, who swept her into his *Follies*. The eyes—and her teenage grace —acted like a powerful magnet on Charles Chaplin, who tramped around Manhattan with her during the heady days of his *Gold Rush* premiere in 1925.

Broadway was full of pretty chorus girls with beautiful bodies, and Louise was one of them, but Brooksie had a brain as well as a body, though she wouldn't use either to get financial security. "I just wasn't equipped to spoil millionaires in a practical, farsighted way," she once said.[1] Louise had no inclination to chase any man for long.

Nor did she chase stardom; instead, it kept chasing her. And she in turn kept chasing it away. If rehearsals got dull, she slipped off to W. C. Fields's dressing room for a private display of comic juggling. If she did the Charleston till 3:00 a.m. and didn't feel like performing the next day, she stayed home.

For such impetuosity, the producers and directors called her an insufferable brat. Louise, on the other hand, called it "that precious quality of youth: indifference to the censure of those whom one did not admire."[2] Precious or pugnacious, her attitude seemed only to fuel, not retard, her meteoric rise.

With Louise Brooks, things happened fast or not at all—and movies weren't even on the list. The twenties were starting to roar, Calvin Coolidge and prosperity reigned, and this lithe Kansas spitfire loved the sheer living and frolicking in New York. Though many a chorus girl yearned to be in "pitchas," Louise was not one of them. But Paramount's headhunters finally got to her.

It was the Jazz Age—cynical and promiscuous and all in good fun. Brooksie's escapades with and without Chaplin were notorious, and people were calling her a trollop, and worse, behind her back. Her front, meanwhile, faced more and more cameras as Paramount turned her into a delightful little trollop on screen: *The American Venus, Love 'em and Leave 'em, Evening Clothes, Rolled Stockings*—the titles told the story. When one of her directors fell madly in love with her, she married him and went West. Everybody said she did it for his money and that it wouldn't last. They were right that it wouldn't last and wrong that she was after his money. Women all over America copied her hairdo, and for two years in Hollywood, every little breeze whispered Louise. But they could never copy her caprice.

"Love is a publicity stunt," she once wrote, "and making love—after the first curious raptures—is only another petulant way to pass the time waiting for the studio to call."[3]

Not that she ever sat around waiting for the studio to call. On the contrary, she did her best to elude the calls. And when talkies hit the movie colony and the stars trembled lest their voices be their death knells, Louise Brooks was not among the terror-stricken. A certain wealthy sportsman desired her company on a European cruise, and she astonished Paramount by simply quitting. And then in a kind of afterthought to unemployment, she accepted an offer to make a film in Berlin for a director she'd never heard of. She was no great authority on American directors, let alone German expressionist–realists. All she knew was that this one wanted her to play—no big surprise—a kind of prostitute. A girl named Lulu.

What she didn't know was that Lulu would be the greatest, most sinless prostitute of them all.

Brooks and Berlin. Louise and Lulu. They were perfect for each other in 1928. Berlin had sex, sin, decadence, and despair; Brooks had everything but the despair. One didn't despair on $2,000 a week, especially if one inclined toward the bisexual. Much later, in a letter to her brother

Theodore, she bit off his head for misquoting her on Berlin's "immorality" at the time.

"Without help from you I can make my own silly observations," she fumed. "And you are either a fool or a liar to say I would comment on the low state of anyone's morals—mine being non-existent."[4]

To this high-spirited wisp of a Kansas girl, Berlin made Hollywood look as tame as Wichita. No doubt about it—studying for the part of Lulu was going to be great fun. G. W. Pabst's casting of Louise Brooks in *Pandora's Box* made a controversial project more so. He could have had Marlene Dietrich, who wanted the part badly, but he thought her too old and too obvious—one sexy look from Marlene "and the picture would become a burlesque." Basking in his recent discovery of Greta Garbo, Pabst had something new in mind: absolute, stunning realism.

Thirty years later, the director of the Cinémathèque Française would proclaim, "There is no Garbo! There is no Dietrich! There is only Louise Brooks!" She and Pabst were hailed as geniuses and *Pandora's Box* as a masterpiece.

Some call it the greatest of all silents.

By 1930, after just three European films, Louise Brooks was the rage of Berlin and Paris. And then she fled from the scene of her triumph—which was typical of her. Time and again, Louise Brooks snatched obscurity from the jaws of fame.

"The career of an actor is the most degrading of all enslavements," she told her brother.[5] She hated the boredom of the film process, and during shooting, she killed the endless waiting time by reading—constantly, voraciously. For bringing Shaw and Schopenhauer onto a movie set, she became the Starlet Scorned.

She reveled in the disapproval. Her friends and enemies thought she was ignoring the movie-making around her, but with one eye, and sometimes two, she was storing everything in an almost photographic memory —not to be retrieved until long after she quit films. "The secret of my failure," she said, was that she had "never been able to work up much of a sweat about films and actors and directors."[6] Indeed, she never even watched her own movies until a quarter century after they were made.

But Louise Brooks never forgot a thing and never stopped searching. It had something to do with Goethe and Proust, who were dead, and a lot to do with the heads and the beds of men who were alive. "There isn't anything wise, clever or tricky about what I do [with a man]," she once confided. "I simply move right to the center of him and whatever phony there is, the phoniness has to go."[7]

That was her approach to film as well and to the craft of writing. For this was a woman who spent the first half of her life as an actress preparing subconsciously for the second half as a writer. During her long later years of seclusion, she scrutinized her own evolution and that of the figures she saw and played on screen. Of all the dark characters in *Pandora's Box*, for instance, the one that most intrigued her was Schigolch, a mysterious old pimp who seduces Lulu as a child, peddles her favors—and just may be her natural father. A strange bond exists between the corruptor and the corrupted.

Louise's own childhood was not quite so Gothic. If ever there were a place to safeguard a little girl's innocence, it would seem to have been the stereotypical southeast Kansas town of Cherryvale, where she was born. Yet at the age of nine, she was molested by a forty-five-year-old house painter with the ominous, or just incongruous, name of Mr. Flowers. Louise Brooks never spoke of it, except to her mother, until half a century later. But the memory of Mr. Flowers powerfully influenced the way she felt about her roots.

Those roots were unbeloved but deep.

The original Brookses were tough, impoverished English farmers who scraped together the passage to America on a merchant ship during George Washington's administration. In the Civil War, Louise's great-grandfather John Brooks fought against the slaveholding plantation owners of Tennessee, a border state whose populace was violently divided between Union and Confederate allegiance. Six years after the war, at the advanced age of sixty-four, John Brooks led his large family—including his three-year-old grandson, Louise's father-to-be—on a thousand-mile odyssey by covered wagon to the free state of Kansas.[8] The Pawnee, Cherokee, and Osage Indians had just been driven out by the U.S. Cavalry and by the white hunters who slaughtered all their buffalo, and so the Brooks clan was free to homestead on 160 acres now made available to white settlers at $1.25 an acre.

The earth was rich but desolate in those parts, and the Brookses ended up near the tiny town of Burdenville, which was later shortened—aptly enough—to just "Burden." By the 1880s, the Brookses had become established as the dominant family there. They donated land for the town's cemetery and established the "Brooks Bros. Bank," Burden's first.

Also residing in Burden was another of Louise Brooks's great-grandfathers, Dr. Havilas B. Rude, a horse-and-buggy country doctor who fell prey to an occupational hazard of the day: morphine addiction. One of the doctor's neighbors recalled seeing him, as an exhausted old man, wander into the Burden drugstore and plunk down fifty cents for powdered morphine: "He could barely drag in. He'd fall down in a chair, take a cork out of the bottle, and lick the whole quarter-ounce of morphine off his palm. He'd settle back and presently begin to jerk, twist and squirm. Then, in a matter of minutes, he would rise, straighten his back and shoulders, and walk out of the place like a 20-year-old!"[9] The doctor's drug problem was no drawback to longevity, at least. He died in 1911 at the age of eighty-six.

Louise's family lines featured maternal and paternal grandfathers whose very names summoned up a feisty, rebellious heritage: Martin Luther Brooks and Thomas Jefferson Rude. Tom Rude followed in his father Havilas's medical footsteps—a single semester at Rush Medical College in Chicago being all he needed to come back to Kansas and set up practice. One of his first patients was ancient John Brooks, Louise's great-grandfather, who finally died in 1884 and was buried next to his wife, Elizabeth, in the Burden cemetery. Their tombstone depicts a pair of clasped hands with the legend "Joined in Death."

"This seems to infer they fought like cats and dogs all of their lives," Louise's brother Theo later concluded, "but one can't be sure of the trend of pioneer thought."

Thomas Rude was a fine doctor of whom it was said that "he could do anything but make money and stay away from a bottle of whiskey." That assessment, while true, hardly did justice to the colorful life and character of Dr. Tom. "Take a good look at a Prince Albert tobacco can," his daughter Eva wrote Louise many years later. "As a child I thought it a picture of our dad."[10]

Before becoming a doctor, Tom Rude was Burden's mayor and its schoolteacher. In 1882 he married Mary Gentry (whose father was talking with the sheriff of Winfield when the sheriff was murdered by the Dalton Gang in broad daylight). He named one of his sons Robert E. Lee Rude, primarily to needle his anti-Confederate in-laws.

All together, Tom and Mary Rude produced ten children; the eldest of the surviving six was a beautiful girl with lovely sad eyes, jet black hair, and a Mona Lisa smile. Her name was an anagram of her mother's: Myra. Due to Mary's constant state of pregnancy, Myra reluctantly took over many of the motherly functions of the household, though she shared her father's passion for horses and the outdoors.

"How beautiful your mother was as a girl," Louise's Aunt Eva wrote her years later. "The Burden natives . . . loved watching her dash by on horseback with her black curly hair flying in the wind."[11] People paid the traveling country doctor "with almost anything but money in those days." Eva and Myra took turns as their father's buggy companion when he made his long rounds. To pass the time at night, he sang "Annie Laurie" and recited verse after verse of "The Lady of the Lake." Eva noticed that he made it a habit to wind up the day at one of the more prosperous farms, where the food and the beds were better.

At home, Dr. Tom tolerated the local ministers invited by his wife to Sunday dinner but pronounced them "mealy-mouthed hypocrites" as soon as they left. One of Louise's favorite stories about her grandfather concerned the night when Burden's good Methodists were convened to discuss ways of paying off the new church building. Myra's mother and grandmother were there, but Dr. Tom opted out, in favor of a big poker game. Suddenly he burst into the church, strode up the aisle to the preacher, and, to the horror of his womenfolk, declared, "I understand you need some money for the building of the church. Well, here's some I just finished taking away from the devil." With that, he dumped a hat full of coins in the clergyman's lap, gave a courtly bow, and strode out. [12]

Less than a mile away lived Martin Brooks, who, like his father, John, had "heeded the call of Lincoln" and fought the Confederates at Shiloh and Missionary Ridge, accompanying General Sherman on the march to Atlanta. In Burden, he settled down to farming and to the begetting and rearing of eight children, including the future father of Louise.

Leonard Porter Brooks, like most of the rest of the prosperous Brookses, grew up to be studious and independent in freewheeling southeastern Kansas. He acquired a mustache and a law degree at the University of Kansas in 1897 and became one of the most eligible bachelors in Burden. He and nineteen-year-old Myra Rude, the effervescent prairie beauty, caught each other's eye and fell in love—though Myra would later observe that, at thirty-six, he was old enough to be her father.

They were married in 1904 and quickly abandoned the burden of Burden in favor of nearby Cherryvale, where Leonard worked in the legal office of the Prairie Oil Company "until it was gobbled up by John D. Rockefeller," according to Louise. Situated near Cherry Creek, it was a classic western boomtown, thanks to the coming of the railroads and the discovery of vast gas and oil fields in the 1880s.

The Cherryvale *Republican*, functioning as an unofficial chamber of commerce, felt that only divine intervention could explain the town's good fortune. "When the boundless natural resources of the oil and gas belt of Kansas are thoroughly investigated," says the paper's 1908 "Souvenir Album of Cherryvale," "one finds himself unconsciously wondering why the all-wise Creator should . . . assemble so many of the great natural gifts in one state or locality."

Cherryvale's population had doubled to nearly 7,000 souls since the turn of the century, and there wasn't a town of its size west of the Mississippi with better railroad connections. The Frisco, Santa Fe, and KCFS&M all stopped in Cherryvale and left loaded down with huge quantities of vitrified brick. Six big plants turned out 500,000 bricks daily, drawing their raw material from the immense shale mounds outside town and fueling their ovens with cheap and plentiful natural gas.

Compared with Burden, Cherryvale was a bustling metropolis, though it was surrounded for miles in every direction by some of the world's

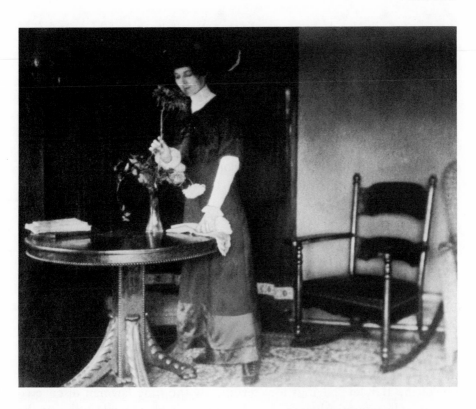

ABOVE: *Myra Rude Brooks in her Victorian parlor, ca. 1910.* RIGHT: *Leonard P. Brooks at about thirty, in Burden, Kansas, ca. 1898*

greatest farmland, where corn, wheat, oats, alfalfa, vegetables, and even cotton grew in abundance.

Louise and every child who grew up there had only to wander a few blocks to find themselves in wide-open terrain that reached a compromise between flat and hilly. That part of southeastern Kansas was famous—and still is—as the haven of a wondrous variety of great hawks which glide lazily over the sunburnt prairie grass, divebombing at their leisure to pluck a field mouse and give it a brief aerial thrill on the way to extinction. Bales and rolls of hay, drying in the sun, dot the fields—the only visual punctuation in a landscape painted more shades of brown than you ever knew existed. To live there is to come to grips with both the beautiful and the godforsaken qualities of its isolation.

Isolated Cherryvale, in fact, was famous for a macabre set of crimes perpetrated in 1872–1873 by "the bloody Benders." The state of Kansas was barely eleven years old, and the Bender family seemed typical of the many thickly accented German immigrants who settled there, operating a roadside inn in their rough-hewn log house just outside town. Ma and Pa Bender had an enticing, flaxen-haired "siren" of a daughter, Kate, who held seances and distributed handbills claiming she could cure "blindness, fits, deafness and all such diseases." Many were lured and after the disappearance of numerous wayfarers, it was discovered that they had checked out of the Bender lodgings for eternity. By the time lawmen discovered eleven bodies, minus their purses, the Benders had escaped south into the Indian Territory, and into the bedtime ghost stories of every child in the area.[13]

Cherryvale's main claim to fame was the Edgar Zinc Company—world's largest zinc smelter—which employed 400 men in continuous day-and-night operation. But bricks and zinc notwithstanding, most folks were farmers, their lives dominated by the weather and the growing seasons.

The main form of excitement in "Smelter Town" and its environs was the recurring string of fires that tended to wipe out every major Cherryvale institution at regular intervals. Two newspapers, the *Republican* and the unfortunately named Cherryvale *Torch*, went up in flames. So did the Methodist Church—Cherryvale's largest—and the bank and the high school.

One of Leonard Brooks's jobs was to console his clients for the absence of fire insurance. Otherwise, his advertisement in that 1908 "Souvenir Album" indicates he was a busy and versatile barrister: "L. P. Brooks, attorney and counselor at law. . . . General practice in all courts, commercial law and collections, real estate, probate, corporation, foreclosure, tax titles, specialties. Personal attention given to all matters connected with the office. Reference: People's National Bank of Cherryvale."

Only one thing dominated his life more than his law practice, and that was his devotion to Myra. Having spent her youth raising five younger siblings, she candidly informed her husband "that he was her escape to freedom and the arts, and that any squalling brats she produced could take care of themselves."[14] Myra's sister Eva put it even more bluntly in a letter to her niece years later:

"The oldest daughter of a large family was not an easy spot to fill in those days when housework was still being done the hard way. It required a lot of inborn mother love which Myra did not have. Her one thought was to get away from it all."[15]

Leonard Brooks took Myra away from it all, but not for long. Their first "squalling brat" to arrive was Martin, born in 1905. Mary Louise was not far behind, on November 14, 1906, and the Cherryvale *Daily News* reported the event on its front page: "Attorney L. P. Brooks is stepping around like a blind horse in a clover patch all on account of a young lady who came to his home this morning where she will reside in the future. All concerned are doing nicely."

The final pair of children, Theodore and June, were born in 1912 and 1914. The three younger children—like Leonard and Myra—were small of stature; in adulthood, no one in the family except Martin exceeded five feet four inches.

The Brookses soon moved from their white frame house to a more respectable red brick one at 320 West Main Street on the edge of "downtown" Cherryvale. Its mini-Victorian roof and gables rose to a point in front, forming a picturesque little dormer window on the second story.

Myra Brooks was as good as her premarital word. She left her children to their own devices, and to Leonard, while she cultivated her wide-ranging artistic interests, particularly her music. She and sister Eva were both talented pianists, and in addition to the popular songs of the day, they played solo and duet piano works of great difficulty. Myra had a maddening desire for perfection, as Eva later recalled for Louise:

"Your mother used to fume and falter because she could not sight read easily," she wrote Louise years later. "She'd say it was completely idiotic to stumble around over a thing like that. Now, I could sight read fairly well, but long before I'd have a page memorized your mother would have the entire composition down pat and [would have] gone on to something else. We enjoyed many a pleasant hour 'dueting'—piano and sometimes voice."[16] *

Louise often observed their sessions together and confirmed Eva's

---

* Louise inherited some of her aesthetic sense from Eva as well as Myra. "Far be it from me to pooh-pooh good technique in music," Eva once wrote Louise, "[but] technique must finally reach that point where it is like breathing—there but not thought of. A medium through which you express the inner emotions. One must learn to live the composition in order for the composition to live."

memory of the pleasure they brought to Myra, despite the technical frustrations. "My most adorable memory of my mother is when she was truly happy at the piano," she wrote Eva's daughter Patricia years later. "And the happiest I ever saw her was when she and Eva played duets."[17]

Their specialty was Schubert, but when alone, Myra more often immersed herself in the dreamy impressionism of Claude Debussy, whose work was still little known and considered highly *avant-garde*. The same could be said for the Verlaine, Baudelaire, and Mallarmé poetry to which much of his music was fused. Myra Brooks sensed and liked what Debussy was doing: challenging the laws that required musical tension to be resolved in prescribed peaks and valleys. With Debussy, every chord seemed to evoke the present fleeting moment of experience.

Debussy's moodiness appealed to Myra's own. The reflective, symbolic nature of the notes, the unpredictable cadences—some of them accidental discoveries at the keyboard—gave expression to her own vague melancholy, which revealed itself in her private ecstatic moments at the piano. Louise often hovered and listened, drinking in that melancholia with an emotional intimacy that neither the mother nor the daughter could ever achieve in their conversations. "It was by watching her face that I first recognized the joy of creative effort," Louise later wrote.[18] Only at such times, in the blessed absence of words, would the distance between Louise and Myra magically vanish.

Myra grew adept at Debussy, and to a lesser extent Ravel, just as she had mastered Bach and Schubert. But she was not unique. There were many good amateur musicians—most of them women—in town. Considering its size and isolation, Cherryvale had more than its fair share of talented pianists who were often showcased in concerts at the Methodist Church. Myra's friend Marcella "Tot" Strickler was one of the best, and newspaper accounts show that she accompanied her violinist daughter Betty in programs that included such difficult pieces as the finale of Mendelssohn's Violin Concerto and César Franck's "O Lord Most Holy." Myra often attended these soirees, but always declined to perform in public herself.

Some people attributed Myra's reticence to snobbishness; others thought it was insecurity; the family thought it had something to do with that same diffident quality that manifested itself in her detached, almost cold, attitude toward her children—the attitude that left a deep mark on Louise, who never lacked attention but often seemed starved for affection.

But if there was a certain void in Louise's early emotional life, it was filled to a large extent by the remarkable Tot Strickler, who lived just a few short blocks away and who provided Louise with the things Myra couldn't give—mostly a lighthearted playfulness and warmth.

"You are the loveliest, strangest fairytale witch who waves the magic wand of beauty over me," Louise wrote long afterward in a rhapsodic letter to this woman, "who gave me standards of excellence, of decency, of individuality, of courage—even of food, those cakes!"[19]

Louise was always welcome in the Stricklers' breathtaking home on West Third Street, just down from the Opera House. Crystal chandeliers glimmered gracefully in the *four* sunrooms, whose windows were hung with gold puffed-silk curtains that could be raised or lowered, in perfect pleats, depending on the time of day. Most of all, Louise loved Tot's mahogany-lined music parlor, an organized riot of Victorian bric-a-brac and potted palms in the high fashion of the day. Almost half a century later, Louise retained a perfect mental inventory of the room's exotic contents: ivory-colored wicker furniture with tapestry upholstery (made in Chicago), a bamboo easel, a plaster bulldog with horsehair collar, a great mounted elk head, the geometrically patterned wood floor designed by Tot to match the hand-painted frieze of roses and harps around the ceiling lattice. And dominating the scene and the life of the place—the rosewood Steinway grand piano.

This setting—plus Tot's vitality and dynamic passion for music—electrified Louise and illuminated her childhood. Tot's infectious sense of humor extended even to regal Myra Brooks, who once shed her dignity long enough to don an organ grinder's monkey costume. The occasion was the Music Club's spring gala, held at Tot's, with a circus theme; Myra was attached to a large music box, while a certain plumpish Miss Dods was "typed for the part of the Dago" organ grinder.

Like Myra, Tot played Bach well and developed a mastery of Beethoven and Liszt, too. But when Louise skipped into her parlor, she would laugh and put away the classics and pound out "Underneath the Stars" and "The Pink Lady" and a host of waltzes for the little girl to dance by. When Tot finally tired of being accompanist, Louise and Tot's daughter Betty would dash upstairs to try on Tot's clothes and fur boas (ordered from New York and from her favorite Kansas City modiste), topping off their costumes with one of Tot's dozens of hats, preferably the imported black velvet toques, crowned with bird-of-paradise and egret feathers—or sometimes the whole bird.

Tot was always in the process of making "improvements," and the Strickler home was such a beehive of activity that no one paid much attention to the painter-carpenter who did a lot of the work. This was Mr. Flowers, a friendly man who was especially friendly to the little girls. Forty years later, Betty recalled him innocently in a letter to Louise: "[Our] living room was pink . . . which reminds me of the time it was painted the WRONG pink by Mr. Flowers. . . . Remember the popcorn he left on his doorstep every morning (must have tasted like moth balls but we all loved it)."[20]

Louise remembered him, all right, despite many years of trying to forget. Mr. Flowers's technique was crude but effective. The other children took his bait and ran away. But Louise was bolder and more curious. Sometimes she went back and knocked on his door for more. One day, inevitably, he asked her to come inside . . .

On the other hand, Louise had forgotten about an incident that Tot later recalled for her in detail:

> Every Monday, while the clothes were soaking, it was Myra's usual custom to [visit] for an extra cup of coffee and discuss politics with Mr. Strickler. [Once], I heard a little voice crying and sobbing as she wades through the deep snow that has drifted on the driveway.
>
> I hastily opened the door and there, shivering and cold, her stockings down, and her shoes full of snow, was my dear little Louise. With tears rolling down her cheeks, she sobbed out her little story—"Mama, you must listen to me." Then she placed her hands on her hips and in an indignant manner stomped her little feet. "Now, Louise, be careful, I am *talking*," [said Myra]. "Yes, you are always talking," [said Louise]. "I came over to tell you Theodore is jumping off the top of the piano and he is so mean, he won't even let me walk on the keyboard. . . . And something else I want to tell you, June is up on the table and has eaten all the chocolate frosting off that cake you baked for Martin's birthday. And I want to tell you something *more* if you will listen—June has chocolate in her hair and all over her face. How do you like *that*? And another thing I just have to tell you, Theodore has a hatchet and is trying to cut a hole in your new washtubs so the water will run out before you get home, and the cake is ruined, and the piano, and maybe the clothes."
>
> In a soft carefree voice Myra told Louise not to cry over such *small things* in life. "You know, my dear, they will be baking better cakes, and there will be much improvement on pianos when you and Theodore get through with that old thing. . . ." At this point I took Louise to the fireside, to caress and warm her tiny feet.[21]

Tot could see the girl was struggling with her mother, who seemed to grow chillier toward her husband, and toward Louise, after the arrival of the two younger children. Many years later, Louise asked if it weren't true that her mother simply hated sex, and men, in general.

"Yes and no," replied Tot Strickler in her eighties. "Myra as I knew her just liked one sex—the sextette from *Lucia di Lammermoor*, Act 2."[22]

Despite her "squalling brats" warning and her husband's generally sympathetic response, Myra Brooks still felt oppressed by the demands of domesticity, for which her music and other intellectual endeavors were only a partial antidote. Myra's reputation was that of the most "cultured" and literary woman in Cherryvale, and she was often called upon to compose verses for bridal parties and Christmas celebrations sponsored by the Thursday Music Club. She also wrote book reviews and lectured on such esoteric subjects as Wagner's *Ring* cycle for the Cherryvale Woman's Library Club.

"For her book reviews," said Louise, "she selected such books as *Nijinsky*, written by the dancer's wife, Romola. Its strange sexual overtones set up a pleasurable creaking of the respectable matrons' chairs."[23] Sister June recalls her mother's chilling rendering of the Mexican emperor Maximilian's death during a review of his widow's memoirs.

The Library Club, which Myra helped found, was a literary society that circulated petitions and lobbied successfully to obtain one of Andrew Carnegie's grant-libraries for Cherryvale. Myra was also instrumental in raising money to add a special reading room where "women from the rural communities might rest and meet" after the long horse-and-buggy journey to Cherryvale. Myra entertained those town and country ladies regularly and royally, though she made light of them behind their backs and dreamed of the world beyond.

But for all the drawbacks of the town and of her domestic situation, Cherryvale was a big step up from Burden, and there were other cultural blessings to count. By 1915 Cherryvale and nearby Independence boasted five movie houses—the Star, Zim, Liberty, Gem, and Snark.[24] (The Snark, run by Martin Johnson, was so named for the famous boat on which Johnson had sailed years earlier with his friend Jack London.)

The silent serials and features of Theda Bara, Tom Mix, Pearl White, and Dustin Farnum were worn and scratchy by the time they got there— but they got there, and Cherryvalians could keep pace with the latest flicker rages. "Louise was only a tiny girl but a great lover of pictures," Myra recalled. "She and her brother and I went often to the first show which got us home for the children's early bedtime. . . . The three of us were admitted for the munificent sum of five cents—five cents for me and nothing for the children. I can see now, in my mind's eye, Louise's little red velvet poke-bonnet bobbing around on the front row, her big eyes beneath it all interest and attention."[25] Louise was especially enthralled by Gloria Swanson—the most exciting new face of 1915.

In April of that year, the Liberty Theater took out large advertisements in the local papers to announce it had engaged a full symphony orchestra for the special two-day run of *The Birth of a Nation*, featuring "3,000 horses, 5,000 scenes, 18,000 people." "It has electrified the world," said the local publicity. Not only that, but "it will make a better American of you."[26] Eight-year-old Louise was among those who went to be electrified, if not bettered.

Cherryvale was also sizable enough to be included on the Western

Redpath Chautauqua circuit, that invaluable bearer of information and culture to the plains. In addition to presenting the Royal Hungarian Orchestra, the All-Black Sterling Jubilee Singers, and the Hesperian Male Quartet, the Chautauqua programs gave the townsfolk a chance to see the likes of Ohio publisher Warren G. Harding long before he became a U.S. senator, let alone President of the United States.

The heart and soul of Cherryvale's cultural life was the local Opera House at Fourth and Neosho streets—an imposing wood structure that still stands today. Myra rarely missed a lecture or a performance there, escaping of an evening to such exotic locales as "Jerusalem," which was the subject of a talk by Madame Lydia Von Finkelstein Mountford "with living picture tableaux." [27] Louise was often in tow.

But most of the time, during the short autumns and springs and the long summers and winters, Myra Brooks could be found reading or practicing her music. Two scenes in particular always stuck in Louise's mind:

> When I was ten, returning home one afternoon with a book chosen by myself at the newly opened Carnegie Public Library, I watched her finish a Cecile Chaminade run, and twirl round on the piano stool like a bird in flight as she took the book from my hand. After reading aloud the title, *Brave Little Holland and How She Grew*, she burst into her lilting laugh, saying, "I'll bet you think it's the story of a little girl!" And of course I did. [28]

Another day, Louise recalled, "while she was seated at the piano, I ran to her to confess that I had just smashed a cup belonging to her best set of Haviland china. Without looking at me she said, 'Now dear, don't bother me when I am memorizing Bach.' . . . My parents' resolute pursuit of their own interests also accounted for my own early autonomy and my later inability, when I went to work in the Hollywood film factories, to submit to slavery." [29]

Many years later, Louise wrote her brother Theo that Myra "was an exquisite person. What do I care that she was no mother and cared less about her children than an alligator? She taught us the love of beauty and laughter. And I would have been dead years ago had she not put great books at my disposal." [30]

It was Myra's finest—perhaps her only—gift to her children, who learned to read by watching over her shoulder.

Myra Brooks's unfeigned love of literature often stunned the townspeople. When the ladies of the Methodist Episcopal Church decided to assemble a booklet called "Favorite Quotations of Cherryvale People," they elicited some predictable Biblical and Shakespearean material, plus a smattering of Tennyson, but mostly the kind of homespun proverbs one might expect from small-town, turn-of-the-century Kansas folks. Nellie Pilkington's favorite quote—"Every cloud has a silver lining"—was typical of the words to live by. But Myra Rude Brooks, when it came her turn, selected a sweeping philosophical declamation by William Ellery Channing (1780–1842), the great Unitarian reformer and minister:

> To live content with small means; to seek elegance rather than luxury and refinement rather than fashion; to be worthy, not respectable; wealthy, not rich; to study hard, think quick, talk gently, act frankly; to listen to stars and birds, to babes and sages with open heart; to bear all cheerfully, do all bravely, await occasions, hurry never; in a word let the spiritual unbidden and unconscious grow up through the common.—This is my symphony.

THERE WERE discordant notes in Myra Brooks's symphony, especially her *symphonia domestica*. But if she lacked many conventional motherly virtues, she had elements of the classic stage mother at heart. On the rare occasions when she turned her attention to her children, it was usually centered on lively Louise, who constantly "bounced around, spinning on her toes" from dawn till dusk.[31] Like all the children in Cherryvale, she attended McKinley School—named for the recently assassinated President—but book learning was not her primary concern.

"Both my mother and I hoped I would become a serious dancer," Louise recalled. Her ever-practical father, on the contrary, pronounced such a career "just silly."[32]

Louise's dancing debut took place at the age of four, in Cherryvale, when she played the bride in a church-benefit production of "Tom Thumb's Wedding." Myra recalled that "she walked up the aisle to the altar and, much to our amusement, manipulated her shower bouquet and bridal veil with all the ease and assurance of a grown-up bride."[33] Among her childhood friends were Venus Jones and Venus's little sister, Vivian, who changed her name to Vance and achieved immortality forty years later as the legendary Ethel Mertz of "I Love Lucy." If Louise was born dancing, "Vivian was born funny," recalled Venus, now retired, from her home in Farmington, New Mexico. "Viv was comical when she was just 2 and 3 years old. We lived across the street from the Brookses for about a year, and I remember Viv and Louise as children playing together." Their romps were often among the tombstones outside the local monument company down the block. On Louise's fifth birthday, Myra threw a party after which six-year-old Venus joined in the cleanup effort.

"Louise helped me with the dishes—I had to stand on a box to reach the sink—so that I'd get through faster and go out and play with her," Venus remembers. "It was a small town and in those days things were very simple, you know. You made your own games. We'd go outside in the evenings and play cops and robbers and blocks and so forth."[34] Louise could usually last longer, and play later, than anybody else. And when

Louise at four, in her first role: as Tom Thumb's bride in a church benefit, Cherryvale, 1910

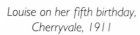

Louise on her fifth birthday, Cherryvale, 1911

there was no one left to play with, the little tornado would keep on spinning and twirling alone.

At eight, Louise performed "The Hesitation Waltz" in the Opera House and took dance lessons from Mrs. Mae Argue Buckpitt, formerly of Buffalo and now—to her mind, regrettably—of nearby Independence, Kansas. Louise remembered Mrs. Buckpitt as "a deserted lady wife who taught me the five positions and little dances from the Chalif book, wearing pleated blue serge bloomers and an immaculate starched white middie blouse."[35]

At age ten, Louise was "what amounted to a professional dancer,"[36] performing at men's and women's clubs, fairs, theaters, and dance halls in the various hamlets of southeastern Kansas. In March 1917, the month before America entered World War I, Myra booked her daughter for four days straight when the Library Club held an unusual mixed-media benefit at the Opera House. More than a hundred paintings and copies of paintings by prominent artists were loaned by the local citizenry and placed on display. The Kansas Gas & Electric Company screened a moving picture depicting the progress of electricity and other wonders, after which—each afternoon and evening—Louise Brooks danced. A total of $191.77 was raised, and all of it went to buy books—181 volumes, including Edgar Rice Burroughs's brand-new *Son of Tarzan*, Arthur Conan Doyle's *Adventures of Sherlock Holmes*, and Irving Bacheller's current best-seller, *The Light in the Clearing*.

Not all of the ten-year-old "professional's" engagements went smoothly, however. "I was given to temper tantrums, brought on by an unruly costume or a wrong dance tempo," she wrote later, "but my mother, who was my costumer and pianist, bore them with professional calm."[37]

At about this time, Myra decided Louise needed a fresh "look" onstage. She took her to a barber and instructed him to chop off the girl's long black braids, leaving her hair in a straight Dutch bob with low bangs nearly touching her eyebrows. People called it a Buster Brown cut.

And thus the little nineteenth-century cherub took on the appearance of a little twentieth-century rascal. The "new look" wasn't really brand-new: family snapshots of little Louise as early as her fifth birthday show her in virtually the same bob that would become her international trademark.

It was the perfect hairdo to fit a devilish personality. Some of her relatives, less charitably, called it a mean streak. Louise fought constantly with her older brother, Martin, and was none too pacific with the rest of the family either. Theodore recalled these battles as monumental tests of will from which Louise usually emerged victorious. His favorite example of the lengths to which she would go to get her way involved her great passion for fudge. Left to her own devices, Louise often repaired to the kitchen to cook up a pan of the chocolate goo—only to become furious when Martin and the others later gobbled it up. Her solution was a masterpiece of nasty simplicity: "She'd spit on it so the other kids wouldn't eat it. That's how she'd keep her fudge." [38]

Seventy years later, the strong impression made by Louise on her Cherryvale neighbors was summed up by Grace Newton, who still runs a hardware store there. "She was quite an attractive little girl—small with very dark hair that she always wore in a Buster Brown cut," recalled Mrs. Newton, rather annoyed at being interrupted from her chores. "But she never came back to this part of the country at all. Evidently, she was very exotic her whole life." The word "exotic" comes out with a note of distinct disapproval; and then the final verdict: "You know, Vivian Vance was raised here too, and I always thought she was ten times the actress Louise ever was." [39]

Cherryvale's heyday was short-lived. Production at the brick and zinc factories declined drastically after the local supply of cheap gas and oil began to dwindle, and by 1919, when Louise was twelve, the population had shrunk to half its peak of 7,000. The Brookses pulled up stakes and set up an interim residence in Independence, where the Prairie Oil and Gas Company was headquartered. Leonard worked briefly in its main office. Louise enrolled as a freshman in Montgomery County High School, where by all accounts she drove the boys crazy and taught at least one girlfriend to roller-skate "by wrapping and tying towels around my knees and a large bed pillow at both my front and back." [40]

During her scant three or four months in Independence, Louise was reunited with her old dancing teacher, the formidable Mae Argue Buckpitt, who operated a dance studio in the YMCA building on East Myrtle Street and who seemed to think highly of Louise, though—as so often with Louise—the feeling was not mutual.

In his "Louise Brooks and the Road to Oz," Kansas historian Charles Cagle notes that she took advantage of National Paramount Art Craft Week, celebrated late that fall of 1919 in Independence, to see the screenings of *Boots*, with Dorothy Gish, and *You Never Saw Such a Girl*, with Vivian Martin. "Obviously, the boys at Montgomery High had never seen such a girl, either," wrote Cagle. "But they had to look fast because by January of 1920, Louise Brooks had vanished completely from their fascinated and flirtatious glances."

The Brooks family's next, and last, move was a big one—125 miles west to Wichita, where Leonard went to work in the legal department of the Sterling Oil & Refining Company and began to build up his sideline law practice with a much larger pool of potential clients from which to draw.

Though the largest city in Kansas, Wichita was still an overgrown cowtown at heart, just a generation or two removed from the gunslingers who prompted the hiring of Marshal Wyatt Earp. It was still a favorite place for hell-raising cowboys in search of liquor and women at the end of the long cattle drives from Texas and Oklahoma. And zealous members of the Women's Christian Temperance Union, fired by the "hatchetations" of Carrie Nation, still made occasional headlines by smashing up bars on dusty Douglas Avenue, the main street of town.

Louise always remembered watching the wild Kansas buggy races as a girl in Wichita and once declared that "my favorite Western character was Wyatt Earp's tubercular friend Doc Holiday. He was the fastest gun of them all, and he didn't care whether he lived or died, so he was utterly without fear."[41]

For Leonard Brooks, it was ideal: There was plenty of legal work. In the long, hot summer evenings he would hold forth on the subject of crooked politicians, firm in the belief that the human condition of southern Kansas would be improved if only he were appointed to a judgeship. In the meantime, he stocked the family's huge fourteen-room frame house on Topeka Street with so many books that the foundation on one side—the side with all the lawbooks—sank eleven inches.

The Brookses' cavernous Topeka Street "barn" was a children's palace of mysterious nooks and crannies and hideaways. It was a realm that Louise ruled, as her sister, June, recalls: "She used to have a doll stove— a real cooking stove for kids—and she'd make itty bitty cakes and cookies and goodies on it, and of course I ate them. She'd plan games for us and she'd give plays, too. She made up one where I was Raggedy Ann—it was performed at the Miller Theatre—and she made all the backdrops and scenery and designed the costumes, too. At home she had her own tiny theater—just about the size of an apple box. She painted beautiful little paper figures and waltzed them around and told stories, and all the neighborhood kids would come and watch."[42]

Louise also roped her siblings and neighborhood friends into dance entertainments, selecting the Victrola records and tirelessly drilling the children until they rebelled. At night, once Leonard and Myra retired to their bedroom, the offspring were free to run amok, generally without detection, until the decibel level of Louise's savage battles with Martin prompted the intervention of a parent.

A number of those battles stemmed from her reading material. Myra had permitted her to subscribe to both *Harper's Bazaar* and *Vanity Fair*, whose graceful models she studied endlessly. For some reason, her magazines "so infuriated my jealous brother Martin that he would tear them up and hide the scraps behind the bookcases in the living room."[43]

Louise, more than her siblings, loved the family library, which, in addition to Leonard's lawbooks, contained all the English Victorians—

Dickens, Thackeray, Tennyson, Carlyle, and Darwin—plus the obligatory Americans, Emerson, Hawthorne, and Twain. Goethe was the token foreign-language author.

"All these books I read with delight," Louise recalled, "not caring in the least that I understood little of what I read." [44]

She cared just as little about her schoolwork, though she brought home better-than-average grades in English, Latin, math, and social studies from Horace Mann Intermediate School. But she cared intensely, at least for a while, about the class play (*Mr. Bob*) and about her extracurricular dance and elocution classes at the Wichita College of Music.

The grande dame of that establishment was Alice Campbell Wriggly, who, like Mrs. Buckpitt before her, also taught the five basic ballet positions, embellished with little dances that involved "tossing artificial roses from gilded reed baskets." Miss Alice's forte was old-fashioned kicks and splits and a "flabby imitation of the technique of the Russian ballet." [45] She was not destined to hold Louise's interest for long.

Louise at fifteen, Wichita, 1921

Nevertheless, Louise performed widely in Wichita. At twelve and thirteen, she was composing and directing little entertainments for local theaters and the Shrine Club, which in turn led to performances at a variety of private parties and benefits. Lila Cornell, whose father was one of the proud founders of the Million Dollar Shrine Band, performed with Louise when they were junior-high schoolmates during World War I.

"We were partners in the art of dance," said the eighty-one-year-old Kansan during an autumn reminiscence. "We were appearing together at the old Forum for the Shriners before they started having the Shrine Circus."[46] They also danced together in the Horace Mann gymnasium to raise money for the Red Cross and for Woodrow Wilson's War Bonds. Lila's fondest memory of Louise was a private-party benefit at the spacious Mead family mansion on Belmont Street—the gala event of the 1919 social season. An entire orchestra was assembled and rented for that magical evening. In the spirit of Isadora Duncan, it climaxed with Louise's Grecian Dance, performed by moonlight around a lagoon in the garden.

That same summer of 1919 she was engaged to dance on a barge at Ozark Beach, Missouri.

But the idyllic nature of such occasions was tarnished for Louise by the strained, inconsistent attitude of her mother, who might encourage her daughter one day and ignore her the next.

"Louise was very likable and not snobbish at all," says Lila, "but her mother didn't pay much attention to her. She didn't give a hoot. Her mother was 'society' and wanted Louise to be the same, but she just wasn't that way. It always seemed like Louise didn't get along too good with her mother."[47]

Perhaps because of that, and the typically rebellious nature of her early teens, Louise was growing more rather than less theatrical. Jayne Milburn, whose family lived two doors south of the Brookses, remembers being startled one day at the sight of Louise sashaying along in a long black satin dress ("piped in red") that swept the sidewalk. This would have been unusual at any time or place in Wichita; it was downright astonishing in the early afternoon.

Jayne, several years younger than Louise, played mostly with June Brooks, who had a marvelous ability—acquired with Louise's help—to take any scraps of cloth and turn them into the most elegant doll clothes. "June could come to our house any time," she recalled, "but I went only once to hers and was told by my mother not to go again."[48] The implication was that there was something not quite orthodox about the Brooks household, namely the presence of Louise.

The step-up in theatricality was a reflection of Louise's increasing status as a solo dancer and her two obsessive interests: performing and boys. On her fourteenth birthday, November 14, 1920, she received her first diary, on the inside cover of which she wrote, "Passed by the Board of Censures [*sic*]." Many passages are erased and there are furious references to the fact that her brother Martin kept finding and reading the volume. But despite such torments, she filled it faithfully, beginning on January 1, 1921, with the triumphs and tragedies of adolescent life. Many entries are prophetic of her adult life.

"I grow very homesick [for Independence, Kansas] sometimes," she writes on January 2, 1921, "but here [in Wichita] I have dancing, and as I someday intend to rise high in the ranks, I must begin now."

A few days later, upon seeing *Once to Every Woman*, starring Dorothy Phillips, she makes her debut as an embryonic critic, dubbing it "a splendid picture, but rather farfetched." And a week later: "I saw *Passion* with Pola Negri. It is wonderful and she is wonderful." By the end of January, her criticism already seems refined for a fourteen-year-old: "I saw Mary Pickford this evening in *The Lovelight*. The thing I think most unusual about her is that she is beautiful in every position and move. Very few actresses are." In February, she saw *Worlds Apart* and *While New York Sleeps*—the latter "because we thought it would be naughty (but it wasn't)." In April, Myra and Louise thought Lillian Gish and Richard Barthelmess "darlings" and *Way Down East* "simply wonderful." And in September she "cried a barrel-full" during *The Four Horsemen of the Apocalypse*. After seeing Valentino again in *The Sheik*, she declared him her favorite, adding, "What female don't admire the con man stuff?"

Wichita also attracted many live productions, and Louise rarely missed one, usually skipping school to attend on matinee days—*The Passing Shows, The Smiles of 1921*, and virtually every vaudeville engagement, whose dance numbers she sized up brutally: "They had a ballet in the show," she wrote on September 30, "and it was rotten. One little girl had talent, but, oh, how crude. The ballerina did a toe dance, which was rotten, and their 'premier danseuses,' oh me oh my!"

And of course the 1921 diary is peppered with dramatic accounts of the battle of wills with Myra:

> I hate Mother, I hate her! Just now I could kill her. It all started last night. I was in the bathroom, and she came in. Always when I am in there she comes in to show that she can. When she walked out, I shoved the door and not knowing that she was still there, I hit her. (I think she stood there to see if I would slam it.) This made her mad, and she got all worked up and bawled and fussed around. This morning she would not speak to me at all.[49]

At other moments, however, Louise could be very clinical about her own behavior, her parents, and her siblings. On Christmas Eve 1921, she made the following diary entry: "It is near the end of the year, and I wish to speak of family relations. Mother and I don't get along very well. I am selfish and stubborn. Theodore is also stubborn, but as a rule, we get along all right. I boss June all the time, so that's all right. Dad and I get along fine."

Also in 1921, the fourteen-year-old Louise became immersed in a relationship with a prosperous businessman and Sunday school teacher by the name of Mr. Vincent—a successor, it seems, to the sinister Mr. Flowers back in Cherryvale. The dozens of Mr. Vincent entries in her diary are intertwined with her dancing and romantic exploits:

Jan. 9, 1921: "Mr. Vincent is crazy about my hair. Last night he mussed it all up, making me look like a —. Lord, how I like him."

Jan. 21: "My dance was the hit of the evening. I received the most applause and everything. Sad, but true, I forgot one part. Mr. Vincent whispered a lovely compliment in my ear (how I love him!)."

Jan. 24: "We had a lot of fun in school today reading 'Midsummer Night's Dream.' All the girls are catty to me. That's what it costs to be the star."

Feb. 8: "Mr. Vincent told Mother last night that he wanted me to dance out at an affair of his at the Shrine Club. 'Sweet Mommo!' "

Feb. 14: "I danced three dances. . . . Everyone liked my 'French Baby' best. Mr. V. said he must model me in my red costume. (He has said that of every costume I wear.)" Mr. and Mrs. Vincent, Louise, and Myra then hurried out to catch the Wheat Show program at Wichita's huge old Forum auditorium. "Mrs. V. and Mother sat in the parquet together, and Mr. V. and I sat in the arena. I loved that. The orchestra was wonderful. Going out, we saw the board of directors of the Wheat Show. They all called to me and called me 'Sweetheart.' Afterwards Mr. V. said he almost lost 'his girl'. . . . I snuggled up to Mr. V. and did not get very cold."

March 6: "At Sunday School this morning, Mr. V. said he wanted me to see him after Sunday School. Some time ago Mother and Father said they were going to join the church. Since then, Mr. Weatherwax [the religious education director] has tried several times to have me come in also. But always I refuse because I do not ever expect to be an angel. That was what Mr. V. wanted to speak to me about. He said, 'Louise! They tell me your mother and father are coming into the church, and you aren't coming with them,' etc. Of course I did just as Mr. V. said. I would do anything he asked. . . . Mr. Weatherwax was very, very glad [and] gave me a card to sign. While signing it, Mr. V. also came in. He patted me on the back. . . . He said that he would begin modeling me in a week."

A diphtheria quarantine put her out of commission for several weeks ("we took the anti-toxin Saturday in the back—gee, it was awful"), but things were back to normal by April.

April 3: "Mr. V. is going to take some Kodaks and get some pictures of me in Grecian poses. He told Mother he was going to have a 'heart-to-heart' talk with me. He will surely romp all over me."

April 7: "At last! I posed for Mr. V. We tried several poses in my red costume and gypsy costume. . . . I found out from Mother that while I was dressing he showed her a nude he was making lifesize. He would not tell the model's name. It spoiled it all for me. I don't believe he wants to model me at all."

Even so, his modeling and picture-taking sessions with her continued —so frequently that her mother couldn't always accompany her. Myra's suspicions were apparently aroused at some point, and she required escorts for Louise, but inconsistently.

Mr. Vincent, all in all, took a more obsessive interest in Louise's physical than in her spiritual development at the First Presbyterian Church of Wichita. Fifty years later, she named him as one of the sexual corruptors of her youth.

But there were more wholesome occupations—or at least occupations with boys nearer her own age. After a Maytide dance and taffy-pull party in Independence, Louise renewed a little teenage romance with a boy named Marene, who was now old enough to drive.

"Marene and I have some affair," she told her diary on May 7. "We were together all evening, and he brought me home in Dinmans' car. We rode around for *quite* a while, and oh, boy! . . . Well, I'm crazy about Marene, and I surely have him going. I suppose I'll be lovesick for a few days."

Marene was replaced by a more long-lasting heartthrob named Meridith Joselyn: "Meridith and I are still devoted," writes Louise on June 14. "We went down to see the river several times"—the euphemism for kissing sessions. A week later, Meridith threw a party and "danced with me a good deal too much to suit some of the girls. Sally Lahey is crazy about Meridith, and she said not a few catty things to me. There was a boy who was hanging about me incessantly. Mercy! Don't boys love con-man stuff. I have let M. knock me around enough to ruin anyone. They love to lord it over us, and I pretend to be so weak."

And the next day, June 23:

"Horrors—I must be boy-struck. I mope around all day now and take no interest in things that used to be so nice. . . . I have been swimming a great deal lately with Campbells and Meridith. We have lots of fun. Robert is awfully rough. He throws me around considerably, but you know what women love. We went out to Hendersons in the evening, and I gave them a dance in the moonlight on the lawn."

A week later: "I have a new one on the string—Everett Fox. I know I have him jolly well." Everett was gone in a few days, replaced by Charles

Corbett, who "kissed me five times—the villain—and some of the other boys tried it."

And so it went . . .

The only thing Louise loved more than boys was dancing. But she and her dance teacher Alice Campbell were becoming increasingly disenchanted with one another. At a loss for what to teach the girl, Miss Campbell let her develop her own lesson plans, but was embarrassed to let the fact be known. Things came to a head one evening during a lesson when Louise told her she didn't like a certain dance she'd been given.

"Well, that set the ball to rolling," Louise wrote in her diary on February 9, 1921. "She gave me an awful lecture, and all I did was to stand there, first on one foot, then the other. I guess I have about had enough of Miss Campbell."

The explosion came the next day: "Some time ago Miss C. asked everybody to quit looking at my lesson for it gave her away. I make or rather make up every bit of my dances, and everybody got onto it. That ruined Miss C.'s reputation, and when blabbed around, the thing for her to do was to remove the cause."

Alice Campbell dismissed Louise from her class for being "spoiled, bad-tempered and insulting"—charges no one could deny. Myra had often tried to curb Louise's critical tongue ("Now, dear, try to be more popular—try not to make people so mad!"), but with a notable lack of success.

"I would watch my mother, pretty and charming, as she laughed and made people feel clever and pleased with themselves," Louise wrote later, "but I could not act that way."[50]

After all the time and effort invested in Louise's creative development, Myra was devastated by the dismissal. She went to everybody at the music school—"weeping and telling the tale," said Louise, and pleading that "yes, Louise *is* hard on everyone, but she is *much* harder on herself."[51] Miss Alice was unmoved and would not relent. Louise was out, and good riddance.

In her remarkable diary entry of February 10, 1921, Louise confided that she was "not a bit sorry" about getting the boot: "It has left me with a curious, relieved feeling, and I am strong for new adventure. I must study, and that means away to broader fields. I've had enough of teaching my teacher what to teach me."

Louise was not quite rid of Alice Campbell yet.

"Mother had another talk with Miss C.," she writes ten days later. "She named the various instances when I have insulted her and showed my temper before her. Most of them are supposed, but Mother believes all. I have a rotten temper, and if I don't calm down, something worse will happen."

. . .

The loss of Alice Campbell's instruction did no harm to Louise's performing. At the end of March she danced for the American Legion show in Independence, and two weeks later there was another posh private garden-party performance:

"Everything went off very well," she wrote in her diary. "My first dance I danced along the terrace, the second down by the pool. The spotlight was flashed from the second floor, and yellow, blue and red lights were flashed. This is the first time I have entirely originated my dances. I had a fine applause, and people raved about it."

In September there was a five-night engagement at the Wheat Show in Wellington, Kansas ("I am an awful hit—the show business is in me"). A new instructor, Alice Mills, helped her spiff up some old dances—the Pierrot, the Spanish, and the Garden numbers—for the Twentieth Century Club. By fall she had graduated to the grandiose stage of the Miller Theater, Wichita's finest. Then came her greatest triumph to date, at Wichita's annual Wheat Show—biggest in the state—where she performed the Bubble Dance, "making my entrance in a pony cart piled high with balloons." At the same show, she caught the performance of the famed Pavley-Oukrainsky Ballet from Chicago.

But as she turned fifteen on November 14 ("had a rotten birthday, as usual"), she was restless and out of sorts and still complaining to her diary that "I am going to die if I can't study under a fine teacher."

Louise Brooks, and American dance enthusiasts in general, were ripe for the innovations of a sensational young company called Denishawn. When Ted Shawn's small company—with Martha Graham and Charles Weidman, but without Ruth St. Denis—came to Wichita's Crawford Theater on November 17, 1921, Louise and Myra were in the audience.

The girl and her mother considered themselves connoisseurs of music and dance, and by Midwest standards they were. They were aware of the free-form dancing of Isadora Duncan, whose abstract improvisations to Beethoven, Liszt, Chopin, and Gluck still shocked most traditional ballet-omanes. But Myra and Louise were not prepared for the more disciplined originality of Ted Shawn, and they sat spellbound by the breathtaking variety of choreography, set to a gamut of compositions from Scarlatti to Erik Satie.

No one in Wichita, it was safe to say, had ever heard Satie's spare, plaintive, eccentric music before. The program was balanced with more accessible fare such as the *Valse Directoire*, a sentimental favorite originally choreographed by Shawn for Carol Dempster. Of great relevance to Wichitans—located as they were in the heart of Plains Indian territory—was Shawn's powerful *Invocation to the Thunderbird*. This highly athletic representation of an American Indian dance was the first serious stage choreography of its kind.[52] Set to John Philip Sousa's "The Red Man" (from his suite *Dwellers in the Western World*), the *Thunderbird* made as great an impact in Wichita as it had at its Los Angeles premiere just two months before.

The long and varied program (twenty-three numbers) also included *Pierrot Forlorn*, the first dance Shawn choreographed for the tragicomic pantomime of Charles Weidman, and *Revolutionary Étude*, set to Chopin's soul-stirring statement of Polish nationalism and featuring Martha Graham—"one of the earliest examples of proletarian ferment in American dance terms."[53] It owed its genesis to Isadora Duncan's *Marseillaise*, but there was no denying its original impact when Shawn leaped straight toward the footlights, one clenched fist upraised, the other behind his back, turning wildly to reconnoiter the stage for hidden enemies. As the music crescendoed with Graham's desperate run into his arms, Shawn personified the despair of the oppressed in revolt.

But none of what preceded it could rival the finale—Shawn's spectacular dance-drama, *Xochitl*. The first American dance based on Aztec-Toltec themes, with lavishly authentic sets and costumes by the Mexican artist Francisco Cornajo, *Xochitl* contained the first solo role created for Martha Graham and marked the first professional appearances of Charles Weidman and of Graham's talented younger sister Geordie—forever in Martha's shadow. Its tale was that of the virtuous Xochitl (Martha Graham), whose father (Weidman) concocts a mind-altering liquor from the maguey plant. When they take the magic liquid to the emperor (Shawn), he becomes intoxicated by the drink and by Xochitl's dancing. In a violent duet, the emperor forces himself upon the girl, who resists ferociously— so ferociously that Graham often left Shawn's face bloody and bruised. Finally returned to his senses, the repentant ruler makes Xochitl his empress as his court celebrates and the curtain falls, to wild applause.

Deeply moved, Myra and Louise went backstage after the performance, and Louise was introduced to Shawn, who was attracted by the mischievous, alluring look of the girl. He invited her to attend his new Denishawn dance school in New York the following summer. Having just seen the miracles of which that school was capable, Louise was excited by the prospect.

"He is awfully goodlooking and has a wonderful personality," she told her diary that night. "I am *crazy* about him!"

Wichita could hold her no longer. Over the next six months, she and Myra worked relentlessly on poor Leonard Brooks: In addition to Mr. Shawn's invitation, $300 tuition was required to attend his school.

Leonard finally provided his money and his blessing after Myra located a suitable chaperone: Alice Mills, Louise's recent dance "consultant." Louise described her as "a stocky, bespectacled housewife of thirty-six

Louise on the eve of her departure from Wichita for Denishawn

who, having fallen idiotically in love with the beautiful Ted Shawn at first sight, decided to study dance with him."[54] Mrs. Mills would accompany her and live with her in New York, where she would have the unenviable job of keeping Louise out of trouble.

When the Santa Fe train pulled out of Union Station in Wichita, heading northeast in the heat of July 1922, fifteen-year-old Louise Brooks shed not a single tear.

*Denishawn Dancer Louise as Hopi Princess Kodeh with
Ted Shawn as Kwahu in* The Feather of the Dawn, *1924*

2 · Denishawn and the Silver Salver

True ease in writing comes from art, not chance,
As those move easiest who have learn'd to dance.
— ALEXANDER POPE

LOUISE was dazzled.

"I was 15 years old in the summer of 1922 when, after getting off the train from Wichita, Kansas, I walked into the Grand Central Station and fell in love with New York forever. As I looked down at the marble floor and then up 200 feet to the great dome arching over my head, a shaft of sunlight from one of the huge, cross-barred windows pierced my heart."[1]

Other than that burst of youthful poetry, not much record of Louise's first exposure to the kaleidoscope of New York City survives.* She appears to have absorbed the experience in silence, keeping her emotions to herself by predisposition and by a determination not to appear unsophisticated.

Any romantic delusions of grandeur were quickly laid to rest by the reality of her new home—an undazzling rented room in a railroad flat on 86th Street near Riverside Drive. There she passed the steamy summer nights tossing and turning in a double bed next to the lumpy Alice Mills. Though contemptuous of Alice, Louise was smart enough to realize how loosely she and her good-natured chaperone were handcuffed.

"I tolerated Mrs. Mills' provincialism because she shared my love of the theatre," wrote Louise years later.[2] Together they saw as many Broadway shows as they could afford, including the Sigmund Romberg hit *Blossom Time*, which was the first Broadway musical to employ classical compositions. In that "biography" of Franz Schubert, he's so hopelessly in love

* Her 1922 diary is lost.

with a girl named Mitzi that he can't concentrate on composing—hence the "Unfinished Symphony."

But Louise's favorite was the *Ziegfeld Follies*.

"In the first act," she remembered, "Fanny Brice's burlesque of Pavlova's swan dance filled the New Amsterdam Theatre with laughter. In the last act, standing motionless in front of a black velvet curtain, with black velvet sheathing her exquisite figure, she broke the audience's heart with her singing of 'My Man.'"

Aside from Fanny Brice, "the rest of my attention was concentrated on the famous *Follies* girls. I was not impressed. Only Anastasia Reilly, with her smooth dark hair and her boyish figure set off by a pageboy costume, showed personality, that faithfulness to nature which I sought, and still seek, in all human beings. The rest of the girls wore smiles as fixed as their towering feather headdresses. I decided right then that onstage I would never smile unless I felt like it."[3]

Even at fifteen, Louise was a hypercritical observer, hungrily sampling the delights of Broadway and already making some significant long-range resolutions concerning her stage persona. She was also laying plans for the creation of "my dream woman"—for "inside the brat who sweated four hours a day at dancing school lived the secret bride of New York whose goal was the sophisticated grace of the lovely women already seen and studied in the pages of *Harper's Bazaar* and *Vanity Fair*."[4]

But first the bride-to-be had to do the sweating. "Horses sweat, men perspire, and ladies glow," went the refrain. Louise did all three in the rigid regimen of the Denishawn School, which afforded little time (and no money) for frivolity. Alice Mills's willing availability for theatergoing was a godsend. Otherwise, "nightlife" was generally discouraged and, in any event, unlikely after the long, exhausting hours of classes. The instruction was demanding, but fabulously creative compared to her primitive dance training back in Kansas.

"Mr. Shawn's lessons consisted of demonstrations of his matchless balance and body control in such creations as his 'Japanese Spear Dance' and his 'Pose Plastique,'" Louise recalled. "Charles Weidman, his most experienced male dancer, took us through barre and ballet exercises. During a sweltering July and August, I went to weekday classes from ten to twelve in the morning and from one to three in the afternoon. Even in the ballet work, we danced barefoot, which was painful for unaccustomed feet on the splintering pine floor. Having gone barefoot during Kansas summers, I was spared the torn soles and blisters that tormented some of the pupils. Sweat! Sweat! Sweat! Exhausted boys stood in pools of their own sweat. Unwashed black wool bathing suits stank with stale sweat."[5]

The only "sweat-free, stink-free pupil," she said, was "a sweet, lonely fat girl, who stood around waiting for one of the three boys in the class to ask her out, which none of them ever did. Most of the students were females from the Middle West, to which, like my chaperone, Alice Mills, they would return to establish Denishawn schools. Kansas-born though I was, 'these hicks,' with their marcelled hair, their blouses and skirts, and their flat, unsyncopated voices describing the wonders of Grant's Tomb and the Statue of Liberty, filled me with scorn."[6]

The scorn did not escape the notice of Miss Ruth when she was in New York. St. Denis practiced something like "holistic supervision" over her students' lives—their dancing, their after-hours reading, and even their spiritual development fell under her purview. Denishawn's ambience was idealistic and ascetic, in sharp contrast to the rest of the contemporary dance scene, such as it was.

"The only [American] ballet was at the Metropolitan Opera and it was so bad you wouldn't believe it," said Ted Shawn. "Dancing then was limited to the lines of chorus girls kicking 16 times to the right, then 16 to the left, embellished by a 'cartwheel,' 'the splits' or kicking the back of one's head, or by the clog, soft shoe and acrobatic dancers of vaudeville."[7] There was no company that regularly toured with a whole evening of dance, which was merely incidental to other theatrical forms.

Not so at Denishawn, where Louise, as one of the newest and youngest pupils, had a lot of work to do just in learning the ropes. The first rope was learning how to deal with Miss Ruth and "Papa" Shawn themselves.

The exotic Ruth St. Denis began life as the less exotic Ruthie Dennis of Eagleswood, New Jersey. As a teenager she did variety-act skirt dancing before being discovered by impresario David Belasco, who in 1900 nicknamed her "St. Dennis" because of her chaste behavior offstage. The canonized surname stuck, and added glamour. In 1906 in New York, she created the East Indian suite *Radha* (or *The Mystic Dance of the Five Senses*) to music from Leo Delibes's *Lakmé*. This first great innovative solo propelled her into a three-year European tour. More important, as Jane Sherman observes, *Radha* was "the spark that started a revolution in the art of American serious theatrical dance."*

During her long career, St. Denis maintained her spiritual-intellectual development through extensive readings in all manner of philosophy and religion. Her inspiration and her aim in dance came from the Kantian precept of "the Good, the True and the Beautiful." She was influenced by Mary Baker Eddy's Christian Science and, even more profoundly, by Eastern religions.

---

* Jane Sherman, a Denishawn student from 1923–1925 and company member from 1925–1928, was a keen observer who in later years became the Denishawn historian, chronicling its important dances, tours, and artistic development in four authoritative books (see Bibliography) from which this account draws heavily.

At a time when "no 'nice' girl would ever display her legs on the stage to the lewd gaze of men," Shawn said later, St. Denis "freed the female human body from the ugly, crippling, unhealthy clothes that prevailed around the turn of the century, . . . enduring ridicule, antagonism, even persecution" in the process. Even more crucial, "Isadora Duncan and Ruth St. Denis freed movement itself from the stylized, artificial crystallizations of 19th century ballet, and from the meaningless acrobatics of the commercial theater."[8]

Ted Shawn was similarly absorbed by religion (for a while he had been a Methodist divinity student) and its rendition in dance. His ballroom apprenticeship took him from Denver to Los Angeles, where he gave exhibitions of the bunny hug, turkey trot, tango, and maxixe. Shawn, too, was intrigued by ethnic dances but, unlike St. Denis, looked primarily to the Americas for inspiration. He found it in Aztec and North American Indian legends, Negro spirituals and the John Brown legacy, New England "contra" dancing, and cowboy lore.

Shawn and St. Denis met in 1911, fell in love, and married in 1914 over the hysterical objections of Ruth's mother. The virginal bride was thirty-five, the groom twenty-two. They immediately embarked on a series of successful tours together. In 1915, a name-that-waltz contest in Portland, Oregon, produced the word "Denishawn" and a lot of good publicity. Soon after that, the "Denishawn Dancers" came into existence, along with "The Ruth St. Denis School of Dancing and its Related Arts" in Los Angeles. The first classes lasted all day and—with lunch included—cost $1, a fee that the students dropped into a cigar box on their way in. In 1916 the renamed "Denishawn School" admitted a Santa Barbara girl named Martha Graham. Miss Ruth had thought her too old (at twenty-two), too small, too overweight, and too homely, but Shawn thought he saw talent there.

The school had pragmatic as well as artistic purposes: Shawn's "dance-dramas" and St. Denis's nonnarrative "music visualizations" were growing increasingly ambitious and required a supply of young dancers trained technically and attitudinally for new challenges. Tuition-paying students, moreover, helped supplement the thin box-office receipts in an era that predated grants or other outside support. Shawn and St. Denis were constantly searching for the delicate balance between their high artistic standards and the demands of commercial theater.

By the end of 1921, Shawn opened the New York branch of Denishawn, soon to be located on West 28th Street, with a summer studio in Carnegie Hall. The proliferation of Denishawn schools had begun, and the creation was four-pronged: dance company, school, new technique of movement, and pedagogic theory—"the first systematic and sustained attempt to provide in Western theater dance a substantial alternative to ballet"[9] and the first to pass such a discipline on to others. By the 1950s, two dozen American dance companies could trace their lineage to Shawn, St. Denis, or their star protégés, Martha Graham, Doris Humphrey, and Charles Weidman.

In effect, Denishawn founded American modern dance.

Louise Brooks, arriving in New York in 1922, was on the ground floor of this phenomenon, or at least the mezzanine. Her recruitment in Wichita was typical of the informal manner by which budding dancers were discovered for Denishawn in the course of Shawn's touring. The most talented of them would be invited, after proving themselves, to become members of the company at a salary of $40 a week, with a $5 raise for each additional year of service. It wasn't a fabulous amount—but then Denishawn was the only modern-dance company that paid *anything* on a regular basis. "Competition to join their ranks was therefore enormous among hundreds of young dance students who could find no other self-supporting outlet for their talents," says Sherman. And most of the chosen few became intensely motivated, rededicating their minds and bodies to the demands of Denishawn professionalism.

St. Denis, while not concerning herself with imparting technique, occasionally visited to watch the students at work or to deliver a little inspirational talk on the Art of Dancing. Some of those words-to-live-by were preserved by the fourteen-year-old Jane Sherman, who scribbled them down. "Any technique is sufficient which adequately expresses the thought intended by the artist," St. Denis said one day. And another time, "You should *think* of the dance as Art although you may have to *do* it as a business." Among her most cosmic declarations: "We dancers reveal your inner selves. We are your dreams made real."

One of Miss Ruth's pronouncements held special relevance for Louise. This was St. Denis's conviction—based on a long conflict of her own—that "a talented girl is the result of a mother who has been repressed and into whom goes all that mother's ambition and culture."

St. Denis's classroom appearances at the New York and Los Angeles schools often included demonstrations that held both novices and veterans enthralled and attracted such celebrity guest-pupils as Lillian and Dorothy Gish, Ina Claire, Myrna Loy, Ruth Chatterton, and actor-director Richard Bennett (with his daughters Joan and Barbara). Miss Ruth's electric presence and philosophy thus influenced not just her own students but other performers beyond the realm of dance.

Yet Louise saw immediately that the real teaching force at the school was Ted Shawn and that St. Denis was content that it should be so. Like all Denishawn dancers, Louise was expected to learn and perform varied dance forms, but first to master a basic technique which, except for lack of *pointes*, was nearly identical to that of classic ballet. Sometimes Shawn himself relieved Doris Humphrey in supervising the strenuous, half-hour barre routine. This was followed by open floor exercises to perfect the dancers' *arabesques, attitudes, fouettés,* and *pas de chat.* After executing solo *tours jetés*, leaps, and spins, the dancers lined up to try brief figurations, always watching themselves in the wall-sized mirror. Each student alone would then do a sequence of Spanish, Hungarian, and Denishawn *pas de basques.*

Next it was Shawn personally who paced Louise and the others through Denishawn's "Arms and Body" exercise, done to the Briar Rose Waltz from Tchaikovsky's *Sleeping Beauty.* Everyone then sat in a circle for the next activity, which was unlike anything Louise had experienced in her Kansas dance training—"hand stretches to force the fingers as far back as they would go, in imitation of Cambodian or Balinese flexibility. Or we would strain to copy the East Indian cobra side-to-side head movements above motionless shoulders." [10] Class always concluded with learning a dance that might—and often did—find its way into the performing repertory. As the exercise combinations were incorporated into dances, the movement became freer and more concerned with interpretations.

Arriving for these classes, Louise sometimes discovered an American or foreign guest dancer-choreographer holding forth. For Shawn and St. Denis prided themselves on giving students "the richest and most varied fare possible—old, new, domestic, foreign, and anything we felt would enlarge their knowledge of dance that had any value (we did *not* include tap dancing!)."

Shawn's energy, perfectionism, and often stinging criticism were counterbalanced by an impartiality that made for good group spirit and morale. He taught passionately and, Louise thought, brilliantly. He had devised his own magic formula by borrowing and embellishing upon ballet, eurythmics, French movement theory, and ethnic gesture. Between 1914 and 1931, he choreographed 185 of 300 Denishawn dances and nine of its sixteen major ballets, co-creating another three with St. Denis—and he danced in most of them himself.

Denishawn's success as both a teaching and performing organization required the presence of a third great artist, Louis Horst, the pianist-composer and musical director who supplied the amazing range of music to which Denishawners danced. After he joined the company in 1915, he quietly began to displace the syrupy compositions of Ethelbert Nevin and Victor Herbert with Bach and Beethoven and the modern music of Satie, Debussy, Ravel, and Scriabin—none of them yet well known in America. Often, Denishawn's audiences in the hinterlands were hearing such music for the first time.

It was a fortuitous coincidence for Louise that many of those "advanced" composers were the ones of which her mother was so enamored. Thanks to Myra's piano efforts, the little five-foot-two hayseed with the pudgy cheeks and the flashing eyes was already on intimate terms with much of this music before she came to New York—a fact that astonished her peers and teachers alike. Back in Kansas, Louise had invented her own steps to some of these same piano works; many of the rhythms and cadences were already "in her feet," or at least in her head. Denishawn pupils were instructed never to count—in rehearsal or performance—no matter how complicated the beat. Just "listen to the fundamental pulse, the sound of phrase endings and beginnings, the overall 'feel,' " Doris Humphrey told them, "because the body can be taught to memorize through the muscles." Louise had a head start, but she was also dancing to a good deal of new music, commissioned specially for Denishawn, by such important American composers as Edward MacDowell, Charles Wakefield Cadman, and Charles Tomlinson Griffes.

While the music, the dance, and the instruction enthralled her, the "off-duty" regulations did not. One of the reasons for the school's success was its reputation for strict morality. The public liked what it perceived as the impeccable conduct of "happily married" Shawn and St. Denis—an image carefully fostered by Miss Ruth. She made it known through her interviews that she lived according to the highest personal ideals; left unspoken, but implied, was a comparison to the scandalous Isadora Duncan. Also unspoken (and unnoticed) was Shawn's bisexuality—as idealistic, in its way, as St. Denis's heterosexuality—and the fact that Denishawn's namesakes spent most of their half century of wedlock living apart.

Denishawn students, Miss Ruth decreed, "must live quietly, read good books, listen to good music, seek an atmosphere of culture." Louise of her own accord did the latter three, but chafed at the first. All of a sudden, in the wild and permissive Jazz Age, she was faced with a moral code unknown to her even in childhood: no boyfriends, no drinking, and certainly no sex. "Miss St. Denis is very strict," Louise told one interviewer. "She wouldn't let us smoke or eat candy or stay up late or anything. We did nothing but work and dance."[11]

Jane Sherman, because of her strict upbringing, was an inadvertent example of the Denishawn "good girl" who conformed to Miss Ruth's model. "A trip around the world is better than a motor ride to a roadhouse," she told a New York *Telegram* reporter on the eve of the company's 1925–1926 Far Eastern tour. But even this good girl rebelled at St. Denis's nagging demand that she lose the adolescent pounds she gained during the early months of that tour. Wrote Jane in a letter from India:

"Mother, something drastic must be done with me when I get home. I now weigh 125 and you know that's too much. I've *gained* four pounds in spite of fasting, dieting, heat, and all. . . . Edith [James] swears it's the climate plus my age and I sincerely hope she's right. Louise Brooks was fatter than I am! And not just around the hips! So I guess there's some hope for me yet."[12]

Photographs of Louise at the time show that Sherman was right. Then, and later in films, Louise with her rather short legs and plumpish thighs never possessed the perfect dancer's figure. "I am on a diet, and it is very hard," she wrote in her diary March 27, after a show in Marshalltown, Iowa. "I must stick to it and get these 'hips' of mine down." It was the very same preoccupation that she "scorned" in her peers.

With grand superiority, she pretended not to care about her appearance and went about immersing herself in Denishawn dance instruction, trying to grasp the theory of movement that suffused it.

François Delsarte (1811–1871) held sway over an unlikely combination of artists, intellectuals, and physical culturists, including the dance pioneers. His motivational science of movement was at the heart of Denishawn's theory and practice, and Shawn imparted it to Louise as to all of his dancers, in simplified form. Delsarte correlated every human movement to an emotional state. His tenet was that movement expresses emotion much more viscerally and directly than speech; that, in fact, it is emotion which produces body movement in the first place.

Understanding human gestures, Shawn believed, could even enable people in everyday life to read each other's emotions. "Every thought and feeling is shown by the movements, attitudes, contours of the human body," declared Shawn, who functioned as the company's psychiatrist. It was no wonder they called him "Papa."

Denishawn students benefited from one highly practical application of Delsarte—the freeing of the dancers' feet from shoes. The naked, unencumbered foot brought far greater emotional expression into dance by increasing flexibility and introducing thousands of new combinations into the gesticular "vocabulary" of the choreographer. Bare feet, perhaps, marked the single biggest difference between classical ballet and Denishawn dance.

Nothing could have been more natural and agreeable to Louise, the barefoot kid from Kansas.

Delsarte's, in truth, was a pan-artistic theory. As preached and practiced by Shawn, it emphasized the interdependence of *all* the performing arts. Denishawn's total theatrical experience—visual, musical, kinaesthetic, speechless—was not unlike another popular entertainment (few called it an art) of the day: silent film. Almost every word of Delsarte, especially his "Nine Basic Problems of Pantomime," was applicable to the movies, and St. Denis's biographer, Suzanne Shelton, would cite Louise along with the Gish sisters, Mabel Normand, and others "who created a language of silent film gesture based solidly on Delsarte."[13]

"Much can be said with little," observed Shawn. "I have seen an almost immobile body, under terrific stress, move an audience almost to tears by a movement of one big toe."

In later years, Louise was fond of saying, "I learned how to act by watching Martha Graham dance." Dozens of times during the 1922–1923 season, Louise watched her onstage from the wings, thrilling to Graham's solo *Serenata Morisca*. More than half a century later, referring to the title of Sherman's 1979 book, *The Drama of Denishawn Dance*, Louise wrote Jane: "You are right to call Denishawn 'Drama.' Martha is a superb actress whose unpopular monkey face in that period of candy-box prettiness kept her out of the theater. So she turned dialogue into dance. What I would give to see her Hedda Gabler. . . ."

Brooks and Graham alike owed a dramatic debt to one of the greatest dancer-pantomimists of all, Charles Weidman, who was already well on his way to becoming the premier male dancer in the country, after Shawn. As instructor to the advanced Denishawners, Weidman often ended his lessons with pantomime exercises. But simply watching his *Pierrot Forlorn* was a subliminal education in itself, and company members took private delight in Weidman's wickedly funny offstage pantomimicry of Miss Ruth.

In fact, all five of the major Denishawn performers—St. Denis, Shawn, Graham, Weidman, and Humphrey—were superb actors in different ways, and impressionable Louise Brooks, the intense observer, would have two whole seasons in which to study their creative processes and ability to project characters across the footlights. The impact of their examples to a large degree shaped the movement qualities that she would later put to good use on the movie set.

In the imaginary gradebook of Denishawn students' development, Louise received high marks. She was a quick study and happily absorbed Ted Shawn's charismatic instruction, transforming herself from a raw novice to a skilled Denishawn actress-dancer in just a few months. There was a special quality about her, an intensity, that projected from behind those burning black eyes and penetrated to those who watched her. Shawn did not fail to notice it. Neither did Martha Graham.

"My first memory of Louise Brooks is still very vivid in my mind," recalls Graham, sixty-five years later. "She stood in the center of a group of girls in Denishawn. They all dressed in the same short dress, the hair the same, and yet Louise stood out in two ways, because she was so extraordinarily beautiful and because of a deep inner power that stood her all of her life."[14]

Louise's rapid progress was just as rapidly rewarded: She was asked to join the company after her first brief summer session as a student—an unusually fast elevation.* The Denishawn schools, of course, had become their founders' own private minor league for the tracking of their best prospects into the real world of "professional entertainment," and Louise was one of the most promising rookies.

Throughout its existence, Denishawn choreography was continuously tested in the box-office crucible—from high-school gyms and small-town movie houses to Tokyo's Imperial Theater and New York's Carnegie Hall. But most of the company's early performances took place on vaudeville circuits. The ultimate vaudeville appearance was Denishawn's 1916 booking at the Palace in New York, where demand for tickets was so great that the management retained the Denishawn Dancers for a second week—Sarah Bernhardt being the only other act ever held over up to that time.

Such glorious engagements were few, however, and most of vaudeville was far from glamorous. Its managers and agents were "the most sadistic, ghoulish, and horrible people encountered in a long professional life," said Shawn, adding that the kind of audiences "who spend hard-earned quarters to watch a seal twirl a trumpet were not *always* receptive to the dance of Denishawn."[15]

Even so, vaudeville paid the bills and helped subsidize the Los Angeles school in its early years. When impresario Daniel Mayer saw a 1921 Denishawn matinee at the Apollo Theater in New York, he was so impressed that he offered to manage a concert tour for the company. Shawn and St. Denis signed a contract in February 1922 for a series of three American concert tours that ranked among the company's highest achievements and initiated Denishawn's "Golden Era," which lasted until 1931.

Numbered among its dancers for the 1922–1923 tour was the fifteen-year-old Louise Brooks, now a full member of one of St. Denis's and Shawn's most impressive companies, consisting of Martha Graham, Charles Weidman, Betty May, Paul Mathis, Robert Gorham, Lenore Scheffer, and five others. This first of the three Mayer concert tours was a grueling one. Previously, the company's vaudeville dates had taken Denishawn to the major cities, where the dance troupe appeared as just one act among many. Now Denishawn would be the featured attraction, sharing the bill with nobody in a phenomenal series of 180 performances in 202 days, between October 1922 and April 1923, in 130 U.S. and Canadian cities.

For Louise, as for the rest of the company, there was only minimal glitter, at best, to performing in places like Shamokin, Altoona, Sandusky, and Ponca City. But Wichita's Crawford Theater was on the list, and Louise got to live out a show-business fantasy: On November 18, 1922,

---

* At least for girls. The double standard whereby boys were more quickly admitted to the company stemmed from the great dearth of male dancers and the need to assimilate them faster.

The Denishawn Company of 1923–1924

she performed with the same dancers who had dazzled her and her mother on the other side of the footlights exactly a year and a day earlier. She was deluged with flowers. Her glory—and Myra's—was complete when Shawn, St. Denis, Graham, and Weidman all went to the Brooks home for a late supper that night to celebrate Louise's sixteenth birthday.

"Another year gone," she wrote in her diary on New Year's Day 1923. "It doesn't seem to me that I have changed so much, only learned a great deal. We are on the sleeper now, leaving Springfield, Ill., where we played a crowded house."

The next day in Toledo, she reports that "it's snowing outside, and everything seems a sort of fairyland"—a theme repeated two days later in Erie, Pennsylvania: "This is a lovely little town. It makes me think of Christmas and storybooks."

But the novelty of the snow and the touring was wearing off by the time the company got to frigid Burlington, Vermont.

"Oh, it's so cold here, and I have a cold," she writes on January 6, 1923. "Bobby [Gorham] is going into the waltz Monday, so we rehearse and rehearse." The all-day train ride of January 7 brought them to Manchester, New Hampshire, but "of course, there are no picture shows."

The worst—the Lyceum in New London, Connecticut—awaited them the following night: "The theater was awful here, and I never saw such rats. I was almost left again today. We changed trains while I slept, and I awoke ten minutes later to find everyone gone. Luckily neither of the trains had left yet, and I grabbed everything and dashed off. They said I was a funny sight as I got on the other train—wild-eyed, white as a sheet, and carrying things in my arms."

But her spirits were lifted twenty-four hours later in Lowell, Massachusetts: "It was the opposite from last night. We played a beautiful auditorium. We are having a hard week. Early morning jumps and all day rides. We are saving, too, and go to the cheap hotels." Louise tended to forget the hardships if she felt she was making progress. "We had a long rehearsal today," she wrote on January 11 in Worcester, Massachusetts, "and Martha helped me with my work quite a bit. It is so nice of her to help me."

For the rest of her life, Louise spoke with awe of Graham:

Martha Graham['s] genius I absorbed to the bone during the years we danced together on tour. She had rages, you know, that struck like lightning out of nowhere. One evening when we were waiting to go onstage—I was sixteen—she grabbed me, shook me ferociously, and shouted, "Why do you ruin your feet by wearing those tight shoes?" Another time, she was sitting sweetly at the makeup shelf pinning flowers in her hair when she suddenly seized a bottle of body makeup and exploded it against the mirror. She looked at the shattered remains for a spell, then moved her makeup along to an unbroken mirror and went on quietly pinning flowers in her hair.[16]

In mid-January, the frozen Denishawners finally boarded a train for the southern part of the tour—the Carolinas, Georgia, Florida, Texas, and Alabama. In Jacksonville, Louise took a boat ride up the St. Johns River, marveling at the Spanish moss–covered trees. "Coming back," she said, "Betty [May], Bobby [Gorham], Mr. [Bill] Burns and myself sat on the back and read Whiz Bang, ate oranges and had a lovely time. Mr. Burns is perfectly adorable." Mr. Burns, a freelance publicist who attached himself to the company for a while, thought the same of Louise. They saw a lot of each other over the next several weeks, ignoring the raised eyebrows of company members.

"Some Georgia Tech boys sent some boys back to see us here," Louise writes in Gainesville. "We went out for a ride very foolishly after the show, and they proved too wild. So we headed them for home at once. Bah! I hate college boys. Give me Billy-boy."

A week later they were back in New England, and so was Billy-boy. "Billy came up to our rooms about 12 o'clock with cigarettes and sandwiches," she writes in Boston on March 1. "It was very late, and he didn't want to go out and run the risk of being seen, so he stayed all night. I sort of think Billy has a case on me." Indications elsewhere in the diary suggest she slept with him that night. But he left again, suddenly, and this time didn't return. "That Billy Burns is often in my mind," she wrote March 10 in Detroit. "I haven't heard a word from him. I guess he has forgotten 'Hell Cat.' "

For Louise, no less than for the other dancers, the travel was exhausting and the routine unchanging: Catch the train at dawn, sleep fitfully on straw or woolen coach seats, and, upon arrival, rush straight to the hotel, and then the theater. Typically, the dancers arrived in the afternoon, located their trunks, ironed, hung their costumes in the dressing rooms, dressed their wigs, and laid out make-up. Only occasionally was there time for a brief rest or light supper. The three-hour concert itself was often followed by a private command performance, for Ted and Miss Ruth were always courting local society angels, and the weary dancers had to oblige.

At this point, Louise felt as close to Ruth St. Denis as she ever would. "Betty, Lenore and I hired a horse and buggy and had a picnic," she writes in Rocky Mount, North Carolina. "Miss Ruth got in and drove a while. Such fun, and we almost wrecked ourselves several times." A few nights later, in Salisbury, North Carolina, St. Denis was at her side in sickness instead of health.

"I am always having trouble with constipation," wrote Louise in her diary, "and tonight I could hardly do the show. Miss Ruth took me home and gave me citrate magnesia, two enemas, and rubbed my stomach. Then she tucked me in bed and kissed me. I just adore her!"

On and on went the tour: to Niagara Falls, Oshkosh, a week in Minneapolis and St. Paul, Cedar Rapids, Waterloo, Dubuque, then back to Chicago, Steubenville, and Philadelphia. The grand finale was twelve straight performances, April 9 through 18, at New York City's Town Hall.

That staggering schedule constituted the professional debut of Louise Brooks—a baptism of fire, under the demands of which many adolescents might have crumbled. But Louise rose to the occasion. It was a heady experience to be dancing in small ensembles with Martha Graham or Shawn himself and to find herself in the very ballet that had most enthralled her—*Xochitl*, with Shawn as Emperor Tepancáltzin in the same enormous cape of orange feathers he had worn when she saw him partnering Graham in Wichita the previous year. Louise was thrilled on March 16, after the show in Eau Claire, Wisconsin, because "tonight Mr. Shawn told me that I was being considered for the solo part in *Xochitl* next year. No one else in the company is being considered, and he said Martha might rehearse me on it, and I must watch it every night. I think it is perfectly wonderful to even be considered, and I will work and work."

Louise's life—like all Denishawners'—was lived out of the suitcase and the two-tiered tin make-up box that each dancer carried on the road. It contained the traditional Leichner's and Stein's cosmetics, two tubes of greasepaint (flesh tone for "music visualizations" and light brown for ethnic numbers), two jars of paste rouge (pale red for cheeks, crimson for lips), eyeshadow, face powder, and solid mascara—which had to be sliced off into a tiny tin frying pan and melted over a candle before it could be applied (quickly before it hardened!) with a matchstick. The dancers paid their own food and hotel bills out of their meager salaries and put up with a multitude of inconveniences. In her theater duffle bag, Louise had to pack a supply of make-up towels (usually "borrowed" from Pullman cars) and rolls of surgical cotton, for nothing like Kleenex or sanitary napkins existed. And of course there were no hair dryers, Band-Aids, zippers, diet pills, birth-control pills, or other such theatrical "essentials." Since body paint was required on all exposed flesh in all performances, everyone had to carry a quart jar of Denishawn's special concoction, hand-mixed by the dancers from powdered zinc, glycerine, and witch hazel.

Because serious dance was in such an embryonic state, there was no such thing as a dance critic. Many newspapers along the route sent sportswriters to "cover" Denishawn, figuring dance was closer to athletics than to anything else. During an interview with one such cigar-chomping reporter, Miss Ruth mentioned Isadora Duncan's contributions to dance. "Miss St. Denis speaks highly of Isadore and Mrs. Duncan," said the next day's write-up.[17] Such ludicrous coverage confirmed Louise's worst prejudices about the provinces. She missed New York, and in more ways than one. Not only was it *the* place to be, but as a practical matter, it was much easier to circumvent the legendary Denishawn Moral Code there. In New York, the city was so huge, she and her activities were easily lost from view.

But on the road—with everyone on the same floor in the same hotel—escaping from her colleagues and returning undetected was much trickier, if not impossible. Although the proper Denishawn Dancer tried to refrain from gossip, Louise provided irresistible fodder by carrying on with the likes of Billy Burns.

Anne Douglas, a colleague of Brooks's during the second Mayer tour, recalls that "Louise wasn't a very happy person" because "she wasn't where she wanted to be, and she'd had a bit more freedom than the rest of us. I got the impression Louise was going out with different men she met on the trip. Maybe it was just to dinner, but in any event she was asserting herself a little more than was comfortable [for the rest of the company]. She just didn't conform and was sort of rebellious."[18]

The Denishawners, like other traveling troupers, tended to break down into small groups. Louise and Lenore Scheffer were almost inseparable; Doris Humphrey, Charles Weidman, and Pauline Lawrence formed a close trio; Anne Douglas roomed with Geordie Graham. But the strain of constant performing, long train rides, and seedy accommodations tried everyone's nerves.

So did Louise's combination of testiness and promiscuity.

"She was very flirty in the hotels," Douglas recalls, "and it was quite easy for men to have a conversation with her."[19] That alone was sufficient to send up a red flag to Miss Ruth. But then came the fatal whisper: "Somebody did say one time that she stayed with somebody one night," Douglas remembers. "We were so excited about that we didn't know what to do!"[20]

Another Denishawner recalled a secondhand report that Louise "slept with all the backstage crew, which upset Mr. Shawn's morals," though Jane Sherman notes that "Denishawn never travelled with a backstage crew of its own much larger than a stage manager and an electrician-carpenter. Other stagehands were recruited locally in whatever theatre they were playing."[21]

It might well have been such a local recruit in whom Louise was interested, but there is no real evidence. The Loose Louise tales later sounded to Sherman "like pretty precocious activity for a 15- or 16-year-old in the early 1920s, particularly in a company noted for its prissiness, its Puritan regulation of behavior, its no smoking/drinking edicts and, it goes without saying, its ban on sexual 'immorality.' "

But the truth mattered less than the perception. Once such rumors got started, they snowballed. Whether or not Louise slept with anyone, the allegation got back to St. Denis and Shawn, whom she viewed as a decided cramp in her style. One night during the tour, in Montreal, Louise noted in her diary that a friend "took us to a lovely cabaret. We could have had a wonderful time, but Miss R. and Mr. S. were along, and we had to be good."

Louise, however, was a fine dancer, and for the time being her personal peccadilloes were overlooked. When the tour ended, in April of 1923, she went, along with most of the rest of the company, for an idyllic summer session at the Mariarden arts colony in Peterborough, New Hampshire.

Greek togas and a wholesome theory of health and culture were the order of the place, founded in 1919 by Guy Currier, a wealthy corporation lawyer, and his wife, Marie, who had once studied dancing with St. Denis. They added the Forest of Arden to Mrs. Currier's first name to produce "Mariarden."* Over the years, various theater and dance groups made use of its ninety sylvan acres, containing the first outdoor stage in America. Eugene O'Neill came to watch a production of his *Emperor Jones* in the forest setting and declared, "At last this has been done as I have written it." [22]

Mariarden's faculty included Ted Shawn as director of the dance department. He taught two dance classes a week in return for free residence and studio and a small percentage of the students' tuition. At this summer theater-school-camp, Shawn put his teenagers through their paces while, simultaneously, he and Ruth worked up material for the next Mayer tour. It was here that he developed *The Death of Adonis*, his masterful "sculpture plastique" which shocked audiences because the soloist wore only the tiniest fig leaf under a coat of white body paint. "Until Shawn attempted it [on the third Mayer tour, 1924–1925]," says Sherman, "no one in this country had yet seen nudity combined with movement. It was too shocking for the cook at Mariarden. When she saw the dress rehearsal, she frantically phoned her employers to inform them that Mr. Shawn was doing an obscene dance."

At Mariarden Louise made an important friendship—with Barbara Bennett, whose actor-father, Richard, she had seen at the Denishawn studio and whose mother, Adrienne Morrison, was also a celebrated actress and, later, literary agent. Barbara's sister Constance was already a

---

* The Peterborough area had been an artistic haven for many years, beginning with the "Trooly Rooral Theater" in 1867. Just across the valley from Mariarden was the Edward MacDowell Artists Colony, sponsored by the composer's wife, which still survives.

young film actress on the rise. Blond, glamorous Constance was the pride of the family; the year before, at eighteen, she had turned out three films, *Reckless Youth, Evidence*, and *What's Wrong With the Women?* Her little sister, Joan, then just thirteen, was also a great beauty who showed theatrical promise. But Barbara, the middle girl, was something of a problem. Neither theater nor film nor much of anything else interested her. She had visited the Denishawn School in New York with her father, who now sent her to Mariarden in the hope that Shawn might guide her toward a career, or at least some semblance of discipline.

Barbara and Louise shared a cabin with two other girls, whom Barbara ignored. "She became my friend," said Louise, "because my strange customs made her laugh." Seated next to Louise at the long institutional tables in the dining hall, Barbara disdained the "disgusting country breakfasts" and merely sipped coffee or nibbled at toast. Her first words to Louise—after watching her devour slab after slab of apple pie—were, "Hello, Pie Face."[23]

"From then on," said Louise, "I participated in her efforts to inject some excitement into her bored existence. Defying the 9 o'clock lights-out regulation, she invited Peterborough boys to our cabin. They brought us cigarettes and applejack. In return, although she permitted no sexual liberties, Barbara entertained the boys with an enviable collection of dirty songs and limericks."[24]

One of the songs stuck so firmly in Louise's mind that, more than half a century later, she quoted it in *Lulu in Hollywood*:

> In Fairy Town,
> In Fairy Town,
> They don't go up,
> They all go down.
> Even the chief of police is queer.
> Oops, my dear,
> Listen here,
> The elevator's there, they say.
> They don't go up,
> Just the other way.
> Holy Bejesus,
> There's lots of paresis
> In Fairy Town.

She also remembered her favorite of Barbara's limericks, but it was edited out of the book, over Louise's objection:

> There was a young man from Kent
> Whose prick was so long that it bent.

To save himself trouble
He put it in double,
And instead of coming he went.[25]

The friendship between Louise and Barbara intensified and continued after the Mariarden session ended in September 1923, when both girls returned to New York City. But for the moment, Barbara went back to her parents' posh Park Avenue apartment to begin work in a play with her father, while Louise began another round of rehearsals for her second Denishawn touring season, which was to begin in a month.

Denishawn's 1923–1924 Mayer tour was similar to the first in its exhausting number of one-night stands spread out over the continent, but differed considerably in programming. Whereas the previous bill consisted largely of shorter pieces, the '23–'24 tour had fewer but more elaborate works and several new ones choreographed to American music. The return of Doris Humphrey to the company, after two years on her own in vaudeville, helped compensate for the defection of Martha Graham, whose sister Geordie now danced Martha's part in Xochitl.*

Louise's role in the company was greatly expanded. Said Denishawn's 1923–1924 souvenir program: "Louise Brooks, who plays the little Hopi Indian girl in Feather of the Dawn, has made swift advancement thru her natural talent and beauty and hard work." In addition to repeating her previous parts in Xochitl, Revolutionary Étude, Valse Brilliante [sic], and Egyptian Ballet, she had new roles in nine music-visualizations and dance-dramas.

Her biggest advance was the assignment to be Ted Shawn's partner and bride in The Feather of the Dawn—the first complete North American Indian ballet ever created for an American audience. Everything about it was expensive, from the two-story adobe set to the authentic costumes, moccasins, and baskets. Artist Earle Frank meticulously based the three-dimensional kachina masks on the real ones at the Smithsonian. And Shawn commissioned Charles Wakefield Cadman, for $1,200, to write an original score based on Indian airs and rhythms.

Shawn drew the narrative theme from a Hopi legend: If a feather is blown into the air at dawn and carried away by a breeze, the day will be auspicious—a perfect day for the brave Kwahu (Shawn) to woo Kodeh (Brooks), daughter of the chief. The thirty-minute drama incorporated eight different Hopi rituals, including Louise's "Dance of the Corn Maiden." In buckskin dress and leggings, wearing heavy silver and tur-

---

* After Broadway producer John Murray Anderson saw her dance Serenata Morisca during the 1922–1923 Mayer tour, he convinced Graham to join his Greenwich Village Follies. Soon after, she was asked by Rouben Mamoulian to head the new dance department at the Eastman School of Music in Rochester, New York. From there, she moved on into a solo career—and dance history.

quoise jewelry, she danced a rapid, stamping pattern with slow, flat-footed turns, alternating between head and body bent forward, then body erect with head thrown back, praising the sun for plentiful corn.

The Feather of the Dawn was the dazzler of the Denishawn show and drew much favorable attention to the beautiful Louise Brooks, whose large, dark eyes gave her a distinctly Indian look. Half a century later, Martha Graham cited this above all other moments of Louise's "deep inner power" onstage: "I remember that power when she stood remote and distant on the top of a Navajo dwelling in *Feather of the Dawn;* again, that curious individuality, beauty and sense of an inner vision."

Brooks was also one of five women selected to dance with Shawn and St. Denis in *The Spirit of the Sea*, originally a St. Denis solo now refurbished as a full ballet. St. Denis was the Sea Spirit, summoned from the deep by Shawn as the melancholic Fisherboy. Louise and the other mermaids are caught in his net—playful, flirtatious sea nymphs, clad only in silk fleshings, with hair made of hip-length cotton streamers dyed all shades of green to resemble seaweed. Years later, when dance critic Walter Terry asked St. Denis to explain the difference between the solo and the ballet version of *The Spirit of the Sea*, she replied, "Not much, dear. I was still the sea. Teddy was a fisherman. Somewhere along the line I drowned him. It was still *my* dance."[26]

And Louise was a part of a ground-breaking new work called *Sonata Tragica*, choreographed by St. Denis and Humphrey to the music of MacDowell—temporarily. Danced by Humphrey, Weidman, and five women in black leotards, *Sonata Tragica* was extremely stark and "modernist." Early in the tour, as an experiment, it was performed without music, and the reception was so enthusiastic that they kept it that way— the first modern American dance to be performed in complete silence.

Louise also performed with the entire company in St. Denis's Babylonian epic dance-drama, *Ishtar of the Seven Gates*, which was as exalted an achievement of St. Denis's art as was *Feather of the Dawn* of Shawn's. The semireligious theme centered on the Babylonian counterpart to Aphrodite, a mother goddess of both love and war. Ishtar (St. Denis) descends into the realm of the Queen of the Underworld (Humphrey) in search of her lover, Tammuz (Shawn), the Adonis-like god of spring and summer who is held captive in hell through each winter. Unless he is freed, there will be no renewal, no fertility. At each gate, Ishtar must yield up a different treasure to gain passage. The original set was monumental. The seven gates were located at center stage beneath a huge arch flanked by flats of thirty-foot griffinlike creatures—men with eagle heads, feathered horses with bearded men's heads. Built at enormous cost, it weighed 800 *tons,* was impossible to transport, and had to be discarded in favor of trompe l'oeil effects.

Sonata Tragica: *Doris Humphrey standing; left to right, Louise, Theresa
Sadowska, Anne Douglas, Lenore Scheffer, Geordie Graham, Martha Hardy*

But *Ishtar* was dazzling nonetheless, as was the totality of the program.
The opening performance on October 15, 1923, at the Apollo Theater in
Atlantic City, featured, in addition to the usual full complement of Deni-
shawn ethnic dances and previous music-visualizations, the world pre-
mieres of four major new works—*Ishtar, The Spirit of the Sea, The Feather
of the Dawn,* and *Cuadro Flamenco*—each of which was dance-historic.
Weidman's *Danse Americaine* was also premiered that night, and so was
Humphrey's *Pasquinade* (also known as *A Creole Belle*), danced to a Louis
Moreau Gottschalk cakewalk.

Louise could not help but be infected by the excitement these creations
generated, and by the satisfactions. As a featured company member, she
was demonstrating a remarkable versatility of movement styles. And offstage, thanks to her exposure to the philosophizing of Shawn and St.
Denis, she was acquiring a deeper range of intellectual interests that
would take root and flower in later literary life.

The beauty and exhilaration of Denishawn combined to make this, in many ways, the most fulfilling artistic experience of her life. A highlight was her triumphant return, for a second straight season, to the Crawford Theater in Wichita on February 13, 1924, where former friends and foes alike gathered to marvel at their hometown girl, already "arrived" at the pinnacle of contemporary dance at the age of seventeen.

But in spite or because of her success on this '23–'24 tour, Louise's petulance was becoming more overt. Signs of trouble between her and St. Denis increased in proportion to Louise's uppity behavior and lurking sense of persecution.

"Miss Ruth preferred compliant girls who sat at her feet and adored her," says Sherman today. "If Louise refused to do this, she could never have been an RSD favorite."[27]

Louise would later say of St. Denis that "I didn't like her either as a dancer or as a person, but as a costumer she had genius, and in posing, both on stage and before the camera, she had no peer. It mattered not whether the photographer was Steichen or a studio hack. Miss Ruth set the scene, directed the lighting, arranged her draperies, struck an attitude, and the photographer was presented with a masterpiece of composition."[28]

But that was a cool, hindsight assessment. By the time the 1923–1924 tour ended, she was convinced that "Ruth St. Denis hated me—[I was] so silent, wicked-looking, no ass-kissing"—although Anne Douglas recalls no manifestation of the "hatred."

"Miss Ruth did not despise Louise," says Douglas. "I think Miss Ruth felt her attitude [was bad]; she didn't despise her as a person."[29] But there was a general feeling that Louise was daring St. Denis, and the world, to cross her—especially after Louise was back in her New York element.

When the ax fell, it fell brutally. In late spring 1924, St. Denis called together her dancers for announcements about the new season. Louise recounted the story:

> We were assembled for word on the following year's tour and I remember everything down to the very smell of the theatre. Barbara Bennett, not a member of the company but my adored friend, went to the call with me. When we sneaked in late and she stumbled in the dark and fell into her seat with her loudest, froggiest Bennett laugh, Miss St. Denis, who didn't care even for polite interruptions, stopped her speech from the stage and started clawing at her long green jade necklace. The next thing I heard was, "Is that you, Louise?"
>
> Then my faint whisper, "Yes, Miss Ruth."
>
> And then, "Well, Louise, to be brief and to the point—not to keep you from your more pressing concerns—I am dismissing you from the company because you want life handed to you on a silver salver."[30]

No other reason, at least in Louise's recollection, was given. She was "thrown out, unwarned and unsuspecting," she said, "At 17, my first and blackest humiliation—and in public too."

A bitter irony of the dismissal concerned Louise's air of superiority—reinforced by St. Denis and Shawn themselves, inculcating their dancers with the belief that their work placed them among the elite.

Half a century later, in a letter to Jane Sherman, Louise's assessment of her Denishawn demise was paranoiac to the point of believing there was a "rule set by St. Denis and Shawn never to speak my name or run the Hopi ballet photos of Mr. Shawn and me. . . . [Many years afterward,] on the phone I asked Shawn why I was blacklisted. He was fittingly embarrassed. The truth is that Miss Ruth detested me, and both of them longed to be movie stars."[31]

She had a few other astonishing notions: "Besides Martha, I thought Denishawn's greatest dancer was Lenore. She left because Doris Humphrey hogged all the lyric roles. I was a lousy dancer and didn't mind at all when Miss Ruth threw me out."[32]

Sherman attributes those views to resentment. "I never heard anything except that [Louise] was a good dancer and beautiful and very talented," she says. "She could not have been so 'lousy' when throughout two tours of the United States she was assigned many group, trio, and at least two solo dances." And Shawn must have liked her a lot, not a little, to have given her the lead in *Feather of the Dawn*, defying the Denishawn tradition of doling out such solos on the basis of seniority. Nor did Sherman ever have any sense that Shawn and St. Denis longed for the silver screen. And it was impossible for Doris Humphrey to "hog" any role that wasn't assigned to her.

St. Denis and Shawn, says Sherman, were "hard-nosed professionals forced to earn a living for themselves, their company and their school." If they thought one of their dancers was negatively affecting the company's morale, let alone reputation, the offender had to go—with or without justice.

Louise's hindsight claim that she "didn't mind at all" was hardly true. The Denishawn experience was critical to her art and her career, and the dismissal would leave a very deep wound. For the moment, stunned to the core by Miss Ruth's words, Louise walked away from Denishawn for the last time and made her way back to the Bennett apartment with a single pathetic question:

"Barbara," she said, "what's a silver salver?"

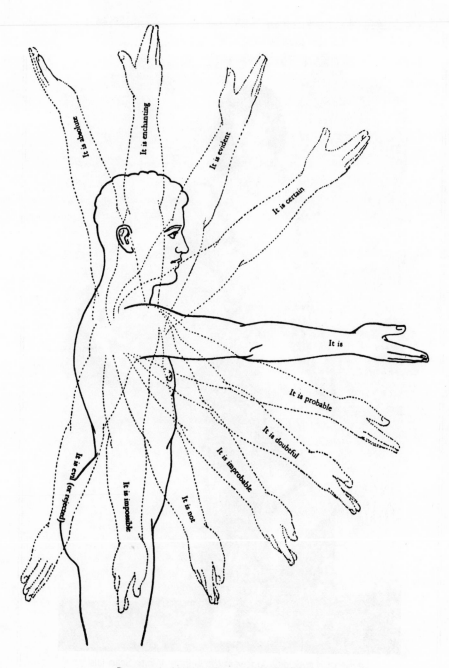

Drawing by William Thomas from Ted Shawn's
Every Little Movement: A Book about François Delsarte

Louise as a specialty dancer in the George White Scandals,
Apollo Theater, 1924; photo by Alfred Cheney Johnston

3 · Scandals

Oh, life is a glorious cycle of song,
A medley of extemporanea;
And love is a thing that can never go wrong;
And I am Marie of Roumania.
— DOROTHY PARKER

I WON'T go back to Kansas!" Louise insisted, over and over, through her tears. She was just the opposite of Dorothy in *The Wizard of Oz*.

Barbara Bennett listened sympathetically and explained that a salver was a tray, but the knowledge did little to cheer up Louise. St. Denis had not only fired her from a plum job with America's preeminent modern dance company; she had done so in the most embarrassing possible manner—in the presence of the whole company, "making an example" of her before the terrified rest of the troupe.

Worst of all, from Louise's standpoint, was the monumental unfairness. The reason for her dismissal had nothing to do with her dancing, which by all accounts—including the reviews and the opinion of Ted Shawn— was quite satisfactory. She had taken it seriously and performed well. No, her dancing wasn't the issue. By St. Denis's own admission, Louise was being kicked out because of her personality, or perhaps her "attitude." All of her hard work, the endless rehearsals and train rides from city to city, the rigors of Denishawn discipline, all the performances—all up in smoke, and why? Just because of her cocky high spirits? At seventeen she had achieved her dream of becoming a professional dancer. Now it was a nightmare, and through no *professional* fault of her own. The wound was deeper than even she herself could know, and she was devastated.

And, incidentally, she was unemployed.

"I won't go back to Kansas!" she kept insisting. But Barbara Bennett—who was three months older and wiser—rose immediately to the occasion.

"Don't be a fool, Pie Face!" said Barbara. "I'll get you a job in a moment."

In the despair of the hour, Louise probably didn't believe her. But it was what she wanted to hear, and if anyone might come to her aid, it was Barbara. Ever since taking the pretty little prairie rube under her wing at Mariarden the previous summer, Barbara had been providing the kind of sisterly advice that Louise never solicited, rarely got, and now desperately needed.

"I worshipped Barbara," said Louise, who didn't use the word loosely. Now almost eighteen, Barbara was everything Louise lacked and admired —"long, elegant, froggy-voiced" and, most of all, sophisticated. At Mariarden, Louise had decided she "must get rid of the Kansas accent and talk like Barbara—eyther, nyther, mattrafact, rahther, lahst, cahn't . . . "[1]

Barbara, for her part, was charmed in just the opposite way by Louise and "for perhaps the only time in her passionate, reckless life, exerted herself in another's behalf: she faced down family and friends in order to protect and instruct 'that obnoxious little Brooks girl.' "[2] By mid-1924, for the better or worse peace of the Bennett clan, Louise was an unofficial member of their household at 950 Park Avenue, near 82nd Street.

The cultivated Bennett women—mother Adrienne Morrison, daughters Constance, Barbara, and Joan—had been educated at the finest schools in America and abroad. As children, the girls stood in the wings and watched their father's triumphs on stage after stage. By the age of twelve, they knew half a dozen Shakespeare plays by heart, turning the Bard's heroes and heroines into their own imaginary playmates. Their lives were full of glamour, and yet at home a certain stodginess prevailed, at least until Barbara's impish friend made her entrances. When Louise came bounding in, the energy level soared.

"I thought she was very, very charming," says Joan Bennett, in those days a fourteen-year-old schoolgirl known only as Richard's daughter and Constance's kid sister. "She came because of her friendship with my sister Barbara, who was a very good dancer. But Barbara was mainly a ballroom dancer—it wasn't what Brooksie did, at all. I didn't know her well, but I recall her as always very humorous."[3]

Louise's extraordinary dancing skill was far greater than that of Barbara, who, unlike the rest of her famous family, was a reluctant performer. She was used to being outshone, especially by the people closest to her. Behind her beauty and elegance lay a fragile psychology and a set of complexes that were aggravated by most of the publicity she received.

"If there's some tinge of incompleteness in the Bennett professional pride, it has to do with Barbara," wrote Harry Lang in a gossipy *Photoplay* piece called "Those Amazing Bennett Girls and Their Pappy." It was

*Louise's friend Barbara Bennett—
troubled sister of Constance
and Joan—ca. 1924*

principally an interview with paterfamilias Richard, "that audience-damning, stormy petrel of the stage," who raved on about the talent and business acumen of Constance but delivered a more somber assessment of "the one whose hair is dark while the others' is golden; the one whose name isn't up in electric lights on theater marquees everywhere."

"Barbara?" echoed Richard Bennett upon the mention of her name. "Barbara? Well, I've always had to force her. She approached everything with fear and trembling . . ."

But she was more assertive when it came to little Brooksie. Getting fired from Denishawn had shaken Louise's confidence and interrupted the plan for turning herself into that "dream woman" and "secret bride of New York"—but only temporarily. Recovering from the shock, with Barbara's help, she saw that her goal was now even more important. There were three basic problems to be tackled.

"I had to get rid of my Kansas accent, to learn the etiquette of the social elite, and to learn to dress beautifully," she said. And since she couldn't attend a fashionable finishing school, "I went for my education directly to the unknown people who were experts in such matters—the people at the bottom whose services supported the enchantment at the top of New York."[4]

A good example was her English professor—"a fresh, contemptuous soda jerk at a Broadway drugstore where I went for fudge sundaes." That Columbia University student mimicked her Kansas twang until one day she disarmed him by saying, "Instead of making fun of me, why don't you teach me how to say it?"

"Not even an unwilling teacher can resist the flattery of extraordinarily close attention," Louise observed (thereby incidentally explaining Ted Shawn's fondness for her). And pretty soon that drugstore elocutionist "began to smile at the fancy of becoming my Pygmalion."

"It's not 'hep,' you hayseed—it's 'help,' 'help,' 'help'!" he would cry. And according to Louise, "within a month of fudge sundaes, this boy had picked his way through my vocabulary, eliminating the last trace of my hated Kansas accent." The goal was not British-sounding "stage" speech, but "clean, unlabeled English" in the pleasant middle range. Her mother, she said, had made her "forever aware of the voice as a manipulative power."[5]

Thus was proper speech achieved. As for "culture" itself, that was "not a prerequisite for becoming a sophisticated New Yorker. It was, in fact, a handicap. The rich men who before long were exhibiting me in fashionable restaurants, theaters and nightclubs shrank like truant schoolboys from the name of Shakespeare, and they looked upon an evening spent at the Metropolitan Opera or at a concert in Carnegie Hall as unthinkable misery."

She solved the problem of being unable to converse with such men by talking "scarcely at all." But Barbara kept introducing her to bankers and stockbrokers, and the dinner invitations kept coming, often to the most exclusive restaurants. One night while Louise was attacking a squab at the Colony, the bird took flight from her plate and crash-landed onto the floor. "From then on," she said, "indifferent to the reactions of my dinner partners, I took instructions from the waiters on how to eat everything on the menu. There was how-to-bone-a-brook-trout night, how-to-fork-snails night, how-to-dismember-artichokes night, and so on, until we came to the bottom of the menu."[6]

When it was all over, she finally felt free to order something she *really* liked—creamed chipped beef.

And now with her speech and her table skills under control, it was time to devote serious attention to fashion. Again, the Bennetts came to her rescue.

"One morning," recalled Louise, "the apartment door was opened by Mrs. Bennett. She looked at me as if I were a stray dog, and said, 'What are you doing here at 8 o'clock in the morning?' I began to cry, so she let me in and left me on a sofa, waiting for Barbara to wake up. In a gray wrapper, without makeup, how worn and unhappy Mrs. Bennett looked. Not a bit like her elegant fashion photographs in *Vogue*." The beautiful living room was "all white with dark touches, uncluttered, like a Chinese painting," but, like Mrs. Bennett herself, it "had the look of something uncared-for and unloved."

An endearing nearsightedness ran in the Bennett family. Still sniffling on the sofa, Louise inquired about it:

> In the dusty white living room, Joan, who was always kind to me, was putting on her glasses to study her history book. "What I can't figure out," I said, "is how, if you can't see without your glasses, you get around without them." Joan took them off and smiled at me. "I can see something without them. For instance, your long black dress. Where did you get that funny, old-lady's dress?"
>
> "A woman in a shop on Broadway sold it to me."
>
> Joan laughed.
>
> At eleven, we heard sounds of rising Bennetts. We heard Constance raging at Barbara: "If you dare to sneak out once more in my white chiffon, I am going to slit your throat." We heard Richard Bennett singing, "I love life and I want to live," followed by his entrance in a blue brocade dressing gown for a trip to the liquor cabinet. After tossing down a glass of whisky, he turned to me, saying, "My God, Joan, where did you get that damned black dress?" Between liquor and his poor eyesight, he sometimes confused me with Joan, who had not yet changed her dark hair to blond . . . Constance, dressed in a perfectly tailored suit of navy blue, flew across the living room and out the front door, leaving behind the perfume of gardenias and a dirty look cast in my direction. . . . Barbara finally appeared, wearing Constance's beige gabardine suit. We lunched on chocolate milkshakes at a drugstore, after which she took me to the smart hairdressing shop of Saveli, where Saveli himself attended to my hair. He shortened my bangs to a line above my eyebrows, shaped the sides in points at my cheekbones, and shingled the back of my head. Barbara was pleased. "As a mattra-fact, Pie Face," she said, "you are beginning to look almost human."[7]

As for the other two Bennett girls, Louise noted that "Joan, younger than I, was no good to me, being in the formative stage herself and busy dying her hair different shades of red and yellow every week." And Constance never gave Louise the time of day, although she served unwittingly as a model for one other important skill. "From Constance Bennett," said Louise, "I was learning to enter a nightclub with my evening wrap clutched high at my shoulders and my head thrown back with an expression of one approaching a smoldering dump."[8]

Barbara was as unenvious of Louise's beauty and talent as of her own sisters'. She tended to her little friend's professional as well as social development. The Bennetts had never thought very highly of dancing in the first place. Even the high art of Miss Ruth, which they all admired, was not reflected in either the social standing or the paychecks of the dancers, and Denishawn's grueling annual circuit through the provinces was not any Bennett's idea of The Theater. "You don't want to spend the rest of your life on tour, washing and pressing costumes," Barbara told Louise.

But could she really get her another job "in a moment"?

Barbara Bennett was exactly as good as her word. Within an hour of Louise's expulsion, as they were walking back up Broadway to the Bennetts' apartment, they found themselves outside the Palace Theater, where Barbara caught sight of the young booking agent and producer, Rufus LeMaire.* Barbara saw LeMaire's eyes widen appreciatively at the sight of the tearful Louise, and quickly introduced them. She wasted no time and no words.

"Rufus," she said, "get Louise a job immediately!"

"A Bennett had spoken," Louise recalled, "and after Barbara agreed that chorus work would do, providing it wasn't a Shubert show, he took me around to the theatre where the chorus was being picked for the new *Scandals* and introduced me to George White who gave me a job on the spot."[9]

Broadway history always casts White in the shadow of his illustrious predecessor and competitor, Florenz Ziegfeld. But by 1924, *George White's Scandals* was just as glittery and almost as popular as Ziegfeld's *Follies*. White had danced two seasons in the *Follies* before breaking away in 1919 to stage his own copycat version, with embellishments. The *Scandals* soon earned a reputation for being less opulent but younger and faster than the *Follies*, and with greater emphasis on the newest dance styles and crazes.

The *Scandals* was also distinguished from the *Follies* in the handling of music. Many composers contributed to every *Follies* show. But the *Scandals* had more musical coherence in that all the songs were entrusted to a single songwriter or team. The most celebrated of its music directors was George Gershwin, who wrote the tunes for all five *Scandals* from 1920 through 1924. Gershwin's first Broadway hit, in fact, was "I'll Build a Stairway to Paradise," composed for the '22 *Scandals*. Less successful but more prophetic in that same show was his "Blue Monday," subtitled "An Opera à la Afro-American." Though removed after opening night, it was a forerunner of the full-length *Porgy and Bess*.

White himself was a colorful and adventurous character, ever on the

---

* LeMaire's brother George was one of the best straight men in vaudeville. Together, the LeMaires produced a revue called *Broadway Brevities*, which enjoyed a good run at the Winter Garden. Even more successful was *LeMaire's Affairs*, another variety show that later co-starred Sophie Tucker and Ted Lewis. Rufus soon moved West to become casting director for virtually every major studio —first Columbia, then Warners, First National, Metro, Fox, Paramount, and Universal.

*Louise in panniered skirt for the George White Scandals, 1924;
photo by Alfred Cheney Johnston*

lookout for a pretty face as long as it had legs to match. After one look at the striking young beauty with the severely cropped hair and piercing eyes, it didn't take him long to give Louise an audition. When he saw her dance, he knew immediately that he wanted her.

And so in the summer of 1924, Louise Brooks—not yet eighteen—became George White's newest chorus girl. Though the youngest member of his cast, she was the only one who was a trained dancer, and that fact —coupled with her stunning appearance and stage presence—soon ignited a little brushfire of newspaper publicity that made her the envy of the chorines.

"The girls hated me," said Louise, and the stage manager wasn't wild about her, either. She feuded with him regularly, and for her overall hauteur he dubbed her "the Duchess of Sidebottom," a nickname that came widely into use backstage. Louise's escalating personality conflicts stemmed from that notorious "attitude," coupled with the fact that her "specialty" dances in the show elevated her slightly but significantly above the rest of the chorus. Given her extreme youth, there were bound to be problems.

Many years later, Louise painted a colorful picture of backstage life in the George White *Scandals* in a chapter of her autobiographical novel, *Naked on My Goat*.* The chapter "Who Is the Exotic Black Orchid?" opens with Louise as the character "Mary" sneaking in the stage door entrance, late as usual, and checking to see if the coast is clear. But she's caught in the act by an assistant stage manager, who berates her for missing the opening chorus yet again. They trade insults before she makes her way to the empty dressing room:

> Ah, how nice to be alone with the rest of the girls on stage. Just like a star. Peace and quiet with plenty of time to put on a really good make-up for the Chinese number. She got into her dressing gown and sat down at the make-up shelf.
>
> Mary put on a different make-up for each number. There was the natural make-up for the Charleston, the Arabian make-up for Araby, the Spanish. . . .
>
> And she didn't do it only because the make-ups were authentic and artistically correct. It also gave her something to do during waits when the rest of the girls were mooching around from dressing room to dressing room, talking about men and sex. And always about John Green. Especially to her.

---

* After finishing the book, she threw it down the incinerator—but later rewrote chapter six and sent copies to her friends James Card and Jan Wahl, both of whom preserved it. She wrestled with the fact that many of her well-known lovers and friends were still living before deciding to write the novel in the third person and to assign the name "Mary Porter" to the character of herself. Details of the writing and destruction of the book (1948–1952) are found in chapters sixteen and seventeen.

The girl who sued him in last year's show. The girl who had the baby the year before. And the girl who tried to commit suicide the year before that. A lot of wild stories Mary didn't care to listen to. Jealous cats. Just because he was so crazy about her. . . .

She pushed her hair under her wig cap and began to coldcream her face, looking in the mirror to see whether her freckles were fading any.

And she wore her Chinese headdress as it should be worn—like a gold helmet of hair with her own hair covered up. The rest of the girls stuck theirs on like hats to show their precious curls. What a bunch of illiterate slobs! They'd never even heard of D. H. Lawrence or Joseph Conrad. All they ever read was the Graphic. As for music! Gladys thought Ravel and Debussy was a French bicycle act.

Her acerbic reverie is interrupted by the sound of the girls tromping back to their dressing rooms at the end of the opening number. Because of its sloppiness, and Mary's lateness, the stage manager yells down the hall that they're going to have to rehearse it again after the show. This produces a great round of resentment against Mary, who hears—is meant to overhear—one of the girls complain as she passes Mary's door: "I could kill her. I could just kill her, I could. Messing up the numbers so all we do is rehearse and rehearse and rehearse. Why doesn't he ever say something to *her?*"

The girls troop into the dressing room without saying a word to Mary, who blithely continues with her make-up. Even "Gladys," her one good friend among the chorines, is mad and hurls a towel at her with the complaint that "you've got your junk spread over half the shelf as it is!"

"Well, you don't have to be so cranky about it" [says Mary]. "Gee whiz, anyone would think it was my fault we're rehearsing tonight."

Gladys looked at Mary for a minute, and then she took a long drag on her cigarette and began singing softly, " 'I'm jealous of the moon that shines above . . .' "

"Jealous" was one of Mary's favorites and she began whistling along with Gladys.

That was when pure, sweet Izzy slammed down her brush and began screeching, "Damn you, Mary Porter, damn you! How many times have I asked you not to whistle in the dressing room. You know it whistles the one nearest the door out of the show, you know it!"

"Oh, don't be such a superstitious ninny."

"It's not superstitious. It's true."

"Then why don't you let me have the place next to the door and I can whistle myself out of the show?"

That shut the little two-faced goody-goody up fast enough. There wasn't any more chance of Isobel's giving up the seat by the door (where she could stick her mug out and see and hear everything that went on) than there was of her getting a date with the Prince of Wales. Dirty little tattle-tale, running to Green with everything she heard.

Thus does Mary demonstrate her disenchantment with the *Scandals* and fail to endear herself to her peers. But now it's time for the Chinese number. After some furious promptings from the assistant stage manager, she makes her way to the wings. The first person she sees is a girl named "Francesca," who is "giggling and wiggling with the press agent Sam Stern's arms around her. The things some girls would do to get their picture in the paper!" Sam is evidently Mary's own beau, or, rather, one of them. He's taking a liberty or two with Francesca, but when he sees Mary, he drops his arm from around Francesca's waist and hustles off. But Mary has seen it all, and as the girls are lining up for the Chinese entrance, she focuses her withering attention on the girl and says:

> "Francesca, about that little argument we were having last night. About Kingsley saying in his column that the most beautiful girl in the show was an exotic black orchid? And you and Honey and the other girls saying he meant you?"
>
> All the girls waiting in line to go on scooted up behind Francesca to hear what Mary was going to say.
>
> "Well, Francesca, I called him today at the paper. And I told him another girl in 'Caprice' said he meant her. And he said no, of course not, he meant me. . . . And then he said he was sorry he didn't know my name yet when he wrote it, so if I liked he would write another thing using my name. But I said no, I just wanted to make sure, that was all. I knew you'd believe me."
>
> As she walked away Mary could hear Francesca beginning to snivel . . .

The chapter concludes when she catches sight of Sam again and decides "as long as she was at it, she might as well give him a piece of her mind too."

> "Sam," [she says,] "I was sure surprised, coming out today and seeing my picture smeared all over the news stands on the cover of that *Police Gazette* magazine."
>
> "What the hell do you mean?"
>
> "I mean I don't want my picture on any common, vulgar old magazine like the *Police Gazette*."
>
> "Is that so. You know, if it was up to me, I wouldn't even put your picture in the men's—"
>
> Two gongs.
>
> She'd better take her entrance position. She had eight whole bars of music to herself and she wanted to get in the mood.
>
> Three gongs.

Mary slipped into the amber spotlight, ready to cross the stage in thirty-two authentic little Chinese steps.[10]

NOT ALL of George White's girls fit that black portrait of pettiness and stupidity, even by Louise's own reckoning. Her colleagues in the 1924 *Scandals* included several of the most remarkable, up-and-coming young women in the business. These included Dolores Costello, daughter of the great stage actor Maurice Costello and the future wife of John Barrymore; Winnie Lightner, the vaudeville and Broadway star who introduced Gershwin's hit "Somebody Loves Me" in this very show; and an especially lovely girl of whom Louise grew quite fond, Dorothy Sebastian—later to become the co-star and mistress of Buster Keaton.

The '24 edition of the *Scandals* was particularly elaborate and got unanimously favorable reviews that September. "There was a bit of confusion due to the great size of Mr. White's show and the short amount of time he has had for rehearsals on the stage of the Apollo," said the *Times* reviewer, "but the occasional aggravations were unable to obscure the beauty and taste of the production."[11]

White went Ziegfeld a step further in the way of near nudity, and his ladies' undress stopped just short of seriously scandalous. That was, of course, the name of the show and the name of the game. But there was quality as well as brevity: Costumes and curtains for the '24 *Scandals* were made in Paris by Max Welty, from designs by Erté.

"There were large quantities of gorgeous costumes," wrote one critic, "much of them on the girls of the chorus from the neck up and the shoes down."[12]

Though Louise was not mentioned by name in the papers—few chorus girls ever were—her exotic orchidlike presence was noted and her word-of-mouth highly flattering. Yet her strange irritability persisted, due to the undiminished sting of her rejection by Denishawn and to all those time-consuming rehearsals for which she herself was partly to blame.

One rehearsal, however, produced a memorable meeting recounted by Louise years later in a letter to James Card. It is a model of the crisp, structured prose for which she strove, and it is reproduced here in its entirety:

> During a rest period one day at rehearsal, George Gershwin wandered into the [Apollo] theatre, sat down at the beat-up old rehearsal piano and began playing through the score. I came over and hopped up on a work table and sat there cross-legged, silent and listening. . . .
>
> I was 17. George was 26. He had just made an enormous success with his Carnegie Hall concert.*

---

* Louise meant the Aeolian Hall premiere of *Rhapsody in Blue* in February 1924.

"Do you know," I said after a while, "the only good thing you've written for the show is 'Somebody Loves Me.' "

Another would have flinched before the face of flaming outrage he turned upon me. But my mother was an excellent pianist. I had lived and danced amid the best music.

We looked at each other for an instant—and burst into laughter.

"I'm sailing for Paris Saturday," he said, turning back to his playing, "and I'll bring you a present. What do you want me to bring you from Paris?"

"Oh, you'll forget."

"No I won't. What do you want from Paris?"

"One of those long wobbly dolls in felt pajamas smoking a cigarette. But you'll forget . . ."

In 1937, a little before he died, when I had become one of the untouchables, I was sitting in the Clover Club one night when he appeared through the heavy black curtains of the door, smiling his lovely luminous smile. And with everybody Hy-Georging him and waving gladly, he walked straight to me and asked me to dance. And it was nearly finished, the music, when he said suddenly, "I've wanted to tell you—it's been on my conscience a long time . . ."

We stopped dancing and looked at each other, remembering.

" . . . I forgot to bring you the doll."[13]

NOW THAT Louise was a bona-fide showgirl, and knew her way around a squab and an escargot, those wealthy bankers and brokers to whom Barbara had introduced her were competing more hotly for the privilege of escorting her to places like the Colony and "21." Soon enough, several of them were also making it possible for her to buy expensive clothes.

"These most eligible bachelors in their thirties," Louise wrote, "finding debutantes a threat, turned to pretty girls in the theater, whose mothers weren't husband-hunting. Café society developed about this time. The theater, Hollywood, and society mingled in the monthly Mayfair dances at the Ritz, where society women could monitor their theatrical enemies and snub them publicly."

The scene, as Louise described it, was positively Gatsbyesque:

All the rich men were friends who entertained one another in their perfectly appointed Park Avenue apartments and Long Island homes. The extravagant sums given to the girls for clothes were part of the fun—part of competing to see whose girl would win the Best-Dressed title. Sexual submission was not a condition of this arrangement, although many affairs grew out of it. For a time, Barbara was kept by William Rhinelander Stewart, who gave her a square-cut emerald from Cartier. One night, when we were swimming off Caleb Bragg's houseboat, the *Masquerader*, she watched it slip off her finger into Long Island Sound. She kept this hilarious accident secret

from Stewart by buying a fake-emerald ring from Denis Smith, whose jewelry business was unknown to innocent lovers. They would have been stag-
gered to learn how many of their gifts were converted into imitations and
cash.[14]

Even Louise suffered a pang or two of conscience, if not quite regret.
"Truly," she said, "ours was a heartless racket. After receiving an ermine
coat from Jaeckel's, the gift of a stockbroker named John Lock, I let him
take me just once to a tea dance at the Biltmore Hotel."

Barbara Bennett had indeed steered her toward the heights. Having secured her entrée into the *Scandals* and made certain she was wined and
dined by wealthy men, Barbara insisted Louise move into the Algonquin
Hotel. The choice was inspired, for at the Algonquin Louise was living
among a who's who of New York's theatrical and literary smart set.

One of the more dashing figures, little remembered today, was Edmund
Goulding, the British film director who "discovered" Joan Crawford and
directed dozens of silent and later sound films including *Grand Hotel*. In
addition to his directorial skills, Goulding was one of the most seductive
ladies' men in New York, with an insatiable appetite for new, and very
young, conquests. But he was no indiscriminate satyr; a man of great
wit and elegance, he preferred intelligence in the women who shared his
bed.

Louise first met Goulding at lunch one day in the hotel. She was "separated by just two years from the Kansas prairie," she recalled fifty-four
years later in an article called "Why I Will Never Write My Memoirs,"
which was eliminated from her book *Lulu in Hollywood*. "As an English
gentleman he must have found me a startling little barbarian."

A startling and very alluring little barbarian. They were both living at
the Algonquin—"Eddie as an honored guest, I as a maddening source of
gossip because Frank Case, who owned the hotel, was positive that I was
14 (I was 17) and had run away from home to join the chorus of *Scandals*.
This, added to my slipping in and out at all hours of the night and the
large amount of money I spent in the dining room, set me beyond the
pale, but since I always paid my bills and never 'entertained' men in my
room, he was driven at last to appeal to my sympathetic sensibilities to
persuade me to throw myself out."

But for now, she was still at the Algonquin and very much savoring
both the boiled Kennebec salmon and the attentions of a very charming
and famous director—"the most extraordinary looking man, with these
brilliant blue eyes and intensity and of course the English accent."

"While he talked about my profile, with which I was perfectly familiar,"
she said, "I watched Robert Sherwood and Dorothy Parker and a lot of

other people jabbering and waving their hands at the Round Table, wondering what made them so famous."*

And then, over their crumpets in the Algonquin dining room, Goulding misjudged the spitfire sitting across from him and popped a question that even a young Kansas girl recognized as both a cliché and a come-on: He asked her if she wanted to come over to Paramount's Astoria studio on Long Island to take a screen test.

"Now I'm a girl in the *Scandals*, and all the girls in the *Follies* and *Scandals* were warned, 'Don't ever have anything to do with a man who offers you a screen test. Never.' "

Still, a screen test was the ultimate goal of every Broadway chorus girl. Except Louise Brooks. "I really wasn't scared because I'd been around a good deal," she said. "I just didn't want to be a movie actress. Lazy and spoiled as I was getting, I still had my mind vaguely fixed on becoming a great dancer like Martha Graham."

She turned Goulding down flat.

"When I said 'No,' after staring at me in a peculiar fashion, he went on, 'Well then, to hell with a movie test, how would you like to spend the afternoon with me?' To that I said 'Yes,' because I was not such a dunce as to dismiss the most joyful being I would ever meet."

It was first things first for Goulding. Upon leaving the Algonquin, they took a taxi straightaway to a house of assignation in the West Sixties, where, in rather ungentlemanly fashion, he left Louise in the cab for half an hour while he paid a visit to the girls.

Next he took her to the Hotel des Artistes, where they visited Ivor Novello's mother, who was a singing coach. Louise was much more interested in getting a glimpse of Ivor, who was comparable to Valentino as one of the great heartthrobs of the day.† But there was no Ivor that afternoon. Instead, Mrs. Novello and Eddie Goulding sang soprano-baritone duets ("and very beautifully, too") for an hour with Louise as solo audience. At the conclusion of this curious drawing room spectacle, she and Eddie drove next to Goulding's apartment, where he was expecting the formidable star Mae Murray for tea—and whatever else might develop. But first there were preparations to be made.

"Having written several films for her, he knew exactly how to set the

---

* She later became a fan when informed that Parker named her canary Onan because "it spilled its seed upon the ground." But the two young stars of the same decade—who had much in common —never met.
† Ivor Novello (1893–1951), the Welsh matinee idol, was then enjoying tremendous success as a playwright, composer, and stage performer as well as film star. His major pictures were *The Bohemian Girl* (1922), *The White Rose* (1923), and British director Adrian Brunel's sensation of the year, *The Man without Desire*, in which Novello plays a sort of Rip Van Winkle who awakens after 200 years to find himself in the sexual dilemma indicated by the title.

scene," Louise recalled. " 'She will sit here,' he said, moving a small table
close to a grey velour chair. 'I'm positive she'll sit here. And Mae is pure
—pure and eternally young.' On the table he set a silver vase holding a
single white rose bud. Then with a wicked smile, beside it he placed a
book of pornographic drawings, very beautifully bound. 'And she is regal,'
he warned me as she rang his door bell. 'You must curtsy when you are
introduced.' Mae Murray came in looking exquisitely pure and young,
wearing white organdie with a pale blue sash and tiny matching blue
pumps. Unfortunately, after I curtsied and she nodded regally, I had to
leave for a theater rehearsal, so I never knew how she felt about the dirty
pictures."[15]

Louise's titillating initiation into the ways of Edmund Goulding that
day proved typical—of Goulding and of her interaction with him. By all
accounts, their relationship remained platonic, in which case Louise
Brooks was virtually the only woman he associated with in theater or film
with whom he never slept. Louise was unpredictably selective about sex,
though at this point in 1924, she was increasingly intrigued by its role in
the careers of aspiring performers. Goulding she continued to regard with
fond irony, observing that he "dragged me around with him like a pet
ocelot to all sorts of places of business and pleasure, but he never said
anything more about my making a screen test."

The theatrical and film worlds were small and overlapping in 1924 New
York, and tied in—then as now—with some of the major figures on Wall
Street. The financiers' interest in show-business profits was matched by
an interest in the beautiful women who constituted their products. Chorus
girls met stockbrokers often and easily in the endless rounds of parties,
and thus did Louise Brooks meet Otto Kahn—one of Paramount's early
backers and a herculean party-thrower.

"When I was in *Scandals*," Louise told British film historian Kevin
Brownlow years later, "naturally, all the girls looked forward to becoming
movie stars, and in the Ritz Hotel, most of the very famous, very rich men
about town in New York kept apartments year-round where they would
give parties. One of these belonged to Otto Kahn, though of course they
would lend them to each other.

"I was invited to a party night [there] with some of the girls from the
Scandals, and among the men were Walter Wanger and Joe Schenck and
Lord Beaverbrook.* So we—all the girls—went up into this little grey suite

* Otto Kahn (1867–1934), banker and philanthropist, was a major partner in the firm of Kuhn,
Loeb & Co., a long-time chairman of the Metropolitan Opera, and an important supporter of many
other cultural and educational institutions. He has been called the greatest patron of the arts in
American history.
Walter Wanger (1894–1968) was a Paramount producer and production chief; he later held

in the Ritz and we were introduced and we had drinks and we talked, and I saw that Lord Beaverbrook was very, very interested in the girl I liked most in the *Scandals*. She was a darling girl from the South, a darling girl —and they were talking and very cosy, and I watched very discreetly and they did disappear into the little grey bedroom in the little grey suite in the Ritz, and then they came out a while later and a few days later she told me that she had a contract at MGM and she did go to MGM and she did do very well, and I say hooray for Lord Beaverbrook!"[16]

She punctuated the anecdote with a great burst of laughter. Louise was inconsistent when it came to protecting her friends' privacy. In this case she chose to keep the name of Dorothy Sebastian a secret. Once ensconced in Hollywood, Sebastian co-starred in *Spite Marriage* with Buster Keaton and became the Great Stone Face's lover. A few years later, speaking to Keaton's biographer Tom Dardis, Louise spoke openly of Sebastian but kept Beaverbrook anonymous, referring to him only as "a diminutive British newspaper publisher." Off the record, she described Beaverbrook as "an ugly little grey man who went directly to his object with no finesse."[17]

To Kevin Brownlow, Louise once wrote: "In New York in 1924 there was a hand-picked group of beautiful girls who were invited to parties given for great men in finance and government. Walter Wanger and Eddie Goulding screened them. We had to be fairly well bred and of absolute integrity—never endangering the great men with threats of publicity or blackmail. At these parties we were not required, like common whores, to go to bed with any man who asked us, but if we did the profits were great. Money, jewels, mink coats, a film job—name it."[18]

But the most shattering seduction scene ever recorded by Louise Brooks was her own, which took place shortly after the Sebastian-Beaverbrook encounter. Like the *Scandals* backstage scene quoted above, it was written as part of *Naked on My Goat* and destroyed—along with the rest of the manuscript—by her own hand in 1952. But James Card coaxed her into reconstructing it.

---

similar posts at Columbia and MGM and also worked as an independent. He married Joan Bennett in 1940 and in 1951, in a jealous rage, shot her agent, Jennings Lang, for which he was sentenced to four months in jail.

Joseph M. Schenck (1878–1961) and his brother Nicholas M. (1881–1969) were early partners of theater-chain magnate Marcus Loew, whose company became the parent of MGM. But Joe left Loew's to become the most influential independent producer in movies. Married to Norma Talmadge, he produced most of her films and those of her sisters, Constance and Natalie—and, most important, those of Natalie's husband, Buster Keaton. This year, 1924, he was elected chairman of the board of United Artists (the Chaplin-Pickford-Fairbanks-Griffith company). He later co-founded 20th Century with Darryl Zanuck and became chairman of the board when 20th Century merged with Fox.

Lord Beaverbrook (William Maxwell Aitken, 1879–1964), the British newspaper baron and cabinet minister under Lloyd George and later Winston Churchill, was also a financial dabbler in movies and a notorious admirer of young stage and screen actresses.

"In my book," she wrote Card, "the seduction scene was as short and inarticulate as [it was in] real life." As before, "Mary" is Louise. "Tony" remains a mystery.

It is Sunday, no *Scandals*, and Mary is sitting in her brass bed in the Algonquin trying to read Mencken's *Prejudices*. When the phone rings, she throws Mencken across the room and grabs the receiver. It's Tony cooing at her like a dove. Tony, her best friend's boyfriend, that lousy English actor who has always been so snotty to Mary and humiliated her and made fun of her Kansas accent. But her best friend is out of town and Tony would just love to take Mary to dinner at the Claremont Inn up the Hudson. And like the silly idiot she is, Mary says yes.

At dinner, though, he was so sweet to her she didn't know what to think. He showed her how to eat steamed clams. And he told her she was beautiful. . . .

It was so cold driving home, and she only had on that little red jacket, why didn't she stop by his apartment and he'd give her a nightcap and build a fire in the fireplace.

The fire was lovely and she sat on a white bear rug looking in the bear's mouth and beginning to see more and more teeth while Tony made drinks and sat in the big flowered chair, stroking her hair. And then she was in his lap, and next thing he'd picked her up in his arms and was carrying her out of the room.

When she woke up the bedroom was empty. . . . Just then Tony opened the bathroom door and stood there with his hands shoved down in the pockets of his white shantung dressing gown.

"Oh, so you're awake. How do you feel. . . . I hope you're not plotting any crying scenes. I've got the devil's own hangover and I'm not up to tears this morning."

He went over and looked into the dressing table mirror, running his hand through his hair that was all straggly now and hanging in his eyes.

"Christ, what bags—look at my eyes, will you—what bags!"

When he turned around, Mary was just lying there staring at him.

"It might be a good idea for you to get up and dress. My wife's closed her damn show in Chicago and her maid will be in at eleven to straighten up the apartment . . ."

He came over and pushed his feet into his red slippers and stood looking down at her.

"And don't think you've taken me in with that ancient virgin business. You've been had before, my pet, you've been had."

Straightening up, he said, "Well, I'm going out to mix a drink. Will you have a drink before you go?"

"No, thank you."

"Well, then . . . Oh, if you're looking for it, you left your red jacket in the living room."

As she crept out the front door, Mary could hear him throwing up in the kitchen sink.[19]

IT WAS around this time that Frank Case ushered the youthful Louise out of the Algonquin—a "humiliating eviction [that] could not have taken place if I'd been wearing a fashionable slinky dress and a hat." She moved to the Martha Washington, "a respectable women's hotel" on East 29th, but was soon asked to leave *there*, too, after people in the next building complained of her exercising on the roof in flimsy pajamas.

"Within a month, my wearing apparel had got me kicked out of two hotels," she said. Then she saw a photo of Marilyn Miller, Ziegfeld's star, in a stunning gown from Milgrim's. The next morning she marched into that store with $500 in cash and put her fashion fate in the hands of a salesgirl from the Bronx. She walked out with a barebacked gown of white crystal beads, slashed to the navel, and silver coat with white fox collar. "Sitting at a restaurant or nightclub table, I was a nearly naked sight to behold," said Louise.[20] Soon, her afternoon dresses were in pastel shades of satin and silk crêpe; her suits, "severely tailored."

And so, by the end of 1924, the secret bride of New York had perfected her "look." But the intensity of the year's events also brought her to the brink of a nervous breakdown: With no time to adjust to the radical shift from dignified Denishawn to raucous *Scandals*, she found herself in great social and sexual demand; she declined the casting couch of an influential admirer and then, in a drunken moment, succumbed to a two-timing cad; in quick succession, she was declared undesirable by the most and then the least chic hotel in town.

Then came the last straw: Adrienne and Richard Bennett decided to ship off the diffident Barbara to a private school in Paris. Louise's best friend and mentor, her Rock of Gibraltar, was being forcibly removed from New York.

It was too much to take. Bored by the nightly performance routine, depressed about her love life, panicky at the thought of losing Barbara— and suddenly smitten by a desire to see the world—Louise marched in and quit the *Scandals* without notice, insulting a few of her enemies for good measure. She would go to Europe with Barbara Bennett.

A clerk in the Manhattan Federal Building was sweet-talked into giving her an emergency passport, and within a week, Barbara and Louise set sail together on the *Homeric*. The voyage was a tonic. Elated at the cosmopolitan prospects of London, Louise experienced a miraculous recovery from the Manhattan blues. A few days out on the ocean, she was her mischievous self again, feeling well enough to send a nasty telegram back to the *Scandals* stage manager who'd given her so much trouble. "Can't wait to find out when White will have to close show due to my loss," she wrote in her diary—only half jokingly.

Back came a cable from the *Scandals* front office: "White says if he knew you'd quit, would have gladly paid passage."

Louise, Leon Errol, and Dixie Boatwright in Florenz Ziegfeld's Louie the 14th, *Cosmopolitan Theatre; photo by Edward Steichen for* Vanity Fair, *June 1925*

4 · Follies

No brains! no beauty! no personality! Can't sing—can't dance—can't act!—stand 'em on their heads and they're all alike—you know!—Who's fucking her?—I don't know—You still here?
— FLORENZ ZIEGFELD at a *Follies* rehearsal, 1925[1]

LOUISE BROOKS was the first girl to dance the Charleston in London.

The time was December 1924. But the destination had been France, not England. During the long voyage on the *Homeric*, Barbara Bennett had been toying with a change of plans.

"On our arrival at the Edouard VII Hotel in Paris," Louise recalled, "Barbara had eaten a ham sandwich with German mustard, over which she decided not to go to the convent school as her mother had intended; she cashed her letter of credit and went back to New York on the return trip of the *Homeric*. I wanted to stay."[2]

So she stayed, but without the slightest idea of what she'd do without money in the middle of Paris. And then as it often did in her teenaged performing years, fate again intervened in her favor. Twenty-four hours later, she was still sitting in the Edouard VII lobby, "just as Barbara had reluctantly left me," when—

> Archie Selwyn, the producer, came across me, friendless, Frenchless, jobless and penniless, but perfectly calm. He was amazed to find me there when he thought me hopping around in the *Scandals*. After painting a grim picture of what happens to 17-year-old Kansas girls in Paris, he persuaded me to go with him to London where he got me a job dancing the Charleston in the Café de Paris.[3]

Located in the West End's Piccadilly Circus, the famous Café de Paris was where the most fashionable Londoners repaired for entertainment and a glimpse of the "Bright Young Things"—male and female—who were roughly the British equivalent of America's flappers. Noël Coward and his friends and hangers-on were at the center of this set, which revolved around the theater world, and vice versa, and democratically welcomed trendsetting Yankees who cared to join the orbit.

Louise suddenly found herself in a prominent solo spot at "London's creamiest calling card" with its padded satin walls, lush décor, and legendary staircase down which the brightest stars of two continents descended nightly. To play there was comparable in vaudeville to heading the bill at the Palace. Top performers such as Beatrice Lillie and Noël Coward, and later Marlene Dietrich and Tallulah Bankhead, were paid lavishly—Tallulah drawing $5,600 a week for six weeks, with free hotel suite and chauffeur-driven Rolls-Royce thrown in. The management desired only the "right" people for clientele, and evening dress was always required. The single show began promptly at midnight.

The London winter was colder and drearier than usual in 1924, but things were hot inside the Café de Paris. Louise was no headliner, but she was equipped with the best of Denishawn training, on the one hand, and a host of fresh new tricks from Broadway's *Scandals*, on the other. She bewitched the crowds who jammed the club to watch her shimmy and crisscross knees into the wee hours. Nobody in England had seen anything like this before. She was a stunning success.

For a while, the black-bobbed teenage rage reveled in the conquest of her second straight cosmopolitan entertainment capital. But the attentions of her British admirers did not quite compensate for the loss of Barbara Bennett's protective presence. Despite all the hoopla and glitter of the Café de Paris, she found her existence lonely and retreated into a soft melancholia not unlike her mother's, nurtured by movie fantasies.

"I was living beyond my means—who doesn't at seventeen?—in a flat at 49A Pall Mall," she wrote film historian William K. Everson years later. "Quite alone, my chief confidant was Nellie, the rosy-cheeked maid with surprised blue eyes and her poor, swollen red paws. One morning, cleaning out the coal basket, with a black smudge on her nose, she sat entranced on the floor with me looking at a picture of Betty [Bronson] descending a staircase while I read to her the *Photoplay* fairytale story of Betty's rise to fame. And then we saw *Peter Pan* and fell in love with her unique beauty and grace and strange impish mind."[4]

Nellie's companionship was comforting but tended to reinforce the girl's gloom. The only antidote was the one she would employ time and again throughout her life, whenever loneliness or disappointment overtook her: the womb of Manhattan.

Louise's decision to go back to New York was as sudden as her decision to leave it. Typically, she hadn't saved a shilling. Captain Lyle Humphreys, who ran the Café, charitably continued to pay her, even after her engagement ended, but that couldn't go on for long. Finally, in January 1925, "I took matters in my own hands," she said, "and invested my last pound in a pathetic cable to Otto Kahn . . . begging him to rescue me from London." Kahn, in turn, cabled Eddie Goulding, who was conveniently visiting his mother in London, and instructed Goulding to pay Louise's rent at 49A Pall Mall and put her on the familiar *Homeric*, bound for New York, on February 14.

So much for London. By the end of February 1925, Louise's Broadway buddies welcomed her back with open arms ("and legs," one of them added) and came quickly to her aid in the matter of employment. One of them announced her return to Florenz Ziegfeld, who had been looking for Louise ever since her mysterious disappearance from the *Scandals* six months before. Ziegfeld was then in the final stages of assembling a new musical and he informed her of an opening for another chorus girl.

"I'm not a chorus girl, I'm a dancer," Louise told the great impresario. So much the better, said Ziegfeld, who had received laudatory reports of her work in the *Scandals* from one of the spies he sent to catch George White's revue. He had an endless supply of sublime female faces and forms, but relatively few of them could do more than look beautiful. Though it was late in the game to be tinkering with the structure of the thing, Louise was not only admitted to the cast but given another one of those enviable "specialty dances" to perform.

The show was not the famous *Ziegfeld Follies*, but rather *Louie the 14th*, a two-act musical farce with music by Sigmund Romberg, produced by Ziegfeld and starring the vaudeville comedian Leon Errol. It was terribly important to Ziegfeld: It would be the debut production in his magnificent new theater, the Cosmopolitan at Columbus Circle. After years of working in somebody else's "house," he finally acquired the Cosmo under a five-year direct lease from William Randolph Hearst, who'd been using it to show Cosmopolitan Company movies. Now for the first time, Ziegfeld had full control of his venue as well as his vehicle, and he was pouring a huge sum of money into the renovation of the place.

Unabashed splendor was the goal. For the remodeling he hired Joseph Urban, who among other things designed a completely new proscenium arch. Urban also painted sixteen gorgeous mural panels (several depicting the triumphant entry of Alexander into Babylon) and supervised their setting into the walls and ceiling. He added twelve new lunettes at the back of the orchestra and hung Flemish tapestries on both sides of the wall above the balcony, with bronze torches beneath them.

The show that opened this palace had better be a knockout.

Louie's plot was as wafer-thin as most musical comedies of that day or this. Adapted by British playwright Arthur Wimperis from a German comedy by Frank and Julius Wilhelm, it was set in the French Alps, which gave the scene designers plenty of grist for their visual mill. Leon Errol in the title role played a drunken American doughboy who stays in France after the Great War, becoming a cook, a mountain guide, and a fake nobleman, and incidentally learning to yodel. Louie is hired by a superstitious French socialite to ward off bad luck by becoming the fourteenth guest at her lawn party.

If this froth were to work, it would have to be carried by the pleasant Romberg tunes, the singing of imported British music-hall star Doris Patston, the tried-and-true vaudeville shtick of Errol, and the dancing of beauties like Louise Brooks. Eighty Glorified Girls and forty-two singers would be on the boards.

Flo Ziegfeld was taking no chances. With opening night just a month away, he ordered trial runs in Baltimore and Washington, D. C., where Louise and the rest of the cast were hastily transported at the end of February. If it worked in D.C.—not the liveliest of theater towns—they'd love it on Broadway.

Actually, the competition in the capital was unusually stiff that week. B. F. Keith's new all-star vaudeville show was playing, and both Fritz Kreisler and the Denishawn Dancers were performing. Shaw's *St. Joan*, Maugham's *Rain*, and *The Lounge Lizard* with Estelle Winwood were on. The movie houses featured Corinne Griffith's *Love's Wilderness*, Mary Pickford's *Dorothy Vernon of Haddon Hall*, Harold Lloyd's *Hot Water*, Norma Talmadge's *Secrets*, and Valentino's *A Sainted Devil*.

And the *Louie* previews went splendidly. On February 23, 1925, Washington *Post* critic John J. Daly, noting that Ziegfeld had "lavished money like a drunken sailor" on his three-hour production, fired a salvo of superlatives:

> In the latest offering from the Ziegfeld laboratories, *Louie the 14th*, which was presented in the National Theatre last evening, there is a transcendentalism—an exaltation of beauty over baseness—that far surpasses anything ever before produced by either Ziegfeld or his rivals of recent years.
>
> *Louie the 14th*, while labeled a musical comedy, comes close to being one of the greatest extravaganzas of the age. . . .
>
> In the closing [patriotic "Jeanne d'Arc"] number of the first act, Mr. Ziegfeld has staged what is undoubtedly the greatest eye spectacle ever seen under the proscenium arch.

The *Evening Star* likewise raved. And it was in Washington one night after the show that Louise had her first fateful encounter with a young baron of the laundry business named George Preston Marshall. She thought it terribly funny that someone should be known as "the rich laundry man." But she also thought Marshall was terribly attractive—if not so terribly gallant.

He was a tall, black-haired man of twenty-eight with a handsome face that was already marked by a subtle play of cruelty. After a party at the Shoreham Hotel, he took me, somewhat drunk, to my room at the Willard Hotel. We had been there only a few minutes when there was a knock at the door. George ran into the bathroom and hid behind the shower curtain, while I opened the door to the house detective. He went directly into the bathroom and came out with George. They chatted pleasantly, leaving the room together after the detective accepted a $20 bill from George. Half an hour later, when I was in bed, a woman employee came into the room and told me to get up, get dressed, and get out of the hotel. Since I was leaving Washington on the morning train for New York, I played dead till she grew tired of shaking me and went away.[5]

Much more would be heard from Marshall later. But for now, Louise was hurrying back to Manhattan for the big opening.

Ziegfeld's publicity agents had done their job well, and by the time the show opened in New York on March 3, 1925, the critics and the public were primed for both the new musical and the new theater.

"A triumph in stagecraft," decreed the normally restrained *New York Times* the next morning, pronouncing *Louie* "an abundant and gorgeously staged musical show. The results certainly met the expectations of all, and exceeded those of most."

"Probably not in his career has Mr. Ziegfeld accomplished anything quite so beautiful to see and to hear," raved "Q.M." of the New York *World*. ". . . Here is, indeed, the world's finest entertainment of its kind." "Q.M." summed up the work of the singers and dancers in a final sweeping sentence that reflected his euphoria as well as his deadline pressure: "With one grand gesture I bow to the chorus."

If opening night was judged a splendid theatrical event, it was equally triumphant as a social one. Outside the Cosmopolitan Theater, hundreds of stargazers and curiosity seekers braved the bitter cold to watch the celebrities enter. They were not disappointed, for the sleek limousines deposited a golden horde of New York's elite, including Mrs. William Randolph Hearst, Mrs. W. K. Vanderbilt, Condé Nast, Adolph S. Ochs, R. S. Rothschild, Bernard Baruch, Paramount's Adolph Zukor and Jesse Lasky, queen of the legitimate stage Ruth Chatterton, and comedy's well-done toast of the town, Bea Lillie. These and other notables made their way grandly to the new "Diamond Horseshoe" inside—sixty-eight elegant loges, freshly carved out of the first few rows of the balcony. From their boxes, the exclusive first-nighters signaled their approval in catered comfort.

Ziegfeld was ecstatic.

Louise, despite the critics' unanimous bow, was less so. She drew only the most favorable kind of critical and audience attention, and even more

publicity. She was happy about that, but again there were backstage problems galore and, as in the *Scandals,* a major personality conflict with the
stage manager–director, the hard-drinking veteran Teddy Royce. Something of a pattern seemed to be developing. At various times, Royce had
insulted her abilities or just sensibilities. Since Louise's best defense was
always a good offense, she set about provoking Royce, who took the bait.

"He was an elfin creature with snapping black eyes, who whisked about
on the coldest winter days dressed only in a tweed suit with a gray cashmere scarf wound around his neck," she remembered. "He detested all of
Ziegfeld's spoiled beauties, but most of all me, because on occasion, when
I had other commitments, I would wire to the theater notice of my non-
appearance."[6]

One spring day, at the end of a matinee, Royce called for everyone to
reassemble onstage, while he himself stood in the orchestra pit sipping a
gin and water.

> Since he was powerless to fire me, he called a special rehearsal, waltzed
> us through our tricks, strengthened himself with a shot of gin, whipped his
> little Oliver Twist scarf over his shoulder, and stepped out to deliver an
> admonition during which he never took his glaring eyes off me. "Some girls,"
> he said in his feisty way, "are breaking down the whole discipline of the
> company—coming late to the theatre, missing performances, in fact using
> the theatre simply as a showcase—a place to publish their wares."[7]

"All the girls looked at me, too, and grinned happily," she added—
shades of her Denishawn dismissal.[8] Although the offending remarks were
on the mild side, Louise felt humiliated, and she ran straight to Ziegfeld's
private den under the Cosmopolitan's stage box to complain bitterly about
her treatment.

Ziegfeld might have been expected to eject this brazen young thing
from both his office and his musical. But he knew a hot property when he
had one. Instead of dismissing her as a troublemaker, "he smiled his
charming, silver-fox smile," told her to disregard Royce, and made the
astonishing, on-the-spot decision to transfer her directly to the summer
edition of his *Follies.*

In all of Broadway, if not all of American entertainment, there was no
greater height than the *Ziegfeld Follies.* It was simply the top show in the
business and its performers were considered to have reached the pinnacle
of theatrical success. The showgirls got between $250 and $300 a week and
they "dripped in furs—not from their salaries, but from the guys that kept
them," remembers one ex-*Follies* girl, Lina Basquette.[9]

Almost from his first show in 1907, Ziegfeld had showcased the most
beautiful women, the best music and dancing, the most spectacular cos-

tumes and staging on Broadway. For nearly two decades he had provided his customers with an endless parade of great performers from Nora Bayes, Mae Murray, Anna Held, and Bert Williams down to Ina Claire, Ed Wynn, W. C. Fields, Marilyn Miller, and Eddie Cantor.

Ziegfeld's *Follies* were undiminished by the increasingly crowded field of competitors and imitators—the George White *Scandals*, *Earl Carroll's Vanities*, the LeMaires' *Affairs* and *Broadway Brevities*, the *Greenwich Village Follies*, the *Music Box Revues*, and the *Garrick Gaieties*, to name a few. The others came and went, but only Ziegfeld had Will Rogers. Only Ziegfeld had Fanny Brice, bringing tears to 2,000 pairs of eyes a night with "My Man." Only Ziegfeld survived, all the way to 1931, because only Ziegfeld proclaimed the simple goal of "Glorifying the American Girl"— shrewdly manufacturing an American ideal of womanhood while exploiting a chief characteristic of male audiences in particular: voyeurism.

Edmund Wilson, in "The Follies as an Institution," tried to fathom the essence of the show's perennial appeal:

> In general, Ziegfeld's girls have not only the Anglo-Saxon straightness— straight backs, straight brows and straight noses—but also the peculiar frigidity and purity, the frank high-school-girlishness which Americans like. He does not aim to make them, from the moment they appear, as sexually attractive as possible, as the Folies-Bergere, for example, does. He appeals to American idealism, and then, when the male is intent on his chaste and dewy-eyed vision, he gratifies him on this plane by discreetly disrobing his goddess.

In Wilson's psychosociological opinion, Ziegfeld's well-trained chorus girls did not represent "the movement and abandon of emotion, but what the American male really regards as beautiful: the efficiency of mechanical movement." Yet despite its resemblance to a military drill, "there is still something wonderful about the Follies. It exhibits the persistent vitality as well as the stupidity of an institution [and] a glittering vision which rises straight out of the soul of New York."

> The *Follies* is such fantasy, such harlequinade as the busy well-to-do New Yorker has been able to make of his life. Expensive, punctual, stiff, it moves with the speed of an express train. It has in it something of Riverside Drive, of the Plaza, of Scott Fitzgerald's novels—though it radically differs from these latter in being almost devoid of wit.[10]

BUT THE PUBLIC was undaunted by such critiques. Not only the newspapers but even the wire services followed Ziegfeld's cast changes breathlessly, and they did not fail to report that as of June 27, 1925, Louise Brooks—who "until a few weeks ago danced a specialty in *Louie the 14th*" —was one of six new members of Mr. Ziegfeld's "beauty chorus." The other newcomers included Hilda Ferguson, "the immortal shimmy dancer,"* and Helen MacFadden, daughter of publisher Bernarr Mac-Fadden (*Physical Culture* was one of his magazines), who would presumably trade some favorable publicity for his daughter's employment. Among the veterans, some special notoriety was reserved for Fritzi LaVerne, a hoofer who, according to Louise, "preferred boys when she was sober and girls when she was drunk, and I never heard a man or a woman pan her in bed, so she must have been very good."[11]

Louise herself was not merely one of the "glorified" girls. She had several solos, including a Gypsy specialty dance, and she was chosen by Ziegfeld himself for an apache dance as well.

The 1925 summer edition of the *Follies* at the New Amsterdam Theater, thanks to Ziegfeld's casting genius, was one of the most popular ever. "New 'Follies' Most Lavish, Replete with Clean Humor," bannered the New York *American* on July 7. "Without a doubt," declared the *American*'s critic, "this twentieth edition of the *Follies* is the most lavish, the most beautiful and the most humorous of all the *Follies* Ziegfeld has ever done." The *Herald Tribune* and virtually all the other dailies reinforced that verdict.

No more stellar cast had ever been assembled for the show. Its headliners were Will Rogers, W. C. Fields, and the wildly popular "child impersonator" Ray Dooley (foil to Fields), plus comediennes Edna Leedom and Ethel Shutta.

"Each one of these five has a different form of clean, brilliant, modern humor," raved one critic. "Each has a personality that fairly leaps over the footlights and holds even the most blasé theatergoer."

Rogers interspersed his lariat tricks with the topical jibes for which he was beloved. The raiding and closing of speakeasies in New York, he felt, were engineered by the Yale Lock Company. The Scopes monkey trial, then raging in Tennessee, also provided a great font of material. As to the reports of his political appeal, the cowboy comedian said he'd accept the Oklahoma draft for governor only if they threw in the Kansas nomination too.

Fields re-created "A Back Porch," his classic effort to take a nap amid a thousand interruptions, and followed it up with "The Naggers," the famous henpecked-husband routine with Edna Leedom as his ball-and-

---

* Also known simply as "The Body," Ferguson was considered the most seductive of all Ziegfeld girls—and one of the most tempestuous. An alcoholic (straight bathtub gin was her drink), she was the mistress of politicians and financiers—but mostly of gangsters, who appreciated her tight-lipped silence in a series of crimes in which she was implicated. Her roommate, chorine Dot King, was murdered in their apartment in 1923—an event which later inspired the story of Louise's last Paramount film, *The Canary Murder Case*. Hilda went AWOL from the *Follies* for two months when the investigation got hot, and the case was never solved. She also refused to testify in later gangland cases in New York and New Jersey. She died of peritonitis at the age of thirty.

chain wife. Louise's own fine account of it focused on the superiority of Fields's stage to his screen comedy:

> The bedroom sketch opens in darkness. Bill and Edna are asleep in a double bed facing the audience. On Bill's side is a night table with a lamp on it; on Edna's side is a night table with a telephone on it. The telephone rings. Bill turns on the lamp and gets out of bed, sodden with sleep, his hair on end, wearing rumpled old white pajamas. He trots around the bed on his little pink feet to answer the telephone. After mumbling a few words, he says, "Good night, Elmer." Then, looking down at Edna, who neither moves nor speaks, he adds, "That was Elmer." Bill turns out the light and gets back into bed. The telephone rings again. This time, when Bill says, "That was Elmer," Edna sits up in a fury. She is lovely. Her blond hair is in perfect order and her lace nightgown exposes her lovely bosom and arms. Her anger does not hide the merriment in her eyes and the dimples in her cheeks. While they fight over the identity of Elmer, nobody in the audience is expected to believe that Edna is Bill's jealous wife. [Eight years later], the film "International House" contains a bedroom sequence played by Bill in the same old white pajamas, with another lovely blonde in an exquisite nightgown—Peggy Hopkins Joyce. But the realistic distaste with which she regards Bill spoils the fun.[12]

In "The Picnic," Fields and Dooley were hailed as "the funniest team the writer of this [review] ever saw on a stage," with a burlesqued war of mutual irritation that "would make a wooden Indian laugh." At twenty-eight, Dooley still had "a body that fitted nicely into a baby carriage," Louise recalled. "Her portrayals of obnoxious kids, aged from two to six, were brilliant travesties."

Shutta's contribution was the elaborate song-and-dance routine "Eddie, Be Good" in which no fewer than two dozen chorines were made up to look like Eddie Cantor.

Among those contributing to the show's script was J. P. McEvoy, a heavy-handed humorist of the Sinclair Lewis school who was Broadway's Neil Simon of the day. Three songs from the show, "Syncopating Baby," "Home Again," and "Bertie," quickly became hits, while the grand finale, "Fine Feathers Make Fine Birds," showcased the scant plumage for which Ziegfeld's girls were most famous.

Now—for the first time—the New York critics singled out the Kansas teenager by name.

"Lina Basquette and Louise Brooks were animated things of joy," wrote "G.V.C." in the New York *American*. "Both beautiful girls, both remarkable dancers and both so vivacious that one's blood tingles within thirty seconds after either one starts a dance."[13] He, and other critics, were especially taken by Louise's dance to "Syncopating Baby."

Louise (right) and fellow Glorified Girl in the "Peacock" number of the Ziegfeld Follies of 1925; photo by International News Photo, Inc.

It was Big Time high praise, and it was followed the next day by another rave for Louise by Bide Dudley in the New York *Evening World*. This article, aside from its praise, delivered Louise the even higher compliment of a two-column caricature—a sure sign of her Broadway "arrival." For good measure, Dudley emphasized that "a distinct hit was made last night by Louise Brooks, who is dancing in several numbers."

The relatively negative New York *Sun* review, by Stephen Rathbun, complained that the show looked too much like the previous *Follies*, "camouflaged with a new opening number, a revised finale for each act, a new sketch, a few other new numbers and the addition to the cast of some principals." But even Rathbun in his pan was moved to note that "last but not least, there is Louise Brooks, a charming brunette, who dances engagingly and has real personality. She would be a welcome addition to any revue."[14]

Variety, too, praised her by name for her Charleston, although the other big trade paper was not so impressed. "You can't make a new quilt by patching up an old one," wrote *Billboard* critic Don Carle Gillette. Eventually he zeroed in on the girl with the black helmet of hair: "There is another instance of unwisely encouraged precocity in the case of Louise Brooks. This snappy little performer has some good stuff in her all right, but she is not ripe enough yet to come out as a principal. In the song number 'Rose of My Heart,' where she poses around while Irving Fisher sings, Miss Brooks is lost and out of place." [15]

Even in her sole negative review she got backhanded compliments. And as a *Follies* performer of increasing reputation, she enjoyed the regular nightly excitement of the audience—the parade of celebrities who came to see the show and notice its wicked-looking acolyte. One night, "looking down from the stage to the front row, I caught my first glimpse of Gloria Swanson," said Louise.

> Walter Wanger told me that he was bringing her and I took infinite care with all my numbers, particularly when I was allowed to rise on 6-inch heels to showgirl height. For that [solo] I painted my face and body as white as a circus horse and—not content with simply getting down the stairs and across the stage in my towering white feather headdress and four-yard train—I wound myself up like a feather duster and exited with a hardly noticeable trip over my tail. Later Walter told me that her only comment on me had been that I looked like a corpse, but I was much too excited with having seen her to mind that. She had looked so stunning in a black suit with her legs crossed and her arms folded and her head thrown back, watching the show like a little general reviewing her troops. [16]

But despite such performing thrills and good reviews, restless Louise could never revel in her own success, and once again she was strangely dissatisfied. Lina Basquette, today a sprightly eighty-two years old and a judge and breeder of champion Great Danes, had been the *première danseuse* of the 1923 edition. Paired with Louise in the '25 edition, she remembers her as "lovely and graceful and very beautiful—but there was always something very sad about her." [17]

Louise revealed at least one reason for that melancholy. "For me, who had danced with Ruth St. Denis, Ted Shawn and Martha Graham, my little dances in the *Follies* were boring," she said. Her only true "moment of delight" came at the end of the show, with the whole company onstage. As if to symbolize her rapid elevation in his organization, Ziegfeld gave her the topmost position on a pyramid of chorines in the grand finale:

> Will Rogers and I climbed a ladder to the top of a fifteen-foot tower set in the middle of the stage. Starting with a tiny noose on his lasso, Rogers would twirl it faster and faster, bigger and bigger, until the rope hissed in a circle around us like an intoxicated snake as the curtains opened and the dazzling spotlight shone on us. [18]

One night in the middle of the run, Rogers was ascending the staircase full of glorified girls, expertly twirling his lariat around the beautiful Louise. Reaching the top, he turned and looked at Brooksie and—in a devilish burst of inspiration—removed his chewing gum and stuck it on the end of her haughty little nose. It got him a big laugh from the audience and a violent tirade backstage.

"You sonofabitch, I'll kill you!" fumed Louise, who never met a cowboy she liked.

He never did it again.

Lina Basquette recalls that Will Rogers was so wholesome, he once threatened to quit in the middle of rehearsals because of all the nudity: "He said he'd leave if they didn't put more clothes on the girls, and so they did." In the public mind, Will Rogers was the darling and W. C. Fields the eccentric. But as far as Louise Brooks was concerned, Rogers was a hayseed with a gimmick and Fields a consummate *artiste*.

She was fascinated by the Great Misanthrope's laconic humor, reliant on the most delicate timing and embellished by his astounding dexterity as a juggler. Most of all she admired his "stately procedures" and "the passionate amount of work he put into his performance."

Though no one knew it at the time, the 1925 *Follies* would be Fields's last Ziegfeld appearance. In the '23–'24 Broadway season, he had scored a major hit with his first sustained character role as a bumbling, two-bit shyster in the musical *Poppy*. Paramount's Astoria chief William Le Baron saw it and loved it and, after testing Fields in the 1924 Marion Davies film *Janice Meredith*, offered him a film contract. Now forty-six, Fields had survived a grueling, twenty-year apprenticeship to reach the threshold of national stardom.

Louise's awe increased nightly as she watched his brilliant comedy turns from the wings. She would have liked to get to know him better, but his solitary nature was as real offstage as on. "Bill adored beautiful girls," she recalled, "but few were invited to his dressing room. He was morbidly sensitive about the eczema that inflamed his nose and sometimes erupted on his hands, so that he had to learn to juggle wearing gloves. After several devastating experiences with beautiful girls, he had decided to restrict himself to girlfriends who were less attractive, and whom he would not find adrift with saxophone players."[19] The amorous advances of chorus girls, he had found, inevitably ended in rejection and humiliation.

Which was where Peggy Fears came in. Like Louise, this sultry Dallas beauty had been transferred from *Louie the 14th* to the *Follies*, but there the similarity ended. Peggy was more a singer than a dancer, and her personality and sunny disposition aimed to please. Louise was attracted to

Peggy Fears in the Lemaire's Affairs of 1927; *photo by Melbourne Spurr*

her fun-loving nature, and "what could be more fun than for Peggy, the most popular girl in the show, to become friends with its most abominated member—me?"

When Louise joined the '25 *Follies*, her reputation had preceded her. The day she arrived for rehearsals, stage manager Billy Strode—much amused—informed her that "I've asked them all and there's not a girl in the show willing to dress with you." Eventually she was assigned to share a dressing room with Dorothy Knapp, the most glorified of all Ziegfeld's glorified girls, and to everyone's surprise, the two coexisted in harmony.

"During the run of the *Follies*," said Louise, "the dressing room of Dorothy Knapp and me became the cultural drop-in of such clowning gentlemen as Walter Wanger, Herman Mankiewicz, Michael Arlen, Charlie Chaplin. It was the biggest dressing room in the building on the top floor of the New Amsterdam, and Dorothy and I shared it because we were so grand and did so few numbers. She had a full-length mirror in which to fill the empty hours."[20] ". . . I was reading things like Aldous Huxley's *Crome Yellow*. The other girls were reading the *Police Gazette*. They would look at me and say, 'Who is this Kansas bitch? How dare she?' "[21]

In addition to the male admirers, Peggy Fears enlivened the dressing room with regular visits, bringing Wedgwood teapots full of corn whiskey and the sleaziest magazines she could find to spoof Louise's literary pretensions.

Brooks and Fears were soon fast friends and living together in the Gladstone Hotel. It was Peggy's idea to stop by a Park Avenue florist shop on the way to the theater and buy a bouquet to present to Bill Fields in his dressing room. The great loner, deeply touched by the gesture, began to invite the girls to his dressing room, where he entertained them royally, making his private bar (inside a wardrobe trunk) available to them.

"While Shorty, the silent dwarf who was his valet and his assistant onstage, went about preparing our drinks," Louise recalled, "Peggy and I would dance around Bill, who sat at his makeup shelf listening to our nonsense with gracious attention." [22]

In the middle of the *Follies* run, a newly upscale Louise Brooks moved to the Marguery, an expensive apartment-hotel at 270 Park Avenue near 47th Street. She was again living above her means, this time "in a large room that looked down on three fine spruce trees crooning peacefully in the courtyard."

John Lock, the stockbroker who had given her the ermine coat, now presented her with a brand-new riding outfit and equestrian lessons at Durland's Riding Academy on 79th Street, where Herr Hugo—formerly of the German cavalry under Kaiser Wilhelm—was her instructor through the mild December of 1925.

Louise, usually in the company of Peggy Fears, was back in the heavy swing of New York social life. In the wee hours, she and Peggy were frequenters of Texas Guinan's notorious speakeasy, where the patrons invariably roared for Louise to Charleston.

Louise adored the outrageousness of Tex Guinan, whose immortal greeting—"Hello, sucker!"—was now the watchword at fast nightclubs everywhere. This lady from Waco proudly advertised the fact that she always went to Mass and never drank, but there her virtue ended. Soon after Prohibition, she became the best-known figure in New York nightlife, reportedly hauling down $700,000 in one ten-month period alone. Her premises were constantly raided, but she insisted that her customers were bringing in their own flasks and that her profits came from the setup and cover charges shelled out by wealthy suckers to see her scantily clad dancers. When the Feds finally slapped her in jail for violating a liquor-selling injunction, she had her orchestra play "The Prisoner's Song" as they led her away. Tex soon returned to her club, healthier than ever, and later had fun staging her own little X-rated Ziegfeldian revue called *The Padlocks of 1927.*

Louise was an amused and amusing participant in such shenanigans.

THE NEW PLAYS

The Summer "Follies"

By BIDE DUDLEY

THE summer edition of the Ziegfeld "Follies," now current at the New Amsterdam Theatre, is just about as good a show as a person could wish to see. The best features of the recent spring edition

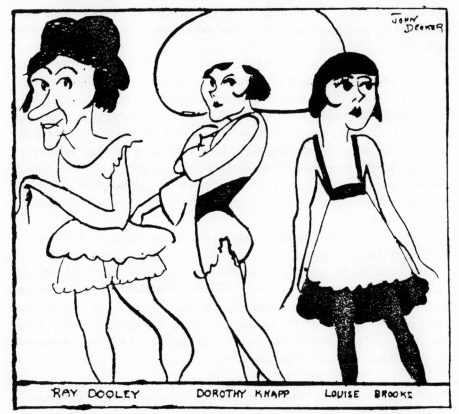

RAY DOOLEY   DOROTHY KNAPP   LOUISE BROOKS

John Decker's caricature in The New York Evening World, *July 8, 1925*

She liked to drink and she liked to dance. She did both things well and could be seen teasing an occasional sucker herself. But even with the racy diversions at Guinan's, she chafed under the occupational hazard of the successful Broadway performer: Working six nights a week, she could never take in anybody else's show or otherwise enjoy herself until after midnight.

Hence, an increase in those "nonappearances" she kept wiring to the *Follies* stage manager. She instantly accepted, for instance, an invitation from Herman Mankiewicz (elder brother of Joseph), who was then the second-string drama critic for the *New York Times*, to attend the long-awaited opening of *No, No, Nanette*.

Louise called Mankiewicz "a marvelous person, a lovely person, my favorite person"[23] and would have accompanied him to a boxing match, let alone the most glamorous Broadway opening of the new fall season. For the previous twelve months, *Nanette* had been delighting audiences in Chicago and the hinterlands. New York critics and theatergoers were tantalized by the show's advance raves and annoyed by its delay in getting to Broadway.

There was no question that Louise would be AWOL from the *Follies* on September 16, the night of *Nanette*'s unveiling, and on the arm of the charming young *Times* reviewer. But she hadn't expected the arm to be so unsteady. Mankiewicz himself was a little overexuberant about the event and about the prospect of squiring one of Ziegfeld's most ravishing beauties. At dinner before the show, he consumed a two-digit number of cocktails; by the time they made their way to the Globe Theatre at Broadway and 46th [now the Lunt-Fontanne] and were ushered to their orchestra seats, Mankiewicz was too drunk to stay awake, much less write a coherent review.

And so the secretly literate Louise rose to the occasion, took notes, and wrote it for him!

The show was "a highly meritorious paradigm of its kind," she opined, aping the arch tone of the *Times*. Charles Winninger as the wayward husband was "extremely mirth-provoking." And there was a mischievous, backhanded compliment for Louise Groody in the title role, who Louise said appeared "to better advantage than has been her lot in an unfortunate number of recent years." She also wrote:

> There is to *No, No, Nanette*, let it be stated for the benefit of those who assemble such statistical material, a plot, in which for the final curtain Nanette, the heroine, embraces Tom, the hero. There is a score, with more familiar quotations from itself—one refers to "I Want to Be Happy" and "Tea for Two"—than even "Hamlet." And there is an energetic cast of well selected comedians.[24]

In spite of its flaws, *No, No, Nanette* overall received positive marks from Louise. She turned in an amazing performance herself, holding her own with the half-dozen other New York critics, who by and large echoed her opinion. To the grateful amusement of Herman Mankiewicz (who was not long for the *Times* staff), no one in or out of the *Nanette* cast ever suspected that an eighteen-year-old chorus girl had written his review.

Louise as Miss Bayport in her first featured film role, The American Venus (1926)

5 · Moving in Pictures

Tensions are vital to life. One should never completely relax unless one wants to feel the poetry of slowly dying. —CHARLES CHAPLIN

The son of a bitch is a ballet dancer! He's the best ballet dancer that ever lived, and if I get a good chance, I'll strangle him with my bare hands.
— W. C. FIELDS on Chaplin

FLO ZIEGFELD was a worldly, easygoing man with an almost endless capacity for tolerance toward his casts. Now in his second decade at the top of the Broadway heap, nothing his girls did could surprise him. He was aware of at least some of Louise Brooks's shenanigans and tended to smile upon them. He could stand and withstand all the tricks of his theatrical competitors and come out from the seasonal rough-and-tumble of the business unscathed. But beginning around 1921, there was one thing that infuriated him: the theft of his best performers by the increasingly aggressive motion picture studios.

By 1925, most of the major film companies had moved production from New York and Chicago to the West Coast, or at least had California branches. They were lured by the constant sunshine, cheap labor and real estate, and the wonderful variety of natural scenic locations. But even when they moved their studios, they usually left their corporate offices and their Manhattan talent scouts behind, and a few of the big companies were slow to leave. The biggest of these was Famous Players–Lasky, now in the process of changing its name to "Paramount." Its sprawling Astoria studios on Long Island remained a hubbub of activity, churning out some four dozen feature pictures in 1926 alone.

Paramount was the most daring of the major movie companies and the one with the most voracious appetite for new talent. There were artistic but mostly economic reasons for this. The shrewd businessmen who ran the place were tightfisted, but they were willing to take risks. If they wanted to stay in the vanguard of public taste, they would have to gamble on the trends and on the stage performers who typified them. It was the not-so-secret dream of almost everyone on Broadway to make movies, and most of them could be had for reasonable sums. And since carfare to Long Island was a lot cheaper than cross-country railroad tickets to Hollywood, Paramount raided the *Follies* and many other New York shows shamelessly and regularly.

Nothing Ziegfeld could do—not even bribery—seemed to hold his talent in place. "Ziggy would have raised the scrubwoman's salary to keep her out of pictures," Louise told an interviewer around this time.[1] Having already lost a few dozen of his most glamorous stars and showgirls to films —Marion Davies, Mae Murray, and Billie Dove among them—Ziegfeld's hatred of the movie headhunters was at fever pitch by 1925.

"One had to be pretty special to get backstage at the *Follies*—Mr. Hearst, or at least the fire commissioner or Paul Block [Hearst's main assistant]," said Louise, "but when Mr. Ziegfeld heard that Paramount was creeping in, he barred everyone."[2]

Indeed, in a rare overt display of wrath, he decreed the backstage areas of all his shows off limits to film company employees, instructing his bouncers to keep them out by force if necessary. But that could hardly deter any cunning movie scout for long. All he had to do was buy a ticket, look to his heart's content, and then track down his prospects by phone the next day.

Two of the most sophisticated Paramount operators were Walter Wanger and Townsend Martin. Both were frequenters of the *Follies*, as much for their own entertainment as for scouting purposes. Wanger was a major studio executive; Martin was a prominent socialite, a buddy of Scott Fitzgerald, and a sometime scenarist who dabbled in the movie industry.

Wanger, in particular, was dazzled by Louise Brooks, that exotic black orchid, the minute he laid eyes on her. He had already heard Eddie Goulding rave about her, and now he and Martin arranged to test her for a bit part in Herbert Brenon's *Street of Forgotten Men*.

Unlike her glorified peers, Louise was not seeking a movie career. She considered "the flickers"* intrinsically inferior to the theater—an accurate judgment as far as social status was concerned. In the phenomenal 1925–1926 season, no less than 178 straight plays and 48 musicals opened in New York. In Gotham, stage was to screen as grand opera was to burlesque. If forced to choose, only a fool would forsake Broadway. For all

---

* So new was the art form, even by 1925, that its name was not yet settled in popular usage, and the anachronistic "flicker" was still common. Thus did *Photoplay* editor James Quirk conduct an opinion poll to determine and ordain a standard term. The winner was the diminutive of "motion picture"—"movie."

her gripes, Louise was having fun, and a Ziegfeld girl's fringe benefits were as bountiful as the checkbooks of her admirers.

But she liked Wanger, who kept showering her with presents, and so she agreed to the test as a lark. Thanks to the proximity of Astoria, it was possible after all to moonlight/daylight—to dance in the *Follies* by night and shoot movies by day.

"Start work on *Street of Forgotten Men*," she wrote in her diary on Wednesday, May 20, 1925. "Allan Dwan, a jolly man, directed [the screen test] in some old D. W. Griffith cellar set, and I ran around like Carol Dempster, being very frightened and graceful and having a lovely time." The test, she said, "was in the afternoon and did not interfere with my social life and my sleep. When you're 18, you're not living unless you go to all the nightclubs every night and stay out 'til four, and then, of course, you've got to have ten hours of sleep at least! So getting up at 7 in order to be made up and ready to work at nine made me cross as a bear."

Brenon, unlike Dwan, "was about as jolly as a double Mickey Finn. He belonged to the old school. He was the tyrant type, and it wasn't only the actors he abused with his sharp Dublin accent and his nasty tongue. Sandbags from the catwalks, carpenters' hammers, electricians' lights, all had a way of falling about him."

But even as a target for missiles, Brenon was imperturbable. Imperturbable—but nasty—and Louise came in for some tongue-lashings, too. Thirty years later, she described it in a letter to James Card:

> The scene I remember working in was awful: a saloon with barroom fight, and I was sitting at a table, far, far more dangerous to the extras if they touched my foot or mussed my hair than were any of the stuntmen with bottles and stools to play with. Why, playing an insignificant bit, I got so much of Mr. Brenon's attention and such an ugly part of it, I can't say. Being frightened of everything else in addition to him, no doubt I clammed up and glowered more than usual—aggravating my worst crime against important people: not giving them the adulation and submission they expect. There, then, is my first experience in movies, and shaking the sawdust from the saloon floor off my Milgrim's suit, I determined to make it my last.[3]

Brenon was one of Paramount's hottest directors, with a preference and reputation for intelligent scripts. His string of hits included *Peter Pan* with Betty Bronson—much beloved of Louise Brooks and her English maid—and would soon be extended with the original silent versions of *Beau Geste* and *The Great Gatsby* in 1926. He was admired for his ability to elicit controlled emotions from such temperamental performers as Alla Nazimova, Norma Talmadge, Pola Negri, and Lon Chaney—all emotional time bombs waiting to go off.

Brenon praised "temperament" as essential to the make-up of great stars, and he was highly temperamental himself. He and Loretta Young got into a legendary battle on the set of her debut picture, *Laugh, Clown, Laugh*. Brenon thought the fifteen-year-old Loretta insufferably spoiled and one day became so enraged at her smugness that he threw a chair at her, mainly to disrupt her composure. She called him "insane" and stomped off the set. (Throwing a chair at the moralistic Loretta Young, said Louise, was "the best thing Brenon ever did.")

In view of Brenon's stature, Louise should have been thrilled by his attentions, especially after he took her to the Kentucky Derby, where by all accounts they had a lovely time. But she never cultivated—or indicated a desire to cultivate—the contact. After the shooting of *Forgotten Men*, she decided she'd done badly and made an unfavorable impression on Brenon.

The opposite was true. Brenon liked her maiden scene enough to keep it in, which he was under no obligation to do. *The Street of Forgotten Men* was his American *Lower Depths*, halfway between Maxim Gorky and Charles Dickens. Its fake beggars were the Artful Dodgers of the contemporary Bowery. Louise, in her brief appearance, is smartly attired in suit and cloche hat with a racy feather in the shape of a question mark. When she flashes a ravishing, close-up smile, no more than the one shot is needed—Brooks nuzzling John Harrington as "Bridgeport White-Eye"— to know this is the bad girl with the bad man.*

Notwithstanding Louise's self-assessment, the test had gone so well that she soon faced a flattering dilemma: not one but two movie offers from the greatest studio rivals, Paramount and MGM.

Paramount had something it called "The Paramount Junior Stars," and, based on Louise's successful bit in *Street of Forgotten Men*, she was invited to junior stardom. Metro submitted a similar offer. Complicating matters was a new organization called the Film Guild.

The Guild was founded in 1922 by the Princetonian Townsend Martin and the Yale-educated director Frank Tuttle and financier Dwight Deere Wiman, together with Fred Waller (later, an inventor of Cinerama). Modeled somewhat on the Theatre Guild, the Film Guild's goal was to break the chains of postwar schlock romanticism that fettered the movies to scripts like *The Tents of Allah*. Guild members made a small number of independent films—most with actors Glenn Hunter and Osgood Perkins —while still retaining affiliations with such big-studio executive friends as Walter Wanger.

Wanger by now adored Louise and was having an affair with her, when-

---

* *The Street of Forgotten Men* was long thought to be lost, but six of its seven reels—including the Louise Brooks footage—were recently rediscovered at the Library of Congress.

Paramount producer and executive Walter Wanger; photo by Associated Press

ever he could book some time around her other romantic commitments. "How sweet he was then," Louise later wrote, "—a brilliant, laughing young man of the world whose heart remained tender. He had taken me under his protection . . . after discovering that my blasé insolence was a masquerade. It amused him to find that the decadent black-and-white Aubrey Beardsley makeup covered a sprinkling of Kansas freckles."[4] Aside from his role of mentor and lover, he was at this point "my best friend," and she went to him for advice:

> It was while I was having supper in Wanger's apartment that I told him about the two film offers. I was sure he would advise me to sign the Paramount contract. . . . I can still feel the pride I took in my new black velvet suit and emerald cufflinks, still smell the russet chrysanthemums in their crystal vase on the table, still see the glowing reds and purples of the fruit compote set in a silver bowl of ice. The compote I never tasted.
>
> Just as I picked up my spoon, Walter said, "You must sign the contract with MGM." I sat back in my chair, speechless, and then began to cry. "Don't you see that your friendship with me would put you in a dangerously vulnerable position at Paramount?" he said. "Everybody would assume that you owed your contract to me, and all the producers would treat you accordingly. If you sign with MGM, you will start fresh—completely independent, on your own."
>
> But I did not see.[5]

Instead, Wanger's sound, altruistic advice cinched Louise's perverse decision to accept the Paramount offer. Years later John Kobal asked her what made her go into films, in view of her indifference to the movie business. Her answer was impatient: "To make money, to make money. To live, for God's sake."[6]

But wasn't she making good money in the *Follies?*

> Well, Ziegfeld wanted me to stay in the *Follies* and be a *Follies* star. . . . I was young then, and they said, "Oh, you're a fool not to go into movies and sign a contract." So I did it. But it was just for the money, that's the only thing. I could spend a week's salary buying clothes, I was mad about clothes for a time. You know, ermine coats and those things eat up a lot of money. I would go out to a nightclub every night in New York and show off my clothes. I had my literary friends. That's what life was in those days. . . .[7]

And so in October of 1925, Louise signed a five-year contract with Paramount. Her first picture would be a flesh spectacle keyed to that year's Miss America contest—*The American Venus.*

Paramount was more deeply rooted and better connected in Manhattan than any other movie company, thanks to a deceptively low-key Hungarian immigrant named Adolph Zukor, who devoted all but a few of his 103 years to the building of an empire. Zukor's was not a rags- but a furs-to-riches story: He left the Chicago mink business for New York at the turn of the century and, with Marcus Loew, got into penny arcades, which were fast on the inflationary way to becoming nickelodeons. Ambitious Zukor was soon bored with distribution and turned to production. Most movies were single-reel "chasers," so called because their main function was to clear out the house after a vaudeville show.

After he and Loew went separate ways, Zukor began to employ stage stars—John Barrymore, Pauline Frederick, and even solid-gold Mary Pickford—as drawing cards for movies. He bought up rights to such staples as *The Count of Monte Cristo, The Prisoner of Zenda,* and *Tess of the d'Urbervilles* and gave his West 26th Street studio the lumpy name of "Famous Players in Famous Plays." By 1914, he was churning out thirty photoplays a year, many of them five or six reels long, but the complex method of selling them to exhibitors led Zukor and producer Jesse Lasky to opt for the central distribution plan of W. W. Hodkinson's Paramount Company.

The "Jesse L. Lasky Feature Play Company" joined Zukor's enterprise in the 1916 merger that produced "Famous Players–Lasky"—no improvement on the name, but a powerful new force in the industry. Zukor, the proto-corporate raider, next bought up a majority of Paramount shares. Hodkinson was squeezed out, with a small consolation: The new studio's name would be Paramount. Hodkinson had also provided its trademark—a mountain and stars he doodled one day on his desk blotter.

Zukor was one of the first producers to integrate production and distribution, but he needed an outside financial network to meet the soaring costs of salaries and theater construction. He and Lasky went to their banker friend Otto Kahn, who helped them float a huge $10 million stock issue for the acquisition of movie show places all over the United States and in Europe.

The transactions involving Kahn were among the biggest of the interlocking relationships that tied the movie industry to Wall Street. Indeed, the New Yorkers' control over the film business increased rather than decreased with the rise of Hollywood, for it was bank accounts and boards of directors that mattered most. Even after East Coast production was dwarfed by that in California, the center of *real* power was still New York. Many of the financiers wanted to participate in the operations of the movie companies they backed, and since Paramount's grand facility at Astoria was just a short hop from Wall Street, the money men could become as actively involved as they wished.

Not even the great scandals of 1921–1922—the Fatty Arbuckle rape case, followed by the murder of director William Desmond Taylor—could slow the momentum of the movie business. By 1925, Paramount's annual profit of about $5 million was twice that of Fox, thrice that of Universal, and more than five times that of Warners. Only Metro-Goldwyn-Mayer rivaled Paramount. In any case, there were profits aplenty to go around.

But money alone did not explain Wall Street's infatuation with the movies. "Power was the most important thing," Louise told documentary filmmaker Ricky Leacock years later.[8] For producers and financiers, she said, money was of interest first as a means to power and, second, because it enabled them "to sleep with beautiful women." The forces that drove the movie moguls of the twenties were the same that drive them today: money, power, sex, fame, and the creation of American popular culture.

Louise had already seen this phenomenon in action in the *Scandals*, when Otto Kahn provided both the introduction and the trysting place for Dorothy Sebastian and Lord Beaverbrook. She would see it again and again throughout her career.

Louise's own career and social life provided an example of how the Hollywood–Wall Street system of owning beautiful women worked, even then, in 1925, when she was just eighteen. While friendly with such struggling young actors as Humphrey Bogart, she was more often to be found on her regular nightclub rounds in the company of Peggy Fears and the high-rolling A. C. Blumenthal, a financier who eventually took over Ziegfeld's business. It was Louise, in fact, who introduced Peggy and "Blumie."

For Peggy Fears, as for most *Follies* girls, the big item on the agenda was to make sure that before their salad days wilted they linked up with a wealthy patron, preferably with a diamond ring to seal the deal.

But for Brooksie, it wasn't all sex and money. She enjoyed but was easily bored by both. She could be dazzled by the expensive trinkets New York had to offer, and she was open to a variety of sexual encounters. But Louise had no interest in the ring or the permanence it implied, and even at eighteen she was more inclined toward "fascinating" people than toward rich ones. When the two virtues coincided, so much the better. But there had to be an element of intellectual stimulation. This was a woman who could sit down and mock up a convincing review in *New York Times* style, and on deadline yet.

Although she never finished high school, Louise was an autodidact extraordinaire, steeped in her mother's artistic revels and her own Denishawn experience. She gravitated toward the intellectuals. The first-chair wits were still seated at the Algonquin and were mostly theatrical in orientation; the movie people were much less homogeneous. But even so, as Louise's own career demonstrated, there was a certain overlap in the two worlds, and Manhattan moviedom had its share of bright lights who formed a kind of suborbital extension of the Round Table. They had less collective glitter and status than the Algonquin's "Vicious Circle" and no regular meeting place. But they existed, and for a time Louise was a peripheral member.

This "Dinette Set," as some wags called it, had an unofficial chieftain in the person of James R. Quirk, long-time editor of *Photoplay* magazine, which in the twenties had nothing in common with the pulp "fanzine" of the forties and fifties. In Quirk's lifetime, thanks to his good taste and fierce independence, *Photoplay* was America's most prestigious film publication, avidly read by producers, actors, and fans alike. Quirk not only chronicled every major movie and star, he also served as father confessor to anyone who sought his counsel—which was almost everyone. Pickford consulted him about changing her "America's Sweetheart" image. The Schencks wanted to know what he thought about this and that trend. Valentino was such a close friend that when the great screen lover died in 1926, Quirk could insist a wax dummy be laid out in the funeral parlor to prevent the defilement of the corpse. (Nobody ever noticed the difference.) Quirk had time for everyone, and with a select few, he exchanged witticisms that often ended up in his magazine. "Assistant producers are mice studying to be rats," was one of his more popular epigrams from *Photoplay*.

Three of Quirk's admirers, and favored associates, were producer Walter Wanger, whiz-kid director Eddie Sutherland, and the great curmudgeon of *The American Mercury*, H. L. Mencken. All were part of that elliptical counterpart to the Round Table, whose other members in the years 1924–1929 included actress Aileen Pringle, director Marshall Neilan and his wife, Blanche Sweet, writers Anita Loos and Willis Goldbeck. Mencken knew the East Coast film people, but "The Low-Down on Hollywood"—written for *Photoplay* at Quirk's request—was his first report on the industry's Pacific branch. One of Mencken's most stylish pieces of reportage, it provided an insightful view of Hollywood:

> I spent my time in Los Angeles studying the Christian pathology of that great city. When not so engaged, I mainly devoted myself to quiet guzzling with Jim Quirk . . . , Walter Wanger and other such literati. For the rest, I visited friends in the adjacent deserts, some of them employed in the pictures and some not. They treated me with immense politeness. Nothing would have been easier than to have had me killed, but they let me go.

In the article's question-and-answer format, Mencken was asked if he'd been introduced to Hollywood's legendary nightlife:

> The wildest night-life I encountered was at Aimee McPherson's tabernacle. I saw no wildness among the movie folk. They seemed to me, in the main, to be very serious and even sombre people. . . . I encountered but two authentic souses in three weeks. One was a cowboy and the other was an author. I heard of a lady getting tight at a party, but I was not present. The news was a sensation in the town. Such are the sorrows of poor mummers: their most banal peccadilloes are magnified into horrors.
>
> Regard the unfortunate Chaplin. If he were a lime and cement dealer, his divorce case [against Lita Grey Chaplin, then raging] would not get two lines in the newspapers. But now he is placarded all over the front pages because he has had a banal disagreement with his wife. I don't know him, but he has my prayers.

The late Valentino was still much on everyone's mind, and so the final bulletin of Mencken's "Hollywood Low-Down" was drawn from the short, hectic life of Rudy le Bien-Aimé:

> Hollywood, I believe, is full of unhappy people. Many of its notables are successful and rich, but I don't think that many of them are satisfied. The sort of attention that falls upon a movie personage is irksome, and, in most of its aspects, insulting. There may be men and women out there who enjoy being pawed and applauded by millions of idiots, but if so I am not acquainted with them. I recall a conversation with the late Valentino. He was precisely as happy as a small boy being kissed by two hundred fat aunts.[9]

H. L. Mencken was sincerely glad to return to the safety of the East Coast.

Louise Brooks was glad not to have left it. She hadn't yet met the cast of characters in California and felt no need to do so. Everything and everybody was in New York, or returned there after a temporary defection. The overlapping leaves of the Manhattan smart set accommodated film people and, compared with the Algonquin crowd, the Quirk-Mencken-Wanger circle was downright democratic and much less sedentary. Their favorite watering hole was Texas Guinan's—a disreputable substitute for the Algonquin. Their transcontinental comings and goings could never be accounted for, but whenever and wherever they did gather, on either coast, the topic of conversation usually turned at some point to the one film man "of genius." Not even Mencken was immune to his spell. On rare occasions, the genius even joined them.

In the theater and film world—in all worlds—nobody was more welcome or more adored than Charlie Chaplin.

All her social, professional, and personal contacts came together for Louise in a monumental way in the middle of the *Follies* run: Charlie Chaplin was coming to town for the New York premiere of *The Gold Rush*.

"You have to remember something about Chaplin at that point," says Ricky Leacock, "and that is that he was infinitely more famous than Jesus Christ ever was—China, Africa, every continent and corner of the world. In 1925, he was the most famous man who ever lived." [10]

And *The Gold Rush* was his most famous movie. A marathon year and a half in the shooting, it was finally completed on May 21, 1925. It had been a traumatic period for Chaplin. Script and production difficulties (many of them chronicled by his young assistant, Eddie Sutherland) were aggravated by the comedian's disintegrating marriage to Lita Grey. To further complicate things, Lita gave birth to Charles Spencer Chaplin three weeks before the film's completion.

The father took no time off to be proud. He had shot a frightening quantity of film—230,000 feet—which he now had to winnow down. Way behind schedule and over budget, he rushed the editing process, cutting the film himself almost up to the day of its premiere, June 26, at Grauman's Egyptian Theater in Hollywood. At 8,555 feet, it was the longest comedy he had yet made.

It was also a major success, but Chaplin was so spent from the effort of making it that he was hardly able to savor the critical triumph. He boarded a train for the six-day trip to New York with the blissful intention of sleeping all the way. It was typical of the way he recharged, and by the time the train pulled into Grand Central Station he was refreshed and girded for the New York premiere on August 17. But first there was the hero's welcome and the round of pre-premiere fêtes to attend.

"As if to receive him, New York had also put on a new glow of luxury, grace and elegance," Louise remembered. [11] Chaplin loved both the new glow and the old glow of New York, and far from dreading this promotion ritual, he enjoyed it. The *Gold Rush* opening would take place at the Strand Theatre on Broadway—just around the corner from the *Follies* show place, the New Amsterdam Theatre on 42nd Street.

"Submerged in my own fascinating being," said Louise, "I was only vaguely aware that *The Gold Rush* had brought Chaplin his greatest triumph; that he was the toast of all intellectual, cultural and social New York; and that for a week the tabloids ran front-page pictures of Broadway beauties, asking 'Who bit Charlie's lip?' Then one afternoon at a cocktail party given by Walter Wanger, I met him."

Then and fifty years later, she thought him "the most bafflingly complex man who ever lived." At thirty-six, he was exactly twice her age; there was an instant chemical reaction between them. His physical presence, she felt, "revealed an exquisiteness the screen could not reflect. Small, perfectly made, meticulously dressed, with his fine grey hair and ivory skin and white teeth, he was as clean as a pearl and glowed all over. Inside he was glowing too with the radiant gaiety released by the successful conclusion of two years' work on his film." [12]

The New York premiere was as spectacular a success as the Hollywood opening. Rave reviews all over America were duplicated in Europe. London audiences were so convulsed that the BBC took the odd, unprecedented step of broadcasting the sound of people laughing inside the Tivoli Theatre "during the ten most uproariously funny minutes." The Germans went crazy over the famous Dance of the Rolls, in which the Tramp sticks a fork in two buns and turns them into starchy starlets, who cavort on a tabletop. The manager of the Capitol Theater in Berlin had to stop the film, roll it back, and play it again *en reprise*.

For the rest of his long life, Chaplin often said *The Gold Rush* was the film for which he most wanted to be remembered. Hardly anyone knew that it had been inspired by two grim historical records—a set of photos showing lines of toiling prospectors in the 1898 Klondike gold rush and a book Chaplin read on the 1846 Donner expedition that ended in cannibalism.

"It is paradoxical that tragedy stimulates the spirit of ridicule," observed Chaplin. "Ridicule, I suppose, is an attitude of defiance; we must laugh in the face of our helplessness against the forces of nature—or go insane." [13]

These were heavy thoughts for a comedy, but Chaplin took time out from such ruminations in New York to sit—stand, actually—for the Edward Steichen portrait, *sans* Little Tramp garb, that appeared in *Vanity Fair*. In Steichen's photo, Charlie grins naughtily into the camera as his curls cast a shadow with faunlike (or satyrlike) horns on the backdrop. The image, like the subject, is bursting with sexuality and energetic humor.

Charles Chaplin at the time of the Gold Rush opening in New York, August 1925;
photo by Edward Steichen

At this point Chaplin and his assistant, Harry d'Arrast, were birds in the gilded cage of the New York Ritz, looking forward to the end of their *Gold Rush* obligations. When the end finally came, they were free to have a good time, and the keen-eyed Chaplin wanted to have it with Louise Brooks. For several weeks, he and d'Arrast double-dated Louise and her best friend, Peggy Fears, squiring them to all the smart clubs: "Swirling in chiffons of pink and blue, Peggy and I danced the tango with them at the Montmartre where the head waiters bowed reverently before Charlie and the haughty patrons pretended that they were not thrilled at the sight of him."

The spontaneous Chaplin was always open to suggestions, and one night Louise wanted to catch the act of a prodigal daughter, recently returned from European exile:

> Charlie and Harry took us, Peggy shining in crystal beads and me magnificent but itchy in gold lace, to the Lido for the opening of the great dancer Maurice [Mouvet] with his new partner Barbara Bennett—my second-best friend. Beneath the composure of his public face, Charlie had a hilarious time because, in the opening waltz, Barbara muffed a step and giggled. Glaring with rage, Maurice did not kick her then only because he was reserving his punishment for their final Apache number at the end of which he sent Barbara skidding on her face to the very edge of the dance floor.[*][14]

The 1925 theater season was a big one in quantity and quality. Aside from *Nanette* and all the new revue editions—*Follies, Scandals, Gaieties,* and so forth—Jerome Kern's *Sunny,* Irving Berlin–George S. Kaufman's *Cocoanuts* with the Marx Brothers, and George and Ira Gershwin's *Tip-Toes* were all in production. But Chaplin and Brooks were more interested in the new straight plays, including *Cradle Snatchers,* at which "we sat in a box . . . looking at Mary Boland, Edna May Oliver and a young actor, Humphrey Bogart, on the stage, while the rest of the audience looked at Charlie."[15]

A few days later, after d'Arrast went back to Hollywood, Chaplin moved to the Ambassador Hotel, and Louise moved in with him. One particularly beautiful night they emerged from the Ambassador, eschewed all the cabbies, and walked no fewer than seventy blocks down to the Greenwich Village Theater for a performance of *Outside Looking In*—"a play about tramps which Charlie had already seen twice," said Louise. Among the cast members were the twenty-five-year-old James Cagney, Charles Bickford, and Blyth Daly as a girl on the lam who disguises herself as a boy.

---

* Maurice Mouvet, described by a contemporary writer as "the sickly, temperamental, much-married dancer," terminated his partnership with Barbara Bennett a few months later. Barbara went to Hollywood where, shortly thereafter, she swallowed half a bottle of lye in the first of numerous suicide attempts.

"Her performance might have interested me more," Louise wrote later, "had I known that I would play her part [Nancy] in the film *Beggars of Life* after the title of the Jim Tully book which Maxwell Anderson had adapted for the theater." [16]

Louise would have been even *more* interested in Blyth Daly had she known the secret behind that lip problem of Chaplin's that the newspapers had made so much fuss about.

"The incident of Charlie's bit lip was made a scandal by himself," Louise later recalled. Walter Wanger, who was present at the scene of the crime, told her that Chaplin had made one too many advances among the bevy of beauties supplied for him that night; one of them bit more than the bait and Chaplin "made a hysterical scene, screaming 'blood poison' and requiring the services of several doctors. But Walter would not tell me the name of the girl who rejected Charlie's sex with such emphasis [and] Charlie has kept it a bitter secret." [17]

It was Blyth Daly.

Chaplin's passion for long walks produced some of the most delightful memories of Louise's life. During one nighttime promenade, they found themselves on the Lower East Side, where they ducked into a little restaurant to shake off a mob of fans.

"Four hours passed before we came out," wrote Louise, "because inside Chaplin had found a wild Hungarian torturing a violin, and Chaplin's absorption in his performance kept us there till closing time. 27 years later I saw the Hungarian violinist come to life again in the person of Chaplin in his variety hall act with Buster Keaton at the piano in *Limelight*." [18]

Chaplin, Brooks, and Fears found themselves in need of a fourth playmate to replace d'Arrast. The role was filled happily by A. C. Blumenthal, "the tiny film financier," as Louise called him. Blumie's attributes, in addition to a certain charm and sophistication, revolved largely around his money. He had a huge penthouse at the Ambassador, and so "most of our time together was spent in Blumie's big, airy apartment."

"Blumie played the piano," said Louise, "Peggy sang, I danced, and Charlie returned to reality—the world of his creative imagination." For Chaplin loved to perform, always performed, and the three lucky New Yorkers were treated to the most lyrical private exhibitions:

> He recalled his youth with comic pantomimes. He acted out countless scenes for countless films. And he did imitations of everybody. Isadora Duncan danced in a storm of toilet paper. John Barrymore picked his nose and brooded over Hamlet's soliloquy. A *Follies* girl swished across the room; and I began to cry while Charlie denied absolutely that he was imitating me. Nevertheless, as he patted my hand, I determined to abandon that silly walk forthwith. [19]

Years later, Louise was discreet in writing of her time with Chaplin for *Film Culture* magazine. But privately, she told a few close friends about one entire weekend the foursome spent in Blumie's suite, ordering up all their meals and rarely even bothering to get dressed. In another day and age—and possibly in that one—it would have been considered an orgy. Afraid of contracting certain diseases, Chaplin had studied the matter and was firmly convinced that iodine was a reliable VD preventive. Normally he employed only a small local application, but one night at the Ambassador he was inspired to paint the sum of his private parts with iodine and come running with a great bright-red erection toward the squealing Peggy and Louise. It had the makings for a topflight sight gag in a Chaplin comedy, were it not for censors and the lack of color stock.

After his death in 1977, Louise spoke more candidly about her relationship with Chaplin. "I had an affair with him for two happy summer months," she told Kenneth Tynan. "He was . . . a sophisticated lover." Chaplin's sexuality and creativity were dynamically intertwined, she thought. By day, he was in constant motion. At night, he required no booze or drugs to facilitate lovemaking or to induce the deep sleep of a child. "His passion for young girls, his Lolita obsession," Louise said, left him "deeply convinced that he could seduce a girl only with his position as director and starmaker." The complexities of the man bordered on the perverse: "He adored his mother's madness," Louise claimed, "and credits her with giving him his comic viewpoint." But in Louise's eyes, nothing could diminish him.[20]

She also paid eloquent tribute to Chaplin's ethical character, even during the Lita Grey divorce. "The truth is that he existed on a plane above pride, jealousy or hate," she said. "I never heard him say a snide thing about anyone. *He lived totally without fear.*"

> He knew [she continued] that Lita Grey and her family were living in his house in Beverly Hills, planning to ruin him, yet he was radiantly carefree—happy with the success of *The Gold Rush* and with the admirers who swarmed around him. Not that he *exacted* adoration. Even during our affair, he knew that I didn't adore him in the romantic sense, and he didn't mind at all.
>
> Which brings me to one of the dirtiest lies he allowed to be told about him—that he was mean with money. People forget that Chaplin was the only star ever to keep his ex-leading lady [Edna Purviance] on his payroll for life, and the only producer to pay his employees their full salaries even when he wasn't in production.[21]

Purviance, a gentle, undemanding lover and performer, played opposite Chaplin in most of his important pictures between 1915 and 1922. She'd been a big part of his life and his career, but even before *A Woman of Paris* (1923), she had begun to drink heavily and show her age—which was then twenty-seven. That was old by youth-worshipping Hollywood standards, and Edna's face and weight fluctuations were making her appear too "matronly" for comedy roles. Yet it was more poignant than awkward when she showed up in New York for *The Gold Rush* premiere —Chaplin's first film without her. Louise met Purviance during that week of August 17–23 and admired the nobility of a still-young woman whose career was already well into its downward plunge.

But Louise could also speak of Chaplin's generosity from firsthand knowledge. She was neither surprised, insulted, nor disappointed by his handling of the end of their relationship. For two months he was her prize and her guide through a fairy tale. Sometimes in the middle of the night, she would wake up next to him and experience bliss just watching the man sleep! Now, inevitably, Chaplin had to leave. It was time to return to Hollywood to begin work on *The Circus*. They parted with great fondness and no false pledges.

"When our joyful summer ended," she said, "he didn't give me a fur from Jaeckel or a bangle from Cartier so that I could flash them around, saying, 'Look what I got from Chaplin.' The day after he left town, I got a nice check in the mail signed 'Charlie.' And then I didn't even write him a thank-you note. Damn me." [22]

Failing or forgetting to acknowledge the check (reportedly for $2,500) suggests that this was not a very calculating woman in terms of cashing in on rich lovers. Instead, years later, she acknowledged a greater debt: "I learned to act by watching Martha Graham dance, and I learned to dance by watching Charlie Chaplin act."

Brooks and Chaplin never saw each other again.

Louise might have lamented, or reflected upon, Chaplin's departure more had she not immediately been thrown into work on *The American Venus*, the first film in which she had a significant role.

Though essentially just a rich slice of cheesecake, *The American Venus* was the perfect vehicle in which to showcase a budding sensation like Louise. From early in the preproduction planning, its every step was accompanied by enormous publicity linking the film to both the Miss America pageant and the *Follies*. Glorifying the American girl was an understatement of its intentions. The pageant was at this point only four years old, and despite the embryonic "liberation" of women, men and women alike were enthralled by it. "Pitted directly against one another for that vital golden band," said Marjorie Rosen, "women submitted meekly to a new institution, the beauty contest." [23]

Adding to the attention was the fact that several sequences in *The*

American Venus were being filmed in a new two-strip Technicolor process then being tried-and-erred on the public.

Louise, at various times and places, attributed her *Venus* role to three different male associates. "Townsend Martin said he got me my job," she wrote in her diary. Elsewhere, she credited director Frank Tuttle, one of her many *Follies* admirers, with lobbying for her. And much later, she recorded a wry scene in which her masseuse inquires about a new beaver coat flung in a chair in Louise's apartment at the Marguery:

> "Oh, that," I said. "Walter Wanger gave it to me." A good Catholic, she knew that Walter was a married man. At that time I was portraying a bathing beauty in *The American Venus*, a film that was being shot at Famous Players–Lasky's Long Island studio in Astoria, and Wanger was an executive in the Famous Players–Lasky New York office.[24]

Evidently all three were instrumental in her selection, and with each other's knowledge. All three were connoisseurs of her stage talent, her conversation, and her wild company—whereas, there was precious little to talk about with Fay Lanphier, the reigning Miss America of 1925 and nominal star of the film.

Townsend Martin's original story, concocted to take advantage of the Miss America location shooting in Atlantic City, was a thin soup about two rival cosmetics manufacturers. The son of one is engaged to marry the daughter of the other, but they have a tiff. The daughter (Esther Ralston) enters the "American Venus" beauty contest to help smash the family rival (Ford Sterling), but then she's forced by her father's illness to go home and miss the big night in Atlantic City. After some soft "suspense," the contest is won by her friend, Miss Alabama.

Louise played the vampish Miss Bayport, an early favorite destined to lose out to one of the blonds. And so she did, in the plot. But she also stole the show from Ralston and Lanphier.

Filming began at the Astoria studios, where the good-natured Frank Tuttle took to kidding Louise from the beginning. "Look for Brooksie in a set with a bed in it," he told his gofers when they complained about never being able to find her. Once, she said, after waiting interminably for a setup, "I crawled up on a high parallel and fell asleep, most peacefully, to the amazement of the electrician and the carpenter working there."[25] With all the late-night *Follies* performances and partying, it was not sex but sleep that she was sneaking off to find. This daylight moonlighting was tougher than she thought it would be. Her Paramount champions expected her to be as delightful to work with as they'd found her to play with. "Coming from the theater where actors were not obliged to love or to pretend to love other actors," she wrote later, ". . . I faced my introduction to a movie set with an awful question. Was the Cocktail Party Spirit to prevail all day, every day for a month, maybe even for six weeks?"[26]

The basic answer was yes:

> Almost at once Frank Tuttle dubbed me "Babbling Brooks" and I knew I was doomed. I had no funny stories, no charming conversation, nothing to make me babble. Double-doomed! because coupled with the Cocktail Party Spirit was the Dog Act Spirit, a rapt devotion to the master which most directors considered essential to their position of command.[27]

Louise's first scenes were with Ford Sterling, who had been a Keystone Comedy star until 1914, when, according to Louise, his salary demands led Mack Sennett to replace him with Charlie Chaplin. Earlier in 1925, after a decade of oblivion, Sterling was given a part in Malcolm St. Clair's *The Trouble With Wives* and was well received. With *The American Venus*, Paramount was trying to build him up for more feature comedy roles:

> To help feed Ford's undernourished *amour-propre*, between scenes I was expected to flirt with him and laugh very hard at his jokes. In this capacity I was such a failure that he sulked and complained loudly about my timing in the chase through the hotel suite. *My* timing in yanking open and banging shut doors, he said, ruined *his* timing. To appease him, time and money were wasted making extra shots of each scene. Frank stopped calling me Babbling Brooks and I started disappearing between scenes.[28]

But sometimes they couldn't even find her in the bedroom sets. Often she would sneak over to see her friend W. C. Fields, who was also filming at Astoria, in *Sally of the Sawdust:*

> I would go to his set to watch him work. He paid no attention to camera setups. For each shot, he would rehearse the same business to exasperating perfection while his co-star, Carol Dempster, and the director D. W. Griffith sat bored and limp in chairs beside the camera. Long shot, medium shot, two-shot or closeup, Bill performed as if he were standing whole before an audience that could appreciate every detail of his costume and follow the dainty disposition of his hands and feet. Every time the camera drew closer, it cut off another piece of him and deprived him of some comic effect. . . . Fields never really left the theater. As he ignored camera setups, he ignored the cutting room, and he could only curse the finished film, seeing his timing ruined by haphazard cuts.[29]

They didn't have to search the sprawling Astoria studio for Louise much longer. Shooting there was completed in a few weeks, and the cast and crew of *The American Venus* were transported to Atlantic City for the pageant sequences on the Boardwalk.

There was a miniature scandal, or an attempt to create one, concerning the 1925 Miss America contest. According to the New York *Graphic*, Fay Lanphier's selection was prearranged. The allegation was never proven, but Paramount by its own admission was deeply involved with the promoters in every phase of the pageant. In exchange for exclusive film rights, the studio agreed to pay half the cost of erecting the main reviewing stand and to award an additional prize—the "American Venus" trophy—to the contestant who, in the opinion of three Paramount judges, had the best photographic possibilities. The two juries inspected the parade rushes filmed by no fewer than eleven cameras, and after some arm-twisting of two holdout judges, Fay Lanphier—Miss California—was the selection of both groups. She had never been professionally photographed or even visited a movie set. But Walter Wanger, then Famous Players–Lasky's production manager, offered her a part in *The American Venus* anyway, and she accepted.

When the bewildered Lanphier reported for shooting, she hadn't any idea what to do about her make-up, coiffure, or costumes, let alone her performance. Esther Ralston was the star, as far as plot and billing were concerned, and she essentially just brushed Lanphier aside. Louise, however, was less easily upstaged.

"I never knew Louise off the set," says Ralston today. "I was so busy with my own scenes. . . . It's too bad no copies of the film have survived. I remember I had to ride down the Boardwalk in a push-mobile, and I had this long blonde wig on that I wore in *A Kiss for Cinderella* [a year earlier]. In the dressing room, I heard some girl say, 'I'd like to put glue in *her* hairbrush!' "[30]

It just might have been Brooksie, who likewise spent her days being rickshawed and paraded.

"The motion picture unit," said a studio publicist on the scene, "was acquiring gooseflesh promptly bestowed by the autumn breezes that swept in on them from the ocean. Louise Brooks, the Ziegfeld *Follies* dancer who plays 'Miss Bayport' in the film, dressed in the regulation bathing beauty outfit, rode in chilly state on an elaborate float up and down the Boardwalk while the cameras registered her pleasure. . . ."[31]

Louise's outfits were a little more—or less—than regulation. For the swimsuit competition she was required, like everyone else, to wear the baggy, U-neck bathing suit of the day. But the most dazzling photo of her from *The American Venus* shows her in full Ziegfeld regalia, with feather-pompom headdress and a calf-length gown that was both backless and essentially topless, save for braided straps that failed to cover her breasts.

In that sensational photograph—published in scores of newspapers throughout the country—she stands defiantly unsmiling, hands on hips, a vamp with no hint of coquettishness. The public never knew that the photo was cropped to remove the half dozen other "Paramount Junior Stars" (including Thelma Todd), who were all staring up at her with thinly disguised resentment. Another junior with a small part and a promising future was eighteen-year-old Douglas Fairbanks, *fils*, who played "Neptune's Son" in a role and a manner that were never mentioned in any reviews.

"The pageant scenes are in color, some well done and some rather garish," said *Variety* on January 27, 1926. "The actual Atlantic City stuff wasn't much of a thrill. The producers tried to stress the undress angle by showing a series of supposedly thrilling 'tableaux vivants.' There was naked stuff in these and it may get censors sore in the more puritanical regions. . . .

"The picture itself is an in-betweener, with a few laughs and no real dry spots, but on the other hand no really hilarious moments. Just lots of female flesh. . . . It may give some of the old boys a kick, and then again it may not."

The Technicolor sequences indeed paid off at the box office, thanks to the massive publicity and despite the mixed reviews. What the feature writers had to say was more important than the critics' verdicts, and they were saying a lot of complimentary things about Brooks. "Louise has one of the three leading feminine roles," said the caption beneath a huge newspaper picture of her in one of those puritanical regions, "and has a better part than even Fay Lanphier. She makes a peppy entry even though she doesn't cop the title 'Miss America.' "[32]

Louise passed Film Acting 101, with the help of Professor Wanger. Early on, she had gone to him with a plea for help: "I said, 'I'm a dancer. How am I supposed to be a movie actress?' And he answered me, 'Anybody can act.' It's true, on the condition that you remain yourself, that you act in accordance with who you are."[33]

Though *The American Venus* attracted attention to her personality, it was primarily intended to showcase her physical attributes. The "naked stuff" advertised both products well.

Too well, as far as Louise was concerned.

Simultaneously with the end of shooting for *The American Venus*, New Yorkers were delighting in a delicious little scandal involving the unclothed body of Louise Brooks, just turned nineteen.

"Follies Girl, Now in Films, Shocked by Own Pictures" headlined the New York *Daily Mirror* on November 30, 1925:

> Louise Brooks, late of the *Follies*, has startled Broadway with an injunction suit to restrain John De Mirjian, theatrical photographer, from further distribution of nude portraits which he has made of her.

The tiny bit of symmetrical perfection who so enthralled Charles Chaplin on his last visit that they were seen together everywhere, is now a budding moving picture actress, which explains many things, among them her desire to turn back the leaves of the volume of her life that include some scores of pictures in the "all together."

Such publicity "encouragers" are all right for *Follies* girls, she believes, but not for future stars of the screen.

In her apartment in the fashionable and expensive Marguery, 270 Park Ave., Louise yesterday gave in no uncertain words her opinion of the growing fad of "undressed photography" to which she subscribed as a necessity in the climb up the theatrical ladder of fame.

The arguments behind Louise's injunctive suit mostly concerned her career, but included a surprise objection—the impact of the nude pix on her hypothetical husband-to-be:

"I intend to be married eventually," Miss Brooks explained, "and what do you suppose my husband would say if every time he picks up a newspaper or walks up Broadway he is confronted with a photograph of his wife clad in only a lacy shawl?

"When I was in the last *Follies* I understood that part of my job was to have these more or less draped things scattered all over. I was never crazy about the idea, but was told that it was necessary to get to the front. So I consented. I went to several photographers many times.

"Now that I have signed a reasonably long-term contract with Famous Players I consider that the necessity is past, so I wish the widespread distribution of those photographs discontinued. The screen public is a curious animal. It likes you to have a pretty form and to show it to advantage during the unraveling of a screen plot, but to see nude stills of a favorite does not suit everyone's fancy."[34]

In her candid fashion, Louise provided the *Mirror* with details of the photo sessions themselves and of the debonair De Mirjian, who was one of New York's most popular portrait photographers—in and out of "society"—during the midtwenties:

"I bear no animosity toward Mr. De Mirjian. He is nice and is a real artist. When I went to his studio on 48th and Broadway he made the photographs himself, instructing me to forget that there was a man in the room and to lose myself in an artistic thought. I did. I pictured myself in the Louvre trying to imitate various works of the old masters.

Mr. De Mirjian was very kind, and as the poses necessitated the gradual removal of the kimono I had brought with me, he very delicately replaced it with other drapes, which he hung about my body.

*Close-up from the controversial John De Mirjian series
of "draped nude" photographs of Louise, 1925*

I was in the studio for about two hours and a half, and when I was dismissed, hurried into my clothes and felt none the worse for my experience." [35]

Since New York was still buzzing about her recent relations with Chaplin, both Louise and the *Mirror* felt the need to address some of the nastier gossip on that subject as well.

"Miss Brooks wants it clearly understood," the article continued, "that her rise has been solely through her own efforts. She resents the report circulated at the time Chaplin was here to the effect that they promised to become more than just good friends. She admits that they saw a great deal of each other, but that she was only acting in the capacity as his guide about the supper clubs."

Her only reason for consenting to the "undraped" pictures, she repeated, was that "I understood it to be a necessity in surmounting the first rung in the ladder to success. Now I am on another rung."

News of the De Mirjian photo scandal was by no means limited to

Manhattan. Thanks to Louise's increasing celebrity in *The American Venus*, the story was picked up by newspapers all over the country. Back in Kansas, her hometown paper ran a censored cutout silhouette of one of the nude shots with the headline, "To Keep a Husband She Hasn't Got, Wichita Girl Sues to Suppress 'Artistic' Photographs." She told the reporter the photos were taken "two years ago [during the *Scandals*], when I was young and silly." The Philadelphia *Inquirer*, on March 21, 1926, devoted an entire page of its Sunday magazine to the subject:

> [The injunction is] certainly a very unusual stand for an actress and former chorus girl to take. . . . But Louise Brooks made it plain that she was in this respect a most exceptional young woman of the stage.
>
> Why should a former chorus girl who has repeatedly capered about the stage in very scanty costumes object to the circulation of pictures of herself posed in the way Mr. De Mirjian and many others think so alluring? And why on earth, if she feels such compunctions against these photographs now, did she ever pose for them in the beginning? . . . Let Miss Brooks explain in her own words:
>
> "I have embarked on a serious career as a motion picture actress, [and] in my new profession I am called upon to play many innocent young heroines, girls who are models of modesty and respect for all the time-honored conventions. In fact, my directors tell me that these are the roles for which I am preeminently suited.
>
> "It would be too great a shock, I fear, for moviegoers who had admired me in one of these roles to come across a photograph of me as I looked when I posed before Mr. De Mirjian wearing little more than a carelessly flung scarf and a pair of sandals. The contrast would be pretty certain to destroy or weaken some of the illusions of innocence and unsophistication my acting has created on the screen."[36]

No one could quite recall any "models of modesty" or of "innocence" she had created, on either stage or screen. The modesty argument was followed by an extended apologia that had more the ring of her attorney's than of Louise's prose:

> "I am not playing the hypocrite as many people seem to think. I am not the least bit ashamed of my chorus girl days. . . . But there would, of course, be shocking immodesty in wearing such costumes out on the street or into the drawing room. . . . Since I have changed my profession I must change my standards of modesty."[37]

"Foolish!" declared De Mirjian, who was outgunned. He made his defense on the general grounds that nude photography had long since achieved artistic and commercial respectability. He complained that he

Seven members of the unofficial "Dinette Set," filmdom's rough, mobile equivalent of the Algonquin Round Table. CLOCKWISE FROM TOP LEFT: *Aileen Pringle, James R. Quirk, Anita Loos, H. L. Mencken, Eddie Sutherland, Mickey Neilan and Blanche Sweet*

never forced Brooks or anyone else to disrobe before his camera and that his artistry had helped build the careers of many such ingrates.

"Have I not photographed a thousand others wearing maybe a shoe, maybe a hat, maybe a shawl?" he asked. "Do not the married women of New York's best society come for pictures of the same kind? They tell me, of course, that the pictures are for private distribution, and that I must not reveal them. . . . But is not the principle the same, from the viewpoint of the matrimonial question? And is it not a vindication of art?"[38]

Apparently not. De Mirjian hinted, in a fit of pique, that he might reveal the names of some of his other famous theatrical and high-society clients. But he never did. The pictures of Louise look tame in 1989, but they were hot items in 1925. The photographer withdrew them to avoid further trouble.

The elegant Louise with reading matter to match—the latest issue of Theatre Magazine, *1927; photo by E. R. Richee*

6 · The Myth of the
Quintessential Flapper

My candle burns at both ends;
  It will not last the night;
But ah, my foes, and oh, my friends—
  It gives a lovely light!
—EDNA ST. VINCENT MILLAY

T H E film industry was ruled by middle-aged Jewish producers, but dominated and transfixed by WASPish, late-adolescent girls. These vibrant, sexy little monsters were of the Frankenstein executives' own creation, and sometimes they got out of control—as was only to be expected in such a volatile business. But the studios were adept at managing the domination-submission syndrome that evolved. It was unlike the theater world, which was inhabited mostly by "professionals," who only occasionally had to be coddled or subdued. The opera world afforded a closer parallel with its problematic prima donnas, but at least they were adult professionals, whereas the prima donnas of the pictures were often not old enough to vote.

The rise of Louise Brooks was thus perfectly in keeping with the central phenomenon of the Flapper Era: youth worship. The youth cult could only have originated in America and could only have been propagated through the aggressive instrument of the movies. The genesis of this obsession with youth was the limited liberation of women after World War I. But in the movies, it started out as strictly utilitarian.

Hollywood's practical reason for using teenagers in grown-up romantic film roles predated the twenties; it had to do with lighting. Klieg lights and Cooper-Hewitt lights (mercury-tube forerunners of fluorescent lights) were merciless uncoverers of every facial pore and imperfection. Only the youngest, purest skin could withstand the close-up scrutiny of their glare.

"A 15-year-old beginner in those first few years of motion pictures was likely to become a star by eighteen or nineteen," said silent star Colleen Moore. "She was also likely to become a has-been by 22 unless she took extremely good care of her complexion or . . . the cameraman obliged by keeping a discreet distance away."[1]

When Moore arrived in Hollywood in 1917, the vast majority of teen-aged female stars faced premature oblivion. They were rescued by an exciting innovation at the D. W. Griffith Studio during the filming of *Broken Blossoms* in 1919. "Word leaked out from the laboratory," she recalled, "that in the rushes Lillian Gish, then an aging 22, looked as fresh and young as a child of twelve. Wanting to believe it, hardly daring to, actresses clamored for information. Was it some new kind of film? A new camera? Different lighting? Nobody could find out. The set was closed to visitors. Billy Bitzer, Griffith's cameraman, was mum."

The rumor was true: Gish was a girl again, thanks to Bitzer. He had covered his camera lens with black maline, a fine silk netting whose tiny holes acted as a retouching device.

Bitzer's visual fountain of youth evolved into the diffusion lens and served to augment the youth fixation that was already entrenched in the industry and in the mind of the public. The cult was everywhere proclaimed. *Photoplay*, for example, made no effort to contain its enthusiasm.

"Youth!" exclaimed reporter Ruth Waterbury. "It's the new battle cry of filmdom. Youth!"

She waxed rhapsodic on the subject: "The motion picture industry deals essentially in commodities and its greatest commodity today is youth. Youth is the common dream of all mankind. Childhood looks forward to it, age looks back at it, but the great and beautiful appeal of it never dies. . . . Paramount has been doing most of the shouting about it—but then Paramount always does shout vigorously. Paramount screams over Clara Bow, rushes forward Gary Cooper, advertises five junior stars, its Paramount school graduates, its fledgling favorites."

The junior stars included "Louise Brooks, Lasky's leading subdeb," whose full-length picture shared the page with Buddy Rogers, Charles Farrell, Janet Gaynor, and Richard Arlen.

The only dissident was Cecil B. DeMille, who still believed that "a young player needs approximately seven years' training before he is ready for stardom . . . A player made overnight dies overnight."

To which the twenty-eight-year-old Irving Thalberg cited the twenty-two-year-old Greta Garbo in rebuttal: "The motion picture public itself is young. Its age range is between 18 and 24. A player who waits seven years to reach them will be too old." Metro, he said, would put such newcomers as Dorothy Sebastian and Joan Crawford on screen without delay and give them "education, leads and publicity simultaneously."

Actually, Sebastian at twenty-four and Crawford at twenty-three were almost middle-aged by Hollywood standards. Many of the new featured players were much younger, including Louise Brooks, age twenty. In any event, the *Photoplay* piece ended with revolutionary fervor: "The fans are young and the new stars are young. Youth calls to youth and the hand that cranks the camera rules the world."[2]

But youth also called to all the parental anxieties. From pulpits and periodicals all over the land, elders decried the laxity of the new manners and morals. Boys had been smoking, drinking, and joyriding for years, but now girls were doing the same—dancing to "that jazz" into the wee hours and ending up at petting parties—and it was time to "do something" about it. But no one knew quite what, since those outrages were inevitable by-products of the two great forces of the day: Prohibition and the automobile. The Eighteenth Amendment, which was subverted from the moment it went into effect in 1920, begat the bootlegger, the speakeasy, and the organized gangster. The car had been around for two decades—but not the *enclosed* car. In 1919, only about 10 percent of American cars were closed; by 1924 the figure was 43 percent, and by 1927, 82 percent.[3] What transpired between boys and girls in closed automobiles was frightening to imagine. The automobile, that symbol of prosperity and technology, was becoming what many Main Street residents considered a bordello on wheels.

The other dubious influence on young people's morals was, in the 1926 opinion of many, the movies—especially flapper movies. The term "flapper" came into use derogatorily as early as 1921, but was soon adopted by champions and detractors alike. It stemmed from the peculiar habit of "smart" girls who left their galoshes unbuckled, flapping as they walked. Thus did the free-spirited flapper girl signify her disregard for convention and her willingness to kick up her boots in the pursuit of pleasure.

Though most moral guardians were upset, a minority of more tolerant observers—influenced by the Freudian vogue—defended flappers and their movies and said it was time to be less hypocritical. "The motion pictures, in showing love scenes and depicting sex episodes, are hastening the day when sex will be neither a secret nor a sin," declared Benjamin Lindsey, a prominent jurist. "Clara Bow may be good or bad. She may be increasing the idea of flirting or easy infatuation . . . for the moment. But if it is to bring the idea of Love and Sex from under cover, if it is opening the subject to all women, it may *look* wrong now, but it is to prove an eventual advantage."[4]

The decade also belonged, after all, to D. H. Lawrence and James

Joyce. And it belonged even more to the music that gave it the name "Jazz Age." You had to *go* to the movies, but *jazz* came to you—on the Victrola, over the radio, out in the streets, and in the speakeasies—and it was there to be danced to.* Its syncopation was the continuo of the twenties, the first purely American musical form—as uncivilized and alluring as the black ghettos from which it came. Only Gershwin tamed it for the concert hall; otherwise, jazz stayed out of harness, ready to accompany booze and blues, dancing and romancing.

Jazz came in with Prohibition and flappers and has outlasted both by a long shot. The flapper reigned for only half a decade, roughly between 1923 and 1928, but she radically changed the styles and standards of beauty.

Above all else was "The Look," and nobody was more attentive to her "look" than Louise Brooks. Photographer De Mirjian wasn't the only one interested in the face and body that it comprised. As her reviews to date affirmed, no young actress looked more strikingly "modern." Louise seemed the very essence of a phenomenon she and her mother had read about in the Independence *Daily Reporter* in Kansas way back in 1919. In an article called "Movies Make Beauty," the writer made the prescient observation that "it is the movies that are molding ever fresh types of native beauty—new American types."[5]

Now, in 1926, it was indeed the powerful *American* essence of Louise's look that gave it its public impact. A case could be made that prior to this girl, and this era, the all-American beauties—epitomized by Ziegfeld's glorified girls—were just variations on European women and European notions of beauty: from Vera Maxwell (the original "Blonde Venus") through Justine Johnson, Mae Murray, Billie Dove, Marion Davies, and Marilyn Miller. Louise Brooks was, first and foremost, an original.

Or was she?

Louise was unique. With a little help from her mother years before, she had created her own appearance. But a number of people took credit for turning it into The Look, including her film mentor and one-time lover, Walter Wanger.

"Why, I took Louise Brooks, a little girl out of the Ziegfeld chorus, who had bobbed hair," he boasted years later. "The whole world copied that."

Brooks was "the girl in the black helmet," all right, and that severe bob was her trademark, but it wasn't patented. It had deep roots in the times, so to speak. The haircut was examined and extolled endlessly in every film and fashion magazine from *Photoplay* to *Vanity Fair*, not to mention the "women's pages" and Sunday supplements of all the newspapers. It was

---

* The word "jazz" itself first appeared in print in 1917, but its origin remains unclear; one source traces it to black Creole patois "jass," meaning "to copulate."

the Haircut of a Hundred Names: the Dutch bob, the pageboy, the Buster Brown, the Prince Valiant, the black helmet, the Cleopatra, the Joan of Arc. . . . no hairstyle before or since captured women's imaginations so fast and ubiquitously. It began around 1920, when women finally got the vote. Cutting off the hair, often in defiance of men's wishes, asserted control over a part of the body hitherto cultivated and fussed with mostly to please the opposite sex. The bob in general—Louise's in particular— was eminently suited to the age. It suggested boyish vigor in tune with the new flat-chested dress lines: The modern girl could fend for herself and either attract a man or get along without one. Her bob was a declaration of independence from the lingering Victorian mores of which long tresses were a vestige.

By the midtwenties, the "Jeanne d'Arc" bob that they saw in American movies and magazines finally motivated the style-setting French to move on the aesthetic-commercial issue of what the haircut *should* look like. The Parisian coiffeur Antoine was received like a conquering hero when he arrived in New York to establish a bobbing salon at Saks Fifth Avenue in early 1927. Most American bobs, Antoine opined, had *"pas de raffine-ment."* He hated Colleen Moore's because its thick, straight cut "gives the face a common expression" that was, frankly, "more than a little vulgar." Clara Bow's bob he thought "piquant, interesting, but slightly heavy." The correct bob must be cut short in back, and the neckline—"which, in unexpert hands, usually makes a woman's neck look like a second base-man's"—must be shaped into a delicate fringe.

The "Louise Brooks bob," as Paramount's publicity department defined it, was "a combination of the Pola Negri, Florence Vidor and Col-leen Moore bobs, retaining the distinctive features of each: . . . Colleen Moore's Dutch cut in front, and the Negri side effect and the Vidor rear ensemble."[6]

Antoine pronounced "the Louise" acceptable and flattering to her face —as if Louise cared what the arbiters of fashion ordained. Socially and professionally, the bob had a crucial advantage that was not lost on Louise and thousands of her sisters: Compared to all other coiffures, it saved an enormous amount of time in preparation and maintenance. Not easily mussed, it was perfectly suited to a fast-and-easy life-style.

The flapper's preferred hairdo dictated other things, such as hats. By far the most popular accessory to the bob was the cloche hat, created in 1923. The smaller the smarter. The close-fitting cloche (from the French word "bell") positively required short hair. It was tightly modeled to the shape of the head and lent itself to a wide variety of angled brims and trimmings and jewelry—a lovely, eccentric creation that flattered most women. On Louise Brooks, it was dazzling, for it functioned as an exten-sion of her clochelike hair itself.

Louise's striking facial look was made even more fashionable by a co-incidental archeological event of the day: the 1923 discovery of Tut-ankhamen's tomb. Tut's fabulous treasures of art and jewelry inspired the "Cleopatra" look, and straight dark hair with square-cut bangs was its hallmark. But for that matter, the whole world of women's fashions was changing. As hair got shorter and more boyish (culminating in the se-verely masculine "Eton crop" devised in 1926), so did women's clothes, which reached mannish extremes of suits and ties that same year. Most women stopped short of that, relying instead on the straight chemise, that staple of twenties fashion, which tended to erase the female form's two most traditionally important attributes: bust and waist.

By 1926, many of these once simple chemises were being tailor-made, and the prices went up as fast as the waistlines went down (eventually to below the hips, which meant no waistline at all). Elongated models glam-orized the vertical, cylindrical look in reaction to the Rubensian "full" feminine ideal of before. It wasn't a good time, or a good fashion, for the pudgies. This volte-face came about quickly: In the half decade between 1918 and 1923, American and European women shed more than three quarters of their prewar clothing. Fashion mathematicians calculated that women's underclothes were reduced to only 10 percent of those worn by their mothers. There were still such strange and mystifying constructions as the corselette and corslo-silhouette and corslo-pantalon-chemise—all designed to convert the female figure into a cylinder. But by and large, lingerie now had more erotic than practical significance.

Beautiful young performers such as Brooksie epitomized the new ideal and millions of women wished to emulate it. By 1926 Louise was one of the film world's most exciting bobbed darlings.

She was by no means its biggest star, however. The most important flapper actress, and the greatest challenger to Louise in terms of who "invented" The Look, was Colleen Moore, then at the peak of her popularity. Thirty years later, in the first major article to resurrect Louise from oblivion, James Card noted that "when [Brooks] is remembered at all, it is usually only to confuse her with Colleen Moore."[7]

Moore was the reigning queen of First National Studios and one of the greatest stars in Hollywood history. In the fall of 1926 the *Exhibitor's Herald* poll of 2,500 theater owners voted her the number one box-office attraction in America—bigger even than Chaplin, Pickford, or Swanson. The same honor would be hers in 1927, when her fan mail reached 10,000 pieces a week.

Colleen Moore wore her hair like Louise Brooks.

Or did Louise Brooks wear hers like Colleen Moore?

"She did copy my haircut," said Colleen Moore in an interview shortly

The bobbed Colleen Moore, reigning box-office star of 1926 and 1927

before her death, adding with a sly little laugh that "I was very flattered." At the time, she paid little attention to Louise and never saw one of her films, during or after the 1920s. "My life was very busy," she recalled. "Oh, I may have said, 'There's another little girl copying my hair,' but then remember, *thousands* of kids cut their hair like mine!"

In 1923, First National had purchased Warner Fabian's best-seller, *Flaming Youth*, a tale of "the beguiling and resourceful tactics of a flapper."[8] The heroine is naïve little Patricia, too sheltered to enjoy all the permissive merriments around her until her mother contracts a fatal illness and goes "to face the great Dim Guess." Then Patricia capers from one affair to another, sampling the full range of flapper illusions and disillusions until the inevitable realization that promiscuity doesn't pay.

Before Moore tested for the part, her mother "picked up the scissors and, whack, off came the long curls. I felt as if I'd been emancipated. Then she trimmed my hair around with bangs like a Japanese girl's haircut —or, as most people call it, a Dutch bob."[9]

Flaming Youth earned an astonishing $1 million and made Moore a star. Audiences flocked to see director John Francis Dillon's lurid portrayal of flapper boys and girls in pursuit of a good time. Future generations won't know its full impact, for eight of nine reels are lost.* But the extant reel contains its most daring sequence: the silhouetted debauch—an adolescent fertility dance worthy of Margaret Mead—in which frantic young bodies run back and forth, throw off their clothes, and leap with abandon into a pool that might as well be the moral abyss.

"The flapper was really born in '23 with that picture," said Moore. "She was like all the young girls my brother used to date. That's where I got her, right off the college campus, from the girls he used to bring around." [10]

Paramount, eager to join the bandwagon, quickly set about developing its "junior stars" and cranked up for its own flapper epics—for which Louise Brooks would become a leading candidate. *Flaming Youth* had set the ball in motion. And since Colleen Moore was making movies before Louise Brooks even left Wichita, that would seem to settle the question of who had The Look first.

But Louise had first been "bobbed" as a little girl; photos of her at age five show her looking almost identical to the actress of the late 1920s. Far from "copying" Moore, Louise's bob was on public view at Denishawn well before *Flaming Youth*. In any case, The Look wasn't everything. A quintessential flapper had to have something else; she had to have "It."

This euphemistic "It" was the Jazz Age term for sex appeal, coined by British novelist Elinor Glyn. Every generation has its popular writers who occupy the pinnacle of vogue until consigned to ridicule or oblivion by the generation that follows. The feminization of popular literature reached a peak in 1925 when eight of the year's ten best-selling books were written by women.† Glyn was not the best of them, but she was the most high-profile—a kind of literary Dr. Ruth, thanks to the steamy sensuality of her books, many of which became films.‡

"Elinor Glyn's name is synonymous with the discovery of sex appeal in the cinema," Sam Goldwyn declared. She defined "It" as the animal magnetism that drew flapper girls and boys to one another and to do the things they did. In 1926, she informed Paramount that Clara Bow was the only actress who really had "It" on screen, whereupon the studio commissioned

---

* A single badly deteriorated reel survives in the Library of Congress vaults. *Flaming Youth* is but one of the countless tragic losses of silent films. A conservative estimate of the devastation is that 85 to 90 percent of all silents have been destroyed.

† Anne Douglas Sedgwick's *The Little French Girl*, Edna Ferber's *So Big*, Margaret Kennedy's *The Constant Nymph*, Edith Wharton's *A Mother's Recompense*, Willa Cather's *The Professor's House*, Mary Roberts Rinehart's *The Red Lamp*, Ellen Glasgow's *Barren Ground*, and Kathleen Norris's *Rose of the World*.

‡ Among the Elinor Glyn stories filmed were *The Great Moment* (1920) and *Beyond the Rocks* (1922), both with Gloria Swanson; *His Hour* (1924), with Aileen Pringle and John Gilbert; the hugely successful *Three Weeks* (1924), with Conrad Nagel and Pringle as the exotic Tiger Queen; and *Man and Maid* and *Love's Blindness* (both 1925).

her for $50,000 to dash off a novella with *It* as the title and Clara as the star.

Bow, in fact, had been popular for two years before she became "The 'It' Girl." Her kinetic unpredictability was first realized in *Black Oxen* and then *Daughters of Pleasure* (1924) and *The Primrose Path* (1925) back when Louise was still hoofing for Ziegfeld. More success awaited Bow in 1926 with *Dancing Mothers* and *Mantrap*. But the role of Betty Lou in *It* was her first to be custom-tailored. As romantic-comedy plots went, *It* didn't seem to have "It": Salesgirl Clara pursues rich, handsome boss Antonio Moreno with ultimate success, no thanks to the title writers who gave her lines like, "Sweet Santa Claus, give me *him!*" But Bow mesmerized everyone, including fellow flapper Louise, who summed her up succinctly: "My God, she was a terrific star!"[11] Later critics, in film-theory jargon, called her *It*'s *auteur*. She was a dynamo of mischievous impulses, as in a scene where she fondles a stuffed dog and suddenly wonders what sex it is.

"She looked at the dog," said Louise. "She turns it around and lifts up his tail and looks at his behind! That was her idea—everything she did was completely original."[12]

All of a sudden, Bow was Paramount's hottest property, commuting between the Hollywood and Astoria studios, where she and Louise crossed paths. The two women liked each other, though all they had in common was impulsiveness—and "It." They also shared a boss, Benjamin P. Schulberg, Paramount's West Coast production chief, who had Bow under his personal contract and whose success as a studio executive was largely tied to Bow's power as a box-office draw. He would, soon enough, become a villain in both the Bow and the Brooks pieces.

For the moment, though, Clara was riding high. When asked to define "It," she answered after a long pause: "I ain't sure." Yet she used "It" to full advantage; it was not her look that propelled her to the heights, but the wild spontaneity of what she did when she heard the cameras whirl.

The wildness was also evidenced in Bow's not-so-private life. Her affair with Gary Cooper was conducted in the openly outrageous flapper mode. "Clara was quite a minx in those days," says Louise's *American Venus* co-star Esther Ralston. "I had a goody-goody reputation, and if she could shock me by saying or doing something, her day was made." Once Clara asked her:

"Esther, do you like Gary?"

"Oh yes," Esther replied, "I think he's going places."

"Yes . . . ," said Clara, "and he always lets me take the dog in the bathtub with us in the morning."[13]

It had its intended effect on Esther Ralston—as Clara did, overall, on the entire country. Bow was a flapper, all right, if not exactly typical. Or was there a flapper "type"?

. . .

That was an important question to the popular press, so Margaret Reid of *Motion Picture Magazine* went straight to the horse's mouth. She wangled a rare formal interview with F. Scott Fitzgerald—the man who in 1920 had essentially "created" the flapper, modeled on his wife, Zelda, in *This Side of Paradise*. The nervous reporter had just arrived at Fitzgerald's tony bungalow at the Ambassador when Zelda burst in, fresh from a Black Bottom dance lesson, and plopped down behind her husband.

She looked "slim, pretty like a rather young boy," Reid wrote, "with one of those schoolgirl complexions and clear grey eyes; her hair as short as possible, slicked back."[14] Starstruck, Reid finally asked Fitzgerald whether he thought flappers had changed in the last six years.

"Only in the superficial matter of clothes, hair-cut and wisecracks," Fitzgerald answered. "The girls I wrote about were not a type—they were a generation. Free spirits—evolved through the war chaos and a final inevitable escape from restraint and inhibitions."

If the virgin and the vamp were the first two basic types of screen heroines (chastity and promiscuity being two sides of the same coin for women restricted to home and boudoir), the flapper was Phase Three: an exuberant "working girl" who had money of her own and affordable, mass-produced fashions to spend it on. Even so, her jobs and her films usually ended in marriage.[15]

Clara Bow and Louise Brooks, however, were saucier and more rebellious than most, even when required to be happily wedded in the end. If they seemed to epitomize the era's dichotomy—euphoria and disillusion—Bow was the more euphoric and ultimately more disillusioned of the two; she had more illusions to start with. Fitzgerald called her "the quintessence of what the term 'flapper' signifies as a definite description: pretty, impudent, superbly assured, as worldly wise, briefly clad and 'hard-berled' as possible." But off-camera, Bow was not so superbly assured as she appeared, and a nervous breakdown would soon belie the devil-may-care exterior.

Fitzgerald was even more taken with Colleen Moore, who represented "the young collegiate—the carefree, lovable child who rules bewildered but adoring parents with an iron hand. . . ." But Moore was a totally different creature off screen: disciplined, conventional, and highly attuned to Hollywood politics. "My career always came before my emotions—almost always, anyhow," said Moore. She was only a flapper on celluloid.

There were other important flappers, too, such as Constance Talmadge, the embodiment of sophistication. Fitzgerald called her "the flapper *de luxe*." Joan Crawford was "doubtless the best example of the dramatic flapper—the girl you see at the smartest night clubs . . . toying iced glasses, with a remote, faintly bitter expression—dancing deliciously —laughing a great deal with wide, hurt eyes." Gloria Swanson, Norma Shearer, and many others had flapper qualities, so that in the end, "It's rather futile to analyze flappers," Fitzgerald concluded. "They are just girls—all sorts of girls. Their one common trait being that they are young things with a splendid talent for life."

Fitzgerald was marvelously right about the "types," but he wasn't concerned with the *real* women behind the screen creations. The quintessential flapper was none of the dazzling creatures he catalogued for reporter Reid. The quintessential flapper was Louise Brooks. She had The Look

Unbobbed Clara Bow, "The 'It' Girl": "My God, she was a terrific star!"

and she had "It" before they became the rage. She had the caprice and the spontaneity.

And she had all these things off-camera as well as on.

A Social Celebrity (1926) was the first of Louise's twenty-four film roles to exploit her overtly as a flapper. Its star was Adolphe Menjou, one of the highest-paid film actors in America.* She'd been cast in a bit part as a

---

* Menjou, the "Frenchman" with *suavité* and *savoir-faire* to burn, was actually a native of Pittsburgh, Pennsylvania, who grew up in Cleveland, where his father operated a French restaurant.

smart-looking manicurist—to give a touch of "It" to some all-male barber-shop scenes. But after filming began in late December 1925, the female star, Greta Nissen, dropped out. Louise remained a manicurist—but her part was rewritten to be the lead. As conceived by Monte Katterjohn (who'd written *The Sheik* for Valentino as well as several Gloria Swanson vehicles), Louise's character was a copy of Clara Bow's manicurist in *Mantrap* the year before.

But that didn't stop Paramount's publicity department from going into a high-gear campaign on her behalf: "Who is Louise Brooks?" asked the press kit. "In New York, if one asks that question he is verbally guillotined for lack of knowledge. . . . If there are such things as meteoric rises in the film world, she has had one. Certainly, to be featured opposite Adolphe Menjou in her second picture is a big achievement."

A Social Celebrity was young director Malcolm St. Clair's third light-comic teaming with Menjou. St. Clair, formerly a newspaper sports cartoonist in Los Angeles, was twenty-nine years old and six feet three inches tall. His biggest credit had been directing Rin-Tin-Tin, the canine wonder, at Warner Brothers before Paramount hooked him up with Menjou for two sophisticated comedies, *Are Parents People?* in 1925 and then *The Grand Duchess and the Waiter* a few months later.

This time around, Menjou is Max the barber in the Delphi, Indiana, shop of his father, Chester Conklin. His specialty is the bob. Paramount was encouraging theater owners to arrange promotions with local barber-shops and to run newspaper ads declaring, "There's nothing greater or finer in this world than being A SOCIAL CELEBRITY."

In the story, Louise, as "Kitty Laverne," stays around Delphi just long enough to make Menjou fall in love with her and then takes off for New York to become a dancer. Soon after, Fate in the form of society matron Josephine Drake lifts Max from the village tonsorial parlor to the Great White Way, where he "scintillates" for a time as a false social celebrity before returning to obscurity, but he's rewarded with the love of that fickle little tart, Louise.

During filming, crowds gathered outside the Park Lane Hotel on Park Avenue (and in Huntington, Long Island, where the barbershop scenes were filmed) to get a glimpse of the popular Menjou and the flapper beauty Brooks, who each did some extracurricular work on behalf of the production. There was a Charleston scene, and Menjou and St. Clair volunteered for the chore of attending the major musicals in search of Broadway's best shimmy dancers. They went to six shows, staying only long enough to catch the obligatory mad jazz number before moving on to the next theater. Sixteen of the best hoofers in New York were thus recruited, most from *Captain Jinx*, a new version of Clyde Fitch's 1901

Louise with Adolphe Menjou in A Social Celebrity *(1926)*

success, *Captain Jinks of the Horse Marines*. And everyone agreed that Louise outpaced them all when she led them through their first rehearsals.

Despite or because of its froth, *A Social Celebrity* garnered favorable reviews, particularly for Conklin, the old Sennett comedian.

"There is a girl in this picture by the name of Louise Brooks," wrote the New York *World* critic. "Perhaps you've heard of her. If not, don't worry. You will. I may have seen in my day a handsomer lady, since they do grow amazingly that way in Kansas, but at the moment I can call forth no specific exhibit for evidence."[16]

Photoplay's minireview of July 1926 opined that "Mr. Menjou plays Mr. Menjou as fascinatingly as usual. Miss Brooks looks more than ever like stellar material."

Praise for Louise and the movie came from everyone but herself.

"I didn't like my acting or my makeup or my clothes," she said. "They almost drove me out of my mind." As for St. Clair, "he neither knew nor cared what life was like in a small town barber shop or in New York society."[17] And in a letter years later to Kevin Brownlow, she tattled on both director and star:

You are right in guessing that Mal St. Clair paid no attention to the camera. He looked into it the way you would okay a dictated letter. If you ever get a print of A *Social Celebrity* you will see that Lee Garmes' lighting is hideous because Menjou, having become a star and a tyrant, demanded, in order to wipe out his bags, that Lee invent a frame lined with big light bulbs for closeups. To match, Lee had to use them on me which showed my freckles under the greasepaint, and more unfortunately, Elsie Lawson's soft mustache. Another demand of Menjou's was our clown white make-up which he connected with youth.[18]

To film writer-historian John Kobal, she was even more brutal about her colleagues:

Mal came from the mugging school of Sennett and he did everything by making faces, and he would mug out a scene for me and then send me into the scene, and I would be so embarrassed. I tried my best to please him and yet not to make all these mugging faces that date so terribly, like Adolphe Menjou.

You know, the old type of film acting in those days was because of the titles, to establish the emotions, let's say, a flirting leer at the girl. So Menjou would begin the scene by making this hideous, grim expression #7 of a grinning leer, and then he knew they were going to cut to some title and then his face would drop to nothing at all and he would go into his next emotion, and that was the kind of acting that Mal tried to direct. And I felt Mal was a really terrible director, although I thought he was a charming man, a lovely man. In those days, anyone could become a director.[19]*

IF LOUISE was disturbed by the acting and directing in A *Social Celebrity*, she was even more disturbed by the reactions of Walter Wanger and Edmund Goulding, whose "pet ocelot" she had recently been. Even before *Celebrity* was released, their interest in her seemed to be waning and they spoke openly of their infatuation with Joan Crawford, who was fast becoming the hottest of the new flapper crop. One such scene made a deep enough impact on Louise for her to record it in detail, summoning

---

* Louise remained fascinated by St. Clair and A *Social Celebrity* even though she had little regard for either. Forty years later, in an effort to gain insight into the film and into St. Clair's formative years as a cartoonist, she spent weeks researching the history and philosophy of comic strips and came to these conclusions in a letter to Brownlow (March 27, 1966):

"Having looked everywhere else for the *Social Celebrity* theme, I find that too in the comics—1913, *Bringing Up Father*. About 1910 the immigrants who had been ditch diggers and servants began to get rich and form 'Society,' copied after the society dramas of the English. An aristocracy of wealth (perfect example—the Irish saloon keeper [Joseph] Kennedy). So Irish Maggie with the sudden wealth from political graft in New York can make the grade if she can keep Jiggs out of the saloon. . . . When I made A *Social Celebrity* and when I saw it [at Eastman House in Rochester] in 1957, it seemed utterly dull and pointless, yet Lotte [Eisner], seeing it in Paris in 1958, found it delightful. Now I see why. She had the historical view of our naïve new world which I lacked."

That sole surviving print of A *Social Celebrity* was later lost in a fire at the Cinémathèque Française.

Caricature of Louise by director Malcolm St. Clair, 1926

"the warm, luxurious smell of Walter Wanger's apartment in New York on a winter's day in 1925":

I see him dressing for dinner, worrying his tie, fixing his sapphire cufflinks from Cartier, as he moved back and forth from his bedroom to the sitting room, listening to the story Paul Bern was telling about Barbara La Marr. Once a big star, she was dying now, broke and alone. And again I feel the story's brooding effect upon us: Walter was a top executive at Paramount, Paul was a producer at M-G-M, I had just signed a five-year contract with Paramount—yet nobody in show business is ever beyond the sound of failure. Far or near, it tolls steadily of scandal, sickness, poverty and rejection. How delightful it was then to see the front door pop open and to watch Eddie Goulding come bounding across the room like an enthusiastic lion about to eat us up. . . .

He had just finished directing *Sally, Irene and Mary*. It was a big hit but he didn't talk about that, nor did he talk about Constance Bennett and Sally O'Neil who were also big hits in the picture. He talked exclusively about Joan Crawford. "She's the find of the year, Walter—the greatest find of the year! Beautiful, wonderful emotional quality—bound for stardom."

What a crust of jealousy those words imposed on my naturally sulky puss. Nobody ever talked that way about me. Walter, when he looked at the rushes in the projection room, actually laughed at my acting. . . . As I listened to Eddie rave on about Joan Crawford, it seemed to me that he had dropped my movie career awfully easy. . . . That Joan Crawford must really be something!

The first chance I got, I went to see *Sally, Irene and Mary*. She was beautiful, all right, in spite of her hair parted in the middle to give her a madonna look. And her legs were beautiful even though she used them to dance the Charleston like a lady wrestler. But she played her part like a chocolate-covered cherry—hard outside, and breaking up all gooey with a sticky center. I didn't care for her. . . . She isn't truly like a chocolate covered cherry; she is like biting into a delectable piece of wedding cake and hitting the brass ring.[20]

LONG AFTERWARD, Louise would debunk the whole thing. "The flapper," she declared in a letter to her brother Theodore, "did not exist at all except in Scott Fitzgerald's mind and the antics he planted in his mad wife Zelda's mind."[21]

Yet the press thought otherwise—and thought Brooks a supreme flapper, consecrated by her very dismissive insouciance.* Only a quintessential flapper would deny the flapper's existence. But there was something ominous for her future in the fact that she was so articulate and opinionated, for male studio executives tended to share Valentino's 1922 view: "I do not like women who know too much."

For the moment, though, Louise was keeping most of her intellectual light under a bushel. The light, instead, was on that face—that "look"—and on the fashions that adorned her body. They contrasted sharply, for example, with the wholesome Colleen Moore's.

"While I was vitally interested in the clothes Colleen Moore wore on the screen," said Moore, who often spoke of herself in the third person, "I never paid much attention to my own wardrobe, going around most of the time in skirts and sweaters and saddle shoes."[22]

Louise would never have said the same. Hers was an intense awareness of every garment she wore: "Dancing for two years with Ruth St. Denis and Ted Shawn had taught me much about the magic worked by authentic costuming."[23] Dressing for her real-life flapper role required the same attention and sense of style. In both spheres she was abetted by the Paramount costumer Howard Greer, whose designs were the talk of the fashion world. His were the first "untheatrical" clothes, elegant but subtle, that were made specifically for the movies. Bow, like Moore, dressed casually—even sloppily—outside the studio. But Louise, beginning in 1926, took her cues from Greer and, soon, from Paramount's other great designer, Travis Banton, in choosing perfectly designed and tailored clothes, for on- and off-camera.

---

* A tally from the 1927 "Dramatic Index" indicates Brooks's importance in terms of major magazine pieces that year:
  Clara Bow—19
  Joan Crawford—14
  Colleen Moore—11
  Louise Brooks—10

Joan Crawford in high flapper form doing the Black Bottom, 1925

Louise's exquisite taste drew increased attention after Banton—undisturbed by any conflict of interest—named her one of the world's best-dressed women in 1927. When interviewed about that honor, she observed that "a well dressed woman, even though her purse is painfully empty, can conquer the world. Compelled to wear last season's turban or shoes that do not blend with her stockings, a girl feels inferior." Her bottom-line piece of advice to the women of America was a flapper classic:

"Don't economize too much on clothes."[24]

Thus far Louise had enjoyed good fortune as well as good fashion, and her long-range career prospects were excellent, even though her paychecks didn't match her rivals'. At this point, Colleen Moore was collecting $12,500 a week at First National and Clara Bow $7,500 from Paramount. Louise was making $250, paltry by comparison, but she was never greedy about money and she knew that, compared to Moore and Bow, she hadn't yet proved herself in films. She couldn't have their salaries, but what she did have—the incomparable "look"—was perhaps

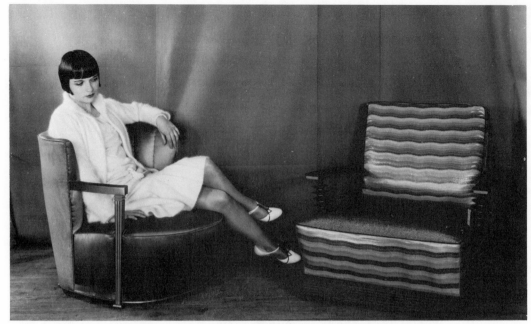

Waiting for a conversation partner: Louise lounges stylishly in 1927

greater. The master portrait photographer John Engstead summed her up in a recollection from his days as a Paramount apprentice:

"I thought she was marvelous. She was as smart as they come. Very few people had her—I hate the word 'chic'; she was just *elegant*. Elegant. Her legs, her ankles, her hands, her body, the way she held her body, the way she walked, the way she dressed, furs over her shoulder, off her shoulder, her hats. . . ."[25]

The quality of elegance. Plus the quality of caprice. When they merged, the result was powerful. "Hollywood had prospered by simultaneously peddling and putting down flapper freedom," says Rosen. "Its glossy ladies, living in the celluloid shadows of a changing society, were at once enhanced by male fantasy and repressed by male prejudices."[26] Erotic, capricious elegance was indeed the Brooks formula. And for now, at least, her caprice was still considered cute.

"Louise Brooks of Wichita Ordering Hollywood About," said the headline of one March 1926 account of her career. When she broke into movies, "she took all her individuality with her," said the report. "Louise is apparently taking what she wants instead of getting what they give her. . . .

"When Paramount put Louise Brooks, of the *Follies*, under contract they also got a lot of fire. Louise may be young, but she has a lot of determination stored in the back of her head. . . .

"When, if ever, Pola Negri, Lya de Putti from Hungary, exploited as 'the rage of Europe,' and the exotic Louise go to work on the same lot there ought to be no dearth of excitement around the Famous Players studio."[27]

Not wishing to miss the bandwagon, *Photoplay* sent its top gun, Ruth Waterbury, to interview Louise at the Marguery on a mild December day in 1925. Earlier that morning, Louise had had an equestrian session with Herr Hugo, and now her masseuse, Mrs. Gard, was working her over:

> She was one of the few people who loved me. And, oddly, I loved her, too. I loved her corpulent figure, in its tight black coat, and her kind, red Irish face under the old-fashioned hat decorated with a bird wing. I loved the tenderness with which she "cracked" my neck, almost snapping my head off, and her concern with my too-short shoes, which were "growing horns" on my heels. I could never get her to gossip about her famous clients—for instance, Mrs. William Randolph Hearst, whose husband was living openly with the movie star Marion Davies. But then neither did Mrs. Gard express her sorrow for my careless disposal of the body over which she sweated, contributing to its seductiveness. . . .
>
> Mrs. Gard had just left me smelling of camphor oil and sitting in bed in a woolly bathrobe when the phone rang announcing the arrival of Ruth Waterbury. . . . The publicity department of the Paramount New York office gave me no guidance in dealing with the press. I got along well enough with the New York journalists I knew as a chorus girl. But I could see I was in trouble the moment Ruth Waterbury, from Hollywood, entered my room, because she looked greatly surprised and greatly displeased to find me in bed. She had obviously expected me to take her to lunch at the chic Marguery Restaurant. . . . Possessing that precious quality of youth—indifference to the censure of those whom one did not admire—I found my composure equal to an hour of Miss Waterbury's hostility.

Let us juxtapose that account, from *Lulu in Hollywood*, with Waterbury's story, which ran in the April 1926 *Photoplay* under the title "Manhattan Technique."

"She was in bed when I called, most of her completely obscured by a bathrobe of Turkish toweling. It was noon, but she had been up earlier horseback riding. After that, Louise explained, she had to receive in bed."

Miss Waterbury was slightly frosted. But after examining the room, cluttered with books and dolls and a huge stuffed dog like Nana in *Peter*

Pan, the veteran reporter was sufficiently intrigued to indulge in a polite sparring match.

"I live only for my art," Louise began. "I read nothing but instructive books."

This one was going to be tough, thought Waterbury, and when Louise "looked up from beneath her long lashes to see how it was going," the writer counseled condescendingly, "Be yourself."

"Her smile is as lazy as her speech," Waterbury wrote, and Louise completed the smile before replying, "Then I won't have anything to say."

"Nothing like that ever stopped a movie interview," returned Waterbury.

It ended in a draw—and an oracular portrait of Brooks.

"Describing Louise presents its difficulties," said Waterbury. "She is so very Manhattan. Very young. Exquisitely hard-boiled. Her black eyes and sleek black hair are as brilliant as Chinese lacquer. Her skin is as white as a camellia. Her legs are lyric. She has been one of the decorative daughters of the night life of New York for three seasons. Georgie White first displayed her in the *Scandals*. Ziegfeld got her next season for the *Follies*. He hung on to her until the movies nabbed her.

"She started in pictures with *The American Venus*. It was only a small part. . . . Nobody intended Louise to be particularly important and Louise didn't bother to mention to anybody that she was. Then Paramount saw her rushes. They signed her for five years. That's how good she is."

At one point Waterbury commented that Louise must have been a very good Denishawn dancer to have been signed on for the main company after just two months' study. At which "another wise glance winged its way upward," Waterbury recorded. " 'They needed somebody in a hurry,' Louise explained. The possibilities of kidding Louise seem very remote."

Waterbury was right, and Louise was merciless.

"[Waterbury's] method of interviewing me was to recount the publicity office's story of my 'sudden success,' expecting to be able to write that I responded with rapture about going to Hollywood. Her notetaking stopped when she discovered that I was not overwhelmed by the magic of Hollywood, and that I hadn't wanted to leave Ziegfeld but had let the screenwriter Townsend Martin persuade me to play a part in his film *The American Venus*."

As for the future, the recumbent Louise allowed to Waterbury that "I want to do things like Gloria Swanson. Most of these movie people—" (she paused and sought the right phrase) "—they slaay [sic] me. I never met any of them until I went to play my first picture. In the beginning I couldn't believe them. They go around saying, 'This is a wow of an idea,'

Louise with unlikely pocketbook in a fashion pose for Meeker Made Handbags

or 'Listen to this gag, baby.' " (a pause and a sigh) "They slaay me. But I admire Gloria. I admire her career. She's gone ahead and got just what she wanted. I like that."

Waterbury then shifted innocently to what, for Louise, was less comfortable ground: "Isn't the family thrilled by your sudden success?"

"She looked at me carefully," Waterbury wrote. "She stirred the bedclothes faintly. 'They don't know about it,' she drawled. She waited and then smiled. 'My mother and father separated when I was a kid,' she explained. 'My father thinks I'm terrible.'

"Her black eyes were languid.

" 'In our family,' she said, 'it was everybody shift for himself.' She smiled once more and waved her little white hand to indicate her apartment. It is a Park Avenue apartment, and in Manhattan there is nothing more utterly utter than a Park Avenue apartment.

" 'Well,' said Louise, 'I have.' "

In fact, everyone in Wichita was following Louise's career closely—especially her mother. Her father thought it silly, perhaps, but not "terrible." And though her parents had marital problems, they were not at this point "separated." Louise was embroidering, either for dramatic effect or just to simplify the story. Overall, she judged her confrontation with Waterbury to have gone very badly: "Whereas she looked upon me as a stupid 'chorus girl' who didn't appreciate her astonishing good luck, I looked upon her as artistically retarded not to know that ten years of professional dancing was the best possible preparation for 'moving' pictures. . . . I didn't realize then that this small cultural conflict with Ruth Waterbury was merely the first instance of the kind of contempt that was destined to drive me out of Hollywood."

And yet *Photoplay*'s treatment of Louise was really quite flattering. "She has magnificent simplicity," wrote Waterbury. There had been an East versus West Coast clash of worldviews, but judging by the two accounts, the "hostility" and "contempt" emanated less from the interviewer than from the interviewee.

Waterbury's article contained one last surprise:

"For my third picture," Louise told her in a rather bored manner, "I'm supposed to play opposite W. C. Fields in *The Old Army Game*. I've played with him before in the *Follies*. Now they want me to play opposite him over there [at the Astoria studio]. But I'm not going to."

Waterbury was stunned. Louise "hadn't disarranged so much as a lock of hair while making this declaration of war." How could she get away with it? Paramount had already announced and widely promoted Louise's upcoming appearance in the film.

"Yes," said Louise, "I know they have. They think I'm going to play it. But I'm not." Summoning all her aplomb, she decreed that she would not allow herself to be misused as a foil, racing around an absurd character named Elmer Prettywillie. Nothing in the world could induce her to change her mind.

And then, of course, in true flapper spirit, she went ahead and made the picture anyway.

Louise and Eddie Sutherland wedding portrait, July 1926

7 · Louise &
"The Boy Director"

You've got to love 'em and leave 'em. If he decides to walk out, beat him to the gate. When one leaves, get another. Aim for the man higher up, and if you can't take an elevator—walk.
— PARAMOUNT PRESSBOOK, 1926

L O U I S E changed her mind about doing *It's the Old Army Game,* or someone changed it for her. She never felt obliged to explain, but it was probably the friendly advice of Walter Wanger that convinced her to be cooperative. For one of the few times in her career, she made a decision based on accommodating her employer in exchange for some future goodwill.

The real question was why she was so huffy about doing the film in the first place, considering how fond she was of the "funnyman" whose foil she would be. The answer lay somewhere in the realm of her ego, which was bruised by the fact that the role was originally announced for Clara Bow. *Army Game* was to be filmed on Long Island, but Clara had a conflict of scheduling and geography: She was committed to making *Mantrap* at Paramount's West Coast studio. This was the first but not the last time in which Louise seemed to be getting Clara Bow's or Colleen Moore's leftovers, and it annoyed her. But she wasn't yet valuable enough to Paramount to do anything other than complain to the press, for which the front office tolerantly forgave her.

Fields himself may have intervened to speak with her, since their fondness was mutual. As Louise had witnessed during their *Follies* days, he was very uncomfortable with beautiful women, and she was a rare exception. Fields, moreover, was nervous about *It's the Old Army Game*—his first starring vehicle for Paramount. He wanted a leading lady he wouldn't have to hate, or feud with. Louise was a known quantity who laughed at

his jokes and didn't threaten him sexually. For her part, having fussed a little and made her point, she could not help looking forward to rekindling her friendship with a man she knew to be the most eccentric and original comedian in America.

Army Game was a considerable risk for all concerned, mostly the studio. Paramount was taking a chance on the not-fully-proven film appeal of Fields, who was forty-seven and worried about the tradition of vaudevillians who flopped in the movies. As for the nineteen-year-old female star, she was up and coming but not yet arrived. Thus in the spring of 1926, Paramount began showering "piquant, pert little Louise Brooks, sensation of the screen" with advance praise: "This girl's a knockout!" exclaimed the publicity department. "Never has any one person—be he male or be she female—achieved movie success so quickly. Her work in [A *Social Celebrity*] convinced the Paramount powers-who-be that the place for Louise was right up with the stars." Paramount decided to entrust its risky *Army Game* project to a handsome, fun-loving director named Eddie Sutherland—soon to become a drinking buddy of Fields and a key figure in the life of Louise Brooks.

London-born A. Edward Sutherland, then thirty-one, was already a veteran of the film industry. His family on both sides was rooted in show business—father Al Sutherland a theatrical manager and producer and mother Julie Ring a vaudeville headliner. His great-grandfather J. H. Ring was a prominent English playwright, his aunt Blanche Ring a major American stage star, and his uncle Thomas Meighan a popular film actor.

Life for Eddie was literally a three-Ring circus. Julie and Blanche worked constantly, and Meighan's star was rising every day in the movies. Eddie's screen debut came in a 1914 Helen Holmes serial on which he served as actor, prop man, and stunt man for $9 a week. Later he became a Keystone Kop, a juvenile lead at Triangle Pictures, and by 1921 a featured player at Famous Players–Lasky in *The Witching Hour*, directed by William Desmond Taylor. But Sutherland was beginning to sour on acting.

Hollywood was a small town, and Eddie had known Charles Chaplin casually for years, often bumping into him at Armstrong & Carlton's Restaurant in the wee hours. It was through Eddie, back in 1917, that Chaplin met a pretty teenager named Mildred Harris, who first became pregnant and then became Mrs. Chaplin. Late one night in 1923 at the restaurant, restless Eddie asked Charlie for a production job, saying, "I don't care what you pay me."[1] Chaplin took him at his word and hired him as an assistant director at $75 a week (he'd been making $400 as an actor) for *A Woman of Paris*, the first film which Chaplin directed but did not appear in.* Eddie watched him shoot a single brief scene with sweet, elderly Lydia Knott exactly eighty times—until the old actress got so angry she finally produced the testy reaction Chaplin was looking for. *A Woman of Paris* didn't fare too well at the box office since the Tramp was missing. But its realistic narrative and restraint profoundly influenced a generation of young directors. Eddie learned enormously from the experience—even if some of the things he learned proved dangerous.

"Charlie shot pictures as we went along," Sutherland told the Columbia University Oral History Research Project in 1959. "We had a basic idea of the story, then we would do the incident every day. We'd shoot for three or four days, then lay off for two weeks and rewrite and perfect it and rehearse it and rarefy it. Charlie had the patience of Job.†

---

* Sutherland was among distinguished alumni. He and Chaplin's other three assistants all went on to important directing careers: Monta Bell (1891–1958), at MGM, would direct Garbo's first American film, *The Torrent*; Jean de Limur (1887–1976), at Paramount, directed the two important Jeanne Eagels films, *The Letter* and *Jealousy*, and co-directed G. W. Pabst's *Don Quixote*; and the volatile Harry d'Abbadie d'Arrast (1897–1968) directed many witty comedies both in Hollywood and France before retiring to the roulette tables at Monte Carlo.

† Years later, when Kevin Brownlow was researching *A Woman of Paris* and planning to interview its assistant directors, he drew some salty advice from Louise: "You can get a positive answer from Harry d'Arrast. Don't ask Eddie. He was brought up on bullshit and will say anything to tell a surprising story." And she was no great fan of the movie itself:

"I am not sure about anything in *A Woman of Paris* except that I, like the rest of the American

Chaplin liked Sutherland's work enough to rehire him as assistant director for *The Gold Rush* in 1925. Among Eddie's jobs was to supervise the building of the spectacular mining-camp set, literally carving it out of a snowy fir forest at 9,850 feet in the Sierra Nevada near Truckee, California. He also had to ride herd on the 600 extras who were real-life tramps, typecast as surly prospectors and hauled up from Sacramento.

Eddie was not only capable, but enterprising. It was his idea for Chaplin himself to play the chicken conjured up in Mack Swain's hungry subconscious—one of the film's funniest scenes. And Eddie originated the brilliant sight gag in which Chaplin and Swain's cabin teeters precariously on the edge of a cliff, depending on how the oblivious characters move about inside.

In *A Woman of Paris*, Sutherland observed Chaplin's use of cameras and lighting; in *The Gold Rush*, he studied the master's pace and timing. In return, Eddie gave Chaplin his skill at people-management, plus some dubious alliances with women—very young women. Chaplin was now interested in yet another teenager. She was Lolita McMurray back in 1921 when she played a bit part in *The Kid*. Now sixteen, she was hanging around the Chaplin studios, where Eddie saw her and mentioned her to the Boss. A screen test followed, Chaplin liked her, and they renamed her Lita Grey.

"When Charlie came up to shoot the [*Gold Rush*] scenes, she came along," said Eddie. "She used to go around the hotel in a very attractive negligee. . . . So I was the one who introduced Charlie to Mildred Harris and then to Lita Grey. In later life he'd say, 'Don't introduce me to any more girls, please, Eddie, if you want things to be fine between us.' "[2]

Now credentialed and ready to direct, Eddie was assigned to "megaphone" three pictures in 1925, none of which revealed spectacular comedic gifts, and then early in 1926 he hit the jackpot. The name of the film was *Behind the Front*, with Wallace Beery and Raymond Hatton. Expectations were as low as the budget for this knockabout burlesque of World War I in which a pickpocket and a detective are vamped by Mary Brian into joining the American Expeditionary Force. But to Paramount's delight, *Behind the Front* became the surprise hit of 1926, breaking box-office records throughout the country.* Beery and Hatton, routine character actors for years, now became stars. Director Sutherland and his

---

public, thought it was . . . as cornball and dated as *Camille*—Edna's clothes and the sets were 1900. We were wearing our skirts up to our knees in 1923. Only Menjou saved something from the corn patch with his elegant performance. . . .

"It was the 'intellectual' critics, bellyaching about censorship, hollering for Freudian sexual freedom, who fastened on the plot of a man with a 'mistress' and blew it up to a 'masterpiece.' "
* Veterans were apparently not offended by its tasteless slogan, "The Sunny Side of the War," or the promotion for exhibitors: "When your audience sees it, they're going to forget that there was anything serious connected with the World War."

screenwriter buddy Monte Brice were hailed as comic geniuses, assured of more money and more films.

Even before *Behind the Front*, Eddie was a favorite of actors and studio executives for his affability and impish humor. Now he was even more popular, and the fact that he was young, handsome, charming, *and* the hottest new comedy director surely contributed to Louise's change of heart about making *Army Game*.

Photoplay's Dorothy Harden was much taken by Eddie's élan in a Manhattan interview around this time: "Eddie is the boy director on the Famous Players lot who, off the set, radiates the roguish allure of a 'Peck's Bad Boy' in the act of getting away with it."[3] Her conclusion was that he "revels in the unusual." His eccentric friends included a six foot four inch German-Japanese art critic and kleptomaniac, Sadakichi Hartmann. Sutherland, she said, "was made a court bachelor years ago and premeditates no matrimonial venture in the near or distant future."

In fact, Eddie had only recently divorced actress Marjorie Daw. As for his rejection of further matrimonial ventures, he would be exchanging vows again within six months, and he would eventually marry a total of five times. As for comedy directing, Eddie said he wanted to do films with humor but without "gags"—rather on the order of A *Woman of Paris*, "but more wholesome in subject matter."[4]

It's the Old Army Game did not exactly fit that description. It had gags galore, and its "wholesome subject matter" dealt with various types of swindling. It was scripted chaotically by Luther Reed from J. P. McEvoy's *Comic Supplement*—the same material on which some of Fields's *Follies* sketches were based. The comedian himself wanted to call the picture *Never Give a Sucker an Even Break*, but Paramount thought that too pugnacious and indelicate for the general tastes of 1926.* For now, he had to settle for the awkward *Army Game* title, a reference to that sleight-of-hand whereby a pea is hidden under a walnut shell faster than the eye can detect. And audiences had to settle for one of the most nihilistic and violently misanthropic comedies produced during the silent era.

The hero of this old army con game is Elmer Prettywillie, played by Fields, and described in the titles as "apothecary and humanitarian—ever ready to administer [*sic*] to those in distress." His drugstore is a magnet for people who do everything but buy drugs. Elmer himself is very fond of his salesgirl (Louise Brooks), described as "a counter attraction at the Prettywillie store." Tessie Gilch, the railroad station agent, is played by Eddie Sutherland's well-known aunt, Blanche Ring. "One look at her," says the

---

* It took Fields fifteen more years and numerous thwarted attempts before he finally got a studio (Universal) to use *Never Give a Sucker an Even Break* (1941) as a title.

Louise and Blanche Ring, Eddie Sutherland's aunt, in a scene from
It's the Old Army Game *(1926)*

title, "and all trains stop." Tessie, for her part, lusts ludicrously after Prettywillie.

Blanche Ring was the buxom dowager type, similar to the foils that Alison Skipworth and Marie Dressler later played for Fields and that Margaret Dumont would soon be playing for the Marx Brothers. Blanche had given Eddie his first stage job many years before, and he was now returning the favor by casting her in her first feature-length movie. It was indeed a family affair and would soon become more of one.

Army Game opens with Fields asleep while, outside, a woman in a car races to his drugstore and frantically rings the night bell. What she is so desperate to obtain, it turns out, is a single two-cent stamp, which she forgets to pay for. She also accidentally sets off the fire alarm. Firemen soon swarm en masse into the store and promptly sit down for ice cream sodas. When they leave, a fire *does* break out—in Fields's cigar box. After a hundred attempts to douse it (including multiple trips with an eyeglass full of water), it finally occurs to him simply to close the lid. The basic plot, once it finally emerges, is a switcheroo on the Florida real-estate boom. William Gaxton plays a "New York go-getter" who is drawn to the drugstore by the sight of Louise and suckers Fields into joining him in the "High and Dry Real Estate" scheme by which Floridians are conned into buying lots in New York—the reverse of the popular land scam of the day.

The picture, overall, is a reliable example of the Comedy of Frustration. Interiors were shot at the Astoria studio, but most of the action was filmed on location in the inland farming town of Ocala, Florida, sixty miles west of Daytona Beach. There, in February 1926, a good time was had by all. For the final chase scene, half the town's population was employed to run crazily through the streets.

That part of central Florida was still on the wild side, and the cast had to do more communing with nature than they planned. A week into shooting, Louise was irate that no local hairdresser had produced soap suds when shampooing her bob. It was just the hard water, they said, but she wanted *suds*, goddammit. Then one afternoon, a love scene between Louise and Gaxton was filmed from a glass-bottomed boat in a broad stream outside town. The area boasted "150 natural springs issuing from the porous Ocala limestone and flowing into a common basin." From the boat, through the lush tropical vegetation, Louise spied a group of Seminole Indian women washing their hair on the banks—and with suds! It was the sole soft-water spring, and the Indians had been using it for bathing since before Ponce de León. Within minutes, Louise's maid was dispatched to engage a squaw, who performed the necessary operation on her hair exactly as Louise wanted it—au naturel and with lots of soap bubbles.

And then there were the wild animals, unscripted. Fields himself had the most bestial encounter, a result of his fondness for camping. While Louise and the rest of the cast went by special train from Astoria to Florida, Fields preferred to motor down in leisurely fashion. It took him four days, during which he cooked his own meals by the roadside. Camping appealed to him for comic as well as scenic reasons, and he continued the practice for a while even after arriving on location. One night, he and his old friend William Grady spread their tablecloth on a soft bed of pine needles in an idyllic setting outside of Ocala. Fields was happily broiling a steak over an open fire when he noticed a large, black, long-snouted boar eating a loaf of bread and looking menacingly toward the steak. Fields gave a swift kick in the big pig's direction, carefully avoiding contact, in view of its evil-looking tusks. A balance of terror ensued until he found a long stick—a *very* long stick—that finally served to chase the grunting animal away.

Another day while Fields was filming a food gag on the edge of a woods, a deer suddenly emerged from the trees, galloped up, and reared on its hind legs. After a moment's dread fear, Fields held out two crackers, which the animal took and ate. Then he offered a third cracker from which he'd already taken a bite, and the animal refused it. Sutherland quickly rearranged his camera, someone whistled, and the deer returned, this time allowing Louise to feed it. The footage was shot, and Eddie said it was so lovely that he'd use it in the picture—but never did.

The Animal Crackers atmosphere continued a few days later when Fields and scenarist Tom Geraghty settled back for their morning shave in a Palm Beach barbershop. Suddenly the barbers, bootblacks, and customers began hurling objects and running out into the street. Fields, who had been dozing, just assumed they had all gone mad. He was one of the last to notice that a skunk had wandered into the shop.

Blanche Ring had no run-ins with animals, but she made an unscheduled comic debut at the Ocala railroad terminal. An engineer threw her a bouquet of flowers as his train raced through the station, the flowers hit Aunt Blanche square in the face, and she toppled backward over the platform. Louise, Fields, and Gaxton all laughed hard, thinking it an intentional stunt. Sutherland loved it.

"Great!" exclaimed Eddie. "We'll do it over again. The next time, please fall toward the camera, Miss Ring." She gazed at him for a moment, decided he was serious, and did the pratfall like a trouper for a second time.

On and off camera, this was a fun-loving cast—to the detriment of the picture. Louise, like everyone else connected with the film, never quite knew what was happening within it.

"We were treated to so much Southern hospitality that the script got lost and the shooting schedule wandered out of sight," she recalled. "Nobody in Ocala seemed to have heard of Prohibition. And if ever there was a company that needed no help in the consumption of liquor, it was ours."[5]

When not drinking, Fields could often be found in the lobby of the Ocala Hotel, where he kept an eye out for a good bridge game (at five cents a point). That he was an expert cardsharp in addition to juggler and comic was often forgotten, or unknown. One night he felt particularly frisky.

"Three hands had been dealt before it came to Mr. Fields' turn to deal," recounted a Paramount publicist on the scene. "Fields smiled. He shuffled the cards, passed them to the man on his right to cut them, and dealt himself thirteen spades. The bidding began with much doubling and redoubling."[6]

From Ocala, the unit moved up to Palm Beach, where the accommodations, not to mention the nightlife, were superior.

"Palm Beach was especially attractive that year," said Louise, "because its millionaires had decided that they could not get through the winter without their *Follies* girls. They had provided Ziegfeld with the money to produce *Palm Beach Nights*, a small edition of the *Follies*. It was housed in an old assembly hall transformed by the famous Viennese designer

Joseph Urban into a nightclub with a full stage. Ziegfeld provided a choice selection of *Follies* girls, including Paulette Goddard, who later married Charlie Chaplin, and Susan Fleming, who later married Harpo Marx. And now every night, at the conclusion of *Palm Beach Nights*, our company (minus Bill Fields) contributed a floor show. Blanche Ring sang 'Rings on My Fingers,' Mickey Bennett sang ballads in a piercing tenor, I danced, Eddie did pratfalls, and Billy Gaxton starred as a comedian. He and Rudy Cameron did an old vaudeville act of theirs, singing and dancing and telling bum jokes with violent self-approval. Then Gaxton appeared alone, playing the violin. This was even worse than the vaudeville act. Trying to recapture the essence of Gaxton's impromptu comedy, I realize now that it was born of despair."

Gaxton, she recalled, was obsessed with his appearance, constantly checking with lens man Alvin Wyckoff "to see whether a scar on the back of his neck was well covered, since it was the only part of him that showed in our two-shots together."

"I knew that our parts as the 'love interest' in a Fields comedy meant nothing," she said, "but Gaxton had convinced himself that this first job in films would launch him on a successful new career, allowing him to escape from years of mediocre vaudeville sketches. At best, it was a mistaken act of friendship—Eddie's giving the part of a boy to a sophisticated actor of thirty-four. Billy Gaxton was so vulnerable, so proud of his good looks, his Spanish ancestry, his acting ability. When he became a great Broadway star in George Gershwin's *Of Thee I Sing* (1931), the deadly bitterness of what he regarded as his failure in *It's the Old Army Game* was exposed by the fact that he refused fantastic contracts, and never made another film."[7]*

It didn't take long in Palm Beach for shooting to get way behind schedule. The front office was frantic, and William Le Baron wired, "All second cameraman's rushes tilted. What are you doing? Sober up and come home." But at precisely that point, said Louise, "Eddie decided that the picnic sequence absolutely must be shot on Mrs. Stotesbury's lawn."

Thus came about *Army Game*'s funniest and most anarchistic scene: the Prettywillie family's picnic outing. The chosen site was El Mirasol, the million-dollar Palm Beach villa of Mr. and Mrs. E. T. Stotesbury, who liked hobnobbing with movie folks. It's the most delicious sequence of a deliciously vulgar and mean-spirited film—a picnic scene memorable for both its groceries and *grosseries*. Fields stuffs himself with food, snap-

---

* This dramatic assessment of Gaxton is one of various factual errors in *Lulu in Hollywood* that are examined in the Appendix. It is true that Gaxton's performance in *Army Game* was not well received—or just not noticed—and that he was bitter about it. But after *Army Game*, he made another silent, *Stepping Along*, and a number of talkies, including *Fifty Million Frenchmen* (1931), *Something to Shout About* (1942), *Best Foot Forward* (1943), and *Tropicana* (1944).

jerking huge spoonfuls to his mouth in between battles with nine-year-old Mickey Bennett. Soon he is spitting pickles, and when the jar gets stuck on his hand, he passes it surrealistically onto the boy's, but without losing sight of the main objective of the scene: to destroy the estate. By the time Fields and Sutherland's crew were done with it, the perfectly manicured grounds were gouged, defiled, and totally covered with garbage.

"What a mess!" Louise recalled. "The whole lawn plowed up. What makes it funny is that Mrs. Stotesbury loved it. Without needing to give a $50,000 ball, she had all Palm Beach talking."[8]

The gross and the grotesque rival each other throughout *Army Game*. Fields at one point extracts a cockroach from a society lady's eye. Later, a cuckoo clock defecates big Ping-Pong balls onto his head. Either the censors were asleep, or Sutherland found a way to purchase their inattention.

Even more surprising than the film's vulgarity is its brutality. Soon enough, in talkies, Fields's laconic verbal humor would eclipse the great physical agility of his comedy. But here and now in 1926, he is still energetic and sociopathic enough to commit violence instead of just threaten it. *Army Game* contains the most savage of Fields's many unpleasant encounters with children. He is tolerant of Mickey Bennett and watches approvingly, so long as the boy is breaking all the windows of the Stotesbury mansion or otherwise destroying or stealing things. But elsewhere in the picture he:

- Binds and gags one squalling infant.

- Gives a mirror and a mallet to another.

- Holds a child over the broken railing of a second-story porch with the intention of dropping him—until Blanche Ring raps reprovingly on the window.

- Tells one child, "Uncle will give you some nice razor blades to play with."

If such virulent misopedia was shocking to 1926 audiences, none of the reviews ever mentioned it. *Variety* said Fields used "nearly every gag he ever saw or heard of" but that this "succession of snappy gags make for a first-class laugh-provoker." From Paramount's standpoint, which was financial, *Army Game* provoked enough laughs to justify two more Fields features in quick succession, *So's Your Old Man* (1926) and the flapper parody, *Two Flaming Youths* (1927).

For Sutherland, it was the beginning of a long association with W. C.

Fields. They would eventually make six pictures together, both silents and talkies.*

"He was a great drinking companion, an earthy man," said Eddie. "We used to go to the fights together and have all kinds of parties together, play good pool, good ping-pong, good golf—a very fine athlete, you know. . . . [But] in all the pictures I made with Fields, from 9 in the morning till 9 at night we were bitter enemies—very polite to each other, but bitter enemies. Mr. Fields wanted to do the story about an ugly old man, an ugly old woman and an impossible kid, and that isn't a very good box-office combination, so we had to outwit him and put in pretty girls, ingenues, leading people, etc., and he hated management. Management meant anybody who said 'no.' "9

But it was the director, not the comedian, who came in for sharp criticism from Louise:

"Eddie didn't know anything about directing, acting, cutting or camera angles," she said. His big problem was in trying to "create" on his feet the way Chaplin did, or the way he *thought* Chaplin did. With Eddie, it didn't often work. In fact, it didn't work that way with Chaplin either. Chaplin directed without a script, but the scenarios were always thoroughly worked out in his head. Though he sometimes experimented with spur-of-the-moment brainstorms, most of his comic inspirations were carefully calculated, many of them years in the germination. Most required twenty-five takes—with meticulous, incremental improvements—to achieve perfection. Imagining that Chaplin really did "think up scenes right there on the set," said Louise, Eddie "would try to make pictures that way . . . with large hangovers, to boot."10

Sutherland had been handicapped by a weak script, but there was something else that was clouding his judgment and breaking up his concentration—something Louise never took into account: Eddie was falling madly in love with her. The minute he met her, he was entranced, and the more she treated him in her capricious way, the harder he fell. Louise was at least infatuated in return. He was no Chaplin, but, for all his shortcomings, Eddie was bright and charming and fun. They both liked to drink and to party, and there were many opportunities to sneak off together.

Even before filming was complete, Eddie was talking about marriage, and Louise was laughing off the suggestion. At nineteen, she still valued her freedom. Her mixed emotions about Eddie paralleled her feelings about *Army Game* itself. She was in this picture to serve as Gaxton's love interest, although the comic hero also fancied her. This, in fact, would be

---

* The others were *Tillie's Punctured Romance* (1928), *International House* (1933), *Mississippi* (1935), *Poppy* (1936), and *Follow the Boys* (1944).

the only picture in which Fields allowed his character to be in love with the leading lady. It was as if he let down his vulnerable defenses just this once for Louise Brooks, whom he knew beforehand.

But if Louise was narratively marginal, she was visually crucial, from her first sexy entrance in tight sweater and cloche hat. She laughs with a rare, irresistible grin. And in the drugstore scenes where Sutherland poses her with Fields in close-ups, her perfect enamel features cause his to light up. There's a fascinating subtext in those two unlikely profiles.

Throughout the film, Brooks's diction is so good, the viewer can lip-read most of her dialogue. Her acting is exemplified by a scene wherein Gaxton finds and destroys her previous boyfriend's letter. Other silent heroines would have mugged in exaggerated hurt or anger. But the muted Louise Brooks merely looks a bit startled—and then gazes back at Gaxton inquisitively. It is the same look of innocent curiosity with which she would regard her men in a much more famous film, *Pandora's Box*, two years later.

Louise's embryonic naturalism in the midst of a frothy comedy was augmented by the stunning way she photographed. Her almond eyes revealed an awareness of artifice—of film in general, of this film in particular —and the freshness of that quality did not escape even the toughest critics. Mordaunt Hall of the *New York Times* said, "Mr. Fields' clever and energetic performance is helped along by the attractive Louise Brooks."[11] *Variety* declared that Louise "photographs like a million dollars," predicting that "this girl is going to land right at the top in the picture racket."

Unbeknownst to Louise—most things unrelated to her amusement were unbeknownst to Louise—the strange, desperate quality of *It's the Old Army Game* matched the international, pre-Crash tendency to make merry for tomorrow we may die. The common thread was alienation, melded somehow with hedonism. Rebellious, free-spirited little moths like Louise were still a safe distance from the flame.

Louise was barely back in her Manhattan apartment, and *Army Game* barely released, when Eddie Sutherland began bombarding her with phone calls in May 1926. Their Florida fling was still much on his mind, and he was uttering the word "marriage" a lot. Louise had enjoyed her time with him and she was flattered by his follow-up attention, but she still didn't take him too seriously as a suitor. Eddie was an unabashed playboy, and his lightning marriage-and-divorce with Marjorie Daw didn't suggest much stability in his concept of matrimony—not that stability was high on Louise's priority list either.

In any case, she was due to start work on her next film, a prestige project this time. It was *The Show-Off*, George Kelly's comedy hit of the 1924 Broadway season, which ran for 571 performances. Heywood Broun went so far as to call it "the best comedy which has yet been written by an American," and Kelly was numbered with Eugene O'Neill, Sherwood Anderson, and Elmer Rice among the most gifted American dramatists. *The Show-Off* was a hot theatrical property much sought by movie studios. Paramount won, and Malcolm St. Clair—Louise's friend and fan from *A Social Celebrity*—was chosen to direct.

Kelly specialized in mixing realistic lowbrow comedy with the pathos of contemporary "problems," the result aspiring to social comment. He had an ear for the idiomatic rhythms of small talk and an eye for American foibles. He won a Pulitzer Prize for *Craig's Wife*, but *The Show-Off* was his best work and Aubrey Piper was his best character—a blowhard railroad clerk who pretends to be a big shot. Aubrey's insufferable personality and compulsive lying get him into progressively deeper trouble with the Fisher family, which he invades. Of such simple material, four different film versions would be made.*

In the title role was Ford Sterling, that rather forlorn leading man whose "undernourished *amour-propre*" Louise had declined to feed in *The American Venus*. Lois Wilson was Amy, the show-off's unhappy wife, and the vinegary mother was expertly played by veteran Claire McDowell. Louise as Clara, the street-smart sister, had a key role that showcased her sauciness. Most of the play's popularity had derived from its dialogue, but St. Claire added some fascinating exterior footage of Philadelphia, including a spectacular car chase, in an effort to liberate the drama from its drawing room. Overall, however, the film's silence was a drawback that Louise was expected to help offset.

And she did her job. St. Clair later said he had only to suggest a certain glance to Louise, and she produced it. A lightning flash of disapproval from her eyes, for instance, suffices to stop Aubrey from stealing a bite of chicken during grace. Juxtaposed with the hapless Lois Wilson, she is all the more striking.

Sterling labored mightily to bring Aubrey to life, stopping short of burlesque. But after *The Show-Off*, said Louise, he "returned to oblivion." [12] †

Louise's growing celebrity, by contrast, contributed to the unusual press interest in the making of the film. In October 1926, shortly after *The Show-Off*'s release, a stunning portrait of her appeared on the cover of *Motion Picture Classic*, the most serious rival to *Photoplay*. Inside the

---

* The four versions are the silent *Show-Off* of 1926 with Louise Brooks, remade for talkies by Paramount as *Men Are Like That* in 1929, the 1934 MGM sound version with Spencer Tracy, and the 1946 MGM remake with Red Skelton.

† Like William Gaxton, Ford Sterling was prematurely buried by Louise. His career continued until just a few years before his death in 1939. He made four silents in 1927 (*Casey at the Bat, The Little Widow, Hearts and Flowers, The Trunk Mystery*), five more in 1928 (*That's My Daddy, Mr. Romeo, Chicken à la King, Oh, Kay!*, and *Sporting Goods*), and six talkies, including Paramount's celebrated *Alice in Wonderland* (1933).

Louise's first cover-girl appearance,
Motion Picture Classic, October 1926

same issue was a major profile of Mal St. Clair, the cartoonist-turned-director, illustrated with his own delightful drawings of Louise, Ford Sterling, Pola Negri, and others. For a publicity-hungry studio, nothing was more important than a cover appearance by one of its rising stars. Paramount was pleased, and St. Clair was thrilled by the treatment.

Louise, on the other hand, never even bought a copy of the magazine.

Paramount wasn't the only studio that was pleased with Louise's work in front of the camera. First National had an eye on her, too, and concluded a deal with Paramount for a month-long loan, July 26 through August 22, 1926. The film was tentatively called *Even Stephen*, to be directed by Al Santell.*

People then and now have wondered why a highly competitive studio such as Paramount would allow its stars and featured players to be borrowed by rival filmmakers. The answer was always as simple as money, and Louise's case was a classic example. Her Paramount salary at this time was $250 a week. But for the period of her loan-out, First National agreed to pay Paramount $1,000 a week. Thus did Paramount make a handsome $750 profit—Louise not receiving a penny more than her contractual $250.

---

* Al Santell (1895–1981), a professional architect before he went into films, was one of First National's busiest and best directors. In the first six months of 1926 before *Just Another Blonde* (as the film with Brooks was eventually named), he'd directed three hits: *Bluebeard's Seven Wives*, *The Dancer of Paris*, and *Subway Sadie*, the latter two with Dorothy Mackaill. The year before, he directed the Corinne Griffith hit, *Classified*, and immediately after *Blonde*, he made *Orchids and Ermine*, one of Colleen Moore's best pictures.

The resulting First National feature had even more title problems than *It's the Old Army Game*. It evolved from *Even Stephen* (the original *Red Book* story by Gerald Beaumont) to *The Girl from Coney Island* to *The Charleston Kid* before its makers finally settled on *Just Another Blonde*—a weak effort to cash in on Anita Loos's *Gentlemen Prefer Blondes* of the year before. The studio urged its distributors to revive the "dumb blonde versus brainy brunette" controversy by encouraging people to write their local newspapers on the subject.

"Get the thing started by writing a few letters yourself, and having your ushers sign them," advised the publicity department.[13]

Billed as a "fast-moving, wise-cracking comedy," the film stars Jack Mulhall and William "Buster" Collier, Jr., as a pair of Bowery gamblers and Dorothy Mackaill and Louise Brooks as their Coney Island sweethearts. Mackaill, the beautiful blonde, and Brooks, the dark-haired imp, play a dance-hall hostess and a shooting-gallery "Annie Oakley" respectively. Mulhall and Collier are occupied with male bonding; they've sworn to split everything 50-50, even Stephen, and to let no dames interfere with their comradeship.

The boys set up a Coney Island gambling joint, but the no-dames pact weakens once Collier gets a look at Brooks. Together they conspire to get Mulhall interested in Mackaill, but not until Mulhall and Mackaill are in an airplane with locked landing gear—expecting to be killed momentarily—do they exchange love vows. The action accompanying this double romance was highlighted by stunning aerial photography and a plane crash, plus some spectacular footage taken from the amusement-park rides in Luna Park—including shots from the front of a roller coaster.

There was equal excitement and romance on the set. Buster Collier, at twenty-four, was the adopted son of the famous stage actor William Collier, with whom he had performed constantly from the age of four. Charming and boyishly handsome, he had an easy grace that came from twenty years in theater. *Just Another Blonde* was his twenty-second film. Though Louise was literally in the process of marrying Eddie Sutherland, she and Collier were instantly drawn to one another, and the result was a brief but torrid affair.

"I don't recall a damned thing about *Just Another Blonde* except some scenes we shot at Coney Island," Louise told Kevin Brownlow many years later. "I was always late, but just too damn stunning for them to fire me." But she added, "I fell in love with the only actor I ever cared for. . . . Buster Collier."[14]

According to Louise, Buster was in love with Constance Talmadge, whose sister Natalie was unhappily married to Buster Keaton. Collier was intimate friends with Keaton and all the Talmadges—a complex set of relationships that Louise would soon learn more about in Hollywood. For

Louise and William "Buster" Collier, Jr., on the set of
Just Another Blonde (1926), New York

Louise and Dorothy Mackaill in a scene from Just Another Blonde *(1926)—*
Brooks's first "loan-out," to First National

now, Brooks and Collier temporarily abandoned their other amours and spent almost every moment together, often posing for joint candid shots on the set.

In charge of all the on- and off-screen lovers was Al Santell, who was both pleasant and efficient on the set. First National spoke beamingly of him: "A cup of tea, a kind word, a ukelele, a song and a keen sense of humor is Al Santell's formula for success as a motion picture director."

The ukelele was important. Whenever Santell was dissatisfied with the studio musicians, he'd sit down and improvise a tune of his own. And a Santell film always stayed on schedule.

"Santell was a very fast director," says Mackaill. "He knew what he wanted and made you see what he wanted. He did have a little trouble with Louise, as far as her acting went. He had to give her a lot of time."[15]

Mackaill was a thoroughgoing professional who had come from England just two years before and landed quickly in Ziegfeld's *Midnight Frolic*—an after-hours show performed on the top floor of the New Amsterdam Theater, where, down below on the main stage, the *Follies* ran nightly. Mackaill was an important First National property at this point, with a clause in her contract stipulating that if her weight went over 130 pounds, she would be fired ("that was in everybody's contract," she says). She was unquestionably the star of this picture, as the publicity material attests ("Dorothy Mackaill may be 'Just Another Blonde,' but gentlemen! how you will prefer her!"), and she was slightly irked at the extra attention devoted to a supporting player.

"Santell was stuck on her," Mackaill recalls, "and Buster Collier was stuck on her, too. All the men liked her. . . . She was a peculiar girl—odd, different. When I say she was not an actress, I mean she didn't have any experience. She had that I-don't-care attitude, probably because she didn't go after these things. I liked Louise, but . . . She didn't know anything about acting, though she knew she was very much admired. She'd go through the picture and—I'm not calling her a Dumb Dora, but it's not far removed. You couldn't give her a big acting part, she wouldn't know what to do with it. . . .

"But she was damned attractive, and I'd say good-humored, not difficult, about it all. She used to laugh and shrug her shoulders and say, 'The hell with it!' But they got what they wanted. All they had to do with Brooksie was turn the camera on."

No actresses' approaches to their craft were further apart than Mackaill's and Brooks's. "If every screen player would use the projection room as frequently as possible [to watch the daily rushes]," Mackaill told an interviewer on the *Blonde* set, "their acting would improve beyond their fondest dreams. For it is on the screen in the projection room that you may sit and study your own work."[16]

Louise, of course, prided herself on never watching either the rushes or even the finished product. But she had a good time during the *Blonde* filming, which was eventful. By day, crowds gathered to watch her at the Luna Park shooting gallery, where she was mastering her Annie Oakley routine. By night, Santell was shooting the dance-hall sequences in the wee hours, after the public was locked out, with a horde of 200 extras literally dancing till dawn. The midsummer night's heat of 1926 was particularly withering; it combined with the hot lights to melt the make-up right off the actors' faces. During the worst of it, Santell was importing 600 pounds of ice daily, placing it in a big vat over which a battery of seven giant electric fans blew the cool air toward the sweltering actors.

The most astonishing event during production involved an aerial tragedy (and cover-up) that was never revealed. "It was on the Mitchell flying Field and we were doing a test [for the aerial photography]," Mackaill recalls. "I was in a 'Jenny'—an open-cockpit plane, you know—when it crashed for real *and the pilot was killed!* The camera wasn't running, they were just seeing how it worked. The camera was strapped on the plane, in back of the pilot, between the pilot and me, shooting me. So it was top-heavy. We only went up about 800 feet, and crashed. . . . For some reason I wasn't strapped in—thank God."[17]

Mackaill was thrown onto the field, somehow escaping serious injury. The strapped-in pilot was killed when the nose and front section of the plane smashed deep into the ground.

"The strange thing was that that was the theme of the picture," says Mackaill—the girl and the pilot thinking they were about to be killed. "I'll never forget it, because it was the same day Valentino died [Monday, August 23, 1926]. . . . What a day! They almost lost me, too."

Not a word of the accident leaked out. The studio's desire to hush it up coincided with that of the military, whose plane and whose turf were involved. Considering that mishap, the newspaper advertisements for *Just Another Blonde* are macabre: Mackaill and Mulhall clutching one another in the downward spiral of a plane, whose broken wreckage is seen below.

But the most striking of the ads shows two gamblers in a struggle while, beneath them, a pair of tumbling dice sport the face of Mackaill on one, Brooks on the other. It's not hard to decide which of the two—the innocent-looking blonde or the black-haired siren—is the "nice" girl and which the minx.

Before he even began filming, Santell got a shock to rival the plane disaster that would soon follow. It came in the form of a casual request from Louise, duly recorded by a First National press agent and confirmed by Dorothy Mackaill.

They fell 5,000 feet
in five seconds—
but that was plenty of time
for him to fall in love!

The wind took his breath away,
but he saved enough to tell her—
what he had thought he
would never tell any girl!

First National
Pictures

First National
Pictures, Inc.
Presents

JUST ANOTHER BLONDE

An
ALFRED SANTELL
Production

with a 4-Star Cast . . .

DOROTHY MACKAILL - JACK MULHALL
Louise Brooks and William Collier, Jr.

"Mr. Santell," Louise said to the director, "I'd like a little time off today. I want to get married."

It was said in true Louise Brooks fashion—"just like that. No hemming or hawing, no preliminary remarks. [She] announced that she was going to wed as nonchalantly as if she wanted a cigarette. . . . The calmness of the young lady and the suddenness of the shock tied Santell's tongue in a knot for a minute. Then: 'Sure, go get married.' And the dashing Miss Brooks was off in a whirl of taxi dust for the Grand Central Station, New York, to meet director Edward Sutherland."[18]

Eddie, for his part, was rushing back by rail to New York from Hollywood on the 20th Century. He arrived just in time for their 4:00 p.m. wedding at the Municipal Building, deputy clerk William McCormick officiating. Actor Allan Forrest, Mary Pickford's brother-in-law, accompanied Eddie and served as his best man. The suddenness of the thing—and the celebrity of the newlyweds—gave the newspapers a field day.

"3,000 Miles Just to Marry" headlined the New York *American* on July 22, 1926, the day after the wedding, above a large picture of Sutherland

*Eddie Sutherland and his slinky bride at the Famous Players–
Lasky studio offices in Astoria, Long Island, 1926*

embracing his sultry bride. The photograph is uncannily like the caricature on the *Blonde* tumbling dice. The *American* got a good quote out of
Eddie: "I was five days on the [West] Coast when I realized how impossible
life would be without her. So I came back—that's all."

"Unexpected Marriage" was the announcement above Louise's picture
in the New York *Mirror*, whose reporter, Dorothy Herzog, reached Sutherland at the newlyweds' hotel. "You're certainly a fast worker," Herzog
quoted herself as telling Eddie. " 'I had to be,' his voice sounded excited
over the wire. 'I was afraid of losing her.' " It was Louise's "initial matrimonial excursion," wrote Herzog, adding that "her army of swains would
make a marine corps look puny." Herzog's conclusion was a classic of the
period:

> Eddie once told us that marriage was a mighty, mighty serious thing and
> he wouldn't try it again unless he was sure of himself and the girl. Though

his courtship of the dark-eyed, dark-haired, vivacious Miss Brooks was comparatively short, it was, nevertheless, thorough, and the forced separation from the seductive emoter did the rest. Eddie is in his late twenties. Miss Brooks is nineteen, but she knows what it's all about. So that's that.

The New York *Daily News* handled the marriage of Eddie and his "seductive emoter" in the style for which it was famous. "Con Game Film Lures Leaders to Love Match," said the headline, while reporter Irene Thirer revealed that "they came together, took out a marriage license and were wed—all within an hour."

As all the newspapers noted, their courtship had been a whirlwind one, most of it telephonic, most of it spent apart. The honeymoon consisted of two days at the Ambassador—scene of Louise's dalliances with Eddie's former boss, Charlie Chaplin. And when the forty-eight hours were up, Eddie rushed back to California to megaphone the new Beery-Hatton comedy, *We're in the Navy Now*. In the wake of the surprise success of *Behind the Front*, the *Navy* sequel took on more importance for the studio, and Eddie was anxious to keep up his short string of hits.

The sequel turned out decently enough, not a smash but respectable at the box office. Only the most sharp-eyed viewers noticed Eddie's inside salute to his new wife: The name of the ship is the S.S. *Louise*.

If Brooksie's famous in-laws celebrated her entrance into the family, there's no indication of it, despite the fact that most of them—Thomas Meighan and the Ring sisters—lived in New York. Their absence or silence at the wedding suggests they didn't take too kindly to Eddie's impetuous choice, and though Louise was henceforth one of their tribe, they made no efforts to include her in their social circle.

But Louise had no inclination to be offended—and no more time for in-laws than for honeymoons. She knew Eddie and his Beau Brummel reputation well enough to know that he wasn't lonely back in California. For her part, she'd been unfaithful to her absentee fiancé-husband both before and after their wedding. Vows of monogamy were neither requested nor exchanged between Louise and Eddie, although they did think in traditional terms at least to the extent of finding a furnished apartment to rent.

During Eddie's quick trip to Manhattan a few weeks before they were married, "the renting agent gave us an address on Central Park South," Louise wrote Kevin Brownlow years later. "The apartment door was opened by Mary Miles Minter. Now, we knew who she was and she knew who we were, but her expression was as remote as that of a nun receiving a couple of plumbers." [19]

It would be sixty years before Sidney Kirkpatrick's book, *Cast of Killers*, purported to "solve" the William Desmond Taylor murder case in which Minter and her mother were deeply involved. Louise had it solved much earlier, and she dismissed Brownlow's suggestion that Minter grew grotesquely fat out of guilt for her mother's crime. The apartment encounter took place in 1926, four years after the Taylor-Minter scandal.

"[Mary's] face and skin were good," Louise continued, "but the body was 50 pounds overweight. The sitting room (we went no farther) was painted in the traditional apple green with three-tiered bookshelves built from the floor on two sides of the room. They were partially filled with current bestsellers and other books were flung about on tables.

"I don't think 'guilt' has anything to do with her fat. I don't think she knows the meaning of the word. She is a unique blend of stupidity and cupidity. When Ma saw she was losing her meal ticket to Taylor and killed him, Mary M. M. took her revenge by getting too fat for pictures. Paramount was delighted to find a way to unload an expensive star who was losing money, at the same time they killed off Mabel Normand and Sennett. Nobody was ever charged with the murder of Taylor."[20]

The Sutherlands didn't rent the apartment.

Louise may not have been madly in love with Eddie, but she liked his style and the excitement that surrounded him, and by the end of the summer she was anxious to see him. A few days after the end of filming on *Just Another Blonde* and the departure of Buster Collier, she hopped a train for California to be reunited with her husband. She arrived on September 5, a Sunday night, and was treated royally by Eddie—for twenty-four hours. On Monday, a Western Union messenger arrived with a telegram from New York: Come back to begin filming again. Leave tomorrow.

The second honeymoon, like the first, lasted two days.

Louise was enraged but she acquiesced, and after another grueling three-day ride on the rails, she was back in Manhattan. Work began immediately on *Love 'em and Leave 'em*—a film project put together by her old Film Guild cronies, the *American Venus* team of director Frank Tuttle (fresh from *Kid Boots* with Clara Bow) and screenwriter Townsend Martin. Tuttle and Martin had secured for Louise her juiciest part yet.

Love 'em and Leave 'em was the last and best movie Louise would make in New York. Paramount called it "a character comedy of the glib children of Manhattan," and *Variety* observed that "the title alone should be enough for the box office."[21] Based on the long-running play by John V. A. Weaver and George Abbott, it was a witty, fast-paced tale of two sisters, department-store salesgirls with opposite personalities. Cast as the "good" sister Mame was Evelyn Brent, whose boyfriend Lawrence Gray is compromised early on by kid sister Janie—a sly little flirt played by Louise.

"LOVE 'EM AND LEAVE 'EM"

PRESENTED BY
ADOLPH ZUKOR
JESSE L. LASKY

with EVELYN BRENT
LAWRENCE GRAY
LOUISE BROOKS
A *FRANK TUTTLE* PRODUCTION
A Paramount Picture

TRAMP! TRAMP! TRAMP!
the boys are marching.
   Learn a lesson in up-to-the-minute
loving from this sweet screen charmer.
   "No wedding *belles* for me," sings
our hero. But he changes his mind in
a hurry, and it's
LAUGHS! LAUGHS! LAUGHS!

RIALTO

Based on the play by John Van Alstyne
Weaver and George Abbott
Adaptation and screen play by Townsend
Martin.

Janie doesn't love 'em and leave 'em so much as she vamps 'em and pets 'em—"modern youth's system of loving," said the ads. Paramount described Janie as "like the crazy flapper you fell for last year."[22]

The sisters live together in a typical West Side hive of a boardinghouse. Among the O. Henry–type boarders is sleazy Lem Woodruff, a racetrack crook who fancies himself a ladykiller. Played by Osgood Perkins, he is introduced by one of Townsend Martin's clever titles as "the man who spent six months curing halitosis, only to find out he was unpopular anyway."

When Brent makes the mistake of leaving town, Brooks moves in on Gray. Upon her return, Brent catches them in the act (of kissing) and decides that her sister's cynical philosophy, "love 'em and leave 'em," shall henceforth become her own.

The plot is thickened by Louise's theft of the "Employees' Welfare League" money, but in the end tough-as-nails Brent makes good for both her traitorous sister and her two-timing boyfriend.

The contrast between the sisters is fascinating: dour, steadfast, self-sacrificing Brent versus cute, fickle, unscrupulous Brooks. Louise is an irresistible bad seed from her opening wake-up scene in bed—hair sexily rumpled, nightgown strap slipping over her shoulder. She continues to

Louise in bed for her opening scene in Love 'em and Leave 'em *(1926)*

Louise and Osgood Perkins in Love 'em and Leave 'em *(1926)*

captivate in every scene, whether lolling gorgeously in Central Park or furtively dipping into a goldfish bowl for some instant, convenient tears.

"This Miss Brooks is beginning to act," said *Photoplay*. And it was true, though she would typically denigrate her own efforts. Louise was beginning to intuit a difference between the acting in films made on the East Coast and those made on the West Coast. Her performance in *Love 'em and Leave 'em* is an example of how little a 1926 film actress needed to know—and how much.

"Frank Tuttle was a master of easy, perfectly timed comedy which demanded that kind of acting rather than the wildly energetic style popular in Hollywood," Louise later wrote in an essay for the Toronto Film Society. "An intelligent man, he never interfered with two classes of actors— great actors and nonactors. In the first class was Osgood Perkins, who needed no direction. In the second class was I, who, had he directed me to be funny, would have become an immobilized personality. Lawrence Gray belonged in the ham class. He required gobbets of comic appreciation to keep him functioning." [23]

Usually, she told Kevin Brownlow, "when I played comedy with directors like Mal St. Clair or Eddie Sutherland we would laugh about a scene before we shot it. Not with Frank Tuttle. I didn't even know I was playing a comedy until I saw [*Love 'em and Leave 'em*] with an audience [in the late 1950s]. I played it perfectly straight, and that's the way he wanted it."

Osgood Perkins had the most profound impact on Louise. He was a tall, homely man with an elastic body and a face capable of a thousand transformations. Even when the face was perfectly motionless, his eyes could express the slightest nuance of thought or feeling.* Louise pronounced him simply "the best actor I ever worked with."

"You know what makes an actor great to work with?" she once asked. "Timing. You don't have to feel anything. It's like dancing with a perfect dancing partner. Osgood Perkins would give you a line so that you would react perfectly. It was timing—because emotion means nothing."

Through Perkins she discovered that in film acting, even more than stage acting, there is no necessary correspondence between emotion and the *appearance* of emotion. Thirty-four years later for Alfred Hitchcock, Perkins's son Anthony would demonstrate the suggestive power of a single twitch in *Psycho*: What he actually feels is irrelevant; the emotion we perceive or imagine beneath his facial tics is what matters.

---

* Perkins had just scored a Broadway stage hit in a George S. Kaufman–Marc Connelly comedy, *Beggar on Horseback*. He was a close friend of Tuttle's from joint theatrical activities during their Ivy League days (Tuttle at Yale, Perkins at Harvard), and he had served in a variety of capacities for Film Guild projects—as general assistant, second cameraman, and, most notably, screen villain extraordinaire in *The Cradle Busters* and *Grit*.

And then there was the mysterious case of Evelyn Brent, making her much-heralded Paramount debut in this film. She and Louise were a study in contrasts not only in the characters they were playing, but in their approaches to acting. Two days before shooting on *Love 'em and Leave 'em* began in September 1926, Louise went to the Astoria wardrobe department to talk with its chief, Herman Smith:

> [Smith] was a big, kind man trying to look fierce while he gave me hell for having had my shopgirl costumes custom-made at Milgrim's, when in came Evelyn Brent who had just arrived in New York from Hollywood. For a shocking half hour I sat amazed watching Herman and her assemble a complete wardrobe for the film in which she played the lead, and my sister. From a pipe stand of worn size 12's they selected her clothes; and from the shoe shelves they selected my castoff slippers (we wore the same size 4). All this time her manner was warm and friendly, but I found later she was like a Baked Alaska—very cold inside.
>
> Evelyn was entering the picture with a big studio build-up and trumpets of enthusiasm usually reserved for top stars. And I had never heard of her. A girl in publicity told me that Evelyn had been in pictures for ten years, most recently in a series of girl crook pictures. . . . Ben Schulberg had recently become head of Paramount's West Coast studio on the strength of his having its newest star, Clara Bow, under personal contract. And Schulberg's assistant was Bernie Fineman, husband of Evelyn Brent.[24]

Brent didn't fit any of Louise's categories of great, ham, or nonactors. She had spent years in stage and film, four of them in London, with moderate success and mixed reviews.

"Evelyn was indeed in a class by herself," said Louise. "After all these years the possibility of stardom put her in an emotional state of anxiety, the result of which being that she acted with an intensity better suited to Mata Hari before the firing squad than a shopgirl in a comedy."

After much careful handling and coaxing, Tuttle was finally succeeding at relaxing her performance, said Louise, "when Schulberg wired from the coast that he had seen the rushes and he wanted Evelyn photographed to look much younger [she was twenty-eight; Brooks was nineteen]. And more beautiful. As a consequence, all her carefully nurtured ease and confidence withered away during the rest of the filming, while the makeup man and our camera man, George Webber, worked on the lines under her eyes and around her mouth."

The film overall was as well received as Louise herself. "At the end of the film she goes to the store's masquerade ball *sans* skirt and does a Charleston," wrote one critic. "Who could ask for anything more?"

Nobody asked for more, but Paramount provided more. *Love 'em and Leave 'em* also featured the first screen performance of the "Black Bottom," a shimmy dance that for a time eclipsed the Charleston and would soon be immortalized by Joan Crawford.

Nobody noticed a slip in the production code that allowed Louise's naughty, amoral character to be rewarded in the end. And nobody seemed to mind the humiliation of the hero, identified at his first entrance as "a 90-million-to-one shot for President of the United States," whose pants fall down when he rushes to his girl's rescue and who is finally elevated to his goal of window dresser (from assistant window dresser) only by taking credit for the superior skills of Evelyn Brent.

The film and the story were successful enough for Paramount to re-make the picture just three years later as a talkie, *The Saturday Night Kid*, with Clara Bow as Mame and Jean Arthur stealing *that* version as Janie.*

Louise Brooks turned twenty on November 14, and as 1926 drew to a close, she might well have contemplated her string of film achievements with satisfaction. But she did not. She contemplated, instead, the unreal sensation of being Mrs. Edward Sutherland and the unpleasant prospect of leaving New York.

Eddie and Hollywood beckoned.

So did the critics. As the reviews of *Love 'em and Leave 'em* trickled in, it was clear that the competition between Louise and Evelyn Brent was *nolo contendere*.

"The cast has three featured members—Evelyn Brent, Lawrence Gray and Louise Brooks," said *Variety* on December 8, 1926. "It would have been just as well to have reversed the order of the names, for Louise Brooks, playing an entirely unsympathetic role . . . , runs away with the picture."

Louise stole the show, and Paramount knew it. The deck had been stacked heavily in her favor from the start: She had the best role, the flapper look, the dancer's grace, the favoritism of the front office, the bulk of the publicity, and now the cream of the critical reactions.

For all practical purposes, she had it made.

---

* The two versions of *Love 'em and Leave 'em* prompted William K. Everson to speculate: "Evelyn Brent is such an unattractive heroine and Lawrence Gray such a dunderheaded hero, that one's sympathy would fall to Louise even if she weren't such a charmer. . . . What a marvelously exciting film it would have been had Clara and Louise been co-starred in the original version. . . . One just can't blame the hero for straying from Evelyn to Louise—but having to choose between Clara and Louise would really provide food for thought."

*Louise greeted by Eddie Sutherland's friend Monte Brice
upon her arrival in Hollywood, January 6, 1927*

8 · Paramount Importance

*Louise Brooks, film actress who holds the world's record for interrupted hon-
eymooning, arrived in Los Angeles yesterday. And it was the same old story.
She was minus her husband, Edward Sutherland, director, to whom she was
married about four months ago.*

—LOS ANGELES TIMES, January 7, 1927

IT WAS by now something of a public joke, this business of the Sutherlands' postponed honeymoon. In half a year of marriage, the newlyweds
had spent less than ten days together. She was making this move to Hollywood, despite reservations, for a combination of professional and personal reasons; perhaps she and Eddie might at least get a closer look at
each other.

But Eddie pulled his usual disappearing act and wasn't there to greet
her when she stepped off the train. He was busy shooting, and it couldn't
be helped. He did arrange, however, for a welcoming committee consisting of Monte Brice, producer Charles Christie, and Tom Geraghty, author of the screenplay for *Army Game*. And the obligatory photographers
and reporters were there.

"We both have spent all our salaries on telephone calls since we were
married," Louise told one of them. "We have had a long-distance telephone honeymoon."[1]

Now that she was more or less in captivity, Paramount was stepping up
its publicity on the young beauty in preparation for its plans to keep her
very busy with movie-making. In 1927, she would make four films—most
of them frothy little entertainments with come-on titles such as *Evening
Clothes* and *Rolled Stockings*. Would she really be as hot a property as the
Love 'em and Leave 'em reviews suggested? And could she be sufficiently
tamed to fit into life on Paramount's Hollywood lot?

If there was any doubt in 1926 about where the American movie capital
was located, it was cleared up in 1927. Paramount was closing down

the Astoria studios—a process completed by July—and concentrating all its production energies at the gigantic new million-dollar facility on Marathon Street in Hollywood. There, on twenty-six acres, West Coast studio chief B. P. Schulberg ruled over an assembly line that churned out its goods at a rate of a movie a week. Brooksie was now joining this organization in a much more formal way, for Paramount was the studio taking the biggest gamble on youth, and she was proving to be the most popular of those Junior Stars about whom Jesse Lasky had recently rhapsodized in *Photoplay*.

"As for the youngsters we are training for stardom," Lasky said, "we have come to regard our lot as a movie university. We are very hopeful for Dick Arlen, Charles ["Buddy"] Rogers, Louise Brooks and James Hall, our junior stars. Our Paramount school people, whom I admit did not look too interesting at commencement, are developing rapidly in Hollywood."[2]

He added the ominous but realistic note that "as in any other university, the majority will fail and one or two will make good . . . And we are frankly experimenting in all lines."

Lasky put his cameras where his mouth was: Nearly a third of Paramount's sixty films of 1927 featured one or more of the "juniors," who often seemed to be getting more promotion than the "senior" stars. In fact, the total number of Paramount contract players was really rather small—about two dozen—and they were used almost interchangeably in the studio's many "programmers."

There was a dark underside, however: For reasons more coincidental than pathological, most of the major scandals that rocked Hollywood in the twenties involved Paramount performers, some of them quite young. The Fatty Arbuckle rape-murder case of 1921 was the first, and seamiest. It was followed six months later by the murder of director William Desmond Taylor in which Mabel Normand and Mary Miles Minter were implicated. That was succeeded by the drug-related death of Paramount matinee idol Wallace Reid in 1923 and other minor disasters, culminating in the heroin addiction and death of actress Jeanne Eagels in 1929.

Despite such setbacks, Paramount stuck with its young folks, keeping a closer eye on them internally and suffering the external scrutiny of Will Hays with resignation. By the time Louise arrived on its Hollywood lot, Paramount was confident that the worst of the scandals had blown over and that the best of the young performers were in high-gear productivity.

Clara Bow certainly was. She had made fourteen films in 1925, eight in 1926, and would star in six in 1927. Currently, she was at work on her biggest blockbuster, *It*. Studio chief Schulberg had a variety of personal and professional reasons to savor her success and her importance to the studio. Paramount was willing to indulge Clara and, for that matter, most of the rest of its players, as long as they produced, retained their popularity, kept the shock value of their private lives to a minimum, and remained alive. The studio at this point in its history seems characterized by the sweet smell of success and the joie de vivre of its performers and executives alike.

Certainly there were opportunities galore for Louise, who, in addition to her assured roles, was talked about for many others, including one for which she seemed to be a natural: *Glorifying the American Girl*, a Ziegfeld film extravaganza. Louise was announced as Ruth Taylor's co-star, but in the end neither of them participated. Paramount cast changes were frequent, but the production delays plaguing this *Girl* were not. It wasn't completed and released until 1929—to bad reviews, despite the can't-lose cast of Eddie Cantor, Rudy Vallee, Helen Morgan, and Irving Berlin, with cameos by New York mayor Jimmy Walker, Texas Guinan, Adolph Zukor, Ring Lardner, Florenz Ziegfeld—and banker Otto Kahn.

Otto Kahn and the rest of Paramount's Wall Street backers could afford a little light-hearted involvement in what was, after all, their own profitable enterprise. Seventy-seven million movie tickets were sold every week, and as the fortunes of the film moguls multiplied, so did their appetites.[3] Louise had opportunities to observe those appetites—ego, sexual, and financial—and the maneuvers they inspired.

"You must not forget," she wrote her brother Theo much later, "as a pussy cat, I sat under many a king's chair (Otto Kahn of Kuhn, Loeb, Nick Schenck, the Phipps, Bill Paley) and absorbed many a business deal that I am only now evaluating."[4]

One of the most controversial series of deals concerned the ambitious William Fox. By 1927, his $200 million Fox Film Corporation was well consolidated in all three phases—production, leasing, and exhibition— and turning out fifty films a year. But Fox wanted more. He bought more theaters, plus a 45 percent interest in Gaumont-British, England's biggest film company; he next moved to purchase a controlling interest in Loew's Inc., MGM's parent company. The other studios were now alarmed— especially MGM and Paramount—and "what to do about Fox" was a frequent topic in the presence of the purring pussycat.

"When Nick Schenck decided to rob Bill Fox of the Fox Film Co., I would hear him lay out his plans in Blumie's apartment," said Louise, "after which Blumie would get Fox to borrow another million from the banks to buy theatres."[5]

Louise's use of the word "rob" was an exaggeration. Schenck and Fox were later even aligned with each other, for a while, in the MGM takeover attempt. But Fox's enormous theater-buying spree did, in fact, end in disaster, and if money men like Schenck and A. C. Blumenthal weren't culpable they were at least catalytic in Fox's demise.

For the moment, though, it was the smaller operators who were being forced out, and among the lawsuits flying in all directions was a big one filed by First National against Paramount. The Federal Trade Commission launched an antitrust investigation, which Paramount fought long and hard but lost. On July 9, 1927, in the FTC's famous "look before you book" ruling, the studio was cited for conspiracy to monopolize the industry through the acquisition of theaters (368 of them) in which it excluded the films of its competitors.[6] Paramount was ordered to stop this and the companion practice of "block-booking" by which exhibitors were forced to take a group of mediocre films if they wished to obtain the two or three really good ones.

Independents and small producers hailed the decision—they could now look before they booked—and the big studios shrugged their collective shoulders and paid lip service to compliance.

Several months earlier, as Paramount's legal department was embarking on its last antitrust defense, Louise Brooks was embarking on her first made-in-Hollywood film and on what might be called the Intensified Cheesecake phase of her film career.

If none of her first seven movies was exactly "emancipated," two of the last three had been legitimate stage vehicles requiring comic and dramatic abilities far beyond the average bathing beauty. Most novice film lovelies had to serve a longer cheesecake apprenticeship than Louise, who was now a bit spoiled by the relatively intelligent roles that had come her way through the good offices of Walter Wanger, among others, in New York.

But no love was lost between Wanger in the New York office and Schulberg on the West Coast. "Whenever Schulberg came to New York, they used to put his picture up on the wall," recalls Paramount assistant director Arthur Jacobson, "and take it down as soon as he left."[7] Now that Louise resided in Hollywood, she was far removed from her champions, whose influence at Paramount was waning anyhow. What resulted was a decline in the quality of her roles and an increase in the superficial "love interest" parts usually assigned to players of her age and rank.

On the other hand, it was a dense year of solid movie-making with barely a breather between films. The first of Louise's 1927 roles was a character who had an inspired name—Fox Trot—but little to do in the new Adolphe Menjou comedy, *Evening Clothes*. This was a Menjou vehicle, pure and simple, designed to showcase his suavity, insouciance, and other attributes best rendered in French, culminating in *pathétique*. The dapper Menjou, said Paramount, was "a man who can suggest heartbreak behind a mask of indifference." His current picture would be aimed at the same fans who made successes out of his last three performances in *A Social Celebrity*, *The Ace of Cads*, and *The Sorrows of Satan*.

If Menjou was an ersatz Frenchman, this time around he at least had a real Gallic scenario—*The Man in Evening Clothes* by André Picard and Yves Mirande. Menjou is Lucien, a wealthy farmer whose marriage to Germaine (Virginia Valli) proves disastrous because she can't stand his rustic interests. True gentleman that he is, he allows her to return to Paris and then heads there himself in order to become the kind of sophisticated *boulevardier* Germaine can love. He spends wildly and tries out his new romantic skills on pretty little Fox Trot, whom he steals from Noah Beery. Lucien is soon down to just a set of evening clothes, but his pathos guarantees that Virginia Valli will have a change of heart in the end.

This was fairly weak material, and Paramount knew it. Not even the publicists could work up much enthusiasm—their faint praise of Valli being that she "is extremely easy to look at." Nor did they quite know what to say about Noah Beery. Unlike brother Wallace, Noah's shift from villain to light comedian was not smoothly accomplished, or often repeated.*

For Louise, the most surprising aspect of the picture was the decision to scrap her trademark—the black bob—in favor of the old-fashioned style of "frizzing," which, it was thought, more befitted a frequenter of Parisian nightclubs. Paramount was a bit worried about the change and felt obliged to comment on it.

"The 'Louise Brooks' bob has been abandoned, temporarily at least, by its creator," said a studio release. "Louise Brooks, whose striking hair dress caused flapper fans to name the style after her, has had her head transformed into a hysteria of curls for her role in *Evening Clothes*."[8]

It was also much commented upon by the critics, fixated as they always were on the most minute changes in the appearance of female players. "Miss Brooks, with a change in her eyebrows and curly hair, is stunning," said the *New York Times*.[9]

"Luther Reed didn't want to direct," Louise told Kevin Brownlow. "He had been a writer. And in those days, a writer was not much more than a means of getting a film down on paper so that it could be budgeted, cast and got into production."[10] Reed made three more films in 1927, four early talkies, and disappeared completely from films after 1930.

But *Evening Clothes* garnered much new publicity for Louise, whose portrait by artist Carl Van Buskirk appeared on the cover of *Photoplay*'s

---

* Noah Beery had always played blood-curdling heavies, most notably the brutal Sergeant Lejaune in *Beau Geste* (1926) a year before. But he had recently been well reviewed as the comic character Hell's Bells in a theatrical road show about Teddy Roosevelt, *The Rough Riders*. Some film historians, including James Card, maintain that—contrary to popular belief—Wallace and Noah Beery were *not* brothers.

*The unsuccessful switch from bob to friz, with Noah Beery,
in a scene from* Evening Clothes *(1927)*

Louise makes the cover of Photoplay,
February 1927

February 1927 issue, two days after *Evening Clothes* shooting was completed. In the same issue, "Cal York" (the magazine's East/West Coast pseudonymical columnist) raved:

> Mal St. Clair says she is one of the finest actresses he has ever seen. Adolphe Menjou agrees. So does the whole Paramount organization to whom she is under contract. The public is now chiming in. All this she has accomplished in a year's time.
>
> It is hard to write about Louise Brooks. You have to see her. . . . The beauty, the personality she had on stage intensified ten fold when she got on the screen. . . .
>
> If there is any more poised young person in the whole movie world than Louise, she is yet to be found. Mere questions to Louise about where she came from, and why, elicit no response and no interest from her. Evidently she regards herself as strong drink. You can either take her, or you can let her alone. Louise is not in the business of selling herself. . . .

To the petulance was added a touch of mystery.

What better complement to *Evening Clothes* than *Rolled Stockings*, the next film in which Louise appeared and the first in which the entire cast consisted of Paramount's Junior Stars.

"Positions unique in the history of motion pictures are occupied by four young players in Paramount's new picture, *Rolled Stockings*," trumpeted the studio. "They are known as Paramount Junior Stars of 1927. This means they have special contracts giving them opportunities never before provided for youngsters of reaching fame in a period of twelve months." Their contracts were awarded after Jesse Lasky and B. P. Schulberg had personally "studied their work and compared it with hundreds of others. This was done to provide new screen favorites for the public."[11]

It was implied that there were only four of them—James Hall, Louise Brooks, Richard Arlen, and Nancy Phillips—and that *Rolled Stockings* was their joint debut. In fact, the Junior Stars were an on-again, off-again phenomenon and hardly so formal. There had been no public mention of Louise's "junior" status in either *The Show-Off* or *Love 'em and Leave 'em*. Three of the four—Brooks, Hall, and Arlen—had been making films for several years. And Hall, twenty-seven, and Arlen, twenty-nine, were not exactly youngsters anymore. Only Nancy Phillips was truly a newcomer —and hers was a shooting star; she made but one or two more movies and then disappeared.

This quartet was billed as Juniors because *Stockings* was being aimed at the college set and advertised as "Paramount's successor to its initial youth picture, *Fascinating Youth*." Audiences were promised "girls, jazz, undergraduate tricks and a thrilling boat race" plus other slices of "life among

"C" is for Colfax College, whose variety show stars Louise in Rolled Stockings (1927). Photo by E. R. Richee

the youngsters." The hype didn't stop there. The Juniors were "entitled to preferred consideration in the casting of roles for which they are suited. All their work is studied by directors. In return, all are compelled to keep in physical trim. Their weight cannot increase five pounds. They have to be able to dance, swim, fence and ride well whenever called upon to do so, and they have to avoid all possibilities of gossip or scandal."

All of which was in *every* Paramount player's contract.

The picture itself was much ado about little. Its slight story concerns two brothers, Hall and Arlen, who both fall in love with Louise at college.

Arlen is losing the battle for Louise's affections, and he turns in frustration to Phillips, a young blonde who welcomes his advances. The frat-dance scene in which Phillips enraptures Arlen with her "jazzy" dance was a source of much amusement to the rest of the cast. When Arlen took her hand before the dance was to begin, he found that it was trembling severely.

"What's the matter—nervous?" he asked.

"No," she lied. "I'm cold."

This was summer in southern California. But it was possible, since Phillips was wearing only a skimpy evening dress. So the ever-gallant Arlen fetched her an electric heater. Someone else came up with a steamer rug. James Hall brought her some coffee. And Louise—whose sympathy for someone afraid to do a simple Charleston was suspicious—thoughtfully draped the heavy steamer rug around her shoulders. Soon perspiring profusely and close to fainting, Phillips had to be hauled off to her dressing room to have her make-up redone—and to be cooled down. [12]

Louise was scornful of actors who couldn't or wouldn't do something a director asked. She compared them, disparagingly, with the tough-as-nails lens man on this picture:

> I never knew a camera man who ever complained about standing on his feet all day, or all night. And while actors, directors and stunt men were making a production out of their bravery, the camera man would take the greatest risks with nothing more than a laconic remark to the boy who brought him his camera refill. . . .Victor Milner, who photographed *Rolled Stockings*, never said hello, goodbye, or kiss my ass to actors. [13]

Eventually in the film, Phillips dances, Arlen takes the bait, and she agrees to go with him to a "roadhouse"—the 1920s version of the No-Tell Motel. Arlen will be kicked off the crew if he's discovered there. In a plot twist filched from Fitzgerald's *This Side of Paradise*, Hall rushes to the den of iniquity and allows himself to be caught and expelled in place of his brother. Arlen can stay and take part in the climactic rowing race—in real life, the annual contest between the universities of Washington and California, filmed at Berkeley.

Director Richard Rosson, who came from a filmmaking family, was a busy man for Paramount in 1927.* "He'd been Allan Dwan's assistant [on such films as the Douglas Fairbanks *Robin Hood*]," Louise later told Kevin Brownlow, "and it was an assistant that he wanted to be. During *Rolled*

* Richard Rosson's (1894–1953) older brother, Arthur (1889–1960), was also a Paramount director and his younger brother, Hal (1895–), a successful photographer, who had just shot *Evening Clothes*. Dick Rosson had recently directed Gloria Swanson in *Fine Manners* (1926), her farewell film as the reigning queen of Paramount after eight years and twenty-seven movies. He directed four more films for Paramount before settling into a successful career in the less pressure-filled post of second unit director.

Stockings he sat sweating, with a trembling script. There wasn't enough Bromo-Seltzer to float him out of his chair."[14] Even so, *Rolled Stockings* seemed to have "It"—the stars, the title, and certainly the aggressive advertising campaign: "We swear to the youth, the whole youth and nothing but the youth of *Rolled Stockings!*" said the ads, which featured some of the best-drawn graphics of any Paramount films of the twenties. But the promotion turned out to be better than the film, or the reviews, and no one connected with it ever achieved much in the way of stardom—except for Richard Arlen.

Arlen was in good shape for his two-mile rowing scenes in *Rolled Stockings*. He had recently gone through seventy-five hours of pilot's training —everything from dogfights to tailspins—for that "road show of the air," *Wings*. While Louise and the Juniors were making B pictures on the back lots, the front lots were occupied with the biggest project in Paramount's history: a grand spectacle of World War I flying aces, featuring Clara Bow, Buddy Rogers, and Richard Arlen—and stupendous aerial photography.

Wings combined the latest in cinematic and aerodynamic technology, and William Wellman, himself a distinguished wartime pilot, was the perfect choice to direct. He would cross paths with Arlen again—and with Louise—the following year, and he was destined for greater fame with *Public Enemy* (1931), *A Star Is Born* (1937), *Beau Geste* (1939), and *The Ox-Bow Incident* (1943). But his success all hinged on the success of *Wings*, which hinged on his ability to harness his planes and his cast into serving a weepy, mediocre script. When it finally played the circuit in late 1927 and early 1928, it was a techno-spectacular hit—breathtaking on 100-foot screens, with full orchestra, synchronized military sound effects, and blue and red tinting of battle sequences.

A new organization calling itself the Academy of Motion Picture Arts and Sciences had just been formed to upgrade the prestige of the profession, and there was private agreement that *Wings* would get its first best-picture award.

Given her feisty personality, another silly comedy under another mediocre director might have finished Louise Brooks in motion pictures. But *The City Gone Wild*, directed by James Cruze, came just in the nick of time. It was a gangster melodrama, inspired by the great success five months earlier of Paramount's first big crime picture, *Underworld*. That film, based on Chicago newspaperman Ben Hecht's observation of Prohibition hoodlums, starred George Bancroft and the tense Evelyn Brent— this time perfectly cast and directed by Josef von Sternberg, master of narrative flow and atmospheric lighting.

The gangster genre (dating back at least to D. W. Griffith's *The Musketeers of Pig Alley* in 1912) was already much beloved. And so Paramount ordered up another action-packed, hard-driving script by Charles Furthman (Hecht's co-author on *Underworld*) and Furthman's brother Jules, the whole production to be supervised by Lucien Hubbard, fresh from enormous success in the same capacity on *Wings*.

The City Gone Wild opens during a great crime wave with the rival gangs of Gunner Gallagher and Lefty Schroeder engaged in a desperate machine-gun battle. The district attorney and the town's top criminal lawyer (Thomas Meighan) are engaged in a friendlier rivalry for Nada Winthrop, daughter of capitalist Luther Winthrop. The D.A. is bumped off after discovering that Luther is the brains behind the syndicate, whereupon Meighan sets out to bring the killers to justice. But he is soon tangled in a web of mobster blackmail. Louise Brooks as "the gunman's honey," Snuggles Joy, threatens to tell all—which would result in the "social crucifixion" of innocent Nada, the girl Meighan loves. Louise ends up double-crossing her own man and, fearing no social crucifixion of her own, tells the whole story for the price of a tombstone on Gunner's grave.

Louise's was just a supporting role, but a juicy one, and she was intrigued to be co-starring with her uncle-in-law, Meighan, and to observe him at close range.* Meighan was the respectable leading-man "type" left over from the 'teens. Off-camera, he was much the same, and it was unanimously agreed that there was no nicer guy in movies. Just how nice Meighan was to his new niece-in-law has not been recorded, though Louise never said anything bad about him, which was rare for her. Most likely after she studied him on the set, the discovery of his goodness bored her.

Of much greater interest to her was James Cruze, one of the most talented of Hollywood directors.† Cruze had recently filmed Meighan's first picture on the West Coast, *We're All Gamblers*, which was successful enough for Paramount to give him greater directorial billing, linking his name with the star's in the promotion: "What a combination! You saw how they hit in *We're All Gamblers*! Here they are—back again—Meighan and Cruze!"[15] Louise's recollection of Cruze on the set was a typically negative but amusing one:

> He was fascinating. The strangest man I ever knew. . . . He almost never talked and he drank from morning till night. He was the man who invented the drink called The Well-digger's Ass. It was a pick-me-up. You asked, "Why

---

* Meighan's first screen hit had been a crook melodrama, *The Miracle Man*, which he convinced Adolph Zukor to make in 1919. It made stars out of Lon Chaney and Betty Compson (who soon became Mrs. James Cruze), and it led Meighan to rival Wallace Reid as Paramount's leading male star of the pre-Valentino era.
† Cruze directed such innovative Paramount hits as *The Covered Wagon*, a "big-scale" western that did much to establish the form, as well as *Merton of the Movies* (1924), *The Pony Express* (1925), and *Old Ironsides* (1926). This last employed a wide-screen device called Magnascope, which, at climactic moments, greatly enlarged the image to the full height and width of the proscenium.

is it called The Well-digger's Ass?" "Well," [he'd say], "you know how cold the well-digger's ass gets!"

Jimmie hardly talked at all during the making of a film, and I never read a script. We were on location in Griffith Park. He said, "Okay, Louise, get in the car."

I got in the car.

"Well, get in the driver's seat!"

I got in the driver's seat.

"Now, drive off, fast—as fast as you can go."

"I can't drive," I said.

"You can't drive!" He glared at me. He absolutely glared at me. "You can't *drive*??"

It was as if I'd said that I couldn't talk. He was infuriated. It had never occurred to him to ask me if I could drive, or to tell me what the scene was about. So that day's shooting was all loused up, because they had to get a double. . . .

But Cruze was a wonderful man. I don't know what ruined him. I don't think it was booze, because it never changed him at all.

He was a very fast director, but that doesn't mean he didn't take his pictures seriously.[16]

Cruze was one of the first directors to give intelligent treatment to the gangster genre. Many assume that the early sound crime films of James Cagney and Edward G. Robinson were the ground-breakers. But at a time when bootlegging gangs were a real public menace, just beginning to "organize" their crime, films like The City Gone Wild paved the way for those of the thirties—heavy on the action and the moral—by defining their structure.

Like all the rest of Louise Brooks's 1927 films, The City Gone Wild is lost.

The great popularity of Wings was not hurt by an event preceding its release by only a few weeks: Charles Lindbergh's solo transatlantic flight of May 20–21, 1927. As if planes and flying were not already the rage, Lindbergh's achievement, and the national and international celebrations that followed it, were perfectly timed to the advantage of Paramount's picture.

Paramount felt that perhaps the aviation craze might help some smaller pictures, too—such as Now We're in the Air, the latest Beery-Hatton comedy designed to complete their armed-service cycle and duplicate the success of Behind the Front and We're in the Navy Now. If the popularity of those vehicles was decreasing, which it was, Paramount wasn't ready to recognize the fact. "Wallace Beery and Raymond Hatton are the greatest stars comedy has ever produced," the studio insisted. Their films always

Wallace Beery, Louise, and Raymond Hatton in a scene from
Now We're in the Air *(1927)*

appealed to "intelligent people as well as [those who] move their lips while reading." [17]

At the crest of their adulation, aviators were certainly ripe for kidding. But even dressed up with Louise Brooks, *Now We're in the Air* never quite got airborne. This episode was written by Monte Brice, the co-inventor of *Behind the Front* and *We're in the Navy Now*. Keene Thompson also worked on the script, much of which was filmed at a Venice, California, amusement pier. Beery and Hatton, employed by the eccentric Scottish lord Abercrombie McTavish, soon find themselves in France, where they are pressed into air service. The boob aviators drift across the battle lines in a balloon and fall into the hands of the Germans. The plot is dominated by mistaken identities, extending even to Louise, who plays twin sisters— Griselle and Grisette—one a fiercely loyal Frenchwoman, the other a patriotic German lass. Beery falls in love with the German twin, and Hatton with the French one, but they can't tell the girls apart. And so it goes. . . .

Though Eddie Sutherland would have been offended to hear it said, directing a Beery-Hatton comedy wasn't the world's greatest challenge.

This time, the job went to Frank Strayer, a Paramount staff director of routine silents between 1926 and 1928, whose claim to fame would not come until talkies when he directed an even dozen of Penny Singleton's *Blondie* comedies. Louise compared Strayer to Luther Reed, noting that "most of the time, they stood silent behind the camera, letting the cameraman, Menjou, or Beery handle the direction. [They] suffered such fear and agony, being forced to direct, that I dreaded going on the set to watch their struggles."[18]

But she had a great fondness for the prolific Wallace Beery, who made thirty-eight feature films between 1920 and the end of 1927 alone. Missouri-born Beery and Kansas-bred Brooks got along famously. Louise particularly enjoyed Beery's skills at hog calling. He won a "sooey" contest as a farmboy and never let the talent get rusty, especially when challenged by the roar of plane engines on the set of *Now We're in the Air*.

In one of the film's more dangerous gags, the "aeronuts" Beery and Hatton wander into a propeller-testing room where six wind machines tear off their Scottish Highlander duds and blow the duo fifty feet out of the shot and into a safety net.

"This is pie for me," said Wally after the first take, preparing to do it again. "I was raised in Missouri where the wind really blows. Kansas cyclones have had lots of publicity, but those cyclones just use Kansas to get a running start. When they reach Missouri, they're really traveling. I stepped out of our cyclone cellar once, thinking the storm was over. The wind tossed me so far that it was four days before I got home. I wasn't hurt a bit because one of our strawstacks traveled along right under me and stopped when I did."[19]

Louise was amused by Beery's tall tales and macabre sense of humor. In one scene, Beery and Hatton had to stand before a wall to await their firing-squad execution. Suddenly Beery complained to director Strayer about the fact that the wall was blank.

"I think it ought to have a little writing on it," he said, whereupon the prop man gave him a piece of chalk. He took it and, around the bullet holes from previous cinematic executions, wrote, "Good shot," "X marks the spot," and other appropriate graffiti. Louise observed that only the masculine sense of humor would appreciate Beery's touch; Strayer liked the idea and kept it in.

Other than the camaraderie with Beery, there wasn't much to hold Louise's interest in making *Now We're in the Air*—nor the audience's interest in viewing it. "When the end of this film finally came at the Rialto," said the New Year's Eve review in the *New York Times*, "a youthful pair of hands alone applauded. The child who did so was obviously quite a few months over eight."

Louise's sole function was to add beauty to a slapstick farce. But there was one important consolation prize. Things were loose on the set, Louise was more sure of herself in general, and her twin roles in *Now We're in the Air* were so undemanding that she felt free to engage in her favorite pastime, reading, which helped kill the endless waiting time between takes and setups. And it was the activity at which she was always happiest.

Almost half a century later, for her book *Lulu in Hollywood*, she labeled a publicity photo of herself and Keene Thompson—the only one she ever posed herself—as her favorite. It shows her lolling with a book, languid and gorgeous, next to the writer, and it reveals more than just the literary aspirations, or affectations, of a starlet-cum-snob. It suggests the way she habitually escaped whatever unpleasant reality was at hand. It also reflects her alienation from most of the people who surrounded Mr. and Mrs. Edward Sutherland of Laurel Canyon. Of the highly circumscribed intellectual scene in Hollywood, Louise later told John Kobal:

> My [New York] friends were all literary people. And in Hollywood there were no literary people. I went to Hollywood and no one read books. I went to the bookstore on Hollywood Boulevard—it's still there—and these Hollywood people would go in and say, "I have a bookshelf, and I want to buy enough books to fill up the shelves." And that was all the reading they did. Don't forget, most people in pictures, they were waitresses, they were very low-class people.[20]

Shades of the stuck-up dancer in *George White's Scandals*—the girl who despised the others for thinking Ravel and Debussy were a bicycle act. Shades of a chip on the shoulder and a superiority complex that guaranteed her unhappiness in Hollywood.

One night Louise met two other literary types who were unhappy in Hollywood. In the lobby of the Ambassador Hotel in Los Angeles, shortly after her arrival in January 1927, she was introduced to Scott and Zelda Fitzgerald.

"They were sitting close together on a sofa, like a comedy team," she told Kenneth Tynan, "and the first thing that struck me was how *small* they were. I had come to see the genius writer, but what dominated the room was the blazing intelligence of Zelda's profile. It shocked me. It was the profile of a witch."[21]

On the home front, Louise was still in a kind of mourning for New York. Her "attitude" toward Hollywood was mirrored in private life and complicated by her always volatile family relationships. She and her mother did not keep up close communications after Louise's departure for New York in 1922. "Myra was restless, ill at ease," her friend Tot Strickler later wrote Louise. "Her high standard of living did not calm her. She longed to

*June and Louise Brooks in Holly-
wood, 1927; photo by E. R. Richee*

travel."[22] The sketchy facts are these: Myra Brooks left Wichita around 1925 and made her way to Chicago. There was a man involved, though Myra always maintained their relationship was platonic. She became associate editor of a Chicago publication called *The Golden Rule*, for which she wrote a weekly column. She also wrote a book called *Health, Beauty and Psychology*, no copy of which survives.

Louise, like the rest of the family in Wichita, was largely out of touch with Myra during this period. But if she wondered whether her mother knew about her career, she had only to pick up a copy of the movie magazines that specialized in coaxing or buying stories from the parents of the stars.

"My Louise," by Myra Brooks, appeared in one such journal—*Screenland*—and raised the wrath, or at least the eyebrow, of Louise.

"When our friends begin to hold forth on the wonderful and unusual promise of their marvelous offspring, we are prone to cast a furtive eye about for the nearest exit," wrote Myra, who could turn a phrase when she wanted. The authenticity of her article was evidenced by the fact that two snapshots of Louise as a child were supplied for it, plus a photo of Myra herself. Also evidenced, loud and clear, is Myra's preoccupation with herself. So rhapsodic is her description of a mother's joy at a daughter's fame that she never even mentions Louise's name until the very bottom of the first page; the article is far more revealing of Myra than of Louise.

"As I sit in a theater watching with absorbed interest one of my daughter's pictures," writes Myra, "my mind runs back over the space of such a few years to the little town in Kansas where Louise was born, with its, what would seem to us now, unspeakably ugly little movie house and its frightfully mediocre pictures then quite the last word in entertainment. . .

"I am told when Louise's pictures are shown at the leading theatre in Wichita, an electric sign flashes out the announcement, 'Wichita's own Louise Brooks.' This is of course lovely, but it always affords me a quiet inner smile and I wonder if anybody remembers what an enormous amount of wire-pulling her mother had to do to get her little picture in the paper for the first time. . . .

"If some day Louise can take a big role and play it with the breadth of sweetness and understanding, the artistry of technique exhibited by Norma Talmadge, for instance, in *Camille*, I shall feel that she has not only justified her own existence and the many good gifts life has laid at her feet, but her mother's ambition as well." [23]

Wichita Eagle society-page announcement of Myra Brooks lecture, ca. 1924

GIVES REVIEW

Mrs. Myra Brooks Will Give a Book Review at the Benefit Mexican Chocolate to Be Sponsored By the Girl Reserve Committee of The Y. W. C. A. In the Home of Will Morris, 136 South Pershing Avenue, Tuesday. Proceeds to Go to the Camp Fund

REED

Myra sounds simultaneously grateful and annoyed that the attention she's getting is reflected from the spotlights on Louise. But Louise's celebrity, coupled with her own writing, was sufficient to gain her a spot on the Redpath Chautauqua circuit, traveling throughout the Great Lakes region to lecture on her favorite subjects, health and beauty. It was amusing, she told the family later, to see herself on a handbill on one side of a pole, and a movie poster of Louise on the other.

"Mother of Screen Favorite Louise Brooks Visits here," read the society-page headline of the Benton Harbor (Michigan) *News-Palladium* in midsummer 1927. Myra was preceded on the bill by singer-dancer Ellenor Cook and pianist Eugenia Folliard, who did an elaborate program of Russian, Ukrainian, and Czechoslovakian folk songs, in full costume.

The *News-Palladium* reporter, much charmed, described Mrs. Brooks as "slim, svelte, gracious" and so youthful and beautiful as to be "often mistaken for her artist-child."

Myra's standard lecture began with her credo: "I believe in the modern girl, in the modern dress, and that if we would eat one-third less and read more we would be a rejuvenated race today." She told her all-female audience that the secret to a young-looking figure was the waist. "Be she 16 or 60, if her figure preserves the waist line any woman can laugh to scorn as to her true age."

To such conventional beauty tips, Mrs. Brooks added an enlightened defense of "the flapper type," criticism of whom was "the latest indoor sport."

"You cannot hope to stem this tide in the youth surging about us," she told the Michiganders, "so the best and only remedy is to meet the boys and girls in their search for TRUTH." She welcomed the entrance of women into the business world and defended the revolution in their dress and she even came out in defense of cosmetics: "Women of today have a right to use every artifice, in reason and with harmony, to make themselves attractive."

Many years later, Myra's sister Eva Calvert helped Louise solve the mystery of her mother's wanderings at this time:

> Your dad was a wonderful person in many ways but not much for social activities, and the little things which delight the hearts of we females never entered his mind. For instance, while Myra was [recovering from an operation], every so often she would remark that it would be fun being cared for and looked after and receiving flowers—with a hopeful gleam in her eye when Leonard was near. I waited most of the first day before asking him if he had thought of flowers. He gave me that "Hmm, flowers? Oh, yes—no, I hadn't thought of it. Would you mind calling for me? Ask them to send a dozen *carnations*." Holy mackerel and catnip tea, carnations! I saw to it that

she received red roses at least every second or third day. She was pleased as punch and never as long as she lived knew that I had had any part in it. Because of a secret yearning for romance she pooh-poohed anything that verged on romance for Pattie or me [her sisters]. I think when she finally had her fling there was very little of the physical but she lapped up all the little attentions and the excitement of going places and doing things with interesting companions. . . .

What made her like she was, in my opinion—first, her never having had a chance to live a life of her own before marriage. She had never enjoyed freedom so she'd be blasted if she'd give freedom to others. She wanted power; to pull a string and have each person dance to her tune. Had she used subtle methods she may have succeeded. Live and let live was completely foreign to her nature. Now I have no idea what happened after I left your home, but what she did she had to do. She had always yearned for freedom, she had to have it or burst. Too bad June and Theo were not older at the time. The "straw that broke the camel's back" was having her grandchildren [by her eldest son Martin] landed on her. . . . Almost every woman who has raised a family dreams of the day when she can take time to think of other things other than the needs of her family. [24]

That document did not reach Louise until 1952, eight years after her mother's death. When it did, it came as an enormous revelation: that by sending her off to Denishawn at the age of fifteen in 1922, Myra Brooks wasn't so much giving Louise her freedom as getting rid of her so that Myra would be a step closer to her *own* liberation. Myra's "fling" had also amounted to the abandonment of her younger son and daughter—as Louise, too, had abandoned them. Louise was left with even deeper ambivalence toward her mother, especially now that she was capitalizing on Louise's fame.*

Myra's continued absence from Wichita was instrumental in Louise's decision to bring her sister to Hollywood. For the first time, she had a large and comfortable home, and she was ready to share it. June was a gangly twelve-year-old in 1927. Her prettiness did not rival Louise's stunning beauty, but her sweet disposition made her beloved of all who met her. There was always a certain pathos to the motherless "Junie." For her brothers, Martin and Theodore, Louise had not felt any great yearning up to this point. But June she missed and romanticized in a way that was close to surrogate motherhood.

Sister June arrived in Los Angeles on June 18, 1927, just four days before Louise began shooting for *The City Gone Wild*. The child had never been out of Kansas, and she spent a dazzling two months in the

---

*The "capitalizing" was hardly very lucrative, and Louise soon began sending her mother a $75 monthly allowance.

middle of the film world, visiting the studio, being entertained, and posing for a gorgeous formal portrait, taken by E. R. Richee, with her famous sister. June loved the Sutherlands' four dogs, the swimming pool, and most of all her sister's undivided attention during their long, rough-and-tumble explorations into the Laurel Canyon woods.

"Louise was a second mother to me," June recalls fondly today, "but she hated the publicity. Once when we were on the train, it stopped and people who recognized her wanted to get her picture and her autograph, and she just pulled down the shade."

Louise wanted not so much to take care of her sister as to cultivate her artistic potential and provide her with the education that Louise had had to acquire on her own. "She and Eddie decided to send me to France for 'finishing,' " says June. Louise chose the Château de Groslay, an exclusive boarding school outside Paris, and Eddie—always accommodating when it came to transatlantic trips—volunteered to accompany the girl there. An ocean liner would be just the place to work on his next W. C. Fields picture (*Tillie's Punctured Romance*), whose writer, Monte Brice, and producer, Al Christie, he invited to go along. Louise would have liked to go too, but she couldn't leave Hollywood.

On August 12, Brooks began filming *Now We're in the Air*, and the very next day, Eddie and June left for Europe—by way of Wichita, where June said goodbye to her father and brothers, and where Eddie had his first and last taste of Louise's Kansas roots. He enjoyed meeting his father-in-law, Leonard—later doing some impressions of the cowtown lawyer for an appreciative audience, his wife.

After a few days in New York (and a trip to Coney Island for June), the Sutherland party boarded the *Ile de France*, where Eddie quickly took charge of shipboard entertainment. Paderewski was on board, and Eddie persuaded him to give a recital. On August 22, he threw a big party for June's thirteenth birthday and filled her stateroom with stuffed animals. In France, he deposited her safely at the beautiful Château de Groslay, once a residence of Napoleon's Josephine. June would spend the next three years there.

Eddie and Monte, after a lively weekend in Paris, hopped the next ship home—but their creative labors were not exactly intense. Sutherland and Brice "could work harder and play harder than any other two men in Hollywood," wrote a reporter in *Collier's*. "They'd disappear for days at a time and unhappy producers never knew whether they were locked up in a hotel room writing a script they had promised or hanging on a bar in a New York night club."[25] Eddie's own account confirms this assessment.

"On the way over I said to Monte, 'Gee, I think Al [Christie] is kind of worried because we haven't come up with anything,' " Eddie recalled. "This was in 1927, when money was confetti and everybody was young, and the gala-galas were going on and it was really a wing-ding. So we got up promptly at 5 in the afternoon, as we'd stayed up till 8 or 9 in the morning, but between 5 and 7 when we met Christie, we dreamed up a story. We came down and Al said, 'How've you boys been all day?' We said, 'We've been working.' You could see his eyes light up at that. He said, 'Did you get anything?'

"I said, 'Yeah, I think this might be pretty good. Listen to this.' So we told him this story we'd dreamed up, I'd tell some and Monte would tell some, and at the end he said, 'Boys, I owe you an apology. I thought that you were loafing and I was getting worried to death. I didn't want to say anything. But now I'm just in heaven, this is great. . . . Let's relax, let's have some wine.' He never drank, but he saw that we did.

"So then work ceased. Nothing happened at all until we got back to New York." [26] Eddie hopped a train to Los Angeles the next day and was home by September 15. The mission with June was accomplished.

The mission of *Tillie's Punctured Romance* was much more problematic, given Eddie's approach to directing. He had a full theoretical understanding of how film comedy worked, based on his close-range observation of the three greatest screen comedians, Buster Keaton, Harold Lloyd, and Charles Chaplin. Eddie was awash in comic concepts, but he seemed unable to settle on any one or to amalgamate them all into an original style of his own. Nor were his organizational skills the greatest, as suggested by his severest critic, Louise, who had an inside view of the making of *Tillie's Punctured Romance*:

> *Tillie* . . . was the worst mess of filmmaking that I have ever observed. Even Fields, who ordinarily had nothing to do with a picture until shooting began, came to our house one afternoon to look into the story, which was told to him by Eddie and the writer, Monte Brice. I remember Bill sitting quietly, listening and drinking martinis from Eddie's two-quart cocktail shaker; I remember him teasing me by dropping my fragile Venetian wine-glasses and catching them just before they hit the floor; but I can't remember one word he said about the idiotic plot contrived for the remake of the film. [27]

Tillie in its original 1914 Mack Sennett version had been a big box-office hit, thanks to Chaplin and Mabel Normand. Remakes were common, but times had changed, and neither the title nor the story had much value in 1927 when Paramount, which bought all the Sennett properties, sold the rights and the services of Fields and Sutherland to Al and Charlie Christie.*

"Temporary insanity brought on by the prospect of losing their com-

---

*The popular Christie Comedies had been movie-house staples since 1916. But the big studios' acquisition of theater chains gradually resulted in the elimination of two-reelers.

pany, their studio, and their Beverly Hills mansion induced the Christies to produce the six-reel *Tillie* with a Paramount release," said Louise. "It was filmed with groans, previewed with moans, shown in a few theaters, and then buried in the vaults. Poor old *Tillie* had not a single mourner."

That disaster was due largely to the breakdown of its ancient vehicle. Louise laid the blame for the equally disastrous results of Eddie's previous directorial effort, another Beery and Hatton pairing, squarely at Sutherland's feet. "He was having a great deal of trouble on *Fireman, Save My Child*," Louise told Kevin Brownlow:

> He'd done no preparation. If he wasn't inspired on the set, he would think of a reason why he couldn't shoot. He would say, "That building is too close to the camera. Now move that building back and we'll shoot tomorrow." And he would come waltzing home at two in the afternoon. Then he and Monte Brice, the writer, would get together with Tom Geraghty, another writer. They'd come into the living room and Eddie would say, "Now, shall we have a few cocktails?" He had a cocktail shaker to hold about a gallon. He'd shake up the martinis and they'd start their story conference. In about an hour, they'd be telling stories about the time they did this or Jack Pickford did that and Tommy Meighan did the other. By that time, I'd be off upstairs, reading a book. But I would hear the conversation getting farther and farther away from what they were going to do the next day. We would wind up all going to a supper club.
>
> The next morning, Eddie would get up and put on a red tie. He used to say, "When I put on a red tie, people don't notice that my eyes look like two Venetian sunsets." Then the building would have to be moved again. [28]

She later amended that story to Eddie's moving "a *whole street*" where the fire was to take place. "This is true and much funnier than moving just a building back and forth. Eddie laughed later, but at the time, his motives seemed to him to be absolutely reasonable and the only thing to do." [29]

In late September 1927, there was a rare period when Louise and Eddie actually cohabited for a full fortnight. She was finally free, for the first time all year, from her own film commitments. But she couldn't stand to be idle for long, and, out of boredom or caprice, she suddenly went back to New York again. When she returned to Hollywood on November 3, the Paramount publicity office put out a story that was widely published around the country. It was uncomfortably ironic, considering where she'd just been:

> Will Louise Brooks and Eddie Sutherland at last get to take a belated honeymoon after 16 months of married life? Or will the exigencies of the movies continue to keep this happily married pair of film celebrities separated by thousands of miles?

These questions demanded answers this morning when Louise came home to Eddie from New York. The petite film star stepped off the Santa Fe Chief, was greeted by her director-husband and was driven to their Laurel Canyon home. Their fifth separation since they were married in New York, July 21, 1926, was ended.

"Will they get to stay together?" is the question filmdom asks. . . .

"It was necessary to close Paramount's Long Island studio to get us together long enough to find a home in Hollywood," Louise said today in recounting their transcontinental romance. "But even that didn't work."

Two months ago Sutherland went to Europe with the Christie brothers, comedy producers, and Monte Brice, scenarist, to plan the Paramount-Christie comedy, *Tillie's Punctured Romance*, which he is now directing. He returned to find his wife packed for a business and clothes-buying trip to New York, from which she returned today.

Louise and Eddie are together at last.

Perhaps Louise did buy some clothes and conduct some business in Manhattan. But she spent much of her time in that familiar suite at the Ambassador Hotel with her old friends Peggy Fears and A. C. Blumenthal. This time, however, there was no Charlie Chaplin to make a quartet.

There was George Preston Marshall instead.

"Mr. and Mrs. Brooks" was Louise's caption for this New York City portrait of late 1927. Photo by Chamberlain & Lyman Brown Theatrical Agency

9 · Every Little Breeze

I wanted a new type. I hired Louise Brooks because she's very sure of herself, she's very analytical, she's very feminine—but she's damn good and sure she's going to do what she wants to do. I could use her today [1967]. She was way ahead of her time. And she's a rebel. I like her, you know. I like rebels. I like people you can look at and you remember who they are.

—HOWARD HAWKS

L OUISE BROOKS was now legal. She was twenty-one, her career was six, and both had a momentum that seemed unstoppable. Her fast-paced professional life was matched by the peripatetic way she conducted her private affairs, burning up the rails that shuttled her and her volatile emotions between Los Angeles and New York.

On her last visit to Manhattan, she sat for a photo portrait that was both lovely and ironic. She had acquired an elegant white-haired terrier, and she brought him to the studio. The resulting double profile she labeled "Mr. and Mrs. Brooks—strangely resembling the pose assumed on the slightest provocation by two of our most famous married stars." The joke was on Alfred Lunt and Lynn Fontanne—but also, rather darkly, on Eddie. Not only was "Mr. Brooks" a dog; he was also a cuckold.

Sutherland's absences had not made Louise's heart fonder. Instead they inculcated first resentment and then indifference. Knowing Eddie was gone and living it up wherever he might be left her the time and the justification to pursue an intense romantic involvement of her own.

George Preston Marshall—often comically confused with George Catlett Marshall (1880–1959), the secretary of state, and plain George Marshall (1891–1975), the director—had been worshipping Louise from afar ever since their torrid first meeting backstage at the Washington preview of *Louie the 14th* in February 1925.* She hadn't seen him again until now, the autumn of 1927, when she was feeling most neglected and irritated by Eddie's travel larks.

The irritation should have been mitigated by the fact that on his latest European junket he at least did her the favor of escorting her sister to boarding school. But perhaps it wouldn't have mattered even if Eddie had stayed home; Sutherland was always far from her mind when George Marshall was around.

Marshall was the antithesis of Eddie. He was big, gruff, decisive, charismatic, and dictatorial. One friend called him "a man who had a thousand ideas a day, two of which were workable.[1]" He was also an amateur vaudevillian and frustrated performer. His trademark was a full-length raccoon coat. At twenty-two, he inherited a small laundry from his father, and from that humble beginning grew the enormously profitable Palace Laundry chain, with fifty-seven outlets ("The Famous Fifty") in and around Washington, D.C.

"Running this dull business occupied very little of his time and a very small part of his brilliant mind," said Louise. "He was passionately fond of the theater and films, and would have become an inspired producer if he had not found professional football a greater challenge."[2]

Louise could never resist making laundry jokes at Marshall's expense. Her pet name for him was "Wet Wash," which he never appreciated, in contrast to his pet name for her—"Scrubbie"—which Louise adopted for a while. He called her Scrubbie, she said, because he had "cleaned her up." But in the course of their long relationship, lasting off and on until the late 1930s, he also bullied her into a series of dubious personal and professional decisions.

For now, though, Louise was happy to be wined, dined, and dominated by this forceful personality, whose love of pleasure dovetailed with her own desire to escape Hollywood as often as possible. The Laundry Baron, in turn, was equally happy to dally and be seen with one of the most beautiful women in America—a woman now in the successful transition from Toast of Broadway to Toast of Hollywood. Their relationship was cemented during that "clothes-buying" trip to New York City, but the tryst had not been calculated. The rekindling of their romance was so accidental as to qualify for the "kismet" label.

"I went to New York to visit Peggy Fears and her husband, A. C.

---

* It was difficult to keep all the George Marshalls straight. When Kevin Brownlow mistook the director for Louise's lover, she replied sharply, on August 11, 1969: "Nobody reads, nobody listens. In three articles and numerous conversations and letters I have said that *my George Marshall was the owner of the professional football team*, the Washington Redskins. I have never seen or met the director, George Marshall. I wonder what dunce has stunned him by telling him about his love affair with me?"

Blumenthal," said Louise. "One night, Peggy, Blumie, Joe Schenck and I went to Harry Richman's nightclub. Feeling bored, I excused myself to go to the ladies' room and went upstairs to the bar, where Helen Morgan was singing on top of her piano. George Marshall . . . was there and bought me a drink. It was the most fateful encounter of my life."[3]

Marshall was instantly enchanted, as he had been two years earlier, by her beauty and intelligence—and now by her much-increased celebrity, a quality on which he placed an ominous importance. During the next passionate month with her at the Ambassador, he could see that every little breeze was whispering Louise Brooks. One example was a recent *Motion Picture Classic* article called "Brooksy: A Credit to Kansas," by Carol Johnston, which both lionized and glamorized the pouty little star:

> At first she was an impudent, sleek-black-bobbed, boyish figure—a little like a gypsy, and a lot like a brownie—swinging into the Algonquin, always without a hat. People used to ask each other who she was. Her name didn't mean anything to me. But she did. Somehow you remembered her. One day I heard someone call her "Brooksy." It seemed to suit her swagger. . . .
>
> Today Louise Brooks is a household word—as famous as Lydia Pinkham, and a lot more fun. . . . My first closeup of her was taken at 10 o'clock in the morning. I had an appointment, but the phone girl refused to wake her up—nothing doing, ringing Miss Brooks so early. So I walked in on her. There she was, the famous Broadway beauty—sleeping soundly, sleek black head pillowed on her arm. She looked all of ten. It was a bright, sunny morning, too. But she wasn't ten: she's 20. She told me so, and I believe her. She could easily get away with a paltry 18 for a couple more years yet. No makeup—she didn't even powder her nose. And she ordered hot chocolate and French pastry, and ate the pastry and drank all the chocolate. So this was the belle of Broadway!
>
> Instead of pink ruffled pillows, ostrich-feather negligee and brocaded slippers—prim tailored pajamas and a plain bathrobe and little red leather mules. Books all about, and a huge stuffed dog. A toast of the town—and she looked like your neighbor's youngest and freshest daughter, only with shapelier legs. New to the movies, but not disconcerted. Her straight black brows would have elevated had you suggested then that the movies could hold much of interest or excitement for her.[4]

But now the piece started to fall apart. Johnston thought she caught a glimpse of "the real 'Brooksy' behind the wisecracking kid with the defiant grin and the swagger." The glimpse consisted of "her new smile since she became Mrs. Edward Sutherland. There's a certain sweetness added to the exciting equipment that made this little girl such a credit to Kansas." The reporter was pleased to witness this "transformation of Broadway belle into devoted little wife, and it is one transformation that took."

Mrs. Sutherland on the grand staircase of her Laurel Canyon home, 1928

And it was one conclusion that sent the occupants of her Ambassador suite into howls of laughter, even as Louise was packing her bags to rush back to Los Angeles for her next movie.

Life at 366 Laurel Canyon Drive had its ups and downs. The transition from capricious flapper archetype to Mrs. Edward Sutherland was not easy for Louise—nor, God knows, for Eddie. Their brief, tempestuous marriage was characterized by two sets of complaints: on Eddie's part, that Louise was violent and abusive and rampantly unfaithful; on Louise's part, that she was abandoned and bored.

But while their marriage lasted, the one thing they both liked to do was entertain, and with two large incomes—Eddie was then making $2,000 a week—it was a luxury and a life-style which they could indulge. This was Louise's one real year of belonging to the Hollywood establishment. Only Beluga caviar, at $14 a pound, was acceptable at the Sutherlands' 1927–1928 parties, which were frequented by the *crème de la crème*. Two of

Louise's favorites were MGM's boy-wonder producer Irving Thalberg and actress Norma Shearer. They could usually be found billing and cooing off in a corner, Thalberg in a chair while Shearer "always sat adoringly at his feet," Louise recalled.

Thanks to Louise, the atmosphere at the Sutherlands' was often tense but never dull. On one memorable occasion, she took it into her head to throw a dinner party with a literary theme.

"We gave marvelous parties—really marvelous," Louise told John Kobal years later:

> [Eddie] was the most wonderful host. We gave that famous, famous party. It was written up everywhere. It was my idea—all books. All the place cards at dinner were books. In front of Irving Thalberg's place I put Dreiser's *Genius*. That's just before he married Norma Shearer.* So in front of Norma's place I put [Enid Bagnold's] *Serena Blandish: The Difficulty of Getting Married*—she'd been trying and trying, and Irving's mother wanted him to marry a nice Jewish girl. It was so funny because Irving walked right in and saw *Genius* and sat right down. But Norma kept on walking around. She wouldn't sit down in front of *The Difficulty of Getting Married*. Not at all! And there was that writer at MGM [Laurence Stallings] who had lost a leg in the war, and I gave him [Alain René Lesage's] *The Devil on Two Sticks*.[5]

Depending on how flattered or insulted they were by her book–place card choices, not all the guests found Louise's humor hilarious. And she never told Kobal which books sat in front of her and Eddie's chairs.

Among the most Runyonesque of the Sutherlands' guests at that time was Wilson Mizner. Though not to be found in a single film encyclopedia, he was a colorful racketeer-raconteur who sold ideas, jokes, gags, and lies to producers and directors, thereby gaining a witty reputation and entrée into the important parlors of the film capital. Nobody quite knew what Mizner did for the studios, but whatever it was, they kept paying him for it. Eddie had known him via Chaplin during *The Gold Rush* and thought he was funny. Louise was alternately amused and annoyed by him, since he had a tendency to steal *other* people's good lines, including those of her friend Grant Clarke, one of the cleverest of the late-silent title writers.†

She captured them both in "Why I Will Never Write My Memoirs," written half a century later for *Focus on Film*:

---

* September 29, 1927.

† Among Grant Clarke's originals was the gangster phrase, "to take him for a ride," written for an early talkie, *The Lights of New York*. Louise loved another of his lines, uttered at a table with Texas Guinan and Brooks at Guinan's El Fay club when Clarke was unable to get a waiter's attention: "Reach down in your heart, Texas, and get me a piece of cracked ice." Back in 1909, Mizner adopted Clarke, then just an eighteen-year-old lyric writer "who kept Wilson in fresh jokes until [Clarke's] death from an overdose of morphine in Hollywood in 1931," according to Louise.

Although [Clarke's] bitter witticisms are woven into film history—'Holly-wood is like floating through a sewer in a glass-bottomed boat'—they are always attributed to Wilson Mizner, the famous raconteur whose gold rush stories, manufactured after five years of larceny in the Klondike, were longer than an Arctic night. He held his audience with the combination of his great physical size and the command of an army general. At my house in 1927, during a repeat of the story of a miner who froze to death while stooping to tie his shoelace and had to be buried in a bass drum, as I rose to mix a cocktail, Wilson circled me with his arm and set me upon his knee, im-prisoned till the end of the story.

Louise's ultimate verdict was harsh. It was tied in with her views on the distortion of film history by means of "the Hollywood literary code, which requires authors and publishers to substitute the names of celebrities for the lesser known names of the originators of jokes and anecdotes."

"Wilson Mizner was a creator of nothing in films," she said. "[But] the obliterated Grant Clarke wrote songs still heard in films. He wrote songs for Al Jolson in *The Jazz Singer,* and for Fanny Brice he wrote her greatest song, 'Second Hand Rose.' "

Louise was extremely fond of both Clarke and Fanny Brice. It was probably through Clarke that she was invited to Brice's home on sev-eral occasions, always wandering off and losing herself in the singer-comedienne's English Tudor library. Unlike those other actors who ordered books for decoration, Brice bought books in order to read them.

"Every volume I took down from the shelves had Fanny's comments written in the margins," she said.

Louise was welcomed just about everywhere. Unlike Eddie, she was no politician, but for a while she made an effort to accompany him to important social gatherings. She watched him operate masterfully and glimpsed the inner workings of the movie business. But she also did some social calling of her own, during which she met Hollywood's two greatest stars.

"I stopped by their house [Paramount writer Benjamin 'Barney' Glazer and his wife, Alice] one day and Garbo was there," Louise recounted. "And also, she would play tennis up at John Gilbert's house."[6] Louise and John Gilbert became good friends; Louise and Garbo had a strange inter-lude, of which more later.

Everybody was curious about Brooksie.

Louise's face was everywhere. She had already appeared on the covers of the two most influential movie magazines, *Photoplay* and *Motion Picture Classic.* And now *Vanity Fair* was stalking her, too, in the person of

*Artist John H. Striebel: self-portrait with Louise as the
model for his long-running cartoon strip "Dixie Dugan,"
based on J. P. McEvoy's* Show Girl

Edward Steichen, America's leading portrait photographer. In 1927 and 1928, she sat for a who's who of Hollywood portrait photographers: E. R. Richee, George Hurrell, James Doolittle, George Hommel, and Otto Dyar among them.

Their striking results [see "A Portrait Gallery"] did more to secure Louise's position in American iconography than all of her movies. For while the films were rather few and rarely played for long, the photos were reproduced in hundreds of magazines and newspapers eager for a fresh face out of Hollywood. Far more people saw Louise's photographs than her movies. And what they were seeing was indelible.

The Hollywood portrait photographer's task, says John Kobal, "was not merely to photograph established celebrities, of which the movies had introduced a rich source, but to help create something entirely new, something that had never existed before—a breed of celebrity with the extraordinary power to transfix."[7] There was a business and product here, and on that crass level, the photographers were simply discovering and marketing "glamour."

But for millions, the impact of the images went mysteriously deeper. In Louise's case, so stunning was the face that it generated a spin-off which outlasted the subject's own fame by a quarter of a century.

This was Dixie Dugan, the chic and sassy comic-strip heroine of John H. Striebel. Her first incarnation was as a character created in 1927 by the ever-popular comedy writer J. P. McEvoy, in a magazine serial called *Show Girl*. Having watched Brooksie in the *Follies*, McEvoy was one of her ardent admirers, once describing her as looking "like a naughty altar boy." He modeled Dixie on Louise in a plot that revolved around a couple of gold-digging Broadway chorus girls and owed an obvious debt to Anita Loos's 1925 best-seller, *Gentlemen Prefer Blondes*.

The authorized (by Louise) story of Dixie's genesis, however, has it that Joseph Medill Patterson, founder-publisher of the New York *Daily News*, handed Striebel a photo of Louise Brooks from *The American Venus* and told him to draw Dixie exactly like her for the comic strip version. The Dixie Dugan stories became so popular that McEvoy assembled them in a book, also called *Show Girl*, which Simon and Schuster published in July 1928.

Dixie dances her way into and out of all the big Broadway shows and twists her hapless boyfriend—Denny from Flatbush—around her little finger, usually via telegram.

> May 15, Denny to Dixie: "GEORGE MORTON WRITES HE SAW YOU DANCING IN JOLLITY NIGHT CLUB (STOP) WHAT DOES THIS MEAN (STOP) WIRE AND TELL ME HE IS A LIAR"
> May 16, Dixie to Denny: "WHAT OF IT?"
> May 16, Denny to Dixie: "I DONT WANT YOU DANCING IN A NIGHT CLUB I WONT HAVE IT"
> May 17, Denny to Dixie: "WHY DONT YOU ANSWER MY WIRE? (STOP) I DEMAND A REPLY IMMEDIATELY"
> May 18, Dixie to Denny: "WHERES THE FIRE?"

Dixie is also being courted by Jack Milton, a stockbroker and manufacturer of "Maid-to-Wear Underthings," who has a little accident and ends up in the hospital. They exchange notes:

> "Dear Miss Dugan: The first thing I saw when I came to were the roses you sent me. Only seeing you could have made me happier. Jack Milton."

> "Dear Mr. Milton: I thought you were dying or I wouldn't have sent them. Throw them out if they annoy you. Dixie Dugan."

The tone here has a certain Brooksian ring. And there was an underlying flapper philosophy that was never better articulated, in or out of Fitzgerald, as when Dixie finally lays down the law to Milton:

> I think you're swell and I like you a lot and I don't know whether you're a bear down in Wall Street or a bull and I wouldn't know if you told me, but Dixie Preferred is one stock you can't manipulate on a margin and the mere fact that I may bite you on the ear once in a while when I'm ginny and think you're someone else must not confuse a sound business man like you. I'm just an old fashioned fool of a girl, big boy, and when I sell out it will be for value received payable in advance in the gold bonds of matrimony. Blue Skies is not an investment—it's only a song by Irving Berlin.

It didn't take long for the movie people to snap up *Show Girl* for filming, and Louise was the obvious choice for Dixie. But the obvious choices were often not made. Louise never played the part—never even tested for it—possibly because the rights were bought by First National instead of Paramount. Though she had been "rented" to First National just a year or so earlier for *Just Another Blonde*, no one tried to obtain her for *Show Girl*—despite the fact that it was directed by Al Santell, who knew and worked with Louise on *Blonde*. Santell ended up casting Alice White, a perky young thing who had just entered films and was briefly touted as a rival of Clara Bow. But her Dixie and Santell's *Show Girl* (1928) both got tepid reviews.*

Louise seems to have been undisturbed by the loss of the part that was made for her; she would in fact lose it again, in another genre, the following year. Meanwhile, she was losing another, even more important role.

Anita Loos's *Gentlemen Prefer Blondes* was an immediate best-seller from the moment it appeared in November 1925. By February of 1926, it was already in its seventh printing, and the whole country knew its irreverent tale of gold-digging cuties among the millionaire set. The theatrical version wowed Broadway audiences in 1926, as the musical version would wow them in 1949. For now, in 1926, the studios were jockeying for position to get the film rights. When Paramount finally won out and assigned the directing duties to Malcolm St. Clair, Louise looked certain to be in line for a major role.

---

* The "Dixie Dugan" strip ran in hundreds of newspapers until 1962, by which time Dixie had turned into an airline stewardess. The Ziegfeld stage production of *Show Girl* in 1929, with Ruby Keeler, Eddie Foy, Jr., and music by George Gershwin, was one of Ziegfeld's few failures, closing after 111 performances. McEvoy wrote a sequel called *Showgirl in Hollywood*, serialized in the U.S. and England from 1929 to 1930 and illustrated with Striebel drawings based on Brooks. The final installment showed Dixie's triumphant marriage, in the presence of Mayor Jimmy Walker, to a millionaire polo player much like the one Louise soon married in real life. The sequel was also made into a movie, in 1930—again with Alice White, directed by Mervyn LeRoy this time. Louise never received a single fee or royalty for serving as the model for a character that made tens of millions of dollars over six decades.

Louise's eyes put the lie to the title; photo by James Doolittle

Speculation to that effect seemed confirmed by a publicity photo released in the fall of 1926 while Louise was making *Just Another Blonde*—a movie whose very title was an attempt to capitalize on the Loos original. That James Doolittle photo, which ran in the December 1926 *Motion Picture Magazine*, showed Louise staring out impishly over her copy of *Gentlemen Prefer Blondes*, with the caption: " 'Is that so?' ask the challenging eyes of Louise Brooks. She has just been chosen as the vamping baby sister whom the gentlemen very frankly prefer—in *Love 'em and Leave 'em*."

Loos, Paramount, and St. Clair took their time finalizing the cast for what they were certain would be the comedy blockbuster of the year. In mid-1927 they got around to screen-testing Louise, but by all accounts, including Louise's, it went badly.

"I stunk," she said simply. She had turned in a natural, straight-faced performance in *Love 'em and Leave 'em*, she said, "because Frank Tuttle, the director, was smart not to tell me that I was supposed to be funny. Because then I would have gotten self-conscious and thought about myself. Anita Loos threw me out of *Gentlemen Prefer Blondes* for this reason. I was supposed to play Dorothy, and she saw my test. I was supposed to be a funny comedienne. I was still my usual self."

Louise was more amused than insulted when she finally bumped into Loos and got the verdict: "I said, 'Oh, Anita, did you run my test? What did you think of it?' She looked up and said: 'Louise, if I ever write a part for a cigar-store Indian, you will get it.' "

Paramount continued to delay, and word of Louise's casting kept being leaked and then denied. In November 1927, *Theatre* magazine carried Louise's picture with a blurb noting that "she was going to be Dorothy in *Gentlemen Prefer Blondes* screen version, but was suddenly booked for something else." James Quirk of *Photoplay*, one of Louise's biggest fans, was sufficiently annoyed to give her another full-page photograph—her fifth, a ravishing E. R. Richee photo—with a sour-grapes caption that seemed to settle the issue once and for all: "Louise Brooks will *not* play the role of Dorothy in *Gentlemen Prefer Blondes* although she was announced, with acclamation, for that luscious part. The producers have discovered that she 'isn't the type.' However, there is just a chance that they might be afraid that the experienced Louise would steal the picture from the less certain Ruth Taylor in the blonde role."

Quirk, as usual, had the inside track. But there were more flip-flops, and as late as April 1928, *Theatre* magazine published a striking full-page photo of Louise with a long caption that concluded: "During the 1928 season Miss Brooks will be co-featured with Ruth Taylor, the 'Lorelei' of *Gentlemen Prefer Blondes*, in a series of gold-digger comedies."

Ruth Taylor indeed got to play Lorelei, but the role of the worldly wise Dorothy was given to none other than—Alice White. It was neither the first nor the last time this would happen. Newspaper and magazine accounts of Brooks's career are littered with announcements of parts she never played, of minds changed, of plans gone awry. This one was especially disappointing. But so was the 1928 film version of *Gentlemen Prefer Blondes*. St. Clair's mugging-clowning approach to comedy was too broad to render Loos's subtler, contemporary humor. And, of course, most of her witty dialogue was lost through the absence of sound.

"Mal met his doom in *Gentlemen Prefer Blondes*," Louise told Kevin Brownlow. "The overhead was terrific. The publicity was terrific. It *had* to be the comedy hit of the year. Mal couldn't fake it anymore. He loused it up. . . . The producers were pretty wary of him. . . . Its failure ended Hollywood's regard for him and his own faith in himself. It was his spiritual death."[8]

It would be exactly a quarter of a century before *Gentlemen Prefer Blondes* got the comic treatment it required, from director Howard Hawks, with the aid of Marilyn Monroe as Lorelei and Jane Russell as Dorothy.

· · ·

Louise's name continued to crop up frequently in the movie magazines and newspapers. An illustrative item concerning her married life, for example, ran in *Photoplay* in late 1927, shortly after a minor earthquake frightened Hollywood:

> Lest you read this story and cry "Breach of good taste to have written it down," it must be explained that Eddie Sutherland and Louise Brooks are man and wife.
>
> It happened that the other morning toward dawn, Hollywood was shaken severely by two sharp earthquakes. Our hero, Mr. Sutherland, was awakened promptly afterwards, not by the shock, but, strangely, by an awfully stiff wallop to the jaw. He opened his eyes in pain.
>
> Miss Brooks was sitting up in bed next to him. She was in a fury and had evidently dealt the jolt to Eddie.
>
> "And if you do that again," she was saying, "I'll move right out to a hotel."
>
> Business of a man apologizing for an earthquake followed. [9]

The earth was moving, all right, but it was unrelated to the Sutherlands' sex life. Eddie's friends, who leaked the tale, thought it a hilarious example of Louise's pugnacity: She could wake up just as ready for a fight as before she went to sleep.

Meanwhile, *Picturegoer* magazine, England's rough equivalent to *Photoplay*, was running full-page montages of Brooks, asking, "Who is this monotony-killer—this provocative eyeful?" and observing that she had so much "It" that "no other star can outshine her in the same picture."

In the States, Louise was now beginning to take some commercial advertising offers. She loaned her elegance to Lux Toilet Soap, allowing Otto Dyar to photograph her in her Laurel Canyon bathroom; the photo ran above her endorsement: "It gives my skin the lovely satin smoothness 'studio skin' must have." In *Photoplay*, Meeker Hand Bags boasted that "Louise Brooks carries one," with a Richee photo of her doing just that. She modeled cute little sailor outfits ("Nautical but Nice") in the *Motion Picture Classic* of October 1928 and posed in some $300 wedding gowns. In the November 1928 *Photoplay* it was engagement rings: "When mother was a girl, any ring would do, just so long as it was a solitaire diamond. And now nothing less than a rock will convince a girl that she ought to give up freelancing and sign a contract. This little sermon in stones is posed by Louise Brooks who—believe it or not—never wears jewelry herself."

Despite her restlessness with movie-making, Louise's roles were getting better, and the one at hand was the most crucial of her career thus far, though she would not know why until the following year. The picture was

Louise was one of the first to model the new "pajama suit" of 1927, this one with a chartreuse velvet jacket and jade green satin pants. Photo by E. R. Richee

A *Girl in Every Port,* directed by Howard Hawks, and it was being made for Fox, not Paramount.

Once again, Louise was on loan, and once again, Paramount was turning a hefty profit. Her salary, in November of 1927, had just risen from $250 to $500 per week. Fox was now renting her for three times that amount, $1,500. Another measure of her growing importance was the proviso that no player's name except Victor McLaglen's could precede Louise's or appear in as large type. Her part, in fact, was not large, but it was memorable.

The story, written by Hawks himself—concerned "the amorous and fistic adventures"[10] of two sailors on a tour of duty in a tramp steamer. McLaglen had come to the movies by way of the boxing ring, and looked it. Here he played the craggy Spike. Robert Armstrong as his whoremongering buddy was named "Salami" up to the premiere in New York City (February 20, 1928), but some censor with an eye for double entendre made Fox change it to "Bill" before the picture went into wide release.

Structurally, the film was divided into a half-dozen segments, each dealing with a girl in a different port. Fox's back lot was a poor excuse for exotic harbors, but the phony ports (low-budget sets, with a few hastily scribbled foreign words on signs) seemed to add to, rather than detract from, the fun. Amsterdam has a couple of cardboard windmills, some bicycles built for two, and girls who say, "Ach! Mine heart goes pitty-pat ven I think of zat sailor."

No matter where McLaglen goes, his girl in every port "is always second-hand goods." Some other sailor has gotten there first and left his tattoo (an anchor inside a heart) on her person. But it's a "buddy" film, and though the star buddies keep scrapping with each other, they also keep bailing each other out of trouble and out of jail.

More than halfway through the picture, there is still no Louise, until the sailors arrive in Marseilles. There, she finally appears—as "Mam'selle Godiva, Neptune's Bride and the Sweetheart of the Sea." By profession, she is a circus performer who dives from a tower into a tank of water. By inclination, she teases and two-times every man she snares. At her first entrance, Louise's dazzling face and dancer's body are shown to great advantage in a tight-fitting swimsuit, nipples clearly outlined, as she climbs up her diving pole for the big jump. The small-breasted beauty dives dramatically—and McLaglen is hooked. He tells his buddy he's quitting the sea for love.

"You ain't in love," Armstrong answers. "You're just all broken out in monkey-bites! Nobody jumps ship for some sexy skirt." When Armstrong is left alone with Louise, the little tart puts the make on him too. He, however, is no fool.

"You used to be Tessie back in Coney Island!" he declares, and we

Victor McLaglen cozies up to high-diver Louise in A Girl in Every Port *(1928).*

know by her face that he's right. But she cuddles him erotically, running a finger up and down his thigh, and tells him she's got most of Spike's dough. She tempts him again in another risqué bedroom scene, hiding his pants. This sexpot is *horny*. But he resists, uttering some immortal words for buddies to live by: "Nothing doing, kid. That big ox means more to me than any woman!"

Louise gives her best hangdog look, revealing the lovely curve of what Christopher Isherwood called "that fine, imperious neck of hers"—the most beautiful neck in all of silent film. The look is one of disappointment rather than contrition; perhaps she's not finished yet. The climax comes with McLaglen's discovery of the anchor-and-heart tattoo on Louise—his unknown rival's "calling card." Finally, thickly, he figures out that the culprit is his best buddy Armstrong.

The inevitable fist fight ensues, as Spike and Bill settle things the manly way. Louise's fate is unknown and insignificant. The important thing is that the buddies are reunited and that "there ain't nothin' ever gonna come between us again."

As "The End" fades up and out, the viewer is left to ponder the misogyny of the piece and the irony of the two pals who remain happily arrested in their unhappy love life, having cemented a "beautiful male friendship" based on violence, deception, and priapic prowess.

"What I remember about this film," Louise once wrote, "is the image of the director, Howard Hawks—tall, elegant, silent, with the face of a conservative satyr." [11]

The film history books are full of declarations about the effect of *A Girl in Every Port* on both Hawks's and Brooks's careers. Hawks was still rather new to directing at the time of *A Girl in Every Port*. He had made *The Road to Glory* and *Fig Leaves* in 1926, followed in 1927 by *The Cradle Snatchers* and *Paid to Love*. But *A Girl in Every Port* was the first of his films to stress his masculine philosophy that "a man is measured by his work rather than by his ability to communicate with women." [12] Hawks's reputation as a "man's director" was as genuine as any such label ever was. He always emphasized action over psychology and dialogue, and he was much admired for his lack of pretensions and his ability to adapt to every technological advance—sound, color, and wide screen. When his eclectic approach matured, he would produce some of Hollywood's most popular films in all genres over four decades.*

He was also "nice and unobtrusive," said Louise. "Every time I arrived on the set I felt like saying, 'Hi! I'm Louise Brooks. You gave me a part in your movie, remember?' " [13] She considered him "the perfect director," as she told John Kobal years later:

> He didn't do anything at all. He would sit, look very, very beautiful, tall and graceful, leaning against anything he could lean against, and watch the scene; and the person who did all the directing was that big ham Victor McLaglen. I mean, when we were shooting, diving into the tank, it was a freezing cold night on the Fox lot, and Howard was walking around in a very

---

* His notable early films include *The Dawn Patrol* (1930), *Scarface* (1932), *Twentieth Century* (1934), and *The Road to Glory* (1936). Later there were fine detective and war films, screwball comedies, westerns—often with Cary Grant, Humphrey Bogart, and John Wayne. Among the best: *Bringing Up Baby* (1938), *His Girl Friday* (1940), *To Have and Have Not* (1944), *The Big Sleep* (1946), *Red River* (1948), *I Was a Male War Bride* (1949), *Gentlemen Prefer Blondes* (1953), *Rio Bravo* (1959), and *El Dorado* (1967).

smart tweed jacket, and I was shivering with the cold coming out of this damn greasy tank, and he smiled at me and he said, "Is it cold?" He was just [like] someone who had wandered on the set and [was] being sympathetic, but I liked him very much as a man and as a director.[14]

She also felt that "Howard Hawks admired me." And she was right, as Hawks made clear to Kevin Brownlow while gazing at a still photo of Louise from *A Girl in Every Port*, forty years after the only time they ever worked together:

> Just think of how modern she looks. Oh God, she was a good-looking girl. . . . I've had a little trouble with women [actors]. I don't blame them. They've found out that they're good doing this and not so good doing that, so they don't want to do the bad things. They're a little bit more afraid to take a chance. When that happened, I quit working with women stars, because I wanted a different type of girl. I didn't want what they'd been playing. I wanted a new type. I hired Louise Brooks because she's very sure of herself, she's very analytical, she's very feminine—but she's damn good and sure she's going to do what she wants to do. I could use her today. She was way ahead of her time. And she's a rebel. I like her, you know. I like rebels. I like people you can look at and you remember who they are.[15]

Kobal suggested Hawks had brought out her sexuality, but Louise demurred. "I use no sex at all," she said. "I never had the feeling of sex. I never try to feel sexy. . . . The people who try hardest to be sexy only fool other fools."

But "It" was there, and the reviewers saw it.

A Girl in Every Port was particularly popular in Europe, where it made a much bigger impact than in America. "Louise Brooks made a charming heartless vamp," said Britain's *Kine Weekly* of March 15, 1928. Henri Langlois of the Cinématheque Française later recalled Louise's "Face of the Century" when he first saw it at the Cinéma des Ursulines in Paris— the Paris of Picasso and the Surrealists and Diaghilev and Gertrude Stein and Les Six composers. The influential Swiss writer Blaise Cendrars went so far as to declare that the Hawks film "definitely marked the first appearance of contemporary cinema."

How could this be—a routine Hollywood action picture that got only a six-paragraph notice in the *New York Times*?

"To the Paris of 1928, which was rejecting Expressionism, *A Girl in Every Port* was a film conceived in the present, achieving an identity of its own by repudiating the past," said Langlois, who was profoundly struck by Hawks's "modernity" and who saved a number of Hawks's silent films from oblivion.[16]

"The film is so precisely designed, developed and controlled," writes Donald G. Willis, "that if you don't know that Hawks later mastered the sound film, you might resent the fact that sound arrived just as he had mastered silent-film technique." As for Brooks, Willis concludes, "her cold-souled predator is a striking creation."[17]

In Berlin, a German director named Pabst thought so, too.

Louise was typically impatient to be done with the film and typically uninterested in the reviews. The filmmaking process itself was getting increasingly on her nerves—besides which, she had travel plans.

On February 23, 1928, less than seventy-two hours after *A Girl in Every Port* was released, Louise left L.A. by train for Miami. She arrived there four days later and left the next morning on a cruise ship bound for Havana, the Caribbean garden spot of sex, gambling, and other pastimes, and the site of a clandestine rendezvous with George Marshall. But it wasn't quite as clandestine as George and Louise thought. It was more like a Feydeau comedy.

"I shall never forget in 1928," Louise wrote Kevin Brownlow, "when I ran away from my husband Eddie Sutherland to meet George Marshall in Cuba, the first people we saw in Havana were John Barrymore and Dolores Costello (running away from her Irish maw [*sic*]), and Florence Vidor (running away from King) and Jascha Heifetz."[18]

Louise found the company and the cavorting a delight, but no more so than Marshall himself. His swaggering presence came equipped with a quick mind and sharp tongue, though he was volatile and prone to mood swings of an almost manic-depressive nature. Among his eccentricities was his refusal to learn to drive; he was always content to travel in a chauffeur-driven Cadillac. In many ways Louise and George were similar. She found him more dashing, more energizing, than Eddie. And she found the tropical partying far more pleasurable than making movies.

Thus for the first but not last time did Marshall take Louise away from her work. Theirs was a hectic odyssey: After a week in Cuba, they went back to Miami on March 5, on to Palm Beach for three days, and then to Washington, D.C., where they lodged at the Wardman Park Hotel. Marshall entertained her there, and vice versa, until March 13, when she moved on to New York City. He may also have visited her in New York, for she was there a whole fortnight, until March 27, before taking the train once more to Washington, back to New York four days later—and then back again to Washington on April 5.

Louise and George could not stay away from each other for long—or from the topic of her disintegrating marriage. Marshall made his opinion clear: Get rid of Eddie. He may or may not have asked Louise to marry him, but the question was at least implied. And thanks to their overt behavior in Manhattan, plus the loose lips of her friends, the possibility of

Photo by E. R. Richee, Hollywood, 1927. The hair defined her character like the hood ornament of a car.

A PORTRAIT GALLERY

For every person who saw Louise Brooks in a film, a thousand saw her in newspapers and magazines. The same is true today. In fixing her image and later icon status, the portrait photographers were more responsible than the cinematographers. With the Nordic beauty of a Garbo, the absence of color could be lamented; but with the jet-black hair and alabaster features of Brooks, color seems irrelevant. The camera neither impressed nor intimidated her. There were more important actresses in Hollywood, but there was none who photographed as magically as Louise.

*Photo by George P. Hommel, Hollywood, 1927.
An elegant formal portrait for* Photoplay

*Photo by M. I. Boris, New York, 1925. Louise and
her naughty eyes were in* The Ziegfeld Follies.

*Photo by Nickolas Muray, New York, 1926. Louise
in garlands looked younger than nineteen.*

Photo by E. R. Richee, Hollywood, 1927. Louise in the Orientalia vogue: "Eugene Richee used to take 60 shots in two hours. We never said a word to each other. Perfect relationship."

Photographer unknown, Hollywood, ca. 1928. A darker view of the flapper as femme fatale

Photographer unknown, ca. 1928

Photo by E. R. Richee, Hollywood, 1928. The Kansas Cleopatra: When Jean Arthur or even Garbo toyed with the pearls, it didn't work. With Louise, it became a classic.

*Photo by E. R. Richee, Hollywood, 1928. Louise called this
first portrait without bangs "that dyke photo of me."*

E. R. Richee came closest to duplicating the lighting effects in
the films themselves. He could reproduce that ephemeral,
frosty quality with the most provocative results.

TED ALLAN, Paramount photographer

Photographer unknown, Hollywood, ca. 1928. Sophistication and sexuality combined: the Jazz Baby at her peak

Louise divorcing Eddie was now being publicly, as well as privately, debated:

> Along Broadway last night [wrote the New York *Telegraph* on April 5, 1928] flew a report that Louise Brooks, Famous Players–Lasky flapper screen star, and Eddie Sutherland . . . are to dissolve the bonds that have held them since July, 1926, in a California divorce court.
>
> Sutherland, a picture director, is in Hollywood, where business has compelled him to spend most of his time since his marriage to Miss Brooks. She is here, staying in an expensive suite at the Hotel Ambassador.
>
> From the picture center in California during the last few days have filtered similar rumors concerning the Brooks-Sutherland domestic affair. The couple, since they have not been together, have reached an amicable separation agreement, it is said in film circles. . . .
>
> Efforts to reach Miss Brooks at her hotel yesterday and last night for confirmation or denial of the Hollywood report failed. She was out, her maid declared.
>
> Since she has been in New York, Miss Brooks has been a colorful figure in Longacre night life. Every evening she has been seen at Texas Guinan's Salon Royale, the 54th Street Club and other gay spots. Peggy Fears, an actress, and Joseph Harriman, a financier, are usually in her party.

The New York gossip columnists did not yet recognize George Marshall, the Washingtonian. Louise was oblivious, anyway, having departed for the capital on the morning that report appeared. After two more days with Marshall in Washington, she finally took her leave of him on April 7, reluctantly bound for Hollywood. The four-day trip gave her plenty of time to make up her mind, and she wasted no time. Shortly after her arrival in Los Angeles, she moved into the Beverly Wilshire Hotel.

Two weeks later, on May 3, she filed for divorce.

Irritated Paramount executives had been trying to track Louise down for weeks, but they were unable to catch up with her during the long trek with Marshall. They wanted her for *Beggars of Life*, the studio's most important dramatic production of 1928, to be directed by William Wellman, who was still basking in the triumph of *Wings*.

"While waiting for the capture of a seemingly reluctant actress he had never met, Billy Wellman came to the unfortunate conclusion that since I did not follow the pattern of the actors who haunted the studio panting after film roles, I did not care about making films at all," Louise wrote years later. She attributed this to the difference between Paramount's East and West Coast ambience. "Because he did not know that sycophancy had no merit in the New York studio where I had begun my career, and because I was unaware that prudent Hollywood actors wooed producers, directors and writers with flattering attention, a coldness was set up between us which neither of us could dispel."[19]

Louise's mentor in the front office, Walter Wanger, had left Paramount early in 1928, and she was left "with no sympathetic studio contact whatever." She could expect no favors from B. P. Schulberg, the imperious West Coast production chief, whom she hadn't even met, and Wellman was Schulberg's protégé. But the rank-and-file personnel at Paramount assumed Louise was still an executive "pet" and regarded her with the mixed fear and resentment that such status—however imaginary—implied. Louise, in turn, was insulted about having to make a screen test for Wellman. She was to play a runaway who disguises herself as a boy, and Wellman told her that Benjamin Glazer, the screenwriter and production supervisor, wasn't sure whether she would photograph well without her trademark bangs. They were testing Arlen, also.

"During the twenties," Louise's account continues, "no director was considered any good who could not make his actors cry real tears, and no actor was considered any good who could not shed real tears on demand. Tears without facial contortions! Luckily, I had acquired this art from my mother, whose soft hazel eyes could overflow at any suggestion of sadness, from the smell of burning beans to a Wagner *Leitmotiv*. However, Billy wasn't only interested in my tears in the scene. He wanted Dick to cry, too, and Dick was not a spontaneous weeper."

After daylong efforts to reduce Arlen to tears, Wellman finally succeeded when "he resorted to the fiction that Dick's mother was dying." Both young stars passed their tests. The redoubtable Wallace Beery didn't have to take one.

The story was a remarkably realistic "tale of Hobohemia"* by Jim Tully, the red-headed, two-fisted "tramp" writer then at the peak of his popularity. Tully's novels† centered on down-and-out heroes endowed with his own rough-and-tumble origins: Tully was raised in an orphanage, often jailed for vagrancy, and spent eight years hopping freights himself. Now in Hollywood, he found a market for his brand of social realism. Half a million drifters occupied "Hobohemia," and there wasn't even a Depression yet. In the year or two since Mencken and others championed him as a "new literary genius," Tully had become a kind of guru in film circles. Many found him charmingly wild, though others called him a bully and a

---

* "Hobo," originally a term for migrant workers, derived from the western "hoe boys" who moved from place to place, usually by hopping freight trains, and harvested with their hoes. At night, they slept beneath "California blankets"—newspapers.
† Other novels included *Emmett Lawler, Jarnegan, Circus Parade,* and *Shanty Irish.*

liar. For a time he worked as Charlie Chaplin's publicist, which was how Eddie Sutherland got to know if not exactly love him. "Jim always thought of himself as a kind of an American Gorky," said Eddie.[20]

But Tully's lower depths did not amuse Louise.

"Jim Tully? He was the most repulsive little Quilp I ever knew," she wrote Kevin Brownlow. "Short and fat with his belly hanging over his belt, yellow teeth to match his face and hair, full of the vanity of *Vanity Fair* and H. L. Mencken. We were sitting on a rock posing for still pictures and he reached over and touched my breast, under my grey flannel shirt. I almost pushed him off the rock."[21]

Tully's Gorkyesque America was the unromanticized tramp camp. His downbeat *Beggars* had begun as a novel and was soon adapted by Maxwell Anderson (co-author of *What Price Glory?*) for the stage: *Outside Looking In*—starring James Cagney and Charles Bickford—was the play that Brooks and Chaplin had taken in during the summer of 1925.

Louise savored that coincidence as she contemplated her role in the film. She played the stepdaughter of a hideous old farmer who tries to rape her. In panic, she grabs a shotgun and kills him. A young hobo (Arlen) who stumbles upon the scene in search of a meal agrees to help her escape from the law, and she dons a disguise of boys' clothes. Soon the "Wanted for Murder" posters with Louise's picture appear on telephone poles.

After a grim first encounter with freight-hopping, the pair wanders hurt and hungry into a camp ruled uneasily by rivals Oklahoma Red (Beery) and Arkansas Snake (Robert Perry). At about the time Snake learns Louise is a girl, the camp is raided, and the bums make a boxcar getaway. But there's more trouble on the train—including a near-gang rape—and Louise escapes only by precipitating a fight between Beery and Perry. Further adventures and narrow escapes climax when the lusty Beery, in an unlikely martyrdom, sacrifices himself on behalf of Brooks and Arlen. "Among the beggars of life they have found their love."

Louise believed that Glazer's "artistic conception" of the film nearly destroyed it. Glazer "wrote for the snobbish *Vanity Fair*," she said. "He had everyone at Paramount—the producers—buffaloed by his 'culture'. . . . Each day's shooting at Jacumba was driven down by car to Hollywood. Billy waited on Barney's okay. Left to himself, Wellman would have made a swell action picture."[22]

She also believed that her own performance was woeful ("I am an embarrassment") and that the only thing that saved the film was Wallace Beery: "Neither God nor the Devil could have influenced Beery's least gesture before the camera. Having been a tramp briefly as a boy, he

Louise and Richard Arlen in Beggars of Life *(1928)*

developed his character with authority and variety. His Oklahoma Red is a little masterpiece." *

Brooks and Beery cemented their friendship on the first day when Beery drove her in his private car to Jacumba, near the Mexican border, to begin the seventeen days of location shooting, May 30–June 15. The film had an ordinary budget ($400,000), but it was unusual in being filmed so largely on location.

> Always [she said] I had been scared stiff when anyone drove faster than 40 miles an hour. But as I sat beside that bear with his open black Packard racing up the treacherous mountain curves, I enjoyed one of the most exhilarating experiences of my life. Wally drove with perfect ease, as if he and

---

* Contemporary audiences can judge these performances for themselves, thanks to James Card. *Beggars of Life* was one of the first three films he rescued from probable destruction in Hollywood, back in 1952. (The others were *Ben-Hur*—the 1926 version—and *The Docks of New York.*)

the Packard constituted a single unit of control and power. . . . After ten minutes, I saw that he was like a great dancer, his sight, his timing, his muscle responses were so perfect that he guessed which way a dog would run across a road and did a ballet around it. Now who could imagine this of the clumsy Beery?[23]

Her confidence secured when he narrowly averted the dog, she suddenly hit him with a typical Brooksian challenge: "Some directors call you a coward," she said.

"That's because I won't do the stunts and fight scenes that my double is hired to do," he replied, unruffled. "Have you got a double for location?"

Louise said she had.

"Then don't let that crazy Wellman talk you into doing any stunts yourself because he says it will make the picture better. That's a lot of bunk. Nobody seeing the picture will know the difference, while you are liable to be dead or in a wheelchair.

"Directors love to kill actors," Beery added.

When they arrived in the boiling heat at the two-story Jacumba Hotel, they found a scummy establishment in which Louise was assigned "a primitive bedroom." Beery refused to stay. During the making of *Now We're in the Air* the previous year, he had learned to fly a plane and bought one of his own. Faced with the prospect of two weeks at the Jacumba Hotel, he now hit upon the happier idea of commuting daily by air from Hollywood.

Jacumba and its 400 inhabitants were situated on the San Diego and Arizona Railway, the main line between San Diego and Yuma. It was photographically ideal for *Beggars of Life* since the tracks ran in a spiral down the mountains, through deep, scenic canyons. The full cast and crew numbered seventy-five, including "twenty riotous hoboes selected by Billy from among the outcasts who financed leisurely drunks by working as extras in films." They took over the town, concentrating on the hotel and the pool hall, whose proprietor, Carlos, was also the local bootlegger.

The star of the location shooting was Locomotive 102, the private freight train on which, and from which, much of the film was shot. The indulgent engineer was tireless in cooperating with Wellman on timing. Within forty-eight hours, he could start and stop the train on a chalkmark, speeding it up or slowing it down to match the needs of the action. There were no undercrankings—cranking the camera at slower-than-normal speed to make the movement appear accelerated on the screen. "[The engineer] was rather astonished with me," Louise observed,—"so beautiful, and so careless; and he had to get used to Arlen pulling out the hairs on his forehead for a hairline." The engineer was also laissez-faire about where people could ride—and what they could do—"astride the cow-catcher, in the engine cab, atop boxcars, inside gondolas, and on flatcars."

"I chose to ride in the caboose," Louise remembered, "with its cozy bunks and fat little black stove, which glowed red in the cold mountain nights." On some dangerously romantic evenings, "she coasted to town on the breeze, with all of us lying out on the flatcars, looking up at the stars shimmering in the black sky."

The close physical contact with Nature that the cast found so exhilarating brought out a kind of D. H. Lawrence sensuality and a desire to flirt with danger, on which the cunning Wellman capitalized. The train crew was shocked at how offhandedly these movie folks regarded their own safety. "They were dazed by the unconcern with which a runaway flatcar and the caboose were plunged into [Carrizo] Gorge, taking with them the second camera and missing the second cameraman by inches," said Louise. "They were dismayed when Billy persuaded me to take the place of my double, Harvey [Parry], and hop a fast-moving boxcar, which nearly sucked me under its wheels."

According to perverse habit, she ignored Beery's advice—spellbound by Wellman's tactics, even as she resented them.

"So fascinated was I by the quiet sadism practiced by Billy behind the camera, especially in his direction of women, that I began to investigate his past life." From Wellman himself, she said, "I learned nothing, because he was extremely shy in conversation with women." But from Arlen, who had just worked with Wellman in *Wings*, she gained some insights.

Brooks and Arlen were superficially friendly, but not terribly fond of each other. "His winning smile concealed a strong dislike for me," she said, attributable to the fact that "when we worked together in 1927 on *Rolled Stockings*, his vanity had made him quickly aware that I did not admire his acting."* But one night over a bottle of whiskey in the seedy lobby of the Jacumba Hotel, "Dick poured two powerful drinks and began a worshipful account of Billy's career."

As a nineteen-year-old adventure seeker in 1917, Wellman had been enthralled by tales of the Lafayette Escadrille. That squadron of American pilots flew some of the first French Nieuport 17s, whose guns were synchronized to shoot through whirling propeller blades. Their glorious dogfights inspired many young Yankees and helped bring about America's entry into the war. Wellman joined a French ambulance corps and then the Lafayette Flying Corps—not to be confused with the Lafayette Esca-

---

* "He was perhaps the worst actor who ever made faces in front of a mirror," she wrote Kevin Brownlow years later. "Jimmy Cagney originated the [*Beggars*] part in the play [*Outside Looking In*, in New York] and Arlen's performance resembled Cagney's like Little Lord Fauntleroy resembled Huckleberry Finn."

drille. He attained the rank of sergeant and shot down two German planes before returning to become a flight instructor in southern California.

But the Lafayette Escadrille and the Lafayette Flying Corps *were* confused with one another—constantly.

"His Croix de Guerre and the fame of the Lafayette Escadrille, which made him a hero in Hollywood, were the foundation upon which he built his career," Louise wrote.*

For the moment, however, high up in Jacumba and fuzzied by bootleg whiskey after a hard day's work, she just let it pass. But when Arlen next told her that he himself had flown with the RAF during the war, Louise laughed at him in disbelief—goading the half-drunk Arlen into a pent-up assault:

> Dick's jaw muscles twitched, as he hunched closer to me to deliver his monologue. "It sure is too bad about your getting a divorce from a swell guy like Eddie Sutherland—and a swell director," he said. "Now that you're not his wife anymore, everybody expects Paramount to fire you. They don't know you're a pet of the front office." He paused for a philosophic sigh. "Funny thing. I've been working at Paramount for three years—a damned fine actor, too—and I make a stinking $400 a week, while you ride around in your damn Lincoln town car with its damn 'black satin' finish. *You*—why, you can't even act! You're not even good-looking. You're a lousy actress and your eyes are too close together." Having concluded his curse upon me and my Lincoln town car, Dick stood up, snatched away his bottle of whiskey, and swaggered from the lobby.[24]

There was no mention of the incident the next day, when Brooks, Harvey Parry, Arlen, and Wellman's seventeen-year-old brother-in-law Jacque Chapin (who had a crush on Louise) met around the town's big cement swimming pool. A show-off diving exhibition by Arlen was soon dwarfed by one from Parry. The stuntman contemptuously bypassed the diving board in favor of a thirty-four-foot tower, climbed to the top of it, and executed a series of dives "that retired Dick to our bench and left me enchanted."

"The vulgar face and mind I knew him to possess formed no part of this Harvey, executing aerial turns and twists comparable in grace to that of some capricious bird in flight," said Louise. He was, after all, performing

---

* By 1931, more than 4,000 men laid claims to membership in the Lafayette Escadrille. Louise later devoured Herbert M. Mason, Jr.'s definitive book, *The Lafayette Escadrille*, and wrote fourteen letters to Kevin Brownlow in an obsessive effort to prove that Wellman was a dissembler: "There was absolutely no reason for Wellman's escadrille being confused with the legendary [Lafayette] unless he put it out and allowed it to be written over and over for the last 40 years. Lying by insinuation and silence is still lying. . . . It is interesting to study the mechanics of the routine commonness of lies—all men are 'heroes,' all women are 'femmes fatales.' "

for her. "My heroes were men of action," she often said, and here was a man of action—a professional daredevil with a loathsome character but a powerfully trained body. This, for Louise, was sexually irresistible. Her admiration increased a few days later when she watched him double for herself in a dangerous scene; he was to fall off the moving train and plunge deep into a canyon below.

A 100-foot dive into water was a routine stunt for Harvey. A 25-foot dive into a rocky canyon was another matter. He agreed to do it on condition that he do the stunt just once. No rehearsals. No retakes. Just once. . . .

Number 102 backed up again and started forward, gaining speed rapidly until the whistle tooted, Billy counted the seconds and yelled "Go!," and Harvey fell away down the gorge. Nobody spoke while the train returned to the spot and we saw Harvey sprawled motionless upon the incline. Nobody spoke after the train stopped until Billy cried, "My God, I've killed him!" At that, Harvey, pleased with his joke, got up, laughing, and waved his arms to indicate no broken bones. . . .

On the trip home that night, I lay out on a flatcar between Jacque and Harvey. As the bell clanged the approach of town, I turned to Harvey, whispering, "At 1 o'clock, come round to my bedroom window. I'll open the screen and let you in."[25]

Lying together in the afterglow of that thrilling stunt "on a warm starry night, pulled by that purring locomotive was what did me in." Harvey came 'round, Louise let him in. Fade out . . .

Fade in brightly to the next morning when Louise was stopped as she crossed the hotel porch after breakfast.

"Just a minute, Miss Brooks," said Harvey—loudly, for the benefit of some hoboes and company members on the porch. "I've got something to ask you."

Holding the door shut with one hand while his other hand held my arm, he said, "I guess you know my job depends on my health." Naming a high film executive whom I had never met, he went on, "Everybody knows you're his girl and he has syphilis, and what I want to know is, Do you have syphilis?" Following an impressive moment of silence, he ended by saying, "Another reason I want to know is that my girl is coming up at noon to drive me back to Hollywood."

He even looked around to size up the effect of his performance. Horrified and humiliated, Louise fled to her room and stayed there as long as she could. Finally, at 1:00 p.m., "praying that everyone had eaten and gone," she went to the lunchroom, which was empty—except for Harvey and his girl:

She was a fat slattern in a yellow housedress. Harvey nudged her, and she swung around on her stool to stare at me and giggle while he spoke to her in an undertone. Just as I finished my ice cream and was preparing to make my escape, Billy came in from location and sat down at my table for lunch. When Harvey came to say goodbye to him, it was obvious that Billy had heard every detail of our sordid affair. . . . He could not resist a small leer in my direction. How the grand Louise Brooks had fallen! It was a sequence he could have directed with relish.

The person she most cared about during *Beggars* had been Robert Perry, as she told Kevin Brownlow:

Making the picture, I told Perry he was gorgeous and a great actor—(why didn't I go to bed with him instead of that smelly little double?)—and why didn't he take his career seriously? We were sitting 'round the fire in the jungle drinking whisky out of tin cups, at night, while Beery was working up on the ridge. Perry looked at his tin cup and said, "This is what I work for—booze. You can't seem to understand—I'm a *bum!*" Later in the caboose he was to even the score when he told me that I was an actress who had made a bum of myself by screwing Harvey.[26]

She summed it up coldly: "I laid my double and lost the respect of my pals, the hoboes." And to Brownlow, she concluded her account with a narcissistic fillip: "Such an ugly but fascinating story about myself."

Beggars of Life gave Louise her first and favorite androgynous role. Her insolent beauty, cold yet fiery at the same time, was a spellbinding blend of masculine and feminine.

"A boy's cap, a woolen shirt, a coat three sizes too large, trousers also too large, and heavy hobnailed shoes made me a different person entirely," she said.[27] Paramount's accountants must have been pleased; compared to the expensive costume budget for Louise's previous pictures, her total tailor's tab on this one was $10.

"Almost all cross-dressing films involve the relationship between authority and freedom," writes Rebecca Bell-Metereau in *Hollywood Androgyny*.[28] If, in fact, masculine behavior is "characterized more by a lack of expressive gestures than by their presence," then Louise was equipped to be a great male impersonator. She tended to lack "submissive" feminine traits in general, and her direct, challenging gaze could rival the deadpan stare of John Wayne any time. And thanks to Denishawn, she understood the nuances of clothes and posture.

Louise's "becoming" a boy was erotic in itself for audiences raised on the sexual allure of the covert. A few years later, Greta Garbo would apotheosize it in *Queen Christina*, but even now, the idea of a beautiful

*Louise the runaway, in boy's disguise, for
William Wellman's* Beggars of Life *(1928)*

woman playing a boy other than Peter Pan caught the fancy of the film
mags.

Beneath the "Beggar and Better" headline on its full-page spread of
Louise (portraits by E. R. Richee) in *Beggars* drag, *Motion Picture Classic*
of August 1928 wrote: "Many a girl has wished—or said she wished—she
were a boy. Louise Brooks goes one better and becomes one in her portrayal of one of the 'Beggars of Life' in Jim Tully's screen story. Any time
Louise wants a nickel for a cup of coffee, she has only to come to us. In
fact, if she'd let us have one with her, we'd go as far as to wrench loose a
dime." *Photoplay* ran similar pictures the same month, noting that Louise

was "a little neat and clean but otherwise a handsome and convincing boy."

Whatever its social and psychosexual implications, Louise's androgyny received a better critical reception than the film itself. "Miss Brooks really acts well," said Mordaunt Hall in the *New York Times* on September 24, 1928, "better than she has in most of her other pictures." But overall, Hall thought the film "rather a dull and unimaginative piece of work," which, in the final analysis, provided no profound insights into the hoboes' existence.

More than one critic pigeonholed *Beggars* as "a man's picture"[29] and judged its social realism as more uneventful than striking. But the public liked the film, and Paramount was satisfied with its "man's director." Like Hawks, Wellman knew when to pull back, especially with Wallace Beery, as Louise recalled: "Much wiser than directors who tried to dominate Wally, Billy let him play his scenes as he liked and, as often as possible, let him work *when* he liked."[30]

Louise also lauded Wellman for "how hard he studied his script and prepared for his day's work. How he always did his best. How sure and fast he worked. How sympathetic he was to the degree that he himself could feel anything. He was not a very sensitive man."[31]

But as that backhanded compliment suggests, she had more criticism than praise for his attitude toward women: "Except for that dive down the embankment when the railroad cop hit my hands, done by my double, I did everything," she told Brownlow. "Wellman risked my legs making me hop a train—and you don't even know that it is I. He might have broken my spine dropping me off the back of a milk cart. But good old Bill was always safe behind the camera."[32]

Louise's feminist psychoanalysis of Wellman held that, by making her risk her life, he was reliving his own fears from the war. "I knew Billy was a phony brave man and consequently a woman-beater—all cowards revenge themselves on women—just by feel, especially when my ass hit the pavement in *Beggars of Life*." Men in his movies often revealed such misogyny, she said, pointing to Cagney smashing the grapefruit in Mae Clarke's face in *Public Enemy* and Gable socking Stanwyck in *Night Nurse*.

"That explains Wellman's love of making men in films weep with his own self-pity," she continued, adding elsewhere that "it is always the 'men's directors' who are the sickening sentimentalists."[33] And for someone who drank as much as Louise, she was quick to criticize the habit in other people. "Billy was an evil, sadistic drunk," she claimed. To Kevin Brownlow, she added an astonishing charge about Wellman during the filming of *Wings:* "He got drunk and Clara got clap. That is not to detract from either of their efforts."[34] If the statement about Clara Bow is true, the disease might have contributed to her subsequent breakdown. If false, it was an ironic slander in view of the nasty lie broadcast by Louise's stuntman in Jacumba.

All in all, the impact of *Beggars of Life* on Louise was greater than that of any film she had yet made. Her boy-girl on the lam was a fascinating, intelligent role; she had worked with a top director and a strong supporting cast in a wild and beautiful location. But the humiliation of the Harvey incident lingered on.

A month later in her suite at the Beverly Wilshire Hotel, she was still wrestling with the mixture of accomplishment and resentment she felt, when the front desk rang to announce the unexpected arrival of Jacque Chapin—the young extra and Wellman in-law who'd fallen desperately for Louise during the Jacumba shooting. Louise said to send him up.

> He entered my sitting room, looking strange and formal, dressed in a blue coat and white pants, his red curls slicked down with some strongly scented oil. He did not talk; he did not drink the Bacardi cocktail I mixed for him. He sat on one sofa before the fireplace, staring at me sitting on the opposite sofa, and then, without warning, leaped at me and grappled me in his arms.
>
> Too astonished to be angry, I shoved him away, saying, "Are you trying to make love to me?"
>
> "Why not?" he said furiously, jumping up and backing away to the door to make his exit. "You go to bed with everyone else—why not me?"[35]

AS LOUISE was losing the front-office protection of Walter Wanger, something similar was happening on a grander scale to the world's second-greatest film comedian, Buster Keaton. Louise saw a lot of Keaton these days, thanks to the other Buster in her life—William Collier, Jr. Brooks and Collier had renewed the romantic friendship that began during *Just Another Blonde* in 1926. Now, in 1928, they often visited Keaton's "Italian Villa" in Beverly Hills, which cost $200,000 to build and another $100,000 to furnish. Louise called it "a magnificent playpen":

> Keaton at home was no different from Keaton in films. He went about each project with the same adorable conviction of a good little boy doing a good thing in the best possible way. After the most idiotically inspired dives off the springboard into the pool, he would go to the patio to barbecue the most perfect steaks. Indoors in the living room above a high balcony, it had pleased him to rig a red velvet curtain on which he could swing down across the room to the top of a grand piano.[36]

Keaton's trademark was his enormous energy—his zest for anything physical, athletic, outrageous. Even Brooks and Collier, ten years younger, had trouble keeping up with him. But they tried, and during

John H. Striebel's "Dixie Dugan" (1928)

their visits they were always struck by the contrast between the comedian and his wife, Natalie Talmadge.

Natalie was the youngest of the three Talmadge sisters, all of them great beauties. But she lacked the charm of Constance, the sensuality of Norma, and the social gifts of both. She had borne Keaton two sons in three years, but now her sisters convinced her she should have no more children, or sex, with Keaton.

"Buster was always 'on,' " said Louise. "I can see how this would be a great trial to such a vacuous lump as Natalie."[37] Natalie, indeed, did not enjoy her husband's pratfall approach to life and art. Nor did she approve of his drinking. And she didn't understand why he wasn't perfectly happy working with Joseph M. Schenck, who was married to her sister Norma.

Schenck had shepherded Keaton's career since 1917. And as his brother-in-law, Schenck not only had to smoke an endless number of exploding cigars, but also to maneuver delicately through the Keatons' domestic affairs. He often found Natalie at home with her lovers instead of Buster, but Schenck was experienced in such matters: He had been looking the other way while his own wife, Norma, carried on with actor Gilbert Roland.

"The Talmadge women were the most natural, comfortable people I ever knew," said Louise of the three Chekhovian sisters. "Connie may have suffered briefly with English royalty fever but she remained naturally delightful; Natalie was a very comfortable lump; Norma, curled up in a chair, was very comfortably bored. And [their mother] Peg—old Buddha —was kept comfortable, as she surveyed the scene, by her attentive daughters. The teaching of old Buddha was sound: Get money, and then get comfortable."[38]

In 1928, Keaton made his worst mistake. He gave up his own studio and signed with MGM to make films over which he no longer had full artistic control. He would be making much more money ($3,000 instead of $1,000 a week) working for Joe's brother, Nicholas Schenck, but Nick spent most of his time in New York, leaving Buster in the hands of Irving Thalberg and Louis B. Mayer, neither of whom could give him much attention. And it galled him to have to get approval for every gag.

"Buster had no one to look after him at MGM, a thing he really needed in a place like that," said his friend Collier.

Suddenly, said Louise, "he seemed unable to deal with people in the real world. That is when, I suspect, booze ceased to be a creative release and became his solution to wretched reality."[39] The reality, at $3,000 a week, might not have seemed wretched to other mortals, but Keaton's agony was his loss of independence.

The state of Buster's mind and career was revealed one late summer evening in 1928 when Brooks and Collier dined at the Keatons'. After midnight, Keaton surprised Collier by asking to be taken to "Keaton's Kennel," his bungalow on the MGM back lot.

It was a lark, thought Louise. Keaton sat silently through the ride. After their arrival, he fixed drinks while Louise and Collier looked around: All the walls were lined with expensive, glass-enclosed bookcases, each divided into many small panes of glass. Keaton suddenly went into the bedroom, returning with a baseball bat. "Strolling neatly around the room," said Louise, he "smashed the glass in each and every bookcase."[40]

Since there were hundreds of panes, it took a while to finish the job, while Louise and Buster Collier watched the attack speechlessly. When Keaton finished, he returned to his chair and resumed the conversation as if nothing unusual had taken place.

Louise told Keaton's biographer Tom Dardis it was a symbolic act of destroying MGM, of "trying to break out of his cage [and] escape to creation. But he never made it."

Keaton did, in November of 1928, enjoy a new affair with Dorothy Sebastian—Louise's friend from the 1924 *Scandals*. Fun-loving "Slam" Sebastian (so nicknamed for her tendency to get falling-down drunk) had secured a Hollywood contract, thanks to Lord Beaverbrook, and co-starred with Buster in *Spite Marriage*. Unlike Natalie, she loved sex and practical jokes alike. But Keaton remained, at heart, an unhappy man.

"Who could foresee that within so short a time his job, his family and his home—all would be lost to him? Thank goodness, he never lost his skill with a baseball bat," wrote Louise.[41]

She might have said the same for herself.

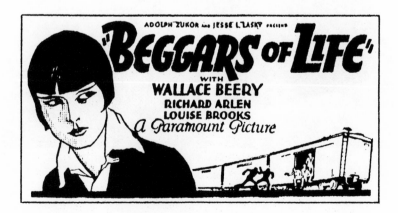

*The mistress of San Simeon: Marion Davies, ca. 1929,
with her beloved dachshund, Gandhi*

10 · "Does Mr. Hearst Know These People Are Here?"

Love is a publicity stunt, and making love, after the first curious rapture, is only another petulant way to pass the time waiting for the studio to call.
— L O U I S E   B R O O K S

I F   A N O T H E R actress had said it, it could be chalked up to the calculated languor of image building. But this was no interview; Louise was writing a private letter in a languid mode, revealing her greatest fear—boredom—which, like its antidote—sex—played a key role in her life during that brief 1927–1928 heyday when every little breeze in Hollywood really did seem to whisper Louise.

The whispers had carried up the California coast and penetrated the lair of publisher William Randolph Hearst, whose long-time companion, actress Marion Davies, wanted a closer look at the little sensation who had married her friend Eddie Sutherland. Thus in December, Eddie and Louise were invited up to the legendary Hearst estate in San Simeon, halfway between Los Angeles and San Francisco, to watch 1927 turn into 1928.

"The Ranch" was Hearst's preferred euphemism for the most extravagant display of wealth in America. Hearst's fairy-tale kingdom covered no fewer than thirty-two miles of the dazzling Pacific seacoast. Two hundred and fifty thousand acres of it were indeed a ranch, with one of the largest herds of cattle in California. Countless beach houses, guest "cottages" the size of haciendas, swimming pools, and other pleasure facilities dotted the fiefdom, but dominating all else, atop a mountain called La Cuesta Encantada (The Enchanted Hill), was Hearst's monumental 130-room castle, lavishly appointed with millions of dollars of antiques and artworks. To

William Randolph Hearst, ca. 1930

this palace, the beautiful, the powerful, and the political made pilgrimages for business and pleasure.

While the real Mrs. Hearst remained discreetly across the country, vibrant Marion Davies was mistress of the manor. She was in charge of approving and assembling an entourage consisting largely of movie celebrities. "I always like people around me," said Marion, the polar opposite of Garbo. "I love to laugh."[1] Augmenting the cast of characters at San Simeon (and helping fill the sixty guest bedrooms) was a more or less permanent group of Marion's relatives, including her mother, her sisters, and a selection of nieces and nephews.

Of this family retinue, Marion was fondest of her eldest sister Reine's two children, Charlie and Pepi Lederer—the most outrageously fun-loving of the crop. The Lederer kids, in turn, preferred Marion to their own mother. And kids they were. Pepi was seventeen when she and Louise first met on New Year's Day 1928 at San Simeon. Her brother Charlie had just turned seventeen the night before, on New Year's Eve. (They were born nine and a half months apart.) During the round of introductions,

Marion announced that Charlie had graduated from the University of California at Berkeley at the age of sixteen. In fact, he had just dropped out.*

Indulged from childhood by Marion and Mr. Hearst, Pepi and Charlie were integral members of the various Hearst-Davies households; their prankishness contrasted sharply with the stuffy world at whose center they lived. San Simeon was Pepi's playground, and Louise—though twenty-one and married—was instantly drawn to the bright, overweight adolescent. Pepi seemed to be the only prisoner of this castle who could get away with breaking the rules—especially the rules about alcohol, laid down by Hearst in an effort to control Marion's heavy drinking.

The Sutherlands were supposed to stay a week at this paradise, with its endless banquets and beach parties, but after three days, Eddie rebelled. "I'll be damned if I'll be rousted out of the hay by a cowbell at eight o'clock every morning for breakfast, and have my liquor rationed as if I were some silly schoolboy," he declared to Louise. "Besides, there's not even a golf course here. I'm going back to Hollywood tonight."[2]

Louise tended to agree that San Simeon was dull indeed "for anyone who did not revel in opulence, who was not a member of Marion's stock company of guests, who was not mentally stimulated by visiting celebrities, and who wanted neither film advancement nor financial aid from Marion or Mr. Hearst."[3] Marion's world was a passive one, said Louise, "in which people literally sat and talked themselves to death," and sober, to boot.

Unlike Eddie, Louise had gotten to know Pepi, who lived up to her energetic nickname. But, she said, "I felt it was my duty as a wife to return to Hollywood with Eddie after he told Marion that urgent business recalled him to the Paramount studio."

Given her marital attitudes and infidelities to date, such solicitude was a bit disingenuous. Taking her aside, Pepi asked, "Why do you have to go with Eddie? You have nothing to do in Hollywood." That argument was compelling enough to dissolve Louise's sense of wifely devotion. There was nothing to do in San Simeon, either, but it was a much grander place in which to do it. Louise stayed three weeks and later provided a revealing account of San Simeon life.† The extravagance there was beyond parody: After a branch of an oak knocked Hearst's hat off one day, he had the tree *moved*, at a cost of $10,000 a foot. Of San Simeon's fictional renderings,

---

* But within a few years, Charles Lederer (1910–1976) would make good. He co-authored or adapted such stories as *The Front Page, Broadway Serenade, His Girl Friday, Kiss of Death, I Was a Male War Bride,* and his own musical *Kismet* for the screen.

† "Marion Davies' Niece," a character study of Pepi Lederer, was published in 1974 in *Film Culture* and incorporated into Louise's 1982 book, *Lulu in Hollywood.*

Orson Welles's *Citizen Kane* (1941) was the most dazzling. But the most perspicacious was Aldous Huxley's novel, *After Many a Summer Dies the Swan* (1939).

In the *Kane* story, written by Louise's friend Herman Mankiewicz, newspaper magnate Charles Foster Kane loves the beautiful but mediocre singer Susan Alexander and tries to turn her into a star. In the Huxley book, Uncle Jo Stoyte, an uncouth multimillionaire, adores the spirited Virginia Maunciple, who pretends to no talent except fun and sex ("a little yum-yum").

Marion matched neither creation, though she inspired both. Said Welles himself: "Kane picked up Susan on a street corner—from nowhere —where the poor girl herself thought she belonged. Marion Davies was no dim shopgirl; she was a famous beauty who had her choice of rich, powerful and attractive beaux before Hearst sent his first bouquet to her stage door."[4]

When he met her in 1918, Hearst was more than three times her age. He stalked her for years, buying front-row tickets to her shows and keeping up an endless stream of expensive presents. He desperately wanted to marry her, but his Catholic wife would never grant him a divorce.

Convinced of her star qualities, Hearst formed Cosmopolitan Pictures to provide Marion with vehicles, but he wanted her to fit the sweetly innocent heroine's mold of the previous decade. No mouth-to-mouth kisses, for example, were permitted. He lavished millions on her films, plus a fortune in free publicity, but they generally failed to ignite the public.

As a couple, they were more feared than adored, but Louise found Hearst disarmingly kind and avuncular in his lair. Inside the twin-turreted castle, the most fantastic room was the 100-foot-long dining hall, which had once been an entire church in Spain! Hearst found that the Spanish were more easily parted from their art treasures, or pieces thereof, than most Europeans.

Ten minutes—no more and no less—were allotted for cocktails before dinner. It was not Eddie Sutherland's kind of establishment, to be sure. But once at the dinner table, an unlimited supply of champagne compensated. The 300-year-old monastery trestle table seated forty, with Hearst and Davies across from each other in the center (not at opposite ends, as in *Citizen Kane*). The most notable guests sat on either side of them, their importance diminishing with distance, and it did not take Louise long to figure out what part of the table was the most fun; she was headed there, anyway: "The morning after Eddie left, I was moved from a seat near Mr. Hearst to the seat next to Pepi at the bottom of the table, where she ruled."[5]

Marion was fond of the "younger degeneration," as she dubbed them:

Two of the leading "Younger Degenerates"
at San Simeon: Pepi Lederer and
William Haines, ca. 1929

Louise, Pepi and Charlie Lederer, actors William Haines and Sally O'Neil, Lloyd Pantages (son of the vaudeville-theater owner), and a "hanger-on" named Chuck Crouch.

Liveliest of all was Pepi. Her practical jokes were designed to deflate large egos, while her twinkling eyes and infectious, toothy smile prevented anybody from staying angry with her for long. "The actress Claire Windsor's false bosom and the writer Madame Elinor Glyn's red wig would vanish from their bedrooms while they lay trustingly asleep," Louise recalled. [6]

Pepi's antics often revolved around liquor, to which she was addicted even then. While swimming with Louise and other friends one day in the huge, clover-shaped marble pool, Pepi learned that a group of Hearst's editors, "solemnly outfitted in dark business suits," was sitting inside at a table loaded with bottles of Scotch and gin: "Pepi organized a chain dance. Ten beautiful girls in wet bathing suits danced round the editors' table, grabbed a bottle here and there, and exited, leaving one of the astonished men to inquire of a Hearst employee, Harry Crocker, 'Does Mr. Hearst know these people are here?' " [7]

Getting around the Hearst liquor laws was Pepi's most challenging vocation. The rules were enforced by a network of informers—maids and servants, part of whose function was to ferret out and confiscate the bottles that Marion hid in the bathrooms and that guests hid under their mattresses. Hearst's spy system was legendary. Over the years, aside from using his own employees, he also patronized detective agencies and often had Marion "watched" in New York. [8]

Louise had been made aware of Hearst's obsessive spying two years earlier during her *Gold Rush* summer in New York. "Walking up Park Avenue one afternoon, I recognized the unmistakable figure of Chaplin more than a block ahead of me," she wrote:

> Swinging his cane, he was strolling with his usual grace except that at intervals he would snap his head back for a quick look behind him. Running to catch up with him I asked, "What in the world is the matter with you?" Looking back once more, Charlie whispered, "Mr. Hearst is having me followed!" and then vanished through the Ambassador's lobby door. Ever since he had become a friend of Marion Davies and Mr. Hearst, because Mr. Hearst guarded Marion so closely, Charlie was sure he too was spied upon. . . . [9]

Louise, who never read newspapers, was evidently unaware of the gossip columns that were linking Chaplin and Davies and inflaming Hearst. A few months earlier, when Marion was making *Zander the Great** and

---

* One of the screenplay writers for *Zander the Great* was Frances Marion, whose father is credited with a memorable line of the era. When he learned she had been hired by Cosmopolitan Pictures

Chaplin *The Gold Rush*, they often met, dined, and cavorted about Hollywood. Hearst was wild with jealousy.

With Pepi filling her in on the delicious details of those intrigues, Louise passed the sybaritic month of January 1928 at San Simeon and scored a hit with Hearst. Marion and Louise got on well, too. Behind Marion's back—and sometimes in front of it—Louise could perfectly mimic her famous stutter and was often called upon by Pepi to do so. But a lot of people did that, and self-deprecating Marion even made fun of herself.

"I couldn't act," Marion once said of her stage days, "but the idea of silent pictures appealed to me, because I couldn't talk either. Silent pictures were right up my alley." [10]

Having known Marion in New York, Louise was impressed with how unchanged she seemed by this fabulous life of luxury. She still called her "B-B-Brooksie," and with affection. But Louise was equally fascinated with Marion's calculating side and with the see-no-evil "moral code" ostensibly laid down by Hearst.

As far as the sexually charged Louise was concerned, the code had less to do with morality than most people thought. Among the San Simeon visitors that year was another precocious adolescent—Louise's sixteen-year-old brother Theodore, a crackerjack tennis player and a soulmate to whom she later confided:

> Nobody, and certainly never Pepi, ever said a word about Marion that did not fit the character of a saint. [They all said] it was Mr. Hearst who was wildly jealous of *her,* whose policing broke up the gatherings in the assembly hall of the castle at midnight (Marion and Mr. H. always left at ten) and herded the men and women into separate beds. Yet Pepi and her group of pansies and dykes could drink and carry on all night. . . . As long as he had Marion's drinking under control and nobody was busting up his objects d'art, he didn't give a damn about their sexual activities. [11]

The impression conveyed by Marion was one of regretful but helpless resignation; she had no choice but to acquiesce to W.R.'s old-fashioned bedtime policy. But Louise saw that as a pose. Marion had her own unwritten rule: "that no girl engage Mr. Hearst's attention for more than 30 seconds." [12] Twice at San Simeon, Louise ran away from casual private encounters with Hearst—once in the castle library:

> The librarian unlocked the brass screen that held the [rare] Dickens edition I wanted to see and then left the room with me sitting in a window seat. Suddenly I heard that sweet high voice: "Well, *hello!*" I looked up to see Mr. Hearst's penetrating, questioning eyes. Whereupon I closed the red vellum

---

and would be writing movie stories for Marion Davies, he sent her a note saying, "So you've gone from bad to Hearst."

*Louise demonstrates more form than substance
in a tennis match with brother Theodore, 1928.*

book and fled from the room. Had Marion come upon us, she would not
only have deported me from the Ranch but have ordered Louella Parsons to
exterminate me in her column. In those days that was film death. Outside
Mr. Hearst, Marion was a most decent woman; but there was very little
outside Mr. Hearst. [13]

"Marion was constantly threatened by the beautiful girls Mr. Hearst
kept in his court," she told Theo, "and it was possible that one of them
might replace her." It wasn't a matter of morals; Hearst and Marion, after
all, "lived in sin" for three decades and even endured a nasty attack on
that account from presidential candidate Al Smith in 1928. It was the more
pragmatic matter of preventing infidelity and the kind of hanky-panky that
produced babies and scandals.

But what most intrigued Louise about the castle's sex code was the
irony of its heterosexual-homosexual double standard. She was fascinated
by sexual experimentation and growing fonder of the openly lesbian Pepi.

"Pansies and dykes"—the favored and not necessarily derogatory terms that Louise stuck by all her life—could get away with anything, protected from pregnancy by biology and from publicity by journalistic taboo.

As Pepi liked to say, "Louise brooks no restraint," least of all in the bedroom. By this time, she had been sexually active for at least five years. Her clear preference for men was revealed in her diaries and her affairs to date with Wanger, Chaplin, Collier, Marshall—and Eddie Sutherland, among others. But she was aware that girls were as strongly attracted to her as boys in a business where homosexuality and bisexuality often seemed more the rule than the exception.

"From the age of 15 I was pursued by lesbians and I was strongly attracted by them, but not much sexually," she said. "While in the *Follies* I lived with Peggy Fears who had already become a lesbian legend, running through the *Follies* beauties like the well-known dose of salts. Every man in New York was jealous of her conquests. How this tickled her!"[14]

Louise would later claim to have had exactly three "explorations" with her own sex—a conservative figure. She allowed the rumor that she was a lesbian to spread, partly out of a desire to shock and partly because she truly did savor feminine beauty, in and of itself. Of Louise's many homosexual friends, one of her favorites was dancer Charles Weidman, who made a light-hearted observation one day in 1923 that she often quoted, and that helps explain her choice of homosexual terms: "Louise," he said, "everybody says you're a lesbian, but you're not really. You're a *pansy*."[15]

Such dizzying ambiguities served to intensify Louise's magnetism. She was boyish and girlish at the same time, and intoxicating to both sexes. There was no doubt that Pepi—madly in love with her—was one of the "explorations." Louise was candid about it, as a friend related: "She told me that Pepi said, 'Let me just fool around a little bit,' and Louise said, 'Okay, if it's anything you're going to get some great enjoyment out of, go ahead,' and so they fooled around. But she said she got nothing out of it."[16]

Louise delighted in Pepi, but not physically. At twenty-one, she approached sex as impetuously as everything else. Her sexuality was an integral part of that adventurous hedonism—the "younger degeneration's" zest for Life, Liberty, and the Pursuit of Pleasure. Some of them were also into drugs (Pepi had an increasing taste for cocaine), but booze was the real drug *du jour*. As an aphrodisiac, it was all most of them needed.

There was a second venue for such youthful scandals and follies: "Ocean House," Marion's beach home in Santa Monica—much more convenient to Hollywood. Marion's retreat was a 200-foot-long colonial mansion that Colleen Moore called "the largest house on the beach—and I mean the beach from San Diego to the Canadian border."[17]* Marion did her "casual" entertaining there, including the annual costume birthday party for W.R. at which he invariably appeared in a Little Lord Fauntleroy outfit and happily rode a merry-go-round imported for the occasion.

Inside the beach house, getting less attention than it deserved, was Marion's breathtaking art collection, purchased for her, of course, by Hearst. When Chaplin visited, he liked to imitate Baron Joseph Duveen, the English art dealer-connoisseur, strolling from painting to painting, making pompous comments as he went.[18] Perhaps the most priceless piece was a fifteenth-century Madonna by Luca della Robbia that was placed above the entrance and inspired a famous bit of doggerel apocryphally attributed to Dorothy Parker:

> 'Pon my honor
> I saw a Madonner
> in a niche
> over the door
> of the No. 1 whore
> of the world's biggest son of a bitch.

The unpleasant word "whore" was a recurring one, to Marion's lifelong chagrin, and Louise was among those who used it. She had been studying the Davies women at close range, and years later, with more admiration than censure, she summed them up—throwing in a psychosexual analysis of Hearst—in her brutal way:

> After many a summer, I read again Huxley's *After Many a Summer Dies the Swan*. He had not the courage to describe Mr. Hearst . . . , but he let himself go describing Mr. Hearst's whore, Marion. . . . They were a hungry lot, old man Douras [Marion's father] and his four beautiful daughters. Reine married George Lederer and acted in musical comedies. Mr. Hearst took up with her first. He had that perversion for going to bed with sisters . . . like some men only get a kick out of going to bed with another man's wife.[19]

The "real" Marion Davies wasn't just that "gay, generous, charitable, tipsy, thoughtless doll," she said. But neither was she the epitome of gold diggers. From the beginning, Hearst had pursued Marion; she merely accepted his gilded cage and stayed in it more or less faithfully until his death. "For 35 years," said Louise, "she had the brains, the iron discipline, to keep this brilliant, fascinating man enthralled. By many years, the longest run in the history of seduction."[20]

---

* After a long battle over taxes, Marion sold Ocean House in 1945 for $600,000—roughly the cost of the thirty-seven fireplaces she had installed. It was huge enough (thirty bedrooms) to be turned into a private beach club and hotel before being razed in 1960.

Louise respected her for that, while Marion in turn seemed fond of Louise and appreciative of her friendship with Pepi. Marion knew full well that most of Pepi's friends only used her as a connection to the Hearst-Davies social set and cash flow. Louise, by comparison, never tried to exploit her in any way.

For that reason, and because she was successful, beautiful, and charming in her own right, Louise was frequently invited to Marion's beach house and came often—with and without Eddie. It was at Marion's, for instance, that she had a memorable encounter, in 1928, with the Hollywood legend who dwarfed all others except Garbo: Gloria Swanson.

Louise was starstruck by very few movie performers. The number could be counted on the fingers of one hand, with vacancies. But Swanson was one of them. "In 1919 when I was 12, I gave up dolls and fell in love with Gloria Swanson," Louise wrote in an unpublished essay on Swanson:

> Her dark hair and blue eyes, her nippy nose, her darling little feet—she was a thousand times lovelier than a bunch of dolls that all looked alike anyhow. . . . She was mine. And when she started changing in her movies, I didn't like it a bit. It was gradual, but by the time I saw *Zaza* in 1924, she was another person. Her face was all makeup. Her eyes . . . seemed to have lost all their shadowy softness. And when she looked straight out of them, her eyes looked like the light behind them had gone out.
>
> Not that she wasn't beautiful in stunning costumes and just as exciting flying about, kicking and fighting and getting away with it. . . . [But] all the delicate seriousness of her Sennett days had been replaced in her comedy scenes by self-approval. At the end of [*Manhandled*] I wanted to give her some dog candy, so much like a charming little black poodle she had been, going through her tricks.[21]

It was soon after *Manhandled* that Swanson went with Walter Wanger to see Louise in the *Follies* (and to say she looked like "a corpse" in her white make-up). In Hollywood, during Swanson's marriage to Marquis Henri de la Falaise, Louise and Eddie were once invited to dinner, but Gloria's presence was minimal: "We had finished cocktails and dinner was announced when she came downstairs in a soft trailing negligee, ate some soup, gave Hank some long thoughtful looks, and went back upstairs again." So much for hostess perfection.

But Louise's most memorable encounter with Swanson took place during a party at Marion's beach house:

> [Gloria] decided to liven up a rather dull Sunday gathering with one of her favorite games. She took all the girls into a room off the big library, sent the butler for a platter of strained honey which was set upon a table with her seated behind it. What the dodge was I forget, but one by one all the men were brought in blindfolded and led to the table. Some question which they

could not answer was put to them, and then as a penalty Miss Swanson told them to bend over and pushed their faces into the honey. It was quite a sight, seeing the men rear back with the honey dripping down over their ascot ties and afternoon clothes.[22]

Though Gloria thought the game hilarious, Louise and the rest of the women were mystified by Swanson's desire to humiliate the men—a vengeful and apparently therapeutic exercise of power. She was, at this point in 1928, having an affair with Joseph P. Kennedy, father of the future President, and rapidly losing her fortune in the Kennedy-financed *Queen Kelly*. That disastrous extravaganza was under the direction of Erich von Stroheim, whose sadistic streak could be contagious.

Eddie Sutherland's was one of the faces that got shoved into the honey platter, and he was not amused. But you never knew what might happen at Marion's, which was why Louise liked the place: "I did not perform, I

Gloria Swanson in high dudgeon, ca. 1928; Barry Paris Collection

did not even talk. I sat and watched other people perform."[23] In February, when Eddie and director Wesley Ruggles went off on a golf trip, Pepi asked Brooksie to spend a weekend at the beach house. The night she arrived, there was no party, no blaze of lights, and no flurry of elegant guests being greeted by Marion and W.R. The huge house was dark and almost empty, except for the library, where she found Marion playing solitaire in her robe and Pepi swooning privately to "When Day Is Done" on the Capehart record player.

The women settled into a boring game of hearts when Marion suddenly put down her cards and told Louise about an encounter with Hearst's wife in the Chicago train station. "We all stared at each other for a second," said Marion, "and then W.R. went over to talk to her, leaving me standing there alone, and she gave me such a look of contempt—I could have killed her."

She then picked up her cards and continued with the game. Louise wondered why Marion would reveal such a painful memory, but not for long. Marion soon put down her hand again and asked Louise sharply, "Were you in *Louie the 14th* with Maybelle Swor?" After Louise said yes, Marion grilled her as to whether Hearst might be seeing the girl at that very moment in New York.

Louise glared up at Marion from beneath the black bangs.

"I was very angry about being placed in such an ugly position and would not answer," she said. "Through her personal spies, Marion knew far more about Mr. Hearst's affair with Maybelle than I did."[24] Marion thought Louise was among the Ziegfeld girls who had attended a certain party on W.R.'s yacht in New York harbor. Maybelle had been there. Louise had not, but her reaction was typical: Rather than say she had no knowledge of Hearst's affair, which was the truth, she clammed up in hostile fashion, leading Marion to think her a collaborator.

After that night, the warmth seemed to go out of Marion's attitude toward her. But Pepi was oblivious as usual and made sure Louise's invitations continued. Eddie's absences also continued, and so Louise went back for another, more fateful weekend in April. The place "had returned to its dream state," Louise recalled. Marion had twenty to lunch on Saturday, and forty more came later in the afternoon to swim in her white marble Venetian pool between the house and the ocean. Still another forty people showed up for a buffet supper on the porch overlooking the pool.

Much like the rules at San Simeon, beach house protocol called for all-day guests to take their leave by midnight. But it was considerably later, after all the coaches had turned into pumpkins, "when I asked Jack Pickford, Mary's brother, with whom I had been sitting in a porch swing, to take me to my room."

Whether their destination was truly the door of the room or a naughtier spot inside it, the night watchman had already found the chamber empty and locked it. According to her elliptical account: "Jack's car and chauffeur were waiting for him, so I went to his house to spend the night." By the time she got home to Laurel Canyon the next day, her brother Theo —still visiting from Wichita—told her Pepi had been playing detective from the moment she discovered Louise's absence and undisturbed bed:

> She telephoned Theodore to pick her up in his roadster, and, in search of me, he drove her to the homes of certain producers, stars and directors selected from Marion's guest list. By Monday morning, everybody in Hollywood, including Eddie and Jack's girlfriend, Bebe Daniels, knew that I had spent the night with Jack Pickford.[25]

BEBE DANIELS, Louise observed, "was a decent woman who rightly hated me for being such a snob and making off one night with her darling Jack Pickford."[26] But Louise claimed this "minor scandal" had nothing to do with her filing for a divorce a fortnight later on May 3.

"I had married Eddie," she said, "because he was a charming man who had besieged me with the gold band. He belonged heart and soul to Hollywood; I was an alien there. He loved parties; I loved solitude."[27]

There were indications to the contrary concerning Louise's preference for solitude, but there was no denying her alienation in and from Hollywood. She was bored with the kind of movie-making that went on there, as opposed to the way things were done on Long Island, and her taste of San Simeon (and of men like George Marshall, Buster Collier, and Jack Pickford) had made her even more bored with the often-absent Eddie.

Eddie, for his part, though not exactly old-fashioned in the matter of extramarital affairs, was outraged at all the gossip over the Pickford escapade which was flooding in to him. Wounded pride was a factor, but so was his real affection for Louise and the betrayal he felt. To his way of thinking, she had broken the unwritten rule that they would look the other way on each other's sex lives, so long as the indiscretions stayed discreet. It was the public humiliation that really hurt. But at heart Eddie knew Louise was not happy with him or with Hollywood. That phony European trip for *Tillie's Punctured Romance*, which so infuriated her, had been a blunder. She had wanted to go along but he had said no. Given Louise's temperament, that virtually propelled her to look elsewhere for sexual and intellectual action—and to find it with Marshall.

"When George and I met again in 1927," she had written, "I fell in love with his mind, which was panoramic. He concentrated absolutely on the business at hand, whether it was reading a comic strip or dipping into Lesage's *The Devil on Two Sticks*." (So *that* was where she got the idea for the amputee's "place card" at her literary dinner!) Marshall, she said, "understood my passion for books, which has made me perhaps the best-read idiot in the world." Eddie had not understood that passion.

> During that fragrant month of October, 1927, spent with George in New York, I was aware of a security I had never known before. From the outside, his life looked like a strenuously disordered striving among conflicting ambitions. It was in fact as perfectly ordered as a Carmelite nun's. I was determined, however, to forget him when I returned to Hollywood. It turned out that I could not, and we met as often as I was able to get away from the studio.

And from Eddie. After her first visit to San Simeon, she had sped to George's side for that exciting odyssey to Havana. A month later, when he finally put her on the train back to California, he left her with a very specific instruction: "Now, the first thing you must do, Scrubbie, when you get back to Hollywood is to start divorce proceedings against Eddie."

Back on the West Coast, she pondered that advice and debated it with Pepi. For six months, she had been leading a double life, and she hated the lie of it. Sneaking around was contrary to her nature. She and Eddie had been unofficially separated since February. He had neglected her, all right, but Louise knew that the marriage was doomed by no particular crime of his and that her own insatiable, or at least intimidating, sexual demands had been making life miserable for him. "She denigrated my manhood!" Eddie complained bitterly, years later, adding that she drove him to impotence and the psychiatrist's couch.[28]

So Jack Pickford was the catalyst, and Louise now did what Marshall told her to do. On April 18, 1928, she moved out, and on May 3 she filed for divorce. Despite all the warning signs and his plausible grounds for relief, Sutherland was hysterical. He threw a series of scenes and at one point swallowed an assortment of pills, but eventually, said Louise, "aided by a flow of parties and pretty extra girls," he recovered.

To Louise, in retrospect, the split had an almost dreamlike quality. "I just went away," she said. "I left a house in Laurel Canyon, a butler and other servants, a Rolls Royce motor car, and, of course, my husband."

When the Associated Press first got a hint of the breakup in mid-April, its wire story ran in the San Francisco *Chronicle* under the deliciously misleading headline, "Louise Brooks, Former Follies Girl, Abandons Love Nest"—meaning her own home. Now papers on both coasts hastened to report the filing of the petition, with a variety of true and false details.

"A. E. Sutherland, film director, was a tired businessman as far as wedding bells were concerned," reported Hearst's Los Angeles *Examiner*. "Louise Brooks, film star, so declared yesterday in her suit for divorce filed in Superior Court. She declared her husband always gave the excuse that he had to work whenever she sought his company in any amusement or recreation." Louise was alleging "cruelty" because whenever she asked to be taken out, "he remarked either that he was 'not interested' or that he was 'too busy.' " Cruelty was relative.[29]

Under the headline "Louise Brooks Tired of Mate's Noisy Friends," the Los Angeles *Times* on the same day reported the same news with a new twist, that it was Louise's tranquillity, rather than her desire for amusement, that went unfulfilled: "Sutherland, Miss Brooks relates, made a practice of bringing boisterous friends home with him and entertaining them at odd hours of the night, to the accompaniment of a lot of noise. This, she said, caused her to lose a great deal of sleep."[30]

It wasn't over yet. They still had to go through the formality of the divorce hearing, which took place six weeks later on June 19, the day after she finished shooting on *Beggars of Life*. Eddie did not attend, choosing to lick his wounds in the comfort of San Simeon. Louise went to the hearing in the company of her lawyer, Milton Cohen, and her star witness, Pepi Lederer.

Pepi's initial reaction to the divorce had been surprisingly negative. "Entrusting my fate to George Marshall she thought was madness," said Louise. But as the hearing date approached, Pepi became absorbed in her role as witness, rehearsing outrageous variants on the theme of Eddie's mental cruelty. On the way to court, attorney Cohen "selected her mildest version and begged her to subdue her performance."[31]

Louise, for her part, told Judge McDill the tragic and now familiar story of the European trip: "I protested when he wouldn't let me go, and he rudely told me I could go to Hades if I wanted to, but not to Europe with him."[32]

The divorce was granted. "Ban on Trip Kills Love of Actress," headlined the L.A. *Times*, barely containing its incredulity. The denouement was crueler than Louise had planned, thanks to Pepi's sense of humor. Back in Louise's Beverly Wilshire suite after the hearing, fueled by a shaker of Bacardi cocktails, Pepi decided to inform Eddie of the decree:

> She sat down at the secretary and composed a telegram to him, ending with the line, "You are now free to diddle with little or no compunction," and signed it with my name. Joe Willicombe received the telegram in his office at San Simeon. He gave it to Marion and Mr. Hearst, who passed it on to Eddie, who read it to everybody, who pronounced me a heartless adulteress who should be stoned.[33]

Despite her carefree attitude, Louise was not really amused by the experience. It had been sad, and so was she. She liked Eddie and bore him no ill will. She had to give him credit for doing the gentlemanly thing —taking the brunt of the blame on the usual grounds of "cruelty" and "incompatibility," despite the fact that in this case the culpability was hardly one-sided. Eddie, of course, could *afford* to be magnanimous since Louise had not demanded any monetary settlement. Due to his lucrative film work and inheritances, Sutherland was a wealthy man. Only a woman as capriciously principled as Louise Brooks would turn down such a golden opportunity. In Hollywood divorce cases, it was positively unprecedented, and he could console himself with the fact that at least it was not going to cost him anything to let her go.

So she was divorced. Indeed, it was Louise who was now free to diddle without compunction, and within ten days she would be in George Marshall's arms again.

Relief mingled with regret after her flighty pal Pepi finally went home, leaving Louise in the lonely suite at the Beverly Wilshire. She wandered over to the window, looked out idly and noticed that A *Girl in Every Port* was playing at the movie house down below. It seemed pathetic instead of glamorous.

"Staring down at my name in lights on the marquee of the Wilshire Theatre was like reading an advertisement of my isolation," she said. "Someday, I thought, I would run away from Hollywood forever. Not just the temporary running away I did after making each of my films—but forever." [34]

11 · Sound and Fury

I'll give the talkies three years, that's all.
—CHARLES CHAPLIN [1]

L O U I S E spent the next six weeks crisscrossing the country with George Marshall, celebrating the divorce in a crazy-quilt itinerary to rival a Denishawn tour: first Chicago, for a quick, unpleasant visit with her mother, then on to Washington and New York to link up with Peggy and Blumie, then back to Washington, returning to Los Angeles for twelve days, back to Washington, north to Atlantic City, and south again to Washington. Finally, on August 9, she was forced back to Los Angeles. There was one more picture to be made before she could escape Hollywood.

The project awaiting her was more important than most. Paramount was making the first of the Philo Vance detective movies: S. S. Van Dine's popular *The Canary Murder Case*, starring William Powell, Jean Arthur, and Louise and directed by that old Brooks admirer Malcolm St. Clair, fresh from his successful Clara Bow picture, *The Fleet's In*. It would be the third time Mal and Louise worked together; since they were known quantities to one another, the picture would be a piece of cake, or so they both thought. *The Canary Murder Case* was in fact a watershed film for both of them, though not for the reasons they imagined.*

Despite her feelings about Hollywood, by the time *The Canary Murder Case* began production, Louise's fan mail and favorable reviews indicated that she was on the verge of becoming one of Paramount's major stars. "I

---

* For the rest of Louise's life, she would be dogged and annoyed by the mix-up between *The Canary Murder Case* and *The Cat and the Canary*, the Paul Leni mystery-horror film made one year earlier. "If Louise Brooks is remembered at all," wrote James Card in 1956 before the big Brooks revival, "it is usually only to confuse her with Laura La Plante in *The Cat and the Canary.*" The beautiful La Plante retired suddenly and early from films in an aura of mystery not unlike that surrounding Brooks.

received an average of 2,000 letters weekly," she told the young publicist Lothar Wolff in Berlin a few months later, archly adding that "friends of mine maintain I didn't use more than a box of stationery to answer them."[2]

The Canary Murder Case was in many ways the perfect vehicle to take her over the top. Then in its eighth printing, the book had sold more than 200,000 copies and was touted as "the Babe Ruth of record-breaking sellers." Van Dine was a pseudonym, and his publishing house, Scribners, was getting good publicity mileage out of the increasing public curiosity about his real identity.*

The story—inspired by the unsolved killing of Broadway beauty Dot King—had sex, murder, and mystery.† The book sales provided massive publicity, and Paramount received hundreds of letters volunteering advice on how it should be filmed. In this hot property, Louise played no less than the title role—a showgirl called "the Canary," who is a ruthless gold digger. After she is found strangled, the police assemble a drawing room full of suspects (Charles Lane, James Hall, Gustav von Seyffertitz), all of whom had sampled her charms and come away with a motive for "croaking" her. Also under suspicion is Hall's jealous girlfriend, played by newcomer Jean Arthur. But the sole witness is strangled, too. It looks like a case for Philo Vance, whimsical socialite and amateur detective *extraordinaire.*

Though Louise is killed off early in the film, her scenes are the highlights of the picture and were advertised as such. In the opening sequence, as star of "The Canary Revue," she is scantily dressed in feathers and backed by seventy beautiful chorines as she swings out over her audience, titillating them with choice views of her legs from below. She never does much more than swing, but the crowd goes wild. In subsequent scenes, she is outfitted in dazzlingly seductive evening clothes that became the talk of the fashion press.

Louise's billing was second only to that of William Powell, hitherto cast only in supporting roles and—with his mustache and dark complexion—usually typed as a villain. It was his first detective role, and Philo Vance was the first of the suave "modern" detectives who worked things out scientifically. The surprise solution to the mystery was such that Paramount told its exhibitors to ask audiences to keep the ending a secret and to "run a notice to this effect on your screen."

---

* S. S. Van Dine, whose real name was Willard Huntington Wright, was a prominent scholar who had written a dozen books on applied ethics, philology, art, philosophy, and music when he suffered a nervous breakdown in 1925. To while away his recovery time, he turned to detective fiction, and by 1928 he had penned *The Benson Murder Case, The Canary Murder Case, The Greene Murder Case,* and *The Bishop Murder Case* and was the most successful detective writer in history, surpassing even Arthur Conan Doyle.
† See chapter 4 note, p. 84.

Louise and William Powell in The Canary Murder Case *(1929)*

From his success in *Canary*, Powell went on to a string of silk-hat detective roles and the apex of sophistication and stardom as Nick Charles in the *Thin Man* series, with Myrna Loy as his equally sophisticated wife, Nora. Louise's friends maintained that she would have made a perfect Nora and was heading in that direction had she played her cards right. But that was in the spacious realm of the might-have-beens.

In the realm of current reality, Louise was present at the birth of the "new" detective genre. Production went well and included a much-publicized visit to the set by the author, who came 3,000 miles from New York to advise St. Clair on "technicalities" but mostly to take a look at the rushes. "I don't know what I expected to see—I had heard many woeful tales from other authors," said Van Dine. He then astonished the studio by declaring, "It is a much better picture than it was a book," and Paramount immediately issued a triumphant publicity bulletin to that effect.

Much was made, too, of a new camera technique invented for the crucial poker-game scene in which the murderer reveals himself. St. Clair wanted an uninterrupted 360-degree close-up pan of the suspects seated at a round table, with the full surface of the table—cards, chips, and ashtrays—visible throughout. Clifford Blackstone, assistant to chief cameraman Harry Fischbeck, devised a rotating overhead camera base that accomplished the feat to the bafflement of everyone.

All in all, it was much ado about more than nothing but less than something spectacular. Louise was a delicious blend of sex and nastiness and Powell a debonair pleasure to watch. But Arthur was shrewish, the other characters were stereotypes, and the pace was sluggish. Though it did moderately well at the box office, the real killer in this mystery was boredom, and blame had to be laid at the large feet of Malcolm St. Clair. He was invariably kind to Louise, and she was always much taken with his exquisite white cashmere suits. But his imitate-my-mugging style of direction, which had irritated her during A Social Celebrity and The Show-Off, was now positively unbearable.

"I hated working with him," she told John Kobal. "[On] the last picture I made with him, Canary Murder Case, he was drunk all the time. Plus a broken leg. He was about 6'4" . . . no, he wasn't. Men then seemed taller. . . .[3]*

St. Clair had been voted the third greatest director of 1926, after Lubitsch and Von Stroheim. But everything had changed after the flop of his Gentlemen Prefer Blondes. Directing Canary, he reminded Louise of a "giant marionette" abandoned by his puppeteer. She employed a similar analogy in her unfinished article, "The Mystery of Mal St. Clair," describing him as once staggering drunk into her room at the Beverly Wilshire and "collapsing over me in bed, looking with his perpetual graven smile like a huge, discarded Pierrot. . . ."

"He was not a calculated mystery like Garbo," she told Kevin Brownlow.[4] "Nobody knew he was a mystery until after his death when we all found that we knew nothing about him. . . . He should have been a film comic. Which brings me to the solution of his mystery. He detested reality. He never talked about himself and his life because he found it so dull and boring. His talk was made up of stories he invented about himself and the people he admired like Sennett." And as usual in Louise's assessments, sexuality was the elusive key.

"What I have not yet worked out is the meaning of my relationship with Mal," she said. "He had no power over me at all, either as a director or as a man who tried to get in my bed on and off for fifteen years. And considering the hundreds of much less attractive men who succeeded in the hay, I can't understand it. The only thing that comes to mind is that the rims of his round blue eyes were bright pink."

There was something unnerving about Mal, and thus for both personal and professional reasons, Louise was greatly relieved when principal pho-

* She was close enough. St. Clair was 6'3" tall. "The last job he had," she wrote later, "was with Zanuck who made it a law that Mal should never stand in the presence of Zanuck, 5'6"."

tography on *The Canary Murder Case* was completed October 1, 1928. In her shoot-and-run tradition, she left for New York that very day, forgetting or ignoring that the cast would probably be called back for retakes, due to a startling technological development.

Louise did not take the novelty of "talking" pictures any more seriously than the rest of her colleagues when the first sound effects crept self-consciously into the movies in 1926 and 1927. Certainly, she did not feel threatened by them. The stars, whistling in the dark, assured each other sound was just another techno-gimmick that wouldn't last. But as it became apparent that the novelty might stick, major and minor stars alike began trembling lest their voices be the death knells of their careers.

Still, Louise was not among the terror-stricken. She was that rare breed of performer who knows virtually no stage fright, no matter what the stage. And besides, her own voice was a melodic, lilting contralto that promised to record well. She would cope with it nicely, thank you. She had mastered every other medium she ever touched. If and when Brooksie had to talk in movies, she'd talk. What was the big deal?

Meanwhile, in the executive offices of Paramount and every other major studio, the opposite of Louise's sanguine disinterest reigned: panic. It is impossible to overstate the turmoil produced by sound in the movie industry, especially in the wake of Warner Brothers's *The Jazz Singer*.

From the uproar, one would have thought Al Jolson's immortal words —"Wait a minute, wait a minute! You ain't heard nothin' yet!"—came out of nowhere. But of course they did not.* Before, during, and after D. W. Griffith, a multitude of disc-recording methods had been devised to synchronize sounds with moving pictures. In 1920, work was spurred by the commercial deployment of that blind "talkie" of the home: radio. The real problem was not synchronization but *amplification* in theaters—for which Lee De Forest's Audion tube led to the solution.

Before its bold move into sound, Warner Brothers was a second-class outfit with shaky finances and few stars other than Rin-Tin-Tin. New sound systems were popping up daily, and the majors were not yet ready to embrace the novelty, let alone the Warners' odious licensing arrangement. But soon after *The Jazz Singer*'s sensational success in October 1927, Warners announced twelve more "talkers."† The new technology could no longer be ignored, and the big studios now scrambled to follow Warners' lead and cash in on the profits.

There would, of course, be no cashing in on profits without a gigantic

---

* That line was not in the *Jazz Singer* script. It was Jolson's cocky catch phrase from vaudeville days when he often had tough acts to follow but always managed to follow them.
† "Talkers" did not give way to "talkies" as the popular term for sound films until 1930.

outlay of capital first ($500 million in 1926 and 1927 alone). It came from the Wall Street bankers, who thereby strengthened their grip on the industry: More than forty bank and utility company presidents would soon be sitting on the boards of major film companies—eight of them at Paramount. Particularly important was Nicholas Schenck, whose brother Joe was in charge of United Artists. It was the brothers Schenck "at whose feet, as a pussycat" Louise sat and listened to many a scheme for dominance in the picture industry.

In May 1928, as Louise began filming *Beggars of Life,* Paramount and most other studios capitulated and made agreements with Western Electric for sound equipment. By the end of the year, 1,000 American movie houses had sound capability.* Warners proclaimed that from now on, *all* its pictures would be part- or all-talking. In September 1928, the Warner conquistadors took over First National and fired 100 employees the first week.

Sound's reign of terror was just beginning. The other wild scramble was for stage actors who "knew how to talk." Studios hardly bothered to find out if their silent stars could do the job first. Nor did they analyze the powerful appeal of Jolson's famous ad lib—its naturalness. The mythical value of "trained" voices took root, along with the morbid fear that all the good ones would be snapped up quickly.

Suddenly there was a bull market in elocution teachers, real and fraudulent: Gloria Swanson lured stage actress Laura Hope Crews to Hollywood and paid her $1,000 a week for voice lessons. Between July and December of 1928, Hollywood's seven "colleges of voice culture" increased to two dozen. Typical of the quackery was a Motion Picture Academy seminar at which the stars' voices were classified as "euphonic, allisophonic, eulexophonic, eurythrophonic, or rhythmophonic"—and the ideal, "dynaphonic."

Hardly noticed was the destruction of an entire subindustry: house orchestras. In two years, 10,000 of 20,000 movie-theater musicians would be thrown out of work and the rest soon followed. Hundreds of silent-title writers—the literati of Hollywood—were also made redundant.

By fall 1928, the stars could no longer ignore the sky falling around them. The novelty of sound was wearing off, but rather than tiring of it, audiences now *expected* it. Many studios were recalling silent films and tacking on sound sequences (a rejuvenation process known as "goatglanding") or switching to sound in midproduction at enormous extra cost. And because of the need for lip synchronization, film speed had to be standardized—the norm arbitrarily set at twenty-four frames per second. †

* At the end of 1929, the figure was an astonishing 8,700.
† A persistent error in film histories is the myth that silent pictures were shot at a standard sixteen frames per second. The silent "standard," in fact, did not exist. Since cameras were hand-cranked, the speed varied wildly according to director and cameraman—ranging from twelve to thirty-six

Perhaps it was just as well for Louise that she had left town during those last hectic months of 1928. If she hated the movie-making process before, she would have been homicidal about it now, for much of the exuberance was going out of picture making. No more technicians bustling about. No more musicians playing mood music to soothe the stars as they worked. No more directors shouting through megaphones; indeed, the quaint verb "to megaphone" (meaning "to direct") henceforth disappeared.

Of many ironies during the transition, the most diabolical was that, when silence went out of the movies, it came onto the set. Above the soundproof doors was a forbidding new command in red lights: "Silence." Economics rigidified things even further: Optical soundtracks soon replaced the wax-disc method, and in the six months ending in February 1929 the studios spent $24 million to upgrade recording facilities, and a phenomenal $300 million was expended for the wiring of theaters. Profits for the government-protected monopoly, Bell–Western Electric, were an outrageous 300 to 500 percent per house. In March, Fox announced the end of all silent-film production, and the others soon followed suit. Looking back in October 1930, *Fortune* magazine called it "the fastest and most amazing in the whole history of industrial revolutions." The retooling of the entire industry had taken place in about twenty-four months.

One reason why this revolution went unnoticed for so long by Louise Brooks and other self-absorbed actors on the West Coast was that much of the sound shooting and most of the sound-film premieres took place in New York. Hollywood performers had felt comfortably isolated, since it still took three days to get from Los Angeles to New York, unless one was willing to risk the air service (just inaugurated in mid-1927) for $450. Many in Los Angeles didn't see and hear their first talkie until *Glorious Betsy*, starring Conrad Nagel, opened there on April 26, 1928.

And so it seemed that, just when Louise finally went to Hollywood in 1927, the great sonic boom was shifting the film industry's attention back to New York again. In a sense, Louise was now in the right place but at the wrong time.

Geography aside, Louise's failure to apprehend Paramount's economic panic over sound was neither uncommon nor inconsistent with the general denial of reality that manifested itself in all aspects of the film colony's existence. Even in the best of times, Hollywood was "an insecure community gripped by chronic self-doubt."[5] A new sign of that insecurity, says Alexander Walker, "was the great influx of star gazers, palmists, crystal

---

frames per second. Many theater owners ordered projectionists to turn up their rheostats and run films faster (in order to squeeze in an extra daily screening); filmmakers learned to frustrate that trick by cranking faster. Some silents were thus shot at a *faster* rate than talkies and are actually slowed down when projected at sound speed.

ponderers and card-readers into the colony. Advice was sought anxiously and expensively from them by those under the threat of speech."[6] A strange mix of naïveté and cynicism aggravated this confusion between illusion and reality.

Canary Murder Case director Mal St. Clair, who "detested reality," was a case in point. Kevin Brownlow later wrote Louise that St. Clair "mirrors the malaise of the first 50 years of motion pictures":

> I can think only of Griffith, of King Vidor (*The Crowd*)—and who else?— who dealt with reality, with real people and with social conditions as they existed outside California. And their moments of reality were very limited. On the whole, Hollywood devoted itself to escaping from reality, and devising more and more intricate ways of permitting audiences to do the same.[7]

To which Louise replied: "You are right, right—EVERYBODY in Hollywood invented romantic characters to hide their dullness and dull backgrounds—pants-pressers, starving actresses and ex-waitresses, starving actors and bums."[8]*

But though Louise was highly attuned to reality-denial in others, she often failed to recognize it in herself. Soon enough she would discover that something more nearly approaching realism did exist in film. For now, though, the one dependable "reality" of movie-making—its silence —was crumbling. But aside from those whose livelihoods depended on the silence, would anybody really miss it?

Silence was golden, and even though all that flickered was not gold, the absence of speech was what required movie audiences to perceive the story and the illusion visually. It was the great fear of those who loved silent films—as it turned out, a correct fear—that words would destroy the enchantment.

The most eloquent voice on this subject was also the most bitter. Asked about talkies in March 1929, Charles Chaplin replied, "I loathe 'em." The rationale behind his loathing was profound: "They are spoiling the oldest art in the world—the art of pantomime," he said. "They are ruining the great beauty of silence. They are defeating the meaning of the screen, the appeal that has created the star system, the fan system, the vast popularity of the whole. . . . It's beauty that matters in pictures—nothing else. The screen is pictorial. *Pictures!*"[9]†

But Chaplin's passionate opposition to sound was dismissed as self-serving. Robert Sherwood of *Life*, for instance—the man who had re-

---

* She added a cautionary and prophetic note: "You speak as if the 'escapist' era had passed forever in films. With TV (which will soon be making all our films), the comic strip world has returned as King."

† Chaplin held out until 1936 (*Modern Times*) before allowing his voice on a soundtrack.

cently championed Mal St. Clair as "the American Lubitsch"—had a much more exciting cause to champion after seeing *The Jazz Singer:*

> Al Jolson as an actor is only fair. But when Al Jolson starts to sing . . . well, bring on your superspectacles, your million-dollar thrills, your long-shots of Calvary against the setting sun, your close-up of a glycerine tear on Norma Talmadge's cheek—I'll trade them all for one instant of any ham song that Al cares to put on.[10]

Behind the humor and hyperbole of Sherwood's effusion was a sobering demonstration—for Chaplin and sympathizers—of how quickly even the intelligentsia, not to mention the general public, was ready to abandon the high art of silent film.

One of the few directors who not only did not tremble in the face of sound, but openly embraced its possibilities, was Louise's old friend Edmund Goulding, who was now making sound tests for Paramount. Few people at the time shared Louise's belief that Goulding was the most brilliant man in films. But in a stunning *Variety* essay of June 13, 1928, Goulding set forth the first thoughtful reply to Chaplin's position—a prophetic, utopian vision of how the new medium would develop:

> [Sound] will not complicate, it will simplify. . . . The new director will be more de Maupassant than Dickens—terse, tense, succinct.
>
> The new actor will bring with him to the screen a new kind of voice. The fallacy of voice training will soon be discovered. The pompous, grandiloquent actor will be a nuisance. . . .
>
> The girl who, in a close-up, can sing a soft lullaby to her baby and whisper —"Good night, my darling"—in such a way that the camera might be listening to her through a keyhole—she will be the new star.
>
> Vocal tricks, screams, sobs, snores, laughter, will be among the valuable tools for story-telling. . . .
>
> The infant industry has taken the ribbons from her hair. She has put away some of her bright toys—she is growing up. She may have a child, one day, and the child's name may be Television, but that's another story.

Another story, indeed—a story that, like the new "talkers," would not require the aid of title writers anymore. The writing and illustrating of titles had been an integral part of filmmaking, particularly in films drawn from literature and the theater. When done well, as in *Love 'em and Leave 'em*, titles provided seamless continuity as well as wit. But in 1928, hardly anyone was lamenting the obsolescence of that craft. Louise was sensitive to the title writer's plight because of her friendship with Ralph Spence, who was one of the best:

> In an effort to be funny, old actors and directors have spread the false belief that any clownish thing coming to mind could be said in front of the

camera in silent films. They forget the title writer had to match his work to the actors' speech. I remember late one night wandering into Ralph Spence's suite in the Beverly Wilshire, where he sat gloomily amidst cans of film, cartons of stale Chinese food, and empty whisky bottles. He was trying to fix up [her own] Beery and Hatton comedy, *Now We're in the Air*, and no comic line he invented would fit the lip action. Silent-film fans were excellent lip readers and often complained at the box office about the cowboy cussing furiously trying to mount his horse.[11]

Now that titles were fast disappearing, it occurred to a few of the more thoughtful observers that sound might not fill the void as easily as they first thought. The problem was both simple and complex: You could put any words in a title and people would "hear" them with exactly the right delivery and inflection. But the same words in the mouth of a real human being were subject to every pitfall from bad acting to bad equipment. And, of course, the internationalism of silent film was lost: Those were Yankee voices crackling through the amplifiers. From now on, universal illusion gave way to national (mostly American) patter.

The very nature of film-going was radically changed. For two generations, the experience was essentially a private one in which the viewer took an active mental and emotional role in apprehending the drama. With dialogue, the experience became collective, shattering the private "emotional communion" between the movie and its viewer. Sounds and words largely replaced the viewer's active cerebral involvement; his viewing became passive. Gone was the private, inviolable trance.

The practice of sound film was both more and less than the theory. *Beggars of Life* was a peripheral example. "During May and June 1928 when the film was shot," said Louise, "the studios clung to their delusion that Warner Brothers' Vitaphone was a passing vogue."[12] It was August before Roy Pomeroy set up Paramount's first sound stage to make tests and add a few dialogue scenes to films such as *Beggars*. David O. Selznick later declared: "I was . . . present on the stage when a microphone was moved for the first time by Wellman [in *Beggars of Life*] . . . The sound engineer insisted that the microphone be steady. Wellman, who had quite a temper in those days, got very angry, took the microphone himself, hung it on a boom, gave orders to record—and moved it."[13]

Louise thought Selznick's account was just "another of those shitty FIRST tales."* But in any event, Paramount was finally taking the sound plunge. It was the first of the majors to get feature-length talkies under

* Among the many others credited with first moving the microphone are Eddie Mannix of the MGM sound department; Gordon Sawyer, who installed United Artists's first sound system; and Dorothy Arzner while working on *The Wild Party* with Clara Bow.

way in the East. Among its projects was a daring one with the Marx Brothers. The boys were enjoying a big Broadway run of *Animal Crackers* by night, while commuting to Astoria to film their previous hit, *The Cocoanuts*, by day. Recording techniques were still primitive at this point (March and April 1929), and during the famous auction scene where Groucho sells worthless Florida swamp lots (in "Cocoanut Heights"), the rattling blueprints repeatedly drowned out his monologue. Retake after retake failed to solve the problem until someone got the bright idea of drenching the blueprints in water to quiet them down.

The Cocoanuts was a brilliant gamble by two of Louise's good friends, producer Walter Wanger and executive producer Monta Bell. Paramount accomplished another coup by signing up the little-known Frenchman Maurice Chevalier for a musical called *Innocents of Paris*, released in April 1929. Audiences loved his happy-go-lucky charm—just the opposite of the aggressive Jolson. They didn't mind the limp tale of a singing junkman. And the whole country began to sing a Richard Whiting tune that became Chevalier's signature song:

> Ev'ry little breeze seems to whisper "Louise"—
> Birds in the trees seem to twitter "Louise"—
> Each little rose tells me it knows I love you, love you.
> Ev'ry little beat that I feel in my heart
> Seems to repeat what I felt at the start . . .
> Can it be true, someone like you could love me, Louise?*

Musicals were good box office and distracted the public from finding out whether their favorite silent actors could handle dialogue. But Paramount did not shirk the challenge of straight drama, either. Its first sound feature at Astoria was Somerset Maugham's *The Letter*, starring Jeanne Eagels and directed by Jean de Limur. Tempestuous Eagels was an early-day "method actress" and a 1922 stage sensation as Sadie Thompson in that steamiest of Maugham stories, *Rain*. When *The Letter* opened in February of 1929, it earned her an Academy Award nomination, and Paramount rushed her into *Jealousy*. The critics hailed her, but she drew equal attention for her erratic behavior and drug encounters. Before 1929 was out, she was dead of heroin at thirty-five.

Eagels's fate seemed a bad omen, for Paramount had invested a lot of precious time and money in her. In the end, she was just one of countless unknown variables in the transition to sound. Paramount, like every other studio, was reinventing the wheel in technology, in personnel, and in the most basic assumptions about making and pacing movies.

---

* The tune was not written for or about Louise Brooks, though many thought it was, and her friends always kidded her about it. Louise, predictably, couldn't stand the song.

Paramount's Pomeroy, for example, was certain that actors would have to pause after each other's lines so that viewers could "have an opportunity to realize the shift in speakers." The concept of the "reaction shot"—in which the listener's face conveyed the necessary responsive emotion—had not yet occurred to anyone.

Among other problems was the audience's expectation that the volume of voices would diminish from close-up to long shot. Peoples' voices diminished with distance in real life. To early talkie audiences, fixed volume was incongruous and unrealistic—and something else to get used to.

And then there was the controversial matter of "dubbing" (short for "doubling") one actor's or singer's voice for another's, which would soon become a major issue for Louise.

If the studios could not stop the progress of sound, they could at least take advantage of it for some other items on their agendas. The moguls' relationships with certain of their major performers seem ambivalent even today. But they seemed downright sinister to Louise Brooks, who thirty years later penned a highly controversial article on the subject, "Gish and Garbo."

Her original (and preferred) title was "The Executive War on the Stars." Its thesis was that the studios were capitalizing on the confusion over sound to "break contracts, cut salaries and tame the stars." As Louise saw it, Lillian Gish and Greta Garbo at MGM presented a perfect dual example of how the war was waged, resulting in one victory and one defeat.

By 1925, two important developments had "finally bound the producers together in a concerted war on the star system." The first was the subjugation of the industry, once and for all, to Wall Street bankers, who generally recognized that it was stars, not producers, who made movies so profitable. That, in turn, led the producers to employ an insidious method of budget-trimming and star-taming—box-office failure. Costly Lillian Gish was the first to be marked for destruction, said Louise: "She was a timely martyr as well, being Hollywood's radiant symbol of purity standing in the light of the new sex star." [14]

The second key factor was the killing of censorship in twenty-four states, thanks to Will Hays's voluntary code and the National Board of Review, which had approved A Woman of Paris, Greed, and von Sternberg's first film, The Salvation Hunters. Such films were leading to public acceptance of more sexual realism—"an acceptance based on the beloved proposition that practically all women are whores anyway," Brooks maintained. Everything was now in place for a box-office bonanza until the producers "were pulled up short by the realization that they had no heroine with youth, beauty, and personality enough to make free love sympathetic." [15]

Lillian Gish in Way Down East *(1920)*

Greta Garbo, 1928; photo by Edward Steichen

Enter Greta Garbo.

When Louis B. Mayer first saw her in the Swedish picture *The Saga of Gösta Berling* in 1925, said Louise, "he knew as sure as he was alive that he had found a sexual symbol beyond his or anyone else's imagining. . . . The suffering of her soul was such that the American public would forgive her many affairs in *The Torrent*, Garbo's first American picture. At last, marriage—the obstacle standing between sex and pleasure—could be done away with! . . .

"The timely coincidence of the advent of talking pictures provided a plausible reason to give the public for the disappearance of many favorites. But there wasn't an actress in Hollywood who didn't understand the true reason. Greta Garbo. From the moment *The Torrent* went into production, no contemporary actress was ever again to be quite happy in herself."[16]

In the Gish case, said Brooks, studio resentment mounted after the release of her *La Bohème*, with John Gilbert, in 1926. It opened the same week as *The Torrent*, which packed the house. *Bohème* did not. This was bad, but not bad enough, according to Louise's conspiracy theory: "It was a question of how to get her to make a real stinker."

The "stinker," produced by Gish herself, was in fact a powerful, sex-charged one called *The Wind*, directed by Victor Seastrom (*né* Sjöström) and written by Frances Marion. Technically brilliant, it had a terrifying cyclone for a climax, but it did poor business. An inexplicable delay in releasing the film did not help, nor did the fact that Mayer put it on the second half of a double bill. After one more film, MGM let her go. Gish's film career, like silent film itself, was gone with *The Wind*.

Garbo, meanwhile, was getting a mere $16,000 a year, compared with Gish's $400,000. Despite enormous pressure—including studio-induced bad publicity and deportation threats—she held out for more money, and she got it: $7,500 a week—exactly what MGM would be saving as a result of no more Gish.

"The victory of one friendless girl in an alien land over the best brains of a great corporation rocked all Hollywood," Louise concluded. But eventually, "Eased out with full approval, in the perfection of their beauty, art and popularity, were Jeanette MacDonald, Joan Crawford, Norma Shearer, and finally Garbo herself."

The revelations of Louise's "Executive War on the Stars" theory were devastating—and not entirely accurate. Both Lillian Gish and her manager, Jim Frasher, for example, maintain it was Gish's preference for a theatrical career, and not MGM's machinations, that derailed her film activity for so long.

"It was *cost* they wanted to bring down, not Gish," insists Lawrence Quirk, author of more than a dozen authoritative books on Hollywood and its stars of the twenties and thirties. "All [Mayer and Thalberg] wanted to do was make a little money! *The Wind* was just box-office death. And she also turned down [Joe] Schenck's offer to go back to the movies because she was influenced by George Jean Nathan, who thought film was way beneath theater."

Quirk has even harsher words for Louise's claim that his uncle, James Quirk, collaborated with MGM to harm Gish and Garbo by publishing critical articles about them. "This is arrant nonsense," said Quirk in a 1986 interview. "Everyone who knew him, or who read *Photoplay*, praised his fierce independence and his disregard of advertising and studio pressures." Louise herself even wrote that James Quirk had a "perfect understanding of . . . how to be friendly but feared, cooperative but alone." [17]

Louise's view is also challenged by Alexander Walker:

> It is often alleged that sound was used as a weapon to ruin the stars. This is baseless. To tame and in some instances humiliate them—yes. But no studio with any corporate responsibility set out deliberately to wreck its own valued and fragile assets in whom so many years of grooming and promotion had been invested and to whom the public stayed extraordinarily loyal. [18]

And yet, having debunked the most sensational aspect of her charges, Walker goes on to support the underlying rationale:

> But the businessmen would not have been acting according to their own initiative if they had not kept their stars in a state of uneasy dependence so that stiffer terms could be exacted from them for an assured future in the talkies. Sound was a great disciplining force: it had arrived at the handiest possible moment when many stars were demanding fees that the box office recession of 1926–27 could not have gone on sustaining. [19]

Privately, the panicked moguls now viewed any practice that saved money as wholly justified: Before talkies, American films monopolized 82 percent of the world market, and foreign exhibition provided 40 percent of Hollywood's gross. Now that the universal language of silence was obsolete, the Tower of Babel would largely wipe that out. The economic crunch was real. Many executives were indeed exploiting the turmoil, but at heart they were groping as much as the actors and improvising as they went. Joseph Schenck summed it up perfectly: "The trouble with the whole industry is that it talked before it thought." [20]

There were three serious flaws in Louise's "Executive War" idea: its premeditation, its gross oversimplification of Lillian Gish's decline, and its flat-wrong assessment of James Quirk's role. But her theory contained some profound truth in its bold analysis of women and power. When they attained it, which was rare, they terrified the rich and often corrupt men in charge. "Garbo was a great threat to Louis B. Mayer because she sat it out for six months [until he caved in]," said Louise. "It was the challenge to their *power* that threatened producers."

Louise, characteristically, left her assessment open to attack because of its hyperbole. What she saw as a conspiracy was in fact just a natural *tendency*—not masterminded, but rather evolving out of what always motivated the movie moguls: money, power, and the selfish idiosyncrasies of their egos.

Even if there was no concerted war against the stars, there were many casualties, and two of them—Clara Bow and John Gilbert—were among the greatest of all. The " 'It' Girl" most fascinated Louise. "All film writers say that Clara failed because of 'talkies,' " she wrote her brother. "They say this about everyone who failed in 1928–29." All film writers were wrong, she said—including the one who would later call Louise "the first natural actress."

> I said, "No, no, you're wrong. The first natural actress was Clara Bow."
> . . . But, for God's sake, she was a half-witted little girl, her father was a busboy, her mother was in a nuthouse, and she wasn't bright.[21]

Even so, Louise liked her, and liked her a lot. Despite the disdainful assessment of her background, Louise was transfixed by her and astonished at how the spunky little star was ostracized:

> Eddie Sutherland gave the best parties in Hollywood. He invited the most amusing people, [but] when I wanted to invite Clara Bow to a party, Eddie recoiled in horror—"Oh, heavens, no, we can't have her, she—we don't know what she'd do, she's from Brooklyn." Her accent and dreadful manners would reproach the producers with their common origins. . . . Everyone at Paramount said of course she's the greatest actress . . . but she wasn't acceptable, and she knew that and it made her feel bad.[22]

Paramount had needed a new star when B. P. Schulberg brought Bow there in 1925. "He'd had an affair with Clara, of course," when he was an independent producer; in those days, according to Louise, "his outfit was the cheapest, and his reputation for the sexual abuse of young actresses who worked for him was the worst." But "coming down from the Brooklyn slums to work for Ben automatically labeled Clara a 'cheap little whore,' a category she was never to escape."

Under Schulberg, Bow was working in as many as three Paramount pictures at a time, thirteen of them in 1925 alone. But once he sold Bow's contract to the studio (for $150,000), and replaced her—in his films and affections—with Sylvia Sidney, his interest in her ceased. "With nobody to supervise her films and take care of her, she went to hell on booze and pills and gambling," Louise wrote her brother Theo.[23]

It was another oversimplification, but one thing for certain was that Clara was extremely fragile and terrified of how her Brooklyn accent would record. Half a century later, in a 1977 filmed interview with Kevin Brownlow and David Gill, Louise recalled a remarkable meeting in the summer of 1928, when Bow was Hollywood's top female star, receiving 30,000 fan letters a month. Louise found her "stunned and helpless" and convinced that her voice would never make it:

> [Schulberg] told her her Brooklyn accent was awful, but it really wasn't at all. Of course, you can always clean it up. . . . When talkies came in in '28, I was told to go over to [Pomeroy's] sound studio. . . . But I wasn't told Clara was going to make the test with me. I'd never met her, and I walked into the studio and there was a big couch and she was sitting in a corner of it, all curled up wearing her usual sweater and skirt, and I sat down and we began to talk and I have no recollection of them lighting the scene, or taking it or stopping it. She just began to talk, she knew all about me, I was supposed to be very sophisticated in Hollywood, that was purely on the strength of my having the magnificent Paris–New York wardrobe and of course being very sniffy. . . . I really was just a hick from Kansas. . . .
>
> [I felt] Clara wanted something from me as we sat talking. . . . She was telling me about how dreadfully Schulberg was treating her and I said, "Well, what's he doing?" This is after she moved to this very expensive house in Beverly Hills and her life was being run by her hairdresser. . . . She says, "Schulberg sent Ruth Chatterton [stage actress-turned-vocal-coach] up to my house on Thursday and . . . I beat it out the back door because they make me feel so terrible that I can't talk." I looked at her, and I have never seen anyone [so] beautiful in her features. She had skin just like a baby, she had this soft fluffy baby hair. And then I said, "Hey, Clara, you haven't any eyebrows, you've shaved off your eyebrows." "Oh," she said, "I did that so I could draw them on anywhere," and if you remember she got to looking worse and worse because she didn't follow the bone structure—she kept moving her eyebrows lower and lower. . . .
>
> It's funny, in 1928 she already knew that she was finished.[24]

In fact, she was mentally ill and her mike fright was now pathological. Perhaps she was doomed anyway. Her "type"—the flapper jazz baby—was giving way to the more mature thirties gold digger of the Jean Harlow mold. In the end, it was executive neglect more than an executive war that did her in.

Of a hundred differences between Brooks and Bow, the most illustrative is that between their attitudes to voice recording. Louise, too, was disappointed by the sound of her own voice when she heard the test results. But she adopted a radically different method of dealing with it, which she incorporated into her speech for life: She began to swear a lot. Forty years later, Kevin Brownlow noted that fact and Louise responded:

"That was a brilliant insight—that I cussed to give my dialogue force. The first time I heard my voice recorded I discovered that I belonged to the never, never, never land. I wasn't believable. So I took to swearing, trying to give my voice some impact—you discerning, nasty little boy— Fuck you!" [25]

Perhaps the meanest phenomenon of the transition period was the taunting of the silent stars. Reflecting the love-hate affair between stars and fans, hundreds of newspaper and magazine stories expressed a kind of sadistic glee at the new vulnerability of a pampered elite. John Gilbert, the screen's reigning and highest-paid male lover, should have been accustomed to taking licks from the press, but he was not amused by H. L. Mencken's good-natured diatribe in the April 1927 *Photoplay*:

> Gilbert is an amiable and tactful young man, and treats me with the politeness properly due to my years and learning. But I heard in Culver City that no less than 2,000 head of women, many of them rich, were mashed on him. Well, I can recall but 15 or 20 women who show any sign of being flustered by me, and not one of them, at a forced sale, would realize $200. Hence I hate Gilbert, and would rejoice unaffectedly to see him taken in some scandal that would stagger humanity. If he is accused of anything less than murdering his wife and eight children I shall be disappointed.

Gilbert's status as MGM's most profitable star had been augmented by his explosive teaming with Greta Garbo in 1926. In *Flesh and the Devil*, as Gilbert's daughter Leatrice puts it, "You can actually see these two terribly attractive people falling in love with each other on the screen." [26] Their relative stardom then was clear: Gilbert, not Garbo, got first billing. Audiences went home reeling, and so did Gilbert. He courted her for the next two years.

That period coincided with Louise's residence in Hollywood, during which she encountered Garbo once or twice at the home of mutual friends.

"In 1928 when I met Garbo at Alice Glazer's," she said, "we sat facing each other closely across a narrow breakfast table. Her gaze was so intense and so eloquent that I left after an hour although I had intended to spend the afternoon."

"We just met those few times," she told John Kobal, but then she dropped a little bombshell: "She made a pass at me." [27]

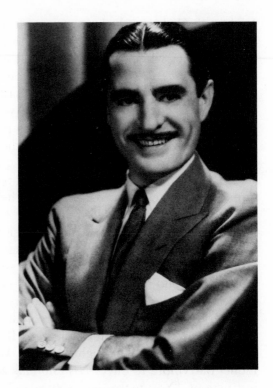

John Gilbert, 1929

Louise, like everyone else, stood in awe of Garbo. Her remark to Kobal was her only published reference to a liaison, but privately, Louise told a confidant that she and Garbo spent a night together and that Louise found her idol charming and tender. Years later, to Kevin Brownlow, she wrote: "When somebody like Dietrich or Bankhead went after her, Garbo took it on the lam." [28]

Garbo took it on the lam from Gilbert, too, after failing to go through with three different wedding plans. On the last of these no-show occasions, MGM's Louis B. Mayer gave the grieving Gilbert a philosophical piece of advice—"Sleep with her, don't marry her"—whereupon Gilbert decked his studio chief. And sealed his own doom. But Louise thought there was more to it: "I think it unwise to put down the Gilbert-Mayer trouble to any particular incident," she said. Mayer never wanted Gilbert at MGM in the first place; Thalberg had insisted. "And Jack was so silly and drunken, hamming it up, letting Mayer bait him into scenes, instead of minding Irving and staying away from him." [29]

Mayer also believed, probably correctly, that Gilbert had planted the seed in Garbo's mind to hold out for more money. That enraged him, but there was little he could do to or about Gilbert—until sound. *His Glorious*

Night with Catherine Dale Owen, a stiff newcomer from the theater, was not Gilbert's first talking picture, but it was the first to be released and it was the one by which his voice would be judged.

His Glorious Night was a moldy romance by Ferenc Molnár, with terrible dialogue. And Gilbert's most disastrous lines were the three most crucial words in the language: "I love you." Over and over he uttered them, in a voice that mismatched his physical virility. When the film opened on October 5, 1929, audiences did the worst thing they could do to a serious actor: They laughed.* The quality of Gilbert's voice was assumed to be the cause. But no one had reckoned on a problem that had more to do with the dialogue than with the delivery.

"Audiences still relatively new to the talkies found it embarrassing to hear, to *overhear*, a man declare his passion for a woman," says Walker.[30] People felt like Listening Toms. A similar example of their discomfort— intimate lines coupled with a performer's speech quirks—was the case of Dolores Costello in Warners' first talkie crime drama, *Tenderloin* (1928). Begged the lisping Dolores of her captors: "Merthy, merthy, have you no thith-ter of your own?" Audiences roared.

In Gilbert's case, the question was whether he had been sandbagged. Louise Brooks hadn't the slightest doubt. When Mayer hired his old friend Lionel Barrymore to direct *His Glorious Night*, she said, he gave simple instructions: "You make that picture and make it *lousy*." Barrymore was then on morphine and "too stoned to worry about anything but money, which Louis Mayer supplied in large, appreciative amounts."[31] Requests by sound engineer Douglas Shearer (Norma's brother) for retakes were denied. MGM director Clarence Brown confirmed the sabotage: "I know what happened. I was there. Doug Shearer told me himself. He said, 'We never turned up the bass when Gilbert spoke; all you heard was treble.' Of course it was a 'mistake.' "[32]

Gilbert was not the only silent actor with a tale of woe in sound. But most bided their time and passed their tests.† What killed John Gilbert was not so much his voice (which was okay in 1933 in *Queen Christina*) as his feud with Mayer, his heavy drinking, and those fatal words, "I love you," repeated over and over. . . . He died three years after *Queen Christina*, mocked and ruined, at the incredible age of thirty-six.

* Or at least that is the legend. There were numerous *reports* to Gilbert (through MGM) that people laughed at his "I love you's," though no contemporary review mentions the fact.
† The smartest waited as long as possible. Joan Crawford's first talkie, *Untamed* (released November 29, 1929), stressed her dancing and bought time for vocal improvement. Swanson waited for Eddie Goulding's help on *The Trespasser* (November 1, 1929). Garbo's first was *Anna Christie* (March 14, 1930). Gish's was *One Romantic Night* (May 20, 1930). Norma Talmadge's delay was one of the few that didn't pay off: Her *Du Barry, Woman of Passion* (November 2, 1930) prompted the possibly apocryphal wire from sister Constance, "Quit while you've still got your looks and be thankful for the trust fund mother set up." Norma did so.

. . .

And then there was Louise Brooks.

She was nowhere near the Clara Bow or John Gilbert league, and it is doubtful whether B. P. Schulberg or anyone else in Paramount's executive suite gave much thought to her. They had many more important things on their minds.

But so did Louise. Shooting on *The Canary Murder Case* was drawing to a close in late September 1928, as was the third year of her Paramount contract. She was at that point making $750 per week and looking forward to a contractual raise—assuming Paramount picked up her option—to $1,000.

A confrontation was brewing between Louise and Paramount, the genesis of which was mutual ignorance. After Walter Wanger left, none of the major executives had any firsthand knowledge of Louise's feistier qualities. She, in turn, had a contempt for studio politics, remained aloof, and prided herself on never lobbying for a part. As she told John Kobal:

> I didn't pay attention to anybody. The clever ones who went around like Richard Arlen wooed all the writers and all the other actors and the producers. And when they weren't working, they were on the lot every day, mooching up and making friends and whatnot. Of course when *I* wasn't working, I was in New York. . . . I didn't even know Schulberg was head of the studio until I was called into his office. I thought Walter Wanger was running the place, but Walter had gone to MGM. . . . I just moved by instinct all my life.[33]

It seems incredible that Louise didn't know who her boss was or that his ruthlessness in personnel dealings led many to consider him "the second biggest bastard in Hollywood, after Mayer." But it may have been true, so out of touch was she.

Louise's call from Schulberg came during *Canary* production, shortly before her September 12 option date. Everyone had been happy with her work, and she figured the conference was a formality. The $250 step-raises in her contract were typical for a Paramount featured player and minuscule compared with what the big flapper stars were making. Colleen Moore was then collecting $12,500 a week at First National, and Clara Bow was getting $7,500. But Louise was never very money-hungry. She had no new demands. She had fulfilled her obligations and was in line for a contractual raise. In that respect, if no other, she was playing by the rules.

Ben Schulberg had never met Louise Brooks, but he knew her reputation as the tartest piece of cheesecake on the lot. He knew she was good and that she was becoming popular, but she was not yet good enough or popular enough to intimidate him. The possibility of losing her never entered his mind.

Even so, when Louise marched into his office for the biggest confrontation of her career, Schulberg might have been slightly wary. His own legal files contained a letter from Paramount attorney Henry Herzblum recounting the difficulties of getting Louise to sign her previous contract renewal and concluding with "Miss Brooks bears the reputation of being a decidedly unreliable person."[34] She had just made mincemeat out of Eddie Sutherland and turned up her nose at alimony. She was palsy with Hearst and Marion Davies, which meant potential publicity—pro or con. Schulberg had heard all about her attachments to Otto Kahn, Wanger, Chaplin, and other high rollers in and out of pictures who could set her up in independent productions if they liked.

But Schulberg was a master at manipulating actors, especially those terrified of talkies. His scam was a simple one—perfectly in tune with Louise's "Executive War on the Stars" theory—and it went like this: All bets and contracts are off. We don't know whether your voice will cut it in talkies. But instead of letting you go, we're willing to keep you at your present salary. Louise recalled his exact words:

"You can stay on at $750 per week or leave."

It was the most naked kind of strong-arming, and she was furious. So this was her reward for playing the game. To Schulberg's total astonishment, she quit on the spot, fixed him with a withering look, turned, and walked out.

She was the only contract player on the Paramount lot to take such a drastic course of action, and as word spread, she was admired for her guts and pitied for her stupidity. But there was a story behind the story, and the *éminence grise* was Marshall.

"I was terribly in love with George Marshall," Louise told Ricky Leacock. The Laundry Baron had called her from Washington the day before her Schulberg meeting to say he had just learned from Monta Bell that she was about to be sandbagged.

"Now look," said Marshall over the phone, "when you go in to see Schulberg, he's going to tell you that he will keep you on at $750 a week, but he won't give you the raise in your option. I also know that some guy called Pabst in Berlin wants you for a very famous picture, and he'll give you $1,000 a week. So you let Schulberg talk, and when he's finished, you say, 'Thank you, Mr. Schulberg, but I'll quit and go to Germany.'"

"And that," said Louise, "is what I did, much to Mr. Schulberg's surprise."[35]

It was a tribute to Marshall and his infinite connections that Louise was tipped off in advance. Pabst's request for Brooks's services was conveyed by telegram to Paramount in Hollywood. Monta Bell was then at MGM

The Edward Steichen portrait for Vanity Fair

but had many friends at Paramount, and as a Washington, D.C. native and newspaperman he had long been friendly with Marshall.*

Louise was a delectable pawn moved by invisible hands on both coasts and two continents. Sick of Hollywood anyway, she saw this as just a new variation on her Denishawn nightmare: She was being screwed, and through no fault of her own. Schulberg could not bully her: "They were cutting actors' salaries just for the hell of it. And just for the hell of it, I quit."

Yet paradoxically, this most rebellious, independent woman was so in love with George Marshall that she was perfectly willing to do whatever *he* wanted her to do.

News of Louise's confrontation spread quickly back East, too. Edward Steichen, the preeminent portrait photographer, had photographed Louise during the *Canary* shooting and now sold the stunning picture to *Vanity Fair*, which ran it in January 1929, with a caption-story headlined "The Rise of Louise Brooks":

> Stranger than fiction is the metamorphosis of Miss Louise Brooks. . . . With her first heavy-lidded glances from the reels of Adolphe Menjou's *A Social Celebrity*, Miss Brooks made her debut as a Lorelei of the cinema. Through a series of boisterous comedies, the nonchalant Miss Brooks pursued her way. Her fortunes in Hollywood have been erratic; after a beginning heralded by the usual publicity fanfare of 'from chorus girl to star' stories, Miss Brooks seemed doomed to routine parts in program pictures. It is only with her recent, glamorous performance as the inadvertent murderess in . . . *Beggars of Life* that she has come into her own. . . . She is now the favored star of the Süd Film Company of Berlin, for whom she will make a film or so abroad before venturing into the "talkies."

So charged was the atmosphere in Hollywood that she literally couldn't wait to get out—leaving on the very day she finished *The Canary Murder Case*—even though she hadn't a clue of what lay in store for her in Germany. The advice that Marshall gave her, and that she routinely took, tended to be self-serving.

"Neither of us had heard of Pabst before, or of the Frank Wedekind play *Pandora's Box*, on which the film was to be based," said Louise. "George's concern at the moment, though, was not my career but his need for a relaxing trip to Europe."[36]

---

* Louise was inconsistent about how she learned that Pabst wanted her for *Pandora's Box*. In her own "Pabst and Lulu," she indicated it was Schulberg himself who told her about the Pabst offer "almost as an afterthought" to their salary confrontation. "I said I would accept it, and he sent off a cable to Pabst." If that was the case, it would mitigate Schulberg's villainy. He could easily have thrown Pabst's telegram in the trash, effecting a delay that could have ruined her chance for the part.

Louise seemed to need the same. They left at midnight, October 6, 1928, aboard the S.S. *Majestic*, bound for Cherbourg and thence Paris and Berlin. The cruise featured much drinking and a heightening of the carefree, careless attitude that characterized them both. In midocean, a cable arrived for Louise from Florenz Ziegfeld, offering her a role for which she had been the model: Dixie Dugan in the Broadway version of *Show Girl*. But Marshall intercepted it and took the liberty of cabling back the reply, "You couldn't offer me enough money to do it," signing Louise's name. He then tore up Ziegfeld's offer and tossed it overboard, not mentioning it until later in the voyage. Louise never got around to contacting Ziegfeld or apologizing for "her" needless insult, and Dixie went to Ruby Keeler instead. "Ziegfeld never forgave me," Louise said later.

The best that could be said of Marshall's action is James Card's speculation that "he was trying to build up her stock," acting as her agent—which he functionally was—albeit in the most arrogant and offensive manner; a potentially great star such as Louise could get away with this, he thought. The worst that could be said is that, not content with possessing her in the present, he was willing to wreck her future in order to keep everyone else away from his prize.

Either way, it was typical of the way Marshall handled Louise's life and career: Another nail was hammered into her professional coffin in the United States, even as he and the S.S. *Majestic* were propelling her toward immortality with Pabst.

Act Two

Lulu

THE MYTH OF PANDORA'S BOX

For a long time, certainly throughout the happy Golden Age, only men were upon the earth; there were no women. Zeus created these later, in his anger at Prometheus for caring so much for men. Prometheus had not only stolen fire for men; he had also arranged that they should get the best part of any animal sacrificed and the gods the worst. . . .

But the Father of Men and of Gods was not one to put up with this sort of treatment. He swore to be revenged, on mankind first and then on mankind's friend. He made a great evil for men, a sweet and lovely thing to look upon, in the likeness of a shy maiden, and all the gods gave her gifts, silvery raiment and a broidered veil, a wonder to behold, and bright garlands of blooming flowers and a crown of gold. . . . Because of what they gave her they called her *Pandora*, which means "the gift of all." When this beautiful disaster had been made, Zeus took her out and wonder took hold of gods and men when they beheld her. From her, the first woman, comes the race of women, who are an evil to men, with a nature to do evil.

Another story about Pandora is that the source of all misfortune was not her wicked nature, but only her curiosity. The gods presented her with a box into which each had put something harmful, and forbade her ever to open it. Then they sent her to Epimetheus, who took her gladly although [his Titan brother] Prometheus had warned him never to accept anything from Zeus. He took her, and afterward when that dangerous thing, a woman, was his, he understood how good his brother's advice had been. For Pandora, like all women, was possessed of a lively curiosity. She *had* to know what was in the box. One day she lifted the lid—and out flew plagues innumerable, sorrow and mischief for mankind. In terror Pandora clapped the lid down, but too late. One good thing, however, was there—Hope. It was the only good the casket had held among the many evils, and it remains to this day mankind's sole comfort in misfortune.

—EDITH HAMILTON, *Mythology*

„DIE BÜCHSE DER PANDORA"
⟨Lulu⟩

Nach Frank Wedekind
Drehbuch: Ladislaus Vajda

Regie: G. W. PABST

Produktionsleitung: George C. Horsetzky / Kameramann: Günther Krampf
Bauten: Andrejeff und Hesch / Aufnahmeleitung: Heinz Landsmann
Regieassistent: Mark Sorkin

Personen:

Lulu	Louise Brooks	Schigolch	Carl Goetz
Dr. Schön	Fritz Kortner	Rodrigo Quast	Krafft Raschig
Alwa Schön	Franz Lederer	Jack	Gustav Diessl
Gräfin Geschwitz	Alice Roberte	Marquis Casti=Piani	Michael von Newlinsky
Braut Dr. Schöns	Daisy d'Ora	Der Inspizient	Siegfried Arno

Herstellung und Weltvertrieb:

Nero=Film=A.G.

VERLEIH FÜR DEUTSCHLAND:

Südfilm=A. G.

BERLIN / LEIPZIG / DÜSSELDORF / HAMBURG
FRANKFURT a M. / MÜNCHEN / BRESLAU / KÖNIGSBERG i P.

12 · The Legend of Lulu

The German soul instinctively prefers twilight to daylight.
— L O T T E   E I S N E R

Imagine Pabst choosing Louise Brooks for Lulu when he could have had me!
— M A R L E N E   D I E T R I C H

M A R L E N E was understandably furious. According to legend, she was in Pabst's office in Berlin, on the verge of being signed by him to play Lulu, at the very moment Louise's telegram arrived accepting Pabst's offer.

There would be many legends associated with Pabst, Brooks, and *Pandora's Box*. The most colorful was the story that Pabst had been conducting an obsessive, two-year, intercontinental search for Lulu—comparable only to the search for Scarlett O'Hara a decade later—and that the European or at least the German film public was breathless to find out who the choice would be. But why would they care so much? It would seem that the Louise Brooks "mystery" and the German "shock" over an American's selection as Lulu were much exaggerated.

It would seem so—but they were not. The legend is not only colorful but true.

"Preparation for *Pandora's Box* was quite a saga, because Pabst couldn't find a Lulu," said assistant director Paul Falkenberg. "He wasn't satisfied with any actress at hand, and for months everybody connected with the production went around looking for a Lulu. I talked to girls on the street, on the subway, in railway stations—'Would you mind coming up to our office? I would like to present you to Mr. Pabst.' He looked all of them over dutifully and turned them all down."[1]

Meanwhile in Hollywood, Louise was quitting Paramount in that climactic confrontation with B. P. Schulberg which lasted all of ten minutes and "left Schulberg somewhat dazed by my composure and my quick decisions":

If I had not acted at once, I would have lost the part of Lulu. At that very hour in Berlin Marlene Dietrich was waiting with Pabst in his office. Pabst later said, "Dietrich was too old and too obvious—one sexy look and the picture would become a burlesque. But I gave her a deadline, and the contract was about to be signed when Paramount cabled saying I could have Louise Brooks."[2]*

Brooks's co-star Francis Lederer validates the legend: "*Pandora's Box* was a German classic. That Pabst would take an American actress for the lead—well, everybody was amazed, because she was definitely not like the other actresses who had played that part. There was nothing German about her."[3]

A trip through the German archives of 1928 confirms that the press attention to Louise and the making of *Pandora's Box* was truly compulsive. Scores of incredulous newspaper and magazine stories declaimed a common theme:

"Endlich die Lulu ist gefunden!" bannered the October 1928 issues of *Sudfilm-Journal* and *Der Film* of Berlin—"The Lulu is finally found!" They called her *Bubikopf*—a boyish scamp with bobbed hair. In the space of four weeks, Louise's face appeared on the front of *Die Filmwoche, Film-Illustrierte, Reich der Frau, Tempo. Elegante Welt, Neue Berliner, Film-Magazin, Neue Zeit, Das Publikum,* and *Funk-Woche* in Berlin, *Cinémonde* in Paris, *Die Bühne* in Vienna, *Das Illustrierte Blatt* in Frankfurt, the *Illustrierte* magazines of Hamburg and Nuremberg, and countless other publications as far away as Zagreb. All expressed astonishment at Pabst's selecting an American and at the incomparable beauty of his selection. F. J. Stefan, for example, recounted the saga in an article called "Two Thousand and One Lulus" for a Hamburg newspaper:

Lulu sprang from a German poetic brain, she is a German figure. . . . Many will ask why none was found among us here in Germany. They will say: today, when America is taking our best talents, do we have to have a Lulu especially brought from Hollywood? . . .

Sixteen hundred out of more than 2,000 applicants were tested. . . . Many of the candidates had the physical attributes of Lulu, but they couldn't act. Others could act, but were either too large or too small, too stiff or too aloof. Lulu is a concept, Lulu could not be shaped anew. . . .

But fortune . . . beamed quite favorably from the wondrous sphinx-eyes

---

* Dietrich was then twenty-five and Brooks twenty-one. "She'd been around for years in Berlin," said Louise, later adding, in fairness: "It must be remembered that Pabst was speaking about the pre–Josef-von-Sternberg Dietrich. She was the Dietrich of *I Kiss Your Hand, Madame,* a film in which, caparisoned variously in beads, brocade, ostrich feathers, chiffon ruffles, and white rabbit fur, she galloped from one lascivious stare to another." But Marlene soon got her consolation prize. Louise thought it ironic that, a year later, another trick of fate catapulted Dietrich to stardom: "It was only because Brigitte Helm was not available that Sternberg looked further and found Dietrich for *The Blue Angel*."

of Louise Brooks. . . . For the first time in film history a great star comes from America in order to conquer here. . . . Louise Brooks, the German Lulu, stands at the beginning of a new epoch in world film.[4]

Stefan's article, reprinted in *Die Bühne* and many other publications, typified the press's ambivalent reaction of annoyance and pride: It was insulting to think that no German actress was good enough to play Lulu, but it was flattering and unprecedented for an American star to make a German film in Berlin. In that regard, Louise was a pioneer. And, of course, the very designation of this Paramount featured player as "a great star" was equally flattering to her.

The European excitement about Brooks's coming to Berlin has been if anything underestimated, not exaggerated. Even the chauvinistic German public, when it saw her photographs everywhere in the autumn of 1928, was fired no less than Pabst by a quality few had appreciated in Hollywood. As James Card put it, "There was unquestionably something in the eyes of Louise Brooks that no American scenarist had yet written a script for."[5]

> In Hollywood, I was a pretty flibbertigibbet whose charm for the executive department decreased with every increase in my fan mail. In Berlin, I stepped to the station platform to meet Mr. Pabst and became an actress. And his attitude was the pattern for all. Nobody offered me humorous or instructive comments on my acting. Everywhere I was treated with a kind of decency and respect unknown to me in Hollywood. It was just as if Mr. Pabst had sat in on my whole life and career and knew exactly where I needed assurance and protection.[6]

Indeed, the fanfare when Louise stepped off the train in Berlin on October 14, 1928, was beyond expectation. In fact, Louise *had* no expectations, so little did she know of Pabst, of German filmmaking, and of the deliciously decadent capital she was about to invade. The train—in proper German tradition—was precisely on time, and an army of autograph seekers and Nero-Film executives, including production chief George Horsetzky and financial backer Seymour Nebenzahl,* was there at the Am Zoo railroad station to greet her. The delegation was headed by Georg Wilhelm Pabst himself.

Photos of the occasion—some taken by Hans Casparius—show a rotund, bespectacled man in a fedora, beaming proudly at a gorgeous flapper in a stylish cloche as she clutches some of the dozens of roses thrust into her arms. Pabst spoke fluent English, and a good thing: Louise hadn't

---

* Louise's summary of the Pabst-Nebenzahl partnership, contained in a letter to Kevin Brownlow, is wry: "Early in his career, after two films at UFA [the dominant German film studio], Pabst found that he could not work within the 'system.' He found a pleasant young Jew, Nebenzahl, who was good at getting money and never came on the set except to look for girls. Pabst made some of his greatest films with good old Seymour."

G. W. Pabst meets and greets Louise for the first time at the Am Zoo
railroad station in Berlin, October 14, 1928. Photo by Hans Casparius

bothered to acquire so much as a German phrase book. Everyone was quite pleased at this first meeting—though Pabst had to work to conceal his disappointed surprise at the presence of George Marshall.

"Pabst looked around, and of course George was a huge, big, handsome, black-haired man, with a drunken English valet," Louise remembered. "The valet [was] staggering around with huge amounts of luggage . . . and George explained who he was and immediately took charge of everything."[7]

All in all, reported the Berlin *Film-Illustrierte*, Louise was greeted "at least as ceremoniously as Pola Negri and Emil Jannings were received in Los Angeles, and certainly better than Greta Garbo was."[8] After the picture-taking session, Louise and George were escorted to the Eden Hotel —Berlin's finest—to set up housekeeping for the next five weeks. Several other *Pandora* stars, including Alice Roberts (who "spoke just enough English to insult me," Louise recalled), were also lodged at the Eden, and so was the impresario Sol Hurok, who signed up Artur Schnabel and Rudolf Serkin there.

After a decent night's sleep, Marshall went off in prosaic search of new German laundry equipment to take back to the States, while Louise had the luxury of two free days to explore the city before filming began.

What a city. And what an exciting time in its life. The thing to do with the National Socialists was to ignore them, which was still possible. "The Nazis we only saw standing in front of railroad stations and other places, selling Nazi magazines, that's all—nobody anticipated it," recalls Lederer.[9] Germany seemed to have recovered at last from the horrendous postwar inflation and unemployment, the strikes and riots, the Spartacist revolt and its bloody suppression by the Freikorps. Now was the time for pleasure-seeking, for tomorrow—who knew?

It was literally a garden spot. More than half the city's land consisted of

At Night, *George Grosz drawing from* Ecce Homo *(1923)*

2 8 3

gardens, parks, and forest. Audiences flocked to Max Reinhardt's fabulous productions of Shakespeare, and three opera companies operated simultaneously under Bruno Walter, Otto Klemperer, and Erich Kleiber. Alban Berg, still basking in the success of *Wozzeck,* was now working on a *Lulu* of his own. Kurt Weill and Bertolt Brecht's *The Threepenny Opera* had just opened on August 28 at the Theater am Schiffbauerdamm, and they were now working furiously on *Rise and Fall of the City of Mahagonny.* Albert Einstein lived in Berlin, and so did young Wernher von Braun, co-organizer of a student group called the Society for Space Travel. W. H. Auden and Christopher Isherwood wrote there. Vladimir Nabokov, amid the giant colony of 50,000 Russian refugees from Bolshevism, was giving tennis lessons in Berlin to subsidize his writing.

"I tell you, Berlin at that time was Paradise for actors, Paradise!" says Lederer, who, at twenty-eight, was eight years older than Louise. "It was completely different from Hollywood, where everything is so spread out. In Berlin, it was all together—a small town. . . . It was much more intimate, like a family."[10]

To Louise, the city's erotic smorgasbord was the most pervasive and intriguing attribute of 1928 Berlin, "where the ruling class publicly flaunted its pleasures as a symbol of wealth and power." No account of the city's sexuality at that time is better than her own:

> Sex was the business of the town. At the Eden Hotel, where I lived, the café bar was lined with the higher-priced trollops. The economy girls walked the street outside. On the corner stood the girls in boots, advertising flagellation. Actors' agents pimped for the ladies in luxury apartments in the Bavarian Quarter. Racetrack touts at the Hoppegarten arranged orgies for groups of sportsmen. The nightclub Eldorado displayed an enticing line of homosexuals dressed as women. At the Maly, there was a choice of feminine or collar-and-tie lesbians. Collective lust roared unashamed at the theatre. In the revue *Chocolate Kiddies,* when Josephine Baker appeared naked except for a girdle of bananas, it was precisely as Lulu's stage entrance was described by Wedekind: "They rage there as in a menagerie when the meat appears at the cage."[11]

BROOKS AND BERLIN. Louise and Lulu. It was the perfect time and place for both to thrive. Who was Lulu? Except for Goethe's Gretchen, she was the single most important woman in German literature, as integral as Camille to France or Hedda Gabler to Norway. And who was Wedekind?

Thomas Mann had an answer: "Wedekind, history will one day say, was in this partly senile, partly puerile, partly feminine epoch—its only man."[12] In literary terms, we can think of him as "the least popular major dramatist" of the twentieth century.[13]

Benjamin Franklin Wedekind (1864–1918) was as dichotomized as his American-German name. His parents moved from Germany to San Francisco, returning to Europe just weeks before he was born. He grew up mostly in Switzerland and, at his father's insistence, went to Munich to study law. But he soon became erotically interested in gynecology, instead, and in the throbbing artistic life of Schwabing, Munich's Bohemian colony.

Wedekind's controversial writing embraced Freud's thesis that civilization is based on the suppression of the most basic human instinct: the erotic. While his contemporaries—Zola, Ibsen, Hauptmann—were decrying social injustice "naturalistically," Wedekind rejected message and medium alike. He preached a "revival of spiritual sensuality and bodily pleasure"—an unattainable freedom of the flesh that outraged late Victorian morality. Even more stunning than his sexual philosophy was his dramatic idiom. He defied the dull, "lifelike" stage language of Naturalism and invented his own unfettered "expressionistic" speech—jarring, outrageous, disjointed, and deliberately unrealistic.

Wedekind also practiced what he preached. He delighted in scandalizing the fin-de-siècle bourgeoisie with his capes and extravagant Mephistophelian garb, and he kept company with *avant-garde* artists and con artists, prostitutes and petty criminals, of whom forgers were his favorites. He loved bordellos, opium dens, and particularly the circus: Clowns, acrobats, and bareback riders he considered the epitome of spiritual and physical equilibrium. They would appear constantly in his writing.

Self-exiled in the demimonde of Paris in 1894, Wedekind met the extraordinary Lou Andréas-Salome, friend and/or mistress of Nietzsche, Freud, Rilke, and many others. She conversed with shocking brilliance on all manner of sexual subjects and then accepted an invitation to Wedekind's room, but refused to sleep with him—a fact which so astonished him that he borrowed her name and certain characteristics for the embryonic "Lulu" he was then struggling to put into dramatic form.

Wedekind also knew August Strindberg, for whom Woman represented all that was evil in humankind. Wedekind, on the contrary, saw her as the embodiment of man's "genuine inner needs"—and of the life instinct itself. Strindberg lamented the victorious sexual power of women. Wedekind celebrated it—and had an affair with Strindberg's second wife. Evidently preferring Wedekind's philosophy to her husband's, Frida Strindberg came to live with him in Munich in 1896 and bore him a child.

Wedekind had finished the first of the two great Lulu plays, *Erdgeist (Earth Spirit)*, in 1895, but had to wait three years for its premiere, in

Leipzig, with the playwright himself in the lead male role. The authorities correctly regarded it as an attack on German society and soon found cause to jail him (for satirically libeling the Kaiser). He became a cause célèbre and, upon his release in 1900, was hailed as a hero throughout Europe.

In 1904, nine years after *Erdgeist*, he completed the second Lulu play, *Die Büchse der Pandora—Pandora's Box*—"a tragedy of monsters" which aroused even more furor than *Erdgeist*. This Wedekind "ideal" of woman came equipped with a sex drive that totally devastated the middle-class society around her. She was the product of a degenerate mind, said the censors, and her creator was attacked as an "arch-pornographer" by church and state. *Pandora's Box* was not performed in Germany until 1918, the year of Wedekind's death. Among those he profoundly influenced was Bertolt Brecht, who compared him to Tolstoy and said, "His greatest work was his own personality." [14]

Wedekind had always longed to go back to the United States, the promised land, where he saw—or imagined—a more liberal morality that permitted the kind of sexuality Europe forbade.

Perhaps, after all, it was fitting that the greatest of all the Lulus would come not from Germany but from America.

The Pandora myth has many variations. All agree that the gods bestowed their gifts upon her—Zeus the power to see and feel, Aphrodite beauty and the charms of love, Hermes the art of flattery. But they differ on the *culpability* of this Eve.

In Padraic Colum's beautiful 1930 version, all is well until the dim-witted Epimetheus takes Pandora from their private Garden of Eden into the world, where men and women already exist:

> At first the men and women looked upon the beauty of Pandora, upon her lovely dresses, and her golden crown, and her girdle of flowers, with wonder and delight. Epimetheus would have everyone admire and praise her. And this they did for a while. . . . But as time went by a change came upon the women: one woman would weep, and another would look angry, and a third would go back sullenly to her work when Pandora was admired or praised.

The women decide that the secrets of Pandora's beauty are kept inside her jar.

> The lid, once tightly fixed down, had been shifted a little. As the hands of the women grasped it to take off the lid, the jar was cast down; the things that were inside spilled themselves forth.
>
> They were black and grey and red; they were crawling and flying things. And, as the women looked on, the things spread themselves abroad or fastened themselves upon them.

The jar, like Pandora herself, had been made and filled out of the ill-will of Zeus. And it had been filled, not with salves and charms and washes, as the women thought, but with Cares and Troubles. . . .

As for Pandora, the Golden Maid, she played on, knowing only the brightness of the sunshine and the lovely shapes of things.[15]

This idea that it was not Pandora's own curiosity but the folly of men and the envy of women that unleashed evil in the world is closer to Wedekind's. His Lulu is driven to express herself through pleasure, free of moral hypocrisy.[16] In a male world where money and sex are the only valid currencies, "Lulu is that which allows both desire and money to circulate," blissfully ignorant of the havoc she wreaks.[17] Her destructiveness is *redemptive*, for she creates the anarchy and death by which society is purged of its sexual repression.*

Lulu was the first of the antisocial heroes—from Brecht's Mother Courage through Tennessee Williams's Stanley Kowalski and Edward Albee's Martha—with whom twentieth-century playwrights would confront the complacency of their audiences.

In the stage plays, Lulu's "idealized bordello" is wherever she happens to be. We know nothing of her origins except that she was a kind of cabaret performer. At the outset, she is married to the jealous Dr. Goll, who has commissioned the artist Schwarz to paint her in a provocative Pierrot pose. Discovering her *in flagrante delicto* with the artist, Goll rushes at them but has a heart attack and dies on the spot.

Now the artist drives himself mad trying to get her to return his love, or at least to reveal her soul. But she is flesh and blood without soul, and certainly without guilt. In fact, she is something different to every man— "the fantasy of each male who associates with her."[18] Schwarz's despairing solution is to rush off and slit his own throat.

He is immediately replaced by the more formidable and cynical Dr. Schön, a wealthy publisher who foolishly believes he owns Lulu. But Schön can't fully possess her, either, and when he attempts to rid himself of her and marry a more respectable girl, the furious Lulu decides to star in a musical revue written by his handsome son, Alwa. Soon Alwa, too, is in love with her—and in rivalry with his own father. Also desperately in love with Lulu is the lesbian Countess Geschwitz.

With lethal caprice, Lulu thwarts Schön's intended wedding and marries him herself, kills him with his own gun, and then makes her escape from the law. She next ruins Alwa and cajoles Geschwitz into buying off

* Wedekind's original inspiration was from two sources: the crimes of Jack the Ripper, who had terrorized London a few years earlier and who was dramatized at Le Grand Guignol in Paris, and a pantomime by Felicie Champsau, "Lulu, une clownesse danseuse," which he saw at the Nouveau Cirque in Paris in the midnineties.

various blackmailers, causing the death of several—and all without a shred of malice or remorse. Finally, she ends up destitute on the foggy streets of London, where the broken Alwa and the mysterious old pimp Schigolch (who may be her father) are all that remain of her retinue. The Earth Spirit has evolved into a hunted animal. Thus far Lulu has avoided actual prostitution, but she now seeks out her first and last customer.

He is Jack the Ripper.

He is the executioner of a sick society.

"Lulu is not a real character," said Wedekind, "but the personification of primitive sexuality who inspires evil unaware."

Pabst had to make her real. His first problem was to combine the two Lulu plays and condense the burlesque quantity and quality of her suitors —eliminating, for instance, an African crown prince who served as comic relief. He also minimized the *grand guignol* violence, modified Lulu's responsibility for Schön's death and reduced the dramatis personae of the last act to just four characters. The greatest task, of course, was to render their complex interrelations in silence, for Wedekind's hysterical dialogue was the chief instrument of his plays—of his Expressionism overall.

But Pabst, at heart, was not an Expressionist—he was an "objectivist" with certain Expressionist trappings of texture and lighting. Perhaps the very silencing of Wedekind's disjointed language would be an aid to him. For he was developing a new cinematic style, and he was more interested in Lulu than in Wedekind. Her speech was unrealistic. Infinitely more "real" for Pabst—and for film—was her visual image.

Wedekind's Lulu had been filmed four times before, most recently by Leopold Jessner in 1923 as *Lou Lou (Erdgeist)* with the great Danish actress Asta Nielsen. Her Lulu was the *ne plus ultra* vamp. She was passionate but hardly erotic—even the passion belonged to another age— and both the lesbianism and the incest were expunged. Nielsen, "the man-eater, devoured her sex victims—Dr. Goll, Schwarz and Schön—and then dropped dead in an acute attack of indigestion."[19]*

Pabst wanted no repeat of such cannibalism. For a while, he didn't even want Louise to keep her trademark black bangs because they too closely resembled those of Nielsen's Lulu.

One thing he knew for certain, though, was that this classic of German literature—of world literature—had never been filmed properly and that the story of Lulu transcended either the presence or absence of speech.

Another thing he knew, the moment he saw Brooks in Hawks's *A Girl*

---

* The earlier silent versions were *Lulu* (1917), directed by Alexander von Antalffy, with Erna Morena and Emil Jannings; the Hungarian *Lulu* (1918), directed by Mihály Kertész (better known later in Hollywood as Michael Curtiz of *Casablanca*), with Claire Lotto and Bela Lugosi; and *Die Büchse der Pandora* (1919), directed by Arzen von Cserepy, also starring Asta Nielsen.

in Every Port, was that she possessed precisely those visual attributes of Lulu that he had always seen in his mind's eye.

If ever there were a fantastic, phantasmagorical twilight zone of film, it was Germany in 1928, and Louise was now stepping into it—about to dazzle herself and film history fleetingly thereby. Louise was more a seeker of truth than of art, but in Pabst she stumbled upon both. He was a major force in the cinema and at the creative peak of his powers.

G. W. Pabst (1885–1967), as a man and as a filmmaker, was full of contradictions—passionate analyst one moment, cold-as-a-fish reporter the next. "His field was psychology rather than sociology," wrote James Card, "his concern more with the battle of the sexes than the struggle of the classes."[20] That concern had drawn him, early on, to the plays of Frank Wedekind.

But Wedekind was the ultimate Expressionist playwright, and Pabst was ambivalent about Expressionism. That dominant stylistic rage of German film in the twenties portrayed the inner life through an exaggeration of the outer, wildly manipulating symbolic objects and stereotyped characters. It began in earnest after the horror of World War I with *The Cabinet of Dr. Caligari* (1919), whose nightmarish sets and disorienting lighting were as "expressive" as its grotesque characters. *Caligari*, like most Expressionist films, was shot in the studio: The artifice was heightened as deliberately as the hysterical acting.

German Expressionist film's heyday lasted an even decade and produced some of the most important films of all time, including *Caligari* (directed by Robert Wiene), *The Golem* (1920, Paul Wegener), *Nosferatu* (1922, F. W. Murnau), *Dr. Mabuse, the Gambler* (1922, Fritz Lang), *Waxworks* (1924, Paul Leni), and *Metropolis* (1927, Lang). The movement had enormous influence, but by 1928, for Pabst, both its efficacy and its novelty had worn off.*

Louise knew, or cared about, none of this. Such theoretical underpinnings were not a part of the American film industry or its way of life in Hollywood. She might have heard of Expressionism. She certainly never heard of *die Neue Sachlichkeit*—the New Objectivity—a movement now developing in reaction to Expressionism. Disillusionment was its emotional source, and indifference its attitude. It was the movement of which Pabst was a leading light.

That indifferent attitude stemmed from the corruption and apparent meaninglessness of European life between the world wars. Coincidentally, it was an outlook that might also have been ascribed to Louise Brooks,

---

* The movement greatly influenced such later directors as Orson Welles and Alfred Hitchcock. *Psycho* (1960), for instance, has been called "the ultimate German Expressionist film."

whose hedonism had a kind of brutal "new objectivity" of its own. In Pabst's case, it was more a reaction against Expressionism (Romanticism gone wild) than a pure thing in itself.

Pabst's artistic restlessness was partly a result of his American experience. He'd gone to New York in 1910 at age twenty-five with the Deutsche Volkstheater, which performed at the Irving Place Theatre. There he acted in and directed plays attended by New York's sizable German immigrant population. Pabst was a latecomer and late bloomer in film. In 1921 he finally left theater and went to Berlin to join director Carl Froelich as an actor, assistant, and scenarist. He didn't direct his own first film, *Der Schatz (The Treasure)*, until 1923, when he was thirty-eight.

In 1925, he burst into international prominence with the first non-Swedish "discovery" of Greta Garbo in *Die Freudlose Gasse (The Joyless Street)*, a grim tale of profiteers, paupers, and misery in inflation-gripped Vienna—traditionally, the city of frivolous operetta. Pabst never got over his awe of Garbo.

"When I met him in '28," Louise recalled, "he said, 'Do you know Garbo very well?' I said, 'Pretty well.' One's always very careful. And he raved about her. And one day we had tea in his apartment, Heinrich Mann, and other people. Very intellectual tea and very boring. But he took me to a big cupboard, and he had just hundreds of stills of Garbo. Oh, he thought she was so marvelous! And he showed me all these stills, and talked about her, and talked about her, and talked about her." [21]

After his Garbo picture, Pabst's inventive *Secrets of a Soul* was hailed as the first overtly psychoanalytical film, on which he had consulted two of Freud's collaborators, Dr. Hanns Sachs and Dr. Karl Abraham. To render the dream sequences and the pathological knife phobia of Werner Krauss, Pabst employed striking, multilayered superimpositions—produced inside the camera, without optical devices, by winding back the film for double and triple exposures.

He polished his realism, instead of his surrealism, in *The Love of Jeanne Ney* (1927), a bowdlerization of Ilya Ehrenburg's harsh romance of a bourgeois French girl and a young Russian communist. It, too, was a virtuosic exercise in technique.

"Every shot [in *Jeanne Ney*] is made on some movement," Pabst told a *Close Up* interviewer in 1927. "At the end of one cut somebody is moving, at the beginning of the next the movement is continued. The eye is thus so occupied in following these movements that it misses the cuts."

Pabst is said to have invented "cutting on movement"—one of those "shitty 'first' stories" that Louise often railed against. He was not, in fact, its originator, just one of its notable early practitioners. He wanted to avoid breaking the narrative flow and provide a visual seamlessness to the action, exactly the opposite of Soviet directors Sergei Eisenstein and Vsevolad

G. W. Pabst's The Love of Jeanne Ney (1927): virtuosic technique with
Expressionist trappings in a "Realist" romance by Ilya Ehrenburg

Pudovkin, Pabst's dynamic contemporaries and champions of the "shock"
cut.

But in the upcoming film (and upcoming legend) of Louise Brooks, far
more important than his technical virtuosity or philosophy was his phenomenal skill with actors. Pabst was deft in his direction of men, but
miraculous with women. The reason—which brings us full circle to Wedekind—was sexual: his fascination with feminine psychology. This was
clear in *Joyless Street* with the fragility of Garbo ("partly due to stage-
fright," says Eisner) and the submissive sorrow of Asta Nielsen. It was
even clearer with Brigitte Helm in *Jeanne Ney*.

"In five out of seven of the films Pabst had directed by 1928, the dominant protagonist was a woman," says James Card. "By 1928 Pabst was ready to pursue his favorite subject into the bowels of Frank Wedekind: he planned to produce the apotheosis of feminine fatality in *Pandora's Box*."[22]

Shooting began on October 17, 1928, and continued for five weeks, until November 23, with amazing precision. Each morning at 6:30, a Daimler limousine arrived to take Louise to work in the west Berlin suburb of Staaken. "On the way, every day we had to stop and wait at exactly the same time and same place while a man and his geese ambled across the road," she remembered. Nero-Film's studio was a former Zeppelin dirigible hangar, where the movie-making process was businesslike, by ethnic instinct and economic necessity. The workday began at 7:00 a.m. sharp and ended at 6:00 p.m., with little time wasted in between—an enormous contrast to Hollywood. One day a bus arrived and deposited no fewer than thirty journalists on the set, all jockeying to get a look at Louise.[23] But the director was undisturbed: Bustling about in his trademark leather jacket, Pabst was a perfect combination of cordiality and efficiency. He had to

Louise with Pandora's Box *cast and crew before shooting the final Jack the Ripper scene: Franz Lederer (Alwa) perched far left, Carl Goetz (Schigolch) with pipe at Brooks's left, director G. W. Pabst on Brooks's right; Staaken studio, Berlin, October, 1928*

be. For one thing, he was directing actors from five nations, communicating with them in their native languages.

"He spoke excellent English," said Louise. "He spoke rather slowly and precisely . . . in German, French, Czech, English and he speaks them all exactly the same—as if he's tacking his words into your brain." Her mental picture of him never faded:

> Pabst, a short man, broad-shouldered and thick-chested, looked heavy in repose. But in action his legs carried him on wings that matched the swiftness of his mind. He always came on the set as fresh as a March wind, going directly to the cameraman, Günther Krampf, who was the only person on the film to whom he gave a complete account of the ensuing scene's action and meaning. Never conducting group discussions with his actors, he then told each actor separately what the actor must know about the scene.[24]

The play *Earth Spirit* opened with a prologue in which the Animal Tamer steps out of a circus tent, a whip in one hand and a revolver in the other, to extend an invitation to the audience: "Walk into my menagerie!" That scene was not in the movie, but Louise perceived something like it on the set: "The finest job of casting that G. W. Pabst ever did was casting himself as the director, the Animal Tamer. . . . Never a sentimental trick did this whip hand permit the actors assembled to play his beasts. The revolver he shot straight into the heart of the audience."[25]

From the beginning, she told James Card, "I adored and worshipped Mr. Pabst. Usually as mean and snarling as a wild cat, I sat up for him and wagged my tail like a little dog."[26] The first thing she adored was that, unlike most directors, Pabst "had no catalogue of characters with their emotional responses."

"D. W. Griffith required giggling fits from all sexually excited virgins," she said. "If Pabst ever shot a scene showing a virgin giggling, it would have been because someone was tickling her. It was the stimulus that concerned him. If he got that right, the actor's emotional reaction would be like life itself—often strange and unsatisfactory to any audience that was used to settled acting conventions."[27]

The legendary Brooks-Pabst rapport—that "mysterious alliance that seemed to exist between us even before we met"—got a big boost on the first day of shooting. Louise hadn't bothered to open, let alone read, the expensive translation of the script which Pabst commissioned for her.* Thus she knew nothing of Lulu's background as a dancer—that, in fact,

---

* The script was ceremoniously presented to her one day as she was "sitting on the set with my maid, Josifine, and my bottle of vermouth. . . . They put it on my lap and I looked at it—I'd never read a script in my life, and I haven't yet—and I opened it and I read a few pages. I thought, 'Oh, my God.' So I put it down by my chair and went away without it, and when I came back it was gone. . . . [Josifine] said, 'You should have kept that.' Gee, I wish I had. It would be invaluable now."

dancing is Lulu's preferred mode of expression and that she performs an impromptu number in one of her first scenes. Pabst marked out a space on the floor, tapped out a fast tempo, then gave Louise a curious look and said, "You can make up some little steps here—can't you?" [28] She nodded, and Pabst went behind the camera to watch her burst into a wildly embellished Denishawn routine.

Pabst was astonished by the perfect grace and skill of her movements. Until that moment, he had known nothing of her dance training, and he was positively joyous at the discovery.

"That I was a dancer and Pabst essentially a choreographer in his direction came as a wonderful surprise to both of us," she said. "As I was leaving the set, he caught me in his arms, shaking me and laughing as if I had played a joke on him. 'But you are a professional dancer!' It was the moment when he realized that his choice of me for Lulu was instinctively right. He felt as if he had created me. I was his Lulu!" [29]

It was also the moment, if such moments can be pinned down, when Pabst fell in love with her. In any case, Louise's knowledge of dance would greatly augment her effectiveness in *Pandora's Box*. Suddenly, after three years of almost nonstop film work, what she'd learned at Denishawn had a deeper, more direct relation to what she could do on film.

Nothing in performance skill was more important to Pabst, whose whole approach to directing (and editing) was, as Louise observed, essentially choreographic. In this he was in tune with the Russian innovators: Stanislavsky, Meyerhold, and most recently Eisenstein preached the integral necessity of "plastic motion" to drama, and Soviet actors, unlike their Western counterparts, were simply expected to have singing, dancing, pantomimic, fencing, and even some acrobatic skills. "The essential thing is rhythm," Meyerhold declared. In stage and film, "there are problems which are *ipso facto* musical problems [and] demand the melody of movement—or its discord—for their solution." [30]

As for music itself, Pabst was so convinced of its catalytic effect that he insisted on hiring a pianist to play for Louise between scenes, even though she told him it wasn't necessary. This wasn't customary in German studios, but he had heard that it was the practice in America. She would have it here, whether she wanted it or not. It was an example of his applied psychology. "Pabst was a great psychologist," said Louise, and he was acutely attuned to her sensitivities. After the first day's shooting, Pabst complimented her and invited her to view the rushes. "I went in and I was just horrified," she said. She thought she hid her reaction, but in the rear of the projection room, she heard Pabst tell assistant director Paul Falkenberg, "Great mistake, great mistake—never do that again, never." [31] And she nevermore sat in on rushes.

All that I thought and all his reactions seemed to pass between us in a kind of wordless communication. To other people surrounding him, he would talk endlessly in that watchful way of his, smiling, intense; speaking quietly, with his wonderful, hissing precision. But to me he might speak never a word all morning, and then at lunch turn suddenly and say, "Louees, tomorrow morning you must be ready to do a big fight scene with Kortner," or "This afternoon, in the first scene, you are going to cry" . . . I liked the way he said it while he was tossing in his food, the usual sauerkraut. . . . That was how he directed me. With an intelligent actor, he would sit in exhaustive explanation; with an old ham he would speak the language of the theater. But in my case, by some magic he would saturate me with one clear emotion and turn me loose. And it was the same with the plot. Mr. Pabst never strained my mind with anything not relating to the immediate action.[32]

In fact, he was studying her "with scientific intensity," on and off the set, to see how she responded, and to what. He was looking for "the shocks of life which released unpredictable emotions."[33]

Every actor has a natural animosity toward every other actor, present or absent, living or dead, Louise declared. "Most Hollywood directors did not understand that." But Pabst did. He exploited such tensions, and Louise, for one, loved it.

"What an exquisite release, what a revelation of the art of direction was the Pabst Spirit on the set!" she enthused. "He actually encouraged actors' disposition to hate and back away from each other, thus preserving their energy for the camera; and when actors were not in use, his ego did not command them to sit up and bark at the sight of him."[34]

Louise, of course, had the best role in the film and the one which most closely matched its performer: "I revered Pabst for his truthful picture of this world of pleasure which let me play Lulu naturally. The other members of the cast were tempted to rebellion."[35] It was *they* who had to play unsympathetic characters motivated solely by lust—characters they were determined to alter for their own and their audience's empathy.

"Fritz Kortner, as Schön, wanted to be the victim," she said. "Franz Lederer, as the incestuous son Alwa Schön, wanted to be adorable. Carl Goetz wanted to get laughs playing the old pimp Schigolch. Alice Roberts, the Belgian actress who played the screen's first lesbian, the Countess Geschwitz, was prepared to go no further than repression in mannish suits."[36]

One by one, Pabst bent them gently but firmly to his will. His handling of Kortner, the great stage actor, was a brilliant example, thought Louise, "of how Pabst used an actor's true feelings to add depth and breadth and power to his performance." Schön had to be in love-hate with Lulu, wildly drawn to her sexually yet maddened by her. Brusque, disciplined Kortner epitomized Reinhardt's high-Expressionist stage-acting technique; as such, he was the perfect foil for Louise's unmannered plasticity—which was essentially the *absence* of technique. Kortner was utterly contemptuous of her even before they met, and when they started working together, his impression of her as a silly starlet was confirmed. "She moved with the grace of an unconcerned kitten," said Lotte Eisner, but wouldn't do a thing to emphasize her feelings. "It irritated him that his partner was just *there*."[37] He was, moreover, jealous of Pabst's attentions to her and infuriated at what he perceived (correctly) as her theft of their every scene.

"But you are only shooting Miss Brooks!" he exploded at one point, after being positioned with his back to the camera for take after take. Like everyone else, said Louise, Kortner "thought I had cast some blinding spell over Pabst which allowed me to walk through my part. To them, it was a sorry outcome of Pabst's difficult search for Lulu."[38]

> Kortner hated me. After each scene with me he would pound off the set and go to his dressing room. Mr. Pabst himself, wearing his most private smile, would go there to coax him back for the next scene. . . . The theatre sequence gave him an opportunity to shake me with such violence that he left ten black and blue finger prints on my arms. Both he and Pabst were well pleased with that scene.[39]

As well they should have been, since it was the most devastating seduction scene in the film. After the violent shaking by Schön in a backstage prop room, Lulu hurls herself on a cot and throws a colossal tantrum, beating her legs in furious scissor-kicks. The camera eye caresses her body, from the white perfect neck, down her bare back and kicking legs. She sneaks a glance at the brooding Schön to gauge the effect of her performance. They wrestle further, but end up entwined—Schön capitulating—after she sinks her teeth into his hand. At precisely the moment of their kiss, the door opens: Schön's shocked son and his fiancé discover them. The scene concludes with the most restrained yet wickedly triumphant expression of conquest on Lulu's face—a volume spoken in two seconds of silence and "one of the highlights of film history, silent or sound."[40]

Louise was lucky that bruising her arms was the worst physical damage done to her. One witness says Kortner's hostility "had nothing to do with Louise as Louise but as simply a very problem-making woman who didn't give a damn about anybody else." Early on, her hangovers sometimes caused shooting to be delayed and Kortner to stomp off. "When she was finally able to resume and Kortner was coaxed back, she would call for a bottle of perfumed spray and give herself a quick spray in the mouth. Kortner flipped his lid every time."[41] But regardless of its source, Kortner's rage accommodated the director's needs.

Pabst was equally deft in his manipulation of Alice Roberts, whose husband was one of the film's financial backers. The implication was that casting Roberts as the countess was a quid pro quo. "She wasn't a good actress," said Louise, "and her fear took the form of hating Berlin, hating her part, and hating me. Any other director would have had to settle for a wooden performance."[42] But not Pabst.

Roberts's first scene to be filmed was the wedding sequence in which she regards her beloved Lulu, the bride, and the odious groom, Dr. Schön, with forlorn jealousy:

> She came on the set looking chic in her Paris evening dress and aristo-cratically self-possessed. Then Mr. Pabst began explaining the action of the scene in which she was to dance the tango with me. Suddenly, she under-stood that she was to touch, to embrace, to make love to another woman. Her blue eyes bulged and her hands trembled. Anticipating the moment of explosion, Pabst, who proscribed unscripted emotional outbursts, caught her arm and sped her away out of sight behind the set. A half hour later, when they returned, he was hissing soothingly to her in French and she was smil-ing like the star of the picture—which she was in all her scenes with me. I was just there obscuring the view.[43]

What Pabst whispered to Roberts was that it would be *him*, not Louise, to whom she would make love. Both in her two-shots with Louise and in her close-ups photographed over Louise's shoulder, Pabst positioned him-self so that she could "cheat" her look past Louise and look longingly at Pabst, who was returning her loving gaze from behind the camera. At other times, "he let her look as cross as possible" at Louise, but wove those shots into the continuity when he needed a reaction shot of her looking at Schön, Alwa, or any of the other men. Roberts's immortal, frustrated glare was "marvelous," said Louise, "because she looked like a very re-pressed lesbian who was hiding it."[44]

Louise was less amused a few days later when Pabst turned his sharp attention to her private life. She wheedled him into giving her a day off to attend the Davis Cup tennis matches. But overall, she said, "his delight in Lulu's character belonged exclusively to the screen," and he was annoyed that she and George Marshall were out every night sampling Berlin's nightlife until three in the morning:

> Marshall had a gift for finery. He would go to Horsch's, a marvelous restaurant, and always in tails. And I don't think Pabst liked to get in tails, and I don't think [his wife] Trudi had many evening dresses. And we had this wild week. I had to be on the set every morning—hot or cold, whether he used me or not. And George would have me up all night, and Pabst was furious, and we'd all go to dinner, and Trudi would glare at me and refuse to speak English! Pabst was furious at George, and George didn't give a

damn. He spent a week there [and went] to all the most expensive brothels. And he had an absolutely marvelous time. He would take me to the theater every night, and I'd come on the set with Klieg eyes. . . . Suddenly one morning, I remember we were shooting the murder scene, and George came on the set in disarray. He said to Pabst, "You'll be very happy, I'm leaving tomorrow."[45]

Happy was too mild a word. Pabst was thrilled. And the next day on the set when he heard Louise accept an invitation to something called "Artist's Ball—Wow!" he put his foot down.

"Müller!" Pabst called to Brooksie's maid. "Louees does not go out anymore at night."

After a howl of protest, Louise tried to reason with him: "But, Mr. Pabst, I have always gone out at night when I worked! I can catch up on my sleep between scenes here at the studio. I always have!"

Which of course was not acceptable to the German studios in general, Pabst in particular. And thenceforth, after each day's shooting, Josifine "returned his Eve to the Eden, where I was bathed, fed, and put to bed till called for next morning at seven. Cross and restless, I was left to fall asleep listening to the complaints of the other poor caged beasts across Stresemannstrasse in the Zoologischer Garten."[46]

Pabst had a way of thwarting the best-laid plans of any performer who interfered with his objectives. Schön's death scene, one of the film's most crucial, provided a consummate example. Schön discovers Lulu romping in their boudoir with Schigolch and the acrobat Rodrigo—and next with his own son, whose head she cradles provocatively in her lap. Lulu fails to notice Schön's rage, and after Alwa leaves, she casually goes about taking off her clothes for their wedding night. Suddenly Schön produces a gun. We assume he is going to shoot her—but no: "Kill yourself," he says in the title, "—it's the only way to save us both!" There is a brief struggle as he tries to force the gun into her hand, and then they freeze. A barely perceptible puff of smoke is all that tells us the gun has been fired:

> Fritz Kortner came on the set with his death worked out to the last facial contortion—with even his blood, the chocolate syrup that would ooze from a sponge in his mouth, carefully tested for sweetness lest it surprise an unrehearsed reaction. Death scenes are dearer than life to the actor, and Kortner's, spectacularly colored with years of theatrical dying, went unquestioned during rehearsal. Pabst left it to the mechanics of each shot to alter Kortner's performance.[47]

Kortner was led to believe the scene was being filmed exactly as he wanted it. But in succeeding takes, Pabst would alter the camera setup or props or otherwise find an excuse to get the angle and effect he had in mind all along: The puff of smoke replaced most of Kortner's carefully rehearsed theatrics. He got to use his chocolate blood, but it appears only for an instant. "So in the end," said Louise, "Kortner wasn't giving his set performance at all." The real impact comes not from Schön but from Lulu's dazed reaction: "Das Blut!"

"Not the murder of my husband but the sight of the blood determined the expression on my face," said Louise.[48]

Pabst had less difficulty with scummy old Carl Goetz as Schigolch—"an enchanting, intelligent, sinister person," as Lederer called him. Goetz, said Louise, "was always getting drunk," which fit his character. "He even smelled the part. He was perfect. He stunk!"[49]

Franz (formerly Frantisek, subsequently Francis) Lederer, the smashingly handsome Czech actor who played Schön's son, did not require much manipulation in order to appear spellbound by Lulu. Though already a popular stage and film actor in his own right, Lederer was in awe of the black-haired beauty to whom he was making screen love. He seemed to melt in her presence, to be overpowered by her—which was exactly what Alwa Schön was supposed to be. Nearly sixty years later, Lederer still refers to her, in his Old World gentlemanly fashion, as "Miss Brooks."

"I absolutely adored her—she was a mysterious person, perfectly cast

Lulu and Alwa (Franz Lederer): Hours after her conviction for his
father's death, his weak will again succumbs to her charms.

for that part," says the last surviving star of *Pandora's Box*. Tanned and sturdy, he looks far younger than his eighty years. Aside from the graying hair, in fact, he is remarkably unchanged from his most famous film of more than half a century ago.

Lederer is absently stirring his coffee at a restaurant in North Hollywood, just a few blocks from the American National Academy of Performing Arts, which he founded twenty-five years ago and where he still teaches and directs. The talk of Louise Brooks is transporting him back to Berlin, and another world: "Veni, vidi, vici—she came, and she was exciting, fascinating, and then . . ." His hand moves eloquently into the thin air. "The thing that was so strange was—her habits. In those days, for a single young lady to have a drink in her hand so often. . . . But that quality, that power—and her looks!

"My relationship with her was very distant," he says, and so are his eyes. "We couldn't talk! She didn't speak a word of German, I didn't speak a word of English. We just looked at each other. After the picture was finished, I was on a train to Paris to make *Maman Calibri* with [director Julien] Duvivier, and she was on the same train—so we looked at each other again. And that was all."

They never met thereafter.

For Lederer, the making of *Pandora* was a peripatetic blur. He knew Pabst and he knew the works of Wedekind from his days as an apprentice in Prague, where Pabst guest-directed the Wedekind play *König Nicolo, oder so ist das Leben* [*King Nicholas, or Such Is Life*]. But as *Pandora's Box* was about to begin, he was immersed in the more demanding and, it seemed, important business of playing Romeo in Max Reinhardt's staging of *Romeo and Juliet*. The timing could not have been worse:

> The day before *Pandora* shooting began was the day of the last dress rehearsal of *Romeo and Juliet*. We had a rehearsal from 10 o'clock in the morning until 6 o'clock the *next* morning! That's how Reinhardt rehearsed. Endlessly, but he was wonderful. . . .
>
> Now, when I was through with the rehearsal at about six, it was too late to go to sleep, so I went to a steam bath, and then I went straight to the studio. And then after the first day of shooting, in the evening I took my car to the theater and did the opening night of *Romeo*.[50]

Young Lederer could be forgiven for having his mind elsewhere that first day. Reinhardt's Shakespearean productions were the gem in Berlin's cultural diadem. Kortner and Elisabeth Bergner were also in *Romeo's* distinguished cast, but Lederer was "not at all happy" with his performance. Reinhardt's direction was stifling: "I didn't have the freedom. I was inhibited."

Pabst was a joy to work with by comparison. After each day's shooting,

*Louise with Lothar Wolff,
Pabst's young publicist who
became her lifelong friend,
at the studio in Berlin,
October 1928*

Lederer had to do *Romeo* at night, which was grueling. But there were compensations: His audiences often included European royalty and the American equivalent—movie stars like Lillian Gish, who liked Lederer's performance enough to arrange a Hollywood contract for him.*

Among the glittery guests one night was Louise Brooks—in the company of her little sister, June, recently arrived for a visit from her Paris boarding school, and Pabst's cheerful publicist, Lothar Wolff. They were waiting for the curtain to go up in the beautiful Deutsches Theater, where paintings of Goethe, Schiller, Molière, and other great dramatists adorned the ceiling.

"Look, June, there's the author of the play," said Louise, pointing to the bust of Shakespeare.

Young June, who had been looking away from Louise, turned to her big sister and said, "Which box is he sitting in?"

Wolff laughed, and in another time and place, Louise might have done

---

* That contract soon fell through when the arrival of sound devalued the utility of non-English-speaking actors. After *Pandora*, Lederer left Germany for Paris and then London, where he learned English and starred in the stage play *Autumn Crocus*. In 1932, he played the same role on Broadway, where he was well reviewed and offered a *real* movie contract. Now "Francis" Lederer, he carved his niche as a Continental leading man in some two dozen American films through the late 1950s, the best of which were *The Man I Married* (1940), *The Bridge of San Luis Rey* (1944), *The Diary of a Chambermaid* (1946), and *A Woman of Distinction* (1950). He then left the movies and made a fortune in real estate, becoming a founder of the Hollywood Museum and a spokesman for world peace.

the same. In this time and place, she flew into a loud rage, berating the girl for her stupidity: "For Christ's sake, June! What the hell am I sending you to a fancy school in Paris for?"[51]

Wolff thought perhaps she didn't want to be there in the first place, listening to three hours of Shakespeare in German. The scene she caused was better than anything in the play—which was "ghastly," Wolff recalls. "Bergner was wrong. Lederer was wrong. Everybody was wrong."* But the blowup *preceded* the show. It was an example of how unpredictably testy Louise could be. Such was her volatility.

And such was her diffidence that she never even told Franz Lederer that she went.

There was another ominous outing. One night near the midpoint of *Pandora* production, Pabst escorted Louise to the opening of a UFA† film at the beautiful Gloria Palast Theatre, apparently to show off his prize Lulu. The UFA officials were polite, but the fans outside were not.

"As we left the theater," Louise recalled, "and he hurried me through a crowd of hostile moviegoers, I heard a girl saying something loud and nasty. In the cab, I began pounding his knee, insisting, 'What did she say? What did she say?' Finally, he translated: 'That is the American girl who is playing our German Lulu!' "[52]

Pabst had tried to protect her from such unpleasantries, suppressing "all overt acts of contempt," at least within his production staff. He gave her the solicitous Josifine, "who had worked for Asta Nielsen and thought she was the greatest actress in the world [and] came to love me tenderly because I was the world's worst actress."[53] But skepticism, or downright hostility, toward Louise existed even in the ranks of Berlin's more intellectual journalists, who thought her literary bent was an act. In a 1967 reminiscence called "Meetings with Pabst," Lotte Eisner recalled her visit to the *Pandora* set:

> In a corner sat a very beautiful girl reading the *Aphorisms* of Schopenhauer in an English translation. It seemed absurd that such a beautiful girl should be reading Schopenhauer, and I thought quite angrily that this was some sly publicity stunt of Pabst's. Some 25 years later, I found out that Louise Brooks really *did* read Schopenhauer.

Lothar Wolff says she read Erich Maria Remarque's *All Quiet on the Western Front*, too. But while Louise was reading, Pabst was attending to

---

* Gottfried Reinhardt, the director's son, called Lederer and Bergner "an embryonic Romeo and an isolationist Juliet."
† Universum Film Aktien Gesellschaft was Germany's giant, government-supported film production and distribution combine, which absorbed many small studios over the years.

yet another extension of Lulu's sexuality. In Hollywood, directors rarely bothered with costumes, and actresses frequently chose their own. At Paramount Louise had played a manicurist in a $500 beaded evening gown, a salesgirl in $300 black satin dresses, and a schoolgirl who attended classes in $250 tailored suits. This most stylish flapper was now irate to discover that her fashion preferences were not even consulted, much less humored. Ignoring her wishes and tantrums, Pabst personally selected all of her costumes "as much for their tactile as for their visual seductiveness. He wanted the actors working with me to feel my flesh under a dancing costume, a blouse and skirt, a nightgown. In turn, he wanted me to love the actors' touch."[54]

There were a few light moments, such as the beer party Louise threw for the company on the London set on her birthday, November 14. But in those last ten days, as filming came to an end, she had a vague sense of something ineffably historical about this transfer of Wedekind's "problem of abnormal psychology" to the screen. The haunting quality of the making of Lulu was unlike anything she had ever experienced in Hollywood.

For the shattering final sequence of *Pandora's Box*, Pabst prepared her brilliantly—by means of costume:

> He went through my trunks to select a dress to be "aged" for Lulu's murder as a streetwalker in the arms of Jack the Ripper. With his instinctive understanding of my tastes, he decided on the blouse and skirt of my very favorite suit. I was anguished. "Why can't you *buy* some cheap little dress to be ruined? Why does it have to be *my* dress?" To these questions I got no answer till the next morning, when my once lovely clothes were returned to me in the studio dressing room. They were torn and foul with grease stains. Not some indifferent rags from the wardrobe department but my own suit, which only last Sunday I had worn to lunch at the Adlon Hotel! Josifine hooked up my skirt, I slipped the blouse over my head, and I went on the set feeling as hopelessly defiled as my clothes. Working in that outfit, I didn't care what happened to me. Anyone else would have bought something and dirtied it up. But he wanted something that was mine and I loved, so that I would feel terrible in it. And I did.[55]

In the fog of London, in those awful streetwalker's clothes, the unsuspecting Lulu picks up Jack the Ripper. He tells her he has no money, but she says, "Never mind. I like you," and leads him up a frightful Expressionistic staircase and into her pathetic garret. Pabst had spent four hours personally spraying blotches of stain onto the walls of those tenement stairs in order to obtain just the right feeling of squalor.

More important, he had chosen his friend Gustav Diessl for the role of

*Lulu and Jack the Ripper
(Gustav Diessl)*

Jack "with adroit perversity." Diessl, said Louise, was the only actor in the cast "whom I found beautiful and sexually alluring. The moment Diessl came on the set [before he was cast], Pabst saw that we just adored each other."[56]

With adroit perversity of her own, she described her time spent kissing and naughtily fondling Diessl as the happiest of the whole picture: "This was very intimate. There was only Diessl and I and the cameraman. And we had a lovely time between each scene. . . . We'd be singing and laughing and doing the Charleston. You wouldn't have known it was a tragic ending. It was more like a Christmas party."[57]

"There was no complexity in Pabst's direction of the Jack the Ripper scenes," she said. "He made them a tender love passage until that terrible moment when Diessl saw the knife on the edge of the table, gleaming in the candlelight."[58] Somewhere in her mind, Louise heard echoes of Ted Shawn quoting Delsarte on the use of the fingers—the delicate shades of meaning conveyed thereby. Lulu and Jack are locked in their embrace, and when the fatal moment comes, Lulu's end is conveyed solely through the soft-focus unfolding of her left hand, graceful as an autumn leaf in slow-motion fall.

One of the most famous endings in the history of film is described best, and most chillingly, by Louise Brooks herself: "It is Christmas Eve, and she is about to receive the gift that has been her dream since childhood: death by a sexual maniac." [59]

In the sixty years since it was made, few other films have elicited as much or as positive critical attention as *Pandora's Box*. But the opposite was true at the time of its release.

When *Pandora* premiered in Berlin on January 30, 1929, it created a modest and negative furor. For its open treatment of lasciviousness and prostitution—Lulu's sexuality, Geschwitz's lesbianism, Schigolch's pimping—it ran afoul of the censors in and out of Germany. It was mutilated even in France, where the normally more tolerant arbiters of morality thought it indecent for a father and son to vie sexually for the same woman. Their solution was to tinker with the titles and convert Alwa from Schön's son to his secretary—which, because of all the paternal-filial embraces, left viewers with the additional impression of a homosexual relationship between the two.

In the United States, the ending was ludicrously changed to let Lulu escape Jack's knife and join the Salvation Army instead—arguably, a fate worse than death.*

Most critics acknowledged the beauty of the film and of its leading actress. But many did something worse than pan it: They ignored it in the shuffle and excitement of the new talkies then dominating public attention on both continents. In an era when there was no such thing as rereleasing a picture after its initial success (let alone failure), *Pandora's Box* was quickly lost in the void between silent and sound pictures.

But before its death, the movie was subjected to a round of critical lumps—and the biggest brickbats were aimed at Louise.

Ernst Jäger in Berlin called her "an inanimate dummy" as Lulu.

At home in New York, *Variety*'s December 11, 1929, review was withering from its opening sentence: "Better for Louise Brooks had she been contented exhibiting that supple form in two-reel comedies or light Paramount features. 'Pandora's Box,' a rambling thing that doesn't help her, nevertheless proves that Miss Brooks is not a dramatic lead. Picture has a difficult time keeping up with itself. Will get by in the sure-seaters and some of the unwired indies."

"Sure-seaters" were art houses. "Unwired indies" was *Variety*speak for independent theaters still unequipped for sound. After a briefly sardonic plot summary, *Variety* observed that "Miss Brooks takes the trial, killing

---

* In New York, *Pandora's Box* played at the 55th Street Playhouse, whose honest management ran an introductory title lamenting the fact that the film had been censored and apologizing for the "added saccharine ending."

lovers and what-nots all with the simple attitude and reaction of a diner who finds the soup just so-so."

It was the same in England. "Louise Brooks [is] a beautiful girl with a very lovely figure," wrote A. Kraszna-Krausz in the British *Close Up*, "[but] her passive decorativeness made us scarcely conscious of any magnetic impulse. . . . In vain one looked for the legendary urging and gaining in her that men desire and fear with a woman."[60]

In the *New York Times*, Mordaunt Hall echoed that view on December 2, 1929: "Miss Brooks is attractive and she moves her head and eyes at the proper moment, but whether she is endeavoring to express joy, woe, anger or satisfaction is often difficult to decide."* Revisionists would later revere Pabst for exploring "the uncharted depths of Louise Brooks, who appears serious yet innocent, sensual yet honest, with an ambivalence the screen had never before reflected."[61] But it was this very ambivalence, for which Pabst had striven, that most annoyed critics at the time.

"Although there are several adroitly directed passages," Hall continued, ". . . one is not in the least concerned as to what happens to any of the characters whose nonchalance during certain junctures is not a little absurd. It is a disconnected melodramatic effusion in which there is an attempt to depict a thoughtless, attractive woman and her unsavory experiences."

So much for any deeper significance. *Pandora* fit none of the half-dozen basic film genres but was closest to melodrama, of which it was a poor specimen. The mordant verdict of Mordaunt Hall was based on Louise's failure to telegraph Lulu's feelings according to accepted silent acting conventions. He interpreted her (and Pabst's) subtlety as an inability to emote.

"Louise Brooks cannot act," wrote another critic. "She does not suffer. She does nothing."[62]

In fairness, the critics were handicapped by the butchered versions of *Pandora* they were forced to view. A measure of the butchery is that the original running length was 131 minutes; the more or less fully restored 1983 version is 110 minutes. The version the *Variety* and *New York Times* critics saw in 1929 was eighty-five minutes. Fully a third removed! But the result was still devastating and all the more surprising to Louise, for whom bad reviews were unprecedented. She had never had anything but raves, and though she claimed not to read papers or care what they said about her, like all actors and actresses, she did.

"Pabst had fired a blank," said Louise, but he was important enough

---

* It is a misfortune for film historians that Mordaunt Hall held sway for so many years (1923–1934) at the *New York Times*, especially during the crucial silent–sound transition period. Because of the *Times*'s standing as newspaper of record, Hall's reviews—rarely insightful or interesting—have been cited and relied upon out of all proportion to their value.

internationally to survive. He didn't even stay to read the reviews, but left Berlin for the Alps immediately after the premiere to begin his next film. "It was I who was struck down by my failure, although he had done everything possible to protect and strengthen me against this deadly blow."[63]

Pabst would have many champions, and successful films, over the next two decades. Brooks would not. She had to wait a quarter century, until the publication of Lotte Eisner's *The Haunted Screen*, for her performance to be fully recognized in Europe—and even longer for such recognition in America, where there was always a stronger element of doubt. The astute American writer Cathy Henkel, for example, recently observed that Brooks as Lulu "gives the impression of being just an extraordinarily beautiful woman who happens to be in a movie." That idea occurred to Eisner in 1952, when she dared to suggest that it was Brooks, and not Pabst, who had truly unlocked *Pandora's Box:*

> [In *Pandora*], we have the miracle of Louise Brooks. Her gifts of profound intuition may seem purely passive to an inexperienced audience, yet she succeeded in stimulating an otherwise unequal director's talent to the extreme. Pabst's remarkable evolution must thus be seen as an encounter with an actress who needed no directing, but could move across the screen causing the work of art to be born by her mere presence. Louise Brooks, always enigmatically impassive, overwhelmingly *exists*. [But] was Louise Brooks a great artist or only a dazzling creature whose beauty leads the spectator to endow her with complexities of which she herself was unaware?[64]

Five years later for a revised edition, Eisner turned that last question into an answer: "We now know that Louise Brooks is a remarkable actress endowed with uncommon intelligence, and not merely a dazzlingly beautiful woman."[65] ("Damn Lotte!" Louise complained. "If I had kept my big black mouth shut, hadn't in 1957 teased her about thinking I was a dunce in 1928, she might not have changed [that] final intuitive question.")[66]

How Eisner came to change her mind is the story of the rest of Louise Brooks's life.

Aside from Louise's acting, the biggest criticism of *Pandora's Box* was a much more basic one, tersely articulated by Kraszna-Krausz:

> Lulu is inconceivable without the words that Wedekind makes her speak.
> . . . The film must give up Lulu's words. It should resign Lulu as a whole.
> For the hundredth time: one should not make films of literature.[67]

Pabst himself never stooped to defend *Pandora*, but eight years later he addressed himself to the crux of such criticism—and to the heart of film art: "Despite the rise of the 'talkie,' I remain convinced that in the cinema the text itself counts for very little. What counts is the image." [68]

He felt strongly enough about that conviction to maintain it in 1937, long after the entrenchment of sound films; how much more deeply had the thought guided him in 1928, when he and his silent art form were at their glorious peak and when *Pandora* was the purest example of image over text.

Louise shaped *Pandora*'s images beyond Pabst's wildest imaginings. But she had shaped something even more profound for her own life and career, which up to now had been charmed and charming but lacked definition. As she told John Kobal:

> I just didn't fit into the Hollywood scheme at all. I was neither a fluffy heroine, nor a wicked vamp, nor a woman of the world. I just didn't fit into any category. . . . I didn't interest them because I couldn't be typed. . . . I wasn't Clara Bow, I wasn't Mary Pickford, I wasn't Lillian Gish and I wasn't anybody, and since they don't know or care to analyze my personality and do something—you see, a Dietrich has to have a Sternberg, and a Brooks has to have a Pabst to establish a personality once and for all, and at the time I made [*Pandora*], I was just as unpopular in Germany as I was in Hollywood. That picture was a huge failure. They expected a *femme fatale*, a siren, a slinking woman with lascivious looks and leers. They expected a man-eater, a sex dynamo with a voracious appetite for men. And lots of people who see that film still insist on looking at it that way, although Lulu does nothing. She just dances through the film; she's a young girl, she leads a life she's always liked. She was a whore when she was 12, and she dies a whore when she's about 18. How can an audience expect a girl at that age to reflect, to suffer? [69]

James Card, too, grappled with the uniqueness of Brooks—that inability to define her, let alone fit her into any film studio's "scheme"—and came to this essence:

> Pabst was not the first to see in the wide, child-like open look of Louise Brooks, a satanic mirror of all the evil in oneself. But he was the first to make effective use of all this reflected evil, cast in a unique frame of black and alabaster beauty, totally unlike whatever quality of sexual charm any other star in the world had ever brought to the screen. [70]

As for the actress herself, here at last was the "type" for which she had been searching, or perhaps not searching: the ultimate type, beyond which there was nothing further. Thus was Lulu both the glory and the bane of Louise Brooks's career, the life and the death of her art. Pabst had been obsessed with feminine psychology and sexuality and with the role of sex in both the social and the personal realm. In Louise, he could not have found a better case study of the phenomena that most intrigued him and drew forth his highest art.

The image-over-text art had now reached its psychoerotic peak. A case can be made that *Pandora's Box* was *the last of the silent films*—not literally, but aesthetically. On the threshold of its premature death, the medium in *Pandora* achieved near perfection in form and content.

It would be many years before the derision of 1929 turned into the superlatives of film historians. For Pabst and Brooks, there are now countless critical tickets into the pantheon—so many, in fact, that we have to ponder the oddity of an obscure young American actress who could so "validate" and elevate a veteran director: Perhaps, notwithstanding *auteurism*, it was Brooks who made *Pandora's Box* and its director great and not the other way around. Without Louise and Lulu, Pabst was a gifted filmmaker, but with her, and *through* her, he was transcendent.

The twenty-two-year-old Louise Brooks, meanwhile, was quite unaware that Pabst had induced her to "reinvent the art of screen acting."[71]

Looking at the broader European cultural context in which Pabst was operating, it can be said that the twenties constituted the Golden Decade of Western art in this century. But the grand sweep of artistic development is rarely visible at the time it is taking place. It may or may not have been evident even to such intellectuals as G. W. Pabst and Josef von Sternberg. It certainly wasn't evident until much later to the women who served to bring their film visions to life—Louise Brooks and Marlene Dietrich.

There is no more fascinating contrast in film history than the images created by and for these two actresses—or, for that matter, their overall careers as well. In image, it is a study in the artificial versus the natural. In career, it is the gradual and careful development of Dietrich as an actress (as well as an image) versus the truncated screen life of Brooks, who simply never developed at all in sound films.

The most celebrated "Lulu-Gestalt" in movies, says Sol Gittleman, was not Pabst's more or less faithful Wedekindian rendering with Louise Brooks, but a mere—one is tempted to say "cheap"—imitation the following year:

> In 1905 Heinrich Mann, the younger [*sic*] of the two famous brothers, wrote a bitingly satirical novel about the German middle class, *Professor Unrat* [*Professor Rubbish*]. In it he created a scarcely concealed imitation of Wedekind's arch-female in Lola-Lola, who manipulates and finally destroys a pompous, middle-aged high school professor. It was Marlene Dietrich who portrayed Lola in the film version, *Der blaue Engel*, which appeared in 1930. Her performance of the heartless seductress epitomized the metamorphosis which Wedekind's Lulu had undergone. From representation of mankind's

subconscious fear of uninhibited freedom, she turned into a vain, petty bourgeois tart.[72]

And thus we come, full circle, back to the nihilism of Louise Brooks. In and out of *Pandora's Box*, Louise, like Lulu, wielded enormous power over men—an unmercenary courtesan, powerfully but capriciously sexual with whomever she fancied, asking little in return save a good time. Marlene and Lola-Lola had an equal sexual power—but wielded it with infinitely greater calculation, on screen and off.

The difference between Lulu and Lola-Lola is as striking as that between Brooks and Dietrich: The former took her erotic nihilism seriously, practicing what she and her silent body preached. The latter exploited it superficially, while—under the enduring guidance of Sternberg—taking seriously the cultivation of her career.*

No such thoughts, of course, occupied Louise at the time she finished *Pandora's Box*. All she knew as she packed her bags was that, aside from Pabst, nobody in Berlin had much liked her or her work. Not until long after did it occur to her that "Lulu's story is as close as you'll get to mine."

The making of *Pandora* was the most important film experience of Louise's life, and the development of her relationship with G. W. Pabst the most profound. But it had been emotionally and professionally exhausting.

"Making the movie was perfect," Louise told Ricky Leacock years later. "He just turned me loose, and I'd be all right. But off the set, he wanted me to be an intelligent woman, a well-disciplined actress, and I wasn't. . . . He approached people intellectually. And you couldn't approach me intellectually, because there was nothing to approach. So he was always a little bit mad at me."[73]

She had an idea that Pabst's own emotions were involved, but she had no inclination to stay and find out. In typical style, she left Berlin hurriedly on November 24, 1928, the day after shooting ended, hopping a train for Paris and then Cherbourg to board the S.S. *Majestic* for the trip home. Back in Manhattan on a dreary December 4, Louise checked into the Elysee Hotel, but she hardly had time for any civilized welcome-home socializing before she found herself in the thick of round two with Paramount.

The studio had been trying desperately to reach her for weeks; either she never received the communications or simply ignored them. In any event, the message was now loud and clear. While she was in Germany,

---

* Some European critics, including R. Paolella in *Storia del Cinema muto*, suggest that, after Sternberg saw and grasped the intimate relationship between Pabst and Brooks in *Pandora's Box*, he consciously set out to cultivate something similar (and more long-lasting) between himself and Dietrich.

the silent–sound conversion had been proceeding rapidly and the studios were grafting sound segments onto a host of films made as silents. *The Canary Murder Case* was one of them, and Paramount wanted Louise to return to Hollywood immediately to make the necessary sound retakes.

Canary was getting the sound treatment, but Paramount was getting the silent treatment from Brooks. After the long ocean voyage, the last thing she wanted was a grueling four-day train trip to California—even if her relationship with the studio had been good. The thought was even more repugnant in view of the rotten treatment she had received from Schulberg and the breaking of her contract. She haughtily declined to return his phone calls, and when he finally got through to her, he took precisely the wrong tack: "Schulberg *ordered* me to return to Hollywood," she said. "Thinking him rather careless about letting me quit, I refused."[74] For its earlier breach of faith, the studio could now go directly to hell.

Paramount thought she was playing hard to get and offered her more money. More offended than ever at what she perceived as a bribe, and apparently egged on by George Marshall, Louise again turned them down. And a third time, and a fourth. Each time, the money increased, and so did Louise's contempt. "Come back, or you'll never work in Hollywood again" was the final ultimatum. "Who wants to work in Hollywood?" was Louise's response. It was much like Dixie Dugan's telegrams to her boyfriend in *Show Girl*. The answer was no, now and forever.

At considerable extra expense, Schulberg was forced to find a substitute not only for the voice recording, but to stand in for Louise in certain retakes. Sixty years later, Arthur Jacobson—assistant director of *The Canary Murder Case*—shook his head in wonderment as he recounted the story:

> We were in a very difficult position. We needed her very badly. Finally, they said they'd give her a bonus of $10,000—but she refused it. . . . So we started to look for a girl her size who had that kind of almost blue-black hair, or whose hair could be cut that way. They looked around for quite a few days and finally found Margaret Livingston [actress wife of bandleader Paul Whiteman], who looked a little like her, and we shot over her shoulder. She was able to turn almost profile to the camera, and she was a good enough mimic, she could almost match Louise's lips.[75]

The bottom-line outcome was costly, awkward, and ultimately very embarrassing. *Variety*, in February 1929, chastised the studios for "the deception of 'looping' voices other than the performers' on to their lip movements in the post-production stage."[76] In the case of *Canary*, few shared Jacobson's high assessment of Margaret Livingston's fill-in performance—least of all Louise: "A cheap Brooklyn accent she gave me."[77] She had the temerity to complain about the voice she forced the studio to hire!

But it was true: Livingston's tough Broadway tones hardly matched the image of that subtle minx on screen. The critics could tell the voice was not that of Louise Brooks, as Alexander Walker relates:

> The first case of voice "doubling" actually exposed publicly was, suitably enough, in Malcolm St. Clair's detective movie *The Canary Murder Case.* . . . Mordaunt Hall suspected [that Louise's] voice did not belong to her; and soon it was admitted that not only was the voice that of Margaret Livingston, but the "doubler" had stood in for Miss Brooks in some scenes when the actress was not available! The magazine publisher George Kent Shuler, sensing or possibly whipping up the fans' outrage at this practice, thundered, "It is bad art and bad entertainment." After which outburst, voice doubling was either more carefully effected, or . . . became unnecessary.[78]

Paramount was doubly furious. Louise's obstinacy not only cost the studio time and money, but was the source of humiliation by the critics and the undermining of audience confidence at a time when it was most needed.

"Odd," she said blithely, "so much rancor after Schulberg had allowed me to leave with less concern than he would drop a crumpled Dixie cup."[79]

She had paid him back, all right. And true to his threats, he retaliated by putting out the story that her voice did not record well—a fabrication which stuck for the rest of her life and career. Louise's voice was just fine, but virtually no one in (or out of) the industry would have any way of knowing it. At this delicate point in the silent–sound transition, first reports were devastatingly permanent.

Louise's "fuck you" to Paramount was lamentable in every tactical and technical way. By the beginning of 1929, sound recording was much improved. Her clear, elegant voice—pitched liltingly in the middle range—recorded beautifully in the few sound films she made later. Moreover, the *Canary* sound retakes were shot by her old friend Frank Tuttle, who had long adored her. She could not have asked for a more sympathetic director to usher her onto the ground floor of the new technology. But she cut off her voice to spite her face, and at the worst possible moment—when Paramount was obsessed and terrified by sound and had neither the time nor the patience to deal with a recalcitrant star.

"By the time *The Canary Murder Case* was made," wrote James Card, "her rapidly growing number of ardent, letter-writing fans indicated that she was about to become one of the major stars of the late twenties."[80] This was true, and the truth of it had not gone unnoticed by the studio, even after her walkout over the broken contract.

Schulberg and Paramount could have forgiven that first act of defiance

—especially since they were in the wrong. Marshall, her unofficial agent and Svengali, had perhaps steered her right during the salary flap, or at least steered her in a way that turned out to her benefit, thanks to Pabst. But the second act of defiance—that was unforgivable, and so was Louise.

With *Pandora* in the can, Louise could have said yes, magnanimously, to the *Canary* retakes, and been a heroine for doing so, with the studio in her debt. No one could take away her European experience or the astonishing film that it produced. Both the cake and the eating of it were hers.

Instead, on the heels of the legendary *Pandora's Box*, Louise Brooks unthinkingly destroyed her American movie career in exchange for some sweet, short-lived revenge.

Louise, Ben Finny, and unidentified friends at Joe Zelli's nightclub, Paris, May 1929

13 · The Lost Girl

Life is a jest; and all things show it.
I thought so once; but now I know it.
— TOMBSTONE OF
JOHN GAY (1685–1732)

I N   L O U I S E ' S   view, she wasn't killing off her movie career, she was merely sticking it to Paramount. There were plenty of other studios—not that she was eager to work for *them*, either, if it meant going back to Hollywood, which of course it did.

George Marshall was pleased with her treatment of Schulberg, having been co-architect of it. But though he wanted her to quit Paramount, he did not want her to quit movies, and it was dawning on him that he might have created a monster. A few days after New Year's 1929, Louise left the Hotel Elysee and moved in with Marshall at the Lombardy Hotel, as she told Ricky Leacock:*

> [George] loved beautiful women and he loved famous women, and my being a famous actress was part of his affection for me. So I got back to New York and he said, "Now, they've opened up a new company, RKO"—Joseph Kennedy had formed the company—"and they want you to sign a contract." And I said, "No, I hate California and I'm not going back." George was a man who never said anything, he never complained to me about anything, he always went into action. He said, "Well, go over and see them anyhow." So I went over and they said, "We'll give you $500 a week." I think they wanted me to do a well-known book then called *Bad Girl.* . . . And I said flatly to them, "No, I don't want to do it." So George didn't say anything.

* In 1973, North German Television (NDR) asked documentary filmmaker Ricky Leacock to interview Louise on film in conjunction with an NDR showing of *Pandora's Box*. Aside from an interview with Gary Conklin for his 1976 documentary "Memories of Berlin: The Twilight of Weimar Culture," and a Kevin Brownlow–David Gill session with Louise in 1977, Leacock's *Lulu in Berlin*, filmed in March 1974, is the only full-length documentary footage of Louise—an invaluable record on which this chapter relies.

He went back to the Lombardy, he had a couple of drinks, and he gave me one shove and knocked me against the bed and I split my head right open. I'd been wearing my hair up, and so I put my bangs back. Then he said, "Well, what do you want to do?" and I said, "I don't know," so he went back to Washington and left me there in a huge suite at the Lombardy, and as usual I was running out of money. Although I made an awful lot of money, it seemed to disappear all the time, and of course he would have to spend a lot of money on me, too, and he didn't like that a terrible lot. So somehow we got into a fight and I disappeared with another man.[1]

Indeed, her expensive tastes had quickly consumed most of the $12,500 she had been paid for *Pandora's Box*, and for the next two months she was in financial as well as professional limbo. But then in April 1929, a fresh communication from Pabst crossed the Atlantic.

"He said, 'René Clair's making a picture called *Prix de Beauté* in Paris and he wants you to play the part, so come at once,' " said Louise. "He always gave me orders, so—although I wouldn't go to Hollywood—I would go to Mr. Pabst."[2]

Once again, she did not have the slightest idea of the story, but her faith in Pabst was supreme—even though he was not going to direct the picture himself. This time, she did not need George Marshall to tell her to accept. She did tell him of the offer, however, and as her unofficial agent, he drew up a contract.

On April 20, 1929, in good spirits, Louise boarded the *Ile de France* for the leisurely spring voyage to Le Havre. Marshall could not accompany her, but she was not lonely. To her pleasant surprise, while still in view of the Statue of Liberty, she spotted Townsend Martin among her co-passengers. He was just as surprised, and just as pleasantly.

They had not seen each other for two years, since *Love 'em and Leave 'em*, whose screenplay Martin wrote. In a November 27, 1928 article that gave Martin's new comedy *A Most Immoral Lady* a lukewarm review, the *New York Times* drama critic wrote that Martin "is better known on Park Avenue than on Broadway." If he had any full-time occupation now, it was that of dilettante and hedonist-at-large. Martin had no particular business in Europe other than to get an early start on the summer social season. And though his sexual preference was for men, he was fond of women too, and very fond of Louise, who knew it.

"He was in love with me," she said simply.[3]

It takes one hedonist-at-large to know another, and the *Ile de France* was a lovely, luxurious setting. Townsend and Louise did a lot of drinking, dancing, and cavorting during the six-day crossing, and of course they slept together.

· · ·

René Clair was waiting to greet Louise in Paris, but their first meeting turned out to be their last. A snag had developed.

"I went to get photographs—still publicity pictures—made with René Clair, who spoke very little English," she said. "He was a very small, demure, rather fragile man, and he took me back to the hotel in a cab afterwards. We finished the photographs and we were riding along the Champs-Elysées and he said, 'Look, you know I'm not going to make that picture.' "[4]

She did *not* know that, and was shocked. Clair went on to tell her that the French-German production company, SOFAR (La Société des Films Artistiques), did not even have enough money to start the picture, let alone finish it, and that, in his opinion, they never would.

"I'm not going to make that picture," Clair told Louise, "and if you're smart, you'll quit, too. . . . You're just going to sit around here in Paris waiting to make a picture that will never be made."[5]

Louise replied that she couldn't back out because "I have a contract, and it's all signed and sealed in New York, and George Marshall made it so I can't get out of it, I'll have to do it." The next scene she described with relish for Leacock:

> Well, exit René Clair. So there I was holed up in the Royal Monceau with nothing to do, I didn't know anybody, and all of a sudden Pabst appeared. He was on his way to London, and he asked me out and I went with him [and several others] and they said, "Where do you want to go?" and I said, "Chez Florence." It was a place with a colored band. I went there every night.
>
> So we went there and we sat down, and Pabst wasn't pleased with me. I was drinking. His idea of a drink for me was a fruit salad in a pitcher surrounded by a little bit of champagne and Kaiser Cup and such things. But I was drinking a brandy or something, and over across the way I saw Townsend Martin. . . . He quit [movies by then], he didn't care, he was rich, and there he's sitting with his great English lady, the Honorable Mrs. Daisy Fellowes. She had a yacht and in consequence loved money like all rich people. So I was very bored with the people I was with and Mr. Pabst was glaring at me . . . and so I told the waiter to tell Mr. Martin to come to my table. He didn't come. Mr. Pabst in the usual German fashion had given me a bouquet of roses, a cluster of roses. Well, finally, Townsend came over— he was a tall, blond man—and he bent over to me and said, "I'm terribly sorry, Louise, but I couldn't leave Daisy alone." Whereupon I took this bouquet and sliced him across the face, leaving a trickle from the thorns.[6]

"Of blood?" Leacock asked, incredulously.

"Of blood, of course," she replied. "He was a gentleman and he laughed, but Mr. Pabst—I thought he was going to kill me right there, and all the men sitting there from SOFAR, and Pabst said, 'Oh, I'm terribly sorry.' He knew Townsend. Townsend said, 'That's all right, all right.' So Mr. Pabst grabbed me and took me back to the Royal Monceau."

For not coming over to her table quickly enough—for waiting until Lady Fellowes left to powder her nose—Townsend Martin got his face slashed. He and Louise had no abiding romance, but they had, after all, been intimate on the *Ile de France* just a few days before. It was a matter of pride, not jealousy. She didn't care whom Martin squired or bedded, but the insulting thought that he thought Daisy a greater "lady" was sufficient provocation for her unladylike attack.

Louise was not exactly contrite. "I thought nothing more about it," she said. But German girls did not do such things, and Pabst was still agitated about the incident when they arrived back at the Royal Monceau. For that matter, he was much agitated about Louise in general, and had been, ever since that first day on the set when her little dance bewitched him and magically vindicated his casting of her as Lulu. During and since the making of *Pandora*, his infatuation remained intense.

"Everyone thought he was in love with me," said Louise. "On the rare evenings when I went to his apartment [in Berlin's Dahlem sector] for dinner, his wife, Trudi, would walk out and bang the door. Mr. Pabst was a highly respectable man, but he had the most extraordinary collection of obscene stills in the world. He even had one of Sarah Bernhardt nude with a black-lace fan. Did you know that in the '20s it was the custom for European actresses to send naked pictures of themselves to movie directors? He had all of them."[7]

Pabst was now forty-four years old and still a handsome, if not exactly animally attractive, man. In addition to a keen interest in women and sex, he had the most fascinating mind she ever encountered; the intense empathy between them transcended even such outrageous social gaffes as the scene at Chez Florence. But at the moment, depositing the tipsy Louise in her room, he was still cross with her about the cabaret incident. Louise, on the other hand, was in high spirits. Feeling less remorseful than kittenish, she decided that the way to cheer Pabst up was with a romp in the hay—the last thing in the world he expected, at that point, but perhaps the thing he most desired. Years later she told Kenneth Tynan it was "the best sexual performance of my career" and that her director-lover was ecstatically pleased with her, with himself, and with the scene.[8]

Pabst departed starry-eyed that morning for London to study British production methods and discuss a film deal that never came to fruition, while Louise now had time on her hands. With no filming yet in Paris, she left on May 23, 1929, for a little vacation on the French Riviera, her fare paid by some unnamed "rich American friends" who set her up in a fashionable hotel.

It was evidently there, at a party in Antibes, that she met Scott and Zelda Fitzgerald for the second and last time. It struck her that they were already considered a bit passé by the fickle breed that summered there: The smart set's literary conversation now ran more to Hemingway, whose *A Farewell to Arms* was just out, than to Fitzgerald, whose *Great Gatsby* was four years old. Sensing the social (and perhaps literary) decline, Scott was apparently depressed—but Zelda was enraged. Though Louise never saw Hemingway and the Fitzgeralds together, she later came to a startling conclusion: "The homosexual hero of war and adventure. A man's man. 'Men without Women.' Zelda Fitzgerald hated Hemingway because he knew she was viciously insane, and Hemingway hated Zelda because she knew he was basically a homo putting on a fighting-and-fucking act to fool himself."[9]*

Such vacationing was fairly tense, and after a week on the Riviera, she returned to Paris, where there was still no budget and no new director for *Prix de Beauté*. It was now June, and she was still cooling her heels. To relieve the boredom, she began accepting invitations to places where her aura of silent mystery was augmented by the fact that she did not speak a word of French. At one such soiree, and subsequently at Joe Zelli's celebrated Parisian nightclub, she got to know a strange young man whom she would refer to thereafter only as "The Eskimo."

"He was half-Swedish and half-English, a darling boy," she said. "They sent him to Paris to work in a bank there, but he would turn up in the morning in tails, so he got fired and was living on a small [family] allowance. I met him at a party and he came to live with me."[10]

It was that simple. His real name appears to have been Karl von Bieck, and he was supposedly an impoverished baron. Louise's 1929 diary indicates that she lent him money. But she never quite nailed down his name, let alone his lineage.

"They called him 'The Eskimo' because his hair was perfectly blond so

---

* Louise called Hemingway "that bloodiest of all killers," but preferred his writing to that of his friend, Gertrude Stein. Her analysis, in an October 18, 1969, letter to Kevin Brownlow:

"I detest liars, not only because they 'insult my intelligence,' but because lies destroy the creative mind. Gertrude Stein finally destroyed her magnificently creative intellect by refusing to face the truth about herself—an old lesbian Jewess whose hatred and jealousy of beautiful women and great contemporary writers were psychotic. In my search for her rare jeweled insights, wading through the miles of her silly, repeating word games in a book such as *The Making of Americans*, substituting her invention of repetitive realism for truth, I could kill her. Even so she didn't fool herself. Hemingway had to type and proof-read the book for her because she herself could not bear to do so. . . . In a viciously brilliant essay in the only book, his last, in which he told some truth— *A Moveable Feast*—he rips the false front off the Stein-Toklas playhouse. Almost no one reads her books; millions of people read his."

it looked like a white fur cap," she said. She herself usually shortened his nickname to "Eskie," and he helped her pass the time until the phone rang on June 9.

"Louees? Mr. Pabst," said the voice. "I'm going to make a picture with you in it. You're to come to Berlin."

More orders, and more acquiescence from Louise, who was undisturbed even when he informed her that since it was his own company (HOM-Film), instead of UFA or SOFAR, he could only pay her $500 a week instead of the $1,000 she was contracted to receive for *Prix de Beauté*.

"You get on the train and come," he said.

"So I got on the train and went," she said, leaving the very next day to star in a picture called *Das Tagebuch einer Verlorenen—The Diary of a Lost Girl*.

Pabst, reliably, was there to meet her at the Berlin station again. But this time, they managed to annoy each other almost on sight, for reasons of real and imagined sexual competition: Louise had brought along the Eskimo, a puppydog figure who was by now permanently attached to his American beauty.

"And who is this?" Pabst asked her immediately.

"The Eskimo," she replied. He was really a baron, she added, but Pabst wasn't impressed. He saw another George Marshall–type distraction to Louise in her work and another rival for her affections.

"He was appalled when I got off the train with the Eskimo," she told Kenneth Tynan. "On top of that, I had a wart on my neck, and Eskie had just slammed the compartment door on my finger. Mr. Pabst took one stark look at me, told me I had to start work the next morning, and dragged me away to a doctor, who burned off the wart. If you study the early sequences of *Lost Girl*, you can see the sticking plaster on my neck."[11]

But Pabst got a bit of his own back on the first day on the *Diary* set when Louise noticed an attractive young woman paying an inordinate amount of attention to him and vice versa. Her name was Leni Riefenstahl; she was later to become the best filmmaker in Nazi Germany and director of that apotheosis of the Third Reich, *Triumph of the Will*—the greatest propaganda film of all time.

Leni and Louise took an immediate dislike to one another.

When he finished *Pandora's Box* six months earlier, Pabst had wanted the Heinrich Mann novel, *Professor Unrat*, for his next project—presumably with Louise as Lola-Lola. But the battle for film rights was won by Josef von Sternberg, the title became *The Blue Angel*, and the role went to Marlene Dietrich. Pabst's second choice was *The Diary of a Lost Girl*, but since he was an independent, the fund-raising process was complex and time-consuming. To tide himself over financially, he signed on with Sokal

Film to co-direct *Die weisse Hölle vom Piz Palü (The White Hell of Pitz Palü)*, starring Leni Riefenstahl and Louise's own Jack the Ripper, Gustav Diessl.

Pabst's co-director was Dr. Arnold Fanck, a physical culturist who since 1920 had been making films dedicated to the beauty and hazards of mountain climbing. Beloved of the German public, the "Alpine films" were a subgenre of the German "health and culture" pictures, which glorified athletic prowess and body-building and in addition to a titillating quantity of adolescent nudity often contained an undertone of racial superiority.

But the Alpine films were a cut above these. Though always built around sentimental rescue plots, the best of them—such as *Pitz Palü*—were redeemed by the breathtaking beauty of glaciers and picturesque mountain chalets and the absence of propaganda.

On *Pitz Palü*, Pabst and cameraman Sepp Allgeier achieved photographic splendor, while Ladislaus Vajda (who wrote the *Pandora* screenplay and co-wrote that of *The Threepenny Opera*) beefed up the story: Mountaineer Diessl loses his bride during an avalanche on Mount Palü, then returns to find a pair of young lovers who insist on climbing the same dangerous peak. Another avalanche, another heroic rescue. But Riefenstahl came across with great allure, and the film was a major success.

"Making *Diary*," Louise recalled, "they were still talking about the dangers of making [*Pitz Palü*], especially the dangers faced by the flyer who risked his life for the aerial shots." [12]* Risking his life in the same plane was cameraman Allgeier. Risking her life now on the ground was Leni Riefenstahl, who continued to see Pabst while Louise burned:

> I was wild with jealousy. Suddenly she started coming on the set every day. She was a strange-looking girl . . . She had rather an oval face, mildly pretty . . . the profile was sharp and intelligent, a hook nose, a strong, strong face. But she came on the set to make love to Mr. Pabst, and that made me mad. I was the star of the picture. She had beautiful legs, and that annoyed me too, and she would always be grabbing him and taking him off to corners, and I watched all the time to see how he reacted to her . . . I knew she was trying to wheedle him, to get him to use her in a picture. He was so clever, and so nice, but he always pushed her away. [13]

Louise later pursued this theme and its variation—the Pabst-Riefenstahl relationship after Hitler's rise to power—with Kevin Brownlow:

> Mr. Pabst was very strange about her. After using her in *The White Hell of Pitz Palü* I thought he would at least give her a constant admiration for the terrible risks she took in filming that picture, but when she came bound-

---

* The pilot was Ernst Udet, later a Luftwaffe general under Hermann Göring. He rebelled against Nazi monstrosities and committed suicide by deliberately crashing his plane.

ing on the set [of *Diary*] to sell him some idea of a new film with her, he would give her more ice than Pitz Palü. The Jews who have blackened Mr. Pabst's name as a Nazi should know how he turned down Leni. . . . Maybe he was bored because she was such a poor actress. Even freezing in the ice, she got into ballet third position.[14]

Riefenstahl's intelligence intrigued Louise—"the way she learned from [Pabst] and picked his brain." She had picked up many pointers about direction from him during *Pitz Palü* and was now "hanging around" the *Diary* set to learn even more.

The Eskimo, for his part, was hanging around hoping to see more of Louise.

"So all the time we made *Diary* I had Eskie in tow," she said. "But Mr. Pabst was very firm about the Eskimo. The Eskimo would come to the studio every day. He would get up about 11, he'd go to the Adlon bar, and then he'd . . . bring out a lot of cold meats to Mr. Pabst and me, and he would have lunch."

They were shooting in Staaken again, in the old Zeppelin hangar, and Pabst allowed Eskie there. But when they moved to Swinemünde, 100 miles north of Berlin, for location shots, "Mr. Pabst took me aside and he said, 'You are not to bring that boy with you, do you understand?' "

Sepp Allgeier, cameraman for The Diary of a Lost Girl *(1929),
beloved of both Louise and Leni Riefenstahl; photo by Lothar Wolff*

Deprived of the Eskimo's company in that romantic setting on the Baltic, Louise began to pay more attention to the other men working on the film. Her eye was most pleased by Sepp Allgeier, the handsome cameraman who was a friend and reportedly a lover of Leni Riefenstahl.* Louise told Leacock:

> I liked Sepp very much. He was the only cameraman I was always really attracted to. He was a beautiful blond, marvelous muscles, a champion skier, and one day he came on the set in his shorts, and Mr. Pabst said, "What are you doing coming out here?" Well, he's showing off his muscles. [Pabst] said, "Go out and put your pants on!" Up in Swinemünde, in this Seacoast Hotel, there was practically no one there except us, and one night everyone had gone to bed except Sepp and I, and we were sitting in the bar, he was drinking beer and I was drinking something, and we were having a lovely time, the whole place to ourselves, enjoying ourselves, suddenly the bar door opened and Pabst stuck his head in and said, "Louees, go to bed!" How he knew we were there, I don't know. He gave Sepp a dirty look, and so we disappeared. . . . Pabst could always guess whom I liked.[15]

Pabst couldn't banish Sepp from the set the way he had banned the Eskimo, nor could Louise banish Leni Riefenstahl, who remained a thorn in her side. The sight of her "gabbing and laughing off in a corner with Pabst," said Louise, "guaranteed my look of gloomy rejection in a close-up"—precisely the look Pabst wanted for that particular shot. But eventually Leni finished her lobbying, and Louise had Pabst to herself.

The Diary of a Lost Girl was based on the moralistic novel by Margarete Böhme. Its heroine is beautiful Thymiane, who is seduced by her father's lascivious assistant (Fritz Rasp of *Metropolis*) and then abandoned by all to bear an illegitimate child in shame. The child soon dies, yet Thymiane must be punished further. She is sent to a reformatory that is brutally run by Valeska Gert and the hideous, leering Andrews Engelmann.† When the authorities try to take away her precious diary, Thymiane sparks a rebellion and escapes. From girls' prison to brothel is a short hop, and she is propelled there by the same bourgeois hypocrisy that got her in trouble in the first place. But still she remains innocent. What happens next is best described by French critic Ado Kyrou in *Amour-érotisme et cinéma:*

---

* Allgeier (1895–1968) worked on a number of Riefenstahl films, including *Triumph of the Will.* But he had to share the honors. In her heyday under the Nazis, Riefenstahl commanded an army of eighteen cameramen for *Triumph* (1934) and no fewer than forty-four for *Olympiad* (1936–1938).

† Engelmann was familiar to American audiences as the U-boat commander in Rex Ingram's *Mare Nostrum* (1926). He later appeared in such Nazi films as Karl Ritter's *Über alles in der Welt* (1941) and *Münchhausen* (1943). Lotte Eisner observed that "the hairless face and almost indecently bald head of Nosferatu haunted German film-makers for a long time. In the more middle-class ambience of *Diary of a Lost Girl*, [Engelmann] looks like Nosferatu's brother."

Louise as Thymiane is menaced by
Andrews Englemann in a publicity
shot for The Diary of a Lost Girl.
BELOW: A stunning display of what
Christopher Isherwood called
"that unique, imperious neck
of hers" in a swoon with
Joseph Rovensky from
The Diary of a Lost Girl (1929)

Not yet 17, inexperienced, [Thymiane] is bewitched by the luxury of the establishment, of whose function she is ignorant. She rapidly removes her prison uniform in favor of a white evening gown.* For the first time in her life she can comport herself like a woman and men look at her. Even a man who has not been presented asks her for a dance. Delighted, she accepts. This dance is beyond doubt the unique sequence in all the history of the cinema in which a woman dares express the poetry of the gradual and marvelous growing of sexual desire. She dances, at first smiling; she is happy. But soon happiness transforms into joy, she closes her eyes, contact with a masculine body awakens her own. Her arms hang down limply, her legs follow an instinctive rhythm, and it is a body overflowing with love which a man carries towards a bed. In the morning Louise cannot understand why she has been paid for doing what she knows is the most marvelous of all human actions.

The brothel scenes—lush and shocking in 1929—indeed show Brooks at her most erotic, dancing, drinking champagne, arching her swanlike neck in full sexual submission. Through it all, the character of Thymiane never loses her innate generosity, and she ends up exposing the evils of the reformatory and delivering a stinging indictment of the system.

In *Diary* as in *Pandora*, Pabst filmed Louise with loving attention to her androgynous beauty—again capitalizing on her quality of "knowing innocence." He captures it best in the early seduction scene with Fritz Rasp —the only German actor, aside from Gustav Diessl, whom Louise found sexually attractive. That sequence, which melds her pudgy-cheeked girlishness and eternal womanliness, was conceived as a ballet and directed "as a series of subtle, almost wordless manoeuvres between an 'innocent' young girl and a wary lecher." [16]

Pabst, said Louise, "chose Fritz Rasp not only for the restraint with which he would play a part verging on burlesque but also for his physical grace and strength. When I collapsed in his embrace, he swept me up into his arms and carried me off to bed as lightly as if I weighed no more than my silken nightgown and robe." [17] As he lays her on the bed, her foot tips over a painfully symbolic glass of red wine, spilling it onto the sheets, after which his body descends to cover hers.

It is the film's most intensely erotic moment.

But the most famous sequence in *Diary* is the reformatory scene in which Gert, the sadistic headmistress, beats a gong in Prussian military tempo by which the girls are forced to exercise. The rhythm gets faster and faster, Gert's face becomes more and more contorted, until she and

---

* Cyd Charisse made an identical entrance twenty-three years later in *Singin' in the Rain*, the definitive film musical set in Hollywood at the time of the silent–sound transition. In this unmistakable homage, Charisse wears a Louise Brooks bob and a white dress and is first seen, as Louise was, about to descend a staircase.

Valeska Gert: mistress of sadistic, orgasmic repression at the girls' reformatory in Pabst's
Diary of a Lost Girl *(1929)*

the scene reach a climax. Louise referred to this as "the orgasm scene"— brilliantly edited by Pabst and luridly acted by Gert.

On and off the set, there were vibrations between Brooks and Gert that did not escape Pabst's notice. He loved Gert, as a person and as an actress, but he was not above manipulating her shamelessly.*

"She asked me out," said Louise, "because I adored going to lesbian and pansy places, and those were among the things that I wasn't allowed [by Pabst]. . . . "[18] "A film is about conflicts. Mr. Pabst, because Valeska Gert might go after me, told her that I did not want to work with her so that she would be properly antagonistic in *Diary*."[19]

The result on film was immortality for Gert and for the scenes she dominates.

But it was death, rather than immortality, that awaited *The Diary of a Lost Girl* at the box office upon its release. What killed the picture was not so much the bad reviews as the timing: In Europe as in America, the talk of the film world was talk. The silent *Diary* couldn't compete with the excitement surrounding any bad new sound film. Even more than *Pandora's Box*, *Diary of a Lost Girl* disappeared in the crevice between the two forms of film. For the most part, it was ignored. But what contemporary attention it did get was uniformly negative.

The influential Berlin critic Hans G. Lustig gave it a single withering paragraph in *Der Tempel*. Others devoted their space to savaging Böhme's novel, "the popularity of which among the philistines of the past generation rested upon the slightly pornographic frankness with which it recounted the private life of some prostitutes from a morally elevated point of view."[20]

Pabst, it seemed, had simply shifted the venue of the Lulu themes from the unspecified theatrical circumstances of *Pandora* to a more realistic 1929 German setting. He was again fixing on the role of sex in society— and again hitting too close to home as far as the German public was concerned. One critic called it a "fictionalized documentary" on the current moral and social climate of Berlin, which it was. Most, like Siegfried Kracauer, chastised Pabst for harping "on the immorality of [Thymiane's] middle-class environment" to such an extent "that the brothel almost appears to be a health resort" by comparison.[21]

---

* Pabst used Valeska Gert (1896–1978) earlier in *Joyless Street* and subsequently in *The Threepenny Opera*. Like Fritz Rasp and Gustav Diessl, she was an unofficial member of his "company," but she appeared in dozens of other films and also operated a cabaret in Berlin before and after World War II. Her swan song was as the living mummy in Federico Fellini's *Juliet of the Spirits*, in 1965. In the sixties, Louise sent her a belated "note of appreciation for her great performances" and later advised Kevin Brownlow to interview Gert: "I hope you can get to this amazing old dyke who screwed Eisenstein." Gert was a lesbian, but she reportedly had a brief affair with Soviet director Sergei Eisenstein when he visited Berlin in 1929.

Kracauer was simultaneously getting and missing the point, for that was just the message: The brothel has more honesty and integrity than the society at large.

But the censors did not miss the point. They butchered *Diary* more brutally than *Pandora*. In the ending Pabst intended, Thymiane was to become the proprietress of her *own* high-class brothel, rejecting respectability in favor of the wealth and power that a rotten bourgeoisie could respect. But the censors insisted that Thymiane embrace precisely the kind of sentimental reformism that Pabst disdained, twisting the film into conformity with German middle-class values. Pabst capitulated because he had to coexist with them and because he would live to fight another day for such subsequent (and better) films as *Westfront 1918* (1930), *The Threepenny Opera* (1931), and *Kameradschaft* (1931). *The Diary of a Lost Girl* was a kind of sacrificial lamb, as its scenarist, Rudolf Leonhardt, affirms:

> Pabst's accommodating nature had already made him prepared to make two different endings—for vice, even involuntary vice, must not go rewarded.
>
> Where the censors had not forbidden passages beforehand, entire filmed sequences were cut without mercy later on. In one version, if I remember rightly, they cut 450 metres, and in either this or another version they made 54 further cuts.[22]

The entire "bedroom ballet" sequence and many others were cut—and not just in Germany. For most Europeans who saw it in 1929, says Leonhardt, "The film comes to an end shortly after the middle of our script, inconclusively and incomprehensibly. I once saw it myself at a cinema in Paris and stayed in my seat at the end because I thought the film had broken."

As for Americans, they never saw it at all—and this was probably just as well. *Variety*'s Berlin correspondent caught the premiere at the UFA Kurfürstendamm Theater on October 24, 1929, and sent back the following obituary:

> G. W. Pabst is among the best of German directors still working here but has had atrocious luck with his scenarios. This one, taken from a best seller of years ago, is no exception. . . .
>
> The discretion which Pabst displays in his direction only softens the comic qualities of the story. This time he has been unfortunate in his choice of his heroine. Louise Brooks (American) is monotonous in the tragedy which she has to present.[23]

No serious criticism of *The Diary of a Lost Girl* could take place until three decades later, when it was finally reassembled more or less as Pabst intended (but still with the "reformist" ending). Lotte Eisner felt it represented "a new and more realistic Pabst." But at the time, *Diary* came in for the same drubbing given to most *Neue Sachlichkeit* films—panned for its "neutrality" and for failing to offer a remedy. Lost on most critics was the fact that Pabst's technique in *Diary* was different from that of *Pandora*. Eisner, virtually alone, recognized a new, semidocumentary restraint: "Pabst now seeks neither Expressionistic chiaroscuro nor Impressionistic glitter; and he seems less intoxicated than he was by the beauty of his actress."

Less so, but still intoxicated. Brooks's dazzling presence now dominates every critical analysis of the film. In 1955, in reference to *Diary of a Lost Girl* a quarter century after its release, Henri Langlois of the Cinémathèque Française rendered one of the most breathtaking homages ever given an actress:

> Those who have seen her can never forget her. She is the modern actress par excellence because, like the statues of antiquity, she is outside of time . . . She has the naturalness that only primitives retain before the lens . . . She is the intelligence of the cinematographic process, she is the most perfect incarnation of *photogénie*; she embodies in herself all that the cinema rediscovered in its last years of silence: complete naturalness and complete simplicity.[24]

Pabst's goal had not been social reform, but the portrayal of contemporary socioeroticism—its sensual beauty no less than its rotten core. His treatment was cynical, to be sure, and much flawed by melodrama, but still a potent blend of brutality and sexuality. In the cabaret party scene, Louise recalled, Thymiane is offered as first prize in a raffle: "Pabst wanted realism, so we all had to drink real drinks."[25] Louise rose to this challenge, on the strength of hot German champagne, and is both intoxicated and intoxicating in the scene.

The Diary of a Lost Girl was Pabst's last silent film and, in at least one respect, the pinnacle of a dying art form. "No director during the silent period," says Lee Atwell, "equalled his ability to create scenes of sustained erotic intensity that appeal to our aesthetic sense as well as our innermost desires."[26]

It was, in fact, Pabst who made that appeal to the aesthetic sense, but it was Louise who appealed to the innermost desires—including Pabst's.

"Louise was pretty much on her own during *Diary*," says James Card. "Pabst almost seemed to lose interest in the film. There's a point in the picture when the cutting goes to hell, even beyond what the censors did to it."[27] For one thing, Pabst was already preoccupied with preparations for his first sound film, *Westfront 1918*. He was also beginning the fierce struggle for film rights to *The Threepenny Opera*—the most revolutionary

German musical of the century—and determined not to lose out on it, as he had lost *Professor Unrat* to Sternberg.

Louise held Leni Riefenstahl partly responsible for Pabst's distraction, as well, and ruminated for years about her nefarious effect on him.* Yet Louise had her own distractions during *Diary*, which were correspondingly annoying to Pabst.

"Every time we met," she said, "I always had a guy, and a different guy, and it was a long series over the years of his getting madder and madder . . . He was mad at George, he was mad at all the succession of men." [28]

Currently, the Eskimo served as the focus of Pabst's irritation, which must have been aggravated by the private sexual tensions between Brooksie and himself. Pabst had been much more disturbed by the rose-slashing of Townsend Martin than she realized. Surely he knew it could only be explained by the fact that she had been having some kind of affair with *Martin*, too, in addition to other known and unknown lovers.

One evening during the filming of *Diary*, Pabst took Louise to a Berlin nightclub, where the conversation turned to Lili Damita, the fiery French actress who later moved to Hollywood and caused a sensation less for her films than for her stormy marriage to Errol Flynn. Pabst had directed her in two films in 1926, and the trauma was still fresh in his mind.

"She had the most beautiful body I ever saw," said Louise. "She never was a success, but she had the temper of an absolute devil. I got into a fight with her once and she damn near killed me."

The subject of Lili Damita's temper was Pabst's entrée to bring up the Townsend Martin incident with Louise.

"You know, I haven't forgotten that," he told her. "You make me think of Lili Damita. Sitting in this very restaurant with her one night, she got mad at someone across the room, and she picked up an iron ashtray. She took it and threw it across and missed this man just by 'that' and broke the mirror!"

To which tale, Louise added: "Somehow, I could tell he forgave me, but he never forgave Lili." [29]

Pabst could always forgive her, even through the sadness of failing to "save" her. All he could do was watch, helplessly fascinated by everything about her and frustrated by his own truncated affair with her. To Tynan, Louise had indicated that the one-night stand with Pabst had been little more than a charade. But to Brownlow she gave the story a different slant: "Pabst! I went to bed with him one night in Paris and it was so exciting that I refused to risk another performance. This made him furious, especially when I always had some bastard on my tail. I do not bring up sex in

---

* A full account of Riefenstahl and Pabst during the Nazi period is found in chapter 17.

Louise cavorts during an outing at Swinemünde on a day off from filming The Diary of a Lost Girl, *July 1929. Photo by Lothar Wolff*

my articles unless it had a direct bearing on relationships—and it always does."[30]

After their night together in Paris, the direct bearing of sex on her relationship with Pabst escalated from the abstract to the unavoidably real:

> He wanted the affair to continue. But I didn't, and when I got to Berlin it was like *Pandora's Box* all over again, except that this time the man I brought with me was the Eskimo—my white-headed boy from Zelli's. . . . I hated to hurt Mr. Pabst's feelings with the Eskimo, but I simply could not bring myself to repeat that one and only night. The irony, which Mr. Pabst never knew, was that although Eskie and I shared a hotel suite in Berlin, we didn't sleep together until much later, when *Lost Girl* was finished and we were spending a few days in Paris. "Eskimo," I said to him the evening before we parted, "this is the night." And it was—another first and last for Brooks.[31]

Surprise! Everyone had assumed she and Eskie were a romantic item when in fact they were just pals. The Eskimo had served as a cover to help her deflect further advances from Pabst, whom she revered too highly to treat as offhandedly as she dealt with most lovers. Townsend Martin, Walter Wanger, Eddie Sutherland—they and their broken hearts could take care of themselves. But Louise was not going to toy with G. W. Pabst.

Beyond sex, there was the issue of Louise's professional attitude—or lack of same. Pabst knew she'd had only a foggy notion of what *Pandora's Box* was all about. He also knew, as Louise later said, "I had no idea at all of [*Diary's*] plot or meaning till I saw it 27 years later, at Eastman House." That lack of interest, once its charming caprice wore off, increased the tension between them. He wanted her to stay and let him turn her into an actress who could rival even Garbo. But Louise's American playmates were making her homesick. For the first and fatal time, she said no to Mr. Pabst. He was furious, and on the last day of filming for *Diary* he spoke his mind:

> We were sitting gloomily at a table in the garden of a little café, watching the workmen while they dug the grave for a burial scene, when he decided to let me have it. Several weeks before, in Paris, he had met some friends of mine—rich Americans with whom I spent every hour away from work. And he was angry: first, because he thought they prevented me from staying in Germany, learning the language, and becoming a serious actress, as he wanted; and, second, because he looked upon them as spoiled children who would amuse themselves with me for a time and then discard me like an old toy. "Your life is exactly like Lulu's," he said, "and you will end the same way."
>
> At the time, knowing so little of what he meant by *Lulu*, I just sat sullenly glaring at him, trying not to listen.[32]

To James Card years later she added that Pabst "came so near to being right that I shudder now a little, thinking of it."[33] It wasn't until the late 1950s—when she saw the similar sexual explorations of Ingmar Bergman in film—that she thought she grasped the essence of this intense, brilliant director: "Pabst's feelings for me were not unlike those of Schön for Lulu. In those two films, *Pandora's Box* and *The Diary of a Lost Girl*, I think he was conducting an investigation into his relations to women with the object of conquering any passion that interfered with his passion for his work. He was not aroused by sexual love which he dismissed as an enervating myth. It was sexual hate which engrossed his whole being with its flaming reality."[34]

One of the Studio Lorelle portraits of Louise on a French postcard, Paris, 1929

14 · Beauty Prize

People who are very beautiful make their own laws.
—TENNESSEE WILLIAMS

ON JULY 31, 1929, Louise left Pabst and Europe again—but not for long. The *Olympic* carried her back to New York, but she was there only a few days when yet another cable arrived, summoning her back to Paris: The money had finally been found to make *Prix de Beauté* (*Beauty Prize*). By August 23 she was in Bremen and five days later in the French capital.

Both the actress and her two Pabst films had been fairly well publicized in Paris, but Louise was totally unprepared for the heroine's welcome awaiting her. In Paris, they considered her a major international star. Augusto Genina, the newfound director of *Prix de Beauté*, was at the station, along with many other well-wishers and a passel of journalists who gave her the kind of treatment Garbo and Dietrich were getting in Hollywood.

"All I could speak was Kansas English, and the French couldn't make heads or tails of it," she said.[1]

But that did not disturb anyone, least of all the reporters, who swooned over her in print. Shop windows were filled with her pictures—gorgeous portraits taken at the famed Studio Lorelle on her previous visit to the city. Hairdressers advertised coiffures "à la Louise Brooks" to Parisiennes.

"By then it was thumbs down for Louise Brooks in Berlin," says James Card, "but in France they were absolutely mad about her. She was more French to them than any French actress."[2]

Cedric Belfrage, one of the better film writers of the day, was the first to internationalize the embryonic Louise Brooks "cult" after talking with Pabst in Berlin. "Some are born European; some achieve Europe; and some have Europe thrust upon them," wrote Belfrage in August 1929. Louise he placed in the hybrid category of those who achieved Europe "as a natural consequence of the fact that they were really born European—though they didn't know it at the time." Other examples of that breed were Anna May Wong, Betty Blythe, and the now forgotten Virginia Bradford. But Belfrage's elaboration was most specifically, and insightfully, tailored to Brooks:

> In Hollywood they were, in a way, square pegs in round holes. They were good, but they weren't happy. They were well on the upward path to the starry heights; some had actually achieved stardom. There was nothing to stop them except their temperaments.
>
> They had restless souls, like Chekhov's heroines who sit on the wide-open steppes and moan all day long: "God! I'm stifling here! I can't breathe! When, oh when, do we go to Moscow?" . . . So, in the end, they packed their grips and lit out for their spiritual home. Hollywood saw them no more—for a time, at least.
>
> There was Louise Brooks, for instance. Charming girl, Louise. Pretty girl. Clever, too. People liked her in Hollywood—those who could understand her. The others thought she was cold, haughty and upstage. But there was no doubt about her ability. Nobody asked her to leave; she just left. The siren voice of Europe called her and held her. She went to work for Pabst in Berlin—at a salary at least double what she received in Hollywood. . . . But I am naive enough to believe sincerely that it isn't the salary that holds Louise in Europe. Of course, it makes a decided difference to her outlook. But fundamentally it is the fact that, at heart, she is a European.
>
> When I say European, I mean as distinct from Hollywoodian—the only other thing one is allowed to be, if one is in the movies. Louise adores New York, and goes back there for a short visit between each picture. But Hollywood? The very mention of the place gives her a sensation of nausea. The pettiness of it, the dullness, the monotony, the stupidity—no, no, that is no place for Louise Brooks.
>
> Or so the eminent Herr Pabst described it to me over a cocktail in the Bristol Bar, Berlin. "Louise," said Herr Pabst, "has a European soul. You can't get away from it. When she described Hollywood to me—I have never been there—I cry out against the absurd fate that ever put her there at all. She belongs in Europe and to Europeans. She has been a sensational hit in her German pictures. I do not have her play silly little cuties. She plays real women, and plays them marvelously."[3]

For a spiritual European who spoke only Kansas English, there was much to worship at the French altar. Once the Pabst-Belfrage hyperbole was stripped away, the essence of Louise was one of great intuitive intelligence—a woman with deep artistic aspirations and sensibilities—but very little grasp of those European intellectual currents in which she was now swimming.

Even after two films in Berlin and a close personal relationship with Pabst, Louise had not bothered to learn much about the German film movement. With no French equivalent of Pabst to guide her, she was even less inclined to explore current developments in the French cinema.

The most conservative strand was an "Impressionist" school, more or less reflecting that pictorial style.* The most outrageous was inspired by the literary-artistic vogue of Dada and Surrealism and epitomized by René Clair's *Entr'acte* (1924)—its script full of amusing nonsense by Francis Picabia ("The greatest invention of mankind is bicarbonate of soda"). Not long before Louise's arrival, Paris was abuzz about *Un Chien andalou (An Andalusian Dog)*, co-written by Luis Buñuel and Salvador Dali, with its shocking images of slashed eyeballs and severed hands. Also at work were Marcel Duchamp and Man Ray.†

But by the end of the decade, many French directors were gravitating toward documentary realism and *populisme*—a preference for real life and real people. And after his flirtation with the avant-garde, it was René Clair who became the most populist, and popular, filmmaker in France.

Louise had heard a lot about Clair and his satirical, tragicomic style— more than she had heard about Pabst before *Pandora*—and was looking forward to working with him. And the feeling was mutual. *Prix de Beauté* had been set up by SOFAR-Film as a one-film contract for Clair, who was to write and direct it specifically for Louise Brooks. But in addition to its financial problems, the film had the drawback of its hybrid status—neither silent nor talkie.

Clair, like his friend Pabst, had gone to London to study the new technology and then returned to Berlin to rework the *Prix de Beauté* script for sound. But SOFAR did not like it. "They cut everything I wrote," he said, "except the last scene."⁴ So instead of the Brooks project, Clair made his first sound film, *Sous les toits de Paris*—which was declared a masterpiece. And *Prix de Beauté*, a supremely French property developed by an Austrian, was now in the hands of an Italian.

But it was all the same to Louise. She was still basking in the unexpected attention, and her nonexistent Italian was no worse than her nonexistent French.

---

* The French intelligentsia took its cinema seriously, and among its pioneering concepts was film criticism. Louis Delluc's "Ciné-Club" was the first to assert the stature of film as an art equal (or even superior) to music, literature, and theater.

† Man Ray (1890–1976), painter, photographer, and *avant-garde* filmmaker, began as Emmanuel Rodnitzky of Philadelphia. He now lived in Paris and was struck by Brooks's face when he saw it in the magazines during *Prix de Beauté* filming. He never forgot her and in the late fifties sent her one of his abstract paintings, which hung thereafter on the wall of her bedroom.

. . .

The cosmopolitan Augusto Genina (1892–1957) was more than just a disciple of René Clair's, as he is usually described. He worked for years in the Italian film business, which was squandering its resources on such ponderous epics as *The Last Days of Pompeii* (1926). Genina had already made twenty films by that year, including a ten-reel version of *Cyrano de Bergerac* (1922) that was hand-tinted—160,000 individually colored frames. But he yearned for more energized filmmaking. He was among the first to propose a consortium of European film artists to produce joint international projects, and soon set out for France and Germany to find such collaborative work for himself.[5] By 1929, he was considered the best of the expatriate Italian directors—a satellite orbiting the major realists.*

Genina now had some large shoes to fill, for the marks of Clair and Pabst were all over *Prix de Beauté*. It was their screenplay he had inherited, and he hoped to inherit a bit of their skill as well. Certainly, he inherited Pabst's preoccupation with Louise's face—by which he was transfixed.

The scenario itself, despite all the wrangling over it, had surprising depth. In later years it would sometimes be called just another "Louise Brooks destroys her man" story, but it was hardly that. If anything, the script and the film were a kind of feminist *cinéma verité* thirty-five years ahead of their time.

The original idea was Pabst's, inspired by the beauty contests then much in vogue in Europe, as in America. But it had nothing in common with the *American Venus* genre coming out of the United States. It was a working-class tragedy.

A happy Sunday swimming outing introduces us to Lucienne (Brooks), her possessive fiancé André (Georges Charlia), and his friend Antonin (Augusto Bandini). Cavorting and tossing sand at the men, Lucienne is a lovely birdlike creature, a fluttering burst of energy who loves being the center of attention, heedless of the fact that André is jealous of his own best buddy.

There are moments in this opening scene when she appears to act *entirely with her neck*—"that incomparable neck, a solid though slender curving alabaster column," wrote one critic. "She twists it in a sudden dynamic flash, or bends it to reveal its strange and enticing convexity. . . ."[6]

Lucienne and André are typesetters for a Parisian newspaper. The next day at work, she comes across a notice announcing the Miss France

* In his forty-year career, Genina made 150 films, often writing his own scripts and starring his wife, Carmen Boni. After Mussolini restructured the sagging Italian film industry, he returned to Italy and made a number of quasi-Fascist films, the most famous of which was *The White Squadron* (1936).

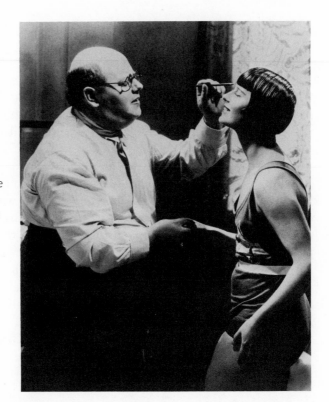

Lucienne gets a last-minute touch-up before the Miss Europe contest in Prix de Beauté *(1930).*

beauty contest—and secretly sends in her photograph. That night, the trio (much like that of *Jules et Jim*) visits a carnival, but there is something loutish about the crowd and its forced jollity and about André himself.

Afraid of his reaction, she now has second thoughts about the contest and tries to withdraw—only to discover she has already won. Before she even has time to inform André, Lucienne is whisked off to Berlin to be France's entry in the Miss Europe competition. Her reception is wildly enthusiastic—eerily akin to Brooks's real-life arrival in Berlin the year before. As she promenades at the beauty contest, Genina caresses her gorgeous profile with close-ups. Lucienne, the hands-down winner, is overjoyed—and then she sees André.

He is furious and demands she come back to Paris to marry him. Sadly, she gives in—and the marriage is just as depressing as she imagined it would be. A caged canary painfully symbolizes her predicament. Only her continuing Miss Europe fan mail provides some distraction from house-wifery—and André is jealous even of that. When he exits, the wealthy Prince de Grabovsky (Jean Bradin) arrives with a film-test offer. If she passes, it means the lead in a movie about a troubled singer (*La chanteuse éperdue*). She must leave André—with regret, not hatred. As he sleeps, she departs, leaving only a note: "I loved you sincerely once, and maybe I'll love you again."

The screen test is a smashing success.

The final sequence, closely adhering to the way René Clair wrote it, is one of the most visually spellbinding climaxes in all of film. It provides *Prix de Beauté* with its suspense, its tragedy, and its profound *film noir* quality. And it has sent critics—the few who have taken the trouble to see it—into raptures for half a century:

Wildly jealous, André watches from the shadows as Lucienne and Grabovsky arrive for the screening. Fans are waving magazines with her face on the cover (the printed caption "Louise Brooks" is not quite concealed on one of them). Settling next to the Prince in the projection room, Lucienne rapturously watches herself singing on screen. André now slips past the guard and peers into the screening room, just in time to see Grabovsky take Lucienne's hand. As Lucienne smiles, André raises a pistol and through the half-open door fires a bullet into her heart.

A brief startled look, and she crumbles into Grabovsky's arms for the last exquisite image: Her upturned profile fills the foreground and flickers

Louise as Lucienne: A beauty queen's work is never done in Prix de Beauté.

René Clair devised the idea for Rudy Maté's exquisite final shot in Prix de Beauté: *Lucienne's film image continues to sing "Don't be jealous . . . " after she is murdered by her husband in the screening room.*

in the light of the vibrant Lucienne on screen—still singing the theme of the film within the film:

> *Ne sois pas jaloux, tais-toi—*
> *je n'ai qu'un amour, c'est toi.*

> "Hush, don't be jealous—I've only one love, it's you."

PRIX DE BEAUTÉ was unusual in many ways: It was antimarriage, proto-feminist, and critical of the working class, the bourgeoisie, and the dilettante rich in equal measure. It was not about "the ruination of her man" but, rather, the attempted liberation of a virtuous woman—for 1929 a fairly advanced theme. Yet as a film, it was neither fish nor fowl: a transition-period silent, doctored up with music and some badly postsynchronized dialogue.

The latter defect canceled out all its virtues as far as the public was concerned. In Berlin, where the film was called *Miss Europe*, the *Variety* correspondent praised Genina's directing and his "natural way of looking at things," but reported the grim fact that "owing to bad synchronization this talker is a failure. After five days it had to be removed. The Titania Palast has at no time done such bad business with a film as with this one."[7]

It was the afterthought of its sound that was important, not the serious theme. Largely overlooked, too, was the superb photography of Rudolph Maté.* The film shimmers with visions, alternately graceful and harsh. In *Prix de Beauté*, says James Card, "the image is still predominant, and the camera still mobile."[8] Genina's attention to visual textures—to lighting and composition—put him, at least this once, in the league of Pabst, Clair, and Sternberg. And his "newsreel" style antedated such Italian neo-realist films as *Open City* by fifteen years.[9]

Also overlooked were the inspired "blue-collar" costumes of Jean Patou, one of Europe's most important designers.

Not overlooked, on the other hand, was Brooks. Henri Langlois would compare the film to a blinking beacon that lights up whenever she appears on screen and goes dead when she is off. Her natural performance here, says Card, is the one that most resembled her in real life. "She was vexed with Genina," Card recalls, "because he kept telling her to smile—smile, smile, smile! He could never get enough of it."[10]

Genina was vexed with Louise, too, as he would later reveal in his memoirs. "She would have been the ultimate actress," he said, if it hadn't been for alcohol:

> She didn't just guzzle cognac and champagne. Her drunkenness began at four in the morning and finished towards evening. But then right away it started again and didn't stop until four in the morning, at which point they brought a new bottle of champagne to her room. . . . In the morning when they came to take her to the set, they had to carry her bodily because she was sleeping. They set her up in a big chair and made her up while she was sleeping. They woke her only to shoot the scene, after which she returned to drinking and put herself to sleep again. . . . The day we were going to shoot the final scene, she disappeared. It was necessary to call the police,

---

* Maté had just done the magnificent cinematography for Carl Dreyer's *La Passion de Jeanne d'Arc*. During the shooting of *Prix*, he performed an important audio as well as visual function for the unilingual Louise. Her translator was "a sarcastic boy" who took advantage of the situation to make mischief. "I would say, 'Ask Genina if I should close the door in this scene,' " Louise recalled, "and he would say to Genina, 'Brooks says it's a stupid idea to close the door in this scene.' " Maté also knew no English when he began the picture. "Poor Genina worked courageously in spite of the difficulties and the disdain he got for being Clair's replacement," said Louise, but he was frustrated. Then one day, "Rudy looked down and said, 'Miss Brooks, I can interpret for you.' He'd learned to speak English in about two weeks! That's how marvelous Hungarians are about picking up the language. So from that time on, Genina would tell him what he wanted me to do. There was really no directing me anyhow. All I needed was choreography. 'You come in this door and you go out that one.' "

Maté was, in fact, Polish.

who found her in a château, naturally drunk. The film cost a lot [more] because of her. . . .[11]

Genina added that Louise was also sleeping with her hotel bartender at the time. Everyone marveled at how well she photographed, considering the hangovers and her method of sobering up from them—three swigs of gin.

But whether Brooks was drunk or sober, Genina, like Pabst before him, was hypnotized by the way her features conveyed feelings for which there were no words, even if the right microphone had existed to record them. She manifested a longing that André Breton once expressed: "All my life my heart has sought a thing I cannot name." Perhaps something in the fictional Lucienne called forth Louise's own unhappy marriage—her real-life walkout on Eddie Sutherland—and motivated the palpable disaffection in her scenes with André.

"Not another actress on either continent would've played it that way," declares James Card.[12]

As for the bravura finale, the verdict is unanimous—typified by Charles Stenhouse's review in the June 1930 issue of London's *Close Up*: "Its remarkable ending redeems the previous passages, whose very mediocrity emphasizes the ending's splendor. At last, a morsel of true sound technique."

Catherine Ann Surowiec speaks of its *"cinéma-verité* lyricism" and calls the ending "a tempting trace of the film's potential" but laments the early departure of René Clair. "Under Genina's direction, because of its transition technique, marvelous climax, and the presence of Louise Brooks, it is an interesting film; however, if Clair had been able to continue working on it, it could have been an outstanding one."

Surowiec's final evaluation of Louise is transcendent:

> More than an Art Deco icon, the youthful Louise Brooks possessed a startlingly original, timeless beauty, the kind of *photogénie* which fascinates and enraptures both the camera and the spectator. We, and the camera, are in love with her. The final flickering images of *Prix de Beauté* are unforgettable: we observe a luminous presence cut off in her prime, but in turn are struck by the immortalized image, isolated in time, preserved by the art of film.[13]

And Ado Kyrou:

> Louise, dying in a cinema while her celluloid image continues to exist up there on the screen, has always been for me the poetic symbol of the permanence of feminine beauty through the medium of the cinema.[14]

"Louise Brooks," wrote Jan Wahl, "never looked more heartbreakingly beautiful than she does at this instant, which also denotes the end of her real career."[15]

"She didn't know how good she was in *Prix de Beauté*," concludes James Card, "because she didn't have the same respect for Genina that she had for Pabst."[16] And as if to verify that, forty years after making *Prix de Beauté*, Louise had a four-word comment upon learning that its producer wanted to reissue it: "He must be nuts."[17]

With the end of *Prix de Beauté* came a new sensation for Louise—a kind of postpartum depression unknown after her previous pictures. For the first time, she did not immediately leave town. "Town," of course, was Paris.

The Eskimo had disappeared some time after his one sexual audience with her, and so had her rich American playmates. But she had no pressing reason to return to the States, and so she stayed on for nearly two months, holing up in her hotel with stacks of books. Breton's Surrealist novel, *Nadja*, was just out, and someone translated a phrase—"the unparalleled joy of committing some splendid sacrilege"—that suddenly illuminated the Townsend Martin rose bouquet incident for her. It seemed a time for pondering such things. And she finally had time to pay some attention to sister "Junie," lavishing stuffed animals, clothes, and toys on her and visiting the boarding school outside Paris. "All the girls were hanging out over the staircases on three floors to get a look at her," June remembers.[18]

And then, in that pleasant, melancholy fall of 1929, she once again found herself in the company of G. W. Pabst, who seemed to have an unusual amount of business in Paris. But if he was still courting her, there was no recurrence of their glorious night the previous spring. They simply enjoyed each other's company, for the first time unconstrained by the actor-director relationship. Those weeks of unwinding were a joy—but so, for that matter, was the whole convoluted making of *Prix de Beauté*.

"The happiest time I ever had, looking back," she told John Kobal, "is when I was making pictures in Paris and didn't speak French. And the reason I was happy was I didn't have to talk to anyone. I didn't have to explain anything. I'd get up in the morning and go to the studio, and didn't have to discuss anything with anyone. I didn't have to talk at all."[19]

On November 27, 1929, she walked up the gangplank of the familiar *Majestic* for the return to New York. She had made three crossings in the space of twelve months. She could not know that this would be her last for thirty years or that she would never work in Europe again. She had just turned twenty-three. At the peak of her fame and beauty, there was something else she could not have imagined: that *Prix de Beauté* would be her last starring role.

"The Brooks success in Europe raises questions why more American stars failed to venture to the more advanced European cinema since language was not a factor," wrote John Roberts. "To the Hollywood powers, the actress' break with Paramount was an unpardonable sin. In retrospect, Brooks was correct in abandoning Colleen Moore's leftovers for three classic films."[20]

Indeed, in moving against traffic and opting for Europe rather than Hollywood, Louise had acted on a good aesthetic instinct—except that she, like everyone else, neglected to foresee just how revolutionary the sound revolution really was. Had she stayed in Europe as Pabst counseled, she would have faced the same problem there that Emil Jannings, among many other Europeans, now faced in Hollywood. Even if they could quickly learn the language, their foreign accents were a handicap.

Yet Garbo proved the obstacle could be surmounted, and Louise's brilliant expeditions into the heart of European cinema might well have continued. Compared with the best films of Germany and France, Hollywood silents were backward. But with talkies, the situation was instantly reversed. And once actors missed the sound boat in Hollywood, they missed it for good.

Louise and Dante: Bangs banished in a Warners publicity photo for
God's Gift to Women (1931)

15 · Booby Prize

Every cliché about Hollywood is disgustingly true.
— JAMES CARD

I T WAS EASY for Louise to ignore talkies in Berlin and Paris, where she didn't understand the languages and where few of the new American sound pictures were shown. It was even easier to ignore the stock market crash of late October 1929.

But once she was back in New York that December, both realities had to be dealt with—talkies more than Wall Street. European silents were even less of a draw than American ones. And though Louise claimed she never read reviews, she sneaked enough looks at *Variety* to know that neither *Pandora's Box* nor *The Diary of a Lost Girl* was well received in New York, let alone Peoria. Mostly, the Pabst films just hadn't been received at all. And *Prix de Beauté* wasn't even considered for an American run.

"At the time these pictures were released as silents everybody wanted to see talkies," she told her brother Theo, "so that my films went unnoticed and I decided I was a great failure."[1] The biggest blow was *Pandora*: "Everyone said I stunk." It had just opened in New York on December 1, 1929, to bad reviews, and, though pretending not to care, she was stung —so much that she refused the offer of a tall, handsome young cigarmaker's son who wanted to escort her to see it.

William Paley was twenty-eight years old. After graduating from the University of Pennsylvania's Wharton School of Business six years before, he had entered his father's Congress Cigar Company as a vice president. In 1928, around the time Louise was filming in Berlin, he became excited about radio after discovering that the company's sales of La Palinas cigars jumped when they were advertised over the air. "I had about a million dollars of my own and I was willing to risk any or all of it in radio," he said.[2] In September 1928, he used $503,000 of it to buy a controlling interest in the money-losing Columbia Broadcasting System, whose office in the Paramount building was occupied by about a dozen demoralized employees. A year later, a stock exchange deal between CBS and Paramount solidified Paley's corporate strength. Overall, his radio revolution was fast, brilliant, and profitable.

Brooks and Paley had met a year earlier, in December 1928, shortly after he came to New York from Chicago to buy CBS, when Louise was in Manhattan between the two Pabst films. Paley rarely missed a major movie or Broadway opening and was often a starstruck guest at the lavish theatrical parties hosted by such business associates as A. C. Blumenthal and Otto Kahn. "As a young bachelor," he wrote in his autobiography, "I met and got to know the gods and goddesses of the silver screen." One of the goddesses was Louise, whose beauty and forceful intelligence dazzled him.

"I knew all sorts of actresses, but she was a different kind of girl," muses Paley, exactly sixty years later, in his CBS office. "I wasn't the least bit sophisticated in those days. She was. She took me by the hand, took me around, told me what to do. Right after we started our romance—I'd just met her, really—I went up to a ski resort in the Adirondacks. I'd only been with her for a few days, you understand, and I was up at that resort a day or two when I got a telegram from her. It said, 'Why aren't you here? I want to see you. Come home.' She ordered me back—and I went! She was a very strong girl."[3]

Between December 1928 and February 1929 they saw a great deal of each other—and of "that lesbian friend of hers [Pepi Lederer]," Paley recalls. "One night the three of us went out together somewhere and ended up in the same house and spent the night. We put Pepi in the other room."

He pauses long before adding: "I think she was very much in love with me, and I was of course extremely fond of her. She didn't want to leave me—she had to keep going back and forth [between Europe and New York]. But I was too young then. I was too unsophisticated to appreciate her the way I should."[4]

If so, it wasn't for want of trying, as Louise herself recalled: "Bill had rented a furnished duplex apartment of Edgar Selwyn in the building across the street from the 55th Street [Playhouse]. One night he announced with delight that *Pandora's Box* was playing there—we must see it at once. I declined. He was completely disgusted with my stupid indifference to my worth and art."[5]*

---

* *Pandora's* incongruous second feature at the 55th Street Playhouse was Laurel and Hardy's *Should Married Men Go Home?*

Pandora's failure in the United States hurt more than just Louise's ego. In the always jittery film industry, a flop could cancel out a string of hits. And *Pandora* was in the bomb league—even worse, it was a *silent* bomb. Never mind that the Salvation Army ending was not her fault. The star, like the captain, would go down with the ship. Europe was thus a double flop: Louise not only failed to gain any sound-film experience there, but she appeared to be faltering even in the obsolete silent medium.

As a result, no offers were pouring, or even trickling, in, and as the new decade turned, she was running dangerously short of cash, if not of beaus. In addition to Paley, one of the men she was now spending time with in New York was, oddly enough, Eddie Sutherland. They were seen several times at the nightclub of Harry Richman, who took the liberty of announcing on January 9, 1930, in the presence of reporters, that Louise and Eddie "have fallen in love again and are shortly to remarry," which was duly reported in the New York *Daily Mirror* beneath a photo of Louise on Eddie's lap.[6]

But Harry Richman was what Louise and everyone else in New York fondly referred to as a bullshitter. He also claimed that Clara Bow was coming to marry him the following week, and he introduced Louise as "the captivating crooner of the stage." The remarriage did not occur.

Most of Louise's nightclubbing was done not with Eddie, but with her old friend Peggy Fears, who had finally married financier A. C. Blumenthal in 1927. But keeping up with Peggy and Blumie was expensive, and in mid-1930, when Louise was nearly broke, Peggy came to her aid. With Blumenthal's help, she arranged for Columbia Pictures to offer Louise a $500-a-week contract. Columbia was smaller and less prestigious than Paramount, but the salary was considerable for an actress with no track record in talkies—and for an economy now spiraling irreversibly downward.

James Card picks up the story at this point:

> Told to report to Jack Cohn in the New York office of Columbia, Miss Brooks waited an hour in the outer office—an experience totally unique in her career. Rather than be late for a date with Winston Guest to watch him exercise his polo ponies, she left Cohn's office without signing her contract —an event totally unique in the careers of the brothers Cohn, Jack and Harry.
>
> When she arrived in Hollywood, still without a contract, by way of discipline Harry Cohn cut her salary in half but granted her the privilege of sitting every afternoon in his office while he, conducting the affairs of Columbia Pictures sans either shirt or undershirt, sat at his desk presenting to all who entered the perspiring apparition of an executive who seemed to be quite uncharmingly naked.[7]

The more startling fact was not that Cohn expected sex in return for movie work, but that Louise went back to Hollywood expecting movie work in return for walking out on his brother in New York. Harry was a former fur salesman and pool hustler who co-founded Columbia in 1920 and ruled it despotically until his death in 1958. The Harry Cohn sex test was so well known as to be considered routine by this time, and neither Fears nor Blumenthal could understand Louise's outrage.

"One night I called them in Larchmont [N.Y.] from Hollywood," she wrote James Card, "screaming about Harry keeping me in his office every afternoon, trying to get me to bed, and Blumie screeched back, 'What the hell, Louise, you've been doing it all your life for nothing! Why don't you do it now when it can do you some good?' " *

The answer was that she thought she didn't have to. She had shared the train ride from New York with Jack—the more decent Cohn—who apparently forgave her for leaving his Manhattan office, or at least held open the matter of her employment. So she kept showing up at Columbia in spite of Harry's unsubtle lust and was persistent enough to be offered a western in August 1930—by which time the newspapers were on the story. You couldn't keep anything from Louella Parsons for very long:

> The sleek, dark-haired Louise Brooks, erstwhile *Follies* girl and former wife of Eddie Sutherland, is in Hollywood. I found Louise perched in a chair in the waiting room at Columbia. She had just come in from New York with Jack Cohn, one of the officers of the Columbia Corporation, and Dugal Stewart, who has been signed to direct plays.
>
> Columbia's plan for the former *Follies* favorite is to feature her in a western opposite Buck Jones, with Art Rosson directing. Both Cohns, Harry and Jack, were working out the plans yesterday. Meanwhile the "starving young actress," as Louise calls herself, is at the Ambassador receiving all her old-time friends.[8]

But the Cohns' plans had not been best-laid, nor had Louise. The Buck Jones film, for which they wanted her to don a frontier woman's wig, was what it sounded like—a punishment. Columbia had not even bothered to get her agreement, so certain were they of her desperation for work, and they were astonished when Louise turned down the part: "Her refusal brought a telephone call to her home from the studio head himself—the call, an ultimatum: wear the wig, play the Western, or Louise Brooks is

---

* The same December 19, 1955, letter to Card rounds out the picture of Brooks and Blumenthal's relationship: "In spite of all his jealousy, Blumie always found me extraordinarily funny, and we always had a good time together. Once when he was fighting some [divorce] suit of Peg's, he invited me to the Sunset Towers and tried to get me drunk and told me that his butler had photographed Peg and me in the act. The picture of a butler in tails, snapping us like a couple of cavorting pheasants, struck him at the same moment I began to laugh, and he burst into laughter too."

finished. But the message was delivered to her mother; Miss Brooks would not come to the telephone."[9]

Her *mother!* As if Louise did not have enough to worry about, Myra Brooks had recently decided to abandon her Chautauqua career and come to live with her famous daughter in Hollywood for a period that stretched to six months.

"I can still see her," Louise wrote, "inspecting the grand piano left behind by the band leader Paul Whiteman when he rented me his Hollywood house. 'My goodness, Louise, there has been enough liquor spilled in this piano to set it afloat,' she said. 'It can't possibly be tuned.' I would gladly have rented a decent piano if she had expressed a wish for one, but she did not."[10]

Part of Myra's way was that she did not *ask*, and this visit was a reminder of everything mother and daughter had and had not been to each other. Many years later, Louise recalled her at this time (Myra was then forty-six) in replying to her friend George Pratt, who had written of attending a Wagner festival:

"It makes me think of my delightful mother," she said, "whom I was going to send to Bayreuth about the time I ran out of money. She was always so expensive, although she always began by demanding so little."[11]

Louise did not share her mother's (or Pratt's) Wagnerian tastes: "To me, Wagner is a series of magnificent passages connected by long dull crap." Myra, in turn, felt pretty much the same about movies: "Films bored her silly, especially mine." Even so, they had their long-postponed rapprochement—though it was strained by Louise's unemployment and the perception of her recent "failure" abroad. The Los Angeles *Times*, for example, welcomed her back with the kind of I-told-you-so that Hollywood loved to read: "Europe no longer has any lure for Louise Brooks. . . . Her experiences abroad convinced her that the actor is far better off under the conditions existing in this country than abroad."[12]

In light of the Harry Cohn experience, Louise's derision can be imagined. But there was more clucking from the press. *Film Daily*'s gossip column of October 10, 1930, led with this item:

> Imagine her embarrassment, when she returned to Hollerword from Paris with several trunkloads of the latest Parisian gowns and sport clothes, to find that the styles represented in her collection were already old numbers in the film capital. That's what happened to Louise Brooks. A little investigation showed her that the creators of fashions in the studios were actually setting the Parisian styles. Over in the frog metropolis, the costumers copy the designs from the Hollywood pictures and they become the "latest Parisian fashions." So Louise had merely dragged back a load of clothes that were

already being discarded among the stars in the film capital where they originated several months before.[13]*

But she was out and about, and being talked about, and one night not
long after the Columbia debacle, David and Irene Selznick escorted her
to a charity fund-raiser at a nightclub that had been turned into a casino
for the event. Louise recalled:

> I detest gambling and wandered off to a room empty except for a pretty,
> rather plump blonde sitting against a pillar. It was Marlene Dietrich. Her
> fine blonde hair was tightly curled and she wore a baby-blue chiffon dress
> with heavy German silk stockings. To my surprise, she said hello to me in a
> warm, friendly voice. She was still recognizably Lola-Lola of *The Blue
> Angel*.[14]

Brooks never recorded her own reply, and—lamentably—there was no
discussion of Pabst or his casting of Lulu. To Louise, the newly arrived
Marlene seemed not much different from the other languid Continental
beauties materializing around town:

> When Marlene Dietrich first went to Hollywood, the whole film industry
> worshipped Greta Garbo. It was unconfessed worship but nonetheless ridic-
> ulously obvious. Producers were importing Garbo imitations from all over
> Europe. Directors (among them Sternberg) were making their actresses as
> Garbo-like as possible. Men stars would take salary cuts and second billing
> to work with Garbo. Short dark actresses went into eclipse. Other actresses
> became blondes, drew their eyebrows in thin arched lines and wore false
> eyelashes. Before the camera, they stared mysteriously in close-ups; flung
> their heads back unexpectedly; and fell supine on unsuspecting beds and
> sofas.[15]

Louise—like everyone else—was mesmerized by Marlene's Lola-Lola
in *The Blue Angel*. But Dietrich's first American film, *Morocco* (1930), left
her cold, and so did the legendary "image":

> By the time *Morocco* was released, all resemblance to that magnificent
> [Lola-Lola] was dead and gone forever. There was no trace of happy vulgar-
> ity or generous impulsiveness in the new refined Dietrich. Her harsh, dy-
> namic movements had been subdued to a stately walk between poses for still

---

* There was as much truth as bitchiness to this item. Earl Luick, the Warners designer who created
ravishing gowns for Louise in *God's Gift to Women* (1931), revealed a trade secret: "Hollywood no
longer has to look to Paris for style dictation as was the case only a few years ago. The world in
general and Paris in particular looks toward the American film for the newest and most striking.

"A great many of my designs are based on rumor. If I hear that Paris is expecting to cut necks
in a certain manner the next year, or are contemplating using trimming in certain places with
certain furs, I do not wait until the fashion really comes in. I at once design them for pictures
which are shortly to be in production. Thus, by the time Paris actually decrees such styles, our film
is on the market."

pictures. She didn't act anymore because she couldn't without opening the round eyes now kept half-closed and heavily shadowed with false eyelashes; and a facial show of emotion would spoil the lighting that sculpted her round cheeks. Faithful fans still insist that her metamorphosis from Dietrich to a slick Hollywood type was the best thing that ever happened to her. But every time I see *The Blue Angel*, I cry a little. [16]*

Dietrich's posing—literal and figurative—also fascinated Hollywood portrait photographer John Engstead, who had a len's-eye view of both Lulu and Lola-Lola. In Louise's case, he told John Kobal, posing was a matter of sheer elegance—"her legs, her ankles, her hands, her body, the way she held her body, the way she walked, the way she dressed, furs over her shoulder, off her shoulder, her hats . . . put anything on her and it was right. Dietrich can do that too if she wants to." [17]

And Dietrich wanted to, much more than Brooks. Dietrich cooperated fully, anticipating her portrait sessions and spending extra, uncomplaining hours on them. Says Engstead of Marlene: "She loved Marlene Dietrich's face. She had made a great thing out of this. This was her creation. She was going to be sure that I helped her as much as I could. She worked harder than anybody else I ever knew."

And then there was Brooks: "Louise always seemed to me to be a little lazy. I don't think she ever thought of being a really big star, I don't think this was in her schedule. Because she was very arrogant. She never sort of worked with [portrait photographers]; if it pleased her she would do it. She just knew what she wanted to do." [18]

Or so it seemed. Socially, her signals were mixed. "The trouble with us," her friend Grant Clarke told her in 1930, "is that we are too degenerate for one part of Hollywood and not degenerate enough for the other." Louise added an exegesis:

> This sour observation covered the fact that we were both Midwesterners born in the Bible Belt of Anglo-Saxon farmers who prayed in the parlor and practiced incest in the barn. And, although our sexual education had been conducted by the elite of Paris, London and New York, our pleasure was restricted by the inbred shackles of sin and guilt. Thus at the same time our reputation for immorality excluded us from the parties of respectable Holly-wood . . . , our reputation for sudden attacks of puritanism excluded us from the delights of the carefully arranged parties which ended for us after lunch or dinner when we were dismissed with a firm goodbye. [19]

Louise's sexual abandon, in other words, was selective.

. . .

* To Kevin Brownlow years later, she put it another way: "Marlene Dietrich made one great picture and only one, *The Blue Angel*. Then she just stopped acting. She became a great entertainer."

The hypothetical film career of Louise Brooks is a fabulous one, and goes something like this: After learning the trade at Paramount and making three gorgeous films in Europe, she returns triumphant to Hollywood, where the studios recognize her perfect voice and snap her up as both a sophisticated light comedienne and as a steamy, uninhibited, more believable new kind of lover who combines many qualities of Bow, Garbo, Crawford, and Dietrich.

The actual film career, on the other hand, was no such fairy tale. Now twenty-four, Louise was as close to broke as she had ever been since leaving Wichita at fifteen. In fact, she wasn't close to broke. She was broke. And forced to swallow her pride. "Garbo talks!" heralded the Swede's first sound film, and similar trumpetings were heard for the others. But no fanfare greeted the first talkie of Louise Brooks—a two-reel comedy called *Windy Riley Goes Hollywood.**

The little studio making *Windy* was Educational Pictures, which had long ceased to make school films and, as "Mermaid Comedy Company," turned to low-budget comic shorts. These it churned out on an assembly line. Many great comedians worked for Educational over the years— Buster Keaton, Harry Langdon, Edward Everett Horton, Bert Lahr, Milton Berle, the Ritz Brothers, and Danny Kaye. But it was a place for people on the way up or down.

Windy Riley, a comic-strip character created in 1929 by Broadway cartoonist Ken Kling, is a cocky, cigar-smoking braggart from the sticks who bluffs his way to New York, or in this case Hollywood, with schemes that always land him in trouble. He was played in the film by Jack Shutta.†

There was nothing surprising, or even interesting, about the movie except for "Educational's crack director, William B. Goodrich"—which was all the studio had to say about him. "Will B. Good" was another of the humiliating pseudonyms required of Roscoe "Fatty" Arbuckle, still in disgrace a decade after his three trials for manslaughter in the rape-death of Virginia Rappe.

Arbuckle was, in fact, a gifted director, and there had long been a movement afoot, led by *Photoplay*'s crusading James Quirk, to let him make and star in his own movies again. Thousands of letters poured in in support, but the industry never forgave him, and *Windy Riley* was a good example of his punishment. Its plot, in view of Arbuckle's fate, was not only ironic, but downright cruel: Film star Betty Grey (Brooks) has been attracting too much adverse newspaper attention. One more front-page

---

* So obscure was this picture that Louise herself could never get its title right. In her own filmography, she called it *Windy Reilly in Hollywood*, a mistake that has since been perpetuated in dozens of books and articles. In England, it was more pointedly retitled *The Gas Bag*.
† Shutta and his sister Ethel were stage actors now working (Jack as manager, Ethel as performer) at George Olsen's club in Culver City.

scandal, and the studio will cancel her contract. But wise-cracking Windy in the publicity department produces all the wrong results.

Arbuckle could not muster even a pretense of enthusiasm for this one, nor for Louise. She spends much of the footage in a bathing suit, but her beauty was unexploited by close-ups. Arbuckle "made no attempt to direct," said Louise. "He sat in his chair like a man dead. He had been very nice and sweetly dead ever since the scandal that ruined his career. But it was such an amazing thing for me to come in to make this broken-down picture, and to find my director was the great Roscoe Arbuckle. Oh, I thought he was magnificent in films. He was a wonderful dancer—a wonderful ballroom dancer, in his heyday. It was like floating in the arms of a huge doughnut—really delightful." [20]

After the dismal *Windy Riley*, Arbuckle made one or two more abortive comeback efforts, going to Europe on an acting tour in 1932. But he returned even more broken-hearted, and before another year was out, he was dead in body as well as spirit.

The best to be said for *Windy* was that it was quick cash and quick to make —$500 for three days' work. ("We shot it bang-bang-bang. Terrible. I never saw it, of course.") She now began a project that looked more promising in terms of reviving her career: a farce called *It Pays to Advertise*, directed by Frank Tuttle. It was, surprisingly, a Paramount film, and Louise speculated that the role only came her way because Tuttle liked her and said, "Let's give Brooksie a job." But there was more than charity involved, says film historian William K. Everson:

> It's true that Paramount had it in for her, and virtually blacklisted her in Hollywood—although one of Paramount's "insults" backfired rather curiously. Apparently after *The Canary Murder Case* she still owed them one picture, and in late 1930 Paramount worked off that obligation by putting her into one last film, *It Pays to Advertise*, where its utilization of the former star in a small part in the opening reel would presumably be an object lesson, and would warn other potentially rebellious stars to retain their humility. But Paramount reckoned without director Frank Tuttle, who was a good friend of Louise's and had worked with her before. Although the part was small, Tuttle did everything he could to make Louise *look* good photographically, and to make the part itself interesting. [21]

In his New York apartment, stacked from floor to ceiling with film cans, Everson prepares to demonstrate his point. He threads *It Pays to Advertise* through his projector, and we are about to see (and *hear*) the twenty-five-year-old Louise Brooks as Thelma Temple, star of the Broadway musical *Girlies Don't Tell*.

Art deco titles and a lush, jazzy score herald the fact that we are now in the film thirties, instead of the twenties. In the first, and rather exciting, air scene, a plane containing Brooks and the scapegrace playboy pilot (Norman Foster) is forced to land (she has been distracting him in the air) and is surrounded by photographers eager to get shots of the famous actress:

"Now just raise the skirt, just a trifle. . . . Oh, boys! Get a look at them gams!"

Someone examines her leg to make sure it hasn't been bruised in the rough landing. Someone else fondles the foot.

"Mmmmmm," she coos, in her most lilting, ironic tone, "pat it all better. . . . What do you think you are, a chiropodist?"

The voice, the leg, and the scene are wonderful.

And then Brooks vanishes completely—supplanted by the labored comedy of Skeets Gallagher ("Voulez-vous vamoose?") and a dull romance between Foster and Carole Lombard. The box-office prospects were modest, said *Variety*, "in the absence of compelling names." Brooks's name was considered so uncompelling that it got fifth billing.

"When Louise disappeared from the film," continues Everson, "the official leading lady took over—Carole Lombard, who was still rather inexperienced (especially in romantic comedy) and who got *no* help at all from Tuttle."

Louise's misfortune was that the critics felt the loss but failed to credit her for it. "The picture starts out at too swift a pace to keep up," said *Variety*. "The trump trick is played first."

At around this time, someone steered Louise toward director Wesley Ruggles. Says James Card, "She went out on a date with him, but she got putout by something he said and ended up knocking him off his barstool." So much for *that* job contact. By January of 1931, Louise's movie work had degenerated from career to occupation, but she still had enough momentum to get one more major-studio role, this time for Warner Brothers in a comedy titled *God's Gift to Women*.

The novice star was Frank Fay, a suave vaudevillian with no film experience.* He plays a notorious Don Juan who pursues, and is pursued by, every beautiful woman in Paris. But it's Yankee lovely Laura La Plante for whom he falls. Her father (Charles Winninger) insists he swear off other women, after which a doctor tells him he has a severe heart condition and will die if he indulges in so much as a single kiss. Now all his former lovers fight for the privilege of being his nurse. "A wild furore of

---

* Fay's wife, Barbara Stanwyck, followed him to Hollywood, where her star quickly outpaced his. But for now, he was thought a hot new discovery. Warners dubbed him "The 'It' Man" and billed him as "the 1932 model lover—built for speed, style and endurance."

Louise with Frank Fay in God's Gift to Women

petticoat domination" results, says the publicity, "and hair-pulling matches are in order" among Joan Blondell, Louise Brooks, and Margaret Livingston (Louise's *Canary Murder Case* "doubler").

Louise had little to do in the film but look elegant, which she did very well, and Warners promoted her royally, both in print and in an extraordinary quantity and quality of publicity photos. By now she had stopped wearing her trademark bangs on screen and though the naked forehead seemed shocking at first, the new look had a more mature allure. In the most stunning of these portraits from *God's Gift*, Louise posed in classic profile with a bust of Dante, with photographic results that are among the finest of her career.

Once again, the film itself was forgettable—but the director, Michael

Curtiz, was not. Though the colorful Hungarian immigrant was still more than ten years away from *Casablanca*, he had already made a name for himself with *Noah's Ark* (1929), a two-hour-and-fifteen-minute epic with Dolores Costello and the young Myrna Loy.*

He terrorized *God's* gifted cast of sixty and demanded endless retakes for tempo, but Louise's chief memory of him concerned his accent and malapropisms ("It would make your blood curl!"). There were guaranteed laughs, she said, every time he went looking for character actor Charles Winninger with shouts of "Mr. Vinegar! Mr. Vinegar!"

One other bright spot for Louise during the making of the film was her new friendship with Howard Shoup, Warners' wild and witty dress designer. He regaled her with anecdotes and shared a note he got from one of the *God's Gift* producers, ordering him to "Do something about Blondell's tits."[22]

But the critics were harsh. "When a two-reeler plot is stretched to feature length," said *Variety*, it was "no gift to audiences."[23] Louise, concludes Everson, "looked enchanting, and it's incredible that further offers didn't follow."[24]

But one offer did follow, and Louise's response to it was typical of her maddening caprice. She had just accepted three small roles in three bad movies. She would now turn down a gem.

Since working with her on *Beggars of Life* in 1928, William Wellman had made seven pictures, steadily honing his skills in the new sound medium. He now offered Louise the feminine lead in a gangster melodrama called *Public Enemy*, opposite the young and still little known James Cagney. As the definitive Prohibition antihero, Cagney established himself explosively, and the film caused an enormous sensation—not least for the famous scene in which he smashes a grapefruit in Mae Clarke's face (the most brutally rude act of man against woman yet filmed). Rejected by Brooks, Wellman offered her role to a blond newcomer who became as legendary as Cagney: Jean Harlow.

And why, exactly, did Louise turn it down?

"In order to make a trip to New York," she said blithely.[25] Specifically, to see George Marshall.

Wellman was incredulous. Louise apparently said yes at first, and the advance publicity included her in the cast.† He respected her as an ac-

---

*Born Mihály Kertész in Budapest, Curtiz (1888–1962) made 100 films for Warners—many routine, some outstanding: *Black Fury* (1935) with Paul Muni; *The Private Lives of Elizabeth and Essex* (1939) with Bette Davis; *Casablanca* , which won him an Oscar in 1943; *Mildred Pierce* (1945) with Joan Crawford; many Errol Flynn adventures; and *King Creole* (1959)—the best of the Elvis Presley films.

†The erroneous inclusion of *The Public Enemy* among Louise's films persists because the *New York Times* review of April 24, 1931, listed her in the credits and because "when people see an extra girl walk through a scene with a black bob and bangs, they say, 'There is Brooks,' " Louise later wrote.

tress. He wanted her. He was willing to defy her "blacklisting." When they met a year later at the bar of Tony's Restaurant in New York, he hit her with the big question: "Why did you always hate making pictures, Louise?"

She was nonplussed for a moment, but finally replied that it wasn't making pictures she hated—it was Hollywood.

"Those were the last words I ever heard him speak," she said. ". . . Bewitched by his own success in Hollywood, he could not imagine my hating the place."[26]

"She just wasn't interested," says James Card. "She was more interested in Marshall."[27] And so she lost not only a role but possibly sex-goddess superstardom, too. In a lifetime of lost and found opportunities, *Public Enemy*—one of the great successes of the early thirties—is somehow the most painful loss, if only because it was her last. She would make a few more minor appearances, but turning down *Public Enemy* marked the real end of Louise Brooks's film career.

Escaping Houdini-like from Hollywood again at the end of January, Louise spent the bulk of 1931 traveling between New York, Washington, Los Angeles, and Wichita, relieved to be free of movie commitments. Marshall not only entertained her but apparently supported her during this period. Then in October, she was suddenly moved to revive her stage career—moved mainly by money. But she also figured a theatrical job would keep her in New York, where she wanted to be.

She was cast in a new Norman Krasna comedy about Hollywood, *Louder, Please!*, under the direction of George Abbott—a promising venture.

Her farcical ingénue role was not unlike "Thelma Temple, star of *Girlies Don't Tell*," but it was the feminine lead and she could play it flashily. Hers was the biggest name there. On October 26, *Louder, Please!* opened in previews at the Boulevard Theatre in Jackson Heights, and Louise was in the cast. But on Halloween, just twelve days before the show's Broadway opening at the Masque Theatre, she was inexplicably fired.

Brooks Atkinson gave the show a lukewarm review in the *Times* ("noisy and breathless and synthetically amusing"),[28] and Louise's presence might not have added to its sixty-eight performances. But it was safe to say she was faring no better in theater than in film. Abbott was easy to work with. If she couldn't get along with him, could all her Hollywood problems have been the studios' fault? Her reputation for failure was spreading.

George Marshall, meanwhile, continued to squire her around town.

As to other claims that she was in Wellman's *Steel Highway* (1931) and Robert Florey's *Hollywood Boulevard* (1936), she says: "I appeared in neither film."

Two days after *Louder, Please!* opened, they double-dated with actor Leslie Howard and his wife for a night of dining, dancing, and gambling at the Central Park Casino to celebrate Louise's twenty-fifth birthday. But she recalled a certain strain in the revelry:

> Leslie, who had evidently accepted the invitation because he enjoyed George's social performances, said nothing. Mrs. Howard, a large English-woman who looked more like Leslie's mother than his wife, tried to inject gracious remarks here and there into the stream of George's witty stories, but his loud voice was as hard on them as it was on Eddie Duchin's orchestra, playing in the background. . . . At the end of each story, he would let out a self-appreciative haw-haw-haw and clap Leslie on the back with such enthusiasm that Leslie crumpled over the table like a paper angel. [29]

Louise had admired Howard ever since seeing him onstage in *The Green Hat* with Katharine Cornell in 1925. Now she was delighted when he told her "he hated films for the same reason I did, the goddamned sitting around most of the time waiting for lights and sets to be fixed." [30]

But people were paid for "sitting around," and nobody was paying Louise to do anything at the moment. She was simply one of the more glamorous among the unemployed, whose ranks were swelling astronomically, from eight million in 1931 to twelve million now, in early 1932. It was beyond the predictions of the worst pessimists. To be given any job at all was a big favor. But Louise had no chits to call in—only old hostilities and vengeful enemies. George Marshall would see that she did not starve, but he was unwilling to assume her debts, which by now were considerable. The creditors could no longer be ignored, and she now took the same step that a multitude of other overextended Americans were taking —not defenestration but bankruptcy.

"Louise Brooks Is 'Flat Broke' " headlined the New York *Graphic* on February 2, 1932.

"Brooksy Broke, Save for Duds" was the *Telegraph's* banner on the same day. The other papers followed suit, pouncing on the news in an amazing burst of publicity.

> "Louise Brooks (Dixie to You) Is Bankrupt"
> "Louise Brooks, Ex-Film Star, in Bankrupt Role"

The New York *Daily News* even put the story and picture on its front page. The face was now known as much from the popular Dixie Dugan comic strip as from the screen:

> Louise Brooks, film favorite of the pre-talkie era . . . , was adjudged a bankrupt yesterday with liabilities of $11,969 and assets—"my wearing apparel." [31]

Before the aptly named bankruptcy referee H. P. Coffin, Louise gave her occupation as "motion picture actress, unemployed," and the Hotel Madison on East 58th Street as her address. Among her creditors were Bergdorf Goodman ($2,361), Saks ($3,440), Jay Thorpe ($1,551), various other posh dress shops in Hollywood and New York, and a hotel or two. None of her creditors appeared to testify. Had they made it a practice to do so, they would have spent all their time at such hearings.

The news stories evinced the usual mixture of sympathy and satisfaction that one so proud had fallen so low. Celebrity bankruptcies, after all, were favorite Depression tales. Misery loved company, and it made common folks feel better to know that certain overpaid, smarty-pants starlets were now in the same miserable boat—the humbling comeuppance of the once rich and still famous.

Within twenty-four hours of the hearing Louise, properly humiliated, her downward mobility now known to all, left town with Marshall for two weeks' consolation in Bermuda.

Nineteen thirty-two was a good year for no one but Franklin D. Roosevelt. The out-of-control unemployment, the devastation of the Dust Bowl, the pervasive hopelessness were manifested by a sharp increase in suicides, many—but not all—related to loss of fortune. The toll in Hollywood was particularly heavy. Among the film colony denizens who killed themselves over the next few years were actors Karl Dane, the goofy soldier of *The Big Parade,* who used a gun, and Lou Tellegen, the matinee-idol husband of Geraldine Farrar, who committed hari-kari with a pair of gold scissors. Director George Hill blew his head off with a hunting rifle. Other actors and would-be actors took similar routes (sometimes by leaping from the huge "Hollywood" sign on Mount Lee above the studios), including John Bowers, Arthur Edmund Carew, James Murray, Peg Entwistle, and Ross Alexander.

But by far the most shocking suicide was that of MGM producer Paul Bern on September 5, 1932. One of the most sophisticated men in Hollywood, he had married Jean Harlow just two months before. He left behind a cryptic note to Harlow* and wild rumors that it was sadomasochism and impotence that drove him to shoot himself. Bern was Irving Thalberg's closest associate, and everyone liked him, including Louise. He had taken her to her first Wagner (*Die Walküre*) at the Met in 1926.

"For no particular reason, one night I went to the opera with Paul," she told a friend. "And except for my entrance in a practically topless

---

* "Dearest Dear, Unfortunately this is the only way to make good the frightful wrong I have done you and to wipe out my abject humiliation, I love you. Paul. You understand that last night was only a comedy."

crystal beaded dress of white and an ermine coat, that was all the good he got out of me."[32]

Despite her tough tone, Louise was much disturbed about Bern's suicide and always dismissed the impotence motive: "All men trusted their wives and girlfriends to sweet little Paul. But he got into more beds with his 'culture' than any wolf in Hollywood. Joan Crawford, Clara Bow, Jean Harlow. . . ."[33] The secret reason he killed himself, she said, had nothing to do with sex and everything to do with marriage:

> The only person I knew out there who didn't [always talk about movies] and whom I was really fond of was Paul Bern. . . . No one ever seemed to understand why he killed himself. They've got the silliest idea. His wife turned up, that's why. He was a bigamist. He married Jean while he was married to this other woman, and she turned up.* And he was a very sensitive little man. . . . He had to tell her that his real wife had turned up. And this would ruin her career at MGM. . . . I was amazed at Paul doing a thing like that. I was so fond of Paul.[34]

As if bankruptcy and suicides weren't depressing enough, there was her volatile relationship with George Marshall. They fought constantly. In 1932 and 1933 the main issues were her extravagance and their mutual ambivalence about marriage. Then, during a trip to Chicago in July 1933, Louise thought she saw a convenient way to resolve both problems.

While nightclubbing with friends one evening, Brooksie was introduced to a Chicago playboy and a polo player named Deering Davis. Photographs clearly testify that he was not a handsome man: thinning hair, dull features, and deep black bags under his eyes gave him a sad, bassetlike appearance.

But he was a terrific dancer—and nothing was more seductive to Louise. She stayed in Chicago almost two months, during which she and Deering "did" the clubs nightly. His family wealth came from Chicago's great farm-equipment firms and mergers (John Deere, William Deering & Company, International Harvester). His father, Dr. Nathan S. Davis, was founder of the Chicago Medical Society. Deering had recently divorced the Philadelphia socialite Peggy McNeal and was now highly eligible, while Louise was on one of many furious rebounds from Marshall. Before she left Chicago in September, Brooks and Davis made whimsical plans for a ballroom dance act—and a wedding.

"Screen Star Weds Society Bachelor" said the headlines two weeks later. The marriage took place immediately upon her return to Chicago,

---

* Shortly after Bern's death, his first wife, the unsuccessful starlet Dorothy Millette, drowned herself in the Sacramento River.

Mr. and Mrs. Deering Davis on their wedding day,
Chicago, October 10, 1933

October 10, 1933, at City Hall. Davis's brother and sister-in-law, Dr. and Mrs. Nathan S. Davis III, were the only witnesses. The groom, at thirty-six, was ten years older than the bride.

The Associated Press reported that, for a honeymoon, the Davises would go by car to a ranch in Tucson, via Colorado Springs. Davis liked the Southwest and wanted to settle there, but it was too close to Kansas for Louise's comfort. Nothing is known of their three months of traveling, except that Davis and Louise—with the aid of a Victrola and the odd nightclub here and there—had plenty of time to work up their dance act.

Returning to Chicago, the Brooks & Davis dance team made its debut at the fashionable Chez Paree on February 23, 1934, and drew rave notices. The Chicago *Evening American* said it would have sent its dance critic, "but when the dancers are listed in the Social Register—and especially when one member of the team is the scion of one of the oldest and most conservative families in Chicago, it's society news." Deering Davis was extremely popular "with men as well as with the ladies, who unanimously agreed he was the best dancer in Chicago," the report continued.

So last night it wasn't surprising to find a large number of our fashionable set [including thirty of Davis's friends from Lake Forest, plus Prince Michael Cantacuzene of Rumania] at ringside tables to lend their support and encouragement to his professional career. . . . They found Deering perfectly calm and showing none of the traditional nervousness of the performer on a "first night."

He said, grinning:

"No. I'm not nervous. You see, I realize nobody's going to be looking at me. They'll be watching Louise all the time, and she's so pretty and so sweet and dances so well, they're sure to like her and I'll just be the fellow she's dancing with! So there's nothing for me to be nervous about."

It was really too modest of Deering! As a matter of fact, he acquitted himself very well in their first number—an adagio—and later they encored a rhumba and still later an apache dance. And Louise was adorable! Her gown for the first number was of turquoise blue crepe with a pleated skirt and sleeves, which was very effective with her shiny black hair and piquant, sunburned face.

The novelty of the society dance team was big, and the Brooks & Davis act lasted a full month at the Chez Paree. The novelty of being married to Deering Davis lasted exactly one week after the conclusion of their club engagement.

"Louise Brooks, one of the best known of the silent film actresses, and now a member of the Brooks-Davis dance team and of the matrimonial team of Mr. and Mrs. Deering Davis, has decided to dissolve both partnerships," said the New York *Mirror* on March 30, 1934. The Los Angeles *Times* on March 28 got a choice detail out of her attorney, Philip R. Davis: "Miss Brooks departed on a train late last night without a good-bye to her husband and leaving only a note of her intentions."

Louise's second and final attempt at matrimony lasted just under six months. "I hated marriage," she told John Kobal. "In the first place, to be called Mrs. Davis or Mrs. Sutherland would simply *inflame* me. My name is Mary Louise Brooks, and don't be calling me Mrs. Davis or Mrs. Sutherland. My ace in the hole, getting married, didn't work out." [35]

Davis had been just "another elegant, well-heeled admirer," says James Card. "She never spoke of him as other than a legal nuisance to be cleared away later." [36] As with Eddie, Louise left without seeking or getting a dime of alimony from a very wealthy man.

She never laid eyes on Deering Davis again.

The "society dance act" had been something of a lark, but now that she was back in New York without visible means of support, dancing became her livelihood. The Chicago routine had at least been useful as a trial run for a more professional dance team that she now formed with Dario Bor-zani, a.k.a. Dario Lee.

This important partnership took them all over the country and lasted more than a year. Its genesis was an April night out in Manhattan, shortly after her flight from Deering Davis, when Louise caught and liked the dance of "Dario and Diane" at the swank Place Pigalle. A week later, Diane stepped out to get married, and Louise stepped in. "Dario & Louise" made their debut on June 29, 1934, at the new Westchester Center Gardens in White Plains, where they danced elegantly to an orchestra led by Meyer Davis, "the society maestro." The only surviving report, from the New York *Sunday Mirror*, paints a moody picture:

> "Here today; gone tomorrow" and "fame is fleeting" are old but true expressions, as witness—out in Westchester County Center there is appear-ing in the floor show a tall, sophisticated, rather weary-looking singer named Louise Brooks. The majority of patrons who look and listen every night never heard of her. She's just another night club warbler. Yet only a few years ago Louise Brooks was a star in the silent films who once enthralled Charlie Chaplin and married Eddie Sutherland, popular film director.

The surprise was not that Louise looked weary but that she *sang*. If true, it was the only time in her professional life. The *Mirror* also ran a color photograph of Louise looking sultry, or weary indeed, in the West-chester Center lobby.*

Nevertheless, Dario & Louise were soon on their way to Detroit for a month's work at the Blossom Heath Inn. From there it was Chicago and a month at the Chez Paree—Brooks & Dario this time, instead of Brooks & Davis. When that engagement ended on October 6, they hastily re-turned to New York for their Place Pigalle opening four days later. The results were excellent.

"The star of Louise Brooks' fortune, after suffering a score of ups and downs, again is in the ascendancy," wrote one paper. "In less than six months after teaming with Dario she has again become the toast of Broad-way." O. O. McIntyre wrote in the New York *American* that "Louise Brooks and Dario threaten to recapture the furore of the Castles," while *The New Yorker*'s "Tables for Two" column by "Lipstick" (Lois Long) was just as friendly:

> Another visit to the Place Pigalle after the theater got me up to Here with ermine capes, smart chit-chat and Names. . . . Dario and Louise Brooks are dancing. I didn't dare look at first, because Brooks has always been a swell

---

* The failure to mention dancing and the description of her as "tall" make the singing reference doubtful; it was probably invented by a rewrite man glancing at the photograph.

girl; when I finally peeked, I was grateful to her for being a swell dancer besides. It is damn nice of her to be so good.[37]

Louise & Dario danced at the Place Pigalle for almost three months—until January 5, 1935—a phenomenal run by dance-act standards. From there they went on tour, performing at the Embassy Club in Miami, the Patio in Palm Beach, and clubs in Indiana and Kentucky, returning to New York in between for engagements at the Central Park Casino and the Capitol Theatre—by which time the toast of Broadway seemed stale. *Variety*'s critic was cranky about the whole program:

The dance team of Dario & Louise, appearing at the Capitol Theatre in New York, April 12, 1935; photo by Maurice Seymour of Chicago

Doubtful show value at the Capitol this week. Picture *Vanessa: Her Love Story* [starring Helen Hayes] is drab and doleful. Stage show lacks comedy. . . . One of the dance acts is Louise Brooks and Dario from the Place Pigalle. Did okay. Miss Brooks is an ex-star of films, but that fact is unmentioned. Her radical change of coiffure makes identification not too easy. . . . Dario handles her smartly and she handles herself with commendable facility. White satin does not appear to be the ideal selection for her.[38]

Following a brief reprise at Place Pigalle in May, Dario & Louise played a two-month grand finale at the Plaza. She remembered the after-hours more than the act itself.

When I was dancing with Dario at the Persian Room in the Plaza, . . . after the midnight show I would walk down to the Gotham Hotel to visit Tallulah Bankhead. She would declaim Phaedre in lousy French and read the Bible in her lovely Alabama accent while everybody said she stunk and tried to do it better; and in a hooded corner sat Estelle Winwood nursing her latest dose of clap from one of her little boys. It was I who reported Bankhead's best line, "Don't tell me cocaine is habit-forming, I've been taking it for 17 years and I ought to know."[39]

Dario & Louise danced at the Plaza from June to August 1935—and then disbanded. Whether the problem was personality conflict, bookings, or Louise's ennui is unknown. Dario soon reunited with Diane, and together they danced on into oblivion.

Louise was in the doldrums of the Capitol Theatre run with Dario when life was brightened by the sudden reappearance of her favorite friend— Pepi Lederer. Just returned from London that day, Pepi and an English girlfriend surprised Louise backstage on April 15, 1935, with a huge basket of roses. The reunion called for a celebration. The story calls for a flashback:

Louise and Pepi had not seen each other for five years—since the winter Pepi came to New York and signed up for a writing course at Columbia University (which she quickly quit) before taking off with Marion Davies and W. R. Hearst for their 1930 European tour. Pepi had been banished from Hollywood to New York due to a little weekend party she threw at the Beach House when Marion and her entourage were absent:

King Vidor was shooting *Hallelujah* with an all-Negro cast at M.G.M. On impulse, while visiting the set on the last day of production, [Pepi] invited the vivacious little Nina Mae McKinney and some other members of the cast to [Marion's]. After three days, a neighbor, shocked by the sight of black people running in and out of the mansion, telephoned Marion, who sent [her sister] Ethel to end the party. . . . "And I shall never forget the expression on Ethel's face when she opened the door and saw me in bed with Nina Mae," Pepi said.[40]

New York City did not exactly reform Pepi's ways. Louise was present one night there when, during a minor crisis, Pepi cried, "Quick, Watson, the needle!" and rushed out to the apartment of actress Alma Rubens in the same building. Beautiful Alma had starred in several Hearst pictures, the last of which was *The Rejected Woman* (1924), but her addiction to morphine by now made it impossible for her to work. Since Hearst and Marion continued to support Alma, Pepi felt free to ask her the favor of an injection—but an hour later, she came back stone sober. Alma had run out of morphine and was a madwoman. "She's nothing anymore," Pepi said. "Nothing but two big black terrified eyes."

Rubens died a year later on January 21, 1931.

Louise recalled another evening in 1930 with Pepi at "21" when "a beautiful boy came to our table, introduced himself, and sat down"—Pare Lorentz, film critic for Hearst's *Evening Journal*. He was immediately caught up in the remedial speech lesson that Pepi had been giving Brooksie, who still retained her native Kansas tendency to drop the final "t" of past-tense verbs.

"Left, kept, slept," Louise enunciated carefully.

"Yes, but incorrectly arranged, Mary Louise," said Pepi. "To be quite accurate, you should say 'slept,' 'kept,' 'left.' "

Lorentz was enchanted by Pepi and asked her for a date—which she evasively declined. When Louise later asked why, Pepi replied: "He works for Mr. Hearst, doesn't he?" *

Besides which, Pepi was a lesbian. Which was why Louise was speechless a few weeks later when she dropped by to see Pepi at the Warwick and found her deathly ill and terrified:

> She had had an abortion and was hemorrhaging badly. This was the most astonishing piece of news since the Virgin Birth because, as far as I knew, she had never gone to bed with any man. . . . "And you honestly don't know who the man was?" I asked, in consternation. "No, I don't," she said violently. "And I don't want to know the name of a man who would rape a dead-drunk woman . . . on New Year's Eve."[41]

Despite that horror, Pepi was back to health and back in Marion's and Hearst's good graces in time for their June 1930 voyage to Europe. In London, she wrote Louise that she had found a lovely new companion

---

* Pare Lorentz (1905–1972) soon after became film adviser to the U.S. Resettlement Administration, in which capacity he made two lyrical and influential documentaries: *The Plow That Broke the Plains* (1936) and *The River* (1937).

named Monica Morris, "who had come to share her flat, her generous allowance, and Marion's charge accounts."

Now in 1935, backstage at the Capitol Theatre, Pepi and Monica insisted that Louise come to their suite—one of Hearst's, of course—at the Ritz Tower Hotel for a late-night supper. Louise agreed, and found Beatrice Lillie and Gloria Morgan Vanderbilt there, too. After the other guests departed, Monica had a burning question for Louise:

> "Will you take me to Harlem to get some cocaine?" She was most urgent.
> . . . I referred her to Tallulah Bankhead, at the Gotham Hotel, and Monica hurried out, leaving Pepi and me alone in the Ritz Tower for what was to be our last serious talk before her death.
>
> As the door of the entrance hall closed behind Monica, Pepi and I stood looking at each other. She had beautiful blue eyes, and they were suddenly dark and attentive; they did not lie to me. Now I understood at least one of the things that had made her want to avoid Marion and Mr. Hearst—cocaine.[42]

They chatted a while about the sagging fortunes of Hearst and Davies, namely *Operator 13*, Marion's last MGM film. At that point, said Louise, "No amount of free Hearst publicity could fill [the] theatres when a Marion Davies picture was shown." Hearst himself was approaching bankruptcy—his debt now about $126 million—and despite his toadying courtesy call on Adolf Hitler in September 1934, the Nazis were banning U.S. films and the whole lucrative German market would soon be shut off. The film industry was preoccupied with the loss of profits, Hearst and Marion with the loss of power and prestige. This was the inauspicious time that Pepi chose to return to Hollywood.

When Pepi and Monica arrived on the West Coast, Marion was at San Simeon, and weeks went by with no invitation to join her. Pepi grew depressed and then, "without warning," said Louise, "Marion and Mr. Hearst decided to have Pepi committed to the hospital for a drug cure. She had time only to slip her diamond ring from her finger to give to Monica before she was taken away."

The day after Louise & Dario opened their last engagement at the Persian Room, Louise got a call from John McClain, a Hearst columnist and friend, with a wire-service bulletin: Pepi Lederer had jumped out a window of the psychiatric section of Good Samaritan Hospital in Los Angeles.

In the growing list of film parts that Louise Brooks *did not* play during the 1930s, the oddest by far is the title role in *The Bride of Frankenstein* (1935). Director James Whale was seriously considering her for that lead, though he was also considering Brigitte Helm, another graduate of German films.[43] In the end, he chose neither, settling on Elsa Lanchester of the electrified hair, who was perfect.

Just as she was not going to be the bride of Frankenstein, Louise was also not going to be the bride of George Marshall. For one thing, she was still legally married to Deering Davis—a marriage which was as much an act of defiance against Marshall as anything else. The Brooks-Marshall relationship had always been volatile and the marriage issue thorny. At the peak of their romance (before and during *Pandora's Box*), they were both married to other people. After their divorces, he "repossessed me for reasons of pride and jealousy," said Louise, but later, "viewed in a sensible light, I threatened to become an expensive burden."

Worst of all, from her standpoint, "he told me with careless truthfulness [that] the excitement of making love to a married woman was no longer present." Worst of all, from Marshall's standpoint, was something Louise kept secret—or at least kept out of print—for the rest of her life, except for a single cryptic reference fifty years later: "[George] had given up all thoughts of marrying me after I had an affair with another man, in 1929."

William Paley was the only one of Louise's many lovers whom she would never name publicly. "The romance only really lasted a year," Paley recalls, but it confirmed Marshall's belief that Louise was a "tramp" at heart, and he was furious. "Marshall was one of those big, aggressive men-about-town," says Paley. "He was outraged that she was seeing me, and that was it—he left her."[44]

But not before he beat her up first. It was his fury over Paley, more than her refusal to sign an RKO contract, that had prompted him to abuse her back at the Lombardy Hotel, when he split her head open (and she had to resume wearing bangs until the wound healed). He used Paley as a real or convenient excuse to rule out marriage to Louise. But when she returned from Europe to stay, Marshall continued to see her, especially in 1930 after Louise sublet an apartment on Park Avenue at 56th Street. He liked that cozy old place with its three fireplaces and fine, wood-paneled library. When in New York, he would spend nights with her there. With no false vows of fidelity, they settled into something more than a sexual friendship, from which Louise derived a large measure of emotional stability. James Card sees Marshall as "a kind of incestuous father figure to her."[45]*

After his wrath over Paley subsided, Marshall seems to have acquired a new tolerance for Louise's sexual activities—such as an encounter with a

---

* Card was also struck by their Freudian, or just Anglo-Saxon, olfactory obsession with cleanliness. Aside from their pet names for each other ("Scrubbie" and "Wet Wash"), Louise often spoke of Marshall's, and her own, incredibly acute sense of smell: "I always had this Welsh stink about me," she said.

distinguished psychiatrist that solidified Louise's lifelong contempt for that profession:

> One rich and famous [psychiatrist] was Dick Hoffman. In 1930 he took me to dinner and upon returning to my apartment made the kind of scene that ended in his getting in the hay with me. He was white and soft like a worm. A week later . . . I was in [Marshall's] bedroom at the Elysee Hotel when the phone rang. It was Hoffman. George purposely spoke to him so that I could understand what Dick said. He told George that he had been to bed with me, that I was a bum, and that George was a fool to keep me. George thanked him, hung up, got into bed with his newspaper while, almost fainting, I ran to hide in the bathroom.[46]

Marshall could still not resist her.

"According to George, it was my truthfulness that made him fond of me," said Louise, "because truthfulness is a form of courage. And it was his obsession with his own cowardice that made him turn from art to rousting-about a team of brave men on the football field." If, as Louise often said, "50% of my value in his eyes lay in my being a movie star," she was becoming less and less valuable as the grim thirties wore on. And meanwhile, as Marshall's interest in her waned, something much more engrossing than the laundry business began to occupy him.

Always enthralled by football, he now decided to fulfill his fantasy of owning a team. It was a good time to buy franchises at bargain-basement

George Marshall in his trademark raccoon coat, at a football game in 1934

prices. His friend Art Rooney in Pittsburgh had purchased the Pittsburgh Steelers (then still called the Pirates), in July 1931 for a grand total of $2,500. In 1932, Marshall bought the Boston Redskins (then called the Braves) for the same modest franchise fee. It was not a very good team, and Boston was not a very good football city. The sports editors and citizens alike preferred their two baseball teams. Marshall complained that even the Radcliffe girls' hockey team got more press. His mounting fury over low attendance climaxed on a November afternoon in 1936 when his Redskins played Pittsburgh in a crucial preplayoff game: Barely 5,000 of Fenway Park's 35,000 seats contained spectators. According to Marshall's friend, sportswriter Shirley Povich:

> His revenge was swift. Marshall announced that if the Redskins got into the playoffs, the title game wouldn't be played in Boston. They did, and it wasn't. He took the game to neutral New York, burning every bridge back to Boston and liking what he had done.[47]

When Marshall moved the team to Washington the next year, the Redskins won the NFL championship in their first season—and the capital was a fanatical football town ever after. But his importance was not just local. He helped mastermind the two-division structure that vastly widened the national popularity and profitability of football. "He took charge of everything," recalled Pittsburgh's Rooney. "George had more to do with the formation of the NFL's rules than anyone I know of. A lot of things we have now he proposed years before—things like the draft system, TV broadcasts. . . . He was the force."[48]*

But those glory days came a little later. The five years Marshall owned the Redskins in Boston were grim—1932–1936, the same five years in which he still owned Louise Brooks. Marshall's foul temper during that time was legendary: His team was a loser, and he was simultaneously fighting with the fans, newspapers, city officials, and, of course, Louise. When he finally made the big break with Boston, he did so with Brooksie, too.

Marshall had had his fill of the bright, mouthy woman whose fierce independence he could manipulate but never dominate, even by occasional beatings. She feigned no interest in football, and her social propriety could not always be trusted. And so he opted for Louise's diametric opposite: Corinne Griffith, another beautiful silent-film actress but a relatively empty-headed one, who would not challenge him but function as

---

* Marshall also asserted himself in more malignant ways: For twenty-five years he maintained a strict color barrier—no blacks allowed on the team. That ban lasted until 1961, when U.S. Secretary of the Interior Stewart Udall threatened to kick the Redskins out of their new federally subsidized stadium unless they integrated.

the kind of hostess and showpiece needed for the business and social obligations of a football team owner. They were married in 1936.*

Marshall's inevitable abandonment of Louise devastated her. Though they had not been as close in recent years, George was always "there"—or somewhere within train's reach. The finality of his marrying Griffith hit her hard; she referred to it later as "betrayal." If, as philosopher Rose Hayden maintains, there is a single emotional turning point for good or ill in everyone's adult life, this was it for Louise Brooks.

"How can I explain George being the rock upon which my self-esteem shattered?" she later wrote. "His direct, plain-spoken cruelty was felt and known to all. From our first meeting, I knew he was dangerously destructive. It wasn't love or sex or respect or a need to be told what to do—my mother turned me loose at birth and autonomous I have remained—what kept me enthralled?"[49]

There was no simple answer to this, one of the key questions of Brooks's life. It lay somewhere in the magnetic attraction-repulsion of one cruelly direct person for another, and in a certain masochism of Louise's: the fact that Marshall bullied her, told her what to do, physically overpowered her, and did not "adore" her the way most men did. Some who knew him at close range—such as his long-time business associate Leonard Viner—render damning assessments of the man:

> Marshall was one of the outstanding con men of his time. He manipulated people right and left, and he could sell the Brooklyn Bridge or the Washington Monument, and charm the birds off the limbs if he set his sights on somebody. He didn't mind who he used or abused. . . . He had no loyalty to anybody. I recoil every time I see that monument to him in Kennedy Stadium.[50]

To the end of her life, Louise's feelings about Marshall swung back and forth like a pendulum, often tormenting her. "That cynical cad . . . had a profound and evil influence over me for ten years," she wrote James Card in 1955, but three months later she mused about "what a bitch I had been, and it came over me that far from being a mean man, [George] had for years kept me and dressed me like a doll and asked to marry me when even the kindest man would have long since thrown me out on the street."[51]

Later still, when she told John Kobal, "I don't think I ever loved any man," he asked if Marshall were an exception.

* Corinne Griffith was called the "Orchid Lady" for her delicate beauty in three dozen silent films. She encouraged Marshall's yearnings for respectability. From 1937 to 1947, he was publisher of a Hearst newspaper, the Washington *Times-Herald*, and, for a time, he was a Democratic National committeeman. He and Griffith divorced in 1958. She died in 1979.

"Well, I was crazy about him, yeah," she said. "But the word 'love'—no, I don't think I ever *loved* the men I knew. It's a very strange thing. I've noticed that very often the men who were the best in bed were the men that I cared the least about. The men who were the worst in bed were the men I liked the most. . . . I don't know why. . . . I always liked the bastards."[52]

If George Marshall was the most important man in her private life, G. W. Pabst occupied that position in her career. In troubled 1935, Louise was surprised to learn that Pabst was in New York and wanted to see her. She went immediately.

The Metropolitan Opera was mounting a new production of Gounod's *Faust*, and Pabst was keenly interested in making a film version—whether of the opera or epic poem itself is unclear. But he was in America to raise funds for the project, whose dream cast was clearly fixed in his mind: Pabst's *Faust* would star Greta Garbo as Gretchen and Louise Brooks as Helen of Troy.

Louise was interested. Her loathing for movie-making did not extend to Mr. Pabst. They met on October 17, 1935, and aside from the film discussion, which went well, they resumed their old tensions, thanks to Louise's choice of nightclub acts—a nudity-filled drag show.

"Mr. Pabst looked upon me as a moral zero," she later wrote a friend. "I took him to Minsky's in New York in 1935. He was outraged—I still can't see why."[53] Two days later she left New York for a visit to Wichita and, after a week at home on Topeka Street, went on to Los Angeles.

She had not set foot in Hollywood for four years, and only Pabst could have lured her. He himself had been lured there two years before by what he thought was a Warner Brothers offer to direct a film on Napoleon. It never materialized, but *A Modern Hero* did: Pabst's one and only American film, based on the 1932 Louis Bromfield novel about an ambitious dreamer with an Oedipus complex (Richard Barthelmess) who gets to the top by exploiting his business partners and his women. "It was just the kind of psychosexual narrative at which Pabst excelled."[54]

But in making *A Modern Hero*, Pabst had run afoul of Hal B. Wallis, the meddling and peremptory producer. Ignorant of Pabst's accomplishments in Europe, Wallis dictated everything from camera angles to the length of shots and otherwise demeaned Pabst as a director.

"I have asked you for close-ups repeatedly and I don't want to have to write you again," said Wallis in one of many insulting memos. "You will have to get used to our way of shooting pictures . . . and I have explained this to you in great detail a number of times and I don't want to go over it again."

Considering such handicaps, Pabst managed to fashion a rather strong picture, and, when released in 1934, it was by no means a bomb. But neither was it a smashing success. Pabst and Warners were glad to part ways. He next obtained a contract with Paramount to direct a script called *War Is Declared* for none other than B. P. Schulberg. This prophetic story concerned a ship-of-fools liner whose passengers divide into two hostile camps—democratic and fascist—after a demented wireless operator (a role Pabst created for Peter Lorre) reports that a war has begun. The passengers are at each other's throats by the time they discover that the "war" was a hoax. But in the tense atmosphere of 1933, this film never had a chance; it was scuttled by fear of European political repercussions.

Pabst had returned home, terribly frustrated. But now he was back to try again with *Faust*, and Louise too returned to the Hollywood she hated, out of loyalty and unemployment. Pabst was working hard on the party circuit (where he was distinctly uncomfortable), even throwing a few himself in an effort to find backers. At one of those gatherings, Louise met Erich von Stroheim for the first and only time: "Stroheim was miserable, talking to Pabst in German."[55] *

But the money for *Faust* was never found, and the project fell through, together with Louise's raised hopes. Pabst soon left, later to write a scathing account ("Servitude et grandeur de Hollywood," 1937) of what he viewed as Hollywood's repressive, deadening way of filmmaking. Jan-Christopher Horak provides the grim coda:

> The psychological wounds of two years of unemployment and the insults suffered at the hands of Wallis and Co. may also explain why Pabst, then faced with a choice between Hollywood and Nazi-run Berlin in 1939, chose the productive slavery of UFA under Hitler to the prospect of joining the Los Angeles *Lumpenproletariat*. In retrospect, it was wrong decision morally, but Pabst [was] too sensitive and thin-skinned to suffer further degradation.[56]

LOUISE ALSO HAD no desire for more degradation, but "having little money and no more faith in myself, I stayed on in Hollywood for lack of a better plan." She settled in at the modest Ronda Apartments and tested for a Republic B picture, *Dancing Feet*, "but they were unsatisfied with the tests, and they hired a blonde who didn't know how to dance," she said.[57]

Within walking distance of her flat was the Garden of Allah, where her old Algonquin friend Robert Benchley had a cottage, and one day Louise strolled over for a visit. She found Humphrey Bogart sitting on the floor,

---

* Louise called Stroheim "the one pure visual genius of film" for *Foolish Wives* (1922) and *The Wedding March* (1928). She never shared the view that he wrecked his own career through mad extravagance; in her opinion, it was "those two vulgarians, [Joseph P.] Kennedy and [Gloria] Swanson, who really destroyed Erich" during the making of the disastrous *Queen Kelly* in 1928.

leaning against a sofa with a Scotch and soda, trying—successfully—to keep up with Benchley's own consumption. The next day, Bogart asked her to join him for a drink—which "coming from Humphrey," she said, "was nothing less than a declaration of love."

She was being ironic, but she hastened to the scene and they evidently slept together. Afterward, she wrote, "I thought about how different Humphrey and I were. He could love only a woman he had known a long time or—what amounted to the same thing—one who was flung at him in the intimacy of a play or film. To me, love was an adventure into the unknown." [58]

In any event, it was Mayo Methot and not Louise who now set fire to Bogart and brought his passions to a boil, "blowing the lid off all his inhibitions forever." When Louise next saw him, in early 1936 at the home of writer Eric Hatch (My Man Godfrey), he was in an agitated state brought on by Mayo's passionate dancing with actor Mischa Auer. Suddenly the maid announced that Methot's husband was on his way to the party, whereupon Humphrey and Mayo hastily prepared to leave.

"But wait!" Louise recalled. "She had taken off her slippers to dance, and now one of them could not be found. Everyone searched for it except me, and that must have aroused Humphrey's suspicions, because quite suddenly he lunged at me with the most hideous face, rasping, 'God damn you, Louise, tell us where you hid Mayo's slipper!' " [59] The real culprit was Auer, who produced the shoe just in time for the pair to make their getaway.

Louise, as usual, would not use her friendship with Bogart to solicit a movie job at Warners, where his star was rising. It was six months later, in August of 1936, before she finally got some $300-a-week work in a low-budget Universal western, Empty Saddles, starring Buck Jones. Jones had had a hankerin' for Louise back in 1930 during her noncontract period at Columbia, when she haughtily declined. This time she said yes.

The sagebrush epic at hand was one of the more ludicrous of the genre —but for what it was worth, she was the leading lady. The film opens with eight measures of clip-clopping cowboy music, endlessly repeated, while a special-effects ghost goes about haunting an empty cabin, if not an empty saddle. A murder has evidently been committed there, but neither the ghost nor the killing is ever referred to again. All we know is that it's "The Ranch of the Empty Saddles," and there is a curse on the place.

"Will ya let that old clock alone, Pop, and come on and eat?" says "Boots Boone," the twenty-nine-year-old Louise Brooks, in a lilting Midwest-cum-cultivated-cum-Midwest-again voice. The old man is out of it, and she advises some handsome strangers, "Don't pay any attention to Pop— he drinks quite a bit. So do I."

The greatest challenge for Louise was to appear interested in, not to mention jealous of, Buck Jones, whose oil-slicked hair is unmussed even after a chaste night in his sleeping bag. "I'm not taking any lessons from the drugstore blonde," she fumes, after he flirts with one. There's a hint of her old petulance in this "take-charge" frontierswoman, but for the most part Louise seems hypnotized. Adding insult to injury, director Lesley Selander would not even let her do her own horseback riding. A grunt-filled fist-fight between Buck and the villain concludes one of the most static and silly westerns in Hollywood history.

In defense of Selander (1900–1979), this was one of his first feature assignments, the result of his friendship with the amiable Jones. Selander's later cowboy pictures (including dozens with Tim Holt and Hopalong Cassidy) improved considerably. But a measure of *Empty Saddles's* quality is that filming began on August 26, 1936, and ended on September 2.

Universal's publicity department now released an amazing "interview" with Louise:

> "I feel that my career is just beginning and that practically all of the rest of the time was wasted."
>
> It was pretty brunette Louise Brooks speaking. She is back again now, as leading lady for Buck Jones in his new Universal picture, *Empty Saddles.* . . .
>
> "I am delighted with my role in *Empty Saddles.* It gives me an opportunity to do something, not just stand around and look pretty. I wouldn't trade it for all the other roles I have ever had because I am really acting now, not just being an ornament, and I feel that, at last, I am on the road toward getting some place in pictures."[60]

The press was not buying it. On September 5, United Press transmitted a one-paragraph item which summed up Hollywood's attitude toward her: "Louise Brooks, who turned up her nose at a Paramount contract several years ago, is back in pictures again."

Restless Louise was changing her residence with some frequency and still living on the financial edge. *Empty Saddles* paid $300 a week, all right— for one week. For a brief period, she lived at the Hollywood Roosevelt Hotel, where her chief recollection was of Mack Sennett, the genius of early film comedy, who, like herself, had fallen on hard times:

> Almost every day, from about noon, he would sit in the lobby for a couple of hours, smoking his cigars, watching the people go by. He was then only fifty-one—a big, healthy, wonderfully handsome and virile man. How could *he* have allowed himself to be discarded to die on the Hollywood rubbish heap? . . . I wondered what thoughts lay behind the expressionless mask he wore in public.[61]

There were many such inhabitants of Hollywood limbo in 1936, and Louise was wandering among them. She checked out of the Roosevelt in September and moved to an apartment at the Villa Italia on North Crescent Heights Boulevard in Hollywood, for about two months. No more chauffeur-driven limos for Brooksie. She now took buses to and from her job hunts, and she was on her way home from one when she had her last encounter—more a surrealistic nonencounter—with Hollywood's greatest legend:

> Walking from Santa Monica Boulevard one late afternoon, I saw an old town car driving toward me. I had never seen it before but I *knew* it was Garbo's. It was going slow but it got *very* slow as it got up to me. Then I saw Garbo. She was sitting very straight in the shadows of the interior, black coat, black turban. Her expression did not change at all when she looked at me, but her eyes said, "I will stop and take you with me." I played like I did not see and walked on to the Villa Italia while the car picked up speed on its way to Beverly Hills.[62]

And that is all that is known of the thoughts that lay behind Louise's own expressionless mask that day.

The entire year 1937 passed in a similar kind of trance as Louise played out the last act of her tragicomic movie career. The biggest landmark of the year for her was a sad one: She danced with George Gershwin at the Clover Club a few nights before he died (July 11, 1937).*

Then her hopes were raised, once again, by a small but flashy part in Robert Florey's *King of Gamblers*. Florey, she said, "specialized in giving jobs to destitute and sufficiently grateful actresses." It was a hard-hitting story about the slot-machine racket, with Lloyd Nolan as the obligatory newspaperman and Claire Trevor as his chanteuse girlfriend. Akim Tamiroff was the evil King of Gamblers, and Buster Crabbe had a featured role. Louise was not the only former star reduced to bits. Evelyn Brent, whose career had become just as badly stalled, was in the film too. They met on the set for the first time in years. "After saying hello, no further words were spoken between us," Louise recalled. "There was nothing to say. . . . When Evelyn's scene was finished we went to the still picture gallery where we were photographed [with] Bob Florey. It took no imagination to guess the caption that would appear under the photograph."[63] Both actresses found the "comeback" theme humiliating.

"New Chance Given to Evelyn Brent and Louise Brooks," said a Los Angeles *Times* headline. "Two stars of former years made a simultaneous

---

* See account on pages 67–8.

appearance on a set at Paramount studio and were handed not an entire script to learn, but just a few lines of dialogue apiece."

Brent thought the humiliation unintentional and went about desperately trying to set it right:

> I'm not making what is termed a comeback. I dislike that word. I haven't been away. I've been here all the time just fooling around and not making any particular attempt to get work. My mind is made up now and I'm going to carve a new niche for myself in films. I'll play any kind of a role offered, bad woman, good woman, young woman or old woman. I'm a bad girl in *King of Gamblers,* and I enjoyed playing the character.[64]

Louise, on the other hand, said nothing. Her role as Lloyd Nolan's fiancé in one of the early scenes was shot in just four hours: She looked smart, in turban and veil, chatting with Nolan in a bar. The scene was cut out entirely. Louise was sure the whole thing had been a cruel charade.

"The studio went out of its way to offer negative comments," says James Card. "In the captions for every publicity photo, the implication was that she'd been forgotten. I think it was a deliberate slight. It wasn't friendly as in, 'Oh, boy, she's making a comeback!' This wasn't the day of 'cameo' roles."

But William K. Everson discounts the conspiracy theory:

> Paramount had made its point back in 1930 and by now had probably forgotten all about Louise Brooks. Florey had wanted to use her in his 1936 *Hollywood Boulevard* but it hadn't worked, and the role [in *Gamblers*] was both a way of making good on his promise, *and,* more importantly, casting a good actress in a good role. . . . Certainly Paramount, the most economy-minded of all the majors, would not have spent time and money to humiliate Brooks.[65]

Florey's Paramount films, says Everson, were tightly paced melodramas, and this one, with its complex plot, was running too long. Louise's episode was the only sequence that could be cut *in toto* without leaving an obvious hole.

But Louise could never believe that, and her persecution complex was confirmed by her next, and penultimate, experience in pictures. In September 1937, she did a screen test for a Grace Moore musical at Columbia, *When You're in Love,* directed by Robert Riskin and co-starring Cary Grant. At this point, says James Card, Harry Cohn was finally able to avenge his rebuffed shirtlessness seven years before:

> Fully believing that she would refuse, he offered her a test for a lead with the condition that she first agree to work as an extra in the dancing chorus. . . . She did not refuse. Columbia released dozens of stills showing Louise

*Louise and cowboy actor Addison "Jack" Randall
at a sporting event, April 10, 1937*

in the chorus; and the publicity department captions on them spoke volumes. "Louise Brooks, former screen star, who deserted Hollywood seven years ago at the height of her career, has come back to resume her work in pictures. But seven years is too long for the public to remember and Louise courageously begins again at the bottom."[66]

Another release said, "Louise Brooks, former star, threw pride aside and resumed her career as a ballet dancer in Grace Moore's current picture." And still another: "Louise Brooks . . . this week launched upon a comeback with hopes of recapturing the success and popularity she once knew." It was not even a bit part this time; it was merely a lowly hoofer's position.

There was little to console Louise at this time, except a singing cowboy named Addison "Jack" Randall. She moved in with him in December 1937, but they had been having an affair for about six months. Randall, a handsome, burly man of thirty, played minor romantic leads as well as cowboys, but never achieved the fame of his younger brother, who performed under the name Robert Livingston. Bob was one of the "Three Mesquiteers" (the others were Max Terhune and Ray Corrigan) and would soon play the Masked Man in Republic's *The Lone Ranger Rides Again* serial.

Randall liked sporting events, and he and Louise were often seen out and about. A *Photoplay* photographer once snapped them in a shot that captured her wearing a kerchief and the biggest grin of any known candid photo. During their time together, what they most shared was an abiding interest in sex. In her blunt fashion, Louise later told a friend that Randall was dedicated to autoeroticism, which she found fascinating: "I have known people like Addison Randall who conduct sex as a series of mechanical experiences, unrelated to bodies or minds, men or women."[67]

They also had a mutual flair for domestic violence, one instance of which was witnessed by her friend Howard Shoup, the Warners dress designer.

"I remember once in Hollywood, Shoupie coming in to take me away from Addison's," said Louise. "For a moment, he stood looking into the dining room at the shattered remains of an intimate little dinner, at Addison glowering at the end of the table with an indestructible shaker of

Louise and her father on the occasion of her Deering Davis divorce hearing in Wichita, December 8, 1937

martinis in his paw, and then Shoup said, 'Well, Mary Louise, whatever else may be said about you, you're never dull.' "[68]

At about this time, another face from the past showed up: Barbara Bennett, happily retired from show business since her 1929 wedding to the songwriter Morton Downey. Barbara had five children by Downey, and their marriage was thought to be of the storybook variety. Barbara was now introduced to Jack Randall, of whom Brooksie was tiring. Louise, for her part, decided it was time to get out of Hollywood for a while and clear up her head—and her marital status—in Kansas.

One of the reasons why her interest in Randall was fading—and why she boarded the train for Wichita at the end of 1937—was that Louise had met another man she wanted to wed. But her ever-ambivalent attitude toward marriage was compounded by the realization that legally she was still Mrs. Deering Davis.

Since she was out of money, she decided to make rare use of her attorney father. A few days after her arrival, the Wichita *Eagle* ran a two-column photo of Louise and Leonard P. Brooks smiling happily at one another in his law office. It looked like a happy family reunion scene and, essentially, it was. L.P.'s charge was "gross neglect," and Davis did not contest. With the final decree on February 10, 1938, her precious maiden name was restored. The Associated Press reported that Louise was making plans "for a third trip to the altar"—but not another word is to be found about it, or the name of the would-be groom.

Other mysterious press stories popped up around Louise. One said she returned to Hollywood immediately after the divorce "to make a test with Henry Hathaway for *Spawn of the North*," a drama about Canadian fisheries. If so, she lost the part to Dorothy Lamour. Another West Coast report claimed Louise was now working on the stage under the name "Linda Carter."

She was, in fact, back in Los Angeles, living in the Hotel Brevoort, but it took her until August 1938 to find a job. Probably through Randall, she met director George Sherman, who offered her another "oater"—two weeks' work for Republic as the leading lady in *Overland Stage Raiders*. It was the latest in the Three Mesquiteers series with Ray Corrigan (as Tucson), Max Terhune (as Lullaby), and—replacing Bob Livingston—the thirty-year-old John Wayne (as Stony Brooke). Wayne's career was stalled in B westerns (eighty of them in the last decade!), but he was finally on the brink of stardom thanks to John Ford's *Stagecoach*, released just a few months later in 1939.

Overland Stage Raiders had an unusual contemporary setting not unlike that of the later "Sky King" series: Seems there's been a wave of robberies on the Oro Grande Stage Line—typical. What's atypical is that our trio, part owners of a little airport, convince the gold mine operator to start making his shipments by plane. Things are fine until a midair robbery makes the Mesquiteers (and co-owner Louise) look like crooks.

"I'll give you just twenty-four hours to make good!" says the boss to John Wayne.

"Well, okay," he drawls, "if that's the way you feel about it." The Mesquiteers have fifty-five screen minutes to recover the gold and their honor.

"Prompted by some inner sense which proved correct," Louise later wrote, "I felt that I was reaching the end of my career in 1938. . . . The sorely needed $300 salary did little to cheer me up at the prospect of working in a typical Hollywood Western whose unreality disgusted me." Growing up in Kansas, close to the "boozing, whoring and gun fighting" of real-life cowboys, "it is not surprising that I did not share Hollywood's romantic view of the cowboy hero." But she held a highly romantic view of this young cowboy actor who was far more compelling than Buck Jones:

> . . . At sunrise one August morning I was driven in a company car to location on the ranch where Republic shot all its Westerns. Where was I supposed to go, I wondered, after I got out of the car and stood alone in a cloud of dust kicked up by a passing string of horses—that damned dust so cherished by Western cameramen. Up the road a bunch of cowboys were talking and laughing with two men who stood slightly apart from them. When the company car honked for them to get off the road, the two men looked around, saw me, and came to greet me. One was a cherub, five feet tall, carrying a bound script; the other was a cowboy, six feet four inches tall, wearing a lovely smile. The cherub, who was the director, George Sherman, introduced me to the cowboy who was John Wayne. . . . Looking up at him I thought, this is no actor but the hero of all mythology miraculously brought to life.
>
> During my 13 years in films I had made a study of the manner in which the reigning stars of Hollywood exercised their power. My first study had been of Queen Gloria Swanson, who knocked people about like bowling pins. My last study had been of King Clark Gable, who wore his crown at a humorously apologetic angle. Now, for the first time I beheld a Duke born to reign. John was, in fact, that which Henry James defined as the greatest of all works of art—a purely beautiful being.[69]

One day on the set, Wayne and Corrigan treated Louise and the rest of the cast to a Colt .45 demonstration, shooting dimes off a tree stump at fifty paces. After six perfect rounds, and the loss of twelve dimes, they called it a draw.

If only the movie had been as interesting. Aside from a parachute jump early on, its primary action is a continuous loop of stock footage of streaking horses and riders. It is odd to see a *bus* in the middle of this hybrid,

Her last screen appearance: Louise and John Wayne in their fadeout pose from Overland Stage Raiders *(1938)*

New Deal western, with its anachronistic emphasis on technology. It is even odder to see Louise with shoulder-length hair, thick lipstick, and thin, arched eyebrows, foreshadowing Veronica Lake's generic forties look; she is barely recognizable. Wayne, the only one of these cowboys without a midriff bulge, is exactly as Louise described him—big, sexy, and magnetic—and having a good time with Brooks on camera. "It never fails," says Lullaby, who keeps a dummy named Elmer on his knee, "—when Stony meets a gal, we meet trouble!"

"*Overland Stage Raiders* is not what you would call a maligned masterpiece," says film critic Richard Geary. "You'd like to be able to say that Brooks redeems it, but she can't and she doesn't." It is a dreadful film from start to finish, with every cliché known to Western man and western genre. Louise adored Wayne but could not stand the humiliation of the film. *Raiders* was the last straw. She never made another movie.

By now, Louise's social life matched her bleak professional life. She had always admired Raymond Griffith, who was now a producer with Fox, because "he was the most marvelous actor and dancer." One night she accepted his dinner invitation but not his after-dinner advances, at which point "he stripped me of every layer of self-respect," berating her as "a cheap drunken tramp, not even good enough to be called a whore. He was right. I shall never forget his delivery in that penetrating whisper."[70]

Soon after, Bill Reviere, the brother-in-law of William Randolph Hearst, Jr., phoned Louise one evening "asking whether I would like to meet David Mdivani, that wicked 'Prince' once married to Mae Murray. I said yes."

> We gathered together in that restaurant across the street from the Beverly Wilshire—another South Seas joint. I was taking my downfall very hard, and when I sneered at Mdivani's lack of knowledge about Russian literature, he sent Billy out to call another girl. In a half hour appeared Barbara Denny [actor Reginald Denny's twenty-one-year-old daughter]. She was lovely and frail. I sat questioning her. I could not believe that her father would turn her loose upon the town. We went to Mdivani's apartment in Beverly Hills. It was filled with photographs of Russian royalty. The next morning we went to collect Barbara. Mdivani had gone out. Still drunk, still lovely, she knew only that she had been done in. A few years later she killed herself.[71]

In Louise's final "phasing out" in Hollywood, one of the precious few humorous moments came during a last meeting with her old friend from Algonquin Hotel days, director Edmund Goulding, whose *Grand Hotel* had won the best picture Oscar for 1932. He was still more interested in "discovering" beautiful actresses than anything else, and this time it was the pretty model Jinx Falkenburg:

> [Goulding] remained most like an ebullient, slightly mad social director on a cruise ship. He had not withdrawn into the clouds of godly genius along with other successful directors. . . . Eddie had invited me to lunch at a charming house rented for our host, the handsome young Earl of Warwick who had come to Hollywood to heal the wounds inflicted by a recent divorce. The other guest was Jinx Falkenburg who moved in an atmosphere of exalted "class." Hollywood producers worshipped "class" and for a time believed that this pretty, big, healthy girl was a potential star. That morning Eddie had seen a test of Jinx which he had directed at Warner Brothers. At the luncheon table she asked how it was. "Terrible," he said, suddenly coldly professional. Then in response to her expression of outrage he added, "But your behind in that nightgown was delectable—like two grapefruits tied up in a napkin."[72]

Jinx failed to join in the laughter but rather, according to Louise, "gave me a look of hatred and got up and left the table."

If Goulding was so fond of Brooks, he might have offered her a part in a movie. But he never did; so far as he knew—never having seen *Pandora's Box* or *Prix de Beauté*—Louise the actress was much like Jinx Falkenburg, only much more fun to be around.

Even if someone *had* offered her another film part, Louise probably would have turned it down. "At the very end in Hollywood," she said, her old friend Malcolm St. Clair "was still trying to get me to come to the Fox studio when he was only an assistant to Zanuck then, to make a test for a picture, and I wouldn't."[73] And so, as she had done after the abortive comeback of 1931, she turned again to dancing in 1939, picking up a few jobs, including a brief engagement at the Victor Hugo Club in Hollywood. But it wasn't enough.

"I was flat broke in a little hotel off Vine," she told James Card, "when I met the beautiful Barry O'Shea, the ballroom dancer. He was just the thing for a dancing school."[74] For students, they drew from such places as the Westlake School for Girls, whose pupils would soon include Shirley Temple. (Louise, who was not among her legions of fans, imposed a wonderfully impossible verdict on the eleven-year-old star: "What a swaggering, tough little slut she was.")

The Brooks-O'Shea Studio, located in Beverly Hills, did not survive long. Neither partner was suited to administration or to the gentle wooing of students' parents. But it got off to a good start after a mysterious, fifty-three-year-old businessman named Fletcher Crandall put up some money for the venture. He was "grey, dapper and soft-voiced," said Louise, "and the third time I saw him I said, 'C'mon Fletcher, confess. You're a con man!' " She was kidding—but not completely:

> You see, he had no background. He didn't come from anywhere, and that was the dead giveaway. Just returned from Africa. The distant, unprovable point. Anyhow, he backed us, and within a month I had an adorable school on Sunset and an apartment at Normandy Village, and Shoup made me some darling clothes, and I got O'Shea out of his pointed shoes and tight suits into soft, loose wools and a decent dinner jacket. But I couldn't stand the bastard. We fought like tigers, and then he started writing checks on the money coming in next week, and I sold the business to him for $2,500. The next day Crandall asked me to lunch at the Cock and Bull, which was strange for there was no sex between us. I kept O'Shea with me every minute. Fletcher asked to borrow $2,000 over the weekend to go up to the Springs with his whore, who was trying to be most expensive, and I said, "Fletcher, I know you. I'll never get the money back, but you made it possible for me to get it, and I feel obliged to give it to you." He got grand, of course, for a minute, but the next minute he was sending his man over to the bank with me to get it out of the safety box.[75]

Crandall had a past, all right, as well as a present scam. He was on parole after serving five years in San Quentin for grand theft and "bunko" —California's quaint name for swindling. Shortly after obtaining the "loan" from Louise, he and a partner were arrested for bilking various women, including a widow of sixty-three, who lost her $65,000 life savings and was "sent to a sanitarium in a nerve collapse."[76] The grand total was $147,000.

All things considered, Louise got off easy. And she was being hailed as a hero for helping to uncover the "Hollywood Facts Corporation" through which Crandall manipulated stocks as well as people in phony investments. "It was the suspicion of the Wichita girl [now thirty-three] which exposed eight months of Crandall's activity in the movie capital," said one report.[77]

She hadn't exactly been Sherlock Holmes; she simply reported that Crandall's $2,000 repayment check had bounced and that he had skipped town. And in her typically unpredictable way, she now felt pity rather than rage toward the man who had conned her—one of life's "lame ducks," she liked to say.

"Funny," she wrote Card years later of Crandall. "Each of us and our morals. I went down to jail to take him some cigarettes [and] looking at me out of that terrible wire cage, he said, 'I don't give a damn about clipping old Mrs. Thing for fifty grand, but if I ever get it back, I'll give you back your $2,000.' "

She wouldn't hold her breath.

The Brooks-O'Shea Studio folded, as it was destined to do even without Crandall's hastening of the event. When his trial came up, she did not want to testify against him, which gave her a good reason to leave town— as if she needed another one. The Big Swindle was a fitting conclusion to her life in Tinseltown. A meeting with an old friend and former lover helped cinch her decision: "Walter Wanger warned me that if I hung around any longer I'd become a call girl."[78]

Enough was enough. Disgusted, depressed, and pretty close to destitute, it was time to say farewell to Hollywood once and for all. It was time to give up. On July 30, 1940, she took the train home to Kansas.

The last portrait in Hollywood, 1939; photo by Autrey

16 · Lulu in Purgatory

Oh, sir, not that! How can you kiss my hand?
It is so ugly and so rough!
So much I have to scour and scrub and sand,
Since for my mother I can never do enough.
— M A R G A R E T E in Goethe's *Faust*

SO I fled to Wichita," said Louise, ". . . but that turned out to be another kind of hell."[1]

During her seventeen-year performing career, Louise calculated that
she had earned exactly $124,600—none of it saved or invested.* Going
back to Kansas now, at age thirty-three, she had no illusions; she was
returning home "in failure and disgrace."

The Union Station in Wichita was only a dozen blocks from the Brooks
homestead on North Topeka Avenue, but it was the longest journey of
her life. The sidewalks simmered in the August heat as the vanquished
heroine and her brother struggled with her luggage to Theo's car for the
short hop home. There, Leonard P. Brooks was waiting for his famous
daughter with an awkward little welcome-home dinner not unlike the
one over which he had presided a few years earlier in honor of her
mother.

For L.P., it was a time of prodigal daughters and wives. After almost a
decade of separation, Myra had returned from her odyssey in some failure
and disgrace of her own. Louise was instantly aware of the "curious new
relationship" between her parents. She and her brother spent years analyzing it: Myra told Theo the source of the problem was that she had been
"led astray" into marrying a much older man. According to Theo, "she
blamed her [own] father for permitting her to be so led by Dad."[2]

---

* The exact breakdown: $104,500 from films, $10,100 from theater, $10,000 from all other sources.
"I was astonished that it came to so much," she said. "But then I never paid any attention to
money." Louise never received any royalties or residuals from subsequent screenings of her films.

That had been the reason for Myra's preannounced rebellion against child-rearing and for her flight to Chicago. But Leonard Brooks was unflappable. Despite his wife's long absence and the reports of her flamboyant activities, "he was tolerant and waited patiently for the return of Myra," her friend Tot Strickler told Louise. Myra simply showed up one evening, found the door unlocked as always, and let herself in.

"Leonard, I am home," she said. "I have come home to stay."

"Well," he replied, "that's just fine, make yourself at home, we have plenty of room."

"It was a triumphant return," Tot concluded.[3]

But Robert Brooks, the grandson who lived with them at the time, thinks it was somewhat less than triumphant. "The way I was told," he said, "things got real bad for [Myra], and he felt sorry for her and took her back in."[4] In any case, she was back. And there was a sense of resignation about her.

"In my opinion Myra was a better person in every way after her fling," wrote her sister Eva to Louise a few years later. "Had we had her life to live, her problems to face, whatever they were, we would have done no better, probably not as well. We all make mistakes. . . . At least your mother's were interesting."[5]

But the fact that Myra's mistakes were "interesting" did not facilitate Louise's painful effort to work out her feelings toward her. From the moment of her arrival, Louise spent these Kansas days in strange atone-

Louise, L. P., and June Brooks at home at 924 North Topeka Street in Wichita, ca. Christmas 1940

ment, scrubbing floors, fighting with everyone around her—and drinking heavily.

There are various accounts of Louise's psychological battles with Myra at this time, but none is so incisive as Louise's own. It was written, typically, in an article that had nothing to do with her mother—an unpublished essay on Joan Crawford. Louise was drawing a parallel between Crawford's on-screen character and her mother's in real life. The connection was tenuous, but the vignettes of the mother-daughter relationship are revelatory:

In August 1940 when I caught up the tattered folds of my Hollywood robe and fled home to Kansas, I grew to hate my mother. Not that she was unkind. She simply laughed—like a person with a happily corrected blind spot. This, after the admiration and solicitude of her way with me in Hollywood, cut me like a knife. And the final jab came one day when we were cleaning out the drawers of her secretary and, coming across a once-cherished pile of my letters and photographs she asked, "Do you want these, Louise, or shall I throw them out?"

From then on our conflict mounted until it broke into the open—with violent tirades on my part, and on hers a kind of performance which always ended with mother laid low, succored by whichever ladyfriend was cast in the part.

In particular, one steaming afternoon, I remember her richest and fattest friend, Zana Henderson, arriving with peonies and a quart of cream for poor starved mother, intending to make a fast Lady Bountiful sick call and remaining to go on active duty. (Mother was a genius at conning people into servitude.) Heaving angrily up the back stairs for the fifth time with some brew, Zana trapped me in the hall and demanded that I carry it to the sick room. And on my refusal her long-hidden contempt truly withered me with, "You won't take this in to your mother? Why, I'd do that much for a dog!"

Having been extremely unpopular when I left Wichita—imagine, that mean freckled little Brooks girl getting into the movies!—and more so for daring to come back a failure, such incidents of additional bad publicity blackened my heart. So while I cleaned and washed and cooked, the free part of my mind was eased by turning our conflict into a play—a sort of Eugene O'Neill thing, I called it to myself. Naturally I was the tragic heroine, flying to the sheltering arms of my once-loving mother, now become the villain of the piece, the hypocrite unmasked.

It went on fairly well, this continuous daydream, until I got to the end—the smashing climax—when I was to denounce my mother with righteous wrath, take up my great courage and bang out the door to reenlist in the battle of life. The curtain fell, of course, on mother alone; broken with remorse. The trouble was, though, as my own best audience, the more I regarded this scene, the less of a hero and the more of a louse I became. All my sympathy went to the poor woman rid at last of a vicious daughter.[6]

There was no way to do battle with an invalid mother. Myra was suffering from emphysema and high blood pressure, and the demands of her ailments seemed to dovetail with her private yearnings. "When Myra visited us in '40," Eva wrote Louise, "she asked me how in the world I managed having my family treat me like a queen?" Louise was many things, but she was not a very good lady-in-waiting.

This grim domestic situation had one bright spot in the form of Louise's nine-year-old nephew, Robert, the son of her divorced brother Martin. Robert had come to live with his grandparents a year before, and his stay in Wichita coincided almost exactly with that of Louise—hers ending in 1943, his in 1944 at age thirteen. With Robert, Louise developed the closest emotional attachment she ever had to a child. Thirty years later, she still spoke fondly, and proudly, of teaching him to read. The patented Brooks method of instruction was to exhort her nephew with correctives such as, "Can't you even spell 'cat,' you son of a bitch?"[7]

"They said I was a 'mirror reader'—the old term for dyslexic—and Louise said, 'Bullshit, he's just a normal nine-year-old boy,'" Robert Brooks recalls. "We went over and over everything. And she taught me my math by metronome! If you missed anything, you started all over again. She tried to teach me the rhumba and the samba, too, but at that age I wasn't too interested in dancing.

"She also used to fix meals for me—she'd make them beforehand and leave them in the refrigerator. They were always nutritious, but some of the combinations were pretty horrible—spinach and oatmeal together, for instance, isn't what a nine-year-old's really after. But if you were hungry enough, you'd eat the damned stuff."

Was she his surrogate mother?

"Yes," he replies. "And I was her surrogate child. With me she had an opportunity to be a mother. She'd say, 'Robert, I'd like to wring your neck.' I didn't know how to take it—and then she'd reach out and hug me. She was a perfectionist. She wouldn't take second—didn't like it from herself and didn't like it in others. There was only one way to do things and that was the right way. She'd bawl me out, but I wasn't scared of her. . . . As a kid I saw more than some grownups."

One of the things Robert Brooks saw was the intense conflict between Louise and Myra. "My grandmother was a strong-willed person," he says, "and of course Louise was too. You put two women like that in the same house, and it's a head-on collision. It was two women trying to dominate not so much each other, but the *situation* and the location."

Even so, the big house on Topeka was "a wonderful home to be raised in," Robert Brooks remembers. "Grandfather never locked his place. The standing rule was that if you were a Brooks, and you were down and out and broke and went to Wichita, you just walked in and found a bed and a meal, and you'd get up in the morning and Grandad would say, 'Well, how're you doin', Robert?' He had a sense of humor that was very dry."

The Brookses rarely displayed much overt affection, but it was there, despite all the fussing, particularly between Louise and Theodore. "They were the closest as brother and sister," Robert says, recalling one battle that ended with Theo seeking refuge in the kitchen and sitting down opposite the boy at the table: "After a minute, Theo looked up at me and said, 'Louise has disowned me, Robert. But it's not the first time.' "

Louise identified intensely with the waiflike Robert; they were seeking shelter under the same roof from the mix-ups of the world. She had never expressed any desire to have children—indeed, she had never expressed anything other than a W. C. Fieldsian annoyance toward children in general. But Robert's role in her life was bigger than anyone ever knew. Thirty years later, Louise copied down a list of biographical questions in her logbook—favorite composer, favorite flower, and so forth. One was more profound than the rest. It asked, "Whom in your life have you loved most?" Beside it Louise wrote, "Robert Brooks."

For the most part, when Louise worked at all after 1932, it was in dance. And though carving out a living as a dance instructor was difficult, it was her only marketable skill in Wichita, Kansas. Once again, Louise decided to open up a studio.

Theodore helped bankroll the project, modestly, and together they scouted sites, settling on the back quarters of the Dockum Building, a drugstore at the corner of Hillside and Douglas. This little structure with its Spanish stucco design and mosaic tilework was charming; Theo and Louise and a few friends worked hard and enjoyably to fix it up, installing full-length mirrors, a barre, and Venetian blinds (that still remain) to keep out the all-penetrating Kansas sun.

But most of all she needed a partner. First she visited a young tap-dance teacher named Jimmy Cavaness, asking him to teach her how to do an acrobatic cartwheel, which he did. But he had other commitments, and so she turned to young Hal McCoy.

"I met her in my freshman year at Wichita University through her sister June," says McCoy, a genial man with a twinkle in his eyes. Knee problems and a little extra weight have altered the lithe dancer's form, but not the folksy outlook that led him to settle down contentedly for a lifetime in Wichita. In his teens, McCoy won a Charleston contest and then got a job with a song-and-dance act for the Santa Fe Railroad, performing in train-station waiting rooms between Kansas and California.

Louise and Hal McCoy in their dance exhibition at the Crestview Country Club, Wichita, September 22, 1940

Now retired and living just a mile or two from the site of the Brooks-McCoy Studio of Ballroom Dancing, he recalls his brief, tumultuous association with Louise:

Sometimes we talked about her film career and she'd tell me stories, but she ran in the jet set—way out of my league. She was very photogenic—though not as pretty to look at as she was in her photos. She had a reddish-bluish blotched skin and longer hair by then, but she still had the bangs. She

was very athletic—the type of build you see now in girls—slim, almost boyish. She was the first girl I ever saw who wore slacks. She had them custom-
made because women didn't wear slacks then and nobody made them.
Louise was built for it, and they fit her like she was poured into them. She
always wore high heels with them. . . .

One thing I can tell you is that she had a vicious disposition. We went
out to dance one night at the 400 Club, and Harry Perkins, one of the boys
she knew in school, came up and wanted to dance with her—he cut in on
us—and you'd have thought I had hold of a tigress! I'll never forget how she
turned around and literally *snarled*, really bared her teeth at him.[8]

"She didn't think much of the people here," adds McCoy in classic
Kansas understatement. Most of their time together was spent teaching
and rehearsing for a series of local exhibitions for such groups as the
College Hill Business Association and the Young Republicans—an awe-
some comedown for the former toast of two continents. She was truly
back at square one—performing in some of the same places where she
had appeared as a precocious thirteen-year-old, such as the high-ceilinged
Innes Tea Room, where civic groups met for monthly lunches. The
Brooks-McCoy duo's first "professional" engagement took place on September 22, 1940, at the posh Crestview Country Club, and got good notices. But these exhibitions were chiefly designed to advertise the
rhumbas, tangos, and fox trots they taught at their studio.

To the same end, for the first time in her life, Louise now composed
some extended prose. Her first published work, printed in Wichita, was
a thirty-six-page booklet called "The Fundamentals of Good Ballroom
Dancing." It cost fifty cents. As its foreword explained, it was a review of
"the essence of good dancing wherever discriminating people gather," and
it was written—with a little help from Theo—in the high Brooksian style.
In the opening "Why Dance?" section, Louise informs the reader that
"the instinct to 'cut a rug' " is ancient, and "the front line enemy of
overweight and old age." Her trade secret she reveals early: "Dancing
beautifully depends upon nothing more involved than the ability to stand,
walk and move beautifully." She then declares that "there is always a
reason for poor dancing, but never an excuse." The stage thus set, Louise
offers a canny predance tip from one who practiced what she preached:

An important point that women rarely think of is their psychological
attitude immediately preceding the dance. During the short walk to the floor
she is the center of attraction. . . . The professional trick of walking to the
floor in time with the music is an excellent habit for both men and women
to cultivate. The rhythm and feel of the music is thus assimilated by the time
the couple reach the floor, and the initial steps become a graceful continuation of the approach.[9]

Louise in her Wichita dance studio, 1940; the photo, by Charles Bartlett, appeared on the cover of her first booklet, The Fundamentals of Good Ballroom Dancing.

In her most memorable passage, Louise teaches that:

> The fundamentals of good dancing are not dictated by a stodgy social order. . . . You do not refrain from the mad excesses of the jitter-bug just because Mrs. Snob-Awful glares at you, but because such styles easily become coarse. Neither do you refrain from kicking your feet in the air because so-and-so says it isn't correct; it's simply because there is no room to spare on the average floor, and most people don't like to be kicked unexpectedly. . . .
>
> If you can pick up your partner and whirl her around your head grace-fully, you are privileged to do so—providing you are in a vaudeville act, in the movies, or that every other dancer on the floor has been paid to stay out of the way. . . . [But] as a dancer you are not so much interested in the tricky steps concocted by Jojo Jumpo at the Ha Ha Club, as in the funda-mental precepts that are in perfect taste, no matter where you may be.[10]

In "Five Hints on How to Follow Any Man," she has savvy advice for the wives of all the Jojo Jumpos of Wichita: "Most men fancy themselves good dancers. If you follow them well, you have proved their point for them and have earned their eternal gratitude. Follow, tho' it kills you— then underscore his weaknesses in this booklet and mail it to him."

Louise's "Fundamentals" conclude in a blaze of glory on the subject of "Dance Floor Etiquette." It is Miss Manners forty years ahead of her time —an arch lecture on "the fundamental basis of all good behavior, whether on the dance floor, street, or at a dog fight"—from the woman who once slashed a beau's face with a bouquet of roses in a nightclub:

> It is the woman's privilege to stop dancing or refuse to dance, but never to request a dance unless she knows her partner intimately (or is married to him, in which case it is a demand, not a request). . . .
>
> "Cutting in" is a practice which, for better or worse, will probably remain with us. It is often abused. . . . The woman can never refuse to be cut. The man should never cut in on the same man who cut him. He must wait until a third man intervenes, then he may cut back. . . .
>
> Few men are enchanted by the woman who fires a continual barrage of conversation while she dances. While occasional remarks are not taboo, both men and women should save their conversational charms for the intermis-sion. Friends on the dance floor are given a smile or slight nod of recogni-tion, but the dancers do not stop in the center of the floor for a fireside chat.[11]

As a postscript, Louise recommends some RCA Victor records to prac-tice by, such as the old Wayne King standby "I'm Forever Blowing Bub-bles" for waltzing and Xavier Cugat's "Siboney" rhumba. About 750 copies were printed, and discount rates were available for those wishing to buy her "Fundamentals" in bulk, but it was not exactly a runaway best-seller in Wichita.

"I finally threw away at least 500 of them a few months ago," said Margaret Brooks, Theodore's wife, in 1987.

The Brooks-McCoy Dance Studio had worse problems than just slow pamphlet sales. Foremost among these was Louise's tendency to alienate the precious few students. McCoy remembers, for instance, that she could never refrain from making fun of an adult couple whose last name was Butts. "Louise insulted them every time they came," he says. "She called them Mr. and Mrs. Bull," Why Bull? "Just because it wasn't the right name. Each time I'd correct her, and the next time they came—it was 'Mr. and Mrs. Bull' again."

Eventually the Buttses became annoyed.

A more basic problem was the difference in temperament between Hal and Louise—and, inevitably with Louise, the issue of sex. "Our personalities didn't mesh," he says. The final break came one night after another Innes Tea Room demonstration that had not gone to Louise's liking:

> I was engaged to be married, so I wasn't interested in anything but the business end of the association. . . . So this night, she was chewing my ass out about being such a lousy dancer. I'm pretty quick on the draw, and so was she. We were in a cab—I didn't even have a car then. The cab stopped in front of her place, and she said, "Well, are you going to come in?" And I said, "No, I'm not coming in, and I doubt if I'm coming back." She probably hadn't been rejected too many times. She got out of the car and the taxi took me home, and that's the last time I ever saw her.[12]

Louise had hoped to make a living from the venture, but her partnership lasted less than a year. With or without Hal, it was the wrong time and place: The Brooks-McCoy Studio of Ballroom Dancing came and went before Pearl Harbor.

Pearl Harbor. After the Japanese attack in December 1941, no American city underwent a greater transformation than Wichita. For years, the Boeing Aircraft Company was one of the few heavy industries in a tranquil community mostly occupied with stockyards and farm services. Boeing employed 4,684 before Pearl Harbor, with no great expansion in sight. By 1943, its Wichita assembly lines swelled sixfold to 29,795, working at a feverish, twenty-four-hour-a-day pace to turn out the B-17s needed to win the war. As more and more young men left town on the troop trains, older men and Rosie the Riveters arrived from Oklahoma and Kansas's own small towns to find the jobs that had eluded them for a decade.

But they did not come to Wichita for dance lessons, and Louise needed a job. She wasn't the assembly-line type, nor was she patriotically mesmerized by the war: Hardly a reference to it can be found in any of her letters. By and by, she heard about an opening at Garfield's, one of Wichita's tonier downtown women's stores. On August 3, 1942, she was hired as a salesgirl at the accessories counter—notions, scarves, purses, and belts.

"The first time I saw her after she lost her studio," says her friend James Kiefner, now of the Wichita Public Library, "she took home stacks of books about leather. She read about it from the time it left the animal, how to tan it, all the various types and finished products. She had to know *everything*. It was an example of her intellectual curiosity, that compulsion to learn all there was to know about a thing." [13]

She lasted six weeks at Garfield's, being little more suited to clerking notions than to assembling airplanes. The employment situation was awful, but she was still in good spirits and dabbling in dance. Kiefner, a Wichita University student like Hal McCoy, asked if she would help him and a group of WU students with a skit they were preparing for the college's Spring Celebration. She did, and their friendship continued:

> I never saw her in anything except a long robe, at home or at the studio. It was probably a relic from one of her movies. She'd get up there with her long cigarette holder in front of the ballet mirror and the barre and direct. . . .
>
> She'd already had problems with the local people—they sort of blacklisted her. But I think her self-destruction probably started with her mother, who was a rather severe-looking woman, a Twentieth Century Club type.* With Louise, there was a wall there, but once in a while you could see it come down. . . .
>
> I didn't visit her that often, but whenever I did, she was always in her bare feet, and her room and bed were always strewn with books—Schopenhauer, Nietzsche, you name it, they were all there, all from the public library. And she always had a bowl of fresh fruit—a couple of grapefruit, a banana, grapes. And that was it. That's the way she lived. It was very, very dark. She had the lamp on her bedside table covered by a towel to diffuse the light. She never went downstairs. There was a long, eerie corridor you went down—you sneaked past wherever her mother happened to be. She was unhappy there. She told me she left Hollywood not because she herself decided to leave, but because she was kicked out. I said, "What do you mean 'kicked out'?" And she said, "I like to fuck and drink too much." She was real frank about that. [14]

---

* The Twentieth Century Club, which still exists, was an organization of society matrons whose charitable activities were overshadowed by social ones. Louise had danced for them as a child, and Myra delivered book reviews at their meetings.

SHE HAD those same appetites in Wichita, and despite the job situation, Louise was still inclined to some hell-raising. In 1942, the person with whom she raised the most hell was an old friend named Danny Aikman, who laid claim to being the most outrageous man in Wichita.

Aikman was an actor and dancer with a fabulous, well-developed body. He came from a wealthy oil family in nearby El Dorado and was accustomed to indulging himself. He was also accustomed to getting in trouble with the police, often for promiscuity. Aikman and Brooks met in 1930, during one of her visits home, when he was still a high-school buddy of her brother Theodore. With Louise's encouragement he soon left Wichita to pursue his dance career, but they saw each other afterward in New York and elsewhere. Danny danced in hotels, nightclubs, vaudeville, cabarets, and transatlantic cruise ships—everywhere. He ran with such beautiful people as Ramon Novarro, and later, as "Brent Hodges," Republic Studios signed him for westerns, thanks to his good looks and Kansas-bred skill with horses.

"He was the Cesar Romero type—an adagio dancer," says a friend, "and Louise was one of his closest friends. In Wichita, he threw the wildest parties. . . . Louise was always invited, of course, and I remember one incident with the football team from North High School—it was like the legend of Clara Bow taking on the USC football team, only I think this one was true. Louise liked boys, and Dan liked boys too. They had a helluva time. It was very notorious."

Today, at age seventy-eight, Aikman proudly retains his Screen Actors Guild card—and his fond memories of Louise Brooks:

> She taught me a lot about dancing [in Wichita and] New York, too. . . . I used to let everybody photograph me in the nude as a model . . . I had a show in London at the Dorchester House, and since I had a gorgeous body, I just wore black tights—you could see through them—and they said, "We can't have that in London" and made me wear a gold girdle sort of dance belt. Louise came to see me. She had a lot of wealthy boyfriends. She was always introducing me to some gay millionaire.
>
> One time she went with me on the *Aquitania*. I was entertaining [and] she got one of her boyfriends to get her a stateroom so we could be together a lot, singing and dancing and swimming in the ship's pool. I don't remember who the boyfriend was—some older man in his sixties. He just stayed in his stateroom all the time and didn't come out except to pay the bills.
>
> I came back to Wichita in '42 because my mother had a stroke. As soon as I got there, I called Louise and went right over to see her. Every time she'd throw a wingding, she'd call and ask me over. Louise liked gay people. One night the police raided her place. Once I was just walking down the

street at Douglas and Broadway, wearing this flowered shirt I got in California. They'd never seen anything like it in Wichita. And the police arrested me and charged me with dressing as a woman. Because I wore a shirt with flowers on it! They hated me. They knew I came from a monied family, that I was a star in Europe, and so forth, and they were after me. I was arrested about a dozen times in Wichita, and each time I had to call my father, who had to pay $100 to get me out. Same old $100 fine every time. He couldn't understand what was going on. . . . I was so wild, I didn't give a damn. Louise and I were two chips off the old block. I guess we were about the two wildest things to come out of Wichita.[15]

By the end of 1942, Aikman had had enough of Kansas and vice versa. He left for California and went to work for the Pasadena Playhouse, where he met Ruth St. Denis. "I talked with her about Louise," Aikman says, "and she said, 'Louise was one of the finest dancers we ever had. If she had continued with me, she'd have been one of the world's greatest dancers.' Louise said Ruth fired her, but if that was true, it didn't stop her admiration for her. When I told her I was from Wichita, she immediately said, 'Isn't that where Louise Brooks is from?' "

He sighs and pauses: "She could've been one of the biggest stars that ever lived. But she didn't care. It didn't mean anything to her. She just didn't desire great wealth and fame."

As far as Wichitans were concerned, Louise already had great fame, and it was getting greater. Those who knew her then describe her as either obnoxious or wonderful. Many recall her fighting with Myra and Theo. One remembers her "being drunk and standing on her head in public"; another says she and Theo "were always drunk and together," cursing and having a good time of it—she was "savagely sarcastic to old school chums." Others say she was "delightful" and had "all the charisma in the world—the most elegant thing I'd ever seen."[16]

But if the locals hadn't really blacklisted her yet, they were about to. Louise eventually moved out of her parents' house and into a rented bungalow at the corner of Third and Broadview. There she had more freedom, and some of her guests remained overnight or longer. Eyebrows were raised. "She was always written up in the paper," remembers Jimmy Cavaness, "usually for being drunk. But the write-up I remember most never even mentioned her name—it was a story about a wife coming home and catching her husband 'being taught a ballroom dance horizontally in bed.' Everybody knew who it was."[17] Eyebrows were raised further. And then came the shocking report that Louise Brooks, former film star, had been arrested for "lewd cohabitation" with an unidentified male.

Only in Kansas could one cohabit lewdly, and only Kansas would have a specific statute prohibiting it: "Every man and woman (one or both of whom are married, and not to each other) who shall lewdly and lasciviously abide and cohabit with each other . . . shall on conviction be adjudged guilty of a misdemeanor."[18] You could get six months or a $500 fine, or both, for it.

Her father's legal services were presumably called upon in this event, and there is no evidence that the case ever went to court. No charges had been pressed in the earlier "wingding" raid either. But the very fact of the arrests was a source of rage to Louise and outrage to her detractors. It was no wonder she identified so strongly with Danny Aikman. "They practically ran them both out of town," said one friend.

"The citizens of Wichita either resented me for having been a success or despised me for being a failure," she said years later. "And I wasn't exactly enchanted with them."[19]

"Louise is the cross I have to bear," said her mother throughout it all—not once but repeatedly, and not just to her "richest and fattest friend," Zana Henderson. Myra Brooks seems to have been neither surprised nor devastated by the scandals Louise was generating. As far as she was concerned, it didn't much matter anymore: All was already lost. Louise later said that her mother never forgave her for throwing away her fabulous career, and by all accounts that was correct.

"Like umpteen other actresses, Louise was a mother-propelled performer," says James Card. "To have achieved what she did and then to come back home and operate a dinky little dance school in Wichita—it was an embarrassment to Myra."

But more than that, it was a deep, personal disappointment. The throwing away of Louise's letters and photos had been the most cutting indication, but her mother's every word and glance seemed a reproof. Louise had hoped that, in view of their reconciliation in Hollywood in the thirties, she might now lick her wounds with some maternal sympathy—as one battle-scarred woman to another. But despite Louise's penances, Myra seemed to be withdrawing even more of her sparse affection. "I remember," Theodore later wrote Louise, "how Mother, thinking only of herself, . . . used to carry on bitterly because you and George [Marshall] didn't marry."[20]

For Louise, it was a gall of guilt and anger. She would keep probing the subject of Myra for years, plaintively seeking help from the one great friend they had in common back in Cherryvale, Marcella "Tot" Strickler:

> Tot, for God's sake, what do you think was the driving force behind Mother's wanting to be flattered and admired and waited on? Did she only want to "Be Somebody"? Or did she have some definite aim with a willing-

ness to work like a bastard to get it?*. . . . Tell me, oh tell me, all you know about Mother. . . . What above all was her feeling toward me? I don't think that she was jealous of me as a person—it was only that I was a symbol of what she thought she should have been. And she should have!

Tot's response was reassuring, if not fully convincing:

> There was no jealousy existing in your dear little mother's makeup. She loved you, *I know above all else.* There comes a time in a mother's life when [she gets tired] after having four *howling brats.* . . . A mother can become so common in her family's estimation, that [she] longs for something. Her mental attitude changes.

Tot's daughter Betty—Louise's Cherryvale playmate—also answered her plea for help in understanding her mother. Of the thousands of letters Louise received in her lifetime, Betty's was one of only a dozen that she kept to the end:

> Look, Louise, you can't put logic to your mother and mine—their world was different, everything in it was different. Myra got out in said world up to her uh-huh, and, as I think back, probably got stung many times. . . . Myra did tell me several times that she wanted for you the things that she felt *she* wanted. Also, that you would have made a wonderful school teacher and if you had been left to your own desires and not pushed, would have been content with whatever your lot. . . .
>
> You were just the one with talent and Myra just wanted to be you; she would have done well on the stage, wouldn't she? I think you are probably a lot like Myra in some ways. . . . By the way, did you know that your father played the violin in the attic?[21]

The consensus is that Myra *was* jealous of Louise's success, though she vicariously enjoyed it—which was what distressed her all the more about Louise's "failure."

"Louise told me that when she first went back home, she spent days scrubbing floors," says James Card. "It was very masochistic. Here was a girl who had her picture in all the world film magazines, reducing herself to this. I'm sure she did it to herself as self-punishment. She spoke not so much of guilt as of remorse—but for what? It wasn't for the career itself. For letting down her mother? For jettisoning her Puritan values? It depends on how psychoanalytical you want to get."

Aggravating Louise's pain was Myra's invalid status—the constant fact of her illness. Myra, in fact, was dying. She had only another year to live.

---

* This plea was written on February 11, 1952, when Louise was seeking childhood details for her autobiography. Her long letter included no fewer than thirty questions. Tot's reply to the one above consisted of an amazing, twenty-one-page handwritten story, "In Retrospect"—a romanticized portrait of the Brooks family at Christmas in Cherryvale when Louise was about six.

Leonard and Myra Brooks at home, 924 North Topeka Street, in Wichita, ca. 1935

As for her father, good-natured L.P. was never very adept at saying the right thing in an emotional crisis: He unwittingly cemented Louise's depression one night by telling her that *Overland Stage Raiders* was his favorite of her films.

There were too many insults added to too many injuries. Earlier in 1942, Louise had been in touch with her friend Albert Ascher, a wealthy New York investment banker. Now, on January 8, 1943, he telephoned her, evidently expressing his desire for her company, and she asked him to wire the money for a train ticket. It arrived five days later, whereupon she fled Wichita instantly, that same day. By January 15, she was back in Manhattan.

Kansas had been the severest kind of purgatory, and the final parting with her mother was wrenching, for they knew they would never see each other again. But Wichita had not been without its exhilarating moments. Aside from the revels with Theo and Danny Aikman, Louise had achieved a certain mysterious artistic ecstasy and "closure" to her life as a dancer. She revealed this only to James Card, and not until a dozen years later, in a letter with few details. Yet the profoundly introspective nature of the experience is a revelation in itself:

> In 1941–1943 in Kansas, I did two perfect dances, and I did them for those farmers and had them breathing with me. Brahms and Debussy, hardly any movement. Back in New York, the night before I was to go to Music Corporation to see about some nightclub jobs, I danced them for Peggy Fears. She has exquisite showman sense. "Brooksie, they're marvelous. I couldn't take my eyes off your face." That was good enough for me. I never went to MCA, and I've never danced since. I'm a ham, but only for a small select audience.[22]

Louise, New York City, ca. 1946

17 · Lulu in Hell

The pain of life, that haunts our narrow way,
I cannot shed with this or that attire.
Too old am I to be content with play,
Too young to live untroubled by desire.
— F A U S T in Goethe's *Faust*

F O R Louise, the next decade was more down-and-out than the one before—a cloudy, gin-drowned, hand-to-mouth existence with generous helpings of despair. "Only Dostoyevsky collaborating with Budd Schulberg could tell the story of Louise Brooks from 1930 to 1955," wrote James Card. "The last years of that time—from 1948 to 1955—were the period of full retreat."[1]

Even the act of retreating was nightmarish. Among the events to which Louise was oblivious was World War II, and in her haste to get out of Wichita, she failed to reckon on troop movements and military rail priority. In Chicago, where New York passengers had to switch lines, she was "thrown off a train . . . which was taken over by soldiers, with only $10 in my pocket." For the next twenty-five years, she told Kevin Brownlow, "I have dreamed nightly of losing my money, my luggage, and all my friends disappearing."[2] It was a traumatic realization of just how broke and alone she really was.

The once-mighty Louise Brooks was frightened and down to her last $10 bill. But another train came soon enough, and on January 15, 1943, after three years of prairie flagellation, she was back in New York, staying at the Wyndham on West 58th Street, courtesy of Albert Ascher. "I had crept to a hole to find out what I had become and how to find the way back to what I was," she said.[3]

Ascher, then forty-four, had recently co-founded the William E. Pollock Company. He evidently met Louise through Otto Kahn, but the only thing known about their relationship is that it was brief and held no long-term prospects. A few days after her return, she applied for an instructor's job at the Arthur Murray Dance Studio, taught a few classes on a trial basis, and was gone within a week. It was time to face the truth: She had exhausted the possibilities of dance, as well as film and theater.

From her earliest years in New York, Louise had had close connections with some of the most powerful press czars—men like Joseph M. Patterson of the New York *Daily News* and Robert R. McCormick of the Chicago *Tribune*, not to mention Hearst and Beaverbrook. She never asked one of them for a favor. Now, however, she called the man she regarded more highly than all the rest: William S. Paley.

Brooks and Paley had communicated rarely, if at all, after 1932. But once she reestablished contact, he responded with amazing speed. She had been back in New York just twelve days when she and Paley met at noon on January 27, 1943, in his office at CBS. He spent that same night with her at the Wyndham, concealing his shock at her condition:

"When she came back from [Wichita] to see me, she looked awful. Her face looked bad, her clothes were horrible. She was ashamed of the way she looked. . . . I called my friend Ben Gimbel, whose wife ran the Saks dress department, and I said, 'Look, ask your wife to do me a favor—pick out some clothes for her. . . .' We had one or two episodes then, but that was it."[4]

"Episodes" notwithstanding, Paley made it a firm practice never to give jobs to friends or relatives; during the entire course of his career, none of his children ever held so much as an internship at CBS, and he would make no nepotistic exception for Louise. He simply directed her to the CBS personnel department where, two days after their tryst at the Wyndham, she met with Louis Schurr. Paley did not intervene and Louise did not mention his name: Her own impressive show-business credentials sufficed to secure her a radio tryout, and exactly one week later, on February 5, she made her first disembodied appearance on a program called "Hobby Lobby." Her voice was mellifluous and a role soon followed in the soap opera "Aunt Jenny," working with such prominent radio voices as Jim Backus and Kenneth MacKenna.

It seemed as though she might find a niche, or at least an income, not to mention a new social life: On June 29, Louise accompanied Paley, Gimbel, and two others to the smash hit of the season, *Oklahoma!* In June, she met up again with Robert Benchley who, to her pleasant surprise, presented her with an inscribed copy of Pascal's *Pensées* ("from Blaise Benchley to Blaise Brooks") that she cherished for life.*

---

* "The saint's name Blaise struck him as very funny," Louise later wrote to Kevin Brownlow. "It would have been more dramatic had Humphrey [Bogart, friend of both Brooks and Benchley] given me the book, since St. Blaise is venerated as the Patron Saint against throat diseases." In

By August 1943 she had graduated to a part in the popular "Ellery Queen" mystery series—but it was her last. Louise's exit from radio was as sudden as her entrance six months before.

"I quit, for [a] hundred reasons, including Wounded Pride of Former Star," she told Kenneth Tynan. One of the hundred reasons was that she had to work "almost incognito," according to James Card: "She claimed to have originated the idea for 'What's My Line?,' though the guy she worked for got credit for it."

Meanwhile in 1943, *The American Weekly* discovered Louise was back in New York. This was a well-heeled magazine but not a very reputable one. Its editors "gave me $1,500 for one of those dreadful, ghostwritten confession stories. But never being able to get a word of sex or men or name-dropping out of me, they never used it. Ethelda Bedford, who wrote it, was delighted with her title, 'I'll Never Grow Old'—because of Dixie Dugan. I found it most depressing."[5]

"I was in love with Louise before I ever met her," says Lothar Wolff—and he was just nineteen when they met.

That was Berlin, 1928. This is New York, 1986, and in his East Side apartment he smiles at the memory of a summons from his boss at PARUFAMET* telling him to go meet G. W. Pabst, who needed help with *Pandora's Box*. There was no one in charge of publicity, and Pabst asked Wolff if he could handle it.

"I couldn't write a sentence," Wolff recalls. "I was completely ungifted. But Pabst was known for his generosity, and so I said yes. I received sixty marks a week—about twenty dollars. As far as I was concerned, I had arrived."

Wolff was dazzled by Louise's pictures—and then by the real thing. In the coming months, he succeeded brilliantly in placing stories and photos of her in every major German publication. She called him "Woofie," and their fond, youthful friendship continued far beyond *Pandora*.

"I couldn't find her when I first came to New York in 1936," says Wolff, who then worked as a film editor for *The March of Time* newsreels, but after the two refugees were reunited, "we were very close. We used to go out together, mostly to restaurants, but also I used to cook dinner for her at my broken-down apartment on East 40th Street. She was very good at adjusting to adversity, and I didn't have much money either in those days. There wasn't much loose change. We were just pleased to be together."

Louise always found Wolff's gentle manner charming: "I remember

---

Benchley's suite at the Royalton that day, Louise noticed a framed photo of a child playing a large stringed instrument. Benchley had titled it "Little Girl Going Down on Cello."
* An acronym for Paramount, UFA, and Metro-Goldwyn-Mayer, PARUFAMET was the European distributor for all three big studios.

once in 1943 in Lothar Wolff's apartment with the first violinist of the Philadelphia Orchestra—Woofie put on a record of one of Beethoven's quartets and then hauled down a book which explained what the quartet meant!"[6] It struck her as delightfully odd that anyone would *read* about a musical composition.

But reading was what Louise did almost all the time these days, even though Lothar did his best to get her out and about:

> She was a joy to be with but always unpredictable. Once, Louise and I and two other people were walking along in front of the Plaza, and suddenly Louise just literally ran away—she dashed across the street without saying anything, and didn't come back. She never said why. She just felt like it. One minute you thought you had a handle on her, and the next you realized she was too complex to fit that. She wasn't ambitious. She never went *after* anything. Some romantic encounter would always have first place in her life and overshadow everything else. Nothing she ever did surprised me. . . .[7]

Wolff was a rare friend to Louise; he was, first of all, one of the few who spanned her whole adult life, but more important than its length was the nature of their friendship—the fact that his affection never varied whether she was a success or a flop. He accompanied her on visits to various new and old acquaintances, such as Syd and Steffie Robbins and the Film Guild crowd—Dwight and Steve Wiman and Townsend Martin of rose-slashing fame. Lothar also instigated a meeting between Louise and Iris Barry of the Museum of Modern Art, the most important figure in film preservation in America. But Louise came away unimpressed:

> In 1943 Iris Barry, who started the Museum of Modern Art film department, had me to lunch with Lothar Wolff and she said she wasn't going to get a copy of *Pandora's Box*—that it had no *lasting* value.[8]

IRIS BARRY'S low opinion of *Pandora's Box* reflected the decline of G. W. Pabst's reputation during World War II. Earlier, he was a darling of the left, for after the apolitical Brooks films, he conquered the sound medium with three triumphantly political pictures. *Westfront 1918* (1930) was a powerful antiwar film that attacked resurgent German nationalism. *The Threepenny Opera* (1931), a striking adaptation of the musical, received high praise from everyone but Bertolt Brecht* and still holds up after half a century. *Kameradschaft* (*Comradeship*, 1931), a mine-disaster tale in which Frenchmen and Germans unite to overcome national chauvinism, won a special League of Nations peace prize.

---

* Brecht fell out with Pabst over the handling and the elimination of certain scenes. He filed a lawsuit, which he lost.

Many hailed Pabst as Europe's single best director—the one who best preserved the essentials of silents while mastering sound. He'd been in Paris directing Fyodor Chaliapin in *Don Quixote* when Hitler came to power in 1933. The Nazis soon banned his pictures, and in 1939, he returned to Austria (since the Anschluss, a part of Germany) in order to sell his family property in Styria and collect his aged mother for their planned emigration to America. But when Germany invaded Poland in September, all travel was curtailed.

Pabst was stuck inside the Reich. He languished there for two years until forced by finances to contact his old mentor, Carl Froelich, at the Reichsfilmkammer in Berlin. Froelich got the ban on him lifted—and so it was that he made two German, if not necessarily "Nazi," films during the war. The first was a mediocre entertainment picture called *Komödian-ten (Comedians)*, with Gustav "Jack the Ripper" Diessl. Because it dealt with the formation of a German National Theater, it won the Gold Medal at the Fascist-controlled Venice Film Festival of 1941. More controversial was *Paracelsus*, filmed in Prague in 1942. This allegory of the sixteenth-century physician-alchemist was construed as pro-Nazi and would prove tremendously damaging to Pabst.

"With Pabst," wrote James Card, "the crime of which Furtwängler was accused seemed even more grievous. His many leftist admirers who, look-ing at his films through rose-tinted glasses, had seen him as their cinema champion in Western Europe, considered Pabst's return to Austria in 1939 an act of outright betrayal."[9]

Louise blamed Leni Riefenstahl for "trying to put Pabst with the Nazis" and defended him staunchly. "Except for getting Goebbels' okay to make films through his friend Froelich, he did not [do] a Nazi thing."[10] But Louise's friend Lotte Eisner was among those who never forgave Pabst for making *any* kind of movies in Hitler's Germany. He had at least "tolerated" the Nazis, she said, and in a letter to Louise, Eisner recounted a postwar visit during which she grilled Pabst about the matter:

> I said, why were you in Vienna during the Munich affair? "Because my poor father died. See, here, the announcement." And why were you in Berlin when war broke out? "Because my father-in-law was very ill—see here the announcement of his death." And why didn't you leave? "Here are the tickets for a boat to the USA for me and my family." And what happened? "I lifted a too heavy trunk and got a hernia. Here is the proof of my being operated." So he had all the proofs carefully kept. I said, "Through Brecht I have read a lot of [English mystery writer] Edgar Wallace—always the man with the best alibis is the culprit."
>
> You see, he had become very slick. It was his bad luck and his bad wife maybe. . . . I know you like Pabst, but that was his fate, alas.[11]

But Lotte and Louise agreed on the subject of Riefenstahl: "In 1932," Eisner wrote Brooks, "Leni came to my office at the *Film-Kurier* and asked me to come to tea with her and a wonderful man. Now, I was always mistrusting Leni's bad taste, so I asked with whom and she replied, 'Adolf Hitler.' And I said, 'I do not want to meet that damned fellow!' "*

Years later, when Kevin Brownlow wrote Brooks that he had just interviewed Riefenstahl in Munich, Louise could not resist asking, "Did she tell you whether she laid Hitler?"

Aside from her fleeting career in radio, Louise had two other wartime jobs, both of which she loathed. The time was 1944–1945:

> Sammy Colt, Ethel Barrymore's son, said to a boy who worked in publicity, "Bobby, get Brooksie a job." And I found myself, with no preparation, no contacts, no nothing, writing items and those smelly little stories for [columnist Walter] Winchell. My success astonished and angered my boss even more because I never opened a paper or read a column, and one day when I told him not to mess around with my stuff after I'd spent hours cutting a story from 200 words to one line, Rumpelstiltskin, screaming that he was a Columbia graduate, fired me, and nothing but the unexpected gratitude with which I accepted my dismissal kept him from jumping up and down through the floor. For it's a nasty, sneaky racket, a black mark against me, I've always felt, 'til the other month when I realized how much I'd learned about good writing, sweating down those stories to a line.[12]

A similar job followed, and a similar firing, after which "I had to move from the decent little hotel where I'd been living to a grubby hole on First Avenue at 59th Street."[13] She was ready to stay in that hole and not emerge, but a few stalwarts such as Lothar Wolff kept tabs on her and escorted her out. On Christmas Eve 1944, he took her to the Royalton Hotel to see her old friend Blyth Daly, the stage actress who had achieved immortality—at least in Louise's estimation—for biting Chaplin's lip and inspiring a scandalous round of speculation in the tabloids during his 1925 visit to New York for the *Gold Rush* opening. "I was fascinated by Blyth," wrote Louise of that evening. "She flattered me at the same time as she defamed me. . . . Woofie and I brought her a bottle of champagne. She was telling a story about me—'that was when Brooksie had clap on 'Handkerchief Hill'—and Jimmie Backus said, 'Blyth, do not tell this lie again.' "[14]

---

* Eisner's comments, quoted by Louise in a January 14, 1977, letter to Herman Weinberg, are followed by Louise's further complaints about "the nauseating lies Leni tells about her friendship with Hitler. I wonder what one day John Wayne, Sammy Davis, Frank Sinatra, Bob Hope and Chuck Connors will be telling about their friendship with Nixon?"

Blyth was a great storyteller, and she got a lot of raw material from Sam Colt and his mother, Ethel.

But Louise had some up-to-the-minute Ethel Barrymore material of her own, thanks to her affair with Sam (whose father, Russell Colt, had left him much of the Colt arms fortune):

"One morning in New York in 1945 when Ethel's son, Sammy Colt, was in my apartment and rang his mother to explain why he had not completed some mission to Wall Street, you could have heard her all over the building as she roared, 'Get out of that damned whore's apartment this minute and come home.' "[15]

Myra Brooks died on April 20, 1944. Her last words were, "God bless Leonard, God bless my children. Oh, God, be merciful, forgive me."

Louise grieved in her silent way, with no outpouring. Their parting fifteen months earlier in Wichita had been unmistakably final. It was Louise's habit to distance herself emotionally from those who were about to leave her; her mother's physical passing thus seemed almost a technicality. But it did not lessen the obsession to "know" her and to "find" her in odd places for the rest of her life. The matter of Myra's sexuality particularly haunted Louise. She asked old friend Tot Strickler two pointed questions about her mother:

"Didn't she really detest sex? And men too?"

To which Tot replied with a cryptic: "Yes and no."

Louise was less interested in her father's sexual attitudes. Brother Theo was the authority on that subject, and he kept her informed of his findings up to the very end:

> Daddy's preoccupation with sex, which continued into his 93rd year, is fascinating to relate. It included such objective expressions as banging the Negro maids, and, when his personal prowess declined, such vicarious delights as listening to other people do it, for which purpose he ultimately bought a hearing aid. Yet, I have mother's testimony to the effect that he was an unsatisfactory partner, though a demanding one.[16]

LOUISE certainly did not detest sex. As the years went by, she manifested a continuing, if not increasing, interest in it. She was, after all, a woman whose beauty and sexuality had played a central role in her creative and private life alike, whose enjoyment of sex was enthusiastic and independent of age.

But at this point, she was also a woman reflecting on the deeper mysteries of sexuality that gave meaning to life itself. As always, she assumed her own experiences to be universal. But if the generalizations were dubious, the self-analysis was razor-sharp: Louise was her own psychiatrist, and her letters became a way of exorcising demons—most of all, a real sexual demon from childhood. To Kevin Brownlow, for example, she wrote of D. W. Griffith's fondness for extremely young girls:

> I know all the marks of that kind of man. When he was making *That Royle Girl* and *The Sorrows of Satan* at Paramount in New York I used to go on his set and meet him around the studio and he *never* spoke to me. But he would always *look* at me. People who have had the same sexual experiences always convey this knowledge between them with their eyes. And further, he was obsessed with the rape of young virgins in his films. When you add his perversion to booze and religious superstition, you have a real nut. . . . This may sound like a superficial approach . . . , but in every work of art the composer is trying to figure out why he did what he did, and what were the injuries that betrayed him. Always it returns to sexual experience. [17]

The thought was borrowed from—or confirmed by—Tolstoy, whose pre-Freudian view she often quoted: "Man survives earthquakes, epidemics, the horrors of war, and all the agonies of the soul, but the tragedy that has always tormented him, and always will, is the tragedy of the bedroom." [18] Louise's post-Freudian view went a step further:

"There can be no doubt about it," she said, "sex is basic to security. If you think you fail in that, nothing else can compensate for this inner sense of humiliation. Thank God, at 35 I banished my shame and Puritan background and learned how to please others and myself." [19]

These days, she was also rethinking her artistic life, with distance, in terms of its sexual sources and implications. Her performing career had begun (and ended) in dancing—the most erotic of art forms. It had been a short step from there to the *Scandals* and *Follies*, the most erotic of Broadway's "legitimate" offerings. Cheesecake eroticism followed in Hollywood and then the sublime erotica of G. W. Pabst. It was still too early, and *Pandora* too little appreciated, for her to know that her own immortality would result from that last great foray into sexuality. Two marriages and many affairs were in ashes, and in the wake of those and other bitter disappointments, it seemed as though all her beauty and sexuality had ever produced was unhappiness.

There was a recurring pattern in Louise's life that was even more galling now, in plain middle age, than in her beautiful youth: Few men had believed that a woman so gorgeous could be so frighteningly and aggressively intelligent, too. Or as her brother Theo succinctly put it: "She scared men shitless." [20]

There were exceptions, of course—men like Wanger, Chaplin, Marshall, Paley, Pabst—though they perhaps had their frightened moments, too. What those exceptional males had in common was a certain intellec-

tual security, the will to dominate, and varying degrees of already established power.

But for Louise, most of the time the battle of the sexes was exactly that.
She viewed most relationships with men as *conflicts* —conflict into which
she plunged zestfully. Various male writers have labeled Brooks (and the
character of Lulu) a "nymphomaniac"—a sexist term Louise addressed
many years later in a remarkable letter containing her empirical views of
men by ethnic breakdown:

> For 35 years I have been studying men's hatred of women. Mary Heming-
> way weighs it out in her book about Ernest. It is the Howard Hawks' [idea
> of] two brave fighting buddies (homos) who "prove" their "masculinity" by
> occasional brutal rampages among women. If I may slip into generalities . . .
> Irish men hate women, fear women—and they win all the lousy lay medals.
> But do not confuse sex performance with "love." Contrary to all this stuff
> women are putting out today about the need for having orgasms, sexual
> satisfaction never holds people together. . . . Among American men, South-
> ern men have always most loved women (as demonstrated by Carter's regard
> for Rosalyn). Southern men grew up among women and felt at home with
> them. . . .
>
> In my unwritten masterpiece, *Men in My Bed*, I would advise all non-
> Jewish women to marry Jews. When I was in the *Follies* (1925) I observed
> that all the Irish Catholic girls from Brooklyn, Bronx, New Jersey, married
> and stayed married to Jews, never rotten Irishmen. When I went to Holly-
> wood I observed that the most intelligent actresses married Jews. (Frances
> Goldwyn gave me excellent advice on this matter which I could not follow
> because then as now, wealth, security, position were not my major goals.
> Alas!)
>
> Now—why do Jews love or at least not fear/hate women? (Stroheim as a
> genius is excepted.) It is because Jews alone are not afraid of women's brains.
> . . . I have never heard of a Jew beating up a woman because he lost an
> argument or doubted his mental competence. Contrarily, whereas Eddie
> Sutherland and George Marshall deeply resented my love of books, Walter
> Wanger first gave me the Russians and Herman Mankiewicz Aldous Huxley,
> and Paul Bern took on the cultural expansion of Sally Rand, Joan Crawford,
> Clara Bow and Jean Harlow. I still have a beautifully bound *Kipling Verse*
> Paul gave me. (Sally and Jean were intelligent women whom he helped to
> self-respect. Joan Crawford made the mistake of trying to read *Elizabeth and
> Essex*, became a literary critic and condemned Scott Fitzgerald. Clara stared
> at the title until she felt like Queen Elizabeth and demanded to play the
> part.) [21]

Louise was no "nymphomaniac," just a connoisseur of heterosexual
men. She was also fond of gay men, and comfortable with them, from her
earliest performing days with Denishawn. She once went so far as to say,

"The best lovers I ever had were homosexuals."[22] At least one intimate friend, however, thought it wasn't a lover she was seeking in her gay friendships: "She wanted a mother, and she sought it in men. But most straight men aren't mothers, and so she sought gay men. . . . She felt a genuine kinship with homosexuals—even to the point of the physical mannerisms, limp wrists, and so forth she used in conversation. In some ways, she was the epitome of what they wanted to be. She knew this and was totally at home with them. She was wary with straight men, but with gay men she was totally at ease."[23]

And, as she repeatedly made clear, she was fond of lesbians, too. Her close friendship with Pepi Lederer had caused tongues to wag about Louise even before *Pandora's Box* dared to display Sapphic love on a movie screen. Thereafter, Louise cultivated an ambivalent, almost coy attitude about lesbianism, as in her comments on the "tense portrait of sterile lesbian passion" that Pabst had tricked out of the unwilling Alice Roberts:

> At the time, her conduct struck me as silly. The fact that the public could believe an actress's private life to be like one role in one film did not come home to me till 1964, when I was visited by a French boy. Explaining why the young people in Paris loved *Pandora's Box*, he put an uneasy thought in my mind.
>
> "You talk as if I were a lesbian in real life," I said.
>
> "But of course!" he answered, in a way that made me laugh to realize I had been living in cinematic perversion for thirty-five years.[24]

Feigned surprise infuses that "realization"; Louise had been aware of the lesbian tag at least since Pepi and San Simeon, where there was a "fierce house law of 'no fucking,' although the fags and dykes were allowed to carry on like crazy."[25] She told Kevin Brownlow that "by the time I got to Hollywood, everyone thought I was a lesbian" and speculated that it may have influenced Pabst's selection of her to play Lulu.[26] She also admitted to a certain calculation on the subject: "Although I always had a batch of [lesbians] around to feed my vanity, I never had an affair with Peggy [Fears]. . . ."[27] There were many variations on this theme, later on, in her articles and correspondence:

> I had a lot of fun writing "Marion Davies' Niece," leaving the lesbian theme in question marks. All my life it has been fun for me.[28]

> When I am dead, I believe that film writers will fasten on the story that I am a lesbian. . . . I have done lots to make it believable. Peggy Fears and I used to hold hands in public and make Blumie and George Marshall wild. All my women friends have been lesbians. But that is one point upon which I agree positively with [Christopher] Isherwood: There is no such thing as

bisexuality. . . . Ordinary people, although they may accommodate themselves for reasons of whoring or marriage, are one-sexed. Out of curiosity I had two affairs with girls—they did nothing for me.[29]

She had previously declared: "Almost all lesbians are bisexual, partly because, just like the homos, they love the other sex too, and partly because a girl has to live and men are still the best bet."[30] She was always playfully inconsistent on the subject. Years later, when she saw that Brownlow's book *The Parade's Gone By* . . . included a photograph of her in mannish suit and hairdo, she wrote him: "You little stinker. How come you follow the Garbo photo with that dyke photo of me?"[31] To which he replied: "I love that picture of you. Far from being Dyke, I think it's terribly sexy." She replied: "Whatever makes you think being dyke is not being sexy? On the contrary, it is double sexy. Same with boys."[32]

Added to the ambiguity was Charles Weidman's assessment: "Louise, everybody says you're a lesbian, but you're not really, you're a *pansy*." What Weidman meant is obscure, but what Louise meant, in frequently quoting it, was that she loved women as a homosexual man, rather than as a lesbian, would love them.

"I never saw any indications of her overtly or covertly making any passes at a woman," says Lothar Wolff, who observed her with equal fascination at twenty-one, thirty-one, and forty-one. "If anything, I got the impression she didn't care one way or the other. I don't think the lesbian-attraction thing was a conscious process. Wherever she went, there wasn't a head that didn't turn—even among the staid Germans. She was breathtakingly beautiful, and something went out from her, a certain sparkle, which enchanted people. They couldn't take their eyes off her."[33]

Louise's petulant unpredictability about sex seemed to mystify herself as much as her lovers:

> Quite early in life I learned to pay attention to what I *did* and not what I *thought*. I would be dressing to go out to dinner with some guy. I would say to myself I am not going to get drunk and lay this bastard and all the time I would be filling my purse, not with the Cartier cigarette case and compact which I might lose drunk, but with lesser items. Or I would have a date with some man who might do me good saying to myself I am going to be enchanting and flattering, all the while rehearsing the vicious truths I would hurl at him.[34]

The operative rule with Louise was neither heterosexuality, homosexuality, or bisexuality. It was just sexuality—often marinated in alcohol. Her highly charged approach to boys and girls alike is summed up by a warning to one of her last lovers: "If I ever bore you it'll be with a knife."

· · ·

Tallulah Bankhead in the late 1940s

As far as the theory and practice of sexuality were concerned, none of Louise's friends was more delightful than Tallulah Bankhead. Their friendship had long predated this 1940s period, stretching back even earlier than Pepi's cocaine searches in the thirties. Before, during, and since that time, Tallulah was noted for her wild parties, to which Louise was often invited. Ethel Barrymore showed up at one of them, and Louise quoted her first words upon entering: "Has Tallulah taken her dress off yet?" Tallulah stories were legion, and it was always difficult to separate the true from the apocryphal. One of the best Bankhead herself told to John Kobal. She was at a Democratic political gathering in honor of her "divine friend," Adlai Stevenson, when she had to go to the bathroom. No sooner was she settled in than she noticed the absence of toilet paper:

> So I looked down and saw a pair of feet in the next stall. I knocked very politely and said: "Excuse me, dahling, I don't have any toilet paper. Do you?" And this very proper Yankee voice said: "No, I don't." Well, dahling, I had to get back to the podium for Adlai's speech, so I asked her very politely, you understand, "Excuse me, dahling, but do you have any Klee-

nex?" And now this quite chilly voice said: "No, I don't." So I said: "Well, then, dahling, do you happen to have two fives for a ten?"[35]

Nowadays, with the end of the war and the onset of something resembling "mature middle age," Tallulah's gatherings tended to be a bit more *intime*. According to Louise, she was particularly enamored of sailors, and not very choosy about name, rank, or serial number. Louise occasionally joined in, but was less impressed by Tallulah's men and drugs than by the vitality of her mind. Tallulah often held forth on the deathly fear of IDEAS in Hollywood—one of many viewpoints she and Louise shared. Neither woman had any real organized set of beliefs of her own, but both were always open to new and sometimes wild ideas about art, sex, and life. Their lesbian attitudes, for example, were strikingly similar: Louise once quoted Tallulah as saying, "I only became a Lez because I needed the publicity—I had to get a job," clarifying that "in the '20s and '30s, a Lesbian was tops in desirability, especially with a girlfriend as a side dish."[36]

Even their film careers were alike, to the extent that neither's talents had been fully utilized; neither had made very many or very good pictures in America; both had been undisciplined and ill-advised, yet they could now view their aimlessly drifting lives with more humor than self-pity. Louise spoke often of Bankhead to her friend William Klein, who says:

> In that whole New York period, I believe her favorite person was Bankhead. She thought Tallulah should've run for President, that she was the most intelligent woman she ever knew. She adored her and spent a lot of time with her—their apartments were not too far apart. Tallulah of course was heavy into the drug scene and would occasionally offer Louise cocaine, but Louise didn't get into that. She just admired her enormously—the fact that Tallulah would give money to people who needed it all the time; it sounded to me like she helped Louise on occasion, too. Somebody could just show up at the door, and Tallulah'd reach for her handbag. Louise thought she had all the elements that were really striking in a woman—she had the intelligence, the generosity, the talent. She told me stories of wild nights out on the town when they'd try out different crazy things. Once they decided to go out to a bar and find a black guy, and they did. They brought him back to Tallulah's, and—afterwards—the three of them agreed they didn't think it was "right" and wouldn't do it again. . . . It wasn't the *ménage à trois* they didn't think was "right," it was that blacks and whites shouldn't mix! She always spoke of those days with Tallulah as being her most "alive."[37]

THE GOINGS-ON with Tallulah were tame compared with the life of another old friend—Barbara Bennett. From 1929 to 1941, while sisters Constance and Joan (now Mrs. Walter Wanger) made three trips apiece to divorce court, Barbara was often quoted on the domestic bliss of being married to Morton Downey and raising five children and 110 chickens on a fifty-acre farm in Connecticut. Perhaps there were marital strains even before she met Jack Randall in Hollywood, but in any event, Barbara became enamored of the cowboy actor just as Louise became unenamored of him.

Louise had an inkling about the developing romance, but she was surprised to learn that the two were married in Ensenada, Mexico, in June 1941—just three days after Barbara's divorce from Downey. In her haste to be free of him, Barbara had given up custody of her children and agreed to be denied visiting rights unless she was in a state of "complete sobriety" and conducted herself "with propriety becoming a good mother"—the bitter Downey to be sole judge of her compliance. Press photos, meanwhile, showed her and Randall at bottle-strewn nightclub tables in Hollywood and New York.

Barbara almost immediately regretted her surrender of custody and began a futile series of lawsuits which succeeded only in dredging up the "unfit mother" charges and her well-known drinking binges. Each court appearance ended in more humiliation than the one before. In the final hearing, Superior Court Judge Edward Quinlan of Bridgeport, Connecticut, denied her any partial custody because she had "permitted volatile infatuation to be substituted for mother love."

The always resilient Louise was on friendly enough terms with both Barbara and Jack Randall to meet them in New York at the Westbury Hotel on June 24, 1943. Barbara told her about landing roles in some westerns with the good-hearted Buck Jones, who, as Louise observed, always had a soft spot for washed-up actresses. If Barbara was happy with Randall, Louise was glad for her—but Barbara's happiness was never to last for long. In the summer of 1945, at the modest peak of his cowboy career, Randall was killed when his head struck a tree as his horse galloped before the cameras on a B western. Six months later, in March 1946, Barbara attempted suicide in New York City. And then, in July 1953, Barbara astonished everyone with her next marriage—to her late husband's brother, Robert Livingston—followed by another, to Canadian journalist Laurent Surprenant. The end of Barbara Bennett's story was recorded by Louise in the cruel tone she reserved for her closest friends—and for herself:

> Barbara made a career of her emotions. Periods of work or marriage were terminated by her frightening, abandoned laughter of despair and failure. Only her death, in 1958, achieved in her fifth suicide attempt, could be termed a success.[38]

AT ABOUT this time, Louise met a woman named Jane Kent, who ran an "escort service" out of the Barbizon Hotel. It is clear that they became good friends over the next decade; what is less clear is whether Louise became professionally "affiliated" with the service. Louise would intimate, but never claim outright, that she had been reduced to prostitution during her 1943–1955 years in New York City. She preferred to leave the question —was she or wasn't she?—in the same nebulous state as the lesbian matter. But various friends say the answer was yes.

"She wasn't a hooker on the *streets*, for God's sake," says one. "But there was a point when she simply didn't know where her next meal was coming from, and a phone call to the right person could produce a lonely gentleman in need of an evening's companionship. It was very discreet, and I think, all things considered, infrequent. She did what she had to do."

Larry Quirk, nephew of *Photoplay* editor James Quirk, recalls conversations with Louise in 1960 in which "she said she was working with a madam for a while. One place she talked about was the Hotel Martinique, where you met sailors or took them, as long as the cops were paid off. She told me once she was 'knocked down' [arrested] by a cop who wasn't getting paid."[39]

Danny Aikman, her friend and fellow exile from Wichita, saw her occasionally at this time: "We'd go to the Waldorf or the Plaza and have a lot of laughs. I always loved Louise, and I felt very badly about some things in her life. I guess you know she became a call girl in New York."[40]

But perhaps "call girl" wasn't the term. Louise left one grim revelation in the form of an autobiographical story called "Amateur Night in Greenwich Village," set in 1943. It opens with "Denise"—an ex–film star, now 37—fretting about her two-month overdue hotel bill as the phone rings. It's Henry Ormond, "a rich old bachelor in the leather goods business [who is] very generous to girls who are nice to him and go to his parties."

> [Denise] still had her beautiful clothes, and her friends didn't know yet that she was busted. It wouldn't be long, though. Rich people smelled a touch a mile away. Only today she had talked about getting a job, acting in radio soap operas. . . .[41]

In Ormond's hotel room, "she saw over his shoulder, neatly on the desk before the window, the well-known tray, loaded with liquor bottles, soda water, ice and glasses." He mixed her a strong scotch and soda, and himself a weak one. "You know," he said, "I never go to movies myself, but [a friend] tells me that you were a big success until you got hard to handle." Denise overcomes her impulse to run away, but, "like boiling water poured into a cut glass bowl, something delicate cracked in her mind. For a moment she didn't know where she was. Where was this room? In what hotel? In what town?"

Ormond is impotent but has other forms of sexual amusement. He takes her to a Greenwich Village club where girls dressed as men fondle him in the dark. A pair of blond sixteen-year-old twins join them, as does a tough cookie named Pat and another woman to whose apartment they adjourn. There, after the other girls perform for him, it is Denise's turn. Dazed though she is, she is about to comply, when Pat approaches with a riding crop and inexplicably slashes it across Denise's face. The blow stuns her into reality instead of sadomasochism. In tears, she flees—turning over to a cabbie the lone $5 bill she got from Ormond.

So ends Louise's darkest piece of fiction—and nonfiction.

It was not morality but inability to feign sexual pleasure that curtailed her career as a prostitute. Anyway, the idea of professional whoredom was too ironic to be borne. People had often accused her of it, but she had always been secure in the knowledge of her own strange form of integrity. It was too late now to learn or turn the tricks of that trade.

In the orgiastic "Walpurgis Night's Dream" of Goethe's *Faust*, there is a taunting exchange that spoke forcefully to Louise at this point in her life:

YOUNG WITCH: You need powder and petticoat,
You matrons old and shoddy;
But I sit naked on my goat
And show my fine young body.
OLD WITCH: Our manners are too good, my dear,
To match your youthful bragging;
Though young and tender now, don't fear:
You'll rot, and soon be sagging.

The ephemeral beauty of youth was a subject dear to the heart of Louise's great dance teacher, Ted Shawn. On his seventy-fourth birthday, Shawn posed for a nude photograph and sent it in his annual newsletter to his friends, explaining that "to a dancer, his body is something from which he cannot depart, and like a painter viewing his painting, or a sculptor his carving, a writer his book, a composer hearing his works played—we are undetachable from our bodies. . . . So I have always had a birthday picture taken every year as a record of how the instrument stands up under increasing years." [42]

Only Ted Shawn (or someone equally well preserved) could so clinically contemplate the erosion of an ideal physique. Louise had more ambivalent thoughts on the subject:

I had always looked upon my beauty as a curse because I was regarded as a whore rather than an actress. Now at least I understand that my beauty was a blessing. It was my lack of understanding the way to merchandise it that was the curse.[43]

Louise was thirty-nine in 1945. If it is difficult for ordinary mortals to lose their youthful good looks, how much harder for someone of truly breathtaking beauty? She could no longer deny the solid onset of middle age. With her gray hairs came the stealthy lines, etched in the corners of her mouth from a hundred thousand little muscle-pulls of tugging in cigarette smoke, and other lines around the eyes, dug by every squint of irony or suspicion cast upon all the lovers and strangers of a lifetime. Missing in action one day was the translucent quality of her skin, replaced by a grayness. If anything stayed unchanged it was her eyes—and yet they, too, were betrayed by their surrounding territory: It was time for the darkening shadows and that barely perceptible deepening—the "receding" of the eyes, an optical illusion in more ways than one.

As if deliberately to negate her world-famous "look"—the shiny black helmet framing the features of a flapper Cleopatra—Louise wore her salt-and-pepper hair long and unkempt. Her small mouth seemed to become smaller, and the sometimes compressed lips were now regularly "pursed." She had also put on a significant amount of weight—30 pounds more than her normal 103.

Louise did not despair about her loss of beauty, but neither was she overjoyed about it. In bouts with self-pity, her ally was the bottle. Gin had been with her in the good times and was still with her in the bad. She had been drinking rather heavily since the age of fourteen; by 1945, if not much earlier, she was a chronic alcoholic and chronically unemployed. What the hell, why not drink and get fat? As she hid away in her "grubby little hole" on First Avenue, her state of mind sharply contrasted with the euphoria outside. Thousands of servicemen were returning. . . . Was that goddamned war finally over? Apparently so. Crowds were wildly celebrating V-J Day in the streets of Manhattan.

Cheers.

"That was when I began to flirt with fancies related to little bottles filled with yellow sleeping pills," she said. "However, I changed my mind, and in July 1946 the proud, snooty Louise Brooks started work as a salesgirl at Saks Fifth Avenue. They paid me $40 a week. I had this silly idea of proving myself 'an honest woman,' but the only effect it had was to disgust all my New York friends, who cut me off forever. From then on, I was regarded as a questionable East Side dame."[44]

The friends who abandoned her were Townsend Martin, Dwight

Wiman, and their immediate set. They preferred a poverty-stricken unemployed actress to a middle-class working woman. But the word "all" was
an exaggeration. Lothar Wolff remained ever faithful, as did her old Denishawn pal Lenore Scheffer (now Mrs. Dennis Bland), and a few others.

She also made some new friends in and around one of the most legendary bars in New York. Louise spent a great deal of time at Jimmy Glennon's Saloon, whose owner took a paternal liking to her, let her run a tab,
and watched out for her welfare and her whims. Without being a "celebrity bar," Glennon's, at Third Avenue and 55th Street, was the favorite
watering hole of such luminaries as Robert Benchley and Humphrey
Bogart.

"It was the kind of place where, the minute they got to town, people
like Bing Crosby and Paul Douglas and Bill Holden and Charles Butter-
worth and John O'Hara would go," says John Springer, long-time agent
and publicist to the stars. Glennon had two pictures over the bar—one
was Nancy Carroll and the other was Louise Brooks."

The story of how John Springer met Louise is a potential film scene
and a candidate for the *Guinness Book of World Records*'s "coincidence"
category. Springer tells the tale with deadpan relish:

> When I got out of the Air Force [in 1946] I moved into a little apartment
> on First Avenue with several guys . . . There was a woman across the hall,
> very strange, we thought, because we'd meet her in the hall and she'd put
> her purse up in front of her face and walk like this [hiding behind the purse].
> Her hair was long and hanging straight down, dark with lots of gray in it. We
> knew her name was Miss Brooks, and that was all.
>
> One night we decided we'd have a movie party and we rented a couple of
> old silent movies just for fun. We had people there like Jack Lemmon and
> Cliff Robertson, who were then waiters and bartenders around the corner
> from us, and Nancy Carroll was there—I loved her and we were good
> friends. We had a movie called *The Lost World* [1925] with Wallace Beery
> and Bessie Love, and we made posters and did a real old-time movie thing.
> The posters said, "Movie Party! Come up!" and had arrows pointing to the
> apartment, and on one of the posters it said something like, "You won't see
> Clara Bow, you won't see Louise Brooks, but you'll see Bessie Love and
> Nancy Carroll." Joke things like that.
>
> And so the party's going strong, and Nancy and I were out in the kitchen
> making drinks and there was a furious knock at the door and I opened it,
> and it was Miss Brooks from across the hall. "How dare you make fun of me!
> How *dare* you!" And Nancy said, "Louise! Brooksie! Come on in!" And she
> said, "Nancy, I'm surprised at you!" and she ran across the hall and slammed
> the door.
>
> And that was the first time I was aware that she was Louise Brooks. I went
> over and tried to convince her that it was only a party, nobody had any

idea she lived there, wouldn't she come—no way. She wasn't about to be mollified.[45]

They were mocking a broken-down actress as far as Louise was concerned. But in time Springer soothed her ruffled feathers and they became friends and fellow patrons of Jimmy Glennon's—separately.

"Louise went to Glennon's on the off-hours, not after the theater when there was a mob scene," he recalls. "She would come in alone and sit at the end of the bar by herself and never talk to anybody except Jimmy. If there were a lot of people there, she'd go right out. People would come on to her, which she'd completely ignore. Jimmy protected her. She was very, very guarded at first, but she started to talk to me and began to realize I was sincerely interested in her. But if I were in there with other people and Louise came in, she would never in any way acknowledge me."

Louise gave her own amusing version of this story to Ricky Leacock: "We were both living at 1075 First Avenue. [John] was working at RKO; I had gone into blackout. Every time he would bring me some old magazine or publicity about myself I would slam the door in his face. This led to our lasting friendship."[46]

One night, Springer and actor Robert Sterling were at a back booth in Glennon's with an old friend named Eddie Sutherland and his *fifth* wife, Edwina. "I saw Louise come in," says Springer, "and all of a sudden I realized she had once been married to Eddie. She saw him. She ordered her drink, drank it and walked right out."[47]

For Louise, aside from the liquor dispensed there, the major attraction of Glennon's was Glennon. She had begun to take up painting—little oil-on-cardboard works over which she labored long and hard. One was a portrait of Glennon, which she gave him and which he hung proudly in the bar. In the flyleaf of her address book under "In case of accident or death . . . ," James A. Glennon was the name she wrote in. Her letters indicate they had an off-and-on affair at least into the late forties and perhaps much longer. "Just now the phone rang," she wrote Kevin Brownlow nearly two decades later. "It was Jimmy Glennon from New York. Drunk. . . . Jimmy came to my aid when all the world had decided I should jump off the 59th Street bridge. And now he announces that he is coming up to go to bed with me. . . . And he will, too, unless I head him off. Which I will. . . . Drunk, he is worse than Dylan Thomas and Brendan Behan combined."[48]

For now, Glennon was an extremely important figure in the life of Louise Brooks, the salesgirl with the celebrated past, the alcoholic present, and the most bizarre customer approach of any Saks employee. "I must have intimidated more women who left the store without buying anything," she told John Kobal.

I'd do funny things. . . . After they put on the dress, I'd stand and they were waiting for me to zip them up or something, and I didn't do anything. . . . I was going to prove a point, that I could go out and get a job and work like everybody else. But it didn't really work out at all. I quit. I wasn't fired.[49]

It was an important distinction: The Saks job was indeed one of the few she voluntarily resigned (on April 13, 1948). By her standards, it was a long tenure—nearly two years. But she considered it just one more redundant object lesson in humility:

> . . . Saks and Harry Cohn made me think how strongly safe secure people advocate humbleness for others, especially if those others might afflict their bank accounts. Perhaps if I ever hear a chambermaid rehearse its benefits, I'll take a new look at it. Until then, I'll just keep in mind what those two experiences did for me. They injured me deeply—got me nowhere—and gained the contempt of all.[50]

Despite her solitary existence, the forty-to-forty-five-year-old Louise Brooks had no shortage of suitors. "Between 1948 and 1953, I suppose you could call me a kept woman," she told Kenneth Tynan. "Three decent rich men looked after me." She often told interviewers that there were "three rich men"—or, alternately, "three millionaires"—who wanted to marry her at this time. But she always declined to name them.

A single cryptic item in Walter Winchell's column at the beginning of May 1947 revealed that Louise Brooks, former silent-film star, would wed "James Mulcahey, San Francisco financier," the marriage to take place "any weekend." But nothing more was ever heard of it, and James Mulcahey cannot be found.

The one man she *did* want to marry was "big-hearted Irishman" James Dunne, a marine engineer she met at Glennon's. But there was a road-block: Dunne was a Catholic, and his religion required that Louise obtain an annulment from the long-gone Deering Davis. "I remember Jimmy devouring her with his eyes when we were eating dinner in New York once," says a friend of that period. "I remember it was halibut! And without warning, she spewed a mouthful of halibut all over him. She wasn't drunk. She laughed and said afterward, 'I don't know what gets into me.' I wondered if these things were intended to provoke a violent reaction in men."

Louise never became Mrs. Dunne. But she took up with two people who fulfilled the yin and yang of her sexual needs on a long-running basis. The first was a young sergeant who had guarded General Douglas Mac-Arthur's wife and was now stationed at Fort Dix. How they met is unknown, but he often came into Manhattan and Louise enjoyed the rough-and-tumble company of "Don the Marine," as she called him, for the remainder of her years in New York City. He was a jealous man, and they were a sadomasochistic couple, often goading each other into physical abuse—usually after a bottle of gin.

Simultaneously, Louise befriended a girl called "Butch"—"a remarkable drinker," said Louise, who was an authority on the subject. Don and Butch knew each other, too, and there were no secrets among them: Don told Louise he was interested in Butch, whose sexual preference was decidedly, though not strictly, for women:

> Butch frightens me. She called at seven in a dead voice, so unlike her. For reasons based on desire, she had counted on us for Thanksgiving. . . . And then Don called . . . mad because I wouldn't go to Butch's—but he wouldn't go alone. This, although he had been brooding over "making it" with her ever since that night a year ago last August when he brought in $20 worth of gin and steak, I fell asleep, and Butch [left]. . . . I do not know the Marine code, but I cannot convince Don that buying gin and steak for a lady does not give him rights over her body.[51]

W H A T E V E R else could be said about Louise's life now, it was safe to say she had obliterated her past. As far as she and her *amours* were concerned, there was no trace of the ex–movie queen about her, her surroundings, or her life. And then one day in 1948, her telephone rang, and the voice was that of G. W. Pabst.

He asked her to lunch at the Ambassador Hotel, but "a half hour before I was to meet him, he phoned me saying, 'Louise, I cannot have lunch with you today.' That was all—he sounded very tense."[52] Pabst was in New York trying to sell *Der Prozess* to an American distributor. What he wanted from Louise she never learned, but he returned in 1950 with two new film projects in mind. This time, a better reception awaited him, including a lavish article in the *New York Times* by Louise's friend, Herman Weinberg:

> No list of the ten directors who most shaped the language of the film and contributed importantly to it would be complete without the name of G. W. Pabst. . . .
>
> [The first of his two current projects] is the much-heralded *Odyssey* of Homer, to be filmed in Italy with, if possible, Garbo as both Penelope and Circe. He would like to get Clark Gable or Orson Welles as Ulysses. . . .
>
> The second project, to be called *The Last Ten Days*, deals with Hitler's last ten days before his death.[53]

Like the Garbo-Brooks *Faust*, the Garbo-Gable *Odyssey* never materialized, but the second project did—its purpose to debunk the persistent rumors that Hitler escaped Berlin alive in 1945. The book was by Michael Musmanno, a presiding judge at the Nuremberg war trials. The script by

Erich Maria Remarque was filmed as *Der letzte Akt (The Last Act)* in 1955 with Oskar Werner as narrator-protagonist and Albin Skoda as the Führer. The film was well reviewed in Europe and America, one critic noting that "its dusky quality remind[s] one of *Pandora's Box*."[54]

Things were going better for Pabst, who this time kept an appointment with Louise—a pleasant if uneventful reunion. Her 1950 meeting with Pabst was Louise's last encounter with the great director who had so changed her life. By now, they were simply old friends. And so they would remain.

"It was his *mind*, in general, that was so fascinating," said Lothar Wolff of Louise's unending regard for her mentor.[55] What a cerebral, universal man and director she knew this Pabst to be! The greatest of twentieth-century and pan-historical literature was fair game for him—from Homer to Faust to Wedekind to Musmanno. And what a pity, she knew, that she would never see him again.

The period from 1947 through 1952 is literally the Lost Years of Louise Brooks. From the age of fourteen, she faithfully kept a logbook for every year of her life—except for those five, which are contained on a single page of her 1953 record. Yet their very "silence" made them five of the most important years of her life; despite the booze and the blues, she was working with more concentrated intellectual energy than she had ever applied to anything—preparing for a second career that would save and redeem her life. Jobless and isolated, Louise was becoming a writer.

It did not begin with such a lofty or even conscious goal. It began as a possible source of income and a way to pass the time and dodge depression after quitting Saks in 1948:

> To earn a little money, I sat down and wrote the usual autobiography. I called it *Naked on My Goat*, which is a quote from Goethe's *Faust*. . . . Then, when I'd read what I'd written, I threw the whole thing down the incinerator.[56]

This was a brutal oversimplification of an undertaking whose form and content consumed her for decades. The work was not a standard autobiography. She was determined that it contain "the truth"—including "the full sexual truth"—and was thus faced with the problem of naming prominent friends, enemies, and lovers still very much alive. Her solution, as noted earlier, was third-person novel form.

"The more people try to explain themselves, the more they entangle themselves in a web of confusion," she wrote much later to Kevin Brownlow. "It is only in fiction that people are 'all of a piece.' Biography and autobiography are the greatest fictions. . . . In reality I do not know anything about myself or why I do anything."[57]

The book's genesis lay in finding her first diary, written at fourteen. "I couldn't believe it," she said. "This wasn't I—this hating, hateful, envious, vengeful, sex-loaded little vixen—but it was!" She soon resurrected the rest of her journals, poring over them, studying the choice of words, and analyzing what she had been and what she was now. Her book, she decided, would move back and forth in time and not even deal with her film career. Working with her diaries, she methodically drew up a list of "mystical moments" in her life, which she planned to incorporate:

1914—age 7, Cherryvale, spring, noon, sitting on porch after lunch. . . .

1916—age 10, radiant gold with love from Mother. . . .

19??—don't forget how she used to look at reflection by the hour in train windows—freckles—mustache. . . .

1924—trees on Riverside Drive, lace panel insertions, flamenco costume, cooking opium. . . .

1924—Book of Job, "the thing I feared has come upon me," Miss Ruth's look. . . .

1929—age 22, Paris, dawn, September, the garden behind the apartment. . . .

1942—age 35, Wichita, in June, speakeasy in the country, the catalpa tree. . . .

1945—age 37, New York, February, Dwight [Wiman's] apartment at the Gotham, 4 a.m., the dream in the apple tree. . . .[58]

A surviving sheet of paper from 1949 shows that she structured these events, and her early life, in ten chapters with telling titles derived from her diary entries:

Chapter 1: As I someday intend to rise high in the ranks.

Chapter 2: I would be ruined.

Chapter 3: What it costs to be the star.

Chapter 4: I do not ever expect to be an angel.

Chapter 5: (untitled)

Chapter 6: Who is the exotic black orchid?

Chapter 7: To be the belle and then to fall.

Chapter 8: Excitement seems to follow me.

Chapter 9: Away to broader fields.

Chapter 10: The silver salver.

She wrote, or planned to write, 400 pages, and the project involved voluminous autobiographical research. Toward that end—a profound desire to apprehend her lost childhood, to find its elusive "Rosebud"—she wrote a fervid letter to her old friend Tot back in Cherryvale, Kansas:

Thank God I found you! . . . Here's the thing, Tot. I'm writing a book, a novel. Not for fame or money or success—it may never be published—but because I must. For two extraordinarily happy years I have been working on it—learning to write—but mostly learning to tell the truth. At first it is quite impossible. You make yourself better than anybody, then worse than anybody, and when you finally come to see you are "like" everybody—that is the bitterest blow of all to the ego. But in the end it is only the truth, no matter how ugly or shameful, that is right, that fits together, that makes real people, and strangely enough—beauty. . . .

The title might well be "The Making of a Shit." For that is what the book shows.

About eight years ago [1944] I took a good look at myself and my little friends and began to wonder what had turned us into bitter, envious phoneys. Further, I decided to grow up, to face reality and truth. But I had spent 30 years of hard work becoming a fool, and you just can't stop like that. Thank God for Age! I am free at last from that life. There's not a living sonofabitch who can get a thing or make a cent out of exploiting this old bag.

That's how the book began.

But it is a History too, of a time, and of places—places like Cherryvale that can never be again. So the amount of research I do on my own life is astonishing. For every fact must be absolutely right, even if I don't use it. And I have never kept a picture or a letter—nothing. This is where you come in. . . . Tell me, oh tell me, all you know about Mother. If I can do her portrait in my book as it should be done it will make the reader laugh and weep.[59]

The two big questions are whether she actually finished writing her book and whether she really destroyed it.

"I feel certain she did have the full text written," says James Card. At the time, she wrote him coldly: "Down the incinerator last April [1954]. Not the *best*. But fine training." Card was incredulous that she could destroy it and told her so. To which she replied:

About *Naked*, you evidently didn't quite believe me when I said I always wanted to be the best. The amount of research I did on my own life and times would lead you to believe I was writing about a stranger in Tibet. The odd thing is that I used almost none of it—but I have to know! From a wealth of knowledge you can pick the one right word; from little, you go on piling words upon words, hoping to hit the mark through sheer abundance. How I hate such writers, Thomas Wolfe—all those gabby daydreamers on paper who don't know their trade. Thinking it over, to paraphrase the inspiration-perspiration line, I say that good writing is 1% illumination and 99% elimination.[60]

She wasn't the least bit sad about the destruction. On the contrary, writing what she called "Incinerator One" confirmed her belief that "nothing is ever wasted," including the gossip-column stint. But there was a deeper reason for Louise's trip to the incinerator. It was tangled up in a problem that no amount of third-person disguise could resolve, and it would take her another quarter of a century—in her brilliant 1978 article, "Why I Will Never Write My Memoirs"—to articulate it:

> In writing the history of a life, I believe absolutely that the reader cannot understand the character and deeds of the subject unless he is given a basic understanding of that person's sexual loves and hates and conflicts. It is the only way the reader can make sense out of innumerable apparently senseless actions. To paraphrase Proust: how often do we change the whole course of our lives in pursuit of a love that we will have forgotten within a few months. We flatter ourselves when we assume that we have restored the sexual integrity which was expurgated by the Victorians.
>
> I too am unwilling to write the sexual truth that would make my life worth reading. I cannot unbuckle the Bible Belt. That is why I will never write my memoirs.[61]

EVER SINCE her adolescent encounters with Mr. Vincent and Mr. Weatherwax at the Presbyterian church in Wichita, Louise's life had been marked by a distinct absence of religion. That lack of interest changed, however, in 1952.

Except for the conversion of Saul on the road to Damascus and similar leaps of faith based on a single mystical experience, religious transformations are hard to pinpoint. In Louise's case, it was the loneliness and apparent pointlessness of her existence that led her to a deep exploration of spirituality.

Her spiritual trek was guided by two New York City priests—Father Thomas Egan and Father Paul Burkort—whom she saw with increasing frequency in late 1952 and early 1953, and by a book about the life of Saint Thérèse de Lisieux, *Storm of Glory*, by John Beevers. Saint Thérèse, "The Little Flower," was a French Carmelite nun who became one of the most beloved of all Catholic figures. Her humble doctrine of the "Little Way" to Christ touched the hearts of millions who could never identify with the harsh dictates of, say, St. Paul. So enamored of Saint Thérèse was Louise that she spent one entire Sunday propped up in bed with her easel, fashioning a portrait in charcoal on canvas from a small photo of Thérèse at age eight. "To fix it," she wrote in her diary, "I brushed on LePage glue which made the charcoal run. I thought the eyes were ruined but I left it alone—and the painting became more like St. Thérèse." It was the best and most haunting of her dozen works of art.

For Louise, there was no such thing as a casual interest in anything— least of all her soul. Just as with something so prosaic as leather, once she became intrigued she had to know everything about it, and that lifelong

*Louise's painting of St. Thérèse de Lisieux, "The Little Flower":
charcoal on canvas, October 1954*

trait she now applied compulsively to religion. She was less concerned with salvation, life after death, or even the existence of God than with her own life on earth—a rather shabby life on earth at that moment.

"Patience is the masterpiece of strength," she quoted in her diary—she who longed for the ability to be patient.

The choice of denomination was easy in view of her fondness for Fathers Egan and Burkort. Her life, for better or worse, had always been full of freedom, of unrestricted activity, and of unanswered questions. It had been for worse, rather than better, she decided. She was now looking for answers; she often said, in other contexts, that she had to be "told what to do." The vagueness of Protestantism had only convinced her of its hypocrisies. Dogmatic Catholicism was sure of itself, and its clarity much appealed to her at this point. The concept of sin, which this Lulu had always rejected, now seemed embraceable—bearable—when balanced with the certainty of forgiveness.

She decided to become a Roman Catholic and, complying with Catholic procedure, wrote home to Theodore in Kansas for a copy of her baptismal certificate, if one existed. Theo was aghast at this turnabout in the one person in the world he thought safe from "Papacy." On July 21,

1953, he wrote back, informing her that no record of baptism could be found. He added his own pungent opinion of what she was doing and of the church that required such things as fifty-year-old baptismal records:

> It seems to me a cruel thing that any institution would be so bound up by dogma as to gamble lives and souls on trivialities devised by men to harry the faithful. Like good merchants, they seem to realize that plenty of sin means good business. Where none exists, they devise it. I cannot help but think that you could find God, peace and happiness under better circumstances. Love, Theo.

Despite Theo's admonitions, Louise was baptized in New York on September 15, 1953, at St. John the Evangelist Church, 55th Street and First Avenue, three blocks from her apartment. After that, she withdrew even further from the world and deeper into a seclusion that now had an element of religious ecstasy in it.

"The only people she would talk to or relate to, other than someone like me and a few others at Glennon's, were the couple of priests she was very close to," recalls John Springer.[62]

Her relationship with Father Burkort was especially enriching. He accepted Louise herself, no less than her unorthodox approach to God, as he told her in a letter: "Louise, you have an intelligent rather than an emotional understanding of the faith."[63] In her replies, Louise's greeting was always "Dear Best of Teachers." But she could also spend an afternoon "hollering at Father Burkort," as she put it. "My big beef with Father was sex—he said I should rise above it. He did. But I am no saint."[64]

When Louise raised the subject of her book and its sexual content, the good priests expressed their concern not so much for the writer as for the impressionable young readers—especially girls—who might be led astray thereby. "Father Egan and I had a rough session on literary integrity," she wrote a friend. "His argument, briefly, was that the exposition of all sin set forth in beauty or ugliness drew the reader to it. I don't know. Thinking it over, I had to admit that reading about drinking made me want to drink, and that reading about sex excited me. . . . Perhaps [now] you understand why my becoming a convert led me to destroy my book. It is very possible that I would have done so anyhow. But that cinched it."[65]

Louise's conversion to Catholicism was a deep source of comfort to her. Its importance is not negated by the fact that she eventually left the Church, in 1964, and later spoke of it irreverently—as in her advice to Kevin Brownlow upon learning of his plan to marry:

> Take instruction and become a Catholic and get married in the church. It doesn't mean a thing except that you are joining up in the richest, classiest

outfit in the world. The best institution for birth, marriage and death. Religious myths are basically alike. The Catholic church has at least some beauty and order.

I like the story about the Catholic who lost his faith and left the church. His friend said, "What Protestant church are you joining?" He answered, "I said I lost my faith, not my mind."[66]

RELIGION and burnt memoirs notwithstanding, Louise now knew she wanted to be a writer—no, more than that: She knew, by 1954, that she *was* a writer. The writing of *Goat* gave her new confidence. The Church gave her a greater measure of serenity than any she had known before. She felt able to take a detached view of people, with the potential aim of writing about them. She could train her extraordinary natural gifts of observation on anything—such as a strange interlude with ZaSu Pitts.

Louise's sole encounter with Pitts took place in 1954 during the run of a play in which ZaSu—in a typical comic-maid role—was attempting a Broadway comeback. Brooks wrote a letter in praise of Pitts to columnist Westbrook Pegler, who quoted from it next day in his column in the New York *Journal-American*. Louise takes over from there:

> Then ZaSu telephoned me. She couldn't figure out why I had written Pegler, but she still wanted to thank me, which got me an invitation to see her play and dine with her afterwards. At the start of the evening, ZaSu only gave a pitiful hint of the character she then played on TV—the eternally indecisive one, forever hesitating among a series of equally absurd choices. She was late, and I was about to knock on the door of her room at the Hotel Pierre when she arrived. She jumped upon seeing me and, for an instant, her eyes would have liked to have fled. She took some things she would need at the theatre, and we went down. In the lobby, another woman was waiting for her—another jump on ZaSu's part, who then remembered that she had invited *her*, too, to come see the play. After the curtain fell, the two of us met backstage where six other people were already waiting for ZaSu. . . .
>
> Once at her place, I discovered that ZaSu wore a thin mask to hide her true character. . . . After everyone ordered his unique whisky-soda, her voice took on a disagreeable tone in the way she added "—and I'll have a double strawberry ice cream soda." When she talked of her husband whom she missed (he had stayed in California), she let out one of those voluptuous sighs that made me smile. Seeing this, she retreated to her armchair. . . . [Then] she turned to her guests and said, "You don't know, of course, but I wasn't always a comedienne. Oh, no! I began as a dramatic actress." And as she was talking to us about von Stroheim and *Greed*, the charming Trina was reincarnated before our eyes, with her luxuriant hair and long, pearly legs—Trina on her way to bed with her 250 gold coins.[67]

This cryptic vignette *in toto* occupied a single page.

. . .

But if Louise by 1954 was a writer, she was still an unpublished one, and even unpublished writers need to eat. Since quitting Saks in 1948, she had had no formal employment of any kind. She existed through the largesse of men who chose to "keep" her, augmenting her income with a few "escort" jobs. She asked for and received a few small loans from her father back in Kansas and from Theo and June. But it was a meager existence, and she was without any foreseeable prospects of income as a writer. She was now forty-eight years old and again on the brink of destitution. She had long since run out of new people from whom to ask favors. There was only the one she had asked before.

William Paley was by now the undisputed electronic-media baron in the United States—a position he has maintained, with occasional forays into retirement, to the present day. Louise had had no contact with him after the end of her abortive radio career. He had done his best for her, and she did not want to bother him again. But in her mind she replayed that night in 1929 when he announced with delight that *Pandora* was playing—and she had refused to go.

"He was completely disgusted with my stupid indifference to my worth and art," she had confided, and he was presumably disgusted with her again for botching her chances at CBS. Her track record made it all the more astonishing and "proof of his fine character," she said, "when, after I made a mess of my life, he came to my rescue in 1954 with a blessed allowance."[68]

At her wit's end for rent money, she had written Paley in a desperate plea for help on December 6, 1954. His response was immediate and heroic, relayed to her by John Minary, who was in charge of the William S. Paley Foundation. This was, and remains, the CBS chairman's private philanthropic arm, dispensing modest sums of money to recipients designated by its founder. Within a week, she was in Minary's office gratefully accepting a check for $1,000 and—more important—the conditions for a *regular* monthly allotment of $200 thereafter.

It was not charity that she would be receiving, but a subsidy or stipend for her new career as a writer. That would be its classification, and Minary made it clear that Paley expected her to produce. Exactly what and when she would produce were left up to Louise; there would be no deadlines. With no great evidence of its existence, Paley was expressing confidence in her writing ability. The allowance would continue indefinitely, subject to a single commandment like that of the mythical John B. Tipton on CBS's own "The Millionaire": She must never divulge her benefactor's name or allow him to be embarrassed in any way by his support of her. Paley's anonymity and her discretion in keeping her love life out of print were all he asked.

William S. Paley—the guardian angel of Louise Brooks's life. His faith was as important as his money—his refusal to abandon a true *abandonnée*. She was convinced that in addition to Paley's goodness, she saw the hand of God at work. There was no reason in the world why she should be given another chance by a man she had so often disappointed. For that very lack of reason, she was determined not to disappoint him again.

"My life between 1935 and 1954 when Bill Paley started giving me an allowance, I would not wish on anybody," she later wrote a friend.[69] Finally, she could see that life behind her, and she was exhilarated. She rediscovered her sense of joy and her sense of humor, revealing both to a confidant in one of the great epigrams, and epitaphs, of the century:

> Every woman should have two foundations and two saloons.[70]

But she was still searching for that thing she could not name: for an inspiration, perhaps; for a catalyst to the literary-artistic redemption awaiting her; for love.

James Card, meanwhile, was searching for Louise Brooks.

Act Three

PANDORA'S BOOKS

Louise at sixty: a photo by her friend Roddy McDowall, in Rochester, 1966

18 · Resurrection

We believe we can change things according to our wishes because that's the only happy solution we can see. We don't think of what usually happens and what is also a happy solution: things don't change, but by and by our wishes change. — MARCEL PROUST

I do not bring up sex in my articles unless it has a direct bearing on relationships—and it always does. — LOUISE BROOKS

I F her conversion to Catholicism represented a spiritual rebirth, Louise was now on the threshold of both a romantic and a cinematic resurrection as well—her artistic rehabilitation integrally linked with the last great love affair of her life.

James Card, thirty-nine, had been film curator at George Eastman House International Museum of Photography in Rochester for seven years. In that time, he single-handedly built the Eastman House collection from a dozen little Edison kinetoscopes into a master collection of more than 5,000 titles, second only to that at the Library of Congress and second to none in private hands. His forte was not just accumulation but restoration, particularly of the most endangered film species, silents. He personally saved some 3,500 films that would otherwise have been lost— obtaining many of them in the Machiavellian ways known only to archivists adept at international wheelings and dealings. And in a day when many great silent stars and directors were still living, he often sought them out, visiting them or bringing them to Rochester.

Card's infatuation with Louise Brooks began long before 1955—and long lay dormant.

"It was *Girl in Every Port* at the B. F. Keith Palace Theatre in Cleveland, 1928 or 1929," he recalls. "I was about 14 years old. The thing that intrigued me was the hairdo. I remember nothing at all about the picture, just that face."

A decade later, Card found himself in Germany making documentary films as a free-lancer on the eve of World War II. He was arrested by the Nazis in Danzig for filming the occupation of that "free city" in 1939. A harrowing escape followed, as did army service and then marriage and career concerns—all of which obliterated further thoughts of Louise Brooks until his first trip to the Cinémathèque Française in Paris in 1953. He asked to see *Pandora's Box* and *The Diary of a Lost Girl*, but Henri Langlois (1914–1977), the institution's founding director, at first refused. "He didn't have any interest at all in either of those films," says Card, but he grudgingly consented to project and watch them with Card, if only to take a look at Brooks.[1] Langlois was thunderstruck. Suddenly he wanted to know everything about her. So did Card, and he left the screening room fired anew with the desire to locate her.

Pandora's Box was itself a candidate for resurrection. It then existed only in a variety of incomplete versions scattered throughout Europe. Any "masterpiece" status it enjoyed was solely in the minority opinion of such critics as Lotte Eisner. But Langlois was now so taken by it that he joined forces with Card for its restoration. Soon, through the combined efforts of the Cinémathèque Française, the Cinémathèque Suisse in Lausanne, and the Danish Film Museum in Copenhagen, a nearly complete print was reassembled according to Pabst's original shooting script.

Langlois was then mounting a major exhibition of cinematic artifacts and photos at the Musée National d'Art Moderne—"60 Ans de Cinéma" —which ran from June through September of 1955. Visitors entering the building were greeted by two gigantic portraits looming down from wires in positions of co-equal honor: Falconetti from Dreyer's *The Passion of Jeanne d'Arc* (1927) and Brooks from *Pandora's Box*. What stunned people was that the two dominant faces belonged to such obscure actresses— "Falconetti as Jeanne, the most spiritual image ever evoked by the cinema, and Louise Brooks as Lulu, the most physically feline destroyer," wrote Card.[2] The former never made another movie; the latter disappeared after 1930. Asked to justify his choice of Brooks over Garbo or Dietrich or a hundred others more worthy of the honor, Langlois made a ringing declaration that became the rallying cry of Louise's resurrection:

There is no Garbo! There is no Dietrich! There is only Louise Brooks!

In his catalogue for the exhibit, Langlois's lavish praise sowed more seeds of the Louise Brooks cult: "She has the naturalness that only primitives retain before the lens. . . . She is the intelligence of the cinematographic process, she is the most perfect incarnation of photogénie. . . . Her art is so pure that it becomes invisible."[3] Ado Kyrou soon after declared categorically, "I do not know of a greater tragedienne of the screen."[4] Interest in *Pandora's Box* was beginning to soar.

Louise hadn't an inkling of what was happening. Card, who had engendered the renaissance, made certain before leaving the Continent to acquire a print of *Pandora*, as well as *The Diary of a Lost Girl*, from the Danish Film Museum. But he still did not know where or whether Louise Brooks lived—until a chance conversation with John Springer in 1955.

Card later recalled the Gothic account of another New Yorker who had recently seen Louise:

> His portrait of her was as dismal as anything in the dreary confessions of Lillian Roth and Diana Barrymore: [She] rarely left her gloomy one-room apartment located within the forbidding shadow of the grimy old Queensboro Bridge. . . . Bitterness and despair had allegedly wrecked her beauty and the abortive consolation of the bottle ruined her figure. On the few occasions when she stirred out of this black cave of forgetfulness, it was only to hurry over to Glennon's Bar on Third Avenue, clad in a long black overcoat which she never removed out of shame for her bloated body. A furious, baleful look repulsed any acquaintances of the past who might have encountered her on one of these excursions. . . . "You look at her face," he told me, "and think—this is a woman who is just waiting to kill herself."[5]

Springer gave Card her address and mentioned Card to Louise: "She was suspicious. She didn't want to meet anybody. But I assured her this was an important man who had the credentials and that, according to him, at the Cinémathèque she was considered in the same league with Garbo, which she just sneered at. She didn't believe a word of it. As far as she was concerned, she was an old has-been who'd been a cute flapper that got the parts Clara Bow and Colleen Moore didn't want."[6]

On July 5, 1955, James Card wrote to tell her that, "after 25 years in limbo, Paris had restored her to stardom."

"I asked her the usual initial questions of the film historian: 'What was your first picture? How did you happen to begin film acting?' and similar inanities," says Card. It was the beginning of a correspondence that changed both of their lives, as Louise's moving reply makes clear:

> The mystery of life . . . that you should, after almost 30 years, bring me the first joy I ever tasted from my movie career. It's like throwing away a mask. All these years making fun of myself with everyone overjoyed to agree . . . away all false humility forever!
>
> You see, they had to hog-tie me in the first place to make me go into pictures. . . . They didn't know what to do with me, I fitted nowhere, so they decided that I was a lousy actress. I, who would be the *best* at everything I did, so vain. After the day I went into the projection room with Walter Wanger and the director to see my second picture, and they laughed and kidded me about my acting, I vowed that I would never see another picture that I was in—and I never have, not even my pictures made in Europe.[7]

Card was instantly struck by the "curious, crackling charge" of her prose. "It was as a result of her *letters* that I started to pour it on," he says. "It was obvious that here was a person who could be writing and should be writing."

As for Louise, it seemed too good to be true—both Card's attentions and the tidings he bore. Had her film work really been so good? Had it been good *at all?* Any lingering value she had placed on it had been erased by Iris Barry's putdown of *Pandora* in 1943. Could the great Barry have been wrong? Brooks sent Card some fragments of her memoirs, and he responded enthusiastically, telling her "the extracts are wonderful" and offering to help her rewrite the book. Both the tone and the frequency of the exchange escalated. On August 1, 1955, she wrote to "Dear Mr. Card." By August 24 it was "Dear Jimmy" and she was "terribly excited about writing again." She had seen a photograph of him and was anticipating their first face-to-face meeting:

> I've been going crazy trying to imagine you. So that I would not be disappointed, I had finally settled on a small, plump man with pale eyes and a faint yeasty smell, but never would I have dreamed of anything so *soigné.* I'll be the one with the witch's mane and the bare feet sticking out. . . . And, sad as it is to disenchant you—I am FAT.[8]

She was bracing him for the worst, and not without reason. The fateful first meeting took place October 23, 1955. Card recalls her "looking like the Witch of Endor, bloated and existing on gin." In the sanitized version, for publication, he wrote:

> The horror story that had been told me about Louise Brooks, I immediately discovered, was only superficially true—which is to say it was not true at all. She received me barefooted, dressed in a nightgown and a faded, well-scrubbed Chinese robe, then promptly returned to bed, where, she admitted, she spent roughly 80% of her time. Of the memorable Brooks visage there remained the exquisite profile and, incredibly, that piquant eyebrow-and-a-half.
>
> What I had been prepared to enter as a dungeon turned out to be a kind of shrine consecrated to cleanliness—Freudian perhaps—but for whatever reason, the room was a perpetual battleground against the oily grime that is unique to Manhattan. And on the walls, three oil paintings by Miss Brooks that looked not at all symptomatic of suicide . . . in particular, an oil of St. Thérèse. . . .[9]

Thirty years later, he still remembers Louise's first-floor flat as "meticulously clean and scrubbed," but he adds:

> One thing about someone who drinks nothing but gin—there's a special scent that emanates from the body because it's so strong. There was a long

corridor leading to her apartment, and the whole first floor was permeated by the smell of that gin. There wasn't any question of sloppiness or uncleanness—just that very strong smell of gin.[10]

Essence of gin notwithstanding, they took an immediate and powerful liking to each other—so much so that he spent the night there. When he returned to Rochester the next day, George Pratt, Card's associate at Eastman House, remembered the Shakespearean exuberance with which he described Louise: "The first thing Jim said to me was, 'I just met the most wonderful woman that ever lived in the tide of time.' " The correspondence further intensified. A week after their meeting, Louise wrote:

> Sunday morning . . . Rain . . . But shall I start writing my book? Shall I, shall I? And don't snow on me. That would be too cruel. If you say yes, I'll set aside all doubts and fears and do as you advise. . . . That is, if you are not too busy to read and correct my manuscript. Knowing me now, you see that I have no more faith in myself than a rabbit staring at a python.
>
> This morning I had the courage to take an old mirror out of the closet and look at myself. Blubber, blubber, toil and trouble. I'm on a DIET.[11]

Card's effect on her was tonic. It manifested itself in a sharp upswing in her mood and a sudden awareness of her past achievements and present capabilities—permeated with a strong romantic surge. In the euphoria, her literary yearnings seemed to coalesce after years of groping experimentation. And in her letters of the next few weeks, she would reveal more of her soul to Jim Card than to any man in her life:

> You did not know what you did for me, telling me to *call the book "Naked on My Goat."* To be told what to do is the root of my attachment to G.M. [George Marshall], and it had a great deal to do with my becoming a Catholic. The trouble is, though, much as I need to be directed, the people before you I would allow to do it numbered just two. Anyhow, with my wavering gaze fixed firmly on the right point, after three days and nights of mental work, the whole book sprang up this morning as neat as a crocus. All the parts of the old book which do not belong to that title have disappeared. . . . Another extraordinary thing is that the book is free now. It has a life of its own. . . .[12]

Thus began Incinerator Two—the second *Naked on My Goat*. Her use of that title to describe the first version was ex post facto; it was Jim Card who picked the phrase out of the Goethe verse when she read it to him. And it was Card for whom she now sat down to reconstruct "the chapter I know best"—her *Scandals* account, "Who Is the Exotic Black Orchid?" Like the first *Goat*, the second never saw print. But her labors would prove fruitful in the perpetual process of learning how to write. She was so excited and energized (and a bit drunk) that she telephoned Card and wrote him a second letter that same day, November 3, 1955:

> No wonder I'm on a diet. I didn't realize . . . how could I have done this to myself, mind and body, these last ten years? I lash about with the accumulation of ten years' energy and ask myself "Why? Why?" Now I understand the look in old friends' eyes . . . that compulsion to abase myself. When did it begin? Why is it? Tell me, oracle.
>
> Damn, damn, damn. Throwing myself at evil people.
>
> It's like being set free from some dark, degrading spell. I can't start my book today. I've got to sober up.
>
> Since you have nothing else to do, I'll play games with you. Do you have one of those books listing foundations? My foundation begins with a "P." If you can guess it, I'll give you an autographed picture of Bessie Barriscale.* It isn't really funny. Maybe that's why I make it a game. It's wonderful and sad.
>
> This is the first time I ever noticed how limited a telephone is. The thing it's really good for is a fight. You can blast away without any danger of getting your brains beaten out.[13]

Card today sees her jubilance in terms of a statement by her friend, Father Henry Atwell: "The worst thing that can happen to a human being is loneliness." Card was rescuing her from the torments of two decades. But soon enough—within a few weeks—they would be arguing and Louise writing anxious lamentations:

> How could I have behaved so terribly? . . . Tell me that you are not utterly disgusted with me . . . Are you truly coming down next week? Oh, joy, and I won't drink. I'll be good. . . .
>
> After you hung up, I went back over the thing that has been driving me crazy—why had I, after 30 years of secrecy, opened up to the one man I ever wanted to think well of me—and gone on and on, pouring out my shame and despair and failure from deeper and deeper channels, some I hadn't known existed? And why, above all, had he allowed it, listening patiently to one degrading story after another, so dull, so alike?

The answer to both questions was that "I had spoken the truth"—and it had set her free. Her ecstasy had its apotheosis on November 23, 1955, when she wrote Card at dawn:

> Darling, waiting for the A&P to open, I was sitting here musing in the laziness of love, talking to you. This morning at Mass, I was so exceedingly happy that all the calm faces, the proud faces, and the sad faces cannot resist looking at me. Oh, darling, how can anything be wrong? I began praying for

* Bessie Barriscale (1884–1965) was a once-important, now forgotten film star from 1914 to 1921.

you after your first letter and all my prayers have been answered. And what of the amazing transformation in me that neither I nor another person nor the church could accomplish? And did not Fr. Burkort give you to me, first in general, and then in fact? He had just heard my confession in the lower church, and I was weeping at the altar rail when I looked up, and there he was, laughing down at me with his usual disregard for the outraged faces turned our way. "Remember this corner, this spot where you're kneeling?" It is the place where he gave me instruction, where he set up his bit of blackboard, and in sheer excess of energy, lashed words and curious lines and circles, covering his cassock in a veil of chalk while the eraser flew off in all directions. "Everything will come right, Louise. You will find a wonderful man." And then, to my amazement, after having heard my confession— "and you *deserve* him."

The next day she added: "I cannot wait to receive your letter on 'why I'm not jealous.' I could write 'why I am' in a single line."

With Incinerator Two under way, it occurred to Louise that she had written Incinerator One for the same reason she took up painting: "To understand it." If her writing failed, she wrote Card, "I can always become a portrait painter. I did one of Glennon [and] since then, July, I've had two urgent commissions offered me, and as Marshall would say, 'Of course she wouldn't do it, she'd get *paid!*' Still, a hundred bucks would hardly pay me for my time. I paint one day and then I think for six weeks, and then I paint another day and think maybe two months before I lay on more oil. To paint a person's insides you have to paint just as God formed him without any current or personal improvements."

She had done eight paintings and would do only four more, most in Japanese style, vertically signed "LUISA"—Jim Card's pet name for her— in pseudo-Oriental script. The one she was working on now infused her with longing and, for the first time, the thought of leaving New York:

> Trees. Looking at that damn painting to think what to do about it made me long to see a tree. Not a tree in a closed-in place, a tree that belongs to somebody, but a strong, independent, alone tree like the big wild cherry I remember in a little wood. . . . When I was little, trees were my life from spring to fall. From the sweet scent of cherry blossoms all around me to the soft patter of rain in the sycamore. Being small and light, I could climb to the highest swaying branches, my long black hair beyond the reach of my brother's claws; my body hidden from my mother's incessant yelling.[14]

Two days later, suddenly doubting Card's affection, she wrote him a farewell letter and ran to the post office, as she often did, to mail it before she changed her mind. "Coming home, I felt fine for awhile," she said. "I found a piece of cardboard, and from the Japanese painted in black and

*"Bird in Snowstorm," oil painting by Louise;
New York City, November 1955*

white a little cold bird on a dry branch. Then it was time to go to Mass, and I was a broken woman. Oh, God, don't let Jim take me seriously. Don't let him be mad. Don't take him away from me."[15]

Her love for Card and her desire to glimpse something other than concrete and steel were leading her to consider his urgings that she move to Rochester, where she could write on film and make use of Eastman House. They met several more times, and the relationship became more ardent. In the four months between November 1955 and February 1956, Louise wrote him a total of forty letters. Love letters. Happy letters, sorrowful letters, yearning letters:

> Jim, Jim, tell me the truth. I can bear anything—but I will have *all* of you—or *none*. I will make no compromise. . . . Be merciful and tell me the truth—do not break my heart. . . .[16]

> Never in my whole life have I truly wanted anything I didn't get. It's a matter of complete attention, absolute concentration, and from the moment I got your second letter I have never taken my mind off you . . . Writing my book was simply a gag (not that I'm not going to knock it out and try to sell it—I've got a reason now). . . . If it would have drawn you to me, I would have taken up wrestling. But I was scared too. I made a point of looking lousy when I met you. . . . That proved that you were just another guy. . . .

I've told you eight hundred ways what a bitch I am. . . . I think what throws people off about me is that they always associate a bitch with jewels and clothes and money, publicity and success. These not being first things in my life, people place upon me virtues belonging to poverty and modesty. That's the only explanation I can find for people's surprise at my true nature —for I don't try to deceive anyone.[17]

From the bottom of a bottle on December 10, 1955:

Lovely whisky. Not mad anymore. Lovely clean room getting all dirty— lovely clean Brooks getting all dirty. . . . Lovely sad whisky—so relaxing— cursing, leaping, praying, waiting, Saturday, Sunday, Monday, Tuesday, Wednesday, Thursday, Friday, Saturday, telephone call, lovely telephone call. . . . "April in Paris" they're playing on the radio. . . .

The same on December 12:

Oh, this is nonsense—being drunk and silly. Sober, I'll be fighting you inch for inch—I love you. Louise.

She told him she did not want to get married; she wanted them both to be free to "always walk out the door." But she was also, by now, actively urging him to leave his wife and two daughters, setting forth her amazing theory of fatherhood and other arguments that seemed obvious to her, if not to Card:

As for the children, that's a woman's business, bringing them up, and it will give her something to do 'til she finds a man to suit her. . . . As for children, again, what do you remember of your father, or care? Unless there's incest involved, I never heard of anyone in their hearts really caring, father for child, child for father.[18]

. . . I will be with you or someone else.[19]

In her usual offhand, outrageous fashion, she had made some nasty generalizations about Jews—as she often did—and Card took her to task for anti-Semitism. Her response revealed her approach to men and the world at large, as well as Jews:

Let me clear up the Jew thing. You're the one who is Jew-happy. If you paid attention, you'd notice that I panned the Irish and Kansans and Germans, in fact everyone and everything. It's a way I have of getting to things. For example, the other night I heard a bunch of kids stink up Sibelius' Second Symphony, and I learned more about its beauty and how it should be played than if I had heard it properly played and conducted a thousand times. If I truly hated Jews, I would be the biggest bitch in North and South America. Bill Paley and Walter Wanger have been a hundred times more

wonderful to me than all the lousy Irish-Catholics and Middle Western Protestants I've known lumped together. . . .

There isn't anything wise or clever or tricky to what I do anyhow. If I am
drawn to a man, I simply move right into the center of him. I know him
immediately and intimately. There isn't room inside him for me and whatever is phony, so the phoniness has to go.[20]

She was still seeing "Don the Marine" and having violent arguments
with him over Card. Full of doubts and alcohol, she sat down after one
such scene at 3:00 a.m. and wrote Jim:

Say, you cured me of Marshall. How lovely. But I am *alone*. I have never
been alone before in my whole life. Give me up, darling, that is the clean
solution. Your wife—I'm not a 100 percent heel. I don't want to louse up
her life. . . . Oh, I look horrible. Bags to here, and thinner and thinner. I
can't remember eating anything but those two apples since Thursday.
Crunch, crunch. . . . Private torture. How can you like me? I am so wicked.
The radio is playing "Threepenny Opera". . . .[21]

She ventured forth with him on his lecture trips to Wilmington and
Niagara in January, and all was well—she was on her best behavior.
"Don't you see how much of my misery comes out of not always being
like that?" she wrote him afterward. "Do you think I want to be an ugly
drunken senseless bitch, a dull screaming bore? That's why there are
things to settle. If I am to straighten out, I must have a reason to live."[22]
Meanwhile, she was in regular contact with Bill Paley's assistant at the
foundation for her monthly "allowance" and her literary progress report:

John Minary was his most severe self. He began, "How's the book coming?" I said I had done nothing, coughing feebly. Then he said either I go to
a doctor or he would have nothing further to do with that excuse. [I talked
about] *Diary of a Lost Girl* . . . how I never had the least notion of what the
picture was about. Now, he said, those things are very funny. "Those are
things you should put in your book. Will [Card] still write the book with
you?" Yes. "Then get started." So, darling, it looks as if I must write The
Damned Autobiography (a good title). Will you help me with it, read and
edit as I go? Oh, you must . . .[23]

He said yes, and the die was cast—leaving unresolved the issues of
marriage and divorce. She would go to Rochester.

"She was eager to get out of Manhattan," says Card. "Her only concern
about leaving was Minary and her checks. But it was actually easier for
the Paley Foundation to justify [the allowance] if she was 'working on a
book' at Eastman House." By charter, the foundation was not supposed to
make grants to individuals, only to tax-exempt organizations. But unbe-

knownst to Card, or even Louise, the money was *not* coming from the Paley Foundation. It was from Bill Paley himself.

"She appeared as an old friend of Mr. Paley's who was down on her luck," says John Minary, an erudite and affable man whose decades of service to Paley began in 1942 when the two men worked in wartime intelligence in the North Africa campaign. "Mr. Paley has a very kind heart; there were a lot of people he knew who had fallen on hard times, and he often helped them out. . . . I think sometimes Louise had the idea it was a kind of prize, a little like the Pulitzer."[24] If Louise thought she was getting an official foundation stipend, Minary saw no reason to disabuse her of the notion nor to discourage her Rochester plans. The Big Move finally took place in March 1956.

"There was a pretty rough period before she got settled in town," says Card. "She stayed at the Treadway Inn on East Avenue, which was the closest to Eastman House. She was there alone for a month or so, and she had that whole place turned upside down. She had so much booze brought to her room—and if they wouldn't bring it to her, she'd go charging out to find some on her own."

When sober, Louise was enthralled with Card's film lectures at Eastman. But when her mercurial temperament was pixilated with gin, the results were explosive.

"She was terrifying as a person," remembers Jan Wahl, a Cornell student and film enthusiast who got to know Louise shortly after she came to Rochester.* "I never knew her to eat anything but oyster crackers. One night I was worried about her being drunk so much and I poured a bottle of gin down the sink, and she almost killed me. I'd say, absolutely, she was a clinical alcoholic then."

In light of current thinking on alcohol dependency, others might say she'd been an alcoholic, if not from the time she took her first drink, at least since she was a teenager in the *Scandals* and *Follies*, when she began going out to speakeasies nightly with her show pals and boyfriends.[25] "I remember waking up next to her once," said one of her lovers, "and being startled by her face staring at me with an absolutely furious look! I finally figured out it was from being an alcoholic—that thing of waking up without knowing right away who the person was you were in bed with."

Card found an apartment for her on East Avenue, selling much of his film collection in order to furnish the place. Despite all her drinking, she was still largely enjoying the novelty of being in Rochester. It was, in a sense, her first real home. But she was not getting much writing done. According to Card:

* Jan Wahl today is the author of some five dozen popular children's books, as well as a film writer and collector.

The first summer in Rochester, she didn't want to be left alone. Or rather, she'd go back and forth—she didn't want to be left alone, she wanted to be left alone. She'd often give me long lectures about how unimportant children were. This is what she expected—that I'd make a break.

That issue would wax and wane constantly in their relationship. But eventually she turned her attention to Eastman House. "General" Oscar N. Solbert, a crusty veteran of both world wars, was the director there—its first. "I introduced her to him," says Card, "and he kept dropping names. Every name he dropped, Louise made it clear she'd been to bed with them. After that, General Solbert always referred to her as 'that woman!' So at first they were hostile to her and then they dismissed her as psychotic. It wasn't until years later that they realized she was an important person."

Louise was winning no popularity contests at Eastman House in 1956, but the staff did all it could to assist her. "We decided we'd do the book together," says Card. "But first she had to see what she was writing about." And so for the first time in her life, Louise began consciously to study films, assaying the silent era and her own critical faculties in a long series of private screenings. "She especially wanted to look at all the Garbos, Gishes, Swansons, Bows and Crawfords," says Card.

And—also for the first time—the Brookses.

Legend, fostered by Louise herself, has it that she could only bring herself to view her own movies at Eastman House when fortified by gin, which she gulped continually in the screening room. Card emphatically denies it.

"She looked at them carefully and analytically, not drunkenly," he says. "She couldn't have written the things she did if she'd been drinking when she saw the pictures."

But surely, in that winter of 1956, there must have been some trepidation before her first viewing of *Pandora's Box*.

"No," says Card, flatly. "Not only did she sit down and watch *Pandora*, but she responded very sharply to everything about it. For instance, I'd arranged a score, and she hated it. 'It's got to be *gritty*—gritty throughout!' she said. So we sat down and taped another score—all Kurt Weill, selected by Louise Brooks herself. Not only *Threepenny* and his light-opera pieces, but from the serious works too, string quartets and the like." As for her acting and the rediscovered beauty of her image:

> Her interest in that was on the level of going through a scrapbook. She was never impressed with her own performances. . . . She was aware that that person on the screen was doing something different from the others, but on the other hand she seemed to have no self-awareness at all. She never felt anything she did was absolutely right. The only time I remember her

remarking on her own beauty was in a reverse-angle shot in *Diary of a Lost Girl*: "Was I sexy! Look at her, look at her!" During the *Pandora* screening, I remember her saying, "Those lights were so hot and Lederer was using this stuff on his hair, you can almost see the steam rising from his head."[26]

THE RESURRECTION of Louise Brooks in Europe was predated by Card's screenings of her films in Rochester, and in New York and Toronto too.* But she was still largely "unresurrected" in America when her first serious profile—written jointly by Card and Brooks herself—appeared in the September 1956 issue of the Eastman House magazine, *Image*: "Out of Pandora's Box: Louise Brooks on G. W. Pabst" consisted of Card's introduction and Louise's three-page essay, "Mr. Pabst."

Word of Louise's reemergence was now spreading fast, as evidenced by a classic 1957 note from Ed Sullivan to Jim Card: "Be sure and give Louise Brooks my very warmest best wishes. She was always a real thorough-bred."[27] Louise was not thrilled by the equine metaphor. But *Sight and Sound*, Penelope Houston's film magazine in London, soon commissioned Card for a much more important article, "The 'Intense Isolation' of Louise Brooks." In that lyrical piece, Card confessed to a hidden agenda in bringing his "lost" actress to Rochester after decades of hibernation: "I had dreamed that, once confronted by the overwhelming evidence of her own effectiveness [on screen], Louise Brooks would at last succumb to the lure of the 'comeback trail' that has brought Lila Lee, Mary Astor and Bette Davis to face the television cameras. [But] instead of falling in love with herself, she became suddenly enraptured with motion pictures."[28]

And with writing.

Card is not modest about his importance to Louise's writing at this crucial point in her life, nor should he be. He gave her advice, assistance, and, most of all, confidence. They would indeed work on her book together—but not the autobiography.

Women in Film was the new project, a collaborative effort of complementary essays by Brooks and Card. "The idea was that I'd 'set up' an actress and then she'd pull her down, or vice versa," he says. "Once in a while we might agree, for the same or different reasons." It was to be a kind of literary "Sneak Preview" before its time, focusing on a dozen subjects: Joan Crawford, Lillian Gish, Greta Garbo, Clara Bow, Gloria

* The first American, post-1920s public screenings of *all* of Louise's major films took place at Eastman House's Dryden Theatre in Rochester, under Card's supervision: *Beggars of Life* (October 18–19, 1952), *Love 'em and Leave 'em* (May 12–13, 1956), *The Diary of a Lost Girl* (April 9–10, 1957), *Pandora's Box* (June 9–11, 1958), and *Prix de Beauté* (June 27, 1958). Before 1960, Eastman House had the only American prints of those films. The Toronto screenings resulted in Louise's fond twenty-two-year friendship with Fraser Macdonald of the Toronto Film Society, for which Louise served as an official "patron" from 1965 to 1982.

Swanson, Marion Davies, Norma Shearer, Joan Bennett, Pola Negri, Betty Bronson, Marlene Dietrich, and—possibly as a finale—Louise Brooks herself. In case anyone wondered about her polemical bent, she described the book as "a study of extraordinary, uniquely beautiful women and the success with which they preserved their originality of face and personality against the vicious grinding of the producers who would reduce them to a commodity as uniform, as interchangeable, as expendable and cheap as canned peas." [29]

The concept was novel in every respect—and therein lay its publishing problem: There was no precedent for such a thing. The serious treatment of film was still in a primitive state in 1957: Among major American universities, only NYU, UCLA, and USC had film-studies departments; there were precious few film histories or critical works in book form. Paul Rotha, Rudolf Arnheim, and James Agee were among the few film writers taken seriously—but so seriously that they were judged to have little general-reader appeal. Nevertheless, Card and Brooks moved forward, completing their Joan Crawford section first. They sent it off quickly to the Macmillan Company, and just as quickly, on July 25, 1957, came the rejection letter from editor Charlotte Painter: "I enjoyed reading the pieces on Joan Crawford very much, and I am sorry that this did not seem a book that Macmillan could undertake." Among Louise's rejected insights was this passage:

> To me Joan Crawford's screen portrayals are all one: a series of transparencies through which she projects her daydream—herself—a wonderful abused kid. On the screen every ladylike effort is stretched by the memory of self-abasement; the salt of every tear is the salt of self-pity.
>
> . . . Leading a life in triplex—the person she was, the person she thought she was and the screen person—she played [her roles] like Joan Crawford imagining herself to be Gloria Vanderbilt playing the part of a poor, kicked-around whore. To be a movie star and not approve of her private self; to feel that Hollywood does not, and the public would not, approve of her private self, makes for a deadly state of confusion. . . .
>
> Like every young girl in pictures, Crawford also must have been influenced in her personal life by that movie concoction called a "sympathetic" starring part. For sex and box office, the heroine is made to look as bad as possible through most of the picture but done up in the end like an organdy apron as a sop to the American myth of womanhood. . . .
>
> As for Crawford's Flaemmchen [the stenographer who sells herself to a rich man] in Grand Hotel and her Sadie Thompson in Rain, they are utterly consumed by her pity. The fate-worse-than-death treatment given the trollop role by the highly emotional actress has always been a wonder to me anyhow. Not that I advocate making a life of shame enticing, but to be so

widespread both in reality and on the screen it must bear some mark of attractiveness.

I once knew a real Flaemmchen [Jane Kent] in New York, and if she ever felt sorry for herself, it was because she missed getting some deserved adornment, not because she wasn't a good girl getting varicose veins behind the counter in the 10-cent store. Through her boyfriend, a bellboy at the Waldorf Astoria, she met and made herself agreeable to a variety of gentlemen ranging from Texas politicians to Hindu princes. In a simple grey suit with her golden curls piled high on the top of her head, done up for a weekend with one of these men, nothing could have been farther from her spirit of delight than Joan Crawford's gloomy preparations in *Grand Hotel* to go away with Wallace Beery. In his place, grown uneasy under her accusing eye, I should have sent her off to the nearest Christian Science Reading Room.[30]

Macmillan wasn't ready for this. "It was top-notch stuff," says Card, despite his basic disagreement with her viewpoint. "She was really getting into the swing of writing." Easily discouraged as always,* Louise threw her copy away and Card stuck his in a drawer, where it has remained until now.

In another drawer—never even submitted to a publisher—was Louise's "Gloria Swanson" of the same year. Louise scrawled "HOLD FOR FACTS" across the top, but never returned to it. The eleven-page portrait has a typically bleak, Brooksian conclusion:

My last sight of Swanson was in the TV show, "This Is Your Life," seen in January, 1957. Brave and bold she came on with scarves like banners flying from her shoulders and a gay little black hat sitting on her head grown so big now for the neat body. And the nose, when they cut to a close shot of her sitting with a grim rein on her poise, the nose that had so endearingly defied the laws of gravity, now hung heavy over her face. . . .

And then the agony began. An aging dandy, once the gallant Rod La Rocque, stalked down stage to say, "Gee, Gloria, remember the old Essanay days in Chicago? You sure were a beauty then." Then Mack Sennett telling her what a great heart she had in the old comedies—making a ten-foot jump off a bridge for as many takes as were needed. And Swanson couldn't get a word in edge-wise to correct him. And then Jesse Lasky, looking diffident and boyish still, speaking in his inoffensive tenor, reminding her of how she left Paramount to produce on her own—left an offer of $17,500 a week. "No, it was $18,000," she answered with her delicate voice all gone now, with her true, almost harsh, but wonderful voice.

---

* "I do not agree with people who think criticism and rejection are good for the development of a strong character," she once wrote Kevin Brownlow. "My soul is shrunken and scarred with rejection. And you may be sure every publisher who turned down your book has robbed you of a little faith in yourself."

They had given her a plug for the Gloria Swanson dresses and all the people were gone and she was telling about her work for her favorite charity but she couldn't wind it up. Ralph Edwards had to pick up the finish. Swanson was buried.[31]

THE SWANSON and Crawford pieces had not worked, but for once Louise did not give up. Her next subjects would be the greatest stars of all —Lillian Gish and Greta Garbo. *Women in Film* as a book concept was more or less dead. But "Gish and Garbo" might stand on its own, because this time she had a unifying theme—her favorite—"The Executive War on the Stars." She was intuitively certain of her theory that the studios wrecked the careers of major stars who threatened their power. All she needed was facts.

Again, though he did not fully share her thesis, Card helped her establish a factual basis for it, pointing her toward the right reference materials, over which she pored for months. The result was the most controversial piece she ever wrote—and the first to be published in a major film magazine, *Sight and Sound*.* After it appeared, Dwight Macdonald wrote to commend her article "because it said exactly what needs to be said about the Hollywood producers and their treatment of artists. You know the truth from the inside and have expressed it poignantly."[32]

But not everyone was so convinced of her "truth." One of those who wrote in protest to Louise was Lawrence J. Quirk, nephew of *Photoplay* editor James Quirk, whom she had accused of collaboration with the studio executives in their "war." In her replies to Larry Quirk, Louise seemed to backtrack:

> Nobody else [but James Quirk] ever wrote the truth about the Academy of Motion Picture Arts and Sciences: "The hands that sign the paychecks directed its first decisions, and justified [my] former statement that it was conceived in insincerity and born with a transparent veil of bunk." (Oct. 1927) . . . . If I did not think he was an extraordinary man of excellence, as zestful as his name, I wouldn't be bothered with him. Whatever my "misinformed" idea is, it is not "anti-Quirk." During my three years at Paramount he was wonderful to me. . . . Remember that this writing racket is new to me and I need your love and help. Everybody blasts me. But Jimmy Quirk thought I was okay.[33]

Yet in later reprintings of the essay, Louise never corrected the characterization of Quirk or gave the main reason Gish left Hollywood (to resume her stage work). Gish herself gave mixed signals. At the time, she wrote to praise Louise:

---

* For the full discussion of Louise's "Executive War on the Stars" theory, see chapter eleven.

I cannot sail for Italy without sending you a note of thanks, admiration and wonder! First my gratitude—then my pride that a woman of our profession had so fine a writing talent—then amazement that you could delve so long and deep as to learn so much of the tactics of the company and people you write about. My own family did not know many of the things in your article.[34]

But asked about "Gish and Garbo" in 1987, the great Gish at age ninety had a more skeptical view: "I always wondered where she *was* and how she *knew* all those things. I must tell you that I never saw her, never met her, and never saw any of her movies. I always thought she was more interested in print."[35]

Louise's first year in Rochester was intense on many levels, and so, by this time, was her curiosity about all the revisionist esteem for her and her films in Europe. She now had a desire to see for herself and to spend some time traveling with Jim Card, which is what they did, in November 1957. It was her first time on Continental soil in twenty-seven years.

The first stop was Copenhagen, where Card's good friend Ove Brusendorff was director of the Danish Film Museum. No homage was scheduled there—just a round of socializing centering on Brooks, Card, and Brusendorff (1909–1986), a Danish resistance fighter in World War II. Ib Monty, Brusendorff's young assistant then, now the museum's director, recalls the lady and her visit:

> I remember her as a hard-boiled, fast-talking, fast-drinking, fast-smoking "American" type. I couldn't catch up with her. She had this drinking problem, I know, because Brusendorff had a bottle of Danish schnapps called *Akvavit,* and she got angry every time Card discreetly removed the bottle. "Don't do that, Jim!" He had a fatherly attitude—I think he was concerned about her condition and was trying to see that she wouldn't be drunk and cause a scandal. She was always chain-smoking. . . . And you couldn't flatter her. Other stars I have met, they want to please and say the right thing. She didn't have that attitude at all. To a young man like me, she was rather frightening. This was a woman of the world, she had a tough life, she'd been through a lot, she had no illusions. . . . We were all in love with this *picture* of Louise Brooks, and then suddenly you see her 25 years later, and she was totally changed. That is a banal impression, I know. But with someone like Claudette Colbert, for example, you could see her and follow her life and she didn't really change. But with Louise Brooks, it was as if she turned into another personality completely.[36]

Every one of the Danish Film Museum's two dozen photos of Louise in Copenhagen shows her with a drink, a cigarette, or both, and usually a sullen glare as well. She did, however, submit to interviews with Vibeke

Broderson Steinthal for the film museum magazine, *Kosmorama*, and with Swedish poet Folke Isaksson, who later wrote a profile of her for Stockholm's *Dagens Nyheter.*

Brooks and Card stayed at Copenhagen's eighteenth-century Hotel d'Angleterre, a five-star establishment catering then as now to crowned heads. Its windows afforded deluxe vistas of fairy-tale harbors and the quaintly garish architecture of Christian IV. Beneath the twelve-foot ceilings of their French Empire–style suite was every luxury, including heated towel bars in the bathroom, but mostly Louise availed herself of the liquor supply and the chance to engage Card in a series of sexual encounters and arguments that were far more heated than the towel bars.

"Both she and Jim were wild people," says Jan Wahl, who was then in Copenhagen on a Fulbright. One day Wahl took Louise to dinner, but the meal did not go exactly as planned:

> I decided on a place called Syv Små Hjem—the Seven Little Houses— one of the nicest in Copenhagen. We were practically alone in the restaurant, and she didn't know what to order, so I ordered lobster thermidor. When the plate came, she did an amazing thing: she just turned it upside down on the floor. The waiter came and without a word, he took away the mess, and then he came back with a bottle of Tanqueray gin—which was exactly what she wanted. I got the idea she was in some kind of telepathic communication with him.[37]

From Denmark, her journey continued to Paris, where Louise met Henri Langlois and spent an amusing evening at the Crazy Horse Saloon —or the "Grazy Orse," as Langlois called it. She was thrilled when "after 27 years the waiters at the Ritz Bar remembered me and came out to kiss me. This brought great snorts from Henri—and much laughter from everyone else enquiring whether the waiters had come out on crutches. None of my other old haunts did I see because Henri kept saying, 'Is finish.' But he was wonderful to me—no one can make me laugh like him. He has an unlimited assortment of ludicrous faces, mostly of a saintly turn, with which to illustrate his text."[38]

In Barcelona, Louise wanted to see the Gaudí architecture, and she met the author Robert Ruark at her hotel. "The last time I ever danced was with Louise in Barcelona," remembers James Card.

From there, it was on to Madrid, where she realized a lifelong desire to examine the El Grecos at the Prado—and then home, bittersweet home, to Rochester.

The European voyage had had its lovely moments, and Louise wrote Brusendorff to thank him for everything from "the beautiful memories" to the herring in wine vinegar (no mention of lobster thermidor). But the trip had increased the tensions between Brooks and Card. Upon his re-

Louise and James Card in Barcelona, 1958

turn, Card came under fire for his semiscandalous relationship with Louise and her tempestuous presence at Eastman House. In a huff, he resigned, but General Solbert refused to accept the resignation. Card stayed on.

Louise, meanwhile, was in a constant tizzy about her Paley allowance. Terrified of losing it, she was convinced she had to collect the money personally. That required a grueling 650-mile round-trip drive from Rochester to New York City, and those monthly runs—six hours down, turn around, six hours back—are among Card's darkest memories of the period. One particular nightmare stands out in his mind: "On the way back from New York, I saw she'd concealed a bottle of gin which she kept nipping from along the way. She was getting drunker and drunker, and all of a sudden as we're speeding along the thruway, she just decided to get out of the car!"[39] She actually opened the door and started to get out. He forcibly restrained her. But that trek—in February 1958—mercifully turned out to be their last. The next month, when Louise phoned John Minary at the foundation to say she could not get down to New York, he was undisturbed. It had all been unnecessary: From now on, the money would simply be mailed.

At this point in a chronology of her life that she prepared years later, Louise wrote "MENOPAUSE" in large capitals. Its physical and emotional changes did nothing to diminish her volatility, but at least she had her writing and her beloved cat Suzy—a recent gift from Card—to look after. Then in September 1958, not long after "Gish and Garbo" went to *Sight and Sound*, Louise got a call from Langlois in Paris: He wanted to mount a full-scale *hommage*, screening *Love 'em and Leave 'em*, *Pandora's Box*, and *The Diary of a Lost Girl*, among others. Would she attend?

She would—this time, without Jim Card. *Variety* picked up the story on October 22, 1958:

> Louise Brooks, film ingenue of the 1920s, will get the nostalgic treatment Nov. 5–7 in Paris when the Cinémathèque Française via its archivist, Henri Langlois, organizes one of its "homages" to stars of yesteryear. . . .
>
> Miss Brooks will fly to Paris Oct. 27 to personally participate in the "discovery" of herself 30 years later.

In Paris, the newspapers were billing her as "the Marilyn Monroe of the silents," and she was given such regal treatment at the Royal Monceau (the site of her glorious one-night stand with Pabst in 1929) that she refused to leave the hotel, except for the main ceremony. After the *Pandora* screening at the Cinémathèque's theater on the Rue d'Ulm, Langlois threw a grand reception in her honor, where she was besieged by several hundred young fans with autograph books. After running that gauntlet, she quickly retreated for the bulk of the month to her bed and its red quilt, admitting only Lotte Eisner, the odd visitor such as Kenneth Anger (pre–*Hollywood Babylon*), Henri Langlois ("I didn't understand a word he said"),[40] and Mary Meerson, his live-in companion and chief assistant:

> Mary decided to hate me because she thought I had designs on Henri—God forgive her! One day alone in my room at the Royal Monceau I nailed her with the truth of our situation and cleared the air. She became my friend and took care of me like a mother. She is the most generous person I ever knew. She arranged for me to see films in an outside projection room which

she paid for; she loaded me with orchids and perfume; she would have had me meet anyone in Paris if she could have gotten me out of bed.[41]

Louise's lethargy—and the comforts of the Royal Monceau—caused her to cancel a trip to the Cinémathèque Suisse and remain in Paris, where she ventured out more than she admitted. On one occasion, she met Man Ray, the surrealist artist-photographer, who had long admired her and soon sent her, upon her return to the States, one of his small abstractions.

"The surrealists were always in love with her," says Robert Benayoun, the editor of the French film magazine *Positif*, in Paris. "Man Ray loved that kind of face and image."[42]

With Thomas Quinn Curtiss, drama editor of the *International Herald Tribune* in Paris, she encountered the great comedy director Preston Sturges, who was so down-and-out that he had pawned his coat and was cadging drinks from friends:

> Whenever I would go out at night it was with Tom Curtiss to the Elysée Matignon where we would meet Preston who was so beautiful, so bitter, so tragic, so brave—it broke my heart. . . . Preston asked for so little—to pay for a brandy, the gas for his teensy car, get his winter coat out of hock. I could not help him because, as a guest of the French government, I could not ask him up to my room for lunch and a drink. Langlois hated Sturges— chiefly because Preston spoke better French than Henri.
>
> After viewing this tragedy of a human being, I find his films of Hollywood superficial nonsense.[43]

By far the most precious thing Louise took home from France was her intimate friendship with Lotte Eisner, which would last until Eisner's death in 1983:

> When I went to Paris . . . I expected to stay at most a week. But Henri became so fascinated by my conduct—I would not go anywhere, meet any- one, go to bed with anyone, buy anything. Amazing! He kept me in Paris for a month to test my authenticity. That was okay with me. He was paying my bills. . . . However, Henri was unwilling to believe that I was happy in my brass bed at the Royal Monceau with books and the radio and gin and tomato juice, and Albert my floor waiter trying to roust me out to go to Mass across the street. As a sop to his "neglect" he started sending Lotte over to entertain me every day.[44]
>
> The first day, she came into my room, gave me a hard look and said, "I do not like women." Perhaps she was concerned about the stories of my being a lesbian. At any rate, she made me laugh so much that she too laughed with the joyful laugh of a child, which made us friends forever. She

brought me black bread and Swiss cheese and yellow apples; I gave her coffee and American chocolate bars. Then we would talk about people and films, but mostly about books—Proust, Goethe, Tolstoy, Dickens, Samuel Johnson, Ring Lardner. Lotte seemed to have read every genius in every language, and Louise got an education. . . .[45]

She became the best friend and the finest person I have ever known. . . . But she never talked about herself except on those rare occasions when I accidentally touched the secret release to her private life. . . .

I do not remember much about her hiding films in the wine cellars of friends around France, except that the weight of the film cans damned near broke her back, and she thought it was a lot of fun. Henri, over a period of months, kept the German officers amused, showing them films and confusing them among piles of unidentified cans while the treasures which they sought disappeared. . . .

Henri's jealousy . . . has prevented her from getting credit for much that is great about the Cinémathèque Francaise. . . . Another time Henri was laughing because I would go nowhere without Lotte. "We are very happy," I said. "Two old maids together."[46]

THE 1958 Paris *hommage* gratified Louise in profound ways. It was conclusive proof of her "resurrection" as an artist, and the unfeigned affection of Eisner, Langlois, and Meerson was proof of her ability to inspire love. The number of outside excursions belied her claim that she never left the brass bed. And the trip apparently satisfied her desire to travel once and for all, for upon returning to Rochester, she became even more of a recluse. Astonishing but true: Louise left Rochester only once again.

That one final excursion was on the occasion of a rare screening of *Prix de Beauté* at the 92nd Street YMHA in New York City, on January 12, 1960. She was to make a short speech. And as she had not seen her New York friends in almost four years, it would be a reunion as well, and so she started early in the day to fortify herself with gin. First item on the agenda was lunch with Lillian Gish—a fact Gish has since forgotten, as Louise was only one of many guests. Brooksie was hitting the wine pretty hard, and Lillian was distracted by phone calls. "At the end," recalls Jan Wahl, "when we were all saying goodbye, Louise really felt out of it and she just said, 'Godammit!' She was summing up her philosophy of the moment—and Miss Gish took her by the shoulders and said, 'Louise, God *bless* it!' It was a perfect moment."[47] And then, said Louise, "[Lillian] gave me an encouraging hug and damn near broke my rib cage."[48]

The turnout at the YHMA was a "This Is Your Life" scene to match Gloria Swanson's. In addition to a large audience, nearly all of Louise's pals showed up to cheer her on, including Peggy Fears (with her girlfriend,

*The reunion of Louise and Richard Arlen at Sibley's
department store in Rochester, 1962*

"Miss Fairweather," NBC's sexy-voiced weatherwoman), Jane Kent, John Springer, Lenore Scheffer Bland, Jimmy Glennon, Jan Wahl, and "Butch." Only "Don the Marine" seems to have been absent; he wasn't much for culture. Though she had been drinking fairly heavily, Louise was in control and well received. Her breathtaking beauty in the film itself —receiving its New York premiere thirty years after it was filmed—left everyone in awe. The evening was a great success, but all the fuss had made her more nervous than the *hommage* in Paris.

"I memorized a 10-minute talk which I delivered without a script or mike," she later wrote. "Every three sentences the audience would stop me with roars of laughter. It was most flattering. But when I got back to Rochester I vowed I would never leave it again."[49]

Louise was true to her vow and her desire for renewed cloistering; her forays outside were fewer, her solitude greater. But among the visitations that could not be prevented were her dreams. One of them was so startling that she recorded it in a sleepy scrawl in her diary, July 16, 1960:

Eddie Sutherland—a fine apartment in New York. He comes in with tramps. I must live with him again. Beekman Place. He is still 30. The apartment is littered by his friends who drink all Scotch and smoke all cigarettes. I scream. A brown-eyed girl clutches me: "But I must find my bag with my money!" Tearing away, I find the apartment much bigger. A dining room, another bedroom with children. I have already thrown out my colored maid who turned white with red pimply children destroying the apartment. Last scene—a room walled in yellow satin with appliqué figures eight feet high, breathing and billowing at me.

The next day, George Marshall phoned to tell her that Eddie was "very ill in London." But he recovered.

A flesh-and-blood face from the past materialized in late September, 1962, when actor-turned-fashion-promoter Richard Arlen came to Rochester to promote a line of dresses at Sibley's department store. Nobody told him Louise Brooks lived there, or that she'd show up for the luncheon in his honor. More than thirty years had passed since their last meeting, and for a minute, reported the local paper, "a slight tempest raged":

> "You didn't know me," stormed Louise, whose silvering tresses are now worn off the forehead and sweeping down behind in ballet style. She had handed him a reminder—some stills from two movies in which they starred. . . .
>
> "You didn't wear your bangs," he told Louise, who now was lightly weeping. "But I knew the instant I saw the picture."
>
> When the reproaches subsided, they talked with a rush about two dozen topics, including their roles in *Rolled Stockings* . . . what's the news of Clara Bow . . . how Arlen wouldn't forget the time Louise sent her new Rolls-Royce back to the shop to be satin-surfaced because she didn't like shiny cars. . . . Louise remembered he was the first to popularize the he-man, no-makeup look. Arlen remembered Louise attracted much attention with her "wicked eyes."[50]

Time had healed this, if not every, wound.

Through the turmoil of the last decade, Louise had clung with surprising tenacity to her Catholicism. Though she was not exactly pious, her faith sustained her in a way to which only her confessors were privy. The absent Father Burkort's role was gradually assumed by Father Henry Atwell, who was not so holy he couldn't take a drink with her on occasion. She also took to visiting Rochester's Cenacle Convent, where she particularly enjoyed the company of Mother Digges and sometimes passed the length of an afternoon with the nuns in such tranquil pursuits as sewing. Their calming influence was important in view of her off- and-ongoing battle with alcohol. Sometimes, as on Easter Sunday 1962, she attained a brief ecstasy.

"A glorious Easter, darling," she wrote her sister June, also a Catholic convert. Inspired by Mother Janet Erskine Stuart's "zest of a glorious fight," she felt that the higher will "that prevents me from drinking is infinitely superior to mine, which is nagging at me continuously to let go —get drunk." Mother Stuart's example helped her see "the sin of thinking, saying, doing things in judgment of others—straightening them out, setting my superiority against their inferiority." The next sentence she underlined heavily: *"The cross is different for each one, so we often make the mistake of thinking that we could bear any other better than our own."* Mother Stuart's revelation was that "we change too easily under joy and sorrow. They take us off our duty. Joys and sorrows are meant to exist in the same soul, they are meant to follow each other in regular succession. Joy is the herald of sorrow, and sorrow of joy."[51]

She seemed almost to be reviving a quality which Father Burkort had ascribed to her spiritual life before:

> Not only did she have an intense devotion to St. Thérèse, she had a really deep insight into mysticism. She was interested in St. Bernard and had written to me about how much she loved his writings. She had a deep inclination toward mysticism—the heights, you know, not just contemplation; not pursuing God, but God's pursuing *you* in a sense. You get to such a degree of feeling and emotion that you become really intense in your love of God. I suspected in her writings that she was arriving at that.[52]

From 1959, Louise kept a prayer card of Pope John XXIII, invoking the success of the upcoming Vatican Council. She spoke to few friends about her faith, but one of them was Jan Wahl, who says, "I always thought the main reason she converted was to stop herself from committing suicide."

Another reason was to find love. But by late 1963 she and James Card had reached their nadir. He would not leave his wife; and by trying to keep pace with Louise, he feared he might be on the road to alcoholism himself. She could no longer tolerate their frustrating situation. A complicated mix-up in October 1963, involving a visit to Rochester by Langlois and Beatrice Couve de Murville, daughter of the French foreign minister, left Louise convinced that Card and Langlois were plotting to humiliate her. In a stroke, she cut herself off from both men, berating Card for his "betrayal" and accusing him of everything from stealing her photographs to depriving her of research materials. She wrote paranoid letters to that effect to Card's friends and employers, demanding that he stay out of her life forever. He said he would do so happily—and when he later wrote to apologize, she renewed the attack, describing his apology as "more doubletalk from a thief and a liar." Nothing could mitigate her rage, which had the tragic ring of a Woman Rejected.

George Pratt, the Eastman House film historian who knew them both intimately and was caught in the middle, had harsh words for both. Brooks he found impossibly willful and Card full of ulterior motives:

> Although he rescued Louise, he also—because he was beginning to be bored with his job and because he was eager to collect erotic legends around himself—later harassed Louise and kept trying to push her back (on a moderate scale and for his own amusement) into the life she had left in New York. He definitely mistreated her. [53]

Card's view is that "she read a lot of things into me in that period that really weren't there, but she wanted them to be." He remembers Pratt warning him, "She'll end up hating you. She's bound to resent you because you brought her back to life after she'd almost succeeded in destroying herself."

Once Louise made a break of any kind, it was decisive. And with the termination of her reliance on Card, she was likewise terminating her Catholicism. Her sister June attributed it to the fact that one day "she went to confession to a young priest who was a greenhorn and said something to upset her, which was unfortunate because Bishop [Fulton J.] Sheen lived just down the street, and he would have been marvelous with her." In any event, "I left the Church in the spring," she wrote Jan Wahl on October 18, 1964, summarizing her disillusionment coldly and disdaining the mystical factor:

> I was an "intellectual" Catholic. I tried hard for 11 years, all the time observing myself and other Catholics. For myself, I found that it led often to great mistakes. For instance, trying to behave like a "Christian" to Card led to his abuse of me. If I had batted him around as he expected and wanted, he never would have gotten out of hand. Then I found that far from simplifying my problems, [Catholicism] increased them. To my personal pride and contempt and prejudices, it added those of the Church. Added to my natural ability to make enemies, it augmented their hatred with people's hatred of Catholics. . . .
>
> Yet, I might have held out a little longer if I had not observed what it did to ordinary people. . . . The better Catholics people think they are, the more intolerant and nastier they are to everybody else. Priests ridden with ambition and envy. Nuns filled with holy superiority. And in the end the whole Church is just another grand financial racket. . . . They have had their last buck from me. . . . And priests wanting to censor my writing! God damn them all. [54]

It was no coincidence that Louise's Catholicism ended almost precisely with her ardor for James Card. If he had betrayed her, so had God. The worst of the Brooks-Card "feud" lasted from 1963 to 1966, after which there was a partial reconciliation. But for now, this last great love had turned to hatred on her part.

Full forgiveness would take twenty years.

The wrenching break with James Card had another dimension—that of the child's breaking away from the parent—which was significant for Louise as a writer. She was now, in the mid-1960s, entering into the full flower of her literary life. She perhaps had to "kill off" her mentor in order to be independently productive after a long apprenticeship.

Between 1959 and 1963 she had, after all, published not a single article —nothing since "Gish and Garbo." Her only outside activity was an appearance on April 12, 1963, before the Catholic Women's Club of Rochester to deliver a feminist speech titled "The Influence of Movie Stars on the Freedom of Women." From now on, she would devote all her mental and emotional energies to writing. "In October 1963," she wrote, "having become increasingly sensitive to all contacts with people, I vowed to stay alone in my toy apartment with my toy typewriter, my toy books and articles, my toy mind."[55] In a therapeutic burst of productivity, she would publish eight pieces in the next four years. At the same time, she became a compulsive letter writer, often cranking out more than a dozen a week —letters that were crucial in helping her think through the subjects of her articles.

"I want to write, not for movie fans but for all who love extraordinary people," she once told Jim Card.[56] But first she had to write for the movie fans. The first three pieces she turned out were for the French-Canadian magazine *Objectif:* "ZaSu Pitts" in August 1963, and then a two-part biographical sketch, "Louise Brooks par elle-même," in the February–March and April–May issues of 1964. They paid little but satisfaction.

What increased her confidence, as well as her correspondence and the quality of her articles, was a powerful new friendship with Kevin Brownlow, the British film writer–historian, then in his early twenties. Brownlow's first letter arrived from London in July 1965 in praise of her "Pabst and Lulu"—a reworking of her earlier essay—in the Summer 1965 issue of *Sight and Sound.* He requested some personal reminiscences from her about directors and films of the twenties, to which she replied that "to give you 'some personal reminiscences' is to write a book. You must ask me specific questions about those directors I knew."

In his answer, and in the 200 letters to follow, he did just that—provoking the single greatest body of Louise Brooks correspondence. She was soon asking as many questions as she answered and initiating a brilliant exchange of views on the process of writing itself.

"In every other art," she wrote Brownlow, "a person, if he will, can judge his work. But I cannot, and evidently nobody else [can] or there would be thousands less scribblers. . . . I write by rules. Is it true? Is it well written as to the choice of words—will it translate? Cut every word and sentence that tickle my vanity and make me feel learned or intellectually superior. Or witty. . . ."[57] "Whenever I get confused in overwriting with words that mean nothing, I get up from the typewriter and act out the scene with the sights and sounds exactly as I remember them."[58] No literary endeavor was so dangerous as film writing, she maintained:

> Just remember these rules in writing film stuff: First, Dryden's law—cut everything "in which fancy predominates, for self-love may easily deceive." Then apply this rule to everything your subjects tell you. Their gags, funny stories, feats of bravery, acts of insolence were all invented by Monty Brice who rewrote them out of ancient barroom lies. (There is nothing quite so damning to integrity as going for a gag, printing it, and then finding it applied to ten other people in ten other books.)[59]

Brownlow rapidly assumed Card's former role as her literary counselor and sounding board—but at a distance. Then in mid-1965, he came to Rochester and taped a ruminative interview with her in which she observed that "Dickens sat down and wrote everything straight off. Somerset Maugham would work over one of his stories for hours and hours. Neither of them could have been any better or any worse if one had been slower and the other faster. . . . I write everything in my head, so that when I sit down to the typewriter it's composed. I'm not talking as if I can write well, I'm just telling you how I work."[60]

The interview was for Brownlow's forthcoming book, *The Parade's Gone By* . . . . When she got the transcript, she sharply pointed out the difference between transcribed conversation and good written sentences, warning him against repetition of the same idea in different sets of words, and comparing the problem to film editing: "As a cutter, if you put three takes of the same shot in a scene, you would be out of work."[61]

As for her own writing, and the method to the madness of where she "planted" her articles, Louise made a grand declaration of independence:

> I write neither for fame nor money. I will not have my work tampered with. *Playboy* asked me to do an article about Sex in the Twenties but called it off when I said they could not change a word in it. They would turn it into tits and free fucking for men. That is what they pay for, either writing cut to their taste or recut by them to their taste. All American magazines pay high for this privilege. . . . They do not give a damn about film history.[62]

She was incensed at the exploitative *Playboy* film articles of Hollis Alpert and Arthur Knight, epitomizing the American journalistic lust for money and cheap thrills. She preferred the little magazines abroad—and was sending off her "Marlene" to Robert Benayoun in Paris at that very moment, April 1966. The French did not censor her nor were they squeamish about *real* sex as opposed to *Playboy* titillation. "I don't feel I know a man [well enough to write about him] unless I've slept with him," she would say. To Kevin she summed it up neatly: "I do not bring up sex in my articles unless it has a direct bearing on relationships—and it always does."[63]

It certainly had a bearing on "Charlie Chaplin Remembered," which she wrote for Jonas Mekas's *Film Culture* in the spring of 1966.* Other than the early "Mr. Pabst" for *Image* in 1956, it was her first article published in the States—a companion piece to Brownlow's "Watching Chaplin Direct *The Countess from Hong Kong*" in the same issue. This time Louise's autobiographical approach was more nuanced—not yet perfected, but evolving in the right direction. There was no existing model for the way she wanted to write, but she admired Josef von Sternberg's bitter 1965 memoirs, *Fun in a Chinese Laundry*, which inspired her to revanchist self-revelation in a conversation with John Kobal:

> All of us write because we have suffered some terrible humiliation and we've got to set the record straight and get even somehow. . . . Instead of giving us that gag title from one of the first Edison pictures, he really should have called it *Why I Am Greater than Marlene Dietrich*. Because the whole thing is this argument to prove that he was a great director of genius and she was his puppet, manipulated and *created* by him. . . .[64]

Sternberg was "the greatest director of women that ever, ever was," thought Louise:

> In telling about Dietrich he solves the terrific mystery of *her* mystery! . . . Dietrich always used to mystify me because I wondered what the hell she was thinking about with that long, gorgeous stare. [Sternberg] tells you in one simple line of direction: he said to her, "Count six, and look at that lamp post as if you couldn't live without it." So, giving her these strange thoughts which she was able to concentrate on to fill her mind, he also gave her this strange air of mystery, which of course she never had with any other director. . . .
>
> He could take the most gauche, awkward, sexless dame and turn her into a dynamo of sex. . . . Sternberg, with his detachment, could look at a woman and say, this is beautiful about her and I'll leave it, not change it, and this is ugly about her, so I'll eliminate it. . . . With this Dietrich, if you ever saw her in those pre-Sternberg films, she was just a galloping cow, dynamic, so full of energy and awkward, oh, just dreadful, and the first time he saw her, he saw her leaning against the scenery, very bored, because she

* This article is quoted at length in chapter five.

was working in a play, *Zwei Kravatten*, and didn't give a damn. And he saw that and it was lovely. But all of her movements were horrible. So he simply cut out the movements and painted her on the screen in beautiful, striking poses staring at a lamp post.[65]

It started out as an attack and ended up as an even-handed appraisal of Sternberg's genius. But overall, she scorned the deification of directors. The *auteur* theory—that the director is the exclusive "author" or creator of a film—left her cold. She recalled that Eddie Sutherland used to "come home every night after work, throw his feet down on the couch, grab a martini and start talking about Bill Fields: what he did at home, what he did in the scene, what he's going to do tomorrow. He wasn't occupied with the lighting or the camera or the costumes or the scenery, but *with his actors*, which is the whole essence of direction."

Louise was now taking on film theory as well as film history—carrying the discursive battle into the home court of the experts, namely Andrew Sarris. With François Truffaut and André Bazin, Sarris was promulgator of the *auteur* theory, which fascinated Louise even as she strove to discredit it.* After the second issue of *English Cahiers du Cinéma* appeared in New York in 1966, full of *auteurism*, Sarris was delighted to receive a letter "from that luminous beauty, Louise Brooks," which he quoted in his next issue—beside a large photograph of her:

> The Bazin translation . . . took me two hours and three dictionaries to get through. Mind, I am no intellectual judge but it did seem a lot of fancy words . . . to get to the simple fact that "the *politique des auteurs*" is "the negation of the work to the profit of the exaltation of its *auteur*." Ever since the beginning of films, writers and directors have been jealous of the actor's glory, trying to find some way of wiping them off the screen with words.[66]

"Well, damn that Sarris," she wrote Herman Weinberg when she saw herself quoted. "If I had had the least idea that he would publish my letter I would have read it over and made it plain." But, not very secretly, she was thrilled. In the same mail with the *Cahiers*, a promotional advertisement for her "Marlene" piece had arrived, and she was bursting with ideas and accomplishment:

> My letter [in *Cahiers*] does sound funny over the "fine" writing of the famous Kenneth Tynan [on the same page]. . . . What a kick like a mule I got out of getting top billing [in *Positif*] for the 340 words I wrote on Dietrich. From dancing and acting and getting my name in lights and having my

---

* The *auteur* theory was hardly new, nor did it originate with the French or the Americans. As early as 1913, German intellectuals were campaigning for the *Autorenfilm*—films to be judged as the work of a single author-director.

pictures seen by millions I got no feeling whatever. This little ad reaching few—I find overwhelming.

If I could write in profound generalities I would set up, in opposition to the *auteur* theory, the *acteur* theory. I was nothing in films. But those two greatest actors, Chaplin and John Barrymore, counted acting as nothing compared to the praise [they received] as intellectuals. Charlie went mad with praise for A *Woman of Paris* in which he did not appear, while you could do nothing but bore him with his art as an actor. While Barrymore spat upon his art in his last pictures, he set himself up as a philosopher.

Even those who shared the best of two worlds as writers and personalities —Johnson, Lord Byron, Shaw, Fitzgerald—never could resolve the *auteur-acteur* theory. No doubt the answer is in the ease with which you do your work.[67]

Louise could never quite resolve it, either. Three years after these forceful attacks on the *auteur* theory, she wrote a French journalist: "Mr. Pabst made me important. The theatre is shaped by actors: films, by directors." But her *Cahiers* letter to Sarris, her assessment of Sternberg, her *Positif* piece on Dietrich, her exuberant homespun *acteur* theory—all were superb examples of her reflective powers. No wonder that, all of a sudden, everybody seemed to want her memoirs.

It was consistent with the perverse sequence of events in Louise's life that a stream of inquiries and offers to publish her autobiography should begin pouring in precisely when—after years of striving—she was abandoning the idea.

"If she had published *Naked on My Goat*," says James Card, "I was going to come out with a sequel called *Memoirs of the Goat*."[68] His quip relates to Louise's biggest difficulty as a memoirist—"the harming of people."[69] Through the painful trial-and-error process of *Women in Film* and her short articles in esoteric film journals, she had been developing a new style and concept—and just when she was on the verge of perfecting it, *now* they wanted her autobiography. It infuriated rather than pleased her. "It's the story of my life," she fumed to Weinberg. "Whatever I did, I was treated as nothing. The reviews of 1929 and '30 of *Pandora, Diary, Prix de Beauté*—nothing."

It is the same today with my writing. Any publisher will do one of those fucking—and I do mean fucking—as-told-to books of me, but for my own work, they ask me to send them a complete book and they will "look at it." The editor of the University of California Press wrote how marvelously I wrote in the UCLA brochure [for Pauline Kael's 1962 lecture-screening of *Pandora* in her "Psychological Masterpieces of the Cinema" series], and would I send a book to him for him to "look at," as if he couldn't tell already, as if I had nothing to do but write books for his okay.[70]

Ghostwritten sleep-and-tell was not the kind of "sexual truth" she had in mind. Ever since that UCLA screening, Kael and other admirers had been inducing publishers to ask for her memoirs "and I have told them to go fuck themselves."* The number of rebuffed editors and would-be collaborators was growing as Louise responded to their overtures with insults or silence. A Doubleday editor, for example, probably thought he was doing her a favor in September 1966, when he wrote a letter that any other autobiographer would have been thrilled to receive: "Dear Miss Brooks: I have recently heard through Pauline Kael that you have been working on a book of your experiences and career in films. As a great admirer of your work, I would be most interested in the opportunity of *considering* this for *possible* publication. Please let me hear from you and if possible, *send along your manuscript*. Sincerely, James K. Ross."

The emphasis was supplied by Louise in relaying the note to Kevin Brownlow, along with her three-word verdict: "This condescending son-ofabitch."[71]

Later, she wrote Herman Weinberg that she didn't want him to do a book on her, either, because "your exquisite kindness would force you to give me a 'beautiful nature' and readers would say, 'That's not the bitch I know.' "[72] But it was all a moot point. There would be no autobiography now for the same reason as in 1952: She couldn't tell "the whole sexual truth." The issue of discretion, moreover, was closely connected to the issue of finances—and to the advice of her secret counselor.

"Bill Paley is the only man who ever wanted me to understand business," she confided to her brother Theodore, "and he is pleased because I had sense enough to turn down a contract from Thames & Hudson, London, for my biography."[73]

The only way around the problem was the way she had already trod—profile-essays that were selectively autobiographical—and these she continued to write. She produced a lovely vignette on Buster Keaton for Roddy McDowall's *Double Exposure* in 1965, and when McDowall made the pilgrimage to Rochester to meet and photograph "this enigma," he came away deeply moved and with a lifelong friendship:

> What struck me was the degree of her intelligence, her humor and the beauty of her speaking voice—a wondrous speaking voice, mellifluous. It's

---

* That statement by Louise, in a September 14, 1968, letter to Kevin Brownlow, was amended two days later: "I see by my last letter that I am still hamming it up [by] telling publishers 'to go fuck themselves.' I didn't say that. I just meant that."

so regrettable that she wasn't in more talking films because the voice was a musical instrument.

We sat and talked, and after I left, I remember getting into the elevator and having the most extraordinary reaction. It was as if I'd been under such a pressure of fascination and beguilement that suddenly I let go and my whole body just became weak and I remember crying. I was only about 37 years old at the time, and being in the presence of that much life, curiosity, intelligence in this cell-like apartment was almost too much. It was as though the walls would burst because the personality of the woman was so tremendous. And the laughter and the wit and the mercurial sadness of her.[74]

Louise, in turn, was charmed by McDowall, whose *Lord Love a Duck* (1966) she went to see and liked. He and friends John and Bill Springer now took a daring step to bring Louise into the 1960s: They bought her, jointly, her first television set. The TV opened up a world of films and stars she'd never seen before, and actually served as a stimulus to her writing: she had a new batch of heroes (Ava Gardner) and villains (Zsa Zsa Gabor) to work with, especially in her letters.

"She wrote like a dream," says McDowall. "She was very succinct about her point of view, even if it wasn't particularly accurate." Hollywood was like *Rashomon*, anyway—you got conflicting stories of every event, depending on each observer's point of view—and Louise now applied her own quirky viewpoint to a major piece for simultaneous publication in the winter 1966–1967 issues of *Positif* and *Sight and Sound:* "Humphrey and Bogey."

Its thesis was located, classically, in the topic sentence: "Humphrey Bogart spent the last twenty-one years of his life laboriously converting the established character of a middle-aged man from that of a conventional, well-bred theatre actor named Humphrey to one that complemented his film roles—a rebellious tough known as Bogey." The article contained some of Louise's most quoted observations on Hollywood:

> In the years since his death, in 1957, biographers catering to the Bogey Cult have transformed him into a cinematic saint—St. Bogart—in whom I can find scarcely a trace of the Humphrey I first knew in 1924 or the Bogey I last saw in 1943. The earliest strokes in the biographers' portraits are those that paint him as a "loner," a man of "self-determination," who makes "all his own decisions," with regard for nothing beyond immediate satisfaction. Such a description will not do for the twentieth-century film star in Hollywood. Being myself a born loner, who was temporarily deflected from the hermit's path by a career in the theatre and films, I can state categorically that in Bogart's time there was no other occupation in the world that so closely resembled enslavement as the career of a film star.[75]

Bogart's sole choice was that "he might or he might not sign a film contract. If he signed the contract, he became subject to those who paid his salary and released his films. If he did not sign the contract, he was no film star." He signed. And having done so, he "determined from the moment he settled at Warner Brothers, in 1936, all his time not spent before the camera would be spent with journalists and columnists, who would invent for him the private character of Bogey." In the process, he cleverly exploited his scarred mouth through "all kinds of lip gymnastics, accompanied by nasal tones, snarls, lisps and slurs," said Louise. "Only Erich von Stroheim was his superior in lip-twitching." She believed Bogart's new persona had been inspired by his awe of Leslie Howard's natural acting style when they made *The Petrified Forest* together in 1936:

> And once Humphrey grasped the idea that he, too, might achieve success with some version of natural acting, he went about contriving it with the cunning of a lover. For all actors know that truly natural acting is rejected by the audience. . . . To be a successful actor, it is necessary to add eccentricities and mystery to naturalness, so that the audience can admire and puzzle over something different from itself. Leslie's eccentricities were his fondness for his pipe and for English tweed. Bogart's eccentricities were the use of his mouth and speech. As for mystery, Leslie would have become less if he had revealed himself; Bogart did reveal himself and became more.[76]

Finally, she drew a striking set of parallels to prove that each of Bogart's wives—Helen Menken, Mary Philips, Mayo Methot, and Lauren Bacall—"was fittingly chosen to accord with the progress of his career." Their real characters shaped the Bogart-Bogey character until, finally, Bacall became "his perfect screen partner, as seductive as Eve, as cool as the serpent."

It was a haunting, original portrait that drew critical raves at the time it appeared. In 1987, it drew a different kind of rave from Lauren Bacall.

"Absolute garbage," growls Bacall in disgust at the mention of the article. "A total lie. That story about Mrs. Bogart [Mayo Methot] and his acquiring a lisp—absolutely false." And the author of the piece? "*Hmmfff.* She was a little—I don't know, cuckoo."[77]

Now at the peak of her writing skill, Brooks was pleased, if Bacall was not, about "Humphrey and Bogey." In March 1967, she allowed herself a rare night out to see Carol Channing in a touring production of *Hello, Dolly!* (and to meet the star briefly backstage), but then she got immediately down to work on her next big project—a profile of director William Wellman and the making of *Beggars of Life*.

"It is going to be very rough and personal," she wrote Kevin Brownlow. "As usual, I thought I would sit down and knock it out, and as usual I can't. I have to know everything I can. And goddamit, I can't even remember the damned picture."[78] There followed a dozen questions about the plot, locations, and actors. All in all, Louise wrote Brownlow twenty-seven letters concerning Wellman and *Beggars* as she gathered her information and found her point of view. Her investigation of Wellman's service in the Lafayette Flying Corps put the FBI to shame. James Price in London called the article "shattering." Denis Marion in Paris called it "a masterpiece."* To a cousin in Kansas she wrote:

> Now, in September, 1967, I have learned how to write my autobiography disguised as a book of essays. . . . My French and my English editor confirm the fact that "On Location with Billy Wellman" has hit the mark in form and style. The reader, assuming that I am writing about other people, is told the truth about myself.[79]

Out of her self-absorption, Louise had fashioned a literary approach that was paradoxically objective and subjective at the same time. Her keen memory and faultless eye for detail were filtered through a righteous, quixotic, irritable worldview that manifested itself in her life as well as her writing. It illuminated what she saw as the dependable treachery of the world at large—William Paley excepted:

> The truth is that I have been spoiled by Bill Paley who is also the head of a great corporation. He has always believed anything I told him and acted upon it. That is my crowning stupidity. I try to tell the truth and I take it for granted that everybody else operates this way.[80]

In fact, with fewer slips than most, Louise did try to tell the truth. But also in fact, she forever doubted the veracity of everybody else. She had attained a considerable mastery of her art and was now, without apologies, a writer. But she was still recovering from the loss of James Card, who had given her a new life—and then left her to live it, as always, alone.

---

* "On Location with Billy Wellman," quoted extensively in chapter nine, first appeared in the March 1968 *Positif* and May 1968 *London* magazines.

*The many moods, and mugs, of Theodore Brooks
at the Wichita Eagle and Beacon, 1969*

19 · Louise & Theo

There is much to be said in favor of modern journalism. By giving us the opinion of the uneducated, it keeps us in touch with the ignorance of the community. — O S C A R   W I L D E

T H E   need for secrecy concerning William Paley was burdensome for a woman so fond of "the truth" and of speaking her mind. But if her publishing was cramped by Paley's role in her life, her correspondence was unrestrained. The epistles of Louise Brooks went far and wide, to a hundred people on a hundred subjects. But only one remained her constant correspondent-confidant from the beginning to virtually the end—a writer to whom she could turn for personal as well as literary advice.

He was her brother Theodore, the popular Kansas journalist who as a sixteen-year-old had spent that glorious summer of 1928 with her at San Simeon and even picked up a little work as a movie extra. In those days, he was every bit as much the buoyant pleasure-seeker as his sister and a masterful tennis player, too: adventurous, quick-witted, and always outgoing.

Third of the four siblings, Theodore Roscoe Brooks was five years younger than his famous sister. While attending Wichita schools in the 1920s, he won every city boys' tennis championship at every age level. From there his father packed him off to Kemper Military School and then to the Vermont Academy, but the slim harvest of his prepping was just three semesters at Wichita University, where journalism and geology were the only subjects that interested him. He would eventually combine both into a distinguished newspaper career—but in unhurried fashion.

After Theo's return from the West Coast, the problem that plagued him for life began to worsen: his hearing. An adolescent case of measles left him deaf in one ear. It was followed by Ménière's syndrome, an inner-ear disease that severely impaired the hearing in his good ear and subjected him to recurring attacks of dizziness. By the time he was twenty-one, he was legally deaf—but his skill at lip-reading often concealed the fact.

Though classified 4F, Theo did his part for the war effort in Boeing's timekeeping department, where, "seized with ambition," he devised a new form of clock cards and was made supervisor. In 1944, he married Margaret Nolan. And then a friend asked him to take over the oil and market desk of the *Wichita Beacon* for two weeks—two weeks that never ended. Thus did Theo enter into one of the great American newspaper battles of the century.

For decades, the Wichita *Eagle* and Wichita *Beacon* had been waging a vicious war for supremacy that consumed two great Kansas publishing families and their employees. Wichitans enjoyed a kind of breathless anticipation each day to learn what new outrage one side would print against the other. Always fond of a squabble, Louise and the rest of the Brooks clan followed the fray keenly over the years, especially during 1940–1943. In addition to their war dispatches, the dueling newspapers also rivaled each other for news of the home-grown movie star who was now back in their midst. Most of those stories reflected the traditional newspaper obsession with star marriages and divorces. But photogenic Louise Brooks, the celebrity iconoclast, made even better copy because of her periodic clashes with the local police and the local morals.

Louise got slightly better treatment from the *Beacon*, and so did the news. It was just the sort of scrappy, underdog paper to attract the crusading Theo, who joined its staff in July 1947—"gladly captured for $50 a week." His job was to assemble the "Oil Briefs" column, which chronicled the latest drilling bonanzas and disasters throughout Kansas. Only Theodore Brooks—always "Ted" to his friends and readers, but "Theo" to the family—could have approached such a task with round-the-clock zeal, and with his peculiar, joyous sense of humor. In 1952, he wrote Louise from the house in which they both grew up:

> There was a lot going on in the kitchen tonight, so, after putting the children to sleep, I wandered to the bathroom where I sat on the can, pulled up a three-legged table and started to write an Oil Brief. . . . This was in order to forget that I was letting my wife mop the kitchen floor and that I was very hungry and forbidden icebox privileges until the floor dried. Margaret came up just in a [sic] nick of time. The Oil Brief was going stale on me, and the toilet was warm, giving my tail a humid, tropical feeling that was not conducive to Oil Briefing. Which makes me explain that we have a Westinghouse automatic washer in the upstairs bathroom as a matter of plumbing convenience. The water exhaust tube empties in the toilet, the lid of which has been lost in the shuffle—thus my warm seat, the time of which coincided with "Rinse, Warm," with some concern on my part lest the bowl overflow and wash me down the front stairs like a turd in a mill race.[1]

The *Eagle* bought the *Beacon* in 1960 and turned the vanquished enemy's headquarters into its own. A few of the best *Beacon* reporters were retained, Theo among them. He was now back where he started—a lowly staff writer—and working for a paper he had always loathed. As a journalist in Wichita, with a wife and two children, he had no alternative. But Theo was resilient, and, all things considered, it did not take him long to resculpt the career that occupied the rest of his life.

Theodore Brooks was as kinetic as his sister Louise. Both were unreconstructed mavericks at heart: assertive, strong-willed, and opinionated. But they were profoundly opposite in temperament. Beneath his sharp-witted attacks in print lay benevolence, beneath hers lay bile; his was a long fuse, while hers was notoriously short. While Louise would often explode and lash out at the thickheadedness of the world, easygoing Theo had time and patience for everybody.

One characteristic Theo story involved an unfortunate next-door neighbor who suffered from terrible facial deformities, not to mention behavioral quirks, and was shunned by everyone. Margaret Brooks tells the tale with relish:

> Poor old Leonard didn't have any partition in his nose and only had one eye and his nose was split up one side. He said it was because his mother had syphilis before he was born—he just looked like a grotesque monster. . . . Anyway, he'd always try to find Theo and engage him in conversation. Theo never would rebuff him, he'd always be friendly. So one time Theo was downtown on a streetcorner talking to some important guy that thought he was somebody, and suddenly Leonard came by and said, "Hello, Theo!" and Theo said, "Why, hello, Leonard, how are you today?" and made a big fuss over him. After a while, Leonard went on his way, and the big-shot looks at Theo disgustedly and says, "Who was that awful-looking creature?" and Theo says, "My father."[2]

Margaret pauses for a hoot of laughter, then adds: "Theo never told him the difference, never bothered to explain later on. He just didn't give a damn what people thought."

Not unlike his sister Louise.

At the Wichita *Eagle*, Theodore Brooks's desk was situated at the very back of the newsroom. By the late sixties, he had only a tiny percentage of his hearing left, and it was thought that—if he were tucked away in a corner—the shouting matches that were his conversations would least disturb his fellow scribes. Wiry little Theo, at 5 feet 3 inches, was almost exactly the same size as Louise. At sixty, he attributed his vigor to the restorative powers of tennis. He played the game so well that he once goaded Jack Copeland, sports editor of the *Beacon*, into a legendary public bet: Theo could beat him with a frying pan instead of a racket. Copeland wrote a story about it, and a crowd turned out to watch the historic event: Theo won, six-love, six-love. He continued to play into the 1970s, for Theo was in better shape than most men half his age. But he had the fatal Brooks family addiction to cigarettes, which was slowly wreaking havoc with his lungs and bringing on emphysema.

Any conversation with Theodore Brooks was difficult. He was adept at lip-reading, but if one mumbled or had a mustache, the task was laborious. His whimsicality was also a factor. If he liked you, or what you were saying, things went fluently. But Theo's hearing device had a heart and mind of its own, forever whistling, humming, and otherwise going haywire. Oddly enough, it malfunctioned most frequently when his interlocutor was a superior. Often the boss would just give up in disgust. Like every good warrior, Theodore knew the strategic advantages of his handicap. The battle at hand was the bitter American Newspaper Guild struggle of 1970–1971 at the Wichita *Eagle and Beacon*—a holocaust of organizing in which forty journalists eventually quit or were fired. Theo was a leprechaunical guru for his young activist colleagues and now, just a few years from retirement and despite misgivings, he lent his unique undercover skill to the union effort: After lip-reading all strategy sessions inside the editor's glass-enclosed office, he gleefully reported every management move in advance.

Everything Theo did, said, or wrote was so full of wry good humor that it often ran the risk of not being taken seriously. For years, people snickered at the concept of an Oil and Gas Editor—people outside the industry, that is. But petroleum and natural gas constitute one of Kansas's largest industries, and Theo was a tireless champion of independents and "wildcatters." The umbrella word "energy" had not yet been applied to a federal department or entered the general lexicon. But with the "energy crisis" of the seventies, Brooks and his expertise suddenly assumed critical importance. He was named "Energy Editor" of the *Eagle* in November 1972—the first such animal in the nation—from which post he tried to explain to an ostrichlike public what the multinational oil companies and OPEC were up to.

Theodore Brooks was the foremost energy writer not just in the Midwest but in America. In the late fifties and sixties, he had been the first to forecast both the crisis and the profiteering behind it. Now the topic was so hot that the national media recruited him. His February 28, 1974, appearance on NBC's "Behind the Lines" with "energy czar" William Simon even stirred Louise's interest in the subject—and gave her the chance to see him, in the video flesh, for the first time in three decades.

"I was terribly worried that you would be cut from the News-Oil production of 'Behind the Lines'," she wrote him the next day. "As excited as I have ever been in my life I turned on Channel 21 an hour and a half early—to be *sure*. . . . By the time you came on I was fit to be tied. Another great fear was that you might be lousy (I never knew before or realized that you were 100% ham and blossomed on camera).

"Remember, I haven't seen you for 31 years. My first shock being to find you so handsome. The next was your style—dramatic, unique. Everybody else on the show was alike—underplaying the scene. And of course I fairly burst with pride when you were introduced as an 'expert.' The implication being that you were the *only* journalist expert in the whole damned U.S. . . .

"Since Watergate and my discovery that I am the stupidest, most ignorant old bitch in the world . . . , I wish that you will tell me whether I got your message right: [that] there is no conspiracy among the oil companies; that as the sunflower follows the sun by nature, so it is by nature that the oil companies rob the world. They do not have to get together to decide to do what they have been doing since they came into existence."

Louise had understood the message precisely, and from that day forward, her interest in national affairs soared. She now plunged into reflection and spent two days formulating an essay for Theo titled "Footnotes on the Education of an Old Actress":

> I had grown so sick of silly film people and writing silly articles. . . . I was growing quite frantic stalking the library looking for green pastures and not finding them when I was hit with politics and money and how these most complex dealings in human mischief are ruled by the most ordinary men who achieve wealth and power simply by fitting neatly into their appointed slots without disturbing the bureaucratic or organizational machinery. From this viewpoint Nixon could not have avoided being elected in 1972.[3]

It was an assessment with which Theo agreed. But he was most pleased simply to be the catalyst for his sister's intellectual involvement in something other than—and larger than—herself.

"She talked about him quite a bit," Jim Card remembers. "She was exceedingly, extremely fond of him. She suffered vicariously over his hearing loss, but she enjoyed his letters and columns immensely."

Theo's deafness was a terrible burden to him, but a boon to posterity: It required these two articulate siblings to exchange their thoughts in letters, which remain, rather than phone calls, which do not. Their literary admiration was mutual. On many a day, Theo would stride chuckling through the *Eagle-Beacon* city room, waving the latest missive. "Oh, she's a bitch," he would declare with undisguised approval. "Read this!"

On one such day in March of 1971 he brandished a letter from Louise fulminating about Pauline Kael, whose latest book and *New Yorker* piece Theo had made the mistake of recommending.

"I haven't read *The New Yorker* since 1945 when some supercilious slut wrote an ignorant and patronizing series on Martha Graham. . . . [Kael] writes very well on a subject about which she knows nothing. She is a person whose gushing pressure to write and write and write excludes her own life and the thought and reflection and the experience which make silly personal views on films worth reading."

Louise still proffered her own critical pronouncements, however: "Bergman to my mind is the greatest film director today."[4] She loved *Bonnie and Clyde*; she admired Mike Nichols's direction of *The Graduate* but hated its "standard man's angle [with] the myth that women are always pursuing men."[5] She thought Vanessa Redgrave "superb" in *The Loves of Isadora*—the last film she went out to a moviehouse to view, in 1969—but she railed against the sentimental falsification of Isadora's character: "There will never be another Redgrave, perfect in acting, poetry, fire, body and dancing, to bring Izzy to life. If I were she, I would challenge the writers to a wrestling match and pound their brains out."[6] Yet generally she believed that all film critics wasted huge quantities of words when in fact "there is only one message—Learn to see."[7]

With acid typewriter, Louise held forth to Theo on friends and foes in and out of film, interspersed with comments on such family news as the wedding of his daughter: "How happy I am for you that, contrary to my prediction, Rosie is not lost to you. . . . Pepi [Lederer] used to admonish me, 'Don't do it without the gold band.' For it takes a very clever woman to operate outside marriage."[8]

In November 1972, she was moved by an article (in that *New Yorker* which she never read) to tell Theo: "The profile of Tallulah Bankhead proves what I have always maintained—that the career of an actor is the most degrading of all enslavements given that he is intelligent as were John Barrymore and Bankhead. Both of them were reduced to hideous grotesques celebrating all their vices."[9]

She could tell Theo things that she hadn't the nerve or the heart to tell some of her friends personally: "Ever since Roddy McDowall came to Rochester to photograph me for his book *Double Exposure*, he has phoned me to get my opinion of his TV performances. Last week he phoned to hear what I thought about his new series, 'Planet of the Apes.' Knowing that I would hate it, I had purposely not seen it. (Why he should care what I think, living among the intellectual elite in Hollywood, is a subject I have ceased to chew on.) However, he was so urgent and seemed so attached to his ape (it takes him three hours to put on the ape face) that I promised to watch the show and write my report.

"Years ago I learned that truth is not the answer when it comes to appraising anybody's creative work; yet when I have praised what I thought bad, I have lived to eat my words. 'Apes' is so silly and so useless as a vehicle for Roddy that I think I will wait for it to be—I hope—canceled, and then I can write a sympathetic burial letter."[10]

With Theo and others, the subject was most often writing. She was constantly invoking the styles of her holy trinity—Ruskin, Proust, Nabokov—and deploring the myriad crimes against the language. "If I could write only anecdotal shitty gags and dead stories in stinking journaleze, I wouldn't write anything," she said. The elusive objective was truth: "Try to set down *one* ugly experience in your life truthfully," she lectured, "and find out how abhorrent it is."[11]

If anyone understood such things, it was Theodore. A close look at Theo's and Louise's writing suggests that each was influenced, or at least reinforced, by the crisp irreverence of the other. Knowing the care he took in his own writing, Louise even sent him rough drafts of some of her articles, including "Marion Davies' Niece," for his critique. This was a rare honor indeed, and Theo knew it: Louise entrusted her raw prose to few. Kevin Brownlow and James Card were among them, but Kevin was in London and she had cut off Card. Theo's function as her private literary consultant thus assumed even greater importance.

Louise and Theo engaged in a variety of arguments over the years, but had always remained enormously fond of one another.

"My favorite Theo story," she reminded him in one good-humored letter, "was when you were working as a shoe salesman and a man with a false limb was your customer. You fitted his live foot and then, overcome with solicitude, you fitted his false foot, asking, 'How does that feel?'

"But then you have a great capacity for love, although where it came from I cannot imagine, since our parents were bereft of that emotion. . . ."

Only in her letters to Theo were there no taboos. With him she was free to explore Goethe, Proust, Shaw, James, and the other writers in whose works she found keys to her own life and family. The correspondence with Theodore was a back-and-forth tennis match of ideas, confessions, and psycho-literary revelations:

> The last place in the world I would expect to find a picture of mother is in Henry James. This morning I was reading *The Spoils of Poynton*. Superficially, the plot deals with an English widow whose son is about to take over the house she has sacrificed so much to make beautiful. James lets the reader think that she is fighting to retain her "things." Then he drops his bomb:
>
> "The great wrong Owen [her son] had done her was his failure from the

Rare hilarity in her Goodman Street apartment, 1972; photo by Jim Laragy

first to understand what it was to have a mother at all, to appreciate the beauty and the sanctity of the character. . . . One's mother, gracious heaven, if one were the kind of fine young man one ought to be, was a subject for poetry, for idolatry. . . . She had the house in Paris, she had the house in Poitou, she had more than in the lifetime of her husband because she had to the end of her days the supreme word about everything."

Reading this I burst into the happy release of laughter. For my battle with Mother (1940–43) was over her will to supremacy—"appreciation," she called it. Her model was her sister Eva, crippled with arthritis, waited on hand and foot by husband and children. And when I was getting ready to go to New York (1943) I remember your running out the back door where I was hanging up sheets on the clothesline in the back yard. Quite suddenly you realized that mother had trapped you, that she might live for years after father's death, binding you to "mother love." [12]

One wonders—as Theo wondered privately to his wife, Margaret— about Louise's *own* will to supremacy and about her willingness to fight tooth and nail with Myra until their mother took to her bed and fought "unfairly" therefrom, thereafter.

Thoughts of their mother often dominated Louise's mind and letters to Theo—certainly more than thoughts of her father, who outlived Myra by many years. Poor Leonard seemed to plague Louise by his longevity, and he received short shrift from her: "How pitiful our poor little father was, playing Judge Brooks, chasing everybody away, snapping at the air with his monologues on the human condition and how to rectify it."*

That was Louise's final assessment of the man. Her only other reference to him in all her correspondence with her brother came in 1971. It was just the reverse with Theo, who often wrote at length about their father and rarely mentioned their mother. In a now lost letter, he had written her an extended reflection on Leonard, to which she responded with two succinct sentences: "Your long letter about father is unanswerable. He fixed my tiny Cartier watch perfectly."[13]

If this seems a bit brutal, it pales by comparison with the epitaph she reserved for her older brother, Martin, whose death on October 3, 1971, was dutifully relayed to her by Theodore.

"Thanks for telling me about Martin's death," she replied promptly, taking the opportunity to gripe that "Charles Brooks [a cousin] had been dead for several years before anyone got around to mentioning the fact to me. I have searched my memory trying to capture in Martin's name one generous thought, one unselfish act, one word of truth—and I find none. He was the most detestable person I ever knew."[14]

But as she always loathed Martin, she always adored Theodore. In an October 14, 1974, letter, she reminded him: "If you are properly amplified and do phone me, be sure to call in the morning. Once a week I drink a pint and go to sleep and you might find me gincoherent after three." To no one else would she make such a request or such a confession. Louise and Theo, in addition to their equally jaundiced outlooks, shared common and uncommon ailments that further united their spirits:

"Interesting that you and I have arrived at the same point—you by deafness, I by self-exile. Ten years ago when I confined myself I found that I had a great deal of time to fill because in ordinary life people spend nine-tenths of their waking hours in senseless talk." There were two kinds of conversationalists: "The people who stare at you, waiting for your lips to stop moving so they can talk; and the people who catch up a word of your talk—death, sickness, marriage, whatever—and launch into a monologue on the subject. Whatever remnants of thought and decent English remained in the 20th century have been obliterated by TV."

Her solution to the problem: not to talk to anybody. But the written word—that was different; that was the superior form of communication which transcended the banalities of speech. The *need* to communicate with Theo on paper appealed to her, and so did the striking parallels she

---

* Leonard Brooks continued his passionate involvement in law and politics to the end. He never attained his longed-for judgeship, but in 1945 he was appointed assistant attorney general of Kansas. He died on October 14, 1960, at the age of ninety-two.

perceived between Theo's "wall of silence," as he called it, and her own self-imposed isolation in Rochester. "In 1963 when I cut off Jimmie Card I erected my own wall of silence," she wrote him.[15]

But she was growing increasingly irascible—partly because "since I went off the sauce in February [1975], my personality has completely changed." In September of that year, Theo reported a discussion with a friend concerning the rise of the Nazi party in Germany, noting offhandedly that "I recalled you mentioning a low state of morality in Berlin at that time."

In her reply, she leapt at him with claws extended:

"I am answering your letter fast and mailing it fast so I won't be able to take it back. . . .

"What is the state of your mind that would allow you to invent a Louise Brooks who would 'mention' [a low state of morality in Berlin]? Without help from you I can make my own silly observations. And you are either a fool or a liar to say that I would comment on the low state of anyone's morals—mine being nonexistent."[16]

She was likewise affronted by his "patronizing" assessment of the connection between smoking and writing: "Try doing just a little bit of writing at a time," he had advised her. "Gradually lengthen it. Finally you'll be hitting on all 8 cylinders again. So it is proving with me. I found that when I thought I was working hard, I was really smoking hard."

Her sarcastic response was withering: "It is amazing how what is right for you is right for me too. Before writing this letter to you I threw away my cigarettes, got out my corncob pipe, wrote a little bit, then lengthened it, and then knocked out the first three chapters of my autobiography. Love, Louise."

Theo took this, as he took all of her outbursts, in stride. He resolved to choose his words more delicately, and when a mutual friend wrote him about not hearing from Louise, wondering if he had said something to offend her, Theo replied: "She goes into long fits of silence. If you have indeed offended her, have no doubt, you will hear from her. She is thinking up hideous ways in which to roast you over a verbal fire."

As Louise's alienation and paranoia mounted, so did the attacks on her friends. Roddy McDowall thought it stemmed from "her lack of respect for herself, which led to a big disturbance in her view of a lot of other things. You'd call and she'd say, 'Why are you calling? Why do you want to talk to me?' It was generated from thinking 'If you like me and want to talk to me, there's got to be something wrong with you.' That never left her. She was so perverse and ambivalent about everything, and of course, she loved a good fight. . . . I just never took [the provocations] seriously. On a wave of self-hatred, she'd write a letter of attack and then by the next post there'd be one rescinding the one before, saying, 'Oh, I'm so full of rubbish.' "[17]

Another friend, composer David Diamond, took a similarly tolerant view of this tough-talking lady who, he discovered, was very knowledgeable about music. They had actually met some twenty years earlier in New York, and Diamond recalls that first conversation:

"I told her right off—I was that kind of a kid—'I think yours are the greatest legs I've seen in my life.' "

"Where did you see my legs?"

"In *The Canary Murder Case.*"

"Oh, for Christ's sake, they're not *that* great."[18]

When they reestablished contact in Rochester, Diamond visited her, usually finding her "in her seedy, see-through peignoir. I said, 'Oh, Louise, you look like you're straight out of Nathanael West.' " And he got away with it, because she admired his acidity as well as his music.

One day Diamond brought her some of his recordings, and in her usual blunt fashion she told him, "I don't listen to records, only the radio." He offered to play for her in his home, and she said, "I never go out." But on the beautiful Fourth of July in 1968, Diamond insisted she come over for a jumbo shrimp dinner and personally flushed her out of her apartment to bring her. Once there, she was unimpressed with the shrimp (because they were still in the shell) but spellbound by Diamond's extensive library and his inscribed Samuel photo of Martha Graham. They reminisced about their mutual friend, and about Louise's own "look" as a performer, which led to a feisty exchange:

"Who the hell thought of those eyebrows? Why do they have to begin over there?"

"Mind your own business."

"Didn't you ever talk to anybody, like Max Factor?"

"That fucking idiot? Why don't you stick to music. Why don't you just shut up and play your piano."

"Louise, I'm a trained violinist. I'm a second-rate pianist, but let me play you something on the violin."

And so he played her the Bach Partita in D Major, "up to the chaconne. She was looking me up and down, up and down, and when it was over, she said, 'You funny little man. You've got these huge shoulders and no hips at all. Come sit by me. . . . ' " Diamond declined an amorous advance, took her home in a cab, and then declined a second advance—at which point, he says, "she became very abusive and anti-Semitic. With the liquor, that viciousness came out."[19]

Another time, Diamond recalls, he made the mistake of mentioning Augusto Genina's account of her drunkenness during the making of *Prix de Beauté*. Louise had not known of it, and was angry and upset when she read the passage from Genina's memoirs.

"She herself would naturally not tell the truth about it. How would she even know it? She was loaded. Drinkers never are very honest about themselves. She never referred to being out-and-out drunk on the set. Louise's reputation for drinking was not an exaggerated one. She of course eliminated every reference to it as a defect in her life." [20]

It was an acutely sensitive subject, as her unwitting brother Theodore would soon discover.

If Louise had always tended to turn on those close to her, the mental and physical anguish of arthritis and emphysema now augmented her cantankerousness and intensified her conflicts with the world. Five years earlier she had confessed to Theo that her right hip was growing more painful and had been doing so since 1967. "Now I must take a cab to drag home the grub from the supermarket," she complained. "Bill Springer, my dentist, tries to get me to a doctor but I resist on the grounds that if it is Arthur Itis a doctor will only eat up my savings without doing any good, and if it is somebody else I don't want to know about it."

Theo, meanwhile, was having similar problems. In June of 1975 he was forced to take early retirement from the *Wichita Eagle and Beacon* because of acute emphysema. By then, he wrote his nephew Robert Brooks, he had become "so deaf I couldn't hear myself break wind." To increase the efficiency of his oxygen intake, he had to take long walks every day, and, to amuse himself, he wrote a pseudoscientific account called "The 40-Minute Mile." The flesh was weak, but his efforts to battle depression were ceaseless.

"I have to jazz myself up with little enthusiasms of one sort or another," he told his old friend Virgil Quinlisk. For years they had shared an interest in the science of "turdology," exchanging photographs and mock-scholarly treatises on the different feces of the species. But he was brought back to somber reality by Louise's frequent requests, in the fall of 1976, for advice on making out her will and disposing of her modest estate:

All this willing business of yours is disquieting to me. My own health is just precarious enough to inspire appreciation of the discomforts, miseries and hazards various afflictions can bring; plus the subjective array of fears and doubts the imagination creates and reason often confirms. What I am getting at is that if you are getting to the place where you are having difficulty crawling out of bed, getting yourself something to eat and so on, you have to have people around to help. And there are times when just reaching out and holding someone's hand does more good than aspirin. Most everyone has to drag on for a while during the last act of the show and one is but foolish to deny it until he is hauled off to a pest house. So when it's no longer any fun for you to attempt to make it alone you simply *must* let me know. We will figure something out, and although I don't have any clear notion of what that might be, I do have some ideas and none of them is dull. Oh, what a blessing it is to be bright and shiny!

He was striving mightily to be cheerful, but betrayed his own dark thoughts in the next paragraph:

> I got to thinking of these things the other day when, while driving down town, a guy threatened to lick me for some imagined traffic insult. As I cussed him back it occurred to me that if a physical confrontation actually ensued I would not have enough stamina to strike but one or two blows, and then, alas, the speed of my retreat would be limited to a slow walk. So I shut up. . . . I am shaken, frightened to find myself so vulnerable. [21]

Her brother's confession of frail mortality had its intended impact on Louise, who replied a week later that "pain and common sense (after four years) are at last driving me to the doctor." Her friend Bill Springer set up an appointment with a specialist, though she fretted about the expense and futility of it all.

"I have not the least hope of help for my arthritis," she continued in her first handwritten letter in years; henceforth, she would never type again. "Doctors don't get Nobel prizes for research into that dull affliction. Doubtless I will be put on drugs which is laughable—following my cutoff on booze. What scares me to death is the fact that I have *never in my life* had a physical examination. . . . I will write you after I get the news." [22]

The news was not good. The long-delayed diagnosis was osteoporosis of the hip, a degenerative disease in which the bones become porous and brittle due to calcium deficiency. This, coupled with her osteoarthritis, was causing increased pain and loss of strength in the spine. Her right hip ball joint had worn down to less than half its normal spherical size and shape—"bone crunching on bone," Louise explained it to Theo. Within a year, they told her, she would be in a wheelchair permanently.

But it need not happen. Implantation of an artificial hip joint was almost a routine procedure by then. There was no damage to her knees, no apparent problem with the left hip at all. The necessary operation would only require a two-to-three-week hospital stay, after which the doctor assured her "I will be free of pain and able to walk and stay in my apartment."

Though full of dread, "I have no choice," she told Theo, and agreed to an operation in January 1977. And she did something else she had never done in the thirty-three years since she left Kansas: She inquired, ever so gently, if Theo could come to visit.

"You anticipated our suggestion," he replied immediately, offering up-beat words of wisdom and a choice of timetables. He was buoyed by her decision and anxious to see her. To sister June he confided his belief that Louise would be "a different person when the constant and gnawing pain of that eroded joint is removed," adding that "I look forward to some old-fashioned comedy when she screams at me and I fail to hear it."[23]

And he continued to bombard Louise with plans.

"Barring a blizzard, we would drive," Theo wrote her, "and . . . we'd duck down through the Holston River valley in Grainger County, north-east Tennessee. There we could look for the early Brooks[es] on the rural tombstones. . . . I say 'we' because you would be with us and on the way back home. One can grow old and one can be alone but not both at once. We want you here."[24]

It was not to be. Louise was confused by all the travel options and annoyed by his Pollyanna picture of what lay ahead. Probably, too, she was horror-stricken at the thought of playing her last act in unbeloved Wichita. Most of all, she was simply terrified of the operation itself. And so she canceled it.

Louise avoided informing Theo of her decision until a late-night phone call December 23. Margaret would have to relay the message, and she could escape facing Theo directly.

The next day, Christmas Eve, she sat down to write him, frantic lest he write her first: "I pray to God this letter reaches you before you have a chance to write me. I canceled the hip operation Nov. 30, but I was afraid to tell you, fearful that you would write me a Godly medical sermon (you had already told me how happy I would be in the hospital). I have been cursed by all the medical-God worshippers here because I refused to have my hip joints chopped out and become a mutilated toy and I can not bear more."

She enclosed an explanatory letter from her doctor, which she asked to be returned, and concluded with a heartfelt plea:

"Since doctors know nothing more about arthritis than did the cave men, and I have had 70 years of experience with my body, I shall play my final role with old age, pain and death from day to day, thanking whatever accident of birth keeps me as active and free of pain as I am, until the final trap.

"I hope you will grant me the same good sense in my decisions on arthritis that I grant you in the management of your ills. Love, Louise."

But as she feared, Theo was writing her simultaneously, and their let-ters crossed in the mail. He was "distraught, depressed and distressed beyond telling" at the sudden turnabout, he told her. It was a sad and beautiful letter, full of aching concern:

"Each of us, I am told, has his own *Götterdämmerung*. Unable or unwilling to escape the compulsions of a lifetime, we give it a false value and rush to embrace it. I think that is nonsense. Do what you can to get your show back on the road and let me know immediately."

And then he added a fatal paragraph:

"The whole thing sounds to me like you became depressed, fell off the wagon and proceeded to declare war, but in this I may be quite wrong. Operation or not, we will visit. I must fix you with my evil eye and read the complexities of your mind. Love, Theo."[25]

George Pratt once mused that "Louise loved to build up to occasions where she could be outraged." Now, despite Theo's hedge that he might be "quite wrong," she took huge offense at his suggestion that a drinking binge had caused her to cancel the operation. Insulted and furious, she sent him the following note on January 3, 1977: "Theo: In your letter 12/24/76, your invention of me was so poisonous that I shall never read another word you write, never write you another word, never see you again. Louise."

He, meanwhile, had received her Christmas Eve letter and resigned himself to doing exactly what she asked—allowing her to manage her own ills. "I am enclosing the [doctor's] letter you asked to be returned," he replied on New Year's Day. "The situation finds me flabbergasted. I don't think there is anything I can now say that would either add or detract from the wisdom or folly of your decision." He told her he still planned to visit.

He had not yet received her cutoff notice. And so two days later, she penned another—on the back of his own letter.

"Theo—It was necessary to open the envelope to get my [Dr.] Willard letter. I did not read this letter—Any further letters will be 'Returned to Sender.' Louise."

His patience finally broke. Hurt and offended himself, he did not try again. "Theo tried to help everybody, especially Louise," said Margaret, "because they always understood each other. He did everything he could to help. But boy, if he got rebuffed, that was the end. You were a sonofabitch from then on."

Thus ended the rollicking correspondence of a lifetime. The Rochester visit never took place, and Theo's emphysema rapidly worsened. On May 26, 1981, he died. He was sixty-nine.

In her living room in Wichita on a hot September evening in 1986, Margaret Brooks glanced up at a framed portrait of the sultry, twenty-five-year-old Louise: "She knew that Theo was not going to live too much longer," mused his soft-spoken widow, who held no grudges and steadfastly kept in touch with Louise until her death. "She had to know that.

Theo and Louise in Beverly Hills, 1928

She wasn't stupid. And Theo was really the only one she had left to cling to. I figure she couldn't stand the idea of him dying. She reacted that way so she wouldn't even know what he wrote or know when he died or know anything more about him. She couldn't stand the thought of losing him, too." [26]

*Lulu in Rochester: a portrait of the recluse at her peak of cult fame;
photo by Jim Laragy, Rochester Democrat and Chronicle*

20 · The Cult

She was the most seductive, sexual image of Woman ever committed to celluloid. She's the only unrepentant hedonist, the only pure pleasure-seeker I think I've ever known. — KENNETH TYNAN

FOR Tynan, whose sexual adventures were legion, that was saying something. "When men bored her," he added, "she walked out on them. When Hollywood bored her, she walked out on Hollywood. She gave it up and went into retirement, from which she's never emerged."

Thus spake the man who, aside from Card and Langlois, contributed more than anyone to the growth of the Louise Brooks Cult—though the Cult existed long before Kenneth Tynan got around to boosting it. Fueled by the Langlois proclamation of 1955—no Garbo, no Dietrich, only Brooks!—Pandoramonium reigned in Europe thereafter. But the domestic reverberations did not hit Louise with full force until much later. In the twenties, she had not cared in the least what "image" the studio publicists created or neglected to create for her; now, the second time around, she would try to assert some control over it.

"Please do not use Catholic Convert Theme—or Poverty and Rescue from the gutter so dear to the sob-and-save story writers," she wrote Theo in 1964 when he inquired how to handle her resurrection in print. The idea of a "Brooks Cult" developing anywhere had seemed preposterous, but as Louise confessed to John Kobal:

> Oh, I got an enormous kick out of it. I was killed dead when *Pandora's Box* failed, so from that time on, I just didn't care. . . . To be suddenly reclaimed from the dead was marvelously exciting. . . . Most people die before things like that happen—to find that you are to a certain extent admired. It's a wonderful blessing.[1]

The "New Wave" obsession with her continued. Jean-Luc Godard paid tribute through his actress wife Anna Karina, whose impulsive character

Louise and Suzy, a gift from James Card, September 1964

in *Une Femme est une Femme* (1961) and again in *Vivre sa Vie* the next year was modeled on Louise. Roman Polanski was eager to meet her; he borrowed John Springer's letters from Louise (and never returned them). Kevin Brownlow, who was supervising editor on *The Charge of the Light Brigade* in 1967, wrote her:

> Did I tell you that I went to a Swinging London party, with a lot of the *Charge* people, which was held in a big Victorian house in Emperor's Gate? One bedroom, with near-Beardsley design and very dark, had a huge blowup of someone who looked awfully familiar and turned out to be you, dark and brooding. Evidently you are very "in."[2]

By the time a wider awareness of Louise spread to America, it was the tumultuous late sixties and her bitchy outlook seemed tailor-made for the times. She addressed the subject of actors and TV talk shows, for example, in an iconoclastic little piece called "Actors and the Pabst Spirit":

> When I made movies there was no television and consequently there were no Talk Shows. But if then I had been told that some day actors would be paid large sums to sit and talk to one another on television, and that an audience of millions would listen to them—I wouldn't have believed it. For the Talk Show is merely a matter of transferring a group of actors from a movie set where they sit and talk behind the camera to a television set where they sit and talk before the camera. This form of entertainment took shape during the production of the first movies when actors found themselves

spending much of their time on the set, unused, ignored or forgotten. And actors cannot exist without an audience. When not working before the camera, they contrived a means of staying alive by putting on a show of their own behind it. Within a short time every actor had a repertory of entertaining routines suitable for directors, producers, and other actors. Seen on a Talk Show, the actor's is so obviously a mechanical performance posing as spontaneous wit that its inanimate spirit cannot engage the attention of a child for an instant. What holds adult attention is the rare electrifying appearance of an actor who smashes his plaster mask and brazenly expresses his natural animosity toward every other actor present or absent, living or dead.[3]

Always accompanied by stunning photos of Louise at the height of her beauty, such articles increased her reputation for candor while enhancing her rediscovery as a "sex goddess." One of the most expansive paeans came from Douglas McVay in the August 1965 issue of *Films and Filming*. McVay compared her favorably to all rival silent goddesses:

It was left to Louise Brooks . . . to unite the spiritual and the carnal. Gish supplied one half of the female equation: the naive gaiety and vulnerable poignancy. Brooks provided the other: the cynically ambivalent, ruthless allure. Yet, because she could herself switch on occasion to sentiment and a sense of purity, her range went, finally, beyond Gish's: so that she is arguably the greatest of all the silent-era goddesses. . . .

Brooks' pathos was always more classically refined—like her looks. [Her] special star quality was that when serious she looked more innocent or pure or virginal or honest (and when . . . smiling, more *carnal*) than any other female star before or since.[4]

At this same time, a documentary film called *The Love Goddesses* appeared, the first to include footage from a Brooks film *(The Diary of a Lost Girl)*; and in London, "T.M." in the May 1965 *Sight and Sound* found similar cause to celebrate her:

What IS it about Louise Brooks, the most haunting face in the history of the cinema? . . . Take a look at those eyes. Just as Garbo was set apart by her mysterious withdrawal, so Louise Brooks was set apart by her eyes. . . .

Men kill or are killed for her sake; and out of the chaos around her, those candid eyes gaze from unimaginable depths of innocent purity, striving to understand.

Less apocalyptic was the local view, from Rochester columnist Henry Clune on May 9, 1965: "In the University Avenue supermarket, where she goes to buy a lamb chop, a can of peas and a box of shredded wheat biscuits, no one, bumping go-carts with this rather squat, middle-aged woman, whose graying hair is slicked back tightly from her brow, and whose clothes give her no distinction whatever, would recognize her as 'one of the living legends of screen history. . . .' "

Clune, dealing with the real 1965 woman rather than the 1929 legend, was no more awestruck now than in 1959 when he wrote: "Miss Brooks wore Murray's Space Shoes, which are therapeutic rather than ornamental. If they had webs, they'd look a little like snowshoes. . . . [She] was utterly without makeup."[5]

"Clune must have been primed with a load of gossip, expecting sex and scandal, dyed hair, a mink stole and spike heels," Louise wrote to George Pratt. "The moment he walked in my apartment and saw the crucifix, my black coat and space shoes I knew I was dead. . . . 'You were never much in pictures and never made any money. Who pays your bills? Tell me about the men you knew (with a nudge). I won't tell anyone.' "[6]

Such pieces were rare, however. Most of her press was so superlative as to lack any critical value. Other than Lotte Eisner's untranslated work more than a decade earlier, Louise had not yet been "captured" in book form by a serious film historian—an omission that was corrected in 1968 by Kevin Brownlow's *The Parade's Gone By* . . . . That magnificent collection of interviews with the pioneers of the silent era had been five years in the making and remains the definitive sourcebook on the subject. Brownlow's primary interest was film production, and Louise was one of only a few performers he included.

"Louise Brooks was not one of the important stars of the silent era," he wrote by way of introduction. ". . . But of all the personalities of that era, [she] has emerged most triumphantly. She has become the object of idolatry for thousands who are too young to remember her in silents, and who base their admiration on revivals at archives and film societies. Louise Brooks fan clubs have started up all over the world. Her youthful admirers see in her an actress of brilliance, a luminescent personality, and a beauty unparalleled in film history."[7]*

Brownlow's *Parade* also legitimized Louise as a film historian, but elsewhere she was treated as an idol. By 1969, of the many worshipful characterizations in print, the one she most enjoyed was S. J. Perelman's reference to "the immortal Louise Brooks" in his *New Yorker* story, "She Walks in Beauty—Single File, Eyes Front, and No Hanky-Panky."[8] Louise read it upon returning from the office of her lawyer, Henry Messina, where she had just signed the latest of her wills. The coincidence amused her, and she wrote Perelman a note asking why he had not let her in on her divinity in time to save her the trip. He replied, advising her to

---

* Brownlow provided her with an advance copy of her quotations. One of the cuts she made—in order to spare an old friend's feelings—was the following: "When Chaplin blends tragedy in with his laughter, it doesn't quite come off, does it? He is a little bit sorry for himself. (I'm thinking of *Limelight.*)"

"touch a match to the will" but "don't bother to burn Harry Messina, he may come in useful to some other client to sue a dry-cleaner." Next, he said, she should charge a new set of clothes and jewels to Harry and then "burst like a Roman candle on the entertainment world, which is dominated by such pallid apologies for womanhood as Jane Fonda and Tuesday Weld. . . . What do you think? A wholly new career for you, the same for Messina—I say, it's worth a try."[9]

But 1969 brought more reminders of mortality than immortality—such as the death of George Marshall on August 9 at age seventy-two. Six years earlier, he had lost his mind after a stroke. "I would not believe it," said Louise. "Every few months, I would call his secretary in Washington, who would tell me again that George was 'senile.' "[10] And she did not learn, until long after the fact, of the death of a director who had fallen into such obscurity that even the *New York Times* ignored his passing: In 1974, Eddie Sutherland had died at seventy-seven. To her friend Bill Klein, Louise would confide a certain wistfulness about Eddie Sutherland: "She talked about him a long time one day. She told me that she did almost love him . . . she wished maybe it had continued a little longer. There was a note of regret, but—it was that double way Louise had of dealing with things."[11]

But in March 1974 Louise, very much alive, finally agreed—with many misgivings and changes of mind—to her first filmed interview. Documentary filmmaker Ricky Leacock had been asked by North German Television to get her recollections of Pabst to accompany a broadcast of *Pandora's Box*. The result was the hour-long *Lulu in Berlin*, a conversation between Brooks and Leacock in her Goodman Street apartment.

Leacock, who began making films at age fourteen, was a pioneer of American *cinéma verité* documentaries and a collaborator with such major names in that field as D. A. Pennebaker and the Maysles brothers. Also the founding head of the MIT film department, Leacock helped develop portable camera equipment that would later be adapted by television and mainstream film studios.*

"You are the first person to make me really laugh—which I adore—since I banned Jimmie Card in 1963," she wrote Leacock after several amusing phone battles.[12] But the next letter was all business—and a classic in the art of reiteration:

> I think it best to write that it has always been my policy to receive a bank check for any film work; and to receive the bank check before I do any film work.

* Leacock's is one of only three extant filmed interviews with Louise. The third was shot in June 1977 by Kevin Brownlow and David Gill, who "brought along Bessie Love to keep me calm while they tore up the joint" and was largely limited to a discussion of Clara Bow. "In reviewing these filming experiences," she later wrote Leacock, "it was most fun fighting with you."

So do not fail to bring me a *bank check* when you come to Rochester to film me.

A bank check for $300.[13]

The lady wanted a bank check. And she got it. And Leacock got his interview—a priceless portrait of Louise in the act of storytelling—clad in unglamorous robe, without make-up, but with her sharp mind, bold spirit, and sense of humor intact.*

"One of the things I like best is that when she's describing *Pandora*, one could swear she's looking at the screen—she 'sees' it so vividly," says Leacock. "How many actors or actresses ever pay attention to how a director works? I never heard any kind of insight like hers. Extraordinary. Always putting herself down, in that funny way she had. Something I never talked to her about but really wanted to was the extent to which *she* changed *Pandora's Box*—Pabst's whole conception of it. It became a film about *her*, rather than about Lulu. . . . She was so aristocratic—how the fuck did she come out of the cornfields? That wonderful *elegance*. . . . Jesus, what a wonderful lady."[14]

The first and only book about Louise Brooks to appear in her lifetime was published by Phébus in Paris in 1977. *Louise Brooks: Portrait d'une anti-star*, edited by Roland Jaccard, consisted of French translations of several of Louise's published articles; one new piece, "Une certaine idée de la liberté" [A certain idea of freedom], on her parents and childhood; Lotte Eisner's essay about her; and other ecstatic homages to her beauty. *Anti-star* also included five pages of an erotic Italian comic strip drawn by Guido Crepax. "Valentina," its title character, was inspired by Louise and drawn in provocative, seminude poses. Valentina is Lulu's contemporary alter ego, the reincarnation of her eternal (rather sadomasochistic) sexuality.

Louise might well have been annoyed by such liberties, but in her contrary fashion, she loved it—and told Crepax so in a deeply revealing letter:

As far as I know no American actress has been the inspiration for a comic strip, and surely never for two. John Striebel drew the syndicated *Dixie* from 1926 till 1966. And you began *Valentina* in 1965 just as if you had found me again where John left me when he died.

Could it be that Valentina is the lost Louise Brooks? Dixie Dugan was not. She was strong and intelligent and always knew how to take care of herself in a world she understood perfectly.

---

* Louise was later furious to discover that the interview was broadcast in Germany with a dubbed German soundtrack: "I hate those goddamned voiceovers—some bitch stealing my face."

Guido Crepax's "Valentina" cartoons, based on Louise in homage to her, 1977

Ortega y Gasset wrote that "We are all lost; only when we confess this do we find ourselves and really live." But I knew what it was to be lost when I was a little girl and my mother could not understand why I wept alone. Making films in New York was okay because I learned so much and discovered Tolstoy and *Anna Karenina*. Then I was sent to do films in Hollywood in 1927. Nobody could understand why I hated that dreadful, destructive place which seemed a marvelous paradise to everyone else. "What's the matter with you, Louise? You've got everything! What is it you want?" For me it was like a terrible dream I have—I am lost in the corridors of a big hotel and I can't find my room. People pass me as if they cannot see or hear me. So first I ran away from Hollywood and I have been running away ever since. And now at 69 I have given up all hope of ever finding myself. . . .[15]

After a further exchange of letters, she paid an even more extravagant compliment to Crepax:

Besides Mr. Pabst, you are the only person who has understood me, and both without even meeting me except in films. . . . I have always grieved because I have a poor brain. Now it seems to me that if the Wizard of Oz could give the Scarecrow a diploma, then the Wizard of Crepax could give Louise a diploma. Will you send me a drawing? I will put it in a frame on the chest of drawers facing my bed—and when a book puzzles me I can look up at the drawing and understand everything.[16]

LOUISE'S last magazine article was also her most important: "Why I Will Never Write My Memoirs," as noted earlier, answered its own question in terms of Louise's inability to "unbuckle the Bible Belt." Written in early 1977, it was a sexual masterpiece—because of which she had trouble getting it into print. "I love writing and can't please anybody," she once complained to Jan Wahl. "It is the truth that makes people fascinating and unique, and nobody wants it." Her newest rejection came from the two-year-old *American Film*, published by the American Film Institute (AFI) in Washington, D.C. Its first editor, Hollis Alpert, who had interviewed her in 1965 for *Playboy*'s "Sex in Cinema" series, now became the object of some old and new wrath:

> He was trying to tell me without exposing his fawning servitude to the establishment that *American Film* did not recognize "sexual degeneracy" in Hollywood. He is a perfect example of the very core of my article—Bible Belt hypocrisy. Isn't that comical? Operating under the fine moral banner of the John F. Kennedy Center.[17]

She was still simmering a month later when the AFI announced its selection of the fifty greatest American films. Louise renewed her attack —this time against the entire theory and practice of the organization itself:

> The nerve of this cheap outfit daring to fake the selection of the "greatest American films of all time." In the first place, how were these 50 films thrown together? By whom? And how can anyone fairly vote on them without having seen all of them? I have only seen 21 of the 50. . . . The first 35 years of film are represented by four films, the last 7-and-a-half years by 11 films (mostly junk). . . . The two Disneys on the AFI list [*Fantasia* and *Snow White and the Seven Dwarfs*] give away the plot. The voters grew up on TV comic strips: no attention is necessary to follow. My friend in the building, Avram Phelosof, 26, Syracuse University—he picked *Kane, Strangelove, The General, Godfather, 2001*. Under my fiendish glare he was afraid to pick *Star Wars*, which he knows frame by frame.[18]

Her worst prejudices against American film publications were reconfirmed, or so—in her rage—it seemed, and once again she had to look abroad to find a place for the swan song and signature piece of her literary

Louise in her kitchen during Kevin Brownlow's filmed interview, 1977; photo by David Gill

life. Finally, in March 1978, almost a year after she wrote it, "Why I Will Never Write My Memoirs" ran in the little London journal, *Focus on Film,* where it was read by a tiny audience of British film buffs.

It was the sort of article in the sort of magazine that English drama critic–author–bon vivant Kenneth Tynan would have read, had he been in London, which he was not. Tynan was wisely wintering in Santa Monica, where, one morning, he flipped through his *TV Guide* and discovered that a local station had scheduled "a film on which my fantasies had fed ever since I first saw it, a quarter of a century before"—*Pandora's Box.*[19]

Tynan, then fifty-one and perhaps the finest critic in the English language, was best known in the States as creator of Broadway's scandalous nude revue, *Oh! Calcutta!* This was his third viewing of *Pandora's Box,* whose star he endowed with the high-spirited beauty and majesty of a wild horse. She had haunted him for years and captivated him more profoundly than any other film actress. Now, in early 1978, he was still in love with that obscure, seventy-one-year-old object of his desire—or at least her twenty-year-old self. And he was fired with an obsession much like James Card's to seek her out. He pitched the idea of a Profile to *New Yorker* editor William Shawn, who approved.

When Tynan called Roddy McDowall and asked him to arrange a meet-

Kenneth Tynan, 1969.

ing, the ever-protective McDowall declined. But after Tynan read him some journal excerpts of his impressions of Louise, McDowall was convinced that "he really absorbed the essence of everything she was on the screen, and I called her up and told her that."[20]

On February 9, 1978, Louise received her first letter from Tynan, requesting an interview and setting in motion an elaborate series of negotiations. Just a few months earlier she had written to Kevin Brownlow, "I won't let John Springer bring Polanski here to see me. I won't see John Gilbert's daughter. I won't do a TV interview with Richard Leacock—I ain't gonna do nutten no more no how."[21] But Louise was aware of Tynan's literary importance, not to mention *The New Yorker*'s, and she wanted to do the Profile. She also knew it would be an in-depth piece and thus a potential problem. She had recently told Brownlow: "Any journalist who quotes me on Paley might get me cut off without a penny."[22] And to Herman Weinberg: "I really must CROW about Kenneth Tynan's asking to visit me for a *New Yorker* profile on me—because that's all the pleasure I'll get out of it. I can't do it."[23]

Indeed, on the very day she got Tynan's letter, she had called the Paley Foundation for permission to do the Profile, and been denied. That prompted an intense lobbying effort and flurry of phone calls among Tynan, Shawn, Paley, Leacock, and Roddy McDowall—at the end of which she updated Weinberg:

After two months of being kicked around between the Foundation and Tynan, Bill [Paley] has finally agreed to let me see Tynan for *The New Yorker* profile. Bill's name is not to be uttered. William Shawn, the great editor, has guaranteed this. (Tynan wasn't going to utter it anyhow.)

Tynan is crazy. He simply would not give up, and of course I am tickled to death. He gets here April 30 to see films and me. [24]

Tynan's visit to Rochester, April 30–May 3, was the most euphoric experience of the last decade of Louise's life. They were drawn to each other like long-lost lovers. Tynan had less than two years to live; Louise had seven. It was a platonic love affair—the last of their lives—as intense as the sexual affairs for which both of them were famous. Tynan spent his first day in town at Eastman House, watching all of her extant pictures, which were freshly pulsating in his mind the next morning when he met her for the first time.

He was a combination of all the contradictory qualities she adored: polite, outrageous, serious, ribald—and brilliantly amusing. She, in turn, dazzled him with her own ebullience and the strength of her mind and character. Despite much pain, she left her apartment, for one of the last times, to accompany him to dinner at Rochester's finest restaurant, the Rio Bamba.

"We are just right for each other—a darling bastard and a 'fascinating monster,' as Isherwood named me," she wrote Brownlow. During their "three glorious days," she said, "we talked about people and sex. . . . What he will write in the *New Yorker* piece I cannot imagine." [25]

It hardly seemed to matter at the time. "She was obviously cuckoo about him and he about her," recalls Adolph Green, who was close to Tynan and had recently begun a friendship with Louise:

It was one of those things like *Peter Ibbetson*,* where if only the two of them could have met in dreams and really made it happen! He was just mad about her, that's all. He thought she was the most unique and interesting woman and—what he liked—really wicked, and someone with tremendous insight into everything. He had a lot of qualities that she responded to instantly. He was such an eccentric and so knowledgeable, and he loved everything from the lowliest corn to the most erudite art. [26]

"It seems clear to me," said Rochester University professor Donald McNamara after a lengthy discussion with Louise about it, "that the Tynan interview was the result of a three-day seduction and that Louise

* That 1935 Henry Hathaway movie, starring Gary Cooper and Ann Harding, was a romantic fantasy based on the George du Maurier novel of two sweethearts torn apart in childhood but reunited years later—and eternally—by fate.

saw seduction as part of the interview process."[27] The ardor continued in a passionate literary manner: During the next fifteen months, Louise wrote Tynan ninety-two letters in which, says Kathleen Tynan, she "tried to unravel her inquisitor. The touching, insistent subtext of all their exchanges and conversations . . . was Louise Brooks' search for Ken." In one letter, Louise went so far as to declare that she had been "suddenly overpowered by the feeling of love—a sensation I have never experienced with any other man. Are you a variation of Jack the Ripper who finally brings me love which I am prevented from accepting, not by the knife but by old age?"[28]

As to the Profile, Louise immodestly believed the letters were more essential than the interviews. "We really just gossiped here," she told McNamara. "Most of the profile was made up from my letters or quotes from my articles. But Tynan puts them together so neatly that you don't realize it."[29]

"The Girl in the Black Helmet," Tynan's biography-in-miniature, was a stunning blend of her past and present. It received extraordinary attention before, during, and after its publication in *The New Yorker* on June 11, 1979. The seventy-page manuscript spent months in transit between Brooks, Tynan, Shawn, and the Paley Foundation, everyone fussing over cuts. "The strain of holding Ken down to satisfy my board of directors [at the Paley Foundation] has reduced me to 88 pounds," she wrote Brownlow. But when the article appeared, the response was unanimous: Both Tynan and Brooks were deluged with praise, and Louise was besieged by more reporters, editors, and fans than ever in her lifetime. James Card and Kevin Brownlow had been the first to write about, and thereby encourage, the Louise Brooks Cult among *cinéastes*. Tynan turned it into a mass phenomenon. Letters and offers flooded in. Dick Cavett wanted her for his TV show. The publisher Alfred A. Knopf asked for her autobiography.

"I didn't dream that [Tynan] would write all that off-the-record stuff, such as my affair with Pabst that I was positive the stuffy old *New Yorker* wouldn't publish, but he did and they did," Louise wrote Brownlow two days after it appeared. "People have been calling me from all over, laughing like hell. I'm always hollering for TRUTH, and it tickles everyone to see me hit in the puss with my own pie."[30] To James Watters of *Life* she wrote that "the sex stuff in it got me piles of high class fan mail calling me a woman of great 'courage' and 'integrity' and for the first time in my life *I like myself*. But don't worry, I'll return to my senses."[31]

For Louise, there was a resurgence of the exhilaration of her first "resurrection" in 1955—but it was brief. An ominous sign had come back in June 1978, a whole year before the Profile ran: "Since Tynan was here my 'life' seems much more useless," she wrote Brownlow in a moment of post-Ken depression.[32] Her anticipation of the Profile had been enormous over the course of that year, and its appearance was climactic and anticlimactic both—the realization that it was the apotheosis of her revival. And while on one level she reveled in the new attention, she was overwhelmed by the burden of it.

She had also worried that Tynan might discard her after the Profile appeared and was relieved that he did not. It made her happy to think that "a little piece of me and a little piece of you will always belong together."[33] He was now trying to lure her to Beverly Hills for a family visit "and 'a small party of 50 in your honor.' He is nuts, too."[34] He also wanted her to come to Spain—an equally preposterous idea, but fun to think about. "Bill Paley should have me flown to Almería in the company plane," she wrote Tynan. "He would, too, if I could see him and bring back laughter, for he has a screwy sense of humor."[35]

But the fond tone changed irrevocably after Tynan's August 25 letter from Puerto Vallarta, Mexico. He was writing to inform her that two independent producers were chomping at the bit to do a film about her life and that, in his opinion, she should waste no time in coming to terms with them on screen rights, lest their interest wane and the deal fall through. He had already laid more than a little groundwork for that deal, which he proceeded to outline for her in hard-sell fashion: No lesser light than Mike Nichols was eager to direct the Louise Brooks story. Tynan and Nichols would collaborate on the screenplay which—like the direction—would be a model of zest and taste instead of the usual Hollywood pathos. Louise and Tynan would have ownership and full control of the project, he assured her, even down to casting. Opportunity was knocking but wouldn't wait long for an answer. Nichols had other deals in the works, Tynan warned, and she must hurry. He pressed her to tell her agent, Robert Lantz, to give the producers an immediate go-ahead on the screen-rights option. Finally, as a kind of afterthought, he disavowed any selfish thoughts of his own potential gain in the project. He hardly needed any additional work, he said, noting that his current commitments would keep him occupied for years.[36]

Louise was frightened and suspicious. The whole thing was too fast and too glib. She felt steamrollered, and for all the assurances that "we" would be in control, it seemed that "Louise" was not. Tynan's jaunty tone did not prevent a terrible thought from creeping into her head: Could he have been interested in exploiting her all along? Making money out of her? She had given him access to her soul and every intimacy of her heart. Could the whole thing have been a fake? She did indeed contact Lantz—but to say no, not yes. From now on she did not want to deal with Tynan at all.

But in the interim, he called her, and she scribbled a frantic cry of distress to Lantz:

> Exactly what I wished to avoid happened. At 8 p.m. Tynan phoned from Mexico. . . . He said over and over that he had *no interest* in getting the release of my life story. I asked him why . . . didn't he let Nichols take care of his own business? "Mike is very shy." Evidently Nichols and [the producer] thought Tynan could get an okay from me—and he did, too—this bully. When I finally said no—that I was disgusted with his crap—he became very grand. . . . He denies everything in [his letter] except his beautiful disinterest—this is a mess—I want nothing to do with *Leacock, Cavett,* ANY-BODY—[37]

She was getting madder at Tynan by the hour and four days later, on September 24, she sent a similar distraught letter to William Shawn, whose gentility and integrity she now clung to and on whom she increasingly relied for advice:

> I hired Lantz to keep Tynan away, after scaring me to death for one year and five months. His last performance before publication was to phone in April saying that if I saw Jim Watters from *Life,* you would probably kill my profile. I did, and you didn't. . . .
> Sept. 22 I phoned Lantz who doesn't seem able to back away from money. It enrages me that nobody but you understands that I AM just like I am.[38]

Louise's wrath was not solely related to the proposed film deal. She was getting retroactively angrier about the portrait Tynan had painted of her —"mad as a hornet about her image," says Leacock, which was the reason she gave for canceling their second interview. Leacock always scrupulously sent her half of every royalty check he received for showings of *Lulu in Berlin*; she had recently written him: "To me, to be a great person is the final work of art, and you are a great person. Total generosity defines it—being gifted and spreading it around."[39] In the B.T. era—Before Tynan —"we'd drink and get mad at each other and then start laughing," recalls Leacock. But A.T., she wrote him, "after being 'celebrated' by Tynan as a drunken whore, I will have nothing to do with you, or Cavett, or Nichols or anybody else without having full control of the product."[40] To Kevin Brownlow, who was safely removed from it all in London, she poured out her escalating feelings of betrayal:

> Ever since old Tynan doublecrossed me by converting sex gossip into *The New Yorker* profile, I have been battered with publishers' offers to print cheap sex memoirs, and offers from three film outfits to place me in film history as "Tynan's drunken whore". . . . [He] has been trying to live in the Hollywood style of the superstar and suffers with debts. . . . I told him I had hired Lantz

to keep him from phoning or writing me—he went on talking for that $20,000 the outfit had promised him if he could get my release. . . . I finally said *my name was not for sale for anybody's dirty picture*, and I didn't give a damn about Nichols.[41]

She was forgetting, or neglecting to mention, that she had read the Profile before it went to press, without requesting that any "sex gossip" be removed. But in one respect, Louise was acting consistently: "When I am finished with a person it is forever. I do not think this is a good way to be. But I endow the people I like with certain beauties and excitement, and when they make me sore all the inspiration dies out of the friendship."[42]

The most intriguing aspect of her reaction, or overreaction, to Tynan was the belated concern about her "image"—as if she were cultivating it in a certain direction that was now threatened. Her young Eastman House acquaintance, Morgan Wesson, thought that was precisely what she was doing: "The great success of that woman was in totally resurrecting her reputation—and from a sickbed, immobilized, and being an alcoholic."[43]

She had created something of a monster, and it was herself.

THE TYNAN tempest took a heavy toll on Louise, who turned seventy-three on November 14, 1979, in the middle of it. Her weight loss was now alarming. "The celebrity brought to me by the *New Yorker* Tynan profile stuns me," she wrote Brownlow at the end of the year. "I am the same old slob, but down to 80 pounds—getting sicker."[44]

She could tolerate the pain and immobility imposed by arthritis; it was her breathing that was driving her wild. And then came a disaster. On January 11, 1980, she awoke with an industrial-strength hangover; getting out of bed, she lost her balance, fell against a chest of drawers, and broke four ribs.

"Eleven days locked up in a madhouse called hospital," she wrote Kevin. "I have emphysema—no cigarettes. Maddening."[45]

Ken Tynan had emphysema, too. The dreadful lung disease was one more common bond, a grim one, between them—as it had been between Louise and Theodore. But neither Tynan nor Brooks knew how advanced his case really was. On July 26, 1980, Kenneth Tynan died at the age of fifty-three. Despite her hostility over film deals and images, Louise was stunned and grieved.* She had loved that bright creature, who barnstormed her world and energized it for the last time. She had found her final soulmate, and had things worked out—a rapprochement, perhaps,

---

* She managed a quote for Jack Garner's obituary feature on Tynan in the July 29 Rochester *Democrat and Chronicle*: "He had the wonderful delicacy of selecting the right word. It's something you don't see in writers anymore. He pawed around very carefully for the exact word he wanted. I don't think he had great insight, but he developed a beautiful portrait of his subject. He painted with words."

or just the natural course of his outliving her—Tynan, of all her literary suitors, would surely have been The Biographer. The ninety-two letters were proof of it, and she had taken secret comfort in the thought that he might help see her through her own death. She felt very tired and very old. Tynan, the intellectual lover par excellence, Tynan, the sonofabitch, had abandoned her too. But still, the fans kept coming. . . .

As a result of the Profile, many people gained the impression that Louise was living in poverty. Some, such as the dancer Katie O'Brien, even sent her small checks—which she promptly returned. It was one more reason to be annoyed with the way Tynan had "poortrayed" her.

Tynan's piece was reprinted in the *London Observer* magazine, and, with the turn of the decade, more articles poured forth from the international press. In 1980 alone, several important magazines devoted entire issues to Louise—*Jeune Cinéma* and *L'Avant-Scène* in France and *Frauen und Film* in Germany, among others. In the United States, even such unlikely publications as *Vogue* joined the bandwagon. *Vogue's* September 1981 story on Louise was written by none other than Anita Loos, who had once called her "a black-headed blonde—she has a blonde personality." It was a description Louise, for some reason, always liked.

Now in 1981 there was something ironic about the eighty-eight-year-old Loos reminiscing fondly about the woman she had rejected fifty years earlier for *Gentlemen Prefer Blondes*. And there was something bizarre about the misinformation that riddled her *Vogue* article. They met, Loos said, "when we were working as novices at the old MGM studio in Culver City." (Louise never made an MGM film in her life.) They were both four feet eleven inches and weighed ninety-two pounds, she said. (Louise was five feet two inches and weighed 103.) George Marshall, she said, "spent fortunes on trying to further a career in the movies which Louise didn't want" (Loos was thinking of Hearst and Marion Davies) because "it interfered with her social life as Queen of the Washington football team" (she was thinking of Corinne Griffith). Louise was most irate to read that "her favorite form of exercise was walking off a movie set."

Anita was playing fast and Loos with the truth, while carelessly hyping the Brooks Cult.* Louise often commented on "her crime [of] corrupting film history" by passing on countless mistakes. She could have written the greatest history of Hollywood and winds up listing all the very tall men she didn't go to bed with."[46] As for Loos's autobiography, *A Girl Like I*: "Every page is a lie and a mess of facts. But I love her and she writes me because

* Perhaps age was a factor. Loos died on August 18, 1981, a month before publication of the *Vogue* story, which was her last.

I think *Gentlemen Prefer Blondes* is a work of art, as good in its way as Jane Austen's *Pride and Prejudice.*"[47]

Yet for all her wild inaccuracies in the *Vogue* piece, Loos came close to the essence of what her subject conveyed on screen: She called it "Louise Brooks' erotic ecstasy." And she made an amazing, sweeping declaration:

> She was by far the prettiest girl in Hollywood, a fact which was only the beginning of her incredible career. For today's film critics all agree that Louise Brooks became the greatest actress in the history of moving pictures.[48]

L O U I S E ' S strength was ebbing; it was too late to begin writing any full memoirs. But as far back as 1966, Louise had thought about assembling her essays into a book. What it would be, she told Kevin Brownlow, "is my autobiography disguised in a series of essays about other people." She was still hoping to use *Naked on My Goat* as a title "because that will be the title of my first essay showing me going naked from the Denishawn Dancers to naked in the *Scandals* to naked in the Ziegfeld *Follies* to naked in my first film, *The American Venus*. This also establishes the producers' view of me as a naked beauty who was not to get any fancy ideas in my head about being an ACTRESS."[49]

By 1980, the body was weak but the mind was sharp, kept active by William Cuseo at the Rochester Public Library, who supplied her with a steady stream of books. ("I am the only woman who ever gave up men for the public library," she said.[50]) Cuseo could locate anything—including "Cinematic Theology," Brownlow's recent article in *The New Statesman* which deplored the obscurantism of semiotics (the science of signs). "It made me so sick," she wrote Kevin, "that I sent it down to William Shawn, asking him to do a piece to help save film from semiology."[51]

Shawn, for his part, refused to give up his gentle insistence that she put together a book, and now it was finally going to happen. Her film-journal pieces over the years had been little read outside film circles and could be magnificently "new" if properly packaged. Shawn recalls the genesis:

> I proposed the book that became *Lulu in Hollywood*. Originally, I urged her to write her autobiography, but all that came of that was what is now the first chapter ["Kansas to New York"]. She was too ill to continue. I then selected, arranged, and edited the pieces she had written over the years for various magazines, and these pieces, together with the new chapter, constituted the book. She asked me to write an introduction—just for her own pleasure, or fun—and I did.[52]

"Knopf is publishing my film articles in a book—with an introduction by William Shawn and his title, *Loulou* [*sic*] *in Hollywood*," she wrote Brownlow, "but nothing tickles me anymore—this goddamned emphysema. Kathleen Tynan just sent me some stuff left by Ken, banned in the U.S., which I can squirt into my lungs for three hours of breathing."[53]

As to that "original" first chapter, Louise could be forgiven for an act of convenience. Unbeknownst to either Shawn or Robert Gottlieb, Knopf's editor-in-chief, she fashioned it largely from three existing pieces. The first two pages of family history were recycled verbatim from "A Certain Idea of Liberty" in the French *Portrait d'une anti-star*, which had never appeared in English. Passages on her Denishawn and *Scandals* experiences were cannibalized from her unpublished "Gloria Swanson" of 1957. Some of the rest came from a first chapter of memoirs she had drafted in the sixties. But all the material was uniquely hers, and new to the thousands who would read it for the first time. Shawn's elegiac introduction set the mood:

> It should not come to us as a surprise that a film actress can write, but, so narrow are our expectations, it does. . . . It may well be that the number of beautiful, eloquently erotic film actresses who have been able to write *is* very, very small. But, whether it is small or large, in my judgment Louise Brooks must head the list. . . .
>
> Her apparently innate ability to offer herself to the screen with nothing held back carries over to her writing. . . . Her directness, her powerful impulse to tell the truth, her refusal to withhold anything provide a literary foundation from which she can readily take flight; and that she does. At one point in this book, she writes of her life, "And so I have remained, in cruel pursuit of truth and excellence, an inhumane executioner of the bogus, an abomination to all but those few people who have overcome their aversion to truth in order to free whatever is good in them." If she had written nothing more than that one sentence, I would be prepared to call her a writer.[54]

Gottlieb had found her "sensible, charming, and—because of her terrible breathing—sad. She was also stubborn, and not as accurate about dates as she thought she was. But it was a happy, efficient, professional relationship, and of course the book did very well."[55]

Very well indeed. *Lulu in Hollywood* was published in May 1982—to an avalanche of rave reviews. Peter Campbell in the *London Review of Books*, for instance, called it "unfailingly perceptive about the arts of acting and film-making":

> Hollywood . . . was profligate with talent. Like a factory that packs lobster tails or goose livers and discards the rest of the beast, it took the bit that it thought it could best exploit. In Louise Brooks' case it was a wonderful

face. What never came to terms with Hollywood, and what Hollywood never had any use for, was the remarkable human being masked by it.[56]

William K. Everson gave her a fine send-off in *Films in Review*, concluding that "not being a historian, Brooks can certainly be forgiven for a few errors." Everson's similar review for *Variety* carried the inimitable headline: "Louise Brooks, Brainy Beauty, Scorned Hollywood: A Hot Read."[57]

James Wolcott in *Esquire* referred to "the warm milk bath" poured for Louise by William Shawn in the introduction and went on to say: "It's a very tart, fleet, gossipy book, a whip-flicking display of wit and spite. The truth is that Louise Brooks is a cool, unrepentant snob—and the snobbery is in fact a finely calibrated crap detector."[58] Walter Clemons in *Newsweek* said, "Her own life now has a dimension besides her appearances on film: She's a brilliant historian."[59] F. X. Feeney in the Los Angeles *Weekly* called it "paragraph for paragraph, as hard and mysterious as a diamond."[60] More raves appeared in the *New York Times*, *New York Magazine*, the Philadelphia *Inquirer*, the Toronto *Star* (which serialized the book, as did the New York *Post*), the Los Angeles *Times*—and most of the other major newspapers in America and England. But the most important review to Louise was an unpublished one: William Paley's. She had not seen him in almost thirty years, and never would again; in all that time, he said, "she phoned me once—maybe twice."[61] But he was much gratified by *Lulu* as final proof of her talent and success at writing, neither of which he had honestly expected.

A few "moderates" such as Stanley Kauffmann in the June 23, 1982, *New Republic*, withheld full beatification. Kauffmann chided Shawn for his awe that an actress could write mentioning Mary Astor's *A Life on Film*. Kauffmann and others also criticized the "catchy but imprecise" title of the book, noting that Lulu's career in Hollywood was "short and insignificant" and that most of her essays dealt with people and events in New York and Germany: "The acting career, except for the European films, is not overwhelming as such, neither is her book. But in both of them, the Brooks [sexual] uranium tingles."

One recurring complaint was that the book contained hardly a word, and nary a picture, of her life after 1940.

The negative reviews were few, but significant. Auberon Waugh's in the London *Daily Mail* challenged the beauty, the morality, and the writing ability of the author. Since 1938 she had been just "hanging around," wrote Waugh. "It sounds rather a miserable life, and she sounds rather a miserable woman. . . . Her book may not teach us much about the cinema, but it provides a gloomy little object lesson in sexual morals: Don't let your daughter on the stage."[62]

The most serious criticism concerned accuracy. Not everyone was willing to forgive Brooks her trespasses of fact. British film historian Alexander Walker, who reviewed *Lulu* in the London *Evening Standard*, said he put "little trust in Louise Brooks as a reliable witness":

> Brooks is responsible for some very serious miscomprehensions—particularly as regards her peers. I find her the equivalent in movies of Lillian Hellman in the politics of a later period. Each rewrites history to the extent of being self-deluding and also misleading others.[63]

Another vocal dissident was Lawrence Quirk, editor of his own feisty *Quirk's Reviews*, who was now angrier than ever about the characterization of his uncle as a tool of Louis B. Mayer. He was further incensed by Knopf's failure to correct errors long since identified in Louise's original essays. Quirk blasted the book as "a disgraceful pot-pourri of blatant falsehoods, distortions and odd biographical omissions—self-pitying, self-congratulatory and self-serving." He called it sour-grapes, mean-spirited, "disorganized and badly edited." As for Louise's celebrated "independence," he called no lesser rebuttal witness than Eddie Sutherland, quoting him from 1963:

> Louise had something up there on the screen, sure, when she was properly handled, but in her offscreen life she never grew up, ducked responsibility right and left, and was totally unfit for marriage. What she calls her "rebellions" were just childish petulance.[64]

Louise's strong philosophical commitment to Truth with a capital T—Proustian or Goethean literary Truth—did not extend to errors of her own. When she read Everson's mention of her mistakes, she wrote him, "Thanks for the corrections of fact—although I was not writing a textbook." * But it was interpretation, rather than facts, that concerned Sara Laschever in the most important of *Lulu*'s negative notices, in the October 21, 1982, *New York Review of Books*. She thought Louise's "incorrigible integrity" a cover-up for something else:

> Her principal undertaking in *Lulu in Hollywood* . . . is to lay claim to a personal truthfulness equivalent to that now-famous image of guileless, automatic candor which she projected on the screen. And just as critics and audiences have loved Lulu in the person of Brooks, she appears to hope that they will love Brooks in the person of Lulu.
> In view of this ambition, her book is, in its way, a triumph of style. Brooks gives the impression of withholding nothing while actually concealing a great deal. She pretends to total frankness while presenting an elaborate myth of herself: the actress as moral exemplar, more honest and uncompromising

* For the errata in *Lulu in Hollywood*, see the Appendix.

than her more successful contemporaries and, it would seem, just about everyone else. . . .

The picture that emerges is of a willful child—both spoiled and neglected —belligerently fighting for her parents' attention. . . . [By 1928] the spoiled child had become a spoiled star—but before she was established enough, enough in demand by audiences, to get away with it. . . . Perhaps this is how, finally, she is like Lulu. Not her much-vaunted honesty but her appetite for pleasure ruined her life. . . .

Still, she is true to the persona she imagined for herself, and her self-portrait is the one undeniable success of the book. . . . Brooks' cranky, muddle-headed personality comes through clearly. By turning her impulsiveness and self-indulgence into a fiery iconoclasm, she has transmogrified the very quality for which Hollywood rejected her so many years ago into one for which she is extravagantly admired today. Where then she was merely unprofessional, now she has become the quirky individualist, willing to sacrifice everything—career, fame, fortune—in her need to flaunt convention. It may be her greatest role.

NO NEGATIVE assessment of her character or motives, however, could prevent thousands of adoring new "Brooksies" from being recruited to the Cult by *Lulu in Hollywood.* She had considered *Escaping with My Life* as the title, and it now seemed even more fitting: The deluge of admirers threatened to finish her off, and she was none too gracious about them. "Fans? I detest them!" she said. "All they want to do is come up and rob you." She began to mark letters "return to sender," unopened, and she declined all new *hommages.* For that matter, she had stated her definitive position back in 1971, when Theo relayed an eager young critic's invitation (on behalf of the Wichita Film Group) to return triumphantly to Kansas for a film festival in her honor:

> I am sending you *Sight and Sound* with my Fields article because it makes clear my attitude towards boys like Barry Paris. I have turned down homages in London, Toronto, California, New York . . . this year Scotland. Not because I think I am grand. I just don't like getting ruffed up by a lot of fools who pay my expenses for the privilege of abusing me.[65]

Now, interviews were granted only rarely, either on a whim of the moment (Professor McNamara and two Topeka high-school students) or out of prior friendship. James Watters was in the latter category. He had interviewed her for a 1980 *Life* piece (the one Tynan said might threaten his *New Yorker* profile) and written that "a mini-industry has grown up in praise of this extraordinary cult figure." Watters now wanted to talk with her again for his current project with the photographer Horst, *Return Engagement: Faces to Remember—Then and Now,* and she agreed.

Watters's earlier portrait of Louise, like Tynan's, relied more heavily on her letters than on conversation. There was no need to gild the lily of her prose. All he had to do was provide the transitions—such as the fact that she invited some friends and a local reporter to be present when Horst took her pictures:

> I wanted them here to keep me from remembering that I am an old hag in front of the camera; I wanted the reporter for a piece in the paper which might impress my landlord to the point of giving me a new stove.

But that was the Louise of 1980. "Nowadays," wrote Watters in 1983, "Louise's letters have dwindled to brief, hand-written notes on colored slips of paper. She plans no more memoirs, though she admits, 'my memories flow so easily, it scares me. I follow the rule of my beloved Proust: *The duty of the writer is not to imagine, but to perceive reality.* My memory is selective, but what I remember is as clear as if it were recorded on film.' "

Louise and her book were also inspiring a minivogue in the hair and fashion world. "Louise Brooks . . . is back in fashion again at the age of seventy-six—in the hairdressing salons," said the London *Evening Standard*.[66] "It seems that after months of her face staring out at them from bookshops, the smart girls of Manhattan are demanding the hairstyle from their crimpers."

Women's Wear Daily confirmed that "Louise Brooks is wielding her influence again. The Lulu haircut is showing up on younger women with their own flapperish style."[67] The *New York Times* said that when the striking cover of *Lulu in Hollywood* appeared, "scissors started clicking. Paris called the straight, ear-length cut *le bob*; it crossed the Channel to London, and now it is to be seen in shops from SoHo to Madison Avenue."[68]

Her photo was now *de rigueur* in any survey of film and fashion "glamour"—in books, TV documentaries, and Andy Warhol's *Interview*. Louise, typically, dismissed the attention with one hand and accepted it with the other: "The fact is, I played no glamorous parts and wore no glamorous clothes. I think I got in [these books] because of the effect I had privately on the women stars' clothes. . . . When I went to Hollywood in 1927 the girls were wearing lumpy sweaters and skirts in the daytime and long, baby blue ruffled dresses at night. I was wearing sleek suits and half-naked beaded gowns and piles and piles of furs (my bills shocked even Walter Wanger and Bill Paley)."[69]

Louise the "icon" would travel beyond fashion and into the wider culture, from "Loulou" perfume to MTV videos and of course film. Melanie Griffith in *Something Wild* and Sabine Azéma in *Mélo* are only two of many Brooks-inspired film heroines. The most overt tribute is Stephanie

Beroes's *The Dream Screen* (1986), a multilayered essay on the mythifica-
tion of women which weaves *Pandora's Box* clips into two stories—one
fictional, one real—of contemporary femmes fatales, both Lulu-Louise
look-alikes.

Lulu in Hollywood, the Beroes film, and the 1980s in general finally
corrected a real or imagined phenomenon Louise perceived in her early
Cult of the fifties and sixties. She expressed it in response to questions
from the French magazine *L'Alsace:*

> I find your opening sentence intriguing: "For millions of men who love
> cinema, you are Loulou." With one exception [Lotte Eisner], as far as I
> know I have never had a single admirer of my films among women. And to
> be a film star of enduring quality, an actress must be not only admired but
> also imitated by women fans. The intriguing question is why some inspire
> women to imitate them, and not others? In the Twenties, why Clara Bow
> but not Colleen Moore? In the Thirties, why Garbo but not Dietrich?[70]

Her appeal now transcended the sexes. But the ultimate manifestation
of her literary and pop-culture trendiness was a parody. "I cannot pay
attention to anything that does not immediately concern me," Louise
once confessed.[71] Veronica Geng's "Lulu in Washington," in the June
1984 *American Film*, mercilessly mimicked the self-absorption and the
style:

> One evening in January 1929, while I was reading a book at supper in the
> expensive Park Avenue apartment of an ugly, vulgar banker, I received an
> urgent cablegram from J. Edgar Hoover, asking me to appear in a clandes-
> tine film of a sex party among government officials. . . . Due to a mere
> accident of birth, which at the time I took no notice of, I was erotically
> irresistible to both men and women, but false humility was a gift I had been
> denied. . . .
>
> I had always been abnormally truthful, though it never occurred to me to
> be vain about it. My integrity, like my sexual beauty, came so naturally that
> I was quite mystified by the attention it drew if I happened to mention it.
> Thus it was that the banker's presumption in questioning my self-knowledge,
> which I specialized in, I saw through as a pathetically ill-disguised alibi for
> keeping me in New York as his private property to flatter his ego. I left for
> Washington, packing only his first editions. Having often told him he was
> too stupid to appreciate them, I could not be so sanctimonious as to leave
> them in his possession. . . .[72]

IN HER heyday, interest in Louise was largely restricted to pockets on
the East and West coasts. Half a century later, the Rochester postman was
delivering letters from all over the world, many addressed simply to
"Louise Brooks, Rochester, USA." Sometimes it wasn't only the letters

that arrived, but the admirers themselves. "I tell people over and over not to come here to see me, that I am a mean old woman," she once wrote Theo, "but they barge up and make sad noises and I let them see me and then they get mad at me for being a mean old woman."[73] Out of curiosity or compassion, she usually let them in.

Some of them took advantage of her. In 1968, a college boy named John appeared penniless at her door, spent the night on her couch, borrowed $50, and was never heard from again. Disturbed, she wrote George Pratt: "I have a contempt for people who shake me down, which ill matches my fortune. . . . These are all kids who seem to have sucker lists of antique movie actresses."[74]

She told Kevin Brownlow she had "always been a collector of lame ducks. Didn't I tell you about my little male whore whom I taught to read with *What Makes Sammy Run?* And the truck driver who wasn't a truck driver but preyed upon the homos in Times Square, beat and robbed them, whom I taught to do exquisite pastels? They both went to hell anyway, but they did it with some knowledge of the beauties of art."[75]

Back in 1969, a more honorable youth named Jeffrey Rolick had asked Louise for an interview for his school newspaper, the Canandaigua County (New York) College *Blue Collar*. At first she agreed to see him, but she later told him she was sick and couldn't. He sent a bouquet to cheer her up, which drew the following letter:

> Today at noon my bell rang and a man presented me with a large hunk of tissue paper which I found to contain a most expensive and beautiful flower arrangement in a basket. . . . You make me feel like the old bitch which I am, because I am not sick. I always say I will do an interview or make a personal appearance, then panic and back out. It is something basic in my personality. Today at 62, 40 years ago when I was making pictures. . . .[76]

She continued at length in a rundown of her career and ended with, "You are welcome to print this letter in your paper if in any way it will make up for my sneaky performance. . . ."

Even in her old age, she could not turn people away. One night in 1984, her bell rang and she made the painful trip from bed to door—a struggle now requiring ten minutes to accomplish. Facing her was a black-bobbed French girl named Isabelle who looked exactly like Louise at twenty. Drenched from a thunderstorm, she said she had come all the way from Paris just to meet Louise, with no particular purpose beyond that. Louise called her friend Marge upstairs, who took her in for the night.

But she was now too ill to be anything other than agitated, upset, and

confused by the visitations of lame ducks. There was only one exception
—one last stranger who touched her heart.

Ross Berkal sits at the piano in his Boston living room, playing the Debussy
"Sarabande." Louise Brooks, from her framed portrait on the piano, is
watching him. The music and the mood are dreamy, Ross Berkal is
dreamy, and so is the story of how Louise changed his life.

Berkal was just eighteen in 1983 when he saw *Pandora's Box* and *The
Diary of a Lost Girl* and fell in love with the girl on screen:

> I felt this really intense need to meet her—it was really important to me.
> I wrote a couple of letters that were "returned to sender," and so I wrote
> another one saying something like, "You know, you should at least be able
> to give me a nasty reply." Still no answer. Then I sent her a postcard that
> said, "If I don't hear from you by such-and-such date, I'll be up at 4 o'clock
> on Saturday." So I didn't hear from her and I just went up there [October
> 28, 1984] and rang Marge's bell and I'm waiting and thinking, "Jesus, I drove
> for eight hours, I don't believe this." I was shaking. Marge took me in and
> Louise was in bed. It was like a first date or something, I was so nervous. But
> she didn't throw me out. Her first question was, "Why did you come out and
> see me?" I told her I had just seen the two films and—I don't know, I tried
> to explain the impact, and we ended up talking for six hours and got off onto
> all kinds of weird topics, like radio shows, for instance, which she listened to
> a lot of. I have a tendency to chatter and get left hanging in mid-sentence
> and I'd done this a couple of times, and she finally got a little irritated and
> said, "I'm supposed to be the one who has the emphysema and forgets"—
> with that little half-smile of hers. She was really sick with a cold, on top of
> everything else, and I said, "I shouldn't stay too long," and she said, "No,
> no, you drove eight hours." She was terrific. One of the churches near
> Louise's apartment has a beautiful set of bells. I remember hearing them in
> the background as the sun was going down. . . . At the end she said, "I want
> you to promise me that you're not going to come and see me again," and I
> promised. She kept repeating it. "Now you understand, you're not to come
> back." I said, "I understand," and I went back to my hotel room and I cried.[77]

At Christmas, he sent her a passionate "farewell" letter and a three-
page love poem. She liked the poem well enough to reply, giving him her
phone number and permission to call. He was thrilled and called her
faithfully, once a week, thereafter.

The subject of their conversations was often music. Debussy was Berkal's favorite composer, as he was Louise's and her mother's. She told him
that Myra had often played "Footprints in the Snow" and "The Girl with
the Flaxen Hair" for her to dance to as a child. And so it was that, during

several calls, Berkal laid the receiver atop his piano and played long-distance renditions of Debussy (the Book One Preludes) for Louise.

"She was my best friend and probably the best friend I'll ever have," says Berkal, whose story ends on a mystical note: A few months before she died, he sent her a picture of himself at the piano, which she put on her bedstand. Her friend Marge said it was one of the few things that Louise didn't throw away. "But when it came time to inventory the apartment after Louise's passing," says Ross, "Marge could not find the photograph. Where had it gone? I would like to think that Louise took it with her."

Ross Berkal was an exception. As a rule, glorious tributes did not impress her. She once wrote her brother about some translated articles she had just received from a friend: "It was very sweet of him to send me the Italian stuff, although I never read anything about myself [which doesn't] make me puke. That doesn't mean that I don't love my latter-day fame; I simply reserve the right to find the whole thing ridiculous."[78]

The attitude was inconsistent, of course, and depended on exactly *what* was being said and by whom. But by and large, the way to Louise's heart lay not through flattery:

> I am asking all the "idolizers" to stop writing bullshit about me—after all, they are really forming me after their own image. . . . When I made films I never read reviews of them. Now I cannot avoid it in letters from my "Cult." They all admire the silliest sequence in *Beggars*, the opening, simply because it matches the scrambled technique of today. And they all hate the long close-ups in all the films. They cannot bear to rest their minds for an instant anymore on what has happened before and what may happen next because nothing beneath the surface happens anymore in films.[79]

She made frequent derogatory references to Ado Kyrou, "the Greek pansy," and to the flamboyant praise heaped upon her by other writers whom she presumed, often correctly, to be gay. "I have a shelf full of that stuff," she would say. "It makes me sick." It was their prose more than their sexual persuasion that annoyed her, but there was no denying that deep ambivalence—her lifelong appreciation-deprecation of homosexuals.

"Another thing that disgusts me," she wrote Brownlow, is "getting mixed up in these pansy cults." If anyone doubted her special appeal to gay people at this point, there was much evidence—such as the front-page *Village Voice* story of June 29, 1982, on how AIDS was affecting lifestyles. It began:

> When the moon smiles down on Christopher Street, the good gay man sets aside his *Lulu in Hollywood*, dabs on a dash of Paco Rabanne, slips into

a Chereskin pullover, and heads for this week's chrome-and-fern bar. A year ago, the same man threw down his *Drummer*, slipped a bottle of Aroma into his leather jacket, and butched out to the Mine Shaft.[80]

Someone sent a copy of it to Louise, who marked it up with X's and thought it important enough to keep.

Trashing her own fans seemed disingenuous for a woman who had always enjoyed nothing better than talking about herself. But by now she had had enough of her own cult to be able—in conversation with John Kobal—to speak eloquently about other people's, in relation to film as art and film preservation:

> It isn't like great literature which very few people can understand and those few people had to pass down from century to century. Anyone who goes to a movie can understand it. . . . All you have to have is an eye and an ear, to have lived, spoken, felt, eaten, drunk and so forth. That's the whole terrible thing about this movie cult, these movie curators, these film archives . . . they go from cult to cult. This year they're mad about Japanese films and everything else stinks, and next year it's Ingmar Bergman and everything else stinks. . . .[81]

A book of film-star portraits, *People Will Talk*, produced by Kobal drew capsule comments on her own personal heroines and antiheroines.

Marilyn Monroe: "She was no fool. She was very smart. What did she do? Accidentally take an overdose? You know, I'm taking that Valium, which is a tranquilizer. And you take more and more because they cease to affect you. And more and more and more and more, like Judy Garland and Elvis Presley."

Claudette Colbert: "I hear the Reagans are visiting Claudette Colbert at her home in the Bahamas. Where'd she get all that dough?"

Bette Davis: "Oh, look, here's my favorite actress. I liked whatever she did. I think she's a real actress."

Debbie Reynolds: "Jesus! She ruined *Singin' in the Rain* for me."[82]

Yet still, even after Tynan and *Lulu* and all the adulation, there was the angry, lingering paranoia that nothing could erase. She was convinced, for instance, that *Variety* had blacklisted her from 1925 to 1963 "because I would not go for the shake of taking an ad in its Anniversary edition."[83] And when the talk with Kobal turned to Denishawn, the paranoia burst forth anew:

> You know what burns me up? For years, John, my whole career as far as these charming United States of America are concerned has been a blank. Ted Shawn and Ruth St. Denis must have given thousands of lectures, and they've written between them 15 books, and they have never found me

worthy of so much as a *mention* of my name, ever having been with them, and it's the same with the Follies.[84]

It was not entirely accurate, but that was her perception. She said the same thing in letters to Denishawn's Jane Sherman and others and complained as well about being isolated in dull, remote Rochester: "I have been exiled in this damned town since 1956 and know only what occasional visitors tell me. Perhaps you can tell me how Charlie Weidman died. . . ."[85] To Ricky Leacock she had said something similar: "It's always been my habit to live very much alone. But once in a while I miss very much knowing brilliant and intelligent people from whom I've learned everything. But I don't meet any brilliant people anymore."[86]

That charge was not well founded. Louise was in constant touch with the outside world by phone and mail and for many years had both the health and the money to go wherever she pleased. Her communications were excellent. George Pratt thought her reclusiveness was an emulation of Proust and kidded her about "Remembrance of Things Pabst." Roddy McDowall had another idea about her misanthropic isolation:

> A lot of older people who live alone over a long period or have secluded themselves or don't trust themselves, make a "temperature" where they think they're safe. If they get out of those parameters, they think they'll spin out, which they probably will because they're emotionally unable to deal with the world on its "normal terms." You get slightly paranoid—those demons, the boogeyman—lying there alone all day long, hearing the sound only of your own brain. A lot of people recognize certain things that will trigger a behavior that they can't afford to express any longer. Louise knew she couldn't drink the way [she used to] anymore, so when she'd go off the wagon, her regret—her disturbance about it—was enormous. She was a person who was always trying to matriculate somehow within herself, and to discipline herself. There's a very profound reason why Louise stayed confined the way she did. . . . I think it was her safety. She made a ghetto for herself where she was safe. It was a very closed oasis. If she'd gone out, she might have gone berserk.
>
> People used to say, "She's foolish, she could be doing this or that, she could be enjoying her late life." But I think she was scared. She could never brook a fool. She had very limited patience. Once the humor about the idiot would subside, then she wanted, in a sense, to kill. To obliterate. That's very dangerous if you're out there in a world with a great many fools. You have to have enormous patience. And she didn't. So I think she was wise [to stay alone]. For her, she was wise.[87]

Whatever else might be said about her exile, there was no doubt that it was self-imposed, and that she had once felt very differently about it:

When I was young, I was unhappy most of the time. The pursuits of my friends: fame, money, power, did not make me happy. Their pleasures, sexual messes, showing off and pushing each other around did not make me happy. Only when I moved to Rochester in 1956 did I find some happiness. Far away from anyone who would care to manage me, I can live as I like and close the door every night saying, thank God I am alone.[88]

But now, the feeling of isolation, the mounting irritability and bitterness—all were exacerbated by the devils of age and infirmity, the same spoilers that prevented her from savoring the success of her book. It was all happening too late. In a shattering letter to Herman Weinberg, she put it into words:

Am I collecting on those hellish years (1935–1955) when I blacked out in my self-imposed ruin without a cent to hold me together? You would think Bill Paley and money in the bank would ease my overwhelming fear now— and it has been two-and-a-half years since I had a drink. I thought *that* would cool me out—it hasn't. But every morning I face the day with dread —putting myself together like some old plastic toy, knowing that a loud TV can shatter my grip on control, *despair*—a jump ahead of straight insanity. And everyone is so decent to me—spoiling me—I have no excuse of neglect or poverty—is it the helplessness of arthritis? Fear of disease and death? It isn't failure—I never had sense enough to make any plans from one day to the next. From that viewpoint my late "celebrity" and financial security are a miracle. But I wish I were dead.[89]

The last outing: "Looks like a ghost, doesn't it?" Louise and her own
portrait of fifty years earlier at the Edward Steichen exhibit,
Eastman House, Rochester, August 5, 1979

21 · The End

There's little in taking or giving,
There's little in water or wine;
This living, this living, this living
Was never a project of mine.
Oh, hard is the struggle, and sparse is
The gain of the one at the top,
For art is a form of catharsis,
And love is a permanent flop,
And work is the province of cattle,
And rest's for a clam in a shell,
So I'm thinking of throwing the battle—
Would you kindly direct me to hell?
　　　　　　　　—DOROTHY PARKER

BRING a gun," Louise told her friends when they called, over and
over. At first they were shocked and frightened, but she said it so often
that they got used to it after a while.

The last years of Louise Brooks—the *very* last years—contained no
more or less pathos than those of any elderly, solitary mortal ravaged by
osteoarthritis and emphysema and, in Louise's case, an overwhelming
desire to die. But she was never a serious candidate for suicide. Like
Dorothy Parker, who talked and wrote about it incessantly, she could
never do it. She was too timid—and too brave.

She was also too desperately tired out even to leave her apartment
anymore. Except for a few doctors' appointments, she had not done so
since August of 1979. That Last Great Outing came about thanks to John
C. Benz, a retired Eastman Kodak employee with a fondness for Rolls-
Royces and old movie stars. After the Tynan Profile appeared, Benz found
Louise's address and sent her, oddly enough, a Susan B. Anthony dollar,

asking her to reply. She did, and they became friends. He offered to take her for a ride in his gorgeous white 1969 Rolls (complete with TV), in which he had recently chauffeured Gloria Swanson to a local screening of *Manhandled*. The Rolls's credentials—having carried Gloria—failed to impress Louise, and she demurred. But Benz kept plugging: "I asked her many times, but she wouldn't go out. The only place I could get her to go to was Eastman House—she didn't want to, at first, and I had to talk her into it."

The date was Sunday, August 5, and the occasion was a centennial exhibition of Edward Steichen photographs at the George Eastman House's International Museum of Photography (July 3–October 28, 1979). Louise had not been there since 1966. Benz would take her in style—picking her up in the Rolls. She wore her black dress—*the* black dress, the only one she ever wore. She could still walk, but it was difficult, and when they got there, Benz procured a wheelchair. They stopped to linger in front of her famous 1928 *Vanity Fair* portrait.

"Looks like a ghost, doesn't it?" she said, within earshot of Jeannie Williams of the Rochester *Times-Union*, whose write-up appeared the next day. And then Louise's lightning glance landed on Charlie Chaplin. "Oh, isn't that marvelous! He's right next to me! . . . Steichen always said, 'You have to see it in the eyes,' and he never photographs anyone who isn't thinking."

Louise had a good time and consented to allow reporter Williams to accompany her back to the apartment, where they talked about her memoir. "Will it be racy?" Williams asked.

"Where necessary," replied Brooks. "Probably every other page."

So rare were Louise's public appearances that the *New York Times* reported this one in its August 7, 1979, "People" column:

> Henri Langlois once said of Louise Brooks: "Her art is so pure that it becomes invisible." Lately, the same thing could be said about Miss Brooks herself. . . .
>
> But on Sunday she made one of her rare outings from her apartment to look at an exhibit of Edward Steichen photos . . . The former actress, in a wheelchair because of an arthritic hip, was dressed in black. "Mourning my youth," she explained.

Thereafter, Louise became a permanent recluse. The main reason was physical, but perhaps too the Steichen show had affected her in a way Dante observed: "There is no greater pain than the remembrance of past happiness in present misery."

For the next two years, she came to rely more and more heavily on John Benz and his wife, Helen, as he remembers:

God rest her soul, she was a bitch, though. I'd do things for her, and she'd give me hell, and I'd talk back to her, and then she'd call me up and apologize. I took her to Eastman House in the Rolls, then later I took her to the dentist in my Grenada. She said, "Oh, now I'm not important—I'm driving in a Ford!"

She'd call up and say to Helen, "Will you make me some chicken salad or some tuna fish sandwiches for dinner?"—it was always cold stuff, no hot food. My wife did that for a year or so, and I used to go up there three times a week, and that's quite a ways from here. . . .

It's funny, she was awful tight. She spilled some water in the kitchen once and she said, "Will you clean it up?" and I said sure. So I went in and took some paper towels and she said, "What are you doing with those?" and I said, "I'm going to clean it up," and she said, "Don't you know those paper towels are expensive? Use a sponge."

One year, I think it was 1981, she wanted to give a Christmas party, which was unlike her. She hadn't been drinking since she fell, and I said, "You won't drink, will you?" and she said no. So we went up there and she had two or three other people and they started drinking and she started drinking, and my wife had to help her into bed. She liked gin. She'd drink it straight, not even an ice cube. She smoked Pall Mall and Lucky Strikes, unfiltered, two packs a day at least—strong and fast, like her gin. She was just skin and bones. I had to weigh her before the doctor appointments, and she was down to 78 pounds. . . .[1]

Helen Benz has been listening in silence to her husband's account of their encounters with Louise. She now makes her first and last utterance: "She'd call and ask me to make her something, and I never minded. I always wondered why she never went into the talking movies. And then when I met her and saw her disposition—I understood exactly. If she couldn't have her way, forget it."

Louise had a tendency to use people, and they knew it. But such was her power to fascinate that she always found the people she needed, or they found her. It was a testament to the medical profession, for instance, that two of its members were concerned enough about her to revive that antediluvian practice known as the house call. William Springer, dentist brother of her New York publicist friend John, came to fix her teeth (and never sent her a bill), while gentle Dr. Joseph Stankitis—the only physician she ever liked and trusted—made periodic check-up visits after her refusal to have the hip-joint operation that might have restored her mobility. "Her illness made it difficult for her to get around," says Dr. Stankitis, "but it wasn't so much that she couldn't as that she didn't want to. I think she didn't want people to see her—to destroy the image people had of her."[2]

A new friend, Barbara Mayberry, came to her through William Shawn, who contacted Mayberry in Rochester and asked her to look in on Louise in the wake of the fall that broke her ribs.

"So I called," says Mayberry, "and she said, 'Well, as long as you have to come, come on down,' and I went. She asked me if I had read the Tynan article and I said no, I had not. So she sent me to the bookcase and said, 'Read it!' And I said all right, I'd bring it back in a couple days. 'No,' she said, 'just mail it back—I don't want to see you again.' And I said, 'No, now Mr. Shawn would like me to look in on you again, to be sure you're all right. I'll be back.' And that's how it began."[3]

Mayberry came by faithfully, once a week, and soon took over a number of chores for Louise, organizing her taxes and sending her own maid in to keep the apartment in shape. As Louise's health worsened, the daily mechanics of living were becoming more daunting. How much longer could she live alone? Mayberry began to look into the idea, proposed by Roddy McDowall and (unbeknownst to Louise) Francis Lederer in Hollywood, that Louise move to the Motion Picture and Television Country Home and Hospital in Woodland Hills, California.

Fifteen years earlier, Kevin Brownlow had paid a visit there. Louise had asked him about a Mack Sennett comic actress named Dot Farley, and he dutifully reported back:

> I had a strange encounter with Dot Farley at the Motion Picture Country Home. I was trying to trace the bungalow of Marion Davies' director E. Mason Hopper. It was pouring with rain, and the man who was driving me had got lost among the line upon line of sad, lonely little cottages. Finally, I got out and went up to a cottage which had a light in the window. The bell-push had a temporary, typewritten card above it: DOT FARLEY. I rang, and after a few minutes a very old, very small woman came to the door. She saw me, and her face lit up; a visitor! I felt dreadful. So I introduced myself, told her that I had [acquired] several of her pictures, that her performances were much admired in England, and that the name Dot Farley ensured entertainment value for any film. She was very charming, and she insisted on coming out into the rain to show me where Hopper's cottage was, and to guide us out of the lane. As our car backed away from her little house, my last view was of Dot Farley standing in the pouring rain, in bedroom slippers and housecoat, illumined by the yellow light from her bedroom.[4]

Louise was spellbound and replied instantly:

> What a fascinating story. . . . But do you think you should feel so sorry for these old actors? Before the Home they were left to die in poverty. Many of them are not poor. Like all actors, they want to be with other actors, especially when they are ill and friendless. I wonder how I will die, cut off

from even my detestable family. Why are all my friends English, or German? To myself I am more American than America. Maybe that is the reason.[5]

But the prospects of the Motion Picture Home and her own death were now more real than hypothetical. Even though she did not have the requisite number of years in filmmaking to qualify, the Home was willing to make an exception—provided, of course, that Louise wanted to come. "At this point I am only waiting to hear from Ms. Brooks regarding her interest," wrote one of the Home's directors to Mayberry. "Experience has demonstrated that we are well advised to wait until we hear from the person contemplating retirement."[6]

The devoted McDowall urged her to go, if only to avoid those severe Rochester winters, and assured her that in California he could be of help to her. Louise was inclined to go, despite her misperception that she would have to turn over all her assets to the Home, which would then parcel out a small monthly amount for her spending money. "That wouldn't even buy me my cigarettes," she complained to John Benz. But still, it seemed like the best course of action.

"It was all set," recalls Mayberry. "And then she decided she should call someone who lived there to find out about life in this home—it was Mary Astor—and when she called, the receptionist said she'd have to have Miss Astor call her back (which she did) because they didn't allow phones in the rooms. And that was it. She decided then and there she wouldn't go. I said, 'Louise, I'll go with you, I'll take you out.' But she absolutely refused because the telephone was her lifeline."

It was, everyone agreed, a stupid rule, and Louise Brooks would take her chances in Rochester rather than submit to that, or any other, indignity.

When, in his last fateful letter, Theo had warned her against that seductive *Götterdämmerung*—begging her not to "give it a false value and rush to embrace it"—she had taken enormous offense and cut him off forever. But now, if not then, embracing her *Götterdämmerung* was precisely what Louise wanted to do.

She made that clear to William Klein, who did not enter her life until late 1981 but became an extremely important part of it when he did. Klein, a Rochester television and radio critic, had been drawn to her as an admiring fan; they "hit it off like gangbusters," he says, and he soon became her correspondence secretary, confidant, gofer, and chief conversation partner during her last three years. A visit or call from Klein is noted on virtually every page of Louise's daily logbooks until her death. As her sounding board, he also took the brunt of many rages and whims that would have driven away a less patient soul.

"She decided to play the role of The Dying Actress," says Klein, "and she played it to the hilt. The 'bring-a-gun' thing. I couldn't count the number of times she said it."

It is midnight, and Klein has just finished a TV broadcast. He is pacing and racing through a six-hour recollection that ends only with the light of dawn. The words tumble out in torrents:

> I knew that at any time Louise could have made the little sandwich that she ate at 5 o'clock or put the Nabisco wafers in a cup. . . . It wasn't easy for her, but she could get around. She had that little walker with the prongs. But after the doctors told her to stop the cigarettes and the liquor and she took to her bed, that was it. "I am now dying." She just took this whole attitude toward The Dying, the wanting to die—and everything was directed toward it. Whenever Jack [Garner] did an article on her, he was encouraged to bring in the emphysema-bedridden-dying Louise thing. She just didn't want to go on—and yet I had this feeling that she did. It was back and forth, the same as when people would send her reviews of her book. She'd act disinterested, like she could never figure out why it was so well-received, but inside her eyes was a little twinkle. It was the same thing with the dying. She wanted to die, but she wasn't about to swallow any of those pills.[7]

In better days, Louise and Bill talked happily about everything. "One of the reasons she liked me," he says, "was because I could give her answers about old films and song lyrics and things. We'd get on a roll and then come to a point where we couldn't remember something and have to call and find out. We drove the library nuts." And like her ninety-three-year-old father, "Louise loved talking about sex—she never shut off that gear of her brain. One of the last things we talked about was the AIDS issue. She had to know everything about it."

Klein was protective and carried out her orders: "Don't let anybody in here. I don't want to see anybody." But she made a few exceptions, and the by-invitation-only Dying Actress performance was sometimes interrupted by pilgrims.

It had been forty years since Louise had seen or heard from the person she identified as the one she had "loved most" in her life—Robert Brooks. The son of her "detestable" elder brother Martin, Robert was the boy she had taught to read in Wichita, and he had disappeared from her life as quickly as he had appeared.

One day in 1984 she got a letter from him, and soon after, he went to Rochester, unannounced and uninvited, to see his ailing aunt in the flesh. "I called her and she said, 'I don't want you to come see me.' Then I called her back and she said, 'Come tomorrow.' When I saw her, there was more bawling out, but it was kind of affectionate. The last thing she said was, 'Don't come back.' "

It was short, and not terribly sweet.

"I don't know . . . ," says Robert Brooks after a long pause. "I think she really did care."

Uninvited members of the Cult also checked in, such as the Italian camera crew that paid a surprise visit for an interview about the "Valentina" comic strip. They spoke not a word of English, and Louise was totally perplexed. But it was a measure of her resilience that she thought to call the superintendent, who was Italian, to come up and translate.

The Cult also had a Celebrity Branch, and in her last years, various luminaries beat a path to Louise's door—José Limon and Christopher Isherwood among them. The biggest flurry took place in November 1982, when seven actress-stars of Hollywood's golden era were invited to Rochester to accept the George Eastman Award for lifetime contributions to movies. Those honored were Joan Bennett, Dolores Del Rio, Myrna Loy, Maureen O'Sullivan, Luise Rainer, Sylvia Sidney—and Louise. The "Georges," which are awarded periodically and not annually, had not been given since 1978, and it was a major event. But Louise was simply too ill to attend. She did, however, tape-record a brief, eloquent statement of thanks that was played during the ceremonies.

Loy and Del Rio were also kept away by illness, but the four others came, and three of them wanted to see Brooksie. Local film critic Jack Garner escorted Rainer to Louise's apartment, where the two septuagenarian actresses "hit it off marvelously," Garner reported in the Rochester *Democrat and Chronicle*. "They compared notes on European acting versus Hollywood stardom and the reasons why they both fled Hollywood after a relatively few films.* Brooks seemed to particularly enjoy Rainer's hilarious imitation of Louis B. Mayer's gruff, flat accent, as she talked about her short-lived MGM career."[8]

In contrast to the quiet, genteel Luise Rainer was the brassy, gregarious, gravel-voiced Sylvia Sidney, who came with her publicist, Louise's old friend John Springer. There are two accounts of that visit, the first from Springer:

> When I got to Rochester, the first thing I did was to call Louise and ask if she'd mind if I brought someone over who was dying to meet her—Sylvia—

---

* Austrian-born Luise Rainer (1910–) was heralded as another Garbo when she arrived in Hollywood in the midthirties. She won back-to-back Oscars for her melodramatic performances in *The Great Ziegfeld* (1936) and *The Good Earth* (1937) and made five more films in quick succession, but by 1938 her career came to an abrupt halt—the result of her tumultuous first marriage (1937–1940) to playwright Clifford Odets and her quarrel with Louis B. Mayer over stereotyped roles. She made only one more film, *Hostages* (1943), and later married British publisher Robert Knittel, with whom she lives in London and Switzerland.

and she said, "I love Sylvia Sidney, she really wants to meet me?" We went to the apartment and . . . told the driver we'd only be five or ten minutes, and at the end of an hour I finally had to say let's go. She was so impressed with Sylvia. She knew all of Sylvia's work, and they gossiped like a couple of schoolgirls. They just had a fabulous visit.

But Bill Klein, who was also present, tells a different story, with the benefit of Louise's private reaction later: "Louise hated her because she had too much jewelry jangling and she smoked in the apartment, which Louise was furious about, and the *mouth*—she just wouldn't stop!"

Sidney declines to discuss the visit.

Last but not least was gentle, good-natured Joan Bennett, who made the pilgrimage to Goodman Street with her husband, David Wilde. Louise had written about the Bennett family in *Lulu in Hollywood*, making fun of their notoriously bad eyesight, among other things. Privately, Louise told Klein that, as far as she was concerned, Barbara was a loser and Joan a fool. "I always thought the talent in the family was Constance," she said. And she wasn't much more diplomatic to Joan's face, according to Barbara Mayberry, who was there:

> It was just awful. Joan had a great deal of trouble seeing; her eyes were gone. And, well, Louise just put everybody in his place. She was very rude. She was saying things like, "Oh, you're still acting? I didn't think you could act originally. How did you ever get this award?" It was embarrassing. Joan was quite flustered. Her husband's a charming man, and he was trying to hang in there with the proper small talk. But Louise persisted in dwelling on some of the terrible things they'd done when they were children—apparently she and Barbara Bennett were real hellions. It was one of those terrible "Oh, Louise! How could you say that?" situations, but afterwards Louise certainly couldn't understand why I thought it was awful.[9]

On another occasion around this time, Bill Klein conveyed a message to Louise from Leslie Caron, whom he interviewed for WVOR in Rochester. Caron, whose many scenes in *An American in Paris* had included an unabashed homage to Brooks, was *sang-froid* through the interview, says Klein, until she learned that he knew Louise and that she lived in Rochester.

"She suddenly became very passionate," he says, "and I remember her words exactly: 'You must tell Louise Brooks when you see her that among the people I hang with in Paris'—that's what she said, 'hang with'—'that we hold her in the very highest regard. I can't begin to tell you what all the writers and the film people think of her talent. She was the most enormous contribution to films.' And then she signed a photo for Louise."

Next came the unlikely combination of Peggy Cass and Susan Strasberg, who were appearing in Rochester in *Agnes of God* in February 1984.

But the most successful—and unlikely—of all the big-name visitors was Joan Rivers, whom Louise at first did not know.

"I kept telling her, 'Louise, this is one of the really big women in show business now,' " says Klein, and at his prodding, she watched Rivers on "The Tonight Show." The ignorance had been mutual until 1982, when Rivers—at Roddy McDowall's urging—read and loved *Lulu in Hollywood* and did a lively review of it for the *Hollywood Reporter*, describing *Pandora's Box* as "a kind of 1929 *Looking for Mr. Goodbar*." [10]

When Rivers came to Rochester in 1983, she called Klein and said, "I'm desperate to meet Louise Brooks." He arranged it, though after the overdose of Sylvia Sidney, Klein was worried about how Louise might react to the frenetic comedienne:

> But when she showed up the next morning, she was totally different—the other side of Joan Rivers. It was a rainy, rainy day and she'd brought her whole entourage—manager, hairdresser, they all wanted to meet Louise. Joan brought croissants, which of course Louise wouldn't touch. We pulled every chair in the apartment into the bedroom, and Joan was just wonderful with her. The one thing Louise always did for guests was give them her best. The best bed jacket went on. We'd take her ancient pink one off and put the sharp blue one on. I'd say, "Now are you sure you feel good enough for this?" and she'd say, "Don't worry, when they show up I'll put on the performance." And she did, though she had a lapse of memory a couple of times on things that Joan could easily have answered. But Rivers was so good with her, she never filled in the spaces. She just waited to hear what Louise had to say. [11]

Three years later in Pittsburgh, after the first of two raucous comedy turns ("Boy George is just what England needs—another queen who can't dress"), Joan Rivers sinks into a chair in her dressing room, and as she speaks of Louise, she is another person indeed, her voice soft and serious:

> I've never seen such a beautiful face in a bed. It was like a porcelain cameo, and you could see why men must have just been crazed. She said, "I've seen you on 'The Tonight Show' and you make me laugh—I think you're much better than Johnny." That just struck me as very funny. And then we talked about Roddy and Hollywood and—oh, it was freezing cold and it was such a dreary apartment. . . . I still see this incredible face. That's what killed me, that incredible face sitting in that bed. [12]

Rivers could not believe Louise's apartment—not squalid, but spartan in the extreme. Afterward, she asked Klein and McDowall what kind of gift she might give Louise: "I said to Roddy, I want to send her some beautiful linens and he said, 'She won't use them.' I want to send her a bed jacket. 'She won't wear it.' I want to send her books. 'There's no point.' Everything I came up with—'she won't use it, she won't want it.'"

Louise had long since given away her stereo and her Kurt Weill records. Rivers offered to send a new one, but Klein knew better: "Louise didn't want a stereo. Why do anything pleasurable like get up and play a record? A lot of times I wanted to bring my VCR over and play something I knew she'd like—but it was too confusing for her. She thought it might jar the TV set or something—do something out of the ordinary."

Joan Rivers sent her a book of paintings by El Greco, once Louise's favorite painter. The present made no special impression, but the visit itself—by a woman whom Louise had not even heard of a few weeks before—seemed to cheer her more than that of any other of her prominent admirers.

"Maybe it was because I was younger," says Rivers. "The others, maybe, were all wrecks of what they were, and you see a wreck talking and you know you're a wreck too."

A bizarre idea occurs to her, and the old Joan is back again: "She was the Pia Zadora of her generation!"

Louise was physically helpless, or believed herself to be so, and she was very calculating in making sure her support systems were in place. As Barbara Mayberry saw it:

> The three "service workers" in Louise's life at this point were Bill Klein, who handled the mail and her contacts with the artistic world; Marge, who handled the day-to-day feeding and caring for her; and Barbara, who was like a business manager. Basically there were the three of us, with Jack Garner added in, that she relied on. . . .
>
> It's funny, I was thinking about the way she was about gifts. When I got her something like the electric blanket, that was grand, she loved it, and she talked about it and would praise you endlessly, keeping you happy. But if you happened to buy her something that she didn't think she needed—one Christmas I gave her some china, just a single setting, because her things were so awful, and she looked at it and said, "What am I going to do with that?" And I said, "You're going to use it instead of what you've got." And she said, "I don't want it, take it back," and handed it to me! You just couldn't get your feelings hurt. Sometimes when she got to be so very difficult, I thought to myself, "Why am I doing this?" but I just couldn't bring myself to leave her. I'd occasionally say, "That's it, I'm not going to have you talking to me that way—goodbye!" And then the phone would be ringing when I walked in my front door. She'd be calling. And the next time I came, she'd have something for me, a little peace offering. She was a bright woman. I didn't really fool myself. I think she was fond of me, but she also needed me. She did that with all of us.

When I'd leave town, it was always a toss-up whether to tell Louise and
have her go into a tailspin or to try to leave and come back before she missed
me. I'd get back and sometimes there'd be 10 or 15 messages from her on
the answering machine, "Barbara, where are you? I don't know where you
are, please call me"—just frantic. She was feeling terribly alone and
frightened toward the end. [13]

Klein's role was getting much harder, too:

Did I tell you about the drummer? That thing went on for a month—
there was someone drumming "constantly" and it was bothering her. I heard
it, and believe me, it wasn't loud at all. Finally I went out and tracked it
down—an innocent young woman playing the drums, turned out she was
with the Rochester Philharmonic. I asked her if she'd ever heard of Louise
Brooks and she hadn't, but I took her over to the apartment and Louise
adored her. It turned out to be a very pleasant experience. The woman was
very sweet with her, and Louise was thrilled—with her and with me. You'd
get rave reviews from Louise for months if you solved something "major"
like that. But she worried about *everything* —there wasn't enough food in
the refrigerator, what if something happened to Marge? And the phone bill.
She made all of her calls collect. Anybody she called—the Paley Foundation, William Shawn, nieces or nephews, it was always "reverse the charges."
They either wanted to hear from Louise, or forget it. And even though
everyone accepted, she was terrified the calls'd be charged to her. She'd sit
there with this worried look on her face that'd just kill you. . . . I'd say,
"Don't worry, my friend Alice at the phone company told me if it's on your
bill, she'd take care of it." She still wasn't convinced. She lived so frugally—
after *Lulu in Hollywood*, knowing the figure she had in the bank, I used to
say, "Louise, the television doesn't get a good picture, get a new TV," or
"get a new bed you can crank up and down with a button—don't live so
ridiculously." But she was petrified. I even brought over a financial adviser,
and made sure he didn't charge her. She was so nervous—she heard on TV
that even if you had Medicaid, it wouldn't cover the whole bill—Art Linklet-
ter wouldn't lie, right?
    And then she decided, for no reason in the world, that she didn't want
The New Yorker to come anymore—she couldn't read it, it was cluttering up
the apartment. She was going to write to Bill Shawn personally and tell him
to stop sending it. Now, believe me, it was in her apartment for three minutes. I'd take it upstairs to Marge, who read it and then gave it to Mr. Shaw,
who got Louise's groceries. Two people got the benefit of it. But she was
adamant. I said, "Why upset Mr. Shawn? Just let the fucking magazine
come, Louise!"—you could use words like that with her. She was all alone in
there, and there was nothing else to think about, and these ideas just came
to her.
    There was a side that drew everybody to the edge with Louise. If you got

the people [who helped her out] and put them on a psychiatrist's couch and made them give one word for Louise, it would be *troublesome*. . . . Being in that room and knowing, or hoping, you were being of some help to her— the challenge of trying to pick up her mood. But toward the end, those last few visits were very hard to endure. I just couldn't chalk up any success at all. There was nothing coming back from her.

The final terror for Louise was neither physical nor spiritual, but mental. "This emphysema . . . ," she told Chris Chase of the *New York Times* over the phone. "It clouds your mind, your memory. I don't know what I'm talking about half the time."[14] Her mind was all she had left, and the loss of memory panicked her. In a brave effort to combat it, she was compulsively writing down every phone call, every conversation, virtually every detail of every day. She constantly asked whoever she talked to to repeat what they just said, slowly. The jotting-down process was so laborious that many of her friends simply stopped calling to spare her and themselves the exertion.

James Watters's last visit, for example, was in March of 1985. "She recorded everything said by longhand," he said. "It was very tedious." Ricky Leacock was more patient and, in his rough, fond way, more adept at distracting her from The Dying: "The only way to get her out of it was to say, 'Louise, when you saw Pabst in the spring of 1929 . . .' and then she'd start. She'd become like a talking machine, and it would take over and you didn't have to worry, and she'd go on and on with it as long as you liked. It became a substitute for actually living."[15]

"We drove the library nuts," Bill Klein had said, and librarian William Cuseo confirms it:

> She was a wonderful, brilliant woman. She used to go through five or six books a week, easily. Any book on any film person, she read it—and most of them she dismissed as packs of lies and distortions. She made marginal notes everywhere. . . . I had to white-out some of the obscenities where she used ink and underlined them . . . Some people were offended, and other people started to realize that these were Louise Brooks notations and they stole the books. I finally told her, "Please, please, Louise, these books have to circulate!" This woman should have been an editor. She was remarkable. She would take a book, and not only would she correct the grammar and names and facts and dates, but she would make corrections in the *index*. . . .
>
> But toward the end, it was the most terrible ordeal for her, it was pitiful. She would call the library 30 to 50 times every day. I am not exaggerating. "Is so-and-so dead?" "How do you spell 'catastrophe'?" And she'd call back a minute or two later—"Please tell me again how you spell 'catastrophe.' " She was very, very concerned about losing her mental ability. It was a way of reaching out and making contact. We all knew why she was doing it—five,

eight times in a matter of five minutes. She really taxed us, but we answered every question.[16]

"Tensions are vital to life," Chaplin had said. "One should never completely relax unless one wants to feel the poetry of slowly dying."[17] But for Louise, there seemed nothing very poetic about it. She would, however, at least see—and be reconciled with—the most important living face from her past.

It had been a long time since James Card had come to call. He now phoned and made a date to do so—and then, so much like Louise herself, he had second thoughts and tried to cancel. To his diary that night, July 9, 1983, he confided:

> Decided to weasel out of the meeting with Louise. When I called her she said she was very disappointed. I said I was surprised. She said, "But I love you very much—have always loved you." So I went in the afternoon. Astonished to realize it was July [1982] when I last saw her. She is even more emaciated and pale. . . . It was a three-hour agony session—forgetting everything in a moment—repeating—repeating—repeating—[18]

He went to see her again two days later. Among other things, they discussed a biography—not autobiography—and she designated him, in writing, as her "sole authorized biographer." But the most important outcome of his visits came a week later in the form of her inscription in his copy of *Lulu in Hollywood*:

> To Jimmy Card—who saved me from First Avenue and the 59th Street bridge in New York and brought me to Rochester where I could write in peace and quiet—All my love—Louise.

They would part, at last, as friends.

By 1984, she could no longer write. A single sentence exhausted her, and she hadn't been able to muster even that for her beloved Kevin Brownlow for a year and a half. On April 3, 1984, in shaky script, she wrote the final entry in their brilliant twenty-year correspondence: "Forgive me for writing no more. This dreadful emphysema. Love, Louise."

But she consented to a last, soulful interview with John Kobal, throughout which she "coughed a lot, grumbled a lot, cursed her illness, then chuckled at the irony of fate that had brought her to this not very pretty pass."

"There would be moments," wrote Kobal, "when she'd sit there fighting for breath, clawing her cane, gritting her teeth. There was nothing to be done. When the spasm had passed, she'd take a sip of juice to help clear her throat. The strain of sitting at the table for so long was telling on her.

But every time I suggested we stop and she go to bed, she brushed it off. Even though her body might show signs of pain, her eyes, sunk back, large, dark, glowed with intelligence and curiosity and life."[19]

Her brutal honesty clashed with self-pity and fear and struggled to keep both at bay:

> Suppose this woman, Marge . . . she's 82, you know . . . suppose she stops coming down and feeding me, what's going to happen to me then? . . .
>
> I'm miserable. If I could think of a good way of ending it all, I'd do it. I'm such a coward. I'd like to be out of the whole thing. What can you expect? . . . The moment I get up and make a move, I can't breathe. It's terrible. And I know that when you go into intensive care in the hospital, you're hooked up with the oxygen tank and with the wheelchair and—God, it's a rotten way to go. Terrible disease. No, I'm utterly miserable.[20]

A silence followed. There was, said Kobal, "not much to be said after that." He covered her hand. She grinned. The burst of self-pity was over, and she disdained the pity of others.

"This woman, Marge" was Louise's elderly upstairs neighbor Marjorie Van Tassell, who was literally keeping Louise alive. It was a case of the eighty-two-year-old taking care of the seventy-eight-year-old.

In previous years, Louise had been standoffish with the solidly working-class Marge, who spent eighteen years as an optical solderer at the Kodak plant. But for that matter, neither woman was exactly warm and cuddly; at one point they quarreled and stopped speaking to one another. But after she fell and broke her ribs in 1980, Louise knew she needed help.

"She asked me if I'd bring her her meals," recalled Marge, "and I said okay"—but only if the services were provided in exchange for friendship. "I don't want to take any pay," Marge told her, "because I don't want you to boss me around." Ever-frugal Louise was only too happy to agree, and from that day forward, Marge was Louise's lifeline. The rigidity of their routine structured both women's lives, as Marge related:

> For breakfast, she wanted a raw egg, two pieces of toast with red raspberry jam, and a cup of coffee with a little milk. After I brought it down to her, I always had to say, "I'll see you at noontime."
>
> For lunch she'd always have half a banana and spoon-sized shredded wheat, and then I'd always have to say, "I'll see you at suppertime." If I didn't say it, she'd call me up to make sure I was coming.
>
> For dinner, she used to have meatloaf and a salad, but then she changed to boiled ham on two pieces of bread, with lots of butter and mayonnaise— and half an apple and half a cookie. Every night it was the same thing. If I put one more crumb on her plate, she'd say, "Take it back."[21]

The dynamic of their relationship was intricate. Marge was averse to foul language. She had her limits with Louise and would not be treated like a servant. Both issues came to a head over the Garbage Can Crisis—still such a painful memory that Marge had to pause now and then to wipe away the tears:

> She wanted me to go out and deal with the garbage cans rolling in the driveway and making noise. I said that wasn't my job, and then—she called me a bad name. [It was "bitch."] I said, "Shhh!" and she said, "Nobody tells me to shut up!" I wasn't ever going to speak to her again . . . but I took the elevator down and I moved the cans, and when I came back she said, "Did you take care of those cans?" I said, "Take a look." She went out there and opened up the window and looked out—oh, I'll never forget it, her hair blowing in the wind, so frail. . . .[22]

Marge and Louise were both very upset—Louise's regret about hurting Marge's feelings outweighed, perhaps, by the fear she might abandon her. A day or two later she told Marge, "I won't use those words anymore"—from Louise, a major apology.

"Louise liked me to be there sometimes when Marge was there," says Bill Klein, "because she knew I was very diplomatic, and that I paid attention to Marge and encouraged her to sit down and take part in the conversation, and she felt that after I was there with Marge, she was going to get two or three days of great Marge. She told me that one time in so many words."

Klein and Mayberry both had to press Louise to give Marge even a Christmas present, but sometimes she surprised them all. One day Marge found Louise rummaging through a trunk. "Here's some gold for you," she said suddenly, handing a little object to Marge. It was her wedding ring from Deering Davis.

Klein watched the ties between them grow stronger:

> There was something Louise liked, but didn't like to admit, about the fact that she could find pleasant moments with somebody who was—well, "beneath" her. Louise was always aware of whom she was talking to, and Marge wasn't a very complex person. She knew she wasn't talking to somebody who'd read Shaw or Proust, and she made adjustments for Marge. I think it was a wonderful relationship. It had a lot of stress and strain, but Marge got a lot out of it, and Louise got a leveling, too.[23]

Louise was fading rapidly now. She was keeping her eyes closed much of the time during the day, and Marge or Bill would have to coax her to open them. Her diary entries of the last few months are a *pathetic* grappling with memory. She wrote certain facts and phrases over and over again—fragments of people and places and memories: "Victor Fleming directed *Wizard of Oz* and *Gone With the Wind*" . . . "Girl in Every Port, H. Hawks" . . . "Mariarden—Peterborough, N.H." . . . "Peggy Fears & Blumie lived in Larchmont" . . . "Joan Rivers" . . . Detached bits of her life were swirling around her brain.

Toward the end, Louise phoned Marge every night for an hourlong talk that seemed to relax both of them before bedtime, and to ease Louise's fearsome worrying. Marge finally told her, "Listen, as long as I'm able to come down here, you don't have to go to that home. Is that what you want me to say?" Louise said yes. Often they rambled on, drowsily, until midnight:

> I'd say, "Are you tired?" and she'd say, "No, let's talk a little longer," or when her voice was bad she'd say, "You do the talking," and I'd tell her about my life, my people. . . . She liked to go back into childhood things. We'd go through the Mother Goose rhymes, and she'd say, "How does 'Blackbirds' go?" and I'd say, "You know, *Sing a song of sixpence, pocket full of rye. . . .*" She liked that old song, "K-K-K-Katie," and sometimes I'd sing it or she'd sing it to me. She just wanted to hear something cheerful. And then I'd say, "Good night, I'll see you in the morning." If I didn't, she'd call back and ask me if I was coming in the morning.
>
> One night she fell asleep while we were talking, and I went down, opened the door, turned on the light, and there she was, so peaceful, asleep, with the phone up to her ear. Toward the last, she was doing that more and more. I was worried about getting down there and hanging up the phone before it started buzzing in her ear.[24]

During the last phone-call lullaby with Marge, Louise asked her, simply, "Will you miss me?"

And Marge, in reply, sang her a little song of long ago:

> I'll forget you when I can live without the sunshine,
> I'll forget you when I can live without the rain,
> When summer roses forget their fragrance. . .
> I'll try to forget you in vain.[25]

LOUISE BROOKS died of a heart attack during the night of August 8, 1985. She was seventy-eight.

In France, and elsewhere around Europe, many newspapers and magazines carried the story on their front pages. In the United States, with few exceptions outside of Rochester, a brief obituary appeared among the usual daily death notices.

She was cremated and the urn interred in Rochester's Holy Sepulchre Cemetery. Two weeks later, a private memorial service was held in Rochester's Blessed Sacrament Church. It was a Roman Catholic Mass conducted by a priest who never knew her but who felt assured of her piety by the crucifix on the wall of her bedroom. It was generally agreed, as Ross Berkal put it, that "if she was listening, Louise got a big kick out of that." Only two dozen people attended.

One nice touch was the playing of Beethoven's "Ode to Joy." Another was Jack Garner's reading of several passages from *Lulu in Hollywood*. The third, and only other, saving grace of the service consisted of the brief remarks of her nephew, Dan Brooks. Theodore's son had often conversed with his aunt by phone but had never, in forty years, met her. Yet in four minutes, he evoked her life, her gifts, and her beauty, concluding with their lesson for the future: "The next time such excellence appears, maybe it will be recognized."

Late that night after the service, an agitated Bill Klein speaks of her for six hours. Then a long pause, and a conclusion: "She had a wonderful sense of humor, you know, and she had a laugh—oh, I could get her to sparkle. I just had the feeling that Louise was going to be around forever."

Her other friends missed her, too, but were less grieved than relieved for Louise. "I honestly feel happy for her," said Jack Garner. "She wanted it very much."[26] Barbara Mayberry said, "I think she was looking forward to seeing what death was going to be like—another stage to go through, and kind of an interesting stage at that."

Only Marge Van Tassell seemed devastated after the service, but later that afternoon, on the arm of Ross Berkal, she went to an Eastman House memorial screening of *Beggars of Life*, which she had never seen. That evening, she agreed to a visit—an hour that turns into three. She cannot stop talking and thinking about Louise, and it is nearly midnight when she startles her guest with a sudden decision: to get the key and go down to look inside apartment 307. She hasn't yet broken the habit of their routine, the instinctive need to check on Louise.

Louise's small apartment is exactly as she left it. If there is a color at all, it is dull pink—walls, carpet, lamps. Even the dim light itself is pink. A chair, a couch, a dinette set, all fifties vintage—neat, sparse, grim. Not enough to fill a single notebook page. "She never gave you the feeling that she felt she was living in a grubby place," Barb Mayberry had said. " 'This is home, this is where I live, I am queen wherever I am, this is where I am reigning, from this bed. . . .' " More dull pink in the bedroom. The Sears bed, and crucifix facing it. The television. Two aluminum canes in a corner. Pill vials on the bedstand, Tranxene, Valium. . . . On the dresser sits her haunting portrait of Saint Thérèse, and on the wall hangs the Man Ray abstract. Except for the works of art, there is no evident character or beauty in the three rooms that belonged to one of the greatest, most individualistic beauties of the century. But the appearance is deceiving; the life and beauty and character have merely compressed themselves into a space where they truly belong—her bookshelves. The dog-eared, super-annotated copies of *Remembrance of Things Past* and *Faust* and Ruskin and Shaw and Saint Bernard; *Lolita, Martin Chuzzlewit,* Mill's *On Liberty,* Cardinal Newman's *Apologia,* Goethe's *Poetry and Truth*; biographies of Cocteau, Keaton, Swanson, Chaplin; all of Brownlow's and Kobal's film books and Jane Sherman's on dance; Ado Kyrou's *Amour-érotisme et Cinéma,* French and German dictionaries; Mencken, Kipling, Montaigne, Colette, Carlyle, Ibsen, hundreds more. All her friends are present and accounted for.

Marge turns out the lights and carefully locks the door. She is very tired now and bids her visitor goodbye.

Marge died eight months later.

Adolph Green gazes out at a Manhattan skyline that looks like the inspiration for *Wonderful Town* and takes his time trying to capture Louise's elusive presence in words. Louise has been cavorting through his consciousness from the time, at the age of eight, he first saw her in *The American Venus.* Finally he gets it: "Instantly you knew she was wicked and independent. The quality that came across was that she wasn't playing according to the rules of anyone else. I was aware of that as a kid, that she had her own rhythm and her own takes that had nothing to do with what anybody else was doing around her, and which—aside from her evident beauty—made her totally arresting."[27]

Some called her "the lost star of the twenties," and it is in fact impossible to think of another actress who produced such a powerful impact in such a short career, and in so few movies, not one decent sound film among them. The secret of that power was so disarmingly simple—"complete indifference to the camera," she called it. "Utter relaxation and freedom of movement," said James Card.

Not everyone was bowled over by her, of course. Ricky Leacock filmed a delightful interview with director George Cukor who, when her name is mentioned, exclaims, "Louise Brooks? What's all this talk about Louise Brooks? She was *nobody.* She was a *nothing* in films. What's all this fuss about her?" That view was shared by many of her contemporaries, including Colleen Moore, but the other view—articulated by Jan Wahl—holds that she is "more modern than any other actress of her time" and that "her art has never aged."[28]

"It is her concentration, her focus, her wonder in things, her gaiety, her fretfulness, that give extraordinary meaning," wrote Wahl. Louise had written "Gish and Garbo." Wahl complemented it with "Garbo and Brooks":

> Louise Brooks was the complete American. She was erotic. She suggested swift intelligence, a shiny spring uncoiling. She suggested terrific restless-

ness. Being a dancer, she talked with her body. Unlike Garbo, she was not aloof. Unlike Gish, she was not fragile. Unlike Clara Bow, she was not from the five-and-dime. . . .

Garbo moves like a sleepwalker through nearly all her films. . . . Tightly isolated, it is weariness that marks the Garbo figure, whereas it is vitality that marks the Brooks.[29]

Louise had corroborated the nub of that comparison herself, years before: "The timing of great actresses is the same as that which marks the rhythm of their real lives. You can neither teach nor learn to act according to any timing other than your own."[30]

The theory of Garbo and Brooks as the yin and yang of Woman on Screen leads to the impenetrable heart of what screen acting really *is*, to the Langlois claim that "her art is so pure that it becomes invisible," and to Tynan's pronouncement that Louise, "with no conscious intention of doing so, reinvent[ed] the art of screen acting."[31] The only certainty is that screen acting has no relation to stage acting, where expansiveness dominates subtlety. Louise once told James Card that the art of film acting "does not consist of descriptive movement of face and body but in the movements of thought and soul transmitted in a kind of intense isolation."[32]

The actor's sole hope, she said, was to set free his honest spontaneity:

> Essentially, what matters is personality. Take a girl like Clara Bow, who wasn't beautiful and really didn't act. She was just herself, and suited to the period. Norma Shearer, Gloria Swanson, I don't know whether they were good actresses, but they were great personalities. You have to have a very powerful personality. That's what makes a star.[33]

Her friend George Pratt said it with a twist: "I've always thought Louise was an erotic presence more than an actress." An ambiguity struck him, he laughed and clarified—"not *a neurotic* presence, an *erotic* presence. But come to think of it. . . ."

Brooks's writing was similar to her acting: A small output produced a great impact. There were only three people she really wanted to write about, she said—Gershwin, Chaplin, and Martha Graham. She made attempts at all three, but was dissatisfied with the results. It took her thirty years to write the 100 pages that became *Lulu in Hollywood*. Her trademark was brevity. Perhaps that's what she was as a writer: a literary *miniaturist*. With what epigrammatic eloquence did she once sum up writing and all other creative endeavor to Kevin Brownlow: "What is art but a close clinging to a bit of life that you have looked into most deeply?"[34]

Even so, certain doubts about her truth as well as her intellectuality remain. "Because she's such a good writer, we think, therefore, she's telling the truth in a way nobody else has," says John Kobal. "That's why it works. But we confuse the real truth with an eccentric, wonderful viewpoint that may or may not be *the* Truth. I think a lot of her pieces are about the art of writing more than about Hollywood."[35]

That would dovetail with the assessment of her nephew.

"She had a good intellect," says Daniel Brooks, "but it was essentially visceral, not cerebral. She didn't have the kind of trained mind to think things through philosophically. It all came from the gut. She was not an intellectual thinker. She was able to *enunciate* a lot of intuitive ideas."[36]

Composer David Diamond, one of Louise's most clear-eyed friends, speaks of her refusal to acknowledge alcohol "in her version of herself—which is the intellectual Louise." But he also authenticates that "intellectual Louise," who one day discovered *The Journal of Eugénie de Guérin* in his library. Guérin (1805–1848) was a brilliant, pessimistic French diarist, and an obscure one. "*Nobody* knows Guérin," says Diamond, "but Louise did!"[37] Among her favorite passages was this one which Louise read aloud to him:

> . . . This globe is an abyss of misery and all we gain by stirring its depths is the discovery of funereal inscriptions and burying places. Death is at the bottom of everything and we keep continually digging as though we were seeking for immortality.[38]

"I think she identified very closely with this woman," Diamond concludes. "In those two volumes, you will find 50 percent of Louise Brooks' philosophy."[39]

If Louise was no academic intellectual, she was profoundly self-educated. And a hinge between the actress and the writer-thinker is provided by David Thomson's highly critical review of *Lulu in Hollywood* in *Threepenny Review:*

> So the book seeks to repair the past, to vindicate the isolation of the present, and to have us honor Lulu as a belle-letrist. . . . To this day, Louise Brooks seems more like the idea of a writer than a real writer. . . .
>
> So much of the book is reticent to the point of deviousness. . . . But Miss Brooks has to deal with old age, retrospect, and trying to believe that there was an order to the fitful mess of her life. . . .
>
> Just as Louise Brooks is sometimes pitched as a woman alone but triumphant—no matter that her life seems to have been at the behest of men who owned, directed, or kept her—so on the screen Lulu is a powerhouse commanding the camera and the moment, and yet she is helpless in the plot, being carried along by others' actions and her own careless rapture. Fact and sequence are no more evident in *Lulu in Hollywood* than they are in *Pandora's Box*. . . . Ecstatic downward motion, the creep of darkness, and the

central light of Lulu are what sustain it, plus the rhythmic wreckage of all the men drawn to her. . . .

But for about 50 minutes in *Pandora's Box*—and no more is needed—Louise Brooks is one of the most important actresses in film.[40]

"*Lulu in Hollywood*," said Thomson, "only intensifies the mystery of Louise Brooks." It was left to her old confessor, Father Burkort, to see the mystery as mystical and to synthesize both careers, both of her lives: "She had the gift of words, but more important, she had a spirit that was arched to eternity and not simply to time."

If in Louise's life there was any "Rosebud"—Orson Welles's device of the sled symbolizing Citizen Kane's lost innocence—the discovery of it begins and ends with two questions. First—what did Louise really *want*?

Her friends and foes alike asked it a thousand times in a thousand ways but never got a clear answer. The question was often accompanied by a lament: "You could have gone into the '30s as a major star," John Kobal said to her, and she responded: "No one can understand how . . . I cannot think of anything . . . you don't know . . . you never. . . ."[41] It was the one subject on which her gift of words always failed her. And the dissolved career reduces nearly everyone who knew her to a mixture of regret and anger.

"What a goddamn *waste!*" says Larry Quirk, caught between "intense admiration for what she had and rage over all her distortions. She could have rivaled Garbo! She was a true *abandonnée*—uninhibited, insatiable curiosity, intelligent, beautiful. Some kind of torment, deep down, made this woman what she was. What was the terrible thing? What was this awful self-destructive urge? Such a waste . . ."[42]

It must have been the same frustration that maddened Ziegfeld and Pabst and Marshall and—the list is long. No one knew what to make of a woman who threw away opportunities as fast and furiously as Louise. But the great irony in her chaotic life is that *Pandora*, her crowning achievement—one of the crowning achievements in film history—came through the very willful caprice that caused her to ditch stardom in Hollywood. Her professional suicide was her redemption as an actress. And thus to lament her career and revere *Pandora* is a contradiction: In practice if not theory, the two were mutually exclusive.

"What did she want?" asks David Thomson. His answer is the obverse, and he is led to it by the theme of her Bogart essay—that Humphrey got lost in his masquerade:

Is it only the belated understanding of *Pandora's Box* that lets her see herself as an outsider, rather than a discard? . . . We may wonder whether it wasn't *Pandora's Box* that stopped Louise Brooks in her tracks. Not just because it was better than she had ever been before, but because it brought her within range of a fictional being she could neither shrug off nor become. . . .

The most sensual, intimate, and credible performance in silent film is also the most inhuman . . . the single most crucial picture of woman in film . . . and Louise Brooks is an old woman in Rochester, New York, as shaken as all of us by the demonic Lulu.

"How do you follow up the act of making it with Denishawn, the Follies, Paramount and Charlie Chaplin by the time you're eighteen?" asks critic and teacher John Barba, a psychologist who has spent long hours developing his own Tynan-like "profile" of Louise Brooks. "Forget about Pabst for a moment. Just think about what came *before* Pabst, and it is staggering. The most you can become after that, later on, is an institution, like Mary Pickford or Helen Hayes at eighty—embalmed in adulation for something you were fifty years ago. I can understand her reticence to go this route."[43]

Other people have other ideas. Anita Loos thought the reason Louise threw everything away was that, at heart, she was just lazy and masochistic, and thus wanted no more than you'd expect a lazy masochist to want —to be hurt and left alone. More likely, it was that traumatic dismissal from Denishawn which provided the rationale, consciously or subconsciously, for always pulling the rug out from under herself before someone else could do it first—her self-destructive career pattern from *Scandals* to *Follies* to Paramount to Pabst and even to CBS radio.

What did Louise really want?

An answer is necessary from James Card:

> Obviously, it wasn't "stardom." If one thing is clear—and it's surprising how many people simply refuse to believe it—it's that she had no ambition to be a popular screen actress. She claimed she wanted to be a good dancer.[44]

She said it to Kobal in so many words: "I wanted to be a great dancer like Martha Graham, that was my ambition."[45] And toward the end she revealed: "In my dreams I am never crippled, I dance . . ."[46] Only another dancer, someone intimately familiar with the joy of the soaring, could measure the full pain and meaning of such dreams.

But in Roddy McDowall's view, the mystery of what Louise "wanted" was submerged in something even deeper than her dancing:

> She was on some personal vendetta against herself, which short-circuited a lot of things for her. I don't know what that heartbreaking element was that set her onto this path of self-destruction. It was part of that volatile, pyrotechnical personality—when she was young she must have been like a whirling dervish. She must have been like a shot of oxygen right into the

brain. If she had a supportive person "gardening" her, there was no end to the heights that she could reach. Pabst pulled all her strings with such extraordinary finesse that she was ravishing. She was an original force of such potency that it was irrepressible, but in the hands of the unsympathetic, she would fragment. She kept saying, "I'm not an actress." She had no respect for herself as an actress. But Pabst did, and had she been less of a hedonist. . . . It was one of the rare great experiences of my life, knowing Louise. She was so difficult because she couldn't accept the full measure of the regard people had for her. [47]

Rose Hayden, viewing Louise psychoanalytically, believes her self-vendetta stemmed from "some serious personality disorders that went beyond eccentric and into dysfunctional." Writer Tom Graves, who interviewed Louise at length in 1982, came away with a strikingly similar opinion: "I think she had a mental health problem that went beyond alcoholism. That compulsive marginal annotation of books, for example —Tynan might say this was the mark of a feral creature, an intellectual super-woman. I might say it's the mark of someone who was mentally ill."

But that is a minority view, and if she was disoriented, so was the industry's response to her. Jan Wahl wrote that "no one at Paramount seemed to realize what they had signed up, although her films became popular and her face became a symbol." Perhaps that was it. Perhaps she just could not live up to that *face*, which was somehow greater than herself. The same could be said of many actors, but the face and beauty of Louise Brooks were surpassing. And yet when Ricky Leacock asked her why she was so "horrified" upon seeing the first rushes from *The Diary of a Lost Girl*, she replied:

> Don't you see? That's why I was never an actress. I was never in love with myself. I would go to a party, and I'd see Dolores Del Rio and Constance Talmadge and Constance Bennett, all these beautiful women, and I'd say to myself, "You're the ugliest one here. You're all black and furry. You've got freckles. Your dress is not as attractive. . . ." And so in the end, you can't be a great actress unless you think you're beautiful. It's of the essence.

"But you're a contradiction of this," Leacock protested.

> No, I'm not. To be a great actress, you must know what you're doing. When I write my little pieces, I know exactly what I'm doing. I was simply playing myself, which is the hardest thing in the world to do. [48]

The logic was flawless, and the "little pieces" were the key. What Louise wanted in her creative life was dancing and writing, in that order. Everything in between was an unsought bafflement, and, inevitably, a disappointment.

A decade later, Leacock mulls over that crucial exchange and starts a sentence he doesn't finish: "This amazing ability to screw up everything . . . this terror of succeeding . . ."[49]

Which leads to the last—and darkest—question in Louise's life: What *was* "the whole sexual truth" she could never tell?

In all of her diaries, letters, and interviews, there is not a single reference to pregnancy or abortion. "She always called herself 'Barren Brooks,'" says one confidant, "and she never took any preventive measures. She was convinced she could never have children." No medical confirmation or refutation exists. Her view of motherhood was that, for her, it would have been a disaster. Her own mother—never a traditional "nurturer"—she viewed as both the curse and blessing of her life:

> Over the years, I brought upon myself both poverty and solitude, and came to the conclusion that my mother had fostered in me an idea of freedom that was totally utopian, and a guaranteed source of disillusionment. In [old age], I found myself imprisoned in a minuscule apartment in Rochester, N.Y., a city alienated from all other cities, without friends to comfort me. . . . Looking around me, I saw millions of old people living the same way, whimpering like a bunch of puppies that they were alone, and with no one to talk to. They were enslaved by their habits, reduced to bodies endowed with the power of speech. But I was free! Although my mother left us in 1944, she never abandoned me. She brings me comfort every time I read a book. Each time I read, it's as if I were reading over her shoulder, and learning the words, just like when she read out loud from *Alice in Wonderland*.[50]

So Louise made peace with the ghost of her mother, even as she "killed off" her brother Theo, execrated the memory of brother Martin, and distanced herself from sister June. In the end, she turned back to family, corresponding with them and naming her sister, sister-in-law, nieces, and nephews as heirs, with Theo's son Daniel Brooks as co-executor of her estate.*

But after Theo's death, she was emotionally tied to none of them. Thomson's description of her way of writing about people could be extended to her way of dealing with them: "They are kept at a distance; prodded away by archness, and by her numbness to affection." Barbara Mayberry could not think of "anyone she felt an emotional closeness to— someone that, if run over by an automobile, she would weep for. Maybe Roddy McDowall, but no . . . Maybe Tynan—no doubt she was very fond of him, but. . . . That was an area of Louise that didn't really exist. There seemed to be no real close emotional attachment to anyone."[51]

The cause lay somewhere in that "whole sexual truth" she spent the

---

* The other co-executor was her Rochester attorney, Benjamin Phelosof.

last half of her life writing around as much as about: her sexuality as both the motivating and the limiting factor of her career, no less than her life. "Sex was maybe the only thing she ever *fully* enjoyed," said one of her lovers. And it was not really true, as she had told Tynan, that she was "never in love." She had been in love many times. It *was* true that, like Lulu, she "drove men crazy without trying." Few men could cope with the fact that a woman so sexually alluring could be brilliant, too.

Brooks's friend Lotte Eisner had the deepest insight: "Her work as an actress was inseparably connected with falling in love, enchantment, conquering the male sex, and she certainly expected more from love than I ever did. Since she continually risked her body, she needed to find a support for her soul and was always disappointed anew." [52]

Finally and inextricably, there was another great brooding element of Louise's sexual consciousness, the determining one—so recurrent in her thoughts as to be labeled an obsession: the concept of the actress as whore, through the ages—and of herself as whore, through her life. The whoredom of the actress, she told John Kobal, went back to ancient Greece. Her own experience reflected it, and publishers' reactions to her writing confirmed it.

> It's simply that I make whoring as ugly as it is, and this is a man's world and they're not going to have it. . . . Men are the publishers, and anything that kills their sexual pleasure is not going to be allowed. . . . It's all right in [Henry Miller's *Tropic of Capricorn* and J. P. Donleavy's *The Ginger Man*] to make up men who beat women and kick them around and give them syphilis and clap and babies. That is fine because that makes the man a *hero* in this kind of world's eyes. . . . I detest what they do to women. And women are forced into that kind of life, and they are not going to let me tell it. . . . That's why they hate [*Pandora's Box*], because it shows this rich man, this rich man like Hearst, whose whole life is to build power, to get rich enough and powerful enough to live a life of sex with women. That is every man's ambition. I don't care who they are or how they hide it or whether they are able to achieve it or not, and I write against that from beginning to end. [53]

She was less angry and more whimsical on the subject of whoring in her talks with Kenneth Tynan:

> I never had anything to show for it—no cash, no trinkets, nothing. I didn't even *like* jewelry—can you imagine? Pabst once called me a born whore, but if he was right I was a failure, with no pile of money and no comfortable mansion. I just wasn't equipped to spoil millionaires in a practical, far-sighted way. [54]

So many people had called her a whore for so many reasons that she believed it; she had always felt like a whore for taking men's money. She had to do it to live, or so she was convinced. The salesgirl alternative she had tried and failed at. Kobal wrote that the allowances she got from rich men were "not obligations to a discarded 'kept' woman, but tributes to her for having been a giving woman." Nor was her generous spirit negated by her latter-day stinginess with money; that was merely the Great Depression syndrome, the result of deprivation. In the monied years, she had been wildly free with her cash—and with herself.

In artistic terms, too, she had a keen recognition of generosity: "Did you ever reflect," she once mused to a friend, "that without generosity in the arts there are no artists perfectly developed? Proust—yes. Henry James—no. Garbo—yes. Dietrich—no. Judy Garland—yes. Sinatra—no." [55]

Generosity and curiosity are related to each other, and to the real "Rosebud" of Louise Brooks's life: a man named Mr. Flowers in Cherryvale, Kansas. Over the years, he sometimes became "Mr. Feathers" for reasons of disguise or faulty memory. Whatever his name—"I was done in by a middle aged man when I was nine," she said. [56] And after her readings in Nabokov: "I was loused up by my Lolita experiences." Mr. Flowers had defiled her in a time and place where child molestation was not even discussed, let alone understood. "[He] must have had a great deal to do with forming my attitude toward sexual pleasure," she told Tynan. "For me, nice, soft, easy men were never enough—there had to be an element of domination—and I'm sure that's all tied up with Mr. Feathers. The pleasure of kissing and being kissed comes from somewhere entirely different, psychologically as well as physically. [57] And most devastating of all, when she bravely told her mother about Mr. Flowers, Myra put the blame on *Louise* for "leading him on."

She was a lonely teenager in New York, lured to her girlfriend's boyfriend's apartment by booze and boredom. She was a *Follies* girl for Ziegfeld, lured into a movie contract by Walter Wanger, and into his bed as well. She was a flapper star-on-the-rise, lured by George Marshall into trading Hollywood for a European cruise. When her youth, beauty, and career evaporated in the Depression, she was lured by her own temperament back to Kansas for penance, then again to New York and the bottle, and lured finally to Rochester for a measure of redemption.

She was all these things, but most of all she was a curious little girl skipping in a dusty street of Cherryvale—lured to some dark corner by candy and a movie.

There is a choice of epitaphs, starting with the one Louise gave to Orson Welles: "To be a rebel is to court extinction." [58]

There was the one Theo composed in 1969, after she sent him one of her many wills:

You remind me of how much of our lives have been spent, how slow the days used to drag and now how fast they fly. . . . I shall put you beside momma and papa in Burden and 1,000 years from now people will stop to read "Louise Brooks, 1908–1988, She Was Our Star."[59]

There is Louise's beloved Proust:

Everything great in the world comes from neurotics. They alone have founded our religions and composed our masterpieces. Never will the world know all it owes to them nor all they have suffered to enrich us. We enjoy lovely music, beautiful paintings, a thousand intellectual delicacies, but we have no idea of their cost, to those who invented them, in sleepless nights, tears, spasmodic laughter, rashes, asthma, epilepsies, and the fear of death, which is worse than all the rest.

And there is the one Louise designated for herself: "I never gave away anything without wishing I had kept it; nor kept anything without wishing I had given it away."

Her eulogists attested to the qualities that made her the uniquely *American* character she was—the paradoxical party girl and recluse; the reckless beauty with her "gift for enraging people"; her riveting expressiveness of movement and words; the dichotomous sexual freedom and bondage.

Except in nineteenth-century romanticism, there is really no such thing as a "free spirit." As Louise said of Bogart, the minute choices are made—especially in money and employment—freedom dissipates. But to the extent that any twentieth-century spirit could soar, Louise's did—in dance and on film, in her artistic and sexual ecstasies, and in her writing. It never soared high enough or perfectly enough to satisfy her for long. But ecstasy and duration are mutually exclusive. It must be enough that there *were* moments and not lamented that there were not more. She sought life and liberty, all right, but not the pursuit of happiness; Elias Canetti's definition would have appealed to her: "Happiness—that contemptible life-goal of illiterates."[60] Happiness and its fickle little handmaiden, "success."

All the epitaphs for Louise speak eloquently of the ceaseless striving and longing in her life, but not of the extraordinary concepts of success and failure that motivated it. After *Pandora's Box* was panned, she said, "I lived for years and years with this terrible sense of failure." The best of her character sketches, "Marion Davies' Niece"—the tragicomic Pepi Lederer story—was the only one whose central figure was a "failure." It was Louise's most bristling and visceral piece because she identified so intensely with her subject and because, in confronting the boogeyman of failure, she saw that she was judging her own life by the same criteria that doomed poor Pepi.

Louise was just a child, really, when she pitched it all—an adolescent wined and dined and sought after by the world. It was all so frivolous, so unreal, so heady and so long ago. If it had never been her idea of "success," how could the loss of it be "failure"? Louise had not "failed," of course. She had succeeded brilliantly as a dancer, an actress, and a writer, and at certain times she had to see and know and admit this. But she always doubted her success, suspected it of being failure in disguise, somehow *felt* it to be so. It was consistent with her forever looking to be disappointed in people, most of all herself. For only by two standards had she "failed"—Hollywood's and, more deadly, her own.

The real epitaph of Louise Brooks was a brutal one, inspired by her merciless self-criticism and intended neither for sympathy nor for public consumption. She confided it in a letter, a dozen years before she died, to her brother Theodore: "I have been taking stock of my 50 years since I left Wichita in 1922 at the age of 15 to become a dancer with Ruth St. Denis and Ted Shawn. How I have existed fills me with horror. For I failed in everything—spelling, arithmetic, riding, swimming, tennis, golf; dancing, singing, acting; wife, mistress, whore, friend. Even cooking. And I do not excuse myself with the usual escape of "not trying." I tried with all my heart."[61]

APPENDIX

CHRONOLOGICAL BIBLIOGRAPHY OF ARTICLES BY LOUISE BROOKS

LOUISE BROOKS FILMOGRAPHY

ACKNOWLEDGMENTS

BIBLIOGRAPHY

NOTES

INDEX

The major and minor errors in *Lulu in Hollywood* cited here have been identified by Kevin Brownlow, William K. Everson, Jane Sherman Lehac, George Pratt, Lawrence Quirk, Anthony Slide, Alexander Walker, and the author, among others:

Page 8: Ted Shawn never performed a dance called *Pose Plastique*. Louise probably referred to his *Adagio Plastique*, which later evolved into *The Death of Adonis*.

Page 16: Jetta Goudal did not appear in *Java Head*.

Photo page 5, after page 38: Louise's photo caption says the "Dixie Dugan" comic strip ran until 1954. In fact, it ran until 1962, the year of artist John H. Striebel's death.

Photo page 12, after page 38: Keene (not "Keen") Thompson.

Page 47: Nina Mae (not "May") McKinney, of King Vidor's *Hallelujah*.

Page 67: Rodgers and Hart did not write the music and lyrics for *The Little Shows*. For the first two *Little Shows* of 1929 and 1930, most of the composing was done by Arthur Schwartz, with words by Howard Dietz. The third show, in 1931, had multiple lyricists, including Noël Coward ("Mad Dogs and Englishmen"), and composers, including Ned Lehac ("You Forgot Your Gloves").

Page 81: Susan Fleming (not "Flemming"), wife of Harpo Marx.

Page 82: William Gaxton "never made another film," Louise wrote. In fact, he made many, as listed in the footnote in chapter seven, page 134.

Pages 86–92: The Lillian Gish controversy. In 1927, Gish "left Hollywood forever," says Louise on page 90. But four pages earlier she wrote: "I could not understand how [Gish] could have gone back to Hollywood in 1929" to make her first talkie, *One Romantic Night*. Gish also made many later films in Hollywood.

Norma Shearer and Joan Crawford were not "eased out" of MGM but, rather, turned down offers from that studio to stay.

The more important mistakes in Louise's assessment of Gish's career derive from the "Executive War on the Stars" theory and are discussed in detail in chapter eleven, pages 221–224.

James R. Quirk of *Photoplay* was hardly a tool of MGM executives, whose films and policies he often criticized, without regard to advertising pressures. Anthony Slide observes that in ascertaining Quirk's attitude toward Gish, and others, Louise tended to quote *Photoplay*'s capsule reviews, which were not written by Quirk, instead of the primary reviews, which often were.

Page 87: The National Board of Review was not an outgrowth of "the Hays Office," which in any event was established in 1922 and not 1925. The National Board of Review was founded in 1909 in New York in a successful effort to preempt government censorship.

Page 88: When Louis B. Mayer saw Garbo in *The Saga of Gösta Berling* in 1925, "he knew as sure as he was alive that he had found a sexual symbol beyond his or anyone else's imagining," says Louise. But Garbo herself has said that "when I met Mr. Mayer, he hardly looked at me," and it is generally agreed that Mayer hired her because he really wanted the director Mauritz Stiller, who wouldn't sign unless Mayer signed Garbo, too.

CHRONOLOGICAL BIBLIOGRAPHY
OF ARTICLES BY LOUISE BROOKS

1. "The Fundamentals of Good Ballroom Dancing," privately published in Wichita, Kansas, 1940.
2. "Who Is the Exotic Black Orchid?" and "Amateur Night in Greenwich Village," unpublished manuscripts, extant sections of the autobiographical novel, *Naked on My Goat*, ca. 1955.
3. "Mr. Pabst," *Image* 5, George Eastman House, Rochester, N.Y., September 7, 1956.
4. "Gloria Swanson," unpublished manuscript, January 1957.
5. "Joan Crawford," unpublished manuscript, February 1957.
6. "Gish and Garbo," *Sight and Sound*, London, Winter 1958–1959.
7. "ZaSu Pitts," *Objectif*, Montreal, August 1963.
8. "Als ich mit Pabst arbeitete" ["My Work with Mr. Pabst"], in *Der Regisseur: G. W. Pabst*, ed. Rudolph S. Joseph, for Münchener Photo und Filmmuseum, Munich, December 1964.
9. "Filmography—Positive and Negative," *Objectif*, Montreal, February 1964.
10. "Louise Brooks par elle-même," *Objectif*, Montreal, no. 26, February–March, 1964, and no. 27, April–May 1964.
11. "Pabst and Lulu," *Sight and Sound*, London, Summer 1965. (Reprinted in *Pandora's Box, Classic Film Scripts* [New York: Simon and Schuster, 1971]. French translation in "Louise Brooks: Portrait d'une anti-star," see number 26 below. Reprinted in *Lulu in Hollywood*, see number 28 below).
12. Louise Brooks Filmography, Checklist No. 27, *Monthly Film Bulletin* (British Film Institute), July 1965. With notes by LB.
13. "Marlene," *Positif*, Paris, no. 75, May 1966.
14. Letter to Andrew Sarris, *English Cahiers du Cinéma*, New York, no. 3, 1966.
15. "Charlie Chaplin Remembered," *Film Culture*, New York, no. 40, Spring 1966, pp. 5–6.
16. "Buster Keaton," in *Double Exposure*, edited by Roddy McDowall. New York: Delacorte Press, 1966.
17. "Humphrey and Bogey," *Sight and Sound*, London, Winter 1966–1967. (French translation in *Positif*, Paris, no. 81, February 1967).
18. "The White Hell of Pitz Palü," Toronto Film Society Program, March 25, 1968.
19. "On Location with Billy Wellman," *London Magazine*, London, May 1968. (French translation, in *Positif*, Paris, no. 114, March 1968).
20. Biographical questionnaire sent to Patrice Hovald, published in *L'Alsace*, July 17, 1969.
21. "The Other Face of W. C. Fields," *Sight and Sound*, London, Spring 1971. (French translation in *Positif*, Paris, no. 125, March 1971).
22. "Actors and the Pabst Spirit," *Focus on Film*, London, no. 8, February 1972, pp. 45–46.
23. "Marion Davies' Niece," *Film Culture*, New York, nos. 58–60, October 1974.
24. "Stardom and Evelyn Brent," Toronto Film Society Program, January 13, 1975.
25. "Duke by Divine Right," introduction to Allen Eyles, *John Wayne* (Cranbury, N.J.: A. S. Barnes, 1976).
26. "Une certaine idée de la liberté," (A certain idea of freedom), only original essay in *Louise Brooks: Portrait d'une anti-star*, ed. Roland Jaccard. Paris: Phébus, 1977.
27. "Why I Will Never Write My Memoirs," *Focus on Film*, London, no. 15, March 1978, pp. 31–34.
28. *Lulu in Hollywood* (New York: Alfred A. Knopf, 1982). (Reprinting "On Location with Billy Wellman," "Marion Davies' Niece," "Humphrey and Bogey," "The Other Face of W. C. Fields," "Gish and Garbo," "Pabst and Lulu," with one "original" chapter titled "Kansas to New York.")

LOUISE BROOKS FILMOGRAPHY

(Production dates and minor credits supplied where available)

1. THE STREET OF FORGOTTEN MEN

Produced by Famous Players–Lasky (Paramount). Directed by Herbert Brenon. Screenplay by Paul Schofield, adapted from the *Liberty* magazine story by George Kibbe Turner. Photography by Hal Rosson. Art direction by Frederick A. Foord. Released August 24, 1925. (6 of 7 reels extant.) An O. Henry-esque underworld romance set in a professional beggars' "cripple factory" in the Bowery.

Cast: Percy Marmont (Easy Money Charlie), Mary Brian (Fancy), Neil Hamilton (Philip), John Harrington (Bridgeport White-Eye), Juliet Brenon (Portland), Louise Brooks (Moll).

2. THE AMERICAN VENUS

Produced by Famous Players–Lasky (Paramount). Directed by Frank Tuttle. Screenplay by Frederick Stowers, from an original story by Townsend Martin. Photography by J. Roy Hunt (including Technicolor sequences). Art direction by Larry Hitt. Released January 25, 1926. (8 reels.) A beauty-pageant comedy set at the 1925 Miss America contest in Atlantic City. The film is lost.

Cast: Esther Ralston (Mary Gray), Fay Lanphier (Miss Alabama), Lawrence Gray (Chip Armstrong), Ford Sterling (Hugo Niles), Louise Brooks (Miss Bayport), Edna May Oliver (Mrs. Niles), Kenneth MacKenna (Horace Niles), Ernest Torrence (King Neptune), Douglas Fairbanks, Jr. (Neptune's son, Triton).

3. A SOCIAL CELEBRITY

Produced by Famous Players–Lasky (Paramount). Directed by Malcolm St. Clair. Screenplay by Pierre Collings, from an original story, "I'll See You Tonight," by Monte J. Katterjohn. Photography by Lee Garmes. Released March 29, 1926. (6 reels.) Comedy of a small-town barber's son who poses his way into New York high society. The film is lost.

Cast: Adolphe Menjou (Max Haber), Louise Brooks (Kitty Laverne), Chester Conklin (Johann Haber), Elsie Lawson (April King), Roger Davis (Tenny), Josephine Drake (Mrs. Jackson-Greer).

4. IT'S THE OLD ARMY GAME

Produced by Famous Players–Lasky (Paramount). Directed by Edward Sutherland. Screenplay by Thomas J. Geraghty and J. Clarkson Miller from a story by J. P. McEvoy. Photography by Alvin Wyckoff. Titles by Ralph Spence. Released May 25, 1926. (7 reels.) Anarchistic comedy of wacky druggist who gets mixed up in a Florida real-estate scam.

Cast: W. C. Fields (Elmer Prettywillie), Louise Brooks (Mildred Marshall), Blanche Ring (Tessie Gilch), William Gaxton (George Develan), Mary Foy (Sarah Pancoast), Mickey Bennett (Mickey).

5. THE SHOW-OFF

Produced by Famous Players–Lasky (Paramount). Directed by Malcolm St. Clair. Screenplay by Pierre Collings, adapted from the Broadway stage play by George Kelly. Photography by Lee Garmes. Edited by Ralph Block. Released August 16, 1926. (7 reels.) Satiric comedy of an insufferable braggart who disrupts the life and values of a middle-class family.

Cast: Ford Sterling (Aubrey Piper), Lois Wilson (Amy Fisher), Louise Brooks (Clara Fisher), Gregory Kelly (Joe Fisher), Claire McDowell (Mrs. Fisher), C. W. Goodrich (Mr. Fisher), Joseph Smiley (Railroad Executive).

6. JUST ANOTHER BLONDE

Produced by First National. Directed by Alfred Santell. Screenplay by Paul Schofield, adapted from the short story "Even Stephen" by Gerald Beaumont. Photography by Arthur Edeson. Edited by Hugh Bennett. Titles by George Marion. Production dates: August 12–28, 1926. Released December 13, 1926. (6 reels.) A love story and action drama, with aerial scenes, about two gambler-hustlers and the Coney Island girls they romance. The film is lost.

Cast: Dorothy Mackaill (Jeanne Cavanaugh), Jack Mulhall (Jimmy O'Connor), Louise Brooks (Diana O'Sullivan), William Collier, Jr. (Kid Scotty).

7. LOVE 'EM AND LEAVE 'EM

Produced by Famous Players–Lasky (Paramount). Directed by Frank Tuttle. Screenplay by Townsend Martin, adapted from the stage play by John V. A. Weaver and George Abbott. Photography by George Webber. Released December 6, 1926. (6 reels.) Fast-paced, topical flapper comedy of "good" and "bad" sisters who have jobs and a common boyfriend in a department store.

Cast: Evelyn Brent (Mame Walsh), Louise Brooks (Janie Walsh), Osgood Perkins (Lem Woodruff), Lawrence Gray (Bill Billingsley), Jack Egan (Cartwright).

8. EVENING CLOTHES

Produced by Paramount. Directed by Luther Reed. Screenplay by John McDermott, adapted from the play *The Man in Evening Clothes* by André Picard and Yves Mirande. Photography by Hal Rosson. Titles by George Marion. Production dates: January 3–29, 1927. Released March 19, 1927. (7 reels.) Comedy-drama of French gentleman farmer, spurned by his bride, who goes to Paris to become sophisticated enough to win her back. The film is lost.

Cast: Adolphe Menjou (Lucien), Virginia Valli (Germaine), Noah Beery (Lazarre), Louise Brooks (Fox Trot), Lido Manetti (Henri).

9. ROLLED STOCKINGS

Produced by Paramount. Directed by Richard Rosson. Screenplay by Percy Heath, adapted from an original story by Frederica Sagor. Photography by Victor Milner. Titles by Julian Johnson. Edited by Julian Johnson. Production dates: April 4–May 5, 1927. Released June 18, 1927. (7 reels.) College-set comedy with racy "roadhouse" adventures leads up to climactic rowing-team race. The film is lost.

Cast: James Hall (Jim Treadway), Louise Brooks (Carol Fleming), Richard Arlen (Ralph Treadway), Nancy Phillips (The Vamp), El Brendel (Rudolph), David Torrence (Mr. Treadway), Chance Ward (Coach).

10. NOW WE'RE IN THE AIR

Produced by Paramount. Directed by Frank Strayer. Screenplay by Thomas J. Geraghty, adapted from an original story idea by Monte Brice and Keene Thompson. Photography by Harry Perry. Titles by George Marion. Production dates: August 1–September 10, 1927. Released October 22, 1927. (6 reels.) Slapstick Beery-Hatton comedy of boob "aeronuts" who stumble into the World War I air battle in France. The film is lost.

Cast: Wallace Beery (Wally), Raymond Hatton (Ray), Louise Brooks (Griselle and Grisette), Russell Simpson (Lord Abercrombie McTavish), Duke Martin (Sergeant).

11. THE CITY GONE WILD

Produced by Paramount. Directed by James Cruze. Screenplay by Jules Furthman, adapted from an original story idea by Jules and Charles Furthman. Photography by Bert Glennon. Titles by Herman Mankiewicz. Production dates: June 22–July 7, 1927. Released November 12, 1927. (6 reels.) Hard-boiled underworld melodrama, with gang wars and gunfights, in which criminal lawyer turns prosecutor to avenge a friend's death. The film is lost.

Cast: Thomas Meighan (John Phelan), Marietta Millner (Nada Winthrop), Louise Brooks (Snuggles Joy), Fred Kohler (Gunner Gallagher), Duke Martin (Lefty Schroeder), Nancy Phillips (Lefty's Girl), Charles Hill Mailes (Luther Winthrop).

12. A GIRL IN EVERY PORT

Produced by Fox. Directed by Howard Hawks. Screenplay by Seton I. Miller, adapted from an original story by Howard Hawks and J. K. McGuinness. Photography by L. William O'Connell and R. J. Berquist. Art direction by William Tummel. Edited by Ralph Dixon. Titles by Malcolm Stuart Boylan. Released February 20, 1928. (6 reels.) Buddy film of two sailors, their fisticuffs, and their amorous adventures with fickle women in various ports of call.

Cast: Victor McLaglen (Spike), Robert Armstrong (Bill), Louise Brooks (Mlle. Godiva, the Girl in Marseilles), Maria Casajuana (the Girl in Buenos Aires), Sally Rand (the Girl in Bombay), Natalie Kingston (the Girl in the South Seas).

13. BEGGARS OF LIFE

Produced by Paramount. Directed by William Wellman. Screenplay by Benjamin Glazer and Jim Tully, adapted from the book by Tully. Photography by Henry Gerrard. Titles by Julian Johnson. Edited by Alyson Shaffer. Production dates: May 18–June 18, 1928. Released September 22, 1928. (9 reels.) Tale of tramp life in which a girl disguised as a boy runs away from the law and rides the rails through the tough hobo subculture.

Cast: Wallace Beery (Oklahoma Red), Louise Brooks (Nancy), Richard Arlen (Jim), Edgar "Blue" Washington (Black Mose), H. A. Morgan (Skinny), Roscoe Karns (Hopper), Robert Perry (Arkansas Snake), Jacque Chapin (Ukie).

14. THE CANARY MURDER CASE

Produced by Paramount. Directed by Malcolm St. Clair. Screenplay by Florence Ryerson and Albert Shelby LeVino, adapted from the book by S. S. Van Dine. Photography by Harry Fischbeck and Clifford Blackstone. Edited by William Shea. Titles by Herman Mankiewicz. Production dates: September 11–October 12, 1928; sound retakes, December 19, 1928. Released February 16, 1929. (7 reels.) The first Philo Vance detective mystery, with many elegant suspects in the murder of a blackmailing showgirl.

Cast: William Powell (Philo Vance), Louise Brooks ("The Canary," Margaret Odell), Jean Arthur (Alys LaFosse), James Hall (Jimmy Spotswoode), Charles Lane (Charles Spotswoode), Eugene Pallette (Ernest Heath), Gustav von Seyffertitz (Dr. Ambrose Lindquist).

15. DIE BÜCHSE DER PANDORA (PANDORA'S BOX)

Produced by Nero-Film, Berlin. Directed by G. W. Pabst. Screenplay by Ladislaus Vajda, adapted from the plays *Erdgeist* and *Die Büchse der Pandora* by Frank Wedekind. Photography by Günther Krampf. Edited by Joseph R. Fliesler. Art direction by Andrei Andreiev. Costumes by Gottlieb Hesch. Production dates: October 17–November 23, 1928. Released January 30, 1929, in Berlin; December 1, 1929, in New York. (9 reels.) Lulu's sinless sexuality hypnotizes and destroys the weak, lustful men around her—and ultimately herself.

Cast: Louise Brooks (Lulu), Fritz Kortner (Dr. Peter Schön), Franz Lederer (Alwa Schön), Carl Goetz (Schigolch), Alice Roberts (Countess Geschwitz), Krafft Raschig (Rodrigo, the Acrobat), Gustav Diessl (Jack the Ripper).

16. DAS TAGEBUCH EINER VERLORENEN (THE DIARY OF A LOST GIRL)

Produced by HOM-Film, Berlin. Directed by G. W. Pabst. Screenplay by Rudolf Leonhardt, adapted from the novel by Margarete Böhme. Photography by Sepp Allgeier. Art direction by Ernö Metzner and Emil Hasler. Production dates: June 17–July 26, 1929. Released October 23, 1929, in Berlin. (8 reels.) Morality tale of a beautiful girl who is seduced, abandoned, and sent to a brutal reformatory, from which she escapes to a brothel, propelled all the while by German bourgeois hypocrisy.

Cast: Louise Brooks (Thymiane), Fritz Rasp (Meinert), Andrews Engelmann (Warden), Valeska Gert (Warden's Wife), Edith Meinhard (Erika), Joseph Rovensky (Thymiane's Father), André Roanne (Count Osdorff), Sybille Schmitz (Elizabeth, the Governess), Vera Palowa (Aunt Frida), Francisca Kinz (Meta), Arnold Korff (the old Count Osdorff).

17. PRIX DE BEAUTÉ (BEAUTY PRIZE)

Produced by SOFAR-Film, Paris. Directed by Augusto Genina. Screenplay by Augusto Genina, René Clair, Bernard Zimmer, and Alessandro de Stefani from an original story by G. W. Pabst and René Clair. Photography by Rudolph Maté. Edited by Francis Salsbert. Set design by Robert Gys. Costume design by Jean Patou. Music by Wolfgang Zeller. Production dates: August 29–September 27, 1929. Released August 20, 1930. (109 minutes.) Retitled *Miss Europa* in Germany; shot as silent, Brooks's voice later dubbed in French. A neorealist, working-class tragedy in which the diffident heroine is chained to her dull job and jealous fiancé until a beauty contest takes her away from it all.

Cast: Louise Brooks (Lucienne), Georges Charlia (André), Jean Bradin (Prince de Grabovsky), Augusto Bandini (Antonin), Gaston Jacquet (the Duke).

18. WINDY RILEY GOES HOLLYWOOD

Produced by Educational Pictures. Directed by William B. Goodrich (Roscoe "Fatty" Arbuckle). Screenplay by Ernest Pagano and Jack Townley, adapted from the cartoon-strip character of Ken Kling. Released August 12, 1931. (2 reels, 21 minutes.) Retitled *The Gas Bag* for release in Great Britain. Short comedy of cocky Windy trying to revamp the publicity department of a Hollywood studio and mucking it all up.

Cast: Jack Shutta (Windy Riley), Louise Brooks (Betty Grey), William Davidson (La Ross), Wilbur Mack (Snell), Dell Henderson (Allen), Walter Merrill (Reporter).

19. IT PAYS TO ADVERTISE

Produced by Paramount. Directed by Frank Tuttle. Screenplay by Roi Cooper Megrue and Walter Hackett. Photography by Archie J. Stout. Released February 19, 1931. (66 minutes.) Ad-agency farce about rival soap manufacturers and the ne'er-do-well playboy son of one of them.

Cast: Norman Foster (Rodney Martin), Carole Lombard (Mary Grayson), Skeets Gallagher (Ambrose Peale), Eugene Pallette (Cyrus Martin), Lucien Littlefield (Adams), Louise Brooks (Thelma Temple).

20. GOD'S GIFT TO WOMEN

Produced by Warner Brothers. Directed by Michael Curtiz. Screenplay by Joseph Jackson and Raymond Griffith, adapted from the stage play

The Devil Was Sick by Jane Hinton. Released April 15, 1931. (74 minutes.) Romantic farce concerning a notorious Parisian womanizer who falls for a Yankee girl but must ward off all his past conquests.

Cast: Frank Fay (Jacques Duryea), Laura La Plante (Diane Churchill), Charles Winninger (Mr. Churchill), Louise Brooks (Florine), Joan Blondell (Fifi), Margaret Livingston (Tania), Yola D'Avril (Dagmar), the Sisters G (Marie and Mabelle), Arthur E. Carewe (Dr. Dumont), Alan Mowbray (Auguste).

21. EMPTY SADDLES

Produced and released by Universal. Directed by Lesley Selander. Screenplay by Frances Guihan, adapted from a story by Cherry Wilson. Photography by Allen Thompson and Herbert Kirkpatrick. Edited by Bernard Loeftus. Art direction by Ralph Berger. Production dates: August 26–September 2, 1936. Released December 20, 1936. (67 minutes.) Confused western about outlaws attempting to take over a haunted dude ranch.

Cast: Buck Jones (Buck Devlin), Harvey Clark (Swap Boone), Louise Brooks (Boots Boone), Charles Middleton (Slim White).

22. KING OF GAMBLERS

Produced by Paramount. Directed by Robert Florey. Screenplay by Doris Anderson, adapted from an original story by Tiffany Thayer. Photography by Harry Fishbeck. Art direction by Hans Dreier and Robert Odell. Released May 3, 1937. (78 minutes.) Underworld crime story about the slot-machine racket and crusading reporter who uncovers it.

Cast: Claire Trevor (Dixie), Lloyd Nolan (Jim), Akim Tamiroff (Steve Kalkas), Larry "Buster" Crabbe (Eddie), Evelyn Brent (Cora), Louise Brooks (Joyce Beaton). Brooks's role is cut.

23. WHEN YOU'RE IN LOVE

Produced by Columbia. Directed by Robert Riskin. Screenplay by Robert Riskin, adapted from an original story by Ethel Hill and Cedric Worth. Music and lyrics by Jerome Kern and Dorothy Fields. Music direction by Alfred Newman. Choreography by Leon Leonidoff. Photography by Joseph Walker. Edited by Gene Milford. Released February 27, 1937. (110 minutes.) Grace Moore vehicle in which the singer journeys from Mexico to her big U.S. concert, falling for a wealthy "tramp artist" along the way.

Cast: Grace Moore (Louise Fuller), Cary Grant (Jimmy Hudson), Thomas Mitchell (Hank Miller), Henry Stephenson (Walter Mitchell), Louise Brooks (ballet dancer).

24. OVERLAND STAGE RAIDERS

Produced by Republic Pictures. Directed by George Sherman. Screenplay by Luci Ward, adapted from a story by Bernard McConville and Edmond Kelso, based on characters created by William Colt McDonald. Photography by William Nobles. Edited by Tony Martinelli. Released September 28, 1938. (55 minutes.) The "Three Mesquiteers' " eighteenth entry— a "modern" western in which they transport gold shipments by airplane but are framed for a robbery.

Cast: John Wayne (Stony Brooke), Max Terhune (Lullaby Joslin), Ray Corrigan (Tucson Smith), Louise Brooks (Beth Hoyt), Anthony Marsh (Ned Hoyt).

ACKNOWLEDGMENTS

Facts and favors, large and small, were provided by virtually everyone from whom they were asked over a three-year research period in Kansas, New York City, California, Rochester, Pittsburgh, London, and Paris, among other places. I thank all the wonderful people below for their help in providing pieces of the Louise Brooks puzzle and for their equally important moral support.

KANSAS

In Cherryvale, Kay Driskel, Audrey Crowder, and Shannon Raush of the Cherryvale Public Library; Imogene Littell, Eva Hills, and Grace Newton. In Pittsburg, Professor Charles Cagle of Pittsburg State University.

In Wichita, *Wichita Eagle and Beacon* editors Davis Merritt, Jr., Fran Kentling, and Diane C. Lewis; stalwart friend and sleuth, Daniel R. Rouser; Dolores Ramsey, Myrna Hudson, and, most of all, James Kiefner of the Wichita Public Library; Dr. Allan Cress, Wichita State University German professor, translator, and mentor; dancers Hal McCoy, Lila Cornell Metz, and Jimmy Cavaness; Elliott Levand, Larry R. Green, Ruth Vawter Rankin, Jayne Milburn, Vida Havner, Edna Aikins Horton, and Kay Hicks. Personally crucial to my task were Pamela Paris Loyle and David E. Loyle, Thelmah G. Dodds, E. Reid and Genevieve Fletcher, Marilynn Gump and her late dog Trinka, Harry and Margaret Saums, Martin and Mary Umansky, Kent and Bonnie Grove, Mike Fizer, and Hal Ottaway. Thanks also to Rhonda Brooks of Lenexa, Kansas.

NEW YORK CITY

Archives and archivists: Ron Magliozzi and Charles Silver of the Film Studies Center, Museum of Modern Art, and Mary Corliss, Daniel Pearl, and Paula Baxter also of MoMA; Dorothy Swerdlove of the New York Public Library's Billy Rose Theatre Collection; Helen Stark, librarian of *The New Yorker*; Carol Shapiro, curator of CBS radio archives; Richard Koszarski of the Astoria Motion Picture and TV Foundation; Peggy Rosenthal, librarian of the New York *Daily News*; Diana Edkins of *Vanity Fair*; and the Columbia University Oral History Collection.

Stars and interviewees: Lillian Gish (and her manager, Jim Frasher); Martha Graham (and Laura Marchese of the Martha Graham Dance Center); Adolph Green, Aileen Pringle, and Lauren Bacall; former *New Yorker* editor William Shawn; current *New Yorker* editor Robert Gottlieb and executive editor Martha Kaplan; Algonquin Hotel manager Andrew Anspach; authors James Watters, Jerry Vermilye, and Tom Dardis; CBS board chairman William S. Paley and John Minary of the Paley Foundation; publicist John Springer; Doris Vinton and Dorothy Begley of The Ziegfeld Club.

Other help was provided by Ira Resnick of the Motion Picture Arts Gallery; Ann Martin of *American Film*; Joan Canale of the New York Public Library; David Pannett of Barnard College; John Loughery, John A. Gallagher, Gene Stavis, Karen Beardsley, Maitlin Peters, Kevin Lewis, Jessica Mitchell, Victoria Page, Earl Levine, Allan Geschwind, Andrew Maietta, and John Allison.

ROCHESTER

James Card was, simply, the single most important contributor to this book: a maverick scholar, historian, teacher, curmudgeon, and unparalleled conversation partner.

William Klein of station WVOR in Rochester was the first to provide guidance and valuable information in the quest.

Composer David Diamond, straddling both New York City and Rochester, gave me profound insights into his friend Louise.

Archives and archivists: At the International Museum of Photography at George Eastman House, marvelous Kaye MacRae, projectionist extraordinaire Ed Stratman, librarian Rachael Stuhlman, Mari Howard, and Francisco Gonzalez; William Cuseo of the literature and arts division of the Rochester Public Library; Peter Ford, library manager of Gannett Rochester Newspapers; Alan K. Brakoniecki, editor-in-chief of *Kodakery*, the Eastman Kodak Company newspaper.

Sebby Wilson-Jacobson of the Rochester *Times-Union*, film critic Jack Garner of the Rochester *Democrat and Chronicle*, retired columnist Henry W. Clune, and Rochester University professor Donald McNamara all gave valuable assists.

Among Louise's friends who cooperated wonderfully were Barbara and Richard Mayberry, Edith Medwin, Benjamin and May and Avram Phelosof, John and Helen Benz, Carol Gambacurta, Jeffrey Rolick, and the late Marjorie Van Tassell, who kept her alive. Thanks also to Marie Weidman and Cecilia Ciaccia; to Dr. Joseph Stankitis, now of Buffalo; and to Peter Hanson and Richard Sisson of Cuba, N.Y., who made their superb photograph collections available to me.

CALIFORNIA

Archives and archivists: Tremendously important help was provided by Sam Gill and Kristine Krueger of the Margaret Herrick Library at the Academy of Motion Picture Arts and Sciences; also by David Shepherd of the Directors Guild; Eleanor Tanin at the UCLA Film, Television and Radio Archives; the Pacific Film Archives; San Francisco *Chronicle* librarian June Delappa; film historian Anthony Slide; Debbie Caulfield and the Los Angeles *Times* library; Bob Pavlik of the San Simeon library; and documentarist Gary Conklin.

Stars and interviewees: Francis Lederer, Esther Ralston, the late Colleen Moore, the late William Collier, Jr., Anne Douglas Doucet, Arthur Jacobson, Dan Aikman, Charles "Buddy" Rogers (and Joyce Aimee), Douglas Fairbanks, Jr., Mrs. Edwina Sutherland, Paramount photographer Ted Allan, publicist Teete Carle, and, most of all, my deepest gratitude to Louise's friend Roddy McDowall.

Special thanks again to June Brooks Lashley for speaking with me, uninvited, on a hot day in San Jose and several times, more willingly, thereafter.

Screenwriter Judd Klinger gave valuable advice and took me in off the streets, while other support was provided by the celebrated *National Lampoon* artist Rick Geary and his wife, Deborah, in San Diego and later New York; Goldie Wolfson in Inglewood; Richard Tussey and David McClelland in Oceanside; and writer Margaret Murray in Concord.

PITTSBURGH

Archives and archivists: William Spinelli of the Duquesne University library and its Michael A.

Musmanno Collection; Pittsburgh *Post-Gazette* librarian Carol Jenkins; Alban Berg authorities and musicologists Frederick Dorian and Judith Meibach; Pennsylvania State University film department head William Uricchio and *Post-Gazette* film critic Marylynne Uricchio; rare-book finders Donnis Decamp and Mark Selvaggio; and Jay Dantry, bookseller to the stars.

The late Art Rooney, grand old man of the Pittsburgh Steelers, was a delightful help.

Support services were kindly provided by Terri Vosco, Polly Schoenberger, Peter Oresick of the University of Pittsburgh Press, and Chris Walsh of Kinko's. Betty Goodwin, International Travel Coordinator of Pitt's Informal Program, made the Copenhagen sojourn possible. Charlie Humphrey, Adrian McCoy, and Scott Mervis of *In Pittsburgh*, Ceci Sommers and Steven Baum of WQED-FM, Bruce Van Wyngarten of *Pittsburgh*, and Robert Gangwere of *Carnegie* magazine were all reliable lifelines.

Dr. Laurie L. Lankin, Mike "Ralphie" Kalina, and Doris Bauer were the inner-sanctum friends who kept me going, along with David Bandler, Michael Vargo, Tara Alexander, John Pappas, Rebecca Willis, Rita Glosser, Tim Ziaukas, Jane and Jonathan Harris, and the dearest teacher of all, Ruth U. Ross.

WASHINGTON

The D.C. investigative team was headed by my friend and advisor, John Barba, working with Paul C. Spehr and archivist Katharine Laughney in the Motion Picture, Broadcasting & Recorded Sound Division of the Library of Congress. Thanks also to ace reporter Kenneth V. Cummins and to the associates of George Marshall—Shirley Povich, Leonard Viner, Everett Bergman, Jack Guy, Sidney Carroll, and Jay Conger.

BOSTON

Ross Berkal was the most faithful of supporters and contributors. Thanks, too, to Maren Kröger of the Goethe Institute of Boston, to the Harvard Theater Library, to Alan Schroeder of WBZ-TV, and, once again, Ricky Leacock and his colleague, Susan Woll, who came through magnificently at the eleventh hour.

Elsewhere around the country, Cathy Henkel of the Seattle *Times* in Washington was always a source of support. My gratitude also goes to National Public Radio commentator Sean Connolly and WJHU-FM program director Dennis Bartel of Baltimore, Md., and Mr. and Mrs. Wyoming B. Paris, Jr., of Bel Air, Md.; Robert Brooks of St. Louis, Mo.; Leatrice Gilbert Fountain of Riverside, Conn.; Joan Bennett and David Wilde of Scarsdale, N.Y.;

Annagreta Swanson of the Peterborough Town Library, N.H.; Marcia Froelke Coburn of Chicago, Ill.; Dr. David and Dr. Sharon Mason of Indianapolis; the very generous photo-collector Bill Hutchinson of Griffith, Ind.; Maxine Fleckner of the Wisconsin Center for Film Research in Madison; the Reverend Paul Burkort of Winter Haven, Fla.; Dorothy Mackaill of Honolulu; the late Venus Jones Speer of Farmington, N.M.; Tom Graves of Memphis, Tenn., editor-publisher of *Rock & Roll Disc*; and to the great teacher-philosopher Reverend Robert R. De Rouen, S.J., of Denver, Colo.

LONDON

Kevin Brownlow, as noted in the Preface, was a mainstay of all my research and writing. His colleague David Gill at Thames Television deserves thanks, too. So do Meredith Etherington-Smith and Jeremy Pilcher; Christopher Sinclair-Stevenson of Hamish Hamilton; film historian Alexander Walker; David Meeker and Allen Eyles of the British Film Institute; Kathleen Tynan, Catherine Ann Surowiec, Nobel Prize–winner Elias Canetti, and last but by no means least—the Peter and Catherine Green family of Hessett, Suffolk.

PARIS

Bethany Haye cheerfully coordinated the French research on Brooks, traveling a variety of blind and sighted alleys. Noelle Giret and Nadine Teneze at the Cinémathèque Française were extremely helpful; thanks, also, to Robert Benayoun and to Katherine Pancol.

COPENHAGEN

Ib Monty, director of the Danish Film Museum, was gracious and helpful; thanks to Kurt Nielsen and the Danish Tourist Board, to April Lane and SAS Scandinavian Airlines, and to Vibeke Brodersen Steinthal.

Elsewhere around the globe, my sincerest thanks to Louise's friend Fraser Macdonald of the Toronto Film Society; to Enno Patalas, film section director of the Münchner Stadtmuseum, Munich, West Germany; and to Rajka Iliscevec, Jugoslovenska Kinoteka, Belgrade, Yugoslavia.

BIBLIOGRAPHY

BOOKS

Allen, Frederick Lewis. *Only Yesterday.* New York: Harper & Bros., 1931.

Atwell, Lee. *G. W. Pabst.* Boston: Twayne, 1977.

Balio, Tino, ed. *The American Film Industry.* Madison, Wis: University of Wisconsin Press, 1976. (Reprinting of "Loew's, Inc.," *Fortune* magazine, August 1939.)

Barlow, John. *German Expressionist Film.* Boston: Twayne, 1982.

Bell-Metereau, Rebecca L. *Hollywood Androgyny.* New York: Columbia University Press, 1985.

Bennett, Joan, and Kibbee, Lois. *The Bennett Playbill.* New York: Holt, Rinehart & Winston, 1970.

Block, Haskell, and Shedd, Robert. *Masters of Modern Drama.* New York: Random House, 1962.

Brooks, Louise. *Lulu in Hollywood.* New York: Alfred A. Knopf, 1982.

Brownlow, Kevin. *The Parade's Gone By . . .* New York: Alfred A. Knopf, 1968.

Case, Frank. *Tales of a Wayward Inn.* New York: Frederick A. Stokes, 1938.

Chaplin, Charles. *My Autobiography.* New York: Simon and Schuster, 1964.

Colum, Padraic. *Orpheus: Myths of the World.* New York: Macmillan, 1930.

Dardis, Tom. *Keaton: The Man Who Wouldn't Lie Down.* New York: Charles Scribner's Sons, 1979.

Davies, Marion. *The Times We Had: Life with William Randolph Hearst.* Indianapolis: Bobbs-Merrill, 1975.

Deschner, Donald. *The Films of W. C. Fields.* New York: Cadillac Publishing Co., 1966.

Dorner, Jane. *Fashion in the Twenties and Thirties.* New Rochelle, N.Y.: Arlington House, 1973.

Eames, John Douglas. *The Paramount Story.* New York: Crown, 1985.

Eisner, Lotte. *L'Écran démoniaque (The Haunted Screen: Expressionism in the German Cinema and the Influence of Max Reinhardt),* 1952. Paris: Terrain Vague, 1965. (English editions: London: Secker & Warburg, 1968; Berkeley and Los Angeles: University of California Press, 1969.)

————. *Ich hatte einst ein schönes Vaterland: Memoiren.* Heidelberg: Verlag das Wunderhorn, 1984.

Etherington-Smith, Meredith, and Pilcher, Jeremy. *The 'It' Girls.* London: Hamish Hamilton, 1986.

Everson, William K. *American Silent Film.* New York: Oxford University Press, 1978.

Eyles, Allen. *John Wayne.* Cranbury, N.J.: A. S. Barnes, 1976.

Farnsworth, Marie. *The Ziegfeld Follies.* New York: G. P. Putnam's Sons, 1956.

Fields, Ronald J., ed. *W.C. Fields by Himself: His Intended Autobiography.* Englewood Cliffs, N.J.: Prentice-Hall, 1973.

Fountain, Leatrice Gilbert, with John R. Maxim. *Dark Star.* New York: St. Martin's Press, 1985.

Friedrich, Otto. *Before the Deluge: A Portrait of Berlin in the 1920's.* New York: Harper & Row, 1972.

Gehring, Wes D. *W. C. Fields: A Bio-Bibliography.* Westport, Conn.: Greenwood Press, 1984.

Gill, Brendan. *Tallulah.* New York: Harper & Row, 1972.

Gittleman, Sol. *Frank Wedekind.* Boston: Twayne, 1969.

Goethe, Johann Wolfgang von. *Faust, Part I,* translated by Philip Wayne. Baltimore, Md.: Penguin Books, 1963.

Grosz, George. *Ecce Homo.* New York: Grove Press, 1966.

Guiles, Fred Lawrence. *Marion Davies.* New York: McGraw-Hill, 1972.

Harriman, Margaret Case. *The Vicious Circle.* New York: Rinehart & Co., 1951.

Haskell, Molly. *From Rape to Reverence: The Treatment of Women in the Movies.* New York: Holt, Rinehart and Winston, 1973.

Higashi, Sumiko. *Virgins, Vamps and Flappers: The American Silent Movie Heroine.* (Monographs in Women's Studies, Sherri Clarkson, ed.) St. Albans, Vt.: Eden Press, Women's Publications Inc., 1978.

Holme, Christopher, trans. *Pandora's Box (Lulu),* Classic Film Scripts. New York: Simon and Schuster, 1971.

Huxley, Aldous. *After Many a Summer Dies the Swan.* New York: Harper & Brothers, 1939.

Jaccard, Roland, ed. *Louise Brooks: Portrait d'une anti-star.* Paris: Phébus, 1977.

Kamin, Dan. *Charlie Chaplin's One-Man Show.* Metuchen, N.J.: Scarecrow Press, 1984.

Kirstein, Lincoln. *Dance: A Short History of Classic Theatrical Dancing.* New York: G. P. Putnam's Sons, 1935.

Kobal, John. *Hollywood Glamor Portraits.* New York: Dover Publications, 1976.

———. *The Art of the Great Hollywood Portrait Photographers, 1925–1940.* New York: Alfred A. Knopf, 1980.

———. *Great Film Stills of the German Silent Era.* New York: Dover Publications, 1981.

———. *People Will Talk.* New York: Alfred A. Knopf, 1986.

Koszarski, Richard. *Hollywood Directors 1914–1940.* New York: Oxford University Press, 1976.

Kracauer, Siegfried. *From Caligari to Hitler: A Psychological History of the German Film.* Princeton, N.J.: Princeton University Press, 1947.

Kyrou, Ado. *Amour-érotisme et cinéma.* Paris: Terrain Vague, 1957 (revised, 1967).

———. *Le Surréalisme au Cinéma.* Paris: Terrain Vague, 1963.

Leprohon, Pierre. *The Italian Cinema.* London: Secker & Warburg, 1972. (Originally published in Paris by Editions Seghers in 1966.)

Loos, Anita. *Gentlemen Prefer Blondes.* New York: Boni & Liveright, 1925.

———. *A Girl Like I.* New York: Viking Press, 1966.

McBride, Joseph. *Hawks on Hawks.* Berkeley, Calif.: University of California Press, 1982.

———, ed. *Focus on Howard Hawks.* Englewood Cliffs, N.J.: Prentice-Hall, 1972.

McClintock, David. *Indecent Exposure.* New York: William Morrow, 1982.

McCreadie, Marsha. *Women on Film: The Critical Eye.* New York: Praeger, 1983.

McDonagh, Donald. *The Complete Guide to Modern Dance.* New York: Doubleday, 1976.

McDowall, Roddy. *Double Exposure.* New York: Delacorte, 1966.

McEvoy, J. P. *Show Girl.* New York: Simon and Schuster, 1928.

Moore, Colleen. *Silent Star.* Garden City, N.Y.: Doubleday, 1968.

Mordden, Ethan. *That Jazz! An Idiosyncratic Social History of the American Twenties.* New York: G. P. Putnam's Sons, 1978.

Myrent, Glenn. *Henri Langlois: Premier citoyen du cinéma.* Paris: 1986.

Paley, William. *As It Happened.* Garden City, N.Y.: Doubleday, 1979.

Pratt, George C. *Spellbound in Darkness.* Greenwich, Conn.: New York Graphic Society, 1973.

Ralston, Esther. *Some Day We'll Laugh.* Metuchen, N.J.: Scarecrow Press, 1985.

Rentschler, Eric, ed. *German Film & Literature: Adaptations and Transformations.* New York and London: Methuen, 1986. (Thomas Elsaesser essay, "Lulu and the Meter Man: Pabst's *Pandora's Box* [1929]")

Robinson, David. *The History of World Cinema.* New York: Stein and Day, 1981.

———. *Chaplin: His Life and Art.* New York: McGraw-Hill, 1985.

Rosen, Marjorie. *Popcorn Venus: Women, Movies, and the American Dream.* New York: Avon Books, 1973.

Rosenberg, Bernard, and Silverstein, Harry. *The Real Tinsel.* New York: Macmillan, 1970.

Roud, Richard. *A Passion for Films: Henri Langlois and the Cinémathèque Française.* New York: Viking Press, 1983.

Russo, Vito. *The Celluloid Closet: Homosexuality in the Movies.* New York: Harper & Row, 1981.

St. Denis, Ruth. *An Unfinished Life.* New York: Harper, 1939.

Sarris, Andrew. *The American Cinema.* New York: E. P. Dutton, 1968.

Schlundt, Christena L. *The Professional Appearances of Ruth St. Denis & Ted Shawn: A Chronology and an Index of Dances, 1906–1932.* New York: The New York Public Library, 1962.

Shawn, Ted, with Gray Poole. *One Thousand and One Night Stands.* New York: Doubleday, 1960.

———. *Every Little Movement: A Book about François Delsarte.* New York: Dance Horizons, Inc., 1963.

Shelton, Suzanne. *Divine Dancer: A Biography of Ruth St. Denis.* Garden City, N.Y.: Doubleday, 1981.

Sherman, Jane. *Soaring: The Diary and Letters of a Denishawn Dancer in the Far East: 1925–1926.* Middletown, Conn.: Wesleyan University Press, 1976.

———. *The Drama of Denishawn Dance.* Middletown, Conn.: Wesleyan University Press, 1979.

———. *Denishawn: The Enduring Influence.* Boston: Twayne, 1983.

———and Barton Mumaw. *Barton Mumaw, Dancer.* New York: Dance Horizons, 1986.

Shipman, David. *The Story of Cinema*. New York: St. Martin's Press, 1982.

Singer, June. *Androgyny: Toward a New Theory of Sexuality*. Garden City, N.Y.: Doubleday, Anchor Books, 1977.

Springer, John, and Hamilton, Jack, eds. *They Had Faces Then*. Secaucus, N.J.: Citadel Press, 1974.

Thomas, Dana L. *The Media Moguls: From Pulitzer to Paley*. New York: G. P. Putnam's Sons, 1981.

Tynan, Kathleen. *The Life of Kenneth Tynan*. New York: William Morrow, 1987.

Tynan, Kenneth. *Show People*. New York: Simon and Schuster, 1979. (Reprinting of "Louise Brooks: The Girl in the Black Helmet," from *The New Yorker*, June 11, 1979.)

Vermilye, Jerry. *The Films of the Twenties*. Secaucus, N.J.: Citadel Press, 1985.

Walker, Alexander. *The Shattered Silents: How the Talkies Came to Stay*. New York: William Morrow, 1979.

Walker, Stanley. *The Night Club Era*. New York: Frederick A. Stokes Co., 1933.

Watters, James. *Return Engagement: Faces to Remember—Then and Now*. New York: Clarkson N. Potter, 1984.

Weaver, John T. *Twenty Years of Silents: 1908–1928*. Metuchen, N.J.: Scarecrow Press, 1971.

Wedekind, Frank. *Five Tragedies of Sex* ("Spring's Awakening," "Earth Spirit," "Pandora's Box," "Death and Devil," "Castle Wetterstein"); translated by Frances Fawcett and Stephen Spender. London: Vision Press Ltd., 1952.

Willis, Donald G. *The Films of Howard Hawks*. Metuchen, N.J.: Scarecrow Press, 1975.

Wilson, Edmund. *Edmund Wilson: The American Earthquake, A Documentary of the Twenties and Thirties*. Garden City, N.Y.: Doubleday, Anchor Books, 1958. (Reprinting of "The Finale at the Follies," from *The New Republic*, March 25, 1925.)

———. *The Portable Edmund Wilson*. Edited by Lewis M. Dabney. New York: Viking, Penguin Books, 1983. (Reprinting of "The Follies as an Institution," from *The New Republic*, April 1923.)

Wood, Robin. *Howard Hawks*. London: BFI Publishing, 1981.

ARTICLES

Amengual, Barthélémy. "Georg Wilhelm Pabst." *Cinéma d'Aujourd'hui*, no. 37, Paris: Editions Seghers, 1966.

———. "De Wedekind à Pabst." *L'Avant-scène*, Paris, December 1980.

Atkins, Irene Kahn. "Arthur Jacobson." A Directors Guild of America Oral History, 1981. (Unpublished.)

Black, C. M. "Man with a Megaphone." *Collier's*, July 16, 1938.

Brodersen, Vibeke (Steinthal), "Pandora i Kobenhavn" ("Pandora in Copenhagen"). *Kosmorama*, the Danish Film Museum magazine, no. 31, December 1957.

Brooks, Myra. "My Louise." *Screenland*, February 1928.

Cagle, Charles. "Louise Brooks and the Road to Oz." *The Little Balkans Review, the Southeastern Kansas Literary and Graphics Quarterly* 3, no. 1, Fall 1982.

Card, James. "Out of Pandora's Box: Louise Brooks on G. W. Pabst." *Image* 5, Eastman House, Rochester, N.Y., September 1956.

———. "The 'Intense Isolation' of Louise Brooks." *Sight and Sound* 27, no. 5, Summer 1958.

———. "Cinema 16 Film Notes," April 29, 1959.

Everson, William K. "Remembering Louise Brooks." *Films in Review*, November 1985.

Falkenberg, Paul. "Six Talks on G. W. Pabst." *Cinemages* 3, May 1955.

Geng, Veronica. "Lulu in Washington." *American Film*, June 1984.

Harris, Dale. "Silents Speaking Loudly." *Performing Arts* 17, no. 12, December 1983.

Herrmann, Lucie. "Louise Brooks." *Frauen & Film* Vol. 26, December 1980.

Horak, Jan-Christopher. "G. W. Pabst in Hollywood, or Every Modern Hero Deserves a Mother." *Film History* 1, 1987.

Isaksson, Folke. "Filmens Vackraste Kvinna" ("The Cinema's Most Beautiful Woman"). *Dagens Nyheter*, Stockholm, July 16, 1961.

———. "Oh Louise." *Chaplin*, no. 52, Stockholm, January 1965.

Joseph, Rudolph S., ed. "Der Regisseur: G. W. Pabst." Munich, 1963. Quoted in Atwell, *G. W. Pabst* (Boston: Twayne, 1977).

Kraszna-Krausz, A. "G. W. Pabst's 'Lulu.' " *Close Up*, London, April 1929.

Langlois, Henri. "Hawks: homme moderne" ("The Modernity of Howard Hawks"). *Cahiers du Cinéma*, January 1963.

Laschever, Sara. "Pandora's Box," *New York Review of Books*, October 21, 1982.

Loos, Anita. "Greatest Actress in Moving Pictures." *Vogue*, September 1981.

Luft, Herbert G. "G. W. Pabst." *Films in Review*, no. 15, February 1964.

McNamara, Donald. "A Conversation with Louise Brooks." *The Missouri Review*, no. 3, Summer 1983.

McVay, Douglas. "The Goddesses." *Films and Filming*, August 1965.

Mencken, H. L. "The Low-Down on Hollywood." *Photoplay*, April 1927.

Pabst, G. W. "Servitude et grandeur de Hollywood," in *Le rôle intellectuel du cinéma*, Cahier 3. Paris: Institut international de cooperation culturelle, 1937.

Pancol, Katherine. "La star rebelle." *Paris Match*, September 13, 1985.

Perelman, S. J. "She Walks in Beauty—Single File, Eyes Front, and No Hanky-Panky," *The New Yorker*, February 22, 1969.

Potamkin, Harry Alan. "Pabst and the Social Film." *Hand and Horn*, January-March 1933.

Povich, Shirley. "Marshall: Impresario of the Redskins." Washington *Post*, September 2, 1986.

Quirk, Lawrence J. "Lulu in Hollywood" (two parts). *Quirks Reviews*, nos. 41 and 42, June and August 1982.

Reid, Margaret. "Has the Flapper Changed?" *Motion Picture Magazine* 33, no. 6, July 1927.

Rivers, Joan. "Lulu in Hollywood" (review). *The Hollywood Reporter*, June 11, 1982.

Roberts, John. "Louise Brooks." *Classic Images*, no. 92, February 1983.

Schutz, Wayne. "Louise Brooks: A Magical Presence" (two-part filmography). *Classic Images*, nos. 94 and 95, April and May 1983.

Slide, Anthony, ed. "Silent Stars Speak," transcript of AMPAS panel discussion, September 8, 1979, with Esther Ralston, Lois Wilson, Jetta Goudal, et al. (Unpublished.)

Surowiec, Catherine Ann. Museum of Modern Art, 1981 program notes for *Prix de Beauté*. (Unpublished.)

Sutherland, A. Edward. Columbia University Oral History Research Project, February 1959. (Unpublished interview transcript.)

Thomson, David. "The Actress Taking the Part of Lulu." *Threepenny Review*, Berkeley, Calif., Spring 1983.

Tynan, Kenneth. "Louise Brooks: The Girl in the Black Helmet." *The New Yorker*, June 11, 1979.

Wahl, Jan. "Louise Brooks: Rising Star, Falling Star" (two parts). *Movie & Film Collector's World*, nos. 165 and 166, July 29 and August 5, 1983.

Waterbury, Ruth. "Youth." *Photoplay*, November 1927.

Weinberg, Herman G. "G. W. Pabst to Dramatize Hitler's Last Days." *New York Times*, March 19, 1950.

NOTES

1. FLASHBACKS

1. LB to Kenneth Tynan, *Show People* (New York: Simon and Schuster, 1979), p. 263.
2. LB, *Lulu in Hollywood* (New York: Alfred A. Knopf, 1982), p. 18.
3. LB letter to James Card, December 17, 1955.
4. LB letter to Theodore Brooks, October 1, 1975.
5. LB letter to Theodore Brooks, November 1, 1972.
6. LB letter to Theodore Brooks, March 12, 1971.
7. LB letter to James Card, December 21, 1955.
8. LB, *Lulu in Hollywood*, p. 4.
9. Quoted in Charles Cagle, "Louise Brooks and the Road to Oz," *The Little Balkans Review* 3, no. 1, Fall 1982, p. 3.
10. Eva Calvert letter to LB, October 13, 1952. Courtesy of Louise Brooks Estate.
11. Ibid.
12. Ibid.
13. Jay Robert Nash, *Bloodletters and Badmen: A Narrative Encyclopedia of American Criminals from the Pilgrims to the Present* (New York: M. Evans & Co., 1973), pp. 53–54. Also various clippings and monographs provided by courtesy of the Cherryvale Public Library, Cherryvale, Kansas.
14. LB, *Lulu in Hollywood*, p. 5.
15. Eva Calvert letter to LB.
16. Ibid.
17. LB letter to Patricia Calvert, September 19, 1967.
18. LB, *Lulu in Hollywood*, p. 7.
19. LB letter to Marcella "Tot" Strickler, February 11, 1952.
20. Betty Strickler (surname unknown) letter to LB, undated, ca. 1952.
21. Marcella "Tot" Strickler to LB, June 4, 1952. Courtesy of Louise Brooks Estate.
22. Ibid.
23. LB, *Lulu in Hollywood*, p. 9.
24. Cagle, "Louise Brooks and the Road to Oz," p. 10.
25. Myra Brooks, "My Louise," *Screenland*, February 1928. Courtesy of Bill Hutchinson.
26. Local circulars, Cherryvale Public Library.
27. Cagle, "Louise Brooks and the Road to Oz," p. 8.
28. LB, "Chapter I, Autobiography," unpublished manuscript, p. 4.
29. LB, *Lulu in Hollywood*, p. 7.
30. LB letter to Theodore Brooks, October 8, 1971.
31. Cagle, "Louise Brooks and the Road to Oz," p. 9.
32. LB, *Lulu in Hollywood*, p. 5.
33. Myra Brooks, "My Louise."
34. Venus Jones Speer to BP, December 3, 1986.
35. LB, autobiographical notes to James Card.
36. LB, *Lulu in Hollywood*, p. 5.
37. Ibid.
38. Quoted by Margaret Brooks to BP, September 13, 1986.
39. Grace Newton to BP, November 12, 1985.
40. Cagle, "Louise Brooks and the Road to Oz," p. 11.
41. LB to Clyde Gilmore, Toronto *Telegram*, September 7, 1968.
42. June Brooks Lashley to BP, October 10, 1988.
43. LB, *Lulu in Hollywood*, p. 9.
44. Ibid.
45. Ibid., p. 6.
46. Lila Cornell Metz to BP, Wichita, Kansas, November 23, 1986.
47. Ibid.
48. Jayne Milburn to BP, Wichita, Kansas, September 14, 1986.
49. LB diary, October 15, 1921.
50. LB, *Lulu in Hollywood*, p. 6.
51. Ibid.
52. Jane Sherman, *The Drama of Denishawn Dance* (Middletown, Conn.: Wesleyan University Press, 1979), pp. 28–29.
53. Ibid., pp. 64–65.
54. LB, *Lulu in Hollywood*, p. 8.

2. DENISHAWN AND THE SILVER SALVER

1. LB, "Chapter I, Autobiography," unpublished manuscript, p. 1.
2. LB, *Lulu in Hollywood*, p. 8.
3. Ibid., p. 9.
4. Ibid.
5. Ibid., p. 8.
6. Ibid.
7. Ted Shawn, *Every Little Movement: A Book about François Delsarte* (New York: Dance Horizons, Inc., 1963), p. 80.
8. Ibid., p. 82.
9. Don McDonagh, *Martha Graham: A Biography* (New York: Praeger, 1973), p. 38.
10. Jane Sherman, *Denishawn: The Enduring Influence* (Boston: Twayne, 1983), pp. 18–19.
11. LB to Ruth Waterbury, quoted in *Photoplay*, April 1927.
12. Jane Sherman, *Soaring: The Diary and Letters of a Denishawn Dancer in the Far East: 1925–1926* (Middletown, Conn.: Wesleyan University Press, 1976).
13. Suzanne Shelton, *Divine Dancer: A Biography of Ruth St. Denis* (Garden City, N.Y.: Doubleday, 1981), p. 137.
14. Martha Graham to BP, July 27, 1987, courtesy of Laura Marchese.
15. Quoted in Sherman, *Denishawn: The Enduring Influence*, p. 63.
16. Kenneth Tynan, *Show People* (New York: Simon and Schuster, 1979), p. 269.
17. Quoted by Ted Shawn, *One Thousand and One Night Stands* (New York: Doubleday, 1960), p. 124.
18. Anne Douglas to Jane Sherman, April 26, 1986; Anne Douglas to BP, January 5, 1987.
19. Douglas to Sherman, April 26, 1986.
20. Douglas to BP, January 5, 1987.
21. Jane Sherman letter to BP, March 1, 1986.
22. George Abbot Morison, *History of Peterborough, New Hampshire* (Rindge, N.H.: Richard R. Smith Publisher Inc., 1954), pp. 351–52. Courtesy of Annagreta Swanson, Peterborough Town Library.
23. LB, *Lulu in Hollywood*, p. 12.
24. Ibid.
25. LB, "Chapter I, Autobiography," unpublished manuscript, p. 11.
26. Quoted in Sherman, *The Drama of Denishawn Dance* (Middletown, Conn.: Wesleyan University Press, 1979), p. 90.
27. Jane Sherman to BP, February 18, 1987.
28. LB to Clyde Gilmore, Toronto *Telegram*, September 7, 1968.
29. Douglas to Sherman, April 26, 1986; Douglas to BP, January 5, 1987.
30. LB, "Gloria Swanson," unpublished manuscript, January 1957.
31. LB letter to Jane Sherman, September 10, 1979. In many other letters and statements over the years, Louise made similar complaints about blacklisting, claiming that her name had been stricken from all of St. Denis's and Shawn's books. In fact, however, she is properly included in the list of 1922–23 company members in Ted Shawn's autobiography, *One Thousand and One Night Stands* (written with Gray Poole), on page 116.
32. Ibid.

3. SCANDALS

1. LB undated letter to James Card, ca. 1955.
2. LB, *Lulu in Hollywood*, pp. 12–13.
3. Joan Bennett to BP, October 12, 1986.
4. LB, *Lulu in Hollywood*, p. 10.
5. Ibid., pp. 10–11.
6. Ibid., p. 12.
7. Ibid., p. 14.
8. LB, "Gloria Swanson," unpublished manuscript, January 1957, p. 2a.
9. Ibid., p. 3.
10. LB, "Who Is the Exotic Black Orchid?," unpublished chapter of *Naked on my Goat*, ca. 1955.
11. *New York Times*, July 1, 1924.
12. Ibid.
13. LB, one-page George Gershwin sketch, undated, sent to James Card, ca. 1955.
14. LB, *Lulu in Hollywood*, pp. 14–15.
15. LB, "Why I Will Never Write My Memoirs," *Focus on Film*, March 1978, p. 34.
16. LB filmed interview with Kevin Brownlow and David Gill, 1977, transcript, p. 18.
17. LB letter to Kevin Brownlow, April 27, 1967.
18. Ibid.
19. LB, "Who Is the Exotic Black Orchid?"
20. LB, *Lulu in Hollywood*, p. 16.

4. FOLLIES

1. Quoted in Edmund Wilson, "The Finale at the Follies," which first appeared in *The New Republic*, March 25, 1925, pp. 125–26. Reprinted in *Edmund Wilson: The American Earthquake, A Documentary of the Twenties and Thirties* (Garden City, N.Y.: Doubleday, Anchor Books, 1958).
2. LB, "Gloria Swanson," unpublished manuscript, January 1957, p. 4.
3. Ibid.
4. Quoted in William K. Everson, "Remembering Louise Brooks," *Films in Review*, November 1985, pp. 537–38.
5. LB, *Lulu in Hollywood*, p. 45.
6. LB, *Lulu in Hollywood*, pp. 75–76.
7. LB letter to James Card, October 3, 1955.
8. LB, *Lulu in Hollywood*, p. 75.
9. Lina Basquette to BP, June 29, 1987.
10. Edmund Wilson, "The Follies as an Institution," April 1923. Reprinted by permission of Farrar, Straus, Giroux, Inc.

11. Kenneth Tynan, *Show People* (New York: Simon and Schuster, 1979), p. 249.
12. LB, "The Other Face of W. C. Fields," *Sight and Sound*, Spring 1971.
13. "G.V.C.," New York *American*, July 7, 1925.
14. Stephen Rathbun, New York *Sun*, July 8, 1925.
15. Don Carle Gillette, *The Billboard*, July 18, 1925.
16. LB, "Gloria Swanson," pp. 4–5.
17. Lina Basquette to BP, June 29, 1987.
18. LB, "The Other Face of W. C. Fields."
19. Ibid.
20. LB letter to James Card, October 3, 1955.
21. LB to Clyde Gilmore, Toronto *Telegram*, September 7, 1968.
22. LB, "The Other Face of W. C. Fields."
23. LB filmed interview with Kevin Brownlow and David Gill, 1977, transcript, p. 12.
24. *New York Times*, September 17, 1925.

5. MOVING IN PICTURES

1. Quoted in Carol Johnston, *Motion Picture Classic*, September 1927.
2. LB letter to James Card, October 3, 1955.
3. Ibid.
4. LB, "On Location with Billy Wellman," *London* magazine, May 1968. Reprinted in LB, *Lulu in Hollywood* (New York: Alfred A. Knopf, 1982), p. 20.
5. Ibid.
6. LB to John Kobal, *People Will Talk* (New York: Alfred A. Knopf, 1986), p. 93.
7. Ibid., p. 94.
8. LB to Ricky Leacock, filmed interview, *Lulu in Berlin* transcript, March 1974, p. 32.
9. H. L. Mencken, "The Low-Down on Hollywood," *Photoplay*, April 1927, p. 36–37, 118–20.
10. Ricky Leacock to BP, Boston, August 11, 1986.
11. LB, "Charlie Chaplin Remembered," *Film Culture*, no. 40, Spring 1966, p. 5.
12. Ibid.
13. Charles Chaplin, *My Autobiography* (New York: Simon and Schuster, 1964). p. 334.
14. LB, "Charlie Chaplin Remembered." p. 5.
15. Ibid.
16. Ibid.
17. LB letter to Kevin Brownlow, July 23, 1966.
18. LB, "Charlie Chaplin Remembered." p. 6.
19. Ibid.
20. LB letters to Kevin Brownlow, March 23, 1966, March 27, 1966, and November 8, 1967.
21. Ibid.
22. Ibid., pp. 272–73.
23. Marjorie Rosen, *Popcorn Venus: Women, Movies and the American Dream* (New York: Avon Books, 1973), p. 91.
24. LB, *Lulu in Hollywood*, pp. 17–18.
25. LB letter to James Card, October 3, 1955.
26. LB, "Actors and the Pabst Spirit," *Focus on Film*, no. 8, February 1971, p. 45.
27. Ibid.
28. Ibid.
29. LB, "The Other Face of W. C. Fields," *Sight and Sound*, Spring 1971.
30. Esther Ralston to BP, July 28, 1986.
31. Gordon, Allvine, Paramount pressbook for *The American Venus*, January 1926.
32. Wichita *Beacon*, January 24, 1926.
33. LB, "Louise Brooks par elle-même," *Objectif*, February–March 1964.
34. New York *Daily Mirror*, November 30, 1925.
35. Ibid.
36. Philadelphia *Inquirer*, March 21, 1926.
37. Ibid.
38. Wichita *Beacon*, December 20, 1925.

6. THE MYTH OF THE QUINTESSENTIAL FLAPPER

1: Colleen Moore, *Silent Star* (Garden City, N.Y.: Doubleday, 1968), p. 34.
2. Ruth Waterbury, "Youth," *Photoplay*, November 1927, pp. 46–47, 134–35.
3. Frederick Lewis Allen, *Only Yesterday* (New York: Harper & Bros., 1931), p. 100.
4. "Judge Ben Lindsey Defends. Flapper Movies," *Photoplay*, November 1927, p. 29.
5. Quoted in Charles Cagle, "Louise Brooks and the Road to Oz," *The Little Balkans Review* 3, no. 1, Fall 1982, p. 12.
6. Paramount pressbook for *Evening Clothes*, May 1927.
7. James Card, "The 'Intense Isolation' of Louise Brooks," *Sight and Sound* 27, no. 5, Summer 1958, p. 241.
8. *New York Times*, November 26, 1923, p. 15, quoted in George C. Pratt's *Spellbound in Darkness* (Greenwich, Conn.: New York Graphic Society, 1973), p. 295.
9. Moore, *Silent Star*, p. 129.
10. Colleen Moore to BP, January 16, 1987.
11. LB to John Kobal, *People Will Talk* (New York: Alfred A. Knopf, 1986), p. 83.
12. LB filmed interview with Kevin Brownlow and David Gill, 1977, transcript, p. 5.
13. Esther Ralston to BP, July 28, 1986.
14. This and subsequent quotes from Margaret Reid, "Has the Flapper Changed?," *Motion Picture Magazine* 33, no. 6, July 1927, pp. 28–29, 104, quoted in Pratt, *Spellbound in Darkness*.
15. Sumiko Higashi, *Virgins, Vamps and Flappers: The American Silent Movie Heroine* (St. Albans, Vt.: Eden Press, Women's Publications Inc., 1978), p. 102.
16. Paramount pressbook for *It's the Old Army Game*, May 1926.
17. LB letter to Kevin Brownlow, October 25, 1967.
18. LB letter to Kevin Brownlow, April 2, 1968.
19. LB to John Kobal, *People Will Talk*, p. 82.

20. Louise Brooks, "Joan Crawford," unpublished manuscript, February 1957.
21. LB letter to Theodore Brooks, March 12, 1971.
22. Moore, *Silent Star*, p. 163.
23. LB, *Lulu in Hollywood*, p. 104.
24. Quoted in "Actress Studies Clothes Economy," Paramount pressbook for *Beggars of Life*, p. 2.
25. John Engstead to John Kobal, *People Will Talk*, p. 528.
26. Marjorie Rosen, *Popcorn Venus: Women, Movies and the American Dream* (New York: Avon Books, 1973), p. 97.
27. Wichita *Eagle*, March 28, 1926.

7. LOUISE & ''THE BOY DIRECTOR''

1. A. Edward Sutherland, unpublished interview transcript, Columbia University Oral History Research Project, February 1959, p. 37.
2. Ibid., p. 59.
3. Dorothy Harden, "The Boy Director," *Photoplay*, May 1926, p. 66.
4. Ibid.
5. LB, "The Other Face of W. C. Fields," *Sight and Sound*, Spring 1971, p. 96.
6. Paramount pressbook, *It's the Old Army Game*, May 1926.
7. LB, *Lulu in Hollywood* (New York: Alfred A. Knopf, 1982), p. 82.
8. LB letter to Kevin Brownlow, January 14, 1967.
9. Sutherland, Columbia Oral History Project, pp. 103–5.
10. Kevin Brownlow, *The Parade's Gone By . . .* (New York: Alfred A. Knopf, 1968), p. 361.
11. *New York Times*, July 5, 1926.
12. LB, "Actors and the Pabst Spirit," *Focus on Film*, no. 8, February 1971, p. 45.
13. First National pressbook for *Just Another Blonde*, September 1926.
14. LB letter to Kevin Brownlow, September 16, 1966.
15. Dorothy Mackaill to BP, April 22, 1987.
16. *Just Another Blonde* pressbook.
17. Dorothy Mackaill to BP.
18. *Just Another Blonde* pressbook.
19. LB letter to Kevin Brownlow, May 7, 1971.
20. Ibid.
21. *Variety*, December 8, 1926.
22. Paramount pressbook for *Love 'em and Leave 'em*, December 1926.
23. LB, "Stardom and Evelyn Brent," Toronto Film Society Program, January 1975, p. 2.
24. Ibid.

8. PARAMOUNT IMPORTANCE

1. Los Angeles *Times*, January 7, 1927.
2. *Photoplay*, November 1927, p. 134.
3. Marjorie Rosen, *Popcorn Venus: Women, Movies and the American Dream* (New York: Avon Books, 1973), p. 108.
4. LB letter to Theodore Brooks, December 23, 1970.
5. LB letter to Theodore Brooks, August 10, 1976.
6. *New York Times*, July 10, 1927.
7. Arthur Jacobson to BP, Los Angeles, January 13, 1987.
8. Paramount pressbook for *Evening Clothes*, March 1927.
9. *New York Times*, March 21, 1927.
10. Kevin Brownlow, *The Parade's Gone By . . .* (New York: Alfred A. Knopf, 1968), p. 360.
11. Paramount pressbook for *Rolled Stockings*, June 1927.
12. Ibid.
13. LB letter to Kevin Brownlow, October 25, 1968.
14. Brownlow, *The Parade's Gone By . . .*, p. 360.
15. Paramount pressbook for *The City Gone Wild*, November 1927.
16. Brownlow, *The Parade's Gone By . . .*, p. 360.
17. Paramount pressbook for *Now We're in the Air*, October 1927.
18. Brownlow, *The Parade's Gone By . . .*, p. 360.
19. *Now We're in the Air* pressbook.
20. John Kobal, *People Will Talk* (New York: Alfred A. Knopf, 1986), p. 79.
21. Kenneth Tynan, *Show People* (New York: Simon and Schuster, 1979), p. 269.
22. Marcella "Tot" Strickler letter to LB, June 4, 1952. Courtesy of Louise Brooks Estate.
23. Myra Brooks, "My Louise," *Screenland*, February 1928. Courtesy of Bill Hutchinson.
24. Eva Calvert letter to LB, October 13, 1952. Courtesy of Louise Brooks Estate.
25. C. M. Black, "Man with a Megaphone," *Collier's*, July 16, 1938.
26. A. Edward Sutherland, unpublished interview transcript, Columbia University Oral History Research Project, February 1959, pp. 111–12.
27. LB, *Lulu in Hollywood*, p. 82.
28. Brownlow, *The Parade's Gone By . . .*, pp. 361–62.
29. LB letter to Kevin Brownlow, October 24, 1966.

9. EVERY LITTLE BREEZE

1. Sidney Carroll to John Barba, Washington, D.C., November 26, 1986.
2. LB, *Lulu in Hollywood* (New York: Alfred A. Knopf, 1982), p. 45.
3. Ibid.
4. Carol Johnston, "Brooksy: A Credit to Kansas," *Motion Picture Classic*, vol. 26, September 1927, pp. 53, 86.

5. John Kobal, *People Will Talk* (New York: Alfred A. Knopf, 1986), p. 94.

6. Kobal, *People Will Talk*, p. 79.

7. John Kobal, *The Art of the Great Hollywood Portrait Photographers, 1925–1940* (New York: Alfred A. Knopf, 1980), p. 16.

8. LB letters to Kevin Brownlow, August 1, 1965, September 28, 1967, and January 11, 1969.

9. *Photoplay*, November 1927.

10. *Bioscope*, Great Britain, March 15, 1928.

11. LB, "Louise Brooks par elle-même," *Objectif*, April–May 1964.

12. Andrew Sarris, *The American Cinema* (New York: E. P. Dutton, 1968), p. 53.

13. *Objectif*, April–May 1964.

14. Kobal, *People Will Talk*, p. 82.

15. Howard Hawks to Kevin Brownlow, quoted in Brownlow letter to LB, August 7, 1967.

16. Henri Langlois, "The Modernity of Howard Hawks," *Cahiers du Cinéma*, January 1963, Editions de l'Étoile & Grove Press, Inc. Translation by Russell Campbell. Reprinted in Joseph McBride, ed., *Focus on Howard Hawks* (Englewood Cliffs, N.J.: Prentice-Hall, 1972).

17. Donald G. Willis, *The Films of Howard Hawks* (Metuchen, N.J.: Scarecrow Press, 1975), p. 102.

18. LB letter to Kevin Brownlow, June 16, 1969.

19. LB, *Lulu in Hollywood*, p. 21.

20. David Robinson, *Chaplin: His Life and Art* (New York: McGraw-Hill, 1985), p. 308.

21. LB letter to Kevin Brownlow, January 12, 1967.

22. LB letter to Kevin Brownlow, November 26, 1966.

23. Ibid.

24. LB, *Lulu in Hollywood*, p. 27.

25. Ibid., p. 30.

26. LB letter to Kevin Brownlow, November 26, 1966.

27. "Actress Studies Clothes Economy," Paramount pressbook for *Beggars of Life*, September 1928.

28. Rebecca L. Bell-Metereau, *Hollywood Androgyny* (New York: Columbia University Press, 1985), pp. 3, 16.

29. Jerry Vermilye, *Films of the Twenties* (Secaucus, N.J.: Citadel Press, 1985), p. 208.

30. LB, *Lulu in Hollywood*, pp. 28–29.

31. LB letter to Kevin Brownlow, January 23, 1967.

32. LB letter to Kevin Brownlow, November 26, 1966.

33. LB letter to Kevin Brownlow, February 10, 1967.

34. LB letter to Kevin Brownlow, August 18, 1967.

35. LB, *Lulu in Hollywood*, p. 31.

36. LB, "Buster Keaton," in Roddy McDowall, ed., *Double Exposure* (New York: Delacorte Press, 1966), p. 161.

37. Quoted in Tom Dardis, *Keaton: The Man Who Wouldn't Lie Down* (New York: Charles Scribner's Sons, 1979), p. 120.

38. Ibid., p. 129.

39. Ibid., p. 146.

40. This quote and account are taken from Dardis, *Keaton*, pp. 168–69, and from LB's "Buster Keaton" in McDowall's *Double Exposure*, p. 161.

41. LB in McDowall, *Double Exposure*, p. 161.

10. "DOES MR. HEARST KNOW THESE PEOPLE ARE HERE?"

1. Marion Davies to Herbert Howe, "The Local Favorite," *Photoplay*, April 1926.

2. LB, *Lulu in Hollywood* (New York: Alfred A. Knopf, 1982), p. 40.

3. Ibid.

4. Orson Welles, foreword to Marion Davies, *The Times We Had: Life with William Randolph Hearst* (Indianapolis: Bobbs-Merrill, 1975).

5. LB, *Lulu in Hollywood*, p. 41.

6. Ibid.

7. Ibid.

8. Davies, *The Times We Had*, pp. 20–21.

9. LB, "Charlie Chaplin Remembered," *Film Culture*, no. 40, Spring 1966, p. 6.

10. Davies, *The Times We Had*, p. 23.

11. LB letter to Theodore Brooks, February 12, 1976.

12. LB letter to Kevin Brownlow, May 7, 1971.

13. Ibid.

14. LB letter to Kevin Brownlow, October 19, 1968.

15. Quoted in LB letter to Kevin Brownlow, June 11, 1969.

16. Quoted by William Klein to BP, Rochester, N.Y., August 25, 1985.

17. Colleen Moore, *Silent Star* (Garden City, N.Y.: Doubleday, 1968), p. 225.

18. Ibid., p. 95.

19. LB letter to Kevin Brownlow, January 18, 1969.

20. Ibid.

21. LB, "Gloria Swanson," unpublished manuscript, January 1957, pp. 1–2.

22. Ibid., p. 6.

23. LB letter to Kevin Brownlow, October 10, 1977.

24. LB, *Lulu in Hollywood*, p. 43.

25. Ibid., p. 44.

26. LB letter to Kevin Brownlow, October 30, 1968.

27. LB, *Lulu in Hollywood*, p. 44.

28. Quoted by Lawrence Quirk, from undated 1960 interview.

29. *Los Angeles Examiner*, May 3, 1928.

30. *Los Angeles Times*, May 3, 1928.

31. LB, *Lulu in Hollywood*, p. 46.
32. Los Angeles *Times*, June 20, 1928.
33. LB, *Lulu in Hollywood*, pp. 46–47.
34. Ibid., p. 21.

11. SOUND AND FURY

1. Quoted in David Robinson, *Chaplin: His Life and Art* (New York: McGraw-Hill, 1985), p. 389.
2. Lothar Wolff, "A Little of Louise Brooks," press release, Nero-Film, 1929. Translated by Wolff, September 1975.
3. LB to John Kobal, *People Will Talk* (New York: Alfred A. Knopf, 1986), p. 92.
4. LB letter to Kevin Brownlow, October 25, 1967.
5. David McClintock, *Indecent Exposure* (New York: William Morrow, 1985), p. 187.
6. Alexander Walker, *The Shattered Silents: How the Talkies Came to Stay* (New York: William Morrow, 1979), p. 130.
7. Kevin Brownlow letter to LB, October 30, 1967.
8. LB letter to Kevin Brownlow, November 8, 1967.
9. Charles Chaplin to Gladys Hall, *Motion Picture Magazine*, March 1929.
10. Robert E. Sherwood, "The Silent Drama," *Life*, October 27, 1927, p. 124.
11. LB, "Pabst and Lulu," *Sight and Sound*, Summer 1965, p. 123, and *Lulu in Hollywood* (New York: Alfred A. Knopf, 1982), p. 100.
12. LB letters to Kevin Brownlow, November 26, 1966, and February 5, 1970.
13. Kevin Brownlow, *The Parade's Gone By . . .* (New York: Alfred A. Knopf, 1968), p. 432.
14. LB, *Lulu in Hollywood*, p. 87.
15. Ibid.
16. Ibid., p. 88.
17. LB letter to Lawrence Quirk, September 17, 1960.
18. Walker, *The Shattered Silents*, p. 143.
19. Ibid., p. 145.
20. Quoted in Alexander Walker, *The Shattered Silents*, epigraph.
21. LB to Kobal, *People Will Talk*, p. 78.
22. LB filmed interview with Kevin Brownlow and David Gill, 1977, transcript, p. 3.
23. LB letter to Theodore Brooks, December 23, 1970.
24. LB filmed interview with Kevin Brownlow and David Gill, 1977, transcript p. 3–4.
25. LB letter to Kevin Brownlow, January 25, 1967.
26. Leatrice Gilbert Fountain, introductory remarks at the Thames Live Cinema Festival screening of *Flesh and the Devil*, Radio City Music Hall, March 6, 1987.
27. Kobal, *People Will Talk*, p. 79.
28. LB letter to Kevin Brownlow, October 19, 1968.
29. LB letter to Kevin Brownlow, July 29, 1977.

30. Walker, *The Shattered Silents*, pp. 169–70.
31. LB to Brownlow, *The Parade's Gone By . . .*, p. 665.
32. Leatrice Gilbert Fountain, with John R. Maxim, *Dark Star* (New York: St. Martin's Press, 1985), p. 184.
33. Kobal, *People Will Talk*, pp. 94–95.
34. Henry Herzblum letter to Louis E. Swarts, September 8, 1926.
35. LB to Ricky Leacock, filmed interview, *Lulu in Berlin* transcript, March 1974, p. 2.
36. LB, *Lulu in Hollywood*, p. 47.

12. THE LEGEND OF LULU

1. Paul Falkenberg, "Six Talks on G. W. Pabst," *Cinemages* 3, May 1955, p. 46.
2. LB, *Lulu in Hollywood* (New York: Alfred A. Knopf, 1982), p. 96
3. Francis Lederer to BP, North Hollywood, California, July 29, 1986.
4. F. J. Stefan, *Der Hamburgischer Correspondent*, October 20, 1928. Translation courtesy of Dr. Allan M. Cress.
5. James Card, "Out of Pandora's Box: Louise Brooks on G. W. Pabst," *Image*, Eastman House, vol. 5, September 1956, p. 133.
6. LB, *Lulu in Hollywood*, pp. 104–5.
7. LB to Ricky Leacock, filmed interview, *Lulu in Berlin* script, March 1974, p. 6.
8. *Film-Illustrierte*, Berlin, October 19, 1928. Translation courtesy of Dr. Allan M. Cress.
9. Francis Lederer to BP.
10. Ibid.
11. LB, *Lulu in Hollywood*, p. 97; originally published in her essay "Pabst and Lulu," *Sight and Sound*, Summer 1965.
12. Sol Gittleman, *Frank Wedekind* (Boston: Twayne, 1969), p. xii.
13. Haskell Block and Robert Shedd, *Masters of Modern Drama* (New York: Random House), 1962.
14. Bertolt Brecht, *Augsburger Neueste Nachrichten*, March 12, 1918.
15. Padraic Colum, *Orpheus: Myths of the World* (New York: Macmillan, 1930), pp. 67–73.
16. Günter Seehaus, *Wedekind und das Theater*, Munich, 1964. The quotation, and aspects of this analysis of the Lulu character, are found in Gittleman, *Frank Wedekind*, p. 65ff.
17. Thomas Elsaesser, "Lulu and the Meter Man," in *German Film and Literature*, ed. Eric Rentschler (New York: Methuen, 1986), p. 49.
18. Gittleman, *Frank Wedekind*, p. 68.
19. LB, "Pabst and Lulu," p. 124.
20. Card, "Out of Pandora's Box."
21. LB to Leacock, *Lulu in Berlin* transcript, p. 28.
22. Card, "Out of Pandora's Box."
23. *Film-Illustrierte*, Berlin, November 16, 1928. Translation courtesy of Dr. Allan M. Cress.
24. LB, *Lulu in Hollywood*, p. 99.

25. LB, "Pabst and Lulu."
26. LB to James Card, quoted in James Card, "The 'Intense Isolation' of Louise Brooks," *Sight and Sound* 27, no. 5, Summer 1958, p. 242.
27. LB, "Als ich mit Pabst arbeitete" ["My work with Mr. Pabst"], in *Der Regisseur: G. W. Pabst*, ed. Rudolph S. Joseph (Munich: Münchener Photo und Filmmuseum, 1964). Quoted in Lee G. Atwell, *G. W. Pabst* (Boston: Twayne, 1977), p. 53.
28. LB, *Lulu in Hollywood*, pp. 96, 102.
29. Ibid., pp. 101–2.
30. Quoted in Lincoln Kirstein, *Dance: A Short History of Classic Theatrical Dancing* (New York: G. P. Putnam's Sons, 1935), p. 320. Courtesy of George C. Pratt.
31. LB to Leacock, *Lulu in Berlin* transcript, p. 26.
32. LB, *Lulu in Hollywood*, p. 105, and LB to John Kobal, *People Will Talk* (New York: Alfred A. Knopf, 1986), p. 92.
33. LB, *Lulu in Hollywood*, pp. 98, 100.
34. LB, "Actors and the Pabst Spirit," *Focus on Film*, no. 8, February 1971, p. 46.
35. LB, *Lulu in Hollywood*, pp. 98–99.
36. Ibid., p. 99.
37. Lotte Eisner, *Ich hatte einst ein schönes Vaterland: Memoiren* (Heidelberg: Verlag das Wunderhorn, 1984), p. 88. Translation courtesy of Dr. Allan M. Cress.
38. Ibid., p. 95.
39. LB, "Actors and the Pabst Spirit," p. 46.
40. Dale Harris, "Silents Speaking Loudly," *Performing Arts* 17, no. 12, December 1983.
41. David Diamond to BP, quoting a cast member, September 14, 1988.
42. LB, *Lulu in Hollywood*, p. 101.
43. Ibid., p. 99.
44. LB to Leacock, *Lulu in Berlin* transcript, p. 14.
45. Ibid., p. 6.
46. LB, "Pabst and Lulu," p. 127.
47. LB, *Lulu in Hollywood*, p. 100.
48. Ibid.
49. LB to Leacock, *Lulu in Berlin* transcript, pp. 11–12.
50. Francis Lederer to BP.
51. Lothar Wolff to BP, New York City, January 28, 1986.
52. LB, *Lulu in Hollywood*, p. 95.
53. Ibid.
54. LB, "Actors and the Pabst Spirit," p. 46.
55. LB, *Lulu in Hollywood*, pp. 103–4, and LB to Leacock, *Lulu in Berlin* transcript, p. 16.
56. LB, "Actors and the Pabst Spirit," p. 46, and LB to Leacock, *Lulu in Berlin* transcript, p. 17.
57. LB to Leacock, *Lulu in Berlin* transcript, p. 17.
58. LB, *Lulu in Hollywood*, p. 98.
59. Ibid., p. 104.

60. A. Kraszna-Krausz, "G. W. Pabst's 'Lulu,' " *Close Up*, April 1929, p. 26.
61. Atwell, *G. W. Pabst*, p. 62.
62. Quoted in LB, *Lulu in Hollywood*, p. 95.
63. Ibid.
64. Lotte Eisner, *L'Écran demoniaque* (Paris: Terrain Vague 1952).
65. Lotte Eisner, *The Haunted Screen: Expressionism in the German Cinema and the Influence of Max Reinhardt* (Berkeley: University of California, 1969), p. 296.
66. LB letter to Kevin Brownlow, February 23, 1966.
67. Kraszna-Krausz, "G. W. Pabst's 'Lulu,' " pp. 27–28.
68. G. W. Pabst, "Servitude et grandeur de Hollywood," in *Le rôle intellectuel du cinéma*, Cahier 3, Paris: Institut international de cooperation culturelle, 1937.
69. Kobal, *People Will Talk*, p. 81.
70. James Card, "Cinema 16 Film Notes," April 29, 1959.
71. Kenneth Tynan, *Show People* (New York: Simon and Schuster, 1979), p. 240.
72. Gittleman, *Frank Wedekind*, p. 79.
73. LB to Leacock, *Lulu in Berlin* transcript, p. 5.
74. LB letter to Patrice Hovald, April 28, 1969; published in *L'Alsace*, July 17, 1969.
75. Arthur Jacobson to BP, Los Angeles, January 18, 1987.
76. Quoted in Alexander Walker, *The Shattered Silents: How the Talkies Came to Stay* (New York: William Morrow, 1979), p. 133.
77. LB letter to Patrice Hovald.
78. Walker, *The Shattered Silents: How the Talkies Came to Stay*, p. 135.
79. LB, "Out of Pandora's Box," p. 136.
80. Card, "Out of Pandora's Box," p. 135.

13. THE LOST GIRL

1. LB to Ricky Leacock, filmed interview, *Lulu in Berlin* transcript, March 1974, pp. 19–20.
2. Ibid., p. 21.
3. Ibid., p. 23.
4. Ibid., p. 21.
5. John Kobal, *People Will Talk* (New York: Alfred A. Knopf, 1986), pp. 92–93.
6. LB to Leacock, *Lulu in Berlin* transcript, pp. 21–23.
7. Kenneth Tynan, *Show People* (New York: Simon and Schuster, 1979), p. 275.
8. Ibid.
9. LB letter to Kevin Brownlow, October 25, 1967.
10. LB to Leacock, *Lulu in Berlin* transcript, p. 24.
11. Tynan, p. 276.
12. LB letter to Kevin Brownlow, February 10, 1968.
13. LB letter to Kevin Brownlow, October 22, 1966.

14. LB letter to Kevin Brownlow, December 5, 1966.
15. LB to Leacock, *Lulu in Berlin* transcript, p. 25.
16. LB, "Actors and the Pabst Spirit," *Focus on Film*, no. 8, February 1972, p. 46.
17. Ibid.
18. LB to Leacock, *Lulu in Berlin* transcript, p. 27.
19. LB letter to Kevin Brownlow, September 5, 1967.
20. Siegfried Kracauer, *From Caligari to Hitler: A Psychological History of the German Film* (Princeton, N.J.: Princeton University Press, 1947), p. 179.
21. Ibid.
22. Rudolf Leonhardt letter to Lotte Eisner, September 17, 1953.
23. *Variety*, November 13, 1929. Courtesy of George Pratt.
24. Henri Langlois, catalogue for "60 Ans de Cinéma," Cinémathèque Française, Paris, 1955.
25. Tynan, p. 256.
26. Lee G. Atwell, *G. W. Pabst* (Boston: Twayne, 1977), p. 70.
27. James Card to BP, Rochester, N.Y., September 16, 1985.
28. LB to Leacock, *Lulu in Berlin* transcript, p. 8.
29. Ibid., pp. 28–30.
30. LB letter to Kevin Brownlow, April 29, 1969.
31. Tynan, pp. 275–76.
32. LB, *Lulu in Hollywood*, pp. 105–6.
33. James Card, "The 'Intense Isolation' of Louise Brooks," *Sight and Sound* 27, no. 5, Summer 1958, p. 242.
34. LB, *Lulu in Hollywood*, pp. 97–98.

14. BEAUTY PRIZE

1. Wichita *Beacon*, May 6, 1956.
2. James Card, Eastman House lecture, Rochester, N.Y., November 10, 1986.
3. Cedric Belfrage, *Motion Picture Magazine*, February 1930.
4. Quoted in Catherine Ann Surowiec, Museum of Modern Art program notes for *Prix de Beauté*, 1981.
5. Pierre Leprohon, *The Italian Cinema* (London: Secker & Warburg, 1972). Originally published in Paris by Editions Seghers in 1966.
6. Douglas McVay, "The Goddesses," *Films and Filming*, August 1965, p. 6.
7. *Variety*, September 3, 1930, p. 44. Courtesy of George Pratt.
8. James Card to BP, Rochester, N.Y., September 16, 1985.
9. Jan Wahl, "Louise Brooks: Rising Star, Falling Star," Part 2, *Movie & Film Collector's World*, no. 166, August 5, 1983.
10. James Card to BP.
11. Quoted in *Il Divismo: mitologia del cinema*, by Giulio Cesare Castello (Torino: Edizioni Radio Italiana [RAI], 1957), p. 169–70. Translation courtesy of John Barba and David Diamond.
12. James Card to BP.
13. Catherine Ann Surowiec, program notes.
14. Ado Kyrou, *Amour-érotisme et cinéma* (Paris: Terrain Vague, 1957; revised, 1967).
15. Jan Wahl, *Louise Brooks*.
16. James Card to BP.
17. LB letter to Kevin Brownlow, July 11, 1967.
18. June Brooks Lashley to BP, October 10, 1988.
19. John Kobal, *People Will Talk* (New York: Alfred A. Knopf, 1986), pp. 91–92.
20. John Roberts, *Classic Images*, no. 92, February 1983.

15. BOOBY PRIZE

1. LB letter to Theodore Brooks, August 18, 1972.
2. William S. Paley, *As It Happened* (Garden City, N.Y.: Doubleday, 1979), p. 35.
3. William Paley to BP, New York, September 12, 1988.
4. Ibid.
5. LB letter to Herman Weinberg, April 27, 1977.
6. New York *Daily News*, January 10, 1930, and New York *Mirror*, January 10, 1930.
7. James Card, "The 'Intense Isolation' of Louise Brooks," *Sight and Sound* 27, no. 5, Summer 1958, p. 244.
8. Louella Parsons, the New York *American*, August 2, 1930.
9. James Card, p. 244.
10. LB, *Lulu in Hollywood* (New York: Alfred A. Knopf, 1982), p. 7.
11. LB letter to George Pratt, September 18, 1969.
12. Los Angeles *Times*, October 5, 1930.
13. "Along the Rialto," *Film Daily*, October 10, 1930.
14. LB, "Marlene," *Positif*, no. 75, May 1966.
15. Ibid.
16. Ibid.
17. John Kobal, *People Will Talk* (New York: Alfred A. Knopf, 1986), p. 528.
18. Ibid., pp. 532, 527
19. LB, "Why I Will Never Write My Memoirs," *Focus on Film*, March 1978.
20. Kevin Brownlow, *The Parade's Gone By . . .* (New York: Alfred A. Knopf, 1968), p. 363.
21. William K. Everson, "Remembering Louise Brooks," *Films in Review*, November 1985, p. 535.
22. LB letter to Kevin Brownlow, April 11, 1969.
23. *Variety*, April 22, 1931, p. 18.

24. Everson, p. 535.
25. LB, *Lulu in Hollywood*, p. 21.
26. Ibid.
27. James Card to BP, Rochester, N.Y., September 16, 1985.
28. Brooks Atkinson, *New York Times*, November 13, 1931.
29. LB, *Lulu in Hollywood*, p. 63.
30. LB letter to Kevin Brownlow, August 23, 1966.
31. New York *Daily News*, February 10, 1932.
32. LB letter to George Pratt, September 18, 1969.
33. Ibid.
34. Kobal, p. 80.
35. Ibid., p. 90.
36. James Card to BP.
37. "Lipstick" (Lois Long), *The New Yorker*, November 24, 1934, p. 32.
38. *Variety*, April 17, 1935, p. 18. Courtesy of George Pratt.
39. LB letter to Kevin Brownlow, July 7, 1971.
40. LB, *Lulu in Hollywood*, p. 47.
41. Ibid., p. 51.
42. Ibid., pp. 35–36.
43. Everson, p. 535.
44. William Paley to BP.
45. James Card to BP.
46. LB letter to Kevin Brownlow, October 25, 1969.
47. Shirley Povich, "Marshall: Impresario of the Redskins," Washington *Post*, September 2, 1986.
48. Art Rooney to BP, Pittsburgh, Pa., July 10, 1986.
49. Quoted in James Watters, *Return Engagement: Faces to Remember—Then and Now* (New York: Clarkson N. Potter, 1984), p. 26.
50. Leonard Viner to BP, July 19, 1987.
51. LB letters to James Card, August 24 and November 22, 1955.
52. Kobal, p. 80.
53. LB letter to Herman Weinberg, October 31, 1974.
54. Jan-Christopher Horak, "G. W. Pabst in Hollywood, or Every Modern Hero Deserves a Mother," *Film History*, vol. 1, 1987.
55. LB letter to Herman Weinberg, February 11, 1976.
56. Horak, "G. W. Pabst in Hollywood."
57. LB, "Louise Brooks par elle-même," *Objectif*, February–March 1964.
58. LB, *Lulu in Hollywood*, p. 67.
59. Ibid., p. 68.
60. Universal Studios pressbook for *Empty Saddles*, 1937.
61. LB, *Lulu in Hollywood*, p. 75.
62. LB letter to Kevin Brownlow, October 19, 1968.
63. LB, "Stardom and Evelyn Brent," Toronto Film Society Program, January 13, 1975.

64. Paramount pressbook for *King of Gamblers*, May 3, 1937, p. 4.
65. Everson, p. 536.
66. James Card, "The 'Intense Isolation' of Louise Brooks," p. 244.
67. LB letter to Herman Weinberg, January 8, 1977.
68. LB letter to James Card, November 23, 1955.
69. LB, "Duke by Divine Right," introduction to Allen Eyles, *John Wayne* (Cranbury, N.J.: A. S. Barnes, 1976).
70. LB to Kevin Brownlow, November 15, 1968.
71. Ibid. In a postscript, Louise added: "The above reads as if Barbara's suicide was connected with Mdivani. It wasn't. She was a little lost girl who was fatally attracted to the brutes who destroyed her."
72. LB, "Why I Will Never Write My Memoirs," p. 34.
73. Kobal, p. 82.
74. LB letter to James Card, December 1, 1955.
75. Ibid.
76. Los Angeles *Times*, June 15, 1940.
77. Wichita *Beacon*, June 19, 1940.
78. Kenneth Tynan, *Show People* (New York: Simon and Schuster, 1979), p. 261–62.

16. LULU IN PURGATORY

1. Kenneth Tynan, *Show People* (New York: Simon and Schuster, 1979), p. 262.
2. Theodore Brooks letter to LB, undated (ca. 1967).
3. Marcella "Tot" Strickler letters to LB, February 11 and June 4, 1952.
4. Robert Brooks to BP, January 15, 1987.
5. Eva Calvert letter to LB, October 13, 1952.
6. LB, "Joan Crawford," unpublished manuscript, February 1957.
7. LB letter to James Card, January 7, 1956.
8. Hal McCoy to BP, Wichita, Kansas, June 18, 1986.
9. Louise Brooks, "The Fundamentals of Good Ballroom Dancing," Wichita, Kansas (1940), privately published, p. 9.
10. Ibid., pp. 14–15.
11. Ibid., pp. 33–35.
12. Hal McCoy to BP, Wichita, Kansas, September 4, 1986.
13. James Kiefner to BP, Wichita, Kansas, June 18, 1987.
14. Ibid.
15. Dan Aikman to BP, September 17, 1986.
16. Charles Cagle, "Louise Brooks and the Road to Oz," *The Little Balkans Review*, 3, no. 1, Fall 1982, pp. 14–15.
17. Jimmy Cavaness to BP, September 27, 1987.
18. General Statutes of Kansas, 1935, Chapter 21, Article 9, no. 21-908, "Adultery; inde-

cency; lewd cohabitation; penalty." Courtesy of Daniel R. Rouser.

19. Tynan, *Show People*, p. 262.

20. Theodore Brooks letter to LB, August 10, 1969.

21. Betty Strickler (surname unknown) to LB, undated, ca. 1952.

22. LB letter to James Card, December 1, 1955.

17. LULU IN HELL

1. James Card, "The 'Intense Isolation' of Louise Brooks," *Sight and Sound* 27, no. 5, Summer 1958, p. 244.

2. LB letter to Kevin Brownlow, September 14, 1968.

3. Card, "The 'Intense Isolation' of Louise Brooks."

4. William S. Paley to BP, New York City, September 12, 1988.

5. LB letter to James Card, August 24, 1955.

6. LB letter to Kevin Brownlow, February 21, 1968.

7. Lothar Wolff to BP, New York, March 29, 1986.

8. John Kobal, *People Will Talk* (New York: Alfred A. Knopf, 1986), p. 84. A transcription error in Kobal's excellent interview has Louise at lunch with "a local wolf" instead of "Lothar Wolff."

9. James Card, "Out of Pandora's Box: Louise Brooks on G. W. Pabst," *Image* 5, George Eastman House, September 1956.

10. LB to Ricky Leacock, filmed interview, *Lulu in Berlin*, transcript, March 1974, p. 35.

11. Lotte Eisner letter to LB, December 18, 1977.

12. LB letter to James Card, September 14, 1955.

13. Kenneth Tynan, *Show People* (New York: Simon and Schuster, 1979), p. 262.

14. LB letter to Kevin Brownlow, November 16, 1968.

15. LB letter to Kevin Brownlow, November 14, 1968.

16. Theodore Brooks to LB, September 21, 1967.

17. LB letter to Kevin Brownlow, September 16, 1966.

18. Quoted in *Lulu in Hollywood*, p. 65.

19. LB to Kevin Brownlow, August 25, 1966.

20. Theodore Brooks to BP, Wichita, Kansas, July 1969.

21. LB letter to Herman Weinberg, January 21, 1977.

22. LB letter to Kevin Brownlow, October 25, 1969.

23. James Card to BP, Naples, N.Y., April 23, 1987.

24. LB, *Lulu in Hollywood* (New York: Alfred A. Knopf, 1982), p. 99.

25. LB letter to Herman Weinberg, January 19, 1977.

26. LB letter to Kevin Brownlow, October 19, 1968.

27. LB letter to Kevin Brownlow, April 29, 1969.

28. LB letter to Herman Weinberg, January 14, 1974.

29. LB letter to Herman Weinberg, January 8, 1977.

30. LB letter to Kevin Brownlow, February 10, 1967.

31. LB letter to Kevin Brownlow, October 24, 1968.

32. LB letter to Kevin Brownlow, October 25, 1968.

33. Lothar Wolff to BP, New York, January 28, 1986.

34. LB letter to Kevin Brownlow, October 25, 1969.

35. Kobal, *People Will Talk*, p. 681.

36. LB letter to James Card, October 29, 1955.

37. William Klein to BP, Rochester, N.Y., August 25, 1985, and October 31, 1988.

38. LB, *Lulu in Hollywood*, p. 13.

39. Larry Quirk to BP, New York, March 30, 1986.

40. Danny Aikman to BP, telephone interview, September 17, 1986.

41. LB, "Amateur Night in Greenwich Village," unpublished story in manuscript, undated.

42. Jane Sherman and Barton Mumaw, *Barton Mumaw, Dancer* (New York: Dance Horizons, 1986), pp. 222–23.

43. LB letter to Herman Weinberg, October 12, 1977.

44. Tynan, *Show People*, p. 262.

45. John Springer to BP, New York, July 14, 1986.

46. LB letter to Ricky Leacock, September 19, 1977.

47. John Springer to BP.

48. LB letters to Kevin Brownlow, August 23 and September 10, 1966.

49. Kobal, *People Will Talk*, p. 90.

50. LB letter to James Card, November 24, 1955.

51. LB letter to James Card, November 23, 1955.

52. LB letter to Dr. Ludwig Gesek, Austrian Society for Film Sciences, February 11, 1974.

53. Herman G. Weinberg, "G. W. Pabst to Dramatize Hitler's Last Days," *New York Times*, March 19, 1950.

54. The Musmanno papers are courtesy of curator William Spinelli of the Michael A. Musmanno Collection, Duquesne University, Pittsburgh, Pennsylvania. The author wishes to acknowledge other valuable comments and insights provided by Claire G. Paris, Justice Musmanno's private secretary.

55. Lothar Wolff to BP, January 28, 1986.

56. Tynan, *Show People*, p. 262.

57. LB letter to Kevin Brownlow, September 5, 1967.

58. Notes courtesy of Louise Brooks Estate, Rochester, N.Y.

59. LB letter to Marcella "Tot" Strickler, February 11, 1952.

60. LB letter to James Card, September 14, 1955.

61. LB, "Why I Will Never Write My Memoirs," *Focus on Film*, March 1978, p. 34.

62. John Springer to BP.

63. Quoted in LB letter to James Card, December 18, 1955.

64. LB letter to James Card, January 7, 1956.

65. LB letter to James Card, October 29, 1955.

66. LB letter to Kevin Brownlow, July 8, 1969.

67. LB, "ZaSu Pitts," *Objectif*, August 1963, published in French in Montreal. The article was never published in English, and the original has been lost. The retranslation from the French is by Teri Vosco and BP. Cautionary note: Nothing is more perilous than translating a translated article back into its language of origin. In the 1986 reissue of *Louise Brooks: Portrait d'une anti-star*, for example, the American publishers were unaware that Louise's "Actors and the Pabst Spirit" existed in English. In their retranslation, Frank Tuttle's characterization of Louise as "Babbling Brooks" becomes "Brooks the Chatterbox"—and is rendered senseless.

68. LB letter to Herman Weinberg, April 27, 1977.

69. LB letter to Kevin Brownlow, June 23, 1967.

70. LB letter to James Card, January 8, 1956.

18. RESURRECTION

1. Glenn Myrent, *Henri Langlois: Premier citoyen du cinéma* (Paris: pub. 1986), p. 262.

2. James Card, "Out of Pandora's Box: Louise Brooks on G. W. Pabst," *Image*, September 1956.

3. Henri Langlois, catalogue for "60 Ans de Cinéma," Cinémathèque Française, Paris, 1955.

4. Ado Kyrou, *Amour-érotisme et cinéma* (Paris: Terrain Vague, 1957; revised, 1967) p. 282.

5. James Card, "The 'Intense Isolation' of Louise Brooks," *Sight and Sound* 27, no. 5, Summer 1958, p. 241.

6. John Springer to BP, New York City, July 14, 1986.

7. Quoted in James Card, "The 'Intense Isolation' of Louise Brooks," pp. 241-42.

8. LB letters to James Card, August 24 and September 14, 1955.

9. Card, "The 'Intense Isolation' of Louise Brooks," p. 242.

10. James Card to BP, September 16, 1985.

11. LB letter to James Card, October 30, 1955.

12. LB letter to James Card, November 3, 1955.

13. Ibid.

14. LB letter to James Card, November 24, 1955.

15. LB letter to James Card, November 26, 1955.

16. LB letter to James Card, November 27, 1955.

17. LB letter to James Card, November 29, 1955.

18. LB letter to James Card, December 19, 1955.

19. LB letter to James Card, January 7, 1956.

20. LB letter to James Card, December 22, 1955.

21. LB letter to James Card, January 8, 1956.

22. LB letter to James Card, February 5, 1956.

23. LB letter to James Card, February 6, 1956.

24. John Minary to BP, New York, December 31, 1987.

25. Marilynn Gump to BP, telephone interview, July 1988.

26. James Card to BP, Rochester and Naples, N.Y., September 16, 1985, and subsequent conversations.

27. Ed Sullivan to James Card, September 17, 1957.

28. James Card, "The 'Intense Isolation' of Louise Brooks," p. 243.

29. LB to Rex O'Malley, quoted in Card, "The 'Intense Isolation' of Louise Brooks," p. 243.

30. LB, "Joan Crawford," unpublished manuscript, February 1957.

31. LB, "Gloria Swanson," unpublished manuscript, January 1957.

32. Quoted in LB letter to George Pratt, November 4, 1959.

33. LB letters to Lawrence Quirk, August 31 and September 9, 1960.

34. Quoted in LB letter to George Pratt, June 22, 1959.

35. Lillian Gish to BP, New York, March 5, 1987.

36. Ib Monty to BP, Copenhagen, March 30, 1987.

37. Jan Wahl to BP, Toledo, Ohio, May 24, 1987.

38. LB letter to Ove Brusendorff, December 20, 1957.

39. James Card to BP, Naples, N.Y., December 5, 1987.

40. LB to Richard Roud, *A Passion for Films: Henri Langlois and the Cinémathèque Française* (New York: Viking Press, 1983), pp. 101-2.

41. LB letter to Kevin Brownlow, March 6, 1967.

42. Robert Benayoun to BP, Paris, France, April 3, 1987.

43. LB letter to Kevin Brownlow, November 8, 1967.

44. LB letter to Kevin Brownlow, October 30, 1975.

45. LB letter to Patrice Hovald, April 28, 1969, published in *L'Alsace*, July 17, 1969. The "lesbian" sentence was edited out.
46. LB letter to Kevin Brownlow, October 30, 1975.
47. Jan Wahl to BP.
48. LB letter to Herman Weinberg, May 3, 1977.
49. LB letter to Jeffrey Rolick, January 24, 1969.
50. Rochester *Democrat and Chronicle*, September 28, 1962.
51. LB letter to June Brooks Lashley, April 16, 1962.
52. Reverend Paul Burkort to BP, telephone interview, October 8, 1987.
53. George Pratt to BP, Victor, New York, November 25, 1986.
54. LB letter to Jan Wahl, October 18, 1964.
55. LB letter to Jeffrey Rolick, January 24, 1969.
56. LB letter to James Card, September 30, 1959.
57. LB letter to Kevin Brownlow, January 18, 1966.
58. LB letter to Kevin Brownlow, May 11, 1966.
59. LB letter to Kevin Brownlow, July 25, 1966.
60. LB to Kevin Brownlow, p. 9 of interview transcript. The passage was removed at Louise's request from Brownlow's first draft.
61. LB letter to Kevin Brownlow, September 30, 1966.
62. LB letter to Kevin Brownlow, December 5, 1966.
63. LB letter to Kevin Brownlow, April 29, 1969.
64. John Kobal, *People Will Talk* (New York: Alfred A. Knopf, 1986), pp. 86-87.
65. Ibid.
66. Quoted in "Editor's Eyrie" column of *English Cahiers du Cinéma*, no. 3, 1966, p. 67.
67. LB letter to Herman Weinberg, May 14, 1966.
68. James Card to BP, October 25, 1987.
69. LB letter to James Card, August 24, 1955.
70. LB letter to Herman Weinberg, February 23, 1962.
71. LB letter to Kevin Brownlow, September 27, 1966.
72. LB letter to Herman Weinberg, November 9, 1977.
73. LB letter to Theodore Brooks, December 23, 1970.
74. Roddy McDowall to BP, telephone interview, September 16, 1988.
75. LB, "Humphrey and Bogey," *Sight and Sound*, Winter 1966–1967.
76. Ibid.
77. Lauren Bacall to BP, New York City, March 7, 1986.
78. LB letter to Kevin Brownlow, November 15, 1966.
79. LB letter to Patricia Calvert, September 19, 1967.
80. LB letter to Kevin Brownlow, January 3, 1967.

19. LOUISE & THEO

1. Theodore Brooks letter to LB, December [no date], 1952.
2. Margaret Brooks to BP, Wichita, Kansas, September 8, 1986.
3. LB letter to Theodore Brooks, March 4, 1974.
4. LB letter to Patrice Hovald, April 28, 1969, published in *L'Alsace*, July 17, 1969.
5. Quoted by Clyde Gilmour, Toronto *Telegram*, September 7, 1968.
6. LB letter to Kevin Brownlow, August 18, 1969.
7. LB letter to Kevin Brownlow, March 11, 1969.
8. LB letter to Theodore Brooks, August 31, 1971.
9. LB letter to Theodore Brooks, November 1, 1972.
10. LB letter to Theodore Brooks, October 14, 1974.
11. LB letters to Kevin Brownlow, January 11, 1969, March 11, 1969, and November 21, 1977.
12. LB letter to Theodore Brooks, August 31, 1971.
13. LB letter to Theodore Brooks, March 12, 1971.
14. LB letter to Theodore Brooks, October 8, 1971.
15. LB letter to Theodore Brooks, February 12, 1976.
16. LB letter to Theodore Brooks, October 1, 1975.
17. Roddy McDowall to BP, telephone interview, September 16, 1988.
18. David Diamond to BP, New York City, September 14, 1988.
19. Ibid.
20. Ibid.
21. Theodore Brooks letter to LB, October 16, 1976.
22. LB letter to Theodore Brooks, October 25, 1976.
23. Theodore Brooks letter to June Brooks Lashley, November 24, 1976.
24. Theodore Brooks letter to LB, November 16, 1976.
25. Theodore Brooks letter to LB, December 24, 1976.
26. Margaret Brooks to BP, Wichita, Kansas, September 8, 1986.

20. THE CULT

1. LB to John Kobal, *People Will Talk* (New York: Alfred A. Knopf, 1986), p. 85.
2. Kevin Brownlow letter to LB, October 30, 1967.

3. Louise Brooks, "Actors and the Pabst Spirit," *Focus on Film*, no. 8, February 1971, p. 45.

4. Douglas McVay, "The Goddesses," *Films and Filming*, August 1965, p. 6.

5. Henry Clune column, "Seen and Heard," Rochester *Democrat and Chronicle*, October 25, 1959.

6. LB letter to George Pratt, November 4, 1959.

7. Kevin Brownlow, *The Parade's Gone By . . .* (New York: Alfred A. Knopf, 1968), p. 356.

8. S. J. Perelman, "She Walks in Beauty—Single File, Eyes Front, and No Hanky-Panky," *The New Yorker*, February 22, 1969, pp. 32-34.

9. S. J. Perelman letter to LB, April 10, 1969.

10. LB, *Lulu in Hollywood* (New York: Alfred A. Knopf, 1982), pp. 45-46.

11. Bill Klein to BP, Rochester, New York, August 25, 1985.

12. LB letter to Ricky Leacock, January 31, 1974.

13. LB letter to Ricky Leacock, March 19, 1974.

14. Ricky Leacock to BP, Cambridge, Mass., August 11, 1986.

15. LB letter to Guido Crepax, January 7, 1976. Retranslation courtesy of John Barba.

16. LB letter to Guido Crepax, May 3, 1976. Retranslation courtesy of John Barba.

17. LB letter to Herman Weinberg, August 23, 1977.

18. LB letters to Herman Weinberg, October 6 and 8, 1977.

19. Kenneth Tynan, *Show People* (New York: Simon and Schuster, 1979), p. 232. Originally "Louise Brooks: The Girl in the Black Helmet," reprinted from *The New Yorker*, June 11, 1979.

20. Roddy McDowall to BP, telephone interview, September 16, 1988.

21. LB letter to Kevin Brownlow, December 25, 1977.

22. LB letter to Kevin Brownlow, October 24, 1977.

23. LB letter to Herman Weinberg, March 15, 1978.

24. LB letter to Herman Weinberg, April 18, 1978.

25. LB letters to Kevin Brownlow, April 18 and May 29, 1978.

26. Adolph Green to BP, New York City, October 20, 1986.

27. Donald McNamara letter to BP, January 10, 1987.

28. Quoted in Kathleen Tynan, *The Life of Kenneth Tynan* (New York: William Morrow, 1987), p. 487.

29. Donald McNamara, "A Conversation with Louise Brooks," *The Missouri Review*, no. 3, Summer 1983, pp. 68-69.

30. LB letter to Kevin Brownlow, June 13, 1979.

31. Quoted in James Watters, *Return Engagement; Faces to Remember—Then and Now* (New York: Clarkson N. Potter, 1984), p. 26.

32. LB letter to Kevin Brownlow, June 10, 1978.

33. Kathleen Tynan, *The Life of Kenneth Tynan*, p. 499.

34. LB letter to Kevin Brownlow, September 19, 1978.

35. Kathleen Tynan, *The Life of Kenneth Tynan*, p. 492.

36. Kenneth Tynan letter to LB, August 25, 1979.

37. LB letter to Robert Lantz, September 20, 1979.

38. LB letter to William Shawn, September 24, 1979.

39. LB letters to Ricky Leacock, March 21 and 22, 1979.

40. LB letter to Ricky Leacock, September 20, 1979.

41. LB letter to Kevin Brownlow, September 22, 1979.

42. LB letter to Kevin Brownlow, January 29, 1966.

43. Morgan Wesson to BP, Rochester, N.Y., September 16, 1985.

44. LB letter to Kevin Brownlow, December 29, 1979.

45. LB letter to Kevin Brownlow, February 11, 1980.

46. LB letters to Herman Weinberg, April 6, 1977, and March 15, 1978.

47. LB letter to Kevin Brownlow, January 12, 1966.

48. Anita Loos, "Louise Brooks," *Vogue*, September 1981, p. 374.

49. LB letter to Kevin Brownlow, August 15, 1966.

50. LB letter to Kevin Brownlow, October 18, 1969.

51. LB letter to Kevin Brownlow, March 31, 1980.

52. William Shawn letter to BP, May 29, 1986.

53. LB letter to Kevin Brownlow, January 4, 1981.

54. William Shawn, introduction to LB, *Lulu in Hollywood*.

55. Robert Gottlieb letter to BP, November 16, 1987.

56. *London Review of Books*, August 5–18, 1982, p. 21.

57. *Variety*, June 9, 1982, pp. 4, 35.

58. *Esquire*, May 1982.

59. *Newsweek*, May 24, 1982.

60. Los Angeles *Weekly*, June 25–July 1, 1982.

61. William Paley to BP, New York, September 12, 1988.

62. Auberon Waugh, London *Daily Mail*, July 15, 1982.

63. Alexander Walker, undated 1983 letter to Lawrence Quirk.

64. Eddie Sutherland, quoted by Lawrence Quirk, *Quirk's Reviews*, June 1982.

65. LB letter to Theodore Brooks, August 31, 1971. The passage referred to in the Fields article: "In the '60s, many schoolboys wrote to me and came to see me. Most of them knew only my name and had never seen any of my films. They approached me with wildly uninformed flattery, after which, presuming me to be a forlorn old actress full of gratitude, they expected me to fill their arms with my most precious still pictures and sit three hours at the typewriter composing material that they could muck about, sign with their names, and present to the teachers of their film classes."

66. London *Evening Standard*, July 15, 1982.

67. *Women's Wear Daily*, October 22, 1982.

68. *New York Times*, February 8, 1984.

69. LB letter to Herman Weinberg, December 17, 1976.

70. LB letter to Patrice Hovald, April 28, 1969, published in *L'Alsace*, July 17, 1969.

71. LB letter to James Price, Secker & Warburg, London, May 8, 1968, carbon copied to George Pratt.

72. Reprinted in Veronica Geng, *Partners* (New York: Perennial Library, 1985).

73. LB letter to Theodore Brooks, June 25, 1973.

74. LB letter to George Pratt, March 15, 1968.

75. LB letter to Kevin Brownlow, September 16, 1966.

76. LB letter to Jeffrey Rolick, January 24, 1969.

77. Ross Berkal to BP, Boston, August 8, 1986.

78. LB letter to Theodore Brooks, August 18, 1972.

79. LB letters to Kevin Brownlow, November 15 and December 25, 1966.

80. Arthur Bell, "Where Gays Are Going," *The Village Voice*, June 29, 1982, p. 1.

81. Kobal, *People Will Talk*, pp. 83-85.

82. Ibid., pp. 89-90.

83. LB letter to Kevin Brownlow, August 4, 1967.

84. LB to Kobal, *People Will Talk*, p. 85.

85. LB letter to Jane Sherman, September 10, 1979.

86. LB to Ricky Leacock, filmed interview, *Lulu in Berlin* transcript, March 1974, pp. 33-34.

87. LB to Hovald.

88. Roddy McDowall to BP, telephone interview, September 16, 1988.

89. LB letter to Herman Weinberg, August 1, 1977.

21. THE END

1. John Benz to BP, Greece, N.Y., November 11, 1986.

2. Dr. Joseph Stankitis to BP, telephone interview, November 1, 1988.

3. Barbara Mayberry to BP, Rochester, N.Y., April 26, 1987.

4. Kevin Brownlow letter to LB, August 18, 1966.

5. LB letter to Kevin Brownlow, August 23, 1966.

6. Richard Hellman letter to Barbara Mayberry, July 15, 1980.

7. Bill Klein to BP, Greece, N.Y., August 25, 1985.

8. Jack Garner, "Curtain Calls from a Hollywood Past," Rochester *Democrat and Chronicle*, November 7, 1982.

9. Barbara Mayberry to BP.

10. Joan Rivers, *The Hollywood Reporter*, June 11, 1982.

11. Bill Klein to BP.

12. Joan Rivers to BP, Pittsburgh, Pa., April 6, 1986.

13. Barbara Mayberry to BP.

14. *New York Times*, September 16, 1983.

15. Ricky Leacock to BP, Boston, Mass., August 11, 1986.

16. William Cuseo to BP, Rochester, N.Y., May 18, 1987.

17. David Robinson, *Chaplin: His Life and Art* (New York: McGraw-Hill, 1985), p. 514.

18. James Card diary entry, July 9, 1983.

19. John Kobal, *People Will Talk* (New York: Alfred A. Knopf, 1986), p. 95.

20. Ibid., p. 96.

21. Marjorie Van Tassell to BP, Rochester, August 23, 1985.

22. Ibid.

23. Bill Klein to BP.

24. Marjorie Van Tassell to BP.

25. "I'll Forget You," copyright 1921 by M. Witmark & Sons, lyrics by Annelu Burns, music by Ernest R. Ball.

26. Jack Garner to BP, August 21, 1985.

27. Adolph Green to BP, New York, October 20, 1986.

28. Jan Wahl, "Louise Brooks: Rising Star, Falling Star," Part 1, *Movie & Film Collector's World*, no. 165, July 29, 1983.

29. Ibid.

30. LB, "Louise Brooks par elle-même," *Objectif*, February–March 1964.

31. Kenneth Tynan, *Show People* (New York: Simon and Schuster, 1979), p. 240.

32. James Card, "The 'Intense Isolation' of Louise Brooks," *Sight and Sound* 27, no. 5, Summer 1958, p. 244.

33. LB to Chris Chase, *New York Times*, September 16, 1983.

34. LB letter to Kevin Brownlow, January 20, 1968.

35. John Kobal to BP, New York City, November 19, 1986.

36. Daniel Brooks to BP, Wichita, Kansas, November 29, 1986.

37. David Diamond to BP, Rochester, N.Y., October 28, 1988.

38. *Journal of Eugénie de Guérin*, edited by G. S. Trebutien (New York: Dodd Mead Company, 1893).

39. David Diamond to BP.

40. David Thomson, "The Actress Taking the Part of Lulu," *Threepenny Review*, Spring 1983, pp. 21–23.

41. Kobal, *People Will Talk*, p. 93.

42. Larry Quirk to BP, New York, July 13, 1986.

43. John Barba to BP, Washington, D.C., June 14, 1986.

44. James Card to BP, September 16, 1985.

45. Kobal, *People Will Talk*, p. 91.

46. Quoted in Charles Cagle, "Louise Brooks and the Road to Oz," *The Little Balkans Review* 3, no. 1, Fall 1982, p. 16.

47. Roddy McDowall to BP, telephone interview, September 16, 1988.

48. LB to Leacock, *Lulu in Berlin*, transcript pp. 27–28.

49. Ricky Leacock to BP, Boston, August 11, 1986.

50. LB, "Une certaine idée de la liberté" ("A Certain Idea of Freedom"), in Roland Jaccard, ed., *Louise Brooks: Portrait d'une anti-star* (Paris: Phébus, 1977), p. 24.

51. Barbara Mayberry to BP.

52. Lotte Eisner, *Ich hatte einst ein schönes Vaterland: Memoiren* (Heidelberg: Verlag das Wunderhorn, 1984), p. 92. Translation courtesy of Dr. Allan Cress.

53. John Kobal, *People Will Talk*, p. 76.

54. Kenneth Tynan, *Show People*, p. 263.

55. LB letter to Herman Weinberg, March 15, 1978.

56. LB letter to Herman Weinberg, October 8, 1977.

57. Tynan, *Show People*, p. 265.

58. LB letter to Kevin Brownlow, May 9, 1969.

59. Theodore Brooks letter to LB, February 28, 1969.

60. Elias Canetti, *Auto-da-Fé* (New York: Continuum Publishing, 1983). Translated by C. V. Wedgwood. [Originally published in 1935.]

61. LB letter to Theodore Brooks, November 1, 1972.

INDEX

Page numbers in **boldface** refer to illustrations.

TEXTUAL

ACKNOWLEDGMENTS

Grateful acknowledgment is made to the following for permission
to reprint previously published material:

American Film: Excerpt from Veronica Gengs's "Lulu in Washington" (June 1984). Reprinted by permission of *American Film.*

A. S. Barnes, Inc.: Excerpt from Louise Brooks's Introduction to *John Wayne* by Allen Eyles. Reprinted by permission of A. S. Barnes, Inc.

Democrat and Chronicle: Excerpt from an article about Richard Arlen and Louise Brooks (September 28, 1962). Reprinted by permission of the *Democrat and Chronicle,* Rochester, NY.

Kevin Brownlow: Excerpts from the 1977 Kevin Brownlow-David Gill filmed interview with Louise Brooks. Reprinted by permission of Kevin Brownlow.

Famous Music Publishing Companies: Excerpt from "Louise" by Leo Robin and Richard A. Whiting. Copyright 1929 by Famous Music Corporation. Copyright renewed 1956 by Famous Music Corporation. Used by permission.

Farrar, Straus & Giroux, Inc.: Excerpts from "The Follies as an Institution" from *American Earthquake* by Edmund Wilson. Copyright © 1958 by Edmund Wilson. Copyright renewed 1986 by Helen Miranda Wilson. Reprinted by permission of Farrar, Straus & Giroux, Inc.

Film Culture: Excerpts from Louise Brooks's "Charlie Chaplin Remembered," *Film Culture,* no. 40 (Spring 1966). Reprinted by permission of *Film Culture.*

Film History: Excerpts from Jan-Christopher Horak: "G. W. Pabst in Hollywood, or Every Modern Hero Deserves a Mother," *Film History,* vol. 1, no. 1. Copyright © 1987. Reprinted by permission of Taylor and Francis, NY.

Films & Filming: Excerpt from Douglas McVay's "The Goddesses," *Films & Filming* (August 1965); excerpts from Louise Brooks's

"Actors and the Pabst Spirit," *Focus on Film,* no. 8 (February 1971) and "Why I Will Never Write My Memoirs," *Focus on Film,* no. 15 (March 1978). Reprinted by permission of *Films & Filming.*

Films in Review: Excerpts from "Remembering Louise Brooks" by William K. Everson, *Films in Review* (November 1985). Reprinted by permission of *Films in Review.*

Image: Excerpts from "Out of Pandora's Box: Louise Brooks on G. W. Pabst" by James Card, *Image,* George Eastman House (September 1956). Reprinted by permission.

Alfred A. Knopf, Inc.: Excerpts from *Lulu in Hollywood* by Louise Brooks. Copyright © 1974, 1982 by Louise Brooks. Rights in the UK administered by Hamish Hamilton Ltd. Reprinted by permission of Alfred A. Knopf, Inc. and Hamish Hamilton Ltd. Excerpts from *The Parade's Gone By . . .* by Kevin Brownlow. Copyright © 1968 by Kevin Brownlow. Rights in the UK administered by Peters Fraser & Dunlop Group Ltd. Reprinted by permission of Alfred A. Knopf, Inc. and Peters Fraser & Dunlop Group Ltd. Excerpts from *People Will Talk* by John Kobal. Copyright © 1986 by The Kobal Collection Ltd. Reprinted by permission of Alfred A. Knopf, Inc.

The Little Balkans Press, Inc.: Excerpts from "Louise Brooks and the Road to Oz" by Charles Cagle, *The Little Balkans Review,* vol. 3, no. 1, Fall 1982. Copyright © 1982 by The Little Balkans Press, Inc. Reprinted by permission.

Macmillan Publishing Company: Excerpts from *The Times We Had: Life with William Randolph Hearst* by Marion Davies, edited by Pamela Pfau and Kenneth Marx. Copyright © 1975 by The Bobbs-Merrill

PHOTOGRAPHIC
ACKNOWLEDGMENTS

Photographs reproduced in this book were provided with the cooperation
and kind permission of the following:

John Benz: 172, 314; A Portrait Gallery 3

Estate of Louise Brooks: 2, 9 (both), 18 (both), 30, 189, 235, 322, 388, 404, 432, 490, 494

Kevin Brownlow: 168 (top), 185, 278, 339, 340, 501

James Card: 120, 160 (both), 168 (bottom), 203, 218, 227, 261 (Garbo), 390, 457; A Portrait Gallery 7

La Cinémathèque Francaise: 32, 282, 324 (top), 363

The Danish Film Museum: A Portrait Gallery 2 (left), 4

Eastman House: 22, 137, 292, 299, 304, 341, 357

Gannett Rochester Newspapers: 461, 482, 492, 522

Estate of George Grosz (Princeton, New Jersey): 283

Peter Hanson and Richard Sisson: 94, 178 (top), 180, 209, 211; A Portrait Gallery 1, 2 (bottom right)

Mike Kalina and Karen Beardsley: A Portrait Gallery 8

Kobal Collection: 218, 224, 291; A Portrait Gallery 6

Barbara Mayberry: 446

Hal McCoy: 394

Roddy McDowall: 438

Museum of Modern Art: 118 (Edward Sutherland), 138, 141, 144, 164, 200, 238, 380; A Portrait Gallery 2 (top right)

New York Public Library at Lincoln Center—Astor, Lenox, and Tilden Foundations (Billy Rose Collection): 63

New York Public Library at Lincoln Center—Astor, Lenox, and Tilden Foundations (Dance Collection): 52

New York Public Library at Lincoln Center—Astor, Lenox, and Tilden Foundations (Theater Collection): 89, 116, 196, 366

Lawrence Quirk: 118 (James Quirk)

Joanna T. Steichen: 106, 271

Vanity Fair—The Condé Nast Publications: 76 (© 1925, renewed 1953)

Jan Wahl: 133, 150, 158, 178 (bottom), 188, 251; A Portrait Gallery 5

Wichita Eagle and Beacon: 381, 406, 474

Wide World Photos, Inc.: 99, 502

Lothar Wolff: 301, 331

A NOTE ON THE TYPE

The text of this book was set in a digitized version of Electra, a Linotype face designed by W. A. Dwiggins (1880–1956). This face cannot be classified as either modern or old style. It is not based on any historical model; nor does it echo any particular period or style. It avoids the extreme contrasts between thick and thin elements that mark most modern faces and attempts to give a feeling of fluidity, power, and speed.

Composed by Dix Type Inc., Syracuse, New York

Printed and bound by Halliday Lithographers, West Hanover, Massachusetts

Designed by Iris Weinstein

SARAH DUCHESS OF MARLBOROUGH

by the same author

BLENHEIM PALACE

GARDENER TO QUEEN ANNE

GRINLING GIBBONS

Sarah Duchess of
Marlborough

DAVID GREEN

CHARLES SCRIBNER'S SONS
New York

Contents

Illustrations

ILLUSTRATIONS

Elizabeth Countess of Bridgwater
By courtesy of His Grace the Duke of Marlborough

Robert Harley Earl of Oxford
National Portrait Gallery

Lady Masham
National Portrait Gallery

Queen Anne
By courtesy of His Grace the Duke of Marlborough

Sarah Duchess of Marlborough: the mantilla portrait
By courtesy of His Grace the Duke of Marlborough

following page 224

Arthur Maynwaring
National Portrait Gallery

Sir John Vanbrugh
National Portrait Gallery

Blenheim: the Grand Bridge

Blenheim from the north-west

Blenheim: the Marlborough monument

Marlborough House

Blenheim: the Column of Victory
Country Life

Lady Henrietta Godolphin, afterwards 2nd Duchess of Marlborough
By courtesy of His Grace the Duke of Marlborough

Francis 2nd Earl of Godolphin
National Portrait Gallery

Mary Duchess of Montagu
By courtesy of His Grace the Duke of Marlborough

Diana Duchess of Bedford
By courtesy of His Grace the Duke of Bedford

Sarah Duchess of Marlborough (the Petworth portrait)
Courtauld Institute of Art (from the Petworth Collection)

ILLUSTRATIONS

Charles 6th Duke of Somerset
National Portrait Gallery

Elizabeth 3rd Duchess of Marlborough
By courtesy of His Grace the Duke of Marlborough

Charles Spencer 3rd Duke of Marlborough
By courtesy of the Earl Spencer

Lady Anne Bateman
By courtesy of the Earl Spencer

John Spencer
By courtesy of the Earl Spencer

Endpapers: Blenheim: north front. Fourdrinier's engraving dated 1745, the year after the death of Sarah Duchess of Marlborough

Acknowledgements

It should be said at the outset that this book is based mainly, as any full biography of the Duchess of Marlborough must be, on the Blenheim Papers; and that without free and frequent access to them one would have been rash indeed, if not hopelessly handicapped, in attempting such a task. Although from long experience I believed I could count upon the Duke of Marlborough for this very big favour, it was none the less deeply appreciated when it was granted. It has increased a debt to Blenheim which I can never hope to begin to repay.

By concentrating on the ninety-three files labelled *Sarah Duchess of Marlborough*, in Blenheim's muniment-room, I had hoped to complete that part of the research in three months. If however I had paid closer attention to Dr Reid's *Report & Classification of the Blenheim Palace Archives* (1891) I would have realised that those ninety-three bundles were by no means all and that important papers, 'discovered in a closet' and handed to Archdeacon Coxe in 1820, had been filed in fat folders in a different place. It meant, in fact, working at Blenheim on this one subject for rather more than four months; and if I outstayed my welcome in the Estate Office, Mr W. L. Murdock and Miss K. M. Gell were kind enough not to show it; while in the Palace I had at all times nothing but kindness and help from the owner, from his secretary Mrs E. M. Sharpe, from Mr A. M. Illingworth and from all the staff.

If Blenheim was, obviously, the first port of call, Althorp was the second. 'I have been at Althorp', the Duchess tells Mrs Clayton in 1722, 'which is a fine place and there is what I call more sense in that house than in any I have yet ever seen, and I had rather have it than Blenheim if I had nothing to consider in it but myself'. I would like now to express my thanks to Althorp's owner, the Earl Spencer, for going out of his way to help me, not only with manuscripts but with answers to my many questions and for allowing me to reproduce portraits from his famous and quite astonishing collection.

While thanking owners of manuscripts in country houses I must say how grateful I am to the Duke of Bedford for permission to quote from the Duchess of Marlborough's letters to her granddaughter Diana Duchess of Bedford; to the Duke of Devonshire and to his curator, Mr Tom Wragg, for information from the Devonshire Collections; and to Mr T. Cottrell-Dormer for letting me examine the manuscripts at Rousham. When I had all but despaired of tracing a rare and interesting pamphlet of 1712—*The St Albans Ghost*—Lord Rothschild was good enough to send me a copy: again my grateful thanks.

In the Manuscript Room of the British Museum, thanks to the Keeper and Assistant Keeper and their assistants, I was directed to unpublished material which threw fresh light on a hitherto misty period (1712–14) when the Marlboroughs were in exile or, as the Duchess preferred to call it, on a sort of pilgrimage. I feel particularly grateful to those who helped me in that and also in my attempts to track down unpublished Masham letters.

But how can I hope to thank at all adequately all those historians, archivists, curators, librarians and others who so kindly and so readily came to my assistance? I can but give their names and trust that they may realise how deeply I have appreciated their co-operation. At the St Albans Library Miss Muriel Wilson the librarian was extremely efficient and helpful; while Mr O. J. Weaver gave up his time to drive me to Sandridge and to Water End. Mr S. W. Shelton, the archivist at Glyn, Mills, was good enough to show me the Childs Bank records and to have them copied for me. Miss Angela Green, archivist, of the Berkshire Record Office, told me of her discovery of correspondence to do with the completion of Blenheim and the Column of Victory. Mr W. A. Speck of Newcastle University drew my attention to an important letter at Blenheim which I might otherwise have overlooked.

For reference to manuscripts in the Harrowby Trust I am grateful to the Earl of Harrowby and to Miss Pauline Adams, archivist, of the Stafford County Record Office; and for similar facilities in connection with the Gorhambury estate archives in the Hertfordshire County Record Office my thanks are due to the Earl of Verulam and to Mr Peter Walen; and also, in connection with the Panshanger Letters in the same office, to Lady Monica Salmond.

To Mr David Piper of the National Portrait Gallery and to Mr Oliver Millar of the Lord Chamberlain's Office I am much indebted for their expert guidance through the labyrinth of portraits of the Spencers and the Churchills and their many connections.

ACKNOWLEDGEMENTS

I would like to say thank you again too to Sir Owen Morshead, Mr Howard Colvin, Mr Laurence Whistler, Miss Audrey Russell, Mr Geoffrey Beard, Mr T. L. Ingram, Miss Pauline Croft and Miss Elizabeth Burton; to the Curator and staff of the National Register of Archives; to the Librarians of the London Library, the Library of the Society of Antiquaries and the Huntington Library at San Marino, California; and to Miss Jill Ross of the Oxfordshire County Libraries for her kindness and patience.

At the most trying stage of all—the collating of material and indexing of fourteen shorthand notebooks, involving more than three thousand entries—I was helped in Cornwall by my wife and son, who devoted many hours to a most tedious and exasperating task.

To the conspicuous end I have left one of my biggest debts of gratitude, that to Miss Anne Whiteman, historian and fellow of Lady Margaret Hall, who at every stage of this biography has unstintedly helped me with advice and encouragement.

It remains only to add that if, in spite of checks and counter-checks, this book still has its shortcomings, they must most certainly be blamed on the author and not on the kind and clever people who have so generously helped him.

13

No more must soothing musick please
  but Sighs & Sorrow fill ye plains.
A tortured mind no Sounds can ease,
  The Nymph is fled, ye Love remains.

Let Nature lye dissolved in night,
  The powerfull sun forbear to rise.
The Spacious world needs want no Light,
  'Twill flow from Lady Marlborough's eyes.

Sir Samuel Garth

Introduction

It was an age of greatness and of littleness, of grandeur and of absurdity, and to evoke it we need sound though it be no more than the notes of a turret-clock, striking today from Townsend's tower at Blenheim as it struck for the first Marlborough and his duchess. But we are not so impoverished. There are Purcell and Handel and Bach; and we have but to listen to an overture to sense the majesty of the reign of Anne, or to their dances—gavotte, bourrée, gigue—to savour the frolic nonsense of those Kit-Cat quipsters Sir Samuel Garth, Sir John Vanbrugh and the rest; or to join in the rustic junketings at the founding of Blenheim.

This is the ambience of Queen Anne's governing (she who, as Johnson said, seemed born for friendship, not for government); and to the strains it may be of a pavane on Anne's harpsichord, the same that was lent to Abigail but given to Sarah, we watch the decline of a once passionate friendship.

But need all this be enacted again? Perhaps not; and yet when crumbs fall from rich men's tables they may be worth gathering; and where the men are of Trevelyan's calibre or Churchill's and the table Blenheim's muniment-room, the answer may be yes. Without such giants as forerunners one's task would have been harder; for they having, biographically speaking, fixed Marlborough on his high pedestal for all time, have left the field that much clearer for his duchess.

As for the Duchess of Marlborough, though not, like Marlborough, determinedly enigmatic ('My actions shall speak for me'), she is more complex and more secretive than she would have us suppose. 'I am of the simple sex', she says, and 'I tumble my mind out on paper without any disguise'; and yet when she chooses she is a past-mistress of the smoke-screen and the red herring; so that

17

sooner or later the reader comes to realise that the path through the labyrinth, along which this most candid of guides is leading him, has been deftly bounded by herself. Dr Johnson of course saw this as plainly as did Pope and Horace Walpole. To Pope she was 'by turns all womankind'; for she was favourite, politician, doctor, lawyer, architect, wife, mother, grandmother and a good deal more.

'I have been a kind of author', she said. She had indeed and to such good purpose that as one slogs through the reams she has written, at Blenheim, one finds oneself wondering whether there can be anything left to say about her which she has not already said, with merciless repetition, herself. But it is because she is such a good letter-writer (her ink, too often acid, is sometimes wine and never water), that she deserves the stage and in this book, wherever possible, she is given it. She leaves nothing to chance. She even remembers to remind posterity, 'As one is the worst judge of one's own simplicity, one is the best of one's sincerity', and adds, 'I will therefore say nothing of the first.'

From time to time, in one generation or another, she has been whitewashed and worshipped and all but canonised; though whether that says more for the whitewasher than the whitewashed it is not easy to decide. Sir Winston Churchill praises her courage, her spirit, her commonsense, qualities which set her niche higher than that of other favourites, if no higher than Queen Anne's. With those virtues too we must list her beauty and her love of Marlborough, which was tempestuous and real.

On the dark side there are the quarrels with everyone from the sister-queens Anne and Mary to her own children and grandchildren; and though at the time they meant heartbreak, they may safely be skimmed now for some insight into her turbulent mind. Her own Green Book of her children's shortcomings, though devoured with palpable horror by her own friends before breakfast (or so they told her), would today hardly rank as bedside reading. No, as a writer she is at her best in letters and on the subject of her own melancholy; though there again, like Mother Hubbard's dog, she stirs our pity only to surprise us next day in the guise of an upholsterer (and 'the best upholsterer in England'), singing a ballad while she stitches away at yards of red damask for a granddaughter's bed.

Though it pleased her to shock the world, her fascination is not in her violence but in her tragedy, in that *hamartia* or tragic flaw which ensured her downfall. For beyond the tragedy common to everyone hers would seem sometimes to approach greatness, in part because of her fall but even more perhaps because of the outrage it meant to her, because she saw herself as frank, conscientious, patriotic and well-disposed and could never for the life of her understand how or why calamity had overtaken her. Was she to be damned for disdain, banished for temperament? Savagely she strikes through the charges—'hard thoughts', 'long absence', 'resentments', 'sullen looks' —and hurls into the scale the £100,000 she claims to have saved Queen Anne in her Wardrobe. Yet even at the death of Prince George she seems to have been thinking more of her own self-justification than of the Queen.

After her fall, that disappointment should succeed disappointment seems natural enough, if only because Sarah was embittered and needed to get even with the world. For the first half of her career she could say, she had served the nation; but in her long widowhood it was her family she slaved for; that and Marlborough's glorification, and her own self-vindication; all of them, to her mind, feverish and desperate tasks.

Time and again, in friendship, in religion, her reason was her enemy, she was so hopelessly self-reliant. Quick to suspect motive and to see what did not exist in hearts and minds, she could never believe in the intangibles of faith or of art, for to have done so would have been to betray her intelligence. She knew herself to be a rational being and if others were less so they were probably fools or knaves.

> On human actions reason though you can,
> It may be reason, but it is not man.

She could never have learned such a lesson, any more than she could have been made to realise that it might be better occasionally to be fooled than to be perpetually suspicious. It was that as much as anything that lost her the love of her daughters Henrietta and Mary. If she had fallen out with them only, we could the better believe in their 'barbarous behaviour' and 'monstrous usage', but sooner or later she quarrelled with most people till at last she found she had grown sick of humanity and of life itself.

And this being so, all might well be dreariness were it not for the presence of such frolicsome spirits as Dr Garth and the Duke of Somerset. For Sarah they were heartening and for us, even when discovered in a windowless muniment-room, they step out from their letters as warmblooded witnesses to her extraordinary charm. The gargantuan doctor, who seems from the first to have been dumbfounded by Sarah's beauty, was happy to remain so for the rest of his life. His championship was unquestioning if not glorious. Not very articulate, he is chanced on at a patient's dinner-table where, 'like one who is forst from the power of truth & the aboundance of his hart, & after he had been silant for a good while, lay down his knife & with a solom aseveration sayed the Duchess of Marlborough was the best woman in the world, the most generous & compassionate & ready to do good when any cause was rightly represented to her, & he pondered how one of so much merit ever came to be a favorit . . .'

Somerset too, at sixty-five (Sarah was then sixty-three), completely, ardently and joyfully lost head and heart. If only she could have taken life as lightly! But no; wit, unless sarcasm, was not to her taste, while hearts, as she well knew, could be desperately wicked. She would shut herself up at Windsor or at St Albans and soothe herself with books. She would do this when in umbrage with Anne; and much later she would retire to Wimbledon, to the house she had meant for the granddaughter she had loved. 'As I am quite alone at this place', she writes at eighty-one, 'I am better pleased than I have been a great while, for I see nobody, & at London one is always in dread of seeing those one wishes never to see or in expectation of seeing some few that are generally better employ'd than to come. Hopes, I think, seldom come to anything & upon the whole I think my situation is not an ill one. I cannot be disappointed when I have no hope & I fear nothing in the world but the French'.

At such times one is inclined to echo Abigail (of the dying Anne): 'This good lady deserves pity'. And yet might she not, as the richest of widows, have won even more sympathy if she had indulged in less self-pity and had done more positive good? After all, there have been women just as ill-used who have scorned to air, even to their intimates, their melancholy. And yet again who are we to sit in judgment or to decide how it was that she found no comfort in God or man? Her courage must have been the greater for it. In solemn mood she would confide to Maynwaring that when she felt devout she would choose 'a little poor church where there were none but plain husbandmen & women in straw hats'; but this mood he might shatter by saying he had noticed that 'even the most devout do still indulge themselves in their favourite inclinations' and that he doubted if Christians had the monopoly of salvation. 'I have seen several even Indians', he wrote to her, '(I don't mean negroes but those of the East Indies) that I have thought better made in all respects both as to body and mind than myself and why they should be destined to be forever miserable I could not possibly conceive . . .'

Such thoughts could be stimulating and at the same time disquieting. She took comfort in the reflection that she had an excellent brain and that sooner or later everything in heaven and earth must yield to reason, as surely as that all the walls of Blenheim must one day meet, no matter where the masons began.

There is the unlikely tale (there are so many apocryphal tales) of her being stumbled over in the dusk, a bundle of black shawls containing an old invalid, prostrate in prayer. It is next to incredible; but if we can believe as we must that a chambermaid supplanted her as Keeper of the Privy Purse, we can surely believe anything; for as Hardy remarked, 'Though a good deal is too strange to be believed, nothing is too strange to have happened.'

In old age, as a diligent seeker, she must have thought she deserved to discover truth, for she read in translation the Greek philosophers and spent many an hour copying into her commonplace-book page after page of the Old Testament. It is there that we find Job and the Proverbs, but never her greatest need of all, St Paul on charity. In fact there were lessons she rejected, and Bishop Hare's home truths on 'resentment' were among them.

If at times her life reads like a bombardment, (Lord Wolseley's 'torpedo in petticoats'), she herself, though appalled, remains resilient; outraged by what has happened, yet ready to be astonished anew at every fresh instance of inhumanity and ingratitude. What had she done to deserve such treatment, she the loyallest of servants, she the kindest of mothers and of grandmothers? Unfailingly the answer is nothing; there was nothing, she calls heaven to witness, to reproach herself with, she had always been right and had acted correctly; it was simply that for the thousandth time the world had let her down. And for this she demands sympathy and keeps on demanding it, like one who insists upon showing operation scars.

But this is not a psychological study. Often enough her own writings reveal her as unbalanced and emotional. At times she seems to border on madness; at times she seems too coldly sane. That she lived to be eighty-four was, for her day, phenomenal and in that time she lived several lives. Indeed, like her descendant Sir Winston, she came nearer than most to knowing the gamut of human experience. She knew favour and disfavour, eminence and exile, happiness and bitterness; she was wife, mother, widow, grandmother, and was forever wishing she had been a man. For years she was often in pain and she died completely disillusioned.

It has been said that Sarah belongs to history and so, for what that is worth, she does. But was she great? If toughness is greatness she was. Her courage was beyond praise. Marlborough had never hoisted a white flag and nor would she. She had never owned one. For the rest, posterity will judge for itself.

CHAPTER I

The Observant Child

1660-1685

———————◆———————

There was little time for childhood. For most, though not for Sarah Jennings, life was short, often very short indeed. If one survived birth and infancy one was popped into grown-up clothes and briskly sent about the business of living.

Schools? Yes there were schools, but a girl was lucky to find in her hand anything more instructive than a hornbook. For what should a woman do with learning? 'Hardly one woman in a hundred', wrote Lord Peterborough, 'can write or read', and who should mind it? It was almost something to be proud of.

'What a scholar would you have been if that had been your business!' wrote Arthur Maynwaring to Sarah Duchess of Marlborough, many years later, 'but I am perfectly of your mind that I never yet saw a lady that was the better for her learning, and very seldom a man.'[1] And Sarah? 'I am no scholar,' she said, 'nor a wit, I thank God.'; and again, 'An ounce of mother wit is better than a pound of clargy.' [book learning].

Sarah Jennings was born on the 29th day of May, 1660* in a small house in that part of St Albans known as Holywell. Her brothers, both of them, died in infancy. Of her sisters, Frances, eight years Sarah's senior, preceded her to court as a maid of honour. The other sister, Barbara, married Edward Griffith and died at the age of 26 in 1678.

* Sarah Jennings was christened in the abbey or (as it is now called) cathedral of St Albans on June 17th, 1660. The baptismal register, lost for 137 years, was found in 1880.

Sarah thought nothing of pedigrees, ('I value nobody for another's merit'), but owned that her father's was reckoned a good one and that 'he had in Somersetshire, Kent and St Albans £4000 a year'.[2] The St Albans estate was at and about the village of Sandridge,* three miles north-east of the city.

The Kent estate of Agney had belonged to her mother when, as Frances Thornhurst, daughter of Sir Gifford Thornhurst, baronet, she had married Richard Jennings (then spelled Jenyns) in 1643.

It is a pity that almost every word that has come down to us of Mrs Jennings is to her detriment. In the seventeenth century it was not hard to acquire a reputation for witchcraft, and in her case it could be that it was based on nothing more sinister than, as one contemporary put it, 'knowing more than the common race of mortals'. Nevertheless it must be owned that in the newly cleaned Kneller† which hangs at Althorp, the face of old Mrs Jennings is disturbing. No gracious chatelaine this, but a gaunt old beldam, the huge manly nose and watchful eyes looming from the darkness, her sandy wisps thrusting from beneath a widow's coif. Next to it in the gallery hangs the Kneller of Sarah which, Queen Anne told her, 'I have at last got home and am so mightely pleas'd with I would not part with it for anything.',[3] and the same which, when all was over, was returned to the sitter.‡

Ignoring the unkind contrast between mother and daughter, for we have nothing of Sarah in old age, we may unreservedly admire herself as, in her prime, she looks slantingly at us with all the confidence of her undeniable beauty, the blue satin setting off the gold of her hair, the lustrous eyes, the cherubic lips. She has her mother's

* 'I know that in old deeds that I have which belong to the Manor of Sandridge that estate came from Sir Ralph Rowlett, and that might have been in William the Conqueror's time for ought I know'.

Sarah to David Mallet, 4 Oct. 1744 (Spencer mss.)

† Sir Godfrey Kneller (1646–1723).

‡ In an undated letter from Campden House Anne tells Sarah: 'I was yesterday at ye picture drawers in leister feilds. There was but a few pictures of people I know but those weare very like and the work methinks looks more like flesh and bloud then Sir Godfrey Nellars. He is to draw ye Prince and if that proves well I shall be tempted to desire my deare Mrs Freeman would once more give her self ye trouble to sitt for her picture, for I would fain have one that is likly to last longer then I doubt this I have will do.' (Blen E 17)

high-domed forehead, but never that nose. Sarah's nose, admired by Marlborough for its straightness, is well modelled and very slightly tip-tilted. The poise of the head is enchanting, while about the whole—head, neck, shoulders, the bust half-revealed by the careful-casual folds of the bodice—there is a bloom and a radiance which, we are told, were in fact quite exceptional.

It was this startling radiance in Sarah and her sister Frances (Grammont's La Belle Jennings) which first astonished all who saw them. Well hidden at Blenheim is a *jeu d'esprit* written for Sarah when she was a maid of honour by a young friend, Mistress Loughry, then in Touraine:

Having ye curiosity to climbe up a pare of steep staires where none of my company would follow mee, I found there in a little high Terrasse an old man setting with a huge perspective [glass] which hee rested on ye wall. Hee was in a strange wild habitt, with a mighty long beard almost to his feet . . . Hee told me it was a perspective left him by an enchantress and he could if it were but rightly placed see what was done at that time in any part of ye world. I began to be half out of my witts to look too. I turn'd it wether hee wold or noe as nigh as I could guess towards England and 'twas very strange I was soe lucky it seems as just to hitt upon St Jeamses Park . . . Hee would not lett mee look for a minet but told mee with amazement that hee saw hundreds of wemen or Angels, for hee could not distinguish which of the two they were, but for his part hee was of an opinion 'twas paridice. 'twas between 6 & 7 aclock at night & there happen'd to bee a great deale of company ๏ . . . But at last, giving a great cry out of a suden, 'I see', said hee, 'a young beuty coming down ye great walk with rayes about her head like a sun, but 'tis impossible for mee to distinguish at this distance whether 'tis the lustre of her complexion or of her eyes that produces them. Shee is in a crowd that follows her wherever shee goes but there is people that never quitts her one minet. She has without doubt a witt & goodness as extraordinary as her beuty, for of these adorers ther's not one that reproches her of any kindness to one more then another.' I shov'd him something rudly from his seat and taking his place I saw you stand-

ing as hee had described you. You can't imagine ye joy I had in
that sight, I was like a thing transported. I shouted, hollow'd
after you. I call'd you by your name a hundred times as lowd
as I could hollow—'Miss Ginings! Miss Ginings!' But Miss
Ginings was cruell to nothing but mee. You never as much as
turned your head that way, and I was only answer'd by ye
Ecoes who all found a pleasure in repeating your name after mee.
I however never seast calling to you till at last I saw you turn
in to St Jeamses House. Ye sun that was about your head was
it seems that which gave light to all ye park for, in a minet
after, all ye Company quitted it and it grew soe dark 'twas
impossible for mee to see any longer.

> Yet oh her beauty shineth as the sun
> And dazzl'd Reason yields as quite undone.

It was this devastating radiance of Sarah's which, from girlhood
to old age, enraptured at sight the hardbitten and the naïve, the
Garths and the Somersets, the Coningsbys and the Cibbers . . . Such
beauty was not long to be hidden at Holywell nor at Water End, her
grandfather's gabled house beside the watersplash near Sandridge.
Like Frances, she must go to court; like her to be ogled by James
Duke of York and, again like her, to resist him.

Sarah, claimed Dr Hare,* was almost born in a court.[5] Long
before she was a maid of honour she visited it; and so she had met
Princess Anne, James's daughter by Anne Hyde, when Sarah was ten
and Anne six.[6] 'The beginning of the Princess's kindness,' Sarah
remembered, 'had a much earlier date than my entrance into her
service. My promotion to this honour was wholly owing to
impressions she had before received to my advantage; we had used
to play together when she was a child, and she even then expressed
a particular fondness for me. This inclination increased with our
years. I was often at Court, & the Princess always distinguished me
by the pleasure she took to honour me, preferably to others, with
her conversation & confidence. In all her parties for amusement I
was sure by her choice to be one.'[7]

The two little girls, the Princess and Miss Jennings, were intro-

* Dr Francis Hare (1671–1740), Marlborough's chaplain and afterwards Bishop
of Chichester.

duced to each other by a Miss Cornwallis, who was related to Anne; not, one might guess, a momentous meeting; a princess meets dozens of little girls and soon forgets them as Anne, we are told, forgot Miss Cornwallis; but with Anne the captivation by Sarah was instantaneous, lasting and profound.

'Very early indeed in these young lives', observes Sir Winston Churchill, 'did those ties of love, kindling into passion on one side and into affection and sincere friendship on the other, grow deep and strong, as yet unheeded by the bustling world. There was a romantic, indeed perfervid element in Anne's love for Sarah to which the elder girl responded warmly several years before she realised the worldly importance of such a relationship.'[8]

Anne, lacking Sarah's vivacity, had quiet charm. Her voice was low and musical, her brown hair curled, her hands and figure were pleasing. Like her sister Mary she suffered from weak eyes which were later to cause a chronic frown. But in temperament the contrast with Sarah was even greater than in looks. Timid, she longed for friendship and assurance. Often morose and pessimistic, even sullen and cold, she turned thankfully to one radiating confidence and fire.

In her own 'character' of Queen Anne, written in old age, Sarah says she had 'a person and appearance very graceful and something of majesty in her look. She was religious without affectation and certainly meant to do everything that was just', although towards the end of her reign she was imposed upon and fell into evil hands.* To which Dr Johnson, after reading the Queen's letters published in Sarah's *Conduct*, adds, 'There is indeed [about Anne] nothing insolent or overbearing, but then there is nothing great or firm or regal, nothing that enforces obedience and respect or which does not rather invite opposition and petulance'.[9] By blood and by upbringing she had every excuse for becoming a bad queen. That she did not, that with certain reservations her reign was glorious was largely owing to the good intentions she set out with and to her

---

* In another paper however (Blen G-I-16) the Duchess enlarged upon this: 'The queen was extremely well breed & never made a harsh or uncivel answer to any body tell that vile woman got so much power over her [Abigail] & she allways ment well but after she grew so fond of that creature & her ministers she often spoak in her stile who tho she was not a fool she had been used to very low company & her nature was brutal'.

strength of will, repeatedly undermined though it was by ill health on the one hand and the faction of parties on the other.

Anne could not remember the face of her mother, Anne Hyde. Her father, James Duke of York, on the death of his first wife, turned Roman Catholic and married a fifteen-year-old Catholic, Mary of Modena who, up till that time, had never heard of England and so, luckily, had no notion of what it would mean to be Duchess of York.

Charles II, James's brother, restored to the throne in the year of Sarah's birth, had the wisdom to realise that his nieces Anne and her elder sister Mary, as potential queens, must be raised as Protestants; and for that reason the girls were closeted at Richmond Palace and later at St James's with staunch Protestants to look after them: Lady Frances Villiers and Henry Compton Bishop of London.

Anne was taught French and drawing, singing and acting (she could strum a guitar) and very little else besides etiquette and religious observance, not forgetting of course the annual day of mourning for her martyred grandfather. Into her world, narrow as a cell, came occasional rumours of plots. Frightened, she hurried to her chaplains. Who were these papists and how could she escape them? They were not altogether reassuring. According to Sarah they were 'Such Divines as could have said but little in Defence of their own Religion, or to secure her against the Pretences of Popery'.[10] Yet with the wisdom of Solomon how could they have convinced her that her only safety lay in the Church of England, when her own father, who with all his failings was kind to her, was a papist repeatedly banished from his brother's kingdom on long, rough journeys—to Brussels, to Edinburgh—when Anne herself would go with him and Sarah too?

Anne's mind, as it chanced, was of the kind that can be captivated by repetition; and once that had been grasped, all bishop and chaplains needed to do was to press home their lesson daily and leave the rest to time. It was a method which worked so well that Anne became a fervent Anglican, recoiling from Dissent on the one hand and hating everything Roman Catholic on the other.

Mary of Modena Duchess of York, Anne's very young stepmother, herself beautiful, chose her maids of honour for their looks. Of these Frances Jennings was the most startling; and it was natural enough that when she was old enough, which meant when she was twelve,* her handsome sister Sarah should follow her into the duchess's service. Both of them of course, in the court of Charles II, were much run after. Frances, spritefull as John Evelyn calls her, and flighty, was soon married to Captain Sir George Hamilton and had had six children when he was killed in action in 1676. After three years of widowhood she married a Roman Catholic, Richard Talbot who, on the accession of James II, became Duke of Tyrconnel. Judging from her scrawls at Blenheim Frances was very different from her sister, scatter-brained, ultra-feminine and sufficiently pious to found an order of nuns.

As for Sarah, she came, as she tells us, 'extream young into the court and had the luck to be liked.'[11] She found herself at first in a nest of queens or potential queens: Mary of Modena (15), Anne (8) and her sister Mary (11) who would marry Dutch William and with him reign as Queen Mary II. To Charles and James, busy with their own affairs, this feminine coterie may have had no more significance than a cage of linnets or, in a phrase of Vanbrugh's, a parcel of foolish plants. Certainly it must at times have seemed like a hothouse for exotics, with the young Duchess of York, a ravishing brunette introduced by James as 'your new playfellow', the most exotic of all.

In the Victoria & Albert Museum one may see a doll said to have been given to Anne by a lady-in-waiting. Its low-necked, full-skirted dress is what one would expect, but the high head-dress of fine lawn, its lace edging sewn on to a wire framework, is perhaps rather surprising;[12] although we find Sarah, on Anne's behalf, sending to France for 'a fine lace headdress agreed for 400 franks (£36 1s. 3d.)'[13] Sometimes these 'heads' took the form of pleated lace fans, hazardous in sedan-chairs or with candles. 'You may tell his lordship', Sarah wrote to a friend, 'that I have burnt the best head I have in writing this letter'.[14]

In play as in dress they naturally aped their elders; and so boredom, with luck, would be kept at bay with endless games of ombre, basset or whist or their childish equivalents. There was very little reading and apart from gossip not much conversation. To divert them

---

* Most authorities give twelve as her age of entry to court. In a letter at Blenheim, however, the Duchess herself says: 'I have known the court since I was thirteen years old'. (Blen G-1-16. Undated)

nothing more exciting could be thought of than to command them to act a play: John Crowne's masque *Calisto the Chaste Nymph*, performed on December 2nd, 1674, with in the cast two queens-in-embryo (Anne and Mary) and in the audience two kings (one reigning, one to be); while a rival claimant, the Duke of Monmouth, danced in the ballet. Sarah took the part of Mercury; Diana being played by the saintly Margaret Blagge. Miss Blagge, ablaze with diamonds one of which she lost, after saying her piece hurried to the wings 'where several ladies, her companions, were railing with the gallants triflingly enough till they were called to re-enter. She, under pretence of conning her next part, was retired into a corner, reading a book of devotion.'[15]

Such frolics fly to the head, yet even in that company Sarah has left it on record that she was bored. 'I think anyone that has common sense or honesty', she wrote long afterwards, 'must needs bee very weary of every thing that one meets with in courts. I have seen a good many & lived in them many years, but I protest that I was never pleased but when I was a child, & after I had been a maid of honour some time, at fourteen I wishd my self out of the court as much as I had desired to come into it before I knew what it was'.[16]

All too well she remembered the tedious company, the endless card-games by candle-light and the stuffy rooms they played in. Even so, fourteen must have been an exaggeration, for she was sixteen when she won a battle with her mother as to which of them should leave the court, and it was she who then chose to stay:

> Mrs Jennings and her daughter, Maid of Honour to the Dutchesse, have had so great a falling out that they fought; the young one complained to the Dutchesse that if her mother was not put out of St James's, where she had lodgings to sanctuary her from debt, she would run away; so Sir Alleyn Apsley was sent to bid the mother remove, who answered, with all her heart, she should never dispute the Duke and Dutchesse's commands, but with the Grace of God she would take her daughter away with her . . . So rather than part with her, the mother must stay, and all breaches are made up again.

But a month later comes the dénouement:

Mistress Sarah Jennings has got the better of her mother, who is commanded to leave the Court and her daughter in it, notwithstanding the mother's petition that she might have her girle with her, the girle saying she is a mad woman.[17]

It has the authentic ring; and further tiffs are more than hinted at in letters at Blenheim. Yet when the old lady lay dying, Sarah sat up with her at St Albans night after night, so that the Queen begged her to have a care of her own health. It was a strange relationship, realistic to the point of cynicism and, like Sarah herself, doggedly unsentimental.

Of London Marlborough was to write later, 'I looked upon it as a place habited by wolves';[18] and in that context it was no bad thing for a young person to be able to assume an air of serene detachment. 'I made it my business', declared Sarah, 'to observe things very exactly without being much observed my self'.[19] And there was plenty to observe. It did not take Sarah long to realise that life at court was a good deal less polite than she had been led to suppose. One evening she was sitting alone in a window-seat when a door opened and a girl scarcely older than herself came out sobbing and wringing her hands. What was the matter? She would say nothing except that her mother had undone her by her advice.* Mrs Jennings's advice, we may be certain, had been far more sensible, and when the testing time came, Sarah would be glad of it. In the meantime perhaps it was as well, though again perhaps not, that her companions, the queens-in-embryo and their tiny circle, were so religiously segregated. Pawns as they were, matches would of course be made for them (a princess customarily married at fifteen); but while they were waiting it was considered wise to make theirs, except for the odd cleric, a manless world; and of course heavy boredom set in. For with every saint's day observed and every card-game played there must still be interminable evenings when all the girls could think of was to play at mothers and fathers or at husbands and wives and to write more or less imbecile letters to their friends.

Strange indeed were the letters written by Anne to Mistress Cornwallis, and stranger still Anne's and her sister Mary's to Frances

* The girl, a Miss Trevor, was, according to Sarah, with the connivance of her mother, betrayed by Thomas Thynne of Longleat.

Apsley and hers to them. There are writings—Swift's letters to Stella, the Brontës' Gondal sagas—which defy classification, and these are of them; and when their editor, Colonel Bathurst, calls them grotesque protestations of devotion, that seems as near the mark as we shall get. Anne's letters to Miss Cornwallis were, according to Sarah, soon censored, but that was of small consequence. Either her father or her stepmother (it is not clear which), reading an unsealed letter, was 'very much displeased at the passionate expressions with which it was filled.' On the grounds of her Roman Catholicism, though that of course would have recommended her to James, he forbade Miss Cornwallis the court and commanded Anne to cease writing to her.* Anne was expected to spend some time in tears, but no. In a fortnight, says Sarah, she seemed to have forgotten that her friend had existed. It was Sarah herself who years later coaxed Anne to grant the unfortunate woman a small pension. Anne however did remember once or twice to send a footman to suggest she stand at her window to see her drive to Hyde Park. 'What became of her afterwards', Sarah muses, 'I could never learn, but that probably she sank unregarded into a state of very low poverty and misfortunes. Thus ended a great friendship of three or four years' standing in which time Lady Anne had written, it was believed, above a thousand letters full of the most violent professions of everlasting kindness'.[20]

Both then and later Anne, in her attempts at the clandestine—letters, secret meetings and so on—was apt to be far less lucky than her sister Mary who, in pursuit of what Sarah called 'pretty Entertainments and Romantick Amusements to help the time to pass away', showed ardour and industry and was never discovered. In her effusions to Frances Apsley Mary's pen flies over the paper without a comma to show a gift for love letters which might well have been better employed. Feigned names taken from the plays in which they had both acted were but a beginning. Mary, signing herself Mary Clorine, writes to Frances as 'dear dear dear dear dear dear Aurelia', and continues,

* In her *Lives of the Queens of England* (1884) Miss Strickland makes no mention of an intercepted letter. She maintains that Sarah, finding that Miss Cornwallis was a Roman Catholic, denounced her as such to Bishop Compton, who had her dismissed.

I may if I can tel you how much I love you but I hope that is not douted I have given you proves anufe if not I will die to satisfie you dear dear husban if al my hares were lives I wold lose them al twenty times over to sarve or satisfie you . . . I love you with a flame more lasting then the vestals fire thou art my life my soul my al that heaven can give deaths life with you without you death to live. What can I say more to perswade you that I love you with more zeal then any lover can I love you with a love that ner was known by man I have for you excese of friandship more of love then any woman can for woman & more love then ever the constanest lover had for his mistress. You are loved more then can be exprest by your ever obedient wife vere afectionate friand humbel sarvent to kis the ground where once you go to be your dog in a string your fish in a net your bird in a cage your humbel trout.

Mary Clorine[21]

Understandably, Anne felt outclassed. 'I am not one of those', she told Frances Apsley,

who can express a great deal & therefore it may be thought I do not love so well, but whoever thinks so is much mistaken, for tho I have not may be so good a way of expressing my self as some peopel have, yet I asure you I love you as well as those that do & perhaps more then some . . . Farwell deare Semandra.

Ziphares[22]

From all of which nonsense Sarah the observant stood aside, so much so that Frances complained of finding her cold as ice; but if she had bothered to read Anne's letters she would have found phrases which might later have echoed with a familiar ring: 'Be as free with me as ever . . . I hope you will do me the justice to beleeve that I will never change . . . I am ye same I ever was & ever will be to ye last moment of my life . . .'

After their marriages, and all three married, their friendships became more ordinary and Frances, as the wife of Sir Benjamin Bathurst, settled decorously at Anne's court. But long before that, in fact when Sarah was fifteen, John Churchill, page to the Duke of York and ten years her senior, had begun his courtship.

The story of John Churchill first Duke of Marlborough has for all time been told by his descendant, Sir Winston Churchill; how he was born at Ashe House near Axminster in 1650 (one of twelve children, seven of whom died in infancy); how his family had been divided against itself by the civil wars; how his father, the gallant but impoverished Sir Winston, rewarded for his part as a royalist by an augmentation to his arms, chose as his motto *fiel pero desdichado* (faithful but unfortunate); and how Churchill himself, after a nominal education at St Paul's School (Lord Chesterfield found him 'eminently illiterate'), was appointed page to James and so entered the court circle where sooner or later he was bound to meet Sarah Jennings.

It is at this point that Sir Winston cautions his readers to 'brace themselves for what will inevitably be a painful interlude', while he deals with the affairs of Arabella Churchill (John's elder sister, born in 1649, who became James's mistress), and of John Churchill himself who for three years was the lover of Barbara Villiers, Duchess of Cleveland, herself the mistress or ex-mistress of Charles II. In Sarah's directions to Marlborough's biographers, as set out in her will, she tells them to begin after the revolution of 1688. Much that preceded it she preferred not to dwell on, and nor need we. She was particularly scornful of those she called 'the Duke of Marlborough's sister and her Train of Bastards' who with some deference had been mentioned by Thomas Lediard in his *Life of John Duke of Marlborough*, a biography she had not commissioned. 'Because they had Titles', she says, 'he seems to think that was an Honour to the Duke of Marlborough. I think it quite the contrary. For it seems to insinuate that his first Introduction was from an infamous Relation, when the whole Truth of that matter was as follows: His sister was a Maid of Honour to the first Duchess of York, Hyde. She had at least two or three Bastards by the Duke of York or others, when her Brother was whipt at St Paul's School for not reading his Book . . . Now I would fain have any Reasonable Body tell me what the Duke of Marlborough could do when a Boy at School to prevent the Infamy of his Sister, or why Mr Lediard could have any Judgment in mentioning King James's Favourite.'

It was as well that the paths of Sarah and her sister-in-law diverged. In Marlborough's biography, Sarah told David Mallet, 'I would have nothing named of her nor of any of the family she produced. I see no reason for giving any account of her husband Godfrey, nor any of the children's promotions . . . There can be nothing said that is good of any of them.'[23] True, Colonel Godfrey, whom Arabella eventually married, was of no great distinction; but no history of Marlborough could be written without mention of Arabella's son the Duke of Berwick, who fought as valiantly for France as Marlborough did for England.

As for the Cleveland affair, it was to be ignored altogether. And indeed in the biography of a hero to show blemishes at the outset—the clay foot protruding from the statue's sheet—is manifestly rash. However, in the event Mallet never wrote a line of Marlborough's history; and when at long last his biographer was found he proved to be not only his own descendant but a fighter after his own heart. 'Audacity', Sir Winston Churchill has written in another connection, 'is the only ticket'; and here too that is his watchword. Stung by the attacks on his ancestor by Macaulay, Sir Winston in battle-dress makes for the ramparts. He admits that the affair with the Duchess of Cleveland lasted three years, that Charles II expelled Churchill from court and that the Duchess gave him £5000 with which he bought an annuity; but what of that? 'How disgusting', he exclaims, 'to pretend with Lord Macaulay a filthy, sordid motive for actions prompted by those overpowering compulsions which leap flaming from the crucible of life itself! Inconstant Barbara loved her youthful soldier tenderly . . . He returned her love with the passion of youth. She was rich and could have money for the asking. He had no property but his sword and sash. But they were equals, they were kin, they lived in the same world. She was now the mother of his child'.*[24]

What has shocked posterity has not of course been the infatuation which, as Sir Winston suggests, was too predictable for comment,

* The child Barbara, born 16 July, 1672, was sent to the convent of the Immaculate Conception in Paris, there to become Sister Benedicta. After having a child, Charles Hamilton, by the Earl of Arran, she became prioress of the convent of St Nicholas at Pontoise.

See A. L. Rowse: *The Early Churchills*, pp. 143–4.

but the careful investment of the lover's gains, for which the receipt survives. It is an unedifying incident and one that might happily be omitted from a biography of Sarah did it not provide the key to her seemingly unreasonable reaction to Churchill's wooing. Their love letters make at Blenheim a pitiful bundle,[25] the more so for Sarah's endorsement: 'Read over in 1743 to burn them but I could not doe it'.*

John is the ardent, sighing lover, Sarah the mocking, elusive nymph. If his are *billets doux*, hers are *billets durs*. John tells her he is sick, his head aches, his heart is ready to break and death must be his ease if she will not love him. 'Had I the will, I have not the power ever to break my chains'. Yet he still fails, in the acceptable sense, to propose. 'If it were true', retorts Sarah, 'that you have that passion for me which you say you have, you would find out some way to make yourself happy—it is in your power. Therefore press me no more to see you, since it is what I cannot in honour approve of, and if I have done too much, be so just as to consider who was the cause of it.' At which her lover exclaims, 'How unjust you are! ... Give me leave to do what I cannot help which is to adore you as long as I live ... Could you ever love me I think ... it would make me immortal'.

Sarah gets cross. He writes only to tease her, 'but 'tis to no purpose to imagine that I will be made ridiculous in the world when it is in your power to make me otherwise'. Finally of course, with groans at being treated like a footman, the lover toes the line. All along, we may be sure, Sarah knew what she was about and played her hand with precision. Everyone at court, including Sarah and her mother, knew about Barbara Cleveland; and now that that liaison was broken, another obstacle had arisen in the shape of Catharine Sedley (heiress of Sir Charles Sedley and later to take her turn as mistress to the Duke of York and to become Countess of Dorchester), on whose behalf Sir Winston and Lady Churchill had, according to Sarah, been making 'a disagreeable noise in the town' because they had a

* A second endorsement in Sarah's hand reads: 'leters from Mr Churchill before & after I was marri'd which I desire Grace Ridly may have to burn without reading them. read over in 1736. read again in 1743.' Grace Ridley, her favourite servant, was in attendance at her death in 1744.

mind to have their son marry this 'strange creature' for money. However, that came to nothing.

Sarah of course had had other proposals, one of them from the Earl of Lindsey, ever afterwards to be jestingly called her lover. Years later she was told of a coffee-house conversation, overheard by Arthur Maynwaring,* between a Mr Hopkins ('Hoppy') and Peregrine Bertie, vice-chamberlain and Lord Lindsey's brother.

Hoppy: Well, here's my Lady Duchess's health. I fancy she must have been the finest woman that ever was.

Bertie: Ay, she was mighty agreeable. My brother Lindsey was in love with her and had like to have thrown himself away upon her.

Maynwaring (to himself): God eternally damn him and sink him —He throw himself away upon her!

Bertie: Why, ay, she was no fortune.

Hoppy: What, was she not? She was worth at least £8000 when she married Lord Marl and has been since the best fortune and the best wife in Europe.[26]

Sarah was annoyed with Lediard not only for his deference to royal bastards (Marlborough, she said, was very much shocked when his children took notice of relations he was ashamed of), but also for saying that Marlborough had 'made a Considerable Figure among the Beau Mond'.[27] 'That', said Sarah, 'I interpret to be a fop. He was naturally genteel without the least affectation, and handsome as an angel tho', ever, so carelessly dress'd.'[28] The good looks of John and Sarah together were long remembered. 'Impartial judges will, I am persuaded, allow that I may without flattery mention beauty to your Grace', wrote Dr Hare to Sarah when she was sixty-six, 'who with your great Consort was beautiful to a proverb and who still retain more of it than any Lady of your age and have shewn it in a race of children that I believe no one family can equal.'[29]

History, as Sir Winston Churchill remarks, cannot proceed by silences, and history is coy about the date of Sarah's wedding. She herself, she who boasted of a good memory but could not remember dates, does not help us. All she says, and that of marriage in general,

* Arthur Maynwaring (1668–1712), M.P., auditor of imprests, member of Kit-Cat Club, writer (contributed to *Whig Examiner* and *Medley*). Lifelong admirer of the Duchess of Marlborough, he called himself her secretary (unpaid).

is: 'If it be necessary, the sooner it's got over the better. I think that where the affection is grounded upon good reason it cannot be too soon, but if one marries from Custom and for Posterity only, I think I should delay that heavy Yoke as long as I could.'[30] In her own case it seems safe to assume that affection was indeed grounded upon good reason, though if for once in her life heart overruled head, no one would blame her.

At Blenheim an undated fragment in the Duchess's hand is endorsed by her: 'My letter to my sister before I was marry'd about my Brother Griffith'. It reads:

> ... who I am more weare of then of any thing in the world. Hee has larnt french ever since my sister deyd & thinks there is no body understands more nor prononceys it beter then him self. I am in admeration every time I see him how my poor sister could have such a passion for him. Then hee is soe ill bred & fancyes him self such a wet [wit] & makes such a noise from morning to night & that as my Mother says hee turns my head. I beleeve I had not had his company but that hee wants mony. I cannot imagin how hee will doe to live being of a humer that makes him uncapable of anything but spending. I confess I have not much concarn for him & all I desire is that hee may not spend all at St Albans without paying the interest which hee will doe if hee bee not prevented I do realy beleeve & then the poor child will bee undun.[31]

The letter, a characteristic one, is addressed to Sarah's sister Frances and refers to her brother-in-law Edward Griffith, then a widower with an infant daughter who died the following year. The child's mother, according to an inscription in St Albans Cathedral, died on March 22nd, 1678; and the wretched Griffith had learned French and paraded it 'ever since', while his young sister-in-law Sarah had to tolerate his maddening company in the same (her mother's) small house.

Yet for the date of Sarah's secret wedding (sponsored and financed, it is said, by Mary of Modena), Dr Reid gives the spring of 1678[32] and Sir Winston Churchill 'some time in the winter of 1677–78'. Added to which we have Archdeacon Coxe in 1847 observing, 'The biographers of the duke, as well as historians in general, place his marriage as late as 1681, which cannot be correct because Henrietta, the eldest daughter, was born July 20, 1681.'[33] Their first child Harriet, who did not live, was in fact born in October, 1679.

When John Churchill, writing to Sarah in April, 1678, addresses the letter to Miss Jennings, Sarah endorses: 'When this was writt I think I was married but it was not known.' From such evidence as we have it seems probable that they were married late in 1678 or early in 1679. Secret weddings were not uncommon. In 1675, the year John Churchill met Sarah Jennings, Margaret Blagge, whom we last saw reading Jeremy Taylor under cover of *Calisto*, quietly married Sidney Godolphin. It was nearly a year before John Evelyn, who regarded her as his adopted daughter and with whom she had signed a pact of 'inviolable friendship', heard of it; and in 1678 she died after giving birth to a son Francis, who would in due course marry Sarah's eldest daughter, Henrietta. A third secret wedding, that of Abigail Hill and Samuel Masham in 1707, would again, for Sarah, have momentous significance.

For the first five years of their marriage the Churchills had no home of their own. For a time, while he attended the Yorks on their journeys of exile, Churchill tried leaving his wife in his bachelor lodgings in Jermyn Street and it was there that their first child was born and died. Later Sarah stayed with her mother-in-law in Dorset, but that did not serve either. John wrote calmingly to Sarah, begging her patience, 'for she is my Mother and I hope at last she will be sensible that she is to blame in being peevish'.[34] It was the old story. 'From the beginning of the world', wrote Sarah in widowhood, 'there has not been two women that were good mothers-in-law'.[35]

And what of her own mother at St Albans? She and John Churchill seem to have liked each other well enough, but the house was small and he could not often be there; nor was it unknown for there to be 'disorder & ell humer' when mother and daughter lodged together. On the whole it seemed better to correspond. 'I was sorry I ded not see you before I came out of town', Sarah writes to her at Lady Anglesey's in Jermyn Street, 'but I never heard one word of your being there tell Munday ... and being in waiting & to goe early the next morning to St Albans it was impossable to get time enough from the hurry I was in all that day to have found you out, except I had known derectly whare you lay & you know that is allways very uncartain. I find somebody has been deverting them selves with my shape which is not yet grown soe slender but I am sure the first thing you will say to me is good god Deare child what makes you soe monstrous big sure you must bee with child tho you dont own it. You will see by this you are to expect noe change in my person but I find my self something free-er from vapours & the waight upon my eyes that I us'd soe often to complain of sence I drank the watters, which is of much more consiquance to me . . .'[36] and so on.

It was an uncomfortable time. James and his duchess, as Roman Catholics harried by the Test Act, were in almost constant exile. When they went to Brussels or to Edinburgh the Churchills went with them, unless Sarah was pregnant (Henrietta was born on July 19th, 1681), when she stayed in England.

In 1682 Churchill, returning with James from Scotland, was ship-wrecked in the *Gloucester*. They barely escaped with their lives. In December James awarded him the barony of Churchill of Aymouth in the peerage of Scotland. In the same year Frances Apsley married Sir Benjamin Bathurst, and John Sheffield (Lord Mulgrave) flirted with the Princess Anne. Anne liked him, and indeed he compared most favourably with the Elector of Hanover (later George I of England) who had approached her the previous year but returned to his country without proposing, a slight she never forgot. In the bleak nunnery Anne then lived in Mulgrave's attentions were welcome and—who knows?—had Anne been as secretive as her sister, she might have married him and had healthy heirs; but it was not to be. Discovery fell upon them like a thunderclap and sent Mulgrave mouldering in a leaky vessel to Tangier.* Though by no means the end of Mulgrave, it was the end of the courtship and the signal to Charles and James for a worthier suitor to be found quickly for the royal princess.

All in all it made an unpromising introduction for Prince George of Denmark, but Prince George was not easily abashed. Blond and handsome, with only a few pockmarks, he looked the part, and little more was expected of him. Anne tolerated him and later, perhaps to

---

* Miss Strickland, echoing Mrs Manley, asserts that it was Sarah who reported the Mulgrave affair to James. She sensibly adds that the leaky vessel can hardly have been deliberate on James's part, since to hazard a whole crew to be rid of one scapegrace would surely be beyond even a Medici's malevolence.

her own surprise, found she could love him. In the summer of 1683
they were married. From the outset, to everyone except Anne it was
obvious that Prince George could never be more than a lay figure,
but in some ways that was as well. Charles II's opinion has been
quoted and misquoted ad nauseam. Sarah's version reads as follows:

> King Charles II had tried him all ways & at last thought he
> might make something of him & best discover of what he was
> made in the way of drinking, but declared upon the experiment
> that he could compare him to nothing but a Great Jarr or Vessel
> standing still & receiving unmoved & undisturbed so much
> liquor whenever it came to its turn.[37]

Anne, now lodged in the Cockpit in Whitehall and beginning her
long and tragic series of births and miscarriages, begged for Sarah
as a lady-of-the-bedchamber and was given her wish. In one of her
many narratives Sarah writes, 'Lord Marl: intended that I should
allways live near London & never see the court, but soon after made
me lady of the bedchamber to the Princess of Denmark'.[38] In the
meantime, perhaps to humour her, he built Holywell House* at
St Albans where, for better for worse, they would be neighboured
by Mrs Jennings, widowed since 1668 and still living in the house
where Sarah had been born. The site, with its holy well and water
meadows beside the Ver and at the foot of the abbey slope, was a
pleasant one. True, as Marlborough was to write from Flanders,
St Albans was 'not famous for seeing far', but the abbey was on the
skyline, the lapping of water in one's ears and in spring perhaps even
the song of the nightingale, of which Sarah was especially fond.†

Of London and court life there Sarah felt she had observed more
than enough; for if the restoration had been gay (and she herself, too
young to remember, had been lucky to escape the plague and the
fire), Charles's reign now looked to be ending in a blood bath. 'I
remember nothing that happened in King Charles's time worth
mentioning', she noted, 'Only ye many executions upon that which

---

* Holywell House. 'However ordinary it may be,' wrote Sarah in 1714, 'I
would not part with it for any house I have seen on my travels.'

† 'This being the season I hear the Nightengales as I lye in my bead I have
wish'd them with all my hart with you, knowing you love them.' John to Sarah,
23 April, 1703. (Blen E 2).

was called Lord Russells plot & a great deal of horror to that I felt. My nature carried to an aversion to ye proceedings in ye end of that reign. I was sorry not to find that compassion in the breast of another [the Princess Anne's]. All I could prevail on my self to do was to say nothing.'[39]

In old age Sarah amused herself by dictating to her favourite granddaughter Lady Diana Spencer a history of England; but what with the gout and 'perpetual interruptions', both resented, grandmother and granddaughter never got very far. Still there it is, bound in yellowing white vellum, with many blank pages, and stored away in its box at Blenheim.[40] 'Charles the 2nd', we read on page one, 'his Restoration . . . Charles profess'd in Publick the Protestant religion but (if he was any) he was the Roman Catholick. He was thoroughly convinced that there was no such thing as Virtue or Sincerity and that everyone acted from interested principles. He had good parts but hated application to business. The Duchess of Cleveland his first mistress us'd him extreamly ill. He was too much led by his brother the Duke of York.

1681. From this time the King began to be absolute. The nation was divided by two parties, viz. Torys & Whigs. The former were for the Court & never thought the King had too much Power. The latter were the greatest ennemies to arbitrary government & to popery, consequently hated by the King. The Bishops, by their aversion to Presbyterians, threw themselves into the Tory party & were protected by the King.

1684. The King makes the people give up to him all their privileges. Jeffreys [Judge Jeffreys] in his Circuit distinguish'd himself greatly by his unheard of cruelty. Charles was become absolute, or rather the Duke of York, for he led the King.

Charles died aged 54. Some suspect he was poison'd.

CHAPTER II

James and the Revolution

1685-1688

◆

Sarah's history of England, dictated to her granddaughter, ends with three paragraphs on the brief, disastrous reign of James II:

1685. James makes no Alterations as to Places, which was not surprising as those already in place were all his creatures and put in by him self in his Brother's reign. The Tory's were arriv'd to the hight of their wishes. James went publickly to Mass & declar'd publickly that his Brother had died in the Roman Catholick faith, which was a very great prejudice to K: Chas II's memory who had in his lifetime so often declar'd him self a Protestant.

The King sends the Lord Cheif Justice Jeffreys to try the rebells [Monmouth's] & Maj: Gen: Kirk went with some troops to keep the people in awe. These two comited unheard of cruelties such as were never before practis'd in any country.

James had now two things in view, to make him self absolute & to establish Popery.

At the time of dictation, in the reign of George II, the sixth reign she had known, Sarah tended to view former monarchs with some indulgence. James's brutality she could never forgive, but as a ruler, she reflected, he could have been worse. He was 'a good Manager for the publick without breaking any Law but what proceeded from his Weakness of having a Mind that every body should attend him in Heaven by establishing Popery here'.[1] And again, 'Hee was under a great temptation of bringing in a Religion which hee was perswaded was so meritorious a thing that it would secure him honour in this world & everlasting happynesse in the next'.[2] For a king damned by most historians as cruel, vicious and blundering, this might almost rank as a reprieve. Bishop Burnet* finds that he had 'no personal vices but of one sort',[3] which again, for a Stuart, was markedly in his favour. John Churchill James had always had faith in and in the year of his accession he made him Baron Churchill of Sandridge.

It was true that James went publicly to mass. Indeed, of all his rash acts few were rasher than, at the very outset, commissioning Wren to build, for his palace at Whitehall, a sumptuous Roman Catholic chapel. The statues and carving for it were entrusted to Grinling Gibbons and Arnold Quellin, the frescoes to Verrio; and Wren was told that, even if it meant calling in hundreds of extra workmen, the building, inside and out, must be finished by the following autumn. It was. The first service was held there on Christmas Day, 1686. 'I could not have believed', wrote John Evelyn, 'that I should ever have seen such things in the King of England's Palace'.[4] Even this however might have been stomached had not James proved a persecutor. Braced by the victory Churchill had won him over Monmouth at Sedgemoor, James sent Jeffreys on his western circuit of vengeance with such effect that wherever one looked there seemed to be, on the skyline, a corpse swinging from a gallows.

'I hope', remarks Lediard gently in his life of Marlborough, 'it will not be look'd upon as foreign to my purpose if I just hint at some of the principal Instances of His Majesty's evil & unhappy Conduct (I may say unhappy as well with regard to the Nation as Himself), as they justify the Conduct of our Hero in the most critical and difficult Scene of his whole Life'.[5] And certainly in the dilemma of divided loyalties which Churchill was soon to find himself faced with, the brutality of James would help substantially to tip the balance.

In the meantime James attacked the Church of England, beginning with Anne's Bishop Compton and Dr Sharp, who was to become Archbishop of York and her favourite churchman. After that James tackled the army or rather, set out to convert it, an attempt which had 'little Effect with the Soldiery, nor did I', says Lediard, 'ever hear that many Proselytes were gained.' It did however sting a

* Gilbert Burnet, Bishop of Salisbury (1643-1715).

parson called Johnson into publishing a pamphlet addressed to 'the English Protestants in King James's Army', and this so maddened the King that 'it gave his Majesty & his Favorites a new Opportunity of gratifying their Revenge. Johnson was immediately imprison'd & arraign'd at the King's Bench Bar before Sir Edward Herbert, who sentenc'd him to stand thrice in the Pillory, to pay a Fine of 500 Marks, and to be whip'd from Newgate to Tyburn; which latter in particular was perform'd with so great Severity & in such deplorable Manner as was of no great Service to their Cause . . . Yet all these Things were but the bare Earnests of more egregious Tyrannies and Follies. Change of Religion was now made the only Step to Preferment, and all who adher'd to their old Principles were soon discharged the Royal Service.'[6]

This last was not strictly true. Sarah and her husband were not discharged the royal service; although Churchill told the Earl of Galway, on James's accession, that 'if the King was ever prevail'd upon to alter our Religion, he would serve him no longer but withdraw from him.'[7] To which Burnet, writing of the Churchills in the reign of Anne, adds, 'He never betrayed any of the King's secrets, nor ever set the King on violent measures . . . but on the contrary gave him always moderate counsels . . . His wife is about the Princess [Anne] and has gained such an ascendant over her that there never was a more absolute favourite in a court. She is indeed become the mistress of her thoughts & affections & does with her, both in her court & in her affairs, what she pleases.'[8]

At their first childhood meeting Anne had found Sarah delightful, an impression reinforced by almost everything that had happened since. Those she had formerly confided in, Frances Apsley and her own sister Mary, had married and, for the time being, left her. They were strange, desolate times. There had been Mary's wedding day when, after a day and a half of weeping, it was all they could do to force the bride to attend the ceremony. Anne, then thirteen, was sickening for smallpox. Even so Mary, in Holland now, seemed like Anne herself to be happier in marriage than she had expected; and certainly George was in almost every way preferable to William. However, in Anne's case, as Sarah tells us, a friend was what she most coveted, someone beautiful, self-possessed and entertaining. someone to shield and love her and lead her through that thicket of vipers which, as she saw it, was the *beau monde* of James II. Flawless, radiant, utterly self-possessed, Sarah was that person. But such harmony is in immortal souls. Anne, ever a pessimist, trembled for it. With Sarah she had all happiness. She was terrified of losing it. By a lucky chance she was soon able to promote her. It happened like this.

When Anne's old 'lady governess' and First Lady-of-the-Bedchamber, Lady Frances Villiers, died, she had been succeeded by Anne's aunt Lady Clarendon. Sarah disliked her, and so it seems did Anne for she wrote, 'My poor Countes growes more & more naucious every day'. Others speak more favourably of her, but Sarah insists she was 'a Lady whose Discourse & Manner could not possibly recommend her to so young a Mistress, for she looked like a mad Woman'. But there, as the same witness testifies, 'Her Highness's Court was throughout so oddly composed that I think it would be making my self no great Compliment if I should say her chusing to spend so much of her Time with me did no Discredit to her Taste'.

One of the old countess's more irritating habits was prayer. 'They called her a good woman', remarks Sarah, 'I suppose because like her lord she made a great rout with prayers'. It was all Church Party window-dressing to impress the Princess Anne. But there it was. No matter how obnoxious an aunt, she could hardly be dismissed for praying. On the other hand, if reasons could be found for getting rid of Mrs Jennings and Miss Cornwallis, surely it should not be beyond the wit of woman to oust Lady Clarendon. When at last the solution was hit upon, it was so brilliant and at the same time so simple and obvious, Anne wondered why she had not thought of it herself. Lord Clarendon was appointed Lord Lieutenant of Ireland, 'to which Country', runs Sarah's record, 'his Lady was to go with him. The Princess received a sensible Joy from this Event as it gave her an Opportunity of promoting me to be First Lady of her Bedchamber, with a Satisfaction to herself that was not to be concealed.'

After that, the next step was to banish any hint of inequality. 'She grew uneasy', Sarah remembers, 'to be treated by me with the Ceremony due to her Rank & with the Sound of Words which implied Superiority. It was this turn of Mind which made her one Day propose to me that whenever I should happen to be absent from her we might in all our Letters write ourselves by feigned Names such as would import nothing of Distinction of Rank between us. Morley and Freeman were the Names her Fancy hit upon; and she left me to chuse by which of them I would be called. My frank, open Temper naturally led me to pitch upon Freeman, & so the Princess took the other; & from this Time Mrs Morley and Mrs Freeman began to converse as Equals, made so by Affection & Friendship.'[9]

What could be more delightful? Yet there was a snag, a warning even in that innocent-seeming proviso 'whenever I should happen to be absent'; for Sarah, with a growing family, had often to be absent, and no matter how Anne might try to content herself with letters (and they both wrote every day), Sarah's absence was to Anne 'in appearance a sort of death'. 'Upon my word', writes Anne to Sarah, 'I cannot live without you, and tho I wish you and Mr Freeman every thing your own harts can desire, you must not think . . . that it is reasonable for you to live out of ye world as long as I am in it'.[10] For weeks, sometimes for months, Anne had to let her stay at St Albans, herself making do with her portrait ('a pleasing thing to look upon when I can't see the original') while impatiently expecting the next letter. If it failed to arrive she would again take up her own pen. 'I hope that next to Lord Churchill', she wrote, 'I may claime ye first place in your heart. I know I have a great many Rivalls, which makes me sometimes feare loosing what I so much value, but knowing that I never have nor never will do any thing to deserve it, I comfort my self that you will not do any thing that is unjust'.[11]

It was a theme to return to: '. . . and give me leave to assure you my happiness or unhappiness depends wholly on my deare Mrs Freeman, for as long as I have the second place in her heart I can never be ye last & if ever I should loos it (which Christ forbid) it would be impossible for me to be ye first tho all other things on erth concur'd to make me so'.[12] And yet again: 'I hope ye litle corner of your heart that my Lord Churchill has left empty is mine.'[13]

What John Churchill thought of all this we shall never know; but when he writes to his wife (and he hated writing) he sounds too pleased with his young family ('the little poppetts', as Anne calls them) to care. 'You cannot imagine', he tells his wife, 'how pleased I am with the children, for they having noe body but their maid, they are soe fond of me that when I am att home they will be always with me, kissing & huging me . . . Miss is polling me by the arme that she may writt to her dear mamma, soe that I will say noe more, only beg that you will love me always soe well as I love you & then we cannot be but hapy'. To which Henrietta adds shakily: 'I kise your hands, my dear mamma. Hariote.'[14]

There was no doubt about it, he was the kind of father every wise child would choose; but then again, was this wise from the parents' point of view? Was there not in such a relaxed atmosphere a danger of discipline and good management being undermined? As Sarah afterwards put it, 'I have heard it much objected of me that I waited so seldom on the queen [Anne] and was so little about her, and because this is so contrary to the practice of all Favourites I shall give a particular account of it. Soon after my marriage, when our affairs were so narrow that a good deal of frugality was necessary, Lord Marlborough, though his inclination lay enough that way, yet by reason of indulgent gentleness that is natural to him he could not manage matters so as was convenient for our circumstances. This obliged me to enter into the management of my family. I likewise thought I owed a great deal of care to the education of my children'.[15] And indeed, as Burnet testified, 'She stayed much at home and looked very carefully after the education of her children.' It sounds sensible in the extreme. Time alone would show how the children responded.

In the family bible[16] at Holywell Sarah wrote the names of her six children (omitting the first, Harriet) and of their godparents. From this we know that the godmothers for Henrietta (born 19th July, 1681) were Arabella (Mrs Godfrey) and Mrs Jennings; that Anne's (born 27th February, 1684) were Lady Sunderland and the princess after whom she had been christened; and that the heir Jack (born 12th January, 1686. He became Lord Blandford) had as his god-fathers Lord Tyrconnel (Sarah's brother-in-law) and Sidney Earl of Godolphin. The godparents of the remaining three children—Elizabeth (born 15th March, 1687), Mary (born 15th July, 1689) and Charles who was born on the 19th August, 1690 and died in infancy —included two of Anne's ladies-of-the-bedchamber, Lady Fretch-ville and Lady Fitzharding.*

* Lady Fitzharding's brother, the Earl of Jersey, married to a Roman Catholic, became a favourite of King William's, and their sister Elizabeth, later Lady Orkney, his mistress. Another sister married William's Dutch favourite Lord Portland.

Though it was a small circle, soon to widen enormously, for the
time being all of Sarah's close friends were there. The Prince and
Princess of Denmark, Lady Sunderland, Lady Fitzharding, all these
were intimates; but to Anne and the Churchills the time was
approaching when no name would have more significance than that
of Sidney Godolphin. Anne affectionately nicknamed him Mr
Montgomery; and with him and the Freemans to protect her she,
perhaps for the first time, felt safe.* Lord Chamberlain to Queen
Mary of Modena, widower of Margaret Blagge (she died in 1678)
and godfather to the Churchill heir, Godolphin (Pope's Patritio) had
a great deal more to him than his looks, or Kneller's versions of
them, would have us believe (p. 97). 'Physiognomists would hardly
discover by consulting the aspect of this lord', wrote Swift, 'that
his predominant passions were love and play, that he could sometimes scratch out a song in praise of his mistress, with a pencil and a
card, or that he had tears at his command like a woman, to be used
either in an intrigue of gallantry or politics. His alliance with the
Marlborough family & his passion for the duchess were the cards
which dragged him into a party [the Whigs] whose principles he
naturally disliked & whose leaders he personally hated as they did
him.'[17] That of course was a biassed view. Godolphin was not
Sarah's lover but her admirer, as she was his. Looking back she all
but worshipped his memory. His was 'the most disinterested and
honest service that ever was, I believe, performed by man'; and at
his death she wrote in her bible: 'the best man that ever lived'.

Godolphin, a short, grave Cornishman, disfigured as were so many
people then by smallpox, was indeed devoted to the Churchills, as he
was devoted too to Anne and to James's exiled queen to whom, says
Swift, he continued to send 'little presents of those things which are
agreeable to ladies, for which he always asked King William's
leave.'[18]

---

* 'The unreasonableness, impertinence & Brutalety that one sees in all sorts of
people every day makes me more & more sensible of ye great blessing God
Almighty has given me in three such freinds as your dear self, Mr Freeman &
Mr Montgomery, a hapynesse I beleeve no body in my Sphere ever enjoy'd before
& which I will allways value as I ought but never can express ye true sense I have
of it tho to my last moment I shall make it my endeavour.' Anne to Sarah
(undated). (Blen E 18.)

In the Estense Gallery at Modena and now disintegrating from the ravages of woodworm there hangs, in carved limewood, an elaborate vanitas.[19] From the skull in the middle is suspended a medallion bearing the self-portrait of the carver, Grinling Gibbons, and near it, among festoons of flowers, fruit and shells, a score lies open at that verse of James Shirley's, here set to music, which runs:

> The glories of our blood and state
> Are shadows, not substantial things;
> There is no armour against fate;
> Death lays his icy hand on kings.
> Sceptre and crown must tumble down
> And in the dust be equal made
> With the poor crooked scythe and spade.

Of the provenance of the panel nothing is known; yet what more likely than that it was one of those presents so thoughtfully sent by Godolphin to Queen Mary? But that is looking ahead. At the time Godolphin stood as godfather to Jack Churchill, James was still on the throne and, according to Burnet, 'saying every day that he was king and would be obeyed . . . He had both priests and flatterers about him that were still pushing him forward. All men grew melancholy with this sad prospect'.[20] One harsh measure succeeded another until, with the Declaration of Indulgence, it seemed clear that James was bent on disaster. Archbishop Sancroft and six bold bishops refused to read it in public and were sent to the Tower. While their trial was pending Mary of Modena gave birth to a son;* but there were more bonfires and bellringings later for the release of the bishops.

While the Queen had been pregnant, Mary in Holland had by letter closely questioned her sister Anne as to symptoms. 'There was a current report', says Lediard, 'that whilst the Queen either was or pretended to be with Child, the Princess Anne being one Day at Her Majesty's Toilet too inquisitive about that Matter, She received a severe Check from the Imperious Queen (or, as some say, She threw Her Glove at Her Royal Highness's Face), upon which She retir'd from Court.'[21] Whether or not the warmingpan in which the child was said to have been smuggled into the royal bedchamber was a

---

* James Francis Edward Stuart (the Old Pretender), born June 10, 1688.

figment of Mary's mind or another's (it was soon discarded), her correspondence with Anne gives an impression of conscience opposed by self-interest and of conscience coming off a poor second. They wanted to believe it and so, by a process well known to modern commerce, they did believe it. 'I shall never now be satisfied', Anne wrote to her sister, 'whether the child be true or false. Maybe 'tis our brother . . . Where one believes it, a thousand do not. For my part, unless they do give a very plain demonstration . . . I shall ever be of the number of unbelievers'.[22]

Few births can have been more public, for James had invited many witnesses and many came, but most of them were Roman Catholics. Anne stayed at Bath; Churchill sent excuses; Sarah's sister Frances was there but Sarah was not. The most she could testify to was the pregnancy, and even in that she seemed full of doubt. She had been, she said, 'an eye-witness of all that proceeding for about seven months and I must say there was great cause given for jealousies. If it was a true child it was certainly very ill order'd, but if it was not I don't see how it could bee better'.[23] Ambiguity was in the air; but one might have thought that Sarah and Anne as mothers would appreciate that were every mother expected to prove her child her own, the judgment of Solomon would be called for every day.

James's time was running out and nothing, nor anyone except himself, could now save him from exile. On the day of the bishops' acquittal the invitation, signed by the Bishop of London and others, had gone to William in Holland. In Whitehall there were as always rumours, but Mary of Modena, nursing her babe, simply could not believe that her friend and stepdaughter, the other Mary, would come over with William to seize the crown. 'That I will never believe', she wrote to her, 'for I know you to be so good that I don't believe you could have such a thought against the worst of fathers, much less perform it against the best, that has always been kind to you & I believe has always loved you better than all the rest of his children. Besides, if you knew anything of this horrid design, I am sure you could never writ so many kind letters & so full of indifferent subjects as you have done of late both to the King and to me. You have too much sincerity'.[24] But Mary's will had become William's and William saw himself as the saviour of Europe.

And so 'a great king with strong armies and mighty fleets fell all

at once, and his whole strength, like a spider's web, was so irre-
coverably broken with a touch that he was never able to retrieve
what for want both of judgment and heart he threw up in a day'.[25]
On November 5th, 1688, with the Protestant wind behind him,
William landed near Torbay.

The desertion of James by Churchill rankled in Sarah's mind for
the rest of her life. It was not of course that she doubted him, but she
hated the thought that posterity might do so. Even in her will she
inserts a note 'for the history' that Churchill left James 'with great
regret at a time when 'twas with hazard to himself, and if he had
been like the patriots of the present times he might have been all that
an ambitious man could hope for by assisting King James to settle
popery in England.'[26]

At Blenheim one can still see the King's warrant for Churchill's
command at Salisbury in 1688, beginning, 'Right Trusty and Well-
beloved We Greet you well . . .' and it gives one pause. Yet remembering all the hangings and whippings and hopeless mismanagement,
what better did James deserve? The defection of his daughter Anne
is said to have cut him to the heart. It was nothing to him that her
weak husband—'Est-il possible?' as he called him—had gone over to
the enemy; it might be an advantage; but Anne he loved and her
going grieved him. In Anne's flight from London Sarah played a
leading part. In her *Conduct* she remembers:

> Upon the landing of the Prince of Orange the King went
> down to Salisbury to his Army and the Prince of Denmark with
> him; but the News quickly came from thence that the Prince of
> Denmark had left the King and was gone over to the Prince of
> Orange, and that the King was coming back to London. This
> put the Princess into a great Fright. She sent for me, told me her
> Distress and declared that rather than see her Father she would
> jump out at the Window. This was her very Expression.
>
> A little before, a Note had been left with me to inform me
> where I might find the Bishop of London (who in that critical
> Time absconded) if her Royal Highness should have occasion
> for a Friend. The Princess, on this Alarm, immediately sent me
> to the Bishop. I acquainted him with her Resolution to leave
> the Court and to put herself under his Care. It was hereupon

agreed that he should come about Midnight to the Neighbourhood of the Cockpit and convey the Princess to some Place where she might be safe.

The Princess went to Bed at her usual Time to prevent Suspicion. I came to her soon after; and by the back Stairs which went down from her Closet Her Royal Highness, Lady Fitzharding and I, with one Servant, walked to the Coach, where we found the Bishop and the Earl of Dorset. They conducted us that Night to the Bishop's House in the City and the next Day to my Lord Dorset's at Copt-Hall. From thence we went to the Earl of Northampton's and from thence to Nottingham, where the Country gathered about the Princess; nor did she think herself safe till she saw that she was surrounded by the Prince of Orange's Friends.

As this Flight of the Princess to Nottingham has by some been ignorantly not to say maliciously imputed to my Policy and premeditated Contrivance, I thought it necessary to give this short but exact Relation of it. It was a Thing sudden and unconcerted; nor had I any Share in it farther than obeying my Mistress's Orders in the Particulars I have mentioned; though indeed I had Reason enough on my own Account to get out of the Way, Lord Churchill having likewise at that time left the King and gone over to the other Party. Quickly after this the King fled into France.

It is a careful account, bettered only perhaps by Pepys who fills in the detail: that Sir Benjamin Bathurst 'heard a sudden outcry of women and ... found it to be a universal cry among the ladies that some[one] or other had carried away the Princess ... Upon Mrs Danvers going into her Highness's chamber to call her & receiving noe answer to her call, she opened the bed and found the Princess gone & the bed cold, with all her yesterday's cloaths even to her stockings & shoes left behind ...'[27] The Bishop had had the gumption to bring with him his sturdy gardener, George London, so that one way and another the women were well protected and the only loss (in the mud) was one of Anne's shoes.

Professor Walcott, commenting on 'the superbly timed defection of Marlborough' adds, 'The defection of his wife was possibly just as decisive. She was responsible for persuading the Princess Anne to forsake her father and . . . contemporaries considered her desertion the final blow that led James to abandon his kingdom.'[28] As for Sarah's contention that the flight was unpremeditated, a contemporary critic of her *Conduct*, called it downright affectation. One wonders too what she thought when she read in Lediard:

About six Weeks before the Princess left Whitehall She had order'd a private Staircase to be made, under Pretence of a more commodious Passage to the Lady Churchill's Lodgings, but in Reality that she might make her Escape that Way when Her Person or Liberty was in Danger. The Night before Her Royal Highness withdrew, the Lord Chamberlain [Godolphin] had Orders to apprehend the Ladies Churchill and Berkeley [Fitzharding]; but the Princess desiring him to defer executing those Orders till she had spoken to the Queen, the Lord Chamberlain did so accordingly.

At Nottingham Colley Cibber was called in to help wait at table:

The post assigned me was to observe what the Lady Churchill might call for. Being so near the table, you may naturally ask me what I might have heard to have passed in conversation at it; which I should certainly tell you had I attended to above two words that were uttered there, and those were "Some wine and water". These I remember came distinguished and observed to my ear because they came from the fair guest whom I took such pleasure to wait on. Except at that single sound all my senses were collected into my eyes, which during the whole entertainment wanted no better amusement than stealing now and then the delight of gazing on the fair object so near me. If so clear an emanation of beauty, such a commanding aspect of grace, struck me into a regard that had something softer than the most profound respect in it, I cannot see why I may not without offence remember it; such beauty, like the sun, must sometimes lose its power to choose and shine into equal warmth the peasant and the courtier . . .[29]

CHAPTER III

William and Mary

1688-1702

———————◆———————

'I know not how it happens', wrote Arthur Maynwaring to the Duchess of Marlborough in 1709, 'that from the beginning of the world to this day it was hardly ever known that any one was called to govern a kingdom, either as principal or deputy, that was extremely fit for the office.'[1]

To the nation and to the world James II had appeared manifestly unfit to govern, but when William landed from Holland the English thought him, at first sight at least, little better. Grotesquely ugly and with a chronic asthmatic cough which hindered conversation, he hated talking and, adds Burnet who knew him well, business of all sorts. He had been, says the bishop, much neglected in his education and had moreover 'a very ungraceful manner of laughing, which he seldom did unless he thought he had outwitted somebody, which pleased him beyond measure'. His favourite pursuit was war and after that, hunting. 'The depression [*sic*] of France was the governing passion of his whole life. He had no vice but of one sort in which he was very cautious and secret. He had a way that was affable & obliging to the Dutch but he could not bring himself to comply enough with the temper of the English, his coldness & slowness being very contrary to the genius of the nation.'[2]

Sarah was from the first poorly impressed by King William's friends. He was 'not very nice in the Company hee keept, for by his choice hee had for the most part men that one should think oneself very miserable to bee condemned often to bee shut up with';[3] but then, as she said, she had not expected William to stay. After saving England from slavery he would, she supposed, return to Holland. 'But I do solemnly protest', she added, 'that if there be Truth in any Mortal, I was so very simple a Creature that I never once dreamt of his being King. Having never read, nor employed my Time in any thing but playing at Cards, and having no Ambition my self, I imagined that the Prince of Orange's sole Design was to provide for the Safety of his own Country by obliging King James to keep the Laws of ours, and that he would go back as soon as he had made us all happy. I was soon taught to know the World better. However, as I was perfectly convinced that a Roman Catholick is not to be trusted with the Liberties of England, I never once repined at the Change of the Government. I might perhaps wish it had been compass'd by some other Man, who had more Honour and Justice than he who could depose his Father-in-law and Uncle and then act the Tyrant himself; but I never once wished that the Change had not been made. And as to giving King William the Crown for Life, at first I did not see any Necessity for such a Measure; and I thought it so unreasonable that I took a great deal of Pains (which I believe the King and Queen never forgot) to promote my Mistress's Pretensions. But I quickly found that all Endeavours of that kind would be ineffectual; that all the principal Men except the Jacobites were for the King and that the Settlement would be carried in Parliament whether the Princess [Anne] consented to it or not. So that in reality there was nothing advisable but to yield with a good grace.'[4]

The gist of it was this. After James II the crown was his elder daughter Mary's and after her Anne's. Dutch William, as Mary's husband, could reign jointly with her only with her consent; and although Mary, utterly submissive, readily gave it, Anne, with every probability of her sister's having an heir, saw her own chance of reigning diminish. In the event, Mary had no child and died young, and William outlived her by only eight years; but if fate had been kinder to them they might easily have outlived Anne, who died in 1714.

If Sarah, loyal to Anne, had been disgusted by the attitude of William, who insisted on wearing a crown as Mary's equal and not, as a courtier put it, as his wife's gentleman-usher, she was equally so by the behaviour of Mary. In her *Conduct* she continues:

On the Arrival of Queen Mary in England, the Princess of Denmark went to meet her, and there was great Appearance of Kindness between them. But this quickly wore off and a visible Coldness ensued, because Queen Mary grew weary of any Body who could not talk a great deal, and the Princess was so silent that she rarely spoke more than was necessary to answer a Question. And indeed, whatever good Qualities Queen Mary had to make her popular, it is too evident, by many Instances, that she wanted Bowels.

Of this she seemed to me to give an unquestionable Proof the first Day she came to Whitehall. I was one of those who had the Honour to wait on her to her own Apartment. She ran about it, looking into every Closet and Conveniency and turning up the Quilts upon the Bed as People do when they come into an Inn, and with no other sort of Concern in her Appearance but such as they express; a Behaviour which, though at that time I was extremely caress'd by her, I thought very strange and unbecoming. For whatever Necessity there was of deposing King James, he was still her Father, who had been so lately driven from that Chamber and that Bed; and if she felt no Tenderness, I thought she should at least have looked grave or even pensively sad at so melancholy a Reverse of his Fortune. But I kept these Thoughts in my own Breast, not imparting them even to my Mistress, to whom I could say any thing with all the Freedom imaginable. And it was impossible for any Body to labour more than I did to keep the two Sisters in perfect Union and Friendship.

Queen Mary's conduct does indeed sound unfeeling until one reads in Burnet that William had commanded her to be 'so cheerful that nobody might be discouraged by her looks or be led to apprehend that she was uneasy by reason of what had been done. This made her put on a great air of gaiety when she came to Whitehall . . . in which she might perhaps go too far because she was obeying directions and acting a part which was not very natural to her'.[5] In any case, to one who studied faces as closely as Sarah did, the performance was a crude one; but what extraordinary people these were! First the warming-pan myth and now a ghoulish forced gaiety to show a clear conscience . . . But one remembers that they were Stuarts and that both Mary and Anne had a strange automaton quality which made them, given their lesson, carry it out almost as though under hypnosis, unfeelingly and to the letter.

As for Sarah's contention that Mary soon tired of anyone not willing to talk, an early critic pointed out that 'no Person in the World can be so agreable to a woman who loves to talk a great deal as another who loves to talk very little'.[6] However, there was plenty of cause for dissension, and not the least Sarah's monopoly of Anne and the certainty that everything Mary said to her sister would be repeated to her favourite.

For his part in the revolution John Marlborough was now rewarded with the earldom of Marlborough.* William also confirmed his rank of lieutenant-general and gave him the task of reconstituting the army.

In May, 1689 war was declared against France and so, at the head of 8000 men, Marlborough set out for the allies' headquarters in Flanders. Sarah was left to labour, as she has said, to keep the two sisters in perfect union and friendship. Both Sarah and Anne were pregnant; Sarah of her last daughter, Mary; Anne of the Duke of Gloucester. There was a small quarrel about lodgings (always a fruitful source of bickering. Anne asked for some and was denied them), and a much bigger set-to about Anne's allowance. She had heard, she told Mary, that her friends had a mind to make her some settlement. And 'Pray', demanded the Queen, 'what friends have you but the King and me?' This of course was deliberate rudeness. 'I never saw her', says Sarah, 'express so much Resentment as she did at this Usage, and I think it must be allowed she had great Reason. For it was unjust in her Sister not to allow her a decent Provision, without an entire Dependance on the King.'[7]

When the question was raised in the Commons, 'all possible Endeavours' were used to get Sarah to dissuade Anne from pursuing it.

* The earls of Marlborough of a former creation had been distant connections on his mother's side of the family.

My Lady Fitzharding, who was more than any Body in the Queen's Favour, and for whom it was well known that I had a singular Affection, was the Person chiefly employed in this Undertaking. Sometimes she attacked me on the Side of my own Interest, telling me that if I would not put an End to Measures so disagreeable to the King and Queen it would certainly be the Ruin of my Lord and consequently of all our Family. When she found that this had no Effect she endeavoured to alarm my Fears for the Princess by saying that those Measures would in all Probability ruin her, for no Body but such as flattered me believed the Princess would carry her Point, and in case she did not, the King would not think himself obliged to do any thing for her. That it was perfect Madness in me to persist and I had better ten thousand times persuade the Princess to let the Thing fall and so make all easy to the King and Queen. But all this was so far from inclining me to do what was desired of me that it only made me more anxious in the Prosecution of it.[8]

Time and again when courage and spirit were called for—to fight smallpox, it might be, or William's meanness to her young mistress (who, after all, had helped him to her father's throne)—Sarah met the challenge magnificently. Anne's sister and brother-in-law were determined that her allowance should come from them as a royal favour. Sarah advised Anne to let Parliament grant it as her own right. Sarah won and Anne was voted her allowance of £50,000 a year, but the resentment of William and Mary was formidable.

Anne was not ungrateful. 'A little above a Year after the Settlement was made', Sarah's record continues, 'I was surpris'd with a Letter from her, wherein she offer'd me the yearly Pension of 1000 l. Some of her Words are these: I have had something to say to you a great while and I did not know how to go about it. I have designed ever since my Revenue was settled to desire you would accept of 1000 l. a Year. I beg you would only look upon it as an Earnest of my good Will, but never mention any thing of it to me; for I shall be ashamed to have any Notice taken of such a thing from one who deserves more then I shall be ever able to return.'[9] It was typical of Anne's gracious way of giving. A thousand pounds was more than many then earned in a lifetime;* and Sarah's own circumstances, she tells us, were not very great. She consulted Lord Godolphin who said there could be no reason in the world for refusing it. She accepted.

Disappointingly, the perfect union and friendship between Anne and her sister deteriorated. In a comic–pathetic Gilbertian way Anne saw her husband, Prince George of Denmark, as admiral, field-marshal and lord-high-everything-else; a fixation which, when Anne came to power, was to prove a nuisance. William, a professional soldier, could not tolerate amateurs in uniform and, in Ireland, snubbed the Prince by refusing to let him travel in his coach. There was but one alternative and it became known as the Prince's Design of Going to Sea. 'You will allow, I believe', Sarah comments, 'that it was very natural for the Prince to chuse a Sea Expedition rather than expose himself again to the like contemptuous Usage'. And we then have the farce of George's volunteering 'and without any Command'; at which 'the King said nothing, but immediately embraced him by Way of Adieu'.[10] Tact was called for, although the word in its present meaning was then unknown.† A desperate attempt at face-saving seems to have been made, even Sarah being appealed to, gently to dissuade the Prince from his Design. It was the sort of ludicrous situation at which only posterity may be allowed to laugh. For want of humour and sensibility Prince George had in the end to be positively forbidden by Queen Mary to go to sea. But the next blow was far more serious. Early in January, 1692, the Queen sent for her sister, again pregnant, and after chiding her about the £1000-a-year allowance, told her that Sarah must be dismissed. Anne meekly but firmly refused and the Queen lost her temper. The following day, recalls Sarah, 'the King was pleased (without assigning any Reason) to remove my Lord Marlborough from his Employments. And I think it is not to be doubted that the principal Cause of it was the Court's Dislike that any Body should have so much Interest with the Princess as I had, who would not

* To give some notion of present-day values one needs to multiply these sums by at least fifteen.

† The O.E.D. gives 1804 as the date of the first usage of 'tact' in its modern sense.

implicitly obey every Command of the King and Queen. The Disgrace of my Lord Marlborough therefore was designed as a Step towards removing me from about her.'[11]

That may have been one of the reasons, but historians have not accepted it as sufficient in itself to warrant the dismissal of Marlborough, whom William had made virtually commander-in-chief. As with outbreaks of war, so in crises of this kind, a number of things will simmer until suddenly some trifle—a rebuff, an intercepted letter, even a barrackroom guffaw—touches off an explosion. 'As a matter of fact', wrote the Marquess of Halifax in 1693, 'he [Marlborough] had been upon secret terms with the Court of St Germains, from which he obtained a written promise of pardon and to which he had succeeded in reconciling his wife's obedient tool the Princess Anne'. After mentioning Marlborough's 'ostentatious jealousy of the Dutch elements' (in particular William's Dutch favourite Hans Bentinck Earl of Portland), Halifax records that the sudden dismissal on January 10th, 1692 aroused the liveliest excitement and considerable sympathy.[12]

On the question of Marlborough's Jacobite dealings, since almost the only contemporary sources are Jacobite, we are on unsure ground; nor can we know how much he told his wife. It is now generally accepted that Marlborough, in common with Godolphin, the Duke of Shrewsbury and others, sought a pardon from James as a matter of insurance, (for after all, if one rash king could lose his throne, so could another), and that for further correspondence with the exiles the Marlboroughs found natural channels in Arabella's son and Marlborough's nephew the Duke of Berwick and in Sarah's exiled sister Frances Duchess of Tyrconnel. Sarah, ever a staunch patriot, is most unlikely to have been directly involved, and the fable concocted at the time about her disclosure of military secrets (a Jacobite invention) has long since been discounted. There remains the belief that in 1689 Marlborough secured a pardon from James on the understanding that Anne too should send a contrite letter, which she did, receiving in return, it is said, forgiveness conditional on her never wearing the crown. For the rest of Marlborough's manoeuvres with St Germains, and they were many, Sir Winston, though perhaps too charitably, dismisses them as so much political expediency and bluff.

At the end of January Anne received from someone who seemed curiously well informed an anonymous letter:

Madam, You may billive if I had not all the respect Imagenable for your Heyness I would not give you this trouble. I begg of you for your own sarke that you will have a care of what you say before Lady Fitzharding, remember shee's lord Portland & Betty Villars is sister. You may depend upon't that these two are not ignorant of what is said and done in your lodgings. Then I leave you to judge whether they make not their court att your expense that's by exposeing you & preserving the King as they call it. You know you are but an Honorable Person being in the hands of the Dutch Gards and should there be anny vilence offerd what cann wee doe for you? or indeed for our selfs. The King & Queen has been tould that there has not passed a day since lord Marleborrow's being out that you have not shed tears. If I durst I could soone convince you that his misfortune coms from your own ffamelly [household]. If it ended in his turning out he meight leave it with patience, but if resolutions hold he will be confined as soone as the Parlement is up, and if you doe not parte with his Lady of your selfe you will bee obliged to it. Would you but inquire where Lady Fitzharding was the weeke before he had his dismission you would feind that her tiers were not verry sinceare ... Upon the whole matter he's the Lookiest Gentleman in England* who's sister governs the King and his wife the Queen & is the entire confidant of poor deluded Lady Marleborrow. If you sleight this advice I wish you may not have cause to repent it.

I am with all respect your
Heyness's unknowen dutyfull humble servant
J.H.

The postscript reads: It has been taken great notice of Lord

* Probably referring to Edward Villiers first Earl of Jersey (1656–1711), brother of Lady Fitzharding, Betty Villiers (Lady Orkney) and Lady Portland (all children of Lady Frances Villiers and cousins of Barbara Villiers Duchess of Cleveland). Lord Jersey was popular with William. Lady Jersey was a close friend of Queen Mary's.

Godolphen & Cherrey Russele's* being at lord Marleborrow's
Lodging so late ye neight he was turn'd out.[13]

There was not much Anne could do about it except to pass on the
letter to Sarah, who kept it as she kept everything. As for Lady
Fitzharding, Anne had long been suspicious of her, even jealous, but
Sarah would not listen. She preferred on the whole to suspect Lady
Fitzharding's sister Betty. 'The world said', comments Sarah, 'that
Lady Fitzharding betrayed my Lord Marlborough to King William
& Queen Mary. I had proofs that she did many things that were
wrong . . .'[14] but she was probably no worse than a trimmer with a
foot in each camp. Betty Villiers, William's mistress, was different.
'There was very good reasons to believe', runs one of Sarah's
endorsements, 'that in the time of King William's anger against
Lord Marl. Mrs Villiers did a great deal of mischief, tho' I had been
extreamly civill to her not out of any design which is allways the
reason that such wemen are courted, but I loved her sister Fitzharding
when I was but a child & living with all the intimacy imaginable
with her, that friendship introduced her sister Mrs Villiers afterwards
my lady Orkney to my lodgings where she heard us talk with
freedom, but nothing that ought to have don Lord Marlb. or me any
prejudice. There was no doubt but she joynd with every body that
were Lord Marlboroughs enemys at that time in order to remove
him from his employments . . .'[15]

Although in the role of wife-kept-in-the-dark Sarah is never
altogether convincing, this does seem to have been a puzzle she
brooded on, as she brooded on Marlborough's desertion of James.
Years later we still find her protesting utter ignorance of the reason
for Marlborough's dismissal although, she owns, she had 'often
thought it might have been compassed by the malice of the tories
who were very well with my lord Portland & he had ever a great
prejudice to my Lord Marl. And my lady Orkney, then Mrs
Villiers, was so great an enemy of mine that it was very probable
she would help forward anything of that Nature . . .'[16]

Of Lady Fitzharding Sarah says frankly, 'Tis certain I had more
fondness & inclination for her then any body I ever knew in my
life'.[17] And later, 'She had a great deal of wit but was interested.

* Admiral Edward Russell, later Earl of Orford (1653-1727).

And Queen Mary showed more inclination for her than any body. I lov'd her extremely tho' I found at last her morals were not good.'[18] The two ladies-in-waiting were often together gossiping or, as one sees in the Kneller at Blenheim (p. 49), playing interminable games of cards. Anne's jealousy, although she was ashamed of it, was not to be hidden.

'I have in another paper', remarks Sarah, 'explain'd something of the Naggs Head & Loupa, which ment Lady Fitzharding & Lady Bathurst. They were both entertaining wemen & I was often with them, but the queen [Anne] did not care for any body that I gave any time to.'[19]

Bewildering indeed is the labyrinth that winds among these nicknames and grisly the snares and pits that beset it. Lady Fitzharding (née Villiers and at one time Mrs Berkeley) sets a double problem in the form of twin nicknames: Loupa* and Mrs Hill; which last (a really monstrous red herring) has understandably led biographers to suppose that Sarah's cousin, Abigail Hill, made a much earlier appearance than she did and that Sarah made such a fuss of her that Anne became jealous. All of which of course is nonsense. Some things are more deeply hidden than others, and it is not to be wondered at that at Blenheim a slight endorsement of Sarah's (one of thousands) eluded Sir Winston's team of experts and those who have followed them. Upon an undated letter of Anne's Sarah has written: 'When the queen† thought I was too kind to Lady Fitz' and 'This letter shews that it was not unreasonable for me to speak to her upon her kindness to Mrs Masham since it appeares that she was uneasy at my kindnesse for Mrs Hill which was the name then that my Lady ffitzharding went by.'

Anne's letter begins:

'tis impossible to be better satisfyed then I am with you in every thing & I hope I have not done any thing lately that should make you think other ways. I must confess Mrs Hill has hereto-

* Loupa. 'Coupa' (as sometimes printed) must surely be a wrong transcription. The obvious interpretation is Lupa: a harlot. The Nag's Head was almost certainly Lady Bathurst, née Frances Apsley.

† Sarah as often as not, when writing of the past, refers to Anne as queen when, at the time in question, she was Princess of Denmark.

fore made me more uneasy then you can emagin but seeing every day more & more how litle reason I had for my feares I should be ye unreasonablest creature in ye world if I gave way to them any longer & what is past I beg may be both pardoned & forgot for I am ashamed & angry with my self that I should have bin so troublesome to my deare lady Marleborough. I fancyed that Mrs Hill had out of Curiosity intercepted my letter* but I beleeve I am mistook . . .[20]

And again:

. . . I can't end this without beging deare Mrs Freeman to have a care of Mrs Hill for I doubt she is a Jade & tho I can't be sure she has done any thinge against you there is too much reason to beleeve she has not bin soe sincer as she ought. I am sure she hates your faithfull Mrs Morely & remember none of her famely weare ever good for any thing. That which makes me say this is becaus I see she begins to talk more freely & to be more with you then she has bin of late & knowing some yeares ago you weare quite fallen out & by degrees you weare made up till at last you weare as much bewitch'd by her as ever & knowing besides your inclination for her & her very agreeable humour I feare you may in time againe grow as fond of her as you have formerly bin. . . . I beg your pardon for saying so much on this subject & if you are angry I will never mention any thing of it more . . .[21]

Since the Villiers set were far too powerful to be ousted, Anne decided on a line of indifference. 'Lady Fitzharding', she complained to Sarah, 'has bin ye spleenatick'st out of humoure creature that ever was seen when she has bin with me but to all others she has bin very easy, but it dos not att all afflict me nor nothing can as long as my deare deare Mrs Freeman continues kind, her freindship being one of the things I valu most & which I would not loos to be empress of the world'.[22]

* Anne's letters to Sarah were so frequently intercepted that to one of them (undated) she added: 'Who's ever hands this lights in I wish they may be so good natur'd after they have reade it to lett it go by this night's post, that my deare Mrs Freeman may not have any cause to think her faithfull Morely neglected writing, for she never will fail her in any thing that lyes in her power . . .' (Blen E 17).

Had the Morley–Freeman friendship needed the cement of shared affliction there was now no want of it. In the spring of 1692, and not for the last time, a false and baseless charge of conspiracy to murder William and restore James was trumped up by one Robert Young, then in gaol, against Marlborough and others. Young was a forger (though not having lost his ears made him, said Sarah, an irreproachable witness) and the net he had prepared was a crude one. There were of course forged signatures, Marlborough's included; and there was also said to be an incriminating note hidden in a flowerpot at the Bishop of Rochester's, but it could not be found. However, Marlborough was arrested, those refusing to sign the warrant were ignored, and he was sent to the Tower, where he stayed from May 5th to June 15th. As Sarah was preparing to visit him there (and she had difficulty in getting a pass), another blow fell. On May 22nd Charles, their younger son, died. All she could do was to write; and so it is that we have that rare thing (for the rest she insisted on his burning) a love letter from Sarah, and one of such feeling as to make us wish there were more:

> Wherever you are, whilst I have life, my soul shall follow you, my ever dear Lord Marlborough, and wherever I am I should only kill the time wishing for night that I may sleep and hope the next day to hear from you.[23]

Later, with the help of a bribe, she was admitted, and in the meantime there were soothing letters from Anne:

> I hear that Lord Marlborough is sent to the Tower; and though I am certain they have nothing against him . . . yet I was struck when I was told it, for methinks it is a dismal thing to have one's friends sent to that place. I have a thousand melancholy thoughts, and cannot help fearing they should hinder you from coming to me; though how they can do that without making you a prisoner I cannot imagine . . . But let them do what they please, nothing shall ever vex me so I can have the satisfaction of seeing dear Mrs Freeman; and I swear I would live on bread & water between four walls, with her, without repining; for as long as you continue kind, nothing can ever be a real mortification to your faithful Mrs Morley, who wishes she may never

enjoy a moment's happiness, in this world or the next, if ever she proves false to you.[24]

Every day Anne sent more encouragement:

I am sorry with all my heart dear Mrs Freeman meets with so many delays; but it is a comfort they cannot keep Lord Marlborough in the Tower longer than the end of the [legal] term; and I hope, when Parliament sits, care will be taken that people may not be clapped up for nothing, or else there will be no living in quiet for anybody but insolent Dutch and sneaking mercenary Englishmen. Dear Mrs Freeman Farewel; be assured your faithful Mrs Morley can never change . . .'[25]

Finding Sarah downcast she begs her, 'For God's sake have a care of your dear self and give as little way to melancholy thoughts as you can . . . I fancy ass's milk would do you good and that is what you might take morning or afternoon, as it is most convenient . . .'[26]

When Marlborough was released there was no return to favour. On the contrary, he was to remain in the wilderness for six years. William, insecure in a strange country, is believed to have been far more concerned about the strength of the Anne–Marlborough faction and the possibility there of a rival court than of any danger from the direction of St Germains. Sarah saw it differently, both then and later, and perhaps it is time to take up the thread of her tale:

I protest that the loss of my Lord Marlborough's Employments would never have broke my Rest one Minute, but the being turned out is something very disagreeable to my Temper; and I beleive it was three Weeks before my best Friends could persuade me to go to a Court which (I thought) had used my Lord Marlborough very ill. However, at last they prevailed. And I remember Lord Godolphin said that it could not be thought I made any mean Court to the King and Queen, since to attend the Princess was only paying my Duty where it was owing. I waited therefore on my Mistress to Kensington. The Consequence was such as my Friends, having no Reason to apprehend it, had never thought of.

The consequence was in fact consternation and fury; and if

Sarah's friends were surprised they must have been as naïve as they were foolish. As a matter of commonsense and common politeness, as well as of etiquette, when a courtier was disgraced his wife stayed from court; so that when Anne entered the drawing-room attended by Sarah, Mary was dumbfounded. It was the strangest thing that ever was done, she wrote to Anne the day after, and the only thing that had prevented a scene was Anne's condition. 'But now I must tell you plainly, Lady Marlborough must not continue with you . . .' It is a long letter and not in its general tone an unkind one. It ends: 'At some other Time we shall reason the Business calmly, which I shall willingly do, or any Thing else that may shew it shall never be my Fault if we do not live kindly together, nor will I ever be other by Choice but your truly loving and affectionate Sister'.[27]

Mary as Queen had a right to exact obedience, but in demanding Sarah's removal she was asking for something Anne felt it would be death to give. Sadly then but with Stuart obstinacy Anne refused, and was promptly told to remove from the Cockpit. This of course on Mary's part was malicious and also probably illegal since the place, on the Downing Street side of Whitehall, had been given to Anne by Charles II. It was Anne's turn to decide not to make a scene. Having begged Syon House of the Duke and Duchess of Somerset, she quietly withdrew there with her modest court. William, says Sarah, tried his utmost to dissuade the owner from letting Anne stay there, 'but his Grace had too much Greatness of Mind to go back from his Promise,* so there was an End of that Matter'.[28]

When, at Syon, Anne gave birth to a dead child, she sent a message to Mary, who visited her, but there was no reconciliation. Sarah's dismissal was again demanded and again denied and Anne was left trembling and as white as the sheets. After that, several snubs were devised for Anne and her husband. They were not saluted. They were no longer to have guards (Anne was robbed). Friends were forbidden to call. At St James's Church the custom of leaving the text of the sermon upon the Princess's cushion was to be discontinued . . . and so on. It was all too spiteful and petty to be bothered with; yet to Sarah it meant much and she brooded on it. Repeatedly she proposed to Anne that she herself should retire and so make things

* This tribute of Sarah's, in her *Conduct* (1742), to the Duke of Somerset was written long after his proposal of marriage to her in 1723.

easier; and each time, with increasing agitation, Anne implored her not to think of it:

> But I beg it again for Christ Jesus's Sake that you would never name it any more to me. For be assured, if you should ever do so cruel a Thing as to leave me, from that Moment I shall never enjoy one quiet Hour. And should you do it without asking my Consent (which if I ever give you, may I never see the Face of Heaven) I will shut myself up & never see the World more but live where I may be forgotten by human Kind.[29]

The Earl of Rochester, uncle to Anne and Mary, offered to act as go-between and was rebuffed. With Stuart pride and obstinacy on both sides the case was hopeless and would remain so until the Queen's death. The only possible link might have been Anne's sickly child the Duke of Gloucester, to whom the Queen sent rattles and other presents, but on those occasions no more notice was taken of Anne 'than if she were a Rocker'.

From Syon Anne and her household moved to Berkeley House, Piccadilly. She can never have felt the need of Sarah's company more than in this winter of 1692–3 when Mrs Jennings had a stroke and her daughter was sent for to St Albans. Although paralysed, the old lady lingered, to die the following May. Anne sent doctors and as usual wrote every day: 'I hope in Christ your Mother will do well & am sorry with all my Soul I have this occasion to serve you. I have nothing more to say but beg my dear Mrs Freeman would always be so just as to beleeve I would go round ye world upon my baire knees to do her or hers ye least service & she may be assured ye least command from her shall be obeyed with all ye hast emaginable by your faithfull Morley'.[30]

As the time dragged on, Anne became concerned for Sarah's health—

> ... your Mother may lye as she is now a good while. I must beg once more that you would try to get a little rest or else you will never hold out; & since your own house is so neare that you may be called in a minute upon ye least accident, in my humble opinion you had better go to bed there every night & get what sleep you can. Nature cannot beare to be so harassed as you do

your deare self but will at last sink under it. For God's sake be perswaided to take some ass's milk, that will not hinder you from any thing but will cool & sweeten your blood which must needs be heated & out of order with sitting up so perpetualy. I have an ass in St James's Park & if you will make use of it send me word & I will take care you shall have it a Saturday morning. I have bin led about my chamber today & was caryed into ye garden for a litle aire . . . but 'tis impossible for your faithfull Morley to be at ease in her mind while dear Mrs Freeman is in such a tormenting condition.[31]

Anne's gout* is already severe (she is only twenty-eight), but she is unselfish enough to say, 'I swaire I could with pleasure endure 10,000 fitts of ye gout or any risk in ye world if it could be but a reliefe to my deare Mrs Freeman when she is in trouble'.[32] When Sarah asks for Dr Radcliffe's† opinion, Anne tells her he is surprised that Mrs Jennings has lasted so long. To which Anne herself adds, 'I cannot see that you have any just cause to reproch your self for any thing. I am confident you never omitted ye least title of your duty to your Mother while she was living & in her sickness you have shown your self ye best & tenderest daughter that ever was'.[33]

Anne offered a horse-drawn litter to bring Sarah and her mother to London, but it was too late. After twenty-five years of widowhood and a trying illness, Mrs Jennings had died. Her will, dated February 12th, 1692, is curious. After directions for burial 'att the Aby church att St Albans as near as I can conveniently be laid by my four first children . . . my daughter's coach to follow my hearse directly to the church gate without any further ceremony', she left everything to her 'dear and loving daughter Sarah Countess of Marlborough' and for her 'sole and separate use and benefit'. As for Marlborough, her 'dear son-in-law', she added, 'tho I love him with all my heart he shall not hereafter have any benefit concern or intermedleing with any part or parts of my estate . . . but shall be therefrom . . . fully &

---

* Gout is not common in women. Both Anne and Sarah may have suffered from it, but it seems more likely that most of the trouble in their hands, knees and elsewhere was due to some form of arthritis.

† Dr John Radcliffe (1650–1714), chosen by Anne as her principal physician in 1686. Later he fell from favour and declined to attend at her death.

wholly debarred & excluded . . . my said dear & loving daughter to be sole executrix'.[34]

When Frances Tyrconnel, exiled in France, heard of the will she was displeased and said so. Of all the many good reasons man has provided for family discord, wills and money have always come first; and in this case there may have been cause for grievance. When in the revolution of 1688 the Tyrconnels had fled to Ireland, 'We came away', Frances reminds Sarah, 'with nothing but close on ouer backs', and for years, again according to herself, they were kept on very short commons. During that time she bombarded her sister, in a huge and all but illegible scrawl, with undated screeds mainly, it would seem, about petticoats and 'father beads'. (Her spelling even for those days is wonderful). But of Sarah and her own nieces she writes from time to time quite fondly. 'I hope the little butys is well though you say nothing of them . . . I think I love mis Harriat & her Mother better then all the world put togather'. Could Sarah possibly send her half-a-dozen 'right worickshire cheses & one chestershire chise'? (At 'Cheshire' she makes three attempts and crosses them out). 'Allso a litle berill of grots or ote mele. I have been mighty happy thus for lent . . .' Cheese? Sarah scribbles on the back of the letter: 'The 3 horse shoes in newgate street over against St Martans the best chese is to bee had', and so the parcel goes off. 'Yuer magnificent parsel of cheses would make me a fraide of begeing', exclaims Frances gratefully, 'Wee will in a privat way drinke yuer helth this lent & do less penance then if wee had not shuch friends'.[35]

And then comes the will trouble, Frances 'not being so much as named in my poore Mother's will. I need not', she tells Sarah, 'believe you contributed to the making so unkind a will . . .' She sends a load of complaints and ends, 'All these things might apeare less heavey then at a time when some are starveing & others not'. To which Sarah replies testily, 'I hope I shall bee in better temper to answer then I beleive you were at the writing'. As for their mother's will, 'I have no reason to find fault with it because it was certainly intended very kind to me, tho I know nothing but debts you are excluded from. I am very far from saying or thinking you had noe reason to expect a share in what my mother left, but I ded not make my mother's will and if she had lived a thousand years I should never have named the settling her estate to her . . .'[36] And so on. Frances must have known what she was up against. She sounds warmhearted, scatterbrained, uncomplicated. This is typical of her:

> Yuer letter made me wet it more then you could have don when a writing & if you can in the least remember the reall passion & inclination I ever had for you 'tis what you will esele belive & I must again aferme that in my hole life I never ded love any thing better then yuer selfe whatever star rained for thes late yers to make all a peare rong . . .[37]

And so for Sarah it was back to Berkeley House for consoling talks with Anne. They had no need to weep over old Mrs Jennings; but in the loss of young children there was deep mutual sorrow, and in William and Mary, or so they thought, mutual tyranny and dislike. In conversation of course it was perfectly safe to refer to William as the Monster or Caliban or the Dutch Abortion. Everybody did it. But when the same epithets appeared in Anne's letters, Sarah thought it best to cross them out. 'What is blotted out', she is careful to explain, 'is something that frighted me where she expresses so much haterid to her sister but', she adds, 'if it were to bee don now I should not bee so carefull'.[38] (The endorsement is undated).

Was Mary so disagreeable? Bishop Burnet, who had known her since girlhood, did not think so. 'She seems', he wrote, 'to be a person raised & prepared by God Almighty to make the nations happy . . . All that I can possibly set against her is that she is the most reserved person alive, unto whose thoughts no creature can enter further than as she discovers them'. As a queen she was all but idolised; as a wife she loved William; her spare time was spent stitching, praying, gardening, building, or arranging porcelain, which last was her passion.

Switzer refers to 'that excellent Princess' [Mary] who 'lost no Time but was either measuring, directing or ordering her Buildings; but in Gard'ning, especially Exoticks, she was particularly skill'd'.[39] At Hampton Court, to set off Wren's new front, Charles II's Great Fountain Garden was perfected; while at Kensington the cottagey palace that had lately been Nottingham House was given the kind of box and yew troytown Dutch William liked.

'The Queen brought in the Custom or Humour as I may call it',

wrote Defoe, 'of furnishing Houses with China-Ware . . . piling
their China upon the tops of Cabinets, Scrutores & every Chymney-
Piece, to the Tops of the Ceilings'.[40] At Kensington the Queen's
Gallery alone displayed 154 pieces of porcelain and in the overmantel-
sketches Grinling Gibbons made for the Queen every inch is packed
with pots of all sizes, even to the cornice.[41]

It all sounds innocuous enough. Queen Mary was popular and the
nation's grief real when in 1694 she caught smallpox and died.
Burnet, who attended, wrote:

> We were, God knows, a sorrowful company, for we were
> losing her who was our chief hope & glory upon earth . . . She
> died on the 28th of December about one in the morning in the
> 33rd year of her age. During her sickness the King was in an
> agony that amazed us all, fainting often & breaking out into
> most violent lamentations. When she died his spirits sank so low
> that there was great reason to apprehend that he was following
> her. For some weeks after he was so little master of himself that
> he was not capable of minding business or of seeing company.[42]

While Mary lay dying Anne, herself ill, sent daily messages, on
one occasion delivered by Lady Fitzharding who 'broke in, whether
they would or not . . . to express in how much Concern the Princess
was'.[43] Burnet records a 'reconciling message' from Mary to Anne,
which Sarah denies; but while Gibbons was drafting Mary's
monument (never erected), Lords Sunderland and Somers were
trying to heal the breach between William and Anne. 'My lord, do
what you will', said the King wearily when Somers found him alone
at Kensington, 'I can think of no business.'

On Anne's side, such was Stuart resentment, there was just as little
enthusiasm. As heir-presumptive she now felt strong enough to
dictate her terms, which meant of course that there must be no
question of Sarah's dismissal. 'Caliban', Anne warned Sarah, 'will
without doubt endeavour to make us yeild rather then make one
step towards it him self', but she will never part with her 'till she is
fast lockt in her coffin'.[44] In the meantime Anne, again referring to
William, trusts 'in Heaven we shall not be better freinds then we are
now unless we chance to meet there'.[45]

When in the following September (1695) William took Namur

somebody, not Sarah, persuaded Anne to write and congratulate him. 'Nobody upon earth could have made me do it', Sarah commented later, 'but I was never the councellor upon such great occasions'.[46] Though William sent no answer it was obvious to everyone that the quarrel must end and so it did. Anne was allowed to move into St James's Palace and Sarah with her; and everyone else flocked there to pay them court.

Marlborough, however, still out of favour, became in 1696 involved in another Jacobite plot to murder William. This was no flowerpot penny-dreadful, but a full-scale conspiracy headed by Sir John Fenwick who, when arrested, accused Marlborough, Russell, Godolphin and Shrewsbury with having written treasonably to the exiled king. According to Macaulay Marlborough, under the long ordeal, remained serene and even slightly contemptuous, Godolphin uneasy but self-possessed; whereas Shrewsbury, who was probably the least to blame, crumpled, resigned and retired abroad. Godolphin too retired for the time being. Yet nothing was proved and the charge recoiled. Fenwick was executed on January 28th, 1697.

In the following October with the Treaty of Ryswick signed, England found herself no longer at war with France. William, his chief occupation gone, 'reassumed his farther Pursuit of Gard'ning, in altering & making a considerable Improvement to the Gardens [of Hampton Court] and making that great Terrass next the Thames, the noblest Work of that kind in Europe'.[47] It could have had a mellowing effect. In 1698 he at long last recalled Marlborough, reinstated him in the army and Privy Council and made him Governor to Anne's nine-year-old son the Duke of Gloucester. The child was delicate (all of Anne's children were hydrocephalic) and subject to fits of 'ague', but Marlborough's appointment was of course a mark of restored favour. and the two young heirs, Gloucester and Jack Churchill, then twelve, could now play at soldiers together. But Sarah was not overjoyed. There was a muddle over the young Duke's household: Anne was to choose whom she pleased and then, later, no she was not to, the King would do it. When Marlborough ventured to tell William 'that the Princess . . . had engaged her Promises to several Persons and that not to be able to perform those Promises would be so great a Mortification as he hoped His Majesty would not give her at a Time when any thing of

Trouble might do her Prejudice, she being then with Child', the King 'fell into a great Passion and said She should not be Queen before her Time'.[48]

It was sad that one so expert at war should prove crude at peace; and it was a great deal sadder that Gloucester should have Marlborough as his guardian for only two years before he died. In the glimpses we catch of him in Anne's letters he is almost always ill. 'Dr Ratcliffe . . . assures me ye child is in no manner of danger but however I can't help being afraid till he has quite lost his ague for methinks 'tis an ugly thing for such a distemper to hang so long upon one of his age . . .' And, 'tho I love him very well, I cant bragg of his beauty'.[49]

Some blamed his death on the cramming he had had from his over-zealous preceptor, Bishop Burnet, who boasted:

I went through geography so often with him that he knew all the maps very particularly. I explained to him the forms of government in every country . . . I acquainted him with all the great revolutions that had been in the world & gave him a copious account of the Greek & Roman histories & of Plutarch's Lives. The last thing I explained to him was the Gothic constitution & the beneficiary & feudal laws. I talked of these things at different times near three hours a day . . . He was then eleven years old . . . He was the only remaining child of seventeen that the Princess had borne, some to the full time & the rest before it . . . His death was a great alarm to the whole nation. The Jacobites grew insolent upon it & said now the chief difficulty was removed out of the way of the prince of Wales's succession.[50]

The close of William's reign saw a handful of seemingly unconnected happenings, all of which were to have great influence in Sarah's life. In 1698 Henrietta, her eldest daughter, married Francis, son of Sidney Godolphin and Margaret Blagge. The following year their son Willigo was born, and Anne, Sarah's second daughter, married the Earl of Sunderland's heir, Charles Spencer. In or about the year 1700 one Abigail Hill was introduced by her cousin Sarah, Countess of Marlborough, to the Princess Anne as a bedchamber-woman; and Bishop Burnet married for the third time. On March 3rd, 1701 the Act of Settlement was passed, to exclude the Pretender from the English throne and to ensure the Protestant succession; and on September 6th Marlborough, as commander-in-chief of the English forces in Holland, signed the Grand Alliance treaty between England, Holland and Austria, at Loo, in Sarah's presence. Ten days later James II died in France and Louis XIV proclaimed the Pretender, James III King of England. In January, 1702 Robert Harley, a moderate Tory, was narrowly elected Speaker of the House of Commons; and on March 8th King William died. Sarah commented:

And now, after all I have related of the King, and after so much Dislike as I have expressed of his Character & Conduct, you will perhaps hardly believe me in what I am going to say. When the King came to die, I felt nothing of that Satisfaction which I once thought I should have had upon this Occasion. And my Lord and Lady Jersey's writing and sending perpetually to give an Account, as his Breath grew shorter and shorter, filled me with Horror. I thought I would lose the Best Employment in any Court sooner than act so odious a Part. And the King, who had given me so much Cause to hate him, in that Condition I sincerely pitied: So little is it in my Nature to retain Resentment against any Mortal (how unjust soever he may have been) in whom the Will to injure is no more.[51]

CHAPTER IV

Hail, Glorious Anna!

1702-1704

◆

The glorious scene opens, the reign that is to see the victories of Marlborough, the capture of Gibraltar, the union with Scotland; in science the discoveries of Newton, in architecture the master-pieces of Wren and Vanbrugh and Hawksmoor, in literature the works of Swift and Defoe, of Addison, Congreve and Pope; the reign that will foster the Protestant Succession and put England herself in the foremost place in the world . . . and all this to be launched by a queen who is very nearly a cripple.

After seventeen pregnancies and numberless attacks of gout or arthritis Anne limped, with assistance, to her coronation. She was thirty-seven and had no heir. Of her four chief assets it might fairly be said that the Marlboroughs and Godolphin made three. The fourth was her Stuart will, reinforced by faith, which meant, beyond obstinacy, that when put to it she could and would force herself to accomplish the near-impossible and so, by example, inspire others to do likewise.

Sarah, though not, like Marlborough, at all times an asset, undoubtedly was so at the beginning of the reign when Anne was groping and Sarah's competence, plus Godolphin's, was worth more than a queen's ransom. And while it would be a shocking thing, as historians warn us, to see Queen Anne only as Sarah saw her, the views of an observant witness, no matter how biassed, are, in the absence of a definitive biography, not to be despised.

Sarah's opinion of Queen Anne—written, printed, incised in marble—ranges from the kindly to the savage and then, in old age, back nearly to the kindly again. When Voltaire, visiting Blenheim in the autumn of 1727, asked if he might see the Duchess's memoirs, she said, 'Wait a little, I am at present altering my account of Queen Anne's character. I have begun to love her again since the present lot have become our governors'.[1] Sarah was then drafting for the Rysbrack statue the inscription which began:

> Queen Anne had a person and appearance very graceful, something of majesty in her look. She was religious without any affectation, and certainly meant to do everything that was just. She had no ambition* . . . She was extremely well bred and treated her chief ladies and servants as if they had been her equals; and she never refused to give charity when there was the least reason for any body to ask it . . .

and so on. 'I have put these facts together', Sarah explained, 'for materials for the person who writes the inscription. They are all true, notwithstanding what she was imposed upon in doing at the end of her reign.'[2]

Bashfulness, a minor weakness of Anne's not inherited from her father, had to be overcome before her first speech, which she made 'with great weight and authority and with a softness of voice and sweetness in the pronunciation that added much life to all she spoke'.[3]

On April 23rd, 1702 Anne was crowned, and on May 4th war was declared against France. Louis XIV's proclamation of 1701, acknowledging the Pretender as king, had given 'a universal distaste to the whole English nation'.[4] It was a challenge William would have leapt at had he lived. It was bequeathed to Anne and to Marlborough, now Knight of the Garter, Captain-General and Master of the Ordnance—a trust formidable enough to daunt any soldier and any queen—to vanquish the seemingly unconquerable power of France.

On May 6th the Queen appointed Godolphin Lord Treasurer, the office most nearly approximating then to Prime Minister. Sarah, looking back from a later reign, says that Godolphin, in his attitude to Anne, was 'like Mentor in Telemachus, Her Majesty being the most ignorant and helpless creature living'.[5] But already she felt well entrenched for here, as Sir Winston observes, was 'a close confederacy which had been slowly and tensely wrought. Anne had

* In another version this reads: She always meant well. She had no false ambition.

78

insisted upon the equality of their intercourse, but this privilege was strictly limited. Mrs Morley, Mr and Mrs Freeman and Mr Montgomery—there could not be a tighter thing. They formed a group as integral and as collectively commanding as anything of which there is record in our annals.'[6] So long as she could count upon those three champions—and that surely must be forever—the Queen felt unassailable.

On May 12th Sarah was appointed Groom of the Stole and on June 19th Keeper of the Privy Purse and Mistress of the Robes; whilst her daughters, Lady Henrietta Godolphin and Lady Anne Sunderland,* joined her at court as Ladies of the Bedchamber. It seemed the ideal plan. Marlborough must be often abroad and so, with her brood all but fledged, what else could Mrs Freeman have to do all day but play cards and talk to Mrs Morley? And when the court was at Windsor, Mrs Freeman would still be at hand because Mrs Morley had made her Ranger of the park and had given her the pleasant lodge that went with it. Anne may have been surprised at how seriously Sarah took her new duties. Zestfully she hurled herself into them and after setting the privy purse in order (no more bribes, no more poundage, no more bought places), she turned to the question of the Queen's clothes.

Some women (Frances Tyrconnel for one) would have lost their heads and ordered wildly. Sarah knew better. She knew that extravagance was senseless and that nothing, not even a queen's wardrobe, could resist the cool, calmly thought out policy of rationalisation she had long since learned to apply to everything. Jewels, for example, could be hired, and doubtless with state robes there could be similar economies; for after all, with the best will in the world, what could be more vulgar and futile than to overdress a martyr to gout? 'Some people', Sarah remembered, 'to be revenged of me for not letting them cheat have said she was not fine enough for a queen, but it would have been rediculous with her person & [one] of her age to have been otherwise drest. Besides her limbs were so weakend with the Goute for many yeares that she could not indure heavy cloaths & she really had every thing that was hansome & proper for her'.[7] For state occasions of course there

* Her husband, Charles Spencer, succeeded his father as 3rd Earl of Sunderland in 1702.

would have to be velvet and ermine, but for ordinary days clothes should be ordinary and good. It is only now and again, in Anne's letters, that one seems to catch a subdued hankering for nonsense. 'I beleeved when I writt to you about my manto* for the thanksgiving day', she wrote, 'it was a hard task, but heavy clôths are soe uneasy to me that I could not help just mentioning it tho at ye same [time] I had a mind to be fine too & in order to be soe I intended to have two diamond buttens & loops upon each sleeve . . .'[8]

At times the Queen could be quickly humoured, at times not. With affection on both sides much can be tolerated; but Sarah had much to do and so, when too pressed for argument, she would resort to finality and put an end to difference with her 'Lord, Madam, it must be so!'† But clothes were frills. There were far more serious things to see to, among them the Queen's politics, which all too obviously needed to be taken more firmly in hand. However, the same policy applied and in the schooling of Anne there was nothing daunting or new. 'I used to pass many hours in a day with her', Sarah recalled, 'and allways endeavour to give her notions of loving her country, of justice & governing by the laws & making her self bee beloved rather then feard & I allways showed her how easy that was to doe when she had [it] so much in her power to doe good and I ever told her that nothing was so great & honourable as to govern upon the conditions that a crown was taken nor no way so certain as that to keep it as long as she lived.'[9]

Excellent, what could be better? 'You shall always find me', declared Anne in her first speech, 'a strict and religious observer of my word'. But then what of parties? Was Mrs Freeman, like Mr Freeman, Mr Montgomery and Mr and Mrs Morley, a true Tory? No, she was not. She was emphatically Whig. How indeed could Mrs Freeman live up to her name and be otherwise? The Whigs were for freedom—free thinking, free acting; no shackles, no popery, no wooden shoes and every man on his own merits. It was because James had mocked at all this that he had lost his crown, and woe betide his daughter if she scorned the same lesson. Ah yes, but

* The manto (*manteau*) was referred to as a new fashion in the reign of William, when it was disapproved by Lady Fitzharding as too informal to be worn on a king's birthday.

† Quoted in the 1712 pamphlet *The St Albans Ghost*.

the rock upon which James had foundered, everyone knew, was the Church of Rome. Anne would never make that mistake. Her rock was the true church, the Church of England, to which the very nation was bound and wedded.* Come now, what had the Whigs to say to that? What sandy foundation had they to offer instead? To one whose grandfather had been beheaded, a Whig might too easily conceal a Roundhead or a republican. And what, pray, was the Whigs' attitude to the divine right of kings?

These were awkward questions. Not of course that Sarah could not counter them, but she knew that the answers would at this stage be unacceptable. She knew too that, as in the case of the warming-pan, Anne could make herself believe or disbelieve exactly as she chose. It was vexing. Conversion might take longer than she had thought. 'I did allways endeavour', she wrote later, 'to give the queen a true notion of our two parties, having had a great deal of experience of the men on both sides and having had certain knowledge of a great many truths and facts which her Majesty could hear from nobody else'.[10]

It was early days for knowing how obdurate Anne could be; yet to one of Sarah's tenacity, even had she known it, the more hopeless the cause, the greater the challenge must always be. She never gave up, never spared herself for an instant and was never to be deflected from what she, quite often misguidedly, thought was right. In her draft self-vindication prepared by Bishop Burnet she makes him say:

> The Duchess was now continually trying all the methods & all the arguments she could think of to remove or soften those violent prepossessions the Queen still retained against those whom the Duchess thought the best part of her subjects. With this view she argued frequently with the Queen & sometimes not without a warmth natural to sincerity which yet hitherto did not appear to leave any uneasyness behind it. To the same purpose she wrote many & long letters & by some expressions in the Queen's answers one would have judged that she had now & then laid down her prejudices, but by more & more it

* The first clause in the Act of Settlement (3 March, 1701) runs: That whoever shall hereafter come to the possession of the Crown shall join in communion with the Church of England as by law established.

appeared that her aversion to the very name of Whig was too deep to be cur'd. The Duchess tried to introduce other names for the opposite parties but to little purpose. For tho she found as yet no alteration in the Queen towards herself on this account, yet the work she had undertaken proceeded but by very slow degrees. Something or other still retarded it and made it go very heavy.[11]

For Anne too it was saddening. It seemed to her such a pity that, in a hitherto flawless sky (the sunshine day they had longed for in gloomier reigns) this plague-ridden cloud of politics should have to appear at all. Why, with everything in the world to talk about, from the weather to clothes, must they always have to argue politics? Yet even so the world seemed duller than ever when Sarah was absent. 'I'me sure you can never doubt of my wishing to be with you every hour in ye day', wrote Anne, 'I am now in great hast to be drest, this being my Company Day tho ye weather is soe bad I fancy no body will come. However I will be in a readiness to receive any body that will give them selves the trouble. Therefore for this time, my deare deare Mrs Freeman farewel.'[12] After the first rush for places courtiers had begun to find Anne's court almost as moribund as William's. Many left off coming.

The Queen's Privy Council, Sarah noticed, was almost solidly Tory. That would not do at all. For the Tories favoured a limited war at sea. Only from the Whigs could Marlborough count on solid support for a full-scale land war in Europe. 'My Lord Normanby (soon after Duke of Buckingham)', Sarah noted, 'the Earls of Jersey and Nottingham, Sir Edward Seymour, with many others of the High-fliers, were brought into Place; Sir Nathan Wright was continued in Possession of the Great Seal of England, and the Earl of Rochester in the Lieutenancy of Ireland. These were Men who had all a wonderful Zeal for the Church, a Sort of publick Merit that eclipsed all other in the Eyes of the Queen. And I am firmly persuaded that, notwithstanding her extraordinary Affection for me, and the entire Devotion which my Lord Marlborough and my Lord Godolphin had for many Years shewn to her Service, they would not have had so great a Share of her Favour and Confidence if they had not been reckoned in the Number of the Tories.

'For my own part the Word Church had never any Charm for me in the Mouths of those who made the most Noise with it; for I could not perceive that they gave any other distinguishing Proof of their Regard for the Thing than a frequent Use of the Word, like a Spell to enchant weak Minds.'[13] If Anne chose to call Tories the Church Party, Sarah preferred to call them Jacobites and to warn the Queen that they were after her crown, or even her life.

'I feared the loss of Mrs Morley's life as well as of her three kingdoms', Sarah remembers, 'and out of these apprehensions, too well grounded, I was perpetually telling her that the Whigs were in her true interest and the Tories out to destroy her; and when I saw she had such a partiality for those that I knew to be Jacobites, I asked one day very seriously whether she had a mind to give up her crown, for if it had been her conscience not to wear it I do solemnly protest I would never disturb her nor struggle as I did, but she told me she was not sure the Prince of Wales was her Brother and that it was not practicable for him to come here without ruin to the religion and country . . .'[14]

In a running battle of this sort, Sarah realised, even the smallest gain was not to be despised; so that when Anne proposed four new Tory peers, Sarah begged for a fifth on behalf of Whig Mr Hervey, who was surprised and never ceased to be grateful. His benefactress ought, he said, to have been born in the Golden Age, for only then could her virtues have been appreciated. He launched into verse:

> Here beauteous Nature all her strength combined
> To form ye finest body, noblest mind.
> No single virtue can we most commend,
> Whether ye Wife, ye Mother or ye Friend.

'In short', the new lord concluded, she was 'one so every way worthy of ye Favour she possesses by her incessant Vigilance and incorruptible Fidelity . . . that ye People as well as we her Friends ought to pray for ye Continuance of it for their own Sakes'.[15]

Whether Marlborough, a moderate Tory who strove to keep clear of parties, approved of his wife's proselytising for the Whigs at the risk of friction with the Queen is extremely doubtful; and that too when he must have known Sarah was being egged on by their violently Whig son-in-law Charles third Earl of Sunderland. Sunderland, whom Sir Winston calls a rasping figure, obnoxious to the Queen, was to be one of the five tyrannising lords, as Anne called them—the others were Wharton, Somers, Halifax and Orford —who, as the Junto, formed a self-appointed Whig Cabinet in which lay much power.

Queen Anne, while begging Godolphin to save her from the merciless men of both parties, believed that she could take her pick of Whigs and Tories (mostly Tories) and so rule with an ideal coalition. With this, in theory at least, Marlborough, loathing faction, showed sympathy; and the Marlborough-Godolphin ministry soon formed, which was to last eight years, was in fact a mainly Whig coalition. But the situation was complicated by two conditions which would not apply today: one, that no politician could afford to ignore the Court Party (those who supported the crown on the principle that all opposition was more or less factious and on the practical grounds that the crown was the source of patronage in church and state); and two, that England, with a total population of less than six million, was ruled by the sovereign with the help of a relatively small company drawn for the most part from a few aristocratic and landed families who between them controlled huge blocks of votes in parliament and in the counties.

What nobody could then of course be expected to realise, let alone rectify, was that the machinery of government was so primitive and antique, the wonder was that it could be made to work at all. The sovereign, no longer omnipotent but still powerful, chose or dismissed her ministers as she would. She was not bound to choose them from the party with a majority in the House of Commons; while the House of Lords had infinitely more power than it has today. There was no Prime Minister, as we know that office, although the Lord Treasurer was sometimes given that name; and the Cabinet system was only just beginning to evolve.

Yet if anyone in Anne's reign could have foreseen the twentieth-century pattern, with the ultimate power vested not in sovereign, Lords or Commons but in Prime Minister and Cabinet, with a handful of Civil Service and trades union leaders, he could scarcely have been expected to understand or to believe it. Even now, to foreigners at least, it seems a strange way of governing; and indeed, as Sir Winston remarked, it is the worst system of government in the world—except for all the other systems of government.

In writing of these times it would be as easy to overestimate the influence of Sarah as it would be to underestimate the power of Anne. Anne lacked humour, vision and intellect, her outlook was insular, but she was not shallow or commonplace and she was not, like her husband, a fool. Once her mind was made up, all the arguments in the world could not shake her; and by the same token, once her confidence had been given—to Sarah, to Marlborough—it took a vast amount of guile and disillusion to undermine it.

In the first year of Anne's reign, as in more recent times, an Englishman needed to be stouthearted. Louis XIV, brazen as Mars, had overrun the Spanish Netherlands (now Belgium) and had taken the line of fortresses there regarded by Holland as her protective barrier. Philip V, Louis' grandson, ruled in Spain, with a prospect terrifying to the whole of Europe including ourselves that the two countries, Spain and France, might be united under one crown; a horror which, it was felt, must at all costs be prevented. Marlborough's first task was to assist Holland and restore her barrier, which meant flinging the French troops back from the fortresses of the Meuse.

At the Hague Marlborough was treated like the prince he was soon to become. 'A finer work of art', says Trevelyan, 'has never been shown there. The statesmen of Europe were received at the top of the staircase by a glorious living portrait of a Milord, every inch a soldier and a courtier; said indeed to be fifty years of age but in the prime of manly beauty, with a complexion like a girl's; talking charmingly in bad French; seeming to understand all and sympathise with everyone.'[16] Already he had won the confidence of Antoine Heinsius, the Grand Pensionary of Holland, the first and by no means the least of his overseas conquests.

Yet in spite of all this and in spite of her own confidence and affection in Marlborough, Anne begged him to ask the Dutch to make her husband supreme commander of the Grand Alliance over Marlborough's head! It was solemnly proposed and with infinite tact rejected. It may have been now or later (the documents are undated) that some wag decided to compensate Prince George for his disappointment by making him Steward of Colchester. It was rather too bad. When the thing broke upon the town there were glum faces at Kensington and titters in the coffee houses. Anne wrote to Sarah:

> I can never thank my dear Mrs Freeman enough for her kindness to Mr Morley & her humble servant on all occasions, espessially for ye Consern you express for this ugly foolish thing about the Princes being Steward of Colchester. I have asked him again about it & he assures me he was never spoke to by any body nor knew nothing of it till Sir Thomas Cook came & offerd him the thing . . . I wish you would ask Lord Treasurer what I can do to putt a Stop to all this Noise that has bin made about this thing for 'tis very disagreeable & I do not doubt but my enemys will improve all things to my disadvantage.[17]

For the sake of peace Prince George was in the end allowed to call himself Lord High Admiral and was voted a huge allowance. Everyone except Anne and himself knew that it was ludicrously too much and Lord Sunderland said so, thus calling down upon himself the wrath of Sarah and the lasting enmity of Anne.

In Flanders, one might have expected that, with Prince George brushed aside, Marlborough would be given a clear field. He was granted the command and with it a squad of Dutchmen called field-deputies who made it their business to prevent engagements and forbid the commander-in-chief to fight battles, for fear of hazarding the Dutch troops. To a grave extent this recurrent nuisance was to thwart Marlborough's plans and to try his singular store of patience to the uttermost. His letters to Sarah speak very little of a triumphant general. To begin with, 'You know of all things', he reminds her, 'I doe not love writting', so much so that, with all the official mail he has to deal with, 'were it not for my Zele for her Majesty's service, I shou'd certainly desert.'[18] Yet he promises his wife, 'You shall never faile of hearing from mee every post.'[19] The labour of writing was bad enough, and when letters had been written there was the agony of waiting, no matter how pressing the message, for a favourable wind. To reach Queen Anne at Windsor the news of the victory at Blenheim took eight days.

In May Marlborough wrote to Sarah from the Hague, 'The Quiet of my life depends onely upon your kindnes & I beg you to believe the truth of my soull which is that you are dearer to mee then all things in this world'.[20] In August he shows concern for her health. 'You naturally have a good constitution & if you take this illness* in time, I hope bleeding some times & your own fisick pretty often will give you health & a long life which I doe from my soull wish you . . . You think your letters miscarry or that I have not time to read them. I doe asure you that your letters are so welcome to mee that if they should come in the time I were expecting the enemy to charge mee I could not forbear reading them.'[21]

In spite of every disadvantage, not least the Dutch field-deputies, Marlborough's campaign against the French on the Meuse was successful and a thanksgiving service, attended by Anne and Sarah, was held in the unfinished cathedral of St Paul's. On October 22nd, 1702 Anne wrote charmingly to Sarah to tell her that she had resolved to make Marlborough a duke. Sarah was stricken. 'When I read the letter first', she tells us, 'I let it drop out of my hand and was for some minutes like one that had received the news of a death of one of her dear friends . . . I was so easy for anything of that kind, having before all that was any use, by which it is plain I have no great taste for grandeur.'[22]

To Sarah the privileges of a dukedom were little more than a matter of precedence ('I like as well', she said, 'to follow five hundred as one') and the obligations were onerous. But Marlborough felt differently and, with the encouragement of Heinsius who maintained that the commander's prestige in Europe called for it, decided to accept. The one serious reservation was money: how support a dukedom without an estate? Anne, foreseeing this, made him a grant of £5000 a year for her lifetime and in December asked Parliament to extend that grant to benefit his heirs; but that they declined to do.†

Privately Anne then offered 'dear Mrs Freeman & Mr Freeman' £2000 a year out of her privy purse, 'besides the grant of the five. This can draw no envy', she added, 'for no body need know it . . . I beg my dear Mrs Freeman would never any way give me an answer

* Illness unspecified.

† Sir Winston Churchill estimates Marlborough's income at this time (Dec. 1702) as £60,000 a year. (Churchill, op. cit. 1, 617).

to this, only comply with the desires of your poor unfortunate faithful Morley* that loves you most tenderly & is with the sincerest passion imaginable yours.'[23] Sarah declined but, as Sir Winston exclaims, 'Alas for the glitter of our story! We shall have presently to record . . . how nine years later in her bitterness she reclaimed this gift with arrears, and how the Queen paid every penny of it.'[24]

In the winter of 1702–3 Anne, who shared Marlborough's loathing for faction, found her government sharply divided over the question of Occasional Conformity, an extension of the Test Act of 1673 whereby only those taking Communion in the Church of England could qualify for state or municipal office. The Test Act had led to cynical lip-service and hypocrisy to such an extent that that professional trouble-maker Dr Sacheverell had 'hung out the bloody flag of defiance' and thundered against it. Though it bore every sign of having come from the Devil, the Occasional Conformity Bill was welcomed as a godsend by political extremists, who determined to make as much mischief with it as they could. Defoe called it playing bo-peep with God Almighty; and at first it fooled the Queen who, taking the bill at its face value, sent Prince George to the Lords to vote for it. Though rejected, it was to prove one of several political themes—The Church is in Danger! Invitations to Hanover! Jacobite Invasion!—twanged repeatedly on the one-string fiddle that was Parliament during Anne's reign; and if, for brief seasons, things seemed to be going smoothly, it was astonishing how quickly a storm could be raised simply by plucking one of those hackneyed notes.

For the Marlboroughs 1703 began tragically with the death of their son Jack, first Marquis of Blandford. He was seventeen and heir to the dukedom. Everyone had found him a delightful young man. 'Your son danced a minuet last night', Anne tells Sarah, 'which upon my word he performed very well & I do realy beleeve in time he will make a very fine dancer, therefore I hope you will encourage him in it'.[25] His godfather Godolphin, with whom he was staying at Newmarket when he died from smallpox, found him 'not only the

* This phrase, with slight variations, the Queen applied to herself after the death of her son the Duke of Gloucester in 1700. It would appear deliberately to echo the Churchill motto: Faithful but unfortunate.

best-natured & the most agreeable but the most free-thinking
& reasonable creature that one can imagine for his age.'26

On January 2nd, 1703 young Blandford wrote to his father:

> I would have answered your last letter sooner if I could have
> thought what to say for myself in defence of so great a fault, and
> I find the longer I think the less I have to say; so that I resolved to
> write this letter to beg my dear Papa's & Mama's pardon for
> what I have done, and to promise them never to do so again. I
> owne that I have done some of the things that my Mama
> complains of but she sais if she had told you them with all the
> agravations [exaggerations] she heard them you would have bin
> much more angry with me than you are, and I can't say any-
> thing to them because I don't know what they are. I would have
> writ to my Mama now but that by what she said to me in her
> letter I am afraid she never will throughly forgive me, which
> has greived me so much that I cannot tell how to write till I have
> some hopes of being freinds with my dear Mama; and I hope
> my Dear Papa will be so kind as to intercede for me with Mama
> and to be perswaded that no body can be more heartily sorry for
> having done amiss than, Dear Papa, your most dutyfull son
> > *Blandford*27

On February 9th he wrote to his mother:

> I received a letter from Mr Godolphin last post and the joy
> I had when I found I had some hopes of being freinds with my
> Dear Mama is not to be express'd; but I can't think my self so
> happy till my Dear Mama can find some time to lett me have a
> letter from her and I am sure there can be no greater pleasure
> than [that] would be to, my Dear Mama, your most dutyfull son
> > *Blandford*

On February 20th he was dead. His death, says Burnet, went very
deep in his father's heart; and as for Sarah friends feared for her
reason*. Anne's offer to go to her ('ye unfortunat ought to com to
ye unfortunat') was declined; nor can Godolphin's words have been of
much comfort. This, he said, was 'the greatest occasion of letting the

* Inconsolable in black she is said at this time to have haunted the cloisters of
Westminster Abbey.

whole world see that God Almighty has blessed you with a Christian patience and fortitude as eminent as ye reason and understanding by which you are most justly distinguished from the rest of your sex.'[28]

Marlborough, after making a new will ('If I must dye without a son') in favour of Godolphin's son Francis,* left for Holland, whence he wrote to Sarah:

I doe conjure you by all the kindness I have for you, which is as much as ever man had for woman, that you will take the best advice you can for your health & then follow exactly what shall be prescribed ... You & I have very great reason to bless God for all wee have, soe that wee must not repine att his taking our poor Child from us but blesse & praise him for what his goodness leaves us.

He urged her to 'live soe as that one should chearfully dye when it shall be his pleasure to call for us', and ended, 'I am very sensible of my own frailtes, but if I can ever be soe happy as to be always with you & that you comfort & assiste mee in these my thoughts, I am then perswaid'd I should be as happy & contented as 'tis possible to bee in this world'.[29] Whether Sarah found consolation in his admonitions or preferred Lady Evelyn's 'Sorrow does not kill soe quick as those that feel it are apt to wish', who shall say? For a time she began to hope that she might have another son, but that too failed her.

In Flanders Marlborough was again being frustrated beyond endurance. His letters are full of troubles, from the cussedness of the Dutch to 'those little inconveniencys of the head eake which are but too naturall to mee'. Sarah, taking her cue from Anne, prescribes ass's milk. It is not a success. 'I was yesterday troubled with the head eake', he tells her, ' & this day have sickness in my stomack which I beleive is occasion'd by the ass's milk'. He will give it one more trial ... Disaster. 'Now that I am well', he writes, 'I may acquaint you that the ass's milk had soe disorder'd mee that I did not stur out of my chamber Sunday Munday & Tuesday last, which has made me

---

* Francis Godolphin, married to Marlborough's eldest daughter Henrietta, was to have been made Earl of Marlborough and to have taken the family name of Churchill. Marlborough's youngest daughter Mary, then single, was left £20,000; and Sarah another £2000 a year.

take a resolution of leaving itt off. I did in my former letters desire that some more Ruborb & Licherish might bee sent mee by some Officer . . . It may bee sent by the first Yacht'. And when Sarah has leisure, will she please call at Sir Godfrey Kneller's and see 'if he has any of the Queens Pictures [portraits] by him. A good Copie will bee as good as an originall. It is for the Princess Sophia I mean the Electoris of Hannover'.[30]

The ageing Electress, a lively, personable woman next in line to the English throne and so, as can be the way with successors, frowned on by Anne, had said she would take it very kindly if someone could procure the Queen's portrait for her; and very kindly she took it. Sarah, who had been able to get her nothing better than what she herself called a very ill copy was dumbfounded by the cornucopia of bounty which cascaded in return. Sophia, vowing that she valued the portrait more than the whole universe, sent her the universe worked in tapestry, then valued at £3000, plus about £3000 in cash 'to lay out in silver table plate or sconces as I liked, to put in the room with the hangings she sent me. I ded not chuse such things as I thought uselesse & troublesome', Sarah explains, 'but I desired that the money might be laid out in plain gold plates for the table & that the Ellectors armes might bee put upon them that Posterity might see the Honour that she had don me, & this plate was given by the Duke of Marlboroughs will, at my request, after my death, to the heirs as they succeeded of his family'.*

As with Anne so with Marlborough, Sarah insists that her letters be burned. How she reacted to his complaints, to what extent she reassured him, we can only surmise from what he writes to her. Thus from Bonn:

If you had not positively desir'd that I should always burn your letters I should have been very glad to have keept your dear letter of the 9th, it was soe very kind & particularly upon the subject of our living quietly togeither, til which happy time comes I am shure I cant bee contented & then I doe flatter my self I should live with as much satisfaction as I am capable off. I wish I could recall twentie Yeares past, I doe asure you for noe other reason but that I might in probabillity have longer time &

* Only one of these gold plates now remains at Blenhein.

be the better able to convince you how trully sensible I am att this time of your kindness which is the only real comfort of my life, soe ~~that shou'd I be so unhappy as to see you return to that indifferency which has been the occation of a great deal of uneasyness, I shou'd then have noe comfort left in this life~~ & whielst you are kind, besides the many blessings it brings mee, I cant but hope wee shall yett have a Son, which are my daily prayers . . .[31]

It is easy to look back and see the victories that lay before him—and even at that time there were those who predicted that though he had lost a son, fame would be his heir[32]—but to Marlborough in 1703 it must have seemed like the end of all things, the end of his dynasty, the end of his career. There was no solution but retirement to the English countryside with a loving wife. Never child longed more impatiently for anything, he assured her, than he did for peace that he might be always with her; but of what fate had left them he must above all be able to count on her love, 'for if you doe not love mee & shou'd use mee ill I should have very little concern for anything in this world, for I believe never anybody's happiness depended soe much upon another's kindness as mine at this time does upon you'.[33] The English Malady—the spleen, the black dog of chronic depression—had him by the heart and was worrying the life out of him; and Sarah of course suffered with him. And what of Anne, she who confessed she was of a temper always to fear the worst? Unexpectedly, she now wrote Sarah one of the finest letters of her life, the letter Sir Winston calls magnificent and momentous and one which ranks her with Queen Elizabeth and the greatest sovereigns of the English line:

*Windsor, Saturday**

The thoughts that both my dear Mrs Freeman and Mr Freeman seem to have of retiring gives me no small uneasiness, and therefore I must say something on that subject. It is no wonder at all that people in your posts should be weary of the world, who are so continually troubled with all the hurry and impertinencies of it; but give me leave to say you should a little consider

* It is rare for Queen Anne to date a letter; nor in writing to Sarah does she include salutation or signature.

your faithful friends and poor country, which must be ruined if ever you should put your melancholy thoughts in execution. As for your poor unfortunate faithful Morley, she could not bear it; for if ever you should forsake me, I would have nothing more to do with the world but make another abdication; for what is a crown when the support of it is gone? I never will forsake your dear self, Mr Freeman, nor Mr Montgomery, but always be your constant faithful servant; and we four must never part till death mows us down with his impartial hand.[34]

With the glory of England at stake, says Sir Winston, Anne subordinated party politics to the supreme need. 'Her magnanimity and her sense of proportion expressed the genius of the English race in adversity'.[35] It remained to be seen how Marlborough and his duchess would respond. Marlborough was profoundly moved: for such a queen he would gladly lay down his life. Sarah was far less deeply impressed; indeed she seems almost to have taken Anne's gesture for weakness. 'She flattered herself', Coxe suggests, 'that little exertion was now wanting to gain a complete victory over the political prejudices of her royal mistress. She therefore teased the queen with her eulogies of the Whigs and her censures of the Tories, whom she involved in one common accusation of Jacobitism'.[36]

Marlborough too, though stubborn, was urged by his wife to change his politics, to back the Whigs who supported the war and to oust the extreme Tories who were steadily undermining him on the home front. It was high time for them to vanish and so make room for the soundly saved. When a cuckoo is in the nest it is not in its nature to be tranquil. Nothing would content Sarah until the Tory high-fliers—Seymour, Jersey and Nottingham—had been forced to fly and, in Nottingham's case, had been succeeded by Robert Harley, Speaker in the Commons and now also Secretary of State; while Henry St John became Secretary at War.

In November Marlborough returned and, with Queen and Duchess, welcomed at Windsor the Archduke Charles, the Austrian claimant to the Spanish throne. From Lady Russell we have a glimpse of Sarah in waiting after the banquet:

Now the service being done, Lady Marlborough stood ready

with her towell & bason of water. Our young King,* risen from the table, offered to take the towell from the lady. She held it fast, but he prevailed, took the napkin, diped in the water, took one of the Queens hands & washed her fingers ends & then his own, gave back the napkin to the lady & with it one of the finest diamond rings, desiring her to ware it.[37]

The winter brought its dreary crop of vexations—an attempt to deprive Marlborough of his command in favour of the Elector of Hanover (George I-to-be); a Tory effort to revive the Occasional Conformity Bill, and so on—and then, as Marlborough was leaving for Flanders and for the campaign which would lead to Blenheim, Sarah sprang a mine as devastating as it was unexpected. While bearing in mind her age, the age for pardonable tantrums, one may still think that few women would have made so much of (apparently) so little or sent a husband into battle so disheartened. Even to read his letters at this time is to feel depressed; and Sarah's of course are missing. He denies her accusation that he has been intriguing with an unnamed woman. She rejects his denial. He is utterly wretched. Her suspicion, he says, must vanish, but he can never forget that she refused to accept his word. It must forever make him miserable. 'I loved you so tenderly', he writes, 'that I proposed all the happiness imaginable in living quietly with you the remaining part of my life. I do to my great grief see that you have fixed in you so very ill an opinion of me that I must never more think of being happy . . .' And his letter ends with a curse which cannot, in Sir Winston's view, refer to anyone but Sunderland:

My heart is so full that if I do not vent this truth it will break, which is that I do from my soul curse that hour in which I gave my poor dear child to a man that has made me of all mankind the most unhappiest.[38]

Of Sunderland's share in the mischief nothing is known; nor can one with any certainty name the woman. All that need be said is that Sarah had a strange habit of keeping letters and that now and again, after centuries of burial, one—unclassified, undated—may surface to find or at least appear to find its place in the jigsaw.

* The Archduke Charles titular King of Spain; afterwards the Emperor Charles VI.

Your letter on four sides of paper', writes Lady Southwell in an undated letter to Sarah, 'I think as rediculous as your whole carriage has been to me . . . and thô in your letter you proclaim your lord an ill husband as I often heard you doe everywhere and are willing to discharge the cause of it upon any body but your self, give me leave to tell you (with the same frankness you use to me) that . . . what you call your misfortunes have proceeded wholly from your self. I should not have had a thought of giving any answer to such a letter, only to shew you I act with more sincerity by assuring you that I neither am nor ever will be Your Graces humble servant

E. C. Southwell*[39]

Edward (Swift's Ned) Southwell had married Lady Elizabeth Cromwell, 'an heiress of 2000 l a year' and daughter of the Earl of Ardglass. They had had three sons when she died in childbirth in 1709.

Nonsensical though it was, the affair had blackened his whole horizon as, on April 8th, Marlborough embarked at Harwich. To make matters still worse Sarah at the last moment handed him a paper containing the things which in the heat of argument she had forgotten to say. It was some days later that remorse overtook her, and it may have been well for England that it did. Marlborough, in his letter to her from the Hague, dated April 29th, refers to the spleen and melancholy occasioned by the Harwich paper, but on May 5th we have a more cheerful picture. 'Your dear letter of the 15th', he tells her, 'came to me but this minute . . . it is so very kind that I would in return lose a thousand lives if I had them to make you happy . . . I took yours that you wrote at Harwich out of my strong box and burnt it; and if you will give me leave, it will be a great pleasure to me to have it in my power to read this dear letter often, and that it may be found in my strong box when I am dead. I do this minute love you better than ever I did before. This letter of yours has made me so happy that I do from my soul wish we could retire and not be blamed. What you propose as to coming over I should

* The next letter in the same bundle at Blenheim is from the Duchess of Ormonde, again undated, in which she bids Sarah 'think seriously how you'd bear any bodys wishing Mr Southwell an ill husband'. (Blen E 39).

be extremely pleased with, for your letter has so transported me that I think you would be happier in being here than where you are, although I should not be able to see you often. But you will see by my last letter . . . that what you desire is impossible, for I am going up into Germany, where it would be impossible for you to follow me; but love me as you do now and no hurt can come to me. You have by this kindness preserved my quiet and I believe my life; for till I had this letter I have been very indifferent of what should become of myself. I have pressed this business of carrying an army into Germany in order to leave a good name behind me, wishing for nothing else but good success. I shall now add that of having a long life, that I may be happy with you.'[40]

It is a hazardous task to attempt to probe the minds of the dead; and in these graphs of the heart one sees strange acrobatics. 'Only Sarah Jennings', wrote the ninth Duke of Marlborough, 'could command the confidence of John Churchill . . . He was a true romantic . . . To him Sarah was a radiant and wonderful being whom he was reluctant to place in this world at all . . . He did not possess intellectual excellencies, but idolized those qualities in a woman. It was his wont to worship things; he worshipped intellect in his wife . . . Her masculine qualities made her the dearer in his eyes because they were the complement of his own nature'.[41]

The letter Marlborough prized (he will have had it by heart) is missing; but with that in his thoughts, and so new-hearted, he set out for the Danube and the greatest battle of his life.

Critics of Sarah's *Conduct* (1742) were quick to point out that although she had made room for such trifles as King William's dish of peas gobbled before Princess Anne, she had scorned to record the battle of Blenheim. But that of course, in her own self-vindication, was not her purpose; for the perpetuation of Marlborough's glory she had made other plans. So now in this present biography of the Duchess, nothing could be more needless than a chronicle of that battle, their descendant, Sir Winston Churchill, having described it superbly and for all time.

'My Lord hath joyned together the safety of Europe & the Honour of England with his own Glory', wrote Lord Methuen to Sarah, 'and trebly rendered it Eternall, since not only the wonderfull execution of so noble a designe is owing to my Lord's conduct but the great designe itself hath been formed by himself alone & carried on thro difficulties thought insuperable & which would have been so to any other'.[42]

The sheer daring of it—the striding across Europe, the bluffing of the enemy, the meeting with Prince Eugene, the battle itself and then the bundling of French generals into Marlborough's coach— took and held the fancy of Marlborough's countrymen. And the last touch of romance had been added by the dusty soldier, Parke, who day after day had galloped with the news. First there was the hurried note for Sarah, pencilled by Marlborough while still in the saddle:

> I have not time to say more but to beg you will give my duty to the Queen and let her know Her Army has had a Glorious Victory. Monsr. Tallard and two other Generals are in my Coach and I am following the rest. The bearer my Aid de Camp Coll Parke will give Her an account of what has pass'd. I shal doe it in a day or two by another more att large.*

And then on to Windsor where the Queen sat in the bow-window of the long gallery overlooking the terrace.† Parke, falling at her feet, handed her the scribble which told of a victory which, in Sir Winston's phrase, opened the gateways of the modern world. Delighted, she questioned and rewarded the messenger before writing to Sarah:

> I have had the happiness of receiving my dear Mrs Freeman's, by Colonel Parke, with the good news of this glorious victory which, next to God Almighty, is wholly owing to dear Mr Freeman, on whose safety I congratulate you with all my soul.[43]

'I do not wonder you are all joy', added Mrs Burnet, 'The bishop said he could not sleep, his heart was so charged with joy. He desires your Grace would carefully lay up that little letter [Marlborough's despatch] as a relic that cannot be valued enough'.[44]

For the second time the Queen and the Duchess drove together to a St Paul's thanksgiving, 'the Queen in a rich coach with eight horses, none with her but the Duchess of Marlborough in a very

---

* The original, written in now fading pencil on the back of a bill for inn expenses, is displayed in a stateroom at Blenheim.

† There is a tradition that the Queen was at dominoes with Prince George.

plain garment, the Queen full of jewels . . . The day before was wet
& stormy but this was one of the most serene & calm days that had
been all the year.'[45]

Serenity was the keynote, for in the most unexpected though not
unprayed for way everything had begun to turn out for the best,
with Marlborough triumphant. Once again as far as the eye could
see the sky had cleared; there was nothing to hint that even there in
the coach, in that contrast of dress which could have been unintentional, lay some of the ingredients of those blue-piled thunderlofts
which were one day to break upon them and speed the wreck of
their friendship, after the thanksgiving for Marlborough's victory at
Oudenarde.

In the muniment room at Blenheim there is an unsigned and
undated letter from one who declares himself too much concerned
for the recipient's beauty not to warn her of the injury she will do it
'in Case you dresse & Sett your Selfe out on the Queens birth days.
Leave ornaments to others', the note continues, 'to such as want a
Supply to their naturall beauty . . . Every ornament you putt on
takes off from your beauty. Every ornament you putt off restores
you a grace & you never are soe well as when one sees nothing in
you but your Selfe . . . Pearls look very well upon some necks that
would look very ill without them, but yours would disgrace the
finest necklace in the world . . . Lett others, then, if they please,
undoe themselves in clothes & jewells . . . and goe your Selfe in plain
Clothes with no other charme but your own beauty . . . The plain-
nesse of your Dresse won't hinder you from outshining all the
Queens in Christendom.'[46]

But these were trifles. Blenheim had shaken the world and made it
'look upon the Duke of Marlborough with a sort of amazement as
upon one destined by Providence to rescue and establish the Liberties
of Europe.'[47] 'May our generals prosper!' ran the thanksgiving
sermon, 'May our Queen live forever!' In an age of miracles when
in the same month Blenheim could be won and Gibraltar taken,
anything could happen.

CHAPTER V

Princess of Mindelheim

1705-1706

———————◆———————

Though crags be stormed and citadels totter, people—queens and generals, duchesses and princesses—still need to dress and eat and dose themselves with spa water or with liquorice and rhubarb.

'If I could tell how to hinder myself from writing to you every day I would', runs in her large, heavy, childish hand a typical undated, unsigned, comma-less note of Anne's to Sarah, 'that you need not be at ye trouble of writing so often to me because you say it dos you hurt but realy I cannot for all I have taken ye purging waters today for when I am from you I cannot be at ease without inquireing after you. Lady Sunderland sayes she hopes time will convince you that she is not base. If you intend to appeare on ye birth day you may be as fine as you please without gold silver point & coulourd peticotes ... Crape linen is worn with gowns & for mantoes you may weare such as you did at tunbridg ... I hope you continue both in body & mind as I left you & that you will never have any more such dismall thoughts as once you had. If my Prayers would do I am sure you should never have ye least unquiet thought but be as happy as 'tis possible for any one to be. I must desire you to send me an under peticote & a botle of ye Queen of hungarys water'.[1]

It was this tedious froth of Anne's—what she herself in others called twitell-twatell—that repelled her Groom of the Stole and now began, for long periods, to keep her from court. Since Marlborough had accepted from the Emperor Leopold, as a reward for Blenheim, the little principality of Mindelheim,* south of the Danube, Sarah

---

* Mindelheim. 'What is offered', Marlborough told his duchess, 'will in history

was technically entitled to call herself a princess; yet in fact it meant nothing. 'If I had been a man . . .' she was always saying. 'If I were a great man I should prefer keeping the best Company I could get with Independancy before any pleasure this world can give'.[2]

For Marlborough to ride in the whirlwind and direct the storm; for her (three times she offered to join him in Flanders and three times was refused) to stay at home and find husbands for her daughters,* or to force herself to be closeted with Anne. For though, as she wrote later, 'it was extremely tedious to be so much where there could be no manner of conversation, I knew she loved me & I suffer'd by fearing I did wrong when I was not with her. For which reason I have gone a thousand times when I had rather have been in a dungeon'.[3] And again, 'I us'd to run from the Court and shut my self up six Weeks in one of my country Hous's quit alone'.[4] But then if she failed to go to court, Anne would pursue her: '. . . Your faithfull Mrs Morley has a mind some time next week to come & inquire how they [the spa waters] agree with you a munday if it be a convenient day or els a fryday sevennight or if you had rather ye later end of this week or ye beginning of ye week after the next whatever time is easiest to you & your deare Mr Freeman do but name it & I shall fly with joy to my deare Mrs Freeman'.[5]

Without reading every one of her letters—'Great bundles of them . . . a prodigious volume', as Sarah said—it is not easy to appreciate the inexorable persistence of Anne's importunity with Sarah, both when she was princess and when she was queen. Some of the early letters, Sarah notes, were lost in the flight of 1688. There are hundreds left. There are the gracious letters of giving, when she offers a dukedom or a 'mite' (£10,000) on a daughter's marriage (Sarah accepted half); letters of condolence, fussy letters about remedies: 'The apothecarys man durst not send me the Hiera Pickra so I sent the doctor to his house but he found there was not quite one dose &

---

forever remain an honour to our family'. And so it has proved, for the princely title and rank remain in the Marlborough family today; but the principality itself was restored to Bavaria in the treaty of 1714.

* In 1703 her third daughter Elizabeth married Scroop Egerton, who became Duke of Bridgwater. In 1704 her fourth and last daughter Mary married the Marquis of Monthermer who became Duke of Montagu.

that at ye botom of a botle. He would have me take some Rubarb but that is so very naucetious to me that he could not prevail with me to take it . . .'[6] Yes there is much of that, but much more—so very much more, repeated thud upon thud in letter after letter—of what Sarah calls expressions backed with vows. These, even for the times, seem extraordinary and one wonders with how much pleasure or how much cynicism they were received.

In the earlier notes Anne contents herself with such unremarkable sayings as, 'I realy beleive one kind word from deare Mrs Freeman would save me if I weare Gasping',[7] and 'Tis not possible for any body to be so faithfully yours as I am';[8] but as time goes on the theme is developed. She implores Sarah, 'for Christ Jesus sake never think of being any where but with me as long as I am above ground',[9] and 'as I have ever had a most sincere & tender kindness for my deare Mrs Freeman soe I will preserve it to my grave & oh beleeve me you will never find in all ye search of love a hart like your poor unfortunate faithfull Morlys',[10] 'a hart soe truly soe sincerly soe intirely without reserve nor soe passionately yours'. 'I am', she insists, 'as unchangeable as fate', and 'To ye last moment of her life your faithfull Morely will ever be ye same'. No letter from Sarah means desolation; and then, when it arrives, 'Just as I had writ thus far I received your deare kind letter which I have kissd a hundred times . . . If I writt whole volumes I could never express how well I love you nor how much I long to see you'[11] . . . and so on and so on.

One such letter a year from a queen might be flattering. One, sometimes two a day became a bore and an embarrassment. Sarah, looking back, remembered Anne's letters as 'very indifferent, both in sense & spelling, unless that they were generally enlivened with a few passionate expressions, sometimes pretty enough but repeated over & over again without the mixture of anything either of diversion or instruction.'[12]

It is a little unfair perhaps that, since she insisted on their destruction, we are never, at the peak of her favour, able to judge of Sarah's letters to Anne.* 'In obedience', the Queen dutifully assures her, 'after having read & kissed your dear kind letter over & over I burnt it much against my will & I do assure you you need never be in pain about your letters for I take such care of them 'tis not possible

* Later, as favour declined, Sarah kept copies of her letters to Anne.

any accident can happen that they should be seen by any body'.[13]

What time-wasting nonsense it all was and, from Sarah's point of view, what a waste of opportunity! All she wanted to hear was that her lessons had sunk in and that Anne would support the Whigs who would support Marlborough: a subject of as little taste to the Queen as was ass's milk to Marlborough. It was high time for some extraneous stroke of fortune and sure enough, if a little late on cue, came a *deus ex machina* disguised as Lord Haversham, a mischievous Tory heartily loathed by Sarah, who in the spring of 1705 put forward in the Lords a proposal that, to ensure the Protestant succession, the Electress Sophia should be invited to live in England. This', like Occasional Conformity, was a cynical manoeuvre to trap the Queen's ministers. If they opposed it they opposed the Hanoverian succession. If they supported it they offended the Queen who had made it clear that only over her dead body should anyone of that house be allowed in England. In this she was positive and firm.

'I remember one day', recalled Sarah, 'I told the queen when she was easy with me that I thought there was nothing in the world so good for her as well as for England as to desire of her own accord to have the young Prince of Hannover & breed him as her own son, which would in the first place secure her own life against the Roman Catholicks & make the young man acquainted with the laws & customs of a country that one day (tho I hoped it was a long way off) hee would govern. To which she answerd, not being very well pleas'd, that she beleivd nobody of her age and who might have children would doe that; which was a very vain thought & I beleive proceeded more from her pride or fear of having any body here to bee courted then that she really could expect children tho she was not fourty, because she had had before seventeen dead ones'.[14]

There were of course other reasons: one the not uncommon abhorrence of harbouring a successor; two, George's (the Elector's) abortive courtship when she was princess; and three, Anne's uneasy conscience about the Pretender—'Maybe 'tis our brother . . .' On this occasion however Haversham's motion took a boomerang turn when Anne, attending incognito, heard her ex-suitor John Sheffield, Earl of Mulgrave (now Duke of Buckingham), recently ousted from his post of Lord Privy Seal, warn his fellow-peers that (to quote Sarah) it was reasonable to have one of that house [Hanover] here because the Queen might live so long as to have no understanding.[15] At this Anne was deeply offended. After seeing the motion rejected she wrote to Sarah:

> I believe dear Mrs Freeman and I shall not disagree as we have formerly done, for I am sensible of the services those people have done me that you have a good opinion of and will countenance them, and am thoroughly convinced of the malice and insolence of them that you have always been speaking against.[16]

It was the moment for the Whigs to bring in their counter-measure, the Regency Bill which, in the event of Anne's leaving no direct heir, would guard the way for a successor from Hanover. Without serious opposition it was carried, but . . . There is no armour against fate; Death lays his icy hand on kings. If Anne died with a Pretender living, anything could still happen. Perhaps she would live forever. Anyway, the Regency Bill was the best they could do. In the meantime for Queen Anne in her glory it must often have seemed indeed a hollow crown:

> O wearisome condition of humanity;
> Born to one law, yet to another bound,
> Doom'd to be vaine, forbedden vanity,
> Created sick, commanded to be sound.[17]

Without comfort oneself, was it possible, she wondered, to share vicariously the happiness of others? As her reward (and the nation's) for the victory at Blenheim Anne had given Marlborough the royal estate at Woodstock, a wild place with a ruined manor house, as the site of a mansion which (so it was understood) she intended to build for him. Her Comptroller of the Works, John Vanbrugh, had already drawn plans for it and a wooden model was being constructed. It was a pleasant thought. Might there not still be hours and days for the Queen to look forward to when she and Sarah would finger brocades and even—oh happy day!—play ombre with Mr Freeman in his castle of Blenheim?

Tattered now is the document by Kneller in which he sets out his project for 'an allegorical picture which Queen Anne design'd to present to the Duke of Marlborough for Blenheim House'. His painting was to have measured twelve feet by eight and no one in it was to have been 'represented by the life' except the Queen's Majesty. Kneller had in fact completed the sketch in oils when, as he puts it, 'State Difference happening betwixt the Queen and the Duke of Marlborough', the whole scheme was abandoned. In the sketch, amidst a plethora of allegorical jumble typical of its date (1708), one sees the Queen, a portly figure, bestowing upon a kneeling figure in armour (Military Merit) a scroll upon which has been drawn the north front of Blenheim. Ceres, prominent among the goddesses, could be Sarah; but the plump female figure of Architecture, on Anne's right, is as unlike Vanbrugh as it would be possible to be. Beside her stands 'a Little Youth, the Emblem of Posterity', while at the foot of all, in the foreground, two smaller *putti* spill 'the Golden Cornucopia Shead by her Majesty's Affections'.[18]

It was a delightful idea, as was also the notion that, down the ages, a quitrent for the castle, as it was then called, should be paid by presenting the sovereign, at Windsor and on the battle-anniversary, with a silk standard emblazoned with three gilded fleurs-de-lys on a field argent;* a condition which has been and continues to be faithfully fulfilled.

On the 18th of June, 1705 the foundation-stone of Blenheim was laid. Vanbrugh of course was there, with his second-in-command Nicholas Hawksmoor, a notable architect in his own right. They and five others struck the stone with a hammer and threw down a guinea; which done, the stone—eight feet square, polished and engraved with the words: In memory of the battel of Blenheim, June 18, 1705, Anna Regina—was lowered into position beneath the site of the eastern Bow Window Room, the only room said to have met with the Duchess's approval. After which of course came toasts and junketings and a dance of old beldames. The honours had been done.

At the time of the foundation, as in Kneller's sketch, Sarah was not recognisably in the picture. 'I mortally hate all Grandeur and Architecture',[19] she said afterwards, and she hated them then. If Marlborough chose to humour the Queen and to practise both, that was their affair. She knew Anne would have 'done nothing with the

* Intended as a facsimile of the standard of the Corps du Roi (depicted in the tapestry of the battle), captured at Blenheim.

money that was better'. Sarah herself was content with Holywell and Windsor Lodge, although her ideal was 'a clean, sweet house and garden, tho' ever so small'—a description which hardly applied to Blenheim.

As for the architect, she had heard of him as a writer of comedies, she had never met him. 'At the beginning of those works', she wrote later, 'I never had spoake to him, but as soon as I knew him & saw the maddnesse of the whole Design I opposed it all that was possible for me to doe . . . I don't know that the queen had any particular favour for Sir C. Wren tho hee had been an old servant, but 'tis certain that old Craggs, who was as ill a man as ever I knew, recommended Sr John Vanbrugh to the Duke of Marl: . . . Sr John, tho hee was in the queens office of Works would not have been employed in the building if hee had not been recommended'.[20]

To suppose, however, that Duchess and architect took against one another at sight would be misleading. She found him at first, as did everyone, entertaining; for Vanbrugh was, as the jingle said, 'a most sweet-natur'd gentleman and pleasant'. Sarah laughed at his rhymes and teased him about Swift's verses on his goose-pie house in Whitehall. Perhaps if Marlborough had not found him such excellent company, Vanbrugh might have stood more chance of keeping on good terms with the Duchess; but his profession was against him, and if over Blenheim an architect had to suffer, as with Sarah every architect must, then it was as well that it was Vanbrugh (not one, as he said, to drop his spirits at every rebuff) rather than the ageing Wren.*

In 1705 Wren was still at the head of Anne's Board of Works as Surveyor, with Vanbrugh as Comptroller, an office he had held since 1702, when the Earl of Carlisle is believed to have sponsored him in reward for planning the Earl's 'top seat and garden of England' at Castle Howard.† In the year Carlisle had come into his title—1692,

* After commissioning Wren, in 1709, to build Marlborough House, the Duchess rid herself of him and directed the finishing herself. According to Vanbrugh, she was prevented by Marlborough from bringing an action against Wren, who withdrew with dignity and without open dispute.

† The Duchess maintained that Vanbrugh owed his comptrollership to Marlborough, with the understanding that he should eventually succeed Wren as Surveyor (see Chatsworth Letters 122-3). This assertion is not confirmed by other sources.

the same that saw Marlborough in the Tower—Captain Vanbrugh, as he then was, was in the Bastille, imprisoned as a spy but in tolerable comfort and busy on his first comedy *The Relapse*. His metamorphosis into architect cannot have been, as Swift gibed, without thought or lecture, but next to nothing is known of it. Genius can be a quick learner, and more especially when genius (Wren) teaches and yet a third genius (Hawksmoor) stands by to make dreams workable.

It is quite possible that James Craggs the elder,* who was a friend of Vanbrugh's, introduced him to Marlborough. At an early stage Craggs became attached to the Marlborough household where, says the Dictionary of National Biography, 'his shrewdness and administrative ability attracted the attention of the Duchess, who entrusted him with the management of her business affairs'; and indeed we shall see how thoroughly (especially when in exile in 1713–14) she relied on him.

Vanbrugh himself says that he first met Marlborough casually at the playhouse; that he later showed him the wooden model of Castle Howard, which he liked; and that he afterwards submitted a plan for Blenheim which, with amendments, was wholeheartedly approved by both Marlborough and Godolphin.

On June 9th Godolphin gave Vanbrugh a warrant which appointed him surveyor of all the works and buildings to be erected at Woodstock. In this document, which was to cause endless dispute, Marlborough was named four times, the Queen not once. At the time it was of course unthinkable to ask for the Queen's promise in writing; but later, when favour cooled, much seemed to have evaporated with it, not excluding Anne's impulsive kindness and her word.

From the outset, before a stone had been laid, Marlborough expressed delight with the Queen's present. It was fitting that the achievements of her arms should be commemorated; and as for the setting, it could not have been better. As with Vanbrugh, his fellow-romantic and fellow-visionary, he rode over it, more and more in that wild tangle appealed to them. There was Rosamund's well, the spring known to Henry II, 'that King whose Scenes of Love he [Vanbrugh] was so much pleas'd with'; there was the manor of

* James Craggs senior (1657–1721).

Woodstock, its battered walls still defiant as they were when Elizabeth I was imprisoned in its gatehouse; while between the manor and the site they had chosen for the castle lay a marsh, threaded by a rivulet, and a chasm which Vanbrugh vowed he would span with a Roman bridge. Could it be that, as marsh, stream and valley came into view, Marlborough was reminded of just such another rugged scene, but by the Danube? 'The ground bordering the Nebel, particularly between Oberglau and Blenheim', runs Coxe's description of the battle-site, 'is generally marshy and in many places impassable . . . The morass expands to a considerable breadth, and nearer Blenheim is a species of islet . . . Near the point of the islet is a stone bridge, over which runs the road from Dillingen to Donauworth'.[21]

And then the garden—how soon could it be ready? Marlborough at fifty-five thought of himself, as men did in those days, as an old man. Henry Wise was Queen Anne's head-gardener; and so Marlborough, says Defoe, pitched on him and had him consider that 'he could not expect to live till the trees were grown up and therefore he expected to have a garden as it were ready made for him. Accordingly Mr Wise transplanted thither full grown trees in baskets, which he buried in the earth, which look and thrive the same as if they had stood there thirty or forty years.'[22]

If Wise was not the perfect gardener, he certainly seemed so. Those who knew him believed that, had he worked in the garden of Eden, there would have been no Fall, for there would have been no serpent. The only snakes he tolerated were those on his coat of arms, to add point to the pun: Be ye wise as serpents and harmless as doves. His crest was a demi-lion argent holding a damask rose, the lion having in his mouth a serpent vulnerating him in the shoulder, for Wise endured much from a rheumatic shoulder and from gout. With his team at Blenheim he dug the foundations of the house and of the bridge and its causeway and planted the huge and complex 'military' garden, the long avenues and the two-thousand-acre park. 'For the Gardening & Plantations', wrote Marlborough to his wife, from Flanders, 'I am at ease, being very sure that Mr Wise will bee dilligent'.[23] And sure enough, Wise was soon able to report, 'The severall Plantacons . . . have Shot to Admiration . . . I have taken such Care of raising from Seeds Nuts & Berrys etc such Number of

Plants that I hope Your Grace will not loose time in deciding upon their disposition'.[24] It was all most heartening. There were times when even Sarah seems to have felt a glow.

'I take ye liberty to give your Grace a litle account of my jorny to Woodstock', John Howe tells Marlborough on September 20th, 1705, 'Hearing my Lady Dutchesse was there, I thought it was my duty to waite on her. I mett her Grace going to ye building whither I had leave to attend her, but am not skillful enough in architecture to pretend to give any judgment on that part. The building is about breast high above ye ground & ye gardens, which promise great beauty, very nere being finisht as farr as ye plantations, which Mr Wise says will be perfect this season so as to be gardens by this time twelve months. I had ye satisfaction besides ye honour of finding my litle compliment well receivd, to see her Grace very well pleasd with ye situation & everything belonging to Woodstock Park. I could not omitt, as I view'd it, to pray heartyly that your Grace may there enjoy, with a vigorous & quiet old age, the fruits of your past labours & services to your country'.[25]

At the beginning of the Blenheim works no fewer than a thousand men were employed there. Indeed, so great was the concentration of skilled labour, it was as well that, apart from St Paul's, then nearly finished, Anne was a modest builder. For Kensington, in this year of Blenheim's founding, she had commissioned, in warm brick and stone, a delightful orangery, which Defoe says she planned as a summer supper-house. It was to be useful in other ways too. Writing from Kensington to Sarah, about touching for the evil,* Anne tells her, 'I do that buisness now in ye Banqueting house which I like very well, that being a very cool room & ye doing of it there keeps my own house sweet & free from crouds'.[26]

It was a season of clear shining, a brief summer calm before the next political storm. Had Sarah been wiser she might have realised even at this stage that she was becoming the tool of extremists, a lever for moving the Queen in whichever direction the Junto wished her to go. This time it was the removal of the incompetent Sir Nathan Wright, the Lord Keeper, and the appointment in his place

* One of Sarah's duties was to see that Coggs the goldsmith kept the Queen supplied with healing gold, given to the sufferers, who on one occasion included Dr Samuel Johnson, from the evil (scrofula: a disease affecting the glands).

of the estimable Lord Cowper. Everything was in Cowper's favour except that he was a Whig and Anne still seemed to believe, as Sunderland said, that all Whigs had cloven feet. At first she said no, but after more pressure she (in Sarah's words) 'at last consented to employ him and the consequence of this was that she had not only the ablest man in England to serve her but one that she was perfectly easy & satisfied with'.[27]

So rare is high and consistent praise from the Duchess of Marlborough that a whole chapter should be reserved for her good opinion of Cowper, and his of her. 'All the time I was at Court', she says, 'and after I was removed no man could possibly behave better to me than he did, not only as a gentleman but as a friend and as if he had been my own brother'.[28] When he tried to thank her for his appointment she called for silence. Whereupon he told her, 'Madam, if I must not speak, yet you can't hinder me from thinking as long as I live'.[29]

It was ironical that such a good turn—to Cowper and to the country, to the Whigs and to Anne—should bring Sarah what she described as the Queen's first peevish letter; a letter now hard to trace among many at Blenheim of a tone that might be considered peevish. This, for example:

Kensington, Wednesday
Your poor unfortunate faithfull Morly was at her deare Mrs Freemans door today just before I came from St James's but could make no body heare & it being past two aclock I durst not venture to send round, the Prince staying dinner for me, soe was forc'd to come away without ye satisfaction of one look of my deare Mrs Freeman, which was no small mortification to her that sincerly doats on you . . . I cannot end this without repeating a request that I have often made, that is that you would leave off that formall word Majesty & lett me heare your faithfull Morly named againe that is greivd at her Soul to find my deare Mrs Freeman allways cold & grave & would give ye world to be restored to ye happyness she has formerly enjoy'd.[30]

In old age Sarah herself confessed, 'I mortally hate Madam and Your Grace which I call Bug Words',[31] and she knew perfectly well that 'Majesty' was a bug word to Queen Anne; but it had its uses.

So she persisted and gained her point and lost a great deal more. 'She not only overrated her influence in public matters with the Queen', observes Sir Winston, 'but she mistook its character. She sought to win by argument, voluble and vociferous, written and interminable, what had hitherto been the freehold property of love'.[32]

Those who, for one purpose or another, still came to court complained that the Queen was inaccessible; for her Groom of the Stole barred the door and when she was absent, the Queen would not choose to appear. There was the case of that staunch Tory James Johnston, who went to pay his respects to the Queen at Hampton Court, 'but observing the Duchess of Marlborough to look upon him with anger, he retired to his country seat & fine gardens, not far off, where he entertained himself with country recreations and the refreshment of the pleasant river'.[33]

Wherever the Queen went she was pursued by scores of importunate people with petitions, and it was one of Sarah's drearier duties to deal with them. 'I did constantly write abundance of letters in answer to petitions',[34] she remembered. The lacemakers prayed for less court-mourning, which was ruining their trade. Scotsmen and Scotswomen wanted or did not want to unite with England. Irishmen wanted back their estates. Still more persistent were those begging for pensions or for reprieves. Mrs Stephens, for example, how she haunted the place ever since her husband was sentenced to stand in the pillory. Stephens, rector of Sutton, had been found guilty of a libel on the Duke of Marlborough; but Sarah, as she often did in these cases, interceded. Three days before the battle of Ramillies Marlborough had written, 'I agree entirely with you . . . I should be glad he were forgiven . . . but I do not love to see my name in print; for I am persuaded that an honest man must be justified by his own actions and not by the pen of a writer, though he should be a zealous friend'.[35]

Anne's note too was typical: 'I have, upon my deare Mrs Freeman's pressing letter about Mr Stephens, ordered Mr Secretary Harley to put a stop to his standing in the pillory . . . Nothing but your desire could have inclined me to it, for in my poor opinion it is not right. My reason I will tell you when I have the happiness of seeing you. Till then, my deare Mrs Freeman, farewel.'[36]

Anne may have been surprised to find Sarah, she who mocked at the Church Party, interceding for a clergyman, but in battles of that sort she was sincere and could be merciful. 'Much as I opposed the Tories', she wrote in her *Conduct*, 'I was no Enemy to the Church they talked of, so far as any thing real and excellent was meant by that Word'.

In May Marlborough's victory at Ramillies again put new heart into Queen and country as well as into Sarah and himself. 'As Blenheim saved Vienna, so Ramillies conquered the Netherlands'.* Holland was saved. Again smiles and congratulations, again bonfires and thanksgivings; and yet from Marlborough's letters we find, in spite of added rewards (the £5000 'pension' made permanent; the title to descend through the female line), that things at home were less tranquil than he had hoped.

'Hetherto', he tells Sarah, 'I really have not had time to write to my children, but when I do, bee assur'd that I shal let them know my heart & soul as to their living dutyfully & kindly with you, & let mee beg for my sake of my dear Soull that she will passe by little then faults & consider thay are very young & that thay can't do other then love you with all their hearts, for when thay consider how good a Mother you have been to them thay must bee barbariens if thay did not make a kind return'.[37] And again a month later: 'It is a very great pleasure to me to find you are satisfied with three of your children & hope in God that 392† will in time bee trewly sensible of all the great obligations she has to you'. And in July: 'It is most mortefying to see that nothing can mend 392. I beg of you to do me the justice & your self the ease to believe that whatever thay say can have no credit with me when you asure me of the contrary. I can & do greive as much as any parent can when a child is unkind. We must hope the best & bee allways carefull not to resent their Carage to such a degree as to make the town judge of who is in the right.'[38] And then, a little peevishly: 'By your saying nothing to me of your going to Woodstock I find your heart is not soe much sett on that place as I cou'd wish. Vanbrook writes me that I shall not see him in the Army, beleiving that I shal approve better of his going into Oxfordshire'.[39]

* The Spanish Netherlands, now Belgium.
† Probably their eldest daughter, Henrietta.

But Sarah had other interests, and that summer a strange thing had happened. A messenger had brought her a small packet and with it a flowery letter, full of expressions (as she called them), from Mr Brydges:*

Amsterdam   16 July 1706

Madam,

I should not have been guilty of so great a piece of confidence as to have troubled your Grace with so inconsiderable a matter as this ring . . . if I did not at ye same time hope that ye picture under it would encline your Grace to pardon my presumption to look upon it with so favourable an eye as to let it find place amongst ye rest of your jewels. It formerly belonged to ye Duke of Orleans & had ye Dauphin's picture in it, but that which makes one hope it will prove acceptable to your Grace is a picture of infinitely more value which I have put in ye room of it & which I have had drawn by one who is esteemed very eminent in this way of painting . . .[40]

She stopped reading the letter and opened the packet . . . Hm, pretty enough, the miniature of Marlborough a fair likeness, but as a ring, like its sender, far too showy. It must go back of course. She looked at it again . . . Then she showed it to Coggs the goldsmith who said yes indeed, the 'glass' covering the portrait was one vast, thin diamond. With a sigh Sarah took up her pen:

Windsor Castle   July 25, 1706

Sir,

Upon the receipt of your letter from Amsterdam and the present you sent me with it I cannot disown that I was at first very much pleased with it, beleiving the nature of it not to be so considerable as that the satisfaction I take in its buyer to be abused† upon that account, but upon a more particular examination of its nature I find it to be by much too considerable

---

* James Brydges (1673–1744), created 1st Duke of Chandos in 1719. Paymaster-General of the forces abroad from 1707 to 1712.

† Wrongly copied into Chandos letterbook? The sense is: '. . . the satisfaction I take in its buyer ran no risk of being abused'.

for me to take & having no opportunity of sending it back I will keep it till you come home & hope you will be pleased to tell me the price of it, in order either to buy or return it.

I am with a great deal of respect, Sir,
your most obedient & most humble servant[41]

He protests. Unless she is resolved to kill him with grief he begs she will be pleased never to make further mention of it. She must bear in mind his obligations to her noble family. 'I design', he concludes, 'by ye services of my whole life to give constant proofs of ye gratitude.' As Duke of Chandos (Pope's Timon) we shall hear more of him later.

For Sarah, amid her more tedious duties, it had been a diverting if slightly embarrassing interlude, a breathing space before the next crisis: a major battle with Anne, which would mean calling out all reserves. It was nothing less than a demand that her son-in-law, Lord Sunderland, be made a Secretary of State. This was not Sarah's notion, nor Marlborough's. The move came from the five tyrannising lords of the Junto, of whom Sunderland was one; political blackmail of the kind the world even then had grown used to. For continued Whig support of the war, one of their number must have power. They threatened Godolphin, who begged Sarah to speak for him; and so Sarah, armed with argument, attacked Anne. So did Godolphin himself, and so, even more reluctantly, did Marlborough. The Queen was resentful and adamant. 'On her throne', writes Sir Winston admiringly, 'she was as tough as Marlborough in the field. She would not have Sunderland, she could not bear him. He was, she felt, a brazen freethinker and at heart a Republican'.[42] Sarah continued to hector the Queen and in August wrote:

... Your security and the nation's is my chief wish, and I beg of God Almighty as sincerely as I shall do for His pardon at my last hour that Mr and Mrs Morley may see their errors as to this notion before it is too late; but considering how little impression anything makes that comes from your faithful Freeman, I have troubled you too much and I beg your pardon for it.[43]

To this sour note she received no answer. Had she gone too far?

The Queen, having read Sarah's 'notion' as 'nation'* thought that she had. Godolphin intervened, but after he had patched things up, Sarah wrote again coldly, almost scathingly; yet she received from Anne a kind reply:

> ... I hope you will not go to Woodstock without giving me one look for whatever hard thoughts you may have of me I am sure I do not deserve them, and I will not be uneasy if you come to me; for though you are never so unkind I will ever preserve a most sincere & tender passion for my dear Mrs Freeman.[44]

To which Sarah's rejoinder is again disappointing. Returning to the 'notion' for 'nation' wrangle she says she cannot for the life of her see any essential difference. Her tone is contemptuous. How very much wiser, at this time, are Marlborough's letters to his wife: 'You know that I have often disputes with you concerning the Queen', he writes from Helchin on August 9, 'and by what I have always observed, when she thinks herself in the right, she needs no advice to help her to be very firm & positive . . . I doubt but a very little time will set this of Lord Sunderland very right but . . . I have my apprehensions he will be very uneasy in it; and that when it is too late you will be of my opinion that it would have been much happier if he had been employed in any other place of profit and honour . . .'[45]

Godolphin, bludgeoned by the Junto, stonewalled by the Queen, was in despair. 'I cannot struggle against the difficulties of your Majesty's business', he told her bluntly, 'and yourself at the same time . . . I have worn out my health and almost my life in the service of the Crown . . .'[46] It was true. He now offered to retire to Newmarket, where he bred racehorses. Marlborough told him he was, like himself, 'in honour bound to undergo all the dangers & troubles that is possible to bring this war to a happy end, which I think must be after the next campaign, if we can agree to carry it on with vigour'.[47]

Anne offered a compromise but the Whigs would not hear of it. Finally she appealed to Marlborough: 'Why, for God's sake, must I who have no interest, no end, no thought but for the good of my

* In the version at Blenheim, in the Duchess's hand, the word appears to be 'nation'.

country, be made so miserable as to be brought into the power of one set of men? And why may I not be trusted since I mean nothing but what is equally for the good of all my subjects?'[48]

The Queen, at the climax as at the close of her reign, was in the toils of faction and of unscrupulous politicians. There was no escape. Sunderland was the last man in England she would have chosen. 'He and I should not agree long together', she wrote, 'finding by experience my humour and those that are of a warmer will often have misunderstandings between one another'.[49] Yet she, Queen of England, was compelled to have him.

By the time this pitiful thing had been accomplished, Anne, Godolphin and Marlborough had been driven to the last extremity of disgust and disillusionment. Marlborough told Sarah, 'I shall from henceforth despise all mankind and think there is no such thing as virtue'. Marlborough himself was now threatening to resign and Sarah sent the Queen his letter. To the end of her own' after referring to 'that passion & tenderness I had once for Mrs Morley' she tacked a postscript: 'I desire you would reflect whether you have never heard that the greatest misfortunes that have ever happened to any of your family had not been occasioned by having ill-advice and an obstinacy in their tempers'.[50]—a remark which she must have known would offend.

In spite of Sarah, in spite of herself and her own better judgment the Queen at last gave way. The course of the river had been forced at the cost of friendship.

There were at this time two Secretaries of State: Sir Charles Hedges and Robert Harley. On December 3rd Sunderland took the place of Hedges. Harley remained. 'And it quickly appeared', says Sarah, 'that the Difficulties raised by her Majesty against parting with Sir Charles Hedges were wholly owing to the Artifice and Management of Mr Harley . . . whose Interest and secret Transactions with the Queen were then doubtless in their Beginning'.[51]

CHAPTER VI

Cue for Vipers

1707-1708

———◆———

How unfair it is and how ruinous to the fame of a politician when, after the struggles of a lifetime, the years of anonymity before the hours of glory, the rise, the fall, the years it may be in the wilderness, the memoirs, the polished self-vindication . . . all this and more may for posterity go for nothing and be totally ignored in favour of one bon mot, one sentence, a catchphrase coined in his cups perhaps by an enemy, yet one which seems conveniently to docket the man and set him forever in his nutshell.

And so it is with Robert Harley, Earl of Oxford and Mortimer. Like William III, like the Duchess of Marlborough, he has his apologists; but there are two hard phrases which no student of history can ever forget: the first, Lord Cowper's—'If any man was ever born under a necessity of being a knave, he was';[1] the second, Sarah's—'That wonderful talent Mr Harley possessed, in the supreme degree, of confounding the common sense of mankind'.[2]

Yet we are assured by kind and impartial writers that if we, with Arthur Maynwaring, damn Harley out of hand as 'the most errant tricking knave in all Britain',[3] we shall be gravely misled; and after all, if Macaulay and others could make a hero of William III, (and in recent times we have seen even less promising examples, including Judge Jeffreys), it should not be hard to say something for Harley. 'To represent him', warns Sir Keith Feiling, 'as a mere self-seeking politician would be a travesty . . . His inconsistency was rooted in something like principle. He disbelieved in the whole scheme of party but . . . his conservative purpose was sincere . . . His characteristics were caution, procrastination, improvisation and secrecy'.[4]

Unlike his friend and colleague Henry St John, Secretary at War, who was a born orator, Harley had a grotesque delivery which, in Sarah's description, makes him sound more like a dervish than Speaker of the House of Commons.

'He was a cunning and a dark man', she reflected, 'of too small abilities to do much good but with all the qualities requisite to do mischief & to bring on the ruin & destruction of a nation. This mischievous darkness of his soul was written in his countenance & plainly legible in a very odd look, disagreeable to every body at first sight, which being joined with a constant awkward motion or other agitation of his head & body betrayed a turbulent dishonesty within, even in the midst of all those familiar, jocular, bowing, smiling airs which he always affected in order to cover what could not be covered. He had long accustomed himself so much to dissemble his real intentions & to use the ambiguous & obscure way of speaking that he could hardly ever be understood when he really designed it or be believed when he never so much desired it.'[5]

At the beginning of the reign Harley, with his quips and cranks, had done his utmost to ingratiate himself with the Duchess; but though a weasel may hypnotise a rabbit, if he tries the same treatment on a tigress, one glare may send him scurrying and in this case it evidently did. With Marlborough and Godolphin he had at first more success. He admired and flattered them. They believed in him and advanced him. It was only when, rebuffed by Sarah, Harley realised that in Marlborough's absence Godolphin's moderation was too mild to resist the Junto, that he made the first cautious moves to strike out on his own. And even then there was still the formidable obstacle of Sarah, for as long as she guarded the Queen's door, so long must he be thwarted. But now Sarah was often absent; and besides that, the 'ill star' which had risen over 1707 and brought the allies disappointment at Almanza and Toulon, proved lucky for Harley and found him a go-between with the Queen, a Tory spy so nearly perfect for his purpose that even his guile could hardly have devised a better. Sarah, though she afterwards thought perhaps she had made too much of a vulgar person, never tired of writing about her poor relation, her cousin Abigail Hill, who later became Mrs

Masham and eventually Lady Masham. Bishop Burnet, looking back to her introduction, says:

> It was observed that Mr Harley, who had been for some years secretary of state, had gained great credit with the queen and began to set up for himself and to act no more under the direction of the lord treasurer. There was one of the bed-chamberwomen who being nearly related to the Duchess of Marlborough had been taken care of by her, together with her whole family (for they were fallen low) in a most particular manner. She brought her not only into that post but treated her with such a confidence that it had introduced her into a high degree of favour with the queen, which for some years was considered as an effect of the Duchess of Marlborough's credit with her. She was also nearly related to Mr Harley and they two entered into a close correspondence. She learned the arts of a court and observed the queen's temper with so much application that she got far into her heart; and she employed all her credit to establish Harley in the supreme confidence with the queen, and to alienate her affections from the Duchess of Marlborough, who studied no other method of preserving her favour but by pursuing the true interest of the queen and of the kingdom . . . This went on too little regarded. The Duchess of Marlborough seemed secure of her interest in the queen and shewed no jealousy of a favour to which herself gave the first rise.[6]

In fiction the irony of it would have been thought too crudely drawn. That the Duchess should, as she said, have taken Cinderella 'from a broom', and that Cinderella should then, once secure, turn into the wicked fairy to cast a spell upon the Queen and supplant her benefactress, seemed altogether too farfetched to be true. And indeed it was hard—a trick worthy of some malicious lord of misrule —that such a sordid situation should force itself upon Queen and Duchess and cause such an upheaval as almost to overturn the throne. As the author of *The Other Side of the Question* puts it:

> From the Intrigues of Parties, the Glitter of Courts, the Mysteries of the Cabinet, the Misunderstandings of Princes and all the Eclat of the great World, which may be called the Eminencies

of human Life, we are now to descend with your Grace to the Flats and Marshes of Family-Affairs to a low Tale of Cousins and their Cousins, brought to Court out of Charity, of ragged Boys cloath'd and put to School, and good-for-nothing Fellows preferr'd to Regiments . . .[7]

No one however has told the tale with more clarity nor with more feeling than Sarah herself:

Mrs Masham was the Daughter of one Hill, a Merchant in the City, by a Sister of my Father. Our Grandfather, Sir John Jenyns, had twenty-two Children, by which Means the Estate of the Family (which was reputed to be about 4000 l a Year) came to be divided into small Parcels. Mrs Hill had only 500 l to her Portion. Her Husband lived very well, as I have been told, for many Years till turning Projector he brought Ruin upon himself and his Family. But as this was long before I was born, I never knew there were such People in the World, till after the Princess Anne was married and when she lived at the Cockpit, at which Time an Acquaintance of mine came to me and said, She believed I did not know that I had Relations who were in want, and she gave me an Account of them . . . [Sarah sent ten guineas and went to see Mrs Hill] . . . She told me that her Husband was in the same Relation to Mr Harley as she was to me, but that he had never done any Thing for her.*

I think Mrs Masham's Father and Mother did not live long after this. They left four Children, two Sons and two Daughters. The Elder Daughter (afterwards Mrs Masham) was a grown Woman. I took her to St Albans, where she lived with me and my Children, and I treated her with as great Kindness as if she had been my Sister. After some Time a Bed-Chamber Woman of the Princess of Denmark's died; and as in that Reign (after the Princesses were grown up) Rockers, though not Gentle-women, had been advanced to be Bed-Chamber Women, I thought I might ask the Princess to give the vacant Place to Mrs Hill . . . and it was granted . . . [Abigail's young sister Alice,

---

* According to Peter Wentworth, Harley 'promoted' Abigail's marriage to Masham. (See *Wentworth Papers*, ed. Cartwright, p. 132).

later to be nicknamed by Swift the Queen of Prudes, was found the job of laundress in the Duke of Gloucester's household (in which capacity she starched Anne's 'heads'), and when he died in 1700 a pension of £200 a year. Thanks to her sister she rose meteorically to become Deputy to the Keeper of the Privy Purse, the Keeper then being Abigail].

Sarah's account continues:

The Elder Son was at my Request put by my Lord Godolphin into a Place in the Custom-House . . . His Brother (whom the Bottle-men afterwards called honest Jack Hill) was a tall Boy whom I cloathed (for he was all in Rags) and put to School at St Albans to one Mr James who had been an Usher under Dr Busby of Westminster. And whenever I went to St Albans I sent for him and was as kind to him as if he had been my own Child. After he had learnt what he could there, a Vacancy happening of Page of Honour to the Prince of Denmark, his Highness was pleased at my Request to take him. I afterwards got my Lord Marlborough to make him Groom of the Bed-chamber to the Duke of Gloucester. And though my Lord always said that Jack Hill was good for nothing, yet to oblige me he made him his Aid de Camp and afterwards gave him a Regiment. But it was his Sister's Interest that raised him to be a General and to command in that ever memorable Expedition to Quebec: I had no Share in doing him these Honours. To finish what I have to say upon his Subject: When Mr Harley thought it useful to attack the Duke of Marlborough in Parliament, this Quebec General, this honest Jack Hill, this once ragged Boy whom I cloathed, happening to be sick in Bed, was nevertheless persuaded by his Sister to get up, wrap himself in warmer Cloathes than those I had given him, to go to the House to vote against the Duke.

I may here add that even the Husband of Mrs Masham had several Obligations to me. It was at my Instance that he was first made a Page, then Equerry and afterwards Groom of the Bed-Chamber to the Prince . . .

As for Mrs Masham herself, I had so much Kindness for her and had done so much to oblige her, without having ever done any thing to offend her, that it was too long before I could bring myself to think her other than a true Friend or forbear rejoicing at any instance of Favour shewn her by the Queen. I observed indeed at length that she was grown more shy of coming to me, and more reserved than usual when she was with me; but I imputed this to her peculiar Moroseness of Temper and for some time made no other Reflection upon it.

The first Thing which led me into Enquiries about her Conduct was the being told (in the Summer of 1707) that my Cousin Hill was privately married to Mr Masham. I went to her and asked her if it were true. She owned it was and begged my Pardon for having concealed it from me. As much Reason as I had to take ill this Reserve in her Behaviour, I was willing to impute it to Bashfulness and want of Breeding rather than to any thing worse. I embraced her with my usual Tenderness and very heartily wished her Joy; and then, turning the Discourse, entered into her Concerns in as friendly a Manner as possible, contriving how to accommodate her with Lodgings by removing her Sister into some of my own.

I then enquired of her very kindly whether the Queen knew of her Marriage, and very innocently offered her my Service if she needed it to make that Matter easy. She had by this Time learnt the Art of Dissimulation pretty well and answered with an Air of Unconcernedness that the Bed-Chamber Women had already acquainted the Queen with it, hoping by this Answer to divert any farther Examination into the Matter.* But I went presently to the Queen and asked her why she had not been so kind as to tell me of my Cousin's Marriage, expostulating with her upon the Point and putting her in Mind of what she used often to say to me out of Montaigne, That it was no Breach of Promise of Secrecy to tell such a Friend any thing because it was no more than telling it to one's self. All the Answer I could obtain from her Majesty was this, I have a hundred Times bid Masham tell it you, and she would not.

* In the version at Blenheim (G-I-9) Sarah says Abigail, before answering, 'looked up to the ceiling a good while in a confused awkward manner & then said yes, the Queen taxed her with it & she believed the Bed-Chamber Women had told it her'.

The Conduct both of the Queen and of Mrs Masham convinced me that there was some Mystery in the Affair, and thereupon I set myself to enquire as particularly as I could into it. And in less than a Week's Time I discovered that my Cousin was become an absolute Favourite; that the Queen herself was present at her Marriage in Dr Arbuthnot's Lodgings, at which Time her Majesty had called for a round Sum out of the Privy-purse; that Mrs Masham came often to the Queen, when the Prince was asleep, and was generally two Hours every Day in private with her: And I likewise then discovered beyond all Dispute Mr Harley's Correspondence and Interest at Court by Means of this Woman.

I was struck with Astonishment at such an Instance of Ingratitude, and should not have believed [it] if there had been any Room left for doubting.[8]

Like one who lifts a stone and discovers a nest of vipers, Sarah recoiled. It was the moment of cockcrow. The intrigue was nasty, the lies were crude, the implications horrible. As a historian she handles her material distastefully, as with gloves; yet deftly too, for nothing—from the teeming swarms of Hills to Masham's monstrous ingratitude—has been omitted. So much for the published version. Other drafts have pleasing detail, as for instance that when Abigail was at St Albans she had smallpox and was nursed by Sarah who dosed her with ass's milk and restored her, although she 'thought she would dye'.[9]

In the matter of the secret wedding Anne, as we see, was no match for Sarah. Her 'I have a hundred times bid Masham tell it you' was clumsy and made Sarah the more suspicious, wondering as she did how a bedchamber-woman came to be on such terms with the Queen as to have had a hundred chats with her.

Odd happenings, only a little puzzling at the time, now fell into place. There had been the occasion, for example, when Sarah went to the Queen at Windsor, 'very privately by a secret Passage', and was alone with her when Abigail 'unlockt the door in a loud familiar manner and was tripping across the room with a gay air, but upon seeing me she immediately stopped short and, acting a part like a player, dropt a grave curtsey when she had gone a good way without making any, and in a faint low voice cry'd, 'Did your Majesty ring, pray?'[10]

As with Harley so with his creature Abigail, the views of contemporaries are too conflicting to be of much help. Even her portrait in the National Portrait Gallery (p. 129), though exactly as one would imagine her, has a questionmark beside its catalogue-entry. According to Swift, whom she befriended, 'My lady Masham was a person of a plain sound understanding, of great truth and sincerity, without the least mixture of falsehood or disguise, of an honest boldness and courage superior to her sex, firm and disinterested in her friendship and full of love, duty and veneration for the Queen her mistress . . .'[11] According to the Earl of Dartmouth she was 'exceeding mean and vulgar in her manners, of a very unequal temper, childishly exceptious, and passionate . . . The queen had a suspicion', he adds, 'that she or her sister listened at the door all the time I was with her'.[12] In which case, why did the Queen tolerate her?

There is much unexplained, not least the secret wedding which sooner or later Sarah must have discovered. Why was she not asked? If all Anne wanted was a comforter, a soothing, useful servant, it is plain enough what balm, after Sarah, she must have found in the wench whom Godolphin, who had a nickname for everyone, called Mrs Still; even though she lacked Sarah's sparkle and was apt to be morose. To Sarah she was a monster, but to history she is of less importance as a personality than as a tool, her chief attribute—unobtrusiveness—negative, herself neither heroine nor very convincing villain. 'Abigail', says Sir Winston, 'was probably the smallest person who ever consciously attempted to decide and in fact decided the history of Europe'.[13] Her letters in an uneducated hand to Harley, full of sly nonsense about her poor Aunt Stevens's [Anne's] want of ready money [courage] give no inkling of veneration for the Queen, but on the contrary leave a sour taste and do her no service.

Of course Sarah should have ignored her and of course, being herself, she could not. 'It was so natural for me that had so much obliged her', she says, 'to resent her ill returns and to endeavour to hinder her from hurting me with the queen'.[14] How could she have sat still and shown indifference while a chambermaid was so basely supplanting her in the Queen's favour? No one could blame her, she maintained, if she expressed herself with warmth, and that she did both to the wretched Abigail and to the frightened Queen herself.

When after an interchange of notes Sarah accused Abigail to her face, she 'gravely answered that she was sure the queen, who had loved me extremely, would always be very kind to me', a reply which left Sarah speechless. 'To see a Woman whom I had raised out of the Dust put on such a superior Air, and to hear her assure me, by Way of Consolation, that the queen would be always very kind to me!* At length', she adds, 'I went on to reproach her for her Ingratitude and her secret Management with the Queen to undermine those who had so long and with so much Honour served her Majesty. To this she answered that she never spoke to the Queen about Business'.[15]

Ingratitude was, by Sarah's reckoning, the deadliest sin of all; for just as fools were often knaves, so an ungrateful person would stop at nothing. And as for discussing state business, Sarah, certain that Abigail and Anne did, took the Queen to task about it, only to be assured that her cousin 'never meddled with anything'. 'I believe others that have been in her station in former times have been tattling & very impertinent', Anne admitted, 'but she is not at all of that temper; and as for the company she keeps, it is with her as with most other people. I fancy that their lot in the world makes them move with some out of civility rather than choice; and I really believe, for one that is so much in the way of company, she has less acquaintance than anyone upon earth'.[16] It was not Abigail's fault that her other cousin was Harley, nor that his circle included Dr. Arbuthnot and Jonathan Swift. Not everyone could afford to be as fastidious as queens and duchesses.

But Sarah was not to be so easily side-tracked. Spies' reports were disquieting, her suspicion was profound. By a thousand signs it was all too obvious that Anne herself had changed, though she vowed she had not. Indeed she begged for reconciliation. Surely they might lay aside wrangling and make a fresh start? Why could they not be

---

* In another version Sarah says if she lived a thousand years she could never forget that piece of patronage from one 'that had affected such a humble way that when she met me would always offer to pin up my coat first, and must now pretend to know the Queen's mind'. (Blen G-I-8).

as they used to be? Because, said Sarah if only to herself, things had gone too far. 'It was so long before I suspected I had a secret enemy that was under trust betraying me', she wrote afterwards, 'that it was past helping before I apprehended it'.[17]

When she did apprehend it she made violent efforts by letter and by interview to oust the interloper and so, as she hoped, win back for herself the Queen's favour. In her long letter to Anne of October 29th, 1707 she refers to a recent interview when there had been no emotional scene (a thing Anne was most shy of), but long and profound silences. Sarah had stood throughout, she reminded the Queen, behind a screen, never once pulled out her handkerchief and only wept a little at parting, when Anne kissed her and Sarah 'answered as Brutus did his friend'.*[18] Yet after this, Sarah tells us, 'that vile woman' Abigail blew up the coals again to such purpose that Anne complained of Sarah to Godolphin.

Undoubtedly there were reconciliations and undoubtedly Abigail was capable of making mischief. Time and again Anne tried to heal the breach. In writing to Sarah ('Don't lett any body see this strang Scrawl') she is not ashamed to give way to emotion, although face to face she is. 'My poor hart is so tender', she writes, 'if I had begun to speak I should not have been fitt to be seen by any body . . .' Will Sarah please write too? Anne cannot trust herself to meet her just now, she would break down.[19] But Sarah is unmoved. 'This letter from the Queen', she comments, 'is extreamly kind, but 'tis plain to me that she was fearfull that I should tax her with her passion for Mrs Hill, and therefore she would not have me speak to her but write, nor shew her scrawl as she calls it which is very well writt, but she did not care that my Lord Marl: or Lord Godolphin should see this letter & she had allways allowd me to shew them any thing. As to her not being fitt to bee seen if I spoak to her, she only feared blushing if I spoak upon the subject of Mrs Hill, for when she loved

---

* *Cassius:* Have not you love enough to bear with me,
  When that rash humour which my mother gave me
  Makes me forgetful?
  Brutus: Yes, Cassius, and from henceforth
  When you are over-earnest with your Brutus
  He'll think your mother chides, and leave you so.
  Julius Caesar, act IV, sc. 3.

me most she was not apt to teares & it was very seldom that she expressed her greif that way either for the Duke of Gloucester or the Prince'.[20]

On the nature of a queen's private grief not many perhaps would care to act the critic. On the point of Anne's handwriting, however, it is true that this letter of hers is neatly written. On occasion emotion can make the Queen's hand tremble visibly.* Here it is the script of a composed child, with rounded letters, no blots and every i dottede a mild hand making Sarah's endorsement look spiky and savage. 'Open your dear hart freely', begs the Queen, 'for I can have no eas, till everything is sett right between us . . . Your displeasure is a thing I cannot support'. But again the dry endorsement: 'This letter seems to bee very kind & tender but it shews that all the ill usage that I had afterwards proceeded from Mrs Hill & not from any fault of mine to the Queen. She loved her at this time & that was the cause of my trouble, which she observed & knew very well the occation of it, but she was ashamed of it & therefore she desires that my answer upon it might bee in writing because she never knew what to say upon that subject if she was not full prepared'.[21]

Such passages make repellent reading; yet to stack all one's sympathy with an innocent queen might not be wise. Anne had, says Sir Winston, immense powers of reserve and dissimulation;† while Sarah 'resembled in some respects the kind of woman we are familiar with in the public and social agitations of our own day. But no personal accommodation could alter the antagonism. Behind the Queen lurked Harley, the Tories and Peace. Behind Sarah stood Marlborough, the Whigs, the Grand Alliance and the War'.[22]

---

* Notably in her letter to Sarah (undated) in which she writes: '. . . to beg you would not mention that person any more who you are pleased to call ye object of my fayvour, for whatever caracter ye malittious world may give her I do asure you it will never have any worth with me, knowing she does not deserve it'. She omits three words in two lines and adds them afterwards. The hand is that of a mind in turmoil. (Blen E 19).

† 'She talks some times as if she thought her self good and keeps a clutter with religion that would make one imagine that she had really devotion & some principles . . . There is nothing she will not disown, dissemble or deny if she bee but prepared for it by those that she has a passion for'. Sarah of Anne (Blen. G-I-16).

Marlborough was at first incredulous. A bedchamber-woman closeted with the Queen? Impossible! And as for political influence, no, no, that was womanish nonsense. He was soon to be disillusioned when Godolphin wrote to tell him that he was meeting with the utmost difficulty and resistance. Even so, society at large might have stayed in the dark a little longer had not Prince George given the game away when somebody remarked on the Queen's sore eyes. 'The Queen had a deflexion in her eyes as to which there happen'd some discourse in the House of Lords. Upon this the Prince said inadvertently Her Majesty would soon be free from that Malady if she did not sit up so late at Nights. This occasioned much speculation'.[23] So runs a contemporary report, to which Cunningham adds: 'About this time many things were transacted at Court in the dead of the night'.[24]

To those in the know it must have been obvious that there must soon be a crisis, and sure enough in the winter of 1707–8 there were two. Sarah, paying her Christmas visit to Anne at Kensington, learned from the page who was to announce her that Abigail had just been sent for. 'The Moment I saw her Majesty', Sarah goes on, 'I plainly perceived she was very uneasy. She stood all the while I was with her & looked as coldly upon me as if her Intention was that I should no longer doubt of my Loss of her Affections. Upon observing what Reception I had I said I was very sorry I had happened to come so unseasonably. I was making my Courtesy to go away when the Queen, with a great deal of Disorder in her Face and without speaking one Word, took me by the Hand: And when thereupon I stooped to kiss hers, she took me up with a very cold Embrace and then without one kind Word let me go. So strange a Treatment of me, after my long & faithful Services & after such repeated Assurances from her Majesty of an unalterable Affection made me think that I ought in Justice to myself, as well as in Regard to my Mistress's Interest, to write to her in the plainest & sincerest Manner possible and expostulate with her upon her Change to me & upon the new Counsels by which she seemed to be wholly governed'.[25]

In the long letter which followed, after referring to 'an Embrace that seemed to have no Satisfaction in it', Sarah issued an ultimatum. Either she was to be treated with the openness of a friend or with the reserve of a court official. After some days Anne returned a soft answer which, although in Sarah's view 'equificating', averted open strife for the time being.

In the meantime Marlborough's calming letters to his wife— surely the Queen must respond to reason?—were nevertheless full of his own weariness and despondency, a kind of fatalistic wretchedness at the futility of striving against enemies at home as well as abroad. The one glimmer of hope comes from the direction of Woodstock, where Vanbrugh and the landscape between them had clearly fired him with heroic ideas. Yet even of this he writes:

It is true what you say of Woodstock that it is very much at my heart, especially when we are in prosperity, for then my whole thoughts are of retiring with you to that place. But if everything does not go to our own desire, we must not set our hearts too much upon that place, for I see very plainly that whilst I live, if there be troubles I must have my share of them. This day makes your humble servant fifty-seven. On all accounts I could wish myself younger, but for none so much as that I might have it more in my power to make myself more agreeable to you, whom I love with all my soul.[26]

He suggests that Sarah should consult Wise about building an ice-house and should taste the fruit of every tree in the Blenheim orchard 'so that what is not good might be changed'.

But when Marlborough returned to England for the winter he found things at court even worse than he had supposed. Queen and Duchess were scarcely on speaking terms. Godolphin, steadily thwarted, yearned for retirement as Marlborough did himself. Stalemate in the war and the onerous land-tax which was paying for it reinforced the clamour of those demanding peace; while trouble at the Admiralty meant more trouble for Marlborough, whose Tory brother George shared the responsibility for its muddles with the Lord High Admiral, Prince George of Denmark.

On February 8th, 1708 the Marlboroughs and Godolphin met the Queen in an apartment adjoining the room where the lords of the council had assembled. Godolphin led by proffering his resignation, a gesture the Queen took coolly. She would give him till next day to consider; she knew many who would be glad to take his staff. Next came Sarah, 'with great duty and submission' and with reminders of

Mrs. Jennings, mother of Sarah Duchess of
Marlborough. Kneller

Sarah Duchess of Marlborough. Kneller

Sarah, Duchess of Marlborough.

Sir Godfrey Kneller.

Sarah Duchess of Marlborough. Described in her will as 'my own Picture drawn by Sir Godfrey Kneller, which is only a Head', and bequeathed to her favourite servant Grace Ridley

Sarah Duchess of Marlborough at cards with Lady Fitzharding. Kneller

John Duke of Marlborough. Attributed to Closterman

The Ladies Henrietta and Anne Churchill. Kneller

Queen Anne. J. Riley

Prince George of Denmark. After J. Riley

opinion to; I have heard of y[e] Almanack you
mention, & should be very glad what it says may
come to pass, y[t] I may be soe happy when I dye
as to leave my poor Country settld upon a lasting
foundation, I am sure nothing shall be wanting
on my part towards it; I will not say any more
now for feare my letter should not be ready against
the Duke of Marl: calls for it, but you may expect
another to morrow from your poor unfortunate
faithfull Morly, who sincerly doats on her dear
M[rs] Freeman ——

Mrs. Freeman and Mrs. Morley: (above) Queen Anne to
Sarah; (below) Sarah to the Queen

part of

this letter was writt before the good
impressions I had made in
her idea she was princess
were worn out, for I used to
pass many hours in a day with
her, & allways endeavoured to
give her notions of loving her
country of Religion & governing

Sidney Earl of Godolphin. After Kneller

Sarah Duchess of Marlborough with her children. Closterman

Anne Countess of
Sunderland. Kneller

Elizabeth Countess of
Bridgwater. Kneller

Robert Harley Earl of Oxford and Mortimer. Kneller

Abigail Hill (Lady Masham). Artist unknown
Identity doubtful

Queen Anne. Artist unknown

Sarah Duchess of Marlborough. Kneller. The Duchess is in
mourning for her infant son

long and faithful service, only to be told (if we are to believe James Stanhope), 'You shall consider of this till tomorrow, then if you desire it I shall advise you to go to your little house in St Albans and there stay till Blenheim House is ready for your Grace'. Lastly Marlborough, who 'lamented that he came in competition with so vile a creature as Harley' and that he too therefore must resign. To which Anne said, should he do so it would be to run his sword through her head.[27]

The Queen then withdrew alone to her council, where Harley delivered a report. 'Upon which the Duke of Somerset rose and said if her Majesty suffered that fellow (pointing to Harley) to treat affairs of the war without the advice of the General, he could not serve her; and so left the Council'.[28] He was supported by Lord Pembroke and others, but the meeting continued and the Queen refused to part with Harley until the Commons, by declining to pass the bill of supply, forced her hand. With him went Henry St John* and Sir Simon Harcourt. But Abigail, Harley's channel of communication with the Queen, remained unharmed.

For Anne's cold advice to Sarah we have only the word of Stanhope who was probably not present. Sarah had asked Anne if she might withdraw to the country until the end of the next campaign, so that she and her husband might then retire together. To this, at the interview, Anne may have made a scathing reply, though scarcely in the words quoted, which are uncharacteristic. All she probably said was, 'I shall advise you to retire to St Albans until Blenheim is ready', implying perhaps that she would prefer not to have her at Windsor.

Stanhope omits to add that Sarah had further asked (though 'much interrupted with tears') for the reversion of her court appointments for her daughters, a proviso to which, according to the Duchess, Anne had agreed.

When Marlborough returned to London to take leave of the Queen he found her more friendly and he understood that she would still be willing for his daughters, Henrietta Godolphin and Anne Sunderland, to succeed when their mother retired. To make doubly sure, however, Sarah herself cornered the Queen upon the subject, thanked her and said she had now by her goodness left them

* To be replaced, as Secretary at War, by Robert Walpole.

nothing to do but pray for her. At this Anne 'looked red and uneasy'
and when pressed said she remembered no such commitment and
would be glad to hear no more of it. This to Sarah was shocking;
and 'what made it the more unaccountable was that the queen had
so very extraordinary a memory that she hardly was ever known to
forget any thing of the smallest moment . . . But thus did words,
assurances & the most serious promises bind or not bind just as
humour, temper or inclination worked, & honour & truth came to
be no more accounted of than her new advisers would permit'.[29]

Before Marlborough left for Flanders the Queen wrote to him:

I have had a great mind to speak to you this week, but when I
have met with an opportunity I have found such a tenderness
coming upon me on the thought of the subject I was to speak of
that I choose rather to trouble you this way with my complaints
than any other. You know I have often had the misfortune of
falling under the Duchess of Marlborough's displeasure, and
now, after several reconciliations, she is again relapsed into her
cold unkind way and . . . has taken a resolution not to come to
me when I am alone, and fancies nobody will take notice of the
change. She may impose upon some poor simple people, but
how can she imagine she can on any that have a grain of sense?
Can she think that the Duchess of Somerset and my Lady
Fitzharding, who are two of the most observing, prying ladies
in England, won't find out that she never comes near me nor
looks on me as she used to do, that the tatling voice will not in a
little time make us the jest of the town? Some people will blame
her, others me, and a great many both. What a disagreeable
noise she will be the occasion of making in the world besides,
God knows what ill consequences it may be of. Therefore for
God Almighty's sake, for the Duchess of Marlborough's, your
own, and my poor sake, endeavour all you can to persuade
Mrs Freeman out of this strange unreasonable resolution. I have
not as yet ventured to make any answer to her letter, nor dare
not, for till this violent humour be over all I can say, though
never so reasonable, will but inflame her more. [30]

A more sensible, reasonable, friendly, sincere letter was surely never written. If this was deceit it showed a diabolical finesse of which no one, except her Groom of the Stole, believed Anne capable. Yet there it was, she did believe it. 'Either Mrs Morley was allways the greatest Decembler in the world', she wrote later, 'or she did not find herself touch'd in consiance after fourty years old';[31] and again: 'When she was prepared by those she had an opinion of, she could so far act a part very well as to say anything that was not true with all the ease & coldnesse imaginable & 'tis plain she never had any sense of honour in anything'.*[32]

In response to Anne's plea there will doubtless have been some gentle remonstrance with Sarah from Marlborough; but those who worship reason seem often the deafest to it; or perhaps in this case suspicion and jealousy had ousted reason, at least for a time. When Marlborough had left, Sarah wrote to the Queen to tell her that she would not be surprised nor displeased to hear that she had gone into the country, 'since by your very hard and uncommon usage of me you have convinced all sorts of people, as well as myself, that nothing would be so uneasy to you as my near attendance'.[33]

If it had been a private quarrel it would have been of small consequence, but Anne knew that sooner or later, if Sarah persisted, they must be the jest of Europe and she dreaded the consequences. 'The effects of these female jars', notes Archdeacon Coxe, 'arising from offended dignity on the one hand and disappointed ambition on the other . . . produced the most sinister effects on the administration of public affairs by the perplexities into which they perpetually threw both the treasurer and general'.[34]

It was to be the supreme test of Marlborough's patience. In his letters to Sarah during this spring and summer two themes predominate: Blenheim and the 'indifferency' of his Duchess. In April he refers to her 'resolution of living with that coldness & indifferency for me which if it continues must make me the unhappiest man alive'.[35] In May he uses cypher to remind her that 39 [himself] can have no content if he must live without the esteem and love of 240 [Sarah]; and in June, 'Upon my word, when you are out of humour and are disatisfied with me I had rather dye than live. So on the contrary when you are kind I covett of all things a quiet life with

* Most of the Duchess's harsher judgments of Queen Anne were written when still smarting from 'ill usage'. In old age she toned them down.

you'.[36] When Anne complained of the Duchess of Marlborough's displeasure, Marlborough knew exactly what she meant.

As for Blenheim, Sarah is to coax the Duke of Manchester, ambassador at Genoa, to send thousands of yards of Italian velvet and damask. Marlborough himself is buying tapestry and paintings and has been 'advised by every body to have the Portico, so that I have writt to Vanbrook to have itt; and which I hope you will like for I shou'd be glad we were allways of one mind, which shall allways be endeavour'd for I am never so happy as when I think you are kind'.[37] After two years of building, Vanbrugh had changed his mind about the principal order and switched from Doric to Corinthian. Now, after nearly three, a Corinthian portico seventy feet high for the northern entrance is begged as an afterthought. Sarah would have liked it better if there had been steps to go with it, which for years there were not.

In the meantime, to Marlborough's dismay, Sarah had begged a site of the Queen at St James's, there with Wren to erect a rival to Blenheim. It would cost twice as much as the estimate, her husband warned her, and in any case she would find as a general rule that it was better to buy than to build . . . From none of which could anyone have suspected that Marlborough was about to fight his third major battle at Oudenarde.

Anne's reaction to the news of the victory—'Oh, Lord, when will all this dreadful bloodshed cease?'—was significant; and when Marlborough's account reached her, it can have given no pleasure. 'The Circumstances in this last Battle', he told her, 'I think shew the Hand of God . . . a visible Mark of the Favour of Heaven to you and your Arms'; and then, plunging further, 'Give me Leave to say that I think you are obliged in Conscience & as a good Christian to forgive & to have no more Resentments to any particular Person or Party but to make use of such as will carry on this just War with Vigour'.[38] The letter was typical and sincere; and yet how very odd it is when a christian general, the groans of the dying in his ears, tells his christian queen that she is bound in conscience to forgive her enemies!

Even so, Marlborough's invocation might have carried more weight with the Queen had his Duchess been reasoning with her on similar lines; but her approach was entirely different. She had contracted the habit of sending Anne letters she had received from others, without their permission and with her own comments. This she did in the case of Abigail when, for Anne's benefit, she compared her to Iago; and now again in the case of Marlborough: his note on Oudenarde, in which he spoke of himself as God's instrument of happiness to the Queen and nation, 'if she will please to make use of it'. This, on Sarah's part, proved a miscalculation. The last phrase offended the Queen who wrote to Marlborough for an explanation. In reply she received from Sarah another long letter in anything but a conciliatory tone [appendix I].

Yet all this was as nothing to the onslaughts the Duchess was planning with the help of him she called her secretary, Arthur Maynwaring. Maynwaring was an honest man. He was popular at the Kit-Cat Club, befriended by Vanbrugh, kept a highly reputable mistress,* sat in the Commons, wrote satire and had been made auditor of the imprests (a remunerative sinecure) by Godolphin in 1705. His health was precarious, and indeed in Kneller's Kit-Cat portrait (p. 164.) he looks at the point of death. He doted on Sarah. None of which would have amounted to much had he not been possessed of a strange, immature, schoolboyish quality of impishness, diverting at Holywell, uproarious at the Kit-Cat but, when it came to letter-writing, irresponsible in the extreme. As a secretary he is tireless. He writes draft after draft and sends them all to Sarah. 'Choose any thing you should like', he begs, 'and though I some-times press your Grace on this subject to do things that you seem averse to, I cannot help confessing that I believe in the main you certainly do what is right, for I do not think you were ever in the wrong in your life . . . When I read over this morning', he continues, 'the letter for Mrs Mor: [the Queen] as I have put it together, I cannot help saying one thing pleased me in it very much, which was that tho above half of it be your Graces own writing & your very words, I am sure nobody that were to read it would guess that it were not all writ by one person, which shews that I have not imitated your style so long quite in vain'.[39]

Together they composed long, anonymous letters to Abigail [appendix II]; and together, for Sarah to sign, they wrote outrageous letters to the Queen. Not all of them were sent, but if that written in

* The actress Mrs Oldfield.

Sarah's hand and dated July 26th, 1708 [appendix III]—between the battle of Oudenarde and the thanksgiving—reached its target, the wonder is that Anne agreed to Sarah's sharing her coach to St Paul's.

On that thanksgiving morning (August 19th) Sarah must have had mixed feelings as, in her office of Mistress of the Robes, she selected the Queen's jewels. In one account she speaks of the many hours it had cost her to do them.[40] Nothing, we can be certain, was left to chance. But this was not to be a repetition of 1704, when the Queen was 'full of jewels'. 'Her Majesty', Sarah herself tells us, 'seldom woar Jewells';[41] so why should she choose to wear them now? In the coach there was trouble; and in the portico, or even possibly in St Paul's itself, there was very nearly a public scene when Sarah, as it was said, commanded the Queen to silence. But this, Sarah insisted, was an exaggeration. Fearing that Anne was about to say something she would not have wanted onlookers to hear, Sarah had begged her in a whisper to be quiet. Whatever the truth of it, the offence was profound. Yet it was Sarah who wrote to complain of the Queen's treatment, 'when I had taken so much Pains to put your Jewels in a Way that I thought you would like, Mrs Masham could make you refuse to wear them, in so unkind a Manner; because that was a Power she had not thought fit to exercise before. I will make no Reflections upon it', she ended, 'only that I must needs observe that your Majesty chose a very wrong Day to mortify me, when you were just going to return Thanks for a Victory obtained by Lord Marlborough'.[42]

Every time Sarah wrote she made matters worse, and in this she was egged on by Maynwaring. If only Marlborough could have been there to check her! 'I cou'd wish,' he wrote mildly, from the siege of Lille, 'that Mrs Freeman would see what she so frequently obsarves that 42 [the Queen] is not capable of being chang'd by reason, so that you shou'd be quiet til the time comes in which she must change'.[43] But that was not, as none knew better than he did, Sarah's way. Reason and candour were her twin gods that everyone must yield to. The Queen might safely be left to them and to her. Anne, Sarah tells us, was at Windsor—

Through the whole Summer after Mr Harley's Dismission the Queen continued to have secret Correspondence with him. And that this might be the better managed she staid all the sultry Season, even when the Prince was panting for Breath,* in that small House she had formerly purchased at Windsor which, though as hot as an Oven, was then said to be cool, because from the Park such Persons as Mrs Masham had a Mind to bring to her Majesty could be let in privately by the Garden.[44]

Yet again, on September 9th, 1708, there seems to have been an attempted reconciliation. Anne writes to Sarah, 'According to my promise I writt this to lett my dear Mrs Freeman know if she can com to me at five aclock this afternoon I will be redy to receive you in my Gallery at ye Castle & shall think my self very happy if that meeting setts every thing right between us, there being nothing I am more desirous off then to have a thorow good understanding between deare Mrs Freeman and her poor unfortunat faithfull Morley who will tell her last moment be Soe, whether you think what I shall happen to say be reasonable or just'.[45] But red eyes and raised voices told of failure.[46] Sarah makes no mention of it. All we have are 'Heads of a conversation with Mrs Morley, Sep: the 9th, 1708', but since these include such firecrackers as 'No body countenanced & trusted by her but who is some way or other influenced by Mr Harley', 'Mr Harley never had a good reputation in the world . . . Nobody alive can either bee more odious then hee is or more contemptable to all parties', and 'Why will she not consider fairly & cooly etc',[47] it is not difficult to guess the rest or at least the tenor of it.

In the following month it became known that Prince George of Denmark† was dying. On October 26th Sarah wrote to the Queen:

Though the last time I had the honour to wait upon your Majesty your usage of me was such as was scarce possible for me to imagine or for any body to believe, yet I cannot hear of so

---

* Prince George was asthmatic.

† 'I think my self more obliged to him then to Mrs Morley. I remember all his justice & goodnesse to me in times past. I have a thousand things to thank him for & noe one to complain of. Hee is still the same (I beleive) to me that hee ever was & will allways bee soe unless Mrs Morley thinks fitt to give him a prejudice to me which I am sure I shall never deserve'. (Sarah to Anne, of Prince George of Denmark, 29 Oct., 1707. Blen. G-1-7).

great a misfortune and affliction to you as the condition in which the Prince is without coming to pay my duty in inquiring after your health, and to see if in any particular whatsoever my service can either be agreeable or useful to you, for which satisfaction I would do more then I will trouble your Majesty to read at this time.[48]

Taking this letter with her Sarah travelled all night to Kensington and delivered it. Next day she was received very coolly but remained and was present on October 28th when the Prince died. 'Then I knelt down to the Queen', runs her account, 'and said all that I could imagine from a faithful servant and one that she had professed so much kindness to; but she seemed not to mind me but clapt her hands together, with other marks of passion; and when I had expressed all I could think of to moderate her grief, I knelt by her without speaking for some time, and then asked her to go to St James's; upon which she answered she would stay there. I said that was impossible; what could she do in such a dismal place? and I made use of all the arguments that are common upon that head, but all in vain; she persisted that she would stay at Kensington . . . I said nobody in the world ever continued in a place where a dead husband lay, and I did not see where she could be but within a room or two of that dismal body'. At last she agreed to go and, handing Sarah her watch said, 'Don't come in to me till the hand of the watch comes to this place', and added, 'Send to Masham to come to me before I go'.*

Sarah continues: 'This I thought very shocking, but at that time I was resolved not to say the least wry word to displease her and therefore answered that I would, and went out of the room with the watch in my hand . . . but as I was sitting at the window, watching the minutes to go in, I thought it so disagreeable for me to send for Mrs Masham to go in to her before all that company that I resolved to avoid that; and when the time was come I went in and told her all things were ready, but I had not sent to Mrs Masham; that I thought

---

* 'The deportment of the Duchess of Marlborough while the Prince lay expiring was of such a nature that the Queen, then in the heights of grief, was not able to bear it, but with marks of displeasure in her countenance she ordered the Duchess to withdraw and send Mrs Masham to her'. Swift: *Prose*, v, 369.

it would make a disagreeable noise when there were bishops and ladies of the bedchamber without that she did not care to see, and that she might send herself to her to come to St James's at what time she pleased.

'To this she consented and I called for her hoods, which I remember Mrs Hill* put on; and as she did it the Queen whispered with her, I suppose some kind thing to her sister, who had not appeared before me at Kensington; but upon the alarm of the Queen's being to go with me to St James's, she came into the gallery with one of her ministers, the Scotch doctor [Arbuthnot], to see her Majesty pass, who, notwithstanding her great affection for the Prince, at the sight of that charming lady, as her arm was upon mine, which she had leaned upon, I found she had strength to bend down towards Mrs Masham like a sail and in passing by went some steps more than was necessary to be nearer her; and when that cruel touch was over, of going by her with me, she turned about in a little passage room and gave orders about her dogs and a strong box'.

In the coach Anne gave orders about the burial (room was to be left in the vault for herself); and at St James's Sarah led her to the green closet and gave her a cup of broth. That evening Sarah found the Queen at table with Mrs Masham, who left immediately 'with an air of insolence and anger'. The Queen took a great deal of trouble with the funeral arrangements and showed 'bits of great tenderness for the Prince. I remember', the Duchess concludes, 'she wrote me once a little note at which I could not help smiling, that I should send to my Lord Treasurer to take care that some door might be taken down at the removing the Prince to Westminster, for fear the dear Prince's body should be shook as he was carried out of some room, though she had gone long jumbling journeys with him to the Bath when he must feel it and when he was gasping for breath. I did see the tears in her eyes two or three times after his death, upon his subject, and I believe she fancied she loved him . . . but her nature was very hard and she was not apt to cry.'[49]

The Queen's note, at which the Duchess could not help smiling, ran as follows:

I scratched twice at dear Mrs Freeman's door, as soon as lord

* Abigail's sister, Alice Hill.

treasurer went from me, in hopes to have spoke one more word to him before he was gone; but no body hearing me, I wrote this, not caring to send what I had to say by word of mouth; which was to desire him that when he sends his orders to Kensington he would give directions there may be a great many yeomen of the guards to carry the prince's dear body that it may not be let fall, the great stairs being very steep and slippery. [50]

CHAPTER VII

Favour Declines

1709-1710

———◆———

The Queen's grief was sincere, but to one who took pleasure in the rules of etiquette there may have been some slight relief in meticulously observing them. For hours and days in the great frost of January 1709 gout kept her in bed, where she lay in a purple nightgown in a bed heavy with hangings of purple and black.

'I must desire you to bespeake a purple quilt & three couchions against I see company', she wrote to Sarah, 'but they must not be of any glossy thing; & if you please send one of your servants to ye upholsterer to know the size of ye bed that they may be made fitt. I cannot end this without beging you once more for God's sake to lett the Dear Picture you have of mine be putt into my Bedchamber for I cannot be without it any longer'.

This Sarah endorses: 'When the Queen writt this she was as much under the power of Mrs Masham as ever . . . The Picture that she mentions was the Princes which I took away because I thought she loved him & if she had been like other people 'tis terrible to see a picture while the affection is fresh upon one'.[1]

Among the royal dead perhaps only Albert the good can have been more thoroughly mourned than George the foolish. The Queen haunted the gloomy closets where he had lived and worked, closets which, Sarah remembered, 'looked only into a very ugly little close space where Mrs Masham used to dry linen . . . one was a water-closet & the other full of his tools which he worked with, and I thought nothing was more natural than to avoid seeing of papers or anything that belonged to one that one loved when they were just dead'. But 'all that time she saw everybody that Mrs Masham pleased'.² In another account (there are always several) Sarah says, 'It was generally thought that she only conversed there with Mrs Masham, which I my self once mentioned to her & I never saw anybody so struck, but now it appears that the great concern she shewed when those closets were mentioned was because she met the governing men there at the same time that she solemnly protested to the Duke of Marlborough & Lord Godolphin that she relied only upon them'.³

Sarah came to court seldom and then only for the business of her office. Princes, nay love itself might die, but petitioners persisted. Soon after Prince George's death Sarah felt it her duty to bring to Anne's notice the case of Mrs Howe, a widow with five young children and no money; for, says Sarah, she thought it would give the Queen 'an air of being greivd for the Prince to bee touch'd upon that melancholly subject', and so it proved. 'My artifice', Sarah continues, 'succeeded just as I expected, for her Majesty put on a very melancholly air as if she felt a great deal upon that subject and said yes indeed, I doe know how to pity her. I will look over a list of the lodgings att Somersett hous; & for the pention she said she would do any thing that was reasonable; but she had a hum which she allways has when she does not really care for what she does & answer'd it would bee time enough to say what she would give her when she had spoken to my Lord Treasurer.'⁴

Perhaps, thought Sarah, she might be luckier in 'the case of poor Mr Griffith, a very old servant to her & the Prince who lately died, clerk of the green cloth.* This gentleman left his family in a very ill condition and . . . recommended his children to her Majesty with the most dutyfull & moving expressions'. But the Queen said that Griffith had in his time won a great deal from Prince George at cards, which Sarah agrees he had, 'and so did a great many others very fairly . . . and it would have been a sad thing to have kept his Highness company if they had got nothing by it'.⁵ Another Griffith shared with Abigail and her brother the gift of mimicry, an accomplishment Sarah detested. 'Lady Howard and Mrs Griffith have bin with me today', Anne in an undated note tells Sarah, 'The first goes

* Dr Reid states that Sarah's brother-in-law Edward Griffith became Comptroller of the Green Cloth. (Reid, op. cit. p. 31)

out of town tomorrow & says she loves ye Country mightely but yet looks very melencoly when she speakes of it. My other visiter at my request mimiked you & severall others. Lady Fretchevill* she does much ye best, but for your self she does over act you'.[6]

Friendship had made way for a time of teasing and to this Sarah was prepared to give full rein. She begged for an old harpsichord, which she almost certainly knew Anne had lent Abigail, and 'with some difficulty' Sarah was given her way.[7] It is doubtful if she played herself. She admits she 'did not love fine Musick & thought nothing so pretty as Ballads';[8]† and in this also she was encouraged by Maynwaring.

'I shall be very glad', he assures her, 'to perform a part in Ballad singing whenever your Grace has occasion for a fine voice. I saw the other day a new Ballad upon Abigal. Mrs Chetwynd had it and if I can get a copy I will try to mend the latter part of it & then I can sing it with becoming impudence, which I could not do if I made one quite myself. I am very glad your Grace can be diverted with a harpsichord & I will be sure to practise upon it against I have the honour to wait upon you in your travels. I heard you borrow one of Lady Fitzharding the other night. If you should ever have occasion again, I have one that I never use & yet would never part with because it was given me by Lord Burlington. It is a pretty one and very good but I make use of a worse because it has an uncommon quality of being very seldom out of tune'.[9]

As ballad-monger Maynwaring found a competitor in Godolphin. Neither was an Addison, but for letting off steam or venting venom their doggerel served its turn:

> Who goes to Court may see with half an eye
> Tis over run with nauseous flattery;
> Scarce one man left who will not be afraid
> To whisper Mashams an ungreatfull jade . . .[10]

But the jade too could take a hand in provocation, as when she coolly moved into Sarah's lodgings at Kensington. Sarah of course made straight for the Queen and taxed her with it. Impossible. 'Masham had none of my rooms, she was sure of it & her Majesty

* Lady Frescheville, a lady-in-waiting disliked by Sarah.
† See appendix IV.

was pleased to repeat it over & over & was so very positive of it that I was really ashamed & begged her pardon . . . But as I went downstairs, going by my own lodgings I could not help asking ye page of ye back stairs that carried the candle to light me if there was any use made of those rooms. He answerd ye bedchamber-woman had one part of em & Mrs Masham the other'. So back to the Queen, who remained unmoved. Next day Abigail apologised and moved out only, according to Sarah, to move back again for her lying-in. It was hardly to be wondered at that when Anne for the third time was confronted with the same grievance she lost her temper and shouted, 'Tis a lie! Tis false!'[11] And so once again Sarah was shocked. Anne would never have made such a scene in the old days, she had always seemed so well-bred. Abigail must be coarsening her. To talk with her was useless. However, one could still write.

In letter-writing as in everything else Sarah was systematic and unsparing. True, she wrote fast and tumbled her mind out on paper, but her mind was clear, she knew what she wanted to say and was indifferent as to how long it took her to say it or the recipient to make it out. A few sides of gilt-edged paper (she preferred thick paper from Paris) were nothing. When a situation grew serious it called for what she called a notum or a narrative: a recapitulation running to a dozen or more foolscap pages. In 1709 the Queen received more of Sarah's narratives than ever before, and though the field was extensive, three topics were given priority: long and faithful service, harsh usage and the shortcomings of Abigail.

Abigail was no fool and, in addition to Harley and St John, she had useful allies in Dr Arbuthnot and Swift and, on a lower plane, in the hack-writer Rivella Manley who, though apt to overreach herself, could at least be counted on for zealous support. In a crude age she relied mainly on the bludgeon where Swift would have used a sword; but she was not contemptible. She could be ingenious, and in her account of Marlborough's amours with Barbara Cleveland, whom she knew, she brings, however scurrilously, her characters and their jasmine-scented seraglio to life. She was not conscious of the ludicrous, but neither were most of her readers. Thus in her *New Atlantis*, a best-seller published in May, 1709, she credited Abigail (Hilaria) with a soul fitted for grandeur, 'a capacious repository for the confidence of royal favour'. Abigail's wit and judgment, she claimed, were of the finest and, more than that, she 'not only wore but loved the Holy awful Robe of Religion'. The long panegyric ends: 'She speaks more correct than others write'. It is to be hoped that she did.

To Mrs Manley the reign of Anne, though eventful, was not eventful enough. She therefore sat herself down, as it were, at her loom of fiction and wove melodrama, which she clearly enjoyed. Queen Anne was made to die in childbirth (Abigail adopted the princess), Marlborough of wounds, Godolphin was exiled with the Pretender, and as for Sarah (Madame de Caria), she would have been lynched by the mob had not Abigail saved her. Even as it was, her 'Superbous Palace' was stormed and looted. But the dénouement was still to come. Hilaria (Abigail) gave the Duchess sanctuary, but when the mob murmured, 'she persuaded her (tho' with much difficulty) to resign herself a Votary to Religion'; and since Sarah's status as a widow 'forbad her retirement among the Vestals', Abigail was magnanimous enough to found and endow a new order of which Sarah became Superior, 'so to atone by her perpetual attendance on & Adoration to the Mother of the Gods for the injustice she had done to Mortals'.

Maynwaring, writing to Sarah of 'that vile and nauseous book', made light of its satire. 'Tis all old incredible stuff', he told her, 'and there is one scene which I think you could hardly help laughing at, which is when 240 [Sarah] is going to be pull'd to pieces by the mob for all manner of ill done to 42 [Anne] and to England, Generous Hilaria [Abigail] sends a troop of guards to rescue her'.[12]

For Sarah it made the excuse for one of her longest letters to the Queen. From drafts at Blenheim it looks as though she at first intended a full-length review, but on consideration relegated the book to the end of her letter, in the form of an afterthought: 'I had almost forgot to tell you of a new book . . .' etc. At the beginning of her letter she asks, 'What is it that prevails with you to oppose the advice of all your old servants & councils if it be not that woman'? and suggests that if she should question the first passer-by as to what had caused so great a change in the Queen, 'he would say that the reason was because you were grown very fond of Mrs Masham & were governed by those that govern her'.[13]

Though long since warned by her husband that 'all truths are not to be spoke', Sarah had never been one for leaving things unsaid. She vaunted her candour and failed to see that no one with judgment and sensibility could have sent such letters as she did to the Queen. She 'hoped it would do good' and that Anne would no longer count it a crime for her to accuse her of 'a more than ordinary favour' for Mrs Masham. It could of course, on the contrary, do nothing but harm, and if Sarah failed to realise it, Marlborough did not.

'It has always been my Observation in Disputes', he wrote to her, 'especially in that of Kindness and Friendship, that all Reproaches, though ever so just, serve to no End but making the Breach wider. I cannot help being of Opinion that however insignificant we may be, there is a Power above that puts a Period to our Happiness or Unhappiness. If any body had told me eight Years ago that after such great Success, and after you had been a faithful Servant 27 Years that even in the Queen's Life-time we should be obliged to seek Happiness in a retired Life, I could not have believed that possible'.[14]

In May, certain of peace, he sent from the Hague for a chair of state—'I beg you will take care to have it made so as that it may serve for part of a bed when I have done with it here'[15]—but for peacemaking it was never to be needed. When the allies demanded that, should Louis XIV's grandson refuse to relinquish the throne of Spain, Louis must go to war with him, the peace preliminaries broke down: a disaster that lost us the peace Marlborough had fought for. In England, dismay and disappointment; in France, famine and fury. Soldiers reached for their arms and trudged on towards the holocaust of Malplaquet.

It was hardly the moment for chiding Marlborough for not, on his duchess's behalf, remonstrating with the Queen, yet that is what Sarah now did. Wearily, from the bloodiest of battlefields, Marlborough replied:

I do assure you upon my honour & salvation that the only reason why I did not write was that I am very sure it would have had no other effect than that of being shewn to 256 [Abigail], by which she would have had an opertunity of turning it as she pleas'd so that when I shal speake to 42 [the Queen] of their harsh Behavior to you thay would have been prepar'd ... You are dearer to me then my whole life, for I am fonder of my

happiness then of my life, which I cannot injoye unless you are
kind.[16]

At St James's, perhaps not surprisingly, the victory of Malplaquet
was not mentioned. Sarah was in a whirl of pettiness not worthy of
record except where some lively detail glints from her page. While
she kept her offices (and Marlborough's going could not be risked
by her dismissal), her duties had to be performed, and one senses the
Queen's embarrassment, if not her own, while she did them. When
for example the Queen of Prudes (Abigail's sister Alice) was promoted to bedchamber-woman, Sarah had most unwillingly to
present her to the Queen at Windsor. She went, she tells us, and asked
Abigail to announce her, whereupon 'she started back & said her
Majesty was in her closset, poynting to it as if she would have me
goe & as if she had not so much liberty as to scrape at the door'.[17]
That summer there was a similar scene at the presentation of Mrs
Danvers's daughter who, according to Sarah, 'did not look like a
human creature'. 'The Queen sent for the Dutchess from London to
present Bell Danvers', reports Peter Wentworth, 'till when her
Grace had not been there since the Queen was at Windsor. The town
talk as if the Dutchess had thoughts of resigning the Groom of the
Stole & that upon the condition Lady Sunderland should succeed
her, but they say the Duke of Somersett contests the matter for his
Duchess, which is what keeps the Dutchess of Marlborough from
quiting ... Her house in the Priory [St. James's] advances prodi-
giously, 'tis now a-covering'.[18]
It was a pity that at the founding of Marlborough House the
words on the first stone, *1709 Anno Pacifico*—'neither truth nor good
Latin'—had had to be altered.[19] Even so there were compensations.
'If the house be set in an equal line with her Majesty's Palace',
Maynwaring told Sarah, 'it will have a view down the middle walk
of her Garden ... and being remov'd from all manner of dust &
from the smoke of the houses in the Pell-mell, you will live & sleep
as it were in the middle of that great Garden'.[20] Precisely so. In
September, after showing the place to Vanbrugh, he wrote again:

He did really commend the inside of it very much, but I must
own for the outside he found several faults there that were very
obvious when he shewd them; and he has talk'd me into an

opinion that he is an able Architect as to what relates to the Fabrick without; and I think you say that Blenheim is very well as to that. I believe you & he could make the best house in the world if you could agree to work together.[21]

Yes but they could not; and already Sarah had dealt him a heart-wound by demanding the destruction of Woodstock Manor. Vanbrugh bided his time against Marlborough's return, but Marlborough had other troubles and was writing to Sarah:

> It is not fitt that any body but your self should know that I have just reason to be convinced that 42 [the Queen] has been made jealous of the power of 39 [himself], so that 39 is resolved not only to convince 42 but all the world that he has no ambition & at the same time be careful not to be in the power of villains nor even of 42. It is impossible to explain this in writing . . .[22]

And in the following month, to show the world that he had no ambition, he asked the Queen to make him Captain-General for life. Whoever put him up to it (the Junto?) it was a false move open, to say the least, to misinterpretation. Abigail, 'in her nauseous bufooning way', dubbed him King John.[23]

To her reply, in which she declined the favour, the Queen added:

> You seem to be dissatisfied with my behaviour to the Duchess of Marlborough. I do not love complaining, but it is impossible to help saying on this occasion I believe nobody was ever so used by a friend as I have been by her ever since my coming to the Crown. I desire nothing but that she would leave off teasing & tormenting me and behave herself with the decency she ought both to her friend & Queen, and this I hope you will make her do . . . Whatever her behaviour is to me, mine shall be always as becomes me . . .[24]

And to Sarah the next day:

> It is impossible for you to recover my former kindness, but I shall behave myself to you as the Duke of Marlborough's wife and as my Groom of the Stole.*[25]

* Commenting upon this in 1710 Sarah writes: 'She takes great care in the letter

Three days later Sarah sent the Queen from St Albans an immensely long letter ('as short as I could make it') in the form of a sermon. She begins by agreeing never to mention Abigail on condition that the Queen reads this 'history'—'a long & particular narrative of a series of faithful services for about 26 years past'—and ponders it before taking her Communion. Then come quotations from *The Whole Duty of Man*, e.g. The Queen should examine herself as to 'unthankfulness to those that admonish or being angry with them for it . . . Ask your own heart seriously', Sarah adds, 'whether you have ever told me of any fault but that of believing as all the world does that you have an intimacy with Mrs M: and whether those shocking things you complain I have said was any more then desiring you to love me better then her & not to take away your confidence in me'. Passing on to 'the warning before the Communion in the Common Prayer-book' she reminds the Queen of its terms and more particularly 'that we make restitution to those that we have done the least injury to' and so 'regain the friendship of those we have used ill'. Next comes Bishop Taylor on repentance; and indeed the whole letter or narrative would be most edifying were it not for the unmentionable Abigail, who somehow slides in towards the end. 'I still hope', concludes the Duchess, 'I have a better charecter in the world then Mrs Masham tells your Majesty of Inveteracy & malice . . . for I do not comprehend that one can properly bee said to have malice & inveteracy for a viper because one endeavours to hinder it from doing mischief'.[26]

Presumption on the grand scale can be stupefying, and from her failure to reply when so ordered it would seem that it had stunned the Queen. The only response, says Sarah, was a gracious smile when they met at Communion, and even that she feared was intended for Bishop Taylor rather than for herself. 'For as for friendship', she adds sadly, 'after all the most terrible vows and asseverations,

---

to tell me 'tis now impossible that her kindnesse to me can return, which is my own opinion & I need not tell you how little I desire it should. All I have don which she calls tormenting is in order that wee may bee safe & I own I have some pleasure in making her see she is in the wrong, tho I know she has not worth enough to own it or religion enough to make any body amends for any wrong, notwithstanding the clutter she keeps about her prayers & my soul'. (Blen G-1-8).

here ended even all pretences to it'.[27] But duty had been done. Both Duke and Duchess in turn had reminded the Queen of her Christian duty. They could do no more.

And now, says Sarah, their enemies' plots began to ripen. For months, 'whilst the Queen's ministers were asleep, they [Harley etc.] were frequently at court, advising in secret how to perplex those affairs of which others had the public direction'.[28] For Marlborough and Godolphin it was indeed an impossible situation and one that could not last. Early in the new year the opposition had grown bold enough for a trial of strength which, resolutely met and countered, could have led to their undoing.

The plan, crude as it sounds, was simply to sail over the head of the Captain-General by promoting Abigail's brother, Honest Jack Hill, who according to Sarah 'had never distinguished himself unless it were over a bottle',* to the head of a regiment. If successful it would show the world that the victor of Blenheim could be ignored in his own command, and at the same time it would be grossly unfair to those officers who had fought at his side and were themselves due for promotion; an injustice bound to cause disaffection and to undermine morale. The insult was deliberate, a malicious plan of which, since she supported it, one cannot entirely exempt the Queen. Sarah saw it as a contest between the Captain-General of the Allies and a chambermaid, 'a strange competition', as she told Anne, 'between one that has gaind you so many battles and one that is but just worthy to brush your combs'.[29] She was not far wrong.

At an uncomfortable interview with the Queen Marlborough protested, but all she would say was, 'You will do well to advise with your friends'. He came away, Sarah noticed, with fear in his eyes. But he was not friendless. The lords of the Junto swore that they would support him. Sunderland the extremist urged him to go to the limit with an ultimatum to the Queen—Abigail must go or he must resign—and in that he was zealously supported by Maynwaring who again and again insisted that this was the last chance and a superb one for getting rid of Carbunculata, the 'little shuffling

---

* 'Drinking & mimicking', Sarah writes, 'was his Inclenation'; but she was seemingly unaware of these habits when she got him an appointment as groom of the bedchamber to the young Duke of Gloucester, 'to run after a child from morning till night.' Disillusionment came later.

wretch' Abigail. The weak link was Godolphin. Like Marlborough he was by nature moderate; and like him, in spite of everything, he still had some tenderness for the Queen. He knew her obstinacy, none better, and remembered the lengths to which she had gone with William and Mary in her refusal to part with Sarah. To oust Abigail now, however desirable, would mean an address in the House and open scandal. It might even cost a throne. It must deeply embarrass the Queen. This could not be. And so at Windsor Lodge the last sentence of Marlborough's letter to the Queen was struck out and the ultimatum cancelled. He ended with the words: 'the malice of a bedchamberwoman'.

Marlborough absented himself from the Council meeting, but there was no repetition of the crisis of 1708; and 'by this neglect to take united action', comments Sir Winston, 'not only the Whigs but Godolphin settled their own speedy downfall'.[30] At court there was much hurrying and scurrying as Anne rallied her friends. It 'gave such a life to the Jacobit interest', says Sarah scathingly, 'that many who had never come to court in some years did now run about with very busy faces as if they thought they should soon get the government into their hands . . . Honest people', she adds, 'laughed at such proceedings or else pitied the Queens misfortune who was thus exposed to be the talk of all courts & countries for so wrong a thing as having such a fondness for a bedchamber woman'.[31]

Somers spoke for Marlborough. Godolphin was 'much distracted', Sarah detached. Marlborough, she agreed with Maynwaring, should stick to his guns and let the world see that 'he served till the war was ended only because he did not think it reasonable to let a chamber-maid disappoint all he had done'.[32]

On January 20th the Queen, much shaken, told Godolphin that 'after deep consideration' she had decided not to insist upon Hill's appointment.* As Sarah read it, Abigail's fear of exposure had communicated itself to Anne, whereupon decisions had been reversed and, very temporarily, Marlborough had been restored to favour. While the glimmer lasted, the Queen 'made the greatest professions to him that were possible, and immediately, when the same lady's fears were over, she let them all fall again and returned

---

* The Queen compensated Hill with a 'pension' of £1000 a year and later made him a general, in which rank he led the disastrous expedition against Quebec.

to her former coldness . . . Tis thought', Sarah concludes, 'she will see her errors when 'tis too late as her father did before her'.[33]

For the Whigs it was a Pyrrhic triumph; for 'never', says Sir Winston, 'did the chance return of taking Abigail by the scruff and Harley by the throat'. For want of resolution they had drifted on to a course of suicide, a career in which they were to be speeded by their rash prosecution of Dr Sacheverell.

The theme of Sacheverell's sermon—'In perils among false brethren'—preached in St Paul's the previous November before the Lord Mayor of London had, not surprisingly, proved inflammable. Sarah called it 'an heap of bombast' and it was indeed a hysterical rage against dissenters and toleration which, in another place at another time, would have been brushed aside. Godolphin (Volpone in the sermon) decided to prosecute and so, with the help of Swift and Dr Atterbury, Sacheverell armed with a speech 'exquisitely contrived to move pity' was inflated from almost nothing to something which passed for a model martyr.

Sarah, not appreciating what this martyrdom might lead to, was far less interested in the defendant—'an ignorant impudent Incendiary . . . a lewd, drunken, pampered man'—than in the etiquette observed or not observed by the ladies-in-waiting who with the Queen, day after long day, attended the trial in Westminster Hall, a place still hung about with Marlborough's trophies. The whole thing —and to Sarah it was important—turned on whether the Queen's ladies should stand or sit. When on February 27th Sarah, having stood for three hours, approached the Queen, who sat incognito behind a curtain in the box Wren had designed for her, and asked if they might sit, as was usual at such prolonged affairs, she agreed at once and they did so. Later however the redhaired Duchess of Somerset arrived with Lady Hyde and they both insisted upon standing.

When, after some whispering, the rival duchess was told that they had the Queen's permission to sit, she 'started back with an air as if we had don something very impertinent' and still insisted upon standing, thus making the rest appear lacking in respect. 'It was easy to see the meaning of all this', adds Sarah, 'and that my gold key was the thing aim'd att, which design I was resolved to dissappoynt as much as I could, and for fear the Duke of Somerset should say something to the Queen or get Mrs Masham to doe it . . . I went to the Queen the next morning . . . I made my entry begging pardon for coming so early but I added that she gave some people leave to doe it & I was uneasy tell I had spoke to her alone upon what had happened the day before. She look'd angry & snap'd me up, saying she had very little time & that she expected my Lord Treasurer. I continued that I had not much to say, but finding that the Dutches of Somerset would not sett down as the rest of the ladys did & which was so known a custome, I was fearfull of doing any thing her Majesty did not like. Upon which she answerd very brutally, "I thought I should have been troubled no more with it".* "Yes, Madam", said I, "I must beg to know what you do really like in this matter, because tho' I can't think as some doe you converse with, I am sure I will never come in the way of doing any thing you don't like, & being to goe to the tryall in a few hours, I desire once more to know if you would bee better pleas'd that wee should not sett down". "If I had not liked it", answerd her Majesty, "why should you think I would have ordered it as I did yesterday?" '34

For the rest of the trial everyone sat except Lady Hyde and the Duchess of Somerset, the latter, Sarah noticed, mightily out of countenance. On March 21st the trial ended with a nominal sentence against Sacheverell, who set out upon a triumphal progress through the country, scattering blessings and kisses to devotees and putting new heart into the Church party.

Sarah brooded on the Somersets. He of course, as the Queen had once said, was a fool and a liar. She, the Percy heiress who had married for the third time at fifteen, pretended to be friendly; as who would not, when Sarah had had her appointed? But now all was clear. She aimed to be Groom of the Stole and her husband abetted her. Very well, Sarah accepted the challenge. All the same her tactics were odd for, says Sarah, 'she never was quite so kind as after she had taken the resolution to supplant me, for then she not only came to dinner & made meetings for play oftener than before, but I remember she took it into her head still to kiss me at parting, which was

---

* In another draft the Duchess writes, 'If any body had heard it I could not possibly have waited on her to the tryall, but we were alone & I was resolved to keep my temper till my Lord Marl: came home'. (Blen G-1-8).

quite new. However', she adds magnanimously, 'I took it all in good part'.[35]

The Queen's anger smouldered. Sarah, herself resilient, could not think that recent events had left deep resentment, yet rumour persisted. Even Abigail, they said (and this was cheering), was finding her mistress unmanageable. At last somebody, a Mrs Darcy, told Sarah that the Queen had been told that she often spoke of her in company disrespectfully.* It was the kind of thing Dr Hare meant when he later charged her with 'ill-grounded suspicions, violent passions and a boundless liberty of expressing resentments . . . in the most public manner and before servants';[36] the kind of indiscretion Sarah would never admit. Mrs Darcy advised her to have it out with the Queen at once and this she decided to do. Easter was approaching. What better time for heart-searching and for candour between friends? She sought an appointment. But now it was Anne's turn to be elusive. She put her off and suggested that what she had to say might better be put in writing. Sarah answered no, that would be difficult if not impossible. She must clear herself with the Queen before receiving her Easter Communion; but there would be nothing to cause dispute or even to oblige Anne to answer. Anne retreated to Kensington and there, on Maundy Thursday as dusk was falling, Sarah ran her to earth.

In her account of this last and most devastating interview with the Queen, in her small, dark closet at Kensington, Sarah as a writer is at her best:

> The Page who went in to acquaint the Queen that I was come to wait upon her staid longer than usual; long enough, it is to be supposed, to give Time to deliberate whether the Favour of Admission should be granted, and to settle the Measures of Behaviour if I were admitted. But at last he came out and told me I might go in.
>
> As I was entering, the Queen said she was just going to write to me. And when I began to speak she interrupted me four or

* In one of several drafts at Blenheim the Duchess says she had been 'informed by a friend, a reasonable woman of a very good charecter, that very false & malicious stories had been told Her Majesty of me, & some instances were named of vile inventions that had never entered into my thoughts'. (Blen G-I-8).

five Times with these repeated Words, Whatever you have to say you may put it in writing. I said her Majesty never did so hard a Thing to any as to refuse to hear them speak, and assured her that I was not going to trouble her upon the Subject which I knew to be so ungrateful to her, but that I could not possibly rest till I had cleared myself from some particular Calumnies with which I had been loaded.

I then went on to speak (though the Queen turned away her Face from me) and to represent my hard Case; that there were those about her Majesty who had made her believe that I had said Things of her which I was no more capable of saying than of killing my own Children; and that I seldom named her Majesty in Company, and never without Respect, and the like. The Queen said, without doubt there were many lies told.

I then begged, in order to make this Trouble the shorter, and my own Innocence the plainer, that I might know the Particulars of which I had been accused. Because if I were guilty that would quickly appear; and if I were Innocent this Method only would clear me. The Queen replied that she would give me no Answer, laying hold on a Word in my Letter, that what I had to say in my own Vindication would have no Consequence in obliging her Majesty to answer etc., which surely did not at all imply that I did not desire to know the particular Things laid to my Charge, without which it was impossible for me to clear myself. This I assured her Majesty was all I desired, and that I did not ask the Names of the Authors or Relators of those Calumnies, saying all that I could think reasonable to inforce my just Request. But the Queen repeated again and again the Words she had used, without ever receding.

I desired to explain some Things which I had heard her Majesty had taken amiss of me, and then with a fresh Flood of Tears and a Concern sufficient to move Compassion even where all Love was absent, I begged to know what other Particulars she had heard of me, that I might not be denied all Power of justifying myself. But still the only Return was, you desired no Answer and you shall have none.

I then begged to know if her Majesty would tell me some other Time?—You desired no Answer and you shall have none.

I then appealed to her Majesty again, if she did not herself know that I had often despised Interest in Comparison of serving her faithfully and doing right? And whether she did not know me to be of a Temper uncapable of disowning any thing which I knew to be true?—You desired no Answer and you shall have none.

This Usage was so severe, and these Words so often repeated were so shocking (being an utter Denial of common Justice to one who had been a most faithful Servant and now asked nothing more) that I could not conquer myself but said the most disrespectful Thing I ever spoke to the Queen in my Life, and yet what such an Occasion and such Circumstances might well excuse, if not justify, and that was that I was confident her Majesty would suffer for such an Instance of Inhumanity. The Queen answer'd, that will be to myself.

Thus ended this remarkable Conversation, the last I ever had with her Majesty. I shall make no Comment upon it. The Queen always meant well, how much soever she might be blinded or misguided.[37]

The interview, as recounted here by Sarah and printed in her *Conduct* of 1742, runs to 611 words. It lasted, she tells us, an hour; in which time two people in ordinary converse would speak about 7000 words. Allowing 2000 words for the two further topics mentioned by the Duchess in other versions, we are still left with at least 4000 words unaccounted for; and one cannot help wondering whether, among those missing sentences, lay the key to two problems: (i) What exactly Sarah had heard she was accused of; (ii) Why, with icy and indeed savage deliberation, the Queen persisted in denying her an answer.

Without that key the reader of the Duchess's *Conduct* must not be blamed for forming his own conclusions, which may not (as Anne once predicted) be favourable either to Queen or Duchess. If a fair verdict is to be given, the jury must have the facts, and when facts are withheld by an eye-witness (there were but two people present) it must consider circumstantial evidence. What was it that the Queen's mind was fixed on throughout the interview? Sarah begged her to say it. 'False stories', Sarah knew, 'had been made of me to her. several of which she [Mrs Darcy] repeated to me and said she was sure the Queen had been told of them. These were some of them nothing else but what we properly call Grub Street stories . . .'[38]

But there must have been something more. We know that to be accused by the Duchess of an unworthy and unbecoming friendship with Abigail was the one thing which, understandably, embarrassed the Queen. More than once and with vehemence she had so accused her and (or at least Anne probably feared so when she turned away her face) might too easily bring the same charge again. There had been tense and stormy interviews of which we know little. This was to be the last. The Queen's mind was at breaking point and there was that in it which froze her heart with fear and fury. No matter if nothing was then said of what she dreaded (though it may have been said);* the recollection of what Sarah had written, of what she had said before or of what they said she had said, would to Anne's predecessors have cried aloud for Tower Hill and the block. The most Anne could do was to slay her with silence and that she did, not pleasurably (she had once loved her) but without quarter and with bitter contempt.

* In her version of this last interview set out in dialogue form Sarah writes, 'I should have said, when I began to speak . . . when she saw I went on to tell her the thing, she turned her face from me as if she feared blushing upon something I might say to her'. (Blen. G-I-8).

CHAPTER VIII

The Great Change

1710-1712

———————◆———————

'I shall make no comment upon it', says Sarah, closing her account of her last interview with Queen Anne; but she thought about it constantly and fretfully—why had the Queen been so brutal?—and kept writing about it; and each time she re-told the story she told just a little more.

From one version we find, for example, that the Queen's 'That will be to myself' (the perfect ending) was not in fact the last sentence Sarah heard her speak. But then of all the women in history, only Sarah perhaps would have dared, after such a dismissal, to return to the Queen's door:

> After I had come out from the Queen & sat me down in the long gallery to wipe my eyes before I came within sight of any body, I went back again to the closet & scratched at the door which, when the Queen had open'd, I told her that I had been thinking whilst I sat there that if when her Majesty came to the Castle at Windsor, where I had heard she was soon expected, it would not be easier to her to see me in public as I was now afraid it would not, I would take care to avoid being at the Lodge at the same time, to prevent any unseasonable clamour or stories that might be occasioned by my being so near her without waiting upon her. To this she readily answered that I might come to her to the Castle & that she should not be uneasy at it, by which I conclude that she had been made to promise that she would not enter into any conversation with me in private for fear she

should not be able to answer what I had to say, when at the same time she showed so much willingness to see me in public.[1]

In yet another draft at Blenheim there are minor variations and one substantial addition:

Then I gave her the whole account of what had passed last summer between the Duke of Somerset & me, upon his making as if hee had a mind to doe me good offices to her, & in that relation I shewed all his falsenesse to me, for some things just before made it appear very plain that hee had been working to doe me all the mischief hee could & I am confydent I was not mistaken in beleiving hee had made an ill use of the conversation I had with him att Windsor, upon the Queen's subject, tho' I had asured him in it that no body living wished her more happynesse then I did, but that I knew she could not change to me & desired him not to mention me to her . . . which hee promised very solemnly, but hee brook that I am pritty sure, for I observed all the time I talkd to the Queen upon that matter she had a more then ordinary attention but answered not a word.

In the summer of 1709 the Dukes of Somerset and of Shrewsbury, before yielding to the blandishments of Harley, had both sounded the Duchess of Marlborough to make sure that there was no chance of a reconciliation between herself and the Queen. Somerset,* as things turned out, was to be fooled by Harley's promises of power; but Shrewsbury, playing a more subtle game, would be more successful. 'When he returned to England with his Roman Duchess', writes Sarah of Shrewsbury, 'he had a mind to come into the Ministry', and so of course it was important to back the winning side. The King of Hearts,† as he was called, then treated Sarah 'like a devinity'; but she was not to be hoodwinked. Though he had, as

---

* Of the Duke of Somerset Sarah has much to say, none of it favourable until after 1723, when he proposed marriage. e.g. 'Capricious & uncertain, lying & vain, fawning & insolent and, to avoid many words, as worthless as hee is disagreeable'; 'He was disgusted at the Duke of Marlborough & Lord Godolphin, tho' hee himself knew not why'; 'He was of no more use than my footman'. Sarah suspected him and his duchess of libelling her to Queen Anne.

† Or alternatively, Polyphemus, on account of a flaw in one eye

she owns, 'a sort of an appearance of wisdom', he was covetous and taken all in all, one of the falsest men living. It took him only a short time to discover where favour lay and to decide that if Abigail ordered it the Queen would, as he expressed it, stand on her head.

But it is upon Shrewsbury's Roman duchess that Sarah makes her sharpest comments. She was, she insists, a courtesan who, after chasing him from country to country, married him and pretended to turn Protestant. In England she had no inkling of behaviour and was soon the jest of the town, chucking her duke beneath the chin in public and, upon finding Anne thoughtful, flying to her with the cry, 'Oh my Queen, you must not think always of the poor Prince!'[3]

'The Duke of Shrewsbury', Sarah remembers, 'took all occasions of making great professions to me ... but at the same time his wife blamed me for my ill behaviour to the Queen in all companys & the Duke of Somerset did the same but greived at it because they [sic] lovd me ... It was impossible', she adds, 'for any body to bee such an idiote as to bee imposed upon by them'.[4] It was because Shrewsbury wanted his duchess to be a lady-of-the-bedchamber, said Sarah, that he blocked a reconciliation between herself and Anne. He denied that he had ever spoken to Abigail, but this in Sarah's opinion was 'very foolish because everybody saw that the Duchess of Shrewsbury was continually with her and made a most low & nausious court to her, which the Duchess of Somerset was too proud to do publickly'.[5] ''Tis certain', she concludes, 'that the Queen never had a thought of taking away my employments ... till the Duke of Shrewsbury thought it convenient for his own scheme to assist the Duke of Somerset in that matter'.[6]

Eight days after Sarah's last interview with the Queen the Marquis of Kent, a simpleton nicknamed the Bug, was dismissed as Lord Chamberlain and consoled with a dukedom, so that the Duke of Shrewsbury might be given his office. This caused astonishment, partly because Shrewsbury was known to have voted against the Government at the trial of Sacheverell, and partly because Lord Treasurer Godolphin was not consulted but was told at Newmarket of the *fait accompli*. With candour he wrote to the Queen, 'Your Majesty is suffering yourself to be guided to your own Ruin and Destruction as fast as it is possible for them to compass it, to whom you seem so much to hearken'.[7] It was literally true. For whatever might be said against the Marlboroughs and Godolphin—the avarice of the Duke, the tantrums of the Duchess, the treasurer's lack of resolution—they had made Anne's reign glorious and only when they had been dispensed with would she as a queen cease to shine. Added to this, a glance at the opposition—Harley, St John, Abigail and the rest—was more than enough to convince the impartial that, for the most part, they were out for themselves and had the Devil on their side. They flourished in the dark. Their plots had been hatched in the stuffy closets of Windsor and Kensington, but now they must come out into the open so that the heads they had blacklisted might begin to roll.

Sarah meanwhile had not been idle. Soon after the Kensington interview she wrote to the Queen and enclosed two other letters: Anne's own congratulations to Marlborough on the victory at Blenheim, and a letter of the Duke of Somerset's to Sarah, to show on what friendly terms they used to be. Not only was all this ignored but Sarah was shocked that Anne failed to return Somerset's letter.* It was only by accident that she happened to have a copy, her chambermaid 'when she writt out one [the Queen's] took the other too without being order'd & 'tis very exact even in the speeling & the nonsense which I have marked'.[8]

Maynwaring urged her to assure the Queen that, in the crisis over Jack Hill, she had not advocated an address against Abigail. She did so and received a cold answer, the Queen at the same time charging her with having broken her promise never to mention Abigail again. This in turn called for another long letter, dated June 13th, in which Sarah explained that her promise had been conditional on Anne's assuring her she had read and pondered her narrative-sermon on *The Whole Duty of Man*, which she never had. It was the sort of profitless bickering that can go on forever. This however was cut short two days later when Lord Sunderland, Secretary of State and Sarah's son-in-law, was dismissed, to be succeeded by Lord Dart-

---

* 'Yr Majesty refusing to send mee back yr letter as I humbly desired obliges mee to take a little better care of the rest, but I can't imagine why you are not pleased to lett mee have the Duke of Somersetts letter again; tho' his carriage to lord M: & me, so very different from that letter, makes no impression upon yr Majesty I am perswaded I can make other people ashamed for him when I shew it them.' Sarah to Anne 13 June, 1710 (Blen. G-1-7)

mouth, a Tory dubbed by Sarah 'a Jester himself and a jest to all others'.

Anne, as we know, had never liked Sunderland and had strongly resisted his appointment. He was, she now said, 'obnoxious to all but a few', a phrase which, said Sarah, was not only untrue but uncharacteristic of the Queen and must therefore have been inserted by someone else. As for Sarah she would not, as her friends kept imploring, see the Queen, but she could and would keep on writing until domesday. Marlborough implored her not to. '39 [himself] begs of 240 [Sarah] that they will not on any account be prevaill'd upon to write any more to 239 [the Queen]'; and in another letter, 'For God's sake lett me begg 240 to be carefull of her behavior for she is in a country amongst Tygers & Wolves'.[9] But Sarah's mood was reckless. 'I am resolved I will write once more to her', she said, 'whatever resolution Lord Marl: takes, tho' I doe solemnly protest I would not have more to doe with her then other ladys for all the treasure upon earth, but I will vex her soe much as to convince even her own stupid understanding that she has used me ill & then lett her shutt herself up with Mrs Masham . . .'[10]

The Queen, after giving assurances that no further changes in her ministry were contemplated, dismissed Godolphin. The manner of his dismissal was particularly shabby. On the evening of August 7th he asked her directly, 'Is it the will of your Majesty that I should go on?' Unhesitatingly she answered, 'Yes'; yet her letter of dismissal, sent by a servant, bore the date August 7; and this for the man who, on her accession, had saved her from her own ignorance and had since devoted his life and health to her service. But there were other signs of deterioration in the Queen. She did not, as is popularly supposed, drink,* but unquestionably she had fallen into ill hands. It was what she herself had dreaded and what Sarah had prophesied in 1706 when she wrote of the uneasiness and grief it would mean to Godolphin if he then had to leave the Queen's service. She 'seemed so desirous he should continue in it, but I see as well as he', she had added, 'the Impossibility of his being able to support it or

---

* 'I know that in some libels she hath been reproached as one who indulged herself in drinking strong liquors, but I believe this was utterly groundless & that she never went beyond such a quantity of strong wines as her physicians judged to be necessary for her'. Sarah, of Anne. (Blen. G-1-9. Undated).

himself or my Lord Marlborough, for it all hangs upon one Thread; and when they are forced to leave your Service you will then indeed find yourself in the Hands of a violent Party who, I am sure, will have very little Mercy or even Humanity for you'.[11]

Godolphin was not rich. (He had, it was said, proved a better treasurer to his country than to himself.) The Queen, in her letter of dismissal, offered him a pension of £4000 a year, but it never materialised. Indeed, had it not been for a timely legacy from his brother he would have been very wretchedly off. He lived for two more years and spent much of that time at Holywell, St Albans. His leaving the Treasury, which was put into commission, meant lack of support for Marlborough and the allies. At home, Marlborough knew, it signalled every sort of misfortune from the dismissal of his duchess to the abandonment of Blenheim,* perhaps even to his own dismissal and disgrace. In August he warned Sarah that her dismissal had, so he was assured, been settled and that she must 'expect very quickly every thing that can be disagreeable personally'. He was, he said, much more concerned for what might vex her than for anything that might happen to himself.[12]

Maynwaring, known to his enemies as Sarah's spy, kept her informed. Harley, he reported, was saying of her, 'Ah, that is the rock all will break upon if care be not taken to avoid it'.[13] He had caught a glimpse of Abigail: '. . . in all the days of my life I never saw so odious a creature, and she was so extream hot that her Fan work'd like a windmill . . . Hopkins told me he did not see one body bow to her . . . I do really believe the creature is rotten & shou'd be removed as Card: Wolsey was design'd to be for his stinking breath least sacred majesty shou'd be infected'.[14] But Mrs Still in herself remained cool and, as Sarah had so often done before her, studied the face of the Queen. 'My Aunt', she tells Harley, 'is not very well . . . She has flying pains about her . . . a fitt of the gout . . . Say nothing of it to anybody, for without she is laid up with it she does not care to have it known till it is soe bad she cannot hide it . . . Whenever I said anything relating to business she answer'd pray goe for if you begin to talk you will make it soe late I shall not gett to bed in any time. Tho I think she is in good humour & had not a disponding countenance as sometimes she has'. [15]

* The Duchess stopped the works at Blenheim in October, 1710.

It would be easy to say that if it had not been for Abigail or if it had not been for Sarah, all would have been well and Marlborough would have continued to triumph; but of course there were other factors both negative and positive. Negatively, everyone in England and in France was sick to death of the war. Positively, there was the new-found power of the Press. Opposed as he was to Marlborough, Harley needed to be lucky. He had been lucky with Abigail; and he was now to be luckier still with Jonathan Swift.

Swift, who had come to England to gain Queen Anne's bounty (the first fruits) for the clergy of Ireland (a most unlikely assignment), had not found favour with Godolphin but was soon being made much of by the Harley–St John set. Sarah, though she afterwards fell for Gulliver,* was particularly scathing about him. Writing of Harley's hacks, as they were then regarded, she says, 'The Reverend Mr Swift & Mr Prior quickly offered themselves to sale (besides a number of more ordinary scribblers), both men of wit & parts, ready to prostitute all they had in the service of well rewarded scandal, being both of a composition past the weakness of blushing or of stumbling at any thing for the interest of their new masters. The former of these had long ago turned all religion into a Tale of a Tub & sold it for a jest'.[16]

The Examiner had been launched in the summer of 1710, but it was not till Swift's famous satire on the comparative cost of British and Roman gratitude, which it published in November, that it shook the world he was aiming at, partly with mirth, partly with anger. In the cost of the Roman triumph Swift remembered to include a chaplet of laurel (twopence); and in the British triumph Blenheim, which he rather modestly estimated at £200,000.† It was a good idea amusingly projected and not grossly unfair until the

* 'The Duchess Dowager of Marlborough is in raptures at it. She says she can dream of nothing else since she read it. She declares that she has now found out that her whole life had been lost in caressing the worst part of mankind & treating the best as her foes & that if she knew Gulliver, tho' he had been the worst enemy she ever had, she would give up her present acquaintance for his friendship'. Gay and Pope to Swift, Nov., 1726, on the publication of Gulliver's Travels. (Swift's Prose Works VIII, xviii).

† When completed, the cost of Ble   as at least £300,000, but of that some £60,000 was contributed by the Marlborough estate.

reader reached the end of it, where he found a thinly disguised Duchess of Marlborough accused of peculation on a colossal scale. That the charge was groundless made it none the less infuriating for the victim. Without knowing who had written the libel (she suspected everyone from Prior to Vanbrugh) she drew up a self-vindication of twenty-two and a half pages that read like a balance-sheet and sent it to the Queen who said, 'Everybody knows cheating is not the Duchess of Marlborough's fault'—a remark depending much for its significance on where, when Anne spoke it, the accent fell.

'Swift's business', says the author of The Pen and the Sword, 'was to change history, not to record it . . . He saw that the grounds of the quarrel must be enlarged, that the war must be stripped of its nobility and exposed as the senseless thing he had always suspected it to be . . . Marlborough must be destroyed!'[17] And as for the duplicity of Swift's master, Henry St John, who pretended still to be Marl-borough's admirer, 'Deceit on such a scale', observes Mr Foot, 'has the quality of grandeur'. 'I have very good reason to believe', wrote Sarah to Sir David Hamilton, 'that Mr St John's is the chief instruc-tion of the person that writes it [The Examiner], who has not one single qualification of any merit & is notorious for being of a scandalous & profligate life & conversation. Now I beg of you to tell me upon this occation whether you do not think it is pritty difficult to be silent under such provocations and . . . very hard & unjust in Mrs Morley to suffer such things'.[18]

Maynwaring with The Medley did his best to meet the challenge, but as antidote to Swift's acid the alkali was too weak. Perhaps Sarah herself might have done better. 'I have read your Grace's account', Maynwaring told her, 'of what passed between 42 [the Queen] and 240 [herself] which, notwithstanding your great modesty, I do think is better put together than anyone else could have done it, & had two very different effects upon me in reading it; for all the time I read what 240 said it affected me extreamly, as 'tis natural when one sees one's best friend ill used to be moved at it & to hate those that do it; & yet when I came to the delicious replys of 42, to hear the same senseless words repeated over & over, & a statue lined with earth & stone speaking like the groaning Board & saying so often that it would say nothing was so very ridiculous that it really made me laugh several times. If you had not said the account was exact I should have known it to be so, 'tis so natural, & I wonder you could remember it so exactly, to put it together in so lively a manner, though I need not say now what opinion I have of your good parts for doing anything you have a mind to. I have a great desire to know the particular reason that made 42 so much more brutal now than ever'.[19]

It was Maynwaring, people said, who was begging Sarah not to resign, and to such purpose that her gold key of office came to be called Maynwaring's key. However, he had lost none of what he called his frolick fancy and, reminding Sarah of Tiberius's retreat to Capri with his favourite, Sejanus, remarked, à propos of Anne and Abigail, 'Tis pity this kingdom has no such delicious retreat near it. What think you of the island of Silly?'[20]

In the summer of 1710 Maynwaring was approached by one of the Queen's physicians Sir David Hamilton* with the earnest request that Sarah be dissuaded from her project of publishing the Queen's letters. Before this, says the Duchess in one of her many accounts, it had not occurred to her to do so. It was an idea. After all, the very threat of publication might be enough to postpone her dismissal until Marlborough was ready for it, which would be at the end of the campaign. She had been stung by *The Examiner* and warned that she lived among tigers and wolves. Cautiously therefore, for she never trusted him, she wrote letters to Hamilton, which he promised to read aloud to the Queen. She was satisfied that he did so, but annoyed when he told her that the Queen had made no comment. All she could get was negative, as in December when Hamilton was told to 'hinder' her from helping with Anne's new outfit; nor was she on any account to be encouraged to nominate (as she had suggested) 'any clergyman of good reputation' to referee their quarrel. On the question of the letters, except that she refused to return them, Sarah held her hand. Coxe believed that at this point Hamilton 'represented to the Queen the danger of provoking to extremity a woman of the most imperious character';[21] while to Sarah he (treacherously as she afterwards supposed) gave the impression that an abject apology might now be accepted. 'I am of

* Sir David Hamilton (1663–1721), physician to Queen Anne and to Queen Caroline. Said to have lost £80,000 in the South Sea Bubble.

opinion', he advised her, 'today is most fitting. There seemed to be great tenderness'.[22]

Accordingly, on January 17th, 1711 Marlborough carried his wife's letter to the Queen. It read:

> Though I never thought of troubling your Majesty in this manner again, yet the circumstances I see my Lord Marlborough in and the apprehension I have that he cannot live six months if there is not some end put to his sufferings on my account makes it impossible for me to resist doing every thing in my power to ease him; and if I am still so unlucky as not to make use of any expressions in this letter that may move your Majesty, it is purely for want of understanding; for I really am very sorry that ever I did any thing that was uneasy to your Majesty. I am ready to promise any thing that you can think reasonable; and as I do not yet know but two things in my whole life that ever I did that were disagreeable to your Majesty, I do solemnly protest that as long as I have the honour to continue your servant, I will never mention either of those subjects to you or do any one thing that can give you the least disturbance or uneasiness. And these assurances I am desirous to give your Majesty under my hand because I would not omit any thing possible for me to do that might save my Lord Marlborough from the greatest mortification he is capable of and avoid the greatest mischief in consequence of it to your Majesty and my country.
>
> I am with all the submission and respect imaginable your Majesty's most dutiful and most obedient subject and servant
>
> S. Marlborough[23]

The Queen at first declined to open the letter and then, having yielded to Marlborough's persuasion and read it, she said, 'I cannot change my resolution'.

'Having delivered this letter', one of Sarah's accounts continues, 'he represented to her Majesty by all the most reasonable arguments and in the most moving manner imaginable how necessary it would be to her service as well as to his own satisfaction not to remove the Duchess of Marlborough till she [the Queen] had no more use of him, which in all probability would be in less than nine months, and then he beg'd that he and she might retire both together, which he could not but think better even for her Majesty than to part with one of them in so extraordinary a manner as would oblige her to be always upon her vindication.

'Then he endeavoured to shew that her Majesty's own character was a little concerned in this matter, since he believed there was no precedent for proceeding in such a manner against a woman to whom she had been pleased to make declarations of her friendship both publick and private for so many years, and who was sorry for any mistake she had ever committed and ready to give all possible assurances of never doing the least thing to make her Majesty uneasy for the future; and since an honourable retreat was all he beg'd for, he hoped that would appear so just and reasonable in all respects that any faithful servant she had must wish it.

'For the Queen's sake, as well as for his and the Duchess of Marlborough's, he added that as no Prince ever used any servant so very hardly that had been guilty of great faults, if pardon was asked and firm promise of amendments were made, so in this case there was something yet more cruel not only because nothing had been ever ill meant and what was desired was so small a favour that it would be barbarous to deny it even to one that had never been capable of doing the least service, but also because her Majesty had never laid any thing to the Duchess of Marlborough's charge, nor given any reason for proceeding so harshly against her, to him or to any other person.

'Only once she said to him, when he pressed her extremely upon that subject, that it was *for her honour* to remove the Duchess of Marl: but what that meant he could never learn, any more than what faults she had committed.

'And now if I may be allowed to speak in this case', interposes the Duchess, 'I cannot help saying it was indeed much for her honour to part in that manner, after a friendship of near 30 years, and give no other account but that wise reason for it, which I neither understand nor comprehend; and I do solemnly protest that I never writ or said any thing to Her Majesty in my whole life that I did not think for her service or that I should have been sorry to have all the world witnesses of'.[24]

As Marlborough himself had said, 'All truths are not to be spoke';

and again, some things—a look, a manner, an attitude—no matter how offensive, are not to be tied down and argued about. There are hints that at this time Anne found the very demeanour of the Duchess frightening and resented her hauteur. 'The word disdaine she makes use of', Sarah scornfully comments, 'to discribe my looks is an expression as if it came from a man & mighty rediculous, for I never looked upon her att all but talked allways to other people when I waited upon her in publick places, which I can't but think a very naturall way & nothing indecent in it considering my cercomstances & the manner she treated me'.[25]

However it was and whatever was uppermost in the Queen's mind, her only response to Marlborough's pleading was to demand Sarah's gold key. It must be handed to her within three days. The Duke, on his knees, pleaded for ten.* The Queen countered by making it two days. 'Let us make haste', writes Sir Winston, 'to draw the curtain upon an unnatural spectacle which reduces the stature of a soldier without raising the majesty of a queen'.[26]

When Marlborough, if only perhaps to change the subject, began to protest against the dismissal of three excellent officers merely for drinking his health (and damnation maybe to his enemies), the Queen cut him short and refused to discuss it or anything else till she had the key. 'As soon as I heard this', says Sarah, 'I begged of Lord Marlborough the very same night to carry this key that was so much longed for. Tho he was undressed I got him to put his cloaths on again;† & the true reason why I was in so much hast to have it given was because I hoped hee might have been allowd to have quited upon the Affront in the affair of the officers & I had a mind to have the key given before this came out, that people might not say hee quited upon the account of my places, which many thought

---

* 'He never had petition'd her before for any thing in his whole life with so much submission & earnestness, which only gave her an occation of shewing him in how inhuman a manner she could now treat him'. (Blen G-I-16. Undated fragment in the Duchess's hand).

† Marlborough would of course have been wearing court dress. 'The manner of her Grace's surrender, as I was told by one who was very intimate in the family was that when the Duke of Marlborough told her the Queen expected the gold key, she took it from her side & threw it into the middle of the room & bid him take it up & carry it to whom he pleased'. Lord Dartmouth (Burnet, op. cit. VI, 33).

was wrong, tho I confess I thought using his wife so ill was as great an affront as any, but could not be sure I was not too partial in that matter . . . I must not forget that when Lord Marl: delivered the key I desired to know what her Ma: was pleased to say upon it, but hee could give me no other account then that she mumbled something which hee could not understand nor make any thing of, by which I concluded that speech was her own; & indeed after they had got the key it was needless for them to make any more speeches for her upon that subject, which would have been so much labour lost, besides the pains of geting them by heart, & she has an easy way that I have often known her practice with great success upon many occations when she has not known what to say which is to move only her lips & make as if she had said something when in truth no words were uttered'.[27]

Sarah remained, so she tells us, puzzled. The Queen 'lookd as if she wishd she could give some reason' for her dismissal, but still gave none. It was a quite extraordinary dilemma. To be faced with the world's most winning diplomat—her personal friend and the nation's hero—and deny him even one good reason for his wife's dismissal, one needed to be made of stone. Again, what tipped the scale? Loathing, we may be sure, plus embarrassment, plus something she would keep forever to herself. 'I must again desire you would excuse my not answering some things in your letters', she told Sarah in an undated letter of 1708 or 1709, 'not for ye reason you give for that is a strange unkind one, but because I know it is better not to do it for both our sakes'.[28] And if she would not tell it to Sarah, how much less likely was she to unbosom herself to a man. Whatever Abigail may have told her of Sarah's prattling, that will not have been enough to harden Anne's heart. There must, one feels, have been confirmation from others which, added to Sarah's letters and tantrums—her long absences, her 'saying shocking things', her ill humour and disdain—succeeded in locking the Queen's heart against her forever. But the last clue or straw is missing—'There are yet many things untold', adds the Duchess darkly, 'for which there wants a name'[29]—and we are left to wonder and at the same time to admire the reserve of a queen.

Now was the moment for Sarah to send in her accounts, and at the same time to claim with arrears the £2000-a-year offered by the

Queen in 1702. 'I am persuaded your Lordship* must have observed', she writes in the introduction to her *Conduct*, 'that all those who declare themselves careless about what the World [may] say of them when they are dead are quite as unconcerned to deserve a good Character while they live . . . My chief Aim has been both in publick & private Life to *deserve* Approbation; but I have never been without an earnest Desire to *have* it from the wise and virtuous'.

What, then, are the wise and virtuous to make of this claim for back pay to the tune of £16,000? 'I did not much like doing this', she admits, 'but I was advised to do it and I did do it'. And the Queen? She 'blushed and appeared to be very uneasy . . . looked out of countinance & as if she had much rather not have allowed it'.[30] But she did allow it and, as with Griffith's winnings from Prince George, when Sarah considered how many of her 'dear hours' had been spent in Anne's tedious company, she was not sure if the Queen might not still be her debtor; for the cost of boredom is not to be measured.

As Keeper of the Privy Purse the Duchess was succeeded by Abigail, and as Groom of the Stole by the Duchess of Somerset. For the latter, as for all his acquaintance, Godolphin had a nickname— Troule-it-away—for which there seems no obvious explanation, unless it may have been a phonetic transliteration of 'truly to weigh',† a phrase she could have used to a half-attentive treasurer or queen. Sarah, who disliked red hair and rivalry, calls her obsequious, insinuating, intriguing and absolutely the greatest liar in the world. She may have been all or none of these things. Swift, who so rashly offended her in his *Windsor Prophecy*, said she 'openly professed the utmost aversions from the persons, the principles & measures of those who were then in power and . . . quickly grew into higher credit than all her (Queen Anne's) ministers together'.[31]

In a period with mistrust as its keynote humour is rare enough to be prized when chanced on; for Sarah's humour is almost always sarcasm. Here then, when the two rival duchesses met at the Meredith‡ christening and a tolerably good joke was cracked, the scene might have been cheering. After deliberation it had been decided

---

* Lord Cholmondeley, to whom the *Conduct* is dedicated.

† I am grateful to Mr R. S. Green for this suggestion.

‡ Meredith was one of the officers cashiered for drinking Marlborough's health.

to give the child the Queen's name, and when this had been settled, says Sarah, 'I turnd to the Duchess of Somerset & said to her in a smiling way that the Duke Hamilton had made a boy a girl & christened it Ann & why should not we make this girl a boy & call it George. This was then understood to be meant no otherwise then as a jest upon Duke Hamilton, as it plainly was, & the Duchess of Somerset laughed at it, as the Queen herself I dare say would have done if she had happened to be present. But this as I had it afterwards from very good hands was represented to the Queen in as different & false a way as was possible, who was told that I said, Don't let the name of the child be Ann for there never was one good of that name. I leave you to judge who was most likely to give this story this rediculous turn & who was to find their account in it'.[32]

In March, 1711 luck for the third time came to Harley, melodramatically disguised as a French assassin. The attempt of de Guiscard is at least outlined in every history book: the spy arraigned before the council; his attack on Harley; the pen-knife stabs which St John claimed were meant for himself. But it is as always the detail that fascinates. 'I believe you remember the waistcoat', Harley's sister writes chattily to another sister, 'it was blue & silver ground with rich gold brocade flowers. Sister had kept it up & that waistcoat served for the birthday & this occasion (only a silver fringe put round it & looked very well) . . . The knife struck first in the turning up of the right sleeve of his coat, which the surgeon says broke the force of the blow . . . It struck thro' his coat, which was open at the breast (and they now so far as the buttonholes put a buckram between the cloth & silk lining); through these three it went & into his waistcoat just in one of the gold flowers, which also must have broken the force of the blow . . . The Queen did not believe they had told her truth, but that he was dead'.[33]

As a contemporary ballad-monger sublimely put it:

Meantime thy Pain is gracious Anna's Care;
Our Queen, our Saint with sacrificing Breath
Softens thy Anguish: In Her Pow'rful Pra'r
She pleads thy Service and forbids thy Death.

The wound, though not deep, took weeks to heal, and in that

Harley was less fortunate because in his absence St John gained ground with Abigail and secretly promised that Honest Jack Hill should lead his expedition to Quebec, an adventure which ended in August in complete fiasco. In his thanks to the Commons for his recovery from the 'barbarous & vilainous attempt' Harley said, 'Whenever I look upon my breast it will put me in mind of the thanks due to God, my duty to the Queen & that Debt of Gratitude & Service I must always owe to this Honourable House'.[34] In May, for his pains, he was made Earl of Oxford and Mortimer.

Sarah now retired, says Lediard, in 'uncommon splendour', to St Albans. There was plenty to do. For one thing she was beginning to plan a 'history' which would run from the Revolution of '88 to Queen Anne. Maynwaring, encouraging her as usual, praised her style. 'You allways write so clearly & properly', he told her, 'and with such natural expressions in which you excel everybody . . . In your letter that lyes now before me, one part is written exactly after Montaigne's manner, so much has your Grace profited by those few Books* which you say you have read!'[35]

In his efforts to please her he confers with her architects and potters about the works at Marlborough House. 'I wish you were well in your own house by St James's', he writes to her, 'for that I dare swear is built strong enough to stand till the General Conflagration & I hope & believe too that you will yet be very happy there & like it better than any of your other houses, because as you observe in the country you are generally quite alone or in too much company, either of which extreams you may avoid here'.[36]

But Marlborough House, rushed though it was, could not be ready until the autumn. Wren (the 'poor old man', she suspected, was imposed upon by his workmen) she had had to part with, but she enjoyed finishing it herself; and even if it had cost £50,000, it had been but two years in the making and was, in her view, the

---

* A list of the Duchess's books at Blenheim, dated Sept., 1719 and now at Althorp, includes *The Anatomy of Melancholy*, *The Whole Duty of Man*, Burnet, Clarendon, Milton, Dryden, Spenser etc. Her books at St Albans in 1721 included Shakespeare, Ben Jonson, *Don Quixote* (a great favourite), Montaigne, Cowley, Waller, St Evremont, Plutarch and Epictetus in translation and several volumes on medicine, architecture and theology. Swift and Addison are represented as are Congreve and Nathaniel Hooke. There is also Young's Spelling Book.

strongest and best house that ever was built.* 'I always disliked Blenheim', she writes in one of her jottings, 'and laughed at Sir John as often as I could, saying that the Duke of Marlborough should be always welcome to see me at my houses, that I would visit him sometimes at Blenheim & that I would fade his furniture in my houses before Sir John had half finished his'.[37]

It would be strange to be home-making next door to a queen—living almost in her garden, one might say—with whom one was no longer on speaking terms; and in the meantime there was this ridiculous affair of the St James's lodgings, which Sarah (moving out) was accused of stripping even to the chimneypieces and the brass locks. Marlborough, in his letter to her of May 25th, after chiding her for writing again so freely of 199 [Harley] when he had begged her not to, referred to the lodgings and said, 'I beg you will not remove any of the marble chimneypieces'.†[38] Sarah owned she had taken the locks, which were hers. The chimneypieces, she insisted, she had not taken, and she had the housekeeper sign a statement to prove it. The Queen, they said, was furious. Whether or not the lodgings were intended for Abigail, the Duchess had no right to leave them as she had. '42 is so angry', Sarah was told, 'that she says she will build no house for 39 [Marlborough] when 240 [Sarah] has pull'd hers to pieces'.[39] If Sarah chose to wreck the Queen's lodgings, no further supplies would be voted for the building of Blenheim.

In his estimate of Marlborough and of his reactions Harley was astute. Sarah's dismissal, he believed, would very nearly but not quite compel him to resign; whatever his agony, Marlborough would not desert Prince Eugene and the allies. Blenheim, on the other hand, was a trump to be played with discretion. Everyone knew that Marlborough had set his heart on it. Nothing then could be plainer but that it must be used as a carrot to tempt him on until peace had been made without him; on which happy day he could be dropped.

---

* Marlborough House, since much altered (a storey has been added), was built of brick with stone dressings, in Wren's no-nonsense style; a well-mannered building which nevertheless showed how dull Blenheim might have been in other hands.

† The probability is that Sarah's letter in which the possibility of removing chimneypieces was mentioned, was intercepted by a spy, and read before being forwarded to Marlborough.

When in the autumn of 1710 Sarah stopped the works at Blenheim, the building was reckoned to have cost rather more than
£130,000, £10,500 of which was owed to the Edward Strongs, the
chief masons who had supplied much Cotswold stone from their
quarries near Burford. The sudden stoppage caused distress among
the workmen and a dilemma for Marlborough, who realised that if
he anticipated a Treasury grant and relieved them he might saddle
himself with the cost of completing the half-finished castle. Rioting
was prevented by Samuel Travers, the paymaster, who paid the most
necessitous out of his own pocket.

Now in 1711 Harley made the seemingly magnanimous gesture
of another £10,000 grant so that the works might be resumed. In
Marlborough's letter to Harley to congratulate him on his recovery
from Guiscard's attempt he says, 'I am extremely obliged to you for
the assurance you give me that the building of Blenheim shall not be
neglected. I cannot dissemble the desire I have to see that monument
of her Majesty's goodness and the nation's acceptance of my service
brought to some degree of perfection. I hope I shall give no just
reason for posterity to reproach you for having been the finisher of
it, and if I have the good fortune to spend any part of my life there I
shall always have in my view a remembrance of the obligations I
owe you on this account. I am with much truth, sir, your most
obedient humble servant'.[40]

This was a little different from his instruction to Sarah four years
before: 'I must beg the favour of the Queen that she will allow Sr
Godfrey [Kneller] to come three or four times to draw Hers & the
Princes pictor for Bleinhem. If I am ever to enjoye quietness it must
be there, so that I wou'd have nothing in my sight but my friends'.[41]

Sarah, while congratulating herself on Marlborough House, where
she proposed elegant assemblies for the autumn, had begun to call
Blenheim 'this unfortunate present', 'a monument of ingratitude' (a
phrase of Vanbrugh's); or she simply adopted Godolphin's sour
disclaimer: 'Let them keep their heap of stones'. Marlborough might
in his optimism be planning to move in 'next summer'—or the one
after—but she told him that since Vanbrugh was busy with bridges
and grottoes miles from the main building, the house would never
be finished. At the beginning of the works Godolphin, after viewing
them with Sarah, had written to Marlborough: 'My Lady Marlb: is

extremely prying-into and has really found a great many errors but very well mended such of them as could not stay for your decision. I am apt to think she has made Mr Vanbrugh a little cross, but you will find both ease and comfort from it'.[42]*

It was not a trait to endear her to a spirited architect who, as his biographer says, liked masculinity in life as much as in art,[43] and was unlikely to take kindly to the interference of women. In time he hoped to humour her, but from the first it must have been plain that she lacked imagination and could never be brought to see that, to perpetuate the epic the place was named after called for architecture and landscape on the heroic scale. At one early stage, in her folly, she transferred all the skilled masons to the garden walls, telling them His Grace wanted the gardens finished, and since all the walls must one day meet, it could not matter where they began.

Along the sanded paths and pleached lime-alleys of Wise's unfinished 'military' garden Maynwaring dutifully wandered, to be able to report his impressions to the owner, as he had at Marlborough House. 'The garden was very pleasant and sweet', he tells her, 'with that one fine day after the rain, and I walk'd in it as long as it was light to try if I could find any of the satisfaction which 240 so well describes in being alone in a sweet place: and 'tis certain there is something very pleasing in it but it is of the melancholy kind'.[44]

Marlborough, Sir Winston reminds us, had set his heart upon Blenheim in a strange manner. Broken in health, he knew he could not live long there but still yearned for it as a monument to stand, if only as a ruin, for thousands of years. 'About his achievements he preserved a complete silence, offering neither explanations nor excuses for any of his deeds. His answer was to be this great house. This mood has characterized dynasts in all ages, and philosophers in none. Remembrance may be preserved to remote posterity by piling great stones on one another and engraving deep inscriptions upon them. But fame is not to be so easily captured'.[45]

Writing to Sarah after Bouchain, perhaps the most brilliant action of his career, Marlborough sounds anything but triumphant. His health he despairs of but—'if I cou'd in quietness & without great

* Godolphin himself was responsible for condemning the ruins of Woodstock Manor and for changing the position of the chapel, which now has its altar at the west.

174

inconveniency of old age injoye two or three Yeares of Yours & my children's Company I shou'd blesse God & think my selfe happy ... I know the intentions of those that now govern is that I am to have nothing to do in the peace. This is what I am extream glad of, but they must not know it, so that I beg you will in your letters by the post never mention the peace, ministers nor the Queen, for your letters are constantly read before they come from England ... I shall take my measures for living a retier'd life; if it may be in England I shall be glad of it. If not, my businesse shall be to seek a good climate, for my constitution is extreamly spoilt'.[46]

For one of the greatest generals known to history, for the hero of Blenheim, Ramillies and Oudenarde the knives were now being sharpened. 'While his friends were engaged in the most spectacular piece of treachery in English history', writes Mr Foot of Jonathan Swift, 'and in defiance of the reputation and policy of the most successful of English soldiers, Swift so turned the tables that the Tory case now appeared in the guise of a more discriminating patriotism pitted against all the forces of avarice and pride'.[47] Swift's friends were of course Harley, now Lord Oxford, and St John, soon to be Viscount Bolingbroke; and Swift's pamphlet—perhaps the most effective ever written—*The Conduct of the Allies.**

It was a direct attack on the Marlboroughs for prolonging the war and exploiting it at the country's expense and to their own advantage. As for the bullied Queen, all but edged off her throne, she had, Swift averred, been driven from Windsor Castle to a cottage, 'pursuant to the advice of Solomon who tells us it is better to dwell in a corner of the housetop than with a brawling woman in a wide house'.[48] From not very promising material—a little truth, a few half-truths—but with much skill and malice a weapon had been forged which, if it did not of itself change history, at least accelerated it. In the humour of the hour—war-weary, sour, splenetic—it struck a harsh yet welcome clang: the knell of Marlborough. Returning in time for Christmas, he was dismissed on the last day of the year. Again out of next to nothing a frivolous charge of peculation was trumped up. The Queen's letter of dismissal is missing, since Marlborough, for the only time in his life, gave way to rage and flung it in the fire. Sarah says it was written 'in a very odd & low manner,

* Published 27 Nov. 1711.

as if all respect & common civility were now become a crime towards a man to whom she owed the security of her life as well as the glory of it; there was something so surprisingly shocking & hard in ye manner of expressing her self'.[49] Marlborough's reply was polished till it gleamed like a rapier.[50] One can only hope that it found its mark.

Few pens could do justice to such a crisis and the strange thing is that Sarah having, with or without assistance, done just that, decided to discard from her printed *Conduct* one of the most telling passages she had ever written. Here it is:

When I reflect upon all this I sometimes think that when Posterity shall come to read the annals of our times: a scene of glory, conquest, victory without intermission, at last ending in this manner, were there not authentick records to the contrary, they must certainly conclude that just in the most unhappy crisis of time Queen Anne the wise, the good, the just, the honourable, unfortunately died & that she was succeeded by another of the same name but of a temper & principles directly opposite, one who loved only those whom her predecessor hated & hated those whom she loved, one glorying in breaking the contracts & unravelling* the scheme in which her predecessor had triumphed, one taking a pride in raising those up whom she had cast down as public enemies & in casting those to the earth whom she had seated on thrones, one in a word untouched with a sense of ye miseries of her country & posterity, unmoved with the unhappiness of the world about her, giving back as it were in sport the glories & victories purchased with her subjects' blood & treasure & abusing them to their own unhappiness & misery; one uncapable of understanding or of following the good counsels which had made her predecessor so great; but selfish, passionate, headstrong, preferring the satisfaction of her own private humour or resentments before the safety of her own people & of all Europe.

But when they shall be assured by all the monuments & records of history that this was one & the same Queen Anne who filled this whole period of time, the same who, after having

* 'Undoing' would be more in context.

fought so long & so successfully against France, raised it to a greater pitch of power than it ever enjoyed before, the same who, after having made Charles King of Spain presently dethroned him, the same who, after having entered into the most solemn alliances & contracts, broke through them with so much resolution & ease, the same who, after having owed the quiet & security of her life to her great General & other faithful ministers, afterwards rewarded them with all the ignominy & disgrace she could heap upon them, who . . . but I am weary of recounting these unpleasing things. When posterity comes to be assured of this, will it not shake & surprise them? And will not many be apt to ask what part her justice had in this procedure? what her pity, what her gratitude, what her honour, what her faith & what her constancy? I will give no further answer . . . Facts speak too plainly to be denied.[51]

CHAPTER IX

A Sort of Pilgrimage

1712-1714

———◆———

'If the fault was mostly Sarah's', writes Trevelyan, 'the tragedy was mostly Anne's. For Sarah was left less forlorn. She had more resources in herself; and she had the unchanging love of her husband, of which she was far more proud than she had ever been of the royal friendship even in its palmiest days'.[1]

For Anne the world had, by a series of mischances with the Devil driving, become second-rate; and where before it had been peopled with giants and heroes, now, wherever she looked—the army (Ormonde), the treasury (Oxford), the privy purse (Abigail)—there seemed to be shuffling dwarfs and puppets.* Where among all these little people was greatness? She was friendless, gout-ridden, insecure. Well may she have envied Marlborough pitching his campaigning-tent in the gardens at Holywell or Sarah who, as she had heard with misgiving, was about to begin her self-vindication.

'The Calumnies against me were so gross', Sarah explained, 'and yet so greedily devoured by the Credulity of Party Rage, that I thought it became me to write and publish something in my own Justification . . . a sort of Memorial which . . . I drew up in 1712'.[2] Two years before she had been urged by Maynwaring to write 'a

---

* 'Of all the nonsense that ever I knew in my life nothing ever surprised me so much as that any Prince that knows hee must ask advise of somebody should not think it more for his honour as well as safty to take it from the best of his country [men] & his great councell that hee appears to adviss with who have generally great stakes than to have it from little od people that come in the dark & that are not own'd.' (Sarah to Lady Cairns Undated. Blen. G-I-16).

178

true history of the present time . . . There is nobody that I know but 240', he told her, 'that is capable to write one or that has so great a love of Truth as to be able to follow a thing so despised & forlorn & to quit all other considerations for the sake of it: honours, profits, courts, and even 42'.[3]

It was tempting. For Mrs Burnet, who had 'such a violent passion for Queen Mary', she had long since set down her account of that queen and the 'Monster' she had reigned with. And now, in her Brown Book, Sarah had all the letters of Queen Anne . . . But it was not until *The Examiner* had goaded her to fury that she decided she must publish no matter who smarted or, as she put it, 'whoever's ears may tingle'.

'I have been a kind of Author', she said later. She had indeed; and there had been a succession of more or less talented and more or less helpful collaborators, beginning with Bishop Burnet ('not well done'), continuing with Maynwaring, St Priest and Hutchinson and concluding with Nathaniel Hooke. There were those too—a distinguished trio—privileged to comment before publication: Pope, Voltaire and Robert Walpole, the last perhaps, in view of her subsequent loathing, the most surprising of all. But in 1712, 'thinking him extremely her friend', as he had been Marlborough's, Sarah sent Walpole her manuscript in the Tower where, in Marlborough tradition, he had been immured on a false charge. He read it and 'persuaded her by no means to do [publish] it, saying that the Ministers would employ all their pens by the most scurrilous people whom they had in pay to write against her & that she had better defer her vindication, tho' 'twas a very good one, to some other time;* & he prevailed upon her much against her inclination; & his argument was rediculous, because at that very time they had printed all the falsities against her that even Malice could invent'.[4]

Maynwaring, who had taken great pains with it and, on Sarah's behalf, clamoured for vengeance, must have been disappointed. He was not to know that the *Conduct* for which he had laid a foundation would not appear until thirty years after his death. All he could do was to predict, 'Whoever shall read it a hundred years hence will think and say, the Lady that writ this had the most honesty & the

* In another version this reads: 'to defer the doing it tell people were less madd'. (Blen. G-1-10).

rightest principles & notions of things in the world'.[5] In the mean-time as the lady herself admitted, 'I have a great deal of pleasure in thinking every day what sad wretches I shall make all these people appear to the whole world a little sooner or later, so much that I doe protest I would not part with it [her manuscript] to have Blenheim finish'd & every thing added to it that is in the power of this infamous foolish Court to give'.[6]

There were times, she said, when she heartily wished Blenheim burned.* She sent Maynwaring and Godolphin down there to try out the wing Vanbrugh had added to High Lodge, the ranger's house on Blenheim's western axis, remote and romantic, where Burnet had heard the deathbed confession of John Wilmot Earl of Rochester. Godolphin reported, 'I never lay in so good a bed'. Everything was perfect, even to a dessert of peaches, nectarines, figs and green plums. The company too, except of course for the owners' absence, could not have been better, since they had with them the architect of Blenheim and author of *The Relapse*: 'allways', as Maynwaring said, 'the best company when his Whym is at its highest, tho' perhaps not the best architect.' Good food, good wine, good company in a lodge set high among oaks above the Evenlode, what could be jollier? Yet even in that Arcady there were shadows. Dr Garth shook his head over the decline of Maynwaring while Maynwaring drank deep and tried to ignore it. He moved on to St Albans. 'Several of the best authors, even Plutarch', he reminded his absent hostess, 'have written the praises of illustrious Ladies, & if I shou'd ever turn author I shou'd say so much upon the subject of one of them that I shou'd deserve to be buried in the same manner that a German writer was . . . The women pour'd so much wine upon his grave that it overflow'd the whole church. Something like this I hope you will live to do over my poor Remains, for I am confident your friendship will extend beyond my life . . . a wearisome life which without it would be a real punishment'.[7]

Maynwaring longed to write but was past writing; and indeed on all fronts the enemy looked to have the field to themselves.† Swift in his own chosen company read *The St Albans Ghost* to Abigail and

* The works at Blenheim were stopped officially on June 1, 1712.

† On May 10, 1712 St John sent secret restraining orders to Ormonde (Marlborough's successor as commander-in-chief), forbidding him to engage the enemy.

her husband, now ennobled as Lord and Lady Masham.* 'I went to Lord Masham's tonight', he records with relish, 'and Lady Masham made me read to her a pretty two penny Pamphlet calld The St Albans Ghost. I thought I had writt it myself, so did they, but I did not. Lord Treasurer [Oxford] came down to us from the Queen & we stayed till 2 a Clock. That is the best night place I have. The usual company are Lord & Lady Masham, Lord Treasurer, Dr Arbuthnot & I; sometimes the Secretary [St John]† & sometimes Mrs Hill of the bedchamber, Lady Masham's sister'.[8]

It was the set Maynwaring had so often jeered at. The ghost in the pamphlet, crudely drawn, was the late Mrs Jennings; but at St Albans itself this was indeed a time for ghosts. Godolphin, visited there on his deathbed by Robert Walpole, is credited with having turned to Sarah and said, 'Madam, if there is such a thing as a possibility of spirits returning from the other world I shall certainly appear to you if you should ever abandon this young man'.[9] When on September 15th he died, Sarah wrote in her bible: 'The best man I ever knew'.

Maynwaring is said to have caught a chill on an evening stroll in the grounds of Holywell but, when he died on November 13th, the post-mortem named tuberculosis. In *The Life & Posthumous Works of Arthur Maynwaring*, published in 1715 and dedicated to Robert Walpole, the anonymous author says:

It is to his Glory that the greatest Lady in England wept often by the side of his Death Bed, which he water'd as often with his Tears, being sensible how much he ow'd to such an Illustrious Mourner, when he was sensible of little or nothing else. He had not Words to express the Transport of his Soul when he was almost in the Agony to see him self so far in the good Graces of a Lady of such high Rank & Merit as that his Danger should strike her Dumb & leave it to her Eyes to express the Sorrow of her Soul. It was suppos'd that he would have endeavoured

---

* Though Abigail's soul might be fitted for grandeur, it was with great reluctance that Queen Anne turned so useful a servant into a Lady, at the risk, as she put it, of 'having a peeress lie upon the floor'. However she did so and for good measure made her two-year-old daughter Ranger of St James's Park.

† In July, 1712 St John was to his fury created Viscount Bolingbroke. He had, like Harley, expected an earldom and blamed him for the disappointment.

to have broke thro' the Excess of his Grief & form'd some Utterance for it but his Sister remain'd in the Room. This Emotion of his was the more extraordinary on account of a slight Misunderstanding at that Time between this Great Lady and him. He had given her some Occasion of Offence but was not conscious to him self in what, and it is thought that his Perplexity about it contributed somewhat to the encrease of his Distemper. He would fain have come to an *Eclaircissement* in that matter but he was too near Death and in a few hours after she left him expir'd in the Arms of his Faithful Servant.

Maynwaring, offering to follow the Marlboroughs into exile, had jokingly suggested Mindelheim or America; but that was not to be. There was little enough now however to keep them in England, and Marlborough, a pall-bearer at Godolphin's funeral, turned his thoughts to living abroad. After one has lived a great many years in a hurry, he had once written to the Queen, it was very natural and very desirable to enjoy some quiet; and that quiet he could no longer count upon in England where, as Burnet observed, he was pursued with malice. There was even talk of prosecution for the cost of Blenheim; and there may have been other reasons.

> When vice prevails and impious men bear sway,
> The post of honour is a private station.

On December 1st he left. Sarah was expected to join him almost at once, but there was much to see to and there were difficulties too about boats and passports. 'I did not know', she wrote afterwards, 'whether I should ever see my own country again'. She had long since remarked to Maynwaring, 'Perhaps travelling and a bottle of Spaw watter every morning may have as good an effect upon the passion of hatred as upon love. I am satisfied they are both very uneasy companions & the first is the worse of the two but I fear I am not clear from it . . . At the same time I am sensible that 'tis a great weaknesse & I can say nothing in my excuse but that I think I doe not hate Mrs Morley for loving another but for being so brutall to me after such professions to me & such very faithfull service . . . but as the great author says that lyes before me, one must not bee angry with thistles that they don't produce apples'.[10] She still found it hard to shake off the shock, the outrage, the unbelievable betrayal of Abigail. 'Surely', she exclaimed, 'there never was any time since Adham that such a woman as Ab: gave so many great & good men so much trouble'.[11]

But now there were other things to think of: keepsakes for friends, luggage, servants . . . 'The Duchess of Marlborough hath given great presents at her taking leave of her friends', Lord Berkeley noted, 'severall fine diamond rings & other jewells of great value, to Dr Garth for one'.[12] Her grandchildren too came in for diamonds —'a lottery of all my fine things', as she put it, 'which I made them raffle for'.[13] It was, as Bishop Hare said, to be a sort of pilgrimage; yet even for a pilgrimage it can be surprising how much one needs. There were all the obvious things like wig-boxes and candlesticks, but in uncivilised countries almost anything might be useful. She took forty mantos [manteaux] and petticoats and a vast quantity of linen. She took a tea-kettle to hold five pints, a chocolate-pot, 'a blew bagg lined with fox skins', a powder-puff and seven leopard-skin muffs. When all had been packed she found she had a hundred and twenty large parcels weighing a hundredweight. She hoped nothing had been left out.

And then just as she was due to leave, two vexing things happened. Mary King the laundrymaid refused to join the pilgrimage and had to be paid off with two months' wages (£1); and even more tiresome, while sifting last-minute oddments Sarah chanced on Queen Anne's miniature set in diamonds . . . Swift gives the sequel:

April, 1713. I dined at Lord Treasurer's . . . who shewed us a small Picture, enamelld work & sett in gold, worth about 20 ls, a Picture I mean of the Queen which she gave to Dutchess Marlborough sett in Diamonds. When the dutchess was leaving England she took off all the Diamonds & gave the Picture to one Mrs Higgins (an old intriguing Woman whom everybody knows), bidding her to make the best of it she could. Lord Treasurer sent to Mrs Higgins for this Picture & gave her a hundred Pounds for it. Was ever such an ungratefull Beast as that Dutchess? or did you ever hear such a Story. I suppose the Whigs will not believe it, pray try them: takes off the Diamonds & gives away the Picture to an insignificant Woman as a thing of no consequence & gives it her to sell like a piece of old fashioned plate. Is she not a detestable Slut?[14]

Writing later from Frankfurt Sarah sent her own explanation:

I have heard lately that there has been a heavy outcry against me & that my Lady Burl:* was very angry with me that I gave her a picture of the queen to give to Mrs Higgins† who has nothing to eat but by a pention of the queen which I got her & even in this ungreatfull age she acknowledged it more then it deserved & I really thought it would doe her some little good & that some flattering fool would buy it; tho I did not forsee that she would have it in her power to oblige Cato,‡ nor that a lady should bee angry that I had lived so long freely with & that parted with me very kindly; & much less did it enter my head that any body should think it reasonable for me to keep a thing that could put me in mind of one that had used the D: of M: & my self so barbarously after such long & faithfull service, but this it seems was a great crime, but I own to you I don't care what such people say or think of me, nor did I ever pretend to bee so good a christian as to love my persecutors; tho' to you I will bee so religious as to make a thorow confession: I did in one of my letters or more say something of the Rt Reverend *The Examiner*, after hee had writt the last infamous one I saw concerning the D: of M: & my self, & every body knowing that the author of that Libell is the new Dean who writt the Tale of

* Lady Burlington. 'I carry'd her my Bird to take care of & desired . . . she would give Mrs Higons from me a little picture of the queens'. (Sarah to Mrs Clayton. Blen. G-1-16. Undated).

† The ever grateful and obsequious Mrs Higgins later became an embarrassment. A letter in which she offers to throw herself at the Duchess's feet is endorsed in Sarah's hand: 'I have don her a great deal more good then she mentions in her letter, with no other design then to assist her because I believed her very poor, but I never cared for her nor could not tast her witt & was so weary of her that when I sent her mony & cloaths I would have put away my porter if he had let her in to me'. (Blen. E 46).

‡ On the first night of Addison's *Cato*, in April 1713, Bolingbroke rose and congratulated Booth (in the name part) for his oration against a dictator: a hit against Marlborough. Here however the Duchess seems to be referring to Harley (Lord Oxford), then Lord Treasurer.

the Tub, a book not only against all religion but against all morality. I writt some thing to this purpose, that I was surprised (I could not say that I was sorry) to see the Rt Reverend Do: Swift so highly preferred in the church just after it had been so piously recommended to punish all men that writt libells & against Religion. Now if this reflects upon the ministers, I am ready to come over & stand my tryall; & you may be sure I will never write any thing that I care who sees as to my own perticular; & as wicked as my enemys are, I think my self very safe because it is not possible for them or any body to counterfeit my hand.[15]

Before she had joined him Marlborough had written, 'I am extremely sensible of the obligation I have to you for the resolution you have taken of leaving your friends & country for my sake'.[16] They met at Maestricht in February, a place full for him of campaigning memories, and from there with a cavalcade of horses and servants they made stately progress to Aix, to Frankfurt, to Antwerp.

At first everything was wonderful. It was soothing to be away from a carping court and among friendly, admiring people who would stop their coaches and take them to see their gardens. Wherever they went they were made much of. Banquets were arranged, regiments turned out, cannons fired; even Mindelheim went en fête to pay its prince and princess respectful if diminutive honours.* Sarah liked it better than she had expected, 'but not so as to think of living there'. And then of course the gradual disillusion: too cold, too hot—'Their manner is Stoves which is intolerable & makes my head so uneasy that I can't bear it'—until after a winter of it Sarah finds herself longing for her friends in a clean sweet house and declares roundly, 'Tis much better to be dead then to live out of England'.[17] What that old campaigner Dr Hare had said was true: 'The elegance & ornaments of life which your Grace has always enjoyed without any interruption have made a thousand things

* 'At Mindelheim they have entertainments too & I think the whole world is but a sort of a popit shew, but sure in noe place there ever was such a farse as in England where men seem to bee giving up with joy & thanks what they preserved at soe much expense for soe many years'. (Sarah to Craggs, 7 June, 1713. BM Stowe 751, f 61).

disagreeable to you which to persons less polite would be tolerable enough, especially considering how much you are a stranger to the language, as well as faces, of the persons you must converse with'.[18]

The sort of pilgrimage was fast becoming a sort of exile, but the Duchess was never starved of news from home. 'What now seems to possess everybody's mind', wrote the lately widowed Lady Mohun, in April, 'is a new tragedy called *Cato* . . . The cause is liberty, the character the Duke of Marlborough, as near as one great, wise & virtuous man can be compared to another . . . Heaven forever preserve our dear Cato, or publick ruin will make every private person's case as precarious as mine'.[19]

Sarah sent for Addison's play and read it. 'It pleased me extreamly', she wrote, 'but it was a melancholly sort of a pleasure that made me drop a great many teares & I fancy'd I saw my children doing the same at many expressions, perticularly when tis said that Cato was allways mild, compassionate & gentle to his friends, fill'd with domestic tendernesse, the best, the kindest father . . .' Had she been at the first performance, she adds, she (like Bolingbroke) would have risen and 'poynted at my Lord Mortimer* whenever a perfidious villian was named that ruind his country to sett up himself. I suppose before this', she concludes, 'you will have seen the conditions of the Peace for it is here in French'.[20] This of course was the Treaty of Utrecht (March 31, 1713), Bolingbroke's triumph, to be later condemned by Pitt as an indelible reproach. Marlborough was, as he had said, thankful not to be concerned in it. He was taking his own measures for the future and had come to an understanding with Hanover upon which not all the wiles of Oxford and Bolingbroke would be able to make the least impression.

Marlborough, his wife tells friends in England, was too lazy to write, (so 'intolerable lazy' he had not even written to his daughters); but that of course by no means applied to herself. She wrote to Robert Jennings, cousin and lawyer (he had seen her off at Dover) about business and politics; to Mrs Clayton, wife of William Clayton the Duke's agent, and to her business-manager James Craggs, whom she called Craggs the Father to distinguish him from James Craggs the Son, who had deeply offended her.† Often, to fox spies, her

* Robert Harley Earl of Oxford and Mortimer.

† James Craggs junior the Duchess suspected as the writer of an anonymous

correspondents are unnamed. Often she uses cypher, which she tends to find confusing. 'My last letter was full of heavy complaints from the inconvenience of this place & the cold I suffered, but now it is warmer', she writes from Frankfurt in May, 1713 to an unnamed friend. 'However, I begin to build a chimney which will be finishd today, & that looks as if we were to stay here a long time . . . My strange hand so much in cypher which I am very likely to mistake puts me in mind of a thing a friend of mine writt me upon the receipt of one of my letters: Is it to try the Eyes, wits & patience of the readers, Madam, that you write in such a manner? Which was a very just repremand & upon the thought of it I will end your trouble'.[21]

It amused her that her handwriting was, as she said herself, ridiculous. It was spiky and characterful and could not be forged. She often apologised for it,* only to be assured by the obsequious that it could easily be read from the other side of the room. 'I am so hurryd & interrupted', she explains, 'that I fear I make many mistakes, & I write so fast that my hand is very rediculous'. And to Craggs: 'If you are peevish at my long leters I can only say that I am sure at first sight they seem to bee much longer then they really are & that there are not more words in this notum then might have been put into two sides of this paper if it were writt in your hand'.[22]

The notum, lengthy indeed, contained as usual 'oridgenal speelings'. In an age that had yet to make up its mind about a number of words, Sarah's spelling was no worse than her friends' and in old age showed improvement, but she was apt to come down heavily upon the 'ill English' and bad spelling of others including Vanbrugh, the Dukes of Somerset and Newcastle and Queen Anne. She herself spelt 'guess' 'ghesse', 'citizen' 'cittyson', 'stratagem' 'strataghem' and 'Adam' 'Adham' or even 'Addham'. Sometimes her spelling gives a hint of her pronunciation, as when she sends for 'pattrons of selver & yellow satin & blew tafaty. I think all selver', she adds, 'will make

---

letter she received in November, 1712; but the evidence on which she based her suspicion (a seal) is unconvincing.

* 'Pray let me know freely & plainly if you can read what I writt, because I could make it much plainer by writing slow if it is necessary to bee understood.' Sarah to Craggs, undated. (BM Stowe 751, *f* 217).

most shew upon yellow by candle light'. Marlborough calls a bird a bord, says the battaile of Rammillie has worsened his head-eake and sends for ruborb and lickerish. Four years after the battle of Blenheim he is still spelling it Bleinhiem; but there could be no better instance of Sarah's self-assurance than when she alters his 'forenur' to 'foruner', when what both were groping for was 'forerunner'. Lady Bathurst bemoans her life, finding 'ye pleasures but very unserting, ye troubles sarting'; while Lady Dorchester confides, 'My Neece is preety & Yong enough to wate for preferment some years, being not foreteen'. Proper names of course were always a stumbling-block: Malbarow, Vanbrook or Vanbrugg, Draydon, St Talbons...*

In the meantime Craggs the Father dutifully wrote by every post and Sarah as unfailingly replied. At Frankfurt in the summer of 1713 she found that neither travel nor the waters of Aix had cured her bitterness. With her vindication in mind she sent for copies of all her papers—'7 or 8 parcells of them so writt with my own fine hand'— and for good measure three ballads to be sent with them, 'that which was first made upon the Credit that wee sang at St Albans so often to poor Mr Escourt's tune; that of giving up Spain; and that of the History of Abigal & the back stairs, to the tune of fair Rosimonde'.[23]†

When in August they moved to Antwerp she continued to brood morosely upon past and future, upon death and exile. 'That which I dread most', she wrote, 'is the power of France'. She was convinced that at Anne's death Oxford and Bolingbroke meant to bring in the Pretender, and then (quoting Steele): 'Farewell Liberty, all Europe will soon be French'. Again: 'I know one must dye some Time or other, & I really think the Matter is not very great where it happens or when; but if I could have my wish it should bee in England, in a clean hous where I might converse with my Children & Friends while I am in the World; but if that must not bee I submitt, & I will own to you that I am not so much to be pittyd as some People, having never seen any Condition yet that was near so happy as 'twas thought. When I was a great Favourite, I was raild at & flatterd from Morning to Night, neither of which was agreeable to me; & when there were but few Women that would not have

* A number of words used by the Duchess have since changed their meaning, e.g. 'aggravation' for 'exaggeration', 'clutter' for 'clatter'.

† See appendix IV.

poysond me for the Happynesse they thought I enjoyd, I kept the worst Company of any Body upon Earth and had Reason to be much more weary then of any [thing] that can happen. Still wee are like a sort of banishd People in a strang Country; and I could say Something to every Part of my Life that would convince you that 'tis only a new sceen of Trouble which few are free from'.[24]

When her papers arrived at Antwerp Sarah called in two writers, St Priest and Hutchinson, to help her with her *Conduct*; but without Queen Anne's letters (too precious to be sent or even copied) she could not hope to complete it. It must still wait for another day.

She did a modicum of sightseeing—churches, convents, processions—and wished 'our wise Cittysons & country Gentlemen could travell & see with their own Eyes the sad effects of Popary & arbitrary Power'.*[25] In all her travels, she told Jennings, she had seen nothing worth telling him about, unless it was the castle belonging to the Elector of Trèves, where the Rhine meets the Moselle. 'There was an air of Greatnesse in every Thing about him'; and as for the Schloss itself, she sent a lyrical description to Kneller, then keeping an eye on Laguerre's fresco-painting at Marlborough House. 'It was a place for Jove himself to live in', she told him, 'my friend Mr Vanbrugh would lay out all the King of France's revenue with the addition of the Indies upon it, without ever finishing of it'.[26]

For the first time since her brief childhood, time was on Sarah's hands. She put on weight.† There were no friends to talk or gamble with; nor could one always be writing ('I doe think tis great goodnesse in me', she told Craggs, 'to consider my friends soe much as not to write to them when I have nothing else to doe'). And this of course resulted on the one hand in introspection—'Living abroad makes one very indifferent whether one's life be long or short'[27]—and on the other in making the utmost of such incidents as the loss of a diamond; an event which afforded scope for Sarah's powers of narration.

Writing from Antwerp she tells Craggs:

* '. . . all the history of our Saviour represented by the trades people of the town twice a week . . . the whole thing more impious then tis possible for any body to imagin that had not seen it'. (Sarah to Mrs Clayton. Undated. Blen G-1-16).

† Of the Elector of Mainz the Duchess wrote: 'His shape is, like my own, a little of the fatest'. (Madresfield, p. 32).

It is the fashion in these countries to wear bracelets of dyamonds & pictures about their rists, buckld on in a manner that they cannot come off without undoing. And I came out of a room one evening, immediatly after it had been seen on my rist, into my dressing room, took it off & layd it down upon the dressing table: and I was thinking to undress me, but while I was setting there alone, Ned the black footman that you have seen came thro my bed chamber by the Duke of Marlboroughs order to let me know that the tea stayd for me. And I call'd him in & bad him stoop down to put on my shoe, which I had just pulld off because it hurt me, by which means he had a full oppertunity of seeing the dyamond, for I satt so close to the table that it was just in his Eyes.

After my shoe was on I rose up & hee lighted me into the other room where the tea was to bee made & where it was very naturall for him to have stayd to have assisted in serving the tea, but hee went out immediatly. And upon my missing my Bracelet, which I ded in a very little time, and examining into the matter, the Gentleman of the house, who has all the appearance of a very honest and sensible man . . . said that he was coming down a pair of stairs by chance out of his lodge that looks upon a back door that opens into my dressing room & hee saw a lacky of Madam's open the door & goe into it in the dark.

This is the fact and I think it a plain demonsteration that Ned must have the dyamond, which is [not?] of a great value, but it was the most agreeable & pritty fine thing that ever I saw in my life & I think I would give the full value of it to have it again.

There needs no more than I have [said?] & did to convince any body that this man must take [have taken] the dyamond, who certainly saw it, & hee knew no body was in the room where I left it & that hee could goe round to the back door in a minute & take it up; and no footman ever went into that room without being call'd. Besides, most of my other servants were abroad; and in the examination of Ned there appeard severall marks of guilt; and the Duke of Marlborough was so sure by these demonsterations which I have repeated that hee sent for the magistrates of this town & told them what could bee given upon oath against this man, upon which they sent him to prison; and the laws of this country are soe severe in these cases that a less evedence would hang one of their own people; but the manner & custome is to wrack them till they confess, which is soe dreadfull a thing that I rather chose to give up my dyamond than suffer it in my owne concerne.

And Ned is soe very obstanate a rogue that while hee had any hope of escaping the torments of this world hee would not confess; soe wee have sent to the magistrats to discharge him, & I fancy hee will come for England, which is the chief reason of my troubling you with this long account, that you may think if by any surprise you can have him searched there & by that means find the dyamond about him, where hee thinks him self secure, for I can't imagine that hee will soe much as aim at selling this dyamond in a country where hee knows no body & where it has made such a noise. But I reckon hee has hid it some where & if hee can't get it from the place him self hee will press some person to assist him; and in soe great a family [household] tis to bee feared there may bee one not unlike him self, for hee had companions that used to drink with him; and since I was abroad I have observd upon some occations a more then ordinary greedynesse to get mony.

Pray do me the favour to consult with Hodges in this matter & desire him to goe to my hous & to give the servants warning to have noe correspondence with him nor suffer him upon any account to come there; and to look if all doors & windowes are all securd for hee knows the hous soe well that there is no doubt but hee will rob it if hee can . . . .

The Duke of Marlborough lost a ring of about 150 ls at Aix; but that being a thing that came off easy & always pulld off when hee washd his hands, hee did not remember enough of it to charge any body with it; so it passed off so easy that I believe it might be some incouragement to Ned in this villiany that hee has don . . . Twas a great temptation to make his fortune . . .[28]

Alas for intuition! 'I have lately sent for near four hundred Pounds', Sarah tells Jennings a month later, 'part of which was to get a Jewell I have lost and to recompense an innocent Servant that had been put into Prison about it and that was soe innocent that it gave me a great deal of Trouble when I saw hee had been wronged'.[29] It is only when one sees the account Sarah sent to Mrs Clayton that one realises that the lost diamond must have been the Marlborough portrait ring, given by Chandos and since made into a bracelet, in which form Sarah bequeathes it in her will. 'Tho I had fancyd when this diamond picture was lost', she tells Mrs Clayton, 'that I would give twice the value of it again, yet when they brought it to me, instead of being pleased I could not help bursting out into a great passion of crying to think how much I had wronged a very inosent man and as soon as I had recovered my self I sent for the footman & gave him 50 pistoles to make amends for his ill lodging in prison, assuring him at the same time that if hee would leave a great fault hee has of drinking that I would bee very kind to him'. 'I am glad your diamond is found & no body guilty', writes Lady Sunderland to her mother, 'I dare say the man thinks you have very well made him amends'.[30] It would be pleasing to think it had taught the Duchess a lesson.

But there was no doubt about it, England was the only place to live. 'I should be very well content', she wrote now, 'with the worst of my country hous's'.[31] If need be, she would live disguised in a cottage; though she would much prefer Windsor Lodge, 'of all the Places that ever I was in the most agreeable'. Marlborough too was impatient to return, 'which', said his wife, 'I beleive you can't blame him for. There was only one good reason for his leaving it that ever I could see & that seems to bee very remote at present'.[32]

And then in March, 1714, as hopes were turning homeward, they had tragic news. Their third daughter, Elizabeth Countess of Bridgwater, had died of smallpox. On hearing the news of his favourite daughter's death Marlborough fainted. Sarah wrote to Jennings:

> The Loss of my poor dear Child is indeed very terrible to me ... That she is happyer I don't doubt then in such a World as this where time generally passes away in trifling, in things that are tedious & in many frights for what may happen, which is yet worse ... but all the Arguments that I can possibly think of cant hinder me from lamenting as long as I live the loss of what

I had soe much reason to love as I did my dear Child, who had a
perfect good mind & every thing I could have wish'd in her . . .[33]

'My grief & my loss are inexpressible', wrote the widower, 'your
Grace's concern for my poor children* is a great comfort to me . . .
having no other thoughts but to tend my children & teach them to
imitate their dear Mother in her love & dutifulness to your Grace &
the Duke . . . I know but little of the Publick', he added, 'but I
flatter myself that ye Monsters will so fall out amongst themselves
that we shall have ye comfort to have your Grace & the Duke of
Marlborough return more belov'd than ever'.[34]

Bridgwater's prediction of dissension among the Tory 'monsters'
of course came true, and their house of cards collapsed at the first
clap of misfortune. Gone were the days when Anne could turn to a
Freeman or a Montgomery. There was only Abigail, who had fallen
out with her Treasurer, Oxford,† who in turn had fallen out with
her Secretary of State, Bolingbroke. They raged even in the royal
presence, even as the distraught Queen approached her death.

But long before she died Anne appeared to be in an advanced
stage of decomposition, like some unfortunate host to a parasite
which grows beneath the skin; as though God had 'sent a worm to
madden his handiwork', or rather, that she were helplessly in the
power of some evil spirit. Mrs Danvers, coming to call her one
morning, found her with her back towards her, gazing fixedly at a
clock. When questioned,—'What is it with the clock, Ma'am?'—she
turned slowly about with 'so woeful and ghastly a regard' that Mrs
Danvers 'saw death in the look' and, frightened, summoned assistance.[35] 'She appeared to be the most despicable mortal I had ever
seen in any station', a shocked visitor reported, 'The poor lady . . .
was again under a severe fit of gout, ill-dressed, blotted in her
countenance & surrounded with plaisters, cataplaisma, & dirty-like

---

* The Bridgwater children were John Viscount Brackley (born 3rd Feb., 1704,
died 30 Jan., 1719), a son who died in infancy and Lady Anne Egerton, who was
taken into the Marlborough household and married (i) the Duke of Bedford and
(ii) the Earl of Jersey.

† In March, 1714 Abigail refused to carry Lord Oxford's offer of resignation to
the Queen. 'She had credit enough to hurt Lord Oxford, by which she destroyed
her own foundation'. (Lord Dartmouth in Burnet, op. cit., VI, 33.)

rags'.[36] It was Abigail who told Swift, 'This good lady deserves pity'.

The Queen had been desperately ill at Christmas and now in July, as the Marlboroughs prepared for their journey home, began to succumb to what Sarah called a complication of diseases. It was an age ago that she had written, 'I realy beleive one kind word from deare Mrs Freeman would save me if I were Gasping'; and Mrs Freeman was no longer within call. During her last days Oxford and Bolingbroke 'played the double game of intrigue with the courts of St Germains and Hanover less expertly than the Duke of Marlborough* . . . and the quarrel between the two Tory leaders, despite all Swift's efforts at reconciliation, ended in a furious clash',[37] that clash in fact in the Queen's presence, which she truthfully said she should never survive.

Oxford resigned that same day (July 27th). On the 29th Anne sank into a coma from which she recovered only enough to let her hand be guided with the Treasurer's white staff, which was given with the Council's approval to the Duke of Shrewsbury. She died on August 1st. 'She had lived long enough', writes Sir Winston, 'to strip the name of Britain of most of the glories with which it had shone . . . She sank into her mortal collapse with her country in the jaws of measureless tribulation. But luckily she expired while there was still time to save it'.[38]

For the second time Somerset had taken the lead in a crisis by suddenly appearing, with Argyll, at the Council on July 30th, to thwart the Jacobite machinations of Bolingbroke. To the end Anne kept her people guessing (and we are guessing still) as to her own intentions for the succession; for although she appeared to favour Hanover, her personal loathing for that family was to the last evidenced by her cold letters, which were said to have speeded the death of the Electress Sophia. There was also that sealed packet which Anne 'always carried about her and put every evening under her bolster. She changed the envelope when it got worn or dirty. It was suspected to be a will concerning the Pretender'. It may have been; yet she must have known James III could not have succeeded without changing his religion, which he commendably refused to do. The packet was burned unread.

* Marlborough sought a pardon from St Germains in February, 1714.

In the event the vigorous measures provided for by the Act of Settlement and now taken to protect the Hanoverian succession were successful; although, in Sir Winston's view, if the Queen had lived six weeks longer, Bolingbroke would probably have plunged the country into civil war. He was soon to show his colours by joining the Pretender as his Secretary of State; while Oxford, who in Sir Keith Feiling's opinion never seriously intended a Stuart restoration, remained to be impeached and to languish in the Tower.

From contemporary accounts it would seem that Abigail behaved disappointingly. After coaxing some of the proceeds from the Asiento slave-trade out of Bolingbroke she is said to have ransacked St James's for something better than brass locks, two days before the Queen's death;[39] but since Anne's will remained unsigned, there could be no provision for her favourite beyond that which she had made for herself. 'Can she', Swift was asked, 'hereafter make any figure in the drama but a *persona muta*?' The answer was no. With her lord she retired in quiet state to Langley in Buckinghamshire.*

And Queen Anne? If greatness lies in the conquest of matter by mind and of weakness by will power, then Anne was a great queen and what befell her great tragedy.

On August 2nd, the day after the Queen's death, the Marlboroughs landed at Dover.

---

* Writing from Langley in 1724 to Swift ('one whose goodness to me has always been abundantly more than I could deserve'), Lady Masham says, 'I do assure you from the bottom of my heart there is not a person living I have a greater friendship for than yourself and shall have to the end of my life . . . I long to see you at my retired habitation, where you will meet with a most hearty welcome and faithful friends'. (Swift Corresp. III, 190). She died in 1734. Langley was bought from the widower by Charles Third Duke of Marlborough and rebuilt.

CHAPTER X

No Armour

1714-1717

———◆———

For Hanover and the Protestant Succession long wars had been fought, fortresses taken, villages burned, friends betrayed, conquerors exiled . . . So that now, with Anne dead, it was felt that the scene called for a prince indeed, for some Olympian Phoebus Apollo, but all benevolence, all virtue, to justify the blood and the anguish and with godlike serenity to land on his sceptred isle and claim his own.

A little late on cue at Greenwich there landed, on September 18th, an elderly German gentleman, to be acclaimed as George I of England. There was it seemed no queen (she had been put away for adultery), but there were mistresses—Frau Schulenburg and Frau Kielmannsegge—one fat, one thin. There was also a son George whom his father disliked. The King spoke German and a little French, no English. England, said Lord Chesterfield, was too big for him. But he was not a Stuart. Turning to Marlborough whom he had, against Sarah's wishes, restored to his post of Captain-General he said, 'My lord Duke, I hope your troubles are now all over'.

In their glass coach the exiles had returned amid cheers and flowers. All was sunshine again. Sarah of course would accept no office, but she saw to it that those of her family who wanted appointments had them: this for Mary Montagu and that for Francis Godolphin . . . though she was sorry that the widower Bridgwater was such a manifest fool that she could get him nothing better than Chamberlain to the Prince of Wales. Vanbrugh was knighted and so was Dr Garth, the fat doctor dubbed, at his request, with Marlborough's sword. Even Mrs Clayton, whom Horace Walpole called a pompous simpleton, was squeezed in as lady-in-waiting to Caroline, Princess of Wales.

For a time they were restless. 'Since my last to you from Windsor', Sarah wrote from St Albans to Jennings on August 23rd, 'I have been at the Bath and at Woodstock, and when I came to this Place I was more tird then [on] any of my Travels'. She praised Holywell ('however ordinary I would not part with it') and seemed happy to stay there for the rest of her life; but that was not to be. For one thing, and to her a most vexatious one, there was Blenheim.

Before going abroad in 1712 Marlborough had left the shell of Blenheim in the care of a young man called Henry Joynes, a skilled draughtsman (he later became an architect) regarded by Vanbrugh as his clerk of the works. Hawksmoor called him Honest Harry. He was twenty-one. According to Joynes, the Duke took leave of him on cordial terms, hand on shoulder, and entrusted the building to him; a gardener, Tilleman Bobart, being left in charge of the grounds. In practice two men responsible for three acres of building and two thousand acres of park and garden must either kill themselves in a frenzy of futile labour or do nothing. Sensibly enough Joynes and Bobart plumped for the latter course, except that they would make hay, occasionally show the house to the curious, and fish in the lake; while Vanbrugh, doubtless blessing his luck, moved into the ruins of Woodstock Manor. It would be safe to say that never in the history of Blenheim has life come nearer to Arcady. 'I was fishing last week', Joynes tells a friend at the Treasury, 'and I can't avoid telling you what I catch't, a Brace of good Trouts about 14 ins, a Chub about the same length and eight Dace ten inches each . . . and since, a brace of Chubs one 17 ins, a brave fish to Catcht tho' course to Eat . . .'[1]

It was good going; too good indeed to last. When the Marlboroughs returned they were angry about the haymaking (the gardens had run to ruin) and still angrier that Vanbrugh, instead of demolishing Woodstock Manor, had gone to live in it. The Duchess alleged that on the roof he had built himself a closet, 'as if he had been to study the planets'; though from that point he was far more likely to be studying the perspective of his own masterpiece, 'the cast and turn of the House' that meant so much to him.

However, Vanbrugh was not, like Wren, easy to be got rid of. He had powerful friends at the Kit-Cat: Carlisle, Newcastle, Manchester, and of course Marlborough himself. 'I have just now been with Lord Carlisle', Vanbrugh tells the club's founder, Jacob Tonson, 'who has named Friday for the Barns Expedition. I have seen Lady Marlborough since & she agrees to it & will order a Bardge at Whitehall. The Company she names are Two Ladies besides her Self, Ld Carlisle, Ld Clare, Horace Walpole, Dr Garth and Mr Benson'.[2] How discharge a man with whom one was on such terms? Besides, he might still be useful, if not as an architect (and she might yet manage him in that), then as a matchmaker.

For her Godolphin granddaughter Harriet, a disappointingly plain girl of fifteen, she had her eye on the young Duke of Newcastle, a rich and foolish young man known to fellow-members of the Kit-Cat as Permis, from the phrase he was fond of using: *Est-il permis?* In this delicate project Vanbrugh, who knew him well and was to build for him, offered his help. Sarah gratefully accepted; but the thing went sluggishly. The Duke, Vanbrugh told Sarah, seemed convinced of the fine attributes he had mentioned but voiced 'a sort of wish (express'd in a very gentle manner) that her bodily perfections had been up to those I describ'd of her mind & understanding'. Vanbrugh had been honest about her face and yet was gallant enough to bet that in two years' time no woman in town would be better liked. While the match hung fire, the Duchess put out a feeler in the direction of Wentworth Woodhouse—'vast woods, a great seat in Yorkshire and a mighty rich family'—but Harriet, after meeting the heir, burst into tears; whereupon her grandmother wept too, hugged her and said she need not marry the emperor of the world unless she liked him.[3]

For Blenheim Marlborough sent for estimates with a view to finishing it himself; but there were disputes as to what was owing, and building was not resumed until the summer of 1716; by which time many of those who had worked on it had died or for one reason or another declined to return. These last included Grinling Gibbons, who had been responsible for all the enrichment in stone and marble; Edward Strong, the chief mason; and Henry Joynes, who was about to succeed Hawksmoor as clerk of the works at Kensington Palace.

It was six years since Marlborough had written to his duchess, 'After the many troubles & dependencies wee have labord thro during almost all our lifetime for the good of our children I think it very reasonable, tho we had met with no ungratefull disapointe- ments, that wee shou'd before wee dye be masters of some litle time for our own ease & quiet'.[4] And it was now, in quiet retirement, that they should have reaped that modest reward.

On April 15th, 1716 their second daughter Anne Countess of Sunderland died of what was then called a pleuritic fever. She was, said Sarah, everything that was good and everything that was charming. To her parents her death brought profound grief and shock. She had inherited Sarah's beauty without her bitterness and had been the toast of the Kit-Cat as the Little Whig. There was a tenderness about her which was said to have a softening influence upon her mother. As a child she could never bear to be in her bad books—'What have I done that you think so ill of poor me that loves you so passionately?'—and on one such occasion tells her she had not been to bed for a fortnight without weeping.*

. Her own children—Robert, Charles, John, Anne and Diana—she loved dearly and, with a seeming premonition of death, wrote movingly about them to her husband. 'As to the children, pray get my mother, the Duchess of Marlborough, to take care of the girls, & if I leave my boys too little to go to school—to be left to servants is very bad for children, and a man can't take the care of little children as a woman can—for the love that she has for me & the duty I have ever show'd her I hope she will do it, & be ever kind to you, who was dearer to me than my life . . . Pray let Mr Flournoys get some good-natur'd man for Lord Spencer's governor, who may be fit to go abroad with him . . . and don't be as careless of the dear children as when you relied upon me to take care of them. But let them be your care, though you should marry, for your wife may

* At Blenheim an undated letter from Anne Sunderland to her mother reads: '. . . I have one of my dear Mama's Colds with very great pleasure, for it was a great uneasyness to me to hear you say you thought it a sign your constitution was broak, but I hope it looks more now like being naturall. I am sure whatever it is I shall like being as you are & indeed I should have more ease in indureing any- thing then I can express if it could take off any pain from my dearest Mama that I adore more then I can ever show'. (Blen E 6)

wrong them when you don't mind it. We must all die, but 'tis hard to part with one so much belov'd and in whom there was so much happiness as you, my dearest, ever were to me . . .'[5]

With a great many tears Sarah read the letter and wrote to the widower, 'You may be very sure that to my life's end I shall observe very religiously all that my poor dear child desired. I was pleased to find that my own inclinations had led me to resolve upon doing every thing that she mentions before I knew it was her request, except taking Lady Anne, which I did not offer, thinking that since you take Lady Frances* home, who is 18 years old, she would be better with you than me, as long as you live, with the servants that her dear mother chose to put about her . . . But I will be of all the use that I can be to her in every thing that she wants me; and if I should happen to live longer than you, though so much older, I will then take as much care of her as if she were my own child. I have resolved to take poor Lady Anne Egerton,† who I believe is very ill looked after. She went yesterday to Ashridge, but I will send for her to St Albans as soon as you will let me have dear Lady Di;‡ and while the weather is hot I will keep them two and Lady Harriet with a little family of servants to look after them and be there as much as I can; but the Duke of Marlborough will be running up and down to several places this summer, where one can't carry children; and I don't think his health so good as to trust him by himself'.[6]

On May 28th Marlborough had his first stroke, which resulted in partial paralysis and loss of speech. By the summer, speech had returned and, with Garth in attendance, he was well enough to be moved to Bath. On the subject of Bath Sarah was in agreement with Queen Anne who had called it stinking. 'Of all the places upon earth', wrote the Duchess, 'tis the most disagreeable'. Nor did she believe in the efficacy of its waters; but when the doctor not only recommended them but insisted on staying there with his patient, what else was she to do?

'I think Sr S: Garth is the most honest & compassionate', she told

* Lady Frances Spencer, his daughter by his first wife Lady Arabella Cavendish. She married Henry Howard Earl of Carlisle.

† Lady Anne Egerton, daughter of Elizabeth Countess of Bridgwater, deceased.

‡ Lady Diana Spencer, Anne Sunderland's second daughter and Sarah's favourite granddaughter.

Craggs, 'but after the minuets which I have seen him dance and his late tour into Italy, I can't help thinking that hee may some times bee in the wrong'.[7] Marlborough's health, she added, was of more consequence to her than all the money in the world. Would he please consult his 'club of physicians' in London and let her know what they thought? The symptoms, some of which frightened her, she observed and, in letter after letter, described minutely:

Hee is vastly better in his head & in his speech, there is not the least doubt of that, but tis certain that his limbs are weaker a good deal then they were even at St Albans. Hee can't come upstairs without uneasiness, & some times hee has some thing that I don't know very well how to express of grunting & bemoaning of him self that looks like sicknesse or want of spirits, but when I ask him if hee is sick hee says no, but hee is uneasy & won't or can't discrib what it is. Hee says his belly is harder then it used to bee & tis certain that his cote does not butten easy that was too big when wee came here . . .[8]

Perhaps it was too much to hope that, with a leading doctor in residence, doctoring by post could produce the remedy; but at one stage it did succeed in making the patient laugh. This was when one of Craggs's club of physicians conjured him to 'keep up the dignity of his stomack'. On a good day he could still be 'pritty chairfull' and take a hand at ombre. Sarah tried him again with ass's milk, which 'hee took two days & left it off, fancying it did not agree with him; but that, I believe', added Sarah, 'could bee nothing but fancy'. It was hard to prescribe for one more used to giving orders than taking them; but since the symptoms were alarming, could it be that the remedies should be also?

'I have been told today', writes Sarah, 'that vipors boyl'd in the Duke of Marlboroughs broath is an Admerable thing & will mend his blood & take off the lownesse of his spirits . . . An apothecary here told me hee had known severall take it with good success but the Dutches of Shrewsbury says there is non good in England & that I must send into France & they have the best in the world that comes from Mumpillio [Montpelier]. She talks of having them come alive in boxes with holes fill'd with bran, but I fancy they have a more easy way of sending them'. Craggs hastens to tell his son in Paris to order vipers, only to be informed next post, 'I have a leter from one I think an oracle who . . . has seen that Broath used by severall a considerable time. They that took it complained that the loathing of the Vipors made their other food less usefull to them & that jelly of heartshorn & calves feet was much better'.[9] It was unfortunate that in Paris Craggs the Son had already popped the vipers into the post.

In Sarah's enormously long letters to Craggs from Bath three themes recur: Marlborough's health, Cadogan and Blenheim. William Cadogan,* formerly Marlborough's companion-in-arms, was his closest friend. When in 1706 he had been reported killed or captured Marlborough wrote, 'He lov'd me and I cou'd rely upon him';[10] and three years later, when he was wounded, 'I hope in God hee will do well for I can intierly depend upon him'.[11] When in 1712 Marlborough went into exile, he asked for Cadogan, who met him at Ostende and went with him to Holland, a gesture which cost him his job. As insurance against the worst that might happen in England, Marlborough then asked him to invest £40,000 for him in Dutch government funds. This he did, later switching the investment to Austria in the hope of better interest there. As things turned out, the rate of interest in Austria fell; and when Sarah got wind of it she wrote to Craggs:

> I must tell you a secret great as the world & I conjure you by all that you value upon earth never to breath the least word of it to any man or woman upon earth, for I would not say what I am going to write even to you if I did not find it was a thing absolutely necessary to have your help in in order to save a vast loss that may very probably happen to the Duke of Marlborough or to his family . . . Lord Cadogan has a great many usefull & good qualities, but hee has a passion for mony that is beyond any thing that ever I knew . . .[12]

And so it all came out, the long sad story which exposed Marlborough's jolly, fat, Irish quartermaster-general as a 'vile creature' and a common thief. Whatever happened, said the Duchess, Marlborough need not know. 'The letters come three hours before hee reads or sees any thing, so that I can easyly take any thing out that

* William Cadogan (1675–1726), M.P. for Woodstock, created first Earl Cadogan in 1718.

hee would bee peevish to see'.[13] In the end, Cadogan paid in full; but the cost in fret and friendship was incalculable.

As for Blenheim, even to think of it, said Sarah, was enough to turn one's brain. It was a chaos which only God Almighty could finish. Nevertheless she would have a try. If while she lived she might hope 'to compass a habitation at Woodstock', she might even attempt to sell her crown lease of Windsor Lodge. Craggs, Vanbrugh's friend who had introduced him, must somehow manage him now and keep him sweet, he seemed so easily offended. 'For I really love the man', she admitted, 'and I never saw any thing that I did not like in him but these high flights in building which I can never tast, especially tell I have a habitation to live in, which [it] is high time at our age to have'.[14]

There was something in that; for there was no denying that, owing to a chain of mischances, though building had begun in 1705 now, in 1716, the Marlboroughs' private apartments were still not habitable;* whereas Marlborough House, inside and out, had been completed in two years. On the other hand they had, in addition to that London house (much smaller than Blenheim but still commodious), two good country houses; and Marlborough, though keen to move into Blenheim, seems to have cared less about his own short time and where he spent it than about posterity and a fitting monument to his armies' achievements. His attitude was impersonal; Sarah's was personal; and as they moved from Bath to Blenheim and put up at High Lodge, she decided it was time to take matters into her own hands. 'I don't tell him the tenth part of the maddnesse of it', she wrote to Craggs, 'for fear of vexing him, which must bee avoided as much as possible upon all occasions'.[15]

All she saw at Blenheim then appalled her and the most daunting thing of all was the bridge with which Vanbrugh had begun to span the valley. Wren had suggested a far more modest approach but had been outvoted. The bridge, Vanbrugh decided, must be worthy of a Roman conqueror and that was what, with enormous courage and brilliance, he prescribed. No matter if, with its rooms and towers and arched superstructure, it was entirely unorthodox and looked more

* Then as now the private apartments are self-contained in the east wing which, following common practice, Vanbrugh completed first. Working westwards, his team was completing the first stateroom west of the Saloon when in 1716 he left.

like a Roman aqueduct than anything normally met with in the English landscape. It proclaimed no local hero but a world figure who had marched across Europe to save it and had frustrated the pretensions of France.

All this Marlborough could see and rise to and Sarah could not. When well enough to ride he rode to the bridge head and asked if Vanbrugh was sure there was enough earth for Wise to link the bridge to the valley. He was assured that there was. But in the meantime Sarah mocked at it as Vanbrugh's 'bridge in the air'— unconnected, isolated, leading from nowhere to nowhere and with next to no water beneath it—and fumed that a skilled mason* and countless workmen must waste their time on it when they might have been finishing rooms one could live in. It was unreasonable. It was madness: 'a prodigious expence to no manner of purpose'. Patience was wearing thin.

The Duchess wrote again to Craggs:

> I will say as little as I can upon Sir Johns subject since I see plainly you are partial to him, & I beleive in that affair of the Building to a great degree, but whatever one says one can't help thinking as one thinks & I am allways of the opinion that I have great difficulties to strugle with in that building. I have no mind to fall out with Sr John & much less so vex the D: of Marl: at a time when his health is so bad. At the same time I think I owe it to him & to my family to prevent if I can having a great estate thrown away in levilling of hills, filling up pricipices & making bridges in the air for no reason that I or any body else can see but to have it said hereafter that Sr John Vanbrugh did that thing which never was don before.
>
> You seem to think that hee & Mr Hawkesmore are the only people to bee consulted with. The last I have spoken to this morning & hee has promised to get a fair computation made of what the charge will bee to finish this unnecessary & rediculous thing. How far hee will be able to perform it I don't know, for hee is but one & not the head, but hee appears reasonable &

---

t Bartholomew Peisley (c.1654–1715), the Oxford mason who, with his son of the same name worked on the Grand Bridge and was 'very proud & overjoyd' when the main arch was keyed, 'it being a great & nice piece of Work'.

allows me that I am in the right to see whether what is intended is more to bee liked then the mony that it will cost, but for Sr John I can't imagine what I can say to him . . .[16]

The cost of Blenheim to date she reckoned at £260,000. 'Tis time', she wrote, 'to put a stop to such a maddnesse'.

In one of many subsequent lawsuits Sarah referred to Vanbrugh as a fish of great size, hard to net. So now at Blenheim, the bridge though gargantuan was not in itself monstrous enough, even in Sarah's opinion, to cause his downfall. There needed to be a number of things—Woodstock Manor, where he had staged a pantomime of demolition while buttressing the parts he most cared for; the pretentious kitchen-court ('covered ways for servants'); the blocked views (Sarah vetoed the western orangery but sadly agreed with Wren that the water would still be visible only from the Gallery);* and for good measure, the muddle over the Newcastle match with Harriet Godolphin, which the Duchess without warning had put into the hands of a professional matchmaker. This last, which had embarrassed Vanbrugh with Newcastle, coupled with Sarah's notum of Blenheim grievances, sent to Craggs's brother-in-law, resulted in Vanbrugh's blunt letter of resignation:

Whitehall, November 8th, 1716

Madam

When I writ to your Grace on Tuesday last I was much at a loss what cou'd be the ground of your having dropt me in the service I had been endeavouring to do you and your family with the Duke of Newcastle, upon your own sole motion and desire. But having since been shewn by Mr Richards a large packet of building papers sent him by your Grace, I find the reason was that you had resolv'd to use me so ill in respect of Blenheim as must make it impracticable to employ me in any other Branch of your Service.

---

* The Gallery, now called the Long Library, runs the whole length of the west front. On August 31, 1705 Marlborough wrote from Tirlemont: 'What Sr Chri: Rhen says as to the watter not being seen in the two apartments [Hall and Saloon] is very trew for that prospect is from the Gallerie'. (Blen E 3) But Vanbrugh reminded the Duchess: 'You cannot see all things from all places'.

These Papers, Madam, are so full of far-fetch'd, labour'd Accusations, mistaken Facts, wrong Inferences, groundless Jealousies and strain'd Constructions that I shou'd put a very great affront upon your understanding if I suppos'd it possible you cou'd mean any thing in earnest by them. But to put a Stop to my troubling you any more, you have your end, Madam, for I will never trouble you more unless the Duke of Marlborough recovers so far [as] to shelter me from such intolerable Treatment.

I shall in the mean time have only this Concern on his account (for whom I shall ever retain the greatest Veneration), that your Grace having like the Queen thought fit to get rid of a faithfull servant, the Torys will have the pleasure to see your Glassmaker, Moor, make just such an end of the Dukes Building as her Minister Harley did of his Victories for which it was erected.

I am
Your Graces most obedient Servant

To which the postcript read:

If your Grace will give me leave to print your paper I'll do it very exactly; and without any answer or remark but this short letter tack'd to the tail of them, that the world may know I desir'd they might be published.[17]

In many ways, notably medicine, the age had its drawbacks, but for writing what it meant, for those few who could write a letter, it was glorious. Not many had acquired such finesse, but in his leave-taking of the Duchess Vanbrugh showed how to combine candour with dignity and at the same time work in a thrust at the new favourite, James Moore the cabinetmaker,* referred to by Sarah as her oracle and cynically watched by Vanbrugh in his versatile acrobatics.

At High Lodge two days later, while the Duchess was still smouldering over Vanbrugh's letter, (resilient herself, she had meant him, she said, to laugh at her notum over a bottle of wine), came Marlborough's second stroke. She summoned three doctors and her

---

* 'I think him very honest & understanding in many Trades besides his own'. Sarah to Jennings, 2 July, 1714. (Madresfield, p. 107).

two daughters, Henrietta Godolphin and Mary Montagu. The last, being ill, could not come; which was as well because the house—'a very little lodge where there were but three rooms to lye in & garrets'—was 'prodigious full'.

Before setting out, Henrietta, in her bold scrawl, had written to her father ('I am extream tenderly as well as most dutifully yours') as she vainly hoped in secret. When she arrived she brushed past her mother to go to his bedside. 'She took no more notice of me', wrote Sarah afterwards, 'then if I had been the nurse to snuff the candles'. Next morning, although barely on speaking terms Sarah, for Marlborough's benefit, took Henrietta in her arms, 'whether she would or no, for he could see nothing of her shy look; and afterwards', she continues, 'when we were alone again I asked her if I had not dissembled very well & begged of her that she would do the same, for in this case I thought it as great a virtue as truth. She would not say anything but looked as if she would kill me, and as soon as her lord came I told him how she had used me. He looked uneasy . . . The Duke of Marl: mended and they soon went away with all the doctors but one; and the morning she took her leave I went thro the rooms with my arm in hers to hide this matter even from the servants; and when she came into her own chamber, as I was talking to her without disguise, she seem'd mighty easy & indifferent & looked in the glass, upon which I said, "You're extream pretty", and so left her . . . When we returned to London we went on in the usual manner—dogged rudeness, and I trying to hide it'.[18]

When most needed Sarah had had too little time for her family; though perhaps too she had strange notions of upbringing. 'A horse not broken becometh headstrong,' she copied from Ecclesiasticus, 'and a child left to himself will be wilful'. Now she had too much time for all of them, and especially, in 1717, for her son-in-law Charles Earl of Sunderland, who decided to remarry.

It was a curious thing that almost always when the Duchess heard of an impending marriage in her family, unless she herself had arranged it, it meant bad news; and this of Sunderland was deplorable. He was of the type that works hard (he was now again Secretary of State), plays hard (a gamble, as for most of the Spencers, was irresistible), and falls repeatedly and passionately in love. His letter to Sarah in the fourth year of Anne's reign (a letter in which he assured her, 'Every honest Englishman will acknowledge that whatever good has been done is entirely owing to 201' [Sarah]) is sealed with a device that shows Cupid shooting at three hearts on an altar; and it was this third involvement which Sarah called a ridiculous match.

It was not of course for her to say that the bride, Judith Tichborne, was unsuitable, but of course she did say so. She was, Sarah found, 'a woman unknown, without a shilling and without a name'. Sunderland told his mother-in-law in what he probably thought her language that he needed 'a companion and one to manage the concerns of his family in order to lessen his expenses'. And so, adds Sarah bitterly, 'he chooses one of about fifteen. Upon this I took the liberty to tell my Lord Sunderland that no body could imagine that those ends could be answer'd by one of Mrs Tichborne's age and that I should think the conversation of such a one could not be agreeable to him; that it was marrying a kitten; and really I do think it is very odd for a wise man at forty-five* to come out of his library to play with puss'.

But her main objection—and here Sarah had a duty—was in the terms of the marriage-settlement, which appeared to prejudice the interests of Anne Sunderland's five children. With alarm their grandmother envisaged 'another brood of children†—beggars with the titles of lords & ladies—that can have nothing but what he almost robs his former children of'. As for Sarah's own grandchildren, she might yet live to see them 'come to London behind coaches, as the Duke of Bolton's children did, to get shoos & stockings from their Aunts'.[19] The more she thought about it, the more indignant she grew. How could he 'so soon forget the passionate expressions in his last dear wife's dying letter to be good and tender to her children?'[20]

Almost invariably with these marriage-settlements, she had found, one had but to scratch the surface to find a bishop; and in this one, sure enough, the abettor turned out to have been the Bishop of Norwich, 'a little mean churchman with a poor understanding'. And indeed, now that Sarah called him to mind she wryly realised that

---

* Sunderland in 1717 was 42. At his death his famous library went to Blenheim, in discharge of a debt. It was sold in the late nineteenth century.

† By his third wife, Judith Tichborne, Sunderland had two more sons and a daughter.

had it not been for her own influence with Queen Anne 'hee had not been a bishop god forgive me for it'.[21] In her letters to him she wastes no time beating about the bush. 'One thing is very sure', he is told, 'that she will be a kind of a Beauty at thirty yeares old when my Lord Sunderland is three score . . . I wish', she added, 'you had said more at first to discourage him from so wild a thought'.[22]

The settlement was amended and they married; and as with Cadogan so now with Sunderland, Sarah wrote off another friend. She searched for the tribute she had paid him years ago—'a man of the most open, undisguised, honest zeal for the interest of his country that could possibly be found'—and crossed it through;[23]* for now he was 'a furious madman without any principle',[24] and 'there was nothing base or foolish that hee ded not do'.[25] For his part Sunderland remained, on the surface, friendly; but his was a complex character, staunch in friendship but, as Swift had found, 'implacable towards those to whom he hath given greatest cause to complain'.[26] To fall foul of him was unwise.

The Duchess now began to discover that to a conscientious grandmother a large family can be a blessing or it can become a kind of hydra, so that no sooner has one member been dealt with but another springs up to threaten crisis or calamity. Now, to almost everyone's surprise, Permis Newcastle married Harriet Godolphin. In this case the settlement asked was £20,000,† and although Marlborough at first demurred and said he never gave more than ten, Sarah coaxed him to agree to it. The reception was at Marlborough House. Laughingly Sarah begged a favour of the bride, that the first day her lord did not go out with her, she would call for her in her fine, gold chariot to drive to Hyde Park. But nothing came of it, and when she did call it was only to sit in a dead way and be pumped for questions. The most she would volunteer was, 'How does my grandpapa?' She was a sad disappointment and had no child. As for her husband, he sided with the wrong people, 'being under a great enchantment by Sir John Vanbrugh' and a friend of Sunderland's. However, he had taken Harriet off her hands, though they were still more than full enough, for there was always her ailing lord, and there was Blenheim.

* At Blenheim. In the version at Althorp the same passage has not been deleted.

† The Duchess maintained that the original demand, via Vanbrugh, was for £40,000, and protested that her granddaughter was 'neither citizen nor monster'.

Marlborough was the better for the waters of Tunbridge, she had told Sunderland at the start of the settlement trouble, 'and hee is always the better for travelling and is so strong that yesterday, after having been at the building in the morning, hee went to see one of Sir John Vanbrugh's last follys, the old mannor hous, where hee went up a vast number of steps while I was glad to take my ease in a chair at the bottom of it. It is impossible for me to bee at this place', she adds, 'without being very melancholly, which has already cost £315,000* without one room in a condition to put a bed in; but the vast bridge in the air, without so much as a possibility to have watter, and the prodigious cavitys, as the workmen call them, which all the hills in the park cannot fill up,† is such a picture of maddnesse & folly as no person can discribe; & I am confydent that if Sr John had been continued in these works hee would have confounded as much mony as any tyrant ever wrackd from his subjects, without a possibility of finishing of it, as hee proposed, even at the expense of £70,000; for all the mony upon earth can't make watter stand in the summer in this sort of ground but in durty little spitts which would poyson the air'.[27]

It is unworthy of her, this defeatist pose; yet what visitor would guess, looking today from the triumphal arch she erected, across the serene lake to the bridge, that it was in spite of rather than because of her that the scene etched for Marlborough by his architect was allowed to become something more substantial and more lasting than a dream? Marlborough was never to see it as we see it, but he was big enough to imagine it and to make it possible.

People said that at Tunbridge he had not known them. At Blenheim he rode a little, talked a little, but the unconquerable Freeman Queen Anne had known had already, as it were, withdrawn into another world. In Kneller's portrait that still hangs at Blenheim he saw the armoured figure he dimly remembered he once was. He studied it sadly and was heard to murmur, 'This was once a man'. They told him the Earl of Oxford and Mortimer was about to stand

* This figure shows an unexplained increase of £55,000 on her last estimate, since when little had been done.

† The hill upon which Woodstock Manor had stood was levelled and the earth used for the causeway joining the bridge to the sides of the valley. Medieval masonry from the manor house was used for rubble filling inside the bridge.

his trial. They meant Harley, Robin the Trickster, the arrant tricking knave who had tricked him into exile. For more than two years he had been in the Tower and now, with Marlborough's help, might be sent to Hell. But what was the use of one invalid's tripping another? In agony from the gravel Harley made his last public speech:

For my own part, as I always acted by the immediate directions and commands of the late Queen and never offended against any known law, I am justified in my own conscience and unconcerned for the life of an insignificant old man; but I cannot without the highest ingratitude be unconcerned for the best of queens: a queen who heaped on me honours and preferments, though I never asked for them, and therefore I think myself under an obligation to vindicate her memory and the measures she pursued, to my dying breath . . . I shall lay down my life with pleasure in a cause favoured by my late dear royal mistress.[28]

It was a speech that 'fetched tears either of rage or compassion from the greatest of his enemies; the Duke of Marlborough himself saying that he could not but envy him that under such circumstances he could talk with so much resolution'.[29] But Harley was not to be executed. A fortuitous muddle in procedure led to his release, and he outlived Marlborough by two years. 'Lady Marlborough', Swift was told by Erasmus Lewis, 'is almost distracted that she could not obtain her revenge'.[30]

CHAPTER XI

The Crooked Scythe

1718-1722

———◆———

Sarah Duchess of Marlborough was of those who are sufficiently literal-minded to believe that genius amounts to no more than an infinite capacity for taking pains. Everything, she was convinced, from a lintel to a lawsuit could and must be rationalised and reduced to plain terms of sensible men and money; and this she would demonstrate to the world in law, in medicine and in architecture. The only mystery in architecture was what architects chose to invent. Now that she was rid of Wren, Vanbrugh and Hawksmoor (though the last would be recalled later),* she could, for the finishing of Blenheim, turn to her oracle James Moore; while a couple of gardeners—Charles Bridgman and John Hughes—could attend to the gardens.

Luckily for Blenheim, two of the master masons had left worthy successors—William Townsend and Bartholomew Peisley junior—and these, directed in the middle twenties by Hawksmoor, would make of the Long Library the noble apartment it is. Moore was a first-rate London cabinetmaker (his pierglasses and consoles still grace the Bow Window Room), who might have done better to stick to his trade. As clerk of the works John Desborough made a

---

* On April 17, 1722 Hawksmoor wrote to the Duchess: 'Your Grace, I am inform'd, is finishing the Bridge and other affairs . . . The Gallery will be a room of distinguished Beauty if rightly managed and on the other hand it may suffer much if it is not finished with Skill'. (BM add. ms 9123, ƒ 158). Evidently, when her amateurs reached the Gallery (Long Library) the Duchess found it essential for a professional to be recalled.

poor substitute for Henry Joynes. Except, then, for two good masons and a gardener (Bridgman was excellent), the works, like Anne's ministry in the Great Change, had become second-rate, and full of conundrums.

Among the discreeter withdrawals of front rank craftsmen had been that of Henry Wise, the 'royal' gardener. Like Wren, he was next to impossible to fall out with; so the Duchess wrote to him and he replied:

> I received your Graces letter last night and should have been very glad to have given your Grace the Draught or Lines of the Court and Causeway which your Grace requires, but those works being Sr John Vanbrugh's and Mr Hawksmoor's design, I never had any perfect Draught of them; and expecting for some time to have received your Graces Commands to wait on you at Blenheim I have forbore coming there, so that I have not been there since the Late Works began and therefore cannot say exactly what part is Sunk or Raised, Sr John himself having given the directions; but as to what your Grace fears of not having a free passage from and through the East and West Courts to the Great Court, I never understood but that Sr John always intended it should be so, and is I believe the present design.[1]

She supposed he meant to be helpful, but she was no clearer than she had been before. She had put a stop to the arcades intended for the bridge, demolished Woodstock Manor and called in an engineer, Armstrong,* to see to the canals and cascades beneath it. They must all work it out between themselves. For her part, in the intervals of stitching bed-curtains, she would come out to superintend. She could do no more. In the meantime of course the lampoonists had been busy and Sarah found this written on the back of a Thornhill sketch:

> "See, sir, here's the grand approach,
> This way is for his Grace's coach;

* Probably Colonel John Armstrong, who served with Marlborough and is painted with him in the double portrait which hangs in the third stateroom at Blenheim.

There lies the bridge and here's the clock,
Observe the lion and the cock,
The spacious court, the colonnade,
And mark how wide the hall is made!
The chimneys are so well design'd
They never smoke in any wind.
This gallery's contrived for walking,
The window's to retire and talk in;
The council chamber for debate,
And all the rest are rooms of state."

"Thanks, sir," cried I, "'tis very fine,
But where d'ye sleep, or where d'ye dine?
I find by all you have been telling
That 'tis a house, but not a dwelling." [2]

It was not the kind of wit that Sarah appreciated; nor did she smile at jests about the bridge—

The minnows, as through this vast arch they pass,
Cry, "How like whales we look, thanks to your Grace!" [3]

'The best thing I have heard since I came to this place', she told Craggs, 'is that the bridge in the air is decaying and I hope it will fall, for one may goe under it but never upon it, no more than one can goe into the moon'. She went on to tell him that Sir James Thornhill* was still offering to paint frescoes in the Saloon, although she had crossed swords with him over his charges for the Hall ceiling. 'I told Mr Thornhill', she added, 'that I was very sure that there never was a piece of painting of the size of that in the Hall even of Rubins or the greatest master that cost so much as this had don at the time that they were painted, tho they were of more value when they were dead. This hee would by no means agree to, and if I should have told him what I believe that there is no great value in his painting which is seen at such a distance from the eye as 78† feet hee would have thought me very ignorant and therefore I keept that to my self &

---

* Sir James Thornhill (1675–1734). His charge for the Hall ceiling at Blenheim was £987. For painting the ceiling of the Banqueting House, Whitehall, Rubens was paid the agreed sum of £3000.
† The actual height is 67 feet.

wee parted very civilly & I am to give him the Duke of Marlborough's resolutions in this affair in the winter. I am in some doubt
as to his great skill in painting, but I never saw any great man more
imposing then hee is in all that concerns his trade'.[4]

In the midst of all this the Duchess was suddenly summoned to
another Vanbrugh house, Claremont near Esher, where her granddaughter Harriet Newcastle was said to be critically ill. Arriving
before ten in the morning Sarah found Permis 'weeping very much
and really in so much sorrow that I believed there was no hopes of
her life, which made me', she owns, 'forget all my ill usage and I sat
down and wept with him'. The young Duchess of Newcastle, said
to be suffering from a malignant fever and attended by three doctors,
had in fact, according to her grandmother, nothing worse than 'a
sore throat taken in coming over the water at four a clock in the
morning from Hampton Court'.[5] Sarah was not allowed to see her
and was not even properly thanked. Driving back in her chaise she
felt rejected and desolate. What had been the use of rushing to the
rescue? Why expose oneself to indifference and ingratitude? She
retreated within herself and found little comfort. Long ago Maynwaring had written:

> One that enjoys so much health & that has nothing to ask of
> Fortune cannot fail of being tolerably happy any where with
> the blessing of so good a mind, and yours does really resemble
> the pleasant place you are in [Woodstock], where there are
> nothing but agreeable objects and plain natural Beauties, so that
> wherever you look into yourself you must allways be pleas'd &
> satisfy'd. This is the true reason why you can better bear to be
> alone than any one that I ever yet knew.[6]

If only it were so! And now, alone, as she had planned the
pilgrimage, so she must begin to make inventories and every kind
of provision for the move to Blenheim. Hitherto they had put up at
High Lodge, but now at last they were to take possession of the
house itself. She listed the plate, heading it: *To go to Woodstock 17
May, 1719*. But even that was anything but straightforward. The big
things—the cistern (1944 ounces), the lesser cistern (467 ounces), the
ice-pails, the large gold ewers, the fountain (420 ounces)—all these
were on the Blenheim scale and could be dumped there; but how

many dishes ought one to take, how many candlesticks, how many silver chamberpots? Though she meant to fill the attic storey with her friends it would be silly to overstock Blenheim and denude Marlborough House. She made a few quick notes: 'When I received the plate that belonged to the commander-in-chief from Mr Cadogan's servants, it was found that there was but 44 dishes, which by the indentures ought to have been 48 dishes . . . Candlesticks to be brought up to see . . . One chamber pot the French fashion & another of the same sort reckon'd in the Groom of the Stole's plate . . . A Tea Kettle & lamp bought at Lord Cadogan's auction'.

And that of course was only the beginning. The pictures and tapestries alone called for several secretaries to list them and a corps of carpenters to hang them: Madonnas by Raphael, Rubens, Van Dyck; Queen Anne's full-length portrait for the dining-room; the vast Van Dyck of Charles I on horseback, for the northern end of the Gallery; and two more women by Rubens, 'one taken in Adultry, the other in a Ruff'. Of the countless pieces of furniture she knew every stick and stitch, from the blue Indian-damask bed 'imbroider'd' for her own bedchamber to the 'Bedstead for a servant of Walnut-tree that looks like a Cabinet'. There were 'an Omber Table, 3 corner'd' and several black lacquer tables made by James Moore, who had his own room and closet with yellow serge hangings; and everywhere, even in the postilion heights, the beds* must be stuffed with 'good & sweet feathers, even for the servants'. For herself she kept an 'extream fine quilt stitched in all manner of colours, all work'd by Mrs Jennings's own Hands'.[7]

For Lady Anne Spencer's apartment Sarah had chosen hangings of 'sprigg'd Indian Callicoe with a border of strip'd green, red & white; the window curtains of white Birds Eye Dimetty'. She hoped she would like them, but in any case that would be of small consequence since she would soon be marrying Mr Bateman. It was vexing that, unlike her own children, Sarah's granddaughters, with one or possibly two exceptions, were unattractive if not downright plain.

* In the course of a lawsuit against Joynes in 1738 the Duchess refers to 'the great allowance he charged for the rent of his own house in Woodstock, tho there was a great room for keeping papers in the house [Blenheim] and 300 Beds at least'.

It had cost her £20,000 to marry Harriet; and now Anne, with her big nose and no-nonsense manner, looked like being just as awkward and costly. This Bateman the child had taken to (she had cried mightily when he was ill—a good sign) was not as rich as Sarah had been led to suppose. In fact he was worth only £200,000 or £9000 a year. 'I find his fortune is not so great as the town reported', she wrote to a go-between, but 'though there must bee mony to make a family easy, I shall allways prefer sence & vertue before the greatest estate or tittles'. As for her granddaughter, 'I have had so much experience', she added, 'of Lady Anne that I am perswaded that she has all the qualities of her dear mother'.[8] It was an opinion that was not to last.

However, the match was made and, with the wedding imminent, the family, in the summer of 1719, moved into Blenheim and did their utmost to enliven what Sarah had begun to call that wild, unmerciful house. By the autumn the grandchildren and their friends had mastered Dryden's *All For Love* sufficiently to perform it before Marlborough in Sarah's Bow Window Room. Lady Anne Spencer took the part of Octavia, her sister Di and cousin Anne Egerton playing Antony's children. Mark Antony, wearing Marlborough's sword, was Sarah's page, Humphrey Fish. Cleopatra was Lady Charlotte McCarthy. Sarah herself censored the love scenes and made it clear that there were to be no embraces. Bishop Hoadly* wrote a prologue. The players were much bejewelled and draped with the Genoese velvets and damasks not yet cut for curtains and covers. Marlborough was so delighted, there had to be three performances.

'I am mighty glad to hear the Duke of Marlborough has been so well all this summer at Blenheim', wrote Sunderland, now head of the Treasury, from Hanover, 'and that he has had so much satisfaction in seeing it made habitable. I pray God he may live long to enjoy it . . . I am glad the dear children are all well. I hope they will ever deserve your goodness & kindness . . . I wish I had had the happiness of being with you at Blenheim to have seen the play acted & to have heard that prologue spoke . . . I love you and your family beyond

---

* Benjamin Hoadly (1676–1761), successively Bishop of Bangor, Hereford, Salisbury and Winchester. An extreme latitudinarian. Never visited Bangor and probably not Hereford. (*D.N.B.*)

everything in this world. If you saw my heart you would believe me'.[9]

It was the kind of 'profession' Sarah had seen much of and in her long experience it meant nothing at all; 'having', as she said, 'had millions of professions under the hands of people I had obliged and some in very great places about court, all which I would sell for sixpence a piece'. In this case her cynicism was to be abundantly justified the following year.

1720 was the year of the South Sea Bubble, wildest of all speculations yet one from which, before it burst, Sarah with what Sir Winston calls her almost repellent common sense creamed something to the tune of £100,000. She was right of course in prophesying disaster,* and when it came, Sunderland, Craggs, Vanbrugh, Chandos and thousands more including the royal mistresses were more or less alarmingly involved.

Sarah was not sympathetic. On the contrary, she cried for vengeance, 'being', as she put it, 'always mighty averse to that scheme and wishing to have the directors punished'.[10] But while men are in power, as Dr Hare ventured to remind her, nothing is got by provoking them. On this occasion, as he happened to know, Sunderland had been driven to fury by 'continued provocations which he could no longer bear'; while 'as for Lord Cadogan, what your Grace says is very natural & pretty, but with submission I would not tell everybody I was robbed on the highway & describe the man if I thought that it would expose me to be robb'd again & perhaps murder'd by him'.[10]

No one gave more sensible advice, but it came too late. Sunderland and Cadogan had put their bludgeoned heads together and decided that their best defence was an attack on the Marlboroughs as Jacobites, the most farfetched charge that could be thought of, but at least it would be certain to enrage the Duchess. When the rumour first reached her she laughed at it. 'It appear'd so extreamly ridiculous', she wrote later, 'that I could not believe it, notwithstanding that at that time I had no opinion of my lord Sunderland's sincerity'. But the charge was more serious than she had supposed.

* When James Craggs senior suggested Marlborough should buy South Sea stock the Duchess told him, 'I had persuaded him to sell out of the South Sea and I would do all that I could to oppose his buying again'. (Blen. G-1-16. undated).

Looking back on the crisis the Duchess remembered 'the great struggle concerning the South Sea affairs and the punishing the Directors, upon which subject I used to talk very freely, thinking there was no way of recovering the credit of the nation but for the parliament to do as much justice as they could. My lord Sunderland hearing of this was in a great passion against me and in a very mad fit (for I don't know what else to call it) sent to the Duke of Marlborough to come to his house where, after he had made great professions to him, he fell upon me most bitterly, quite left out the Duke of Marl: in this plot, and told him that I carried on a treasonable correspondence abroad and that I had remitted a great sum of mony when the last fright of a Scotch invasion was I think from the Spaniards, and at that part of the discourse he held up his hand in a great fury and added that the King could prove it.

'When the Duke of Marlborough came home to me he gave me this whole account.* 'tis easy to believe that in his distemper anything of trouble has a great effect upon him. He was half dead when he came into the room, but before I knew what was the occasion of it I revived him with a great glass of strong wine and toast, upon which he had spirits to make this relation, but he was so ill when he went to bed that I sat up with him two or three hours and recovered him by a double dose of Sr Walter Rawleigh's cordial.†

'There is something so foolish & so barbarous in this proceeding that I know of no words that can express it . . . Knowing that there was no possibility of the King's knowing the truth but from myself, I went to the Duchess of Kendal‡ & desired she would do me the favour to obtain for me a very short audience of His Majesty, not letting her know what my business was'.

When the audience had been granted, Sarah took with her a letter

* When Marlborough returned from Lord Sunderland's Sarah was, according to Lady Blayney, playing ombre with the Duke of Buckingham and Lady Burlington. Next day Sarah asked Lady Blayney's mother to accompany her to the royal drawing-room and to observe the King's face closely, since she herself was shortsighted. (Blen E. 49).

† Sarah's favourite remedy for everything and especially for smallpox. Its 31 ingredients included ambergris, to be ground by a strong man. The prescription is at Blenheim (Blen G-I-17).

‡ Née Schulenberg. George I's favourite mistress at this time.

and gave it to the King, who was gracious and 'looked very good-natured . . . And as I was going away', her account continues, 'the Duchess open'd the door and in a mighty obliging manner took me by the hand and desired me to go in to the King, which I excused saying that by no means I would not trouble His Majesty anymore at that time. This I think was the simplest [stupidest] thing that I ever did in my life or that any body could do, for had I gone in then I dare say the King would have told me that he had never heard of any accusation against me, but I was delighted to think that I had done my business effectually in giving my letter into his own hand, not reflecting that my lord Sunderland & others could make him in a minute do what they pleased, & it being an awkward thing to me to talk by an interpreter to two persons that I had never had any conversation with, I indulged my self in the ease of going away. How wrong that was, the King's letter will show . . . after he was advised what he should answer. By what I have heard of this matter', she concludes, 'I believe they did not even then tell him that I was in this terrible plot, but that I was a madwoman & that I did him a great deal of mischief'.[11]

George I's note, in answer to hers, was brief:

17 December, 1720

Whatever I may have been told upon your account, I think I have shown on all occasions the value I have for the services of the Duke your husband; and I am always disposed to judge of him and you by the behaviour of each of you in regard to my service. Upon which I pray God, my Lady Marlborough, to preserve you in all happiness.[12]

It was far from satisfactory. 'I think His Majesty seems to be satisfied with the Duke of Marlborough's and my past services', Sarah comments, 'and to desire the continuance of them; but the middle part of the letter is very haughty & what I know to be my Lord Sunderland's style, and therefore I thought it best not to write any more to the King'.

She might do better, she thought, to write to the mistress and so she did, at the same time apologising to anyone who might after-wards read it for its sycophantic tone: expressions which went much against her inclination, 'but those', she explains, 'are things of form, and they say one must thank kings even when they injure one, and tell them that one is mortified to the last degree upon things that are so preposterous that they can only make one laugh . . . You will observe', she points out, 'that I don't name my Lord Sunderland in either of my letters, but I thought it not amiss to name Secretary Craggs, having heard that the King was of a humour not to believe anything to the prejudice of another if it came from their enemy, and I knew Craggs was in all my Lord Sunderland's councils and was wicked enough to do anything'.[13]

As she had implored Queen Anne so now she begged her successor for a chance to vindicate herself and as before she was to be denied. To the King she described herself as 'the most unhappy of all your Majesty's faithful subjects', and to the Duchess of Kendal she offered to defy the whole world; throwing in for good measure the information that she had not allowed Craggs [junior] to speak to her for nine years. To her dismay she found that neither King nor Duchess would show a glimmer of interest. She was left with silence, which in itself might have taught her not to lay herself open to dusty answers.

She found little satisfaction in Blenheim, 'so vast a place that it tires one allmost to death to look after it and to keep it in order'; and the very year they moved in, the Barons of the Exchequer gave their verdict in favour of the workmen: the debt was the Duke's and not the crown's. For this verdict the Duchess blamed Vanbrugh and his friend 'Old Craggs', once her only true friend with understanding but now as ill a man as ever she knew. She appealed of course, but before the appeal had been heard and lost, both Craggs, father and son, had died. The handsome son, praised by Pope, was thirty-four when he died of smallpox in February, 1721. A month later his father, who had been so faithful to the Marlboroughs in their exile, died from an overdose of laudanum.

The Duchess wrote to the Earl of Carlisle:

The counsel on Sr John's side laid great weight upon my Lord Treasurer Godolphin's warrant to Sir John Vanbrugh, and the Judges ran into that very willingly, for to my certain knowledge two of them were gained by old Craggs' interest & artifices. I thank God he is now no more able to do any mischief, and the Parliament seem to be dissatisfied with his illgotten estate & have a mind to recover what they can of it for the use of the unfortunate South Sea people. I know it was very difficult to get the better of Mr C when he was living, but perhaps his ghost may not have so much influence upon the members of Parliament.[14]

At the appeal, as at the first hearing, everything turned upon the warrant Vanbrugh had been granted by Godolphin at the beginning of the works. The Marlboroughs denied all knowledge of it, but Vanbrugh, in a long document referred to by the Duchess as his libel, wrote:

Will any one believe that in so many quiet, fireside, evening Conferences as happen'd between those two great Lords and her Grace, the manner and method of receiving in & laying out those Hundreds of Thousands of Pounds should never be part of the Amusement? Sure there's some great forgetfullness in this matter.[15]

At the cost of much chaff from fellow-members of the Kit-Cat Vanbrugh had, at fifty-five, married Henrietta Yarburgh, a great-niece of Margaret Blagge and second cousin to Harriet Newcastle. 'I find all his works are large', writes Lady Lechmere,* of Vanbrugh, to Sarah, 'for I hear his Child is ye biggest that ever was seen of its age. I think you may ye easier forgive him his vast designs at Bleinheim since it appears to be so much ye tendency of his Nature'.[16] And in the following month she returned to the same theme:

I hear you are about finishing ye Bridge. I hope it pleases as well as employs you, for I believe you don't proceed in ye manner Sr John did, but calculate an end of your labours, which is an agreeable thought in ye progress of them. For by what I have heard you say, some parts of Bleinheim were so vast in ye designs that tho' they were form'd by a man, they ought to have

---

* Daughter of the Earl of Carlisle. Married (i) Lord Lechmere, whom Sarah called 'the worst man that ever I knew in my life'; (ii) Sir Thomas Robinson, who completed Vanbrugh's Castle Howard asymmetrically so that the west wing is out of keeping with the rest. 'It is impossible to hear and see him', wrote Sarah of Sir Thomas, 'without thinking she must have been mad'. She [Lady Lechmere] gambled, borrowed from Sarah, and died in 1739.

been executed by ye Gods, if one could hope to have seen them finished; and since Jupiter has forgot to come down among us, as one has heard he has sometimes done, Sr John is not quite so proper a builder for this Age as he might have been when ye Gods were in better humour & made nothing of a jant from Heaven to Erth, as I have been told.[17]

Any disparagement of Sir John was welcome, Sarah's own attitude towards Blenheim now hovering between the cynical and the sardonic. That a man should have to pay for a building to compliment himself was the most bizarre thing she had ever heard of; although, as she added, she could never 'enter into ye flattery of having the publick finish it. I was always contented', she told her counsel, Pengelley, 'that that misfortune should fall upon ye Duke of Marlborough as a punishment for having consented that Sr John should have ye management of it'. She reminded him of all she had gone through with Vanbrugh; and even now she was faced with the labours of Hercules to finish a building in which she never had nor ever could have any pleasure.[18]

This her friends found hard to understand. 'Tho' I know Dear Lady Dutchess is not fond of being at Blenheim', wrote Mrs Clayton, 'yet I must own I cannot help admiring of it extremely & wondering you don't like it more; but maybe that may be from my never having had any of those uneasinesses that I believe always attend great Grandure'.[19] The woman was a fool and Sarah had her to thank too for having introduced their 'sacred domestick', the obsequious chaplain Dean Jones, at this moment at whist with Marlborough, who found him witty. Laguerre had caricatured the fellow on a wall of the Saloon . . . The Duchess was watching him. But Marlborough was failing. It was worth much to be able to keep him entertained.

'I hope My Dear Grandfather finds Blenheim air agree with Him as well as this does with me', Henrietta's son Willigo, now twenty, wrote to Sarah from Amsterdam, where he was enjoying the pictures and the canals with Sunderland's heir, Lord Spencer, 'extremely kind and good-natured, which you know he has by inheritance from his mother'. Their governor or tutor, Mann, had, it seemed, to be apologised for. 'There is not an honester man breathes upon the earth', Willigo assured his grandmother, 'and I am sure what faults there were in his behaviour were owing purely & unavoidably to a Scholar's education which hindered him from knowing enough the rules of politeness & behaviour'. Mann never missed an opportunity 'to speak with all the most passionate tenderness & fondness imaginable for the memory of one Dear Person that he formerly belong'd to, Whom You will guess but too well without naming him'.*[20] Yes indeed, the loss of a son is a wound that can never heal. And now Willigo's companion, Robert Spencer, was hurriedly sent for; his father, Lord Sunderland, had suddenly died.

Sarah acted promptly but, it seemed, not promptly enough. Sunderland's study was sealed and everything locked until the heir should return; but to her consternation court officials marched in, broke seals, demanded keys and, in the King's name, helped themselves to whatever they pleased. If she had at the time any inkling of what was behind it, she kept it to herself. She suspected them, she says, of conniving in the South Sea swindle in which Sunderland had been involved, and was even prepared to believe that they stole cash; but she says nothing of Atterbury,† whose Jacobite plot was in fact the chief cause of the excitement. Sunderland died on April 19th and it was not till May 8th that the plot became public and arrests were made. 'There can be little doubt', says Professor Plumb, 'that Sunderland had been in close negotiation with Atterbury before his death'.[21]

The Duchess had her own notions. To explain why Robert Spencer had inherited at his father's death nothing but debts she says this was by no means Sunderland's intention, but 'upon a terrible struggle there was at the South Sea time in the House of Lords, the Court & he [Sunderland] were very much frighted & to prevent sad things being discovered he parted with his own mony to bribe the Parliament that it might be done with more secrecy & quicker than

* Nicholas Mann had been tutor to the Marlboroughs' son Jack, 1st Marquis of Blandford, who died in 1703.

† Francis Atterbury, Bishop of Rochester (1662–1732) and Dean of Westminster. Succeeded Aldrich as Dean of Christ Church. Friend of Pope, Swift and Addison who called him one of the greatest geniuses of his day. Convicted of treason and banished, he left England in 1723 and died abroad.

Arthur Maynwaring. Kneller

Sir John Vanbrugh. Attributed to Thomas Murray

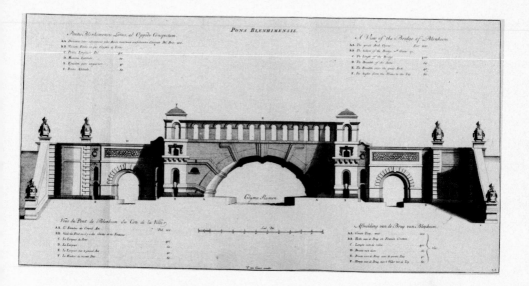

Blenheim: Vanbrugh's Grand Bridge, as planned with arcaded
superstructure and eighty-foot towers

Blenheim: the canal-and-pool scheme west of Vanbrugh's truncated
bridge. The project supervised by the Duchess in the seventeen-twenties

Blenheim: The Kent-Rysbrack monument in the chapel. The first Marquis
of Blandford stands next to his father, John first Duke of Marlborough

Marlborough House: South elevation overlooking St. James's Park

Blenheim: the Column of Victory

Lady Henrietta Churchill
(afterwards second Duchess of Marlborough). Kneller

Francis second Earl of Godolphin. Kneller

Lady Mary Churchill (afterwards Duchess of Montagu). Kneller

Diana Duchess of Bedford. Attributed to Thomas Hudson

Sarah Duchess of Marlborough. Kneller. The Petworth portrait

Charles Seymour sixth Duke of Somerset. Kneller

Elizabeth third Duchess of Marlborough (née Trevor). Artist unknown

Charles Spencer (afterwards third Duke of Marlborough)
as a Roman consul. Stephen Slaughter

Lady Anne Bateman. Enoch Seeman

The Honourable John Spencer with his son, the first Earl
Spencer, and their negro servant Caesar Shaw. Knapton

from the Treasury from whence he was paid again, but he died before that was done'.[22]

Whatever the truth of it, this was a tragic time at Althorp. Sunderland had loved his son and yet now, Robert at his homecoming must set to and reckon his father's debts. The list in his handwriting is at Blenheim: 'Debts for building the Library, and booksellers—£3000 . . . South Sea Bonds—£20,000 . . .' and so on. He made the total £101,000. For himself, as his grandmother put it, he could not have a silver spoon without paying for it; and the Sunderland Library, which he could not bear to sell,* was packed off to Blenheim to compensate Marlborough for what Sunderland had owed him.

But Marlborough himself was now on his deathbed at Windsor Lodge. Garth was dead and so other doctors attended while Sarah, in Sir Winston's unforgettable phrase, prowled around his couch like a she-bear guarding its slowly dying mate, and tearing all, friend or foe, who approached.[23] And what could be more fitting, what more redolent of predestination, than that a great man's great descendant should, though centuries later, write of his life and of his death? Shadows fall upon shadows, so that even as one reads Sir Winston's words, thoughts inevitably dwell upon his own going, however timewasting and futile such thoughts may be:

> The span of mortals is short, the end universal; and the tinge of melancholy which accompanies decline and retirement is in itself an anodyne. It is foolish to waste lamentations upon the closing phase of human life. Noble spirits yield themselves willingly to the successively falling shades which carry them to a better world or to oblivion.[24]

Writing of Marlborough's death, in her Green Book,† Sarah says she thought her soul was tearing from her body. She had never

---

* 'I hope his father's estate will come out . . . considerable enough to prevent his books from being sold, for if they are worth what is said, near £30,000, I must own I think that too much to part with for a curiosity when his own estate is small & so many younger children that I am desirous to make easy'. (Sarah to Mrs. Clayton, 1722. Blen G-I-16).

† The Duchess of Marlborough's account of the shortcomings of her children and grandchildren. It was originally bound in green vellum. (Blen G-I-9).

needed comfort more, and yet those who might have given it—her daughters Henrietta and Mary—though present, were estranged from her and 'like enemies that would report to others whatever I did in a wrong way . . . I desired Mrs Kingdon to go to them', Sarah continues, 'and tell them that I did not know what disorder it might give their father to go to him now . . . but I begged of them that they would not stay long in the room because I could not come in while they were there, being in so much affliction.* Mrs Kingdon† delivered this message & she told me that the Duchess of Montagu answered that she did not understand her, but that if she meant that they were not to see their mother, they were very well used to that.

'They stayed a great while, as I thought, and not being able to be out of the room longer from him, I went in though they were there & kneel'd down by him. They rose up when I came in & made curtseys but did not speak to me; & after some time I called for prayers. When they were over I asked the Duke of Marlborough if he heard them well & he answered yes & he had joined in them'. After which he was carried to the bed in his own room where, adds Sarah, to her great surprise, both daughters followed with young Harriet Newcastle, so that the small room, containing a duke, four duchesses, five grandchildren, surgeons, doctors, apothecaries and servants, was pretty full. Sarah dismissed the children, but neither that, nor her message by Mrs Kingdon, could make the others stir. 'Upon which', says the Duchess, 'I desired Grace‡ to go to the Duchess of Montagu & tell her that for many days I had been mightily harass'd & I must lie down, & I desired her to go into another room with the other two. She answered, "Will our being here hinder her from lying down?" Then I sent Grace to her again to ask her if she had such an affliction & was in my condition whether she would like to have me with her. She said no, but did not go out till I sent to her a third time, & then they all three went out of the

---

* In another version Sarah writes: 'I could have said a great deal to him had not such cruel people been by'. (Blen G-1-17).

† Mrs Kingdon, the Duchess of Marlborough's companion. She afterwards lived with Sarah's granddaughter Diana Duchess of Bedfod.

‡ Grace Ridley, Sarah's favourite servant. She was the daughter of an Oxford-shire vicar.

room & the Duchess of Newcastle went quite away but the others stayed in the drawingroom & hall till four in the morning'.[25]

For some hours Marlborough lay in a coma and died with the dawn of June 16th, in his seventy-third year. For his duchess there was to be no comfort, as she said there had been for Queen Anne, in the funeral arrangements; and her distress was increased by rumours from London, where the town talk was that she had illtreated her daughters at Windsor Lodge, while their father was dying; and that Dean Jones had written to Walpole to ask if the King would pay for Marlborough's funeral. The daughters she would deal with later. Jones she would dismiss; and the funeral of course she would pay for herself.

Dean Jones she was glad to be rid of, she had never liked him. Even Mrs Clayton who had recommended him now owned he had abundance of intolerable great faults; and Lady Lechmere was delighted that he had given himself away. 'I allways believed his being poor & sometimes making the Duke of Marlborough laugh (for he would now & then say a comical thing) was ye reason you bore with him, but I must repeat it again that I am heartily glad accident has shown you what he is, that your compassion to him may cease, & if there are any other people in ye world that are false to you I am earnest & zealous in my wishes that they may be discovered . . . & if we were to stand up for ye honour of our nation in looking for true Englishmen, we must find them in ye silent Tombs. This is a mellancholly prospect for posterity'.[26]

It would have been a melancholy prospect for Dean Jones had it not been for the curious practice in the Marlborough family of taking in each other's dismissed servants. By this system Henrietta had only to have a dishonest footman jailed for her mother to fly to the prison and bail him out; and by the same token, although the household of the new young Duchess of Marlborough (as Henrietta Godolphin now was) was too unorthodox even for Dean Jones to find sanctuary there, she sent him £100, which maddened the dowager and sent the dean into transports. Her noble bounty, as he called it, had reached him by the hand of 'Sr John Van Brugg' and had wellnigh stunned him. As for the note that had accompanied it, 'I find myself', he assured her, 'altogether unable in the least to express ye very transporting sense I have of it; in my whole life I never read anything so transcendently Benigne and Good, for every line breathes the most condescending sweetnesse, ye most emphaticall Goodnesse . . . And I shall constantly & earnestly beseech The Infinite Goodnesse', he concluded, 'which only could Inspire so Divine a likenesse in your Grace's breast, to give & continue to Your Grace all the Blessings of this Life, that you may long enjoy the most comfortable Reflection of your owne Good Actions here & the certaine Reward of them in a Blissfull Eternity'.[27]

In the opinion of the new Duchess's mother, to whom the letter was mistakenly delivered, this amounted to 'something like blasphemy in comparing her to God'. Luckily she did not see the Dean's other letter to her page, Humphrey Fish, asking for the return of a book she had borrowed—Pliny's *Panegyric of Trajan*. The note ended: 'I pray God to give her a Better Temper'.[28]

The lying-in-state was to be at Marlborough House and the temporary burial in Westminster Abbey, since the chapel at Blenheim, Marlborough's ultimate destination, was far from finished. 'Here is a pompous funeral preparing', wrote Vanbrugh to Lord Carlisle, 'but curb'd & crippl'd by her Grace, who will govern it by her fancys . . . I don't know whether it won't cost her Ten Thousand pounds. What a Noble monument wou'd that have made, whereas this Idle Show will be gone in half an hour & forgot in two days. The other wou'd have been a Show & a Noble one to many future Ages. I shew'd the Young Dutchess what your Lordship writ about so great a Fortune falling into such generous hands; which she took mighty well. She says Covetousness has happen'd to appear to her so very odious in some other people that she is sometimes frightened lest she shou'd have seeds in her blood that may spring up one time or other . . . This Will was made but in March last & hurts nobody but her. I don't find however that either she or my Lord Godolphin have the least disposition to dispute it, and I hope nobody else will . . . Her Grace has by this Will (for to be sure that was her doings) made my Lord Blandford independent of his Father & Mother, depriv'd her Daughter of the Jewells & cater'd bravely for herself . . . The whole amounts to a great deal above two millions . . . 'tis a great pitty, as your Lordship observes, that the Duke made no disposition to publick uses, the want of which reflects cruelly upon him . . .' And to his old friend Tonson of the Kit-Cat Vanbrugh wrote: 'He has given his Widdow (may a Scotch Ensign get her) £10,000 a Year to Spoil Blenheim her own way, and £12,000 a Year to keep her Self clean, and go to Law'.[29]

'They say', wrote Dean Jones naughtily to a friend, 'that the Duke has left a letter seald, with the Lord Cadogan, not to bee opend till after his funerall, commissioning his Lordship to dispose of 60,000 l which hee had in the bank of Holland, towards the relief of soldiers' widows that were killed under his Grace's command; but I have some reason to look upon this as satyrical banter'.[30]

It was not etiquette for the widow to attend the funeral. Sarah sent her black coach* containing the Duke of Montagu as chief mourner, to be followed by eight other dukes and a long procession of soldiers and horses, not forgetting the 'Horse of Honour, richly caparisoned, led with a silken Rein by Captain Fish in his Military Mourning, walking on foot'.[31]

'I cannot help touching upon the Melancholy Ceremony that was perform'd yesterday', an eyewitness reported to the Duchess, 'nothing could be finer nor better executed, no disorder whatever, nor one Stop from the beginning to the End; and Everybody agreed that the Musick that Bononcini made was the finest & the most proper for the occasion that could be immagined. A more Generall concern was never seen. Even the Mobb were touch'd for the loss of the Glorious Assertor of their Liberties. Notwithstanding my Lady Scarborough died so lately, Lord Scarbrough attended and march'd all the way with his Regiment . . .'[32]

Other observers sent other accounts. One had noticed that, contrasting with his glossier brethren, the Dean of Winchester was wearing an old black coat grown grey with years. Sarah, taking her cue it might be from Henrietta, sent him £100, 'at which, astonisht', she was told, 'he repeated the words "a hundred pounds?" Then vail'd his Reverend Hatt and slowly raising it up to his melting Eyes he with true Devotion ask't God's Blessing on your Bounty'.[33]

A third informant had been invaluable in checking everything and, doubtless in the privacy of a black coach, noting it down. It was thus that the bill for the funeral (£5265 if household-mourning was

* The Duchess found herself charged for 48 yards of black cloth to line and cover the mourning coach and 6 for harness, 'which', she said 'is enough to cover my Garden'. (Madresfield, p. 149).

included) came by its endorsements showing that no fewer than seven trumpeters and two chaplains charged for had simply not been there; while 'ffeathers for the horses' had been invoiced twice over.[34] Everyone said Bononcini, in the anthem, had been good, but he was expensive. For a similar engagement the Duchess of Buckingham had paid him £100 and so, Francis Godolphin advised his mother-in-law, they had better do the same, 'tho had there not been that precedent for it, perhaps half the sum would have been very thankfully accepted'.[35]

The Duchess, after sending for Bishop Hopkins' *Death Disarmed of Its Sting*, turned her attention to her recalcitrant daughters. It had been more than unkind of Providence to take her favourites, Anne Sunderland and Elizabeth Bridgwater, and leave her with two duchesses, Henrietta Marlborough and Mary Montagu, both of them self-willed and intolerant and impossible to live amicably with. Henrietta at this moment was at Bath with Congreve; but Sarah had long since desisted from warning both daughters against low company. Mary was almost as bad. From her youth she had been immodest, followed by a train of fops as she walked of an evening in St James's Park, or sitting at an assembly 'with many fine ladys in a row as if it were a market for sail', a habit that invited sniggers. Sarah herself, at basset, had overheard a beau say, 'Here will bee fine doings ere it bee long I'le warrant you', or to that purpose.[36] She was scandalised. What had she done to deserve such children? 'I chalenge all the world', she wrote sadly, 'to shew a woman that has don what I have don for all my children from their birth, & loved them so many yeares notwithstanding their terrible usage of me, all which time I loved them enough to have dyed to have saved their lives & to have made them hapy.'[37]

It was a tragic situation if, in an extreme form, a familiar one; for it was not in the big things that Sarah had failed her children but in the small ones, as their tearstained scrawls at Blenheim still show. Mary, when a child, for example, was forever mislaying her clogs. 'I can't help thinking my case very hard', she writes to her mother (and why should she have to write?) 'that you will give me over for so small a thing & which is not my fault, for if I should buy a pair every day I should never have any, for the moment I take them off they are lost. So I don't know what to say since it is not in my power to say what I would, that you should never see me without them any more; but since you won't have me ask you to go out, I am sure I shall have very little ocasion for clogs. I believe you could not be so angery with me for this but that you are angery for so many other things that if I should begin to speak of now I should never have don, so I will say no more but that since you have been so angery with me I have been so misarable that I have wish'd & pray'd for nothing so much as to dy that I might be no trouble to my dear mama & I hope much happier my self'.[38]

And later, 'I am so unfortunate that you take so many things ill of me without saying what . . . I think I always make a chursy or a bow when I see you, and that I ought not to be taken out of Bedlam if I could think it not reasonable to doe so'.[39]

And her sister Henrietta: 'I was the gladdest in the world to receive a letter from my Dear Mama, little thinking upon my word it would bee such a one as I found it, and ever since I have read it I have allmost wished myself dead . . . Dear Mama reproaches mee so much about the company I keep. I really know but of one that you yourself can dislike and hee is one that the people you think best off are very often with . . .'[40] And later, 'Anything that I can do as long as I live I shall never think too much if my dear Mama were but satisfied, which I can't but think she would easily bee if she did but remember she was once of my age her self'.[41]

It surprised only Sarah when her 'poppets' grew into wilful, eccentric, unmanageable women. 'Go tell the fool', Henrietta is reported to have said, 'that I have got him an heir'.[42] And the wilder she became, the tamer and steadier seemed her husband Francis, the worthy offspring of 'Patricio' Godolphin and the saintly Margaret Blagge.

When Sarah's friends reported to her the account London had had of the deathbed scene at Windsor she pronounced it a monstrous distortion. As the gossip ran, Henrietta and Mary, with young Harriet in tow, had been offered nothing to eat or drink, had been treated throughout abominably and all but turned out of doors before their father's death. Sarah wrote and re-wrote her account *in extenso*; she went further. With the help of grandchildren and servants she reconstructed the scene in a full-scale post mortem, though without of course Marlborough and the three duchesses;

and there was close interrogation as to the parts they had all played. Thus—'Mr ffyshe was the first person they saw & that helped them out of the coach. They asked him how their father did . . . Little Di said that she ran to meet them & went with them to the diningroom where she asked if they would have any wine and bread . . . Mrs Kingdon said she sat in the window . . . about two in the morning & that I came down to fetch a cordial & begged of her that if she would do anything for me as long as she lived that she would go out & go to bed . . .'[43] and so on for many long pages.

There had of course to be a scapegoat and the Duchess decided it must be Mrs Kingdon. Either she had muddled her message to the duchesses, when Sarah begged them not to stay, or else—worse and more probable—she had softened it, for she was far too much inclined to take their part. She was even suspected of having shrugged. 'All that malice can invent', protested Mrs Kingdon, 'is only that I made some motion that they interpret their own way. I know of no such motion I made* . . . There is nothing I would not do to obtain your pardon . . . I thought I had found in your Grace every thing that was desirable in a freind & I had no aprehensions of loseing you unless by my own fault. I had for a long time treated you with all the respect & distance that was your due & it was by your own repeated commands I had laid it quite aside & lived with you as with the kindest freind . . .'[44] As for Sarah's daughters, Mrs Kingdon could not think it wrong to wish that they might yet all live in amity with each other, nor that Sarah would object to its being said that the two duchesses, particularly Henrietta, whom Mrs Kingdon loved and who had done a thousand obliging things for her, had a great many virtues and might one day see and mend their faults.

'With this way of thinking', Mrs Kingdon concluded, 'it was natural to say I wished that what faults they had could have been concealed even from you, & if that was not possible, at least from all the rest of the world, for when once things of this nature are made publick a reconcilement is almost impossible . . . nor could I believe it necessary for your vindication'.[45]

This was disloyal thinking and she must go; but it was Mrs King-

* A version in Sarah's hand reads: 'She ded not know what interpretation could bee made of a motion in her shoulders . . . I do think that a shrugg upon this occation is more malicious then any thing that can bee said'. (Blen G-I-17).

don herself who insisted on the last candid interview, when Sarah calmly told her that she had not the same pleasure in her she had once had, 'for tho I beleivd she could never do anything that she thought wrong, & was more agreeable then most people, I thought she could not bee so good a friend as I could bee'. And so, for that and other reasons, the friendship had to end. Sorrowfully Sarah told her, 'since friends were so hard to bee found I must content my self in doing what I knew my self was right without minding what people said'.[46] The woman had even found nerve enough to say that if the poor Duke of Marlborough were still living he would have been on her side! That certainly made it easier to write her off with a light heart.

Directly their last interview had ended, as in the more celebrated case of Queen Anne, of which in this there were echoes, the Duchess sat down and wrote it all out, 'having been so often represented as a very cholerick & angery person; Mrs Kingdon has the good luck to have an other charecter of being all goddnesse & sence'. Come to think of it, she had only tolerated her for her conversation, and that one could always cull from books. As for the dropping of her, it was so gentle and Mrs Kingdon 'had softened her self so much at parting that when I waited upon her to the door she desired to take leave of me with a kiss'.[47]

There was only one thing that still rankled a little with the Duchess and that was the suggestion that she had made her family quarrels public. 'It is not my fault', she protested, 'I was not the aggressor, & am the mother, & by the long patience which I have had I have shewn that nothing but what human nature neither can nor ought to bear could have made me complain of children to any body but a friend in private. There are not many people yet that know this story, but as many as do, weep and tell me that I ought not to trouble my self, having done what I could to prevent these misfortunes, and every body that is good I believe wishes that my children may see their errors and repent'.[48]

The Duchess reached for her Green Book.

CHAPTER XII

Provocations and Proposals

1722-1727

———◆———

The Duchess of Marlborough's Green Book was a book that could not easily be put down; and this applied to the writer as well as to the reader. In spite of gout—'I have no strength in my hands but my heart is as good as any body's'[1]—she wrote rapidly, yet so thickly did events crowd upon her widowhood, incident upon incident, outrage upon outrage, that she could not close the green covers without hearing and having to note yet more distressing news of her family.

The full title of the book—*An Account of the Cruell Usage of my Children*—barely did it justice, since several sons-in-law and grand-children played prominent parts. It was written, she explained, with reluctance and only for particular friends, to vindicate herself and to make them judge of her patience and sufferings; and let it be said at once that almost without exception the reactions of those carefully chosen friends were all she had hoped for. They were, so they told her, appalled; though whether in fact her family squabbles could mean more to them than the bickerings of sparrows or something to smile at, was not her concern. What she wanted was their shocked sympathy and that they readily gave.

Sarah is seldom dull. When her theme is humdrum, the detail is still likely to sparkle. When things seem at their worst she will suddenly rally and mend her mood; as when Henrietta Godolphin calls for her in her chariot and they drive to Hyde Park. 'She did not call me till it was almost dark and I remember we met the company coming out of the Ring. However I never reproached her, loving

234

her and seeing her of a careless temper, and we sang all the way'.[2]

This is poignant; and indeed it was sad that her sufferings, no matter how well earned nor how trifling to others, were real. 'Tis not to be expressed', she writes in old age, 'how much I suffered before I could overcome the tenderness I had in my heart for them; but thank God I am now at ease as to that matter, and if I have done any thing wrong I am sorry for it . . . and if there is any mother that has had more patience I wish I could see her, for I have yet met with no such person'.[3]

The Green Book, then, is something more than a venting of spleen; it is a Domesday, a book of judgment from which nothing has been omitted, from the youngest daughter's childhood—'She would often snap me up'—to the death of Marlborough, not forgetting a postscript to include 'that very great hypocrite' Dean Jones. *En route* we attend assemblies, go to the opera or stay at home while the masquerade comes to us.* We meet the sons-in-law: Francis Godolphin in tears for his wife's shortcomings; Montagu stout and loyal ('If I liked not to see his wife, he liked it better'); and Sunderland the sorrowing widower who soon married again and came out of his library to play with puss.

There is Henrietta as a child with smallpox (Sarah nursed her through it); Henrietta as a young wife living with her husband and babies at Sarah's lodgings in St James's; and Henrietta with Congreve and Gay, 'the worst company a young lady could keep'.† There is Mary Montagu offending Lady Hervey in 1711 (Sarah took Mary's part; the rift lasted for years); and Mary inviting her father to meet

---

* The masquerade when one of the mummers disguised as a monk warned Sarah that she might be harbouring her own estranged daughters in disguise. Although he denied it, Sarah was convinced that the monk was Craggs junior and never spoke to him again.

† 'I am setting just now before her picture when a child', Sarah writes to Mrs Clayton in 1722, of Henrietta, 'which has a gentle good natur'd look as ever I saw & it amazes me to think that such a face, with such kindnesses as I have express'd to her, could bee made by ill company such a creature as she is now. This shews that the saying does not allways hold that put nature out with a pitch forke it will come in again, for I am sure there can never bee any alteration in her for the better after so many yeares'. (9 Oct., 1722. Blen G-I-16).

her friends, including Vanbrugh (or so Sarah guessed) in 1721. There
are storms and absurdities and a great many tears and hysterics of the
kind known to have been cured at one stage or another by a good
spanking.

In the farce over Harriet's mourning for Lady Waldegrave
Arabella's daughter by James II) we learn of Marlborough's disapproval (and of course Sarah's) of mourning for all royal bastards
and their connections: 'And if the Duchess of Cleveland and the
Duchess of St Albans don't mourn for such sort of relations, they
have very few to mourn for'. And in the still more trivial incident
of the cup of tea we get an insight into children's upbringing in the
reign of Anne.

This was when Sarah, on the verge of exile in 1712, made her
grandchildren raffle for diamonds and afterwards gave them tea. 'I
called for some tea and milk to please the children', she remembers,
'and at the second cup they told me that Mama [Henrietta] had said
they should drink but one cup, upon which I made the second half
milk and said they might drink it, for I would take it upon me that
it should do them no hurt . . . The next day when I was melting in
tears at the thought of parting from my children & to go in a packet-
boat to Flanders I received a letter from Lady Godolphin:

> Dear mama you have bid mee allways when I took any thing
> ille to tell you, and I can not help for severall reasons beeing
> concerned that after the children said I had told em not to drink
> two cups of tea, that you made em, for I remember wee was
> allways brought up to know what you said to us was law, as I
> think it was very fitt it should bee to all children, and that they
> should bee brought up to think so, and since it cant bee of any
> use to their health, and may make em venture, and sertinly will,
> to do other things that I forbid, I hope you will grant this request
> from your most Dutyfull Daughter.

A tactless note, one might think, to tear up or even to smile at, but
humourlessness on both sides did nothing to help; nor did, many
years later, Henrietta's cold note to her mother, within a month of
Marlborough's death, crudely signed 'Marlborough'. Towards the
end of Marlborough's life both sides had appealed to him. Sarah, in
her role of kindest of mothers, knew how to make her case and to

shape his answers, herself dashing off a letter to which in a shaky hand he might add one sorrowful line. 'I am sure it is my duty not to complain of her', Mary wrote to him, 'but I believe she will tell you herself some things she has done to me that were never done before by a mother kind or unkind'.[4]

After Marlborough's death there was of course even less hope of a lasting reconciliation, so that mother and daughters settled into a chronic state of mutual disgust which did no good to anyone. 'I have seen such behaviour from them to her', wrote Lady Blayney, 'that, young as I was, it shocked me . . . but the Duchess used to say she had made them all such great Ladies that it turned their heads'.[5]

Other loyal friends held similar views. 'In Bed we began to read ye Account* you were pleased to send', wrote Robert Jennings. 'Ye extraordinariness of it prevented our rising till we had made an end of it . . . so much ffolly & undutyfullness . . . I conclude there can be no reconciliation at present, since he is removed that indeavourd it & cou'd not'.[6]

Mrs Boscawen, a Godolphin connection, was appalled, as indeed nobody that, as she put it, had either children or bowels could fail to be. 'Ye Behaviour is certainly most monstrous and, if I may have ye liberty to say it, not only despicable but detestable too in a person of Quallity with a grain of sence'.[7] Without question it was a book to set old heads wagging. 'I can't tell what reigns in this age', wrote Lady Portland, 'for respect & regard for parants seem extinguisht & people have a pleasure to do what they can to make children fly in their face'.[8]

Notes like these were to be treasured, and none more perhaps than poor Lady Bristol's, for she herself with a house full of in-laws which she called her Kennell of Vermin, knew what such suffering meant. Lady Bristol, then, having read Sarah's notes of 'monsterus behaveour', handed them to her husband and—'My lord', she tells Sarah, 'all the while he was reading them often cry'd out O Monsterus! O vile wretches!'[9] A *cri du coeur* so spontaneous and so soothing that it made it all seem worthwhile, all the writing and re-writing, and all the trouble Sarah had long since gone to in getting him his title.

* Sarah's Green Book.

It was a pity books needed to be bound within covers, there was already so much more to add, some of it perhaps even more startling than what had been recorded. This of Bridgwater,* for example. Could anything be more barbarous than the way he had snatched his daughter from under her grandmother's nose? For years Sarah had cared for the motherless child, Anne Egerton, as her own daughter and would have married her to Chandos† if her rich father had agreed to the settlement, but he would not. Now, soon after Marlborough's death Bridgwater, who was dissatisfied with the will and had pointedly absented himself from the funeral, married‡ Lady Rachel Russell and commanded his daughter to come to Ashridge to wish him joy. Sarah saw through his scheme at once. He wanted Anne to marry the Duke of Bedford, a match which should make the Bridgwater coffers still heavier. But she would nip it in the bud. The child should not go. After some thought she dictated what she herself called a very dutiful and good letter:

> My Grandmama hopes you will excuse her for not sending me now, I have had so great a cold & pain in my ear that my head is now wrapt up in Flanel . . .

As soon as she is well she will go to him. In the meantime, 'My lady Dutches is in a melancholly condition which makes her unwilling to part with me'.[10] It sounded reasonable enough. And so what did the Duke do? Without warning and at eleven o'clock at night he strode into the forecourt of Marlborough House, 'with a candle & lanthorn before him, a footman's coat upon him for fear of catching cold, and the air of being quite mad'. He demanded his daughter. Sarah's account continues:

> The first person that saw him was Lady Anne's woman, who made as much haste as she could to come & tell the Dutchess of Marl: that she might not be surprised. My Lord ran after her & bid her say to the Dutchess that he desir'd she would not make his child undutiful to him. The Dutchess of Marl: was appre-

* Scroop Egerton, Duke of Bridgwater, widower of the Marlboroughs' third daughter Elizabeth.
† James Brydges, 1st Duke of Chandos (1673-1744).
‡ On August 4th, 1722.

hensive that he would have come in to her, which would have been extream disagreeable, & therefore ... sent the woman out with this answer, that she would obey him.

It is a scene from Hogarth: the alarm of a sick child, head swathed in flannel, reflected in the face of her grandmother, herself a bundle of black nightclothes and nightcap, with wobbling candle-sticks. Bridgwater left but returned next morning before anyone was up. More scurrying, more pleas for postponement; but the furious Duke 'made the servant come in to the Dutchess of Marl: who was in bed, to tell her that if Lady Anne was sick, it was she that had made her so & that he would have her away; upon which she said, For God's sake let him take her. He would not go into any room, tho' he was desired to do it, but walk'd about in the Hall like a madman with the most ill natur'd Countenance that ever was seen in any humane Creature. As soon as Lady Anne was dress'd she came down, but being half dead with grief, the servants gave her some water & drops, & after that he took her away in his coach'.[11]

In the life of every woman of robust common sense there must inevitably be times when, except for herself and a few close friends, the whole world seems to have gone mad; when, as Sarah put it, there is some tincture more or less of madness in almost everybody that one knows. The curious thing was that this latest epidemic, in the first months of her widowhood, seemed confined to the aristocracy, since it had begun with the Duke of Bridgwater before, in various forms, infecting the Duke of Chandos, the Earl of Coningsby and the Duke of Somerset.

Chandos, the same who as James Brydges had sent Sarah the diamond portrait-ring mislaid at Antwerp and had supported Marlborough in the Lords, was now the fully-fledged Timon, his villa at Cannons, near Edgware, the wonder of England. In the South Sea calamity of 1720 he had lost heavily and had borrowed from Sarah; 'after which', she remarks, 'he was so mean as to refuse to let me have a Statue of the Duke of Marls tho I offerd to pay ... His Grace had got it by a trick'.[12]

This was not quite true. Chandos, finding in 1721 that two marble statues commissioned in 1710 of Baratta by Vanbrugh for Blenheim were still languishing at Genoa and still not completely paid for, wrote to Sarah: 'They represent Fame & Glory* . . . there being no personall resemblance in either to his Grace† . . . I'l entret your Grace will honnour Cannons so far as to come & see them & if you like Either or Both they shall be at your service on no other Terms than that you'l have ye Goodness to leave them to my Family at your decease'.[13] Sarah, who in 1716 had told Craggs, 'Tho I would give 73 pounds for a dead fly as soon as for these statues I think the Duke of Marl: is oblidged to pay for them since they are don',[14] now turned them down; only, two years later, to change her mind and send for them. In his reply Chandos sadly tells her that they are now heirlooms entailed upon his title. 'Mean and ungratefull', was Sarah's comment, 'full of compliments & prodigious professions but of no reall worth & ment nothing but his own interest'.[15] And so another old friend is shown the door and regretfully walks out of her life.

Earl Coningsby's‡ madness was of quite another kind. This seventeenth-century lord, who had moved the impeachment of Harley, had been twice married, having divorced his first wife and buried his second. Of his ten children, five daughters were living but there was no male heir. One of his sons had died from choking on a cherrystone, in 1708. In 1722, within five months of Marlborough's death, Coningsby proposed to the Duchess.

'I live in hopes', he declared, 'that the Great & Glorious Creator of ye World whoe dos & must direct all things will direct you to make mee ye happyest man upon ye face of the Earth and Enable mee to make my dearest dearest Lady Marlborough as she is ye wisest & ye Best, ye happyest of all Wemen. I am Yr Grace knows I am with ye Truest, ye Sincerest & ye most faithfull hart Yr Graces most dutifull, most obedient humble servant'. And to this he added the postscript: 'There is no such Cattle as Sheep as yr Grace desires to be had tell July next'.[16]

For his proposal Coningsby could not have chosen a worse time nor a worse approach. He and the Duchess had but one thing in

---

* One of these statues is now in the Fitzwilliam Museum at Cambridge. (See also Webb, op. cit., pp. 38–40).

† Marlborough.

‡ Thomas Earl Coningsby (1656–1729).

common and that was love of litigation, a hobby she had only now begun to enjoy. Otherwise there was nothing at all to tempt her to throw in her lot with the sad and irritable father of five new recruits for her Green Book. Her reply is not extant; but it would be surprising if any such offer made to the world's richest widow, as she was now said to be, was not viewed with suspicion. Their correspondence ceased.

Her second suitor was more surprising, more important, more decorous, more persistent and altogether more difficult to shake off. Even in an age when pride was a virtue and snobbery something to be proud of, Charles Seymour sixth Duke of Somerset was, says Sir Keith Feiling, one of the most arrogant oligarchs even of the eighteenth century. Nicknamed the Sovereign, the legend of his vanity is well known: how a daughter was disinherited for sitting in his presence, how servants were instructed by signs, and the roads scoured by outriders before his progresses, to protect him from the gaze of the vulgar. Yet there was another side to the man and it was surprising. He was Chancellor of the University of Cambridge and a great patron of the arts (witness Gibbons' carvings at Petworth and in the library of Trinity College, Cambridge); and he had a sense of humour.

Sarah's early dislike of him was twofold. She had found him a fool and a trimmer who, having failed to impress Marlborough had, temporarily at least, gone over to Harley, in the vain hope of power. She suspected too that Troule-it-away, his redhaired duchess, had for years had her eye on her gold key of office as Groom of the Stole and Mistress of the Robes, posts in which she did in fact succeed her; and that neither of them had done her anything but harm with Queen Anne.

If, then, Sarah's invective had lighted upon the Sovereign—'false', 'malicious', 'insolent', and 'working to doe me all the mischief hee could'—it had played like summer lightning about his duchess who was, she said, plotting and insinuating, mean of soul and the greatest liar in the world; yet—and perhaps that was her greatest shortcoming of all—Queen Anne liked her and was prepared to defend her as she had defended Mrs Freeman and, afterwards, Abigail. Sarah remembered her conduct at the trial of Sacheverell . . . such venomous rivalry, such intensity of hatred; and now death had made nonsense of it all, for Marlborough and the Duchess of Somerset had both died in the same year.*

In the following summer the outriders sped from Petworth to clear the lanes for the glorious equipage emblazoned with bull and unicorn, heading for Blenheim. And what a sight that must have been for those bold enough to gaze at it! The gleaming coach-and-six jingling between the green hedgerows, the horn calling and winding in the clear air over the unpoisoned fields; and within the coach Lord Foppington in full splendour, the periwigged beau, the ardent impatient lover, heaving huge sighs, at sixty-five, for the woman he already called his *souveraine*, now sixty-three.

Sarah was still beautiful. Though gout and gravel attacked her (Coningsby was shocked at how ill he had found her at Blenheim), her hair kept its colour and, except for plumpness, her looks were unchanged. 'If I durst show youer pictors', Frances Tyrconnel wrote from France, 'I wish I had youer one in litle by some sure hand, just as you are, which I heare is mighty well for a grandmother'.[17] We have nothing of Sarah however to compare with Kneller's portrait of Mrs Jennings; and even in the Kneller at Petworth (p. 272) we find her still wearing her gold key.

In the eyes of Somerset she was flawless. His proposal, a dignified document not at all like Coningsby's, speaks of unalterable love and affection, deep rooted and of long standing. 'I will not have a thought', he vows, 'but what shall bee to make you Happy & Easy in all things whatever. Your Grace shall command & make your Tearmes & Conditions. Give mee but your most charming Person, I neither covett nor desire more nor greater riches, for that is the onely & most valuable Treasure to mee . . . Apoynt mee an hour when I may lay my selfe at your ffeett, never to rise till my Pardon is sealed'.[18]

Sarah's answer was less harsh and histrionic than Horace Walpole and his followers supposed. She did not say, 'If I were young and handsome as I was, instead of old and faded as I am, and you could lay the empire of the world at my feet, you should never share the heart and hand that once belonged to John Duke of Marlborough.' What she wrote to him was firm but gentle:

* Marlborough died in June, the Duchess of Somerset in November, 1722.

My lord,

I am at a great loss to know how to express my self upon the subject of your Grace's letter of yesterday. There cannot possibly bee a greater mark given of your esteem then in the offers which you have been pleased to make to me and I am confydent that there is very few wemen (if any) that would not bee extreamly pleased with what your Grace proposes to me; but I am resolved never to change my condition and if I know any thing of my self I would not marry the Emperor of the world tho I were but thirty yeares old.

I hope your Grace will not dislike my truth in this declaration and that you will reward it by giveing me the honour of your friendship, which I am extreamly desirous of, and I asure you that I will never do the least thing to forfeit it as long as I live, but I will endeavour upon all occation to deserve it as much as I can by shewing that I am with all the respect imaginable

Your Grace's most faithfull and
most humble servant[19]

Had the Sovereign been of the kind that readily takes no for an answer he might perhaps have admitted defeat, but he was of different mettle. Living up to his supporters of bull and unicorn he took it as a challenge and pursued Sarah with all the ardour of a fullblooded man passionately in love.

Surprisingly though slowly, Sarah softened. Had she not lectured Queen Anne on his disloyalty and sent her his illiterate letter? And had he not secretly visited the Sorcerer, Robin the Trickster,* in a chair with the curtains drawn? There was a great deal to pardon, and that on both sides. There were talks and explanations. She lent him her Brown Book of Queen Anne's letters, to which his response was unexceptionable. 'It is most notoriousely plain', he declared, 'that the latte Queen's treatment of your Grace was the very reverse of the expressions in most of Her letters to you, for Her expressions were generally kind & tender but her treatment was hard & very unjust to you the most faithfull of servants & best of women. Such are your perfections in Body & in mind that I am every day in a

* Robert Harley Earl of Oxford.

continuall admiration how the Queen could bee soe prevayled with to treat you in soe ungrattefull & soe Barbarouse a manner'.[20]

This was encouraging. She decided to try him with the Green Book, and again the reaction was gratifying. 'Your Grace', he assured her, 'dosse show throughout the wholle a more than ordinary tenderness for all your children, but your children in return doe seem to affect a most unnaturall & most Barbarouse part to the best of mothers & very best of women'.[21]

In everything, she was to find, she could count on him, whether savouring her broth of vipers or, in milder mood, taking a hand at ombre with her favourite granddaughter Di.* There is, again in contrast with Coningsby, some pleasing chaff about a prayer. Somerset tells Sarah, 'I never was in more need of a good prayer than now . . . My words may ffly up to Heaven but my thoughts will forever remain with you Below, and words without thoughts, Shakespeare sayes, will ne'er to Heaven goe'. And so he steals a prayer of Di's and owns to it—'that I may not lye under your Ladyship's youthfull censure that an old man is a heathen & doe want a Prayer & all other good things, when I stole yours the other night off from your Mama Dutchesses Table. I confess I did want that very Prayer, I doe admit it'. Di copies it out for him and, at his bidding, ends with 'Diana' instead of 'Amen'.†[22]

It is a playful duke, and then again, a too serious one. 'Madame', he exclaims, 'you declare to have the courage of a Roman & I doe joyn in opinion with the wholle world to declare that you have likewise the wisedome of a Minerva, & that Divine Providence did at your birth very liberally bestow all Perfections of Nature in forming your body & mind and your Grace dosse mee now the Honour to confess that I doe love & adore you with an inviolable passion. Madame, my life, my heart & my soul now are & must bee forever with you, they are noe more mine . . . Give mee your most charming Person as the reward'.[23]

Something had to be done. For a time it had amused Sarah to toy

* Lady Diana Spencer.

† This prayer is missing, but on another occasion Sarah copies out a prayer she likes for Mrs Clayton: Great God, give us the good things that are necessary for us and keep evil things from us, even when we ask them of thee. (Blen G-I-16 Undated).

with him in light flirtation, but Somerset was too obviously in earnest and determined enough to sweep her off her feet if not deflected. To save all faces and feelings there was but one way out and that was to find him another wife. This she did in the person of Lady Charlotte Finch, daughter of the Earl of Nottingham, with whom Somerset appears to have been delighted. They married and had two daughters.

Replying to Sarah's letter of congratulation Somerset begged for the continuance of their friendship. 'Noe change in the way of life or of ffortune', he insisted, 'shall ever change mee from beeing the same man I have many years professed to bee'. It would not have been the moment to remind him that he had not long since assured her, 'You are the woman, the very woman, the only woman I doe love, I doe value, I doe adore the most & that I doe & will forever seek for all occasions to give Prooffes & Demonstrations of it to you & to the wholle world, my most Dear Dear Dear charming Souveraine'.[24]

It says much for his charm that he succeeded in changing Sarah's mind as to his character, a revolution borne out by her frequent deletions of disparaging references to him at Althorp and at Blenheim. 'I think the historian has been a little too severe in this part', she writes after one such passage, 'for which reason I have blotted it out, the Duke of Somerset having acted a very handsome part to the Duke of Marlborough after the queen's death & likewise done me a great deal of service after the Duke of Marlborough's death'.[25]

For both of them it must have been a heartening interlude and now that minds had grown tranquil Somerset, as the builder of Petworth, could still be helpful with Blenheim. 'You have very right thoughts', he told her, 'to make Blenheim Beautifull & worthy to perpetuate the memorys of the Duke & of the Dutchesse of Marlborough'. They exchanged long letters about it, he consulting Hawksmoor and Pope, while she with James Moore, John Armstrong the engineer and the masons struggled to tame not only the wild house but the landscape. He approved of her plan to channel the Glyme into a canal and to give it three waterfalls as it passed under the middle arch of Vanbrugh's bridge and into a large oval pool on the western side (see p. 172).

Because these waterworks were not Vanbrugh's but Armstrong's under her supervision she found something approaching enthusiasm for them. 'I beleive', she told Somerset, 'it will bee very beautyfull, the Canal & Bason (which is allready don) look very fine. There is to bee a lake & a cascade on the side of the Bridge next Woodstock, which I think will bee no inconvenience & bee a great addition to the place. Sr John never thought of this cascade which will bee the finest & largest that ever was made & the watter constantly fall from it without any trouble. The fine green meadow between the hous & the wood is to remain as it is, & I beleive your Grace will think in that, nature can not bee mended, tho Sr John formerly sett his heart upon turning that into a lake as I will do it on the other side & I will have swans & all such sort of things in it. All the marble Pillasters except three are put up in the Gallary . . . Upon the whole I believe everybody will allow that there is a great deal very fine in this house, as well as many great faults which I can bee very well contented with since they were not by my derection . . . I have reduced the stables to one third of what was intended by Sir John and yet I have room for about fourty fine horses . . . but what I value myself most upon is the fourniture which I have don at home & have made very little use of upholsterers, which has made it cost less by a vast summ & is ten times more agreeable & hansome then if it had been done by them . . .'[26] *

It would have been too much to expect the Duchess and her friends to realise how far Vanbrugh the visionary was in advance of his time, with his love of ruins and of lakes; and it was an ill chance that snatched Blenheim from its creator and gave the credit for its lake to Brown, who did little more than cut through a causeway-dam in the seventeen-sixties. Sarah, as she said, laboured like a packhorse, but it was a packhorse in blinkers, at times almost totally

* 'All the hills that you see from under the great Arch of the Bridge will bee in a deep sloop of green like those at Windsor Castle. There will bee a canal of sixty foot wide which watter will run thro the great Arch of the Bridge & on each side of this watter under the Arch there will bee a fine grass walk of twenty foot broad & there will bee a room paved that comes into this Arch which will bee very pleasant by the watter to sett in in a very hot day & the sight of the woods from that place beyond the watter that will run thro that beautyfull green meadow will certainly bee very uncommon & a very pleasing prospect allways. At Rosamonds Bower I will have something like those temples which they talk of that are at my Lord Burlingtons country house'. (Sarah to Lady Cairns. Undated. Blen G-I-16).

blind; for on the one hand she thought it her duty, with the world's deepest coffers and best craftsmen to draw on, to save money, and on the other to raise to the glory of Marlborough monuments which were more personal than he would have wished.

There was Hawksmoor's triumphal arch at the Woodstock entrance, erected soon after Marlborough's death. The obvious place for it would have been on the east to west axis at what is now called the Hensington Gate, but tradition insists that a gardener whose cottage occupied that site defied the Duchess with 'Go round the other way!'[27] The Roman arch as built Sarah thought too narrow and she was told that its inscription read better in Latin than in English. However, there it was. It kept the secret of the prospect till one had passed through it and it served as pointer to the great obelisk or Column of Victory, with its all-important inscriptions, which had yet to be determined and built.

A book could be written and not a dull one on the trouble that was taken and the people that were consulted for that monument; and indeed there is at Blenheim a portfolio entitled *Explanation of the Obelisk*, though by no means all of the project has been explained. For the monument itself, whether obelisk or column, Hawksmoor drew a dozen or so sketches, some based on the Column of Trajan, others on Bernini's river-gods fountain, only to find at the eleventh hour the commission snatched from him and given to Lord Herbert and his protégé Roger Morris.*

But the problem of the panegyric was far more formidable. Three sides of the dado were for the Acts of Parliament† which had bestowed the estate upon Marlborough and ensured the succession through the female line; the fourth, facing Blenheim, being for the panegyric itself. And who should write it? Who was big enough to extol the greatest of all heroes? Somebody (Marlborough himself?) had suggested Pope ('except that his inclinations are so different from ours as to Liberty'), but that was long ago, before Vanbrugh had lost

---

* Roger Morris (1695–1749), employed by Sarah at Blenheim and at Wimbledon and by Charles 3rd Duke of Marlborough at Althorp. His most celebrated work was the Palladian Bridge at Wilton (1736–7).

† 'The Acts of Parliament inscribed on this Pillar shall stand as long as the British name and language last, illustrious monuments of Marlborough's glory and of Britain's gratitude'. (Part of the inscription on the Column of Victory at Blenheim).

favour and when the obelisk might have commemorated Woodstock Manor and the amours of Henry II. It was not in the least what
Sarah now had in mind; for if, as she had written above that proposal, obelisks were to be raised to 'all our kings have don of that
sort, the countrey would bee stuffed with very odd things'.[28]

But now in 1723 Somerset was asked to approach Pope and did so.
'Mr Pope is mighty well pleased with the Honour your Grace
designs him', Sarah was told, 'and promises to doe his utmost to
please you, thô hee sayes hee never did doe any thing of this kind
before . . . Hee alsoe hasse one condition to make. Hee prays that if
hee should bee so fortunatte as to please your Grace, it may not bee
known hee is the auther. This last condition supports your Grace's
first apprehension of him, but yet lett that bee my care, hee shall very
strongly exert all your thoughts & directions'.[29]

The Duchess thought, consulted others and thought again. 'I
believe', wrote Lady Lechmere, 'you could engrave some mighty
sentences, but the times are dangerous & 'tis not worth going to the
Tower for it, or else one might—cut deep'.[30] Sarah strongly agreed.
'If I should have a mind', she mused, 'to expose the ingratitude even
of those that reaped the advantages of these successes, the whole park
& gardens would not hold pillars sufficient to contain the infamy of
that relation'.[31] Yet tempting as it was, it could not have been called
typical of Marlborough. She resisted it.

We hear no more of Pope's attempt at the panegyric; nor was
Bishop Hare's effort any more successful. As the months and the
years went by in the vain quest for a worthy writer Sarah saw only
too plainly, with the great column rising and no fit inscription ready
for it, the makings of a desperate if not a ludicrous situation. And
nothing short of desperation, surely, could have persuaded her
ultimately to accept, for Marlborough's panegyric, an inscription
written by one of his greatest enemies and betrayers, Henry St John
Viscount Bolingbroke.

On the death of Anne and the collapse of the Tories Bolingbroke,
it was said on Marlborough's prompting, fled to the Pretender, to
help plan the Jacobite rising of 1715, which Marlborough helped to
quell. In 1716 he was dismissed by James and it was not until 1723
that, partly by bribing the Duchess of Kendal, he was granted a
pardon by George I and, in 1725, allowed to return to England. His

one possible claim to Sarah's favour and that a strong one was his opposition, with William Pulteney and Sir William Wyndham (Somerset's son-in-law), to Sir Robert Walpole, and in that, though excluded from the House of Lords, Bolingbroke was influential and sincere.

Sarah's attitude was equivocal and interesting. Of Bolingbroke she had written, 'I have no notion of my lord Bullingbrooks honour, after all the mischeifs which hee did his country & the publick professions which hee made every day in a most solemn manner, which the whole earth knows since to have been all false . . . hee has forfeited all pretentions to any one single vertue'.[32] But on the other hand she had written too: 'I am grown to bee wonderfull fond of usefull knaves, which some people would push into the pond as soon as they had lent their hand to help the person out . . . but that is not my humour at all, for if I thought it fitt & necessary to make use of an ill man or to bee reconciled to my enemy in appearance I would certainly never fail him in any thing that hee could expect from me'.[33]

On July 25, 1728 Pulteney wrote to the Duchess:

I have enclosed sent your Grace the Draught of the Inscription which I received a few days ago from Lord Bolingbroke, and also those other Draughts which I formerly had from you. I have taken the liberty likewise to send you his letter to me, because as it may be of service to those who are to engrave the Inscription (who should take the utmost care to be extreamly exact in the manner of performing it), so will it also convince your Grace with how just and sincere a Regard for the memory of the Duke of Marlborough my Lord undertook it . . .

It was formed, Pulteney added, on classical models and 'not writ by an Able Hand only but done with a good Heart'.[34] Sarah, blind to the merits of heroic architecture, instantly recognised this as the heroic prose she had for years been seeking. The writer's heart was no matter. His sentences, crisp as words of command, were indeed from an able hand:

The Battle was Bloody: the Event decisive. The Woods were pierced: the Fortifications trampled down. The Enemy fled. The Town was taken . . .

Whenever she read it, she said, she wet the paper. Bolingbroke's hero-worship of Marlborough, begun in youth, had run full circle and now his long panegyric was published in full in *The Craftsman*, the paper he ran with Pulteney. If, as he had said, he really wished to remain anonymous, that was a mistake because it gave the *Gentlemans Magazine* the chance to observe that 'as no monumental Marble or Inscriptions could add to Marlborough's Glory, so no Recitals of those Inscriptions in *The Craftsman* could take away from B-l-ke's Ingratitude'.[35]

And even then, Sarah found, her difficulties with the column were not over. There was frost. There was delay. Boards with black lettering were raised to the dado so that she, half crippled with gout, might be carried to see them. The lines were too long; the marble was uneven. In 1730 she tells Townsend the mason she is very much disappointed and troubled to find that after all her pains the inscription is still not finished. 'But I am tired out', she adds, 'and I must now make an end of it as well as I can . . . It will be cruel if I should be disappointed in every thing'; and later, 'I hope you will take effectual care that there is no more Blunders made; for it will be a most terrible thing if there is, to me who have so long set my heart upon this Pillar's being well performed'.[36]

So there it is, the 'lasting monument of his glory and her affection to him'.* Hawksmoor, passing through Woodstock the following year found, as he told Lord Carlisle, no great matter added 'either of good or any more mischief don' since his last visit. 'The Historicall Pillar is set up in the park (conducted by my Lord Herbert).† It is . . . above a hundred feet high. Ye inscription is very long but very legible . . . The Lake is beautifull but ye Cascade does not play, all ye Rivers are almost dry. I forgot to tell your Lordship', he ended, 'that her Grace at Blenheim was not so Gratious as to see me, and I did not ask her only to try what she wou'd doe. I don't know whether I did right in it or not'.[37]

It was six years since Vanbrugh, with perhaps even greater curiosity, had tried to see his own masterpiece and had been turned

* From the inscription on Hawksmoor's triumphal arch at the Woodstock entrance.

† Henry Herbert, 9th Earl of Pembroke (1693–1751), succeeded to the earldom in 1733. Owner of Wilton. Known as the architect earl.

away. Arriving with Carlisle's party he had found 'an order to the Servants, under her Graces own hand, not to let me enter any where. And lest that shou'd not mortify me enough, She having some how learn'd that my Wife was of the Company, sent an Express the Night before we came there with orders, if she came with the Castle Howard Ladys, the Servants shou'd not Suffer her to see either House, Gardens or even to enter the Park, which was obey'd accordingly, and She was forc'd to Sit all day and keep me Company at the Inn'.[38]

Closely watched, Vanbrugh, the Duchess was told, 'went up by the Cock Pitt, expecting to get in at the litle gate that used to be there & when he found he could not get in he walked back again down to Old Woodstock & looked over the wall to see the watter'.[39] However, it would be surprising if a man of Vanbrugh's resource let himself be thwarted by toadying servants, even if it meant scaling the wall by moonlight, which very possibly it did.

That was in August, 1725. Two months later Vanbrugh wrote to Jacob Tonson:

Being forc'd into Chancery by that B.B.B.B. Old B. the Dutchess of Marlb: & her getting an Injunction upon me by her Friend the late Good Chancelr. who declar'd I never was employ'd by the Duke of Marlbh: and therefore had no demand upon his Estate for my Services at Blenheim, I say since my hands were tyed up from trying by Law to recover my Arrear, I have prevail'd with Sir Rob. Walpole to help me in a Scheme I propos'd to him by which I have got my money in Spight of the Huzzys teeth, and that out of a Sum She expected to receive into her hands towards the discharge of the Blenheim Debts, and of which She resolv'd I shou'd never have a farthing. My carrying this point enrages her much, and the more because it is of considerable weight in my Small Fortune, which She has heartily endeavour'd so to destroy as to throw me into an English Bastile to finish my days as I began them in a French one.[40]

He was not to enjoy his triumph long, dying as he did of a quinsy on the 26th of March, 1726 at the age of 62. Like Wren, who had died three years earlier, he had raised his own monuments; and though the Duchess might bar him from Blenheim she could not keep out his name and fame which for all time must be linked with it. If his gay spirit dwells there, its lodging is surely the bridge, where a vast V is incised over a sealed-off window.

The Chancellor Vanbrugh referred to was Lord Macclesfield who, in the case against the Blenheim workmen (four hundred and one 'confederates') had worked himself into a righteous passion against them and had forbidden Vanbrugh ever to sue for the £1660 he was owed. Indeed, had it not been for a letter of Marlborough's which showed that he had had 'a kindness for Sir John', Vanbrugh would have been ordered to pay back even that which he had had. 'It is to be hoped,' comments Dr Coxe, 'no undue share of the immense wealth of the Duchess influenced the judgment of this impeached Lord Chancellor. It appears that he was shortly afterwards fined £30,000 for bribery and embezzlement in the discharge of his official duties'.[41] Sarah, delighted with his decree, in due course rescued him from prison.* His grateful letters to her are from the heart.[42]

In her sixties, then, we watch the machine that is the Duchess of Marlborough, well fuelled with time and money and without the brake once applied by Marlborough, running to dangerous extremes. Semi-invalid though she is, she still has courage and zest enough to challenge the world, if the world will only give her a hearing. As always she enjoys a fight. Disappointed in George I she turns to his son, only to find him and his wife Caroline ('I really love her') committed to Sir Robert Walpole, with whom she must always be at war. She talks, writes, dictates, buys land, hurls herself into elections and lawsuits and into endless family quarrels. From friends all she asks is sympathy and confidence. They must tell and keep telling her she is right and has always been right and this very nearly all of them do. The courageous exception is Marlborough's ex-chaplain Francis Hare, Bishop of Chichester. His long letters to

* 'I own I love him [Mecklesfeild, as she spells him] for the justice which hee ded in so hansome a way to the Dear Duke of Marlboroughs memory & for exposing the knaves as hee ded in the Blenheim cause, but nothing can ever make me do injustice & I think the suiters mony should bee every shilling made good to them . . . I beleive nothing wants reformation more then the courts of law.' (Sarah to Lady Cairns, 25 Feb., 1724. Blen G-1-16).

her glint with the gold of sense. And so from a welter of broken friendships, recorded at Blenheim, the heart lifts as he tells her:

> You say you can't think you are obliged upon any account not to say the truth or to deny yourself the pleasure of speaking your mind upon any occasion, which opinion is the Foundation of all I think wrong in your Grace's conduct. You seem to think nothing ought to be censured as evil speaking if it be speaking truth, but your Grace will find every writer of morality against you and with great reason, for if people were at liberty to vent in all places all the ill they thought true of others, it would destroy Society and there would be no living in the world . . .

If only she could even now be taught to hold her tongue! He cites Godolphin and Marlborough who, provoked to distraction, yet said nothing. 'Where Lord G: said ten words at table before servants or in mixt company your Grace will give me leave to believe you say 10,000. But . . . his silence was very particular and . . . perhaps would not become your Grace; it would take too much off from ye life of conversation & destroy the pleasure you give your friends by saying perpetually things which are extremely diverting & agreeable.* But your Grace will have no exception to make to the example of the Duke of Marlborough, who was always agreeable in conversation & yet always inoffensive & whatever resentments he had, suppressed them to that degree as made him universally beloved & the idol of all who had the honour to be near him. There was in his whole Behaviour an inimitable sweetness which was not only easy to himself & delightful to others, but what he abundantly found his account in . . . If your Grace would in any measure imitate either of those examples, 'tis impossible but that you should have the most friends & the greatest interest of any subject in the nation'.[43]

But of course she would do nothing of the kind. Her friends, to remain friends, must accept her as she was. Why, should the Duchess of Marlborough cease from speaking her mind of everybody to everybody she would no longer be herself, she would be unrecognis-

* On another occasion Dr Hare tells the Duchess: 'It is as impossible for your Grace to converse without warmth & force as it is for you to be dull or ugly, to whom God has given so fine an understanding & so much beauty'. (Blen E 38).

able. The man was a fool and a grossly impertinent one. He even had the effrontery to censure her for forbidding her daughters to enter Blenheim.* 'I am so far from defending them', he had said, 'that I am persuaded they are extremely to blame, but yet I must own I always thought this was carrying things to too great an extremity . . . One must wink hard and connive at many faults to preserve peace & love in familys . . .'[44]

The advice came too late.

---

* 'I don't know what your friends mean by the difficulty in their seeing this house', Sarah writes to Lady Cairns from Blenheim, 'for no one mortal is ever refused it'. (Blen G-I-16. Dated Sept. 29—no year given but in Marlborough's lifetime).

CHAPTER XIII

The Fruitful Vine

1727-1735

There could be no denying that under the Hanoverians family quarrels were the fashion. Not that everyone chose to follow the royal lead, but for those that did the standard was very high or very low according to how one viewed it. In the reigns of the early Georges fathers and sons were at loggerheads; and there were subsidiary squabbles and rivalries among seconds and mistresses, which made for diversion in distant and otherwise stodgy courts.

Sarah, with so small an opinion of the whole pack that she had all but forgiven Queen Anne, would have scoffed at the notion of apeing them in anything. Yet her large family now rivalled if it did not outdistance theirs in what seemed to her outrageous and unforgivable behaviour.

By an understandable law of nature the most scandalous thing of all, as the world thought, she wrote least about, going no further than passing references to her eldest daughter as Congreve's moll. After her father's death in June, 1722 Henrietta Godolphin Duchess of Marlborough went to Bath, where most of her time was spent with Congreve who, at fifty-two, suffered cruelly from gout and cataract. Henrietta, who was forty-one, had had four children two of whom, Willigo Blandford and Harriet Newcastle, survived. In November, 1723, having ceased bearing for nearly twenty years, she gave birth to a daughter, Mary. If when Congreve died in 1729 any doubt remained about paternity it was dispelled by his bequest to the immensely rich duchess of £10,000, leaving only £200 for his former mistress Mrs Bracegirdle.

The strange fancies of Henrietta's monument to Congreve in Westminster Abbey, where she herself was to be buried,* and her wax-effigy of him at her dinner-table are too well known for repetition.[1] Her eccentricity bordering on madness, diverting at a distance, must certainly have been hard to live with, and there can be no doubt but that her dull husband's patience, inherited from both father and mother, was stretched to the uttermost.

Less than two months after the birth of Mary Godolphin (a charming girl nicknamed Minos, who became Duchess of Leeds and died at forty) Sarah, writing to Mary's brother Willigo—'My letters are the longer from tumbling out every thing that I think without study'—said, 'Concerning your mother living with me as she has don for many years,† I am her mother & never yet was the agressor, but she is in so ill hands that she finds new ways every day of surprising the world with her behaviour or rage against me, which is much increas'd since the death of her father'.[2] A sad situation which would drag on till the younger duchess's death in 1733.

Early in the seventeen-twenties Sarah, battling with ill health and litigation, had decided to write her two daughters off. Godolphin's assurance long ago that she (Sarah) had been the best mother in all respects made Henrietta's behaviour the more monstrous. 'But no more of that', she wrote in 1730, 'it is now all over & I shall never have no more to do with her'.[3]

Henrietta's sister, Mary Montagu, Pope's Angel Duchess, was as bad or worse. A fancied slight over the eve-of-exile diamond-raffle of 1712, from which Mary's children had been excluded ('because I knew', explained Sarah, 'you had at your marriage diamonds enough to cover a table'), had led to a lasting coldness which reconciliation-attempts by go-betweens (a Mrs Hammond was the latest) did little or nothing to thaw. Nor did it cheer Sarah to find the quarrels

---

* '. . . and it is my desire & express will that my Body be not at any time hereafter or on any pretence whatsoever carried to Blenham . . . I also give to my said daughter Mary all Mr Congreves Personal Estate that he left me & all my own money or which I enjoyed as such'. Excerpt from the will of Henrietta Duchess of Marlborough dated 11 July, 1732 (BM add ms 28071 ff 34–9).

† The two duchesses, Sarah and Henrietta, did not of course live in the same house. The reference here is to the bad terms on which for many years they were to each other.

carried to the next generation: Willigo on bad terms with his
mother, and Bella Montagu, who in 1723 married the Duke of
Manchester, likewise out of favour with hers. 'I have been told by
several', wrote Sarah, 'that she longed to be rid of her. The Duke of
Manchester had a very small estate and in half an hour's conversation
with him the Duchess of Montagu must know that a woman that
had sense must be very miserable with him . . . Most mothers would
have been touch'd to have reflected upon her being married to such
a man . . . but when she was like a bird out of a cage & knew nothing
of the world, the Duchess of Montagu never minded her . . . How
cruel must a heart be not to be reconciled to a child that had made
such submissions!'[4]

However, there was always for a Marlborough grandchild the
consolation that to be out of favour with mother meant being in
grandmother's good graces; and in this case Sarah set to work,
furnishing Bella's house as she did many another. 'I think myself,'
she wrote gaily, 'the best upholsterer in England. You may do what
you please', she added, 'with the old soldier's verses,* for I have got
them by heart and after my fashion can sing the Ballad'.[5]

With Bella's mother Mary, Sarah's only child to survive her, there
could be no lasting reconciliation; for now, to top all her former
misconduct, she had behaved most extraordinarily in of all places the
workshop of Rysbrack the sculptor. 'She went to see the Tomb for
Blenheim (p. 173) at Mr Rysbrack's', Sarah explains, 'they always
make a Model in Clay to make that in stone by & what is done first
in Clay is often more like than that in marble. She lik'd that extreamly of Lord Blandford & got Mr R: to tell her she should have it,
which I suppose he was not unwilling to gratify her in as she would
pay him for it . . . But when I saw that of my Son it was so extream
like that I was fond of it & desir'd him to bake it & send it to me,
which he did. And liking that model so well I ask'd Mr R: for that
of the Duke of Marls Statue . . . but he excus'd giving it me, saying
that some accident had happen'd to it. I beleive he had let the Duchess of Montagu have it, but that I am not sure of as I am that she was
in a most violent rage when she heard I had got Lord Blandford's
model & said it was only out of Crossness to her that I had taken it,

* The verses, to the tune of *To All You Fair Ladies*, were sent to Sarah by an
ex-ADC of Marlborough's. See also appendix IV.

257

tho' I never had heard the least word of her having a mind to it till some time after I had it . . .'[6] The Green Book began to burst its covers as Sarah scoured her vocabulary. Such conduct wanted a name.

'I married her', Sarah patiently told Mrs Hammond, of Mary Montagu, to the chief match of England . . . and if it had not been for my favour she must have been married to some country gentle-have of 1500 or 2000 pounds a year, which for ought I know might have been better both for her & for me; at least 'tis probable it would have made her behave better . . . But now I have taken my resolution unalterable that I never will have any thing more to say to her. My life is very near run out & I am sure she can now never give me any Pain or Pleasure, & therefore I desire that you would never name her more to your most faithfull humble servant'.[7] And again later: 'I am what is called Bedridden & Dying & tho' I beleive her Wit entertaining I can read that out of any Book & am content with the very few friends I keep company with when I am out of Pain & at my age 'tis impossible to love any body with passion as I did her a great while, but I own that has been long burnt out & I have now nothing to do but to be as quiet as I can'.[8]

There could be no question but that it had been the more lovable and dutiful of her daughters, Anne and Elizabeth, who had died; yet even they had left daughters who, to the kindest of grandmothers, could and did give infinite trouble. It was not enough, Sarah found, to take them into her home, teach them, tend them, dress them and make matches for them. Ingratitude on a more or less monstrous scale was almost always the reward. No one could have been kinder than she had been to Elizabeth's daughter Anne Egerton, the same who had been snatched by an infuriated father intent on her marrying the sixteen-year-old Duke of Bedford. But her behaviour since had proved disappointing, and on Christmas Day, 1724, her grand-mother wrote to tell her so:

I can't help saying that I should have taken the message you sent me very kindly had it been sincere, that you were very sorry that you did not stay long enough in town to come to me, but as I know you had been with several people to whom you never had the least obligation . . . and that you did protest to me that your father never restrained you from expressing your affection to me by letter, so long ago when you were taken away in so very strange a manner, I can impute this last neglect of me to no body but your self, and certainly it would have been better in you not to have sent me any message at all than one that was plainly so insincere to one who, you must be sensible, has been so good a friend to you as well as a parent.

When you left me I had reason to believe that you felt a great deal by the tears which you shed and the expressions which you made to me, and tho' I could not like that you took no manner of notice of me in so many months when you writ to others, I was very easy to you when you came to me in town the following winter, and what has occasion'd this last behaviour I can't imagine; but I am sure that you could not possibly apprehend that I should not be very well pleased that you were to marry the Duke of Bedford, so that I must impute it to your want of Nature to me and add what the world calls it, indecent.

You will remember that allways from a child I endeavoured to convince you that you must never depart from the truth upon any account whatsoever and that no fault that you could commit was so bad as any sort of falseness. I am sure you will never have better advice or instructions given you than that and according to that principle I can assure you with the greatest sincerity that I was, as long as it was possible, your most affectionate grandmother.[9]

The account continues:

In answer to this letter the Duke of Bridgwater sent for the servant that carried it to Lady Anne and then called for one of his own servants into the room, saying that he was to be a witness to what he said to the Duchess of Marlborough, which was as follows: 'Tell her that I have commanded my daughter never to go to her, nor to write or to send her any message, nor to receive any from her; and I desire that she never will send any servant to my house; and tell her that I understand the duty to a mother better than she does her duty to her children'. The servant that brought this message said that he observed that his Grace was in a great agony and tho' he pronounced all this he seemed to be very much out of breath.[10]

The truth was the Duke was as near combustion as a man is ever likely to get. Silence ensued, and it would be pleasant to suppose that afterwards Anne Egerton settled happily with the Duke of Bedford, whom she married in 1725. Her grandmother was delighted with him, and dubbed him her secretary; but he gambled astronomically, fell out with his wife and died young, leaving his title to his brother who, in 1731, married Sarah's favourite granddaughter Lady Diana Spencer. The widow, Anne Duchess of Bedford, married the Earl of Jersey.

Manifestly, to be a Marlborough grandchild and remain on good terms with the dowager was not simple. To love and cherish one's grandmother was one thing, to hate her enemies quite another, particularly when those enemies happened to be one's brothers and sisters. Sarah was fond of Di Spencer, adopted as 'a pritty talking child' of six when her mother died in 1716, but she made it clear to her from the first that there could be no half-measures about loyalty; it must be all or nothing. Her brothers, Robert, Charles and John, drifted in and out of their grandmother's favour while they were at Eton and later while they were abroad. Her unremitting displeasure was reserved for the other sister Anne, married to Mr Bateman in 1720 and now a viscountess.

Though Sarah had never liked Anne Bateman and accused her of 'a thousand mean tricks, even from 14', there may until 1732 have been some possibility of a reconciliation. After that there was none, because Sarah was convinced that she had 'sold' her brother Charles in marriage to Elizabeth Trevor, of whose grandfather she strongly disapproved. If there was matchmaking of that order to be done (and Charles was by then the Marlborough heir), Sarah would do it. For Di she had chosen Frederick Prince of Wales, a project thwarted at the eleventh hour, it was said, by Sir Robert Walpole; and though other more or less unworthy suitors followed—Lord Middleton, the Earl of Chesterfield*—she kept her Cordelia, as she fondly called her, for Lord John Russell, who soon afterwards became fourth Duke of Bedford.

Behind her, in her early training of Di, Sarah had had the benefit of the mistakes she had made in the upbringing of her own children.

---

* In his proposal from the Hague, dated 14 Aug. 1731, Chesterfield writes: 'The honour I should have of being so nearly related to you is not one of my least temptations'. (Blen B 37).

She taught her history and obedience and nursed her through small-pox; and at the age of twelve Di was writing to her French gover-ness, at Sarah's dictation, 'My Mama Dutchess is resolved to let every fool & every wicked person say what they will without giving herself the least trouble'; and later, to Sarah herself, 'The study of my life shall be to deserve the kindness you shew me & to acknowledge my gratitude'.

Thus, when the harsh test of loyalties came—loyalty to her sister Anne or loyalty to her grandmother—Sarah knew she could count upon her. In a typically long letter, sent a week after the burial of Di's son who lived only a day, a letter in which she refers to 'the monstrous treatment I have met with from the rest of your family, which I do believe you have been sorry for, tho I have often observed that you have been very partial to them', Sarah explains, 'I don't mean that you should not see your brothers, but she [Lady Bateman] is a Disgrace to any body's sister. It has been the custom of all times to put a mark upon the person that has been the contriver of any great mischief, & as to my two grandsons, they can't help their weakness . . . But for lady Bateman I must declare that I can never have any satisfaction in the conversation of any body that has any commerce with her . . . I desire, my dear, you will consider very well before you take your resolution . . . You must be very plain with lady Bateman in letting her know that you can have no commerce with her, that you are very sorry that she did not reflect upon the ill consequences of what she has done before it was too late; that all people that are either good or reasonable are & must be sensible that there is no precedent of such a treatment to a grandmother that for thirty years has been labouring to assist & serve a whole family & that has done it with great success; & that you could not live with any ease if you did any thing that was grievous to me. I think I am not in my Nature at all partial . . . There is no acting by halves or trimming in such an affair as this, but I do again protest to you that I would have you do in it as you like best. I only desire to be as easy as I can make my self & whatever you do I shall allways be most affectionately yours'.[11]

Though Di's answer is missing, Sarah vouches for it herself that she was not disappointed. 'I could not bear the thought', she says, 'of her coming to me in the same manner she us'd to do, when I

knew she came from such a viper . . . I press'd her extreamly to do
what would make her most easy and she chose to take leave of her
sister and to come to me with the same friendship & openness she
us'd to do'.[12] From the age of six Di had been learning her lesson, so
that later she could assure her grandmother, as it would seem almost
mechanically: 'Anybody must have a very bad heart indeed that does
not endeavour to make all possible returns to anybody who has
shewn a perpetual kindness to them their whole lives as my dear
Grandmama has done to me & which I shall ever study to deserve'.[13]

After marriage, as *Letters of a Grandmother*[14] show, the correspondence increased. Sarah wrote fast and often, sometimes twice a
day. 'Pray tell me sincerely', she begged, 'if you can read all I write,
for I beleive no body ever before writt so long a letter without
stoping & so fast that the letters are worse shaped I think then
usual'. From court gossip to architecture, from music to medicine,
there is hardly a subject left untouched. It is the one delight left to
the ill and ageing Duchess, to pour out her thoughts and troubles to
the one person she loves, her dear Cordelia, and to build and furnish a house at Wimbledon for her to live in.

In the summer of 1732 the dowager took Woburn on her way to
Scarborough and for Di wrote down her impressions of both. She
was carried round Woburn, she told her, in a chair with short poles
and noticed that, in the picture-gallery especially, the young Duke of
Bedford, who had married Anne Egerton, kept sitting down. 'If I
had time & spirits', she added, 'I could tell you a thousand pretty
things he said & there is nothing so amazing to me as to see a man
that seems to have so much sense & yet to have made such a havoc
of his constitution & of his estate'.[15] When someone remarked that
part of the house was in danger of falling, he said it would outlast its
owner, and he was right.

At York Sarah made time to see and disapprove of Lord Burlington's Assembly Rooms before taking coach to Scarborough which,
like Bath, she found noisy and dirty. She had gone there (she was
seventy-two) to see if the waters could help to make her 'tolerably
easy . . . but whether life is long or short, I think 'tis a very indifferent
thing to me.'[16] The lavatories shocked her. Lord Chesterfield pleased
her . . . and so on. She had observed at York 'a vast deal of what they
call architecture', and she was to see more of it, by Vanbrugh and

Hawksmoor, at Castle Howard. 'My Lord Carlisle', she reported to Di, 'is laying out a mint of money in making an extraordinary place to bury his own family in a finer manner than I have ever heard of & for a great number of them which are yet to be born'.*[17]

While she looked at the plans and buildings of others, Sarah had in mind her own projects at Wimbledon, where in 1723 she had bought an estate from Sir Theodore Jansen, a bankrupt South Seas director; and at St Albans, where she was planning almshouses for 'forty miserable old Creatures' who had never known happiness. Blenheim and Marlborough House had had to be finished without help from their architects; but now surely, at Wimbledon where she had a free hand, a reliable architect might be expected to stay the course. Lord Herbert's success with the Column of Victory naturally led her to consult him; whereupon she found herself landed with his protégé Roger Morris, whom she soon came to dislike.

Long long ago, at the start of the Blenheim works, it may be remembered, Godolphin had told Marlborough that his wife, as she viewed them, was proving extremely prying-into. She had not changed. 'For tho I am not an architect', as she explained to Lady Cowper, 'I find one can't bee long from any building without the danger of having a window or a door or somthing or other that one does not like, & yet I think I am in the best hands we have, but their rules does not allways agree with my fancy, & I am forced to bee perpetually on the watch'. For some reason she suspected that Morris meant to crown Wimbledon with a turret, a thing she could not abide. Asked for a drawing of it Morris, so Sarah told Lord Herbert, refused to leave it with her and this gave offence for though, as she said, her taste might be faulty, she was certainly at seventy-two old enough to know what she liked. When she dismissed him he had the impudence to ask £300 for plans Wren would, he said, have charged £2000 for. This was asking for trouble, for Sarah happened to know that 'for the whole direction & management of St Paul's' Wren had had only £200 a year, 'and was pull'd up in a basket twice a week to the top'.[18]

In one of her twenty-six draft-wills at Althorp Sarah directs that Wimbledon be finished without carving, gilding or foolish ornaments, 'nor a Turret upon the top of the house . . . I desire', she adds,

* Hawksmoor's masterpiece, the mausoleum, now in need of restoration.

'that Mr Bridgman may finish the ground & gardens . . . a nd positively direct that nothing be done by the direction of my Lord Herbert or Mr Morris & I desire that Mr Smith of Warwickshire the builder may be employed to make Contracts and . . . complete the work as far as the distance he is at will give him leave'.[19]

It was bad enough that Morris had embarked on works at Wimbledon without her direction. Only later did she discover that Di's brother Charles had allowed him to lead him into huge expense at Althorp, with a replica of an Inigo Jones church for stables, an elaborate dwelling for a gardener and a great deal of work in the house itself, leaving it, in her opinion, much the worse, when all it needed was sash windows and a plain, useful stable for thirty or forty horses. Morris, who had in fact done work of distinction still to be seen at Althorp, was referred to as infamous, his name added to the black list; so that we find Di's younger brother John promising not only to have no truck with the Batemans but none, too, with Morris. For just as she had long since seen through almost all doctors and lawyers so now, Sarah decided, she had seen through all architects. For her almshouses* she would manage without them.[20]

It could be that that excellent builder Smith of Warwick, whom she may not have regarded as an architect, helped her. The alms-houses, as they stand today, look pleasing enough and may be comfortable. All, with one exception, is modesty; and that a central pediment worthy of Blenheim, bearing on its tympanum the arms and supporters of Churchill and Mindelheim, embosomed by a two-headed eagle on the heroic scale.

In Sarah's letters now there is much about illness: gout not only in hands but in knees, which she remembers Garth calling incurable; and scurvy which drives her mad with itching; and there is much too about death. Her own, come when it may, Sarah views with indifference, but the death of a young man is always shocking and, though she had expected it, she was shocked to hear of the death at Corunna, on October 23rd, 1732, of the young Duke of Bedford.†️ From their first meeting she had been charmed with his behaviour—

* The St Albans almshouses were begun in February, 1733. A fine cedar, said to have been planted by the Duchess, in the forecourt, was recently felled.

† Wriothesley 3rd Duke of Bedford, not to be confused with his brother John 4th Duke of Bedford who married Lady Diana Spencer. (See pedigree at p. 312).

'just as I should have wishd had hee been my own son'—so that she was prepared to believe Providence must have sent him to make up for those others who had been 'like wild creatures without sense or nature'. Now that Providence had taken him she sorrowed more than the widow who had not found the marriage a happy one. She thought, to Sarah's alarm, of marrying John Spencer but, luckily, thought again.

In the following October came the death of Henrietta Duchess of Marlborough. 'I am sure', wrote Di to Sarah, 'you feel more upon this subject than you thought you should yourself'.[21] Sarah owned that she did. She had, she added, vainly attempted reconciliation. Henrietta in youth had been so goodnatured, 'the modestest young creature', till 'flattered & practised upon by the most vile people upon earth'.[22] How often had she herself warned her against that rabble—Lady Oxford and her daughters, Lady Sandwich, yes and Lady Fitzharding, 'for though she had a great deal of wit & humour that was diverting, her house was a dangerous place for young people'.[23] But all to no purpose, 'and I think the consequences of conversing with such ill people', she wrote sadly, 'has sufficiently justified me . . .'[24]

There were rumours that at the last she had turned Roman Catholic. Sarah refuted them. 'What was don about the peice of wood', she assured Di, 'was only folly, for as to religion she had none. It is better to be a Roman Catholick or any thing then to have [no] religion at all, but 'tis certain the company she had long keept, both men & women, had corrupted all her morals & she shewd at last that she had no principle of any sort & was vastly ill natur'd to every body but la: Ma:* . . . but familys seldome agree to live easyly together'.

This was the gloomy side and there would be more of it: yet if gout abated, the dowager could still rally and cry, 'Nobody upon earth ever governed me nor ever shall!' It was the same spirit that she admired in her grandson Charles Spencer, now third Duke of Marlborough,† when he refused to vote the way he was bidden.

---

* Lady Mary Godolphin, aged ten, went to live with her sister Harriet, Duchess of Newcastle at Claremont near Esher in Surrey.

† Charles Spencer, 5th Earl of Sunderland (1706–1758), became in 1733, on the death of his aunt Henrietta 2nd Duchess of Marlborough, 3rd Duke of Marl-

Charles was large and ponderous and not brilliantly clever, but this show of resistance, said his grandmother, 'was so much after my own heart that I believe it would have animated me enough to have given me strength to have lifted him up from the ground and kissed him'.

At times she sounds positively gay as when, for Di's benefit, she recalls the marriage of Dutch William. 'I saw both the weddings of the two last queens', she writes to her, 'which was all private as yours, but I remember one thing that deverted the young people: the Prince of Orange came to bed in a blew sattin wascoat which was the Dutch fashion'.

She goes on to tell Di about her Jacobite house-guests, the Ladies Dillon* and Muskerry,† 'neither of them entertaining', whom she will see only at mealtimes. The devout Lady Muskerry,—'so extreme simple'—has been teased about the thirty-nine articles. 'I made Mr Stephens read them', Sarah writes, 'but after she had said she would defend them all by Scripture, upon consideration I found she was afraid of the debate for she would not own that they were in her Bible, when upon producing it we found them'.

The Duchess seldom descends to bawdy, but when she does the anecdote is worth telling: 'I was told another very foolish thing last night, which I believe is true', she confides, 'that a woman is taken up for having wished the wind was in the King's arse. I must own it was not a very polite expression, but the poor woman has explained it very well, for every body wishes him in England, & he can't be here till the wind is in his back. If the magistrate happens to be a very simple man there may possibly be another subject for a Ballad, but I have not yet heard what they have done with the woman'.

Evidently there were other ways of getting even with the Georges besides plotting with the Jacobites. Sarah scoffed at them and at their

---

borough. He left Althorp in 1734 and lived mainly at Langley, Bucks. In 1817 the 5th Duke of Marlborough was authorised to add the name of Churchill to that of Spencer, 'to perpetuate in his Grace's family a surname to which his illustrious ancestor John first Duke of Marlborough added such imperishable lustre'.

* Lady Dillon, one of the three viscountess-daughters of Sarah's sister Frances Tyrconnel who died in 1730.

† Lady Muskerry was the daughter-in-law of the Earl of Clancarty.

supporters, her arch-enemy being Sir Robert Walpole. It was many years since, as a friend, she had sent him the manuscript of her *Conduct*, though his rejection or postponement of publication may have sown the first seed of animosity. It was to be followed by many more: the dismissal of Marlborough's secretary Cardonnel (for which Sarah held him responsible); the taxing of the £5000-a-year Marlborough grant; his refusal to extend Sarah's lease of Windsor Lodge or to bar the Duke of St Albans from driving through Windsor Park. . . Even her grant of £500-a-year as Ranger of Windsor had been withdrawn; and there had been a rumpus too over Wimbledon, where Queen Caroline, needing a short cut to Richmond, demanded rights Sarah was not prepared to concede. When the Queen threatened to sue, Walpole, as always, supported her. Sarah had not forgotten that when Walpole was responsible for the post-office (or its equivalent), in Henrietta's lifetime, letters for the two Duchesses of Marlborough were constantly delivered at the wrong address. She was certain it was deliberate.*

If in Sarah's view Walpole was the successor of Harley, then Permis Newcastle was the equivalent of St John, with Mrs Clayton (the same of whom she had written, 'God Almighty bless my dear dear Mrs Clayton and all that she loves') an unconvincing yet nevertheless noxious Abigail. And indeed, to one of her many accounts of Abigail's shortcomings Sarah adds: '. . . but I think the mischeifs that have been don since by Q: Car: assisted in all vile things by Mrs Clayton are much greater and seems impossible to be recover'd'.[25]

Newcastle she felt competent to jeer at for his spelling. 'I know', she writes, 'his Grace affects to be a great scholar, which for ought I know may be the reason of his writing Honour out of the common way [Honor] & likewise for writing At with a duble t, but as I am ignorant I may not be right in my remark'.

As for Mrs Clayton, it was disappointing indeed that after all Sarah had done for her (had she not recommended her to Caroline as 'of a perfect good understanding, a reputation without the least blemish, good principles of all kinds and of an extream good family'?),[26] she should toady to royalty as she now so blatantly did. In order that the two ladies (Queen Caroline and Mrs Clayton)

* For Walpole's teasing of the Duchess over the approach to Marlborough House etc. see Hugh Phillips: *Mid-Georgian London*, pp. 49-51.

might play at cards together, or so Sarah alleged, it had been found necessary to confer upon Mr Clayton an Irish title. In her description, for Di, of the pretentious portrait of the newly created Lord and Lady Sundon, as the Claytons now were, Sarah enjoyed herself to the utmost:

> It is drawn in the manner of Hogarth's conversation pieces, but not by him, nor with a design to ridicule; but seriously directed to be done by my Lord and Lady Sundon, who are sitting at a table in their supposed library. My Lord has a book in one hand, a paper in the other . . . There are some books lying on the table besides . . . There stands by Mr Clayton a bookcase with the doors thrown open; and a servant, who I suppose is a page, with a book taken out of the bookcase, which my Lady Sundon holds out her hand to take . . . My Lady's picture I should not have known. Her dress is a fine pink colour with diamond buckles and a great deal of ruffled lace upon her head, and a bunch of pink coloured ribbons on the top of it, and a white apron. For you are to suppose she is undressed early at her studies. And in short I think nothing can be added to make these two figures better if I were to draw them myself, but to put two crowns on their chairs and to dress them in Irish robes.'[27]

At less frivolous times, when gout tortured her as it had tortured Queen Anne, her secretary and doctor, Stephens, would write to Di, 'I think her in no manner of danger, but she is not only in too much Pain to write but so low spirited that she cannot dictate'. On a good day Sarah would write in her own hand, 'I thank God I am never weary of being alone'; and on a bad one, 'It is dismal to be always alone, and the generality of company one meets with is yet worse. Most people are disagreeable for one thing or another, and I think if I could walk out of life without the pain one suffers in dying I would do it tomorrow. For go I must, a little sooner or later, and when pleasures are very small & troubles many there is no reason to be solicitous for the continuation of such a life'.

But she could not be tranquil, she could never relax. It was her duty, she told Di, to save her brother Charles from the cheats; and that meant, among other things, lawsuit after lawsuit against every-one who had been concerned in the building of Blenheim; or if, like

Vanbrugh and Travers, they happened to be dead, then with their executors or assigns. 'You know', she told Lady Cowper, 'I pretend to be a great lawyer' and so, in a sense and by much practice, she had become. For one slight reason or another she had worked herself into a lasting passion against Honest Harry (Henry Joynes), who at twenty-one had been recruited as clerk of the works some thirty years ago and was now an architect of some standing. One might have thought Lord Macclesfield's decree against Vanbrugh and the workmen inviolable, but since he had so sententiously pronounced it, things had taken a different turn. Vanbrugh by a trick had snatched his earnings, Macclesfield had been clapped in the Tower; and now in 1734 another Chancellor, Talbot, had had the effrontery to over-rule Macclesfield's decree. How could this have happened? 'All the reason that appears to me for my lord Chancellor's extraordinary Proceeding', Sarah wrote to Di, 'is that Mr Joyns who has been the vilain in all this affair of Blenheim building has been his architect and built his house for him in Lincolns Inn Fields'.* All the Chancellor had said and done was 'extream indecent', but then what was to be expected of the son of a weak father who, because he happened to be a Whig, Sarah had persuaded Queen Anne to advance from 'a small Bishoprick of Oxford' to the glittering glories of Salisbury?

She prattles on . . . Does Di approve of the tomb Kent has designed and Rysbrack sculpted for Marlborough in Blenheim chapel?† She does. (Not for her to remark that no daughter is mentioned nor depicted). And will she help translate the Latin inscription for Marlborough's bust in the Great Hall? She will. Oh and one last thing: she must see and approve the Blenheim statue (and its inscription) to Queen Anne. 'I am going to Rysbrack to make a bargain with him for a fine statue of Queen Anne', she tells her, 'which I will put up in the bow window room at Blenheim with a proper inscription.‡ It will be a very fine thing & though but one figure will cost

* Joynes built what are now numbers 57 and 58 Lincolns Inn Fields for Lord Chancellor Talbot in 1730. (See Colvin: *Biog. Dic. Eng. Architects*, p. 329.)

† The chapel was consecrated in 1728. The tomb, bearing the date 1733, shows Marlborough in Roman dress, the Duchess in robe and coronet, and their two infant sons. Fame and History are prominent. Envy is crushed by the sarcophagus which bears a relief of Tallard's surrender at Blenheim. (p. 173)

‡ In 1738 the statue is recorded as standing not in the eastern bow but in the

me £300. I have a satisfaction in showing this respect to her, because her kindness to me was real, and what happened afterwards was compassed by the contrivance of such as are in power now'.[28]

It was typical of Sarah, in her long inscription, to score a left and a right by making her forgiveness of Anne the excuse for a reflection upon George II's queen Caroline who, by backing Walpole and Mrs Clayton and in other matters such as Wimbledon, the veto on Sarah's driving through St James's Park, Sarah's four-hour wait in her ante-room and a libel on Marlborough spoken in the Queen's drawing-room,[29] had proved herself worthless and without manners or breeding. True, as Sarah said, she had never flattered anyone living and she could not be accused of flattering Anne when she was dead. In private she made it clear to her friends that she might have said very much more of Anne's shortcomings; yet even so, she pointed out, they still made her a goddess in comparison with the reigning Queen. 'As I had great obligations to the Queen [Anne]', she explained, 'I thought it unbecoming in me to relate anything to her disadvantage'.

For the public at large, then, Queen Anne's blemishes were to be hidden; but for the more private record squeamishness might be flung aside: 'She certainly, as is said on the inscription, meant well & was not a fool; but nobody can maintain that she was wise, nor entertaining in conversation. She was in everything what I described her; ignorant in everything but what the parsons had taught her when a child . . .'[30] And so on. Once—nay twice—and for all, the Duchess had spoken. Queen Anne had not after all been succeeded by another of the same name. In her public image and in her private image Queen Anne of immortal memory was one.

So much for the castle of Blenheim, which Queen Anne never saw and where the Duchess, on her visits, used but one of its hundreds of rooms. And what of the grounds? 'You say nothing', she wrote to Di, 'of the garden and court being so ill kept, though it has cost me a great deal every year; and I will take another method of doing it, which will make it better & with a great deal less charge'.[31]

---

western one of the Gallery or Long Library, in which position it would be seen immediately one entered the Great Hall. It now stands at the south end of the Long Library, without the original inscription.

The charge was then £250 a year and for that John Hughes the head gardener had undertaken

to keep the Gardens & Courts at all Times so neat that at all times of the Year they may look hansome if that any Company comes to see them & with the greatest Nice'ty when My Lady Dutchess is at Blenheim. And I likewise promise to cutt any Weeds that looks ugly . . . all round the Courts . . . If any great Tree falls downe or is taken up in the Garden, that is for my Lady Dutchess's use . . . and I am to raise whatever she Directs & to keep the Walls allways full of good fruit . . . all sorts of Roots for the Kitchin, Sparragrass etc. . . . all sorts of Sallad-tings & usefull herbs & a great deal of Lavender & Roses & Borders of Pinks, Jessamin, Lilly of the Valley, Clove gilly-flowers, Rosemary, Honey-Succles, White Lillys & in Short any thing that my Lady Dutchess shall think proper to Order & in the places which she shall direct . . .[32]

When, smarting under 'the Disgust of my Lady Dutchess', Hughes left, visitors were shocked. 'My wife was much Surpris'd at the Story of Hughes', wrote one of them. 'She says if she could envy anyone it would be Mr Hughes, he had soe quiet & soe plentifull a Situation that she thought he had nothing to wish & therefore nothing to doe but to be honest & thankfull'.[33]

It had been Sarah's boast that in the finishing of Blenheim she had saved the Marlborough trust £20,000; but now she felt less sure. 'I would leave nothing there', she told Di, 'to be done by Mr Morris. Nor do I think it of any use to save money now as I have formerly done for the trust estate, which I am sure no good use will ever be made of '.[34] After all her struggles she found herself in the mood of the psalmist:

For man walketh in a vain shadow and disquieteth himself in vain: he heapeth up riches and cannot tell who shall gather them.[35]

Di attempted to cheer her by offering to take her to the opera. 'It would please me', Sarah replied, 'a thousand times more then any musick that can ever be perform'd, but I fear I shall never be able to go . . . because I can't get out of my chair without two people to help me & when I am got out I can't stand nor goe one steep without two chair men to hold me up'. She would content herself with her chamber-organ which played eight tunes and had cost less than many a bishopric.

In spite of music and pet dogs and of all Di could do for her, however, Sarah lapsed into gloom, wished she could have pre-deceased Marlborough and, with all her vast possessions and wretched health, compared her lot to Job's. 'I can't say I am quite living, nor am I dead, which perhaps is the best state that one can be in. But I can say with Job that my eyes are dim with sorrow & my nerves are as shadows, & indeed I think my circumstances is more like his than anybody's that I have heard of or read of'.[36] Addressing Di as she did as Cordelia, it was surprising that she never saw herself in the role of Lear.

Throughout 1734 the letters continue, the gloom deepens. Over Di's 'very kind expressions' she weeps: 'Perhaps too I may feel it the more from the dreadful usage I have met with from others'. In December there are hints of friction, not with Di but with her husband the Duke of Bedford, who has differed with Sarah over the parliamentary election of John Spencer. Something—an explosion?*—happens and, after letters-by-every-post year in year out, suddenly, for five months, there is nothing at all; and when in June, 1735, we are again allowed an insight, the shadow of anxiety falls across every line. Sarah has found 'full employment in furnishing Wimbledon for dear Cordelia', while growing more and more concerned about her health. Di is said to be pregnant, but is she? The symptoms Sarah hears of bring nothing but worry.

Oh for a charm to ward off evil, some spell or philtre, some con-soling thought, some sanctuary for what was left of happiness, to keep it safe. 'I wish', writes Sarah, 'you could send me a receip to think upon all occasions what will make one most happy, that would be a charming thing'. With an effort she rallies for Di's birthday, 'keept in my family [household]', she tells her, 'with great splender, all my servants had joyful faces & all the wemen made a much better figure, in my mind, then any of her Majesty's maids of honour upon the great days at court. As for my self I need not say

---

* In her letter dated March 16, 1737 to the Duke of Bedford Sarah refers to it as a storm which blew over. (Scott-Thomson, op. cit., p. 177)

how much I wish you may live as long as 'tis possible to do . . . but I must own I am extreamly uneasy at the account you give me of the way you are in'.

She wrote to Di's doctor and sent Marlborough's campaigning tent for Di to lie in. At the end of August she insisted on her coming to London, but nothing could be done. On September 27th, in her twenty-sixth year, Diana Duchess of Bedford died of tuberculosis.*

From what Sarah wrote to the widower eighteen months later one suspects that, at the last, she desperately tried to act the doctor and was prevented. 'Your Grace knew very well', she says, 'that I must have [had] more experience than any body about her. It would be too much to repeat the monstrous usage which I received . . . But I sat silently in outward rooms, bathed in tears; and I own I flattered you . . . which was out of fear that if I did not take that way, you would order the porter not to let me in . . .'[37]

It was a most miserable end to Sarah's last, deep friendship. 'I need say nothing of my heart', she had once told Di, 'for you know that has allways been yours and will be so till I dye and after to all Eternity, if that can bee . . .'

Wimbledon, finished and furnished, was now meaningless. There was nothing to do but burn bundles of Di's letters and this she did, having most of them by heart.

Long ago, in the year of Marlborough's death and in the lifetime of her two daughters Henrietta and Mary, Sarah had written to her kinswoman Mrs Ann Jennens:

> You have stated my misfortunes kindly in hopes to make me feel them the less, but you ded not consider that I have no children, for tho I love these poor grandchildren & will take care of them for their Mothers' sakes, yet that is nothing like having good children of one's own, & I beleive that Dear Mrs Jennens will allow that whoever has been once so happy as I have been & have nothing left but mony, which from my humour I don't want much of, deserves to bee pittyd.[38]

* Several references to a swelling in the neck suggest that Lady Diana Spencer may have suffered from tubercular glands. Although today with proper treatment she would almost certainly have been cured, in 1735 her case was hopeless.

But without counting on pity Sarah had long since become fatalistic. Even as long ago as in the reign of Anne, when peace was imminent, she had told Lady Cowper, 'I pray heartily for it, and whenever that is [comes], I think I shall live without hope or fear, which I really beleive is the best condition'.

CHAPTER XIV

The Grandsons

1720-1740

———◆———

It has often been observed to what a striking extent the regular features of Marlborough, 'handsome as an angel', have been transmitted to his descendants, even to the tenth, to the eleventh, to the twelfth generation. All his grandsons had charm and some were handsome, though none showed more brilliance than most of his Eton contemporaries, nor did any display that ineffable sweetness discerned by Dr Hare in their grandfather.

Charles and John, Di's younger brothers, followed Robert, the Spencer heir, to Eton, after a brief stay at a school in Hampstead. 'I have heard Hampstead school found fault with', wrote Sarah to their father, Lord Sunderland, in 1720, 'and Eaton commended, but I don't know which is best. If they are at Eaton I shall have opertunitys of seeing them oftener then at any school, for as I have alterd Windsor lodge 'tis a thousand times more agreeable then Blenheim & I shall pass the greatest part of my life there, but I fear Eaton is not a wholesome place. One of the children* has got over that terrible destemper the smallpox. Poor little John has not had it. I hope you will leave such orders that hee may not bee murderd as poor dear Ld Barkely was, beeing blooded & removed after the smallpox was on & had not the least cordial to support nature in such an extremity. If hee has it when I am at Windsor hee may as easyly bee brought to me as his brother was to London, and Mr Gerney has more sense & more experience then most of the doctors at this time'.[1]

No school was ideal, but in handiness and cheapness Eton manifestly scored over others, ('Children can be put there for about

———

* Charles Spencer.

threescore pounds a year'); and so without further argument the motherless brothers were packed off to it. At such times a stout-hearted and unsentimental grandmother can be, on the surface at least, a greater asset than an emotional mother, no matter how beloved. How embarrassing, for example, to have a mother like Lady Scarbrough! She had written to the Duchess:

> I will goe to Windsore to pay my duty to the Princess, which I designed doing ye day I settled my children at Eaton . . . but play'd ye foole soe much when I parted with them that I was ashamed to make my Court, but I think truly I should have overcome that if you had bin there.[2]

Charles, who was ten when his mother died and was little marked by the smallpox, inherited from his grandmother a forthrightness and a stoutness of spirit which, with lack of imagination, made ideal material for the soldier he was to be. John, far more sensitive, was a typical Spencer, a lover of cards, a lover of music; one could not be sure that his heart would be ruled by his head. Though occasionally out of favour, as when he declined to have 'no commerce' with Charles, he won, in spite of herself, his grandmother's heart and became her *Torrismond* and chief heir; while his brother lost favour, regained it and then lost it forever.

In Sarah's experience it was almost always the most lovable that were snatched from her. Her sons, her favourite daughters, her favourite granddaughter, and now her favourite grandson Robert Spencer, Lord Sunderland, who at twenty-eight died in Paris, unmarried, in 1729. It was true, she admitted, that he had gambled excessively, but to her he had been kind and goodnatured and, in sharp contrast with others, had done 'very little mischief to the estate'. As to his premature death of a 'fever', that was scandalous. 'There is no such thing', she declared, 'as a good physician in France, or medecine . . . What they did was directly contrary to the methods of our physicians here in the same destemper. I lament extremely', she added, 'that at the beginning of his illness I was not acquainted with it, because as he had strength to hold out for so many days, notwithstanding so much Bleeding & Purging, always thought prejudicial in a fever . . . I cannot but think there was time for me to have sent medecines & a physician from England that might in all probability have saved him. But it is now too late to make these reflections & all the comfort I have at present is that his brother who succeeds him [Charles] is perfectly honest, goodnatured & has as many vertues as I could wish. But still I have lost one that I passionately lov'd of a Branch who have all very good sense'.[3]

It only remained to 'do him all the honour with Decency without Follies even to his Grave'; and it was astonishing how costly, in Paris, such modest honour could be. Without quibble Sarah settled the account of £8430, which included £650 for embalming, an apothecary's bill for £1379, 'un nécessaire de porcelaine' £144, a £200 coffin and a further £600 for bringing it home.[4]

The Duchess was now left with two daughters, seven granddaughters and only three grandsons: Charles and John Spencer and their cousin Willigo Blandford; the Bridgwater heir Viscount Brackley having died at Eton in 1719 at the age of fifteen.

After Eton, in the usual course of things, every young nobleman not at a university needed to be sent abroad. It was a pattern—the Grand Tour—first laid down in the sixteenth century and now, though scoffed at by Pope and others, considered *de rigueur*.

'Most of our travelling youth neither improve themselves nor credit their country', complained Lady Hartford, writing from Florence in 1740. 'This I believe is often owing to the strange creatures that are made their governors, but as often to the strange creatures that are to be governed. Travelling is certainly carried a great deal too far among the English . . . and the fortune which should be increasing . . . is often decreasing in dress, equipage and sometimes in worse things. Could you see the inundation of poor creatures from all the three kingdoms that at the regular seasons overrun the different parts of France and Italy you would with me lament the approaching month of July in which I am destined to receive them here'.[5]

Charles was eighteen months senior to his brother John, and Willigo seven years older than his cousin Charles; so Willigo, with Mann his governor, went ahead to Holland and Switzerland, meeting Charles in Geneva in 1723. When Willigo returned to Utrecht, Charles remained boarded with a Swiss tutor, Gallatin, to be joined there by John with Sarah's ex-page, Captain Humphrey Fish, in 1725.

In their grandmother's opinion all three grandsons were poor correspondents, and Willigo, though he blamed the mailboats, hardly ever wrote at all unless for funds. Then his rare scrawls, in an alarmingly unbalanced hand, would reach the dowager from Utrecht, from Antwerp, from Rome . . . 'Lord Blandford', Sarah learns from Mrs Boscawen,* 'is not for hurrying and especially [not] out of Italy, which country he prefers to all ye world besides & I find intends to visit all ye little courts & states of it . . . They are very busie in viewing all ye paintings of ye greatest masters, but . . . musick is ye thing in ye world in which he expresses ye most delight'.[6]

But the Duchess, like Marlborough before her, had spies throughout Europe, and the reports she was now receiving from them were not reassuring. Concerned, she compared notes with Mrs Boscawen, who replied:

> I really hope & believe those common malicious reports of many are alltogether groundless . . . His delight is in seeing antiquities & curiosities of all sorts & that place [Rome] abounds with them; & consequently does not spend his time as most other young men doe . . . Lord Blandford was gone into ye mountains to visit some old convents . . . Whatever becomes of their letters & how they manage them, there must be a great many lost . . . God send him well home in his owne good time with ye same good principles of honour, vertue & piety that I'm sure he carried out with him & all will doe well.[7]

When Sarah did at last hear from him she remained unconvinced. He wrote from Rome of church music, adding, 'I believe there is no town in the world that is better fitted to give one an abhorrence of the tricks & nonsense of popery'.[8] She hoped he meant it. She had heard he had leanings in that very direction. On the back of his letter (for she is finishing the chapel at Blenheim) she scribbles: 'The panel of wanscoat for the cloath at the Alter 3 yards high wanting 3

---

* Mrs Boscawen, related to the Godolphins and at this time nearly 80, refers to herself as 'very simple' and 'a worn out insignificant old creature'. As the Blenheim records show, she had the courage to take the Duchess gently to task for having appointed herself Queen Anne's mother-confessor and for having sent her *The Whole Duty of Man*.

inches, broad 2 yards 2 inches . . . 2 black steeps of marble up to the Alter'. From Antwerp Mann, himself frowned upon for not writing more often, writes of Willigo, 'His chief business is usually to view everything that is rare and remarkable, but not to engage much in the conversation of the natives'. Even so, he was not allowed to be solitary. 'I was entertained very civilly and handsomely', wrote Willigo, 'by some English officers who . . . enquired much after Lady Tyrconnel and drank her health often'. He had admired the 'extremely pretty & handsome house' in which the Marlboroughs had made their 'long and melancholy stay', a sight which had led him to reflect on 'the great vicissitudes that attend all human affairs'; but otherwise Antwerp and its society held small appeal. 'I cannot say', he ended, 'that there was anything to recommend it to any person that desired to live as he should do & at the same time not lock himself quite up from company. For all the gentlemen there are the heartiest drinkers & the most entirely given up to it that ever I saw in my life'.[9]

The tone was just a shade too shocked to deceive a sharpwitted grandmother. Sarah suspected that Willigo was himself becoming a hearty drinker. While he stayed abroad there was little she could do but hope that he would come to his senses. In the meantime, though opposed by his mother, she squeezed from the trust a separate settlement which would make him, if he lived, one of England's richest men. It was asking for trouble and sure enough, as the years went by, the reports of Willigo became more and more disturbing.

'I have been told from a very good hand', Sarah writes from Bath in 1727 to her ex-page who signs himself Hum: ffyshe, 'that Mr Montgomery's relation has a very great inclination to a lady who I doubt is a sad tawdry creature & that the journey into Holland was chiefly to see her . . . Pray let me know if you think young Mr M is in danger of being drawn into any thing mischievous of that sort'.[10]

It was only too true. Willigo, now referred to even by his sister Harriet as Lord Worthless, had taken up with a burgomaster's daughter at Utrecht. Sarah, who had had her eye on a daughter of the Duke of Bedford's, wrote desperately by every post. Surely he could not be such an ungrateful fool? Surely he would at least return to England first and consult his father? 'I do protest', she writes on thick, gilt-edged paper, 'that I never was so much afflected at any thing that has ever happened to me as I am at what you have written except the death of the Duke of Marlborough and my only son. Since that I have had no sort of pleasure but in doing every thing in my power to perpetuate the glorious actions of the first & before his death I took more pains than you can easyly beleive . . . to establish you in the place of a son . . . and when I am dead, which I beleive is not far off, you will have a better estate than most people have in England . . . I hope you will not return this by breaking my heart, which it will certainly do to see the Duke of Marlborough's heir marryd to a burgomaster's daughter. As to what you say that she is as good a Gentlewoman as any in Holland, which I think is not saying much . . . I have heard several say that she is neither hansome nor so much as agreeable & therefore I must conclude that there has been many artifices used to bring you to such lengths as you seem to bee in so disadvantages & impudent a match without so much as consulting your father . . .'[11] and so on for eight pages. That Marlborough's heir should think of marrying 'a woman unknown to all the world but low people' was unthinkable. It was 'as if a daughter were run away with and had lost her reputation'. It wanted a name.

In his replies Willigo, now twenty-nine, sounds collected and dignified. His girl is the sister of the Countess of Denbigh, very beautiful and altogether one of the finest women of her time. But Sarah remains sceptical. Most people in English society, she says, are too shocked even to mention it to her. Indeed, it was by the merest chance that she had heard the rumour of his engagement to this 'very low and odd woman'. And as to beauty, 'I must say', she wrote frankly, 'that in all the time that I was in Holland I never saw but one woman that looked like a human creature & that was the dowager Lady Albemarle. If this person is no more tempting than Lady Denbigh, you must allow that people will wonder at your choice, who might have had any person undisposed of . . . and as for her birth . . . if you had said wee were all Adhams children & twas no matter for birth, it had been better'.[12]

Sarah consulted Willigo's father, Francis Godolphin—'the most worthy man in the world'—and Sir John Evelyn. Nothing could be done. On the 25th of July, 1729, in Utrecht, Willigo married Maria de Yonge.

Surprisingly, when the worst or what she considered the worst had happened, Sarah simmered to calmness; so much so that in 1730 we find Willigo thanking her for a very kind and affectionate letter. To her pleas to return he says he would like to, 'but as my Mother's long ill conduct towards my Father & Me had obliged me to take a resolution never to see Her, I was Willing to have my Father's Consent to return upon that condition & applied myself lately to the Duchess of Newcastle* to intercede with him for that purpose, which with much Reluctancy she has at last done but without any effect, for instead of consenting to what I thought & shall ever think I most reasonably desired, he only upbraids me for what he calls Indecent Omissions towards my Mother & has told my Sister 'tis a Proposal he can never come into . . . When you reflect', he reminds his grandmother, 'how Good a Daughter she has made to You, a Wife to my Father & a Mother to Me, you will see what reason she can have to complain of my want of duty'.[13]

Francis Godolphin, writing to his mother-in-law of his son's 'weak, improper, ill-judged step' (the kind of folly he himself would never have dreamed of), adds, 'As he has baked, so he must brew'.[14] Neither he nor his wife would take any hand in the brewing.

But Willigo was not to brew for long. Two years after his rash marriage, while drinking heartily at of all things a Tory meeting at of all places Balliol, he suddenly collapsed and died. Sarah, arriving too late with Di, is reported to have said, 'Ay, I suppose he's dead. I would have given half my estate to have saved him. I hope the Devil is picking that man's bones who taught him to drink'. And then, turning to Di, 'Where is my basket, Di? Did I not charge you to bring it?' Di ran to the coach for a heavy basket which may have held money. For two hours Sarah then discussed the case with the doctors and sympathised with the widow, who had since arrived. Which done she left for Blenheim, murmuring as she did so that she would take some other opportunity of satisfying the woman of the house.[15]

The widowed Lady Blandford complained of poverty, but it seems that her jointure provided her with £3000 a year, mainly drawn from the rentals of Holdenby, a large estate Sarah had bought within sight of Althorp. She soon married *en deuxième noces* Bolingbroke's friend and Somerset's son-in-law (then a widower) Sir

* His sister Harriet.

William Wyndham,* who took up her cudgels and sued the Marlborough trust for a better settlement. Her father-in-law refused to see her, while her mother-in-law, Henrietta, directed in her will that on no account was her daughter Mary to give her anything.[16]

Sarah wrote: 'I am told the Duke of Somerset did all he could to hinder Sir William Wyndham from beginning this suit & that when he first saw my Lady Blandford he looked as if he was amazed that such a woman should be married for beauty, but that was not Sir William's case. And poor Lord Blandford was always drunk & in the hands of robbers & people brought out of gaol to make a prey of him'.

In 1734, on hearing that Lady Blandford was pregnant, though in fact she was not, Sarah told Di, 'If it be true, I think your brothers have had as great an escape as another Duke [Bedford] you love very well, for if she had brought a son to my Lord Blandford it would have been a sort of Regency for the use of a Dutch family, & your brothers are got very well off by only paying a great jointure. Who will be heir to your grandfather's great estate at last God only knows. I can only say that I have taken a great deal of pains both in getting & preserving it from abuses, tho' in the last I have not been very successful'.

What Sarah kept asking herself was, were the grandsons worth it? Abroad, Charles and John had been so reckless with time and money —with clothes, for example: 'As rediculous', commented their grandmother, 'as if I should go into Wales & lay out a great deal of money to dress my self up on King George's birthday'—she often wished she had never sent them. 'Dancing gives men a good Air', she wrote to Fish in Geneva, 'and fencing should be learnt . . . Drawing may be useful and is a pretty entertainment, but as to architecture I think it will be of no use to Charles or John, no more then Musick,† which are all things proper for people that have time upon their hands & like passing it in idleness rather then in what will

---

* Sir William Wyndham (1687–1740), baronet, Secretary at War (1712). Chancellor of the Exchequer (1713). Jacobite, implicated in the 1715 rising and sent to the Tower but never brought to trial. Sarah, meeting him in 1734, was surprised to find him 'extream agreeable & of much good sense'.

† 'Wee have as good mussick as there is any where, & some people think as good conversation'. Sarah to Gallatin, 18 Sept. 1726. (Blen E 31).

be profitable'.[17] She was cross when she heard that Johnny, as she called him, had been playing the flute. This he knew was forbidden, for fear it distorted his face.

The boys were stoutly stuck up for by their governor, Fish, who unlike Mann wrote sympathetically and often. Time, he admits, was wasted in Switzerland (a country, in Sarah's opinion, to be passed through on the way to somewhere else), 'because it was very natural for men so young & so full of fire to have a much stronger bent for pleasures than labour . . . However, they understand French very well & speak it & write it very fluently & intelligably but there is room for improvement . . . They have read & understood the best part of Horace,* which is an author your Grace has heard of more than once . . . Mr Charles has very little curiosity & looks upon all travelling as a very insipid entertainment & thinks of Italy with great dread . . . but Mr John is far from being in the same case'. Both have readily and he believes steadily resolved to dedicate all their mornings to useful improvements. 'Mr Charles', he concludes, 'gave his voice strongly for Paris'.[18]

'I cannot with a good conscience blame Charles's want of curiosity', replies his grandmother, 'because I have none my self for such things as you mention . . . You tell me that the expence at Paris will scarce be less than £200 a month. That is more than the Duke of Marlborough and I spent when we were abroad with more than twenty horses & a house full of servants . . . I have been told lately by a great traveller that there is fixed prices for seeing the greatest curiosities & that six people may see them for eighteenpence & an opera for three halfpence'. She suspects that they gamble and if they do, she warns Fish, either abroad or in England, 'unless it be in my company, I will never give them a shilling, either living or dying, tho' I am tenderly theirs'.[19] And again, 'All the French wemen are cheats & they will bee much ceviller if you don't play with them'.

* In March Fish, writing to Sarah, had referred to Horace as 'an Author mightily esteemed by all people of good taste & famous for writing good sense agreeably & genteely'. In April Sarah wrote to him: 'Talking lately to men of very good understanding they named an Author to me which if I don't mistake was Horris & I think in one of your letters lately you said that you were all to bee employ'd in that study . . . I am told that when young people begin it, if they have any good tast they cannot leave it off'. (Blen E 31).

From Paris the brothers send Sarah and Di two *mantilles* (Sarah: 'We don't know what it means'), with instructions how to wear them, for which Sarah returns thanks. The 'directions how to dress my self' were 'very particular . . . and yet I doubt we have not yet attain'd to putting them on in the best air'. But Charles is disappointed in Paris and makes for home, while John moves on with Fish to Dijon.

At Windsor Lodge Sarah looked forward to welcoming Charles warmly and to hearing him prattle away in French to Di; but once again she was expecting too much. To begin with, he looked 'not near so well as he did when he went out of England'; and what was worse, he was inarticulate in all languages not excluding his own. She was disgusted. 'He speaks', she complained to Fish, 'without opening his mouth, thro' his teeth,* & it is difficult to know even whether he says yes or no, without a great attention, which few things are worth . . . There are several wemen in this country who don't articulate & who think it pritty to make a noise like a bird, & this has troubled me so much to find in Charles that I am very desirous to know whether Johnny has got into the same manner of speaking. If he has, I think it is very indifferent what language he talks in'.[20]

Why, even an old Frenchman could put them both to shame! 'Here is a Frenchman', she tells Fish, 'that I believe is about three-score, who has learned in a year's time to read all the English authors & both to write & speak English: his name is Voltaire'.[21]

The more she sees of Charles the more her affection warms towards distant Johnny, and again she confides in Fish. 'I ever liked him', she owns, 'from a little child & tho' there used to be many complaints against him, I must own that I never saw any thing my self that I could bee really angrey with him for, tho' I affected to be so often. I allways thought hee had a great deal of spirit & quickness & has much good nature, which are charming qualities . . . I will not restrain him in the pleasure which hee takes in playing upon the flute.

* To preserve their teeth Sarah recommends the brothers to chew tobacco for 'half an hour or thereabouts' before spitting it out. 'If it be from the scurvy which most people have more or less there is nothing in the world that will preserve them so much as chewing tobacco. Tis what most people do now in this country & if I had known this sooner I should have lost none of my teeth'. (Blen E 31).

The reasons you give for his doing it have convinced me, since you say it does not hurt his face'.[22] But how unselfish she had been to send him abroad, 'not to see him perhaps [again] while I live; but as the gout does not always kill in a few years I will still hope to live to see him, & so well accomplished as to answer all my wishes'.[23]

Certainly when a few months later crisis came and Humphrey Fish died of a fever in Paris, John Spencer, at twenty, proved remarkably competent. 'I have had his body embalmed', he tells his grandmother, 'till such time as I know whether his father would have it sent into England. If he has no mind for that, I can get him buried here. Sir John Dolbin . . . read the burial service over him yesterday & I have sent his body to Dijon till I know his father's resolutions. I am at present at Plombières with the Duke of Kingston. I dare not venture to Dijon as yet upon account of a malignant fever, very common there at present, of which no one has as yet recovered. Mr ffish had this fever, but I believe he could not have lived other-wise, for when he was opened they found several ulcers in his lungs & his heart full of polypuses'.[24]

Sarah was shocked—'He had all things that I could wish for'—and told Johnny, 'I have sent the dismall account of poor ffyshe to his father and . . . will let you know . . . I hope in God you will come to England as soon as you receive this letter, for I am so terrify'd with what has happen'd that I shall not sleep one night in quiet till I see you here . . . No words can express how dear you are to me & I shall be in torture till I see you . . . who am with all the tenderness that ever was in any heart my Dear Dear Johnny yours . . . And for the gold watch, you will bring it in your pocket, which I will pay his father for & you'll wear it for his sake'.[25]

It was one thing to cock a snook at death oneself and quite another to sit by while he snatched these young men, one after another, from under one's very nose: today Humphrey Fish, tomorrow Willigo Blandford, and the day after—? It was intolerable. By 1730 death had taken all male heirs (Sarah made it 'about a dozen') except the two grandsons Charles and John, who kicked over the traces as only rich young Spencers could. They had vowed, it was said, never to soil their fingers with silver, and they unloaded the guineas hoarded by Marlborough, as though they were tiddlywinks. 'What he has spent', Sarah told Di, of her brother Charles, 'is a great deal more than his Grandfather Marl: & I spent when he was at the head of the Army & allmost in the place of a King'. He gambled wildly. Sarah, watching him play at Tunbridge, was wounded at his incompetence. 'It was impossible for him to win', she groaned, 'and if he loses but one hundred pounds in a week . . . it comes to £5000 a year & 200, but alass that summ is nothing in such company . . .' What nonsense it made of all her lawsuits and estate-buying. She kept him as short of cash as she could; but there is no armour against folly.

With Charles for pattern Johnny, to whom Sarah had given the pet name *Torrismond*,* was not to be outrivalled in scandalous escapade and managed to 'make the town ring with some wild frolic every day';[26] although it must be owned that when the frolics are particularised they make tame reading. By a singular law of history the slightest of incidents involving male nudity has almost always been exaggerated and immortalised. Rochester's frisk in the meadow below High Lodge, after swimming in the Evenlode; Bolingbroke's nude scamper through St James's Park; the race between two naked footmen in Woodstock Park ('ye Height of Impudence & ye greatest Affront to the Ladies');[27] these trifles and many like them have for no good reason been perpetuated; while Queen Anne's sealed packet goes into the fire. And so it was that for even less cause one still senses Society's *frisson* when John Spencer, surprised in his bath, 'out of a sprightly & frolicsome humour leaped out of it naked as he was & waited on his visitor down to the very street door.' In a court starved of wit it was considered sensational enough to be told to the Queen at her levée; whereupon Lord Peterborough, on the top of his form, remarked that Mr Spencer was a man of extraordinary breeding to acknowledge the favour of a common visit in his birthday clothes,[28] a quip that must surely have all but brought down the palace.

It was no effort for the Duchess to treat all such nonsense with the contempt it deserved; but the frailer she became, the shorter seemed the intervals between major crises; and that of Charles's bride, Elizabeth Trevor, seemed quite the most shattering of all. Of the girl herself she knew nothing, though she gathered from friends that she had bad teeth, a very indifferent person, was ill bred and obviously not used to the best company. It was her background to which she

* From Dryden's *The Spanish Friar.*

violently objected. 'As to the woman', she told Charles's brother, 'I
don't know what she is nor I don't care, but I do beleive, as bad as
the world is, there are men that have honour enough not to have
lik'd to have marryd the granddaughter of a remarkable Prosecutor
of their own Grandfather who gave him such a title and such an
estate'.[29] It was not one of her plainer statements. The girl's grandfather happened to have been one of the twelve Tory peers created
by Queen Anne to ensure the safe passage of the treaty of Utrecht.
And on top of that, said Sarah, the whole family of Trevors were
'sad people'. It was worse than the case of Willigo. Why, Charles
might have married anyone on earth, yet here he was, ready to link
himself with a family, 'every one of which are so mean & rediculous
that no man of sense but must be ashamed to have any of them seen
in the house'. One of their connections, she had heard, was Sir
Richard Steele—'a most illustrious alliance!'

At the bottom of it all, Sarah felt certain, was Lady Bateman, that
falsest of granddaughters, that Iago who plotted in the dark and sent
her grandmother abusive, anonymous letters. She who was capable
of anything had now, for her own purposes, sold her brother to a
nobody. Sarah had long since ceased to have commerce with Anne
Bateman, but her own duty was clear. She must attack Charles and
she must certainly investigate the marriage-settlement. Charles was
obdurate, defiant, indignant. From his grandmother's letter he
learned that he could not possibly be in love with Elizabeth Trevor,
'for they say she is not at all handsome & has a mean, ordinary
look. I beleive her Grandfather was not a Gentleman . . .' Charles
replied:

Madam, I receiv'd Your Grace's extraordinary Letter last Night
& I own my Discerning won't let me see any Reason in what
Your Grace is pleas'd to say against my Marrying; unless
Invectives are to be look'd upon as Arguments. I shan't
endeavour to convince Your Grace that it is a Match of my own
seeking & not of my overbearing sister's (as you are pleas'd to
call her) because in the Passion Your Grace must be when you
wrote such a Letter all Arguments would be of very little use.
As for your putting me out of your Will, it is some Time since I
neither expected or desir'd to be in it. I have nothing more to

add but to assure Your Grace that this is the last time I shall ever Trouble You by Letter or Conversation.[30]

How extremely brutal and rude; yes and muddled too, for Charles, as Sarah commented, clearly misunderstood the meaning of 'invective'—'for I take Invectives to be Falsities; but my letter was nothing but plain Facts which every body knows to be true'.[31] She could not prevent the wedding. It happened on May 23rd, 1732. But she sent for the marriage-settlement, read it, scratched it and found 'one of the greatest Rogues of any Coat', the Bishop of St Davids.* At her interview with the Bishop Sarah, having nothing to lose, set out to tease him and, as her narrative shows, thoroughly enjoyed it:

Saturday morning the good Bishop came to me to give me an account of his negotiation with my Lord Trevor. He began my Lord's answer, which I interrupted saying, My Lord, I desire to see his letter. He answered he could not do that.

Duchess: Why, my Lord?

Bishop: I have left his letter at home.

Duchess: Then you may show it me another time.

He put his hand in his pocket & took out a paper which he had writ & call'd the minutes of my Lord Trevor's letter.

Duchess: Pray, my Lord, give it me. I'll read it myself.

Bishop: No, Madam, I can't do that.

The Bishop read the minutes: The match not his seeking but the Duke's desire . . . Her Grace's threatening had not been a right way etc.

Duchess: Pray, my Lord, give me that paper.

Bishop: No, I can't possibly do that.

Duchess: Then, my Lord, let a servant of mine write it out.

He was extremely averse, but I rang the bell and with great difficulty persuaded him to let it be copied & at last he did permit Loft to do it, but kept it in his hand as if he had been with pirates that would force it from him. And it being so tedious & awkward to have Loft reach over to look upon every line he was to write, I said:

* Nicholas Clagett, Bishop of St Davids from 1732 to 1742 when he was translated to Exeter. Ob. 1746.

Duchess: Pray, my Lord, let it lie before him, it will be done much sooner. What are you afraid of? You are able to get the better of us two if we should offer to force it from you.

Bishop: Is this talking to me like a bishop?

After it was done he went away and said he was my Grace's humble servant, to which I answered I could not say I was his or that I ever would be so.[32]

All this and more was written down for John Spencer's benefit, although as his grandmother said, 'I know you don't love writing, nor perhaps to receive letters, & I don't wonder that you should love the company of those little hounds, for I think them much more agreeable than the greatest part of those whom I am obliged to converse with here.' In a classically characteristic sentence she explains (sic): 'There is no possibility of any body's loving three persons that mortally hate one another and especially when two of them have done such things to one of them as no person that knows what a principle is but must abhorr'. By which she tries to convey her disappointment in Johnny, who has attended the wedding and is still on good terms with brother Charles and sister Anne Bateman.

The most Johnny would do at this stage was to promise to renounce the Batemans; nor would he marry without his grand-mother's consent; but to Charles he would remain loyal, no matter what the cost. This was in 1732. In the following year, on his accession to the dukedom,* Charles was advised to make his peace with the dowager and did so in a tearful scene which saw not only her acceptance of his apology but, still more surprisingly, her apology to him. She was even gracious to his wife Elizabeth. 'I really love them both', she told Di, 'and am convinced that the Duke of Marl: has many vertues'. She was glad she had agreed to see them, she so nearly had not. To Charles's request for the interview, which had found her in low spirits, she had replied:

I am as much pleased as I can be with any thing to read such a letter as I have received from you, but it is for your own sake,

* In 1729, on the death of his brother Robert, Charles Spencer became 5th Earl of Sunderland. In 1733, on the death of his aunt Henrietta Duchess of Marlborough, he became 3rd Duke of Marlborough and, by agreement, surrendered Althorp to his younger brother John, ancestor of the Earls Spencer.

for as to my self I am so humbled & worn out with continual afflections & desappointments that I can never more be sensible of any great joy, and as I expect non I grow fond of entertaining my self with my own melancholy & nothing is so desagreeable to me as what go's about to devert my mind from it. This is a sort of nonsence that one must feel before one can understand, but I grow so well acquainted with this desmal kind of ease that I shall not goe to London till somthing calls me that I cannot avoid, having noe tast for any thing that is there; but when I must go I shall be glad to see you, who was allways your affectionate grandmother

S: Marlborough[33]

It would have been a good moment for the Duchess to die, and it was no fault of hers that she had to go on witnessing and chafing at Charles's extravagance: at Althorp (the stables etc.), at Langley (the Mashams' 'retired habitation' rebuilt),† at Bray (Monkey Island),[34] at Windsor (mounts and a serpentine river for Little Lodge)‡ ... On all sides he spent wildly, and gambled like a maniac. The Spencer estate was Johnny's and in the meantime, while Sarah lived, Charles could not touch his ducal inheritance. His large allowance went nowhere and he soon found himself begging loans on the expectation of the dowager's death. 'This contented the lenders', Sarah, who had been dangerously ill, commented, 'but I unluckily recovered'. Their friendship deteriorated.

When an heir was born to Charles and Elizabeth, Charles 'came in his chair to Marlborough House, call'd for my porter', notes the Duchess, 'and desir'd him to tell the Dowager Dutchess of Marlborough that his wife was brought to bed of a son, & went away the same moment without asking to see me. This was extreme rediculous

---

† Abigail Masham died in 1734. Charles Duke of Marlborough bought Langley of Lord Masham in 1738.

‡ Sarah accused Charles of providing Little Lodge in Windsor Park with 'serpentine rivers deep enough to hold his ship, & two mountains, one very high which was to have a large room on the top of it; the other lower, only for a tea-room'. Charles protested that he had done nothing more ambitious than 'cut a narrow ditch a little broader to hinder it from stinking'. A plan for his ship survives at Blenheim.

& stupid, to call me Dowager Dutchess to my own Servant, which look'd as if he apprehended otherwise that my Porter might go to the other Dutchess to tell her she was brought to bed'.[35]

In his efforts to handle his grandmother Charles, bluff and straight-forward, certainly lacked finesse. He was, as Sarah said, wonderfully unbusinesslike, useless at cards, hopeless at money. His wife adored him, and he her. When in 1740 Sarah heard that he had kissed the King's hand and set a cockade in his hat to lead a regiment, she could not believe it. This indeed was folly. In her will she had stipulated that on pain of forfeit none of them was to take office nor 'put on a fool's coat & take posts from soldiers of experience & service, who never did any thing but kill pheasants & partridges'.[36] It was too late.

'Your Brother', Sarah told Johnny, 'has done a thing lately that I am sure must be purely his own, without the assistance of any counsel. Whood the painter* has drawn his Picture in the figure of an old Roman Consul with a truncheon in one hand & one arm drawn quite naked, I suppose going to do some great execution. A gentleman that saw it found fault with the arm, saying that it seemed to him to be drawn too large. "Pardon me", replied Mr Whood, "it is as it should be, for my Lord Duke sate himself naked to have it done exactly by the life". This makes several people merry & I must own I think it would have been as well if he had deferred the drawing this graceful figure till he had been in some battle'.[37]

In contrast to Sarah's rift with Charles, which ended in the law-courts, it is pleasant to turn to Althorp and find his brother Johnny happily married, and with not only a wife (Lady Georgina Carteret, chosen by Sarah) but with children of whom his grandmother could approve.

I saw Mrs Spencer and your children last night', Sarah writes from Windsor Lodge in 1742, 'They are both of 'em charming & they talk enough & I find they are mighty fond of coming to me, for I play at drafts with 'em & they both beat me shame-fully. I beleive really they like to come to me extreamly, tho' I

---

* Lord Spencer assures me that the portrait, which hangs above the main stair-case at Althorp, is not by Whood but by Stephen Slaughter. With the owner's kind permission it is reproduced here facing p. 289. D.B.G.

heard they had been told I intended to give them a present; upon which they press'd Grace mightily to know what it was, and after she had acquainted me with their curiosity, I asked 'em if they would have a kiss or gold & they both cried out very eagerly mony.

I am always yours,

S: Marlborough[38]

CHAPTER XV

Without Hope or Fear

1740-1744

———◆———

Although Sarah, with but little reserve, was prepared to welcome it, there seemed no time for death. With three cases still pending ('Sure there is nothing so horrid as the Law') she was sick to death of litigation; sick to death of suffering; sick to death of buying estates and of managing them and the Marlborough trust, this last an onerous chore of which Francis Godolphin refused to relieve her. And yet ... 'You express so much goodness', she had written to the Bishop of Exeter, 'in wishing the continuance of my wretched life, which I assure you I am very weary off, and yet perhaps I should start at death, tho' tis not reasonable because it must come sooner or later ...'[1]

And to Willigo, six years since:

I have two terrible distempers, the Gout & the Gravell, but I thank God my pain is almost gone & nothing remains now but weakness, so that I beleive (for this time) the danger is over, but I must expect returns, & to die a little sooner or later, as one's friends will have it by the assistance of doctors. When I am well enough to reason I think it very indifferent when this happens, and yet there is somthing in nature that contradicts reason & makes one start at pain, & then one takes nautious medecines in hopes they may keep one longer in a world I have been a long time very weary off, and if I could have walked out of it I am confident I should have been gone many yeares ago, for I can have no notion that any place can be worse then this, as the

Generallity of the world is made. This will appear strange nonsence to so young a man as you are, but I tell you very sincerely my thoughts.[2]

Since then Willigo had died* and she herself had been dangerously ill. 'She must be blistered or she must die', whispered a doctor in 1742; whereupon she sat up and declared, 'I won't be blistered and I won't die!'[3] And she lived for another two years.

Prognostications of her death were frequent and not always kind. 'Since this last winter I find people think she won't last long', Lady Vanbrugh wrote to Henrietta in the late seventeen-twenties, 'and they say here, whenever she goes 'tis impossible any body can be sorry and all the Spencers must rejoice'.† And yet in very old age—and to live to eighty was then phenomenal—she was, at the back of the nation's mind, an institution to be preserved with amused tolerance. At the coronation of George II, when she was sixty-seven, she had raised a cheer by walking in the procession in her robes until, exhausted, she had subsided upon a drum. Death was now overdue but, as with our treasured antiques today—a building it may be or a magazine or a politician—the machinery for despatch is missing or seems too crude to use. As Pope put it:

> Old politicians chew on wisdom past
> And totter on in business to the last.[4]

For the grandsons, at Woodstock and at St Albans, Sarah had, sometimes without even bothering to tell them, fought election after election, if only to keep a Walpole candidate off home ground. Woodstock, she maintained, was the Marlborough birthright; and after some trouble, when he was declared by a rival to be under age, Johnny was returned for that borough and continued to sit for it for some years.

As for litigation, experience had shown that the Law was slow and

---

* William (Willigo) 2nd Marquis of Blandford (1699–1731) is buried at Blenheim. In the chapel vault his coffin closely neighbours those, covered in red leather stamped with coronet brasses, of John and Sarah first Duke and Duchess of Marlborough.

† An undated and unclassified letter at Blenheim addressed to the younger Duchess but probably delivered to the dowager.

corrupt and she was disgusted with it. At one time she had thought of reforming it herself but from that she had been discouraged. 'If your Grace will please only to reflect', Francis Godolphin had written in 1730, 'that no less a Man than Oliver Cromwell, when in the height of his Grandeur & Authority, was seriously bent upon redressing not only the delay but many other grievances & abuses that by degrees had crept into the practice of the Law, & had made some steps in Parliament towards it, yet was soon obliged to quit the design as finding it attended with more difficulty & opposition than either his great abilities or unbounded power could get the better of, I believe you will easily give up any sudden thought or hope you might have entertained of success from any attempt of that kind'.[5]

As a business manager Sarah—more capable of business, as Maynwaring had said, than any man—had met with incompetence and (or so she maintained) dishonesty; for the two men of business she had trusted most—Craggs and Guidott—had (again in her view) proved the greatest rogues. Investment had been just as troublesome. True, she had creamed her £100,000 from the South Sea Bubble, but she had been much shocked by the whole enterprise and said so. For years, in the trust's interest and with Charles Spencer's approval, she had bolstered Government funds until rifts with Walpole and with her grandson ruled out all such investment.* The only alternative was to buy land and so she bought it and went on buying until she had, in various counties, thirty estates† which brought with them the oddest and most tiresome responsibilities. Here for example was the vicar of Willington writing to tell her:

* The well-known anecdote of the Duchess of Marlborough's 'rescue' of Childs Bank, by writing that bank a cheque for £700,000 on the Bank of England, said to be threatening foreclosure, appears from *An Old Legend Examined* by S. W. Shelton, archivist of Glyn, Mills & Co., to be, like many another tale of the Duchess, apocryphal. The Blenheim records make no mention of it; although in an undated fragment (G-1-16) she writes, 'If by giving £100,000 immediately I could save my country, I should think it better laid out then in any other way'.

† In addition to Blenheim, Wimbledon, Holywell, Marlborough House and Windsor Lodge (the last two crown-leases), the Duchess died possessed of estates in Bedford., Berks., Bucks., Herts., Huntingdon., Kent., Leics., Middlesex., Norfolk, Oxon, Staffs. and Surrey. John Spencer, her chief heir, already owned Althorp in Northants. His brother Charles was to have Blenheim but he was forbidden in Sarah's will to take goods or furniture from Althorp.

Next July it will be sixteen years since you was pleased to put me into the vicarage of Willington with thirty pounds a year & no more . . . My wife is now ready to lye in of her tenth child . . . Sr Will: Gostwick's family has a Vault under the Chancel, part of which is fallen in & all ye Coffins lie open to all Spectators, which is a very dismal & melancholy sight.[6]

Would her Grace be pleased to order Mr Rudd to make it decent? 'I think Land is the troublesomest thing in the world to have to do with', she writes to John Spencer in 1742, 'and I believe when we are undone 'twill be all alike whatever one's fortune is in. Therefore when I have any money I had rather avoid the troubles of land & have it where I can easily get at it that I may give it away when I see the storm near & disappoint any Government from taking it away from me'.[7]

Infirm as she was, it was simply not worth the struggle. Posterity was a spendthrift and herself a fool to fight for it. 'I am quite tired out', she wrote, 'with struggling against knaves that 'tis impossible to get the better of, without any help or any hope of return from those that I have taken so much pains for . . . I have nobody or but few to take care of when I am dead, [so] I will venture to play [at ombre] with Mr Neville & my Lord Cardigan all the time I am at Woodstock if I can keep them so long with me'.[8]

At one time not only had she looked forward to filling Blenheim's attic storey with her friends, she had even gone to the lengths of inviting royalty.* 'I beleive you will see her Royal Highnesse [Queen Caroline] before me', she had written to Mrs Clayton, 'and if you do I desire you will tell her with my humble duty that I am now come to the end of my leabours of near 22 yeares which I shall think quit thrown away unless she & his Royal Highnesse will bee prevaild upon to doe me the honour, which I flatter my self that they will not refuse, because this place was Erected to bee Built in memory of the servises which the Duke of Marl: ded to the Publick & of

---

* 'There is 20 apartments with all sort of convenience fit to lodge any body, but upon the principal floor there is three that are really so fine that they are too good for any body to make use of except their R: Highness's & the Dear Prince William'. (The Duchess, writing of Blenheim to Mrs Clayton. Undated. Blen G-I-16).

which I hope they & their posterity will allways have the advantage'.[9] But that visit was never paid and now she felt differently. People had died or she had fallen out with them; and she blamed Blenheim too for gout. 'I never design to see Blenheim again', she wrote in 1736, 'In a lodge I have every thing convenient & without trouble'. She had always loved Windsor Lodge. Without the Duke of St Albans, who constantly baited her by careering through Windsor Park, that place would have been perfect.

She had even tried harbouring poor relations; but sooner or later, she had found, they only increased one's spleen. She often wondered, rich and independent as she was, whether it was worth bothering with people at all. 'The kindness & good opinion of one's general acquaintance', she noted, 'are so far from being absolutely necessary to one's happynesse that they are somthing like fair weather which makes one's days pass a little more pleasantly but is of no reall importance to one's satisfaction'.[10] When all was said and done there was still much to be said for good servants, and of course for dogs. As Lady Howard had so sensibly written:

> As to the generality of friendships, those are commonly sincerest & most to be depended upon which are bottom'd upon interest . . . My own relations are all of them as good people as any are in the world, but my notion is that people often find more comfort in their old age from a goodnatured servant that they give good wages to than from all the relations they have.[11]

In the goodnatured Grace Ridley Sarah was certainly lucky and would show herself grateful; and for amanuenses she had the excellent if sometimes peevish Stephens, Loft, and her porter, Walter Jones. She found plenty for them to do. There were letters. There were inscriptions. There were narratives: An Account of the Duke of Bridgwater's Proceedings; An Account of the Present Duke of Marlborough . . . and so on, running to a great many pages. There was the Green Book to be kept up to date. There was the Duchess's will—in need of constant revision—and its codicils. There was, until 1742 when it was published, her own vindication; and there was the groundwork for the biography of John Duke of Marlborough.

For this last Sarah had chosen two recommended historians, Mallet* and Glover,† but she was not prepared to hand them the documents until she had read and endorsed every one, and there were thousands. At Blenheim, to come upon a letter bearing five separate endorsements, all in Sarah's hand, is not uncommon; and at Althorp her Instructions to the Historians for Beginning the Duke of Marlborough's History[12] are as original as everything else she undertook. The biography was to begin: 'I write the History of the Duke of Marlborough', and it was to continue in that same flat manner, for it would require 'no Flourishes to set it off, but short plain Facts'. They must remember to say how cheaply Marlborough had managed the war, and how generous she knew him to have been with pensions. He had, she could honestly say, left King James 'with the greatest Regret imaginable', though doubtless he would have won still greater renown had he helped him establish popery. But 'No King', she added, 'is to be trusted'.

The biographers would be rewarded with £500 each, their work being supervised and approved by Lord Chesterfield and her executors. 'And I desire', she concluded, 'that no Part of the said History may be in Verse, and that it may not begin in the usual Forms of writing Histories but only from the Revolution'. About the latter end of the reign of Charles II too much had been written already; and she had had more than enough too of lampoonists and balladmongers. Besides, as in mock-modesty she had told Charles Spencer, 'You know that I am so very stupid as to have very little taste for poetry'.

The wretched Lyttelton‡ had been gauche enough to show her his poem on liberty, in which she could find no reference to Marlborough at all. Luckily, catching her glance, he had instantly realised his mistake. 'He looked a little out', she noticed, 'took his verses away and later returned them'. But then as she herself remarked, 'Painters, poets and builders have very high flights, but they must be kept down'.[13] And the same went for historians and biographers.

---

* David Mallet (1705?–1765). Literary executor of Lord Bolingbroke.

† Richard Glover (1712–1785). M.P. for Weymouth and opponent of Walpole. Published much blank verse.

‡ George Lyttelton, 1st Baron (1709–1773). Opponent of Walpole. Friend of Pope.

Mallet, recommended by the Duke of Montrose and dubbed by Dr Johnson 'the prettiest drest puppet about town', told the Duchess a month before she died:

> As I am thoroughly sensible both of the dignity & difficulty of the undertaking your Grace has honoured me with, I will throw all other business aside, even the work I have been so long engaged in, that I may enter upon this with my whole attention & application. This I dare promise because it is in my power. Could I add with equal certainty that my abilities are in some degree equal to the task, your Grace might then hope to see a history of the Duke of Marlborough not inferior perhaps to any history that ever yet appeared in the world.[14]

For that biography, as we know, the world had in fact to wait very nearly two hundred years. 'Mallet, I believe', said Dr Johnson, 'never wrote a single line of his projected life of the Duke of Marlborough, but groped for material and thought of it till he had exhausted his mind'. Glover too made no beginning and is said to have returned his £500.

With Nathaniel Hooke, the last of the collaborators in her *Conduct*, Sarah was luckier. Introduced by Pope he proved competent and industrious, which was as well since Sarah, directly she saw him, though bedridden, dictated without stopping for six hours. Without the aid of notes, says a contemporary, she delivered her narrative in a lively and connected manner, and gave Hooke £5000 for which, having lost his all in the South Sea Bubble, he was thankful.

'I shall leave this place with true regret', Pope wrote to Sarah from Twickenham, 'but as you said you liked it so well as to call here in my absence, I have deputed one to be ready to receive you whose company you own you like and who I know likes yours to such a degree that I doubt whether he can be impartial enough to be your Historian. Mr Hook & his daughter (I hope) will use my house while your Grace is at Wimbledon. You see what artifices I use to be remember'd by you'.[15]

All went well until Hooke, a man of courage, attempted to convert the Duchess to Roman Catholicism; after which of course he was *persona non grata*. The *Conduct* however was out and, as

Johnson said, showed an unaffected dignity of style and an artful simplicity of narration. He was shocked at Hooke's 'inserting so profligate a maxim as that to tell another's secret to one's friend is no breach of confidence',* but that, he supposed, was at the Duchess's dictation. Of the Duchess herself Johnson had formed a poor opinion: she 'had not superior parts but was a bold, frontless† woman who knew how to make the most of her opportunities'; and in his brilliant review of her *Conduct* he gently cautions the reader of the possibility that this suppliant for esteem may have indulged to some extent in disguise and suppression. 'Every man that is solicitous about the esteem of others', he points out, 'is in a great degree desirous of his own and makes by consequence his first apology for his conduct to himself; and when he has once deceived his own heart, which is for the greatest part too easy a task, he propagates the deceit in the world without reluctance or consciousness of false-hood'. The successful salesman sells to himself first and squares his conscience before beginning on the customer.

Johnson's judgment on Queen Anne, as he reads her in the letters published by Sarah, is interesting. He finds in those letters 'un-common clearness of understanding, tenderness of affection and rectitude of intention', but discerns too 'a temper timorous, anxious and impatient of misfortune, a tendency to burst into complaints, helpless dependancy on the affection of others and a weak desire of moving compassion . . . She seems', he concludes, 'born for friend-ship, not for Government'.

Horace Walpole, as might be expected, is more frivolous and less polite. 'Old Marlborough', he writes, 'has at last published her *Memoirs*. They are digested by one Hooke . . . but from her materials, which are so womanish that I am sure the man might sooner have made a gown and petticoat with them'.[16]

But the *Conduct* is better than that. Indeed, had it been published in 1712, when Robert Walpole advised against it, it must have burst like a bombshell. In 1742 it could be no more than a squib. The

---

* Referring to Sarah's remonstrating with Queen Anne for not having told her of Abigail Masham's wedding: 'putting her in mind of what she often used to say to me out of Montaigne, that it was no breach of promise of secrecy to tell such a friend anything, because it was no more than telling it to oneself'. (*Conduct*).

† Frontless: unblushing, shameless, audacious. (O.E.D.)

Press as a whole was not reverential. *The Other Side of the Question* (not very good) was countered by Fielding at his most fulsome: 'Why, if this be true', he hopefully quotes a *Conduct* reader as saying, 'the Duchess of Marlborough is one of the best as well as greatest Women ever born'. What a glorious woman! No name should be so dear as hers to the people of England. And as for her pride, that too was a virtue. Fielding himself was prepared to vouch for it that 'no such Pride hath ever been shewn to those who have acknowledged themselves to be her Inferiours, to whom none can equal her in Affability and Condescension'.[17]

After which, one might think, there was nothing left to be said. Horace Walpole however continued to be scathing:

> From her Grace of Marlborough we may collect that Queen Anne was driven to change her ministry and in consequence the fate of Europe because she dared to affect one bedchamber-woman as she had another. The duchess could not comprehend how the cousins Sarah Jennings and Abigail Hill could ever enter into competition, though the one did but kneel to gather up the clue of favour which the other had haughtily tossed away and which she could not recover by putting *The Whole Duty of Man* into the Queen's hands to teach her friendship.

The Duchess's *Conduct*, for the most part 'the annals of a wardrobe rather than of a reign', did contain, he owned, 'a few of those sallies of wit which four score years of arrogance could not fail to produce in so fantastic an understanding'. But it was a pity it had been so much altered and edited and withal was so petty. However, 'Little circumstances indeed convey the most characteristic ideas, but the choice of them may as often paint the genius of the writer as of the person represented'.[18]

Sarah's contempt for the critics was of course Olympian. 'Some', she observed, 'have writ a foolish book to find fault with the *Conduct* and the same person has writ another to answer himself . . . I have done what I had great pleasure in, vindicated myself by incontestable proofs from the vile aspersions that had been thrown upon me by the rage of parties . . . This I have done very clearly and I do not care what fools or mad people say of me, which will always be a great majority'.[19] She admitted that, in an earlier draft at least, she had suppressed much; but what she had written she had written 'with a sincerity that had not so much as the least mixture of art or dissimulation in it'.[20]

Like Blenheim's Column of Victory, the *Conduct* was for posterity. Of her contemporaries Sarah at eighty-two expected nothing. Tiffs of former reigns, no matter how volcanic, had long since been buried beneath the huge mounds of dead leaves which were the squabbles of the royal Georges. The self-vindication of an old duchess, a relic of the reign before last, could be of no consequence.

Towards the end few saw her, but those that did testified to her beauty. 'She had still at a great age considerable remains of beauty', wrote Lady Mary Wortley Montagu,* 'most expressive eyes and the finest hair imaginable, the colour of which she said she had preserved unchanged by the constant use of honey-water'.[21] Again it is tantalising to have no portrait. One of the last things she did was to send one to Pelham's secretary,[22] though whether it showed a lined face or a smooth one ('like a white candle in a holy place') or even the radiant bloom of that unageing Groom of the Stole, we are left to guess. Lady Lechmere, in the steps of Frances Tyrconnel, begged for a portrait 'as you are now . . . Ye knowing you now', she explained, 'makes me wish to have you what you now are, since I find in you what is so agreeable to me that I am unwilling to give it up for a younger face'.[23] Kindly meant no doubt, but perhaps it was just as well she had not complied with it; for she had since fallen out with Lady Lechmere and had no more to do with her.

Just as Sarah believed that ingratitude was the deadliest of all sins, so she esteemed friendship the greatest of all blessings and virtues; and yet, through no fault of hers, the firmest of friendships, if not broken by death, disintegrated. From exile she had written, 'I long to embrace my dear Mrs Clayton and I hope I shall never part from her again for any long time . . . I would fain end my

---

* It was Lady Mary Wortley Montagu who first told the since much told story of the shorn locks. (How in a rage Sarah had once, to spite Marlborough, cut off her hair; how at the time he had ignored it; and how after his death she had found the hair carefully kept in his private drawer). The connection however between this anecdote and Kneller's 'shorn locks' portrait of the Duchess at Althorp has not been substantiated.

life in England with my friends if I can . . .'[24] But then Mrs Clayton (now Lady Sundon) had changed and proved unworthy of her friendship, as had so many more. 'I think the generallity of people in England are rediculous', Sarah decided, 'and I had reather bee shut up between four walls then converse with them, and I have seen people of very good sence that came out of Ireland . . .',[25] though there again, Lady Muskerry had proved a fool. Perhaps she herself just happened to be unlucky, for there could be no doubt, as she wrote, that 'some people are born to receive all the back strocks of fortune'.[26]

With Di gone and Johnny married, Sarah could no longer say she was devoted to anyone; although of course there were more or less loyal servants and more or less entertaining callers and friends. There had been Voltaire, who had asked to see her memoirs before her *Conduct* was published. 'Wait a little', she had told him, 'I am altering my account of Queen Anne's character. I have begun to love her again since the present lot have become our governors'. After which, according to Goldsmith, she asked Voltaire to collaborate and he, reading the manuscript, not only declined but went so far as to remonstrate with her for her bitterness and indiscretion. 'I thought the man had sense', she is quoted as having then said, 'but I find him at bottom either a fool or a philosopher';[27] a remark that hardly rings true.*

Only one of her friends could be as outspoken as Sarah herself without wrecking friendship and that was Lady Mary Wortley Montagu. She was, or so she boldly boasted, out of the Duchess's hurricane-latitude, and eccentric enough to be excused anything and everything. 'I had this day', Sarah told Di, 'a very great dispute with a woman that has more wit than any body I ever knew, my Lady Mary Wortley, and tho' she said a great many pretty things, I stood to my point as most people (you know) do & would not seem to be convinced. She talked mighty prettily, but it is too much for a letter . . .' What a pity! No topic, it seems, was barred, though of Queen Anne Sarah spoke guardedly and far less readily than of the Hanoverians, of whose arrival in England she enjoyed making an *opera bouffe*. None knew better than Lady Mary, however, just how

* Nor would Sarah have used the expression 'the present lot'. Both phrases suggest mistranslation but the sense is probably correct.

thin the ice was. 'The most vindictive Highland chief', she wrote later, 'never had so many feuds, but her deadliest were in the bosom of her own clan'.

Who else ventured near her? Lord Chesterfield ('civiller', she found, 'than any body in the present age'), the pious Lady Hunting-don ('all goodness & kindness'. See appendix v), Lord Marchmont (her executor),* James Stephens (now styled 'Doctor in Physick'. He too was to be an executor and to vet Marlborough's biography); and at the last, of all people, Alexander Pope. For both poet and Duchess, one suspects, this was a playing-at-friendship, a tongue-in-cheek diversion to enliven old age; for what had they else in common (certainly not poetry) but sense and bitterness and an un-dying distrust of Walpole? But Pope chose to pretend otherwise. 'What can I say to your Grace?' he writes to her, 'You think the same things, read the same books, like the same people that I do . . . Be but so good as to like me a little and be assur'd I shall love you extremely'. And again, 'You are directly kind to me and I shall love you. This is very ill bred but it is true and I cannot help it'.[28]

His failure with Marlborough's panegyric has been forgotten and all is lighthearted banter. She sends him the Green Book. He reads it or says he has read it three times and cautiously comments, 'I wish everybody you love may love you, and am sorry for everyone that does not'. He invites her to Twickenham to spend 'a few hours' in his grotto (that obsession of which Dr Johnson said 'His vanity produced a grotto where necessity enforced a passage'). Amazingly, she accepts.

'The Duchess of Marlborough makes great court to me', Pope told Swift, 'but I am too old for her mind and body'.[29] (He was by twenty-eight years her junior). Sarah, while distrusting his malice (had he not turned against Sappho,† his former friend?), was yet sufficiently fascinated to try to humour him; though whether she bribed him on the understanding that *Atossa* was not to be published has never been proved. Pope is supposed to have told the Duchess of Buckingham that *Atossa* in his *Moral Essays* was Sarah; and then to have assured Sarah that it was intended for the Duchess of Bucking-

* Alexander Earl of Marchmont died in 1740 and was succeeded (in the earldom and as Sarah's executor) by his son.

† Lady Mary Wortley Montagu.

ham. It is easy to believe that the trick proved irresistible, for

> Whether the charmer sinner it or saint it,
> If folly grow romantic I must paint it.

For better for worse, *Atossa* was too good to scrap. Posterity must decide for itself who it was meant for:

> But what are these to great Atossa's mind?
> Scarce once herself, by turns all womankind!
> Who, with herself or others, from her birth
> Finds all her life one warfare upon earth:
> Shines in exposing knaves and painting fools,
> Yet is whate'er she hates and ridicules.
> No thought advances but her eddy brain
> Whisks it about and down it goes again.
> Full sixty years the world has been her trade,
> The wisest fool much time has ever made.
> From loveless youth to unrespected age,
> No passion gratified except her rage;
> So much the fury still outran the wit,
> The pleasure miss'd her and the scandal hit.
> Who breaks with her provokes revenge from hell,
> But he's a bolder man who dares be well.
> Her every turn with violence pursued,
> No more a storm her hate than gratitude:
> To that each passion turns, or soon or late;
> Love, if it makes her yield, must make her hate.
> Superiors? Death! and equals? What a curse!
> But an inferior not dependent? Worse.
> Offend her and she knows not to forgive;
> Oblige her and she'll hate you while you live;
> But die and she'll adore you—then the bust
> And temple rise, then fall again to dust.*
> Last night her lord was all that's good and great;
> A knave this morning, and his will a cheat.

* Said to allude to a bust of Queen Anne, within a temple, erected by Sarah (site unspecified), which by 1740 had crumbled to dust.

Strange! By the means defeated of the ends,
By spirit robbed of power, by warmth of friends,
By wealth of followers! Without one distress
Sick of herself through very selfishness!
Atossa, cursed with every granted prayer,
Childless with all her children, wants an heir.
To heirs unknown descends the unguarded store,
Or wanders, heaven-directed, to the poor.[30]

Not every line fitted, but those that did, and they were many, were too close to be doubted. No wonder Sarah showed anxiety.†
'I am not arrived at so much philosophy', she wrote to Lord March-mont, 'as not to think torturing pain an evil; that is the only thing I now dread, for death is unavoidable and I cannot find that anybody has yet demonstrated whether it is a good thing or a bad one. Pray do not think me wicked in saying this, and if you talk to Mr Pope of me, endeavour to keep him my friend: for I do firmly believe the immortality of the soul as much as he does, though I am not learned enough to have found out what it is'. And later: 'I have a great mind to believe that kings' and first ministers' souls, when they die, go into chimney-sweeps'. This last because, while bedridden at Marl-borough House, she had had the sweep and 'One of the chimney-sweepers', she found, 'was a little boy, a most miserable creature without shoes, stockings, breeches or shirt. When it was over', she remembered, 'I sent a servant of mine to Windsor with him, to equip this poor creature with what he wanted, which cost very little, not being so well dressed as the late Privy Seal [Lord Hervey]. And as I could not be sure the souls of these chimney-sweepers had [not] come from great men, I could not repent of their being so much overpaid as they were'.[31]

'I hear you live', Pope wrote to her in the summer of 1743, 'and I hope with all that spirit with which you make life supportable both to yourself and those about you'.[32] And early in the following year, 'What a Girl you are! . . . I sincerely wish your health better than my own and you younger than I that the Tables may be turn'd and I leave you a Legacy at my death'.[33] In a sprightly joint-letter with

† According to the D.N.B., Nathaniel Hooke was authorised by Sarah to offer Pope £3000 for *Atossa's* suppression. See also Pope's works (Twickenham edition, ed. F.W. Bateson).

Marchmont Pope assures Sarah that her soul is certainly immortal and, judging by her last letter, her mind unaffected by her body and her body in tenantable repair.[34]

But she knew she was dying—'No physicians can be of any use to me'—and as Abigail said, in like case, of Queen Anne, 'This good lady deserves pity'. 'I am going soon out of the world', she told Johnny Spencer, 'and am packing up'[35] (for eternity one needed so little); and again, within two months of her death, to Francis Godolphin, 'I am packing up to be gone'.[36] To her own way of thinking she was more than ready. Among the scores of maxims, proverbs and aphorisms copied into her commonplace-book she had noted: 'Not to grow weary of oneself'. She had now reached that stage.

Of her death almost nothing is known except date and place: October 18th, 1744 at Marlborough House. Smollet baldly records: 'Mr Pope, the celebrated poet, died in the month of June. In October the old Duchess of Marlborough resigned her breath in the 85th year of her age, immensely rich and very little regretted either by her own family or by the world in general'.[37] Having seen six reigns, or part of them, most of those who had known her in her prime and might have regretted her going were themselves long since dead.

On the death of Marlborough Princess Caroline, in Hanoverian French, had tried to console his widow with the assurance: 'Il y aura un tems ou vous le rejoindrais et ou vous melleres vos louanges pour ce grand Dieu plain de misericorde avec le mari qui a fait la sattisfaction de votre vie'.[38] Had she known her better she would have realised that the Duchess was less fond of hymns than of ballads; but there it was, for better for worse the day she wrote of had arrived.

Every detail of funeral and will had of course been thought of: the interment 'only decent and without Plumes or Escutcheons'; the will itself to be on paper, not parchment, and to be written (the last of the twenty-six versions) by someone that would not tattle. After years of cogitation and vacillation she had finally decided, with certain safeguards, to leave as much as possible to John Spencer, who survived her by only two years, and as little as she decently could to his brother Charles Duke of Marlborough, then in debt, as she reckoned, to the tune of half a million pounds. The chief surprises were in the codicil, where she left £20,000 and her 'best & largest brilliant Diamond Ring' to Lord Chesterfield, and £10,000 to William Pitt 'upon Account of his Merit in the noble Defence he has made for the Support of the Laws of England and to prevent the Ruin of his Country'. Substantial indeed were the rewards of opposing Walpole.*

It must too have surprised her youngest and only surviving daughter Mary Montagu to find herself mentioned and not un-favourably: 'I give to my Daughter Mary Dutchess of Montagu my Gold Snuffbox that has in it two Pictures of her Father the Duke of Marlborough when he was a Youth. Also a Picture of her Father covered with a large Diamond & hung to a String of small Pearls for a Bracelet. And two enamelled Pictures for a Bracelet of her Sister Sunderland and her Sister Bridgwater'. The diamond-covered miniature was of course Chandos's present to Sarah, lost at Antwerp, found again, and spitefully labelled by Lord Dartmouth (quoting Harley) as the gift of Queen Anne.[39]

It was pleasing to find that from Dr Stephens to the chairmen ('the best that I ever knew') and the porter ('I employ him to copy my papers') all her staff had been remembered and recommended to John Spencer;[40] while to her favourite servant Grace Ridley she left a fortune (£16,000), her striking watch, a miniature of Marlborough 'and my own Picture drawn by Sir Godfrey Kneller, which is only a Head'.† Three hundred pounds was to be distributed among the poor of Woodstock.

Marlborough's diamond-studded sword was to go with the title, though she feared it would not stay bejewelled for long. 'What makes me the more uneasy about the diamond sword', she had written, 'is that I do think Lady Bateman is capable of getting it to make buckles for stays'.[41]

John Spencer, Lady Bolingbroke told Lady Denbigh, might count upon a lump sum of £94,000 plus an income of £27,000 a year. 'Vangeons nous de la fortune', she urged, 'par la mépriser et par en médire, comme dit Montagne de la grandeur'.[42] These were sour grapes indeed, and it was disappointing to find that when the Duchess had boasted, 'I think I am lucky in having so much that

* Sir Robert Walpole died the following year.
† Now in the Gallery at Althorp. (p. 48)

every knave may have a bit of me' she had not meant it literally.

On October 30th Marlborough's body was brought from Westminster Abbey to lie with Sarah's in the chapel vault at Blenheim. The journey was by no means as costly as the funeral had been twenty-two years before; but even so there was a coach-and-six to be paid for, bearers, cloaks, a room hung with mourning, sconces, fourteen crêpe hatbands and fourteen pairs of men's black-topped gloves;[43] but none of that was now his widow's concern. Of her own journey we hear nothing; nor was there need for inscription, since over and over again in various forms she had written it herself. Her chief aim, she had often declared, was to deserve approbation and to have it: 'Of all human creatures upon the earth I would not bee the person that no body speaks well of'.[44] And she wished posterity to speak well of her too.

At Blenheim there is a small, undated scrap of paper bearing on both sides writing in the Duchess's hand. On one side it has this:

I forsee the world will interpret whatever I do that may look descontented & perticular to my having lost the queens favour & my great Employments. That may vex me a little, to be soe much mistaken, but I hope you will never think my misfortunes can be one graine heavier upon that account, for as long as I can live in quiet & safty with the Dear Duke of Marlborough I shall have very little more to wish for.

And on the other:

As one is the worst judge of one's own simplicity, one is the best of one's sencerity, I will therefore say nothing of the first.[45]

'There is nobody like her', Arthur Maynwaring had long ago written, 'nor ever will be'.[46]

Appendices
Bibliography
References
Index

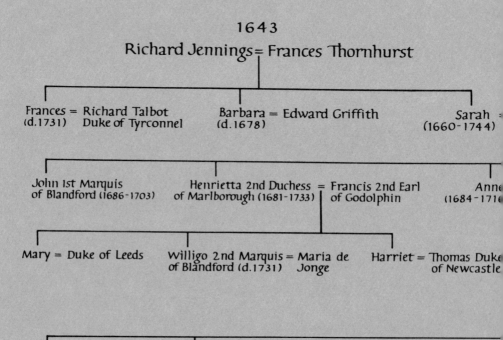

1643

Richard Jennings = Frances Thornhurst

Frances = Richard Talbot   Barbara = Edward Griffith   Sarah =
(d.1731)   Duke of Tyrconnel   (d.1678)   (1660-1744)

John 1st Marquis   Henrietta 2nd Duchess = Francis 2nd Earl   Anne
of Blandford (1686-1703)   of Marlborough (1681-1733)   of Godolphin   (1684-171(

Mary = Duke of Leeds   Willigo 2nd Marquis = Maria de   Harriet = Thomas Duke
                        of Blandford (d.1731)   Jonge   of Newcastle

Robert 4th Earl   Charles 5th Earl of Sunderland = Elizabeth Trevor
of Sunderland (d.1729)   3rd Duke of Marlborough (d.1758)

N.B. The two other children born to the first Duke
died in infancy, as did two boys and a girl be
✳ Hon. John Spencer (1708-174(

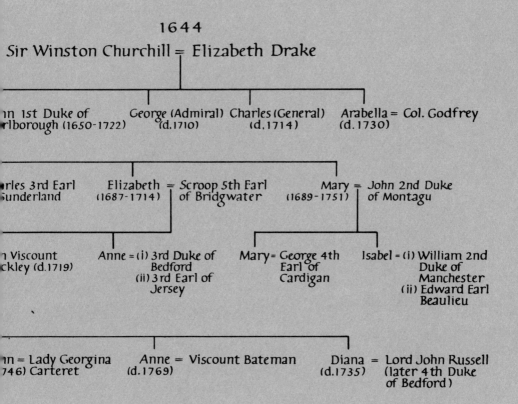

1644

Sir Winston Churchill = Elizabeth Drake

...n 1st Duke of
...rlborough (1650-1722)

George (Admiral)
(d.1710)

Charles (General)
(d.1714)

Arabella = Col. Godfrey
(d.1730)

...rles 3rd Earl
...underland

Elizabeth = Scroop 5th Earl
(1687-1714)   of Bridgwater

Mary = John 2nd Duke
(1689-1751)   of Montagu

...n Viscount
...ckley (d.1719)

Anne = (i) 3rd Duke of
         Bedford
      (ii) 3rd Earl of
         Jersey

Mary= George 4th
       Earl of
       Cardigan

Isabel = (i) William 2nd
           Duke of
           Manchester
        (ii) Edward Earl
           Beaulieu

...n = Lady Georgina
746) Carteret

Anne = Viscount Bateman
       (d.1769)

Diana = Lord John Russell
(d.1735)   (later 4th Duke
           of Bedford)

...hess of Marlborough (Harriet born 1679 and Charles born 1690)
...e second Duke and Duchess of Montagu.
...stor of the Earls Spencer.

Sarah Duchess of Marlborough to Queen Anne*

(Undated)

Tis so natural a thing for one that has served you so many years (not to mention anything else) to say what was possible might bee of use to you that I have noe reproaches to make my self upon anything in my last letter, which was express'd with so much tenderness & respect that I might reasonably have hoped that it could not give your Majesty any offence tho it had come from any of your subjects that has not had the happiness of knowing you soe long as I have don, but I see it put your Majesty into soe much passion that you quit mistook the whole meaning of the letter, which you will find if you will please to look upon it again.

I ded not take a copy of it because I could not dream of what has happen'd, but I am sure I can repeat the meaning of it and I believe the very words without any materiall alteration, which was upon my lord Marlboroughs letter in which hee thanked God for his goodness in making him the instrument of soe much good to the queen and the nation if she would be pleased to make use of it, and I added that it made me melancholly when I reflected that after three such battles wone for your servisses hee aprehended that hee had not much credit with you or that the influence of some ill meaning people might disappoint whatever your most faithfull servants could doe; that I knew your Majesty's answer to this would bee that there were noe such people, but everybody knows that impressions must be given by somebody, that the object of the Princes favour† had so sad a charecter in the world that it could not bee supposed to take informations from him; and since you would not indure to have one think you suffered your own faverit to talk to you upon anything of businesse, what account could bee given of your Majestys doing contrary to the advise of soe many of your most considerable subjects and old experienced friends?

* (Blen G-1-7.) Marlborough's letter, sent to the Queen and here quoted by Sarah, was dated July 12, 1708.

† Admiral George Churchill, Marlborough's brother (ob. 1710).

This was the part of my letter which you disliked & I find by yours that your Majesty thought when I spoke of my brothers* sad charecter & the credit hee has with the Prince that I ment another person who it seems your Majesty thinks is uncapable of any error, & yet I am sure everybody else will allways think she has committed a great many to me, which I could forgive very easyly if she had not been the occation of soe many reflections upon your Majesty; and tho you are pleased to say you will never change the good impressions that I once gave you of her, I hope you will remember that my commendations went noe farther then being handy & a faithfull servant & I ded think she had more sence & honour then 'tis possible for anybody to beleive she has now; but I never thought her Edducation was such as to make her fitt company for a great queen. Many people have liked the humour of their chamber maids & have been very kind to them, but 'tis very uncommon to hold a private correspondence with them & put them upon the foot of a friend & support them in all things right or wrong to the mortifycation of one you had honoured soe long with your kindnesse & who never ded nor never will doe anything to deserve the change.

Your Majesty now sees plainly who was ment by the sad charecter, but I beg of you not to think I am making my court to Abigail, who must never expect to have one good word from me, tho her being a woman & her being so low & inconsiderable in all things (after people have said she has had an ungreatfull behaviour to me) will [would] hender her from ever beeing named or soe much [as] thought of if it were not for her friendship with the enemys to the Government & your Majestys unaccountable aversnesse to soe many reasonable things. . . .

[The Duchess concludes by urging the Queen to dismiss Admiral George Churchill.]

---

* 'my brothers' means here 'my brother-in-law's'.

An Anonymous Letter (undated) to Abigail Masham*

(Written in the hand of Sarah Duchess of Marlborough and endorsed by her, 'A copy of a leter by an unknown hand to Abigal'; and further endorsed—in another hand—'Penny post leter to Mrs Masham when she was in the height of her insolence'. For the composition the Duchess is known to have had the assistance of Arthur Maynwaring).

I am very sensible that the letter which I now take the liberty of writing to you is not likely to have all the effect that is intended and desired. There are such powerful charms in greatnesse that one can hardly hope to perswade you not to like it or to convince you of the danger that it will bring upon you. Tis like telling a lover what ill consiquences will attend a present passion, and to think that any arguments of mine will bring you to reason or moderation would bee to have a better opinion both of you and of my self then I am afraid either of us deserve.

But yet there are some things which I am resolved to represent to you, if not to inform your mind, att least to discharge my own. It is not my design to shew you what a hopeless project you are engaged in whilst you think of carrying on this government by the torrys. The queen tried the use & power of that party att the beginning of her reign & whenever you bring her Majesty back into their measures she will soon bee convinced that the weight of the nation & the force of truth will again prevail & that those lords & gentlemen who have already stood the shock of a stronger ministry will never bee brooken in peices by you & that wretched dabbler in politicks Mr H,† for all the scheemes that you & hee can lay will bee only like soe many plots which can never bear the light. But I only give you this hint which you may think of at your leisure, since I intend not soe much to shew the folly of your present undertaking as your maddnesse in pretending to meddle at all.

Tho you seem to have forgot your obligations of all kinds you must needs remember your origenal & your first enterance into the court. You must allsoe remember where you lived before & what was your employment, which I neither care nor need to mention, it beeing so fresh in

* (Blen G-1-9).   † Harley.

315

everyones memory. You must have heard too that Britain is naturally averse to faverites, let them have deserved ever soe well, and do you think that this nation, which sometimes murmur'd att the power even of the Duke & Duchess of Marlborough, the greatest generall & the best servant that ever any queen had, will patiently indure one Mrs Abigal & squire H? Will people who repined att the greatnesse of those who contributed so much to settle our present government set still to see your power which they know will bee employed to overturn it? What maddnesse, what witchcraft has possessed you? If you had really some of those good quailitys which you want, yet don't you know that your crying sin of ingratitude would bee alone enough to sink you, the most odious of all crimes & you of all persons the most guilty of it; but you are soe far from having any of the vertues which are necessary to support a faverite that you have not soe much as the generous vices which made some which went before you less intolarable in other reigns. And yet dare you pretend to bee att the head of our affairs & to dispose of employments & in short to give up our government into the hands of its enemys in oppossiscion to all those great & noble persons who compassed [composed?] her Majesty's councell & who joyn'd with her att the time of our hapy revolution!

Bee asured the kingdom will not long bear this. Our libertys which have been settled with soe much wisdome & defended with soe much blood & treasure must not bee all given away by your management, nor the fruit of all our pains & hazard blasted by such an influence. When the Parliament meets there will bee a sad account required from you of all the uneasinesse that has happen'd in her Majesty's affairs, of all the difficulties which her ministers have undergone & of all the dangers to which the nation has been exposed.

All these things will certainly bee laid att your door because it is universally known that nobody else has any interest att this time and that you are indeed the only faverite & therefore if you doe not make as much hast to disclaim that tittle as you ded to get it & convince the world that you will never more meddle with any businesse but that of your low station, you may certainly expect before christmas to hear your self declared a common enemy to the state & a firebrand which all men will join to extinguish who have honesty, wisdome or courage or honour & who regard their own or their country's hapynesse & safty.

You cannot but have heard your master Harley often talk of the Greekes & Romans because hee is allways shewing his small learning out of season & [he will] tell you how those great & wise nations proceeded against persons that they thought indangerd their state. Death was allways the reward of such people & if it could not be compass'd by accusing them to the citizens, it was sure to bee brought about by some other practice & those who ded it were soe far from being counted infamous that in some places even their statues were erected, for it was a maxim of those famous nations that against a traytour to the state every man is a souldier, & if you & your oracle H are not traytours to this state 'tis certain there never were any.

However, I am not for punishing you after the example of those people I have mentioned. All I desire is that you will either please to doe noe more mischeif or else that a period may bee put to your rediculous greatnesse, in a parliamentary way & by methods more suitable to that christianity which wee profess.

Wee read in scripture of an namesake of yours one Abigal who had a great deal of sence, which has since been given very sparingly to some of her name; but this woman allsoe had a foolish husband who had heinously offended David, and when that great king was coming to distroy her family, Abigal got upon an ass to meet him & bow'd to the ground & fell on her face, beseeching him to forgive the trespass of his handmaid, upon which David hearkened to her voice & bed her goe home in peace.

This example I must humbly propose to your imitation, that when the Duke of Marl: (who is our David & deliverer) is coming against your family, you may noe longer think to oppose him & ruin his credit with the queen, but may reather get upon an ass & meet him in his way to London & fall down upon your frightfull face before him to try if by any submission you can escape that vengeance which you most justly deserve from him.*

---

* 'What your Grace is pleas'd to say about the letter to Abigail is much more than either that or I deserve. My onely reason for desiring it might not be shown was because I did not think it fit to be seen. But if you please to say that having mention'd to me the writing of such a letter, not as from a friend but from one that would vex & fright her, you receiv'd from me soon after that imperfect scrawl, I have not the least objection to any body's seeing it . . . I only design'd to give some hints which you might make use of or not as you pleas'd . . . The Duke of Marlborough himself has hardly more military courage than I have civil fortitude; nor can I ever care how much I offend those that I am sure I never will please & of whom I think every thing that is ill'. (Maynwaring to the Duchess. Undated. Blen E 26).

Sarah Duchess of Marlborough to Queen Anne*

26th July, 1708

I found plainly when I had the honour to shew your Majesty the two Ballads† that you never see any of them but from me, tho the town and country are full of them, and therefore I take the liberty to send you this, for 'tis noe more to bee expected that your Majesty's new favorit should shew you any of these things of which she herself is generally the subject then that she should inform you right of any other matter; and tho your Majesty was pleased to desire me not to speak any more of her, which I know to bee her own request & what would bee of great advantage to all her designs if she could obtain it, yet I must humbly beg pardon if I cannot obay that command the rather because I remember you said att the same time of all things in this world you valued most your reputation, which I confess surpris'd me very much, that your Majesty should so soon mention that word after having discover'd so great a passion for such a woman, for sure there can bee noe great reputation in a thing so strange & unaccountable, to say noe more of it, nor can I think the having noe inclenation for any but of one's own sex is enough to maintain such a charecter as I wish may still bee yours.

But to the preserving a great reputation severall great vertues are certainly necessary, such as justice & wisdome & constancy, and I hope your Majesty will forgive me if I cannot think it was very just to disgrace your faithfull servants for the sake of some that had betray'd you, nor very wise to disoblige all the honest part of the nation for a few inconsiderable people of ill principles & noe interest; nor if I may bee allow'd to say so was it any great proof of your Majesty's former constancy to leave Lord Marlborough & me for Mr Harley & a woman that I took out of a garrett. One of us I am sure long served your Majesty very honestly, and the other, I may venture to say, has don it successfully; nor can your Majesty say in good earnest that you have not left us or that Lord Marlborough still has the same creditt with you that hee used to

* (Blen G-1-7.)   † See appendix IV.

have, since you have not been pleased to approve of any one thing of consiquence that hee has advised in his letters this year out of Flanders, which I think is a pritty good proof how his creditt stands att present notwithstanding the many victories hee has gaind. And therefore Mr Harley may well assure his correspondents in Holland, as hee does every post, that Ld Marl: & Treas. & I are quit out of favour; and since that is our case 'tis easy to know who are in favour & who they use that obstruct what your ministers & all your councel adviss. For your Majesty does certainly not determine things wholly upon your own judgment, and tho you were pleased to say once that you consulted the Prince in your affairs, I can't but think that his R: Highnesse is too reasonable to meddle soe much as some people would have it thought hee does in things that it is impossible for one in his high station and way of living to bee perfectly informed of.

There can therefore bee no visible cause of all this disturbance in your affairs but that base woman & the creatures that govern her. It is a melancholly thing to remember that your Royall Father was in a manner sung out of his kingdomes by this very tune of lilly burlaro,* especially since your Majesty seems allso inclined to hazard them all reather then displease Abigal; but hee was under a great temptation of bringing in a religion which hee was perswaded was so meritorious a thing that it would secure him honour in this world & everlasting happynesse in the next, & mistakes of that kind, I beleive, there have been instances of, but no history, I am confydent, in any age does give an account of a queen that was brought into such misfortunes as threaten your Majesty because she would beleive no body but a chambermaid, who of herself must bee alltogether ignorant of what is fitt for you to do of any kind; & whenever she does give you any advise it must bee from some of those whose charecters are so truely discribed in this Ballad.

Your Majesty would pardon my returning so often to this odious subject if you would but once reflect on the strange mortifying circumstances that there are to me in this affair. I took her from a broom, as the

* Lillibulero—'A foolish ballad was made at that time, treating the papists and chiefly the Irish in a very ridiculous manner, which had a burden lero lero lillibulero that made an impression on the army that cannot well be imagined by those who saw it not. The whole army and at last all people both in city and country were singing it perpetually. And perhaps never had so slight a thing so great an effect.' (Burnet, op. cit. III, 319). The ballad on Abigail, sent by Sarah to Queen Anne, was to be sung to the tune of Lillibulero. The words of Lillibulero were written by Lord Wharton.

ballad says very rightly, hoping the greatness of the obligation would have made her a faithfull servant to your Majesty & not unmindfull of what she ow'd to Lord Marl: & me. Yet you had no sooner a very ill man in your businesse but this wretch enterd into a strict league with him & became his creature, & so far she forgot me as even to marry without my knowledge, & at last to turn out Lord Marl:, for that was really the case, Madam, & will never be forgott; tho the necessity of your affairs & the discontents that were breaking out in both houses of Parliament obliged your Majesty to call him back to your Councill out of which Abigal & her new master had shut him & your Treasurer. But the wound that this gave some where will never bee eased, nor will the reflections cease that are still made upon it; but this is fitter for others to mention than my self, and many there are that doe it every day.

You cannot but remember, Madam, how many affronts King Charles had, that was a man, upon account of the Duchess of Portsmouth; & I think I need not say a great deal to shew how much worse it is for your Majesty, whose charecter has been so different from his, to bee put in print & brought upon the stage perpetually for one in Abigals post. And if by tiring out Ld Marl: & Ld Treas: you oblige them to quit your service, what can the consiquence of that bee but bringing all your businesse into confusion & exposing her charming person to bee pull'd to pieces; for as long as they are able to continue in their employments, tho with all the disagreeableness & drudgery imaginable to them selves, people only laugh at a queen's forsaking her old servants for such a favorit & are too apt to censure them for not doing what your Majesty makes it impossible for them to doe; but there is nothing more certain than that the moment they are forced to quit, after all the services the world knows they have don your Majesty & their country, she that will justly bee thought the occasion of it will pass her time but very ill & non will come into their places that will bee able to carry on your government two months. And therefor I earnestly desire of your Majesty not to make a second tryall of removing them, which will certainly cost you much dearer than the last. Tis dangerous to provoke the Whigs to make an invitation to the hous of Hanover, which they once hindered but have not had much thanks for it; and tho your Majesty told me very lately that you beleiv'd the people of England might lay you & the Prince aside but you ded not care, or to that purpose, I hope you will please to think better of that matter, for it will bee hard to find out another country where you can bee so well, & in this tis certain you may bee as happy as you please.

Tho I have writt so much I can't help taking notice of one thing, which is how much more easyly your Majesty talks now of this fine passion then you ded not long since; for when I first mentioned it you were pleased to tell me that in your life you had never been half an hour alone with Hill & disownd that you saw her but as a bedchamberwoman; and in six or eight months after you could tell me you thought you might love who you pleased; att which time tis certain you spoke her own words, because that is an expression that is used every day by those that see her. And indeed if she had no influence upon your affairs & did not make your ministers uselesse, there is no doubt but you might make her as dear to you as you pleased & might quietly injoy that inestimable blessing till you were tired of it; but whilst nothing is don that your councill adviss & whilst your Treasurer, who by his post is in a great measure answerable for your administration, presses the same things twenty times over without success, tis certain your people will not long bear patiently the ills that arise from such a passion, which if it bee not better governd for the future must prove fatal to your Majesty & them selves; & therefore you may depend upon it that all the mischief that happens will bee laid upon her, because it will bee impossible to conceive that such dangerous efects should proceed from any thing but so very bad a case.

I hope your Majesty will forgive the freedom of this letter, since you have so ordered matters for me that I can no longer bee of any use to you otherwise then by telling you such truths as these, which no body else will mention, tho most people think as I doe upon this subject. And I doe assure your Majesty that I have no view of any thing but your serviss in what I have written, which however disagreeable it may bee will I hope prove of real advantage to you in the end & that is all I aim att by it.

I remember I have formerly desired your Majesty to burn my letters. Now I make it my humble request that you will please to lay this in your cabinit & I wish that all the notams that I have writt to you were there in hopes some accident or other, when I am dead, might make you remember me & think better of me then you doe att this time. Att least sooner or later it would shew that your Majesty had once a very true friend & a most faithfull servant. I had allmost forgot to let your Majesty know that upon Wednesday, after my Lord Haversham* had waited upon you, his next businesse was to pay his duty to Abigal. I know your Majesty's answer to this beforehand will bee this, that who can help what a madman does & that is true in some measure; but one may help giving occasions for such redicules.

* Lord Haversham had warned the Queen of the Whig plan to invite the Electoral Prince to England. See Churchill, op. cit. II, 412–13.

Ballads

On the 26th of July, 1708 the Duchess of Marlborough wrote to Queen Anne (see appendix III) and enclosed two ballads. Of the ballads about Abigail Masham, then current, the two she seems likeliest to have sent were:

(I) *Verses Upon Mr Harley Being Lord Treasurer**

. . . But then if you ask by what cunning or fate
This last of mankind is grown first in the state,
I answer, 'By neither. His titles and station
Are all the blind work of a strange princely passion;
And thus the whole secret of Britain's undoing
Is nothing but incomprehensible wooing.
Bright Masham's the whirlwind that turns us about,
One whiff of whose breath can bring in or put out . . .'

(II) *A New Ballad To the Tune of Fair Rosamond†*

When as Queen Anne of great Renown
Great Britain's Sceptre sway'd,
Besides the Church she dearly lov'd
A Dirty Chamber-Maid.

O! Abi—— that was her Name,
She stich'd and starch'd full well,
But how she pierc'd this Royal Heart
No Mortal Man can tell.

However for sweet Service done
And Causes of great Weight
Her Royal Mistress made her Oh!
A Minister of State.

* Blen G-1-4.
† Bodl. Firth b 21/94 f 91.

Her Secretary she was not
Because she could not write,
But had the Conduct and the Care
Of some dark Deeds at Night . . .

. . . And so on for thirty-five not very good verses. The Duchess, writing to Sir David Hamilton, the Queen's doctor, on December 6th, 1710, commented:

'. . . 'tis certain that the town & country are very full of prints that do Mrs Morley great hurt because she has given so much ground for such papers, and I hear there is some lately come out which they said were not fit for me to see, by which I guess they are upon a subject that you may remember I complained of to you and really it troubl'd me very much upon my own account as well as others because it was very disagreeable & what I know to be a lye by something of that disagreeable turn there was in an odious ballad to the tune of fair Rosamond, printed a good while agoe, in which the Queen gives an account of Mr Harleys & Mrs Mashams base designs against all those that had brought them to court, and ridiculed her very justly; but that which I hated was the disrespect to the Queen & the disagreeable expressions of the dark deeds of the night. Since that I saw another paper of verses, which was a great ridicule upon all Mrs Morley does, but it was more gentle . . .'*

In the same collection in the Bodleian Library (Firth b 21/94) other contemporary ballads touch upon such subjects as *Harley Wounded by Guiscard*, *The South Sea Whim* (to the tune of *To You Fair Ladies*), *On the Dutchess of Marlborough* ('. . . for Magick Arts do now surround ye Throne: Old Mother Jennings in her Grace is known . . .') and *On ye Dutchess of Marlboroughs Rooting Up a Royall Oak in St James's Park*:

Be cautious, Madam, how you thus provoke
This sturdy plant the second Royall Oak,
For should you fell it or remove it thence
When dead it may avenge the proud offence
And build a scaffold in another place
That may e'er long prove fatall to your Grace . . .†

* Blen G-1-8.
† Bodl. Firth b 21/94 ƒ 67.

APPENDIX V

Two Letters (undated) from Sarah Duchess of Marlborough to Selina Countess of Huntingdon*

My dear Lady Huntingdon is always so very good to me & I really do feel so very sensibly all your kindness & attention that I must accept your very obliging invitation to accompany you to hear Mr Whitefield tho' I am still suffering from the effects of a severe cold. Your concern for my improvement in religious knowledge is very obliging & I do hope I shall be the better for all your excellent advice. God knows we all need mending & none more than my self. I have lived to see great changes in the world—have acted a conspicuous part my self— & now hope in my old days to obtain mercy from God, as I never expect any at the hands of my fellow-creatures. The Duchess of Ancaster, Lady Townshend & Lady Cobham were extremely pleased with many observations in Mr Whitefield's sermon at St Sepulchre's Church, which has made me lament ever since that I did not hear it, as it might have been the means of doing me some good— for good, alas, I do want, but where among the corrupt sons & daughters of Adam am I to find it? Your Ladyship must direct me. You are all goodness & kindness & I often wish I had a portion of it. Women of wit, beauty & quality cannot bear too many humiliating truths—they shock our pride. But we must die—we must converse with earth & worms. Pray do me the favour to present my humble service to your excellent spouse. A more amiable man I do not know than Lord Huntingdon. And believe me, my dear Madam, I am your most faithful & most humble servant.

S. Marlborough

* Selina Hastings, Countess of Huntingdon (1707–1791), supporter of George Whitefield, the Wesleys and the Methodist movement. These letters are reprinted from *The Life & Times of Selina Countess of Huntingdon*, published in 1839 (vol. I, pp. 25–6).

Your letter, my dear Madam, was very acceptable. Many thanks to Lady Fanny for her good wishes. Any communications from her & my dear good Lady Huntingdon are always welcome & always in every particular to my satisfaction. I have no comfort in my own family; therefore must look for that pleasure & gratification which others can impart. I hope you will shortly come & see me & give me more of your company than I have had lately. In truth I always feel more happy & more contented after an hour's conversation with you than I do after a whole week's round of amusement. When alone my reflections & recollections almost kill me & I am forced to fly to the society of those I detest & abhor. Now there is Lady Frances Saunderson's* great rout tomorrow night—all the world will be there & I must go. I do hate that woman as much as I do hate a physician, but I must go if for no other purpose than to mortify & spite her. This is very wicked I know, but I confess all my little peccadillos to you, for I know your goodness will lead you to be mild & forgiving, & perhaps my wicked heart may gain some good from you in the end. Make my kindest respects to Lord Huntingdon. Lady Fanny has my best wishes for the success of her attack on that crooked perverse little wretch at Twickenham.† Assure yourself, my dear good Madam, that I am your most faithful & most obliged humble servant

S. Marlborough

---

* Lady Frances Saunderson, probably daughter of the Earl of Orkney and married to Thomas Lumley, later 3rd Earl of Scarbrough, who had assumed the name of Saunderson by Act of Parliament in 1723.

† Alexander Pope.

BIBLIOGRAPHY

1. MANUSCRIPT SOURCES

Althorp: The Spencer Papers (Marlborough volumes)
Blenheim Palace: The Marlborough Papers
British Museum: Stowe ms 751; Portland ms 29/38; Additional mss
Chatsworth: The Devonshire Collections
Harrowby Trust: The Ryder Papers (Stafford County Record Office)
Huntington Library, California: Chandos and Waller Papers (mss HM
   16600–16635)
Panshanger Papers: Hertfordshire County Record Office
Public Record Office: State Papers (Domestic)
Rousham: The Cottrell-Dormer Papers
Stevens of Bradfield Papers: Berkshire County Record Office

2. PRINTED SOURCES

(I) Reports of the Historical Manuscripts Commission

The following were referred to: The 7th, 9th and 10th Reports.
Appendices to the 3rd, 5th and 8th (Marlborough mss) Reports. Also the
Reports classified as: Ailesbury, Astley, Bath, Buccleuch, Carlisle,
Cottrell-Dormer, Cowper, Dartmouth, Denbigh, Dillon, Downshire,
Egmont, Fortescue, Hamilton, Hodgkin, Lyttelton, Ormonde, Portland,
Puleston, Rutland, Sackville, Townshend, Trevor, Verney, Verulam,
Webb; and the Stuart Papers.

(II) Biographies etc.

ANNE, QUEEN: *Letters* (ed. Beatrice Curtis Brown. 1935)
ASHLEY, MAURICE: *The Stuarts in Love* (1963)
BATHURST, BENJAMIN: *Letters of Two Queens* (1924)
BAXTER, STEPHEN: *William III* (1966)
BROOKE, IRIS: *English Costume of the 17th Century* (1958)

BURNET, GILBERT: *History of His Own Times* (1823) and Supplement (ed. Foxcroft, 1902)

CAMPBELL, KATHLEEN: *Sarah Duchess of Marlborough* (1932)

CHANCELLOR, FRANK: *Sarah Churchill* (1932)

CHURCHILL, Sir WINSTON: *Marlborough, His Life & Times* (2 vols. 1947)*

COLVIN, HOWARD: *A Biographical Dictionary of English Architects* (1954)

COXE, Dr W. C.: *Memoirs of John Duke of Marlborough* (1820)

DELANY, Mrs: *The Autobiography & Correspondence of Mary Granville, Mrs Delany* (1861)

DOBREE, Prof. BONAMY: *Sarah Churchill* (*Three 18th Century Figures.* 1962)

FEILING, Sir KEITH: *A History of the Tory Party* (1924)

FIELDING, HENRY: *A Full Vindication of the Dowager Duchess of Marlborough* (1742)

FOOT, MICHAEL: *The Pen and the Sword* (1957)

GINSBURY, NORMAN: *Viceroy Sarah* (a play. 1935)

GRAMMONT, Comte de: *Memoirs* (late 17th century)

GREEN, DAVID: *Blenheim Palace* (1951)
  Gardener to Queen Anne (1956)
  Grinling Gibbons (1964)

HAILES, Lord: *The Opinions of Sarah Duchess of Marlborough* (1788)

HART, JEFFREY: *Viscount Bolingbroke* (1965)

HARTFORD-POMFRET: *Correspondence* (1806)

HENDERSON, NICHOLAS: *Prince Eugene of Savoy* (1964)

HERVEY, JOHN, Earl of Bristol: *Letter-Books* (1894)
  Memoirs of the Reign of George II (1884)

HIGHAM, C. S. S.: *Wimbledon Manor House* (1962)

JOHNSON, Dr SAMUEL: *Works* (1825)

KENYON, J. P.: *Robert Spencer Earl of Sunderland* (1958)

KRONENBERGER, L.: *Marlborough's Duchess* (1958)

LEDIARD, THOMAS: *The Life of John Duke of Marlborough* (1736)

LEVER, Sir TRESHAM: *Godolphin, His Life & Times* (1952)

MACAULAY, T. B.: *History of England* (1861)

MALLET, DAVID: *Memoirs of the Life of Viscount Bolingbroke* (1752)

MANLEY, MARY DE LA RIVIÈRE: *The New Atlantis* (1709)
  The Secret History of Queen Zarah (1743)

* I am most grateful to the publishers, George G. Harrap & Company, for allowing me to quote so freely from the signed copies of the two-volume edition given to me by the author in 1952. D.B.G.

MARLBOROUGH, SARAH Duchess of:

Account of the Conduct of the Dowager Duchess of Marlborough from her First Coming to Court to the Year 1710 (1742)

Letters from Madresfield Court (1875)

Life of Sarah Duchess of Marlborough (anon. 1745)

Life & History of Sarah Duchess of Marlborough (anon. c.1710)

Private Correspondence of Sarah Duchess of Marlborough (2 vols. 1838)

MONTAGU, Lady MARY WORTLEY: Letters (ed. Wharncliffe. 1893)

OLDMIXON, JOHN: The Life & Posthumous Works of Arthur Maynwaring (1715)

PHILLIPS, HUGH: Mid-Georgian London (1964)

PLUMB, J. H.: Sir Robert Walpole (2 vols. 1956, 1960)

RALPH, JAMES: The Other Side of the Question (1742)*

REID, Dr STUART: John and Sarah Duke & Duchess of Marlborough (1914)

ROBB, NESCA: William of Orange (vol. II. 1966)

ROWSE, A. L.: The Early Churchills (1956)

The Later Churchills (1958)

STRICKLAND, AGNES: Lives of the Queens of England (1884)

SUTHERLAND, JAMES: Background for Queen Anne (1939)

SWIFT, JONATHAN: Journal to Stella & Prose Works (ed. Williams. 1948)

THOMSON, A. T.: Memoirs of Sarah Duchess of Marlborough (2 vols. 1839)

Memoirs of Viscountess Sundon (1847)

THOMSON, G. SCOTT: Letters of a Grandmother, 1732–35 (1943)

Life in a Noble Household, 1641–1700 (1937)

TREVELYAN, Prof. G. M.: England Under Queen Anne (3 vols. 1932, 1965)

WALCOTT, ROBERT: English Politics in the Early 18th Century (1956)

WALPOLE, HORACE: Correspondences (ed. Lewis) (14 vols. 1937–48)

Memoirs of the Reign of King George II (1847)

WENTWORTH PAPERS 1705–39 (ed. Cartwright. 1882)

(III) Pamphlets

A Dialogue in the Shades between Mrs Morley and Mrs Freeman (1745)

A Full Vindication of the Dowager Duchess of Marlborough (1742)

Remarks Upon the Account of the Conduct of a Certain Dutchess (1742)

The Story of the St Albans Ghost (1712)

* James Ralph is named as the compiler of The Other Side of the Question. The author ('A Woman of Quality') was anonymous.

BIBLIOGRAPHY

(IV) Articles

GREEN, DAVID: *The First Mistress of Blenheim* (The Listener, 25 May, 1950)
Sarah Duchess of Marlborough (The Listener, 9 June, 1960)
The Sovereign Proposes (Country Life Annual, 1966)
STRAKA, GERALD: *The Final Phase of Divine Right Theory in England, 1688-1702.* (The Eng. Hist. Review, October, 1962)

Works of general reference have included the *Oxford Companion to English Literature* and the *Dictionary of National Biography*.

REFERENCES TO MANUSCRIPTS
AND PRINTED BOOKS

CHAPTER I—*The Observant Child*

1 Blen E 25 (undated)
2 Corresp. II, 112*
3 Blen E 19
4 Blen E 53
5 Corresp. II, 26
6 Churchill: *Marlborough* I, 166
7 *An Account of the Duchess of Marlborough's Conduct*
8 Churchill, op. cit. I, 166
9 Johnson: *Essay on the Account of the Conduct of the Duchess of Marlborough.*
10 *Conduct*†
11 Blen G-I-10
12 Brooke: *Eng. Costume of the 17th Century*, p. 86
13 HMC Buccleuch & Queensbury I, 361
14 Bathurst: *Letters of Two Queens*, p. 247
15 Evelyn: *Life of Mrs Godolphin*
16 Panshanger (undated)
17 HMC Rutland II, 32, 34
18 Blen E 5
19 Blen G-I-9
20 Blen G-I-9
21 Bathurst: *Letters of Two Queens*, pp. 60–1
22 Bathurst, op. cit., p. 108

23 Spencer (4 Oct. 1744)
24 Churchill, op. cit. I, 92
25 Blen E 1. Churchill op. cit. I, 110–11 & 121–8
26 Blen E 28
27 Lediard: *The Life of John Duke of Marlborough*, I, 38
28 Spencer (To Mallet, 4 Oct. 1744)
29 Blen E 38 (24 Sept. 1726)
30 BM Add ms 29549, *f* 126 (16 Nov. 1725)
31 Blen F-I-30
32 Reid: *John and Sarah Duke & Duchess of Marlborough*, p. 30
33 Coxe: *Memoirs of John Duke of Marlborough* I, 9 f.n.
34 Blen E 2 (16 Jan. 1679)
35 Blen E 51
36 Blen F-I-30 (undated)
37 Blen G-I-9
38 Blen E 1
39 Blen G-I-10
40 Blen XIII (45)

CHAPTER II—*James and the Revolution*

1 Glyn Mills archives (15 June 1734)
2 Blen G-I-7 (26 July 1708)
3 Burnet: *History of His Own Times*, IV, 525
4 Evelyn: *Diary* (29 Dec. 1686)

* *Private Correspondence of Sarah Duchess of Marlborough.* (1838. 2 vols.)
† *An Account of the Conduct of the Dowager Duchess of Marlborough from her First Coming to Court to the year 1710.* (1742)

5 Lediard, op. cit. I, 57
6 Lediard, op. cit. I, 63–4
7 ibid, 73
8 Burnet, op. cit. supp. 291–2
9 *Conduct*
10 Blen (Long Library MSS)
11 Blen E 17
12 ibid
13 Blen E 18
14 Blen E 2
15 Blen G-I-10
16 Bible now at Althorp
17 Swift: Prose Works, x, 26
18 ibid
19 Green: *Grinling Gibbons*, pp. 52–3
20 Burnet, op. cit. III, 184
21 Lediard, op. cit. I, 69
22 Churchill, op. cit. I, 239
23 Blen G-I-10
24 Spencer (28 Sept. 1688)
25 Burnet, op. cit. III, I
26 Thomson: *Memoirs of Sarah Duchess of Marlborough*, p. 572
27 Bathurst, op. cit. pp. 215–19
28 Walcott: *Eng. Politics in the Early 18th Century*, p. 77
29 Cibber: *An Apology For the Life of Mr Colley Cibber*, pp. 57–9

CHAPTER III—*William and Mary*

1 Corresp. I, 208
2 Burnet, op. cit. III, 123, 125
3 Blen G-I-10
4 *Conduct*
5 Burnet, op. cit. III, 384–5
6 *Remarks Upon the Account of the Conduct* etc., p. 26
7 *Conduct*
8–11 ibid
12 Foxcroft: *Life & Letters of Halifax*, II, 150
13 Blen E 48

14 Blen E 45
15 ibid
16 Spencer
17 Blen G-I-10
18 Blen G-I-9
19 Blen G-I-8
20 Blen E 19
21 ibid
22 Blen E 17
23 Churchill, op. cit. I, 130
24 Churchill, op. cit. I, 354
25 *Conduct*
26–29 ibid
30 Blen E 12
31 Blen E 18
32 Blen E 17
33 ibid
34 Spencer
35 Blen E 16
36 Blen E 16
37 ibid
38 Blen E 18
39 Switzer: *Nobleman, Gentleman & Gardener's Recreation*, pp. 57–8
40 Defoe: *A Tour Through England & Wales*
41 Green: *Grinling Gibbons*, plate 85
42 Burnet, op. cit. IV, 241
43 *Conduct*
44 Blen E 18
45 Blen E 17
46 Blen E 48
47 Switzer, op. cit. p. 57
48 *Conduct*
49 Blen E 17
50 Burnet, op. cit. IV, 440
51 *Conduct*

CHAPTER IV—*Hail, Glorious Anna!*

1 Goldsmith: *Works*, IV, 24
2 Hailes: *Opinions of Sarah Duchess of Marlborough*, pp. 2–7

3 Burnet, op. cit. v, 2
4 ibid, IV, 530
5 Blen G-I-8
6 Churchill, op. cit. I, 528
7 Blen G-I-8
8 Blen E 17 (undated)
9 ibid
10 Blen G-I-8
11 Blen G-I-9
12 Blen E 19
13 *Conduct*
14 Blen G-I-8
15 *Lord Hervey's Letterbooks*, no. 247
16 Trevelyan: *England Under Queen Anne*, I, 154
17 Blen E 19
18 Blen E 2
19 Blen E 5
20 Blen E 2
21 ibid
22 Churchill, op. cit. I, 614
23 Churchill, op. cit. I, 619
24 ibid
25 Blen E 17
26 Blen E 20
27 Blen E 6
28 Blen E 20
29-31 Blen E 2
32 HMC Coke, p. 53
33 Blen E 2
34 Coxe, op. cit. I, 132
35 Churchill, op. cit. I, 700
36 Coxe, op. cit. I, 133
37 HMC Rutland II, 179
38 Churchill, op. cit. I, 723-4
39 Blen E 39
40 Churchill, op. cit. I, 735-6
41 Reid, op. cit. Introduction
42 Blen E 45 (16 Sept. 1704)
43 Coxe, op. cit. I, 231
44 Coxe, op. cit. I, 232
45 Evelyn: *Diary* (7 Sept. 1704)
46 Blen F-I-53

47 Blen G-I-9

CHAPTER V—*Princess of Mindelheim*

1 Blen E 18
2 BM Add ms 35853 *f* 17
3 Blen G-I-8
4 *Letters of the Duchess of Marlborough at Madresfield Court*
5 Blen E 17
6 Blen E 18
7-10 Blen E 19
11 Blen E 17
12 Corresp. II, 120
13 Blen G-I-7
14 ibid
15 Blen G-I-8
16 *Conduct*
17 Blen E 18 (An unsigned fragment). The poem evidently derives from the well-known verses by Brooke, Lord Cobham
18 Blen (unclassified)
19 Blen E 13
20 Blen F-I-24
21 Coxe, op. cit. I, 190
22 Bodl. ms Top Oxon d 173
23 Blen E 3
24 Blen A-II-31
25 Blen A-I-20. I am obliged to Mr W. A. Speck for drawing my attention to this manuscript
26 Blen E 18
27 Blen G-I-8
28 Corresp. II, 148
29 Blen F-I-24
30 Blen E 17
31 Blen E 13
32 Churchill, op. cit. II, 33
33 Campbell: *Sarah Duchess of Marlborough*, p. 166
34 Blen G-I-9
35 Coxe, op. cit. I, 375
36 ibid

37-39 Blen E 3
40 Chandos Letterbooks in Huntington Library, California
41 ibid
42 Churchill, op. cit. II, 196
43 ibid, 198
44 Churchill, op. cit. II, 199
45 Churchill, op. cit. II, 200–1
46 ibid, 202
47 ibid, 203
48 ibid, 205
49 ibid
50 ibid, 209
51 Conduct

CHAPTER VI—Cue for Vipers

1 Trevelyan, op. cit. II (Ramillies) p. 99
2 Conduct
3 Blen E 25
4 Feiling: A History of the Tory Party, p. 334
5 Blen G-I-9
6 Burnet, op. cit. v, 326
7 Ralph: The Other Side of the Question, p. 301
8 Conduct
9 Blen G-I-8
10 Blen G-I-9
11 Swift: Prose Works v, 449–50
12 Burnet, op. cit. VI, 32–3
13 Churchill, op. cit. II, 286
14 Blen G-I-8
15 Conduct
16 Churchill, op. cit. II, 284
17 Blen G-I-10
18 Corresp. I, 92–3
19-21 Blen E 17
22 Churchill, op. cit. II, 420
23 Bolingbroke Memoirs, pp. 129–30
24 Cunningham: Hist. of Gr. Britain II, 141–2

25 Conduct
26 Churchill, op. cit. II, 288–9
27 P.R.O. 30/24/21/150. Stanhope to Sir John Copley 19.2.1708 (See Speck & Holmes: 'Fall of Harley in 1708 Reconsidered.' Eng. Hist. Review Oct. 1965)
28 ibid
29 Blen G-I-9
30 Reid, op. cit., pp. 275–6
31 Blen G-I-7
32 Blen G-I-8
33 Coxe, op. cit. II, 204–5
34 ibid
35 Blen E 4
36 ibid
37 ibid (29 April 1708)
38 Conduct
39 Blen E 26
40 Blen G-I-7
41 Blen G-I-9
42 Conduct
43 Blen E 4
44 Conduct
45 Blen E 18
46 Burnet, op. cit. v, 440 (Dartmouth)
47 Blen G-I-8
48 Coxe, op. cit. II, 360–1
49 Corresp. I, 412–16
50 Coxe, op. cit. II, 362

CHAPTER VII—Favour Declines

1 Blen E 19
2 Corresp. I, 411–12
3 Blen G-I-9
4 Blen G-I-8
5 ibid
6 Blen E 17
7 Blen G-I-9
8 BM Add ms 35853. f 14
9 Blen E 27
10 Blen G-I-4

11 Blen G-1-8
12 Blen E 26
13 Corresp. I, 231–8
14 *Conduct*
15 Churchill, op. cit. II, 548
16 Blen E 4
17 Blen G-1-8
18 Wentworth Papers, p. 98
19 Cunningham, op. cit. II, 227
20 Blen E 26
21 Blen E 27
22 Blen E 4 (7 Sept. 1709)
23 Blen G-1-7
24 Churchill op. cit. II, 640–1
25 ibid, 651
26 Blen G-1-7
27 Blen G-1-9
28 ibid
29 Blen G-1-7
30 Churchill, op. cit. II, 665
31 Blen G-1-8
32 Corresp. I, 289
33–35 Blen G-1-8
36 Corresp. II, 455
37 *Conduct*
38 Blen G-1-9

CHAPTER VIII—*The Great Change*

1 Blen G-1-9
2 Blen G-1-8
3 Blen E 26
4 Blen G-1-8
5 ibid
6 Blen G-1-7
7 *Conduct*
8 Blen G-1-8
9 Blen E 5
10 Blen G-1-8
11 *Conduct*
12 Blen E 5
13 Blen G-1-8
14 Blen E 25

15 BM Portland 29/38 (undated)
16 Blen G-1-9
17 Foot: *The Pen and the Sword*, pp. 304–6
18 Blen G-1-8 (Nov. 1710)
19 Blen E 27
20 ibid
21 Coxe, op. cit. III, 170
22 ibid, 175
23 ibid, 175–6
24 Blen G-1-8
25 ibid
26 Churchill, op. cit. II, 797
27 Blen G-1-8
28 Blen E 19
29 Blen G-1-8
30 Blen G-1-9
31 Swift: *Prose Works* V, 463
32 Blen G-1-9
33 HMC Harley II, 669–70
34 Blen E 46
35 Blen E 25
36 Blen E 27
37 Blen G-1-17
38 Blen E 5
39 Blen E 25
40 Blen F-1-48
41 Blen E 3 (4 Aug. 1707)
42 Thomson, op. cit. II, 521
43 Whistler: *Sir John Vanbrugh*, p. 33
44 Blen E 27
45 Churchill, op. cit. II, 754
46 Blen E 5
47 Foot, op. cit., p. 292
48 ibid, p. 301
49 Blen G-1-9
50 Churchill, op. cit. II, 912–13
51 Blen G-1-9

CHAPTER IX—*A Sort of Pilgrimage*

1 Trevelyan, op. cit. IV, 66
2 *Conduct*

334

3 Blen E 27
4 Blen G-1-10
5 Blen E 26
6 BM Stowe ms 751, *f* 3
7 Blen E 27
8 Swift: *Journal to Stella*, p. 494
9 *Horace Walpole Corresp.* XXVIII, 390
10 Blen G-1-4
11 Blen E 20
12 *Wentworth Papers*, p. 313
13 Blen G-1-9
14 Swift: *Journal to Stella*, pp. 658–9
15 BM Stowe ms 751 *f* 54 (to Craggs, 4 June 1713)
16 Churchill, op. cit. II, 978–9
17 Madresfield, p. 64
18 Blen E 38
19 Corresp. II, 92
20 BM Stowe ms 751, *f* 39
21 ibid, *f* 29
22 ibid, *f* 150
23 ibid, *ff* 58–9
24 Madresfield, p. 72
25 ibid, p. 100
26 BM Stowe ms 751, *f* 54
27 Madresfield, p. 66
28 BM Stowe ms 751, *ff* 83–7
29 Madresfield, pp. 45–6
30 Blen E 6
31 Madresfield, p. 74
32 BM Stowe ms 751, *f* 48
33 Madresfield, p. 94
34 Blen E 6
35 Strickland, op. cit. VI, 409
36 *Memoirs of Sir John Clarke*, pp. 71–2
37 Foot, op. cit., p. 361
38 Churchill, op. cit. II, 1012
39 Swift Corresp. II, 222

CHAPTER X—*No Armour*

1 BM Add ms 19,609

2 Webb: *Sir John Vanbrugh (Letters)*, p. 63
3 Blen G-1-9
4 Blen E 5
5 Coxe, op. cit. III, 395–6
6 Coxe, op. cit. III, 397
7 BM Stowe ms 751, *f* 142
8 ibid, *f* 136
9 ibid, *ff* 144 & 150
10 Blen E 3
11 Blen E 4
12 BM Stowe ms 751, *f* 129
13 ibid
14 ibid *f* 136
15 ibid *f* 144
16 ibid *f* 150
17 Webb, op. cit., pp. 84–5
18 Blen G-1-9
19 Blen F-1-31
20 Blen E 51
21 Blen F-1-31
22 Blen E 51
23 Blen G-1-9
24 Blen E 24
25 Blen E 15
26 Swift: *Prose Works* X, 27
27 Blen E 15
28 Memoirs of the Life of Viscount Bolingbroke, pp. 310–11
29 Churchill, op. cit. II, 1024
30 Swift Corresp. II, 391

CHAPTER XI—*The Crookd Scythe*

1 Green: *Blenheim Palace*, p. 147
2 Attrib. Dr Abel Evans
3 Ballard: *Chronicles of Woodstock*, p. 108
4 BM Stowe 751 *f* 205
5 HMC Morrison IX, 473
6 Blen E 26
7 Blen box XXII
8 Blen E 46

9 Blen E 15
10 Churchill, op. cit. II, 1033
11 Blen E 52
12 Churchill, op. cit. II, 1034
13 Blen E 52
14 HMC Carlisle, p. 31
15 Webb, op. cit., p. 184
16 Blen E 44
17 ibid
18 BM Add ms 38056 f 3
19 Blen E 35 (22 Aug. 1721)
20 Blen E 8
21 Plumb: *Sir Robert Walpole* II, pp. 40 & 48 *f.n.*
22 Blen F-I-34
23 Churchill, op. cit. II, 1032
24 ibid, 1036
25 Blen G-I-9
26 Blen E 44
27 Blen E 43
28 ibid
29 Webb, op. cit., p. 146
30 Blen E 43
31 Lediard, op. cit. III, 422
32 Blen E 46 (10 Aug. 1722)
33 Blen E 53
34 Blen Long Library (portf. II)
35 Blen E 21
36 Blen E 7
37 Blen (unclassified)
38 Blen E 7
39 ibid
40 & 41 Blen E 6
42 Manley: *New Atlantis*, p. 145
43 Blen G-I-9
44 & 45 Blen G-I-17
46, 47, 48 ibid

CHAPTER XII—*Provocations and Proposals*

1-4 Blen G-I-9
5 Blen E 49
6 Blen E 43

7 Blen E 35
8 Blen E 45
9 Blen E 39
10 Blen E 6 (20 Aug. 1722)
11 Blen F-I-32
12 Blen E 37
13 ibid (20 Sept. 1722)
14 BM Stowe 751 f 150
15 Blen F-I-31
16 Blen E 41
17 Blen E 16
18 Blen E 34 (17 July 1723)
19 ibid (18 July 1723)
20-24 ibid
25 Spencer (Book B)
26 Blen G-I-17 (20 Aug. 1723)
27 Bodl. d 173 (III)
28 Blen Long Library ms
29 Blen E 34 (10 Oct. 1723)
30 Blen E 44
31 Blen Long Library ms (To Pengelly, 3 Oct. 1728)
32 BM Stowe 751 f 127 (To Craggs, 1716)
33 ibid f 62 (1713)
34 Blen Long Library ms
35 Gent's Mag. May 1731
36 Bodl. Warwick c 2/4. See also Berks County R.O.: Stevens of Bradfield mss F 29-30
37 Walpole Soc. XIX, p. 127
38 Webb op. cit., pp. 166-7
39 Blen E 46
40 Webb, op. cit., pp. 170-1
41 Wade: *Brit. Hist.*, p. 375
42 Green: *Blenheim Palace*, p. 268
43 Blen E 38 (7 Oct. 1726)
44 ibid

CHAPTER XIII—*The Fruitful Vine*

1 Lever: *Sidney Godolphin*; and DNB (Congreve)

2 Blen E 8
3 ibid
4 Blen F-I-35
5 BM Add ms 35853 *f* 16
6-8 Blen E 7
9 Blen F-I-32
10 ibid
11 Blen F-I-31
12 Blen E 13
13 Blen E 10
14 Scott-Thomson: *Letters of a Grandmother* (1732-35)
15 ibid, p. 34
16 ibid., p. 41
17 ibid, p. 58
18 Blen G-I-20 (25 Mar. 1732)
19 Spencer (undated)
20 Scott-Thomson, op. cit., p. 52
21 Blen E 10
22 Scott-Thomson, op. cit., p. 96
23 Blen G-I-9
24 Blen E 21
25 Blen G-I-7
26 Blen G-I-16
27 Scott-Thomson, op. cit., p. 155
28 ibid, p. 152
29 Blen G-I-11
30 Corresp. II, 146
31 Scott-Thomson, op. cit., p. 118
32 Blen F-I-49
33 Blen Long Library ms
34 Scott-Thomson, op. cit., p. 62
35 Psalm 39, v. 7
36 Scott-Thomson, op. cit., p. 96
37 ibid, p. 177
38 Blen E 43

CHAPTER XIV—*The Grandsons*

1 Blen F-I-32
2 Blen E 41
3 Blen E 12
4 ibid

5 *Hartford-Pomfret Corresp.* I, 275-6
6 Blen E 35
7 ibid
8 Blen E 8
9 ibid
10 Blen E 31
11-13 Blen E 8
14 Blen E 22
15 Reid, op. cit., p. 435
16 BM Add ms 28071 *ff* 34-9
17 Blen E 31 (12 Oct. 1727)
18 ibid
19 ibid (21 Jan. 1727)
20 ibid (25 Mar. 1728)
21 ibid (21 Jan. 1727)
22 ibid (12 Apr. 1728)
23 ibid (1 May 1728)
24 Blen E 13 (14 Sept. 1728)
25 ibid
26 Lady Mary Wortley Montagu: *Letters*
27 Hearne: *Diary* VII (20 Sept. 1720)
28 HMC Egmont I, 279
29 Blen E 13
30 Blen (unclassified ms)
31 ibid
32 ibid (duplicated in Spencer mss at Althorp)
33 ibid (29 Oct. 1733)
34 *Hartford-Pomfret Corresp.* I, pp. 33-4
35 Blen F-I-33
36 Corresp. II, 171
37 Blen F-I-34 (8 Jan. 1738)
38 Spencer

CHAPTER XV—*Without Hope or Fear*

1 Blen F-I-35 (undated)
2 Blen E 8 (10 Jan. 1724)
3 Horace Walpole Letters (ed. Toynbee) I, 140
4 Pope: *Epistle to Lord Cobham*
5 Blen E 22 (15 Dec. 1730)

6 Blen E 47

7 Spencer (8 Sept. 1742)

8-10 Blen G-I-16

11 Blen E 44

12 Spencer (reprinted in Churchill, op. cit. I, Appen. II)

13 Scott-Thomson, op. cit., p. 134

14 Blen G-I-9 (23 Sept. 1744)

15 Blen E 42

16 Horace Walpole Letters I, 139

17 Fielding: *A Full Vindication of the Duchess of Marlborough*

18 Walpole: *Catalogue of Royal & Noble Authors* IV, 189

19 Corresp. II, 482

20 Blen G-I-10

21 *Letters of Lady Mary Wortley Montagu*, p. 101

22 Thompson, op. cit., Appendix

23 Blen E 44 (undated)

24-26 Blen G-I-16

27 Goldsmith's Works IV, 24

28 Blen E 42

29 Swift Corresp. VI, 131

30 Pope: *Moral Essays*, Epistle II (To a Lady): 'Of the Characters of Women'

31 Pope's Works I, 439-40

32 Blen E 42 (6 Aug. 1743)

33 ibid (18 Jan. 1744)

34 ibid

35 Spencer (26 Nov. 1743)

36 Blen F-I-34 (3 Aug. 1744)

37 Madresfield, p. xviii

38 HMC Bath II, 181

39 Burnet, op. cit. VI, 30

40 Spencer (To John Spencer, 18 Aug. 1744)

41 BM Add ms 29549

42 HMC Denbigh, p. 142

43 Blen F-I-52

44 Blen G-I-16

45 Blen ms (unclassified)

46 Blen E 26

INDEX

The initials M and SM denote Marlborough and Sarah Duchess of Marlborough

INDEX

DATE DUE

SE 25 '77			
OC 11 '77			
MAR 12 '84			
GAYLORD			PRINTED IN U.S.A.